STRATEGIC
MANAGEMENT
Text, Readings, and Cases
Fifth Edition

STRATEGIC MANAGEMENT

Text, Readings, and Cases

Fifth Edition

Paul W. Beamish

Professor of International Strategy
Richard Ivey School of Business
The University of Western Ontario

C. Patrick Woodcock

Assistant Professor
Faculty of Business Administration
University of Ottawa

McGraw-Hill Ryerson

Toronto   Montreal   New York   Burr Ridge   Bangkok   Bogotá   Caracas   Lisbon   London
Madrid   Mexico City   Milan   New Delhi   Seoul   Singapore   Sydney   Taipei

McGraw-Hill Ryerson Limited

A Subsidiary of The **McGraw·Hill** *Companies*

Strategic Management
Text, Readings, and Cases
Fifth Edition

ISBN: 0-07-560537-6

1 2 3 4 5 6 7 8 9 10 GTC 8 7 6 5 4 3 2 1 0 9

Printed and bound in Canada.

SPONSORING EDITOR: Evelyn Veitch
ASSOCIATE EDITOR: Lenore Gray Spence
MANAGER, EDITORIAL SERVICES: Susan Calvert
SUPERVISING EDITOR: Margaret Henderson
PRODUCTION EDITOR: Rodney Rawlings
PRODUCTION CO-ORDINATOR: Nicla Dattolico
INTERIOR DESIGN AND PAGE COMPOSITION: Lynda Powell
COVER DESIGN: Sharon Lucas
COVER PHOTO: Pete Turner/The Image Bank
PRINTER: Transcontinental Printing

Canadian Cataloguing in Publication Data

Beamish, Paul W., date —
    Strategic management : text, readings, and cases

5ᵗʰ ed.
Includes bibliographical references.
ISBN 0-07-560537-6

1. Strategic planning — Canada. 2. Industrial management — Canada.
I. Woodcock, C. Patrick. II. Title.

HD30.28.B413 1998   658.4'012'0971   C98-932269-6

To the memory of two splendid teachers:
John and Catherine Beamish

ABOUT THE AUTHORS

Paul W. Beamish is professor of International Strategy at the Richard Ivey School of Business, University of Western Ontario. He served as editor-in-chief of the *Journal of International Business Studies (JIBS)* from 1993 to 1997, and is Director of Ivey's Asian Management Institute. He is the author or co-author of over 20 books, 50 articles or contributed chapters, and 60 case studies. His articles have appeared in such journals as *Strategic Management Journal, JIBS, Academy of Management Executive, Academy of Management Review,* and *Journal of World Business.* His consulting and management training activities have been in both the public and the private sector for such organizations as the World Bank, the Canadian Foreign Service Institute, Northern Telecom, and Valmet. He has received best research awards from the Academy of Management, the Academy of International Business, the European Foundation for Management Development, and the Administrative Sciences Association of Canada. He worked for the Procter & Gamble Company of Canada and Wilfrid Laurier University before joining Ivey's faculty in 1987.

C. Patrick Woodcock is an assistant professor at the University of Ottawa where he teaches Strategic Management and International Business Strategy. He is author or co-author of a number of articles, some of which have appeared in *Business Quarterly, Group Decision and Negotiations,* and the *Journal of International Business Studies.* Prior to entering the academic world, he worked for over a decade as a mergers and acquisitions analyst and consultant. Some of the large multinational companies he worked with include Steetley Plc., Holderbank Corporation, and St. Lawrence Cement. He has received business research awards from the Academy of Management in the United States, the Canadian Exporter's Association, and the Administrative Sciences Association of Canada.

CONTENTS

Chapter 8   Organizational Forms   92

Chapter 9   Managing Strategic Change   105

Chapter 10   Corporate and International Strategies   114

PREFACE AND ACKNOWLEDGEMENTS

As with the previous four editions, this book was made possible only through the academic and intellectual support from colleagues at Ivey, the University of Western Ontario (UWO), University of Ottawa, and others across the country. The primary stimulus for this book was our own ongoing need for new, high-quality Canadian material.

Having made the decision to produce a book of Canadian cases in strategic management, a number of other decisions were made: (1) to bring together Canadian cases written not only by ourselves, but by faculty across North America; (2) to include only decision-oriented cases, which we believe provide the best training for future managers; (3) to include cases dealing with international business, high-technology industries, service industries, not-for-profit industries, and business ethics; (4) to provide text material including a basic conceptual framework for use with all the cases; and (5) to include a section on how to do case and financial analysis.

We solicited and received much useful feedback on the fourth edition from colleagues at the more than 40 institutions in Canada and the United States where the fourth edition has been used. From this feedback, we retained the basic structure of the fourth edition, but have changed the majority of the cases and updated the text material. This edition contains 17 new cases and 5 new readings.

We are indebted to several groups of people for assisting in the preparation of this book. First, we are grateful to the case contributors from Ivey, Wilfrid Laurier (particularly Mark Baetz), University of Ottawa, and other institutions. At Ivey, we wish to thank Mary Crossan, Ann Frost, Tony Frost, Nick Fry, Bud Johnston, John Kennedy, Don Thain, Allen Morrison, and Rod White; the doctoral and research assistants Azimah Ainuddin, Fred Chan, Jennifer McNaughton, Detlev Nitsch, Doug Reid, and Ian Sullivan.

Cases were also contributed by colleagues from other institutions:

Bill Blake, Memorial University
John Banks, Wilfrid Laurier University
James Bowey, Bishops University
Wesley Cragg, York University
Walter Good, University of Manitoba
Peter Killing, IMD Switzerland
David Large, University of Ottawa
Kent Neupert, Chinese University of Hong Kong
R.K. Gupta, Memorial University
Diane Hogan, Memorial University
Andrew Inkpen, Thunderbird: AGSIM

Louise Jones, Memorial University
M.D. Skipton, Memorial University
Andre Morkel, University of Western Australia
Mark Schwartz, York University
Joanne Simpson, University of Western Australia

From the above list it is clear that the effort to produce the book has been both a national and an international effort.

With regard to the textual material, the footnotes throughout each chapter indicate the source of the material in the chapter. We wish to acknowledge, in particular, the assistance of Art Thompson and A. J. Strickland on Chapter 2.

Others who provided helpful comments on the outline of the fifth edition include Jack Ito, University of Regina; Scott Carson, St. Mary's University; and Brooke Dobni, University of Saskatchewan.

We are indebted to the strategy area teaching groups, past and present, at Ivey and Wilfrid Laurier University. At Wilfrid Laurier, our special thanks to Larry Agranove, John Banks, Ruth Cruikshank, Elliott Currie, Tom Diggory, Ken Harling, Peter Kelly, and Ray Suutari.

The efforts of many people are needed to develop a book and improve it from edition to edition. The following colleagues from across the country were instrumental in the preparation of the previous edition of this book:

James W. Alsop	Stephen Drew	Greg Libitz
R.W. Archibald	Dwight Dyson	Rich Mimick
Michael Bellas	Gordon Fullerton	Wojciech Nasierowski
Robert Blunden	Christopher Gadsby	John Oldland
Pierre Brunet	George Gekas	Vicky Paine-Mantha
Donald Buskas	Barry Gorman	David Pringate
James Butler	Ann Gregory	Bob Sexty
Mick Carney	Louis Hebert	Reza Sina
John Charmard	G. V. Hughes	Michael Skipton
Ron Correll	John Knox	John Usher

Invaluable in-depth comments were provided to us by manuscript reviewers—feedback which we found to be enormously helpful in the preparation of this fifth edition. This group of reviewers included

Donald Buskas, Selkirk College
Alfie Morgan, University of Windsor
Terry Seawright, McMaster University
Lee Swanson, Lakeland College

We would also like to thank those professors who took the time to respond to a questionnaire early in the revision process and, in doing so, were helpful in the preparation of this edition. Our thanks are extended to:

Allen Backman, University of Saskatchewan
Michael Bellas, Mount Royal College
Robert Blunden, Dalhousie University
Barry Boothman, University of New Brunswick
Ruth Cruikshank, Wilfrid Laurier University
U. Daellenback, University of Calgary
Gary Davis, University of New Brunswick
C. B. Dobni, University of Saskatchewan
Cathy Driscoll, Saint Mary's University
Pat Fitzgerald, Saint Mary's University
Christopher Gadsby, British Columbia Institute of Technology
Jack Ito, University of Regina
John Lille, Centennial College
Beverly Linnell, Southern Alberta Institute of Technology
Alfie Morgan, University of Windsor
Doug Taylor, University of Victoria
Roger Wehrell, Mount Allison University

Financial assistance for some of the case writing at Ivey was received through the Plan for Excellence.

In addition, we wish to thank the various executives who gave us the required access to complete the cases in this book. Finally, we wish to recognize our students on whom we tested the cases for classroom use. Some students served as research assistants; their contributions are duly noted in each case.

Any errors or omissions in this book remain our responsibility. We look forward to feedback from its various users.

Paul W. Beamish
C. Patrick Woodcock

STRATEGIC
MANAGEMENT
Text, Readings, and Cases
Fifth Edition

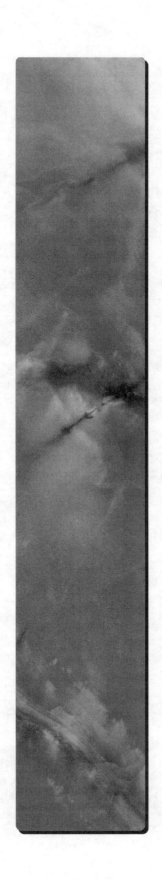

SECTION

I

Chapters

Strategic Management— An Overview

The CityTV philosophy is galactic vision, local touch.

Moses Znaimer, President and Executive Producer of CityTV

Only the paranoid survive.

Andrew Grove, Chairman of Intel Corp.

Nothing energizes an individual or a company more than clear goals and a grand purpose. Nothing demoralizes more than confusion and lack of content.

Tony O'Reilly, CEO of H. J. Heinz Co.

Businesses are successful for a variety of reasons. Some are the first to do something. Some do a very good job on the one or two things that are most critical to their success. And some have developed complex skills, technologies, and systems to support their success. Yet, how do managers consistently develop successful business plans and implement them effectively? The study of strategic management attempts to formalize concepts and approaches that have been observed to produce business success over the long term. These strategic approaches are not a substitute for hard work or functional skills. Rather, they are general management tools aimed at improving a firm's long-term prosperity.

Does strategic planning result in higher performance? Many studies have examined this relationship and the majority have concluded that firms having a formal strategic planning process outperform those that do not. Furthermore, firms taking a proactive strategic approach have better performance than those taking a reactive strategic approach. This evidence demonstrates the usefulness and, in fact, necessity of having a formal, proactive strategic planning process in a firm, whether it be large or small.

The Strategic Management Process Defined

The study of strategic management has been steadily evolving. The original emphasis was on the functions of the general manager—still an integral part of the field. More recently, the strategic management field has broadened to include the study *"of the organizational systems and processes used to establish overall organizational goals and objectives and to formulate, implement, and control the strategies and policies necessary to achieve these goals and objectives."* [1]

The common element in discussions of strategic management is an emphasis on strategy. Derived from the ancient Greek *strategos* or "the art of the general,"[2] strategy has military roots. In fact, not surprisingly, strong similarities exist between the responsibilities of the military general and the general manager of an organization. Their definitions of strategy often overlap as well. In a military context, strategy has been defined as "the employment of the battle as the means to gain the end of the war."[3] In a corporate setting, strategy can be defined as the implementable management scheme for achieving corporate ends. Alternatively, corporate strategy has been viewed as "the pattern in the organization's important decisions and actions, and consists of a few key areas or things by which the firm seeks to distinguish itself."[4] In a broader context, strategy has been defined as "that which has to do with determining the basic objectives of an organization and allocating resources to their accomplishment."[5] A contemporary view of a strategic manager is a facilitator, coach, team builder, and motivator who establishes direction, builds the organization's capabilities, and implements change in the firm on a continuous basis.

To provide the student with a broader understanding of the strategic management concept, eighteen major subfields are summarized in Exhibit 1-1.

The strategic management processes of planning and implementing strategy are complex and evolutionary. The dynamic nature of these processes is important to understand because they are not always completely planned. Rather, they are processes where managers attempt to plan and manage a firm's strategy in an ever-changing competitive environment. In this context, the firm's strategy evolves in a direction that is sometimes planned and other times influenced by unforeseen external competitive forces. Managers plan a strategy on the basis of assumptions about their competitors and their own organizational capabilities. However, as various competitive and organizational influences depart from their expected course, managers must abandon part of the strategy (i.e., unrealized strategy) and adopt new strategies (i.e., emergent strategy). This process, shown in Exhibit 1-2, illustrates the dynamic nature of the strategic process—a process that requires continual learning, review, flexibility, and renewal to meet the needs of the ever-changing competitive environment. This continual evolution of strategy is necessary to produce a sustainable "realized strategy"—one that produces long-term success.

[1] "Common foreword," Charles W. Hofer, consulting ed., West Series in Strategic Management (St. Paul, Minn.: West Publishing, 1986), p. xi.

[2] Jay R. Galbraith and Robert K. Kazanjian, *Strategy Implementation: Structure, Systems and Process*, 2nd ed. (St. Paul, Minn.: West Publishing, 1986), p. 3.

[3] Carl von Clausewitz, *On War* (Middlesex, England: Pelican [Penguin] Books, 1968). Originally published in 1832. Translation published by Routledge and Kegan Paul, Ltd., 1908.

[4] Michael Kamis, *Strategic Planning for Changing Times* (Dayton, Ohio: Cassette Recording Co., 1984).

[5] William Curry, "A condensed version of business policy," mimeographed (Waterloo, Ont.: Wilfrid Laurier University, 1980).

EXHIBIT 1-1   **Some Major Subfields of Strategic Management/Business Policy**

Groups
- Board of directors
- General management
- Stakeholder analysis

Conceptualizing Strategic Management
- The strategy-structure-performance linkage
- Corporate-level strategy (including mergers, acquisitions, and divestiture)
- Business-level strategy

Elements of Strategy Formulation
- Organizational goals
- Corporate social policy and management ethics
- Macro-environmental analysis
- Strategic decision making (choice of strategy)

Elements of Strategy Implementation and Review
- The design of macro-organizational structure and systems
- Strategic planning and information systems
- Strategic control systems
- Organizational culture
- Leadership style for general managers

Organizations
- The strategic management of small businesses and new ventures
- The strategic management of not-for-profit organizations (including governments)
- The strategic management of international business

Source: Reprinted by permission from West Series in Strategic Management, Charles W. Hofer, consulting ed. (St. Paul, Minn.: West Publishing, 1986). © 1986 by West Publishing Co. All rights reserved.

The Levels of Strategy

Business strategists have developed several levels of strategy. These levels, although intimately interwoven in reality, can be considered separately for analytical purposes. The levels, illustrated in Exhibit 1-3, are differentiated on the basis of the nature of the decisions under consideration, who makes and implements the decisions, and how the decisions impact the firm. Exhibit 1-4 describes the various characteristics of these strategic levels.

EXHIBIT 1-2   **The Strategy-Making Process**

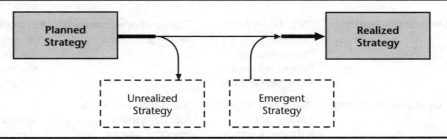

Source: Adapted from "Strategy formation in an adhocracy," by Henry Mintzberg and Alexandra McHugh, *Administrative Science Quarterly,* vol. 30, no. 2 (June 1985).

EXHIBIT 1-3   Levels of Strategy

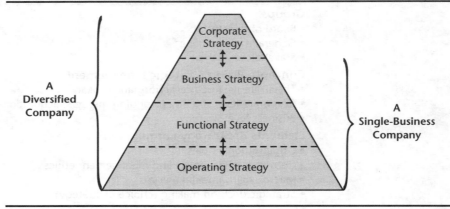

Corporate strategy focuses on decisions related to what businesses a firm is in. For example, whether the firm should enter a new business or get out of an old business, and to which of its businesses it should allocate resources (capital, equipment, skills, etc.) in the future. This level of strategy is most important for the diversified firm (i.e., a firm in several different businesses). The text addresses this strategic level using the same frameworks as are discussed at the business strategy level. However, the pertinent decisions and relationships to corporate strategy are described in the relevant chapters.

Business strategy focuses on decisions about how a specific business competes in its particular market for product or service emphasis. This strategy is the principal strategic concern of a manager who is in only one business or manages a single business division in a diversified firm. The business-level strategy will be the primary focus of this book.

EXHIBIT 1-4   Description of Levels of Strategy

Level of Strategy	Level of Influence	Strategy Makers	Types of Decisions
Corporate Strategy	Corporate strategies	Corporate managers and board members	• Allocation of resources to businesses, and scope of business diversification
Business Strategy	Business strategies	Top business managers in company or business division	• Types of products/markets to be in and the organizational and resource-specific attributes required to support the product/market focus
Functional Strategy	R&D, finance, marketing, manufacturing, human resource strategies/functions	Top functional managers within a business	• Type of operational technique, approaches, and resources that best support the overall business strategy
Operational Strategy	Plants, teams, sales groups, and individuals within functions	Individuals within the functions that have responsibility for tasks or decision-making units	• Specific operational tactics, approaches, and resources that support the business and functional strategies

Functional and operational strategies are the strategies occurring in the functional and operational levels of the business. They provide critical input into the formulation of a business strategy and are important tools for implementing the business strategy at the functional and operational levels within the firm. These latter two strategies will not actively be studied, because they are covered elsewhere in the business school curriculum. However, the student must understand these strategies; it is at this level that managers must eventually translate the corporate and business strategies for effective implementation.

Another type of strategy, international strategy, is important both at the corporate and at the business level. International strategy is concerned with where, when, what, and how to enter and develop businesses in international regions. International strategies are addressed in several sections of the text.

A Conceptual Framework for Strategic Management

The basic underlying paradigm in the strategic management area for over 30 years has been the strategy-structure-performance relationship.[6] This relationship tells us two things—one that is immediately obvious and one that is not. The first and obvious point is that strategy affects performance. Whether one is attempting to organize a fundraiser, increase sales, start a business, or allocate resources in a large organization, strategy matters.

The second, perhaps less obvious point is that organizational structure matters also, as it can support or hamper the strategy. To implement any strategy, certain organizational actions must be taken: certain tasks must be carried out; reward and information systems put in place; people hired, trained, and managed; and reporting relationships established. An unlimited number of potential organizational actions exist. However, they are not all equally appropriate in all situations. Depending on the strategy chosen, some organizational structures are more appropriate than others. In fact, possibly the greatest challenge in the strategic management area is fitting an appropriate organization to the strategy that has been formulated.

A sports analogy can illustrate this second point most effectively. While any hockey team can put six players on the ice with a playing strategy, the organization of the players into three forwards, two defensemen, and a goalie appears to be critical in enabling the team to strategically react both defensively and offensively in a balanced manner. Thus, it is the organization of the players that allows the various strategies to be carried out most effectively.

In the balance of this chapter, we review several well-accepted strategic management models that form the basis for the conceptual framework used in this text. Keep in mind that all of these models have as part of their origins the same underlying paradigm, depicted in Exhibit 1-5.

---

[6] Alfred D. Chandler, *Strategy and Structure* (Cambridge, Mass.: MIT Press, 1962).

EXHIBIT 1-5   **The Underlying Paradigm in Strategic Management**

Exhibit 1-6 details one of the dozens of published models of strategic management. Like many approaches, this model is divided into sections on strategy formulation and implementation. Although formulation and implementation are inextricably linked, for analytic purposes they can be considered separately.

The major variables influencing strategy formulation are:

1. Top management's mission, vision, and objectives for the company

2. The external environment, including competitive opportunities and risks

3. The internal environment, which focuses on the organization's managerial, financial, and technical resources and capabilities

4. Organizational responsibility to society

The conceptual framework used in this text includes the first three of these variables. The fourth variable is subsumed here under managerial preferences and values.

In Exhibit 1-6 there are a large number of arrows between the variables used to illustrate the interrelationships that exist. While in the general case strategy influences structure, certainly in many instances the relationship can be in the other direction or, in fact, in both directions.

The strategy implementation half of the model in Exhibit 1-6 is composed of a separate group of variables. Typically, the major organization design variables are (a) information and control systems, (b) reward systems, (c) people, which includes leadership style, (d) organizational structure, and (e) resource allocation task. This last variable, task, is sometimes viewed as a bridge between formulation and implementation. In this text, all five of these variables are included as part of strategy implementation, although using a slightly different configuration. The role of these variables in the strategic management process will be discussed in detail in Chapters 7 and 8.

The above framework enunciates the differences between strategic formulation and implementation. Strategic formulation involves deciding what to do and where to do it, while strategic implementation involves doing it. In the case analyses, students generally will be asked to describe recommendations and plans specific to both the strategic formulation and the implementation issue. Exhibit 1-7 considers these two dimensions and their characteristics. In particular, the exhibit delineates the descriptive and planning questions that the student should focus on when considering strategic formulation versus implementation. In general, formulation is focused on the what and where questions, while implementation is focused on the when and how questions.

EXHIBIT 1-6   Strategic Management Process

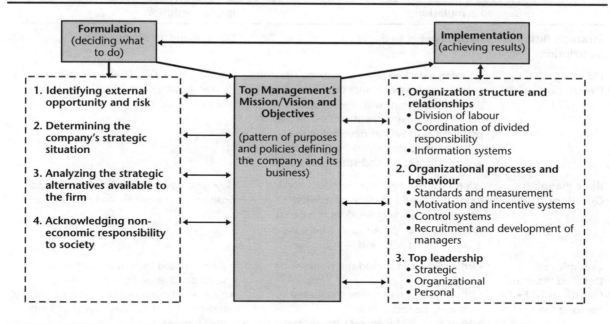

Source: Adapted from Kenneth Andrews, *The Concept of Corporate Strategy*, rev. ed. (Burr Ridge, Ill.: Richard D. Irwin, 1980).

Exhibit 1-8 illustrates the conceptual framework and the key variables used in this text. The environment is largely an uncontrollable influence in this framework, while the other influences or components are more managerially controllable. Therefore, managers, in the short term, must exert influence on the other components in this framework and position themselves in the environment so as to maximize performance. It is for this reason strategic analysis normally begins with the environmental analysis.

The Major Components of Strategy

Every firm has a strategy. Implicit or explicit, effective or ineffective, as intended or not—whenever a firm allocates the resources of people or capital, it is making a statement about its strategy.

Three components are present in a strategy: (1) mission/vision/objectives, (2) competitive position (i.e., market/product/service emphasis), and (3) competitive advantage (i.e., basis of competition).

Mission/Vision/Objectives

In many of the more successful organizations there is a clear sense of "who we are and where we are going." A firm's *mission* answers the questions "Who are we?" and "What business are we in?," while a firm's *vision* is the top management's perspective of what direction the firm should take in the future. It is important the management have a good understanding of both of these

EXHIBIT 1-7   **Planning the Formulation and Implementation in Strategic Management**

	Formulation	Implementation
Strategic Business Description	Deciding what to do	Doing it and achieving results
Planning Description	Planning a desired set of objectives, strategic position, and set of competitive advantages that are consistent with the forecasted competitive environment and management preferences as well as developing the appropriate resources, and organizational systems, processes, and structure	Planning how and when to implement the desired strategy in a logical and doable manner
Basic Planning Questions	What business or market/product/service emphasis should the firm take, what competitive advantages does it have to take such an emphasis, and where should it take such an emphasis?	How and when to implement strategic positions, advantages, components, and tactics
Examples of Detailed Planning Questions to Be Focused On	• What products should the business be focusing on? • What type of customers should the business be focusing on? • What geographic market should the business be focusing upon? • What competitive advantages or skills, capabilities, etc. should the business be attempting to develop?	• When should various aspects of the strategic change be implemented? • How will the managers overcome political resistance and get employees to embrace the change? • How should the company develop? • How should the resistance to change be handled? • How does the firm control and review strategic action?

strategic dimensions and that they communicate them clearly and effectively to the firm's other stakeholders such as the owners, customers, and employees.

The organization's vision or purpose can be translated into specific, measurable performance targets. These objectives typically relate to profitability, growth, return on investment, market share, technological strength, and so forth. In addition, there are "soft" goals and objectives. These might include such things as benefits to society, employee welfare, and management autonomy. Knowledge of the existence of a "soft" counterpart to "hard" terms is essential if one is to have a more complete understanding of an organization.

A firm's vision and objectives are intimately linked to the other strategic variables because the vision and objectives describe the desired strategic results, yet the other strategic variables govern what, how, and when the various objectives are attainable. An example of a firm's objectives is described in Exhibit 1-9.

A clear strategic mission and vision are particularly important in a not-for-profit organization, because these types of organizations are driven by their duty to the community and society. Translating the mission and vision into a clear statement can be very messy, there being no clear underlying profitability

EXHIBIT 1-8   The Strategic Management Process: Basic Conceptual Framework

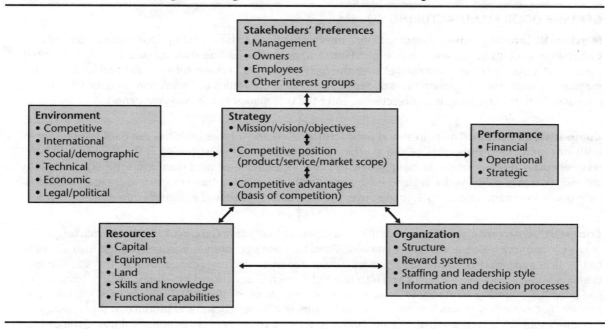

motive. It is vital that all employees, volunteers, donors, and customers understand and agree with the mission and vision statement.

Competitive Position

A second component of strategy is a firm's competitive position, or positions if the firm is diversified into several businesses. Competitive position is defined as the firm's market/product/service emphasis and it can be described as the location and type of customer it services, the product and service attributes its customers value, and its market/product/service emphases relative to its competitors. A firm's competitive position relative to its competitors will be discussed further in Chapter 3.

Business research suggests that there are three generic competitive positions that firms can profitably seek in a market: customer focus, low cost, and differentiation. All of these strategies are aimed at focusing the strategy on a specific competitive position so that you can use your resources and organizational capabilities efficiently and effectively. Very few companies can be everything to everybody in a market. A customer focus strategy entails having a competitive position that focuses on specific customers. An example would be a travel agency that focuses on high-risk adventures, or skin divers. A low-cost strategy naturally focuses the firm to be competitively positioned in the low-cost market of the industry. An example of a low-cost strategy is Wal-Mart or Costco. Firms that take a differentiation strategy are attempting to provide the customer with valued yet distinctive products or services that other competitors are not providing. Examples of this strategic approach are Holt Renfrew, Birks Jewellery Stores, and the Concorde air service between New York and London.

EXHIBIT I-9

GENUINE DOOR MANUFACTURING CO.

Mission/Vision/Objectives. Genuine Door's mission has been to be a leading door manufacturer in the Canadian market. Its future vision is to expand into and become a leading door manufacturer in the United States and a player in the Asian market over the next decade. Objectives for the next two years are to maintain annual revenue growth rates of over 15 percent and a return on investment of over 10 percent annually. Furthermore, there is an objective to enter the U.S. market in this two-year period.

$\updownarrow$

Competitive Position. The market and products that Genuine focuses on is the standard house door in both steel and wood throughout Canada. Their products are the lowest-priced in the market, and are relatively plain in presentation, coming in only five colours. Genuine services their doors through an on-site ten-year warranty policy, which is standard in the industry. Genuine's future competitive position is dynamically going to expand into the U.S. market over the next several years and eventually into Asia.

$\updownarrow$

Competitive Advantages. The competitive advantages that allow Genuine to hold this market position are its economies of scale and production capabilities. Genuine's economies of scale (or large size) allows it to buy steel and wood in volume discounts that other door manufacturers cannot match. This size also gives Genuine access to the most efficient and effective distribution channels and the largest dealers, because they can provide advertising assistance to dealers. Genuine also has developed a highly automated manufacturing process that minimizes production costs, material waste, quality rejections, and production time. Finally, Genuine's supplier and dealer ordering and billing is done by computer connection, minimizing the delivery times and inventory quantities. Future competitive advantages are going to have to be developed that support the U.S. and Asian expansion.

The term *market* refers to both geographic and customer groups. Geographic markets can be local, regional, national, or international in scope. Customer groups, which are defined in terms of customer scope and focus, are an important characterization of a firm's business and focus.[7] Specifically, a business can be defined in terms of (1) customer groups (Who is being satisfied?), (2) customer needs (What is being satisfied?), and (3) alternative technologies (How are customer needs satisfied?). This then describes the competitive position of the firm in the eyes of the customers. Therefore, competitive position is a description of the firm's strategy in relation to its environment, as shown in Exhibit 1-8.

The example in Exhibit 1-9 defines Genuine's competitive position in terms of both geographical and customer group focus. The geographic market encompasses all of Canada, and the pertinent attributes that define the customer group are the low price, limited designs, materials choice (i.e., steel and wood), and warranty period and service.

The firm's objectives and competitive position are linked because managers must decide whether the firm's competitive position (i.e., market/product/service emphasis) is going to provide it with the desired growth and performance levels. If the competitive position is not going to provide such growth, then either the objectives must be changed or the competitive position must be

---

[7] Derek F. Abell, *Defining a Business: The Starting Point of Strategic Planning* (Englewood Cliffs, N.J.: Prentice Hall, 1980), p. 169.

changed. Both the existing and the potential range and focus of market/product/service alternatives must be considered in analyzing possible competitive positions. Exhibit 1-10 delineates some of the alternative market and product/service alternatives one should examine when considering possible new competitive positions.

Competitive Advantages

The third component of strategy is the firm-specific competitive advantages that enable the company to compete effectively in a specific competitive position. These competitive advantages represent the basis upon which a firm competes in its industry and market. Clearly the competitive advantages are important, because they allow the firm to occupy a competitive position. However, these advantages also are important because they characterize how easily and quickly a firm will be able to meet its strategic objectives. A firm with stronger competitive advantages will be able to achieve more challenging strategic objectives than a company with relatively weak competitive advantages. In this context competitive advantages are relative. However, examples of strong competitive advantages include highly valued product patents, highly trained managers and workers, or a mix of capabilities that provide synergies other companies have trouble duplicating. The competitive advantages in a company originate from the resources and organizational design and capabilities as illustrated in Exhibit 1-8.

The example in Exhibit 1-9 describes Genuine Door's intrinsic competitive advantages. These are principally related to economies of scale. More specifically they are high-volume, automated production, volume purchasing discounts, access to efficient and effective distribution channels, and a computer-automated supplier/buyer ordering system. These advantages allow Genuine to be the largest, lowest-cost door manufacturer in Canada (i.e., its competitive position). These advantages will also hopefully allow the firm to achieve its desired growth and profitability objectives.

The five elements of competitive advantage pertinent to industry structure, discussed in greater detail in Chapter 3 (see Exhibit 3-1), show that the

EXHIBIT I-I0 Competitive Position Growth Alternatives

		Market Alternatives			
		Reduced Market	Existing Market	Expanded Market	New Market
Product/Service Alternatives	Reduced Products/Services				
	Existing Products/Services				
	Modified Products/Services				
	New Products/Services				

competitive forces that shape strategy arise not only from internal indus-try competition rivalry,[8] but also from competitive forces generated by sup-pliers,[9] customers,[10] substitute products, and potential new entrants. This framework for analyzing competitors (and industries) is useful for under-standing how a firm competes now and in the future.

Some of the questions related to the various levels of strategic decision making at the corporate, business, and international levels are described in Exhibit 1-11. These questions attempt to illustrate the practical decision-making emphasis from both a firm competitive position(s) and a competitive advantages perspective at these various levels.

■ Evaluating Strategic Performance

The ultimate evaluation of a firm's strategy is its performance over the long term. This is illustrated in Exhibit 1-8. When assessing a firm's strategy, differ-ent performance outcomes should be examined, because they provide evidence of the quality of a strategy—both the formulation and the implementation.

There are three basic types of performance indicators: financial, operational, and other strategic indicators. Exhibit 1-12 describes these various perfor-mance indicators. Financial indicators are broad performance measures that provide one with an indication of how the firm is doing financially. Operational performance indicators allow the analyst to focus on evaluating and compar-ing specific operational aspects of the firm that are relevant to its operational competitive advantage. For example, a service firm depends upon the effi-ciency and effectiveness of its people. Therefore, sales per employee may be an important operational indicator to examine. Furthermore, it is critical to look at both static comparative indicators as well as their trends over time. Other strategic (non-numerical) indicators involve subjective examination of information provided to the manager. This information could be in the form of dissatisfied customers, unhappy employees, or strategic changes or misalignments. This information usually requires subjective assessment, yet it is useful because it is often a precursor to financial or operational per-formance deterioration.

A relatively new performance evaluation tool is benchmarking. Bench-marking is a technique that is being used by companies to evaluate their func-tional and operational-level efficiencies and effectiveness relative to the best in the world. Establishing a benchmarking program involves comparing your operations to firms deemed to have the best of the different types of operations being assessed. For example, if a firm wants to benchmark its purchasing func-tion, it would find a firm having a world-class purchasing operation and assess the differences between its operations and the deemed-best operation. This

---

[8] Michael E. Porter, *Competitive Strategy: Techniques for Analyzing Industries and Competitors* (New York: Free Press), 1980.

[9] Henry Mintzberg, *The Nature of Managerial Work* (New York: Harper & Row, 1973), pp. 91–93.

[10] Derek F. Abell, *Defining a Business: The Starting Point of Strategic Planning* (Englewood Cliffs, N.J.: Prentice Hall, 1980), p. 169.

EXHIBIT I-II   The Relationship Between Strategic Variables and Strategic Level

Level of Strategy	Questions Related to Competitive Position	Questions Related to Competitive Advantages
Corporate Strategy	• Is the firm's competitive position(s) good from an investment perspective, will the portfolio of competitive positions satisfy the corporate objectives, and should they consider either investing in or divesting a business?	• Do the competitive advantages in the various businesses that the firm holds provide synergy to one another? • Can the firm provide corporate-level competitive advantages such as financial acumen to the individual businesses?
Business Strategy	• Would the business's performance be enhanced if the competitive position was changed and does the business's competitive position satisfy the firm's objectives?	• Do the competitive advantages support the business's competitive position, and can the firm improve its business competitive advantages?
International Strategy	• When entering a new country what competitive position should the firm be seeking, and does the new international competitive position satisfy the firm's objectives?	• Does the firm have adequate home-based competitive advantages to move into international markets, and does the firm have enough international competitive advantages such as organizational control capabilities, and market and cultural knowledge to enter an international market?

type of program not only allows the firm to compare its performance with another's, but also allows the firm to observe and learn about how possible improvements can be implemented.

Some other key questions that should be asked as part of the process of reviewing and evaluating a strategy are:[11]

1. Is there internal consistency between the components of the strategy (i.e., do the goals/objectives, product/market scope, and basis of competition all fit together)?

[11] Some of these questions were derived from Seymour Tilles, "How to evaluate corporate strategy," *Harvard Business Review*, July–August 1963.

EXHIBIT I-I2   **Performance Indicators**

Type of Performance Indicator	Measurement Tools
Financial Indicators	Financial values and ratios based on standards or competitive comparisons. *Examples:* Debt-to-quity ratio, profitability ratios (see Chapter 2 for more).
Operational Indicators	Operational measures are values and ratios that indicate the operational efficiency and effectiveness of the firm. These measures are often used to measure comparatively the firm's key operational competitive advantages relative to their prime competitors. *Examples:* Sales to employee, sales to assets, R&D expenses to sales, market share (see Chapter 2).
Other Strategic Indicators	Strategic measures and non-numerical measures are more abstract and subtle in nature. They involve such things as the perceived strategic fit between the various components by various experts in the field, the enthusiasm of employees or employee complaints, supplier or customer complaints, etc.

2. Is the strategy appropriate in light of threats and opportunities in the environment?

3. Is the strategy appropriate in light of the available resources?

4. To what extent does the strategy satisfy managerial preferences and values?

5. What are the key tasks arising out of the strategy and has the organization been designed so that these tasks are performed?

The case studies in this text were chosen to illustrate the impact/role of some or all of the variables in the conceptual framework. They are all decision-oriented, requiring students to analyze and make recommendations as to a course of action for the organization. Achievement of a defensible overall strategy for the organization means that errors in tactics (the specific means of exercising the strategy) may not be fatal. Although the perspective we employ here is that of the general manager, it is important to acknowledge that effective functional managers are also called upon to adopt a strategic orientation. All functions in an organization include both strategic and

---

EXHIBIT 1-13   The Balanced Scorecard

The Balanced Scorecard is a technique that translates strategic vision into action. It does this by communicating, incenting, and tracking the achievement of an organization's strategy. The approach uses a four-step process. The main elements of this process are as follows:

1. Clarifying and translating the vision and strategy
   - Clarifying the vision with the top management team
   - Gaining consensus between top managers about the vision and strategic direction

2. Communicating and linking
   - Communicating and educating the employees about the vision and strategy
   - Setting goals for functions, teams, and activities in the value chain
   - Linking rewards to performance measures at the team and personal level.

3. Planning and target setting
   - Setting targets for business and functional activities to attain
   - Aligning strategic incentives ensuring that the incentives reflect the targets
   - Allocating resources so that activities have the necessary resources
   - Establishing milestones

4. Strategic feedback and learning
   - Articulating the shared vision from various parts of the organization to the top
   - Supplying strategic feedback to all parts of the organization
   - Facilitating strategy review and learning

The Balanced Scorecard has become important because it not only links strategy to performance, but also provides management and employees strategic and operational performance indicators as well as financial performance indicators. By using these precursors to financial performance, managers can develop a causal logic that allows them to understand when and why financial performance is being impacted. It also provides management and workers an early indicator (i.e., prior to financial performance) that they can fix immediately. Finally, the approach does a good job of translating the higher-level strategic vision to the lower-level functional and operational activities including developing incentives, priorities, and goals for specific activities.

Source: Based on Robert S. Kaplan and David P. Norton, "Linking the balanced scorecard to strategy," *California Management Review*, vol. 39, no. 1 (Fall 1996):53–79.

non-strategic activities (non-strategic activities would be made up of more routine activities that require little attention from the general manager or other senior managers). Wherever possible, the effective functional manager will approach tasks strategically rather than operationally. Exhibit 1-14 provides an example of how a particular function can be characterized as strategic rather than operational.

A manager analyzing strategy in a firm does not necessarily do it in an orderly manner. Usually it is a complex ongoing process, as is indicated by the strategic process described in Exhibit 1-2. In this book, however, we will consider the issues in an orderly manner, moving from the external environment, to the companies strategy and characteristics, through to strategic implementation. In Chapter 2, a detailed framework for conducting a case study analysis is provided—including financial analysis ratios. This material is included in order to provide some direction in developing "better" case analyses.

The Strategic Management Process

The process of developing a strategy in a company is not necessarily linear. Often many stages are done simultaneously and feedback discussions can occur at any point. Furthermore, there are both formal and informal strategic planning processes. The informal process supports the formal process by providing information prior to the actual making of the decision. In this text we follow a relatively generic approach to developing a formal strategic management

EXHIBIT 1-14   **Purchasing as a Strategic Function**

Characteristics	Operational Approach	Strategic Approach
Organization Structure	Low visibility, lengthy reporting chain	High visibility, direct reporting to top management
Organization Perception	Isolated, ineffective clerks; a necessary administrative expense	Active, effective material supply managers; possible source of additional profit
Information Access	Limited exposure to critical reports and meetings; added only occasionally to distribution lists of key material	Access to library of material, some of which is generated at the request of purchasing
Decision Issues	Makes decision based on price	Provides expert analysis of forecasting, sourcing, price, availability, delivery, and supplier information, and even outsourcing recommendations
Supplier Network and Relationships	Works superficially with many suppliers; arm's-length, often adversarial, relationships	Focuses on fewer suppliers, cooperative relationships
Frame of Reference	Local, provincial, or at best international	International, with regular investigation of non-domestic sources
Strategic Management	No direct input to the strategy process	Provides critical input to strategy process

Source: Adapted by P. W. Beamish from John N. Pearson and Karen J. Gritsmacher, "Integrating purchasing into strategic management," *Long Range Planning*, vol. 23, no. 3 (1990): 91–99.

EXHIBIT 1-15   The Strategic Management Process Model

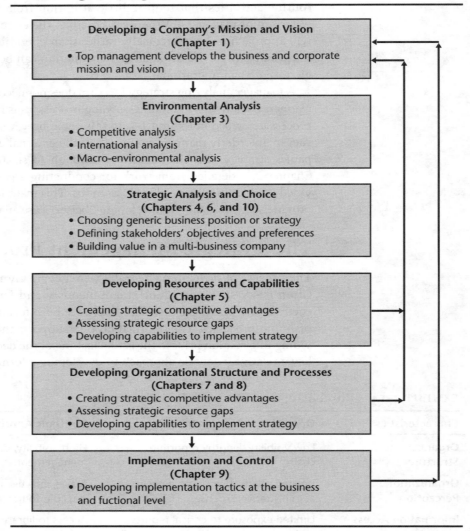

process, and it is illustrated in Exhibit 1-15. The text moves through these strategic stages as is illustrated in the model.

RECOMMENDED READINGS

Adkam, J. D. and S. S. Cowen. "Strategic planning for increased profit in the small business." *Long Range Planning*, December 1990, pp. 63–79.

Hahn, D. "Strategic management—tasks and challenges in the 1990s." *Long Range Planning*, February 1991, pp. 26–39.

Hitt, M. A., R. E. Hoskisson, and J. S. Harrison. "Strategic competitiveness in the 1990s: challenges and opportunities for U.S. executives." *Academy of Management Executive*, May 1991, pp. 7–22.

McMillan, Ian C., and Patricia E. Jones. *Strategy Formulation: Power and Politics.* 2nd ed. St. Paul, Minn.: West Publishing, 1986.

Mintzberg, Henry. *The Rise and Fall of Strategic Planning*. New York, The Free Press, 1994.

Tenaglia, Mason, and Alistair Davidson. "A directory of strategic management software tools." *Planning Review*, July–August 1993, pp. 38–94.

Watson, Gregory H., "How process benchmarking supports corporate strategy." *Planning Review,* January–February 1993, pp. 12–15.

Kaplan, Robert S., and David Norton, "The balanced scorecard: translating strategy into action," Harvard Business School Press, 1996.

Collins, James C., and Jerry Porras, "Built to last: successful habits of visionary companies," HarperBusiness, 1997.

Case Analysis*

I don't know if there have been many mistakes, but their have been lots of lessons. ... Make sure you focus on your core business.

Jim Shaw, President & COO of Shaw Communications

Solve the problem or you don't have a business; solve it or you don't have a job.

Bob Woods, President of Zeneca Agricultural Products

Management is an action-oriented activity. It requires doing to achieve proficiency. Managers succeed or fail not so much because of what they know as because of what they do. A person cannot expect to succeed as a manager and become a "professional" simply by studying excellent books on management—no matter how thoroughly the text material is mastered, nor how many A's are earned at exam time. Just as a skater needs to practise at being a better skater, a person who aspires to become a manager can benefit from practising at being a manager.

Practising Management via Case Analysis

In academic programs of management education, students practise at being managers via case analysis. A case sets forth, in a factual manner, the events and organizational circumstances surrounding a particular managerial situation. It puts the readers at the scene of the action and familiarizes them with the situation as it prevailed. A case can concern a whole industry, a single organization, or even just a part of an organization; the organization involved can be either profit-seeking or not-for-profit. Cases about business organizations usually include descriptions of the industry and its competitive conditions, the organization's history and development, its products and markets, the backgrounds and personalities of the key people involved, the production

---

*This chapter has been adapted by the authors *or* incorporates material from Arthur A. Thompson and A. J. Strickland, *Strategic Management: Concepts and Causes* (Plano, Tex.: Business Publications, 1984), pp. 272–289. Used with permission.

facilities, the work climate, the organizational structure, the marketing methods, and the external environment, together with whatever pertinent financial, production, accounting, sales, and market information was available to management.

The essence of the student's role in the case method is to diagnose and size up the situation described in the case and to think through what, if any, actions need to be taken. The purpose is for the student, as analyst, to appraise the situation from a managerial perspective, asking: What factors have contributed to the situation? What problems are evident? How serious are they? What analysis is needed to probe for solutions? What actionable recommendations can be offered? What facts and figures support my position?

It should be emphasized that most cases are not intended to be examples of right and wrong, or good and bad management. The organizations concerned are selected neither because they are the best or the worst in their industry, nor because they present an interesting and relevant analytical situation. The important thing about a case is that it represents an actual situation where managers were obligated to recognize and cope with the problems as they were.

▧ Why Use Cases to Practise Management?

Charles I. Gragg's classic article, "Because Wisdom Can't Be Told,"[1] illustrates that the mere act of listening to lectures and sound advice about management does little for anyone's management skills. He contended it was unlikely that accumulated managerial experience and wisdom could effectively be passed on by lectures and readings alone. Gragg suggested that if anything has been learned about the practice of management, it is that a storehouse of ready-made answers does not exist. Each managerial situation has unique aspects, requiring its own diagnosis and understanding as a prelude to judgement and action. In Gragg's view and in the view of other case-method advocates, cases provide aspiring managers with an important and valid kind of daily practice in wrestling with management problems.

The case method is, indeed, *learning by doing*. The pedagogy of the case method of instruction is predicated on the benefits of acquiring managerial "experience" by means of simulated management exercises (cases). The best justification for cases is that few, if any, students during the course of their university education have an opportunity to come into direct personal contact with different kinds of companies and real-life managerial situations. Cases offer a viable substitute by bringing a variety of industries, organizations, and management problems into the classroom and permitting students to assume the manager's role. Management cases, therefore, provide students with a kind of experiential exercise in which to test their ability to apply their textbook knowledge about management.

---

[1] Charles I. Gragg, "Because wisdom can't be told," in *The Case Method at the Harvard Business School,* ed. M. P. McNair (New York: McGraw-Hill, 1954), p. 11.

◼ Objectives of the Case Method

As the foregoing discussion suggests, using cases as an instructional technique is intended to produce four student-related results:[2]

1. Increase your understanding of what managers should and should not do in guiding a business to success

2. Build your skills in sizing up company resource strengths and weaknesses and in conducting strategic analysis in a variety of industries and competitive environments

3. Get valuable practice in identifying strategic issues that need to be addressed, evaluating strategic alternatives, and formulating workable plans of action

4. Enhance your sense of business judgement, as opposed to uncritically accepting the authoritative crutch of the professor or "back of the book" answers

5. Gaining in-depth exposure to different industries and companies, thereby acquiring something close to actual business experience

If you understand that those are the objectives of the case method of instruction, you are less likely to be bothered by a question that puzzles some students: "What is the answer to the case?" Being accustomed to textbook statements of fact and supposedly definitive lecture notes, students often find that discussions and analyses of managerial cases do not produce any hard answers. Instead, issues in the case are discussed pro and con. Various alternatives and approaches are evaluated. Usually, a good argument can be made for more than one course of action. If the class discussion concludes without a clear consensus on what to do and which way to go, some students may, at first, feel frustrated because they are not told "what the answer is" or "what the company actually did."

However, cases where answers are not clear-cut are quite realistic. Organizational problems whose analysis leads to a definite, single-pronged solution are likely to be so oversimplified and rare as to be trivial or devoid of practical value. In reality, several feasible courses of action may exist for dealing with the same set of circumstances. Moreover, in real-life management situations when one makes a decision or selects a particular course of action, there is no peeking at the back of a book to see if you have chosen the best thing to do. No book of provably correct answers exists; in fact, the first test of management action is *results*. The important thing for a student to understand in case analysis is that it is the managerial exercise of identifying, diagnosing, and recommending that counts rather than discovering the right answer or finding out what actually happened.

To put it another way, *the purpose of management cases is not to learn authoritative answers to specific managerial problems but to become skilled in the*

---

[2] Ibid., pp. 12–14; and D. R. Schoen and Philip A. Sprague, "What is the case method?" in McNair, *The Case Method at the Harvard Business School,* pp. 78–79.

process of designing workable action plans through evaluation of the prevailing circumstances. The aim of case analysis is not for you to try to guess what the instructor is thinking or what the organization did, but rather to see whether you can support your views against the opposing views of the group or, failing to do so, join in the sense of discovery of different approaches and perspectives. Therefore, *in case analysis you are expected to bear the strains of thinking actively, of making managerial assessments which may be vigorously challenged, of offering your analysis, and of proposing action plans—this is how you are provided with meaningful practice at being a manager.*

Analyzing the case yourself is what initiates you into the ways of thinking "managerially" and exercising responsible judgement. At the same time, you can use cases to test the rigour and effectiveness of your own approach to the practice of management and to begin to evolve your own management philosophy and management style.

Use of the Socratic method of questioning-answering-questioning-answering, where there is no single correct answer but always another question, is at the heart of the case process. A good case can be used with student groups of varying qualifications. With the more highly experienced qualified groups, the other questions become tougher.

Preparing a Case for Class Discussion

Given that cases rest on the principle of learning by doing, their effectiveness hinges upon you making *your* analysis and reaching *your* own decisions and then in the classroom participating in a collective analysis and discussion of the issues. If this is your first experience with the case method, you may have to reorient your study habits. Since a case assignment emphasizes student participation, it is obvious that the effectiveness of the class discussion depends upon each student having studied the case *beforehand.* Consequently, unlike lecture courses where there is no imperative of specific preparation before each class and where assigned readings and reviews of lecture notes may be done at irregular intervals, *a case assignment requires conscientious preparation before class.* You cannot, after all, expect to get much out of hearing the class discuss a case with which you are totally unfamiliar.

Unfortunately, though, there is no nice, neat, proven procedure for conducting a case analysis. There is no formula, no fail-safe, step-by-step technique that we can recommend beyond emphasizing the sequence: *identify, evaluate, consider alternatives,* and *recommend.* Each case is a new situation and has its own set of issues, analytical requirements, and action alternatives.

A first step in understanding how the case method of teaching/learning works is to recognize that it represents a radical departure from the lecture/ discussion/problem classroom technique. To begin with, members of the class do most of the talking. The instructor's role is to solicit student participation and guide the discussion. Expect the instructor to begin the class with such questions as: What is the organization's strategy? What are the strategic issues and problems confronting the company? What is your assessment of the company's situation? Is the industry an attractive one to be in? Is management doing a good job? Are the organization's objectives and strategies compatible with its skills and resources? Typically, members of the class will evaluate and test their opinions as much in discussions with each other as with the instructor. But irrespective of whether the discussion emphasis is instructor-student or student-student, members of the class carry the burden for analyzing the situation and for being prepared to present and defend their analyses in the classroom. Thus, you should expect an absence of professorial "here's how to do it," "right answers," and "hard knowledge for our notebook"; instead, be prepared for a discussion involving your sizeup of the situation, what actions you would take, and why you would take them.[3]

Begin preparing for class by reading the case once for familiarity. An initial reading should give you the general flavour of the situation and make possible preliminary identification of issues. On the second reading, attempt to gain full command of the facts. Make some notes about apparent organizational objectives, strategies, policies, symptoms of problems, root problems, unresolved issues, and roles of key individuals. Be alert for issues or problems that are lurking beneath the surface. For instance, at first glance it might appear that an issue in the case is whether a product has ample market potential at the current selling price; on closer examination, you may see that the root problem is that the method being used to compensate salespeople fails to generate adequate incentive for achieving greater unit volume. Strive for a sharp, clear-cut sizeup of the issues posed.

To help diagnose the situation, put yourself in the position of some manager or managerial group portrayed in the case and get attuned to the overall environment facing management. Try to get a good feel for the condition of the company, the industry, and the economics of the business. Get a handle on how the market works and on the nature of competition. This is essential if you are to come up with solutions that will be both workable and acceptable in light of the prevailing external constraints and internal organizational realities. Do not be dismayed if you find it impractical to isolate the problems and issues into distinct categories that can be treated separately. Very few significant strategy management problems can be neatly sorted into mutually exclusive areas of concern. Furthermore, expect the cases (especially those in this book) to contain several problems and issues, rather than just one. Guard against making a single, simple statement of the problem unless the issue is very clear-cut. Admittedly, there will be cases where issues are well defined and the main problem is figuring out what to do; but in most cases you can expect a set of problems and issues to be present, some of which are related and some of which are not.

Next, you must move toward a solid evaluation of the case situation, on the basis of the information given. Developing an ability to evaluate companies and size up their situations is the core of what strategic analysis is

---

[3] Schoen and Sprague, "What is the case method?", p. 80.

all about. The cases in this book, of course, are all strategy-related, and they each require some form of strategic analysis, that is, analysis of how well the organization's strategy has been formulated and implemented.

Uppermost in your efforts, strive for defensible arguments and positions. Do not rely upon just your opinion; support it with evidence! Analyze the available data and make whatever relevant accounting, financial, marketing, or operations calculations are necessary to support your assessment of the situation. Crunch the numbers! If your instructor has provided you with specific study questions for the case, by all means make some notes on how you would answer them. Include in your notes all the reasons and evidence you can muster to support your diagnosis and evaluation.

Last, when information or data in the case are conflicting and/or various opinions are contradictory, decide which is more valid and why. Forcing you to make judgements about the validity of the data and information presented in the case is both deliberate and realistic. It is deliberate because one function of the case method is to help you develop your powers of judgement and inference. It is realistic because a great many managerial situations entail conflicting points of view.

Once you have thoroughly diagnosed the company's situation and weighed the pros and cons of various alternative courses of action, the final step of case analysis is to decide what you think the company needs to do to improve its performance. Draw up your set of recommendations on what to do and be prepared to give your action agenda. This is really the most crucial part of the process; diagnosis divorced from corrective action is sterile. But bear in mind that proposing realistic, workable solutions and offering a hasty, ill-conceived "possibility" are not the same thing. Don't recommend anything you would not be prepared to do yourself if you were in the decision maker's shoes. Be sure you can give reasons that your recommendations are preferable to other options which exist.

On a few occasions, some desirable information may not be included in the case. In such instances, you may be inclined to complain about the lack of facts. A manager, however, uses more than facts upon which to base his or her decision. Moreover, it may be possible to make a number of inferences from the facts you do have. So be wary of rushing to include as part of your recommendations the need to get more information. From time to time, of course, a search for additional facts or information may be entirely appropriate, but you must also recognize that the organization's managers may not have had any more information available than that presented in the case. Before recommending that action be postponed until additional facts are uncovered, be sure that you think it will be worthwhile to get them and that the organization can afford to wait. In general, though, try to recommend a course of action on the basis of the evidence you have at hand.

Again, remember that rarely is there a "right" decision or just one "optimal" plan of action or an "approved" solution. Your goal should be to develop what you think is a pragmatic, defensible course of action based upon a serious analysis of the situation and appearing to you to be right in view of your assessment of the facts. Admittedly, someone else may evaluate the same facts in another way and thus have a different right solution, but since several good plans of action can normally be conceived, you should not be afraid to stick by your own analysis and judgement. One can make a strong argument for the view that the right answer for a manager is the one that he or she can propose, explain, defend, and make work when it is implemented. This is the middle ground we support between the "no right answer" and "one right answer" schools of thought. Clearly, some answers are better than others.

■ The Classroom Experience

In experiencing class discussion of management cases, you will, in all probability, notice very quickly that you will not have thought of everything in the case that your follow students think of. While you will see things others did not, they will see things you did not. Do not be dismayed or alarmed by this. It is normal. As the adage goes, "Two heads are better than one." So it is to be expected that the class as a whole will do a more penetrating and searching job of case analysis than any one person working alone. This is the power of group effort, and one of its virtues is that it will give you more insight into the variety of approaches and how to cope with differences of opinion. Second, you will see better why sometimes it is not managerially wise to assume a rigid position on an issue until a full range of views and information has been assembled. And undoubtedly, somewhere along the way, you will begin to recognize that neither the instructor nor other students in the class have all the answers, and even if they think they do you are free to present and hold to your own views. The truth in the saying "There's more than one way to skin a cat" will be seen to apply nicely to most management situations.

For class discussion of cases to be useful and stimulating, you need to keep the following points in mind:

1. The case method enlists a maximum of individual participation in class discussion. It is not enough to be present as a silent observer; if every student took this approach, there would be no discussion. (Thus, do not be surprised if a portion of your grade is based on your participation in case discussions.)

2. Although you should do independent work and independent thinking, don't hesitate to discuss the case with other students. Managers often discuss their problems with other key people.

3. During case discussions, expect and tolerate challenges to the views expressed. Be willing to submit your conclusions for scrutiny and rebuttal. State your views without fear of disapproval and overcome the hesitation to speak out.

4. In orally presenting and defending your ideas, strive to be convincing and persuasive. Always give supporting evidence and reasons.

5. Expect the instructor to assume the role of extensive questioner and listener. Expect to be cross-examined for evidence and reasons by your instructor or by others in the class. Expect students to dominate the discussion and do most of the talking.

6. Although discussion of a case is a group process, this does not imply conformity to group opinion. Learning respect for the views and approaches of others is an integral part of case analysis exercises. But be willing to "swim against the tide" of majority opinion. In the practice of management, there is always room for originality, unorthodoxy, and unique personality.

7. In participating in the discussion, make a conscious effort to *contribute* rather than just talk. There is a big difference between saying something that builds the discussion and offering a long-winded, off-the-cuff remark that leaves the class wondering what the point was.

8. Effective case discussion can occur only if participants have the facts of the case well in hand; rehashing information in the case should be held to a minimum except as it provides documentation, comparisons, or support for your position. In making your point, assume that everyone has read the case and knows "what the case says."

9. During the discussion, new insights provided by the group's efforts are likely to emerge. Don't be alarmed or surprised if you and others in the class change your mind about some things as the discussion unfolds. Be alert for how these changes affect your analysis and recommendations (in case you are called on to speak).

10. Although there will always be situations in which more technical information is imperative to make an intelligent decision, try not to shirk from making decisions with incomplete information. Incomplete information is a normal condition managers face and it is something you should get used to.

◼ Preparing a Written Case Analysis

From time to time, your instructor may ask you to prepare a written analysis of the case assignment. Preparing a written case analysis is much like preparing a case for class discussion, except that your analysis, when completed, must be reduced to writing. Just as there was no set formula for preparing a case for oral discussion, there is no ironclad procedure for doing a written case analysis. With a bit of experience, you will arrive at your own preferred method of attack in writing up a case, and you will learn to adjust your approach to the unique aspects each case presents.

Your instructor may assign you a specific topic around which to prepare your written report. Common assignments include: (1) Identify and evaluate company X's corporate strategy. (2) In view of the opportunities and risks you see in the industry, what is your assessment of the company's position and strategy? (3) How would you size up the strategic situation of company Y? (4) What recommendation would you make to company Z's top management? (5) What specific functions and activities does the company have to perform especially well in order for its strategy to succeed?

Alternatively, you may be asked to do a comprehensive written case analysis. It is typical for a comprehensive written case analysis to emphasize four things:

1. Identification
2. Analysis and evaluation
3. Discussion of alternatives
4. Presentation of recommendations

You may wish to consider the following pointers in preparing a comprehensive written case analysis.[4]

Identification. It is essential that your paper reflect a sharply focused diagnosis of strategic issues and key problems and, further, that you demonstrate good business judgement in sizing up the company's present situation. Make sure you understand and can identify the firm's strategy (see Chapters 1, 3, 4, and 5). You would probably be well advised to begin your paper by sizing up the company's situation, its strategy, and the significant problems and issues that confront management. State problems/issues as clearly and precisely as you can. Unless it is necessary to do so for emphasis, avoid recounting facts and history about the company (assume your professor has read the case and is familiar with the organization!).

Analysis and Evaluation. Very likely, you will find this section the hardest part of the report. Analysis is hard work! Study the tables, exhibits, and financial statements in the case carefully. Check out the firm's financial ratios, its profit margins and rates of return, and its capital structure and decide how strong the firm is financially. (Exhibit 2-1 contains a summary of various financial ratios and how they are calculated.) Similarly, look at marketing, production, managerial competence, and so on, and evaluate the factors underlying the organization's successes and failures. Decide whether it has a distinctive competence and, if so, whether it is capitalizing upon it. Check out the quality of the firm's business portfolio.

Check to see if the firm's strategy at all levels is working and determine the reasons why or why not. An initial analytical tool that can be used is *SWOT analysis,* which involves appraising the firm's internal *strengths* and *weaknesses* and assessing external environmental *opportunities* and *threats;* see Exhibit 2-2 for suggestions of what to look for. It must be stressed that SWOT analysis is just a preliminary analytical tool. It must be supplemented

---

[4] For some additional ideas and viewpoints, you may wish to consult Thomas J. Raymond, "Written analysis of cases," in McNair, *The Case Method at the Harvard Business School,* pp. 139–163. In Raymond's article is an actual case, a sample analysis of it, and a sample of a student's written report on it.

EXHIBIT 2-1 A Summary of Key Financial Ratios, How They Are Calculated, and What They Show

Ratio	How Calculated	What It Shows
Profitability Ratios		
1. Gross profit margin	$$\frac{\text{Sales} - \text{Cost of goods sold}}{\text{Sales}}$$	An indication of the total margin available to cover operating expenses and yield a profit.
2. Operating profit margin	$$\frac{\text{Profit before taxes and before interest}}{\text{Sales}}$$	An indication of the firm's profitability from current operations without regard to the interest charges accruing from the capital structure. (Helps to assess impact of different capital structures.)
3. Net profit margin (or return on sales)	$$\frac{\text{Profits after taxes}}{\text{Sales}}$$	After-tax profits per dollar of sales. Sub-par profit margins indicate that the firm's sales prices are relatively low or that its costs are relatively high or both.
4. Return on total assets	$$\frac{\text{Profits after taxes}}{\text{Total assets}}$$ $$or$$ $$\frac{\text{Profits after taxes} + \text{Interest}}{\text{Total assets}}$$	A measure of the return on total investment in the enterprise. It is sometimes desirable to add interest to after-tax profits to form the numerator of the ratio, since total assets are financed by creditors as well as by stockholders; hence, it is accurate to measure the productivity of assets by the returns provided to both classes of investors.
5. Return on stockholders' equity (or return on net worth)	$$\frac{\text{Profits after taxes}}{\text{Total stockholders' equity}}$$	A measure of the rate of return on stockholders' investment in the enterprise.
6. Return on common equity	$$\frac{\text{Profits after taxes} - \text{Preferred stock dividends}}{\text{Total stockholders' equity} - \text{Par value of preferred stock}}$$	A measure of the rate of return on the investment that the owners of common stock have made in the enterprise.
7. Earnings per share	$$\frac{\text{Profits after taxes} - \text{Preferred stock dividends}}{\text{Number of shares of common stock outstanding}}$$	The earnings available to the owners of common stock.
Liquidity Ratios		
1. Current ratio	$$\frac{\text{Current assets}}{\text{Current liabilities}}$$	The extent to which the claims of short-term creditors are covered by assets expected to be converted to cash in a period roughly corresponding to the maturity of the liabilities.
2. Quick ratio (or acid-test ratio)	$$\frac{\text{Current assets} - \text{Inventory}}{\text{Current liabilities}}$$	A measure of the firm's ability to pay off short-term obligations without relying upon the sale of its inventories.

EXHIBIT 2-1 *continued*

Ratio	How Calculated	What It Shows
3. Inventory-to-net-working-capital ratio	$$\dfrac{\text{Inventory}}{\text{Current assets} - \text{Current liabilities}}$$	A measure of the extent to which the firm's working capital is tied up in inventory.
Leverage Ratios		
1. Debt-to-assets ratio	$$\dfrac{\text{Total debt}}{\text{Total assets}}$$	A measure of the extent to which borrowed funds have been used to finance the firm's operations.
2. Debt-to-equity ratio	$$\dfrac{\text{Total debt}}{\text{Total stockholders' equity}}$$	Another measure of the funds provided by creditors versus the funds provided by owners.
3. Long-term-debt-to-equity ratio	$$\dfrac{\text{Long-term debt}}{\text{Total stockholders' equity}}$$	A widely used measure of the balance between debt and equity in the firm's long-term capital structure.
4. Times-interest-earned (or coverage) ratios	$$\dfrac{\text{Profits before interest and taxes}}{\text{Total interest charges}}$$	A measure of the extent to which earnings can decline without the firm becoming unable to met its annual interest costs.
5. Fixed-charge coverage	$$\dfrac{\text{Profits before taxes and interest} \div \text{Lease obligations}}{\text{Total interest charges} \div \text{Lease obligations}}$$	A more inclusive indication of the firm's ability to meet all of its fixed-charge obligations.
Activity Ratios		
1. Inventory turnover	$$\dfrac{\text{Sales}}{\text{Inventory of finished goods}}$$	When compared to industry averages, provides an indication of whether a company has excessive or inadequate finished goods inventory.
2. Fixed-assets turnover	$$\dfrac{\text{Sales}}{\text{Fixed assets}}$$	A measure of the sales productivity and utilization of plant and equipment.
3. Total-assets turnover	$$\dfrac{\text{Sales}}{\text{Total assets}}$$	A measure of the utilization of all the firm's assets. A ratio below the industry average indicates that the company is not generating a sufficient volume of business given the size of its asset investment.
4. Accounts receivable turnover	$$\dfrac{\text{Annual credit sales}}{\text{Accounts receivable}}$$	A measure of the average length of time it takes the firm to collect the sales made on credit.
5. Average collection period	$$\dfrac{\text{Accounts receivable}}{\text{Total sales} \div 365}$$ *or* $$\dfrac{\text{Accounts receivable}}{\text{Average daily sales}}$$	The average length of time the firm must wait after making a sale before it receives payment.

EXHIBIT 2-1   *continued*

Ratio	How Calculated	What It Shows
Other Ratios		
1. Dividend yield on common stock	$$\frac{\text{Annual dividends per share}}{\text{Current market price per share}}$$	A measure of the return to owners received in the form of dividends.
2. Price-earnings ratio	$$\frac{\text{Current market price per share}}{\text{After-tax earnings per share}}$$	Faster-growing or less-risky firms tend to have higher price-earnings ratios than slower-growing or more-risky firms.
3. Dividend-payout ratio	$$\frac{\text{Annual dividends per share}}{\text{After-tax earning per share}}$$	The percentages of profits paid out as dividends.
4. Cash flow per share	$$\frac{\text{After-tax profits + Depreciation}}{\text{Number of common shares outstanding}}$$	A measure of the discretionary funds over and above expenses available for use by the firm.
5. Break-even analysis	$$\frac{\text{Fixed costs}}{\text{Contribution margin/unit}}$$ (Selling price/unit – Variable cost/unit)	A measure of how many units must be sold to begin to make a profit; to demonstrate the relationship of revenue, expenses, and net income.

Note: Industry-average ratios against which a particular company's ratios may be judged are available in the following:
1. Statistics Canada, *Corporation Financial Statistics* (15 ratios for 182 industries).
2. *Key Business Ratios*, published by Dun and Bradstreet Canada (11 ratios for 166 lines of business).
3. Statistics Canada, *Market Research Handbook* (7 ratios for 23 industries).
4. The Financial Post, *Industry Reports* (35 ratios for 19 industries and latest quarterly results for top public firms in industry).
5. *Almanac of Business and Industry Financial Ratios* (14 ratios, 13 trend indicators, and 23 average balance sheet and income statement values, for over 180 industries).

with more rigorous competitive, resource, financial, organizational, etc. analysis. An analysis should also possibly incorporate a competitive analysis of the competitive forces impinging on the firm (you may want to draw up a strategic group map as in Exhibit 3-3 and/or do an industry analysis as in Exhibit 3-1, in Chapter 3). Decide whether and why the firm's competitive position is getting stronger or weaker. Subsequent chapters develop more detailed and specialized analytical tools to assess many of the relationships. Review those chapters to see if you have overlooked some aspect of strategy evaluation. Try to decide whether the main problems revolve around a need to revise strategy, a need to improve strategy implementation, or both.

Using the Internet to Research Companies and Industries

The Internet is a very good tool for getting specific information on companies and industries. Many large companies have Internet sites, and there are many business news and information services that provide supplementary

EXHIBIT 2-2   The SWOT Analysis, with Suggestions of What to Look For

INTERNAL COMPANY ANALYSIS

Strengths
- Adequate financial resources?
- Well thought of by buyers?
- An acknowledged market leader?
- Well-conceived functional area strategies?
- Access to economies of scale?
- Insulated (at least somewhat) from strong competitive pressure?
- Proprietary technology?
- Cost advantages?
- Product innovation abilities?
- Proven management?
- Other?

Weaknesses
- No clear strategic direction?
- Obsolete facilities?
- Lack of managerial depth and talent?
- Missing any key skills or competencies?
- Poor track record in implementing strategy?
- Plagued with internal operating problems?
- Falling behind in R&D?
- Too narrow a product line?
- Weak market image?
- Unable to finance needed changes in strategy?
- Below-average marketing skills?
- Other?

EXTERNAL ENVIRONMENTAL ANALYSIS

Opportunities
- Serve additional customer groups?
- Enter new markets or segments?
- Expand product line to meet broader range or customer needs?
- Diversify into related products?
- Add complementary products?
- Vertical integration?
- Ability to move to better strategic group?
- Complacency among rival firms?
- Faster market growth?
- Other?

Threats
- Likely entry of new competitors?
- Rising sales of substitute products?
- Slower market growth?
- Adverse government policies?
- Growing competitive pressures?
- Vulnerability to recession and business cycle?
- Growing bargaining power of customers or suppliers?
- Changing buyer needs and tastes?
- Adverse demographic changes?
- Other?

information for your case analysis. The best way to find a company site is to use a search engine. Some of the more popular web catalogues and search engines are the following:

Site	Description		Address
AltaVista	Digital Equipment's search engine	Canada:	http://www.altavistacanada.com/
		United States:	http://www.altavista.digital.com/
Yahoo!	A catalogue of valuable web sites	Canada:	http://www.yahoo.ca/
		United States:	http://www.yahoo.com/
Lycos	Another web site catalogue		http://www.lycos.com/
Excite	A full-text search engine		http://www.excite.com/
Infoseek	A natural-language search engine		http://www.infoseek.com/

In addition, there are a variety of web sites that should be of interest to the student—some include company financial reports, some include business news, and some include articles on business issues and techniques. A few of the important sites are given in Exhibit 2-3.

EXHIBIT 2-3

Canadian Information
- Canoe News   http://www.canoe.com/
- Globe and Mail News   http://www.globeandmail.ca/
- Les Affairs   http://www.lesaffaires.com/
- Canadian Industry Information   http://strategis.ic.gc.ca/engdoc/main.html
- Canadian Business Magazine   http://www.canbus.com/
- Canadian Financial Network   http://www.canadianfinance.com/
- Canadian Deposit Insurance Corp   http://www.cdic.ca/
- Toronto Stock Exchange   http://www.TSE.com/
- Vancouver Stock Exchange   http://www.VSE.com/

U.S. Information
- SEC EDGAR database   http://www.sec.gov/cgi-bin/srch-edgar/
- NASDAQ   http://www.nasdaq.com/
- The Financial News Network   http://cnnfn.com/
- Hoover's Online   http://hoovers.com/
- American Demographics/Marketing Tools   http://www.marketingtools.com/
- Industry Net   http://www.industry.net/
- Wall Street Journal   http://update.wsj.com/
- Business Week   http://businessweek.com/
- Fortune   http://www.pathfinder.com/@@cUyeVQQAtmYhdMyb/fortune/
- International Business Resources   http://ciber.bus.msu.edu/busref.html/

Analysis and Evaluation

In writing your analysis and evaluation, bear in mind:

1. You are obliged to offer supporting evidence for your views and judgements. Do not rely upon unsupported opinions, overgeneralizations, and platitudes as a substitute for tight, logical argument backed up with facts and figures.

2. If your analysis involves some important quantitative calculations, then you should use tables and charts to present the data clearly and efficiently. Don't just tack the exhibits on at the end of your report and let the reader figure out what they mean and why they were included. Instead, in the body of your report, cite some of the key numbers, summarize the conclusions to be drawn from the exhibits, and refer the reader to them for more details.

3. You should indicate you have command of the economics of the business and the key factors that are crucial to the organization's success or failure. Check to see that your analysis states what the company needs to concentrate on in order to be a higher performer.

4. Your interpretation of the evidence should be reasonable and objective. Be wary of preparing a one-sided argument that omits all aspects not favourable to your conclusion. Likewise, try not to exaggerate or overdramatize. Endeavor to inject balance into your analysis and avoid emotional rhetoric. Strive to display good business judgement.

Discussion of Alternatives.   There are typically many more alternatives available than a cursory study of the case reveals. A thorough case analysis should include a discussion of all major alternatives. It is important that meaningful differences exist between all of them. In addition, the discussion of alternatives must go beyond the following:

- Doing nothing
- Doing something obviously inappropriate
- The alternative recommended

Each alternative discussed should be analyzed in terms of its associated pros and cons.

Recommendations.   The final section of the written case analysis should consist of a set of definite recommendations and a plan of action. Your recommendations should address all of the problems/issues you identified and analyzed. If the recommendations come as a surprise, or do not follow logically from the analysis, the effect is to weaken greatly your suggestions of what to do. Obviously, your recommendations for action should offer a reasonable prospect of success. State what you think the consequences of your recommendations will be and indicate how your recommendations will solve the problems you identified. *Be sure that the company is financially able to carry out what you recommend.* Also check to see if your recommendations are workable in terms of acceptance by the persons involved, the organization's competence to implement them, and prevailing market and environmental constraints. Unless you feel justifiably *compelled* to do so, do not qualify, hedge, or weasel on the actions you believe should be taken.

Furthermore, state your recommendations in sufficient detail to be meaningful—get down to some operational-level details. Avoid such unhelpful statements as "The organization should do more planning" or "The company should be more aggressive in marketing its product." State *specifically* what should be done and *make sure your recommendations are operational and provide the manager with specific considerations that he or she can implement.* For instance, do not stop after saying "The firm should improve its market position"; continue with exactly how you think this should be done.

Finally, you should say something about how your plan is to be implemented. Here you may wish to offer a definite agenda, stipulating a timetable and sequence for each action, indicating priorities and suggesting who should be responsible for doing what. For example, "Manager X should take the following steps: (1) _____, (2) _____, (3) _____ and (4) _____." One way to organize your recommendations is in a one-page summary according to the chart in Exhibit 2-4.

A key element in the recommendation summary is to assess the financial implications of each recommendation. Any proposed strategy must be feasible, which means, among other things, that the organization must be able to afford it. In addition, when there are major uncertainties, particularly in the medium-to-long term, contingency plans should be specified, that is, "If such and such transpires, then do X."

In preparing your plan of action, remember there is a great deal of difference between, on the one hand, being responsible for a decision that may be costly if it proves in error and, on the other, expressing a casual opinion as to

EXHIBIT 2-4   **Organizing Recommendations**

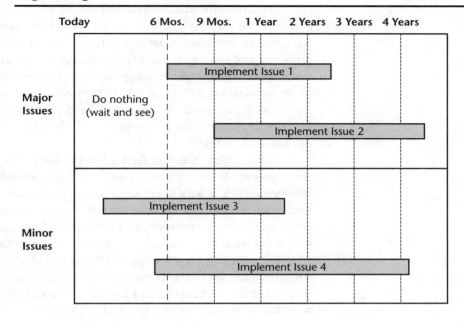

How to Use This Framework: After separating the major from the minor issues, each issue is plotted according to timing. The bar indicates the period over which this issue will he resolved. Inside each bar should be noted the title of the issue and the cost (financial, managerial, and so forth) of implementation. This framework allows us to assess on one page the reasonableness of whatever organizational recommendations are being made.

some of the courses of action that might be taken when you do not have to bear the responsibility for any of the consequences. A good rule to follow in making your recommendations is to avoid recommending anything you would not yourself be willing to do if you were in management's shoes. The importance of learning to develop good judgement in a managerial situation is indicated by the fact that while the same information and operating data may be available to every manager or executive in an organization, the quality of the judgements about what the information means and what actions need to be taken do vary from person to person.[5] Developing good judgement is thus essential.

It goes without saying that your report should be organized and written in a manner that communicates well and is persuasive. Great ideas amount to little unless others can be convinced of their merit; this takes effective communication.

◖ Keeping Tabs on Your Performance

Every instructor has his or her own procedure for evaluating student performance, so, with one exception, it is not possible to generalize about grades and the grading of case analyses. The one exception is that grades on case analyses

---

[5] Gragg, "Because wisdom can't be told," p. 10.

(written or oral) almost never depend entirely on how you propose to solve the organization's difficulties. The important elements in evaluating student performance on case analysts consist of (1) the care with which facts and background knowledge are used, (2) demonstration of the ability to state problems and issues clearly, (3) use of appropriate analytical techniques, (4) evidence of sound logic and argument, (5) consistency between analysis and recommendations, and (6) ability to formulate reasonable and feasible recommendations for action. Remember, a hard-hitting, incisive, logical approach will almost always triumph over a seat-of-the-pants opinion, emotional rhetoric, and platitudes.

One final point. You may find it hard to keep a finger on the pulse of how much you are learning from cases. This contrasts with lecture/problem/discussion courses, where experience has given you an intuitive feeling for how well you are acquiring substantive knowledge of theoretical concepts, problem-solving techniques, and institutional practices. But in a case course, where analytical ability and the skill of making sound judgements are less apparent, you may lack a sense of solid accomplishment, at least at first. Admittedly, additions to one's managerial skills and powers of diagnosis are not as noticeable or as tangible as a looseleaf-binder-full of lecture notes. But this does not mean they are any less real or that you are making any less progress in learning how to be a manager.

To begin with, in the process of hunting around for solutions, very likely you will find that considerable knowledge about types of organizations, the nature of various businesses, the range of management practices, and so on has rubbed off. Moreover, you will be gaining a better grasp of how to evaluate risks and cope with the uncertainties of enterprise. Likewise, you will develop a sharper appreciation of both the common and the unique aspects of managerial encounters. You will become more comfortable with the processes whereby objectives are set, strategies are initiated, organizations are designed, methods of control are implemented and evaluated, performance is reappraised, and improvements are sought. Such processes are the essence of strategic management, and learning more about them through the case method is no less an achievement just because there is a dearth of finely calibrated measuring devices and authoritative crutches on which to lean.

RECOMMENDED READINGS

Reid, Beverly. *Essentials of Business Writing and Speaking: A Canadian Guide.* Mississauga, Ont.: Copp Clark Pitman, 1989.

Treece, Malra, and Larry Hartman. *Effective Reports for Managerial Communication.* 3rd ed. Boston, Mass.: Allyn and Bacon, 1991.

CHAPTER 3

Strategy Formulation and Environment

After a small period of organized order in the telecommunications industry, we are now in a period you could almost call chaos.

Jean Monty, President and CEO of BCE

Its only the second inning and this is a world that can change overnight. ... I'm not going to let you sneak up on me like we snuck up on Compuserve or Prodigy.

Steve Case, CEO of America Online

In formulating a strategy, the effective general manager makes strategic choices that are consistent with the industry and competitive environment the firm operates within. This chapter will consider a variety of analytical approaches that help managers assess the strength of the competition and the attractiveness of an industry. The first step in the analysis requires the student to gain some understanding of the general trends in the industry. This step is used to gather basic industry and economic information related to the industry and most managers have much of this overview information at their fingertips because of their experience in the industry. After becoming familiar with industry basics, the analysis looks at factors that influence the competitive nature in the industry. Next critical industry characteristics are analyzed to give the manager an understanding of what might be strategically important in the future. The final step in the analysis assesses both the overall strength of the competition and the attractiveness of the industry. This final step provides a solid basis upon which internal strategic analysis can then be formulated and eventually implemented.

◖ Overview of the Industry

All managers must understand the environment in which they are doing business. Prior to getting into the details of an environmental analysis one must understand the basic economic characteristics of an industry. Such a basic understanding allows the manager to better understand the subsequent competitive and industry analysis. Basic economic characteristics that should be identified include the market size and growth, the industry's geographic scope, the number of competitors in an industry, the number and sizes of the buyers and sellers, the pace of technological change and innovation, scale economies, experience curve effects, capital requirements, etc. The question that must always be in the mind of the manager when studying these basic economic characteristics is "What are the industry's dominant economic traits?"

Analysis of Competition

When analyzing the industry's competitive environment, students must consider two strategic notions: the industry *competitive forces* and industry *competitive positions,* which create strategic groups. Normally, it is advantageous to initially examine and fully describe the competitive positions in an industry. Then the competitive analysis can be completed by examining the competitive advantages of the industry and firm, as well as the competitive forces impinging on them. This section will adhere to this stepwise competitive analysis approach. The goal of this section is to answer the question "What is the competition like and how strong are each of the competitive forces?"

Analyzing Industry Competitive Forces

One of the most fundamental tools for assessing competitive advantages is Porter's Five Forces Model, shown in Exhibit 3-1.[1] This model describes five forces that influence the competitive pressures a firm experiences given its competitive position and advantages: (1) the threat of new entrants, (2) the threat of substitutes, (3) the bargaining power of buyers, (4) the bargaining power of suppliers, and (5) internal industry competition and rivalry. Each of these forces, in turn, can be broken down into various intrinsic elements of competition as outlined in Exhibit 3-2.

---

[1] Michael Porter, *Competitive Strategy: Techniques for Analyzing Industries and Competitors* (New York: Free Press, 1980), Chap. 11.

EXHIBIT 3-1   Competitive Forces in an Industry Structure

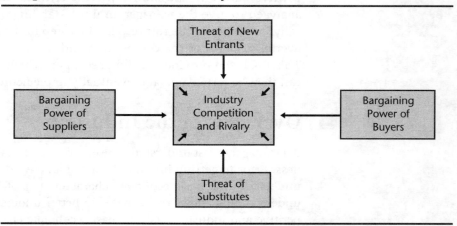

Exhibit 3-2 also illustrates how one can do a "quick and dirty" analysis of the competitive forces impinging on an industry, and thus, a firm. To use this worksheet, select the applicable elements of competition and then rate them on competitive advantage (strength) or disadvantage (threat) as either high or low (i.e., from 1 to 5). Then each competitive force can be assessed as well as the overall competitive tension in the industry now and in the long term.

This framework also provides some clues about how a firm can attempt to change the way business is done in an industry so as to minimize competitive forces. For example, if a business can develop competitive advantages that increase the barriers to entry, the competitive forces will be reduced for the firm and the industry. A *barrier to entry* is a costly obstacle that firms must overcome if they want to compete in an industry. Thus, the competitive forces framework provides a good analytical point for the manager to start assessing the industry's present competitive situation.

International Competitive Analysis

In analyzing an industry, it is useful to determine if the industry has international competitors. Often managers focus on local competition and neglect international competitors who may be changing the way the industry is competing.

Some industries are intrinsically international. These are called global industries and competitors must have globally competitive operations to compete effectively. An industry can be considered global if the product/service has worldwide demand, production economies of scale exist, there is no complex segmentation within markets, and few trade barriers exist. Firms in global industries must generally be true multinationals (that is, production and marketing are carried out in several foreign countries) in order to compete successfully. Examples of globally oriented Canadian firms are Northern Telecom, Alcan, and Bombardier.

In addition, tracking international competition may allow a firm to understand how an industry and specific regional groups of firms within an industry are developing competitive advantages. Competitive advantages at the firm level can be enhanced or developed by country-based competitive advantages—advantages derived from regional specific advantages that tend to increase the competitive capabilities of firms operating in the region. The main types of country-based advantages are the following:[2]

- Natural resource advantages: lumber, water, minerals, agricultural, tourism attractions (e.g., beaches), etc.

- Infrastructure advantages: transportation routes, educational capabilities, government support, economic stability, telecommunications, etc.

- Market and customer advantages: sophistication, size, growth, inquisitiveness, willingness to try new things, desire for unique qualities, etc.

---

[2] Michael Porter, *The Competitive Advantage of Nations* (New York: Free Press, 1990).

EXHIBIT 3-2 Worksheet for Competitive Forces in an Industry

Elements	Competitiveness Rating				
Determinants of Threat of New Competitors (i.e., entry barriers)	Low				High
1. Economies of scale	1	2	3	4	5
2. Proprietary; product differences	1	2	3	4	5
3. Brand identity	1	2	3	4	5
4. Switching costs	1	2	3	4	5
5. Capital requirements	1	2	3	4	5
6. Access to distribution	1	2	3	4	5
7. Absolute cost advantages					
• Proprietary learning curve	1	2	3	4	5
• Access to necessary inputs	1	2	3	4	5
• Proprietary low-cost product design	1	2	3	4	5
8. Government policy	1	2	3	4	5
9. Expected retaliation	1	2	3	4	5
Determinants of Industry Internal Competitive Rivalry					
1. Stage of industry growth	1	2	3	4	5
2. Fixed (or storage) costs/value added	1	2	3	4	5
3. Intermittent overcapacity and fixed costs of capacity	1	2	3	4	5
4. Product/service differences or differentiation	1	2	3	4	5
5. Brand identity and reputation	1	2	3	4	5
6. Costs of switching brands to the customer	1	2	3	4	5
7. Number of competitors and equality of competitive advantages	1	2	3	4	5
8. Difficulty of knowing about competitors	1	2	3	4	5
9. Diversity of competitors	1	2	3	4	5
10. Corporate risk and stakes	1	2	3	4	5
11. Exit barriers	1	2	3	4	5
Determinants of Substitution Threat					
1. Relative price performance of substitutes	1	2	3	4	5
2. Switching costs of customers to substitutes	1	2	3	4	5
3. Buyer propensity to substitute	1	2	3	4	5
Determinants of Supplier Power					
1. Differentiation of inputs	1	2	3	4	5
2. Switching costs of suppliers and firms in the industry	1	2	3	4	5
3. Presence of substitute inputs or suppliers	1	2	3	4	5
4. Supplier concentration	1	2	3	4	5
5. Importance of volume to supplier	1	2	3	4	5
6. Cost relative to total purchases in the industry	1	2	3	4	5
7. Impact of inputs on cost or differentiation	1	2	3	4	5
8. Threat of forward integration relative to threat of backward integration by firms in the industry	1	2	3	4	5
Determinants of Buying Power					
Bargaining leverage					
1. Buyer concentration versus firm concentration	1	2	3	4	5
2. Buyer volume	1	2	3	4	5
3. Buyer switching costs relative to firm switching costs	1	2	3	4	5
4. Buyer information	1	2	3	4	5
5. Ability to backward-integrate	1	2	3	4	5
6. Substitute products	1	2	3	4	5
7. Pull-through marketing	1	2	3	4	5
Price sensitivity					
8. Price/total purchases	1	2	3	4	5
9. Product differences	1	2	3	4	5
10. Brand identity	1	2	3	4	5
11. Impact on quality/performance	1	2	3	4	5
12. Buyer profits	1	2	3	4	5
13. Decision makers' incentives	1	2	3	4	5

Source: Adapted from Michael E. Porter, *Competitive Advantage: Creating and Sustaining Superior Performance* (New York: The Free Press, a Division of Macmillan Inc., 1985).

- Buyer and supplier advantages: relationships, competencies and skills developed, unique value of product or service provided, etc.
- Industry-specific advantages: competitiveness, sophistication, skills development, strategies developed, unique value of product or service, etc.
- Cultural and social advantages: Motivation, creativeness, cooperation, and innate skills of people, etc.

Examples of companies using these locationally specific advantages are resource-based industries (e.g., ones located in resource-rich regions), high-tech industries (e.g., ones located in Silicon Valley where certain high-tech knowledge is particularly abundant), and industrial design industries (e.g., ones located in Italy where creativity and art are particularly valued cultural attributes). Managers can benefit from trying to define international competitors' locational or country-based sources of advantages.

Analyzing an Industry's Strategic Groups and Competitive Position

In Chapter 1, competitive position was described in terms of a company's competitive and customer focus relative to its competition. Such an analysis is also very helpful at the industry level of analysis. It helps define patterns of competition and customer focus, and allows managers to further assess the competitive pressures as well as the market opportunities that may be present because of certain competitive patterns in the industry. There are a variety of ways in which one can assess firms' competitive position in an industry. Two of the most common techniques are the competitive position matrix and the strategic group map or analysis.

The *competitive position matrix* compares the competitors in an industry, highlighting each firm's relevant competitive dimensions. To develop a matrix, we must first discern the important competitive dimensions consequential to potential customers; these could be price, product/service characteristics, product/service scope, or geographic scope. In addition, many managers also consider competitive advantages that differentiate the competitors; these are used to further differentiate the firms in the industry. Exhibit 3-3 provides an example of a competitive position matrix for part of the Canadian newspaper industry.

When an industry has many similar firms, it is often more useful to combine the firms into groups having comparable competitive characteristics and market positions. These groups are called *strategic groups* and they represent firms that compete in the same market segment, for similar customers, and using similar competitive advantages. This *strategic group analysis or map* approach serves the same purpose as the competitive position matrix. The strategic group map tends to emphasize competitive dimensions that are barriers to entry between the various groups, thus making it costly to move between groups. Exhibit 3-4 provides an example of a strategic group map using the Canadian furniture retail industry.

EXHIBIT 3-3   Competitive Position Matrix: A Sample of the Canadian Newspaper
             Industry, 1994

Competition	Geographic Scope	Price	Delivery Schedule	Editorial Policy	Customer Focus
Toronto Star	National	$0.75	Daily—Morning	Liberal	Broad
Globe and Mail	National	$0.75	Daily—Morning	Conservative	Broad, business
Vancouver Sun	Regional—B.C	$0.65	Daily—Morning	Very liberal	Broad, blue-collar
Ottawa Citizen	Regional—Ottawa region	$0.65	Daily—Morning	Conservative, regional and local news	Broad, regional and local readers
Oshawa Times	Regional/local—Oshawa region	$0.65	Daily—Evening	Conservative, regional and local news	Broad, regional and local readers
The Penny Saver	Regional	Free	Weekly	Advertisements	Buyers of new and used goods and services
University Students Gazette	University campus	Free	Weekly	Very liberal	Young—students
Computing Times	National	Free	Monthly	Computer focus	Computer users and literate

One constraint of the strategic group map is that only two dimensions can be represented simultaneously. This limits the descriptive capacity of this approach and it means the analyst must carefully select the dimensions in the map to represent the key strategic dimensions in the industry. The competitive dimensions that were deemed to be important in the Canadian furniture retail business were price/quality and product/service scope or mix.

Once a manager has defined the competitive position of the firm, he or she should attempt to delineate some of the fundamental characteristics of the customers being served in that competitive position. Some of the important characteristics would be the size of the market, the firm's market share, the market growth, and the buying characteristics and desires of the customers being serviced in that competitive position. The manager may also want to look at some of the characteristics of "nearby" competitive positions to see if a movement in some direction might improve their performance.

After having described the competitive position of the firm and its competitors, we should have a good understanding of the business/market focus of the firm and its competitors. It is important to have this understanding before moving on to analyzing the competitive influences and pressures in the industry.

Not-for-Profit Organizational Competitive Position Analysis

Analyzing a not-for-profit organization's market and competitors is a little different from a for-profit organization because the former faces competition from

EXHIBIT 3-4   **Illustrative Strategic Group Map of Competitors in Canadian Furniture Retail Business**

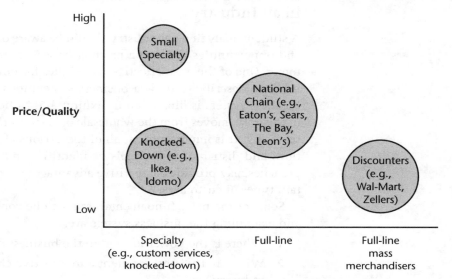

two directions, customers and fundraising. Customer needs (e.g., community needs) may be satisfied by a number of competing organizations. Hence, the not-for-profit organization has to find a unique set of needs that it can satisfy most effectively in the community. Often a market analysis, called a *needs assessment,* is completed prior to setting up new not-for-profit organizations and programs. A needs assessment uses community focus groups, interviews, and questionnaires to evaluate the community's needs in specific areas such as health care or social assistance. During this process, it is important to clarify where other competing organizations overlap or make redundant the need being assessed. The managers can then decide if there is a viable market position that has not been satisfied in the community. Another alternative is for the competing organizations to co-operate and, thus, improve the delivery and content of needs provision to the community.

Competition for fundraising is also an issue for competitive analysis. Some organizations are privately funded while others are publicly funded. In addition, organizations take on different marketing approaches. Certain not-for-profit programs rely on the community member's philanthropic values for funding while other, more entertainment-based organizations, such as theatres, tend to rely on advertising and the quality of the product and service to get funding. Whether it is a value-based or product/service-based pitch, a manager must clearly map out various funding sources, and attempt to position their organization so that new sources and techniques for fundraising are successful.

Analysis of Critical Industry Characteristics

Analyzing the Supply and Distribution Systems in an Industry

A student analyzing an industry should be aware of all of the various options and opportunities to move a product or service from inception to the customer. One of the most effective techniques for developing this understanding is to describe or draw a business system for the industry. An industry business system is illustrated in Exhibit 3-5. Notice how the product, a rug in this case, moves from the wholesale operations right through to after-sales servicing. It is important that all of the various channels of supply, product flow, and distribution channels be identified in an industry, as certain approaches may provide competitive advantages to companies focusing on certain types of customers.

Some of the more fundamental issues to be considered when developing and examining the business system are:

1. Where is the power located in the business system?
2. What are the most efficient and effective channels to use in the industry?
3. Are specific channels more effective and efficient for targeting specific customers (i.e., competitive positions in the marketplace)?
4. Have any of the firms vertically integrated into different activities of the business system and will this provide an advantage or disadvantage?
5. Are there any new types of channels of supply or distribution that are not being used in the industry, but might prove to be effective?

Product Life Cycle

Another major element of industry environment analysis is the product/market life cycle. This analytical tool, illustrated in Exhibit 3-6, assumes that all products move through stages of growth and decline. The cycle has different

EXHIBIT 3-5   A Generic Business System for the Oriental Carpet Retail Industry

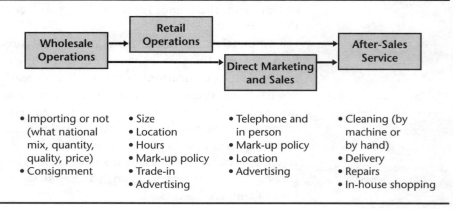

Wholesale Operations	Retail Operations	Direct Marketing and Sales	After-Sales Service
• Importing or not (what national mix, quantity, quality, price) • Consignment	• Size • Location • Hours • Mark-up policy • Trade-in • Advertising	• Telephone and in person • Mark-up policy • Location • Advertising	• Cleaning (by machine or by hand) • Delivery • Repairs • In-house shopping

stages and these tend to beget different patterns of competition, revenue growth, profitability, and cash flow. The strategic concerns and competitive pressures at each stage vary considerably. For example, during the embryonic stage, the strategic concerns are the ultimate demand potential and the scale and timing of commitment; while at the decline stage, the concerns are milking resources to employ elsewhere, timing of a possible exit, and developing niche or value-added strategies.

In summary, the life cycle model and its associated stages allow a manager to predict what competitive forces his or her industry is going to encounter over the next period of time. This in turn allows the manager to develop a strategy appropriate for that stage and set of competitive forces. Chapter 4 will consider this relationship between life cycle stage and competitive actions more thoroughly.

EXHIBIT 3-6   Product/Service/Market Life Cycle Stages

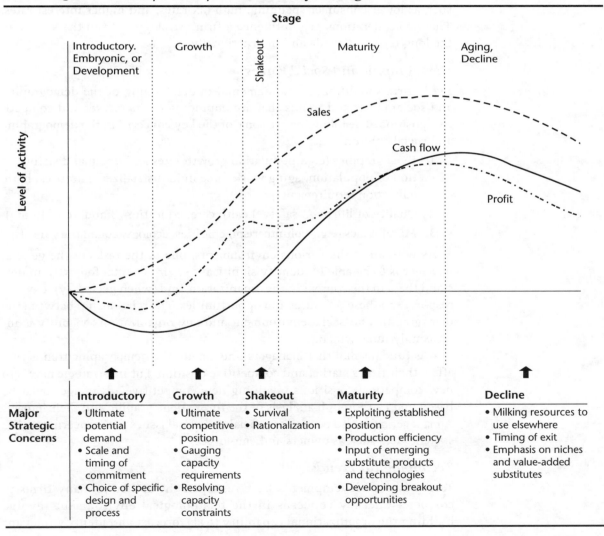

Analyzing a Firm's Macro Environment

A firm also faces a macro environment that includes other influences, some of which may directly or indirectly change the competitive forces and pressures on an industry. These include economic, social and demographic, technical, international, and legal and political forces. These forces will now be briefly commented on.

Economic Trends and Cycles

Economic cycles and trends can influence competitive pressures dramatically. For example, in a recession many firms have to become more cost-efficient due to lower levels of sales. It is important to understand short-term economic cycles and the influence that it might have on strategic plans such as raising capital or increasing plant capacity.

Long-term economic trends are also important strategic considerations. In Canada, our high public debt may create long-term economic implications such as lower consumer spending, high tax rates, and higher interest rates. These considerations may influence a firm's strategy both in the short and the long term in Canada and internationally.

Demographic and Social Forces

Every firm should have a fundamental understanding of the demographic and social forces and trends that are impinging on its market and competitive position. The following are some of the key concerns in the demographic and social environment:

1. Demographics (e.g., population growth rates and unequal distribution of population, aging work force in industrialized countries, high education requirements)
2. Quality of life (e.g., safety, health care, education, standard of living)
3. Moral issues (e.g., volunteerism, charities, ecology, community needs)

As with all of the various environments, one of the tasks of the general manager is to be able to identify significant environmental forces, to understand them in the context of the organization, and (when necessary) to create responses to these pressures and opportunities. The relationship between the demographic and social environment and any organization's viability is increasingly intertwined.

It is fundamental that managers understand the demographic trends that affect their firm's market and competitive position. Future strategic moves to new competitive positions involving new competitive advantages must be based upon a thorough analysis of the future demographic and their impact. A manager must also be aware of social and moral issues that concern its other stakeholders such as owners and employees.

Technological Trends

Technological developments have reshaped the ability of many firms to compete. The key concerns in the technological environment involve building the organizational capability to (1) forecast and identify relevant developments—both within and beyond the industry, (2) assess the impact of these developments on existing operations, and (3) define opportunities. Technological strategy deals with choices in technology, product design and development, sources of technology, and R&D management and funding.[3] Developing a technical strategy is one of the most uncertain aspects of strategic formulation. Not only is the manager dealing with market uncertainty, but there may also be considerable product and process uncertainty attached to such a formulation. Managers must either possess or have access to technological expertise to make such strategic decisions.

The Legal and Political Considerations

The legal and political environment of Canadian business is particularly important given the scale and scope of government activity in Canada.[4] Governments act in a wide variety of ways to create both opportunities and threats for business. Among the most important government actions are: (1) *regulation,* which can increase costs but also control competition or even give a competitive advantage (if firms have adapted to particularly stringent regulations in one location and are therefore better able to handle such regulations elsewhere); (2) *taxation,* which can reduce returns but also increase competitive advantage if a firm faces lower taxation than its competitors; (3) *expenditure,* which can create competitive disadvantage or advantage depending on whether government grants and subsidies received are larger than what competitors receive; (4) *takeover*—for example, the creation of a Crown corporation can produce an unpredictable competitor that also has deep pockets; (5) *privatization,* which can increase competition but also result in a more level playing field; (6) *consultation,* which can become an opportunity for business to influence government policy but also provides government an opportunity to manipulate (i.e., co-opt) business by using the consultative process to justify decisions already made.

International Environmental Considerations

The fifth and final macro-environmental concern to firms in Canada is the international environment. Given Canada's open economy, high levels of foreign ownership, high levels of international trade, and small domestic market, Canadian firms, as seen in many of the cases in this book, are forced to be aware of the trends and market opportunities in countries outside Canada, particularly the United States.

Some of the many differences between the environment in Canada and the international environment concern such variables as currencies (which differ in value and stability), political and economic stability, data availability and its reliability, types of regulatory (legal and accounting) systems, market homogeneity, stage of economic development, and language and cultural mores.

---

[3] See R. A. Burgelman and M. A. Maidique, *Strategic Management of Technology and Innovation* (Homewood, Ill.: Richard D. Irwin, 1988).

[4] See, for example, Mark C. Baetz and Donald H. Thain, *Canadian Cases in Business-Government Relations* (Toronto: Methuen Publications, 1985).

There are, then, at least six environments important to strategic decision making in Canada: (1) industry and competitive, (2) economic, (3) demographic, (4) technological, (5) legal and political, and (6) international. Each of these must be considered in making strategic choices, since analysis of these environments will indicate various opportunities and threats facing the organization. The objective in assessing the various environments is to formulate a strategy that best fits these environments. This is an ongoing challenge, because environments change continually.

Driving Forces

Driving forces are ones that may change, or are changing, the nature of business in an industry. It is important to analyze driving forces in an industry, because it better prepares the manager and company for inevitable change in an industry. Some common driving forces are:

- Changes in long-term growth rate
- Changes in buyers' needs
- Technical innovation resulting in product or process innovation
- New methods of marketing, of distributing, or in the supply chain
- Change in competitor makeup
- Internationalization in the industry
- A change in barriers to entry
- Increases in risk and uncertainty
- Changes in government policy or societal attitudes
- New managerial techniques
- New ways of developing efficiencies or low cost

The strategist should be trying to define what factors will be major causes of change in an industry and which will be minor causes. Then he or she can consider them in the context of potential impacts on their firm's present and future competitive position and advantages as well as on competitors'.

Key Success Factors

Key success factors are those that tend to define the important potential competitive advantages in an industry. Managers must know what they are and understand them. In some industries it is having low-cost raw material supply sources, while in others it is having highly capable R&D personal or economies of scale. Most industries have a variety of key success factors. In addition, certain competitive groups have unique key success factors.

The student should assess whether the company in question has the key success factors, whether they can get them, and how they can get them strategically. Often future key success factors in an industry are highly-sought-after competitive advantages. For example, establishing your product as the standard in the industry is a very important key success factor in the high-tech industry.

◼ Industry and Competitor Assessment

Finally, the student must assess the competitive and industry issues in a meaningful way. Competitive assessment should attempt to answer the following questions:

- How intensive is competition now and in the future?
- Will there be any preferential (or adverse) competitive positions in the industry? Where are they?
- Who are the important competitors to watch and why?
- What types of strategies could competitors adopt and what is their probable strategy?
- What driving forces and key success factors would dramatically alter the competitive situation in this industry and how would it impact your firm?

Industry-level assessment takes a much broader perspective. Important questions for the manager to ask are:

- How will the industry evolve over the longer term?
- Is this an attractive or unattractive industry for new investment and why?
- What are the major problems and opportunities that the industry will or might face in the future?

A summary of the environmental process as described in this chapter is shown in Exhibit 3-7.

Scenario Planning

An environmental approach used by many firms that face considerable environmental or non-controllable risks is the *Scenario Planning* approach. This approach was developed by Shell Oil to strategize appropriate business plans that protected them against the variety of risks they faced including oil price changes, uncertainty of drilling for oil, etc.

The Scenario Planning approach involves developing different scenarios for an industry and competitive environment. The numerous scenarios developed should consider any radical change that could dramatically alter the industry or competitive environment. The previous analysis of the environmental factors should provide ample input for developing these scenarios. Once scenarios have been developed, managers then can assess how their strategy would fare if such a scenario took place and what strategies would be better. After the managers have gone through all of the scenarios, the strategy that best addresses the potential uncertainties is usually adopted.

This exercise is not only useful for developing strategy; it also prepares a company and its managers for the potential of radical change in their environment. If such change does occur, the managers have previously considered the possibly options and outcomes. This planning process also provides managers who are involved in the process with an overall appreciation of the strategic issues facing the firm and some of them may be outside of their responsibility.

EXHIBIT 3-7   A Summary of the Industry and Competitive Analysis and Assessment

Overall Industry Economic Evaluation

- Evaluate market size, market growth, geographic scope, number and sizes of buyers and sellers, pace of technological change and innovation, scale economies, experience curve effects, capital requirements, internationalization

Analysis of Competition

1. **Assess Competitive Forces**
   - Analyze rivalry among competitors in industry
   - Analyze threat of potential entry
   - Analyze competition from substitutes
   - Analyze power of suppliers
   - Analyze power of buyers
   - Analyze the international competitive forces
2. **Assess Competitive Position or Strategic Groups**
   - Analyze the favourable and unfavourable competitive positions or strategic groups in the industry. What might change this?

Analysis of Industry

1. **Business System Analysis**
   - What are channels of supply and distribution are used in an industry and which are most efficient and effective?
   - Are there any potential new approaches to supply or distribution that may be useful in this business?

2. **Life Cycle**
   - Assess future impacts of life cycle forces on the business and products.
3. **The Industry's Macro-environment**
   - Assess the macro-environmental issues such as economic cycles, technology, government policy, international issues (e.g., legal, taxes, duties, etc.)
4. **Driving Forces**
   - Produce a list of critical driving forces that may influence the industry in the future
5. **Key Success Factors**
   - Develop a list of the critical success factors for the industry now and in the future

Industry and Competitor Assessment

1. **Competitor Assessment**
   - Guess what future strategy your competitors will adopt and then assess the impact
   - Who are the strong and weak competitors (now and in the future) and why?
2. **Industry Assessment**
   - Characterize the attractiveness of the industry
   - What major problems and opportunities will the industry face in future?
   - Develop industry scenarios and assess your company's strategy against the scenarios

RECOMMENDED READINGS

Clarkson, Max B. "Defining, evaluating and managing corporate social performance: the stakeholder management model." *Research in Corporate Social Performance and Policy,* vol. 12 (Greenwich, Conn.: JAI Press, 1991).

Mockler, Robert. "Strategic intelligence systems: competitive intelligence systems to support strategic management decision making." *SAM Advanced Management Journal,* Winter 1992, pp. 4–9.

Porter, Michael E. *Competitive Advantage: Creating and Sustaining Superior Performance* (New York: Free Press, 1985), Chap. 2.ß

Thompson, Arthur A., Jr., and A. J. Stickland Inc., *Strategy Formulation and Implementation,* 3rd ed. (Plato, Tex.: Business Publications, 1986), pp. 135–137.

Williams, Jeffrey. "How sustainable is your competitive advantage." *California Management Review,* Spring 1992, pp. 29–51.

Zahra, Shaker, and Sherry Chaples. "Blind spots in competitive analysis." *Academy of Management Executive*, May 1993, pp. 7–28.

CHAPTER 4

Generic Business Strategies and Decisions

Have a real strategy, but the devil is in the detail.

Roberto Goizueta, Chairman of Coca-Cola Corp.

Every new change forces all the companies in an industry to adapt their strategies to that change.

Bill Gates, Chairman of Microsoft Corp.

We changed the rules of the game in a number of ways, and whenever you do that, it's hard.

Andrew Grove, Chairman of Intel Corp.

This chapter considers a variety of generic business strategies. And although we describe all of these generic approaches, it must be remembered that firms should take an approach appropriate to their unique competitive circumstance and environment. Furthermore, the generic strategies that are discussed are known to most managers in an industry, and thus, to be better than the competition, firms must continuously search for new wrinkles to apply to these strategies and implement them creatively and skillfully to ultimately gain a competitive advantage. In other words, firms must continuously strive to improve their competitive position and advantages relative to their competition. This necessitates a constant search for new strategic directions and initiatives. Constant improvement, what the Japanese call *kaizen,* is the only way a firm will sustain its long-term competitive advantage.[1, 2]

In particular, these generic strategies address situations where the firm's environment has created certain competitive pressures that must be addressed by the firm. These environmental situations arise because of high competitive pressures due to low barriers to entry, as well as changing competitive conditions due to product life cycle transitions. In general, a firm in a difficult competitive situation must refocus in its competitive position by becoming a lower-cost or more differentiated producer in the products that it has the most

---

[1] W. E. Deming, *Out of the Crisis* (Cambridge, Mass.: MIT, 1986), p. 31.

[2] See Michael E. Porter, *Competitive Advantage: Creating and Sustaining Superior Performance* (New York: Free Press, 1985), Chap. 9.

competitive advantages in. The firm should also strive to enhance its competitive advantages to support the newly focused competitive position. The above approach is a manner of creating entry barriers and decreases the ability of competitors to replicate the firm's approach.

Generic strategic positions can be viewed broadly as having four dimensions: (1) overall cost leadership, whereby the firm strives to be the price leader in the industry by using a range of functional policies compatible with industry economics, (2) differentiation, whereby the firm strives to be distinctive across the industry in some aspect of its products or services that is of value to the customer, such as quality or style, (3) focus, whereby the firm concentrates its efforts on serving a distinctly defined market segment, which may include some combination of a portion of a product line, particular customer segment, limited geographic area, or particular distribution channel, and (4) breadth, whereby the firm attempts to provide all various products in a specific business market. Exhibit 4-1 illustrates the various possible generic strategic positions. Managers must note that these positions tend to require very different competitive advantages, and so it is very difficult for a business to be in more than one generic position simultaneously. Profitable companies generally focus on one of the four quadrants.[3]

Each of the four positions involves risk. Cost leadership is vulnerable to imitation by competitors or technological changes (e.g., "technological leapfrogging"). Differentiation may not be sustainable if the bases for differentiation become less important to buyers or if competitors imitate the product or service. A focus strategy is also vulnerable to imitation, or the target market segment may disappear as customers' tastes change. Finally, some competitive advantages have shown to be important in all of the competitive positions. For example, Deming has shown that quality is a critical element of both the low-cost and the differentiation competitive position. Improved quality can result in lower costs due to "less rework, fewer mistakes, fewer delays or snags, better use of machine time and materials."

---

[3] See Michael E. Porter, *Competitive Strategy: Techniques for Analyzing Industries and Competitors* (New York: Free Press, 1980), Chap. 11.

EXHIBIT 4-1   Generic Industry Competitive Positions

		Market Value	
		Low Cost	Differentiation
Market Scope	Breadth	Breadth and Low Cost	Breadth and Differentiation
	Focus	Focus and Low Cost	Focus and Differentiation

Examples in Clothing Retailers
- *Breadth and Low Cost:* Biway (low-priced clothes and other items)
- *Breadth and Differentiation:* Holt Renfrew (high-priced clothes and personal goods)
- *Focus and Low Cost:* Cotton Ginny Plus (cotton clothes for large women)
- *Focus and Differentiation:* Harry Rosen (high-priced men's clothes)

Highly Competitive or Fragmented Industries

Industries that have a large number of competitors are called *fragmented industries,* because many small firms having very similar competitive positions and advantages fragment the market. Competition in these industries is intense due to the number of competitors and the inability of competitors to differentiate from one another. Characteristically fragmented industries are easy to enter because of low entry barriers, as delineated by Porter's Five Forces model (see Exhibit 3-1). Examples of highly competitive or fragmented industries are dry-cleaning, bicycle couriers, and small corner stores.

Approaches to competing in fragmented industries are often limited by the very nature of the industry. However, potentially effective strategic initiatives include the following:

- Focusing very carefully on low costs and process innovations that minimize costs. When a firm is expanding, it should apply a "formula" approach to duplicating plants and offices. This will minimize both the capital and the operating costs of the expansion.

- Looking for unrecognized market niches where customers are not having their needs met. A firm may be able to take a focused–differentiated or focused–low cost approach to such a small market.

- In smaller, less dense markets, where competition is sometimes less intensive, focusing on these markets in an efficient and effective manner. This is one of the strategic approaches that Wal-Mart took when it established itself as one of the top competitors in the very competitive merchandise/retailing industry.

- Constantly looking for new trends in technology, government policies, international relations, etc. that allow your firm to take advantage of a newly created market, or allow your firm to build new competitive advantages and barriers to entry.

- Asking "Are there any alternative approaches to the business that would provide the company with a competitive advantage?" Examine Porter's Five Forces Model and look for ways to change the way business is done so that the competitive intensity in the industry is reduced. (For example, can you increase barriers to entry in the industry?) Often firms in fragmented markets become lethargic and miss opportunities for competitive improvement. Such things as economies of scale, forward or backward integration, economies of scope, etc. may enable a company to change the nature of the business, and thus the competitive forces. This approach often requires considerable creativity combined with certain environmental or industry-based changes that allow an aggressive firm to take advantage of a unique opportunity.

Generic Strategies Based on the Life Cycle
Emerging Industries

Emerging industries are recently formed industries resulting from technological changes, changes in customer needs, legal and political changes, etc.

Characteristically, firms in an emerging industry are facing considerable uncertainty in key competitive dimensions such as technology. If the environment conspires to change the nature of that competitive advantage and it is no longer effective, the firm loses its ability to support its competitive position. For example, a firm may have a strong technological advantage that is nullified when a new, better technology becomes available. Examples of emerging industries include the biotechnology industry and newly developing high-tech industries.

Strategies for coping in an emerging industry include the following:

- Ensure that the firm has a strong technological capability, or capability in whatever other environmental uncertainty exists. It is critical that top managers be knowledgeable and aware of the competitive advantages and associated environmental forces. This ensures rapid action if changes appear to be taking place. The firm may also want to supplement its in-house strengths with external forecasting capabilities.

- Concentrate initially on the competitive advantages vital to learning and creating better products and services for the customer. Avoid costs and investments not associated with the critical advantages and success factors in the industry if at all possible. For example, many technology companies avoid the costs of manufacturing, concentrating their limited resources on product/service improvement. Manufacturing can be subcontracted to low-cost manufacturers in low-cost countries. It must be noted that this assumes that manufacturing process development is not a critical part of the emerging industry.

- Cooperate with other companies in the industry in an attempt to build a product or service standard and create customer awareness. Many emerging industries have successfully done this, including the firms behind the VHS tape format and the original IBM PC.

- If the market is initially quite fragmented, attempt to select and focus on a customer base or segment that will be a reference point for customers that might adopt the product or service. Such reference groups are quite often large companies, ones that are very demanding and have a reputation for buying the best. If your initial strategy is to design your product and service for this market, it will allow easier market entry and adoption. These high-quality customers also allow you to attract interim resources such as financing and knowledgeable/capable workers.

- Strive for an early entry into an industry if there appear to be potential entry barriers such as brand awareness that will develop over time. Otherwise, wait until the costs of uncertainty have been eliminated.

High-Growth Industries

A high-growth industry is one that has gone through the emerging stage and is now facing fewer technical uncertainties, but many market and competitive uncertainties. Examples of this type of industry are many sectors in the high-tech industry; in fact, many people call this high-tech industry strategies.

In high-growth industries, market growth is very high, and this tends to moderate competitive forces because competitors are just trying to meet market demand. However, despite the moderated competitive climate, it is a period wherein winners' and losers' competitive positions are shaped. Therefore, it is critical for companies to develop specific competitive advantages that enable them to be winners when demand slows and competition becomes very intense. During the emerging stage, core competencies are often technologically related, but in the high-growth stage marketing competitive advantages increase dramatically in importance.

Some strategies that enable firms to best position themselves to be a winner during the high-growth stage are the following:

- Focus on production volumes and economies of scale. Focusing on high volumes of production and broad distribution channels may allow you to grab the largest market share, and if market share is important (as it is in many industries), then your company has the initial advantage. Furthermore, customers are often just looking for the product at any price because demand is outstripping supply. Such a high-volume and high-market-share strategy is particularly important in industries that have high fixed costs such as high tech. In these industries, high volume enables the companies to cover fixed cost activities such as research and development much more effectively than companies that do not have high revenues.

- Attempt to make your product or service the standard in the industry. To do this a company must gain market share, which can be done by concentrating on production and broad distribution as suggested previously. In addition, companies can increase their effective market coverage by licensing their technology to other competitors. Such cooperation can be very effective and may also overlap into marketing and R&D alliances.

- Try and develop marketing competitive advantages or capabilities. This would include broad channels of distribution, brand recognition, etc. Again this strategic focus may help the company develop market share and a product that is the standard in the industry.

- Constantly consider new technologies and trends that may move the industry in a new direction. Such technologies could dramatically influence acceptance of their product, particularly if the company that develops the new technology has marketing strength.

Maturing Industries

A maturing industry is an industry facing no or minimal market growth, and lower growth often means intensive price competition. Often prior to and during this stage, power in the value chain evolves forward to the distributor, retailer, or customer, leaving the firm with less competitive influence. International competition increases and the ability to effectively differentiate oneself may decline. Therefore, firms must build competitive advantages that maximize cost advantages and/or seek focused markets that are looking for specialized services or products. New customer or product trends may also allow a company to differentiate itself for some period of time.

An example of an industry in the mature stage is the clothing industry, whose firms must continually reinvent themselves in an effort to maintain a competitive advantage. Such reinventing includes moving production to low-cost overseas locations, integrating forward into retail operations, and constantly trying to adjust to new product, production, and service trends.

Some of the alternative strategic approaches to a mature environment include the following:

- The strategy of a firm must focus on low costs and improved customer service. This is a difficult transition, because many of these activities, such as manufacturing and customer service, are not ones the firm has concentrated upon in the past. Those it has concentrated upon, such as R&D, are not required or are much less critical to the survival of the firm now. If a firm cannot make this transition in activities, possibly they should look to merge with a firm that has these capabilities.

- The firm may have to consider aggressively competing internationally to gain the economies of scale and scope that are necessary in a mature business.

- The organization must evolve into a disciplined, cost-efficient, and effective operation where managers focus on controlling costs, quality, and service—things that have become important to the customers. This change often is not easy, because the organization, during the emerging and growth stages, has accumulated unnecessary departments, people, and managers.

- Firms could also consider establishing forward-focused alliances or integrating forward. This strategic approach may preempt the evolution of power forward in the value chain. However, the manager is cautioned to analyze carefully the pluses and minuses of forward integration before doing so.

- The firm may have to concentrate more on process innovation compared to product innovation. During the growth stage, product design and getting the product out at any cost is the critical concern. However, in the mature stage, cost competition will force companies to concentrate on process innovations that make their overall operations more efficient and effective.

- A final option is to recreate the growth cycle by adapting resources and capabilities to new market needs. This strategic alternative is discussed more thoroughly later in the chapter.

Declining Industries

A declining industry faces a shrinking market volume. Competition in such an industry becomes extremely intense, particularly if high barriers to exit exist—that is, impediments to getting out of an industry. An example of a high exit barrier is a firm's huge capital investment in a production capacity that is not useable in another industry. Owners will natually be reticent about writing off such a large investment. An example of a Canadian industry in decline is the fisheries industry, which is facing low fish stocks and a moratorium on fishing in many regions.

In general, four alternative strategies are available to a firm in this situation: to take a leadership position, to seek a niche position, to harvest, or to divest. A firm that takes a leadership position must decide if it can capture such a competitive position given its competitive advantages relative to its rivals. The leadership position must clearly put the firm in a low-cost or better-value leadership position relative to its competitors. Furthermore, the managers must be fairly certain that it can attain such a position; otherwise, it is a very-high-risk strategy given that considerable investment is often necessary. Reinvestment strategies are particularly effective if the decline is not permanent (i.e., demand eventually stabilizes). One tactic firms often use when confronted with a declining market that has no clear leader is to merge or acquire other firms in the industry. This may create a clear leader if economies of scale and scope are important in the industry.

One firm using the *industry leadership approach* in a declining industry is Fisheries Products International (FPI). Vick Young, the CEO, completely redefined the company's competitive position in the industry by refocusing the company from a fish-catching to a value-added fish processing company. The company now concentrates on importing fish, then it processes the fish-making specialty products and reexports them to customers demanding such value-added products.

Seeking a niche position is a good strategy for a firm that does not have a leadership position in the overall market, but can develop a leadership position in a niche market. An important consideration for the firm adopting this strategy is that the characteristics of the niche (e.g., small size or unusual customer demands) and competitive advantages developed by the firm must make it very difficult for the overall industry leader to attack this niche. Sometimes this strategy is combined with a harvest strategy.

A *harvest strategy* is one in which the firm has decided to eventually discontinue the business. However, in the short term, the firm keeps its prices high, minimizes reinvestment costs, and allows its market share to slowly decline while maximizing its profits. If forecasts for the industry are for long-term decline, a harvest strategy is the only viable option for a portion of the companies in the industry.

A *divestment strategy* is the most obvious strategic alternative in a declining industry. Yet, it is often one of the most difficult ones for managers and owners to adopt, because the managers may be without a job and the owners may have to accept a low price. The task of a manager using this strategy is to make the firm look valuable to other firms in the industry.

Small Business or Entrepreneurial Generic Strategies

Entrepreneurs must develop unique competitive advantages, because they do not have the breadth of competitive advantages that a larger business has in the same industry. The successful small business must focus its capabilities on developing very specialized competitive advantages. Some of the more generic strategies and competitive advantages used by small firms are:

- Focus on small niche markets—ones that are small enough not to attract the attention of the larger companies. Such an approach may mean focusing on a specific customer or type of unique product. Some small businesses also focus on a particular part of the value chain (as seen by a larger company) and they provide a unique product or service for companies willing to use them as part of the chain.
- Small companies often provide better service to the customers. Focusing on specific customers and services can enable the entrepreneur to provide more value.
- Small entrepreneurial companies are often faster at making decisions and providing products and services, particularly if they are made-to-order products or services. Speed can be important as a competitive advantage because of its dynamic nature. Decision-making and R&D speed, for example, could provide a small company an ongoing competitive advantage over some of its larger rivals.
- Small entrepreneurial firms have tremendous flexibility in formulating and implementing strategy. This may provide them with a competitive advantage if change or flexibility is required.
- Some small companies, such as specialized consulting firms, are extremely efficient and effective in businesses that require a lot of top management control.

Strategic Evolution in the Life Cycle Process

Businesses plagued with products in the latter stages of their life cycle may be able to revitalize the products by adding new technological advances or redesigning the products for specialized markets. Such an action may create a growth stage by appealing to customers and needs that have not been fulfilled yet. This process can delay the decline of a product and in some cases may lead to a completely new life cycle.

Exhibit 4-2 illustrates how the Canadian telecommunications service industry is evolving. The leading companies are developing new products, new technologies, and new customer segments in their quest for continued market growth. As shown in the Exhibit, the average telephone service is a mature and possibly declining product. However, several years ago the companies developed new growth products (e.g., call waiting, Internet services, and local mobile services) that are growing very rapidly. Many of these same companies are now developing emerging technologies and products that will be the growth of tomorrow (e.g., ATM data services, integrated voice/data networks and lines, and global mobile satellite phone services).

The Exhibit illustrates how telecommunication companies are attempting to evolve into new life cycle stages by redefining their product, customer, and service focus. They are altering their competitive position by refocusing their competitive advantages on these new products and markets. This, of course, requires parallel changes in competitive advantages (e.g., resources, knowledge, and capabilities) within the firm.

EXHIBIT 4-2   **Product Evolution in the Canadian Telecommunications Industry**

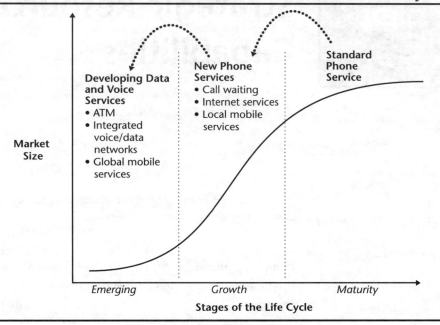

The difficulties of reinventing one's life cycle are not minor. First, a firm that refocuses on a new product may devote so many resources to its refocusing effort that the old products and competitive position are neglected. This may leave the firm worse off if the new market segment does not develop as predicted. Second, sometimes new products require resources and capabilities (i.e., competitive advantages) that the entering firm does not have enough of compared to potential competitors. This makes the firm less competitive in the new market segment. (Witness Kodak's difficult evolution into digital photography at a time when many other companies may have more appropriate competitive advantages and positions.) Therefore, firms must be careful when refocusing their efforts on emerging products. Firms should adopt strategies that develop products that maximize their intrinsic competitive advantages, and should take care to not neglect underlying mature products.

RECOMMENDED READINGS

Adler, P. S., D. W. McDonald, and F. MacDonald. "Strategic management of technical functions." *Sloan Management Review*, Winter 1992, pp. 19–38.

Foster, John. "Scenario planning for small businesses." *Long Range Planning*, February 1993, pp. 123–129.

Moore, Geoffrey. *Inside the Tornado.* New York: HarperBusiness, 1995.

Moore, Geoffrey. *Crossing the Chasm.* New York: HarperBusiness, 1991.

Nutt, Paul, and Robert Backoff. "Transforming public organizations with strategic management and strategic leadership." *Journal of Management,* Summer 1993, pp. 299–348.

Waalewijn, Phillip, and Peter Segaar. "Strategic management: the key to profitability in small companies." *Long Range Planning*, April 1993, pp. 24–30.

CHAPTER 5

Strategic Resources and Capabilities

All we can do is hire the right managers. So my job is picking the right people as managers.

Jack Welch, Chairman of GE Corp.

Knowledge management is critical. It's one of our core processes—sell work, do work, manage people and manage knowledge.

John Patz, CKO of Ernst and Young

A firm's resources represent the assets and capabilities that support its competitive advantages and position. Resources can be physical assets (e.g., land, equipment, buildings, cash, etc.), intangible resources (e.g., brand name, market share, product patents, technological know-how, etc.), or capabilities (e.g., learning proficiencies, product development processes, fast delivery times, managerial abilities, etc.). Analyzing a firm's resources is an important step for a manager when formulating and implementing strategy.

A successful strategy must be supported by strong resources, and when a strategy changes, accompanying changes in competitive advantages and, therefore, resources are usually necessary. When formulating strategy, managers must decide what resources are necessary for a firm's strategy, and how to develop or acquire these resources over time. In this chapter, we consider the analysis of resources and their relationship with strategy.

Strategy's Fit with Resources

Managing resources requires that the manager analyze what resource gaps must be filled to ensure that the firm's present strategy and competitive advantages are maximized Therefore, the selection and quality of resources is critical to the firm's competitive advantages and competitive position. Exhibit 5-1 illustrates the managerial thinking during this process.

Two questions must be kept in mind when determining the specific resources required to pursue a strategy: Do the resources support a firm-specific competitive advantage? and Do they allow the strategy to be implemented? Starting with resources held, the strategist determines the unique characteristics

EXHIBIT 5-1   **The Relationship Between Strategy and Resources**

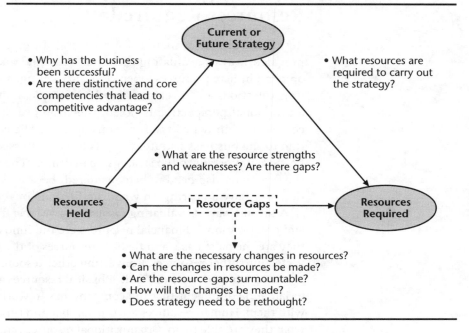

• Why has the business been successful?
• Are there distinctive and core competencies that lead to competitive advantage?

Current or Future Strategy

• What resources are required to carry out the strategy?

• What are the resource strengths and weaknesses? Are there gaps?

Resources Held   **Resource Gaps**   **Resources Required**

• What are the necessary changes in resources?
• Can the changes in resources be made?
• Are the resource gaps surmountable?
• How will the changes be made?
• Does strategy need to be rethought?

of the firm's current resources—ones that differentiate it from its competitors. These broad-based differences are called *distinctive competencies*. A firm also has *core competencies*, which are resources that give a firm its clear leadership competitive position, in the eyes of its competitors and customers. More specifically, core competencies are the resources or capabilities in an organization that truly distinguish it from its competitors both today and in the future, and on which performance depends.

The difference between distinctive and core competencies is subtle. In a nutshell, distinctive competencies are resources and capabilities that broadly differentiate it from the competitors, while core competencies are just a few vital resources and capabilities that provide the firm with its most consequential competitive advantage, and therefore its superior competitive position. For example, Honda Motor Company has many distinctive competencies, such as its trained work force, plant location, and international skills. However, its core competency is its ability to design and manufacture engines. It has successfully used this ability to broaden its product scope into a wide variety of products from Formula One racecars to lawnmowers to portable motorized electrical generators.

Once it is established what both these competencies are, a strategy is then developed that makes good use of them. *Resource gaps* are the differences between the resources required for the strategy and the resources held. If the gaps can be reduced, the probability of executing the strategy is improved. However, if the gaps are large and cannot be reduced, the strategy has to be revised so that the competitive advantages of the firm conform more readily to the competitive strategic position of the firm.

◼ Evaluating Resources Held and Determining Resources Required

Resources can be evaluated from several different perspectives. The most prevalent way of evaluating them is *by function:* finance, research and development, human resources, operations, marketing, and so forth. For each function, questions are developed, of which samples appear in Exhibit 5-2. When a functional perspective is taken, the strategist also needs to consider the context within which the functions operate. The contribution of each function to the business's strategy needs to be addressed, as some functions may be more important to the strategy than others. The interrelationships among the functions also need to be considered, because what is done in one function may have a bearing on what can be done in another function.

A second way of evaluating resources is *by type:* financial, physical, human, and organizational. Financial resources are the funds that the company raises; they are the most basic and flexible resources of the business, and can be converted into other resources. Converting other resources into financial resources is less certain and more difficult. Physical resources are the buildings, raw material, and equipment that the company has to work with and what it can do with them. Human resources are the number and type of people in the firm and what they are able to do. Organizational resources are the procedures and techniques the firm has developed that are necessary for success in the business.

A third way of evaluating resources is *in terms of their breadth.* A resource is essentially broad/wide when it is easily transferred to other situations and narrow/specialized when it is not. Sales staff with knowledge of many different products is an example of a broad resource, while specialized product knowledge is an example of a narrow resource. A broad resource base facilitates a business's expansion of its product, market, and industry scope, while a narrow resource base serves to limit the firm's ability to increase its scope.

EXHIBIT 5-2   An Overview of the Functional Perspective

Function	A Partial List of Questions to Answer
Finance	What is the apparent capacity of the firm to generate internal and external funds? What funds are required for each strategic alternative?
Research and development	How important is technology to the firm's processes and products? What percentage of the firm's resources is devoted to research and development?
Human resources	What is the ambition, depth, drive, loyalty, and skill of the managerial/administrative group in the firm?
Procurement	What is the cost, flexibility, motivation, productivity, and skill of the work force? How important is the procurement function to the firm?
Operations	Does the firm have good relations with suppliers? What is the capacity, cost, and productivity of operations? What is the age, condition, and flexibility of the plant and equipment? What is the quality of the products produced?
Marketing	Does the firm command a premium price and, if so, why? How well does the firm know its customers and its competitors?

A fourth way of evaluating resources is *in terms of the activity or value chain*. This approach is similar to the functional approach, but it focuses the analysis on the value chain activities.

Value Chain Analysis

A *value chain* is defined as the path that the product or service moves along as value is added, prior to reaching the end consumer. A generic value chain is shown Exhibit 5-3. A value chain is made up of primary activities (inbound logistics, operations, outbound logistics, marketing and sales, and service) and support activities (firm infrastructure, human resource management, technology development, and procurement). Firms try to gain competitive advantage by increasing the value to customers in one or more activities relative to competitors. *Value* is defined as improving the worth of the product or service to the customer through either lowering the price or increasing the product or service characteristics. Managers must focus on increasing the value to the customer while attempting to minimize the costs to the firm—this, of course, maximizes total profits to the firm. These two issues are called *strategic value* and *cost* analysis.

Strategic value analysis focuses on a firm's relative value position vis-à-vis its rivals. The analytical approach must combine an analysis of the firm's total industry value chain and the firm's competitive position. The manager must appreciate the relationship between the customers served by the firm's competitive position and the value provided to these customers by the various activities in the firm's value chain. The analysis can include value provided by assets not owned and controlled by the firm, including such things as the quality of service provided by their chosen retail distribution channels and the quality of raw materials provided by suppliers. All of these factors may influence customer value.

Strategic cost analysis focuses on a firm's relative cost position vis-à-vis its rivals. The primary analytical tool of strategic cost analysis is the construction of a total firm value chain showing the makeup of costs all the way from the inception of raw materials and components to the end price paid by ultimate customers.[1] The activity-cost chain thus includes more than just a firm's own internal cost structure; it includes the buildup of cost (and thus the "value" of the product) at each stage in the whole market chain of getting the product into the hands of the final user, as shown in Exhibit 5-3. Constructing an integrated activity-cost chain is more revealing than restricting attention to just a firm's own internal costs. This is because a firm's overall ability to furnish end users with its product at a competitive price can easily depend on cost factors originating either *backward* in the suppliers' portion of the activity-cost chain or *forward* in the distribution channel portion of the chain.

It is important to note that value chain analysis and decisions must be directed at the competitive position of the firm. In other words, increasing the

---

[1] Joseph L. Bower, *Managing the Resource Allocation Process* (Boston: Harvard Business School Press, 1986), p. 80.

EXHIBIT 5-3   Generic Value Chain in an Industry

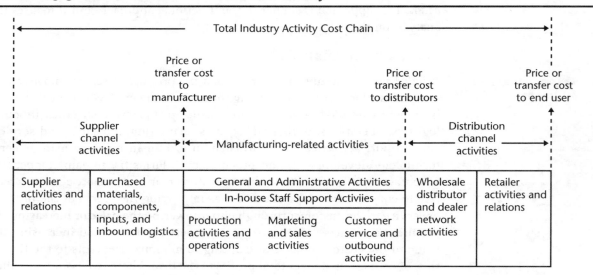

Activity	Specific Cost Activities and Cost Elements	
General and administrative activities	• Finance and accounting • Legal services • Public relations • General management	• Interest on borrowed funds • Tax-related costs • Regulatory compliance
In-house staff support activities	• Payroll and benefits • Recruiting and training • Internal communications • Computer services • Procurement functions	• R&D • Safety and security • Supplies and equipment • Union relations
Supplier channel activities	• Managing and controlling suppliers • Ingredient raw materials and component parts supplied by outsiders • Energy	• Inbound shipping • Inbound materials handling • Inspection • Warehousing
Production activities and operations	• Facilities and equipment • Processing, assembling, and packaging • Labour • Maintenance • Process and product design and testing	• Quality control and inspection • Inventory management • Internal materials handling • Manufacturing supervision
Marketing and sales activities	• Sales force operations • Advertising and promotion • Market research	• Technical literature • Travel and entertainment • Dealer/distributor relations
Customer service and outbound logistics	• Service representatives • Order processing • Service manuals and training • Spare parts	• Transportation services • Other outbound logistics costs • Scheduling
Distribution channel activities	• Includes all of the activities, associated costs and markups of distributors, wholesale dealers, retailers, and any other forward-channel allies whose efforts are utilized to get the product into the hands of end users/customers	

value of an activity must be related to a firm's competitive position (i.e., be valued by a company's customers). For example, if a firm is in an expensive and highly differentiated market position, customers may not want cheaper activities; they may in fact just want higher-value products and services that more thoroughly cover their needs.

Benchmarking, a technique described in Chapter 1, is a very effective tool used by companies to assess the costs and effectiveness of activities in a firm's value chain. Benchmarking allows the firm to measure and compare their activities to other firms that are considered value leaders in a specific activity.

Constructing a complete value chain for a firm is not easy. It requires breaking a firm's own historical cost accounting data down into several principal cost categories and developing cost estimates for the backward and forward channel portions of getting the product to the end user as well. It also requires the manager to estimate the same cost elements for rivals and then estimate their overall value chains—an advanced art in competitive intelligence in itself. But despite the tedium of the task and the imprecision of some of the estimates, the payoff in exposing the cost-competitiveness of one's position and the attendant strategic alternatives makes it a valuable analytical tool.

In Exhibit 5-3 observe that there are three main areas in the cost chain where important differences in the *relative* costs of competing firms can occur: in the suppliers' part, in their own respective activity parts, and in the forward channel part. To the extent that the reasons for a firm's lack of cost-competitiveness lie in either the backward or the forward sections of the cost chain, its job of reestablishing cost-competitiveness may well have to extend beyond its own in-house operations. When a firm has a cost disadvantage in the area of purchased inputs and inbound logistics, five strategic options quickly emerge for consideration:

1. Negotiate more favourable prices with suppliers.
2. Integrate backward to gain control over material costs.
3. Try to use lower-priced, substitute inputs.
4. Seek out sources of savings in inbound shipping and materials logistics costs.
5. Try to make up the difference by initiating cost savings elsewhere in the overall cost chain.

When a firm's cost disadvantage occurs in the forward end of the cost chain, there are three corrective options:

1. Push for more favourable terms with distributors and other forward-channel allies.
2. Change to a more economical distribution strategy, including the possibility of forward integration.
3. Try to make up the difference by initiating cost savings earlier in the cost chain.

It is likely, of course, that a substantial portion of any relative cost disadvantage lies within rival firm's own activity-cost structures. Here, five options for restoring cost parity emerge:

1. Initiate internal budget-tightening measures aimed at using fewer inputs to generate the desired output (cost-cutting retrenchment).
2. Invest in cost-saving technological improvements.
3. Innovate around the troublesome cost components as new investments are made in plant and equipment.
4. Redesign the product or service to achieve cost reductions.
5. Try to make up the internal cost disadvantage by achieving cost savings in the backward and forward portions of the cost chain.

The construction of a value chain is a valuable tool for competitive diagnosis, because of what it reveals about a firm's overall cost/value competitiveness and the relative cost/value positions of firms in the industry. Examining the makeup of one's own value chain and comparing it against the chains of important rival firms indicates who has the most efficient and/or effective activities.

Assessing the Quality of Resources

As stated previously, resources are important for the support of a firm's competitive advantage. A manager must assess the quality of the firm's resources and their ability to provide long-term, sustainable competitive advantages to the firm. Several qualities managers should consider when assessing a firm's resources are shown in Exhibit 5-4.

The more quality characteristics a resource has, the more important it is to the firm—the only caveat being that all resources must be at the very least valuable (the first resource quality) to the firm. A resource or capability that has all of these qualities is clearly a core competency for the firm. Highly profitable firms tend to have an abundance of resources having these qualities. That is why it is so difficult for other firms to copy their strategy (i.e., competitive advantages)—the resources are essentially impossible to duplicate.

Resource Gaps

Rarely is the precise combination of resources needed to pursue a strategy in place. Furthermore, usually a firm is constantly trying to improve its competitive position and advantages, thus requiring new resources. This makes resource gap analysis critically important for a manager. When assessing the resources, a useful approach is to construct a table with entries down the side for the activities or functions and headings across the top for (1) current resources, (2) projected resources, (3) gaps between those two, and (4) how the gaps might be filled (Exhibit 5-5). The body of this table is then filled in with the analytical details.

Resource gaps do not only occur when a firm adopts a new strategy. Just maintaining an ongoing strategy creates resource gaps. New resources must be developed when existing resources deteriorate, depreciate, or turn over. In addition, success with the existing strategy can create resource gaps as additional resources are required for growth. Ocasionally more resources are generated than can be

EXHIBIT 5-4 **Assessing Resource Characteristics and Quality**

Resource Quality	Explanation Question
Valuable	Is the resource or capability valuable in delivering the firm's service or product to its customer? This is a necessary resource quality.
Durable	Is the resource or capability very temporal (i.e., will it disappear over a period of time) in nature? That is, is it a limited natural resource?
Inimitable	Is the resource or capability unique to your firm relative to the competition?
Non-substitutable	Can a resource or capability be replaced by another one in your business or industry?
Inappropriable	Can a resource or capability move to another firm in your industry (e.g., an employee)?
Fungible	Does a resource or capability have a breadth and scope in your company that makes it difficult for others to both imitate and understand (e.g., organizational culture)?

employed profitably in a business. Underutilization of existing resources is a negative form of resource gap analysis. Overproduction of resources can be problematic also—for example, when a firm generates more cash than it can use in the business, making itself an attractive takeover target.

Identifying the Gaps

Resource gaps are identified through strength-and-weakness analysis as part of the SWOT analysis described in Chapter 2. Determination of strengths and weaknesses involves a relative comparison those resources the company has and those it needs. In-depth analysis of resources gaps details the magnitude and type of resource needed, the availability of such a resource, methods for obtaining the resource, and the timing or priority of need for such a resource. It should be noted that some resources, may have to be sold and some acquired to meet the needs of one's competitive strategy.

Reducing the Gaps

The ability of the business to reduce resource gaps is influenced by the magnitude and nature of the changes required, as well as the firm's ability to implement these changes. Reallocating, developing, buying, and selling resources can reduce these gaps. Depending on how the gap is reduced, cost, ease, and timing will differ. Resources can be acquired from the outside, but

EXHIBIT 5-5 **Assessing Resource Gaps**

Activity or Functional Area	Current Resources	Required Resources	Resources Gaps	Filling the Gaps: Tactics and Risk
Finance				
R&D				
Human resources				
Procurement				
Operations				
Marketing				

their high market cost can make it more desirable to develop them internally. Developing resources is usually cheaper, but slower; but it can have other positive benefits, such as providing for the development of a continuous stream of resources (e.g., managers). Moreover, development of resources may be required if sufficient quantities or qualities are not available, either elsewhere in the business or in the marketplace. Obviously, many tactical issues have to be addressed when considering how gaps might be filled.

It should also be noted that the ability to reduce a resource gap will depend on the particular country in which the firm is located. A firm's resource base is not simply a function of its own operational regime, but also a function of the location and country it operates within.[2] In other words, there is an interaction between firm-level and country-level sources of resources and competitive advantage.

Changing a firm's resources carries certain risks. These risks are associated with the number and magnitude of the resources and the quality of resources demanded by the strategic change. The manager must be careful that he or she does not make such a radical strategic change as to render the present firm resources ineffectual and create resource demands impossible for the firm to fulfill in the required time frame. It may be more acceptable for the firm to take a more incremental strategic approach to change, developing resources appropriate for the firm's intermediate competitive positions and associated competitive advantage.

Resource Allocation in Corporate, Business, and Operational Strategy

Understanding the role of resource allocation in the strategic management process is critical. Resource allocations communicate and allow managers to carry out the firm's strategy.

A firm grasp of the resource allocation process is necessary to appreciate its role in the strategic management process. As the matrix in Exhibit 5-6 indicates, the resource allocation process has three phases and three sub-processes. The first phase is the *initiating* phase—where many product/market ideas and proposals originate, and where many new business graduates will spend their first years of employment. The other two phases are *integrating* (i.e., middle management) managerial and *corporate* (i.e., senior management level) managerial levels. The integrating management level is where vertical and lateral strategic issues are integrated. More specifically, the integrating level of management conveys corporate goals and plans down through the organization, and it communicates operational proposals (from the initiating phase) through a screening stage up to the corporate level.

The three sub-processes in the resource allocation process are definition, commitment, and organization. In the *definition* process, the underlying economic and technical considerations of a proposed investment are examined and

---

[2] See M. E. Porter, *The Competitive Advantage of Nations* (New York: The Free Press, 1990).

the overall competitive environment and strategy of the firm are reviewed. During the *commitment* process senior manager commit (or don't commit) to investments on the basis of the prior stage's identification of strategic direction and the deemed quality of investment opportunities. Because the general manager's reputation for good judgement may rise or fall depending on the outcome of the investment, the required commitment will be given only after careful consideration of the various demands at the corporate and operational levels.

The final process, the *context,* sets the organizational context upon which the investments are implemented, including formal structure, reward system, and information and control systems. This flow from the definition to the commitment and finally the context stage is not completely a rational process. Not surprisingly, internal organizational political power and pressures can influence it considerably.

The process of improving a firm's resources requires the manager to identify, invest, leverage, and upgrade its resources. The first two processes have been considered in this chapter. The leveraging process entails trying to get resources working more effectively and efficiently. This in an important managerial and leadership issue, because if resources can be made to produce more output, and thus capital (i.e., resources), the last process of upgrading resources can take place. Good managers realize that a firm's long-term sustainable competitive advantage relies on the continuous improvement of a firm's resources and capabilities.

EXHIBIT 5-6   The Resource Allocation Process

Phase	Definition (goal/plan/result definition and measurement)		Commitment (project/plan impetus)		Context (determination of organizational context)	
Corporate (senior management)	• Macro strategy • Company environment aggregate system		• Terminal decision yes or no		• Design of corporate context • Overall structure, personnel assignment and development, incentive and control systems style	
Integrating (middle management)	• Financial aggregate goals • Strategic thrust ↓	↑ • Product-market strategies	• Filtered company needs (the company's "wants") ↓	↑ • Filtered product/market needs (the business's "wants")	•Corporate needs • Implementation (differentiation, integration) ↓	↑ • Subunit needs • Interpretation, adaptive needs
Initiating (operating level)	• Product-market strategies • Operational plans and execution		• Competing plans/proposals • I've got a "great" idea		• Product/market not served by structure	

Source: Adapted from Joseph L. Bower, *Managing the Resource Allocation Process* (Boston: Harvard Business School Press, 1986), p. 80.

Summary

Finding an acceptable fit between the strategy and the resources available to the business is a major step in formulating strategy.[3] First, the firm's resource must be examined in terms of what is available and what is needed. Resources can be evaluated in several ways: by functional area, by type, by tangibility, by breadth, and by activity costs. Resource gaps must be identified and evaluated to determine the likelihood of their being overcome. Whether they can be overcome depends on the gaps' size, number, and nature; the ways in which the gaps can be reduced; and the time available. When the likelihood of filling the resource gaps poses too great a risk to be acceptable, the strategy has to be modified in order to bring its resource requirements closer to current resources.

---

[3] For more discussion on the analysis of resources, see R. B. Buchele, "How to evaluate a firm," *California Management Review,* Fall 1962; J. H. Grant and W. R. King, *The Logic of Strategic Planning* (Boston: Little, Brown, 1982), Chaps. 4–7; M. E. Porter, *Competitive Advantage: Creating and Sustaining Superior Performance* (New York: Free Press, 1985); W. E. Rothschild, *Putting It All Together: A Guide to Strategic Thinking* (New York: AMACOM, 1976), Chap. 6; R. S. Sloma, *How to Measure Managerial Performance* (New York: Macmillan, 1980); and H. H. Stevenson, "Defining corporate strengths and weaknesses," *Sloan Management Review,* Spring 1976, pp. 51–68.

RECOMMENDED READINGS

Augustine, Lado, Nancy Boyd, and Peter Wright. "A competency-based model of sustainable competitive advantage: toward a conceptual integration." *Journal of Management*, March 1992, pp. 77–92.

Stalk, George, P. Evans, and L. E. Shulman. "Competing on capabilities: the new rules of corporate strategy." *Harvard Business Review,* March–April 1992, pp. 57–69.

Strategy, Stakeholders' Preferences, and Ethics

It's not enough just to treat employees well because by focusing only on them, you forget about delivering superior value to customers and rewarding shareholders. All three are essential to great performance.

Frederick Reichheld, Consultant at Bain & Co.

It is essential that our business practices take social effects into consideration.

Kentaro Aikawa, Chairman of Mitsubishi Heavy Industries.

Strategy formulation may seem to be a highly rational process of analyzing environmental opportunities and weaknesses, competitive positions and advantages, organizational capabilities, and resource strengths and weaknesses. However, managers and others associated with a business may have different assessments of the firm's environment and resource base. They may also use different criteria when evaluating strategic alternatives, and have different perceptions of the need for change. Or the organization may have groups having different preferences and values within it.

In this chapter, the role of stakeholder preferences and ethics in strategy formulation and implementation are considered. The chapter will also describe the concept of corporate culture, corporate ethics, and stakeholder pressures, since they influence and are influenced by managerial preferences.

Managerial Preferences

Everybody has individual preferences that influence his or her decisions and ultimately behaviour. Preferences are derived from an individual's basic values. These values are modified through a person's experience, personal goals, beliefs, attitudes, and competencies.[1] In this context, a manager's task is to unify the preferences and ultimately the employees' behaviours, in a way that supports the competitive advantages and the strategic direction of the firm.

---

[1] Discussion of the personal system in relation to needs and behaviour is found in most texts dealing with organizational behaviour. One good example is A. R. Cohen, S. L. Fink, H. Gadon, and R. Willets, *Effective Behaviour in Organizations,* 4th ed. (Homewood, Ill.: Richard D. Irwin, 1988), Chaps. 7 and 8.

To do this, a manager must confront two issues. First, managers must develop a shared set of preferences and behaviours for their organization, and second, they must ensure that the shared organizational preferences are appropriate for the strategic direction of the company.

Managing Organization-Wide Preferences and Behaviour

Personal preferences must be assimilated into group preferences if management is to have a consistent set of preferences to guide strategic decision making. Managers attempt to guide their organization's preferences, and inform their stakeholders of their preferences, by developing a vision and mission statement. A *vision statement* is a statement that describes the top management's vision of what the firm should represent and strategically be sometime in the future (e.g., five or ten years hence). A *mission statement* sets the guidelines and describes in very general terms how the firm is going to accomplish its vision. Within these statements one often finds a description of the firm's corporate ethics, preferences, and desired business culture. One of the goals of these statements is to provide all the stakeholders with a general description of the company's preferences and ethical principles, and demonstrate how they apply to the overall strategy of the company.

Getting agreement on preferences in an organization is not easy. It is accomplished through a complex process in which power and leadership are often instrumental. Power and leadership enable certain individuals in a business to dominate the formation of group preferences and culture.[2] For this reason, any assessment of firm and group preferences must consider who the powerful people in the organization are, how they see the situation, and what they think should be done. There are both formal and informal leaders in an organization, and both can shape the culture and preferences of a group within the organization. Managing this process requires considerable top management skill and leadership. This process and the participating groups are described more thoroughly below in the stakeholders and corporate ethics sections in this chapter.

Stakeholders' Preferences

Managers are increasingly expected to consider a growing number of stakeholders when formulating strategy. A stakeholder is an individual or a group with a personal interest in the business. Each stakeholder depends on the business in order to realize goals, while the business depends on them for something they provide to the business. General classes of stakeholders who directly influence managers' decisions include shareholders, management, employees, financiers, suppliers, customers, community, and government. Illustrative preferences of these stakeholders and how they encourage managers to meet them are presented in Exhibit 6-1. Managers often reflect the preferences of stakeholders they see as important to their performance. Thus, the marketing

---

[2] Additional coverage of this topic can be found in I. C. MacMillan and P. E. Jones, *Strategy Formulation: Power and Politics*, 2nd ed. (St. Paul, Minn.: West Publishing, 1986).

EXHIBIT 6-1   The Interests of Stakeholders

Stakeholder	Preferences and Expectations	Ways They Exert Influence on the Business
Shareholders	• Appreciation in the value of stock dividends • Social responsibility	• Buying and selling stock • Election of directors • Proxy fights • Public expression of satisfaction or discontent through the press or at annual meetings
Managers	• Participation in decisions • Authority/power • Compensation (salary, bonuses, benefits) • Opportunity for advancement • Job security	• Taking/leaving jobs in the firm • Commitment to work • Quality of work
Employees	• Compensation (wages, benefits, profit sharing) • Participation in workplace decisions • Safe working conditions • Opportunity for advancement • Job security	• Taking/leaving jobs in the firm • Strikes • Absenteeism • Workplace grievances • Quality of work • Union activity
Financiers	• Orderly repayment of principal and interest • Further opportunities for sound investment of monies • Timely disclosure of events	• Willingness to lend additional funds • Covenants in the loan agreements • Enforcement of covenants • Credit rating interest rates charged
Suppliers	• Continued, consistent orders • Prompt payment	• Prices charged • Credit terms • Delivery performance • Willingness to meet special demands • Supply priority during periods of shortage • Technical assistance • Recommendations to other suppliers
Customers	• Satisfactory products or services • Satisfactory price/quality relationship • Fair adjustment practices (warranties, responses, etc.)	• Amount purchased • Word-of-mouth advertising • Complaints, returns, claims • Product liability suits • New product ideas
Community	• Continuity of employment • Continuity of payment of taxes • Environmentally sound activities • Actions socially sound • Participation in community activities	• Boycotts, protests, demonstrations • Awards by community groups • Pressure on government
Government	• Continuity of employment • Continuity of payment of taxes • Environmentally sound activities • Advance national objectives (ROD, exports, job creation) • Satisfy regulations	• Subsidies, tax concessions • Regulations • Licences, permits • Awards by government • Enforcement of regulations
Other interest groups	• Interested in social, moral, environmental, cultural, and community issues	• Boycotts, protests, demonstrations • Educating consumers and the public

manager will tend to reflect customers' interests, and the financial manager will tend to reflect financiers' interests. Stakeholders often have interests in common, because of their involvement in the business.

Which stakeholders' preferences management seeks to satisfy involves difficult choices. Sometimes compromises must be made among the various competing stakeholders' preferences. It is management's responsibility to conciliate and ultimately decide between competing stakeholder groups' preferences. This clearly requires strong managerial abilities. However, sometimes management decides to favour one stakeholder preferentially over another. Such a decision may be based on rational considerations or on the stakeholder's power. Factors influencing the potential power of stakeholders are outlined in Exhibit 6-2. When executives in large firms were asked "Who is really important to the business?" customers were seen as most important, followed by themselves, subordinates, employees, and bosses. Those who were least important, in order of declining importance, were stockholders, elected public officials, government bureaucrats, and other interest groups.

The following questions are relevant when determining the influence of stakeholder interests:

1. Which stakeholder interests are most important?
2. Will any stakeholders be injured by the proposed decisions?
3. Should and can strategy be changed to accommodate stakeholder expectations?
4. Is it possible to negotiate a compromise?
5. Should and can certain stakeholders be replaced?

These questions also raise ethical considerations about "what is right" and "what is wrong"[3] which is addressed later in the chapter.

Managing Corporate Culture

Corporate culture is defined as the common preferences held by those working in the firm about the way things are done. It gives rise to norms, routines, and informal rules that people follow in the firm. It also provides them with a common understanding of what is considered important and standards of performance. Good managers attempt to influence and shape the firm's culture so that it provides the firm with a competitive advantage in either efficiency or effectiveness.

From the strategic perspective, a corporate culture must be closely linked to a firm's business strategy.[4] A culture that is closely linked to the firm's strategy and environment often produces stellar performance results. For example,

---

[3] Additional sources of information on ethical questions are R. E. Freeman and D. R. Gilbert, Jr., *Corporate Strategy and the Search for Ethics* (Englewood Cliffs, N.J.: Prentice Hall, 1988); S. W. Gellerman, "Why 'good' managers make bad ethical choices," *Harvard Business Review,* July–August 1986, pp. 85–90; and L. L. Nash, "Ethics without a sermon," *Harvard Business Review,* November–December 1981, pp. 79–90.

[4] According to T. Deal and A. Kennedy, a strong culture has almost always been the driving force behind continuing success in American business. In *Corporate Cultures* (Reading, Mass.: Addison-Wesley, 1982), p. 5.

EXHIBIT 6-2   **Potential Power Held by Stakeholders When Seeking to Influence Strategic Decisions**

Stakeholder	Degree of Potential Power	
	Is High If:	Is Low If:
Shareholders	• Controlling block of shares with an active interest in the company decisions • Many shareholders have a common interest in what the company does • Shareholders hold stock so they can exert influence over management	• Shares are widely held by uninterested shareholders • Shares are widely held by shareholders with heterogeneous interests • A dominant CEO strongly influences elections to the board
Managers	• A dominating CEO leads management • The management team has been in place for a long time • Compensation is heavily influenced by performance-based bonuses	• The board of directors dominates decision making
Employees	• Belong to a strong union • The company has a tradition of good employee relations	• Unskilled labour force • High unemployment
Financiers	• The company is highly leveraged • The company has defaulted on the covenants in the loan agreements	• The company generates the investment money it needs internally
Suppliers	• Limited sources of supply • Switching costs are high	• Many alternative suppliers
Customers	• Few possible customers • A few customers buy a significant proportion of the output • Customers possess a credible threat for backward integration	• Many possible customers • The company's product is unique
Community	• A single-industry town	• The company has facilities in many locations
Government	• Regulations provide government with control over company activities • Government approval is required for mergers and acquisitions • The government can provide grants, licences, and special tax benefits	• Firm is an international firm with the ability to move operations outside of the country • The country does not have any attractive resources or markets
Other interest groups	• They can influence the actions of some of the other stakeholders such as customers and government	• They cannot influence other stakeholders

firms in the advertising business benefit from a very creative culture, while a firm in health care may benefit from having a caring, yet efficient culture. In particular, organizational culture has a direct impact on how well a strategy is implemented. Consequently, many managers try to proactively manage their organizational cultures by hiring the appropriate people and putting in place organizational environments, rewards, and systems that promote a specific culture. The only downside to having a strong culture is if the strategy has to change; changing an organization's culture is not easily or quickly done.

Organizational culture may also be detrimental when two firms merge and their organizational cultures are different. Examples are abundant. Almost all the major Canadian banks have acquired and merged with investment brokerage firms that had very different cultures. This has forced the merged firms to treat the two organizations as independent entities. Exhibit 6-3 contrasts the cultures in the banking and investment brokerage industries.

The Exhibit illustrates how an organizational culture is often related to the business environment and ultimately the strategy. For example, we see that the banks' organizational decision making, systems, and style are focused on economizing and efficiency, while the investment brokerage firms are focused on customer satisfaction.

Culture in an organization can range from strong to weak. A strong culture greatly influences the behaviour of organizational members. Evidence for the strength of a culture is found in Exhibit 6-4. In general, businesses with strong cultures are likely to have better performance.[5] However, a strong culture is not

---

[5] The role of culture in successful business organizations has been popularized in Great Britain by W. Goldsmith and D. Clutterback, *The Winning Streak* (Harmondsworth, Middlesex, England, Penguin Books, 1985) and in the United States by T. Peters and R. H. Waterman, *In Search of Excellence* (New York: Harper & Row, 1982). Additional sources of information on corporate culture are J. Barney, "Organizational culture: can it be a source of sustained competitive advantage?", *Academy of Management Review,* July 1986, pp. 656–665; S. Davis, *Managing Corporate Culture* (Cambridge, Mass.: Ballinger, 1984); and T. Deal and A. Kennedy, *Corporate Cultures* (Reading, Mass.: Addison-Wesley, 1982).

EXHIBIT 6-3   **The Impact of Culture on Merger Strategy and Implementation**

Organizational Trait	Major Canadian Banks	Canadian Investment and Brokerage Houses
Demographics of organization	• Very large organization • Employee age range 15–65 • Most don't have university degree	• Small to medium-sized organization • Employee age range 30–65 • Most have university degree and further investment certificates
Organizational style	• Hierarchical, staid, and steeped in boss fear. For example, most of the branch workers never get to talk to top management. There are clearly different levels of employees and the lower levels are represented by unions.	• Flatter organization with an aggressive and freewheeling style. For example, employees at all levels must make their own decisions and are in charge of their own work schedules. Employees often meet managers at higher levels in organization.
Organizational systems	• Highly centralized information systems • Most employees paid on a straight salary basis	• Centralized and decentralized information systems • Most employees paid on commission basis
Leadership style	• Career banking executive who has a very formal style	• Career investment executive with an aggressive, demanding style
Decision-making style	• Centralized and bureaucratic. Most lower-level decisions have specific rules of process and constraints. More complex decisions take considerable time and may require written authorization.	• More decentralized, aggressive, and entrepreneurial; very fast at making decisions, as investment managers can make many of their own decisions.
Corporate strategy	• Appears to be to get into all types of financial services globally	• Really concentrates on investment service businesses because of the profitability
Business environment	• Core banking business is mature and has low growth • Moderately profitable	• Investment business has relatively high growth • Extremely profitable

EXHIBIT 6-4   Evidence of the Strength of a Culture

Character of the Culture	Evidence of Character
Strong	• Members share preferences about how to succeed • Members know the activities the business must carry out well to be successful • Standards of achievement are well established • "Heroes" in the organization personify values and provide tangible role models to follow
Weak	• Members have no clear preferences about how to succeed • Members do not agree on beliefs that are important • Different parts of the business have different beliefs or preferences • "Heroes" of the business are destructive or disruptive • Rituals are disorganized, with organizational members either "doing their own thing" or working at cross purposes

a sure road to success. It may even become a liability if it does not fit with the requirements of changing business environment and strategy. Nor is a strong culture necessarily self-sustaining. It can break down when rapid growth brings in new people faster than they can be socialized into the culture.

The compatibility between culture and strategy, sometimes called *cultural risk,* can be examined using a logical process. First, the key tasks arising from the strategy are determined. Next, the behaviour required to perform the tasks satisfactorily is determined. This is compared with the behaviour arising out of the current corporate culture. If required behaviour is similar to the actual behaviour, culture poses no risk to the implementation of strategy. If it is different, culture can present so much risk that it is a barrier to the pursuit of a strategy.

The strategist can deal with cultural risk in several ways. One approach is to ignore culture and plunge ahead. Since a good fit is needed between culture and strategy, this approach nearly always invites disaster. Another approach is to manage around culture, either by performing the tasks in ways more in line with the current culture, or, more drastically, by modifying the strategy so that different tasks are required. A third approach is to change the selected components of culture that affect critical organizational activities. For example, one company facing a more competitive environment found that it needed to improve its relationships with customers. It reoriented the culture to fit its new strategy and environment by promoting the slogan "The customer is always right" to employees and customers, and by training employees to respond courteously and promptly to customer requests.

Managing Business Ethics

Business ethics are related to a society's ethics. Some people know when they are acting unethically, yet they are motivated to do so by various incentives. What are ethics? Ethical decisions and behaviour are concerned with acts that impact the welfare, personal rights, and justice of other people or things. Ethical behaviour is what society considers right and the norm to ensure that social calm and order are maintained.

Some national cultures can have ethical norms different from those of others. For example, in some countries giving ex gratia payment (i.e., bribes) is considered entirely acceptable, while in other countries it is both immoral and illegal. Therefore, it is critical that managers fully understand what the ethical norms are for the country they are considering doing business in.

Managing ethical behaviour in a company is not an easy task. One way in which large companies attempt it is through a "Statement of Ethical Conduct and Behaviour" that lays down appropriate behaviours and potential penalties for employees. Yet the most important ethical influence in a firm is provided by the managers' day-to-day conduct with employees and customers. If managers participate in marginal activities, employees will be encouraged to do so. In addition, managers must be fully versed in ethical conduct and discipline measures, so that they can provide guidance to employees when necessary. Ultimately, managers must attempt to demonstrate consistent implementation of ethical business conduct and punish those that deviate from such behaviour.

Formulating ethical guidelines can be difficult, because of the differences in what is viewed as ethical behaviour in different regions. Nonetheless, a good starting point is to strive to satisfy the ethical norms of all of your stakeholders. For example, if your business is carried out in several countries, the most stringent ethical principles should be adopted—otherwise, those stakeholders, including customers, owners, and employees, could take issue with your ethical standards, and business performance could suffer. Ultimately all people must take responsibility for their actions and must consider the long-term consequences of their behaviours to their career, family, and personal prospects.[6]

Questions that should be asked when assessing a company's ethical guidelines are:

1. Would the manager like to have that behaviour directed at him or her?
2. Is there evidence that any of the firm's stakeholders have adopted or oppose this ethical belief?
3. Has an ethical principle been ignored because of short-term profitability? And has the manager considered the long-term consequences and arguments for such behaviour?
4. Are the committees and organizational processes that establish and control the ethical guidelines democratic?

Managing the Fit Between Preferences and Strategy

Preferences, at both the group and individual level, are directly related to the components of strategy. Some organizations, particularly not-for-profit organizations, have preferences for kindness and cooperation. Yet other organizations, particularly those in tough competitive situations, have preferences for efficiency, effectiveness, getting the job done, and aggressive competitiveness.

---

[6] B. Z. Poster and W. H. Schmidt, "Values and the American manager: an update," *California Management Review,* Spring 1984, p. 206.

These preference differences are related to an organization's competitive environment and strategy, and they must be mirrored in the management's preferences. Yet, some managers have their own preferences that push the company in a specific strategic direction. For example, an entrepreneur often has gambling instincts and wants the company to grow at all costs, often using highly risky strategies. However, a bureaucrat is risk-averse and more willing to curtail short-term growth by taking strategies that maintain long-term stability. The entrepreneur perceives the environment to be full of opportunities, whereas the bureaucrat sees mostly threats and danger. This difference in perceptions, and thus preferences, must be understood by anybody who works with or employs the manager. Understanding the preferences of your manager allows you to cater arguments and strategic formulations to them. For example, if you are asked to assess a risky growth strategy by an entrepreneur, you would be well advised not to simply discredit the strategy to him or her, unless the evidence is overpowering; rather, you should make him or her aware of the concerns, suggest strategic tactics to ameliorate them, and advise him or her to delay the growth until certain strategic concerns and objectives are met. This approach does not bluntly confront the manager's preferences, but forces him or her to consider modifying the strategy to lessen the risk.

Managers have preferences for the types and levels of goals, and where and how the company competes (i.e., competitive positions). Managerial preferences are important to strategy in other ways as well. Preferences for uncertainty influence the tradeoff between risks and rewards, and determine the margin of safety sought to ensure competitive success, financial continuity, and organizational survival. Preferences about self-sufficiency influence the degree of independence sought from key stakeholders. And finally, preferences about how to lead and manage will influence the culture of the firm, as these preferences shape decisions about how to keep employees committed, motivated, and loyal, and decisions about how to best use employees' talents.

Other preferences that influence manager's decisions may be related to power, friendship, or personal gain. Advisors, employees, and employers to top managers must understand the managers' preferences so they can take them into account when providing advice. The advisor should either understand the manager's preferences and perspective of the firm's environment, resources, organizational capabilities, and strategic "fit" or attempt to convince the top manager that his or her perspective, and therefore preferences, are errant. But it is often easier to change top managers than to convince them a different preference would be appropriate.

Managing the Relationship Between Strategy, Preferences, and Culture

Managerial preferences and culture influence strategy. For example, a preference for growth to satisfy a need for achievement or recognition can encourage managers to follow a strategy of diversification. However, the firm may lack the resources, or there may not be environmental opportunities to follow such a strategy. Therefore, there must be a fit between a firm's environment and strategy and its preferences and culture (Exhibit 6-5).

When there is a major gap between the preferences and cultures held versus those required, either the strategy must change or the preferences and culture must change.[7] As stated previously, it is not easy to change stakeholders' preferences or the organization's culture. Making such changes should be considered carefully, as they require considerable effort and may upset the strategic/organizational fit of the company even more. However, if changes in stakeholders' preferences and the organizational culture are deemed necessary, managers should begin making the changes as soon as possible. Some issues that must be addressed in this process are:

- *Leadership*. Often a change in leadership is necessary, not only because it signals to the organization and stakeholders that a change is going to take place, but also because the business can select a leader who embraces the desired preferences and cultural attributes.

- *Signalling a change in preferences and culture*. Quite often it is necessary for the management to overtly signal to stakeholders and employees that a change is going to occur specific to preferences and culture. Changing leadership, changing personnel in the organization, changing the organizational structure and systems, or just informing the relevant parties can do this. However, sometimes shocks are necessary for organizational cultures to initiate change.

- *Changing the organizational culture*. Subtle cultural change can occur over time by changing an organization's structures and systems, by strong and coercive leadership techniques, and by bringing in workers having the desired cultural values. More radical change may require wholesale changes in employees and organizational attributes. However, in both cases it is imperative that management understand how it wants to change the culture, and that it monitor behaviour in the organization to ensure the correct changes are occurring. All too often a company attempts to make these changes without controlling the process.

- *Changing external stakeholders can be done by clearly indicating a change in products, services, or business objectives*. Again, the magnitude of the change will dictate how fast and in what numbers stakeholders will abandon the company. Managers must control this process also. For example, if some investors abandon a company due to changed objectives, management must manage the transition to new investors. In fact, some companies are continuously trying to coerce good (e.g., loyal, quality-based, and long-term-focused) external stakeholders to get involved with their company.

---

[7] Additional sources of information on managerial preferences are G. Donaldson and J. W. Lorsch, *Decision Making at the Top* (New York: Basic Books, 1983), Chaps. 5 and 6; J. N. Fry and J. P. Killing, *Strategic Analysis and Action*, 3rd ed. (Scarborough, Ont.: Prentice-Hall Canada, 1995), Chap. 8; and C. R. Schwenk, "Management illusions and biases: their impact on strategic decisions," *Long-Range Planning*, vol. 18, no. 5 (1985), pp. 74–80.

EXHIBIT 6-5   **Strategic Gap Analysis: Culture and Preferences**

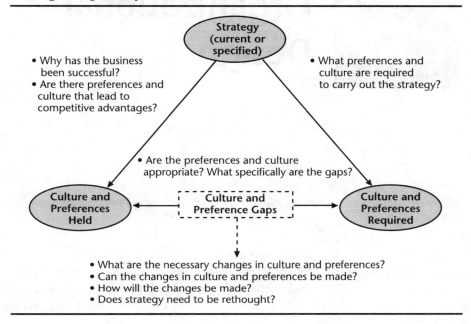

Summary

This chapter has emphasized the human element in the strategy formulation process. What seemed to be a highly rational and analytical process up to this point no longer seems so with the introduction of managerial preferences, corporate culture, and stakeholder pressures. Corporate culture reflects preferences shared by all in the firm. A culture in which many preferences are shared is said to be strong, and may be a major source of success for the firm. Every firm has stakeholders who exert power in varying degrees in order to get the firm to satisfy their preferences and expectations.

RECOMMENDED READINGS

Badaracco, J. L. "Business ethics: four spheres of executive responsibility." *California Management Review*, Spring 1992, pp. 64–79.

Morgan, Malcolm. "How corporate culture drives strategy." *Long Range Planning,* April 1993, pp. 110–118.

Savage, G. T., T. Nix, C. J. Whitehead, and J. D. Blair. "Strategies for assessing and managing organizational stakeholders." *Academy of Management Executive,* May 1991, pp. 61–75.

Stark, Andrew. "What's the matter with business ethics?" *Harvard Business Review,* May–June 1993, pp. 38–48.

CHAPTER 7

Organizational Design

This place was entrepreneurial to the point of confusion.

Steve Case, CEO of America Online

Most companies have created a sketch of the culture they want to build. By contrast, the most admired companies have closer to a detailed architectual blueprint, and they are constantly referring to it.

Bruce Pfau, Managing Director of Hay Group

To implement any strategy, certain organizational actions must be taken. In this chapter, we review the major components of organizational design.

The major organization design variables significant in implementing strategy are structure, information systems, decision processes, reward systems, and staffing and leadership style (see Exhibit 7-1).

Structure

Structure can be viewed as "the design of organization through which the enterprise is administered."[1] Structure is more than an organizational chart. It represents the configuration upon which the organization functions and it influences responsibilities, cooperation, competition, integration, and ultimately the organization's efficiency and effectiveness. Structure is described as having three elements: hierarchy or division of labour, shape (i.e., span of control and number of layers), and distribution of power (i.e., vertical or horizontal, explicit or implicit).

Organizational structure is considered more fully in Chapter 8. This chapter will concentrate on the organizational processes and systems that a manager must consider.

This section has been adapted in part from Arthur A. Thompson, Jr., and A. J. Strickland III, *Strategy Formulation and Implementation,* 3rd ed. (Plato, Tex.: Business Publications, 1986), pp. 330–334.

[1] A. D. Chandler, *Strategy and Structure* (Cambridge, Mass.: MIT Press, 1962), p. 14.

EXHIBIT 7-1   Relationships Between the Major Organization Design Variables

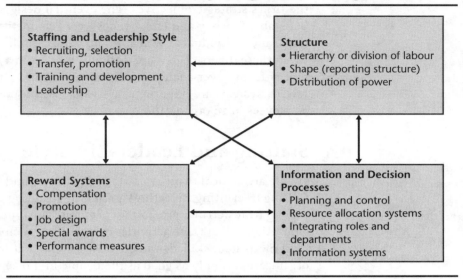

Information and Decision Processes

"Processes are overlaid across the structure to allocate resources and coordinate activities not handled by the department structure."[2] These information and decision processes include planning and control systems (for such things as budgets, schedules, and forecasts), integrating mechanisms (to enable coordination and cooperation to take place between tasks and functional areas), and information systems (to collect, analyze, and disseminate information and knowledge both formally and informally throughout the organization). In any organization it is critically important that the information and knowledge pertinent to a specific decision be provided to the decision maker. This means that either decision processes must be decentralized or information processes must convey critical information to the individuals making the decisions.

Reward Systems

Perhaps the most easily understood element of organization design is reward systems. Decisions on compensation packages (however composed), on promotions (accompanied by any combination of such things as bigger offices, more status, a free parking space, increased holidays, a private secretary, and so forth), on ways of awarding outstanding performance, and on the design of jobs (and who gets the more interesting or high-profile assignments) all can be designed in such a way as to reinforce desired behaviour.

---

[2] Jay R. Galbraith and Robert K. Kazanjian, *Strategy Implementation,* 2nd ed. (St. Paul, Minn.: West Publishing, 1986), p. 114.

Managers design reward systems so that individuals and teams focus on the firm's strategic objectives. The eventual design must consider and support job efficiency and effectiveness, core competitive advantages and positions, and individual as well as group values, preferences, and expectations. Often these diverse needs are difficult to fulfill in a large, complex company that is facing ever-changing environmental and strategic forces. However, reward systems are important motivators and useful tools for evaluation of employees in an organization.

Staffing and Leadership Style

People are critical to an organization's success and long-term performance. Getting (recruiting, selecting), grooming (training and developing), and retaining (transferring, promoting) personnel are crucial activities in every organization. All of these activities ensure that a company hires and retains the most motivated, skilled, and effective people in its organization, because an organization is only as good as the people in it over the long term.

Training and developing skills is becoming particularly important to firms, because of the advent of new technology and processes. Pertinent skills for personnel in a firm range from general business skills to industry-specific knowledge, firm-specific knowledge, and job- or task-specific knowledge and skills. As one moves higher in the organization a broader spectrum of theses skills is required, but it is the more task-specific skills that often have to be taught at the lower levels in an organization.

Top managers also have leadership styles that help motivate and direct employees to fulfill the firm's objectives. The classic leadership dimensions in the business literature are identified in Exhibit 7-2. These dimensions are autocratic, democratic, structural, considerate, transactional, and transformational. It should be noted that the second and third dimensions are not necessarily mutually exclusive. In other words, a leader can have qualities of both structural and considerate, or both transactional and transformational, simultaneously. In contrast, the first dimension of autocratic and democratic is mutually exclusive—a leader cannot be both simultaneously.

Other dimensions that are important to consider in a leader are their knowledge and experience in the industry and company, their risk preferences, their creativity, and their intrinsic motivation to get the job done. Since leadership styles are not easily changed, it is important for a firm to select an appropriate leadership style for its particular strategic situation and organizational characteristics.

Probably the greatest failing when organizations are designed is the lack of consistency between the organization design variables and the strategy variables. Often companies develop problems when their strategy changes, but the organizational design variables are not commensurately adjusted to maintain the desired consistency and fit.

Specific examples of normative configurations of strategy and organizational variables that constitute a fit are shown in Exhibit 7-3. The strategic approaches

EXHIBIT 7-2   Dimensions of Leadership Style

The Autocratic Versus the Democratic Leadership Dimension

An **autocratic leadership** dimension involves a tendency to make unilateral decisions, dictate work methods, provide only short-term goals, and give feedback only when things go wrong. This leadership style is sometimes necessary when a firm faces a crisis and immediate action is required.

A **democratic leadership** dimension involves a tendency to involve group members in decision making and determination of work methods, provides longer-term objectives, and gives complete information feedback and coaching. This leadership style is almost essential when the critical knowledge in the organization is dispersed throughout the employees. This is the case in law and consulting firms, for example.

Note: These two dimensions are mutually exclusive, although most leaders would vary somewhere between the two extremes.

The Structural and the Considerate Leadership Dimension

A **structural leadership** dimension involves focusing on basic managerial functions such as planning, coordinating, and controlling. The focus is on achieving activity results. Typical behaviour includes emphasizing deadlines and the quantity and quality of work to be accomplished. Such an approach is particularly useful if employees know what they have to do, little interaction is required between tasks and the manager, the job can be objectively measured and evaluated, the task is mundane and repetitive, or the organizational culture and employees are very logical and structured in their social thinking and activity patterns.

A **considerate leadership** dimension involves focusing on building mutual trust with subordinates, respecting their ideas, and showing concern for their ideas. The leader is friendly toward subordinates, engages in two-way conversations, and expresses concern about their welfare. Such an approach can be appropriate when the task is very difficult to measure and evaluate, the employee is learning about the task and social structure in the organization, the task involves intimate contact with others including the manager, or the organizational culture and employee are emotional in their social, thinking, and activity patterns.

Note: A leader can have both of these dimensions, as they are not mutually exclusive.

The Transactional and the Transformational Motivational Leadership Dimension

The **transactional leadership** dimension involves motivating employees to perform to expected levels of performance by clarifying responsibilities, and the means to achieve their goals, and by exchanging rewards for performance. This type of leadership style may be best suited to motivating employees that are involved with repetitive, mundane tasks and whose output is easily measured.

The **transformational leadership** dimension involves motivating employees to transcend expected levels of performance by articulating a compelling vision of the future which is consistent with their values, and inspiring them to focus on broader missions that go beyond their immediate self-interest. Transformational leaders provide subordinates or "followers" with individual consideration by engaging them in activities that are tailored to their individual needs and will contribute to their personal development. They stimulate followers intellectually by offering them new ideas and encouraging them to think in new ways about old problems. This type of leadership dimension may be particularly important for firms going through change or taking a leadership role in the development of its industry.

Note: A leader can have both of these dimensions, as they are not mutually exclusive.

EXHIBIT 7-3   Strategy-Organization Fit

Strategy	Dominant Business (vertically Integrated)	Unrelated Diversified (growth through acquisition)	Related Diversified (growth through internal development, some acquisition)
Strategic focus and task focus	• Degree of integration • Market share • Product line breadth	• Degree of diversity • Types of business • Resource allocation across discrete businesses • Entry and exit businesses	• Realization of synergy from related products, processes, technologies, markets • Resource allocation • Diversification opportunities
Structure and decision-making style	• Centralized functional • Top control of strategic decisions • Delegation of operations through plans and procedures	• Highly decentralized product divisions/profit centres • Small corporate office • No centralized line functions • Almost complete delegation of operations and strategy within existing businesses • Control through results, selection of management, and capital allocation	• Multidivisional/profit centres • Grouping of highly related business with some centralized functions within groups • Delegated responsibility for operations • Shared responsibility for strategy
Information and decision process	• Coordination and integration through structure, rules, planning, and budgeting • Use of integrating roles for project activity across functions	• No integration across businesses • Coordination and information fows between corporate and division levels around management information systems and budgets	• Coordinate and integrate across businesses and between levels with planning, integrating roles, integrating departments
Rewards	• Performance against functional objectives • Mix of objective and subjective performance measures	• Formula-based bonus on ROI or profitability of divisions • Equity rewards • Strict objective, impersonal evaluation	• Bonus based on divisional and corporate profit performance • Mix of objective and subjective performance measures
People and careers	• Primarily functional specialists • Some inter-functional movement to develop some general managers	• Aggressive, independent general managers of divisions • Career development opportunities are primarily intradivisional	• Broad requirements for general managers and integrators • Career developments cross-functional, interdivisional, and corporate-divisional

Source: Reprinted by permission from *Strategy Implementation,* pp. 116–117, by Jay Galbraith and Robert Kazanjian. © 1986 by West Publishing Company. All rights reserved.

considered are three different product strategies: single or dominant business, unrelated diversified, and related diversified.

◼ How Organizations Evolve as Strategy Evolves: The Stages Model

In a number of respects, the strategist's approach to organization building is governed by the size and growth stage of the enterprise, as well as by the key success factors inherent in the organization's business. For instance, the type of organization that suits a small specialty steel firm relying upon a regionally focused strategy is not likely to be suitable for a large, vertically integrated steel producer doing business in geographically diverse areas. The organization form that works best in a multi-product, multi-technology, multi-business corporation pursuing unrelated diversification is, understandably, likely to be different yet again. Recognition of these differences prompts researchers to formulate a model linking changes in organizational characteristics to stages in an organization's strategic development.[3]

The underpinning of the stages concept is that enterprises can be arrayed along a continuum running from very simple to very complex organizational forms, and that there is a tendency for an organization to move along this continuum toward more complex forms as it grows in size, market coverage, and product-line scope and as the strategic aspects of its customer-technology/business portfolio become more intricate. Four distinct stages of strategy-related organization structure have been identified:

- **Stage I.** A Stage I organization is essentially a small, single-business enterprise managed by one person. The owner-entrepreneur has close daily contact with employees and each phase of operations. Most employees report directly to the owner, who makes all the pertinent decisions regarding objectives, strategy, daily operations, and so on. As a consequence, the organization's strengths, vulnerabilities, and resources are closely allied with the entrepreneur's personality, management ability and style, and personal financial capabilities. Not only is a Stage I enterprise an extension of the interests, abilities, and limitations of its owner-entrepreneur, but its activities are typically concentrated in just one line of business. For the most part, Stage I enterprises are organized very simply and the owner-entrepreneur makes most top-level functional decisions.

- **Stage II.** Stage II organizations differ from Stage I enterprises in one essential respect: the increased scale and scope of operations create a pervasive strategic need for management specialization and force a transition from a one-person management to team management. However, a Stage II enterprise, although run by a team of managers with functionally specialized responsibilities, remains fundamentally a single-business operation. This is not to imply that the categories of management specialization are uniform across large, single-business enterprises. In practice, there is wide variation. Some Stage II organizations prefer to divide strategic responsibilities along classic functional lines—marketing, production, finance, personnel, control, engineering, public relations, procurement, planning, and so on. In vertically integrated Stage II companies, the main organization units are sequenced according to the flow from one vertical stage to another. For example, the organizational building blocks of an oil company usually consist of exploration, drilling, pipelines, refining, wholesale

---

[3] See, for example, Malcolm S. Salter, "Stages of corporate development," *Journal of Business Policy,* Spring 1970, pp. 23–27; Donald H. Thai, "Stages of corporate development," *Business Quarterly,* Winter 1969, pp. 32–45; Bruce R. Scott, "The industrial state: old myths and new realities," *Harvard Business Review,* March–April 1973, pp. 133–48; and Chandler, *Strategy and Structure,* Chap. 1.

distribution, and retail sales. In a process-oriented Stage II company, the functional units are sequenced in the order of the steps of the production process. Stage II companies are have also developed more formal reporting and information systems upon which to manage and make decisions.

- **Stage III.** Stage III embraces those organizations whose operations, though concentrated in a single field or product line, are large enough and scattered over a wide enough geographical area to justify having *geographically decentralized* operating units. These units all report to corporate headquarters and conform to corporate policies, but they are given the flexibility to tailor their unit's strategic plan to meet the specific needs of each respective geographic area. Ordinarily, each of the semiautonomous operating units of a Stage III organization is structured along functional lines.

  The key difference between Stage II and Stage III, however, is that while the functional units of a Stage II organization stand or fall together (in that they are built around one business and one end market), the operating units of a Stage III firm can stand alone (or nearly so) in the sense that the operations in each geographic unit are less dependent on the other units to carry out businesses. Firms that could be characterized as Stage III include many large breweries, cement companies, and steel mills having production capacity and sales organizations in several geographically separate market areas.

- **Stage IV.** Stage IV is typified by large decentralized, multi-product, multi-market enterprise. Corporate strategies emphasize diversification. As with Stage III companies, the semiautonomous operating units report to a corporate headquarters and conform to certain firm-wide policies, but the divisional units pursue their own respective line-of-business strategies. Typically, each separate business unit is headed by a general manager who has profit-and-loss responsibility and whose authority extends across all of the unit's functional areas except, perhaps, accounting and capital investment (both of which are traditionally subject to corporate approval). Both business strategy decisions and operating decisions are thus concentrated at the business unit level rather than at the corporate level. The organization structure at the business unit level may be along the lines of Stage I, II, or III types of organizations. A characteristic Stage IV company would be Canadian Pacific.

Movement Through the Stages.   The stages model provides useful insights into why organization form tends to change in accordance with product-customer-technology relationships and new directions in corporate strategy. As firms progress from small, entrepreneurial enterprises following a basic concentration strategy to more complex strategic phases of volume expansion, vertical integration, geographic expansion, and line-of-business diversification, their organizational structures evolve from a simply unitary form to functionally centralized to multi-divisional decentralized organizational forms. Firms that remain single-line businesses almost always have some form of a centralized functional structure. Enterprises predominantly in one industry but slightly diversified typically have a hybrid structure; the dominant business is managed via a functional organization, and the diversified activities are handled through a decentralized divisionalized form. The more diversified an organization becomes, irrespective of whether the diversification is along related or unrelated lines, the more it moves toward some form of decentralized business unit form.

However, it is by no means imperative that organizations begin at Stage I and move in lock-step toward Stage IV.[4] Some firms have moved from a Stage II organization to a Stage IV form without ever passing through Stage III, while other organizations exhibit characteristics of two or more stages simultaneously. And finally, some companies have found it desirable to revert to more focused and centralized forms of organizations after having been a decentralized organization.

About 90 percent of the Fortune 500 firms (nearly all of which are diversified to one degree or another) have a divisionalized organization structure with the primary basis for decentralization being line-of-business considerations. Exhibit 7-4 summarizes some of the common organizational changes required in the transition from Stage I to Stage IV.

One final lesson that the stages model teaches is worth reiterating. A reassessment of organization structure and authority is always useful whenever strategy is changed.[5] A new strategy is likely to entail new or subtly different skills and key activities. If these changes go unrecognized, especially the subtle ones, the resulting mismatch between strategy and organization can pose implementation problems and curtail performance.

Organizational Reengineering

Organizational reengineering is a management technique that has been efficient and effective at focusing the organization on satisfying the customers' demands. Organizations that are particularly appropriate for reengineering include organizations that are large and bureaucratic, have not changed in many years, or have not adopted modern technological and business system changes. The objective of organizational reengineering is to make the organization more efficient and effective at focusing on the customers' needs and desires. Some of the characteristics of the reengineered organization can include:

- Customer satisfaction drives all processes in the organization.
- The company is organized around processes, not functions.
- The organization has a flatter structure.
- Interdisciplinary teams are used to manage many things across functional boundaries.

---

[4] For a more thorough discussion of this point, see Salter, "Stages of corporate development," pp. 34–35.

[5] For an excellent documentation of how a number of well-known corporations revised their organization structures to meet the needs of strategy changes and specific product/market developments, see E. R. Corey and S. H. Star, *Organization Strategy* (Boston: Division of Research, Harvard University Graduate School of Business Administration, 1971), Chap. 3.

EXHIBIT 7-4   Common Organizational Changes Required in Transitions

	Entrepreneurial Single Business, Stage I, to Professional Single Business, Stage II	Professional Single Business, Stage II, to Professional Multibusiness, Stages III and IV
Structure	Move from ill-defined functional specialization to well-articulated functions. Almost total centralization converted to substantial functional responsibility, authority. Integration by entrepreneur gives way to various integrating devices.	Move from functional to product/market (business unit) specialization. Development of corporate functions to manage business unit portfolio. Delegation of operating and some strategic discretion to units. Integration across units by corporate functions.
Business-decision processes	Move planning and resource allocation from an extension of entrepreneurial preferences to more objective processes. Increasing use of functional (sales, costs to budget) performance criteria.	Move planning and resource allocation focus from functional departments to business units. Strategic goals (market share, profits) used to assess and control businesses.
Personnel-decision processes	Move to more systematic procedures and objective criteria for staffing, training, and assessing individual performance. Rewards less subject to personal relationships, paternalism.	Further development of systematic procedures with broadening to emphasize the development of general managers. Rewards variable in relation to business unit performance.
Leadership style	Move from a personally oriented, hands-on domination of operations to a less-obtrusive style emphasizing leadership and integration of functional units relative to strategic needs.	Senior management further distanced from operations. Symbolic and context-setting aspects of style become more critical. Leadership in relation to corporate business unit strategic needs.

Source: Adapted from J. N. Fry and J. P. Killing, *Strategic Analysts and Action,* 2nd ed. (Scarborough, Ont.: Prentice-Hall Canada, 1989), Fig. 10.8, p. 226. Used with permission.

- Teams and personnel are rewarded on the basis of process performance.

- Responsibility and appropriate training is provided to all members.

Many companies are now considering the organizational reengineering process in place of downsizing or just layoffs. The process for completing reengineering involves the following steps:

1. Get all of the top managers enthusiastically committed to making the move from a nonintegrated orientation to an integrated process orientation. This is often one of the most difficult steps.

2. Analyze and identify key processes that support core competitive advantages and that support customer product and service desires. Each of the processes should be linked to a customer product or service outcome.

3. Organize the business around the processes, not functions. This means that the processes will normally be completed by multi-functional teams. All processes should be directly linked to the customer in some way. They are often designated as key processes.

4. Eliminate unnecessary activities or steps in these processes, and eliminate unnecessary processes in the organization that do not support these objectives.

5. Appoint a manager or supervisor as the "owner" of each key process, and empower employees by giving them the necessary information and allow them to have responsibility for the changing the process and achieving its goals.

6. Revamp the reward system so that it supports the team who get the process done most efficiently and effectively. Rewards should also be given for retraining, flexibility, and creativity in designing and accomplishing the process. Performance objectives must be set on a regular basis and must be linked to customer satisfaction.

RECOMMENDED READINGS

Fry, Joseph N., and J. Peter Killing. *Strategic Analysis and Action.* Scarborough, Ont.: Prentice-Hall Canada, 1986, p. 202.

Garvin, David. "Building a learning organization." *Harvard Business Review,* July–August 1993, pp. 78–91.

Ghoshal, Sumantra, and Christopher Bartlett. "Changing the role of top management: beyond structure to process." Two-part series, *Harvard Business Review.* Part I: November–December 1994. Part II: January–February 1995.

Hammer, Michael, and James Champy. *Reengineering the Corporation.* HarperCollins, New York, 1993.

CHAPTER 8

Organizational Forms

We were bureaucratic, inward looking, complacent, self-satisfied and arrogant. We tolerated our own under-performance. We were technocentric and insufficiently entrepreneurial.

Cornelius Herkstroter, Chairman of Shell

The most important part of the GE value to us is its management structure.

Gary C. Wendt, Chairman, President and CEO General Electric Capital Services

There are essentially four strategy-related approaches to organization: (1) functional specialization, (2) geographic organization, (3) decentralized business/product divisions, and (4) matrix structures featuring *dual* lines of authority and strategic priority. Each form relates structure to strategy in a different way and, consequently, has its own set of strategy-related pros and cons. Each of these forms will now be discussed.

The Functional Organization Structure

A functional organization structure tends to be effective in single-business units where key activities revolve around well-defined skills and areas of specialization. In such cases, in-depth specialization and focused concentration on performing functional area tasks and activities can enhance both operating efficiency and the development of a distinctive competence. Generally speaking, organizing by functional specialties promotes full utilization of the most up-to-date technical skills and helps a business capitalize on the efficiency gains to be had from using specialized personnel, facilities, and equipment. These are strategically important considerations for single-business organizations, dominant product enterprises, and vertically integrated firms; moreover, they account for why the firms usually have some kind of centralized, functionally specialized structure.

The text in the first half of this chapter has been adapted in part from Arthur A. Thompson, Jr., and A. J. Strickland III, *Strategy Formulation and Implementation,* 3rd ed. (Plano, Tex.: Business Publications, 1986), pp. 334–345.

Deciding what form the functional specialization will take in a firm must account for variations in customer-product-technology. For instance, a technical instruments manufacturer may be organized around research and development, engineering, production, technical services, quality control, marketing, personnel, and finance and accounting. A municipal government may, on the other hand, be departmentalized according to purpose—fire, public safety, health services, water and sewer, streets, parks and recreation, and education. A university may divide up its organizational units into academic affairs, student services, alumni relations, athletics, buildings and grounds, institutional services, and budget control. Two types of functional organizational approaches are diagrammed in Exhibit 8-1.

The Achilles' heel of a functional structure is getting and maintaining tight strategic coordination across the separated functional units. Functional specialists, partly because of how they are trained and the technical "mystique" of jobs, tend to develop their own mindset and ways of doing things. The more functional specialists differ in their perspective and approach to task accomplishment, the more difficult it becomes to achieve both strategic and operating coordination between them. They neither "talk the same language" nor have an adequate understanding and appreciation of one another's strategic role and problems. Each functional group is more interested in its own "empire" and promoting its own strategic interest and importance (despite the lip service given to cooperation and "what's best for the company"). Tunnel vision and empire-building in functional departments impose an administrative burden on a general manager, who spends time resolving cross-functional differences, enforcing joint cooperation, and opening lines of communication. In addition, a purely functional organization can be myopic when it comes to promoting entrepreneurial creativity, adapting quickly to major customer-market-technology changes, and pursuing opportunities that go beyond the conventional boundaries of the industry.

Geographic Forms of Organization

Organizing according to geographic areas or territories is a rather common structural form for large-scale enterprises whose strategies need to be tailored to fit the particular needs and features of different geographical areas. As indicated in Exhibit 8-2, a geographic organization has its advantages and disadvantages, but the chief reason for its adoption is that it normally improves performance when a market-oriented geographically divergent focus is important strategically.

In the private sector, a territorial structure is typically utilized by chain store retailers, power companies, cement firms, railroads, airlines, the larger paper box and carton manufacturers, and large bakeries and dairy products enterprises. In the public sector, such organizations as the Canadian Red Cross and religious groups have adopted territorial structures in order to be directly accessible to geographically dispersed clienteles.

EXHIBIT 8-1   Functional Organizational Structures

A. THE BUILDING BLOCKS OF A "TYPICAL" FUNCTIONAL ORGANIZATION STRUCTURE

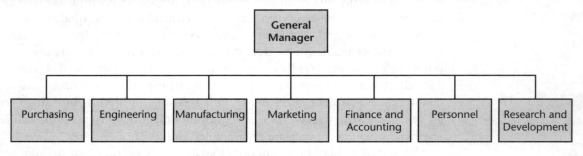

B. THE BUILDING BLOCKS OF A PROCESS-ORIENTED FUNCTIONAL STRUCTURE

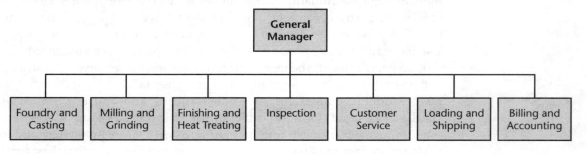

Advantages	Disadvantages
• Enhances operating efficiency where tasks are routine and repetitive	• Poses problems of functional coordination
• Preserves centralized control of strategic results	• Can lead to inter-functional rivalry, conflict, and empire-building
• Allows benefits of specialization and learning/experience curve effects to be fully exploited	• May promote overspecialization and narrow management viewpoints
• Simplifies training of management specialists	• Limited development of general managers
• Promotes high emphasis on craftsmanship and professional standards	• Forces profit responsibility to the top
• Well suited to developing distinctive competencies in one or more functional areas	• Functional specialists often attach more importance to what is best for the functional area than to what is best for the whole business
• Structure tied to key activities within the business	• May lead to uneconomically small units or underutilization of specialized facilities and manpower
	• Functional myopia often works against creative entrepreneurship, against adapting to change, and against attempts to restructure the activity-cost chain that threatens the status of one or more functional departments

Decentralized Business Units

Grouping activities along business and product lines has been a trend among diversified enterprises for the past half-century, beginning with the pioneering efforts of Du Pont and General Motors in the 1920s. Separate business/product divisions emerged because diversification made a functionally specialized manager's job incredibly complex. Imagine the problems a manufacturing executive and his or her staff would have if put in

EXHIBIT 8-2   A Geographic Organization Structure

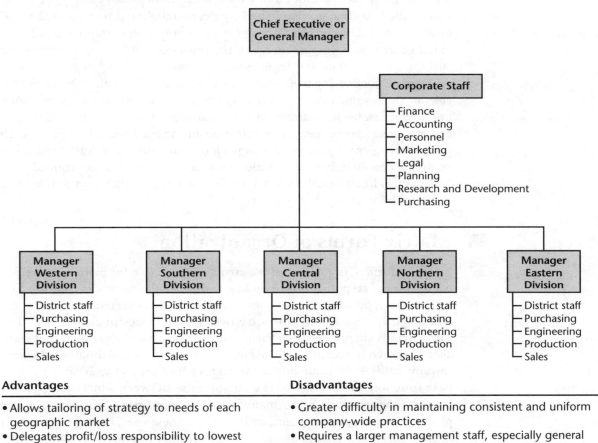

Advantages	Disadvantages
• Allows tailoring of strategy to needs of each geographic market	• Greater difficulty in maintaining consistent and uniform company-wide practices
• Delegates profit/loss responsibility to lowest strategic level	• Requires a larger management staff, especially general managers
• Improves functional coordination within the target geographic market	• Leads to duplication of staff services
• Takes advantage of economies of local operations	• Poses a problem of headquarters control over local operations
• Area units make an excellent training ground to higher-level general managers	

charge of, say, 50 different plants using 20 different technologies to produce 30 different products in 8 different businesses/industries. In a multi-business enterprise, the needs of strategy virtually dictate that the organizational sequence be "corporate to line of business to functional area within a business" rather than "corporate to functional area (aggregated for all businesses)." In the latter case, making sense out of business strategy and achieving functional area coordination for a given business becomes a nightmare.

From a business strategy implementation standpoint, it is far more logical to group all the different activities that belong to the same business under one organization roof, thereby creating line-of-business units (which can then be subdivided into whatever subunits suit the key activities/critical tasks making up the business). The outcome is a structure that not only fits strategy but also makes the jobs of managers more doable. The creation of separate business units, or strategic business units (SBUs) as they are sometimes called, is then accomplished by decentralizing authority to the SBU business-level manager. The approach, very simply, puts entrepreneurially oriented general managers in charge of the business unit, giving them enough authority to formulate and implement whatever business strategy they deem appropriate, motivating them with incentives, and then holding them accountable for the results. However, when a strong strategic fit exists across related business units, it can be tough to get autonomy-conscious business unit general managers to cooperate in coordinating and sharing related activities; each general manager tends to want to argue long and hard about "turf" and about being held accountable for activities not totally under his or her control.

A typical line-of-business organization structure is shown in Exhibit 8-3, along with its strategic pros and cons.

Matrix Forms of Organization

A matrix form of organization is a structure with two (or more) channels of command or responsibility. The key feature of the matrix is that product (or business) and functional lines of authority are overlaid (to form a matrix or grid). Managerial authority over the activities in each unit/cell of the matrix is shared between the product manager and the functional manager as shown in Exhibit 8-4. In a matrix structure, subordinates have dual responsibilities: to their business/product line/project head and to their base function.[1] The outcome is a compromise between functional specialization (engineering, R&D, manufacturing, marketing, accounting) and product-line, market segment, or line-of-business specialization (where all of the specialized talents needed for the product line/market segment/line of business are assigned to the same divisional unit).

A matrix-type organization is a genuinely different structural form and represents a "new way of life." One reason is that the unit-of-command principle is broken; two reporting channels, two bosses, and shared authority create a new kind of organization climate. In essence, the matrix is a conflict resolution system through which strategic and operating priorities are negotiated, power is shared, and resources are allocated internally on a "strongest case for what is best overall for the unit"-type basis.[2]

The impetus for matrix organizations stems from growing use of strategies that add new sources of diversity (products, customer groups, technology, and lines of business) to a firm's range of activities. Out of this diversity come product managers, functional managers, geographic-area managers, new venture managers, and business-level managers—all of whom have important *strategic*

---

[1] A more thorough treatment of matrix organization forms can be found in Jay R. Galbraith, "Matrix organizational designs," *Business Horizons,* February 1971, p. 29.

[2] An excellent critique of matrix organizations is presented in Stanley M. Davis and Paul R. Lawrence, "Problems of matrix organizations," *Harvard Business Review,* May–June 1978, pp. 131–142.

EXHIBIT 8-3   A Decentralized Business Division Type of Organization Structure

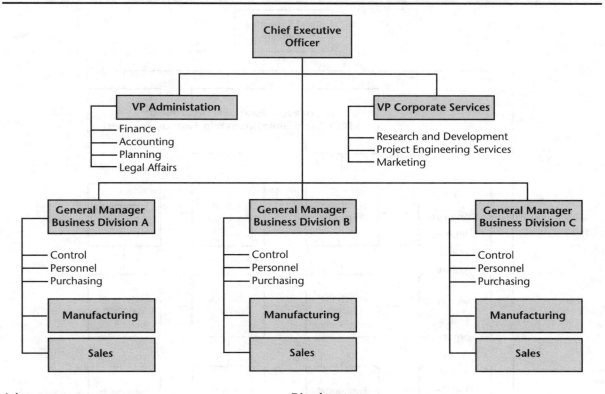

Advantages

- Offers a logical and workable means of decentralizing responsibility and delegating authority in diversified organizations
- Puts responsibility for business strategy closer to each business's unique environment
- Allows critical tasks and specialization to be organized to fit business strategy
- Frees CEO to handle corporate strategy issues
- Creates clear profit/loss accountability

Disadvantages

- Leads to proliferation of staff functions, policy inconsistencies between divisions, and problems of coordination of divisional operations
- Poses a problem of how much authority to centralize and how much to decentralize
- May lead to excessive divisional rivalry for corporate resources and attention
- Raises issue of how to allocate corporate-level overhead
- Business/division autonomy works against achieving coordination of related activities in different business units, thus blocking to some extent the capture of strategic-fit benefits

responsibilities. When at least two of several variables (product, customer, technology, geography, functional area, and market segment) have roughly equal strategic priorities, then a matrix theoretically can be an effective structural form. A matrix arrangement promotes internal checks and balances among competing viewpoints and perspectives, with separate managers for different dimensions of strategic initiative. A matrix approach thus allows *each* of several strategic considerations to be managed directly and to be formally represented in the organization structure. In this sense, it helps middle managers make tradeoff decisions from an organization-wide

EXHIBIT 8-4   A Matrix Organization Structure

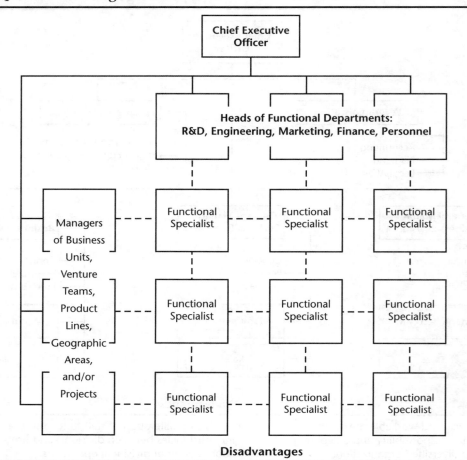

Advantages

- Permits more attention to each dimension of strategic priority
- Creates checks and balances among competing viewpoints
- Facilitates simultaneous pursuit of different types of strategic initiative
- Promotes making tradeoff decisions on the basis of "what's best for the organization as a whole"
- Encourages cooperation, consensus building, conflict resolution, and coordination of related activities

Disadvantages

- Very complex to manage
- Hard to maintain "balance" between the two lines of authority
- So much shared authority can result in a transactions logjam and disproportionate amounts of time being spent on communications
- It is hard to move quickly and decisively without getting clearance from many other people
- Promotes an organizational bureaucracy and hamstrings creative entrepreneurship

perspective.[3] Most applications of matrix organization are limited to covering certain important functions rather than the whole of a large-scale diversified enterprise.

A number of companies shun matrix organization because of its chief weaknesses.[4] It is a complex structure to manage; people often end up confused

---

[3] Davis and Lawrence, p. 132.

[4] Thomas J. Peters and Robert H. Waterman, Jr., *In Search of Excellence* (New York: Harper & Row, 1982), pp. 306–307.

over to whom to report for what. Moreover, because the matrix signals that everything is important and, further, that everybody needs to communicate with everybody else, a "transactions logjam" can emerge. Actions turn into paralysis, since with shared authority it is hard to move decisively without first considering many points of view and getting clearance from many other people. Sizable administrative costs and communications inefficiency can arise, as well as delays in responding quickly. Even so, there are situations in which the benefits of consensus building outweigh these weaknesses.

Combination and Supplemental Methods of Organization

A single type of structural design is not always sufficient to meet the requirements of strategy. When this occurs, one option is to mix and blend the basic organization forms, matching structure to strategy, requirement by requirement and unit by unit. Another is to supplement a basic organizational design with special-situation devices such as project manager/project staff approaches, task force approaches, or venture teams.

International Organizational Forms

A manager can design for international activities in the firm in a variety of ways. The most common are described briefly below.[5]

International Division

The international division is an international business division that is simply added onto the domestic structure, as shown in Exhibit 8-5. This type of structure is typical of a firm having a relatively simple product or functional structure that requires a manager to look after the international operations, which are often sales and marketing related. The structure is appropriate for a firm that is not highly geographically diversified. An international division is usually the first international structural form adopted by a firm as it develops an international strategy. The formation of the international division is an acknowledgement that the international market has become important enough to warrant a top decision maker who focuses entirely on its strategy and performance. Managers are also acknowledging that they must establish an organizational form that links them more closely with their international customers.

Multidomestic Structure

The multidomestic structure, a more evolved international geographical structure, is shown in Exhibit 8-6. It segments the markets according to similarities

---

[5] Paul Beamish, Peter Killing, Donald Lecraw, and Allen Morrison, *International Management*, 2nd ed. (Burr Ridge, Ill.: Richard D. Irwin Inc., 1994).

EXHIBIT 8-5　　The International Divisional Structure

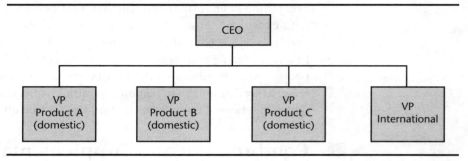

EXHIBIT 8-6　　The Multidomestic Divisional Structure

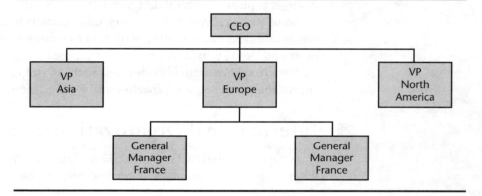

of culture, language, product desires, distribution channels, etc. Divisions are established in markets that have similar characteristics. It should also be noted that activities such as product research and development, marketing, purchasing, and finance are often relegated to the local/head office divisional level. The objective of the multidomestic structure is to move the key functional processes and activities to a location close to the customer.

Managers use the multidomestic structure when they are using a multidomestic strategy, as described in Chapter 10. This structure allows the firm to carry out the decentralized market specific strategy in the most effective manner possible. The role of head office in the multidomestic structure is to provide management personnel, skills, and direction to the international divisions and to coordinate the sharing of technology and information between the divisions.

Global Product Structure

The global product structure is illustrated in Exhibit 8-7. In a global product-division structure the firm is focusing each of its product lines on a broad scope of international markets. This structure allows each business product-division to locate its value chain activities in international locations that maximize the business's overall competitive advantages. For example, in one division, production may be done in Asia, R&D in North America, and marketing in

EXHIBIT 8-7   The Global Product-Division Structure

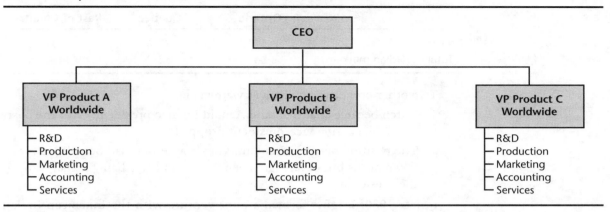

various regions around the world, all of which maximizes the efficiency and effectiveness of the different functions globally for the company. The objective of this structure is to locate parts of the business where they will be most competitive globally.

The global product-division structure is applied to firms that are taking a global strategy internationally (see Chapter 10 for a more thorough description of global strategy).

MINI-CASE   Illustration of Structure-Strategy Linkages*

The following case can be used to assess alternative organizational structures. Suggested discussion questions follow.

T. G. Bright and Co., Limited, 1986

In 1977, T. G. Bright and Co., Limited (Brights) of Niagara Falls, Ontario, sold a wide range of wine products in Ontario in eight categories—sparkling, rosé, white table, port, sherry, appetizer, red table, and other (which included such diverse products as Muscatel, Mazel Tov, and sacramental wine). Through wholly owned subsidiaries, Brights also offered additional selections in many of these eight categories in other provinces.

It was a small firm ($14 million in sales) with over half its sales volume in Ontario (see Exhibit 8-8), most of its manufacturing in Ontario, and a product line that had not digressed from wine. Its 1977 organization is reflected in Exhibit 8-9.

By 1980, Brights' organization was modified to include a second regional operations manager (see Exhibit 8-10). A third production facility in Quebec had been acquired in 1979. With this acquisition, the proportion of sales in Quebec—27 percent in 1979—was expected to increase so that Brights would have the largest non-government operation in Quebec.

*This case was prepared by Professor Paul W. Beamish as a basis for classroom discussion. © 1986 by Paul W. Beamish.

EXHIBIT 8-8   Percentage Share of Canadian Wine Market

	Ontario	Quebec	Rest of Country
Sales	55%	27%	18%
Total Canadian market	34	32	34

Two other organization changes were made:

1. Hatch became chairman and Arnold became president, with the position of executive vice-president dropped.
2. The position of vice-president, sales/marketing, had been filled for a few months but of late had been vacant and was being managed by the president.

In late 1980, Brights formed a joint venture with the Inkameep Indian Band of Oliver, British Columbia, to establish a winery in B.C.'s Okanagan Valley. In 1984 and 1985, small winery operations were established in Manitoba and Nova Scotia, respectively. Sales in 1984 were nearly $38 million, net of excise and sales tax.

In 1985 a limited import operation in wines and spirits under the name of Wines of the Globe was established. (In 1984 the province of Quebec modified its regulations to permit the bottling of imported wines by local wineries.)

Brights' non-restaurant sales were through provincial government outlets, small grocery stores (in Quebec), and company-owned retail outlets. The company operated over 20 retail outlets in Ontario, with perhaps half being located in Toronto.

In order to keep pace with changing consumer tastes, Brights' product mix had been steadily shifting away from fortified wines to those with lower alcohol levels. In addition, a greater proportion of sales was in white rather than

EXHIBIT 8-9   1977 Organization

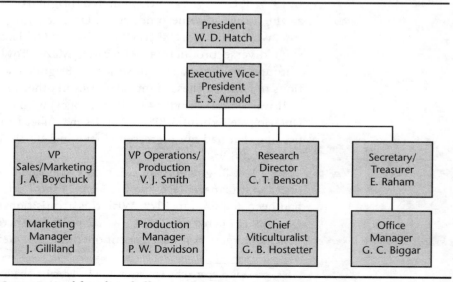

Source: Derived from list of officers and executives in 1977 annual report.

EXHIBIT 8-10   **1980 Organization**

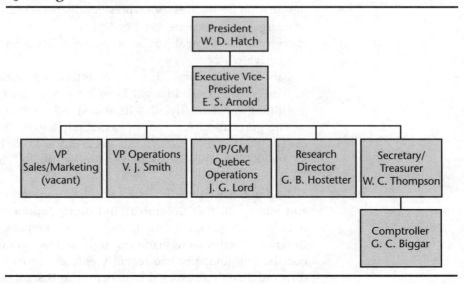

red wines. With the purchase of a Quebec cider company in 1978, Bright acquired the ability and licence to produce cider. Brights had also introduced a wine cooler, which combined specially fermented wine and pure spring water.

Grapes were supplied from three sources—company-owned vineyards, purchases from other grape growers, and concentrate and bulk purchases from other countries. Grapes purchased from local growers in Southern Ontario (and, to a lesser extent, the Okanagan region in B.C.) were the primary source of supply.

By 1985, Brights had once again modified its organization structure (see Exhibit 8-11).

The chairman, W. D. Hatch, died in 1985. The chairman's position was not reflected in the 1985 annual report list of fixers and executives. In lieu of a vice-president, sales/marketing, a staff director of marketing was appointed to work with the regional vice-presidents. The previous vice-president/general manager of Quebec Operations had left the company. His replacement held the title of vice-president/general manager, Eastern Division.

EXHIBIT 8-11   **1985 Organization**

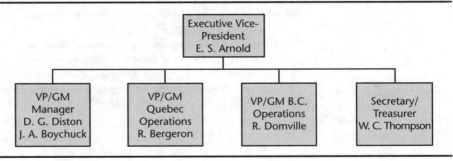

Source: List of officers and executives from 1985 annual report.

In 1986, W. C. Thompson resigned and G. C. Biggar became secretary. The designation for the three vice-president/general managers changed from being in charge of Operations, Quebec Operations, and B.C. Operations to being in charge of the Central Division, Eastern Division, and Western Division, respectively.

Carling O'Keefe Limited, Toronto, Ontario, announced on June 26, 1986, that its wholly owned subsidiary, Jordan & Ste-Michelle Cellars Ltd., had been sold (including substantially all of its assets) to T. G. Bright and Co., Limited.

The purchase price was approximately $30 million. It was estimated that the transaction resulted in a loss to Carling O'Keefe Limited of approximately $7,750,000 after tax, or $0.36 per common share. The business had been unprofitable in 1986.

Jordan & Ste-Michelle Cellars Ltd. had wineries in St. Catharines, Ontario, and Surrey, British Columbia, and, until September 1985, had operated a winery in Calgary, Alberta. Except for 33 company-operated retail stores in Ontario, all sales were made through outlets operated by provincial liquor boards. The company had recently entered into a joint venture to manufacture and distribute cider products for the U.S. market.

At the time of the sale, the gross income for Jordan & Ste-Michelle Cellars Ltd. was almost identical to that of Brights. The acquisition meant that Brights was now the largest winery in Canada by a large margin.

Discussion Questions

1. In 1986, Brights had a regional structure. What alternative forms could it have adopted?
   a. Why, then, did it adopt a regional structure?
   b. How big does a company have to be to justify a regional structure?

2. Why did Brights have a functional structure in 1977, given the arguments for a regional?

3. Why was the position of executive vice-president eliminated in 1980? Why was the position of vice-president, marketing, kept vacant in 1980/81? Why was the position of vice-president, marketing, ultimately eliminated and replaced with a staff director of marketing?

4. What might occur now that the acquisition has occurred?

RECOMMENDED READINGS

Bahrami, Homa. "The emerging flexible organization." *California Management Review*, Summer 1992, pp. 33–52.

Krackhardt, David, and Jeffrey Hanson. "Informal networks: the company behind the chart." *Harvard Business Review,* July–August 1993, pp. 104–113.

Spitzer, Quinn, and Benjamin Tregoe. "Thinking and managing beyond the boundaries." *Business Horizons,* January–February 1993, pp. 36–40.

CHAPTER 9

Managing Strategic Change

In today's world there are two kinds of companies: the quick and the dead.

Al Dunlap, Turnaround Specialist and CEO of Sunbeam Corp.

Act 1 is recognizing the need for change, Act 2 is crafting the vision and Act 3 is reactivating the organization. The transformation of a very large company is a five to ten year journey.

Noel Tichy, Professor, University of Michigan

Transformation is messy. ... If we don't change our leadership style, our behaviors and mindsets, we aren't going to be able to get results.

Mac McDonald, Manager of Shell's Leadership and Performance Division

Organizations must constantly deal with change. Managers wishing to make changes in their organization must be both effective implementers and champions of change. The ability to commit to a change and see that it is adopted has become a highly valued skill in an organization.

The Three Phases of Strategic Change

In broad terms, the process of strategic change can be thought of as having three phases. The first phase is awareness and capability building; the second, commitment and adoption; and the third, reinforcement and recycling (see Exhibit 9-1). The most exciting phase for most managers, and certainly the one that receives the greatest emphasis in the popular press, is the second. Managing this phase well is important, but not necessarily sufficient for overall success.[1]

Phase One: Awareness and Capability Building

The first phase in the strategic change process is awareness and capability building. Without widespread awareness of the need for change, most employees will resist change. Such a reaction is understandable given the uncertainty and potential negative outcome that individuals may face.

---

[1] Gary Hamel and C. K. Prahalad, "Strategic intent," *Harvard Business Review,* May–June 1989, p. 67.

Even when there exists wide awareness of the need for change, there may not be a shared view of the appropriate direction of change. For example, everyone may be dissatisfied with the firm's performance and recognize the need for change. But should the solution be to retrench, or to take an aggressive, growth-oriented approach? It is important that the employee groups not only be aware that change is necessary, but also agree on the type and direction of change required.

Assuming that widespread awareness of the need for, and agreement on the direction of, change does exist—and this is a big assumption—management can then proceed with examining whether it has (or can develop) the necessary capabilities to permit the change to take place. Building capabilities through staff or systems development can be a time-consuming and (in the short term)

EXHIBIT 9-1   Achieving Readiness for Strategic Change

Change Target Development	Potential Obstacles	Common Management Tactics
Awareness Understanding		
• Establishing a general appreciation of the need for and direction of change	• Ambiguous change requirements	• Informal contact, lobbying
	• Inertial resistance	• Loosening-up exercises—target exposure, involvement
• Building a greater depth of knowledge of the situation, its consequences, and potential remedies	• Information bottlenecks	• Short-term task forces
	• Limited capacity to understand	
Capability		
• Developing capacity to perform new tasks	• Personnel bottlenecks—inadequate training and experience	• Training programs
	• Support systems bottlenecks	• Support systems development
	• Behavioural resistance	• Personnel changes
		• Direct coaching
Commitment		
• Developing genuine agreement about and support for the required changes	• Displacement of the problem	• Involvement activities
	• Behavioural resistance	• Partial solutions and demonstrations
	• Inadequacies, inconsistencies in support and incentive systems	• Negotiations
		• Coalition building
	• Weak position of power	• Coercion
		• Personnel changes
Adoption		
• Achieving change in behaviour, effective performance	• Tangible risk	• Close monitoring
	• Lagging resistance, support factors	• Intensification and recycling of readiness efforts
	• Poor readiness	• Mop-up action
Reinforcement		
• Sustaining effort and diligence in performing new tasks	• Loss of commitment	• Rewards for new behaviour
	• Resource and organizational inconsistencies	• Adjustment of resource and organizational factors
Recycling		
• Defining and implementing improvements and new directions	• Problems in linking a series of changes	• Training and structuring for flexibility
	• Complacency	• Continuous challenges for improvement

Source: Adapted from J. N. Fry and J. P. Killing, *Strategic Analysis and Action*, 2nd ed. (Scarborough, Ont.: Prentice-Hall Canada, 1989), Figs. 13.5 and 13.6. Reprinted by permission.

not immediately gratifying process. Nonetheless, it is absolutely essential. Just as a hockey coach needs players who know how to skate and who possess hockey sticks, managers must ensure that the organizational capability for change exists.

Phase Two: Commitment and Adoption

With the proper groundwork laid, the manager, as change agent, can begin placing greater effort on the development of widespread support and enthusiasm for the proposed change. Organizational champions cannot enact changes themselves, particularly in larger firms. They require support throughout the organization from both above and below. Through negotiations and coalition building they need to get other managers to "sign on," or if this is too slow, they need to consider various coercive tactics or ultimately personnel changes.

After wider commitment has been developed (and where possible the principal sources of resistance addressed) attention can turn to actual adoption of the change; people can be hired or moved, money can be spent, assets and resources can be put in place, and people can begin to take on new responsibilities.

What characterizes the commitment and adoption phase is an escalating sense that change is necessary and it is happening. Decisions are being made and acted upon. In contrast, during the awareness and capability phase—even though some resources were being allocated—management still had the option to change their mind, or slow the process.

Phase Three: Reinforcement and Recycling

Even with the change having been adopted, the change process does not end. Followup effort and reinforcement are typically required. It may be a less glamorous phase, but it is no less important. Just as a newly purchased automobile will subsequently require scheduled maintenance, service, and parts, so also does a company change require ongoing attention, both to reinforce change and to ensure that the organization keeps pace with changes in the environment. Only through continuous reassessment can the organization improve overall prospects for success.

Types of Change

One of the most significant influences on the way in which the three phases of the change process are managed is the degree of urgency required. When the impact of urgency on change is considered, we are left with three principal types of change: urgent change, reactive change, and proactive change (see Exhibit 9-2).

Urgent Change

When the necessity for change is urgent, comprehensive action is required, and there is little time for languid decision making. Action is required now. Urgent change is when the company is facing a crisis and the long-term success and

EXHIBIT 9-2 **Pressure for Change**

	Type of Change		
	Urgent	**Reactive**	**Proactive**
Necessity for change	Pressing or immediately	Tangible, but not pressing	Forecast or sometime in the future
Action required	Comprehensive	Diagnostic, plus some clear needs	Uncertain, but diagnostic at a minimum
Timing for required change	Immediate	Soon	Uncertain
Range of options available	Quite constrained due to an erosion of competitive position and advantages	Possibly constrained due to a slight erosion of competitive position and advantages	Unconstrained accept for competitive options available in the industry

possibly viability of the organization is at stake. Usually there are clear signs that change is required—for example, sales and profits have been declining, cash flow is drying up, and other financial and operational performance indicators are poor.

Urgent change often requires a manager who understands the situation clearly and makes the necessary changes quickly, often in a non-participatory manner. That said, employees usually are well aware that change is necessary and may even understand the direction of change required.

Some academics and managers have proposed creating a crisis if there isn't one, to instill the need for change in employees. But the use of a contrived crisis is inadvisable, because the need for change may be questionable, and employee resistance may develop. As well, the general manager who throws his or her organization into a crisis, and is seen to have contrived it, runs a serious risk of losing credibility.

Reactive Change

Unlike with urgent change, in a reactive change situation the necessity for change is not as pressing. Action is clearly required, but sufficient time is available to permit the organization to respond to conditions in a more planned fashion. Abrupt realignments of a firm's strategy or organization are not required.

Generally, the need for reactive change is preceded by some financial and operational performance warnings, but the financial and operational health of the company has not yet been compromised. Some employee groups may be aware that change is necessary, but often they do not understand what type of change will be made or in what direction it will go.

Proactive Change

Proactive change allows the company the luxury of developing over time a strategic plan and implementing it, because the need for change is forecast. Often financial and operational performance has not been affected, but there may be some strategic performance indicators that are providing some feedback to the managers that change is necessary.

At first this type of change seems easier, for management has more degrees of latitude and more time to implement change. However, the difficulty in carrying out this type of change is in understanding the extent, timing, and kind of change required given the uncertainty of future events. Furthermore, employees may be more resistant to change when there is no clear evidence that change is necessary.

Given the uncertainty that surrounds it, change is often implemented step by step. This allows the managers to edge toward their ultimate goal, but adjust plans and objectives as the uncertainty declines.

Most good managers recognize the value of getting practice with change through small, logical incremental steps rather than major one-time realignments. As one writer noted:

> An organization that is used to continuous small changes and that has balanced strategic expertise at the top with operating expertise and entrepreneurship at the bottom is probably better prepared for a big leap than is an organization that has gone for several years without any change at all, but now requires a change.[2]

Further, these managers recognize that dealing with change will always create some level of stress in an organization, and too much change all at once, with the stress this entails, can be fatal. The process of incremental change, or *incrementalism*,[3] allows the managers to continually adjust to new realities in the competitive environment while also maintaining the organization's ability to implement change.

■ The General Manager and Change

The general manager (GM) is the person most responsible for managing change. His or her task is influenced by:

- Experience and skill in the organization and industry
- Political position in the organization
- Preferences and values
- Style
- Urgency
- Available resources

The obvious implication of such a complex list is that key stakeholders may very well hold different perceptions about what type of change situation exists. As Exhibit 9-3 suggests, by plotting an estimate of how each stakeholder may perceive the change situation, it is possible to focus on areas of potential disagreement. The specific type of change, which is obvious to you, may not be obvious to someone else, and vice versa. Further, others may not perceive the need for any change.

---

[2] Robert A. Hayes, "Strategic planning—forward in reverse?" *Harvard Business Review,* November–December 1985, p. 117.

[3] For further discussion, see James Brian Quinn, *Strategies for Change: Logical Incrementalism* (Homewood, Ill.: Richard D. Irwin, 1980).

EXHIBIT 9-3   Key Stakeholder Perceptions of Type of Change Situation

	Type of Change			
Stakeholder	No Change	Proactive	Reactive	Urgent
A				
B				
C				
D				

Tactics for Change

The general manager has a variety of tactics available for implementing change. These will depend in part on his or her skill in coercing people into committing to change, the level and preference for the use of power, and whether this power can or should be exerted directly or indirectly. Exhibit 9-4 lays out four basic tactics for change: giving orders, changing the context, persuasion, and opening channels. Each has advantages and disadvantages and unique characteristics.

This approach is characterized by the forceful, top-down unambiguous issuance of orders. It has the advantage of being fast, and requiring little senior management time. However, low organization commitment and high resistance may result from such an approach. As well, it places heavy reliance on the abilities of the GM to have correctly surmised what change is needed. Not surprisingly, "giving orders" is a tactic frequently observed in an urgent change situation.

Persuasion

Persuasion is a less formal and more time-intensive than "giving orders." It involves negotiation and is more participative in nature. It is a tactic employed by GMs who either do not have a great deal of power, or have the persuasive skills to get commitment. In order to persuade, additional information may have to be collected to educate the target group on the advantages of the change. If the target groups or individuals see the change as being in their self-interest, greater motivation and commitment will result. Focusing people's attention on the long-term positive goals as well as an external target (such as the customer, competition, etc.) can be helpful. The problems associated with this change tactic are that it may require a lot of GM time, is much slower than giving orders, and may require more of a compromise.

Opening Channels

The subtlest of change tactics has been called "opening channels." It is characterized by a low use of power and by indirect actions. It is slow, informal, consensus-oriented, and takes an evolutionary approach. The objective is to open the channels of communication and interaction in such a way that employees are guided in a particular general direction. The task of the GM is to put in

EXHIBIT 9-4   Tactics for Change

HIGH USE OF POWER	
Direct Action: Giving Orders	**Indirect Action: Changing Context**
Characteristics	**Characteristics**
• Forceful, top-down, unambiguous, power-based	• Formal or informal, power-driven; if the organization or resources are changed as a means of driving a change in direction or behaviour, great attention must be placed on implementation
Pros	**Pros**
• Fast	• Fast (but not as quick as "giving orders")
• Desired direction clear	• Useful approach when management power cannot be used directly on principal targets
• Requires little senior management time	
Cons:	**Cons**
• Low organization commitment	• High resistance possible
• High resistance possible	• Risky, since action is indirect but power-driven
• Places heavy reliance on abilities of the GM	• Timing important

LOWER USE OF POWER	
Direct Action: Persuasion	**Indirect Action: Opening Channels**
Characteristics	**Characteristics**
• Less formal; time-intensive, participative, negotiated; may require information to "educate" the employees and/or to permit employees to see that change is in their self-interest	• Subtle, evolutionary, informal; slower; consensus-oriented
Pros	**Pros**
• Higher organization commitment likely	• High commitment likely
• Greater motivation	• Draws ideas from maximum number of people
Cons	**Cons**
• Slower implementation	• Very slow implementation
• Requires a lot of GM time for communications	• Requires a GM with foresight, patience, tolerance for ambiguity
• May require compromise	• Will require compromise

place the conditions (through such means as task forces and training programs) that will enable the organization to more openly consider a particular change.

Realistically, the GM will be unable to exert a great deal of control or precision over the pace at which the change occurs. This is not typically a problem, however, since here the GM has a longer-term focus. Not surprisingly, this tactic for change is often associated with proactive change.

The principal benefits of opening channels are that you often get high commitment, and input will be received from the maximum number of people. It has the disadvantages of being slow and requiring a GM with foresight, patience, tolerance for ambiguity, and a willingness to compromise.

Changing Context

Changing context as a tactic for implementing change that is characterized by high use of power and by indirect action. Changing the organization and/or resources are the principal methods employed. Some of the advantages of this tactic are that it is fast (but not as fast as "giving orders") and useful when management power cannot be exerted directly on the change target. For example, a GM wishing to make an important acquisition may wish to make the acquisition with the support of senior management. He or she may have wide support, but face some resistance, particularly from one key head office manager who will likely be involved in the acquired company. One organizational solution would be to transfer the resisting manager to an unrelated or distant division. Then the acquisition can proceed with support of management. The GM exerts his or her power by moving the resisting manager, and by this indirect action achieves the GM's acquisition objective. While moving a manager is a direct action, this tactic is considered indirect, as it was not strictly a requirement of achieving the principal change (i.e., making the acquisition). The organization context was changed so as to facilitate achievement of the change.

There are inherent risks in this change tactic. It may not eliminate all sources of resistance, and may create new ones. Furthermore, changing the context may be more detrimental to the business than allowing the resistance to be present while continuing with the change.

Conclusion

This chapter has provided an introduction to managing change. The process of a strategic change has three phases: awareness and capability building, commitment and adoption, and reinforcement and recycling. As Exhibit 9-1 noted, there are potential obstacles and common management tactics for each phase.

A significant influence on how the change process is managed is the degree of urgency required. In this context there are three main types of change: urgent change, reactive change, and proactive change.

A strategy has not been implemented until the targeted behaviour has changed. In most instances, the task of installing the new strategy and seeing that the behaviour of people in the organization changes is a formidable one for the GM. Yet with creativity and determination, it is possible.

The tactics available for implementing change will depend in part on the GM's skill, status, and degree of preference for the use of power, and on whether this power should be applied directly. Exhibit 9-4 noted four basic tactics for achieving change: giving orders, persuasion, opening channels, and changing the context.

RECOMMENDED READINGS

Berling, Robert. "The emerging approach to business strategy: building a relationship advantage." *Business Horizons,* July–August 1993, pp. 16–27.

Brache, Alan. "Process improvement and management: a tool for strategy implementation." *Planning Review*, September–October 1992, pp. 24–26.

Floyd, Steven W., and Bill Wooldridge. "Managing strategic consensus: the foundation of effective implementation." *The Executive,* November 1992, pp. 27–39.

Fry, Joseph N., and J. Peter Killing, *Strategic Analysis and Action.* Scarborough, Ontario, Prentice-Hall Canada Inc., 1995.

Pearson, Christine, and Ian Mitroff. "From crisis prone to crisis prepared: a framework for crisis management." *The Executive,* February 1993, pp. 48–59.

Starr, Marting. "Accelerating innovation." *Business Horizons,* July–August 1992, pp. 44–51.

Wilhelm, Warren. "Changing corporate culture—or corporate behavior? How to change your company." *The Executive*, November 1992, pp. 72–77.

CHAPTER 10

Corporate and International Strategies

I don't know of anybody else who has had the same format or the same vision of how a diverse company could operate. Most people who've had a holding company actually try to run the operating businesses, move people from one to another and move cash. We really insist that each of Onex's businesses run as an autonomous unit.

Gerald Schwartz, Chairman of Onex Corp.

We must not only think beyond our traditional borders, but build there as well. ... If we don't become a strong, global force, we will just be eaten up by the American multinationals. Quite frankly, they'll eat our lunch.

Don Loewn, CEO of Saskatchewan Wheat Pool

This chapter considers a variety of generic corporate and international strategies. There are dozens of ways of categorizing strategic decisions. Not all are appropriate for each organization. Nonetheless, there are typically more viable alternatives available than are actually considered by most managers.

Corporate Strategy

Corporate strategy focuses on the task of selecting what businesses to be in, what businesses not to be in, and what businesses to invest in further. Therefore, it really represents an investment or resource allocation strategy for the firm. This section will describe the following basic categories of corporate strategic choices:

1. Diversification
2. Integration
3. Cooperation
4. Retrenchment

1. Diversification

Based on product-line characteristics, the following four types diversification in a firm have been identified: single-product, dominant-product, related-product, and unrelated-product. Each type represents a distinct corporate strategy, and there are measurable differences between them in terms of their deviation from an original product technology or marketing emphasis.

In turn, the original product technology or marketing emphasis suggests an underlying skill base within the firm. This skill base or core competency is defined as "the collective knowledge, skills, habits of working together, as well as the collective experience of what the market will bear, that is required in the cadre of managerial and technical personnel if the firm is to survive and grow in a competitive market."[1]

These four categories of firms have been subdivided into a total of nine types, each of which is then related to performance. Significantly, firms adopting a single-business, dominant-product or related-product strategy were observed to have above-average profitability. This held true in both a domestic context (United States, Canada) and an international context (U. S. multinational, European multinational).[2]

The higher performance associated with firms having a single-product, dominant-constrained, or related-constrained product diversification is intuitively consistent with the "core competency" concept, because all of the products are related to a core business skill or competence. This is why it has been frequently emphasized that successful firms should focus and "stick to their knitting."[3] On the other hand, the above-average profitability associated with active conglomerates is not as obviously associated with the core competency argument until one realizes that these firms' core competencies exist at the corporate level. Such competencies are often financially or administratively related. Research has consistently shown that firms that have businesses and product lines that consistently do not share the core competency of the company have poor performance.

There are important implications for general managers because of differences in the profitability levels associated with the degree of product diversification. Internally, whether a firm is considering an acquisition, a merger, or simply a change in product emphasis, the likely impact of the change upon profits can be better assessed. External to the firm, product diversification strategy represents another tool which bankers, accountants, and investment dealers can use to assist them in assessing a firm's future profitability.

From a diversification perspective, a firm has a variety of avenues that it can select for growth, as shown in Exhibit 10-1. The top four approaches to growth may be suitable if they build upon a core competency in the organization at a business or product level. The lower two approaches to growth (horizontal and conglomerate diversification) and even the related diversification approach must rely on core competencies at the corporate level. It should be noted that very few companies have developed core competencies

[1] Wrigley Leonard, "Divisional autonomy and diversification," doctoral dissertation, Harvard University, 1970.

[2] For more details, see J. M. Geringer, Paul W. Beamish, and R. da Costa, "Diversification strategy and internationalization: implications for MNE performance," *Strategic Management Journal,* vol. 10, no. 2 (March–April 1989), pp. 109–119.

[3] See Thomas J. Peters and Robert H. Waterman, *In Search of Excellence* (New York: Harper & Row, 1982).

EXHIBIT 10-1   Product/Market Growth Strategic Choices

		Market/Customer Growth	
		Existing	New
Product/Service Growth	**Existing**	Market Penetration	Market Development
	Modified/Improved	Product development	
	New but Related	Concentric diversification	
	New and Unrelated	Horizontal diversification	Conglomerate diversification

at the corporate level. Some examples of the successes, among many failures, are the Irving Companies, KKR, and GE.

Market penetration involves seeking increased market share for present products or services in present markets through greater marketing efforts. It is appropriate when:

- Current markets are not saturated with the firm's particular product or service.
- The usage rate of present customers could be significantly increased.
- The market shares of major competitors have been declining while total industry sales have been increasing.
- The correlation between dollar sales and dollar marketing expenditures has historically been high.
- Increased economies of scale provide major competitive advantages.

Market development involves the introduction of present products or services into new geographic areas. It is appropriate when:

- New channels of distribution are available that are reliable, inexpensive, and of good quality.
- An organization is very successful at what it does in its present geographic markets.
- Untapped or unsaturated markets exist.
- An organization has the needed capital and human resources to manage expanded operations.
- An organization has excess production capacity.
- An organization's basic industry is rapidly becoming global in scope.

Product development involves seeking increased sales by improving or modifying present products or services, for either existing or new customers. This strategy is appropriate when:

- An organization has successful products that are in the maturity stage of their life cycles; the idea here is to attract satisfied customers to try new (improved) products as a result of their positive experience with the organization's present products or services.
- An organization competes in an industry that is characterized by rapid technological developments.
- Major competitors offer better-quality products at comparable prices.
- An organization competes in a high-growth industry.

- An organization has especially strong research and development capabilities.

Concentric diversification involves the addition of new, but related, products or services for either existing or new customers—for example, Gillette's development of an array of shaving supplies and products to supplement its blade product strategy. This strategy is appropriate when:

- An organization competes in a no-growth or slow-growth industry.
- Adding new but related products would significantly enhance the sales of current products.
- New but related products could be offered at highly competitive prices.
- New but related products have seasonal sales levels that counterbalance an organization's existing peaks and valleys.
- An organization's products are currently in the decline stage of their life cycles.

Horizontal diversification involves the addition of new, unrelated products or services for present customers. This is one of the more risky strategies, but it is appropriate when:

- Revenues derived from an organization's current products or services would significantly increase by adding the new, unrelated products.
- An organization competes in a highly competitive and/or no-growth industry, as indicated by low industry profit margins and returns.
- An organization's present channels of distribution can be used to market the new products to current customers.
- The new products have countercyclical sales patterns compared to an organization's present products.

Conglomerate diversification involves the addition of new, unrelated products or services for new customers. This is one of the more risky strategies, but it is appropriate when:

- An organization has the corporate capital and managerial talent needed to compete successfully in a new industry (i.e., the organization has the corporate specific skills and competencies to compete in a diverse set of businesses).
- The organization has the opportunity to purchase an unrelated business that is an attractive investment opportunity.
- There exists financial synergy between the acquired and the acquiring firm. Note that a key difference between concentric and conglomerate diversification is that the former should be based on some commonality in markets, products, or technology, whereas the latter should be based more on profit considerations.

To create shareholder wealth with any form of diversification, Porter[4] suggests the need to meet three essential tests:

---

[4] For more details see Michael E. Porter, "From competitive advantage to corporate strategy," *Harvard Business Review,* May–June 1987, pp. 43–59.

1. *Industry attractiveness test*. The industry chosen for diversification must be an attractive one.

2. *Cost-of-entry test*. The cost of entry must not capitalize future profits.

3. *Better-off test*. Either the acquiring or the acquired company must gain competitive advantage.

On the basis of a sample of the diversification records of 33 large U.S. companies, Porter found that companies had ignored at least one or two of these tests, and "the strategic results were disastrous."[5] Almost all of the 33 companies that he investigated had divested many more acquisitions than they had kept, indicating that the acquisitions had not been a success.

2. Integration

There are two basic types of integration: vertical and horizontal. Vertical integration involves a choice of integrating backward to the original supplier of goods or services, and/or integrating forward to the ultimate customer. Horizontal integration means seeking ownership or increased control over competitors in very similar markets.

Some advantages of vertical integration are to reduce vulnerability by securing supply and/or markets, or to reduce transaction costs by absorbing costs upstream or downstream in the value chain. In general, vertical integration helps a business to protect profit margins and market share by ensuring access to consumers and/or material inputs. Some of the advantages and disadvantages of vertical integration are summarized in Exhibit 10-2.

Backward integration, that is, seeking ownership or increased control over suppliers, is appropriate when:

- An organization's present suppliers are especially expensive, or unreliable, or incapable of meeting the firm's needs for parts, components, assemblies, or raw materials.

- Suppliers are few and competitors are many.

- An organization competes in an industry that is growing rapidly. This is a factor because integrative-type strategies (forward, backward, and horizontal) reduce an organization's ability to diversify in a declining industry.

- An organization has both the capital and the human resources needed to manage the new business of supplying its own raw materials.

- The advantages of stable prices are particularly important. This is a factor because an organization can stabilize the cost of its raw materials and the associated price of its products through backward integration.

- Present suppliers have high profit margins, which suggests that the business of supplying products or services in the given industry is a worthwhile venture.

- An organization needs to acquire a needed yet limited resource quickly.

---

[5] Porter, p. 46.

EXHIBIT 10-2 Some Advantages and Disadvantages of Vertical Integration

Advantages	Disadvantages
Internal Benefits	**Internal Costs**
• Integration economies reduce costs by eliminating steps, reducing duplicate overhead, and cutting costs (technology-dependent).	• Need for overhead to coordinate vertical integration increases costs.
• Improved coordination of activities reduces inventory and other costs.	• Burden of excess capacity from unevenly balanced minimum-efficient-scale plants (technology-dependent).
• Avoid time-consuming tasks such as price shopping, communicating design details, or negotiating contracts.	• Poorly organized vertically integrated firms do not enjoy synergies that compensate for higher costs.
Competitive Benefits	**Competitive Dangers**
• Avoid foreclosure to inputs, services, or markets.	• Obsolete processes may be perpetuated.
• Improved marketing or technological intelligence.	• Creates mobility (or exit) barriers.
• Opportunity to create product differentiation (increased value added).	• Links firm to sick adjacent businesses.
• Superior control of firm's economic environment (market power).	• Lose access to information from suppliers or distributors.
• Create credibility for new products.	• Synergies created through vertical integration may be overrated.
• Synergies could be created by coordinating vertical activities skillfully.	• Managers integrated before thinking through the most appropriate way to do so.

Source: Reprinted by permission of the publisher from *Strategic Flexibility: A Management Guide for Changing Times,* by Kathryn Rudie Harrigan (Lexington, Mass.: Lexington Books, D. C. Heath and Company). © 1985, D. C. Heath and Company.

Forward integration, that is, gaining ownership or increased control over distributors or retailers, is appropriate when:

- An organization's present distributors are especially expensive, or unreliable, or incapable of meeting the firm's distribution needs.
- The availability of quality distributors is so limited as to offer a competitive advantage to those firms that integrate forward.
- An organization competes in an industry that is growing and is expected to continue to grow markedly. This is a factor because forward integration reduces an organization's ability to diversify if its basic industry falters.
- An organization has both the capital and the human resources needed to manage the new business of distributing its own products.
- The advantages of stable production are particularly high. This is a consideration because an organization can increase the predictability of the demand for its output through forward integration.
- Present distributors or retailers have high profit margins. This situation suggests that a company could profitably distribute its own products and price them more competitively by integrating forward.

Horizontal integration, that is, seeking ownership or increased control over competitors, is appropriate when:

- An organization can gain monopolistic characteristics in a particular area or region without being challenged by the federal government for "tending substantially" to reduce competition.
- Increased economies of scale provide major competitive advantages.

- An organization has both the capital and the human talent needed to successfully manage an expanded organization.
- Competitors are faltering due to a lack of managerial expertise or a need for particular capabilities or resources that your organization possesses. Note that horizontal integration is not appropriate if competitors are doing poorly, because that means the overall industry is in decline.

A frequently observed method of horizontal integration is acquisition or merger, in which four postures exist: rescues, collaborations, contested situations, and raids (see Exhibit 10-3). The most adversarial acquisition is the raid, and the most cooperative the rescue. The degree of resistance rises steadily from rescues through to raids. The need to consider carefully how to integrate a newly acquired business is often overlooked. Numerous stresses exist which, if not managed, can result in failure.

3. Cooperation

One of the predominant trends in the past decade has been the increased use of cooperative strategies. Whether in the domestic or international market, more frequent use of joint ventures, licensing, countertrade, and technology/R&D collaboration has been observed. These arrangements are characterized by a willingness to either share or split managerial control and possibly ownership.

Several opportunities for sharing can come from a cooperative strategy, including sharing a sales force, advertising activities, manufacturing facilities, and management know-how.[6] A number of potential competitive advantages are associated with each type of opportunity for sharing, including gaining economies of scale in some activities, using another company's specialized assets, knowledge or skill, and lowering the financial risk or increasing the resources put on a project. However, cooperative strategies have an associated management cost, and sometimes the strategic fit can be more illusory than real: for example, salespersons may not be as effective as expected in representing a new product. But despite the difficulties that can arise, a recent trend is the increase in cooperative arrangements between hitherto competing organizations.

---

[6] For more examples, see Michael E. Porter, *Competitive Advantage: Creating and Sustaining Superior Performance* (New York: Free Press, 1985), Chap. 9.

EXHIBIT 10-3   Four Acquisition Postures

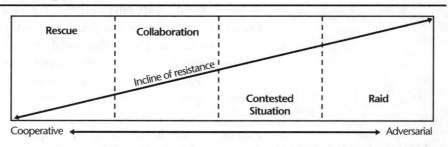

Source: Price, Pritchett, Pritchett and Associates, Inc., *After the Merger: Managing the Shockwaves* (Homewood, Ill.: Dow-Jones Irwin, 1985). Reprinted by permission.

Cooperative strategies may be particularly appropriate for Canadian companies because of our small size in the global competitive environment. Cooperative strategies may allow Canadian firms to compete effectively globally.

There are conditions, however, which would suggest the use of one form of cooperation over another. Some of the considerations before deciding on the form of cooperation would include assessments of:

- Level of risk (e.g., creating a competitor)
- Synergies/complementary skills to be gained
- Regulations influencing type of involvement
- Managerial and financial resources available to go it alone
- Speed of innovation required

Licensing

The advantages to be gained by licensing depend on the technology, firm size, product maturity, and extent of the firm's experience. A number of internal and external circumstances may lead a firm to employ a licensing strategy:

1. The licensee has existing products or facilities but requires technology, which may be acquired more cheaply or quickly from third parties (licensers) than by internal R&D; the need may be of limited extent or long duration.
2. The licenser wishes to exploit its technology in secondary markets that may be too small to justify larger investments; the required economies of scale may not be attainable.
3. The licensee wishes to maximize its business by adding new technologies.
4. Host-country governments restrict imports and/or foreign direct investment (FDI), or the risk of nationalization or foreign control is too great.
5. Prospects of "technology feedback" are high (i.e., the licenser has contractually assured itself of access to new developments generated by the licensee and based on licensed knowledge).
6. Licensing is a way of testing and developing a market that can later be exploited by direct investment.
7. The licensee is unlikely to become a future competitor.
8. The pace of technological change is sufficiently rapid that the licenser can remain technologically superior and ahead of the licensee, who is a potential competitor.
9. Opportunities exist for licensing auxiliary processes without having to license basic product or process technologies.
10. A firm lacks the capital and managerial resources required for exporting or building a regional plant, but wants to earn additional profits with minimum commitment.

Joint Ventures

Joint ventures are appropriate when:

- A privately owned organization is forming a joint venture with a publicly owned organization. There are some advantages of being privately held, such as close ownership; there are some advantages of being publicly held, such as access to equity markets as a source of capital. Therefore, the unique advantages of being privately and publicly held may sometimes be synergistically combined.

- A domestic organization is forming a joint venture with a foreign company; a joint venture can provide a domestic company with the opportunity for obtaining local management in a foreign country and the managers' knowledge of the foreign economy, politics, and culture. This may also have the residual advantage of reducing risks such as expropriation and harassment by host country officials.
- The distinctive competencies of two or more firms complement each other especially well.
- Some project is potentially very profitable, but requires overwhelming resources and risks.
- Two or more smaller firms have trouble competing with a large firm.
- There exists a need to introduce a new technology quickly.

Outsourcing

A recent strategic alternative, from an investment perspective, is outsourcing. Outsourcing involves contracting out, on a long-term basis, critical competencies or tasks. An example of outsourcing is the contracting-out of the computer and information services (CIS) by banks to companies specialized in these businesses. The banks realize that they do not have the expertise or the strategic focus to provide the CIS services to their organization or customers. Therefore, they outsource the task to computer service firms such as IBM and EDS, which have core competencies in this particular business. In this case, the outsourcing provides lower costs and better services. Critical questions to think about when considering the outsourcing option are the following:

- Is the competency or task being outsourced a core competency for the outsourcer, and will this activity or core competency provide critical competitive advantages in the future?
- Will outsourcing allow the insourcer to compete with you more directly? (For example, Intel is now competing with PC computer assemblers such as Compaq.)
- Will outsourcing provide lower costs and higher effectiveness or efficiency, and is this a critical competitive advantage for the firm?
- Do the outsourcer and insourcer trust each other? How can this trust be established or built?

Integrating Corporate and Business Unit Strategy

As stated earlier, corporate and business strategy in reality cannot be separated. Here we look at how business strategies must be addressed when a corporate strategic decision to either divest or invest in a business has been made. A corporate decision to *harvest* an ailing business (i.e., divest or liquidate) versus *invest* (i.e., retrench or turn around) is based upon the firm's competitive position and advantages as well as future prospects for the industry. The retrenchment and turnaround strategies are based upon establishing stronger business-based competitive advantages and competitive positions.

When a business is in trouble—whether as a result of such factors as strong competition, technological turbulence, or escalating interest rates—a different set of strategic choices faces the general manager. An attempt can be made to turn the business around, or the business can be immediately divested or liquidated. The business can also be harvested, which involves optimizing cash flows through such tactics as curtailing all new investments, cutting advertising expenditures, or increasing prices, until the business is sold or liquidated.

The decision of whether to attempt a turnaround depends on the kind of turnaround strategy likely to be successful and then whether the firm is willing to bear the risks, devote the resources, and make the management commitment associated with this particular turnaround strategy.

Three corporate strategies for dealing with ailing businesses are discussed further below.

Turnaround strategies can be classified as follows:[7]

1. Efficiency-oriented
   a. Asset reduction (e.g., disposal of assets)
   b. Cost cutting (e.g., cutbacks in administrative ROD, marketing expenses)
2. Market-oriented
   a. Revenue generation (e.g., increase sales by product reintroduction, increased advertising, increased selling effort, lower prices)
   b. Product/market refocusing (e.g., shift emphasis into defensible or lucrative niches)

Turnarounds can follow definite stages: (1) change in management, (2) evaluation, (3) emergency, to "stop the bleeding" or "unload," (4) stabilization, emphasizing organization, that is, building, and (5) return-to-normal growth.

Turnarounds are appropriate when an organization:

- Has a clearly distinctive competence, but has failed to meet its objectives and goals consistently over time.
- Is one of the weakest competitors in a relatively prosperous growth industry.
- Is plagued by inefficiency, low profitability, poor employee morale, and pressure from stockholders to improve performance.
- Has failed to capitalize on external opportunities, minimize external threats, take advantage of internal strengths, and overcome internal weaknesses over time—that is, the organization's strategic managers have become complacent and failed.
- Has grown so large so quickly that major internal reorganization is needed.

---

[7] For a more complete analysis of these turnaround strategies, see Donald C. Hambrick and Steven M. Schecter, "Turnaround strategies for mature industrial product business units," *Academy of Management Journal,* June 1983, pp. 231–248.

Divestiture, that is, selling a division or part of an organization, is appropriate when:

- An organization has pursued a turnaround strategy and has failed to accomplish needed improvements.
- A division needs more resources to be competitive than the company can provide.
- A division is a misfit with the rest of an organization. This can result from radically different markets, customers, managers, employees, values, or needs.
- A large amount of cash is needed quickly and cannot be reasonably obtained from other sources.

Liquidation, that is, selling all of a company's assets, in parts, for their tangible worth, is appropriate when:

- An organization has pursued both a turnaround strategy and a divestiture strategy and neither has been successful.
- An organization's only alternative is bankruptcy; liquidation represents an orderly and planned means of obtaining the greatest possible cash for an organization's assets. A company can legally declare bankruptcy first and then liquidate various divisions to raise needed capital.
- The stockholders of a firm can minimize their losses by selling the organization's assets.

International Strategies and Modes of Entry

International strategic decisions cover a wide variety of problems and issues. However, some basic international strategies are related to selecting an entry mode for entering a new international market, and defining how the company should coordinate and manage their regional strategies from a corporate perspective.

International Strategies

Strategies for coordinating international business units present managers with two issues: Should the businesses be coordinated globally to produce efficiency or should they be coordinated locally so that effectiveness in the local markets is maximized? (See Exhibit 10-4.)

The globalization approach requires managers to coordinate strategy from a global perspective so that the firm's global competitive advantages from an efficiency perspective are maximized. This approach, called the *global strategy,* involves providing a standard product or service in all geographic regions. An example of a global strategy would be a firm that designs its products in United States because of the technical and design capabilities that exist there, manufactures products in China because of the low cost of manufacturing, and sells the products worldwide. Managers select a global strategy to try to maximize the overall global competitive advantage of the firm. Good examples of global industries are the consumer electronic and computer industries, in which different parts the companies' value chain activities are distributed throughout the world in locations where they are most efficient and effectively carried out. The real challenge for a manager using this strategy is to coordinate the different value chain activities so as to maximize the firm's overall global competitive advantage.

The localization approach requires managers to coordinate and manage different strategies in different international regions. This approach, called the *multidomestic strategy,* emphasizes the different regional aspects of business and market demands. A manager would take the multidomestic approach if all of the firm's regional markets had different customer tastes, distribution systems, marketing techniques, and/or product standards. In this situation, each region must be treated differently. To do this, each is given the responsibility to carry out its own product development, manufacturing, and selling so that it most effectively meets the needs of the customers. A good example of this type of business is the packaged food processing industry. Many of the products in this industry vary regionally according to contents, packaging, and distribution channels. The challenge facing a manager using this strategy is to coordinate the various local strategies so that the brand image is strongly supported, but to diversify decision making and primary value chain activities into the regions in an effective yet economic manner.

The forces that dictate whether a firm takes a global, a multidomestic, or an intermediate international strategic position depends upon the pressures of globalization and localization. Pressures for globalization are associated with industries that have very intense international competitive pressures and

EXHIBIT 10-4   International Strategic Positions and Coordination

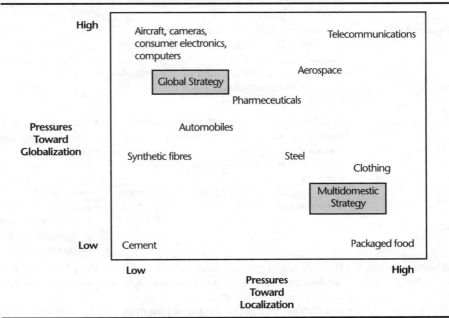

Source: This diagram is used with permission from *International Management: Text and Cases,* 3rd ed., by Beamish, Morrison, and Rosenzweig (Burr Ridge, Ill.: Irwin, 1997).

widely adopted international product standards. Pressures for localization are associated with industries having very pronounced regional market differences. Product, service, and knowledge-transferability in the industry are also quite important in the global business position, because if you manufacture goods in Asia but cannot transport them effectively or efficiently to North America, a global strategy becomes less viable.

Some companies take the *dual strategic* approach. For example, in the telecommunications industry firms must use global technological competitive advantages, yet cater to individual market tastes, product standards, and distribution requirements. This often puts extra pressure on the managers, who must coordinate a much more complex set of strategic alternatives.

It must also be noted that the global and multidomestic strategies are associated with different types of international organizational structures. These structures are delineated in Chapter 9.

EXHIBIT 10-5   International Strategic Modes of Entry

Mode	Reasons for Taking Mode	Risks of Using Mode
Licensing agreement	• Requires few resources particularly capital. • Potentially can get an agreement with a firm having the missing resources (e.g., manufacturing, sales force, etc.) • May be the only way for a small company to enter international markets if the product or service does not transport easily. • Circumvents import duties and quotas. • The licensing firm has minimal risk of income loss, because the operational costs are being supported by the licenser.	• Neither party has complete long-term strategic control over the development of the product. • One party may put in more effort than the other party.
Exporting	• Requires more resources than licensing but fewer than joint venture and wholly owned subsidiary. • May be a good method for a small company to take if the product or service does transport easily.	• May incur extra costs associated with transporting, duties, or volume restrictions related to quotas.
Joint venture	• Requires more resources than licensing or exporting, but fewer than a wholly owned subsidiary. • The firm shares any income losses with its partners. • The potential for learning from the partners is maximized.	• The relationship may not last because of differing long-term objectives or values. • Operational and capital losses can be higher than in the licensing and exporting options because of greater ownership and operational involvement. • The joint venture partner(s), and possibly future competitor(s), may have access to proprietary information and resources in your company.
Wholly owned subsidiary	• The firm has complete control of the product or service from inception through to sales and distribution. • The firm captures all of the profit potential of the product or service.	• The firm risks income losses if the product or service does not do well.

International Strategic Entry Mode Alternatives

A major decision managers must face when they are expanding internationally is how to enter a new market. Entry mode selection involves a complex tradeoff decision between having enough market knowledge, having sufficient resources to support the entry mode, and minimizing risks. Some of the concerns specifically related to the various entry modes are delineated in Exhibit 10-5.

RECOMMENDED READINGS

Beamish, Paul, Allen Morrison, and Philip Rosenweig. *International Management.* 3rd ed. Burr Ridge, Ill.: Irwin, 1997.

Deming, W. E. *Out of the Crisis* (Cambridge, Mass.: MIT, 1986), p. 31.

Hu, Yao-Su. "Global corporations are national firms with international operations." *California Management Review*, Winter 1992, pp. 66–87.

Porter, Michael E. *Competitive Strategy: Techniques for Analyzing Industries and Competitors.* New York: Free Press, 1980, Chap. 11.

Sadtler, David R. "Brief case: the role of today's board in corporate strategy." *Long Range Planning*, August 1993, pp. 112–113.

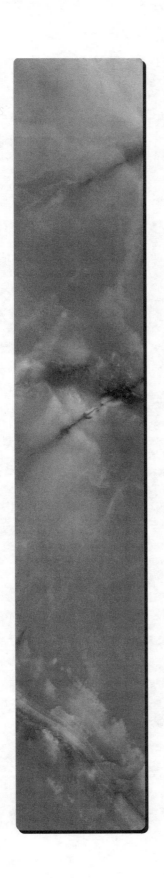

SECTION

II

Readings

A Manager's Guide for Evaluating Competitive Analysis Techniques

JOHN PRESCOTT

JOHN GRANT

Virtually all managers acknowledge the importance of understanding their industries and their competitors. As a result, interest has grown rapidly in the use of various competitive analysis techniques to help formulate and implement strategy. However, managers who want to conduct competitive analyses are faced with perplexing choices among a wide variety of techniques with different strengths and weaknesses, an abundance of internal and external data sources, an array of computer software packages, and constraints in terms of time, money, information, and personnel. Many managers are asking, "Where do I start?"

The efficient selection of appropriate techniques for a particular situation depends on a three-phase process of awareness and choice. First, what relevant techniques are available and how do they relate to one another? Second, what is the focus and scope of the competitive arena of interest? Third, what constraints on time and other resources limit the extent of analyses that can be undertaken? Our extensive review of the literature and of applications in several industries can help managers and analysts complete these three phases effectively.

Utilization Profiles

In order to assist managers to select and apply competitive analysis techniques, we developed a reference guide consisting in part of profiles describing various competitive analysis techniques (Exhibit 1). These profiles can assist managers in several ways. We chose a broad array of techniques to illustrate the increasing variety of analytical options available. The key characteristics of

Source: Reprinted with permission from *Interfaces*, vol. 18, no. 3 (May–June 1988). © 1988. The Institute of Management Sciences, 290 Westminster Street, Providence, Rhode Island, 02903, U.S.A.

each technique have been highlighted along with their typical advantages and limitations. This should help managers to identify the techniques best suited to their situations. Few competitive analyses can be successfully completed using a single technique; the guide can help managers to choose the combination of techniques that will address the issue most effectively and efficiently. We provide references that present additional operational details for each technique.

Competitive Analysis Techniques

The utilization profiles array a diverse set of 21 techniques and evaluate them along 11 important dimensions. The techniques described below are sequenced beginning with broad industry-level techniques and moving to narrower functional area techniques. However, most of the techniques are applicable at either the corporate or the business-unit level. Detailed descriptions of the techniques can be found in Hax and Majluf [1984], Grant and King [1982], Porter [1980], and Prescott [1987].

Political and country risk analysis assesses the types (asset, operational, profitability, personnel) and extent of risks from operating in foreign countries.

Industry scenarios develop detailed, internally consistent descriptions of what various future structures of the industry may be like.

The economists' model of industry attractiveness analyzes the five basic forces (bargaining power of suppliers and customers, threat of substitute products, threat of entry, and industry rivalry) driving industry competition.

BCG industry matrix identifies the attractiveness of an industry based on the number of potential sources for achieving a competitive advantage and the size of the advantage that a leading business can achieve.

Industry segmentation identifies discrete pockets of competition within an industry. The bases of segment identification are often product variety, buyer characteristics, channels of distribution, and geography.

PIMS is an ongoing database of the Strategic Planning Institute which collects data describing business units' operating activities, their industries and competitors, their products and customers. The purpose is to assist planning efforts of the participating businesses.

A technological assessment develops an understanding of the technological relationships and changes occurring in an industry.

Multipoint competition analysis explores the implications of a situation in which diversified firms compete against each other in several markets.

Critical success factor analysis identifies the few areas in which a business must do adequately in order to be successful.

A strategic group analysis identifies groups of businesses which follow similar strategies, have similar administrative systems, and tend to be affected by and respond to competitive moves and external events in similar ways.

A value chain analysis and field maps identify the costs, operating characteristics, and interrelationships of a business's primary activities (that is, inbound logistics, operations, outbound logistics, marketing and sales, service) and supporting activities (that is, firm infrastructure, human resource management, technological development, procurement).

Experience curves show that the costs of producing a product (service) decrease in a regular manner as the experience of producing it increases. The decrease in costs occurs over the total life of a product.

Stakeholder analysis and assumption surfacing and testing identify and examine any individual or group goals that affect or are affected by the realization of the businesses' goals.

Market signaling is any action by a competitor that provides a direct or indirect indication of its intentions, motives, goals, or internal situation.

Portfolio analysis locates a corporation's businesses along dimensions of industry attractiveness and competitive position to help managers to make resource allocation decisions and to evaluate future cash flows and profitability potential.

Strengths and weaknesses analysis identifies advantages and deficiencies in resources, skills, and capabilities for a business relative to its competitors.

Synergy analysis examines tangible (raw material, production, distribution) and intangible (management know-how, reputation) benefits of shared activities among business units.

Financial statement analysis assesses both the short-term health and long-term financial resources of a firm.

Value-based planning evaluates strategies and strategic moves in light of their probable stock market effects and financing implications. (It does not refer to managerial values in our usage.)

Management profiles examine the goals, backgrounds, and personalities of the individuals making strategic decisions in a competing firm or institution.

Reverse engineering is purchasing and dismantling a competitor's product to identify how it was designed and constructed so that costs and quality can be estimated.

Dimension Descriptions

For each of the 11 dimensions developed to evaluate the techniques, we selected criteria to enhance its meaningfulness. The criteria reflect our experience and understanding of what considerations are important for evaluating a particular technique. While firms often use external consultants for some aspects of competitive analysis, we assume that internal personnel will be conducting all phases of the analyses.

Time.   The time required to implement a technique can be separated into development and execution phases. The developmental phase involves specifying objectives and determining any initial constraints that will be imposed on the project. The execution phase involves the collection of data, analysis, and dissemination of the findings to the appropriate individuals.

EXHIBIT 1   Utilization Profiles of Competitive Analysis Techniques.

Twenty-one techniques are evaluated along 11 important dimensions. To use the table, locate the technique and evaluate dimension of interest. In the row and column intersection (cell), our assessment of a technique's characteristics as they apply to the dimension will be summarized.

Dimensions / Techniques	Resource Needs				Data Needs		
	Time		Costs	Managerial Skills	Sources	Availability	Timeliness
	Development	Execution					
1. Political and country risk analysis	Long	Long	High	Conceptual Analytical Diagnostic	Literature search Informants Personal Interviews	From analysis	Historical Current
2. Industry scenarios	Long	Long	High	Conceptual Analytical Diagnostic	Focus groups Literature search Personal interviews	Customized	Future
3. Economists' model of industry attractiveness	Moderate	Long	Medium	Technical Conceptual Diagnostic	Case study Personal interviews Literature search	Off-the-shelf but basically derived from analysis	Current
4. BCG industry matrix	Short	Moderate	Medium	Technical Conceptual Diagnostic	Literature search Personal interviews	From analysis	Current
5. Industry segmentation	Moderate	Moderate	Medium	Conceptual Diagnostic Analytical	Case study Personal interviews Literature search	From analysis	Current
6. PIMS	Moderate	Short	Medium	Technical Analytical	Databases	Off-the-shelf	Current
7. Technological assessment	Long	Long	High	Technical Conceptual Analytical	Direct observation Participant observation Databases Documents	From analysis Sometimes Customized	Future
8. Multipoint competition	Short	Moderate	Low to medium	Conceptual Diagnostic	Literature search Personal interviews	From analysis	Current

The techniques are arranged in descending order from a broad industry level to a narrower functional level. Multiple entries for the managerial skills and sources and evaluate dimensions are in descending order of importance and priority, respectively.

Accuracy Constraints	Updating Requirements		Advantages	Limitations	References
	Frequency	Difficulty			
Availability	Periodic	Reanalyze	Understand other cultures or political positions and potential problem areas	Often evaluated using own norms Language problems Data often difficult to evaluate and can change rapidly if power positions change	Desta [1985] Hofer and Haller [1980]
Assumption of sources	Ad hoc	Reconceptualize	Sensitize management to the need to adapt to industry evolution	Based upon assumptions subject to change Costs	Wack [1985a, b] Porter [1985]
Managerial skills	Ad hoc	Reconceptualize	Structured approach to examining industries Identifies competitors Basis for other in-depth analysis	Basic assumption that economic structure of industry is root of competition Drawing of industry boundaries	Porter [1980]
Managerial skills	Ad hoc	Reanalyze	Primarily a diagnostic tool for identifying profitable industry segments	Needs to be used in conjunction with other techniques such as industry analysis and CSFs	Pekar [1982]
Conceptual skills	Ad hoc	Reanalyze	Identifies pockets of opportunity Identifies pockets of future profits or areas under attack	Choosing segmentation dimensions Piecemeal approach to competition	Bonoma and Shapiro [1983] Porter [1985]
Representativeness of businesses in database	Periodic	Repetitive	Flexibility of use Variety of operations	Lack of organizational variables	Wagner [1984] Schoeffler, Buzzell, and Heaney [1974] Ramanujam and Venkatraman [1984]
Financial support	Continuous	Reconceptualize	Keep abreast of key technological drivers	Expensive, continuous, difficult process	Petrov [1982] Hayes and Wheelwright [1979a, b]
Sources	Ad hoc	Reanalyze	Identifies areas where a competitor may retaliate (vice versa)	Typically ignores motives, skills, etc., of competitor	Karnani and Wernerfelt [1985]

EXHIBIT 1 *continued*

Dimensions / Techniques	Resource Needs				Data Needs		
	Time		Costs	Managerial Skills	Sources	Availability	Timeliness
	Development	Execution					
9. Critical success factors	Short	Moderate	Medium	Conceptual Diagnostic Analytical	Literature search Case study	From analysis	Current
10. Strategic group analysis	Moderate	Short	Low	Conceptual Diagnostic	Literature search Personal interviews Case study	From analysis	Current
11. Value-chain analysis and field maps	Short	Long	High	Technical Diagnostic	Case study Personal interviews Literature search	Customized	Current
12. Experience curve	Short	Moderate	Medium	Technical Diagnostic	Documents Personal interviews Direct observation	From analysis	Current
13. Stakeholder analysis and assumption surfacing and testing	Short	Moderate to high	Medium	Conceptual Diagnostic Analytical	Personal interviews Focus groups Literature search	Customized	Past Current
14. Market signaling	Moderate to long	Continuous	Low	Conceptual Diagnostic Analytical	Documents Personal interviews Direct observation	From analysis	Future
15. Portfolio analysis	Moderate	Short	Low	Technical	Literature search Case study Personal interviews	From analysis	Current
16. Strength and weakness analysis	Short	Long	High	Interpersonal Technical Diagnostic	Personal interviews Direct observation Case study	Customized	Current
17. Synergy analysis	Moderate	Long	High	Technical Diagnostic Conceptual	Documents Case study Personal interviews	Customized	Current

Accuracy Constraints	Updating Requirements		Advantages	Limitations	References
	Frequency	Difficulty			
Managerial skills	Periodic	Reanalyze	Fast, inexpensive method for focusing efforts	Often is superficial	Rockart [1979] Leidecker and Bruno [1984]
Managerial skills	Periodic	Reanalyze	Fast, cheap, easy way to understand key competitors	Superficial; ignores firms outside industry	McGee and Thomas [1986] Porter [1980]
Sources	Ad hoc	Reanalyze	Best techniques for understanding operating details of a competitor or one's self	Data often difficult to obtain Slow, expensive	Kaiser [1984] Porter [1985]
Sources	Ad hoc	Repetitive	Provides an understanding of cost and thus pricing dynamics Gives a picture of whether to compete on basis of costs	Based upon history which may not carry through to future	Hall and Howell [1985] Hax and Majluf [1984]
Managerial skills	Periodic	Reanalyze	Introspection Attempts to get at underlying causes of behavior	Subject to misinterpretation	Freeman [1984] Rowe, Mason, and Dickel [1985]
Managerial skills	Continuous	Reconceptualize	Early warning indicator	Misinterpretation Get off in the wrong direction	Porter [1980]
Sources	Periodic	Reanalyze	Visual summary Requires managers to think systematically about industry and competitive position Heuristic method of decision making	Superficial Assumes cash flow/profit drives decision	Hax and Majluf [1984] Grant and King [1982]
Sources	Ad hoc	Reanalyze	Provides in-depth understanding of entire business's capabilities Provides feedback for remedial action	Costly; long; cooperation of personnel essential Hierarchical position of manager influences perception	Stevenson [1985, 1976]
Sources	Ad hoc	Reanalyze	Shows cost or differentiation advantage as a result of sharing —staying power, exit decisions, response times	Data difficulties Time-consuming	Porter [1985]

EXHIBIT I *continued*

Dimensions / Techniques	Resource Needs				Data Needs		
	Time		Costs	Managerial Skills	Sources	Availability	Timeliness
	Development	Execution					
18. Financial statement analysis	Short	Short	Low	Technical Analytical	Documents Historical records Databases	Off-the-shelf From analysis	Historical
19. Value-based planning	Long	Moderate to long	Medium	Technical	Historical records Databases	From analysis	Historical
20. Management profiles	Short	Short	Low	Interpersonal Technical	Personal interviews Informants Documents	From analysis	Current
21. Reverse engineering	Short	Varies	Varies	Technical	Product purchasing	Off-the-shelf	Current

Financial Resources. The financial resources required to conduct an analysis with a given technique can be categorized as low (under $10,000), medium ($10,000 to $50,000), or high (over $50,000).

Managerial Skills. To complete an assignment a manager may need a number of specific skills; these may be classed in five groups: technical, interpersonal, conceptual, diagnostic, and analytic. Technical skills are those necessary to accomplish specialized activities. Interpersonal skills involve the ability to communicate with, understand, and motivate both individuals and groups. Conceptual skills are the abilities of a manager to think of the abstract and understand cause-and-effect relationships. Diagnostic skills allow a manager to study the symptoms of a problem and determine the underlying causes. Analytical skills involve the ability to identify the key variables in a situation, understand their interrelationships, and decide which should receive the most attention.

Sources. Sources are persons, products, written materials, anything from which information is obtained. Sources are of two primary types, "learning-curve" and "target" [Washington Researchers, 1983]. Learning-curve sources are those that provide general rather than specific knowledge; they are used when time is not critical and to prepare for a target source. For example, industry studies and books are typical learning-curve sources. Target sources, on the other hand, contain specific information and provide the greatest volume

Accuracy Constraints	Updating Requirements		Advantages	Limitations	References
	Frequency	Difficulty			
Sources	Periodic	Repetitive	Fast, easy, cheap handle on financial picture	Data problems Usually limited to public corporations	Hax and Majluf [1984] Hofer and Schendel [1978]
Sources	Periodic	Repetitive	Simplicity—ability to compare alternatives and competitors	Basic assumption that maximizing stock price is primary goal Difficult to implement for individual business units of multidivision company (private firm)	Reimann [1986] Kaiser [1984] Fruhan [1979]
Recency of sources	Continuous	Repetitive	Development of management profiles and manpower (succession) charts Managers do not always act in a rational manner	Past is good predictor of future	Ball [1987]
Managerial skills	Ad hoc	Reanalyze	Best way to understand a competitor's product characteristics and costs	Can be time-consuming May not be critical success factor	

of pertinent information in the shortest period of time. Trade associations, company and competitor personnel are typical target sources. They are often one-shot sources that cannot be used repetitively.

The sites from which one obtains information can be classified as either "field" or "library." By combining the sources and sites of information, we developed a typology of data collection techniques. Exhibit 2 contains 15 data collection techniques that can be used for competitive analysis assignments [Miller, 1983]. For each, we have recommended the most appropriate sources. If a particular technique presents problems in availability or application, then nearby techniques in the exhibit should be considered. For example, if product purchasing is desired but is too expensive or unavailable, then direct observation or a literature search should be used.

Availability.   While data can be obtained for almost any project for a price, the ease with which one can secure data can be classified. Three categories we have found useful are "off-the-shelf," "derived from analysis," and "customized." Off-the-shelf refers to data in the form the manager needs. If the essential raw data are available but require some analyses to put them in the desired form, then we classify the availability as "derived from analysis." When the information for a study must be developed, we call it "customized."

Timeliness.   Data, analysis, and implications that deal primarily with the past are historical; those that address the present or future, we call current or future.

Accuracy Constraints.   The value of a particular technique is limited by the quality of the resources and validity of the data used. Using the above dimensions, we identified the key constraint that would potentially hinder the usefulness of the given technique. This dimension is analogous to a warning label for the user.

Updating Requirements.   Competitive analyses are seldom one-time phenomena. In order to understand the updating requirements for each technique, two useful dimensions are "frequency" and "difficulty." The frequency dimensions can be divided into ad hoc (when the need arises), periodic (according to an established schedule), and continuous.

The difficulty dimension addresses the extent and nature of skills that may be required during an update. If the same analysis can be performed again with no modifications, then we have labeled it repetitive. If modifications must be made because the format or content of the information has changed, we describe it as reanalysis. If the assumptions of the analysis need to be challenged or changed, then the updating requires a reconceptualization.

Advantages and Limitations.   The final two dimensions summarize the major advantages and limitations of the technique. While these assessments are implicit once the preceding criteria have been applied to a specific analytical assignment, they are intended to underscore special considerations.

EXHIBIT 2   **A Typology of Data Collection Techniques**

Note: The exhibit shows the options available for collecting data, given the desired source and location. A source of data can either provide specific target information or general learning-curve information. The location of the data can reside in a field setting or in a library.

Examples of advantages could be insight into cultural constraints or an industry's evolution; whereas limitations could be communications difficulties or conflicting assumptions, either of which may lead to misunderstandings.

References.   The publications chosen are from a much broader list of strategic management references. We based our choice on their availability, managerial orientation, and relative recency. Most contain bibliographies that further extend the resources.

While these evaluation dimensions vary in importance across competitive analysis assignments, recognizing them can greatly facilitate choices when groups of managers and analysts are working together.

Selecting and Using the Techniques

The transition from a description of techniques to their selection for application is best conveyed by an actual example.

The competitive environment of an electric utility company has recently been undergoing significant changes. A great many industrial customers, the utility's "bread-and-butter," have been closing or reducing operations. Other industrial and commercial customers have been threatening partial backward integration into cogeneration systems. Residential customers have been voicing concerns before the public utility board because they pay some of the highest rates in the country. Because of potentially low returns and increasingly high risks, the investment community seems less willing to finance the large capital expenditures necessary in this industry. The utility's geographic service area, vigorously engaged in attracting new businesses, is looking for high-technology and service businesses, which typically consume modest amounts of electricity.

To further complicate its competitive problems, a variety of governmental bodies is openly discussing the benefits of deregulation. Since electricity can be distributed cheaply over wide geographical areas, the need to restrict the boundaries of each utility is being questioned. Deregulation, some argue, would benefit consumers by allowing them to choose among a wider set of competitors.

The managers in the company are faced with an internal situation of severe financial constraints, top management's desire to take immediate corrective action, and a lack of skills in formal strategic planning. The newly hired planners charged with addressing the above issues need a method for organizing their competitive analysis efforts. They must choose techniques for understanding their industry and competitors.

Selecting Techniques

Many competitive analysis assignments begin when top executives become dissatisfied with their firm's prevailing emphasis and understanding of the competitive environment. This was the case in the electrical utility company described above. Management initiated a series of meetings which focused on the strategic planning efforts at the firm. One of the outcomes was an assignment to conduct an analysis of the industry and competitors. The planners, facing the constraints of a limited budget, perceived urgency, and after a series of meetings, an inexperienced support staff decided to focus on two fundamental issues: first, to understand the contemporary dynamics of the broadly defined electrical utility industry; second, to address the strategic position of the firm relative to its key existing and potential competitors. The managers needed to identify those competitive analysis techniques that would best answer their questions within their existing constraints. The outcome is shown in Exhibit 3.

Exhibit 3 also illustrates several important aspects of the process of initiating a competitive analysis assignment. Even the most basic assignments, like those described in the table, present the manager with a variety of choices. The firm in this case concentrated its efforts on basic analyses that would lay the foundation for later in-depth studies. As a result, several possible alternatives were rejected because they were too costly, time-consuming, complicated, or not relevant to the circumstances at that time. For example, industry scenarios were deferred for two interrelated reasons. The team needed to understand the industry better before it could address more sophisticated issues. Second, developing industry scenarios would have been too costly and time-consuming. Techniques, such as political and country risk analysis, multipoint competition, synergy analysis, and market signaling were viewed as not relevant to the immediate issues. The competitive analysis team examined each of the 21 techniques and chose those which best suited the assignment and the constraints imposed on the project.

The team applied three interrelated techniques in order to better understand the industry. First, the economists' model of industry attractiveness provided a comprehensive picture of the industry. It revealed that competition should be viewed from both a regional and a national perspective. Further, deregulation (a concern of top management) was not likely to occur for another three to five years, and then the transmission systems of electrical utilities would be the first area to be deregulated. Finally, while the bargaining power of electrical utilities is not strong, their profitability was expected to increase over the next five years due in part to a construction cycle coming to an end.

Second, using the industry analysis as a foundation, strategic group analysis identified those key competitors important in identifying the firm's relative position. Strategic groups were developed on a national level using publicly available operating and financial data for a set of about 70 firms. On a regional

EXHIBIT 3   A Competitive Analysis at an Electrical Utility Company

Needs	Techniques	
	Chosen	Rejected/Deferred
To understand the dynamics of the industry	• Economists' model of industry attractiveness • Strategic group analysis • Critical success factors	• Industry scenarios • Industry segmentation • Stakeholder analysis
To identify its strategic position relative to its key competitors	• Financial analysis • Management profiles • Strengths and weaknesses analysis	• Value-based planning • Value-chain analysis

level, a group of eight electrical and gas utility firms were selected, which were either in the firm's transmission grid or which competed in their geographical territory.

Third, critical success factors (CSFs) were identified at two levels. During the industry analysis, CSFs were identified for the industry as a whole. Then CSFs were identified for the strategic groups. The layering or combining of techniques within an analysis allows managers to address multiple aspects of a question.

Having narrowed the field of competitors to a manageable number through the strategic group analysis, the team turned to the second issue. It sought to build profiles of the competitors to depict the relative positions of the firms. The choices were to conduct a financial analysis of the firms, to examine their management teams' profiles, and to analyze their strengths and weaknesses. These methods were chosen because the data were easily available, the time for the analysis was relatively short, and the result would be a set of reports that other managers in the firm could use easily. This last point was very important. Since most managers were not really convinced that it was necessary to consider the competition, the competitive analysis team felt it extremely important to choose those techniques that were understood by virtually all managers. When the managers saw the usefulness of these analyses, the team would then move to other analyses that were less familiar but which could provide additional intelligence. Most of the techniques rejected or deferred (Exhibit 3) fit in this category.

From this example, it is clear that even seemingly simple competitive analysis assignments pose important issues and questions. In this case, questions concerning the relative position of the firm could not be tackled until the managers understood the industry as a competitive arena. This new perspective on the environment required customer feedback, technical appraisals, and regulatory understanding.

The assignment in this case took approximately three months to complete, with approximately one-third of the time being spent on the developmental aspects of the study.

◼ Conclusions

Growing competitiveness in many markets and along many combinations of dimensions is increasing the complexity of competitive analysis problems facing managers. Our descriptions of techniques, evaluation dimensions, and information types should provide managers with helpful guidance in making competitive analyses.

REFERENCES

Ball, Richard. "Assessing your competitor's people and organization." *Long-Range Planning*, vol. 20, no. 2 (1987), pp. 32–41.

Bonoma, Thomas V., and Bensen P. Shapiro. *Segmenting the Industrial Market*. Lexington, MA: Lexington Books, 1983.

Desta, Asayehgn. "Assessing political risk in less developed countries." *Journal of Business Strategy*, vol. 5, no. 4 (1985), pp. 40–53.

Freeman, R. Edward. *Strategic Management: A Stakeholder Approach.* Boston, MA: Pitman Publishing Company, 1984.

Fruhan, William E., Jr. *Financial Strategy: Studies in the Creation, Transfer and Destruction of Shareholder Value.* Homewood, IL: Richard D. Irwin, 1979.

Grant, John H., and William R. King. *The Logic of Strategic Planning.* Boston, MA: Little, Brown, 1982.

Half, Graham, and Sydney Howell. "The experience curve from the economist's perspective." *Strategic Management Journal*, vol. 6, no. 2 (1985), pp. 197–212.

Hax, Arnoldo C., and Nicolas S. Majluf. *Strategic Management: An Integrative Perspective.* Englewood Cliffs, NJ: Prentice Hall, 1984.

Hayes, Robert H., and Steven C. Wheelwright. "The dynamics of process-product life cycles." *Harvard Business Review*, vol. 57, no. 2 (March–April 1979a), pp. 127–36.

Hayes, Robert H., and Steven C. Wheelwright. "Link manufacturing process and product life cycles." *Harvard Business Review*, vol. 57, no. 1 (January–February 1979b), pp. 133–40.

Hofer, Charles W., and Terry Haller. "Globescan: a way to better international risk assessment." *Journal of Business Strategy*, vol. 1, no. 2 (1980), pp. 41–55.

Hofer, Charles W., and Dan Schendel. *Strategy Formulation: Analytical Concepts.* St. Paul, MN: West Publishing, 1978.

Kaiser, Michael M. *Understanding the Competition: A Practical Guide to Competitive Analysis.* Washington, DC: Michael M. Kaiser Associates, Inc., 1984.

Karnani, Aneel, and Birger, Wernerfelt. "Multiple point competition." *Strategic Management Journal*, vol. 6, no. 1 (1985), pp. 87–96.

Leidecker, Joel K., and Albert V. Bruno. "Identifying and using critical success factors." *Long-Range Planning*, vol. 17, no. 1 (February 1984), pp. 23–32.

McGee, John, and Howard Thomas. "Strategic groups: theory, research and taxonomy," *Strategic Management Journal*, vol. 7, no. 2 (1986), pp. 141-60.

Miller, Delbert C. *Handbook of Research Design and Social Measurement.* New York, NY: Longman, 1983.

Pekar, Peter P. "The strategic environmental matrix: a concept on trial," *Planning Review*, vol. 10, no. 5 (1982), pp. 28–30.

Petrov, Boris. "The advent of the technology portfolio." *Journal of Business Strategy*, vol. 3, no. 2 (1982), pp. 70–75.

Porter, Michael E. *Competitive Strategy.* New York, NY: Free Press, 1980.

Porter, Michael E. *Competitive Advantage: Creating and Sustaining Superior Performance.* New York, NY: Free Press, 1985.

Prescott, John E. "A process for applying analytic models in competitive analysis." In *Strategic Planning and Management Handbook*, eds. David I. Cleland and William R. King. New York, NY: Van Nostrand Reinhold, 1987, pp. 222–51.

Ramanujam, Vasudevan, and N. Venkatraman. "An inventory and critique of strategy research using the PIMS data base." *Academy of Management Review*, vol. 9, no. 1 (1984), pp. 138–51.

Reimann, B. C. "Strategy valuation in portfolio planning: Combining Q and VROI ratios." *Planning Review*, vol. 14, no. 1 (1986), pp. 18–23, 42–45.

Rockart, John F. "Chief executives define their own data needs." *Harvard Business Review*, vol. 5, no. 2 (March–April 1979), pp. 81–92.

Rowe, Alan J.; Richard O. Mason; and Karl E. Dickel. *Strategic Management and Business Policy*, 2nd ed. Reading, MA: Addison-Wesley Publishing, 1985.

Schoeffler, Sidney; Robert D. Buzzell; and Donald F. Heany. "Impact of strategic planning on profit performance." *Harvard Business Review*, vol. 52, no. 2 (1974), pp. 137–45.

Stevenson, Howard H. "Defining corporate strengths and weaknesses." *Sloan Management Review*, vol. 17, no. 3 (Spring 1976), pp. 51–68.

Stevenson, Howard H. 1985. "Resource assessment: Identifying corporate strengths and weaknesses." In *Handbook of Business Strategy*, ed. William D. Guth. Boston, MA: Warren, Gorham and Lamong, Chap. 5, pp. 1–30.

Wack, Pierre. "Scenarios: shooting the rapids." *Harvard Business Review*, vol. 63, no. 6 (1985a), pp. 139–50.

Wack, Pierre. "Scenarios: uncharted waters ahead." *Harvard Business Review*, vol. 63, no. 5 (1985b), pp. 73–89.

Wagner, Harvey M. "Profit wonders, investment blunders." *Harvard Business Review*, vol. 62, no. 5 (1984), pp. 121–35.

Washington Researchers. *Company Information: A Model Investigation*. Washington, DC: Washington Researchers Ltd., 1983.

The Strategy Concept I: Five Ps for Strategy

HENRY MINTZBERG

Human nature insists on *a* definition for every concept. The field of strategic management cannot afford to rely on a single definition of strategy, indeed the word has long been used implicitly in different ways even if it has traditionally been defined formally in only one. Explicit recognition of multiple definitions can help practitioners and researchers alike to maneuver through this difficult field. Accordingly, this article presents five definitions of strategy—as plan, ploy, pattern, position, and perspective—and considers some of their interrelationships.

Strategy as Plan

To almost anyone you care to ask, *strategy is a plan*—some sort of *consciously intended* course of action, a guideline (or set of guidelines) to deal with a situation. A kid has a "strategy" to get over a fence, a corporation has one to capture a market. By this definition, strategies have two essential characteristics: they are made in advance of the actions to which they apply, and they are developed consciously and purposefully. (They may, in addition, be stated explicitly, sometimes in formal documents known as "plans," although it need not be taken here as a necessary condition for "strategy as plan.") To Drucker, strategy is "purposeful action"[1]; to Moore "design for action," in essence, "conception preceding action."[2] A host of definitions in a variety of fields reinforce this view. For example:

Source: H. Mintzberg, "The strategy concept I: five Ps for strategy," *California Management Review*, Fall 1987, pp. 11–24. Reproduced with permission of the copyright owner. Further reproduction prohibited without permission.

[1] P. F. Drucker, *Management: Tasks, Responsibilities, Practices* (New York, NY: Harper & Row, 1974), p. 104.

[2] Moore, in fact, prefers not to associate the word strategy with the word plan per se: "The term *plan* is much too static for our purposes unless qualified. There is not enough of the idea of scheming or calculation with an end in view in it to satisfy us. Plans are used to build ships. Strategies are used to achieve ends among people. You simply do not deal strategically with inanimate objects." But Moore certainly supports the characteristics of intentionality. D. G. Moore, "Managerial strategies," in W. L. Warner and N. H. Martin, eds., *Industrial Man: Businessmen and Business Organizations* (New York, NY: Harper & Row, 1959), pp. 220, 226.

- in the military: Strategy is concerned with "draft[ing] the plan of war ... shap[ing] the individual campaigns and within these, decid[ing] on the individual engagements."[3]

- in Game Theory: Strategy is a "a complete plan: a plan which specifies what choices [the player] will make in every possible situation."[4]

- in management: "Strategy is a unified, comprehensive, and integrated plan ... designed to ensure that the basic objectives of the enterprise are achieved."[5]

- and in the dictionary: strategy is (among other things) "a plan, method, or series of maneuvers or stratagems for obtaining a specific goal or result."[6]

As plans, strategies may be general or they can be specific. There is one use of the word in the specific sense that should be identified here. As plan, *a strategy can be a ploy,* too, really just a specific "maneuver" intended to outwit an opponent or competitor. The kid may use the fence as a ploy to draw a bully into his yard, where his Doberman Pinscher awaits intruders. Likewise, a corporation may threaten to expand plant capacity to discourage a competitor from building a new plant. Here the real strategy (as plan, that is, the real intention) is the threat, not the expansion itself, and as such is a ploy.

In fact, there is a growing literature in the field of strategic management, as well as on the general process of bargaining, that views strategy in this way and so focusses attention on its most dynamic and competitive aspects. For example, in his popular book, *Competitive Strategy,* Porter devotes one chapter to "Market Signals" (including discussion of the effects of announcing moves, the use of "the fighting brand," and the use of threats of private antitrust suits) and another to "Competitive Moves" (including actions to preempt competitive response).[7] Likewise in his subsequent book, *Competitive Advantage,* there is a chapter on "Defensive Strategy" that discusses a variety of ploys for reducing the probability of competitor retaliation (or increasing his perception of your own).[8] And Schelling devotes much of his famous book, *The Strategy of Conflict,* to the topic of ploys to outwit rivals in a competitive or bargaining situation.[9]

---

[3] C. Von Clausewitz, *On War,* translated by M. Howard and P. Paret (Princeton, NJ: Princeton University Press, 1976), p. 177.

[4] J. Von Newmann and O. Morgenstern, *Theory of Games and Economic Behavior* (Princeton, NJ: Princeton University Press, 1944), p. 79.

[5] W. F. Glueck, *Business Policy and Strategic Management,* 3rd Edition (New York, NY: McGraw-Hill, 1980), p. 9.

[6] *Random House Dictionary.*

[7] M. F. Porter, *Competitive Strategy: Techniques for Analyzing Industries and Competitors* (New York, NY: The Free Press, 1980).

[8] M. E. Porter, *Competitive Advantage: Creating and Sustaining Superior Performance* (New York, NY: The Free Press, 1985).

[9] T. C. Schelling, *The Strategy of Conflict,* 2nd Edition (Cambridge, MA: Harvard University Press, 1980).

Strategy as Pattern

But if strategies can be intended (whether as general plans or specific ploys), surely they can also be realized. In other words, defining strategy as a plan is not sufficient: we also need a definition that encompasses the resulting behavior. Thus a third definition is proposed: *strategy is a pattern*—specifically, a pattern in a stream of actions.[10] By this definition, when Picasso painted blue for a time, that was a strategy, just as was the behavior of the Ford Motor Company when Henry Ford offered his Model T only in black. In other words, by this definition, strategy is *consistency* in behavior, *whether or not* intended.

This may sound like a strange definition for a word that has been so bound up with free will ("strategos" in Greek, the art of the army general[11]). But the fact of the matter is that while hardly anyone defines strategy in this way,[12] many people seem at one time or another to so use it. Consider this quotation from a business executive:

> Gradually the successful approaches merge into a pattern of action that becomes our strategy. We certainly don't have an overall strategy on this.[13]

This comment is inconsistent only if we restrict ourselves to one definition of strategy: what this man seems to be saying is that his firm has strategy as pattern, but not as plan. Or consider this comment in *Business Week* on a joint venture between General Motors and Toyota:

> The tentative Toyota deal may be most significant because it is another example of how GM's strategy boils down to doing a little bit of everything until the market decides where it is going.[14]

A journalist has inferred a pattern in the behavior of a corporation, and labelled it strategy.

The point is that every time a journalist imputes a strategy to a corporation or to a government, and every time a manager does the same thing to a competitor or even to the senior management of his own firm, they are implicitly

---

[10] H. Mintzberg, "Research on strategy-making," *Proceedings After the 32nd Annual Meeting of the Academy of Management*, Minneapolis, 1972, pp. 90–94; M. Mintzberg, "Patterns in strategy formation," *Management Science*, 24/9 (1978):934–948; H. Mintzberg and J. A. Waters, "Of strategies, deliberate and emergent," *Strategic Management Journal*, 6/3 (1985): 257–272.

[11] Evered discusses the Greek origins of the word and traces its entry into contemporary Western vocabulary through the military. R. Evered, "So what is strategy," *Long Range Planning*, 16/3 (1983):57–72.

[12] As suggested in the results of a questionnaire by Ragab and Paterson; M. Ragab and W. E. Paterson, "An exploratory study of the strategy construct," proceedings of the Administrative Sciences Association of Canada Conference, 1981. Two notable exceptions are Herbert Simon and Jerome Bruner and his colleagues; H. A. Simon, *Administrative Behavior*, 2nd Edition (New York, NY: Macmillan, 1957); J. S. Bruner, J. J. Goodnow, and G. A. Austin, *A Study of Thinking* (New York, NY: Wiley, 1956), pp. 54–55.

[13] Quoted in J. B. Quinn, *Strategies for Change: Logical Incrementalism* (Homewood, IL: Richard D. Irwin, 1980), p. 35.

[14] *Business Week*, October 31, 1983.

defining strategy as pattern in action—that is, inferring consistency in behavior and labelling it strategy. They may, of course, go further and impute intention to that consistency—that is, assume there is a plan behind the pattern. But that is an assumption, which may prove false.

Thus, the definitions of strategy as plan and pattern can be quite independent of each other: plans may go unrealized, while patterns may appear without preconception. To paraphrase Hume, strategies may result from human actions but not human designs.[15] If we label the first definition *intended* strategy and the second *realized* strategy, as shown in Figure 1, then we can distinguish *deliberate* strategies, where intentions that existed previously were realized, from *emergent* strategies, where patterns developed in the absence of intentions, or despite them (which went *unrealized*).

Strategies About What?   Labelling strategies as plans or patterns still begs one basic question: *strategies about what?* Many writers respond by discussing the deployment of resources (e.g., Chandler, in one of the best known definitions[16]), but the question remains: which resources and for what purposes? An army may plan to reduce the number of nails in its shoes, or a corporation may realize a pattern of marketing only products painted black, but these hardly meet the lofty label "strategy." Or do they?

As the word has been handed down from the military, "strategy" refers to the important things, "tactics" to the details (more formally, "tactics teaches the use of armed forces in the engagement, strategy the use of engagements for the object of the war"[17]). Nails in shoes, colors of cars: these are certainly details. The problem is that in retrospect details can sometimes prove "strategic." Even in the military: "For want of a Nail, the Shoe was lost: for want of a Shoe the Horse was lost ..." and so on through the rider and general to the battle, "all for want of Care about a Horseshoe Nail."[18] Indeed one of the reasons Henry Ford lost his war with General Motors was that he refused to paint his cars anything but black.

Rumelt notes that "one person's strategies are another's tactics—that what is strategic depends on where you sit."[19] It also depends on *when* you sit: what seems tactical today may prove strategic tomorrow. The point is that these sorts of distinctions can be arbitrary and misleading, that labels should not be used to imply that some issues are *inevitably* more important than others. There are times when it pays to manage the details and let the strategies emerge for themselves. Thus there is good reason to drop the word "tactics" altogether and simply refer to issues as more or

---

[15] Via G. Majone, "The uses of policy analysis," in *The Future and the Past: Essays on Programs*, Russell Sage Foundation Annual Report, 1976–1977, pp. 201–220.

[16] A. D. Chandler, *Strategy and Structure: Chapters in the History of the Industrial Enterprise* (Cambridge, MA: M.I.T. Press, 1962), p. 13.

[17] Von Clausewitz, op. cit., p. 128.

[18] B. Franklin, *Poor Richard's Almanac* (New York, NY: Ballantine Books, 1977), p. 280.

[19] R. P. Rumelt, "Evaluation of strategy: theory and models," in D. E. Schendel and C. W. Hofer, eds., *Strategic Management: A New View of Business Policy and Planning* (Boston, MA: Little Brown, 1979), pp. 196–212.

FIGURE I   **Deliberate and Emergent Strategies**

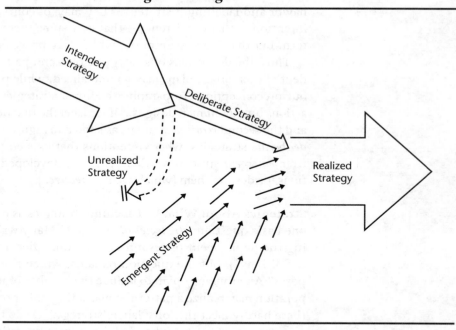

less "strategic," in other words, more or less "important" in some context, whether as intended before acting or as realized after it.[20] Accordingly, the answer to the question, strategy about what, is: potentially about

---

[20] We might note a similar problem with "policy," a word whose usage is terribly confused. In the military, the word has traditionally served one notch in the hierarchy above strategy, in business one notch below, and in public administration in general as a substitute. In the military, policy deals with the purposes for which wars are fought, which is supposed to be the responsibility of the politicians. In other words, the politicians make policy; the generals, strategy. But modern warfare has confused this usage (see Summers), so that today strategy in the military context has somehow come to be associated with the acquisition of nuclear weapons and their use against non-military targets. In business, while "policy" has been the label for the entire field of study of general management (at least until "strategic management" gained currency in the 1970s), its technical use was as a general rule to dictate decisions in a specific case, usually a standard and recurring situation, as in "Our policy is to require long-range forecasts every four months." Accordingly, management planning theorists, such as George Steiner, describe policies as deriving from strategies although some textbook writers (such as Leontiades, Chang and Campo-Flores, and Peter Drucker) have used the two words in exactly the opposite way, as in the military. This reflects the fact that "policy" was the common word in the management literature before "strategy" replaced it in the 1960s (see, for example, Jamison, and Gross and Gross). But in the public sector today, the words "policy" and "policymaking" correspond roughly to "strategy" and "strategy making." H. G. Summers, *On Strategy: The Vietnam War in Context* (Carlisle Barracks, PA: Strategic Studies Institute, U.S. Army War College, 1981); G. A. Steiner, *Top Management Planning* (New York, NY: Macmillan, 1969), p. 264 ff; M. Leontiades, *Management Policy, Strategy and Plans* (Boston, MA: Little Brown, 1982), p. 4; Y.N.A. Chang and F. Campo-Flores, *Business Policy and Strategy* (Goodyear, 1980), p. 7; Drucker, op. cit., p. 104; C. L. Jamison, *Business Policy* (Englewood Cliffs, NJ: Prentice-Hall, 1953); A. Gross and W. Gross, eds., *Business Policy: Selected Readings and Editorial Commentaries* (New York, NY: Ronald Press, 1967).

anything. About products and processes, customers and citizens, social responsibilities and self interests, control and color.

Two aspects of the content of strategies must, however, be singled out because they are of particular importance and, accordingly, play major roles in the literature.

Strategy as Position

The fourth definition is that *strategy is a position*—specifically, a means of locating an organization in what organization theorists like to call an "environment." By this definition, strategy becomes the mediating force—or "match," according to Hofer and Schendel[21]—between organization and environment, that is, between the internal and the external context. In ecological terms, strategy becomes a "niche"; in economic terms, a place that generates "rent" (that is "returns to [being] in a 'unique' place"[22]); in management terms, formally, a product-market "domain,"[23] the place in the environment where resources are concentrated (leading McNichols to call this "root strategy"[24]).

Note that this definition of strategy can be compatible with either (or all) of the preceding ones: a position can be preselected and aspired to through a plan (or ploy) and/or it can be reached, perhaps even found, through a pattern of behavior ("the concept of strategy need not be tied to rational planning or even conscious decision-making assumptions. Strategy is essentially a descriptive idea that includes an organization's choice of niche and its primary decision rules ... for coping with that niche")[25].

In military and game theory views of strategy, it is generally used in the context of what is called a "two-person game," better known in business as head-on competition (where ploys are especially common). The definition of strategy as position, however, implicitly allows us to open up the concept, to so-called n-person games (that is, many players), and beyond. In other words, while position can always be defined with respect to a single competitor (literally so in the military, where position becomes the site of battle), it can also be considered in the context of a number of competitors or simply with respect to markets or an environment at large.[26] Since head-on competition is not the usual case in business, management theorists have generally focussed on the n-person situation, although they have tended to retain the notion of

---

[21] C. W. Hofer and D. Schendel, *Strategy Formulation: Analytical Concepts* (St. Paul, MN: West Publishing, 1978), p. 4.

[22] E. H. Bowman, "Epistomology, corporate strategy, and academe," *Sloan Management Review*, 15/2 (1974):47.

[23] J. D. Thompson, *Organizations in Action* (New York, NY: McGraw-Hill, 1967).

[24] T. J. McNichols, *Policy-Making and Executive Action* (New York, NY: McGraw-Hill, 1983), p. 257.

[25] Rumelt, op. cit., p. 4.

[26] R. P. Rumelt, "The evaluation of business strategy," in W. F. Glueck, *Business Policy and Strategic Management*, 3rd Edition (New York, NY: McGraw-Hill, 1980), p. 361.

economic competition.[27] But strategy as position can extend beyond competition too, economic and otherwise. Indeed, what is the meaning of the word "niche" but a position that is occupied to *avoid* competition.

Thus, we can move from the definition employed by General Ulysses Grant in the 1860s, "Strategy [is] the deployment of one's resources in a manner which is most likely to defeat the enemy," to that of Professor Rumelt in the 1980s. "Strategy is creating situations for economic rents and finding ways to sustain them,[28] that is, any viable position, whether or not directly competitive.

Astley and Fombrun, in fact, take the next logical step by introducing the notion of "collective" strategy, that is, strategy pursued to promote cooperation between organization, even would-be competitors (equivalent in biology to animals herding together for protection).[29] Such strategies can range "from informal arrangements and discussion to formal devices such as interlocking directorates, joint ventures, and mergers."[30] In fact, considered from a slightly different angle, these can sometimes be described as *political strategies,* that is strategies to subvert the legitimate forces of competition.

Strategy as Perspective

While the fourth definition of strategy looks out, seeking to locate the organization in the external environment, the fifth looks inside the organization, indeed inside the heads of the collective strategist. Here, *strategy is a perspective,* its content consisting not just of a chosen position, but of an ingrained way of perceiving the world. Some organizations, for example, are aggressive pacesetters, creating new technologies and exploiting new markets; others perceive the world as set and stable, and so sit back in long established markets and build protective shells around themselves, relying more on political influence than economic efficiency. There are organizations that favor marketing and build a whole ideology around that (an IBM); others treat engineering in this way (a Hewlett-Packard); and then there are those that concentrate on sheer productive efficiency (a McDonald's).

Strategy in this respect is to the organization what personality is to the individual. Indeed, one of the earliest and most influential writers on strategy (at least as his ideas have been reflected in more popular writings) was Philip Selznick, who wrote about the "character" of an organization—distinct and integrated "commitments to ways of acting and responding" that are built right into it.[31] A variety of concepts from other fields also capture

---

[27] E.g., Porter, op. cit. (1980, 1985), except for his chapters noted earlier, which tend to have a 2-person competitive focus.

[28] Expressed at the Strategic Management Society Conference, Paris, October 1982.

[29] W. G. Astley and C. J. Fombrun, "Collective strategy: social ecology of organizational environments," *Academy of Management Review*, 8/4 (1983):576–587.

[30] Ibid., p. 577.

[31] P. Selznick, *Leadership in Administration: A Sociological Interpretation* (New York, NY: Harper & Row, 1957), p. 47. A subsequent paper by the author (in process) on the "design school" of strategy formation shows the link of Selznick's early work to the writings of Kenneth Andrews in the Harvard policy textbook. K. R. Andrews, *The Concept of Corporate Strategy*, Revised Edition (Homewood, IL: Dow Jones-Irwin, 1987).

this notion: psychologists refer to an individual's mental frame, cognitive structure, and a variety of other expressions for "relatively fixed patterns for experiencing [the] world"[32]; anthropologists refer to the "culture" of a society and sociologists to its "ideology"; military theorists write of the "grand strategy" of armies; while management theorists have used terms such as the "theory of the business"[33] and its "driving force"[34]; behavioral scientists who have read Kuhn[35] on the philosophy of science refer to the "paradigm" of a community of scholars; and Germans perhaps capture it best with their word "Weltanschauung," literally "worldview," meaning collective intuition about how the world works.

This fifth definition suggests above all that strategy is a *concept*. This has one important implication, namely, that all strategies are abstractions which exist only in the minds of interested parties—those who pursue them, are influenced by that pursuit, or care to observe others doing so. It is important to remember that no-one has ever seen a strategy or touched one; every strategy is an invention, a figment of someone's imagination, whether conceived of as intentions to regulate behavior before it takes place or inferred as patterns to describe behavior that has already occurred.

What is of key importance about this fifth definition, however, is that the perspective is *shared*. As implied in the words Weltanschauung, culture, and ideology (with respect to a society) or paradigm (with respect to a community of scholars), but not the word personality, strategy is a perspective shared by the members of an organization, through their intentions and/or by their actions. In effect, when we are talking of strategy in this context, we are entering the realm of the *collective mind*—individuals united by common thinking and/ or behavior. A major issue in the study of strategy formation becomes, therefore, how to read that collective mind—to understand how intentions diffuse through the system called organization to become shared and how actions come to be exercised on a collective yet consistent basis.

◨ Interrelating the Ps

As suggested above, strategy as both position and perspective can be compatible with strategy as plan and/or pattern. But, in fact, the relationships between these different definitions can be more involved than that. For example, while some consider perspective to *be* a plan (Lapierre writes of strategies as "dreams in search of reality"[36]; Summer, more prosaically, as "a comprehensive,

---

[32] J. Bieri, "Cognitive structures in personality," in H. M. Schroder and P. Suedfeld, eds., *Personality: Theory and Information Processing* (New York, NY: Ronald Press, 1971), p. 178. By the same token, Bieri (p. 179) uses the word "strategy" in the context of psychology.

[33] Drucker, op. cit.

[34] B. B. Tregoe and J. W. Zimmerman, *Top Management Strategy* (New York, NY: Simon & Schuster, 1980).

[35] T. S. Kuhn, *The Structure of Scientific Revolution*, 2nd Edition (Chicago, IL: University of Chicago Press, 1970).

[36] My own translation of "un rêve ou un bouquet de rêves en quête de réalité." L. Lapierre, "Le changement stratégique: Un rêve en quête de réel," Ph.D. Management Policy course paper, McGill University, Canada, 1980.

holistic, gestalt, logical vision of some future alignment"[37]), others describe it as *giving rise* to plans (for example, as positions and/or patterns in some kind of implicit hierarchy). This is shown in Figure 2a. Thus, Majone writes of "basic principles, commitments, and norms" that form the "policy core," while "plans, programs, and decisions" serve as the "protective belt."[38] Likewise, Hedberg and Jonsson claim that strategies, by which they mean "more or less well integrated sets of ideas and constructs" (in our terms, perspectives) are "the causes that mold streams of decisions into patterns."[39] This is similar to Tregoe and Zimmerman who define strategy as "vision directed"—"the framework which guides those choices that determine the nature and direction of an organization."[40] Note in the second and third of these quotations that, strictly speaking, the hierarchy can skip a step, with perspective dictating pattern, not necessarily through formally intended plans.

Consider the example of the Honda Company, which has been described in one highly publicized consulting report[41] as parlaying a particular perspective (being a low cost producer, seeking to attack new markets in aggressive ways) into a plan, in the form of an intended position (to capture the traditional motorcycle market in the United States and create a new one for small family motorcycles), which was in turn realized through an integrated set of patterns (lining up distributorships, developing the appropriate advertising campaign of "You meet the nicest people on a Honda," etc.) All of this matches the conventional prescriptive view of how strategies are supposed to get made.[42]

But a closer look at Honda's actual behavior suggests a very different story: it did not go to America with the main intention of selling small, family motorcycles at all; rather, the company seemed to fall into that market almost inadvertently.[43] But once it was clear to the Honda executives that they had wandered into such a lucrative strategic position, that presumably became their plan. In other words, their strategy emerged, step by step, but once recognized, was made deliberate. Honda, if you like, developed its intentions through its actions, another way of saying that pattern evoked plan. This is shown in Figure 2b.

Of course, an overall strategic perspective (Honda's way of doing things) seems to have underlaid all this, as shown in the figure as well. But we may still ask how that perspective arose in the first place. The answer seems to be that it did so in a similar way, through earlier experiences: the organization

---

[37] Summer, op. cit., p. 18.

[38] G. Majone, op. cit.

[39] B. Hedberg and S.A. Jonsson, "Strategy formulation as a discontinuous process," *International Studies of Management and Organization*, 7/2 (1977):90.

[40] Tregoe and Zimmerman, op. cit., p. 17.

[41] Boston Consulting Group, *Strategy Alternatives for the British Motorcycle Industry* (London: Her Majesty's Stationery Office, 1975).

[42] E.g., H. I. Ansoff, *Corporate Strategy* (New York, NY: McGraw-Hill, 1965); Andrews. op. cit.; Steiner, op. cit.; D. E. Schendel and C. H. Hofer, eds., *Strategic Management: A New View of Business Policy and Planning* (Boston, MA: Little Brown, 1979), p. 15.

[43] R. T. Pascale, "Perspectives on strategy: the real story behind Honda's success," *California Management Review*, 26/3 (Spring 1984):47–72.

FIGURE 2 **Some Possible Relationships Between Strategy as Plan, Pattern, Position, Perspective**

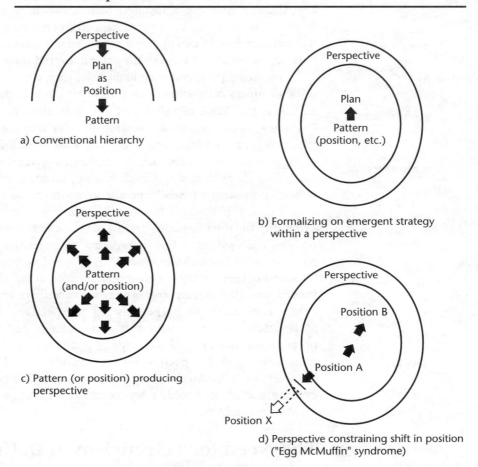

a) Conventional hierarchy

b) Formalizing on emergent strategy within a perspective

c) Pattern (or position) producing perspective

d) Perspective constraining shift in position ("Egg McMuffin" syndrome)

tried various things in its formative years and gradually consolidated a perspective around what worked.[44] In other words, organizations would appear to develop "character"—much as people develop personality—by interacting with the world as they find it through the use of their innate skills and natural propensities. Thus pattern can give rise to perspective too, as shown in Figure 2c. And so can position. Witness Perrow's discussion of the "wool men" and "silk men" of the textile trade, people who developed an almost religious dedication to the fibers they produced.[45]

No matter how they appear, however, there is reason to believe that while plans and positions may be dispensable, perspectives are immutable.[46] In other

[44] J. B. Quinn, "Honda Motor Company case," in J. B. Quinn, H. Mintzberg, and B. G. James, *The Strategy Process: Concepts, Contexts, Cases* (Englewood Cliffs, NJ: Prentice-Hall, 1988).

[45] C. Perrow, *Organizational Analysis: A Sociological View* (Belmont, CA: Wadsorth, 1970), p. 161.

[46] E.g., N. Brunsson, "The irrationality of action and action rationality: decisions, ideologies, and organizational actions," *Journal of Management Studies*, 19/1 (1982):29–44.

words, once they are established, perspectives become difficult to change. Indeed, a perspective may become so deeply ingrained in the behavior of an organization that the associated beliefs can become subconscious in the minds of its members. When that happens, perspective can come to look more like pattern than like plan—in other words, it can be found more in the consistency of behaviors than in the articulation of intentions.

Of course, if perspective is immutable, then change in plan and position is difficult unless compatible with the existing perspective. As shown in Figure 2d, the organization can shift easily from Position A to Position B but not to Position X. In this regard, it is interesting to take up the case of Egg McMuffin. Was this product when new—the American breakfast in a bun—a strategic change for the McDonald's fast food chain? Posed in MBA classes, this earth-shattering (or at least stomach-shattering) question inevitably evokes heated debate. Proponents (usually people sympathetic to fast food) argue that of course it was: it brought McDonald's into a new market, the breakfast one, extending the use of existing facilities. Opponents retort that this is nonsense, nothing changed but a few ingredients: this was the same old pap in a new package. Both sides are, or course, right—and wrong. It simply depends on how you define strategy. Position changed; perspective remained the same. Indeed—and this is the point—the position could be changed so easily because it was compatible with the existing perspective. Egg McMuffin is pure McDonald's, not only in product and package, but also in production and propagation. But imagine a change of position at McDonald's that would require a change of perspective—say, to introduce candlelight dining with personal service (your McDuckling à l'orange cooked to order) to capture the late evening market. We needn't say more, except perhaps to label this the "Egg McMuffin syndrome."

◼ The Need for Eclecticism in Definition

While various relationships exist among the different definitions, no one relationship, nor any single definition for that matter, takes precedence over the others. In some ways, these definitions compete (in that they can substitute for each other), but in perhaps more important ways, they complement. Not all plans become patterns nor are all patterns that develop planned; some ploys are less than positions; while other strategies are more than positions yet less than perspectives. Each definition adds important elements to our understanding of strategy, indeed encourages us to address fundamental questions about organizations in general.

As plan, strategy deals with how leaders try to establish direction for organizations, to set them on predetermined courses of action. Strategy as plan also raises the fundamental issue of cognition—how intentions are conceived in the human brain in the first place, indeed, what intentions really mean. Are we, for example, to take statements of intentions at face value? Do people always say what they mean, or mean what they say? Ostensible strategies as ploys can be stated just to fool competitors; sometimes, however, those who state them fool themselves. Thus, the road to hell in this field can be paved with those who take all stated intentions at face value. In studying strategy as plan, we must somehow get into the mind of the strategist, to find out what is really intended.

As ploy, strategy takes us into the realm of direct competition, where threats and feints and various other maneuvers are employed to gain advantage. This places the process of strategy formation in its most dynamic setting, with moves provoking countermoves and so on. Yet ironically, strategy itself is a concept rooted not in change but in stability—in set plans and established patterns. How then to reconcile the dynamic notions of strategy as ploy with the static ones of strategy as pattern and other forms of plan?

As pattern, strategy focusses on action, reminding us that the concept is an empty one if it does not take behavior into account. Strategy as pattern also introduces another important phenomenon in organizations, that of convergence, the achievement of consistency in behavior. How does this consistency form, where does it come from? Realized strategy is an important means of conceiving and describing the direction actually pursued by organizations, and when considered alongside strategy as plan, encourages us to consider the notion that strategies can emerge as well as be deliberately imposed.

As position, strategy encourages us to look at organizations in context, specifically in their competitive environments—how they find their positions and protect them in order to meet competition, avoid it, or subvert it. This enables us to think of organizations in ecological terms, as organisms in niches that struggle for survival in a world of hostility and uncertainty as well as symbiosis. How much choice do organizations have, how much room for maneuver?

And finally as perspective, strategy raises intriguing questions about intention and behavior in a collective context. If we define organization as collective action in the pursuit of common mission (a fancy way of saying that a group of people under a common label—whether an IBM or a United Nations or a Luigi's Body Shop—somehow find the means to cooperate in the production of specific goods and services), then strategy as perspective focusses our attention on the reflections and actions of the collectivity—how intentions diffuse through a group of people to become shared as norms and values, and how patterns of behavior become deeply ingrained in the group. Ultimately, it is this view of strategy that offers us the best hope of coming to grips with the most fascinating issue of all, that of the "organizational mind."

Thus, strategy is not just a notion of how to deal with an enemy or a set of competitors or a market, as it is treated in so much of the literature and in its popular usage. It also draws us into some of the most fundamental issues about organizations as instruments for collective perception and action.

To conclude, a good deal of the confusion in this field stems from contradictory and ill-defined uses of the term strategy, as we saw in the Egg McMuffin syndrome. By explicating and using five definitions, we may be able to remove some of this confusion, and thereby enrich our ability to understand and manage the processes by which strategies form.

Canada at the Crossroads: The Reality of a New Competitive Environment

MICHAEL E. PORTER

MONITOR COMPANY

Canada and International Competition: Theory and Evidence

Setting the Context

The principal economic goal of a country is to provide a high and rising standard of living for its citizens. By this yardstick Canada's economy has performed well over the last 30 years. It has achieved one of the world's highest standards of living while creating and maintaining a generous and socially progressive state. Adjusted for purchasing power, Canada ranked second among Organization for Economic Cooperation and Development (OECD) countries in per capita gross domestic product (GDP) in 1989, up from fourth in 1960.

We believe, however, that Canada today is at an economic crossroads and that the core of its economic prosperity is at risk. Canada's rich natural resource endowments, its proximity to the United States, and a history of insulation from international competition have combined to allow Canadian industry to achieve an enviable economic performance. These same advantages, however, have led to an array of policies, strategies, and attitudes on the part of governments, business, labour, and individual Canadians that leave the economy in many respects ill-equipped to respond to a rapidly changing competitive environment.

Canadian industry now is undergoing a rapid structural change. As this process continues, signs are already accumulating that Canadian industry is encountering difficulties as it confronts a changed and more competitive environment. If the current trajectory continues, the standard of living of Canadians seems destined to fall behind. Yet there is nothing inevitable about this outcome; Canadians have in their own hands the power to change it.

Source: Excerpts from a study prepared for the Business Council on National Issues and the government of Canada, October 1991, by Michael E. Porter, Harvard Business School, and Monitor Company.

Threats to Prosperity

The underpinning of competitiveness, and thus of a country's standard of living, is productivity. Productivity is the value of output produced by a day of work or a dollar of capital invested. In the long run, productivity determines the standard of living by setting wages, profits, and, ultimately, the resources available to meet social needs. To achieve sustained productivity growth, an economy must continually *upgrade* itself. An upgrading economy is one that relentlessly pursues greater productivity in existing industries by improving products, utilizing more efficient production processes, and migrating into more sophisticated and higher-value industry segments. It is also an economy that has the capability to compete in entirely new industries, absorbing the resources made available from improved productivity in existing industries. The capacity of an economy to upgrade—its competitive potential—depends on underlying structural and institutional characteristics, such as its work force, its infrastructure, its postsecondary educational institutions, and its public policies. Cyclical factors, such as shifts in world commodity prices or exchange rates, can create the illusion of prosperity, but in reality yield only temporary advantages.

The Changing Competitive Environment

Traditionally, Canadians have lived in a relatively insulated environment brought about by paternalistic government policies, a history of market protection, and the accumulated attitudes and experiences of both individuals and businesses.

This old economic order, as we call it, was a system where many prospered. However, because the old order generally provided insulation from external pressures and fostered limited internal pressures, many of the critical requirements for upgrading to more sophisticated and sustainable competitive advantages in Canadian industry have been missing or are only weakly present.

Increasing globalization of trade and investment, accelerating technological changes, rapidly evolving company and country strategies, and—more recently—the Free Trade Agreement with the United States, represent significant discontinuities in the nature of international competition confronting Canadian-based industry. Together, these forces are pushing Canada away from the "comfortable insularity" of the old order. They will both magnify long-standing competitive weaknesses and hasten the pace of structural adjustment to a new competitive reality. What is most troubling is the fact that in essential areas such as science, technology, education, and training, significant barriers stand in the way of effective upgrading.

Owing to Canada's extensive trading relationship with the United States and its unusually high degree of foreign ownership, the shifting character of international competition poses particularly daunting challenges for Canadian firms and public policymakers. Many companies are currently in the process of determining how to reconfigure their North American and international activities, including deciding where to locate what we describe as their "home bases" for individual product lines and even their entire corporate operation.

Typically, a company's home base is where the best jobs reside, where core research and development is undertaken, and where strategic control lies. Home bases are important to an economy because they support high productivity and productivity growth. In the context of the changing global economy, we believe that Canada is in danger of losing much of its capacity to attract and retain home bases.

So far, many industries and sectors show few signs of upgrading. In addition, as we discuss below, macroeconomic indicators have begun to manifest the weaknesses that exist at the industry level. Though Canada's status as a wealthy country is not in doubt, the risk is of a slowly eroding standard of living over the coming years.

Worrisome Performance Trends

Over the 1980s, Canada's economy performed quite well. Real economic growth between 1983 and 1989 was second only to Japan among the seven leading industrial countries (the G7). Canada also enjoyed the second fastest rate of employment growth among the G7 over the same period (the United States was first). Yet despite these favourable macroeconomic indicators, there is mounting evidence that Canada suffers from underlying economic weaknesses that could undercut its ability to achieve a higher standard of living in the future.

- The most serious weakness is *low productivity growth*. Since the early 1970s, Canada has ranked near the bottom of all major industrial countries in productivity growth. From 1979 to 1989, total factor productivity (TFP)—which measures the growth in productivity of both labour and capital inputs—rose by a mere 0.4 percent per year, tying Canada with the United States as the worst performer among the G7 countries. Over the same period, manufacturing labour productivity growth in Canada was the lowest among the G7 countries, averaging only 1.8 percent per annum.

- A second and closely related concern is Canada's record in the area of *unit labour costs*. Unit labour costs measure labour costs adjusted for productivity. They are a key indicator of competitiveness, especially for industries and firms that produce tradeable goods and services. Between 1979 and 1989, Canada's unit labour costs in the manufacturing sector rose more quickly than those in most other industrialized countries, and increased more than twice as fast as costs in the United States, which is the most important competitive benchmark for Canadian industry.

- *Unemployment* is a third danger signal. Despite robust employment growth over the past two decades, the unemployment rate in Canada has exceeded that in most other industrialized countries. In recent years, long-term unemployment has become more of a problem, and the average duration of unemployment has risen. Although the unemployment trend is a separate issue from that of productivity growth, growing numbers of workers with marginal or intermittent attachments to the labour force, and the rising average duration of unemployment, point to underlying problems that could affect Canada's capacity to upgrade its economy and respond successfully to changes in technology and global markets.

- *Lagging investments in upgrading skills and technology.* Canada's poor record in productivity growth and unemployment is disturbing. More worrisome in many ways, however, is that the investments that will drive productivity and employment growth in the future have been lagging. While aggregate investment growth has been quite strong, Canada trails competitor countries in private sector investments linked directly to enhanced productivity. Between 1980 and 1989, investment in machinery and equipment as a percentage of GDP was lower in Canada than in most other major industrialized countries. Similarly, Canadian private sector investment in research and development as a percentage of GDP is the second lowest among the G7 countries (slightly ahead of Italy). Moreover, investments by Canadian firms in worker training fall well short of levels registered in the United States, Germany, Japan, and many other advanced countries.

- Finally, the *macroeconomic environment* is not sufficiently supportive of investment. The ability of government to create a stable macroeconomic environment is being hampered by chronic government deficits and rapidly growing public debt. Combined federal and provincial government debt has been growing more quickly than the economy for a decade and now exceeds 70 percent of GDP. Among the G7 countries, only Italy has a higher government debt level. Servicing these massive government debt obligations lowers Canadian income and places constraints on the ability of Canadian governments to maintain an environment that encourages investment and the upgrading efforts of Canadian industry.

Canada's Position in International Competition

This study provides a detailed examination of Canada's position in international competition between 1978 and 1989 and how this compares with the positions of other industrialized countries. Here, we can only summarize the key findings and conclusions that flow from this in-depth analysis.

Focus on the Traded Sector

A country's performance in the traded sector provides a unique window into the sources of national economic prosperity. The traded sector is a large and increasingly important component of the economies of all industrialized countries. It has particular leverage for productivity growth, especially in smaller and mid-size countries such as Canada, where the ability to trade frees productive local industries from the constraints of the domestic market. Thus freed, these industries can grow and absorb resources from less productive industries, whose products can then be imported. In addition, the traded sector is where firms from a multiplicity of countries compete. It is the place where one can best analyze the ways in which the economic context in different countries creates advantages or disadvantages for firms.

This study takes a detailed look at Canada's export sector. It explores Canada's position in international competition, both over time and relative to other industrialized countries. The basis for our statistical analysis is the United Nations Standard International Trade Classification (SITC) statistics. These trade statistics, which measure exports and imports in approximately 4,000 narrowly defined industries, allow us to compare the trade performance of many countries over time at the level of strategically distinct industries. The UN trade statistics were also used in the original 10-nation research reported in *The Competitive Advantage of Nations*.

The export sector is a vital component of Canada's economy, representing 25.2 percent of GDP in 1989. Among the G7 countries, Canada is second only to Germany in the importance of trade to its economy. Canada's share of world market economy exports has varied between 4 and 5 percent over the past three decades. The trend for the period as a whole has been one of slow decline. More important than the trend in Canada's world export share, however, is how the composition of Canadian exports has evolved.

The remainder of this section summarizes the main characteristics of Canada's exports—a subject explored at much greater length in the full study report.

Significant Natural Resource Dependence

Perhaps the most striking feature of Canada's export profile is the prominent role of natural resource-based exports. These accounted for 45.8 percent of Canada's total exports in 1989. In fact, Canada's share of world resource exports rose from 5.0 percent in 1978 to 8.3 percent in 1989. Of nine major trading countries, Canada has by far the largest share of country exports based on unprocessed and semiprocessed natural resources; these comprised more than one third of all Canadian exports in 1989, compared to 20 percent in the United States and 11 percent in Sweden.

Exports of natural resource-based products are by no means undesirable—indeed, they have done much to make Canada wealthy. However, a high proportion of exports concentrated in relatively *unprocessed* resources suggests that, on the whole, Canadian industry has failed to upgrade or extend its competitive advantage into processing technology and the marketing and support of more sophisticated resource-based products. Dependence on semi- and unprocessed resources also leaves Canada vulnerable to commodity price shifts, technology substitution, and the emergence of lower-cost competitors, often in less developed countries. Why this pattern exists and what it means for the future is therefore a critical issue.

Exports Concentrated in Five Broad Clusters

Understanding the underpinnings of Canada's competitive advantage is aided by examining the nature of its industry *clusters*. To do this, all export industries are grouped into distinct clusters defined by end-use applications. Each cluster contains a number of distinct industries (with forest products, for example, consisting of market pulp, newsprint, sawmilling, and many other industries related to the forest sector). *Upstream industries* produce inputs used by many other industries. Most upstream industries are resource-based, with the exception of semiconductors/computers. There are six broad sectors connected to *industrial and supporting functions*. Industries at this level typically compete on the basis of technology and are often the industrial core of the economy. Another six sectors are associated with *final consumption goods and services*. Industries at this level are connected to end consumer needs. Resource-rich countries typically begin at the top level of upstream industries, while resource-poor countries start from the bottom level of labour-intensive final consumption goods. Most gradually grow toward the middle (industrial and supporting) level as they upgrade and lay the foundation of an industrial core.

Canadian exports are highly concentrated in three of the 16 clusters—materials/metals, forest products, and transportation—which together account for nearly 62 percent of Canada's exports. These three clusters, along with petroleum/chemicals and food/beverages, represented more than 82 percent of total Canadian exports in 1989. Looked at by end-use application, Canadian exports are concentrated at the level of upstream industries, where three of the five main clusters are located. At the level of industrial and supporting goods, Canadian exports consist largely of transportation equipment. Here we see the effect of the Canada–United States Auto Pact, which has had a profound influence on Canada's manufacturing sector (and, especially, its manufacturing exports). In 1989, fully 79 percent of transportation sector exports were from industries related to the Auto Pact. (Other cluster exports included aircraft and related parts and urban mass transit equipment.) Final consumption goods and services represent a relatively small share of Canada's exports (15 percent in 1989), the most significant cluster being food/beverage products, which consists largely of minimally processed products such as fish and grain.

Key Role of Foreign-Controlled Companies

Foreign ownership is relatively high in Canada, although it has been declining since the 1960s. In the manufacturing sector, for example, approximately 45 percent of assets in Canada are foreign controlled. Foreign ownership is quite widespread in most of Canada's five leading export clusters. Exhibit 1 shows the share of corporate assets controlled by foreign firms in selected industries within the various clusters. Among Canada's five main export clusters, foreign ownership is highest in transportation equipment and lowest in forest products. Many of the strategic decisions in important Canadian sectors are made outside of Canada, based on the overall global strategies of parent companies. How the choices made by these parent companies with respect to the location of home base activities for all or segments of their businesses will evolve in response to changes in international competition is a critical issue for the Canadian economy.

Very Limited Machinery Exports

Canada has few internationally competitive machinery industries. In total, machinery exports accounted for just 3.4 percent of all Canadian exports in 1989, up slightly from 3 percent in 1978, but substantially lower than in other

EXHIBIT 1   Foreign-Controlled Share of Assets of Selected Canadian Industries, 1987

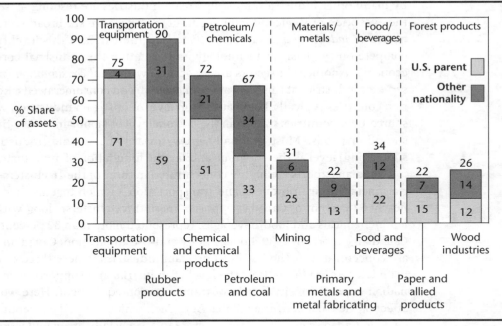

Source: Statistics Canada; Calura.

major industrialized countries. In fact, Canada's share of competitive machinery exports fell from 1.3 percent of world exports in 1978 to 0.7 percent in 1989.[1] In addition, Canada's trade deficit in machinery increased 31 percent in real terms since 1978, to U.S. $3.3 billion.

Machinery industries are a sign of healthy economic upgrading. They give a country's core industries quicker access to and more control over fast-changing process technologies. Superiority in machinery and related and supporting industries can help to sustain competitive advantage in primary goods. Primary goods producers can often work closely with machinery firms located in their home country to upgrade and improve productivity. This relationship tends to be more difficult to build with foreign suppliers. In short, with few competitive machinery industries, many Canadian businesses are deprived of the dynamic interactions that foster process innovation and upgrading.

Principal Clusters Exhibit Limited Breadth or Depth

In looking in more detail, we find that even the most significant export clusters exhibit limited breadth or depth. For instance, in the forest products cluster, three industries—sawn wood, newsprint, and market pulp—account for 75 percent of total exports. There is almost no export position in more sophisticated segments such as fine paper. Most significantly, in analyzing the patterns of change in export composition from 1978–1989, we see little

---

[1] The definition of international competitiveness employed in this study was consistent with that of the 10-nation study: a world export market share greater than Canada's overall share of market economy exports in 1989.

evidence to suggest exports have shifted into more sophisticated industry segments within these clusters.

Few Service Industries Are Internationally Competitive

Services represent about 68 percent of Canada's GDP and account for upwards of 70 percent of total employment. Among the G7 countries, Canada is second only to the United States in the relative size of the service sector. Although most services are not traded, they do represent a significant portion of the inputs of all goods exported by Canada. Uncompetitive domestic service industries can undermine the competitive position of a country's goods-producing sectors. The need for constant productivity improvements and upgrading thus applies equally to service industries, regardless of whether the output of such industries directly enters international trade.

International trade in services has been growing rapidly and now amounts to more than U.S. $700 billion per year (out of total world trade of $3.3 trillion). However, relatively few industries in the Canadian services sector have reached international standing and Canada's service exports as a percentage of total exports are the lowest of the G7.

Deteriorating Trade Balances Outside of Resource Sectors

Canada's overall mix of exports has remained quite consistent in the recent past, with resource-dependent industries maintaining a 45–46 percent share of total exports between 1978 and 1989. Four out of Canada's five dominant export sectors enjoy positive trade balances—materials/metals, forest products, petroleum/chemicals, and food/beverages. Canada's strength in resource-based sectors is reflected in its growing positive trade balance in upstream industries, reaching $23 billion in 1989 (measured in U.S. dollars), up sharply from $9 billion in 1978. A rising trade surplus in the forest products sector (from $5.3 billion in 1978 to $16.4 billion in 1989) largely accounts for Canada's strengthening position in upstream industries.

Canada's trade balance is negative, however, in most of 16 industry clusters. Overall, Canada has recorded growing trade surpluses in resource-dependent goods, and rising trade deficits in nonresource sectors. Higher deficits in most nonresource industries point to weaknesses in Canada's competitive profile. Imports are fulfilling Canadian demand in a growing range of sophisticated industry segments. Canada remains extremely dependent on exports of resource-based products (and transportation equipment) to sustain its wealth and standard of living.

Export Economy Divided into Four Main Categories

Looking closely at Canada's trade patterns suggests another way of picturing the Canadian economy. In particular, it is possible to divide the export sector into four broad industry groupings:

1. *Resource-based industries.* These are industries in which Canadian exports are derived wholly or largely from natural resource advantages. Pulp and paper, lumber, and copper are examples.

2. *Market access-driven industries*. These consist of industries where Canadian exports come from plants established by foreign companies primarily to gain access to the Canadian market. Indicators used to identify such industries in our research were a high share of assets controlled by foreign companies and/or historically high tariffs. Auto Pact industries are the most important example and currently represent about 60 percent of all exports from market access-driven industries. Other industries in this category are rubber products, commercial refrigeration, office and business machines, electrical appliances, and some areas of industrial chemicals.

3. *Innovation-driven industries*. These are defined as either Canadian-owned indigenous industries or foreign-owned industries where competitiveness has been driven largely by Canadian-based innovation. Manufacturing industries in this category include telecommunications equipment, aircraft and aircraft parts, and electronic components.

4. *Other industries*. These represent the balance of Canada's export sector. Industries falling into this group tend to be uncompetitive or marginally competitive based on world export share. Industries in this group consist mainly of foreign-controlled firms with modest exports or indigenous industries involved in trade solely with bordering states of the United States.

To approximate how Canadian exports are divided into these groups, we used UN trade data. Unfortunately, this data covers goods-producing industries but not services. Canadian goods-producing industries were classified using the above categories, and the industries in each category were then aggregated (as measured by shipments). Exhibit 2 displays the trends by category in terms of exports and balance of trade. (Note that exports are valued in 1989 U.S. dollars.) The estimates are crude, but they are consistent with earlier data. As shown, the most significant growth in Canadian exports of goods between 1978 and 1989 was in the resource sector, which markedly increased its exports and its trade surplus over the decade. In the innovation-driven industries, exports have increased slightly and the trade balance is slightly negative, while in the market access sector, exports are up and the trade balance relatively steady. However, the size and trajectory of the "other industries" category is troubling. It is a significant part of the economy but has been contributing to worsening trade balances. This again underscores the fact that the resource sector is the strongest part of the export economy.

Canada's International Competitive Position: Conclusion

This brief overview of Canada's position in international competition and its export economy highlights a number of real or potential weaknesses. Canada's high dependence on exports of relatively unprocessed natural resource-based products signals a lack of breadth even in the country's most prominent export clusters. Likewise, Canada's very weak position in machinery indicates a lack of depth within key industry clusters. Most importantly,

EXHIBIT 2   Canadian Goods-Producing Export Economy by Type of Industries

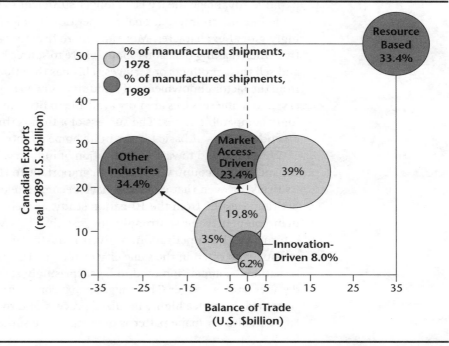

Source: UN Trade Statistics; Statistics Canada; Monitor Company Analysis.

our analysis found little evidence that either the breadth or the depth of Canada's major export clusters is increasing. Taken together, this evidence is consistent with the brief macroeconomic picture, previously presented, which points to an economy that shows limited signs of upgrading, and suggests that productivity growth—the critical driver of prosperity—may be increasingly difficult to achieve.

Determinants of National Competitive Advantage: The "Diamond"

Competitiveness has emerged as a preeminent issue for firms and government policymakers in every industrialized country. Most efforts to explain national competitiveness have taken an aggregate perspective, focusing on factor endowments, macroeconomic indicators, or government policies. Patterns of international trade have traditionally been explained within the framework of comparative advantage. The best-known variant of this theory begins with the premise that all countries employ equivalent technologies but differ in their endowments of so-called factors of production—land, labour, natural resources, and capital—which are the basic inputs of production. The traditional theory holds that particular countries gain advantage in those industries that make the most intensive use of the productive factors they have in abundance.

Recently, however, there has been a growing realization that traditional comparative advantage theory is no longer sufficient to understand the patterns of trade in modern international competition. Competition is becoming increasingly global in character. More and more firms are adopting a global perspective when making decisions about where to source raw materials, manufacture, and sell their products or services. This has the effect of "decoupling" the firm from the factor endowments of a country. Raw materials, components, machinery, and many services are now available to firms in most countries on increasingly comparable terms. The success of a firm is thus less and less dependent on endowments of basic factors in its home country.

With the trend toward globalization of industry, it is tempting to think that the individual country is no longer important to the international success of its firms, or even that countries have become irrelevant to international competition. Results from the 10-nation study, as well as from our study of Canadian competitiveness, strongly suggest that this view is mistaken. Leading international competitors in a given industry are often located in the same country and often in the same city or region. The positions of countries in international competition tend to be surprisingly stable, stretching over several decades or even longer. This suggests that competitive advantage is created and sustained through a highly localized process, and that the attributes of particular countries do shape patterns of competitive success.

The Diamond of National Advantage

What is needed is a new paradigm that presents a consistent and holistic explanatory framework. This paradigm must explain several empirical facts. First, no one country is competitive in all or most industries; rather, countries are competitive in particular industries and industry segments. Second, each country exhibits distinct patterns of international competitive success and failure. Third, countries tend to succeed in clusters of industries rather than in isolated industries, and the pattern of competitive clusters differs markedly from country to country.

The principal conclusion from the 10-nation study is that sustained international competitive advantage results from ongoing improvement and innovation, not from static advantages. Here, innovation is defined very broadly, to encompass technology and the full spectrum of activities relevant to competing in the marketplace. Creating competitive advantage requires that its sources be relentlessly upgraded and broadened.

Against this backdrop, the critical questions then become: What is it about a country that supports high and rising levels of productivity in individual industries? In what ways does a country provide a dynamic environment for its firms? How do countries differ in the competitive environment created for their industries? The results of the 10-nation study suggest that the answer to these questions lies in four broad attributes of a country that, individually and as a system, constitute the "diamond of national advantage." This can be thought of as the playing field that each country establishes for its industries and companies (see Exhibit 3). The four attributes are:

- *Factor conditions.* The country's position in basic factors of production such as labour, land, natural resources, and infrastructure. Also included are highly specialized and advanced pools of skills, technology, and infrastructure tailored to meet the needs of particular industries.
- *Demand conditions.* The nature of home-market demand for the output of local industries. Particularly important is the presence of sophisticated and demanding local customers who pressure firms to innovate and whose needs anticipate needs elsewhere.
- *Related and supporting industries.* The presence (or absence) in the country of supplier industries and other related industries that are internationally competitive. This determinant includes local suppliers of specialized inputs (e.g., machinery, components, and services) that are integral to innovation in the industry, as well as innovative local companies in industries related by technology, skills, or customers.
- *Firm strategy, structure, and rivalry.* The conditions in the country affecting how companies are created, organized, and managed, as well as the nature of domestic rivalry.

Two additional variables, government and chance, also influence the national competitive environment in important ways. *Government policy* is best understood by examining how it has an impact on each of the four determinants of competitive advantage included in the diamond. The role of government is analyzed by looking at its effects on factor creation and the goals and behaviour of individuals and firms, its role as a buyer of goods and services, and its influence on the competitive environment through competition policies, regulation, and government ownership of enterprises.

EXHIBIT 3   **National Determinants of Competitive Advantage: "The Diamond"**

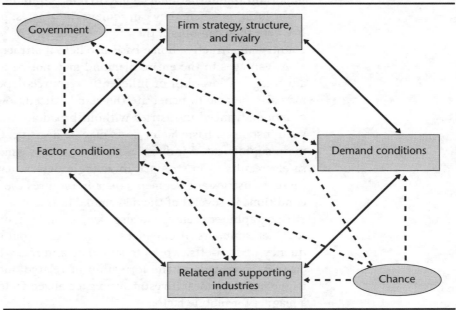

Chance events are developments outside of the control of the country's government and its firms, but which affect the competitive environment. Examples include breakthroughs in basic technologies; external political, economic and legal developments; and international war and conflict. Chance events can create opportunities for a country's firms to acquire or strengthen competitive advantage.

The Diamond as a System

Each of the four determinants of competitiveness influences the capacity of a country's industry to innovate and upgrade. Together they constitute a dynamic system that is more important than its parts.

The ability to benefit from one attribute in the diamond depends on the state of the others. The presence of sophisticated and demanding buyers, for example, will not result in advanced products or production processes unless the quality of human resources enables firms to respond to buyer needs. There must also be a climate that supports sustained investment to fund the development of these products and processes. At the broadest level, weaknesses in any one determinant will constrain an industry's potential for advancement and upgrading.

The four determinants are also mutually reinforcing. For example, the development of specialized supporting industries tends to increase the supply of specialized factors that also benefit an industry. Vigorous domestic rivalry also stimulates the development of unique pools of specialized factors. This is particularly likely if the rivals are all located in one city or region.

The diamond also bears centrally on a country's ability to attract mobile factors of production, a final form of mutual reinforcement. Mobile factors, particularly ideas and highly skilled individuals, are becoming increasingly important to international competitiveness. Mobile factors tend to be drawn to the location where they can achieve the greatest productivity, because that is where they can obtain the highest returns. The same features that make a country an attractive home base also help it attract mobile factors.

Advantages in the entire diamond may not be necessary for competitive advantage in low-skill or inherently resource-dependent industries. Firms may also be able to penetrate the standardized, lower technology segments of more advanced industries without broad advantages in the diamond. In such instances, basic factor costs may be decisive. Competitive advantage in more sophisticated industries and industry segments, on the other hand, rarely results from strength in a single determinant. Sustained success in these industries and segments usually requires the interaction of favourable conditions in several of the determinants and at least parity in the others.

Geographic concentration also elevates and magnifies the interaction of the four determinants. It enhances the pressure from local rivalry and the frequency of spin-offs, works to stimulate and raise the sophistication of local customers, stimulates the formation of related and supporting industries, triggers greater local investment in specialized factor creation, and provides a magnet for mobile factors.

These same forces explain another important finding of the 10-nation study with particular relevance to Canada. There is often a marked disparity between the economic success of regions within countries. The striking difference between the industrial success of northern and southern Italy, northern and southern Germany, and eastern and central Canada are three such examples.

One manifestation of the systemic nature of the determinants is in the phenomenon of clustering. Clusters involve supplier industries, customer industries, and related industries that are all competitive. Such clusters are characteristic of every advanced economy—American entertainment, German chemicals, Japanese electronics, Danish foods. Countries tend to be successful in clusters of linked industries. It is rare that an isolated industry or firm achieves international success.

Clusters grow and transform themselves through spin-offs and diversification of firms into upstream, downstream, and related industries and activities. The fields where several clusters overlap are often fertile grounds for new business formation. In Japan, for example, the interstices among electronics and new materials are spawning new competitive strengths in fields as diverse as robotics and displays.

Vital clusters of industries are often at the heart of a country's economic development, and especially its capacity to innovate. As suggested by the earlier trade analysis, however, the creation of more dynamic industry clusters represents a major challenge facing the Canadian economy.

Applying the Diamond in a Canadian Context

In applying this framework to Canada, four features of the Canadian economy must be addressed: the prominence of natural resource industries in Canada's exports, the role of rivalry in the relatively small Canadian market, the high degree of foreign ownership of Canadian industry, and the effects of Canada's location next to the huge U.S. market.

1. *Natural resources.* Canada's economy, and especially its export economy, is heavily based on natural resources. Some argue that resource industries are inherently less desirable than manufacturing or "high-tech" industries. This logic is flawed. There is nothing inherently undesirable about resource-based industries, provided they support high levels of productivity and productivity growth. Such industries can make a country wealthy if its resource position is highly favourable, as has been the case for Canada during most of its history. If resource-based industries continually upgrade their sophistication through improvements in their processes and products, competitive positions can be sustained and productivity growth assured. In many resource-based economies, however, resource abundance contributes to a set of policies, attitudes, and institutions that reduce incentives to upgrade and make it difficult to move beyond the factor-driven stage of development. This can leave resource-based economies vulnerable to adverse shifts in technology, markets, and international competition.

The key test we must apply in appraising Canada's resource-based industries is their record in upgrading competitive advantage and their capacity for upgrading in the future.

2. *Domestic rivalry*. Domestic rivalry is critical to innovation and to the development of competitive advantage. Yet some commentators contend that Canada's relatively small market precludes the coexistence of strong Canadian-based rivals. Others argue that the proximity of the United States—and thus of U.S.-based competition in the form of imports of American goods—can compensate for limited rivalry at home. Previous research, however, has shown that vigorous domestic rivalry encourages international success not just in large countries, but also in small and mid-sized economies such as Denmark, Sweden, Switzerland, and Taiwan. The number of local firms needed for effective local competition will vary by industry, depending on economies of scale and other factors. In every country studied in the 10-nation research, some firms were found that had achieved a measure of international success without the benefit of local rivalry. Sometimes government policy has limited local competition in virtually all countries (as in telecommunications). Local rivalry may also be less important to competitive advantage in pure commodity businesses in which advantage derives from factor costs rather than innovation. However, the great preponderance of evidence suggests that local rivalry plays a powerful role in competitive advantage. Weak domestic rivalry in many industries in Canada, then, will tend to diminish the odds of achieving sustained international success.

3. *Foreign investment*. There are three main types of foreign investment. Factor-sourcing investment typically seeks access to a country's natural resources, labour, or other basic factors. Foreign firms making such investments have their home bases outside of the host country. Market access foreign investment arises when companies are required—for example, by tariffs or government regulations—to develop a presence in a country in order to gain access to its domestic market. In these cases, too, the home base remains in the country of the parent firm. Most foreign investments in Canada have been motivated by a desire to source Canadian resources or gain access to the Canadian market.

The third, and most beneficial, type of foreign investment is that which establishes or acquires a home base for a particular business or business unit in the host country. In these cases, the management and other core activities are located in the host country, which signals that that country possesses true international competitive advantage in the industry. The home base is where the firm normally contributes the most to the local economy in a particular industry, by establishing the most productive jobs, investing in specialized factor creation, acting as a sophisticated buyer for other local industries, and helping to create a vibrant local competitive milieu.

Canada has witnessed a good deal of debate on the issue of foreign investment and its impact on the country's economy. Much of this debate has been wide of the mark. We believe that in most circumstances, a country is better off with foreign investment than without it. And Canada, in our view, has been a net beneficiary. Foreign companies bring to the host country capital, skills, and technology—all of which boost productivity. Yet the pattern of foreign activities in Canada also signals circumstances that create vulnerabilities for the future. Though there are exceptions, few foreign-controlled firms have made Canada a home base for product lines.

As competition becomes more global and trade and investment barriers fall, the location of firm activities will reflect true economic advantage. The key challenge then is to create the conditions under which foreign—and Canadian—firms will *want* to locate home bases, and perform sophisticated activities, in Canada.

4. *The importance of Canadian diamonds given North American and global competition.* Canada and the United States share a lengthy, easily permeable border as well as many social and cultural attributes. Why, then, should we focus our attention on the Canadian diamond? Wouldn't it make more sense to look at the larger North American diamond, and ask how Canadian firms can take advantage of circumstances in the United States to achieve competitive success? The most basic reason to be concerned about the Canadian diamond is that Canada's standard of living largely depends on the activities that take place in Canada. The location of the most productive economic activities, especially home base activities, is determined by the health of the Canadian diamond in any given industry compared to other locations. And while there are many similarities between Canada and the United States, there are also significant differences—in institutions, trading patterns, tax policies, customer behaviour, economic structure, and labour force composition, among other areas. It is these differences that serve to create distinctive Canadian diamonds in industries. Although the Canada–United States Free Trade Agreement is likely to lessen some of the differences between the two countries, it will also magnify the competitive impact of those that remain.

   Competitive advantage tends to be highly localized within countries. Locations differ in the environment they provide for innovation and upgrading. Proximity to customers, suppliers, rivals, and sources of specialized factors is crucial to the innovation process. The geographic locus of competitive advantage can cross national borders. In the case of Canada, the relevant arena of competitive advantage for a particular industry may encompass adjacent parts of the United States. In addition, it makes sense for Canadian firms to reach into the U.S. diamond to strengthen their competitive position or overcome weaknesses in the Canadian diamond—for example, by selling to and getting feedback from more sophisticated American customers. But

Canadian firms can only take advantage of the U.S. diamond selectively. Basic factors and demand are easiest to access. In contrast, industry-specific infrastructure, a highly skilled workforce, and certain types of supplier and customer relationships are difficult for a country's firms—including Canada's—to source at a distance.

In short, there is no single North American diamond in industries which allows us to ignore Canadian circumstances. Our attention must therefore be directed to the strength of Canadian determinants.

Directions for Change

The Comfortable Insularity of the Old Order

The preceding section presents a picture of an economic system that had served Canada well in many respects but leaves the economy ill-equipped for the future. This old economic order was an internally consistent system in which the determinants were mutually consistent and reinforcing. This makes change exceedingly difficult.

Canada's abundant factor resources have been the bedrock of the economy. In many cases, these resources allowed Canadian firms to be profitable by exporting relatively unprocessed commodities rather than through upgrading. Strategies based on basic factor advantages often limited the demand for advanced technology. This in turn constrained investment in R&D and demand for highly skilled employees, which was reflected in enrolment patterns in universities and in the nature of educational programs. The virtual absence of leading-edge related and supporting industries inhibited another possible source of technology.

These tendencies spilled over into other sectors of the economy where Canada did not have such advantages. Many firms, insulated from external and internal rivalry, were content to exploit the profitable home market. The rate of innovation was slow. What emerged was a tendency to administer existing wealth rather than to invest vigorously to create new wealth.

Canada's wealth also provided little incentive for labour, management, and government to work together to improve national competitiveness. Significant chasms now exist between the three constituencies and within government itself. The relationship between labour and management has often been confrontational. At the same time, management has seldom treated labour as partners. Labour and government have also not worked well together, with labour often taking on an adversarial role with respect to many aspects of economic policy, while governments' relations with their own workforce have also sometimes been strained.

Canadian companies have sought government assistance in export promotion, investment in specialized infrastructure, government procurement, and other forms of support. They rarely have cooperated, however, with governments in areas that have important impacts on international competitiveness, such as R&D, training, and education. The federal and provincial governments have struggled over roles and mandates. This has led to conflicting and overlapping programs that have worked to the detriment of the economy.

These attitudes and behaviours reflect the old competitiveness paradigm. Business acted as if economic rents would go on forever and moved to exploit the sheltered Canadian market. Labour acted as if jobs and high and rising wages could be taken for granted, because business profits were high and secure. Governments held the view that ample resources would continue to exist to fund social needs.

Government's Overall Effect on the Old Economic Order

Government's proper role is to challenge and raise the sights of industry by improving the quality of the inputs that firms draw upon, and creating a competitive context that promotes upgrading. Effective government policies create an environment which stimulates companies to gain competitive advantage, rather than involving government directly in the process.

As we have discussed, government policies in Canada have often not measured up. Those policies that have most hampered competitiveness in the Canadian economy can be grouped into a small number of major themes that are outgrowths of the old economic order.

1. *Insulation from external and internal competition.* Historically, considerable effort has been directed at insulating the Canadian economy from external pressures by protecting firms from international competition and safeguarding national autonomy. Similarly, weak competition policies were a natural outgrowth of the view that companies had to be large to compete with foreign firms.

2. *Forestalling the need for upgrading.* Canadian government policies have often sought to remove the need for upgrading rather than encourage it. Artificially constrained factor input costs—in industries as diverse as transportation, hydroelectric power, and agriculture—lessen pressures for upgrading and reflect a static, cost-based conception of competition. In fact, it could be argued that the current Canadian preoccupation with bringing down exchange rates is a reflection of the same mindset.

3. *Direct intervention instead of business action.* Canadian governments have had a strong tendency to intervene directly in competition rather than stimulate upgrading by industry itself. In many policy areas, particularly in science and technology, and education and training, private sector participation has not been well leveraged. Direct intervention in the form of subsidies and bailouts has also been a prominent feature of the Canadian economic landscape.

4. *Programs to distribute wealth and improve welfare needlessly undermine the economy.* There is a strongly held belief in Canada that all citizens have a right to essential services such as health care and education, a minimum standard of living maintained by social welfare programs, and the opportunity to be employed. Yet the implementation of programs has often proven counterproductive. Canada's commitment to employment has frequently been used to justify protective strategies

that preserve jobs in the short term but simultaneously distort rivalry and delay necessary adjustment. In addition, the effectiveness of the substantial resources devoted to the task of narrowing regional economic disparities has often been undermined by programs which emphasize diversification rather than building on regional strengths.

5. *Conflicting government policies and objectives.* No one level of government in Canada controls a full set of variables in any given policy area, which complicates the process of policy development and implementation. A high level of policy coordination is necessary to make Canada's decentralized system work, but such coordination has been lacking. For example, in labour market programs, the provinces set and enforce employment standards, while the federal government maintains responsibility for training and unemployment compensation. Furthering Canada's science and technology capabilities has also been hampered by a lack of coordination between federal and provincial research bodies. Jurisdictional overlap has often added a layer of complexity and compounded the level of uncertainty that firms face in anticipating changes in the business environment.

Forces of Change

As we have seen in our discussion of the determinants of competitive advantage, the Canadian economy is coming under increasing external pressures. Forces of change are disintegrating the old order. New competitive realities—including globalization of production, finance and markets, accelerating technological change, lower tariffs worldwide, and free trade between Canada and the United States (and perhaps Mexico)—call for a more dynamic and flexible set of responses than those typical of the old Canadian order. Canada's future competitiveness, therefore, must be driven by a new paradigm, based on productivity and innovation.

Major structural adjustment in Canada is inevitable. The question is whether the adjustment is positive or whether it leads to an erosion in the standard of living. Also at issue is how long and painful the restructuring process will be, even if business, labour, and government move in the right direction. How long will it take for Canada to transform itself from the old paradigm to a new one? And how much will it cost?

As external pressures are increasing, Canadian firms are beginning to experience greater internal pressures. This is due partly to a number of government policies that are increasingly oriented toward providing a more challenging competitive domestic environment, and partly as a result of positive initiatives taken by firms themselves.

At the federal level, positive government steps include the recently strengthened competition laws, privatization of crown corporations, and efforts to deregulate industries, including energy and transportation. Government is also beginning to employ policies that encourage, and even pressure, firms to upgrade. Tax reform has reduced past distortions, and generous R&D incentives are in place. Increasing the private sector's commitment to training is at the heart of the federal government's new Labour Force Development Strategy. Reform of unemployment insurance has improved incentives to upgrade skills and return to the workforce, though more must be done. In the area of science and technology, a rising number of government programs are being oriented to priorities driven by the private sector.

In response to the significant external and internal pressures facing the economy, we have also seen signs of positive change in a number of industries studied, including industries in the resource sector. For example, Inco has taken significant steps to upgrade its mineral extraction and smelting technologies and improve labour-management relations. A number of companies in the pulp and paper sector are beginning modernization programs. Other firms have begun to reposition their activities in light of intensified competition by becoming more focused and effective producers.

Systemic Barriers to Change

With increasing external pressures and some positive internal initiatives, one might be tempted to believe that Canada's weaknesses will be corrected naturally. However, the vestiges of the old economic order in Canada have imposed significant barriers to upgrading. These barriers are systemic, not isolated. They reside in policies, institutions, and attitudes that permeate the economy. The challenge is heightened by the fact that the diamond is an interdependent system, in which the weakest link constrains progress.

While some necessary steps are being taken, the current extent of change is inadequate. Our analysis of the determinants of competitive advantage in Canada revealed both tangible and intangible barriers to upgrading. Though each industry has a unique diamond, the strength of which is driven by features specific to that industry, virtually all industries we have examined are affected by at least some of these barriers.

Canada's workforce is not well equipped for upgrading and change. The basic skill levels of many citizens are inadequate, in spite of high per capita spending on education. Shortages exist or are looming in skill- and technology-related occupations. Specialized skill development is lagging due to poor vocational apprenticeship training and weak links between educational institutions and industry. Finally, company investments in training are low compared to other industrialized countries.

Canada's R&D infrastructure is not well aligned with requirements for upgrading. Too much R&D spending takes place through government laboratories. The links between publicly funded research institutes and industry are poorly developed. The supply of highly qualified personnel may be inadequate for future research needs.

The level of sophistication of Canadian home demand also works against upgrading. Weak related and supporting industries, as well as inadequate cluster development, constrain innovation and new business formation in Canada. The lack of Canadian process equipment manufacturers is particularly striking and contributes to the weakness in process technology development and adoption in this country.

Firm strategies and structure and the extent of local rivalry in Canada have done little to enhance domestic productivity. Too many Canadian firms continue to maintain an insular focus, concentrated almost exclusively on the domestic market. Finally, a number of Canada's "safety net" programs continue to diminish personal incentives to upgrade skills.

In many ways, however, the most significant barriers to upgrading are attitudinal. Too often, the old mindsets are still in place in business, labour, and government. Canadians still see competitiveness in terms of the old paradigm, which points to inappropriate responses to the current difficulties.

Threats to Canadian Industries

The forces we have described in general terms can be translated into specific threats in the broad categories of Canadian industries identified earlier. These individual threats differ from group to group, though their underlying causes and implications are similar.

Resource-Based Industries

Given its abundant factor endowments, Canada's heavy emphasis on resources is not surprising. Yet the sustainability of these industries' competitive advantage is in question. Depletion of resources is a threat to both renewable resource industries, such as fisheries, where a number of factors can upset projected equilibrium levels, and nonrenewable resource industries, where new sites are often more remote and therefore more expensive to exploit.

Canada's biggest problem is likely the emergence of lower cost competitors. Basic factor advantages are increasingly replicated by countries such as Venezuela in aluminum or Brazil in pulp and paper. Apart from the resource costs themselves, Canada does not generally have strong cost positions in activities that are driven by labour rates, productivity, or the age and efficiency of capital stock. In these areas, Canada has often failed to make the necessary investments, such as upgrading process technology to increase the efficiencies in production, that would yield a stronger position. Unless Canada upgrades its resource-based industries, it will be trapped in segments where investments tend to be inflexible and where its marginal costs are higher than major competitors'.

Market Access-Based Industries

Many of Canada's market access-based industries, initially spawned to overcome high tariff barriers, are seriously threatened by the increasingly open trading environment. As trade barriers continue to fall, market access no longer requires a major production base in Canada. Many firms are now in the process of reconfiguring their North American and, in some cases, global operations. Some have made decisions to move production out of Canada, taking with them not only jobs but also valuable skills and expertise.

One particularly unattractive aspect of many Canadian industry diamonds is interprovincial barriers to trade: By moving to the United States, firms may encounter virtually no penalty in terms of access to other Canadian provinces, given present trade barriers between provinces. Clearly, if effective barriers remain, firms that choose to stay in Canada are unlikely to invest as much in upgrading their existing domestic facilities than if these barriers were removed.

Innovation-Driven Industries

Canada's innovation-driven industries are tangible proof that Canada can achieve an innovation-driven economy. Yet these industries may also be at risk. Firms that have prospered in spite of weak Canadian clusters may find this weakness increasingly eroding their competitiveness. Firms in such industries may move their home bases outside of Canada to take advantage of more favourable diamonds elsewhere. Even those Canadian industries within strong clusters are at risk because of systemic barriers to upgrading discussed earlier.

Moving to a New Order

We believe Canada is at an economic turning point. Its old economic order is outmoded and in the process of being dismantled. Canadians can respond in one of two ways. One path is to cling to the old order and actively resist the process of change. The other is to continue building on recent economic reforms and seek to further the process of systemic adjustment in the economy. We are convinced that this second path will better ensure Canada's continued prosperity in the fast-changing global economy. Moving to a new economic order will be uncomfortable for many and actively resisted by some. Inevitably, it will involve short-run costs. Yet we are persuaded that these costs are less than might be supposed. It is not that Canadian business and government must spend more, but that they must act and spend differently. More importantly, however, the shift to a new economic order will require a different mindset on the part of government, business, labour, and many individual citizens, one which recognizes and adopts a new paradigm of competitiveness.

The mandate of this study has been to diagnose the state of competitiveness in Canadian industry and highlight key priorities for change. We have not sought to generate detailed policy recommendations. The task of fashioning specific policies and responses must fall to Canadian policymakers and private sector leaders themselves. The final part of this study seeks to provide some guidance by outlining a new economic vision for firms, labour, and governments. We begin, however, by briefly reviewing Canada's major economic strengths.

Strengths to Build On

As it faces a shifting competitive environment, Canada is in the favourable position of having a solid foundation on which to build. In particular, Canada is in many respects better placed to respond to changing global competition than other resource-rich countries such as Australia and New Zealand. Canada has a large export sector that accounts for more than one quarter of GDP and represents a significant share of world trade. It also enjoys preferred access to the world's largest and richest economy, the United States. Canada has a large, diversified natural resource base and ranks among the world's leaders in a range of renewable and nonrenewable resources. It also benefits from having a relatively young and well-educated labour force.

Many Canadian firms have proven that they can compete in global industries. Canada's success in a number of highly contested global industries—including telecommunications, consulting engineering, and nickel—illustrates the intrinsic potential for continued prosperity. Canadian firms have proven that they can compete on the basis of innovation. Northern Telecom, CAE Electronics, Inco, and Canstar are a few examples of firms examined in our research which are at the leading edge of technological sophistication in their industries. They have built and sustained internationally competitive positions through a commitment to R&D and technology adoption. They have created and drawn upon strengths in their home diamonds to achieve international success. Innovation and upgrading are at the core of their business strategies.

There is, in short, a foundation in place in Canada that should allow more firms and industries to achieve sustained advantage in international competition. Canadian industry enjoys a good basic infrastructure, a core of university and other research capability, and an educated human resource base with demonstrated potential. The challenge is to redirect government policies and company strategies to develop and build upon these strengths. Free trade will play a positive role here. With the advent of the Canada–United States Free Trade Agreement, Canadian firms can increasingly benefit from proximity and ready access to the U.S. market. The United States represents not only a significant and growing export market but also a source of products, technology, and ideas. Free trade will hasten the process by which the Canadian economy specializes in those areas where it performs best, thereby boosting productivity. At the same time, Canadian firms will be able to tap selectively into stronger U.S. diamonds to overcome weaknesses in Canada's competitive context in areas such as home demand conditions and related and supporting industries—although, as we have stressed, this is not a panacea.

Elements of an Economic Vision

We believe that a new vision for the Canadian economy is needed, one in which Canada's natural resource abundance is fully exploited, in which firms and governments focus on creating advanced skills and technology, in which sophisticated home demand drives more firms to create advanced products and processes, in which many more Canadian firms compete globally, and in which competition provides a key stimulus for continual upgrading. This does not mean that Canadian firms must compete in different industries than they do today. But it does suggest that they will have to compete in different ways. Firms in Canada need to employ different and more effective strategies, rely on more advanced methods and technologies, and migrate into more sophisticated segments of their industries. In cases where industries cannot be upgraded, resources should flow to more productive uses.

While many specific steps are necessary to raise productivity and improve the dynamism of the economy, we believe that a new economic vision for Canada is best defined in terms of a small number of overarching imperatives:

- *Become an innovation-driven economy.* Innovation—in its broadest sense—is the critical requirement for economic upgrading and increased prosperity. Canadian enterprises in all sectors must move to develop innovation-based advantages. This includes firms in nontraded service industries as well as in the traded sector. Governments must align their policies to support this strategic objective.

- *Increase the sophistication of the natural resource sector.* Resource-based industries have been and will remain a mainstay of Canada's economy. But threats exist to the sustainability of Canada's position in many resource-based industries—threats such as declining real commodity prices, the emergence of low-cost foreign suppliers, and technologically driven changes in end-markets. In the future, Canadian resource producers will be under unprecedented pressure to increase productivity, use more sophisticated technology and specialized skills, and develop more sophisticated and differentiated products.

- *Tackle barriers to upgrading throughout the economy.* Eliminating barriers to upgrading productivity must be a priority for firms and governments. Strategies to develop more advanced and specialized factors must be implemented. Incentives must be shifted, wherever possible, to encourage a greater focus on work, investment, and skill building.

- *Build on Canada's regional strengths.* Many government policies in Canada have put a higher priority on economic diversification than on competitive advantage. A different concept of regional and industrial development is needed, one that focuses on building industry clusters where they already have established or nascent strengths.

- *Move quickly and decisively to achieve complete free trade within Canada.* The fruits of greater specialization will not be fully realized unless Canada becomes a true single market. Competitiveness in a variety of industries has been hindered by the existence of internal nontariff barriers to trade, investment, and labour mobility. These have worked against the development of sufficient scale in some industries and dulled the rivalry necessary to achieve competitive advantage. It is encouraging that the federal government's recent proposals for constitutional reform promise to move toward internal free trade and a strengthening of the Canadian economic union.

- *Transform foreign subsidiaries into home bases.* Given its high levels of foreign investment and large number of branch plants (especially in manufacturing industries), transforming foreign subsidiaries into home bases is one of the most critical challenges facing Canada in the 1990s. Branch plants whose sole raison d'être has been to serve the Canadian market will relocate if their productivity does not match or exceed operations elsewhere. Multinationals will make choices about where to make investments in new skills, technologies, and product lines according to whether or not the Canadian environment is conducive to innovation and productivity growth.

- *Create and maintain a supportive and stable macroeconomic climate.* Finally, sound macroeconomic policies are central to any vision of a competitive, dynamic Canadian economy. Fiscal, monetary, tax, and regulatory policies should all be geared to attaining low inflation, balanced and manageable public finances, and a stable overall economic climate. This will result in a lower cost of capital, encourage investment, and neutralize the tendency for companies to be distracted by exchange rates and interest rates instead of concentrating on the true underpinnings of long-term competitiveness.

Implications for Canadian Firms

Business, labour, governments, and other public sector institutions must all play a role in responding to these imperatives. A particularly heavy responsibility, however, falls on companies and their managers. Firms, not governments, are on the front lines of international competition. Forced to compete in a more global, open, and fast-changing environment, Canadian firms must focus on setting strategies that will allow them to create and sustain competitive advantage. They should move now to reexamine their strategies, not wait for government or outside forces to intervene. While each Canadian industry will present different challenges, many firms will need to take steps in several important areas.

Assess the Canadian Diamond

Canadian firms must begin by understanding their competitive position by product area as well as how their Canadian home bases create competitive advantages and disadvantages. In analyzing their competitive position, the most formidable international competitors in an industry should be the key reference points. Internationally successful firms, as well as the national diamonds in which they are based, provide the benchmarks against which Canadian conditions must be assessed. Canadian companies should be addressing the following questions:

- *The boundaries of the home diamond.* What are the geographic boundaries of the "home" diamond? Does it appear to cross the border with the United States and, if so, what are the key differences for firms operating on either side?
- *Sustainability of basic factor advantages.* How sustainable are Canadian advantages in raw materials, electricity, or other natural endowments? To what extent does the firm rely on explicit or implicit subsidies rather than real factor advantages? How are evolving international trade rules and foreign circumstances likely to alter existing advantages?
- *Quality of human resources.* How does Canada compare in terms of specialized skills relevant to the firm's industry? Are Canadian workers as well trained and well motivated as their foreign counterparts?
- *Technology access.* Where does Canada stand in specialized technologies related to the industry? Are there research institutes or programs in Canada that will assist Canadian firms to innovate?

- *Infrastructure access.* How supportive is Canada's basic and specialized infrastructure in terms of the requirements for competitive advantage in the firm's industry? How does Canada compare with other countries?
- *Canadian demand for sophistication.* Is Canadian demand for the firm's products/services sophisticated? Does it anticipate international needs?
- *Supplier access.* Compared to foreign rivals, does the Canadian firm have better or inferior access to local suppliers in important technologies?
- *Related industries.* What are the related industries that will most influence industry competition? What strengths does Canada have in these industries?
- *Competitor diamonds.* Who are the most significant foreign competitors in the industry? What is the state of their diamonds?
- *Potential entrants.* Who are the emerging potential entrants? What is their cost position? How dependent are they on low-cost natural resources, inexpensive labour, or government support?
- *Capacity for differentiation.* What are the sources of differentiation relative to rival firms? Are there products or segments in which the Canadian firm is more innovative?

Move Toward Innovation-Driven Advantages

Many Canadian firms have long pursued static, cost-based strategies in which they produce "me-too" products and depend on factor costs or pure scale to provide advantages. A large number of such firms are now under pressure from foreign rivals with more efficient processes or cheaper basic factors. To respond to these challenges, firms need to compete in more sophisticated ways. A broader, more dynamic view of cost makes sense for many firms. More investments must be channeled into efficient and innovative processes to increase productivity. Firms facing low-cost foreign competitors may need to reorient their strategies from producing unprocessed and semiprocessed products (where competition is necessarily based on cost) to more highly processed and differentiated products in related segments.

Focus on Areas of True Competitive Advantage

After looking at these issues and questions, many Canadian firms will conclude that they should adopt more focused strategies. In a world of soft economic competition and tariff protection, the proliferation of product lines and businesses may have made sense. The new imperative is to focus on those product lines, market segments, and businesses where Canadian firms can achieve sustainable advantage. Often, this will call for a rationalization of product lines and a concentration on lines that draw on unique competitive strengths. A number of firms in Canada have begun this process. GE Canada, for instance, has narrowed its Canadian product line and increased production of selected products to supply other GE operations worldwide. Similarly, Culinar, a Quebec-based consumer snack food producer, has moved to reduce the breadth of its core product line, divest weaker peripheral businesses, and focus on areas of advantage.

In addition to rationalizing product lines, many businesses will need to reevaluate their degree of vertical integration and exit from products where vertical integration does not provide advantage vis-à-vis rivals. For some companies, a reevaluation of growth-through-diversification strategies will also be required. In a world of more open trade and tougher competition, a greater focus on core businesses will make sense for most firms.

Upgrade the Canadian Diamond

Upgrading the Canadian diamond takes on special importance as firms move toward more sophisticated business strategies. Canadian firms need to act in several areas:

- *Increase investment in specialized human resource development*. Like any asset, employees at all levels require investment to keep them up-to-date. In an environment characterized by more open competition, Canadian firms will have to rely more on advanced skills and improved labour force productivity and less on traditional basic factor advantages.

- *Forge closer ties with educational institutions*. Canadian firms must take a more pro-active approach if they want educational institutions to produce employees with both the general and specialized skills required for competitiveness. Canadian business, like its counterparts in Germany and several other countries, should be providing more direct input into course development at universities, colleges, and technical institutes. Business in Canada should be looking at ways to enhance the status of community colleges to ensure they are not viewed as "second-best" alternatives. Firms should also actively promote and participate in more cooperative educational programs where students work part-time or alternate periods of work and schooling. More businesses are becoming involved with co-op programs. For example, Inco entered into a partnership with Cambrian College in Sudbury to develop an innovative 48-week course that combines academic studies with training at Inco.

- *Improve technology development and adoption*. Firms should also be playing a more active role in ensuring that work conducted at university research institutes or centres and government laboratories is commercially relevant. Many successful firms contract out a great deal of their basic research and perform applied and developmental research in-house. Unfortunately, Canada has few specialized "centres of excellence" within its universities or community colleges where leading-edge research takes place, where the world's best professors come to teach, and where students are attracted from around the world. Firms should consider jointly funding and influencing the research conducted in such centres through trade associations, with related industries, and with government.

- *Transform trade associations into factor-creating mechanisms*. For the small- and mid-sized enterprises that dominate in many sectors of the Canadian economy, the need to upgrade in the areas of human resources and technology development and adoption may appear to pose daunting challenges. Cooperative ventures can be a fruitful path to upgrading factor capabilities for such companies. For example, firms can expand technical assistance and provide more funds to trade associations to develop training programs relevant to their industry. They can support the development of training consortia in which labour and government may participate as partners to industry—as has recently taken place in the electrical/electronics industry. Trade associations can also be a critical liaison between industry and educational institutes in helping to ensure the relevance of curricula discussed above. Finally, in the area of technology development and adoption, trade associations can also represent a valuable clearing house for dissemination of precompetitive research into common areas of concern such as the environment.

- *Nurture Canadian supplier industries.* The absence of dynamic clusters of competitive industries in Canada has been detrimental to innovation. Many firms have sourced abroad, while others have backward-integrated to compensate for the lack of indigenous supporting industries. Canadian companies should be taking steps to strengthen domestic supplier industries. Encouraging domestic suppliers, through local sourcing and the transferring of technology and skills, has become integral to the strategies of prominent Canadian companies such as IBM Canada and Nova Corporation.

- *Strive to develop and serve demanding Canadian buyers.* Firms should strive to serve the most sophisticated and demanding buyers in their home market. Selling to demanding local buyers will strengthen their ability to compete in global markets.

- *Establish links with Canadian-based firms in related industries.* Related industries are those linked to an industry by common technologies, distribution channels, skills, or customers. Canadian firms should strive to develop links with Canadian-based firms in related industries in order to increase technical interchange and information flows in a variety of areas.

- *Develop labour-management relations centered on productivity.* To improve productivity, many Canadian firms will have to adopt less authoritarian approaches to workforce management and a broader view of employees' potential to contribute to firm goals. Labour should be treated as a partner, not an adversary. Employees should be rewarded for productivity growth but should also expect to share the pain in periods of economic adversity.

- *Rely more on performance-related compensation.* In structuring compensation schemes, Canadian companies should move toward making both individual and company performance a significant part of remuneration at all levels.

Adopt More Global Strategies

More than 70 percent of Canadian manufacturers do not serve any export markets, and the majority of those that do export sell solely to the United States. Canada's reliance on the United States as an export market has grown over the past decade, at a time when globalization of many industries has increased. Given a more open global trade and business environment, firms in Canada need to develop global strategies if they are to compete successfully against foreign rivals in many industries. Competing globally means competing beyond North America. First and foremost, it means penetrating foreign markets both through trade and, ultimately, foreign investment. To succeed in international markets, Canadian firms must move more aggressively to satisfy the needs of foreign buyers and establish foreign sales and service channels. They must have the patience to make the investments necessary to build foreign market positions. Northern Telecom's recent acquisition of STC, a U.K.-based supplier of switches and transmission equipment, should enhance Northern's ability to sell into the post-1992 European market.

Competing globally can bring many advantages aside from increased sales. No country has a unique advantage in all the determinants of competitive advantage. Firms can selectively tap into sources of advantage in foreign diamonds, both to compensate for deficiencies at home and to exploit unique characteristics abroad. Canadian firms will benefit by serving the most sophisticated and demanding buyers in foreign countries. Given the ease of access to the U.S. market and the cultural similarities between the two countries, Canadian companies have an unusual ability to benefit from American buyers. The essential foundations for innovation must be present in the home base, however.

Define a North American or Global Mandate

Many foreign-owned or -controlled subsidiaries in Canada are today faced with urgent questions about their future role. Foreign subsidiaries in the manufacturing sector tend to be the firms with the broadest product lines, which overlap with those of subsidiaries in other countries. They also face the need to conform to their parents' global strategy. The potential consequences of a weak Canadian diamond are particularly acute for these firms given the ease and speed with which Canadian operations can be downsized and operations in other countries reconfigured to compensate.

Canadian subsidiaries must try to define a new role that is consistent with the evolving nature of the global strategies being pursued by many of the world's most advanced multinationals. This role is to have the Canadian operation become a North American or global headquarters for a particular product line or business segment in order to exploit particular advantages and strengths in the Canadian diamond. A number of foreign firms operating in Canada have moved in this direction. IBM Canada, for example, has the worldwide mandate for hardware power supplies. Hewlett-Packard Canada's Edmonton-based Idacom division manufactures computer-based protocol analyzers for the worldwide market, while its Calgary operation has the world mandate for supervisory control and data acquisition software. Campbell Soup is reconfiguring its Canadian operations to fit a North American manufacturing strategy. Canada is taking responsibility for a series of small-batch, specialty product lines that are especially well suited to the small yet flexible Canadian plants. The British firm ICI, after taking full control of its Canadian subsidiary ICI Canada, located the world headquarters for its industrial explosives business in Canada.

Redefine the Relationship with Government

Canadian firms must reevaluate their expectations of government and place different demands on government than in the past. First, they should insist that government activity not substitute for business initiative. Second, they should no longer look to government to provide traditional forms of assistance—subsidies, artificial cost structures, lax regulations, guaranteed procurement. Third, Canadian firms should pressure government to contribute to competitiveness through the provision of high-quality infrastructure, advanced factor creation, and appropriate incentives. Government-assisted R&D centres and training programs, for example, can be significant assets for firms. More generally, Canadian firms should promote government policies that promise to improve the home diamond in the industry or industries in which they compete.

Implications for Labour

With some 37 percent of the labour force unionized, organized labour in Canada plays a significant role in the country's economy as well as in a host of individual industries (especially in the resource and manufacturing sectors). Unions also exercise influence by adopting strategies and objectives that affect workplace relations in the broader private sector. The attitudes, policies, and approaches of organized labour can either help or hinder competitiveness. Far-sighted union leaders understand that efforts to increase productivity, upgrade skills, and facilitate shifts into more sophisticated jobs are the best guarantee of good wages in the long term.

In the old Canadian economic order, breakdowns in labour-management relations generally carried little cost. Large resource rents were there to be divided. Market protection and weak rivalry allowed cost increases to be passed on. Companies could prosper without paying much attention to their workforce. Finding themselves in a comfortable competitive environment, many companies accepted wage demands unconnected to productivity performance and tolerated work practices that impeded innovation. These behaviours and attitudes no longer fit the new competitive realities facing Canadian industry. New approaches to labour-management relations are needed. For organized labour, several implications follow from this:

- *Focus on productivity*. Canadian unions have sometimes been hostile to the imperative of productivity improvement, seeing it as a threat to jobs or a veiled attempt to reduce wages and benefits. To varying degrees, they have resisted developments geared to achieving higher productivity—such as workforce reorganization, multiskilling, and compensation systems more closely tied to performance. Today, more than ever before, the future viability of many Canadian industries and firms depends on their success in upgrading productivity. Unions can make an important contribution by assisting firms to identify and remove obstacles to productivity improvement by pressing for job enhancement and flexibility and by supporting advancement based on training and merit.

- *Skills upgrading.* Broadening and increasing workers' skills should be a central objective of labour. In recent years, there have been encouraging signs that unions have come to accept the inevitability of technological change and the necessary skills upgrading that accompanies it. Most of the onus for developing a "training culture" within Canadian business, however, must fall on managers, not workers or their unions.

- *More cooperative labour-management relations.* Shifts in production technologies and increasing competition call for a deeper reevaluation of the traditional labour-management framework. A more collaborative approach is essential. For their part, unions should embrace opportunities to participate in firm planning and encourage more information exchange. If Canadian industry is to compete successfully in the future, labour must move beyond its traditional and deeply rooted inclination to see management as the "opposing team."

Implications for Governments

Both the 10-nation study and our Canadian research have demonstrated that government can improve or detract from national competitive advantage. The question is not whether government should have a role, but what that role should be. Government's role in shaping competitiveness is inherently partial. Government policies in a particular area will generally fail unless they work in tandem with other determinants of competitive advantage. Government policy should be directed to building the skills, research infrastructure, and other inputs on which all firms draw. Through regulations, tax legislation, competition policies, and policies in other areas, government should seek to fashion an environment that supports upgrading and productivity growth. In this section, we summarize the broad implications of our findings for Canadian policymakers. We begin by outlining several general principles for sound policy and then focus on a number of specific areas in which changes are needed.

Some General Principles

Canadian governments should be guided by a limited number of principles as they seek to develop policies to assist Canadian industries and companies achieve international competitive success:

1. *Encourage adjustment and upgrading.* Competitive success grows out of dynamism, not static advantages such as cheap labour or subsidized input costs. Too often, government policy reflects a static mindset. In the next several years, many industries in Canada will be forced to restructure and refocus—rationalizing product lines, exiting from peripheral businesses, shifting away from some industries

and segments and toward others. Government should facilitate these adjustments, not stand in the way. This will involve a government commitment to retraining, building infrastructure appropriate to changed circumstances, and providing an overall environment conducive to restructuring.

2. *Minimize direct interventions.* Direct interventions in the economy often have unfortunate consequences. Ineffective use of expenditures results in wasted resources. In addition, direct intervention frequently leads to an unhealthy dependence on government by industry. Federal and provincial governments should be using indirect means rather than direct interventions to promote competitiveness. Indirect policies encompass programs designed to improve infrastructure and human resources, as well as economic policies that encourage investment and upgrading.

3. *Rely on incentives instead of grants.* Subsidies and grants to specific firms rarely translate into durable competitive advantage. There is little evidence that governments can successfully "pick winners" by targeting support to particular enterprises. Broader incentives that encourage individuals and firms to upgrade skills, or that create advanced factor pools and improved infrastructure, are more effective policy tools.

4. *Reengineer social policies.* In the long run, competitiveness and social goals tend to be mutually reinforcing. More productive industries lead to a stronger national economy, which in turn is better able to meet diverse social policy objectives. At the same time, an effective social infrastructure helps to underpin economic success. The design of social programs can have profound and often unanticipated consequences for the economy. In New Zealand, for example, a noncontributory pension scheme reduced national savings, while the structure of social assistance payments encouraged young people to drop out of school and militated against skill upgrading. Aggregate social spending in Canada is not out of line compared to most other industrialized countries. However, to create an attractive environment for competitive advantage, it is crucial that social goals be pursued in a way that does not sacrifice incentives, upgrading, and productivity growth. Consideration must be given to redesigning social programs that do not meet this test.

5. *Improve intergovernmental policy coordination.* Government imposes an increasingly heavy burden on Canada's economy. This burden is magnified by inadequate coordination of federal and provincial government policies in areas such as economic management, tax policy, training, education, the environment, and procurement. Canadians today are paying a high price to maintain elaborate bureaucracies at both the federal and provincial levels, yet are not receiving the benefits of either strong central control or effective decentralized decision making. The ultimate structure of a potentially reformed Canadian confederation is now under active discussion. This subject lies outside the scope of our study. However, we are convinced that improving Canada's

international competitiveness will necessitate a substantially greater degree of collaboration and coordination between Ottawa and the provinces than has been typical in the past.

6. *Maintain an open policy toward foreign investment.* We strongly believe that efforts to restrict foreign investment in Canada, or to legislate foreign company behaviour, should be avoided. Except in rare cases, foreign investment contributes to the economy through new products, processes, assets, and skills that boost productivity. A substantial body of Canadian research supports this view. Foreign-owned companies are often more efficient and more technologically advanced than domestic firms; many invest as much, if not more, in R&D as their Canadian counterparts. However, while Canada is better off with foreign investment than without it, the existing pattern of foreign activity in the economy reflects weaknesses that are cause for concern. Because of deficiencies in Canadian industry diamonds, foreign operations in Canada are too often limited to sourcing raw materials or performing the minimum activities needed to gain access to the local market. An important objective of government economic policy must be to improve the Canadian economic environment so that foreign companies will, over time, change and broaden the nature of their Canadian activities.

7. *Promote a sound and stable macroeconomic environment to complement other initiatives.* While a stable macroeconomic environment assists in achieving international competitiveness, it does not create or ensure it. Devaluing Canada's currency also does not provide a long-term solution to the country's underlying competitiveness problems. There is, however, little doubt about the types of macroeconomic goals that governments should be setting in order to support competitiveness: low inflation, which works to lower the real cost of capital; a high rate of national saving; and balanced public sector finances. The size of government deficits, and the rapid growth of government debt which has resulted from many years of large deficits, is perhaps the most critical macroeconomic problem facing Canada today. Chronic public sector deficits contribute to higher inflation, interest rates, and taxes. Determined action to reduce government deficits is imperative if Canada is to compete successfully through the 1990s and beyond.

Priorities in Specific Policy Areas: Factor Conditions

The number of government policies that affect the competitiveness of a country's industries and firms is almost limitless. Based on our Canadian research, we have identified some specific priorities for improvement in each part of the Canadian diamond. Because Canadian competitiveness has been mainly rooted in factor advantages, government policies bearing on factor conditions are particularly important.

Investment in Education and Specialized Skills.   Upgrading human resources will be critical to Canadian firms' ability to become more competitive. Canada has a relatively well-educated workforce, but its education and training systems have failed to respond adequately to the challenges posed by the contemporary global economy. Ensuring that the education system does a better job imparting basic skills is one priority. Improving and expanding private sector training is another. Governments should be considering new initiatives in several areas:

- *Provide more training for the unemployed.* Recent moves by the federal government to direct a larger share of labour market program funding to training the unemployed are a promising beginning, but more must be done to shift from passive income support to "active" labour market programs that encourage adjustment and skill upgrading.

- *Promote private sector training.* Canadian firms, in general, spend significantly less on workforce training than their counterparts in other industrialized countries. Governments should consider providing incentives to stimulate more training. One option might be to give UI premium rebates to firms that undertake training (possibly targeted at small and mid-sized firms). Another option would be to develop tax exemptions or credits to encourage training.

- *Set high national educational standards.* Canada's relatively generous spending on education has not translated into superior performance. Canada is virtually alone among advanced countries in having no national education standards of any kind. In other countries, such standards are an important ingredient in fostering high achievement. National standards are not inconsistent with a decentralized education system. In Germany, for instance, national standards coexist with an education system administered by the states, not the central government. A national standard need not require a full-fledged national system for testing, provided an appropriate level of intergovernmental cooperation exists. Provincial governments should move quickly to collaborate in developing agreed standards and testing mechanisms.

- *Put more emphasis on practical curricula and science skills.* Compared to other countries examined in our research, Canada has relatively few scientists, engineers, and technical workers in its labour force. Evidence points to declining interest in the sciences among elementary and high school students, declining enrollment in trade and vocational programs at the postsecondary level, and flat or falling enrollment in college-based technology-oriented programs. School curricula should be redesigned to put more emphasis on science, mathematics, and technology disciplines.

- *Expand apprenticeship programs and update curricula.* Many apprenticeship programs in Canada suffer from limited access, lack of standardized certification criteria, and high drop-out rates. Cooperative efforts on the part of governments, industry, and labour to update apprenticeship programs and extend such training into more occupations are urgently needed if Canada is to expand its pool of highly skilled workers.

- *Work more closely with trade associations.* As discussed above, trade associations represent a potentially high leverage mechanism for upgrading Canadian factors, particularly in the areas of education and training. Governments at all levels should seek to work more closely with these associations to strengthen factor conditions.

- *Promote cooperative education.* Cooperative education programs have proven to be an excellent vehicle for linking education to the workplace and for facilitating the transition from school to the labour force. Participation in these programs should be broadened.

- *Align university funding to support competitiveness.* As currently structured, government funding mechanisms for universities may not adequately underwrite the cost differentials that exist between science- and technology-related courses and other fields of study. Governments should reevaluate existing funding mechanisms and take steps to ensure that adequate resources are available for programs directly linked to competitiveness. Provincial governments should also reexamine the appropriate role of tuition in the overall university funding mix and the potential for school autonomy in setting tuition fees. The privatisation of some programs or even institutions should be seriously considered.

More Focused Technology Development and Faster Adoption. Technology development and adoption are areas where Canada suffers from significant weaknesses. The problem lies more with the private sector than with government, however. Stimulating more research and development and faster adoption of technology in the private sector must be a priority objective of government. Among the specific steps we recommended are the following:

- *Improve coordination of government R&D programs.* Our research revealed a number of areas where excessive fragmentation of government expenditures has limited the effectiveness of science and technology programs. Duplication of research between universities and government labs is also of concern given the overall scarcity of government resources. Expenditures and research efforts in federal and provincial government research organizations must be better coordinated and tied more closely to university research activities.

- *Forge stronger links among government laboratories, provincial organizations, universities, and the private sector.* Government policy on science and technology has attached a high priority to advancing science and to training qualified personnel. While these goals are important, in the future, government policy in this area should put a greater emphasis on fostering more intimate linkages with industry.

- *Increase the proportion of government-funded R&D performed in the private sector.* While government R&D spending has increasingly emphasized private sector and university performance, federal laboratories still accounted for 55 percent of government expenditures of $2.7 billion in 1990, while provincial laboratories accounted for 41 percent of provincial government expenditures of $664 million. Given the funding issues which currently exist within the university system in terms of science and technology infrastructure, as well as the issues of ensuring commercial relevance and technology diffusion associated with government labs, we believe governments at the federal and provincial levels should continue to reduce the proportion of their funds spent internally, in addition to increasing the linkages with industry with respect to the activities that remain.

- *Encourage greater specialization among universities.* Current government policies and funding mechanisms often discourage specialization among Canadian universities. To create the specialized skills and other advanced factors necessary to achieve competitive advantage, more specialization in university programs and research activities should be encouraged.

- *Expand information available on intellectual property.* Intellectual property laws, and the information infrastructure that supports them, play an important role in fostering technology diffusion. The federal government should move rapidly to complete the automation of the patent search process.

Increase the Pace of Regulatory Reform in Infrastructure Sectors.   Regulatory reform in Canada has generally lagged the pace set in the United States. This has resulted in higher service costs to Canadian producers of many goods and services. Canada should continue to move ahead with regulatory reforms in key infrastructure areas such as transportation and communications. In addition, the federal and provincial governments should renew efforts to achieve a greater degree of harmonization of policies that restrict interprovincial competition and rationalization in areas such as trucking.

Strengthen Resource Conservation and Renewal Policies.   Effective natural resource conservation is vital to sustaining the competitiveness of resource-based industries. Canada's record to date has been mixed, although improvements are evident in areas such as forest replantation. With close to half of Canada's goods sector exports dependent on natural resources, governments must ensure that their resource policies promote long-term conservation, not short-term exploitation.

Priorities in Specific Policy Areas: Demand Conditions

Governments have a significant impact on a country's home demand conditions. Their leverage over demand is greatest in the areas of government procurement, regulation of product safety and standards, and environmental standards. The aim of government policy should be to encourage home demand that is early and sophisticated and that anticipates international needs and trends.

Restructure Government Procurement.   The effectiveness of government procurement policy in spurring innovation and competitive advantage in Canada has been undermined by several factors: blurred policy objectives, provincial government restrictions on out-of-province bidding, and a common preference for off-the-shelf products. Only infrequently have governments acted as a sophisticated buyer and sought to pressure Canadian companies to upgrade or created an early market for new products. While some progress in reforming procurement practices has been made in recent years, further efforts are required:

- *Encourage more open competition for government contracts.* Discriminatory purchasing practices, especially at the provincial level, have resulted in significant economic costs. All governments should strive to ensure that competition is open to out-of-province and out-of-country bidders.

- *Use challenging performance specifications.* Use of "make to blueprint" design specifications still appears to be widespread in government procurement in Canada. Wherever possible, governments should move toward performance-based specifications in order to encourage suppliers to develop and proliferate innovative products and processes.

Adopt Stringent and Forward-Looking Regulatory Standards.   Strict, anticipatory regulatory standards can be a potent force for spurring upgrading in industry, provided they are designed and administered effectively. Strict product quality and safety standards pressure firms to improve products in ways that are eventually demanded by international markets. High regulatory standards in areas such as construction, telecommunications, and transportation can stimulate early and sophisticated home demand. Tough standards for energy efficiency and environmental impact trigger innovations in products and processes that are highly valued elsewhere. In all of these areas, governments in Canada should be continuing to move toward more stringent standards and regulations.

Priorities in Specific Policy Areas: Related and Supporting Industries

Our research has found that the presence of home-based related and supporting industries is often critical in stimulating and facilitating innovation and productivity growth. The lack of depth and breadth in most Canadian industry clusters represents a significant weakness as the country and its industries seek to respond to a new competitive environment. Canadian government policy in areas such as regional and industrial development has frequently worked against the objective of building strong, geographically concentrated clusters. Government policies should be tailored to meet the following guidelines:

- *Ensure that programs and policies in all areas are consistent with the development of stronger industry clusters.* Governments should critically examine the full range of policies to determine whether these policies support the growth of clusters.

- *Employ policies that build on existing regional strengths.* The presence of an industry or cluster in a region is generally a sign that some competitive advantage already exists. Government policies should be geared to enhancing clusters rather than—as has so often been the case in Canada—subsidizing existing, inefficient industries and activities or trying to create industries unrelated to local economic strengths.

- *Focus on promoting the development of specialized factors.* The most effective way for governments to reinforce cluster development is to focus on investments that assist in creating specialized factors such as technical institutes, training centres, and other infrastructure related to the needs of specific industries. Importantly, many of the policies and programs that most effectively promote specialized factors are provincial or local in origin.

Priorities in Specific Policy Areas: Firm Strategy, Structure, and Rivalry

Governments can strengthen the competitiveness of their industries by fostering a stable economic environment and creating incentives for investment, skill upgrading, and risk-taking, and by ensuring that a healthy degree of competition prevails in the home market.

Create Stronger Individual and Corporate Incentives for Investment and Upgrading.   Through tax policies and its actions in other policy areas, government helps to structure the incentives for individuals to work, save, and invest in skill building. Government policies also influence the goals and strategies of firms. To strengthen this important determinant of competitive advantage, governments in Canada should be looking at initiatives such as the following:

- *Reengineer "safety net" programs to ensure they are well targeted to those in need and provide appropriate incentives.* Some existing social programs should be restructured so that clear incentives always exist for individuals to work and improve skills. In particular, consideration should be given to reforming social assistance programs to allow recipients to keep a greater portion of earnings from employment, thereby encouraging them to participate in the labour force and upgrade their skills.

- *Encourage stronger linkages between performance and compensation.* Canada currently trails a number of competitor countries in linking compensation to productivity or firm performance at both the managerial and worker levels. Governments can assist in promoting compensation linked to performance through its policies toward its own workforce and also by encouraging appropriate behaviour in the private sector. Providing further incentives for employees to invest in their companies would be one way to strengthen linkages between pay and performance in the private sector.

- *Provide more favourable tax treatment for long-term equity investment.* To increase its international competitiveness, Canada must invest heavily in training, technology, machinery, and equipment. Yet the payoff from such investments is often realized only over the long term. There is concern in Canada (and the United States) that investors— individual, corporate, and institutional—are often guided by a shorter-term outlook. Current tax policy may contribute to a short-term view. While the tax treatment of capital gains in Canada is somewhat more favourable than that in the United States, this is largely offset by higher marginal tax rates. In addition, a number of other countries have introduced measures specifically designed to encourage long-term investment. We believe that Canada should also be exploring ways to restructure capital gains taxation in order to increase incentives for long-term investment in productive assets.

Extend Efforts to Increase Rivalry.   Canada has made significant strides in recent years toward instituting policies that enhance domestic rivalry. Freer trade, deregulation, and the modernization of competition laws are all important steps that have moved the country in the right direction. Now the federal and provincial governments must make an extraordinary effort to eliminate interprovincial barriers as expeditiously as possible. The federal government's recent constitutional initiative should provide a useful impetus to achieve progress in this field.

Move Aggressively to Restore a Favourable Macroeconomic Environment. All levels of government must share in the burden of bringing deficits and debt under much better control, by reevaluating spending programs and increasing the effectiveness of dollars spent. The underlying philosophy of the federal government's recent proposals, contained in its report *Canadian Federalism and Economic Union*, which calls for increased fiscal coordination among the federal and provincial governments, is a sound one and the proposals deserve serious consideration. Finally, despite recent proposals by some, devaluing Canada's currency is not a long-term solution to Canada's competitiveness problems, even if it might temporarily improve the competitive position of some Canadian industries.

Implications for Canadian Citizens

Perhaps the most important factor in Canada's ability to move forward is the attitudes and the mindset of individual Canadians. Unless individual citizens can accept and internalize the new reality, positive programs will be undermined. Canadians must better understand the foundations of their past prosperity and the fact that the comfortable old order is disintegrating. They must also recognize that the sources of Canadian competitiveness are at risk. Most importantly, Canadians must understand that they cannot return to the old order. Instead of looking longingly at the past, Canadians must adopt the new paradigm for what will determine future Canadian competitiveness. They must respond to this new paradigm in their roles as employees, as managers, as voters, and as members of their communities.

Sustainable Competitive Advantage—What It Is, What It Isn't

KEVIN P. COYNE

I shall not today attempt to define the kinds of material to be embraced within that shorthand description; and perhaps I could never succeed in intelligibly doing so. But I know it when I see it.

Supreme Court Justice Potter Stewart
(Jacobellis v. State of Ohio)

Although it was pornography, not sustainable competitive advantage, that the late Justice Stewart doubted his ability to define, his remark neatly characterizes the current state of thinking about the latter subject as well. Explicitly or implicitly, sustainable competitive advantage (SCA) has long occupied a central place in strategic thinking. Witness the widely accepted definition of competitive strategy as "an integrated set of actions that produce a sustainable advantage over competitors."[1] But exactly what constitutes sustainable competitive advantage is a question rarely asked. Most corporate strategists are content to apply Justice Stewart's test; they know an SCA when they see it—or so they assume.

But perhaps an SCA is not always so easy to identify. In developing its liquid hand soap, Minnetonka, Inc., focused its efforts on building an advantage that was easily copied later. In the wristwatch market, Texas Instruments attempted to exploit an advantage over its competitors that turned out to be unimportant to target consumers. RCA built barriers to competition in the vacuum tube market in the 1950s only to find these barriers irrelevant when transistors and semiconductors were born. CB radio producers built capacity to fill a demand that later evaporated. In each case, the companies failed to

---

Source: Reprinted with permission from *Business Horizons* (January–February 1986). © 1986, by the Foundation for the School of Business at Indiana University.

[1] *Competitive strategy,* as the term is used in this article, is exclusively concerned with defeating competitors and achieving dominance in a product/market segment. It is thus—in concept, and usually in practice—a subset of business strategy, which addresses the broader goal of maximizing the wealth of shareholders.

see in advance that, for one reason or another, they lacked a sustainable competitive advantage.

Perhaps it is because the meaning of "sustainable competitive advantage" is superficially self-evident that virtually no effort has been made to define it explicitly. After all, it can be argued that the dictionary's definitions of the three words bring forth the heart of the concept. But every strategist needs to discover whether an SCA is actually or potentially present, and if so, what its implications are for competitive and business strategy.

Therefore, this article will describe a number of established strategic concepts and build on them to develop a clear and explicit concept of SCA.

Specifically, we will examine:

- *The conditions for SCA*. When does a producer have a competitive advantage? How can the strategist test whether such an advantage is sustainable?
- *Some implications of SCA for strategy*. Does having SCA guarantee success? Can a producer succeed without an SCA? Should a producer always pursue an SCA?

Conditions for SCA

Any producer who sells his goods or services at a profit undeniably enjoys a competitive advantage with those customers who choose to buy from him instead of his competitors, though these competitors may be superior in size, strength, product quality, or distribution power. Some advantages, however, are obviously worth more than others. A competitive advantage is meaningful in strategy only when three distinct conditions are met:

1. Customers perceive a consistent difference in important attributes between the producer's product or service and those of his competitors.
2. That difference is the direct consequence of a capability gap between the producer and his competitors.
3. Both the difference in important attributes and the capability gap can be expected to endure over time.

In earlier strategy work, these conditions have been jointly embedded in the concepts of "key factors for success" (KFS), "degrees of freedom," and "lower costs or higher value to the customer." In the interest of clarity, however, they deserve separate consideration.

Differentiation in Important Attributes

Obviously, competitive advantage results from differentiation among competitors—but not just any differentiation. For a producer to enjoy a competitive advantage in a product/market segment, the difference or differences between him and his competitors must be felt in the marketplace: that is, they must be reflected in some *product/delivery attribute* that is a *key buying criterion* for the market. And the product must be differentiated enough to win the loyalty of a significant set of buyers; it must have a *footprint in the market*.

Product/Delivery Attribute

Customers rarely base their choice of a product or service on internal characteristics of the producer that are not reflected in a perceived product or delivery difference. Indeed, they usually neither know nor care about those characteristics. Almost invariably, the most important contact between the customer and the producer is the marketplace—the "strategic triangle" where the producer meets his customers and competitors. It is here that the competitive contest for the scarce resource, the sales dollar, is directly engaged.

Just as differences among animal species that are unrelated to scarce resources do not contribute to the survival of the fittest, so producer differences that do not affect the market do not influence the competitive process. Differences among competitors in plant locations, raw material choices, labour policies, and the like matter only when those differences translate into product/delivery attributes that influence the customers' choice of where to spend their sales dollars.

"Product/delivery attributes" include not only such familiar elements as price, quality, aesthetics, and functionality, but also broader attributes such as availability, consumer awareness, visibility, and after-sales service. Anything that affects customers' perceptions of the product or service, its usefulness to them, and their access to it is a product/delivery attribute. Anything that does not affect these perceptions is not.

Having lower costs, for example, may well result in significantly higher margins. But this *business* advantage will become a *competitive* advantage only if and when the producer directly or indirectly recycles the additional profits into product/delivery attributes such as price, product quality, advertising, or additional capacity that increases availability. Only then is the producer's competitive position enhanced. Two examples illustrate this point.

1. For years, the "excess" profits of a major packaged goods company—the low-cost producer in its industry—have been siphoned off by its corporate parent for reinvestment in other subsidiaries. The packaged goods subsidiary has therefore been no more able to take initiatives or respond to competitive threats than if it did not produce those excess profits. Thus, business advantage may exist, but competitive advantage is lacking. If risk-adjusted returns available from investments in other business exceed those of additional investment in the packaged goods subsidiary, the corporate parent may be making the best business decisions. However, the packaged goods subsidiary has gained no competitive advantage from its superior position.

2. The corporate parent of a newly acquired, relatively high-cost producer in an industrial products market has decided to aggressively expand its subsidiary. This expansion is potentially at the expense of the current market leader, an independent company occupying the low-cost position in the industry. The resources that the new parent is willing to invest are far larger than the incremental profits generated by the market leader's lower costs. Because the new subsidiary can invest more than the market leader in product design, product quality,

distribution, and so forth, it is the subsidiary that has, or soon will have, the competitive advantage.

In short, it is the application, not just the generation, of greater resources that is required for competitive advantage.

Key Buying Criterion

Every product has numerous attributes that competitors can use to differentiate themselves to gain some degree of advantage. To be strategically significant, however, an advantage must be based on positive differentiation of an attribute that is a *key buying criterion* for a particular market segment and is not offset by a negative differentiation in any other key buying criterion. In the end, competitive advantage is the result of all net differences in important product/delivery attributes, not just one factor such as price or quality. Differences in other, less important attributes may be helpful at the margin, but they are not strategically significant.

Key buying criteria vary, of course, by industry and even by market segment. In fact, because market segments differ in their choice of key buying criteria, a particular product may have a competitive advantage in some segments while being at a disadvantage in others. Price aside, the elaborate technical features that professional photographers prize in Hasselblad cameras would baffle and discourage most of the casual users who make up the mass market.

In any one product/market segment, however, only a very few criteria are likely to be important enough to serve as the basis for a meaningful competitive advantage. These criteria are likely to be basic—that is, central to the concept of the product or service itself, as opposed to "add-ons" or "features." For example, in the tubular steel industry, there are just two key product/delivery attributes: a single measure of quality (third-party testing reject rate) and local availability on the day required by the customer's drilling schedule.

Texas Instruments (TI) apparently did not fully understand the importance of differentiation along key buying criteria when it entered the wristwatch market. Its strategy was to build upon its ability to drive down costs—and therefore prices (the products attribute)—beyond the point where competitors could respond. But this competitive strategy, which had worked in electronic components, failed in wristwatches because price, past a certain point, was no longer a key buying criterion: customers cared more about aesthetics. TI had surpassed all of its competitors in an attribute that did not matter in the marketplace.

"Footprint in the Market"

To contribute to an SCA, the differences in product/delivery attributes must command the attention and loyalty of a substantial customer base; in other words, they must produce a "footprint in the market" of significant breadth and depth.

- *Breadth.* How many customers are attracted to the product above all others by the difference in product attributes? What volume do these customers purchase?

- *Depth.* How strong a preference has this difference generated? Would minor changes in the balance of attributes cause the customers to switch?

Breadth and depth are usually associated in marketing circles with the concept of "branding." Branding can indeed be a source of competitive advantage, as shown by Perrier's spectacular advantage in a commodity as prosaic as bottled mineral water.

But the importance of breadth and depth are not limited to branding strategies. Even a producer who is pursuing a low-price strategy must ensure that his lower price will cause customers to choose his product and that changes in nonprice attributes by competitors would be unlikely to lure them away.

Durable Differentiation

Positive differentiation in key product/delivery attributes is essential to competitive advantage. However, a differentiation that can be readily erased does not by itself confer a meaningful advantage. Competitive advantages described in such terms as "faster delivery" or "superior product quality" are illusory if competitors can erase the differentiation at will.

For example, Minnetonka, Inc., created a new market niche with "Softsoap." As a result, its stock price more than doubled. Before long, however, 50 different brands of liquid soap, some selling for a fifth of Softsoap's price, appeared on the market. As a result, Minnetonka saw its earnings fall to zero and its stock price decline by 75 percent.

An advantage is durable only if competitors cannot readily imitate the producer's superior product/delivery attributes. In other words, a gap in the *capability* underlying the differentiation must separate the producer from his competitors; otherwise no meaningful competitive advantage exists. (Conversely, of course, no meaningful advantage can arise from a capability gap that does not produce an important difference in product/delivery attributes.)

Understanding the capability gap, then, is basic to determining whether a competitive advantage actually exists. For example, an attribute such as faster delivery does not constitute a real competitive advantage unless it is based on a capability gap such as may exist if the company has a much bigger truck fleet than its competitors can afford to maintain. Higher product quality does not in itself constitute a competitive advantage. But unique access to intrinsically superior raw materials that enable the producer to deliver a better quality product may well do so.

A capability gap exists when the function responsible for the differentiated product/delivery attribute is one that only the producer in question can perform, or one that competitors (given their particular limitations) could do only with maximum effort. So defined, capability gaps fall into four categories.

1. *Business system gaps* result from the ability to perform individual functions more effectively than competitors and from the inability of competitors to easily follow suit. For example, differences in labour union work rules can constitute a capability gap resulting in superior production capability. Superior engineering or technical skills may

create a capability gap leading to greater precision or reliability in the finished product.

2. *Position gaps* result from prior decisions, actions, and circumstances. Reputation, consumer awareness and trust, and order backlogs, which can represent important capability gaps, are often the legacy of an earlier management generation. Thus, current competitive advantage may be the consequence of a past facilities location decision. BHP, the large Australian steel maker, enjoys important production efficiencies because it is the only producer to have located its smelter adjacent to its iron ore source, eliminating expensive iron ore transportation costs.

3. *Regulatory/legal gaps* result from government's limiting the competitors who can perform certain activities, or the degree to which they can perform those activities. Patents, operating licenses, import quotas, and consumer safety laws can all open important capability gaps among competitors. For example, Ciba-Geigy's patent on a low-cost herbicide allowed it to dominate certain segments of the agricultural chemical market for years.

4. *Organization or managerial quality gaps* result from an organization's ability consistently to innovate and adapt more quickly and effectively than its competitors. For example, in industries like computers or financial services, where the competitive environment is shifting rapidly, this flexibility may be the single most important capability gap. In other industries, the key capability gap may be an ability to out-innovate competitors, keeping them always on the defensive.

Note that only the first category, business system gaps, covers actions that are currently under the control of the producer. Frustrating as it may be to the strategist, competitive advantage or disadvantage is often the result of factors he or she is in no position to alter in the short term.

The broad concept of a capability gap becomes useful only when we succeed in closely specifying a producer's *actual* capability gap over competitors in a *particular* situation. Analysts can detect the existence of a capability gap by examining broad functions in the business system, but they must then go further and determine the root cause of superior performance in that function.

Individual capability gaps between competitors are very specific. There must be a precise reason why one producer can outperform another, or there is no competitive advantage. The capability gap consists of specific, often physical, differences. It is likely to be prosaic and measurable, not intangible. Abstract terms, such as "higher labour productivity" or "technological leadership," often serve as useful shorthand, but they are too general for precise analysis. Moreover, they implicitly equate capability gaps with marginal performance superiority, rather than with discrete differences—such as specific work rule differences or technical resources capacity—that are not easily imitated.

For example, if marginal performance superiority constituted competitive advantage, one would expect "focus" competitors—those who have no capability advantage but excel in serving a particular niche through sheer concentration of effort—to win over more general competitors who decide to invade that niche. But as American Motors learned when Detroit's "Big Three" began producing small cars, and as some regional banks are learning as money center banks enter their markets, "trying harder" is no substitute for the possession of unique capabilities.

Only by understanding specific differences in capability can the strategist accurately determine and measure the actions that competitors must take to eliminate the gap and the obstacles and costs to them of doing so.

Lasting Advantage (Sustainability)

If a meaningful advantage is a function of a positive difference in important attributes based on an underlying capability gap, then the sustainability of the competitive advantage is simply a function of the durability of both the attributes and the gap.

There is not much value in an advantage in product/delivery attributes that do not retain their importance over time. Manufacturers of CB radios, video games, and designer jeans saw their revenues decline and their financial losses mount not because their competitors did anything to erode their capability advantages, but because most of their customers simply no longer valued those products enough to pay the price. In each case, industry participants believed that they had benefited from a permanent shift in consumer preferences and began to invest accordingly. In each case they were wrong.

Whether consumers will continue to demand a product over time, and how they can be influenced to prefer certain product attributes over time, are essentially marketing issues, subject to normal marketing analytical techniques. How basic is the customer need that the product meets? How central to its function or availability is the attribute in each question? These may be the key questions to ask in this connection.

The sustainability of competitive advantage is also a function of the durability of the capability gap that created the attractive attribute. In fact, the most important condition for sustainability is that existing and potential competitors either cannot or will not take the actions required to close the gap. If competitors can and will fill the gap, the advantage is by definition not sustainable.

Obviously, a capability gap that competitors are unable to close is preferable to one that relies on some restraint. Unfortunately, a producer cannot choose whether a particular capability gap meets the former or the latter condition.

Consider the two cases more closely.

Case 1

Competitors Cannot Fill the Gap.   This situation occurs when the capability itself is protected by specific entry and mobility barriers such as an important product patent or unique access to a key raw material (for example, DeBeer's Consolidated Mines). In a Case 1 situation, sustainability is assured at least until the barrier is eroded or eliminated (converting the situation to

Case 2). Barriers can erode or be eliminated over time, unless they are inherent in the nature of the business.[2]

A more significant danger to Case 1 advantages, however, probably lies not in the gradual erosion of barriers, but in the possibility that competitors may leapfrog the barriers by a new game strategy.

For example, the introduction of the transistor in 1955 did nothing to erode the barriers that RCA had created in vacuum tubes; it simply made RCA's leadership irrelevant. Therefore, although sustainability can be estimated by (1) considering all the changes (environmental forces or competitor actions) that could erode the barriers, and (2) assessing the probabilities of their occurrence over a specified time horizon, there will, of course, always be uncertainty in the estimate.

Case 2

Competitors Could Close the Capability Gap but Refrain From Doing So.   This situation might occur for any one of four reasons.

a. *Inadequate Potential.* A simple calculation may show competitors that the costs of closing the gap would exceed the benefits, even if the possessor of the advantage did not retaliate.

For example, the danger of cannibalizing existing products may preclude effective response. MCI, Sprint, and others were able to create the low-price segment of the U.S. long-distance telephone market largely because AT&T did not choose to respond directly for some time. Most likely it considered that the cost of cutting prices for 100 percent of its customers in order to retain the 1 to 2 percent in the low-price segment was simply too high, and that only when the segment grew to sufficient size would a response become worthwhile.

Other examples of situations where a payoff is not worth the required investment include investing in capacity to achieve "economies of scale" when the capacity required to achieve the required economy exceeds the likely additional demand in the industry; and labour work rules, where the additional compensation demanded by the union in return for such changes would more than offset the potential savings.

The inadequate-potential situation represents a sustainable advantage because the "end game" has already been reached: there are no rational strategic countermoves for competitors to take until conditions change.

b. *Corresponding Disadvantage.* Competitors may believe that acting to close the capability gap will open gaps elsewhere (in this or other market segments) that will more than offset the value of closing this one.

---

[2] For example, if the business is a "natural monopoly." A natural monopoly exists where either (1) economies of scale cause marginal costs to decline past the point where production volume equals market demand (that is, where the most efficient economic system is to have only one producer); or (2) the social costs of installing duplicate production/distribution systems outweigh the benefits, a situation usually leading to the establishment of a legal monopoly by government fiat.

For example, a "niche" competitor relies on this factor to protect him against larger competitors, who (or so he hopes) will reckon that an effective attack on his niche advantage would divert resources (including management time) needed elsewhere, destroy the integrity of their own broader product lines (opening gaps in other segments), or create some other gap.

A "corresponding disadvantage" situation constitutes at least a temporarily sustainable advantage, because for the moment an "end game" has been reached. However, as the attractiveness of competitors' other markets changes, so does their estimate of whether a corresponding disadvantage is present in the niche (as American Motors learned to its cost). In addition, competitors will always be searching for ways to fill the capability gap without creating offsetting gaps. Only if the creation of offsetting gaps is an automatic and inevitable consequence of any such action will the producer's advantage be assured of sustainability in the long run.

c. *Fear of Reprisal*. Even though it initially would appear worth doing so, competitors may refrain from filling the capability gap for fear of retaliatory action by the producer. The sustainability of the producer's existing advantage depends, in this case, on the competitors' continuing to exercise voluntary restraint, accepting in effect the producer's position in this market segment.

For example, Japanese steel makers voluntarily refrain from increasing their U.S. market share for fear that American producers can and will persuade the U.S. government to take harsh protectionist measures.

"Fear of reprisal" is probably among the most common strategic situations in business, but it must be considered unstable over time, as competitor's situations and managements shift.

d. *Management Inertia*. Finally, there are cases where competitors would benefit from closing the capability gap but fail to do so, either because management has incorrectly assessed the situation or because it lacks the will, the ability, or the energy to take the required action.

For example, Honda's success in dominating the British motorcycle industry is generally attributed to Norton Villiers Triumph's failure to respond to a clear competitive threat until too late.

Psychologists tell us that managers will implement real change only when their discomfort with the status quo exceeds the perceived personal cost of taking the indicated action. This may well explain why competitors often tolerate a performance gap that they could profitably act to close. But it is risky for a producer to rely for long on the weakness or inertia of competitors' management to protect a competitive advantage; by definition, the end game has not been reached.

In all four cases, how long competitors will tolerate capability gaps they are capable of closing depends largely on the relationship between the value of the advantage created by the gap and the cost (to each competitor) of closing it. The worse the cost-to-benefit ratio, the longer the advantage is likely to be sustainable, because greater changes in the environment are required before value would exceed cost. Coupled with an informed view of the rate of environmental change in the industry, this ratio thus allows the analyst to estimate sustainability.

SCA and Strategy

The classic definition of competitive strategy as "an integrated set of actions designed to create a sustainable advantage over competitors" might suggest that possessing an SCA is synonymous with business success—that those producers who have an SCA are guaranteed winners, and that those competitors who lack one should simply exit the business to avoid financial disaster.

This apparently reasonable conclusion is, however, incorrect. Although an SCA is a powerful tool in creating a successful business strategy, it is not the only key ingredient. In fact:

1. Possessing an SCA does not guarantee financial success.
2. Producers can succeed even when competitors possess an SCA.
3. Pursuing an SCA can sometimes conflict with sound business strategy.

Losing with an SCA

Although an SCA will help a producer to achieve, over time, higher returns than his competitors, there are at least three circumstances where its possessor can fail financially:

1. If the market sector is not viable. In many cases (including most new product introductions), the minimum achievable cost of producing and selling a particular product or service exceeds its value to the customer. In this situation, an SCA will not guarantee the survival of its possessor; it will tend merely to ensure that his competitors will fare even worse.
2. If the producer has severe operational problems. An SCA can allow management the luxury of focusing more fully on achieving operational excellence, but thousands of companies have failed for operational, rather than strategic, reasons.
3. If competitors inflict tactical damage. An SCA rarely puts a producer completely beyond the reach of competitor actions such as price cuts and "buying" market share, which may be unrelated to the SCA itself. A producer will be particularly vulnerable to such competitive tactics if the SCA is not very important, either because the depth of the "footprint" described earlier is shallow or because the gap in capability is minor.

In these cases, producers must select their actions very carefully. Actions that can and will be imitated may result only in intensified competitive rivalry. And, where the producer's advantage is unimportant, he will have little cushion against the competitive repercussions. For example, recent airline pricing policies and "frequent flyer" programs have done nothing to contribute to the long-term profitability or competitive positions of their originators. Unimaginative direct cost-reduction efforts (cutting overhead or staffs, for example) may improve profitability in the short term. But if competitors can and will imitate these efforts, the only long-run effect may be to raise the general level of misery throughout the industry.

Competing Against an SCA

By definition, not all producers can possess an SCA in a given product/market segment. Other competitors face the prospects of competing (at least for some time) from a handicapped position. Under certain circumstances, however, it is still possible for some to succeed.

Rapidly growing markets constitute one such situation. As long as real market growth over a given period exceeds the additional capacity advantaged competitors can bring on line during that time (due to organizational constraints, risk aversion, and so forth), even competitors can thrive. For example, the booming market for microcomputer software over the past five years has enabled many weak competitors to grow rich. Only when market growth slows or the advantaged competitors increase the rate at which they can grow will true competition begin and the impact of an SCA make itself felt.

In markets where true competition for scarce sales dollars is taking place, the number of disadvantaged competitors who can succeed, the degree to which they can prosper, and the conditions under which they can prosper will vary, depending on the value of the advantage held by the "number-one" competitor.

If the number-one competitor has only a shallow or unimportant advantage, many disadvantaged competitors can prosper for long periods. As noted earlier, each competitor is unique. When all attributes are considered, each will have a competitive advantage in serving some customers. The disadvantaged competitors are more likely to receive lower returns than the number-one producer, but they certainly may be viable.

If the number-one competitor has an important advantage in a given product/market segment, some theorists assert that over the long run there will be only one viable competitor. Others may remain in the segment, but they will be plagued by losses and/or very inadequate returns. If there are six different ways to achieve a major advantage, this reasoning runs, then the market will split into six segments, each ruled by a different competitor, who uniquely excels in the attribute most valued by the customers in that segment.

Be that as it may, in practice other strong competitors may also profitably exist alongside Number One under two conditions:

1. *If the number-one producer's advantage is limited by a finite capacity* that is significantly less than the size of the market; that is, he may expand further, but will not retain his advantage on the incremental capacity. Obstacles to continued advantaged expansion are common: limited access to superior raw materials, finite capacity in low-cost

plants, prohibitive transportation costs beyond certain distances. Antitrust laws also tend to act as barriers to expansion beyond a level by number-one competitors.

2. *If the size of the individual competitors is small* relative to the size of the market. In this case, a number of strong competitors can expand for many years without directly competing with each other, by taking share from weak competitors rather than each other.

Weak competitors, of course, are likely to fare badly when competition is intense and the depth of the advantage enjoyed by others is great. Their choices are:

1. To leave the business.
2. To endure the situation until the advantage is eroded.
3. To seek to create a new advantage.

If a weak competitor chooses to pursue a new advantage, then he must ensure that it will be preemptive, or that competitors will not notice his move and will fail to respond until he has consolidated his position. Otherwise, his action is virtually certain to be copied and the intended advantage erased.

Pursuing the Wrong SCA

Although its attainment is the goal of *competitive* strategy, sustainable competitive advantage is not an end in itself but a means to an end. The corporation is not in business to beat its competitors, but to create wealth for its shareholders. Thus, actions that contribute to SCA but detract from creating shareholder wealth may be good strategy in the competitive sense but bad strategy for the corporation. Consider two examples.

1. Low-cost capacity additions in the absence of increased industry demand. Adding low-cost capacity and recycling the additional profits into product/delivery attributes that attract enough customers to fill that capacity is usually a sound business strategy. However, as industry cost curve analysis has demonstrated, if the capacity addition is not accompanied by increases in industry demand, the effect may well be to displace the high-cost, but previously viable, marginal producer. When this happens, prices in the industry will fall to the level of the costs of the new marginal producer, costs which by definition are lower than the costs of the former marginal producer. Thus, the profit per unit sold of all participants will be reduced.

   Depending on the cost structure of the industry, the declines in the profit per unit sold can be dramatic (for example, if all the remaining producers have similar costs). In this case, even the producer who added the new capacity will face declining profitability on his preexisting capacity; in extreme cases his total profit on new and old capacity may fall below the profit he had previously earned on the old capacity alone. While gaining share and eliminating a competitor (good competitive strategy), he has invested *more* to profit *less* (bad business strategy).

2. Aggressive learning-curve pricing strategies that sacrifice too much current profit. Under these strategies, prices are reduced at least as fast as costs in order to buy market share and drive out competitors. The assumption is that the future payoff from market dominance will more than offset the costs of acquiring it. The value of new business, however, is likely to be very sensitive to the precise relationship between prices and costs. This is true particularly in the early stages of the learning curve, when the absolute levels of prices, costs, and margins are relatively high and the profit consequences are therefore greater for any given volume. Especially in high-tech industries such as electronics, where the lifetime of technologies is short, the long-term value of the market share bought by overly aggressive learning-curve strategies can be less than the profit eliminated in the early stages by pricing too close to costs.

The framework for SCA proposed in this article is far from complete. Its treatment of product/delivery attributes and capability gaps (notably organizational strength) is impressionistic rather than detailed. It leaves other aspects of the topic (for example, the sustainability of competitive advantage at the corporate level) unexplored.

But a major concern of the business unit strategist is to determine whether the enterprise (or a competitor's) possesses or is in a position to capture an SCA, and, if so, to examine its strategic implications. The conditions for SCA and the implications of SCA for strategy that have been proposed provide an initial framework for these tasks.

From Warning to Crisis: A Turnaround Primer

P. SCOTT SCHERRER

Long before a business fails, warning signals start flashing. But managers often don't notice the red lights, or even ignore them. When they finally do acknowledge something's amiss, some managers will treat the problem as a temporary phenomenon, putting out the fire but not remedying the hazard.

With a bit of education, however, managers can train themselves to perk up and recognize the bad signs, whether they are activated from within the organization or from the outside. Once managers learn the signals, they also can differentiate between the various stages of organizational decline. No matter what phase a company is in, managers need to act—fast.

Following is a turnaround primer that identifies warning signals, categorizes decline phases, and provides a framework to help managers reverse the direction of an organization that may well be on its way to hell in a handbasket.

External Influences

Many managers believe a downward trend will dissipate when bad news from the outside improves. The external elements that cause them trouble range from increased competition to legal/political vacillations (see Exhibit 1).

Among these external, uncontrollable elements are market changes, customer preference changes, foreign competition, capital market movements, legal precedents, and the political climate. Since all businesses in an industry are similarly affected by external elements, each business survives these changes only because of the ability of its management. Some businesses come through external changes with increased market share and profitability; others fail.

A major problem with the uncontrollable elements is their interaction with each other. A cultural/social change, for example, can result in a legal/political change. This, in turn, can affect the economic environment, leading to a shift in technological developments. The rate of technological development affects the status of the competition, which in turn influences the cultural/social environment, and the circle is complete. What managers often do not

Source: Reprinted with permission of publisher, from *Management Review*, September 1988.
© 1988, American Management Association, New York. All rights reserved.

EXHIBIT 1   **Nine External Warning Signals**

1. Economic growth activity gives management an indication of the economic climate and influences expansion plans.
2. Credit availability and money-market activity are barometers of trends in commercial and investment banking that will alter the cost of funds.
3. Capital market activity gives a clear signal to management of investor attitudes toward any given industry and the state of the business climate.
4. Business population characteristics show the numbers of businesses entering and exiting any given industry, signaling market expansion and contraction and the degree of competition within the industry.
5. Price-level changes indicate the rate of inflation and impact production considerations.
6. Changes in the competitive structure of the marketplace affect products, pricing, and marketing/distribution.
7. Breakthrough technology also causes changes in products, marketing/distribution, and production.
8. Cultural/social changes alter consumer preferences or the conditions under which a product can be sold.
9. Legal/political changes can adversely affect the marketplace or have an impact on the production, sale, and distribution of a product.

realize is that they can create a similar chain reaction within their businesses to combat the external elements. Foresight and flexibility will help management safeguard against uncontrollable elements, using tactics such as promotion, education of the consumer, accelerated research and development, product improvements or elimination, changing expansion plans, changing markets, and changing channels of distribution.

Consider the tobacco companies. They have known for many years about the external changes taking place in their industry—most importantly, the discovery of smoking's serious health hazards. They have been affected by cultural/social and legal/political changes for the past several decades, and recently experienced severe tests in the court system. To offset declining product sales, they developed new products, such as smokeless tobaccos. They also invested in new businesses: RJR Nabisco, Miller Beer, and other consumer products companies that would use established channels of distribution to gain competitive advantage. The tobacco producers understood the early warning signals of the external, uncontrollable elements and acted to offset them. The ability to cope with external, uncontrollable elements requires that management plans for the unexpected and implements that plan when the unexpected occurs.

Internal Elements

Only 20 percent of business failures are caused by external elements. The other 80 percent are the result of mishandled internal elements. Management is the force that drives the internal functions of finance, production, and marketing/distribution, and yet these elements are at the root of the majority of business failures.

When management does not recognize the internal signals of decline, it pretends that slowdowns are caused by external elements. A shortage of cash is often attributed to poor collections or lack of sales. In fact, the shortage of cash is usually a signal pointing to a deeper problem buried within the firm's management and accounting information systems. It may be that the firm is selling its products or services at a price that does not cover the variable costs of making the product or service. The firm may not have calculated contribution margins, actual product costs, and the direct cost of sales to determine the amount of profitability in the product or service.

Like external forces, the internal elements can interact with each other, and any one of the internal, controllable elements may spark a decline. Production techniques can become antiquated. Marketing/distribution can be in the wrong market with the wrong product. Finance can be unaware that the financial requirements of the other departments have changed. (Poor information flow between departments is another signal of decline.)

Coping with Internal Elements

Management often does not use the managerial tools at its disposal to control internal forces. Many managers do not utilize cash projections, but are only aware of balance sheets and income statements. The heart of any company is the synergy developed between the efficient operations of its various departments. The pulse beat for that synergy is the financial statements. Businesses should run on budgets and cash projections. Budgets are the foundation of financial statements, which reflect the success or failure of the business. For many businesses, however, budgets are mystery stories couched in scenarios that allow managers to hedge their positions. Managers create budgets that cannot be wrong, and consequently they cannot be accurate.

Balance sheets may show adequate working capital even when a company is in decline. When the balance sheet is overly burdened with inventory and accounts receivable that are inaccurate, obsolete, or uncollectable, a company is in trouble. The manager should know the status of accounts receivable. If they are increasing on the financial statements, is it because sales are increasing or collections are slow? If inventory is increasing, is it because sales have decreased and production has not? Managers can reduce a firm's reliance on banks by increasing accounts receivable collections, reducing inventory, and paying accounts payable within the discount period to avoid penalties.

Internal elements require constant monitoring. Since management may be unable to understand the dynamic nature of the internal elements, it is not surprising that declines go unnoticed.

Management often doesn't understand its relationships with stakeholders—the people who work for, live near, invest in, or are affected by a company. Customer service, for example, is often a low priority. In most businesses, 80 percent of sales come from 20 percent of customers. Often the cost of servicing a customer and the cost of a sale are unknown. Customers are not classified into categories to determine the most favorable customers to the business.

Management may perceive that the best customers are those who order the most, although these may be the same people who pay the slowest. In many companies, channels of information—from customers, competition, employees, vendors, and other managers—are not open. Without this information, the business cannot adapt to change. Information and the ability to react to it are the most powerful weapons a business has against decline.

Early Internal Warning Signals

Danger signals can be used by management to begin an internal corporate renewal. There are distinct phases of decline, and the danger signals vary within the stages (see Exhibit 2). Not all of the symptoms of decline will appear; there is sufficient cause to worry if some of them occur.

Also, internal warning signals take on different meaning depending on the company's growth rate. In stabilized companies, managers may continue to manage as if the growth will continue in the near future. When plans are not modified to address the new situation, the business courts trouble. Many companies religiously draft strategic plans. All too often, however, the plans are carved in granite and are not adaptable to changing situations. When shifts occur (internal, external, or both), the business is unable to cope with them, and instead continues to follow its strategic plan. Managers believe the strategic plan represents the very best of their creative abilities, and therefore are loathe to deviate from it. The strategic plan becomes part of the problem, rather than the solution.

Financial Predictors

Many financial ratios are tip-offs to a downturn, but management often considers them accounting busywork and pays no heed. Five ratios useful throughout all phases of decline and the turnaround process are:

1. Working capital to total assets
2. Retained earnings to total assets
3. Earnings before interest and taxes (EBIT) to total assets
4. Market value of equity to book value to total debt
5. Sales to total assets

These ratios are especially useful when they are used for at least three years. The business will begin to establish a pattern within the ratios, and deviations from the pattern can be corrected quickly. More mature businesses have long histories, and the ratios should have reached a point where they are consistent annually. A deviation is as good as a red flag.

The ratios noted by turnaround managers generate a picture of the company. They indicate the ability of the business to survive on its own. When they are extremely low, it is time to approach the bank for bridge capital. The bank will not be willing to have any further involvement unless the plan for the turnaround is valid and based on the business's actual ability to support itself after the turnaround.

EXHIBIT 2   Common Danger Signals and the Stages in Which They Occur

Early Decline

- Shortage of cash
- Strained liquidity
- Reduced working capital
- Stretched accounts payable
- Late accounts receivable
- Reduction of ROI by 20 to 30%
- Flat sales
- Several quarters of losses
- Increased employee absenteeism
- Increased employee accidents
- Increased customer complaints (product quality, delivery, back orders, stock-outs)
- Late financial and management information

Mid-Term Decline

- Increasing inventory
- Decreasing sales
- Decreasing margins
- Increasing expenses
- Increasing advances from banks
- Additional requests for consideration from banks
- Late and unreliable financial and management information
- Eroding customer confidence
- Accelerating accounts payable from vendors
- Overdrafts at the bank
- Delayed accounts receivable from opportunistic customers
- Violation of loan covenants
- Bank used to cover payroll

Late Decline

- Little attention paid to decreasing profit
- Staff is cut back without analyzing cause of problems
- Overdrawn bank account substituted for a line of credit
- Cash crisis
- Accounts payable are 60 to 90 days late
- Accounts receivable are more than 90 days late
- Sales decline further
- Employee morale is extremely low
- Company credibility is eroding
- Inventory turnover has decreased excessively
- Supplier restrictions are initiated
- Fewer reports to bank are submitted
- Auditors qualify opinions
- Cheques bounce
- Credit is offset
- Accounts receivable continue to age
- Margins decrease further
- Sales volume decreases further
- Uncollectable receivables increase
- No liquidity
- Working capital is depleted
- Lack of funds for payroll
- Ineffective management
- Attempts to convince lenders that company is viable and liquidation is not necessary

Signals That Can Occur in Any Stage

- Decreased capital utilization
- Decreased market share in key product line(s)
- Increased overhead costs
- Increased management and employee turnover
- Salaries and benefits growing faster than productivity and profits
- Increased management layers
- Losing market share to competition, which is not keeping up with marketplace changes
- Management in conflict with company goals and objectives
- Direction of management and company are different
- Sales forecasts predict company can sell its way out of difficulty
- Poor internal accounting
- Credit advances to customers who do not pay on time
- Nonseasonal borrowing
- Sudden overdrafts
- Increased trade inquiries

 # Double Decline

Often a company suffers a decline thanks to a combination of internal and external elements. Some common signals when both forces are at work include:

- Management by exception rather than flexible planning
- Delegation without inspection, control, feedback, or reinforcement
- Vertical organization chart, with little if any interaction between departments
- Managers with responsibility for more than five direct reports
- Employees with more than one boss
- Broken chain of command
- Overreliance on management by objectives
- Senior managers' abuse of perks
- Marketing the wrong products
- Marketing in the wrong markets
- Inadequate research and development
- Inappropriate channels of distribution
- Unresponsive financial information systems
- Loss of competitive advantage
- Changing technology
- Regulatory changes
- Inadequate understanding of customers' needs
- Allowing one department or business function to dominate and dictate the mission, goals, and objectives of the business

Crazy Eddie, Inc., is an example of a company that has suffered from both internal and external problems. Internally, there were too many layers of management, excessive wages, corporate waste, cost overruns, employee morale problems, and information flow deficiencies. The company had almost every signal of decline.

Externally, new competitors entered the market. Since Crazy Eddie's had damaged its relationships with appliance suppliers, it could not receive the necessary merchandise to compete. The company is now undergoing a turnaround; part of the strategy is to cut costs and payroll by a minimum of $25 million. There is also a slump in the company's markets, so revenue has decreased. The internal elements were changed by laying off unnecessary managers, reducing wages, adding a profit-sharing plan, settling the lawsuits on corporate waste, reducing costs, and adding a computer system to prevent selling items below cost. The external elements are being addressed by rebuilding relationships with suppliers, banks, and consumers.

◼ The Turnaround Process

Turnaround managers bring order to chaos, which usually means they must take control of every function in the business. They create budgets from the bottom up and strictly enforce accountability. They analyze products and markets to determine which have the most profitability. Those that generate losses are terminated quickly and permanently, regardless of the company's relationship with the customer or product. The turnaround manager cuts costs, increases the business's adaptability, and saves the profitable products and markets. Actual costs replace standard costing, and product contribution margins are used to determine which products contribute the most to the fixed costs of the business. Cash flow reports are used continually; at first they may be used daily, then weekly, then monthly, and finally semiannually. The reports are used in developing the operating plan. The time line and the amount of cash flowing in will determine how the business can survive.

The classifications of customers and the aging of accounts receivable determine which customers are profitable. The business may have many customers with repeat orders, but they all may be delinquent in paying their accounts. The business cannot afford to carry them any longer. Reviewing accounts receivable is an essential task of turnaround managers. They decide which customers to keep and which to pursue for more business.

Get Everyone Involved

Banks, vendors, customers, employees, boards of directors, and others affected by the decline of the business need to be made part of the solution. Banks and boards of directors are usually the parties that suggest the use of a turnaround manager. Normally, by the time they notice a problem exists, the situation is approaching crisis proportions. This is a common situation because bank executives and boards tend to be chiefly concerned with balance sheets and income statements driven, despite the fact that healthy looking balance sheets and income statements can disguise many problems. Bank managers and board members do not visit the business and review operations. They do not walk the plant floor and talk with employees. They do not review basic financial information, such as accounts receivable and payable. They only learn about employee morale, customer service, equipment condition, and other on-site situations from a report generated by management.

Trade vendors also need to be included in the situation. They are the business's lifeline to its suppliers. When payments to them are delinquent, the business is in jeopardy of losing its supply line. Management may argue that it can find other suppliers, but unless the underlying problem causing delinquent payments is addressed, suppliers will evaporate along with the company's credit. New suppliers require credit references, and changing suppliers has substantial switching costs. The new supplier has to produce or acquire the supplies requested, schedule deliveries, and obtain payments. As the business adds new suppliers, the bank will receive credit report requests. This is another signal of decline.

Employee participation is essential in the turnaround process. Turnarounds often require asking for pay concessions. Hours on the job and working conditions may be affected. When employees are part of the restructuring plan, they tend to accept painful concessions with more ease. When the restructuring is complete, management should consider itself indebted to these people and should reward them financially.

SRC, a leveraged buyout from International Harvester, is an example of a turnaround where employee participation was the key ingredient for success. In 1979, the company was losing $2 million per year on sales of $26 million. In 1983, 13 employees of International Harvester bought SRC. They developed a detailed reporting system and a full-blown, daily cash flow statement. In 1986, sales reached $42 million. Net operating income increased to 11 percent and the debt-to-equity ratio has been reduced from 89-to-1 to 5.1-to-1. The appraised value of a share in the company's stock ownership has increased from 10 cents to $8.45. Absenteeism and serious workplace accidents have almost disappeared. The company attributes the turnaround to allowing employees to reach their highest potential.

To facilitate a turnaround, union cooperation is essential. It also can greatly influence morale. A turnaround can be accomplished despite the unions, but may require drastic steps such as bankruptcy or massive layoffs. Concessions regarding pay rate, hours, working conditions, raises, vacations, accumulated sick leave, and benefits will be granted only when the union is convinced that the company can survive. That this is possible is indicated by the arrival of the turnaround manager and by the turnaround plan. The cooperation of the other stakeholders also places pressure on the union to cooperate.

Customers must also be taken into account during the turnaround, but businesses in decline tend to forsake customer service. Quality control diminishes, which causes more order returns. This adds expenses to an already strained financial condition. Orders are taken and delivery dates missed, causing loss of credibility with the customers. The inventory, which was a main part of the balance sheet, becomes obsolete and therefore not usable to meet the current demands of the customers. The end result is the loss of the customer base.

Types of Turnarounds and Strategies

A turnaround can take several forms. It can be *strategic* if the business needs to be redefined because of changing markets and products. In the General Nutrition turnaround, for example, the company moved away from its core of vitamins and specialty health foods to the much wider category of health in general. The stores needed items that would make people come to them rather than grocery stores. The company searched for new products and new lines. Brookstone, the specialty gadget store, inspired many of the changes made at General Nutrition. Prior to the turnaround, the stock had plummeted from a high of $29^5/_8$ to a low of $3^7/_8$.

An *operational* turnaround involves changing a business's operations, which could include cost cutting, revenue generating, and asset reduction. In the case of General Nutrition, the turnaround was also focused on the operations of the business. (It is very common for turnarounds to be mounted on several fronts and combine strategies.) At General Nutrition, the management team was strengthened and the company divided into three distinct segments: retailing, manufacturing, and specialty services.

Another example of an operational turnaround is Black and Decker. The company had more than 200 different motor sizes. It had split consumer and professional tools into two separate groups that seldom communicated with each other. This made it easy for the competition to find niches where Black and Decker did not make tools. To remedy the situation, the company organized plants around motor sizes, reduced product variations, and streamlined manufacturing. The number of plants was reduced from 25 to 19. Excess capacity utilization increased by 75 percent. In addition, the company began producing new products to meet consumer demand.

The *financial* turnaround restructures the financial operations of a business. The object is to utilize the financial strength of the businesses as an asset. ITT, for example, divested itself of 23 businesses for almost $1.5 billion and increased return on equity from 8 percent in 1979 to 12 percent in 1987. Management slashed expenses by abandoning its lavish lifestyle, renting out full floors at its Park Avenue headquarters, and cutting the work force by two-thirds.

Each different type of turnaround may focus on a particular strategy. These include:

- *Revenue generating.* Management tries to increase sales, advertising, and markets while decreasing prices.
- *Product/markets refocusing.* Managers analyze products and markets to determine their profitability. Customers are analyzed to determine the nature of their purchases, payment history, and ability to purchase more. Channels of distribution are analyzed to determine their effectiveness. Products are analyzed further to determine their saleability, contribution margins, actual cost of production, cost of sale, cost of distribution, manufacturing efficiency, inventory carrying costs, and cost of customer service. Businesses may have reached the limits of their growth in products and markets, in which case they need to analyze potential moves into other product and market areas.
- *Cost cutting.* Managers reduce administrative costs, R&D, and marketing.
- *Asset reduction.* Management removes unnecessary assets that usually look nice on the balance sheet but actually produce only costs of maintenance and no revenue stream.
- The combination of any of the above.

Using the correct strategy is part of the art of successfully turning around a company. As the turnaround progresses, the strategy may change. Cost cutting may be superseded by revenue generating, and so forth. Strategies may be combined and used in various sequences, but using an inappropriate strategy can be a terminal error. Here are four pointers to choosing the correct strategy:

- Mature businesses should use retrenchment and efficiency strategies, not product/marketing refocusing.
- Businesses with low capacity utilization should pursue cost-cutting strategies.

- Businesses with high capacity utilization should also pursue cost-cutting strategies.
- Businesses with high market share should pursue revenue-generating strategies and product/market refocusing.

The time frame for a turnaround varies depending upon the business, industry, market, severity of the crisis, cooperation of stakeholders, and turnaround manager. A business that has been in decline for several years cannot expect to be renewed quickly. Its reputation for low credibility will have permeated all of its stakeholders and will take some time to reverse. A business that recognizes signals of decline in the early stage can be renewed more quickly.

In general, turnarounds occur in five stages:

1. Evaluation of the situation, which can take from one week to three months
2. Creating a plan, which can take from one to six months
3. Implementation of the plan, which can take from six months to one year
4. Stabilization of the business, which can take from six months to one year
5. Return to growth of the business, which can take from one to two years

Astute managers constantly monitor the health of their businesses and act on the warning signals. Often, managers can see the signals but need outside help to cure the problem. The need to address decline and failure is obvious. The waste of corporate assets and employees' talents that can stem from managerial ignorance can be astronomical. This waste can be minimized if management can notice and address decline in its early stages.

READING 6

Keeping the Engine Humming

ANDREW CAMPBELL
Managing Partner, Campbell & Associates Inc.

Imagine the instrument panel on a car. While there is a lot going on both inside and outside the car, the basic performance measures are shown by the speedometer, odometer, tachometer, battery charger and oil pressure gauge. The driver can get a quick update on the car with minimal confusion.

Similar to the driver who monitors a car's performance, the managers and employees need to constantly monitor their company's performance. However, not all of the performance measures they need are found in the traditional monthly financial statements.

It is no wonder that one of today's hottest management trends is the balanced scorecard. It is an idea whose time has come. Simply stated, the balanced scorecard presents financial as well as non-financial information in a logical format. It measures what is important to the company's overall performance.

The balanced scorecard takes the company's mission, translates each key statement into measurable steps and then presents information so that the critical success factors can be evaluated and compared. In other words, the scorecard highlights the questions that good business managers would normally ask about the performance of a company while driving awareness of the importance of these measures throughout the whole company.

The balanced scorecard provides answers to four basic questions about corporate performance, namely:

1. What is the *customer's perspective* and how do they perceive us?

2. What are the essential *internal elements* that we must do excellently?

3. What do we have to do to *continually innovate* and *add value* to the overall operations?

4. What are the *shareholders' expectations* in terms of financial returns and long-term viability?

Source: Andrew Campbell, "Keeping the engine humming," *Business Quarterly*, Summer 1997, pp. 40–46. One-time permission to reproduce *Ivey Business Quarterly* articles granted by Ivey Management Services on June 9, 1998.

Andrew Campbell is the managing partner of Campbell & Associates, which specializes in business planning consulting. He is the author of *One Step Ahead*, and will have another book published this year about the challenges faced by entrepreneurs as they grow their businesses.

IVEY

Richard Ivey School of Business
The University of Western Ontario

Origins of the Balanced Scorecard Idea

The idea for the balanced scorecard originated with Robert Kaplan and David Norton around 1991 (published in *Harvard Business Review* in early 1992). They concluded that, while traditional accounting measures involving balance sheets, profit performance and selected ratios, were appropriate for the Industrial Age, these measures do not always serve the needs of management to make appropriate decisions in the Information Age. Traditional information is often too inadequate and misleading for the decision-makers to make well-rounded business decisions. They argued that the value of a company was more than just the equity on the balance sheet. For example, historical measures of return on investment and earnings per share can give misleading information to managers if they are making decisions related to more future-oriented areas of customer satisfaction and innovation. Kaplan and Norton believed that some of the shortcomings of traditional accounting methods could be overcome by using a more sophisticated approach.

What Is a Balanced Scorecard?

The balanced scorecard is part of a performance management system. It is a link between each employee and the vision of the company. It is a way to measure the degree to which the vision and mission are being achieved. A good scorecard:

- *Reflects the strategic plan.* It measures the key elements (such as brand equity, consumer intent to repurchase, key staff retention, and return on investment) that determine whether the plan is successful or not.
- *Provides a framework that helps shape work behavior.* It provides meaningful production and quality statistics that can be calculated either daily or monthly.
- *Allows each person to measure their individual performance.* As the scorecard is prepared, each person determines exactly how to measure the performance that is critical for their success and hence, for the company's success.
- *Gives them data to make changes immediately performance is enhanced.*

Strategy is the heart of the system, not just control.

What Does It Measure?

In short, the balanced scorecard can measure what you want, reflecting the nature of your business and your business strategy. Each company would, therefore, have a different scorecard since each corporate strategy is different. Each management team will weight each tactic differently and have a different target. Sample types of measures would include, but are not limited to:

- *Financial*. Including measures of operating profit, key ratios (such as percentage return on investments), and key issues (such as inventory shrinkage).
- *Operational*. Including measures of administration (overhead as a percentage of sales), customer service (number of calls handled) and human resources (percentage of jobs accepted).
- *Customer*. Including product development, order processing and inventory measures.
- *Soft measures*. Including shortages, late shipments and delivery errors.
- *Employee measures*. Including staff turnover, morale and surveys.

Why Have a Balanced Scorecard?

The balanced scorecard approach allows executives to compare fairly the performance of one business unit to another, locally, nationally and internationally. For example, the executives of a company with operations on five continents were trying to compare the performance of their business units in each country. They wondered just how the executive team would "put it all together" and make sense out of financial information that only provided part of the story about how well each business unit was performing. Further, they knew that a limitation of their approach came from them sitting in their "ivory tower." They wanted to involve people "on the line" in making decisions so that these employees could take corrective action when needed in order to improve quality immediately. Their solution was the balanced scorecard.

In my experience, while accounting systems help to measure a company's performance, they have many shortcomings. For example:

- In software companies, the real assets include the people, software and R and D. Traditional accounting methods do not record these "off-balance sheet" assets.
- In automotive companies, sales revenue does not always give a valid picture of how satisfied customers are. It is no wonder that one of the most important ratios that signals future sales growth and market share is "customer's intent to repurchase." This ratio is calculated by companies, such as J. D. Power, that survey customers. But this information is never revealed in traditional accounting information.
- In food companies, brand equity reflects the degree to which a food product has differentiated itself from the competitor's product. Yet, a measurement for this concept never shows on the financial statements.

The intent of a scorecard is to balance financial and non-financial measures, promote alignment, identify the critical success factors, help people manage by focusing on what is vital, and link to strategic objectives so people can understand how "what they do" links to "company success."

EXHIBIT 1   Traditional Performance Measures

PRESIDENT Return on investment					
Finance and Administration	**Sales**	**Production and Projects**	**Human Resources and Administration**	**Marketing**	**Design and R and D**
Meet budget	Meet budget	Meet budget	Meet budget	Meet budget	Meet budget
Return on assets	Dollar sales volume	On-time shipments		Market share	Sales from new products
	Margin percentage				

Some Examples

The concept of a balanced scorecard is easier to grasp when looking at an example. Consider the balanced scorecard of a small manufacturing company (see [Exhibit 1]). The company has two distinct business units: a special projects design and installation business, and a standard product line that is mass produced. They sell to customers around the globe and have a special team that ensures appropriate installation. Innovation and R and D are particularly important to them. Before implementing the scorecard, their monthly performance review examined basic financial data, such as whether each department met budget and one or two measures distinct to each department. For example, the sales department also measured sales volume and margin percentage.

But there were limitations in what they could do with this limited amount of information. They needed something that would include indicators related to productivity, customers, innovation and people, in addition to financial matters. Each department expanded on the measures it needed to effectively monitor what was happening in its area (see [Exhibit 2]). In our example, the sales department added a productivity indicator (the number of proposals delivered to target customers), three customer indicators (order backlog versus forecast sales, the mix of easy to hard sales efforts and a customer satisfaction index) and an innovation indicator (the number of new customers).

Of course, you have to know the company to really understand why some measures were chosen and why others were not. You have to understand the nature of the business before seeing why one indicator is placed under the category of customer satisfaction as opposed to, for example, financial.

The balanced scorecard is particularly useful for those larger multinational companies that want to stay attuned to what is going on, whether in several local branches or in companies around the world.

Best Foods Canada is a part of an international company called CPC. A scorecard must be completed by each of Best Foods' divisions, and is then linked to the corporate scorecard. Each divisional scorecard builds on the organization's core business, core values and core strengths. When divisional scorecards are consolidated, the consolidated scorecard measures the corporate performance. CPC summarized its approach on a diagram that it now uses worldwide. [See Exhibit 3.]

Their diagram is the guide to how their scorecard is to be prepared. As a result, a balanced scorecard has been developed by the Canadian management team for its operations. The scorecard consists of elements, strategic drivers, goals and measures for each key area including consumer satisfaction, customer satisfaction, people development, innovation and learning, best business practices and financial performance [see Exhibit 4]. CPC man-

EXHIBIT 2   Performance Measures with Balanced Scorecard

PRESIDENT

Return on investment • Management team development • Order backlog • Sales diversity/product and geographical mix • Project/order risk • Market share

Finance and Administration	Sales	Production and Projects	Human Resources and Administration	Marketing	Design and R and D
Financial Indicators					
Meet budget	Meet budget	Meet budget	Meet budget	Meet budget	Meet budget
Asset management Return on assets	Dollar sales volume	Product profitability	Turnover of key personnel	Market analysis Sales leads	New products ideas and development
Foreign currency gains	Margin percentage and dollars		Use of grants	Market share	Project profitability
Productivity Indicators					
	Number of proposals to target clients	Plant utilization			Design/sales conversion ratio
		Standard cost variances			Conceptual designs on time
		Warranty cost			
Customer Indicators					
Budget comparison and reporting including projects	Order backlog and forecast sales	Product delivery (on-time shipments and quality)	Social functions attended		Project management (project budget time-lines and customer satisfaction)
Management information system setup	Sales mix (easy/hard jobs)	Drawing accuracy, timeliness and on budget	Overall morale index		Overall effectiveness (R and D/sales percentage)
Banking relationship and ratio compliance	Customer satisfaction index	Project management (labor/other costs)			Overall effectiveness
Innovation Indicators					
	Number of new Customers				Sales from new products
					New ideas and development
Human Resource Indicators					
			Training program Performance appraisal		

EXHIBIT 3   CPC Scorecard

Customer satisfaction + People development +
Business practices + Innovation and learning
= Financial performance

agement believes that if the indicators for customer satisfaction, people development, business practices and innovation and learning are achieved, then financial performance will follow.

After completing the overall corporate scorecard, the managers for each of the 12 Canadian departments/operations were able to complete their own scorecard. These departments report to the management team in the U.S.

How Do You Measure?

It is easy to measure some indicators manually, but virtually impossible to measure all of them this way. Fortunately, software is available to help. Indeed, when you start to measure the information and realize the benefits of having and using prompt, accurate and timely data about all facets of the business, it becomes clear that the only way to make the scorecard work is to use a computer system to gather the data and have people perform the analysis.

How Do You Implement a Scorecard?

A smaller company with a strong entrepreneur at the helm successfully implemented a scorecard using a top-down approach. The president simply announced that the scorecard was going to be used—and it was implemented within one month. The executive group met for two days and defined the approach to performance measurement, agreed on the framework to use and defined the top levels of measures. A pilot project team then spent the same amount of time defining the overall principles and capturing the relevant historical data. The IS department was called in next to set up measures and compile the pilot data. A system administrator then installed the software and integrated the individual scorecards. Finally, an internal person was chosen to be the "change master," his role being to drive the acceptance of the scorecard through the organization.

However, it is not always so easy. In another company, with more than 1,000 people and with locations across Canada, the approach had to be different. The company had gone through a significant reorganization, leaving

EXHIBIT 4   Balanced Scorecard Measurement

Corporate Strategy	Grouping	Measure
Financial	Operating profit	• Total revenue • Percentage increase year over year • Dollar costs • Percentage increase year over year • Taxation
	Key ratios	• Profit as a percentage of sales • Percentage return on assets • Percentage return on investments • Debt-to-equity ratio
	Key issues—inventory	• Percentage of inventory shrinkage • Amount in dollars that are obsolete/expired components
Operational	Administration	• Total overhead expense • Overhead as percentage of sales • Percentage on-time reporting
	Customer service	• Overhead expense as a percentage of sales • Order-entry cost per order • Number of calls handled • Cost per call handled
	Human resources	• Overhead expense as percentage of sales • Dollars per employee per annum • Benefit dollars cost • Benefit cost per employee • Recruitment cost per employee • Percentage of job offers accepted
Customer Measures	Product development	• Number of product proposals government approved • Artwork turnaround time • R and D response time
	Order processing	• Average time credit held • Credit release to stock allocation time • Stock allocation time to shipment
	Inventory	• Supplier lead time • Custom clearance time • Quality control release time
Soft Measures	Shortages	• Percentage shorted on orders • Amount short shipped (in dollars) • Percentage of orders missing delivery date • Number of items shorted
	Late shipments	• Percentage of order shipped late • Average delay time
	Delivery errors	• Percentage of orders incorrectly shipped • Cost of incorrect shipping
Employee Measures	Staff turnover	• Turnover rate • Average length of service • Absenteeism rate • Sick leave utilization rate • Number of requests for transfers
	Morale/camaraderie	• Number of social events • Number of sports events • Attendance at social events • Employee satisfaction index
	Employee surveys	• Communication • Leadership practices • Other issues

a high level of fear and apprehension in the company. Indeed the resistance was so great that certain preparatory employee survey and team-building work had to be done.

Five workshops were run over a 12-month period with the executive team and culminated in all employees across Canada being brought in to a half-day special event launch. The management team then took the message across Canada, with special events at each of the manufacturing and marketing locations. From start to finish the project took 18 months.

Who Is Using It Now?

The balanced scorecard concept started out as just that—a concept. But then, some larger companies evaluated the shortcomings of their business information. Some of the more progressive business leaders in Canada and the U.S. started using the balanced scorecard idea and refined it. These have included managers from American Express, Canadian Tire, Molson, Nynex, Texas Instruments, BC Rail, Rockwater, Apple Computer, Advanced Micro Devices and Best Foods—all companies that have sales greater than $50 million and that are often multinationals.

Three significant trends have allowed this concept to gain wider use and acceptance:

1. The power of computers has now made it possible to link operations locally, nationally and internationally.

2. Participative management, which encourages all to be involved in goal setting, came into vogue.

3. Quality is now being measured by everyone. And the faster employees have such statistical information, the quicker the response time when taking corrective action.

While the balanced scorecard is not perfect, it is a step in the right direction to help businesspeople make well-rounded and generally better business decisions. It is a helpful management tool for those executives who want to shape their company's management information system into something that is suitable for the Information Age.

Leveraging Intellect

JAMES BRIAN QUINN

PHILIP ANDERSON

SYDNEY FINKELSTEIN

What Is Intellect?

Webster's defines intellect as "knowing or understanding; the capacity for knowledge, for rational or highly developed use of intelligence." The intellect of an organization, in order of increasing importance, includes: (1) cognitive knowledge (or know what), (2) advanced skills (know how), (3) system understanding and trained intuition (know why), and (4) self-motivated creativity (care why).[1] Intellect clearly resides inside the firm's human brains. Elements of knowledge, skill and understanding can also exist in the organization's systems, databases, or operating technologies. If properly nurtured, intellect in each form is both highly leverageable and protectable.

Source: J. B. Quinn, P. A. Anderson, and S. Finkelstein, "Leveraging intellect," *Academy of Management Executive*, vol. 10 (1996), no. 3, pp. 7–27.

James Brian Quinn is emeritus professor of management at the Amos Tuck School, Dartmouth College and Leo Block Visiting Professor at the University of Denver. He has published extensively on corporate and national policy issues involving strategic planning, research and development management, the management of entrepreneurial organizations, and the impact of technology in services. His book, *Intelligent Enterprise,* was named Book of the Year in Business and Scholarship by the American Publishers Association and Book of the Year for Outstanding Contribution to Advancing Management Knowledge by the American Academy of Management.

Philip Anderson is an associate professor of business administration at the Amos Tuck School, Dartmouth College. His scholarly interests include organizational evolution, strategic management of technology, and the dynamics of the venture capital industry. His research has been published in the *Academy of Management Journal, Administrative Science Quarterly,* and other journals.

Sydney Finkelstein is an associate professor of business administration at the Amos Tuck School, Dartmouth College. He has conducted extensive research on strategic leadership, in particular on executive compensation and corporate governance. He has published in the *Academy of Management Journal, Administrative Science Quarterly, Harvard Business Review,* and *Strategic Management Journal*. He is co-author with Donald C. Hambrick of *Strategic Leadership: Top Executives and Their Effects on Organizations*.

[1] This structure was first published in an interview article, J. B. Quinn with A. Kantrow, *McKinsey Review,* Spring edition, 1995.

The value of a firm's intellect increases markedly as one moves up the intellectual scale from cognitive knowledge toward motivated creativity. Yet, in a strange and costly anomaly, most enterprises reverse this priority in their training and systems development expenditures, focusing virtually all their attention on basic (rather than advanced) skills development and little or none on systems, motivational, or creative skills. (See Chart 1). The result is a predictable mediocrity, and a failure to match training with value creation or profits.

Characteristics of Intellect

The best managed companies avoid this failure by exploiting certain critical characteristics of intellect at both the strategic and operational levels. These critical characteristics include the exponentiality of knowledge, the benefits of sharing, and the opportunities for expansion it offers.

Exponentiality of Knowledge

Properly stimulated, knowledge and intellect grow exponentially. All learning and experience curves have this characteristic.[2] As knowledge is captured or internalized, the available knowledge base itself becomes higher. Hence a constant percentage accretion to the base becomes exponential total growth. The strategy consequences are profound. Once a firm obtains a knowledge-based competitive edge, it becomes ever harder for competitors to catch up.[3] Because the firm is a leader, it can attract better talent than competitors. The best want to work with the best. These people can then perceive and solve more complex and interesting customer problems, make more profits as a result, and attract even more talented people to work on the next round of complexity. Driving and capturing individuals' exponential learning has been the key to strategic success for most intellectual enterprises, from Bell Labs and Intel to Microsoft, McKinsey, and the Mayo Clinic. For example:

- Microsoft, realizing that software design is a highly individualistic effort, interviews hundreds of candidates to find the few most suited

---

[2] For a thorough discussion of the learning curve literature, see J. M. Dutton, J. E. Butler, "The history of progress functions as a managerial technology," *Business History Review,* vol. 58, no. 2 (1984): 204–233.

[3] J. B. Quinn, *The Intelligent Enterprise* (New York. NY: The Free Press, 1992) develops the arguments for this in detail.

CHART I **Skills Value vs. Training Expenditures**

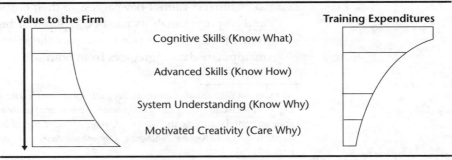

Value to the Firm **Training Expenditures**

Cognitive Skills (Know What)

Advanced Skills (Know How)

System Understanding (Know Why)

Motivated Creativity (Care Why)

to write its advanced operating systems. It then places its new members directly onto small (3-7 person) teams under experienced mentors to design complex new software systems at the frontier of user needs. Microsoft's culture drives everyone with the unstated expectation of 60-80 hour weeks on intensely competitive projects. The best commercial programmers seek out and stay with Microsoft largely because they believe that Microsoft will determine where the industry moves in the future and that they can share the excitement and rewards of being at that frontier. Each Microsoft success in turn builds the experience base and recruitment attractiveness for the next wave of challenges.

Benefits of Sharing

Knowledge is one of the few assets that grows most—also usually exponentially—when shared.[4] Communication theory states that a network's potential benefits grow exponentially as the nodes it can successfully interconnect expand numerically.[5] As one shares knowledge with other units, not only do those units gain information (linear growth), they share it with others and feed back questions, amplifications, and modifications that add further value for the original sender, creating exponential total growth. Proper leveraging through external knowledge bases—especially those of specialized firms, customers, and suppliers—can create even steeper exponentials. There are, however, some inherent risks and saturation potentials in this process. The choices about what knowledge is to be protected, what knowledge is to be shared, and how, are critical elements in intellectual strategies. For example:

• The core intellectual competency of many financial firms—like Fidelity, State Street Boston, and Aetna—lies in the human experts and the systems software that collect and analyze the data surrounding their investment specialties. Access to the internals of these centralized software systems is tightly limited to a few specialists working at headquarters. These HQ specialists leverage their own specialized analytical skills through close interactions with other financial specialists, "rocket scientist" modelers, and the unique access the firm has to massive transactions data. These companies then leverage their systems' outputs as broadly as possible through their extensive brokerage outlets, which in turn yield more information. Nevertheless, the structure of sharing must be carefully controlled. For security and competitive reasons, sales brokers cannot have access to their corporate system's analytics and corporate analysts must be kept out of brokers' individual customer files. Yet for maximum impact the system itself must capture and manipulate data aggregates from both sources. The managing of this

---

[4] An excellent discussion of group and organization-level learning as opposed to individual learning is contained in L. Argote, "Group and organizational learning curves: individual, system and environmental components," *British Journal of Social Psychology,* vol. 32 (1993): 31–51.

[5] E. M. Rogers, R. Agarwala-Rogers, *Communications in Organizations* (New York. NY: Free Press, 1976).

sharing is a major source of competitive edge as is its integration into the software and support systems of the firm.

Opportunities for Expansion

Unlike physical assets, intellect (a) increases in value with use, (b) tends to have underutilized capacity, (c) can be self-organizing, and (d) is greatly expandable under pressure.[6] How can a company exploit these characteristics? Arthur Andersen Worldwide (AAW) offers some interesting insights.

- Andersen attempts to electronically interlink more than 82,000 people in 360 offices in 76 countries. Its ANET, a T-l and frame relay network, connects 85 percent of Andersen's people through data, voice, and video interlinks. ANET allows AAW specialists—by posting problems on electronic bulletin boards and following up with visual and data contacts—to instantly self-organize around a customer's problem anywhere in the world. It thus taps into otherwise dormant capabilities, and vastly expands the energies and solution sets available to customers. The capacity to share in AAW's enormous variety of problems and solutions is enhanced through centrally-collected and carefully-indexed subject, customer, and resource files accessible directly via ANET or from CD-ROMs, distributed to all offices. These in turn expand the intellectual capabilities AAW field personnel have available to add value for future customers.

Effective leveraging of intellectual processes requires attention to (all opportunities for expansion. The techniques used for leveraging these resources closely resemble successful coaching.[7] The critical activities are: (1) recruiting and developing the right people; (2) stimulating these recruits to internalize the information knowledge, skills, and attitudes needed for success; (3) creating systematic technological and organizational structures that capture, focus, and leverage intellect to the greatest possible extent; and (4) demanding and rewarding top performance from all players. Much can be learned from how successful (and failing) practitioners have handled the leveraging of their intellectual resources. Our conclusions draw on an extensive literature search, hundreds of personal interviews, and numerous published case studies of the leading professional and innovative companies of the U.S., Europe, and Japan.[8]

---

[6] J. B. Quinn, *Intelligent Enterprise* (New York, NY: Free Press, 1992).

[7] Our discussion draws heavily from the literature on managing professionals. See for example D. H. Maister, *Managing the Professional Service Firm* (New York, NY: Maxwell Macmillan International, 1993) or J. A. Raelin, *The Clash of Cultures: Managers Managing Professionals* (Boston, MA: Harvard Business School Press, 1991). The best book of readings covering a broad range of issues in managing professionals is R. Katz (ed.), *Managing Professionals in Innovative Organizations: A Collection of Readings* (Cambridge, MA: Ballinger, 1988).

[8] Made in connection with National Academy of Engineering, *Technology in Services: Policies for Growth, Trade and Employment* (Washington, DC: National Academy Press, 1988); and Computer Science and Telecommunications Board, National Research Council, *Information Technology in the Service Society* (Washington, DC: National Academy Press, 1994).

Professional Intellect

There are important differences between professional and creative intellect. Professionals are an important source of intellect for most organizations, but little has been written about managing professionals.[9] What characterizes the management of such professionals?

Perfection, Not Creativity

While no precise delineation applies in all cases, most of a typical professional's activity is directed at perfection, not creativity. The true professional commands a complete body of knowledge—a discipline—and updates that knowledge constantly.[10] In most cases, the customer wants the knowledge delivered reliably with the most advanced skill available. Although there is an occasional call for creativity, the preponderance of work in actuarial units, dentistry, hospitals, accounting units, opera companies, universities, law firms, aircraft operations, or equipment maintenance requires the repeated use of highly developed skills on relatively similar, although complex, problems. People rarely want their surgeons, accountants, airline pilots, maintenance personnel, or nuclear plant operators to be very creative, except in emergencies. While managers clearly must prepare their professionals for these special emergency circumstances, the bulk of attention needs to be on delivering consistent, high quality intellectual output. What are the critical factors?

- Hyper-selection. The leverage of intellect is so great that a few top flight professionals can create a successful organization or make a lesser one billow. Marvin Bower created McKinsey & Co.; Robert Noyce and Gordon Moore spawned Intel; William Gates and Robert Allen built Microsoft; Herb Boyer and Robert Swanson made Genentech; Einstein enhanced Princeton's Institute of Advanced Studies; and so on. The cultivation of extraordinary talent is thus the first critical prerequisite for building intellectual capital. McKinsey long focused on only the top one percent of graduates from the top five business schools, and screened heavily from these. Microsoft typically interviews hundreds of highly recommended people for each key software designer hired, and tests not just their cognitive knowledge but their capacity to think under high pressure. Similarly, experienced venture capitalists spend as much time on relentlessly pursuing and selecting top people as on the quantitative aspects of projects.

- Intense training, mentoring, and peer pressure literally force professionals to the top of their knowledge ziggurat. The best students go to the most demanding schools. The top graduate schools—whether in

---

[9] H. Mintzberg, "The professional bureaucracy," in *Mintzberg on Management: Inside Our Strange World of Organizations* (New York, NY: The Free Press, 1984).

[10] D. Schon, *The Reflective Practitioner: How Professionals Think in Action* (New York. NY: Basic Books, 1983).

law, business, engineering, science, or medicine—further re-select and drive these students with greater challenges and with 100 hour work weeks. Upon graduation the best of the graduates go back to even more intense boot camps in medical internships, law associate programs, or other demanding training situations. The result is that the best professionals drive themselves up a steep learning curve. People who go through these experiences quickly move beyond those in less demanding programs, becoming noticeably more capable—and valuable—than those facing lesser challenges. The best programs stimulate professional trainees' growth with constantly heightened (preferably customer induced) complexity, thoroughly planned mentoring, high rewards for performance, and strong stimuli to understand and advance their professional disciplines. The great intellectual organizations all seem to develop deeply ingrained cultures around these points.

- Constantly increasing challenges. Intellect grows most when challenged. Hence, heavy internal competition and constant performance appraisal are common in well run professional shops. Leaders tend to be demanding, visionary, and intolerant of half efforts.[11] At Bell Labs, 90 percent of carefully selected basic researchers moved on (voluntarily or through so-called stimulated changes) within seven years. Microsoft tries to force out the lowest performing five percent of its highly screened talent each year.

    And at Andersen Consulting, only one in ten associates ever makes it to partnership. Leaders often set almost impossible stretch goals, as did HP's Bill Hewlett (improve performance by 50 percent), Intel's Gordon Moore (double the componentry per chip each year), or Motorola's Robert Galvin (six sigma quality). Top professionals, having survived the rigors of their training, relish competition and want to know that they have excelled against peers. The best organizations constantly challenge their young professionals to perform beyond the comfort of catalogued book knowledge, learned models, and controlled laboratory environments. They relentlessly encourage associates to deal with the more complex intellectual realms of live customers, real operating systems, and highly differentiated external environments and cultural differences. They insist on mentoring by those nearest the top of their fields. And they reward associates for learned competencies. Mediocre organizations do not.

- Managing an elite. Each profession tends to regard itself as an elite. Members look to their profession and to their peers to determine codes for behavior and acceptable performance standards.[12] They often disdain the values and evaluations of those outside their discipline. This is a source of many problems since professionals tend to surround themselves with people having similar backgrounds and values. Unless

[11] See, for example, J. M. Kouzes and B. Z. Posner, *The Leadership Challenge* (San Francisco. CA: Jossey-Bass, 1995).

[12] D. Schon, op. cit., 1983.

consciously fractured, these discipline-based cocoons quickly become inward-looking bureaucracies, resistant to change, and detached from customers. Many professionals are reluctant to share knowledge without powerful inducements. Even then the different values of other groups become points of conflict. Hence, in manufacturing, researchers disdain product designers (who don't understand the physics), who disdain engineers (who aren't concerned with artistry and aesthetics), who disdain production personnel ("who just bang out stuff"), who disdain marketers ("who don't really understand the product's complexities"), who all disdain accountants ("who are only bean counters"). The same thing happens among the specialties of medicine, law, education, and so on.

These professional values—and the elitism they inculcate if not consciously ameliorated—cause contentiousness in professional organizations. Many professionals are reluctant to subordinate themselves to others, or to support organizational goals not completely congruent with their special viewpoint. This is why most professional firms operate as partnerships and not hierarchies, and why it is so hard for them to adopt a distinctive strategy. It is also why successful enterprises use multipoint cultivation—(1) by peers for professionalism, (2) by customers for relevance, and (3) by enterprise norms for net value—to limit the bias induced by professional orientations. Later sections illustrate how successful organizations accomplish this.

Few Scale Economies?

Conventional wisdom has long held that there are few scale economies—other than obtaining a critical mass for interactions—in professional activities.[13] A pilot can handle only one aircraft; a great chef can cook only so many different dishes at once; a top researcher can conduct only so many unique experiments; a doctor can diagnose only one patient's illness at a time, and so on. In such situations, adding professionals simply multiplies costs at the same rate as outputs.

In fact, for years, growing an intellectual organization actually seemed to involve diseconomies of scale. Most often, increasing size brought even greater growth in the bureaucracies coordinating, monitoring, or supporting the professionals.[14] Universities, hospitals, personnel, accounting groups, and consultancies seemed to suffer alike. The only ways firms found to create leverage were to push their people through more intense training or work schedules than competitors or to increase the number of associates supporting each professional. This even became the accepted meaning of the term *leverage* in the legal, accounting and consulting fields.

---

[13] G. Loveman, "An assessment of the productivity impact of information technologies," *Management in the 1990s Program,* 88-054 (Cambridge, MA: MIT, July 1988); W. Baumol, S. Blackman, E. Wolff, *Productivity and American Leadership: The Long View* (Cambridge, MA: MIT Press, 1989).

[14] S. Roach, "Services under siege: the restructuring imperative?" *Harvard Business Review,* September–October 1991.

But new technologies and management approaches now enable firms to capture, develop, and leverage intellectual resources. The keys are: (1) organizations and technology systems designed around intellectual flows rather than command and control concepts, (2) performance measurements and incentive systems that reward managers for developing intellectual assets and customer value—and not just for producing current profits and using physical assets more efficiently. Companies as diverse as Arthur Andersen, Sony, AT&T, Merck, Scandia, State Street Bank, and Microsoft have found ways to do this.

■ Core Intellectual Competencies

The crux of leveraging intellect is to focus on what creates uniquely high value for customers. Conceptually, this means disaggregating corporate staff activities and the value chain into manageable intellectual clusters of intellectually-based service activities (See Chart 2). Such activities can either be performed internally or outsourced. For maximum leverage, a company should concentrate its own resources and executive time on those few activities (most desired by customers) where it can perform at best-in-world levels.[15] Managers need to look behind their products to identify those intellectually-based skills, knowledge bases, or systems that enable the firm to produce higher value outputs per unit cost than its competitors. With rare exceptions, these resources (and not products or physical assets) are what create unique value for customers. By developing these unique core competencies in depth as a secure strategic block between its suppliers and its customers, the company can more aggressively outsource or enter alliances with the world's most effective external suppliers to leverage its fiscal and intellectual resources in other areas.[16]

External Leveraging

Through core competency with outsourcing strategies, managers can serve customers substantially better, simultaneously decreasing risk and size while increasing flexibility. Many entrepreneurial ventures like Apple Computer, Sony, Silicon Graphics, Nike, or Novellus have started in highly-concentrated and heavily-outsourced fashion, leveraging their fiscal capital by factors of three or more—and their intellectual capital by 10s to 100s—as compared with integrated companies. If a company is not best-in-world at an activity (including all external and internal transaction costs involved) it gives up competitive edge by performing that activity in-house. Today, most venture capitalists realize they can obtain bank returns only on fixed assets (unless these embody the company's core competencies). They seek to invest in and leverage the unique intellectual resources of a company, and not to undertake the investments and risks of activities others could perform better. Larger companies—from Continental Bank and Wal-Mart to MCI, Honda, and Boeing—operate in this fashion too.

---

[15] J. Quinn, T. Doorley. P. Paquette, "Technology in services: rethinking strategic focus," *Sloan Management Review,* Winter 1990, was the first published expression of this theme.
[16] J. Quinn, R. Hilmer, "Strategic outsourcing," *Sloan Management Review,* Summer 1994, develops this argument in depth.

- When interviewed, MCI had only 1000 full-time technical people internally, but had 20,000 professionals working for it full time on vendor promises. MCI did not have to invest in facilities, overhead, and benefits costs for these people on a permanent basis and many outside professionals were said to be higher quality than those MCI could hire internally. These specialized suppliers could afford to invest in elaborate facilities to attract top talent to work with their firms on the frontiers of their particular specialties. Besides outsourcing software, construction, and system maintenance, MCI also actively sought out and exploited the innovations of thousands of small firms to attach to its core software and electronic hardware, thus leveraging its own innovative capabilities by hundreds of times.

Once strategists define each activity in their value chain or staff services as an intellectually-based service, managers often see many new opportunities to refocus the company's strategic commitments, restructure internal operations, or create external coalitions to leverage their fiscal and intellectual resources.[17]

[17] J. Quinn, T. Doorley, P. Paquette, "Beyond products: services based strategies," *Harvard Business Review,* developed this concept in depth, as did J. Quinn, *Intelligent Enterprise,* op. cit., 1992.

CHART 2

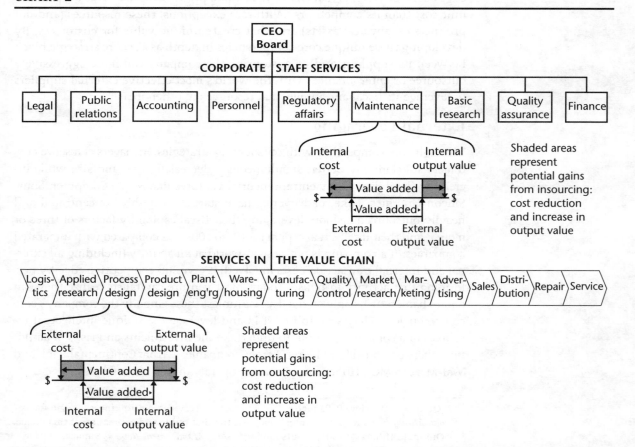

Generally, there are many external providers who, by specializing, can provide greater depth in a specific service and produce it with greater quality or lower cost than the company's internal department possibly could. No company can hope to be better than all outside specialists in all elements of its value chain. And new technologies and management systems have dramatically shifted the balance between what it pays to outsource and what the company can effectively produce internally. Strategic outsourcing of services has become a major means for leveraging intellect.

In today's hypercompetitive[18] climate, such core competency with outsourcing strategies let companies be simultaneously the lowest cost, broadest line, most flexible, and most highly differentiated producer in their markets. No other strategy supports: (a) efficiency (through focus), (b) innovative flexibility (through multiple sourcing), and (c) stability (through market diversity) to the same extent. Many enterprises in financial services (State Street Bank or Continental Bank), retailing (L. L. Bean or Toys "R" Us), or communications, entertainment, and lodging services (Paramount, Turner, or Marriott) operate in this fashion. So do industrial giants like the oil majors, Boeing, Sony, or 3M. Integrated oil companies often outsource many intellectually-based service elements in their value chains to great advantage. (See Chart 3). For example:

- Boeing outsources many parts of its commercial airliners to those who have greater skills in specialized areas. It produces internally mainly those portions of the craft that contain the critical flight control and power plant interfaces. It concentrates its own intellectual capabilities on understanding aircraft technologies and its customers' needs. Boeing focuses its operations on the design, logistics, and flexible assembly processes necessary to coordinate and control the quality and performance of the aircraft.

- 3M's extensive growth has rested on its R&D skills in four related historic technologies: abrasives, adhesives, coating-bondings, and non-woven technologies. In each it has developed knowledge bases and skill depths exceeding those of its major competitors. When combined with two other core intellectual competencies—its remarkable entrepreneurial-innovation system and its strong, broad-based marketing distribution system—these historic technologies have allowed 3M to create and support over 50,000 products for a variety of markets, to maintain a flexible innovative culture, and to sustain continuous growth for six to seven decades.

Organizing Around Intellect

The exploitation of intellectually-based strategies calls for new organization concepts. In the past, in order to enhance efficiencies, most companies formed their organizations around product clusters, process investments, geographical

---

[18] R. D'Aveni, *Hypercompetition* (New York, NY: Free Press, 1994).

needs, or specialized management functions.[19] These clearly optimized the capacity of power holders to direct and control the organization. However, rapidly changing customer demands and increasingly independent professionals require entirely new structures. The extended capabilities of new technologies now enable design and management of much more highly disaggregated organizations, capable of responding to the needs of both customers and professionals. The term network organizations has been widely used to embrace a variety of these new forms, varying from flat, to horizontal matrix, to alliance, to cross-disciplinary team, to holding-company structures that merely finance a number of unrelated divisions self-coordinating on an ad-hoc basis.[20] This categorization reveals little about how the various forms differ, when to use them, or how to manage them for maximum effect.

The main function of organization in today's hypercompetitive environment is to develop and deploy—i.e. attract, harness, leverage, and disseminate—intellect effectively. Each of the truly new organization forms does this in its own way, and should be used only for those particular purposes it handles best. Not only is no one form a panacea, many different forms can be used to advantage within the same company. Because they are useful for certain purposes, hierarchies will doubtless continue in many situations. But we expect much greater use of four other basic organizational forms that leverage professional intellect uniquely well. These are the infinitely flat, inverted, spider's web, and starburst forms. Table 1 summarizes the primary differences among these organization forms and their utility in leveraging intellect. The key variables in choosing among the new forms are:

1. *Locus of intellect.* Where the deep knowledge of a firm's particular core competencies primarily lies

2. *Locus of customization.* Where intellect is converted to novel solutions

3. *Direction of intellectual flow.* The primary direction(s) in which value-added knowledge flows

4. *Method of leverage.* How the organization leverages intellect

All the forms tend to push responsibility outward to the point at which the company contacts the customer. All tend to flatten the organization and to remove layers of hierarchy. All seek faster, more responsive action to deal with the customization and personalization that an affluent and complex marketplace demands. All require breaking away from traditional thinking about lines of command, one-person-one-boss structures, the center as a directing force, and management of physical assets as keys to success. But each differs substantially in its purposes and management. And each requires very

---

[19] One of the best discussions of organizational design is by J. R. Galbraith, *Designing Complex Organizations* (Reading, MA: Addison-Wesley, 1973). A more recent analysis, J. R. Galbraith, *Designing Organizations: An Executive Briefing on Strategy, Structure, and Process* (San Francisco, CA: Jossey-Bass, 1995) extends this earlier work by focusing on new organizational forms.

[20] For a cogent discussion of the different ways the term network is used, see the introduction to N. Nohria, R. G. Eccles, *Networks and Organizations* (Boston, MA: Harvard Business School Press, 1992).

CHART 3   Value Chain—"Integrated" Oil Companies

Finding and Development

Research for techniques / Structure scanning / Seismic studies / Experimental drilling / Developmental drilling / Infastructure development / Transport

Processing and Distribution

Plant engr. / Pre-refining / Refining / Trading / Mixing blending / Transportation out / Marketing / Distribution / Service

Specialized Support

Legal / Real estate mgt. / Corporate intelligence / Logistics integration / Taxes / Finance / Personnel training / Govt. relations / Long-range planning / Accounting

different nurturing, balancing, and support systems to achieve its performance goals.

Infinitely Flat Organizations

In infinitely flat organizations—so called because there is no inherent limit to their span—the primary locus of intellect is at the center, e.g. the operations knowledge of a fast-food franchising organization or the data analysis capability at the center of a brokerage firm. The nodes of customer contact are the locus of customization. Intellect flows primarily one way, from the center to the nodes. The leverage is arithmetic: the amount of leverage equals the value of the knowledge times the number of nodes using it. Single centers in such organizations presently can coordinate anywhere from 20 to 18,000 individual nodes. (See Chart 4). Common examples include highly dispersed fast-food, brokerage, shipping, mail order, or airline flight operations.

Several other characteristics are also important. The nodes themselves rarely communicate with each other, operating quite independently. The center rarely needs to give direct orders to the line organization. Instead, it is an information source, a communications coordinator, and a reference desk for unusual inquiries. Lower organizational levels generally connect into the center to obtain information to improve their performance, rather than to get instructions or

TABLE 1   Outline of Four Forms of Organizing

	Infinitely Flat	Inverted	Spider's Web	Starburst
Definition of node	Individual	Individual	Individual	Business units
Locus of intellect	Center	Nodes	Nodes	Center and nodes
Locus of customization	Nodes	Nodes	Project	Center and nodes
Direction of flow	Center to nodes	Nodes to center	Node to node	Center to nodes
Method of leverage	Multiplicative	Distributive	Exponential	Additive
Examples	Brokerage firms, aircraft operations	Hospitals, construction engineering	Internet, SABRE	Major movie studios, mutual fund groups

specific guidance. Most operating rules are programmed into the system and changed automatically by software. Many operations may even be monitored electronically.

- For example, each of Merrill Lynch's more than 500 domestic brokerage offices connects directly into the parent's central information office to satisfy the bulk of its information and analytic needs. Although regional marketing structures exist, business is conducted as if each of Merrill Lynch's more than 18,000 branch-office contact people reported directly to headquarters, with their only personal oversight being at the local level. Technology permits the overall company to capture data with the full power and scale economies available only to a major enterprise. Yet local brokers manage their own small units and accounts as independently as if they alone provided the total service on a local basis.

Infinitely flat organizations operate best when the activity at the node can be broken down and measured to the level of its minimum repeatable transaction elements (as for example, the cooking and operating details in fast-food chains or the basic components of financial transactions in brokerage operations). Control can be exercised at the most detailed level, yet, if desired, systems can eliminate most of the routine in jobs, free up employees for more personalized or skilled work, and allow tasks to be very decentralized, individually challenging, and rewarding.[21] Under proper circumstances, the electronic systems of such organizations capture the experience curve of the entire enterprise, allowing less trained people quickly to achieve performance levels ordinarily associated with much more experienced personnel. Well designed systems simultaneously offer both highest responsiveness and maximum efficiency. Such has been their effect in firms like Fidelity Securities, Federal Express, Wal-Mart, or Domino's Pizza.

Infinitely flat organizations present certain inherent management problems. Without hierarchy, lower level personnel wonder how to advance in a career path.[22] Traditional job evaluation ("Hay Point") systems break down, and new compensation systems based upon individual performance become imperative. Reward systems need to include a great variety of titles, intangible performance measurements and rewards, and constant training and updating by

---

[21] For an extended discussion of the relationship between and work and information technology, see S. Zuboff, *In the Age of the Smart Machine: The Future of Work and Power* (New York, NY: Basic Books, 1988).

[22] In fact, this is one of the classic defenses of bureaucracy. See for example C. Perrow, *Complex Organizations: A Critical Essay* (Glenview, IL: Scott Foresman, 1979).

CHART 4   **Infinitely Flat Organizations**

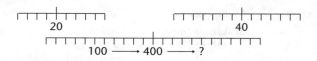

TABLE 2   How Different Organizing Forms Develop Intellect

Type of Intellect	Infinitely Flat	Inverted	Starburst	Spider's Web
Cognitive (know-what)	Deep knowledge and information at center	Primary intellect at nodes, support services from center	Depth at center (technical) and (markets) at the nodes	Dispersed, brought together for projects
Advanced skill (know-how)	Programmed into systems	Professionalized skills informally transferred node to node	Transferred from center to node, then node to mode via the core	Latent until a project assembles a skill collection
Systems knowledge (know-why)	Systems experts at the center. Customer knowledge at the nodes	Systems and customer expertise at the nodes	Split: between central technical competency at the core, systematic market knowledge at nodes	Discovered in interaction or created via search enabled by the network
Motivated creativity (care-why)	Frees employees from routine for more skilled work	Great professional autonomy	Entrepreneurial incentives	Personal interest, leveraged through active interdependence stimulation

advisory teams from the central office.[23] There is a tendency for systems to rigidify with time if companies continue use of the same measurement and control systems. Consequently, external scanning systems, customer sampling, or personal observation systems must supplement the structured hard information linkages of these very flat organizations. Note that this form of organizing is neither horizontal nor a network in the true sense. It is hierarchical, but with only one level of hierarchy.

The Inverted Organization

In the inverted form, the major locus of *both* corporate intellect and customization is at the nodes contacting customers, not at the center. Hospitals or medical clinics, therapeutic care-giving units, or consulting-engineering firms provide typical examples. The nodes tend to be highly professional and self-sufficient. Accordingly, there is no need for direct linkage between the nodes. When critical know-how diffuses, it usually does so informally from node to node or formally from node to center—the opposite of the infinitely flat organization. The leverage of this form is distributive, i.e. the organization efficiently distributes logistics, analysis, or administrative support to the nodes. But it does not give orders to the nodes.

In inverted organizations, the line hierarchy becomes a support structure, not intervening except in extreme emergencies—as might the CEO of a hospital or the chief pilot of an airline in crisis situations. (See Chart 5.) The function

---

of line managers becomes bottleneck breaking, culture development, consulting upon request, expediting resource movements, and providing service economies of scale. Hierarchy may exist within some groups because members of this support structure must ensure consistency in the application of specialized knowledge (like government regulations or accounting rules) that the organization needs. Generally, however, what was line management now performs essentially staff activities.

- A well known example of an inverted organization was SAS after Tan Carlzon became CEO. He utilized the concept of inverting to empower SAS's contact people and to bypass heavily entrenched bureaucracies. Another example is NovaCare, the largest provider of rehabilitation care in the U.S. With its central resource—well trained physical, occupational, and speech therapists—in short supply, NovaCare, through the NovaNet, provides the business infrastructure for over 5,000 therapists, arranging and managing contracts with over 2,000 nursing homes and care giving facilities in 40 states, handling accounting and credit activities, providing training updates, and stabilizing and enhancing therapists' earnings. However, the key to performance is the *therapists'* knowledge and their capacity to deliver this individually to patients.

The inverted organization works well (1) when servicing the customer at the point of contact is the most important activity in the enterprise, and (2) when the person at the point of contact has more information about the individual customer's problem and its potential solutions than anyone else. Experience suggests that because they present unique problems, inverted organizations should be used sparingly, and not as gimmicks to improve empowerment. While seeming to diminish line authority, intermediate line members' roles often increase in importance as they are freed from their traditional information-passing routines and perform more influential activities—such as strategic analysis, resource building, or public policy participation.

The inverted organization poses certain unique challenges. The apparent loss of formal authority can be very traumatic for former line managers.[24] Given acknowledged formal power, contact people may tend to act ever more like specialists with strictly professional outlooks, and to resist any set of

---

[24] For example, see W. G. Bennis, *Why Leaders Can't Lead: The Unconscious Conspiracy Continues* (San Francisco, CA: Jossey-Bass Publishers, 1989).

CHART 5   **The Inverted Organization**

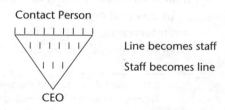

Contact Person

Line becomes staff

Staff becomes line

CEO

organization rules or business norms.[25] Given their predilections, contact people often don't stay current with details about the firm's own complex internal systems. And their empowerment without adequate controls can be extremely dangerous. A classic example is the rapid decline of People Express, which enjoyed highly empowered and motivated point people, but lacked the systems or computer infrastructures to let them self-coordinate as the organization grew.

A frequent cause of failure in both the inverted and the infinitely flat modes is inadequate segmentation and dissemination of information into detailed elements that monitor and support individuals' actions at the nodes.[26] Many such organizations fail because they attempt to make a transition from their more traditional hierarchies to the new forms without thoroughly overhauling their measurement and support systems. In our recent study of over 100 such situations in major service organizations, less than 20 percent had changed their performance measurement systems significantly; and only about five percent had yet changed their reward systems.[27] The complications were predictable. People continued to perform against traditional norms, and at a bureaucratic pace.

The Starburst

Another highly leverageable form, the starburst, serves well when there is very specialized and valuable intellect at both the nodes and the center. Starbursts are common in creative organizations that constantly peel off more permanent, but separate, units from their core competencies. (See Chart 6.) These spin-offs remain partially or wholly owned by the parent, usually can raise external resources independently, and are controlled primarily by market mechanisms. Examples of different forms and ownership relationships include: movie studios, mutual fund groups or venture capitalists, among service firms, and Thermoelectron, TCG, or Nypro, among industrials.

In operation, the center retains deep knowledge of some common knowledge base (e.g. specialized plastic molding technology for Nypro, managing no-load funds for Vanguard, or risk-taking and resource-assembly skills for movie studios). Unlike holding companies, starbursts are built around some central core of intellectual competency. They are not merely banks that collect and disseminate funds. The nodes—essentially separate permanent business units, not individuals or temporary clusters—have continuing relationships with given marketplaces and are the locus of important, specialized market or production knowledge. The nodes may in time spin out further enterprises from their core. The flow of intellect is typically from the center toward the outer nodes. The organization rarely transfers knowledge from one node laterally to another, but feeds back to the core specialized information that other nodes may find useful (without direct competition among their marketplaces). The nodes both

---

[25] For a managerial discussion of coping with such problems, see H. Donovan, "Managing your intellectuals," *Fortune,* October 23, 1989, pp. 177–80.

[26] Quinn, *Intelligent Enterprise,* op. cit.

[27] National Research Council, op. cit., 1994.

CHART 6   The Starburst Organization

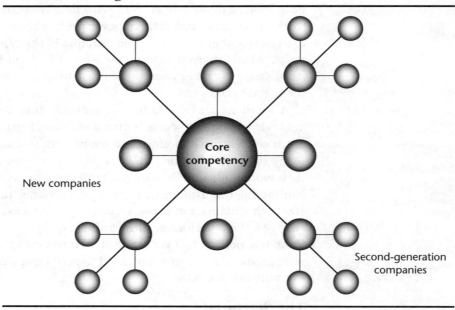

multiply the number of outlets using the firm's core competency and leverage it (a) through their access to specialized market expertise, and (b) through the independent relationships and external financing they can generate as separated entities.

Starburst organizations work well when the core embodies an expensive or complex set of competencies and houses a few knowledgeable risk takers who realize they cannot micro-manage the diverse entities at the nodes. They work well in very ambiguous environments where it is difficult to estimate outcomes without undertaking a specific market test. Usually they occur in environments where entrepreneurship—not merely flexible response—is critical. To be effective, the nodes require the economies of scale and new opportunity spin-offs that only a large, specialized, knowledge base can provide. The center usually maintains and renews its capacities to develop these opportunities by charging the market units a fee or taking a share of their equity. In addition to maintaining the core competency, the corporate center generally manages the culture, sets broad priorities, selects key people, and raises resources more efficiently than could the nodes. Unlike conglomerates, starbursts maintain some cohesive, constantly renewed, and critical intellectual competencies at their center.

The classic problem of this organizational form is that managements often lose faith in their freestanding spin-offs. After some time, they try to consolidate functions in the name of efficiency or economies of scale—as some movie studios, HP, TI, and 3M did to their regret—and recover only by reversing such policies. Starbursts also encounter problems if their divisions move into heavy investment industries, or into capital-intensive mass production activities where one unit's needs can overwhelm the capacity of the core—as HP's computer division overwhelmed its test equipment groups. In most starburst environments, the nodes are so different that even sophisticated computer systems cannot provide or coordinate all the information needed to run these firms from the center. Rather than try, managers must either live with quasi-market control or spin-off the subsidiary entirely. Starbursts tend to work extremely well for growth by innovating smaller scale, discrete product or service lines positioned in diverse marketplaces.

The Spider's Web

The spider's web form is a true network. The term spider's web avoids confusion with other more network-like forms, particularly those that are more akin to holding companies or matrix organizations. In the spider's web there is often no intervening hierarchy or order-giving center among the nodes. In fact, it may be hard to define where the center is. The locus of intellect is highly dispersed, residing largely at the contact nodes (as in the inverted organization). However, the point of customization is a project or problem that requires the nodes to interact intimately or to seek others who happen to have the knowledge or special capabilities that a particular problem requires.

The purest example of a spider's web is the Internet, which is managed by no one. Common operating examples include most open markets, securities exchanges, library consortia, diagnostic teams, research, or political action groups.

The organization's intellect is essentially latent and under-utilized until a project forces it to materialize through connections people make with one another. Information linkages are quite complex; intellect flows from many nodes to many others. Nodes typically collaborate only temporarily in delivering a specific service or solution in project form to a particular customer. The intellectual leverage is exponential. Even with a modest number of collaborating nodes (eight to 10), the number of interconnections and the leverage of knowledge capabilities multiplies by hundreds of times. (See Chart 7.)

Individual nodes may operate quite independently, when it is not essential to tap the knowledge of other sources to solve a problem efficiently. On a given project, there may or may not be a single authority center. Often decisions will merely occur through informal processes if the parties agree. Occasionally, however, the various nodes may need to operate in such a highly coordinated fashion that they delegate temporary authority to a project leader—as when widely dispersed researchers present a contract proposal or an investment banking consortium services a multinational client.

The spider's web form has existed for centuries (among universities and scientists, or within trading groups), but was overlooked in the mass production era, which sought the greater stability, predictability, and control that military or clerical hierarchies seemed to offer. In today's highly competitive environments it offers unique advantages because it can simultaneously support high specialization, multiple geographic locations, and a disciplined focus on a single problem or customer set.[28] It is particularly useful in situations

---

[28] H. Mintzberg, A. McHugh, "Strategy formulation in adhocracy," *Administrative Science Quarterly,* June 1985.

CHART 7   Spider's Web Organizations

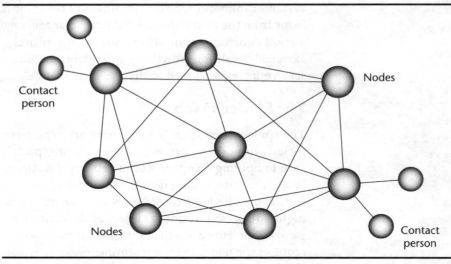

where problem sites are very dispersed and radically different specialties need to be tapped. Often no one person in a given organization knows exactly what the problem's dimensions are, where issues may be located, or who may have potential solutions. The spider's web form releases the imaginations of many different searchers in diverse locations, multiplies the numbers of possible opportunity encounters, and encourages the formation of entirely new solutions from a variety of disciplines.[29]

While it is usually effective for problem finding and analysis, a spider's web presents important challenges when used for decision making. Dawdling is common, as nodes refine their specialist solutions instead of solving the complete problem together. Assigning credit for intellectual contributions is difficult, and cross-competition among nodes can inhibit the sharing necessary in such networks. Extreme overload can emerge as networks become jammed with trivia. Significant changes at both the network and local levels are usually essential to make a spider's web effective in professional situations. The first change is to create a culture for communication and willing sharing. How groups communicate and what they are willing to communicate are as important as the knowledge they have. Overcoming the natural reluctance of professionals to share their most precious asset, knowledge, usually presents some common, and difficult, challenges. One enterprise exemplifies many patterns:

- Arthur Andersen Worldwide (AAW) found that effective use of its ANET required major practice shifts. Despite the large sums it initially spent on hardware, travel, and professional training to encourage utilization of the network, results were disappointing. Major changes in incentives and culture were required. To stimulate wider use of the system, senior partners deliberately posted questions into

---

[29] An interesting discussion of cross-functional synergy is contained in M. Jelinek, C. B. Schoonhoven, *The Innovation Marathon: Lessons from High Technology Firms* (Oxford, UK: Basil Blackwell, 1990).

employees' e-mail files each morning "to be answered by 10 o'clock" and followed up on queries in their own units. Most importantly, participation on ANET began to be considered in all compensation and promotion reviews. Until these and other supporting structural changes achieved cultural modifications, ANET—despite its technological elegance—was less than successful.

Because a spider's web is so dependent on individual goals and behavior, there is no best way to manage one except to stimulate a sense of interdependency and identity with the problem at hand. Shared interest of participants, shared value systems, and mutual personal gains for members are, of course, the essential starting points for any network relationship. However, research suggests that effective network managers generally: (1) force team overlaps in order to increase learning and shared information, (2) purposely keep hierarchical relations ill-defined, (3) constantly update and reinforce project goals, (4) avoid over-elaborate rules for allocating profits to individual nodes, (5) develop continuous mechanisms for updating information about the external environment (e.g. tax code changes, customer needs, or scientific results), (6) involve both clients and peers in performance evaluations, and (7) provide node members with personal and team rewards for participation.[30] These active management interactions are usually needed to avoid the most common failures and frustrations. The other key leverage factor, technology, requires special attention.

Integrating Diverse Forms

Special technology structures are required to support each organizational form. If they are properly designed, they will also enable integration of forms across the entire company. We expect most enterprises to require a mixture, not just a single form, of these basic building blocks, combined with more traditional hierarchical structures. Integrating and leveraging diverse forms within the same firm is very complex.[31] The critical non-organizational element in the process is software. The key is to develop a software framework that can capture, mix, match, and manipulate the smallest replicable units of tasks, customized data, and transactions. When information and measurement systems are developed around these micro-units, a properly designed technology structure can enable both maximum flexibility and lowest cost for the firm and its customers. In today's hypercompetitive environment these are essentials for success.

The Smallest Replicable Level

In earlier years, the smallest manageable unit of measurement for organizations and data seemed to be an individual store, office, or franchise location.

---

[30] E. Giesler, A. Rubenstein, "How do banks evaluate their information technology," *Bank Administration,* November, 1988; S. Harris and J. Katz, "Organization performance and information technology investment in the insurance industry," *Organization Science,* vol. 2 (1991): 263–296.

[31] P. R. Lawrence, J. W. Lorsch. *Organization and Environment: Managing Differentiation and Integration* (Homewood, IL: Richard D. Irwin, 1969).

Later, as volume increased, it often became possible for a parent corporation to manage and measure critical performance variables at individual departmental, sales counter, activity, or stock-keeping-unit (SKU) levels. Then the successful formula approaches of McDonald's, Pizza Hut, H & R Block, and insurance companies pushed the repeatability unit to even smaller micro management levels, such as cooking processes, detailed work schedules, maintenance cycles, accounting transactions, and document phrases. Proper management around these units permits franchisees, agents, and headquarters to continuously guarantee quality and desired service levels and to make corrections within minutes when something goes wrong.

In banking, publishing, communications, structural design, entertainment, or medical research, it has become possible to disaggregate the critical units of service production into digitized sequences, electronic packets, data blocks, or bytes of information that can be endlessly combined or manipulated for new effects and to satisfy individual customer and operating needs. These micro units permit the highest possible degrees of segmentation, strategic fine-tuning, value-added, and customer satisfaction at the lowest cost.[32] The larger the organization, the more refined are these replicability units, and the greater their leverage for creating value-added.

Systems that capture and leverage such data from the outset can build up an information base that provides an insurmountable edge. By constantly updating and analyzing data patterns from these detailed sources, successful IT systems automatically capture the highest level of experience available within the enterprise.[33] Effective dissemination of data throughout the firm allows inexperienced people to vault over normal learning curve delays and enables customer contact people to provide greater quality, customization, personalization, and value-added. Wages can be higher and managers and workers can concentrate on the more conceptual, personalized, and human tasks that provide greater satisfaction for both employers and customers. Properly collecting and distributing such information also provides the basis for integrated lateral coordination among highly diverse organization forms. For example:

- American Airlines' well-known SABRE and its associated operating systems are interlinked to provide consistent data for the airline's very different reservation service (spider's web), flight operations (infinitely flat), financial controls (conservative bureaucratic), ground operations and maintenance (decentralized bureaucratic), personnel training (specialized functional), and other operating modes. The organization structure, operating style, and culture within each unit can remain unique and appropriate to its tasks. Yet the software system ensures coordination among the units, minimizes costs, and ensures that desired service levels and consistency are delivered to customers.

---

[32] For example, see G. Gilder, *Microcosm: The Quantum Revolution in Economics and Technology* (New York, NY: Simon and Schuster, 1989).

[33] For an extended discussion of how IT systems capture experience, see T. J. Allen, M. S. Scott Morton, *Information Technology and the Corporation of the 1990s: Research Studies* (New York, NY: Oxford University Press, 1994).

- Similarly, NovaCare (described above) keeps track of the activities of its 5,000 therapists in 15 minute units of detail. These units provide the basis for scheduling, compensation, billing, and follow-up on all therapies. They enable NovaCare to ensure that all its customers (patients, nursing homes, hospitals, hospital directors, doctors, nursing directors, payers, and regulating bodies) are properly served, charged, or compensated. The system serves a variety of centralized functional (accounting), geographical hierarchical (hospital), inverted (therapy), and spider's web (professional knowledge exchange) structures. Although it collects information in immense detail, the system has unburdened caregivers (who hated detailed paperwork), and freed up regional coordinators (who earlier spent enormous amounts of time in collecting, analyzing, and relaying activity reports) for more personalized and higher value-added activities. The same detailed information about individual operations and transactions also helped to coordinate the purchasing, logistics, financial, and regulatory compliance groups that support these operations.

Far from depersonalizing operations, software provides a framework that allows professionals to behave independently, responsibly, and consistently even though they do not understand major portions of the system outside their realm. It leverages their individual capacities to perform to the point where specialists—like scientific researchers, lawyers, accountants, designers, doctors, market researchers, reporters, authors, or logistics experts—are totally noncompetitive without such systems. Such software systems are also the glue that welds together the highly dispersed service delivery nodes that characterize large-scale intellectual organizations. Leading companies invest heavily in their software to attract, retain, and leverage their very best talent. Software is a key element in managing intellect for competitiveness. Properly developed, it becomes the major proprietary repository of the firm's intellect.

Measuring Outputs

Recognizing that the fundamental building blocks of such systems are objects—integrated packets of data with built-in instructions for manipulation, many information technology producers and users are moving toward object-oriented systems as the preferred solution.[34] Whether these (or their packet surrogates in more conventional systems) are used to implement the minimum replicable units concepts suggested above, many important quantitative aspects of intellectual and service output can now be measured in real-time, and new sensing devices will capture more in the future.[35] Such sensing, of course, is the basis for the direct output measures now used in

---

[34] A good, managerially-oriented overview appears in D. A. Taylor, *Object-Oriented Technology: A Manager's Guide* (Reading, MA: Addison-Wesley, 1990).

[35] For a fairly technical discussion of sensors and real-time data processing, see P. LaPlante, *Real-Time Systems Design and Analysis: An Engineer's Handbook* (New York, NY: Institute of Electrical and Electronics Engineers, 1993).

most communications, airlines, retailing, wholesaling, banking, health care, fast foods, and electric power systems. Monitored in this way are many aspects of quality—e.g., signal quality, signal strength, power variations, fluid flows, service cycle times, error rates, delays, down times, credit-worthiness, variability costs, inventory levels, environmental and operating conditions, and vital systems performance in health care. New technologies, particularly software systems, for capturing such detailed data about customers, operations, and the environment are becoming the most valuable competitive tools of intellectual management.

However, effective management systems typically must go well beyond just software. They must encompass four critical dimensions of (a) peer review of professional performance, (b) customer appraisal of outputs received, (c) business evaluation of efficiency and effectiveness, and (d) measurement of the intellectual assets created. While such measurements would appear critical to professional success, surprisingly few firms perform all four. Merck's and AT&T's approaches to measuring intellectual outputs have been widely publicized, but incompletely explained. Although we cannot provide a detailed treatment here, a few examples will suggest how certain leading enterprises attack individual aspects of this problem.

- After each project, a major investment banking concern asks each team member, its customer group, and a team head to rank all important participants on the project in terms of their demonstrated professional knowledge, specific project contributions, and team support. Customers rate their overall satisfaction with the project and with the firm as a service supplier. Annual surveys, which rank the company against the performance of all competing firms on 28 critical dimensions, supplement this. The firm collects costs and profits for each project and allocates the latter among participating groups on a simple formula basis. Annually, for each division, it calculates the net differential between the market value of each division (if sold) and its fixed asset base. This net intellectual value of the unit is tracked over time as a macro measure of how well management is growing its intellectual assets.

- McKesson Drugs, at the strategic level, emphasizes five major themes for competitiveness: customer-supplier satisfaction, people development, market positioning, relative net delivered cost, and innovation. For each factor it uses internal and external metrics to track its position relative to competitors. It has 42 so-called customer satisfactors that it measures on a routine basis with, among other things, a seven-page questionnaire that goes to more than 1000 customers each year, and with quarterly updates on a smaller set of factors it considers most important. Through its ECONOMOST system, which links its warehouses directly to PCs on druggists' desktops, it can track all costs and such measurable quality features as fulfillment accuracy, delivery times, or stock-outs at both customer and warehouse levels. The same system tracks detailed costs and profits by SKU, and uses market feedback data to advise customers on how they can improve their own productivity. The profits from such services and measures of McKesson's probable costs and profits without its various ECONOMOST software packages give the company a measure of this system's enormous value as intellectual property.

We observed similar systems in our studies of over 100 of the most effective U.S. service companies. Not only must a company design its recruiting, organizing, outsourcing and software support systems to focus and leverage its intellectual capabilities, it must also develop its measurement and reward infrastructures to reinforce its strategic intentions in four critical dimensions. These are professional skill development, customer value creation, internal productivity, and intellectual asset appraisal.

Summary

While managing professional intellect is clearly the key to value creation and profitability for most companies, few have arrived at systematic structures for developing, focusing, leveraging, and measuring their intellectual capabilities. Based on careful research, we have tried to provide some practical guidelines suggesting how successful enterprises have designed their strategies, organizations, training, and measurement systems to maximize the value of their most critical asset, intellect. Technology has created new opportunity and rules for organization design. Customers quickly discover and reward those organizations that understand these new rules.

Values-Based Management

CARL ANDERSON

The highest levels [of creativity] can be expected in those lines of endeavor that involve man's emotions, judgment, symbolizing powers, aesthetic perceptions, and spiritual impulses.

John W. Gardner, Self-Renewal (1971)

An organization in almost all its phases is a reflection of competing value choices. Owners want a return on their investment. Employees want secure jobs and career development. Managers want growth and industry leadership. Government regulators want minimal pollution, safety, work opportunities for a wide variety of groups, and tax revenues. For top managers, this competition comes to a head because they must unravel complex problems whose solutions benefit some groups but have negative consequences for others. Framing these decisions inevitably leads to some crucial dilemmas for managers, who must answer the broad question, "What is a convincing balance among competing value choices?"

In the past, the question has been answered too simply. For example, the financial argument that managers should increase shareholder wealth provides a solution, but at the expense of other stakeholders, such as employees who lose jobs through downsizing. Emphasizing protection of the environment may not allow owners to realize a high return on their investment.

Source: Carl Anderson, "Values-based management," *Academy of Management Executive*, vol. 11 (1997), no. 4, pp. 25–46.

Carl Anderson is a professor of business administration at the Kenan-Flagler Business School, the University of North Carolina at Chapel Hill. After receiving his Ph.D. at Penn State, Anderson taught at the University of Maryland—College Park. His teaching and research interests are in strategic thinking, planning systems, organization design, and executive leadership and decision making. Anderson teaches in the undergraduate, MBA, executive MBA, and Ph.D. programs and in executive education. He has won several teaching awards. Anderson has written four books and his research is published in a wide variety of academic and professional journals. He is currently working on *Strategic Thinking*, which describes the decision-making skills people will need in the complex world of the next century.

Simple rules lead to simplistic solutions that inevitably pit one stakeholder group against another, solutions where something seems to be missing.[1]

Simplistic solutions also play a much larger role in defining what values society embraces. There is no better evidence for the influence of business practice on widely held values than the 1980s' label as "the decade of greed" and the 1990s' label as "the decade of meanness." For better or worse, work has become the principal way most men and women gain satisfaction from doing something more than sustaining their lives. People will always search for frameworks of support and it appears that the recent value frameworks adapted by many organizations are inadequate. The value choices managers make as a group have effects that reach far beyond the borders of their organizations.

Simplistic solutions also do not fit the emerging trend toward a relaxation of the rules regulating business. While this trend simplifies decision making, it places responsibility for a variety of problems on the shoulders of managers rather than government. Businessmen and business women are, for the most part, conservatives who appeal to neutral market forces when opposing government involvement in social programs based on value judgments such as health care or fair hiring practices. This opposition raises the question of who will provide this social support?

For all of these reasons, it is important that managers understand complex problems in terms of value choices.[2] Ideal choices result in fulfillment for all stakeholders, who then coalesce with the organization. Many would say this state of perfection can never be achieved, given that value preferences cannot avoid harming one group or another. To build a value consensus amid these competing pressures, managers should frame choices among important alternatives as value judgments, which have a well-defined place in the managerial decision making framework. Managers may make value choices based on economic performance, competence, the learning organization, and the organization as community.

Experienced managers have worked out a variety of analytical and prescriptive methods for resolving dilemmas created by goals and competition that others can use to their advantage. Some methods are more likely to result in value choices that build compatibility between the individual and the organization. Compatibility is built when consistency is achieved between people's economic and moral nature, beliefs, and goals. Stabilizing an organization through

---

[1] Peter Drucker (1984) "The theory of the business," *Harvard Business Review,* September–October, 95–104.

[2] C. Barnard (1939) *The Functions of the Executive* (Cambridge, MA: Harvard University Press). Barnard strongly emphasized the role of values when he pointed out that effective managers "inspire cooperative personal decisions by creating faith in common understanding, faith in the probability of success, faith in the ultimate satisfaction of personal motives, and faith in the integrity of common purpose" (p. 259). T. E. Deal and A. A. Kennedy (1982) *Corporate Cultures: The Rites and Rituals of Corporate Life* (Reading, MA: Addison Wesley); A. Etzioni (1965) "Organizational control structures" in J. G. March (ed.) *Handbook of Organizations* (Chicago, IL: Rand McNally, pp. 650–677; T. Parsons (1956) "A sociological approach to the theory of organizations," *Administrative Science Quarterly*, vol. 1, 63–85; 225–239.

compatible value choices results in increased entrepreneurial action, heightened entry barriers, additional sources of competence, and sustained growth. Stability through mutually agreeable choices also serves the important purpose of maintaining community in the face of methods like reengineering, which are creatively destructive and unpredictable, but necessary.

The following sections raise deep and difficult arguments that lead to major moral positions and counter positions and, possibly, more questions than answers. Answering the questions thoughtfully rather than simplistically increases the probability of positive outcomes. Leadership is likely to be more consistent and trusted and the organization more attractive to people.

Value Choices and Ethical Dilemmas

Value choices have a specific, well understood place in the framework for making ethical decisions (one group will be harmed by the choice while another will benefit).[3] Ethical principles lay the foundation for all other moral reasoning and behavior, and value choices are built on ethical principles.[4] Quinn and Jones suggest that four moral principles (avoiding harm to others, respecting the autonomy of others, avoiding lying, and honoring agreements) must be met before profit or shareholder interests are satisfied.[5] Managers decide which principles are relevant to a situation and then use these principles as a basis for choosing values and developing standards that make sense in terms of the organization's tasks. Principles are constant from culture to culture and individual to individual, are non-negotiable, and define what is commonly meant by a good society.[6] Managers cannot find or invent new principles and principles cannot be abandoned because of competing analyses; they are prescriptive, universal, overriding, provide truths on which to base attitudes and actions, and provide a compelling reason for doing one thing rather than another. For example, every culture teaches that self-sacrifice to better the common condition is a good thing. Teamwork is, for the most part, grounded in this principle. Other examples of principles used at industry-leading organizations are listed in Appendix 1.

---

[3] Larue Tone Hosmer (1994) "Strategic planning as if ethics mattered," *Strategic Management Journal,* vol. 15, 17–34.

[4] This is most evident in family businesses where founders formally write down what they believe in, developing community by uniquely describing economic and moral/philosophical end results. Well known examples include Johnson & Johnson, The Body Shop, Lincoln Electric, and Ben & Jerry's. These founders had a much easier job than a modern professional manager faces since they combined value judgments and business objectives in the same person; the founder has an opportunity no professional manager has to prepare and develop means for the end he or she has in mind. For a recent example see Russell Mitchell and Michael Oneal (1994) "Managing by values: is Levi Strauss' approach visionary—or flaky," *Business Week,* August 1, pp. 46–52.

[5] Dennis P. Quinn and Thomas M. Jones (1995) "An agent morality view of business policy," *Academy of Management Review,* vol. 20, no. 1, 22–42.

[6] For a discussion of the universality of individual values see J. M. Burns, *Leadership,* (New York: Harper & Row, 1978), p. 20. According to his transformational leadership model, leaders choose and then inspire a sense of common purpose based on values deeply held by society.

To translate principles to practice when problems are complex, decision-makers rely on value judgments of goals or purpose. Value choices are subjective interpretations of ethical principles and vary with what society and individual managers prefer. A decision to protect the habitat of a rare species or to harvest timber to provide jobs and profits involves a value choice. Such choices are far more complex than simple goal statements or standards; they represent management decisions to resolve ethical dilemmas.

Value choices define the area of freedom for managerial action and subsequent organization performance. Ethical principles are constants and serve as building blocks. Value choices influence what people do and how they will do it.[7] The ideas of what is right and what we do usually merge with one another. Empowering workers, for example, increases individual motivation and eventually profit, an important organization goal, while preserving individual dignity, an important principle. Thus management choices define the organization and the performance achieved.[8]

Value choices always present dilemmas. A decision to downsize, which undermines the dignity of the workforce and the organization's culture but increases efficiency, short-term profits, and stockholder returns, is grounded in a conflict between moral and economic choices. There are no readily accepted guidelines for resolving value dilemmas, which vary widely from organization to organization with the goals, priorities, and relative decision freedom of senior managers. How managers resolve these dilemmas defines the values and performance of the organization and many of society's values as well.

Goals and Inherent Dilemmas

Four goals are routinely framed as incompatible by many organizations.

Economic Performance

Profit is a clear goal and reward in a free enterprise economy. Inherent in economic performance goals and measures is the idea that some individuals and organizations will succeed and some will fail. As a result, the higher levels of competition that characterize the late twentieth century have increased the importance of economic performance in most organizations' goal hierarchies.

Competence

Competencies are the tangible or intangible assets that yield sustainable competitive advantage.[9] Many organizations have begun to concentrate on building

[7] C. McCoy (1985) *Management of Values: The Ethical Difference in Corporate Policy and Performance* (Pitman: Marchfield, MA). This book defines the primary task of senior management as setting a clear listing of value priorities when choosing among competing purposes.

[8] N. Nohria and S. Ghoshal (1994) "Differentiated fit and shared values: alternatives for managing headquarters-subsidiary relations," *Strategic Management Journal,* vol. 15, 491–502.

[9] C. K. Prahalad and Gary Hamel (1990) "The core competence of the corporation," *Harvard Business Review,* May–June, 79–91; David J. Collis and Cynthia A. Montgomery (1995) "Competing on resources: strategy in the 1990s," *Harvard Business Review,* July–August, 118–128.

competence and some important advances have been made. Methods like restructuring, reengineering, quality control, process redesign, and especially downsizing emphasize the competencies surrounding efficiency to solve modern competitive problems. Technologies have been enhanced, streamlined, and applied to new markets. Older markets have been redefined. As a result, competence has yielded such notable results as productivity and efficiency, focused organization structures, and enhanced workforce skills that lead to unique competitive advantages.

The Learning Organization

Managers must also build the capacity to change current strategies, tactics, or performance. Decisions affecting learning are concerned with continual improvement, meaningful criticism, individual learning and creativity, and corporate renewal. Improved strategies and tactics are invented to provide more rapid and effective responses to external threats. Learning avoids narrow and rigid dependence on precedence, unquestioning adherence to a common set of assumptions, and the trap of overconfidence that comes with success. All of these are especially necessary in highly competitive situations.

The Organization as Community

In the ideal community, every right is respected and every duty fulfilled.[10] Moral positions are congruent with economic and other positions. Decisions affecting community create situations in which people willingly cooperate for the benefit of all. A strong community frames the work of the organization in a context that elicits significant levels of trust and respect. Because of higher trust, strong communities should have a clear sense of goals and purpose, attract people with a high level of commitment to these goals, improve internal integration and coordination, open communication, increase risk taking, and build leadership that relies on expertise rather than legitimate authority. Overall, a stable community improves and buffers institutional structure and performance.

These four goals are, in fact, interdependent. Over the long run, competence and learning are necessary to sustain economic performance. A strong community is fundamental to all three. Dilemmas occur because decisions that improve competence, learning, and performance can easily hurt community. As a result, a decision process for making value choices so that all four goals can be achieved is highly desirable. Because optimizing all four goals is very difficult, managers often make choices that sacrifice one for another. Defining, understanding, and resolving these dilemmas provides depth and meaning to values-based problems and creates a value structure for the organization.[11]

---

[10] This definition is part of Immanuel Kant's philosophy.

[11] Boris Kabanoff, Robert Waldersee, and Marcus Cohen (1995) "Espoused values and organizational change themes," *Academy of Management Journal,* vol. 38, no. 4, 1075–1104.

Experienced managers know these problems personally; they underlie some of their most gut-wrenching decisions. Here are three of the many dilemmas surrounding the organization as community.[12]

The Organization as Community and Economic Performance

Economic performance has often been elevated above community in recent years. General Motors outsourced jobs in a year of record profits, precipitating a national strike. At the New York *Times,* a bid to change organization culture and management style brought the two issues to the forefront.[13] An initial attempt by the CEO to implement a less authoritarian management style in the newsroom quickly escalated into a conflict with the need to get the paper out quickly and accurately ahead of competitors. Profit and cost goals were put in opposition to the values inherent in a free press; editors argued for a "great paper" as journalists, while business managers argued for cost control and profit. What was never made clear was why the business and news operations needed to work together, what opportunities working together gave them, and what values drove important decisions.

The Organization as Community and Competence

The emphasis on building efficiencies through restructuring, reengineering, and downsizing has come at the expense of community. Reports depict a shell-shocked workforce driven by the need to survive a hostile environment and a ruthless workplace. Decimating and overburdening staffs has put a damper on new product ideas and risk taking. Organizations have not realized their growth objectives. Profits rose at 51 percent of the companies that downsized between 1989 and 1994; 34 percent showed an increase in productivity (only 22 percent increased productivity to their satisfaction); but 86 percent showed a decline in employee morale.[14] Furthermore, downsizing often eliminates people with crucial skills that are the roots of competence.[15]

The Organization as Community and the Learning Organization

A stable community can be a serious liability when things need to be changed. Procedures and behaviors become an obstacle when accepted by people and

---

[12] For example, these problems usually present value dilemmas as decisions are framed as choices among competing goals: environment/pollution, environment/jobs, diversity/discrimination/affirmative action, wage policies (U.S. vs. overseas), productivity/wages (managers vs. employees), employee testing (polygraphs, drug testing), product safety, and truth in advertising.

[13] Ken Auletta (1993) "Opening up the *Times*—restructuring of the NY *Times*," *The New Yorker,* June 28, vol. 69, no. 19, p. 55(16).

[14] Bernard Wysocki, Jr. (1995) "Some companies cut costs too far, suffer 'corporate anorexia,'" *The Wall Street Journal,* Wednesday, July 5, A1; William McKinley, Carol M. Sanchez, and Allen G. Schick (1995) "Organizational downsizing: constraining, cloning, learning," *Academy of Management Executive,* vol. 9, no. 3, 32–42.

[15] L. T. Perry (1986) "Least cost alternatives to layoffs in declining industries," *Organizational Dynamics,* Spring, 48–61; Deborah Dougherty and Edward H. Bowman (1995) "The effects of organizational downsizing on product innovation," *California Management Review,* Summer, vol. 37, no. 4, 28–44.

translated to policies. At Ben & Jerry's, for example, the overriding purpose of serving as a model for other business organizations was implemented through a widely publicized pay scale: top executives could only earn seven times (originally five times) the salary of entry level employees. The company recently hired a series of outside executives at competitive pay in order to expand internationally. The effects of this shift remain to be seen.

Changing values may also stimulate conflict in the ranks, since people have unique interpretations of how the same values should be translated to actions and priorities on the job. What top executives want to accomplish may conflict with middle management and workforce preferences. An educational institution that says it wants to develop students so that they can lead productive and fulfilling lives is likely to encounter conflicts over the meaning of "develop," "productive," and "fulfilling."

It is often argued that insiders, rooted in the stability of community, are seriously hampered when implementing change. An often-used option for change and renewal, therefore, is to bring an outsider in at the top. Recent examples have caused a major debate over the role of community in organizations like IBM, The New York Times, Chrysler, and several computer software companies.[16] While these situations usually begin with a downturn in economic performance, the person brought in to correct the financial and organizational problems is also expected to develop a new long-term vision or to articulate clear values that are widely shared.[17] A value statement may be put forward as a public relations platform and insiders who present obstacles may be moved out.

The root of all three of these dilemmas is framing decisions as choices between competing economic, competence, learning, and community goals. Once value choices among these goals are made, they are extraordinarily difficult to change. Managers trying to implement new value choices often find themselves running into stone walls.

Philosophical Positions

How these dilemmas are answered depends on the decision-maker's philosophical position. Five positions and decision processes are described below in an order that increases the probability of successfully resolving value dilemmas.

The Invisible Hand

Businessmen and women have often untangled value dilemmas by resorting to the old and powerful idea that value choices should be grounded in mar-

---

[16] Gilbert Fuchsberg (1994) "'Visioning' missions becomes its own mission," *The Wall Street Journal,* January 7; Steve Lohr (1993) "For computer convention, be sure to pack vision," *The New York Times,* September 25; Michael W. Miller and Laurie Hays (1993) "Gerstner's nonvision for IBM raises a management issue," *The Wall Street Journal,* Thursday July 29, p. B1; Douglas Lavin (1993) "Robert Eaton thinks 'vision' is overrated and he's not alone," *The Wall Street Journal,* Monday, October 4, p. A1.

[17] This is certainly true at IBM where Louis Gerstner was widely criticized for a lack of vision in 1993. In 1994, as one of his first corporate wide vision/value moves, he changed IBM's statement of "Basic Beliefs." See Laurie Hays (1994) "Gerstner is struggling as he tries to change ingrained IBM culture," *The Wall Street Journal,* Friday, May 13, p. A1.

ket forces. Adam Smith's invisible hand philosophy theorizes that no one chooses the social outcome, yet it emerges through profit seeking by individuals.[18] Managers are solely agents for shareholders, the value of the firm should be maximized, and a healthy organization is defined as one that primarily increases shareholder wealth.[19] Organization problems, with all their intricate economic, social, emotional, and cultural aspects, are reduced to financial problems. Solutions that show a direct link to short term profit are given precedence over all others. Community is good only in the sense that it can show an improvement in shareholder wealth and any real costs from building community should be avoided.[20]

This mechanistic approach has three clear flaws, the first of which can be shown with a simple prisoner's dilemma matrix like the following.

		Firm A	
		Do Not Expand	Expand*
Firm B	Do Not Expand	20,20	22,16
	Expand	16,22	18,18

*The assumption is that expansion by both firms leads to industry over capacity. The first number in each set is A's payoff and the second is B's.

Given these alternatives, research suggests that most players would expand most of the time since this choice maximizes their profit regardless of the decision made by an uncontrollable opponent. It is also clear that both parties (and society in general) will be better off as a pair if each resists the temptation to maximize personal payoff and instead takes a systems viewpoint. If both parties pursue their own interests exclusively, the outcome is worse for both of them than if they cooperate. The uncertainty, of course, is that each competitor is an independent agent, free to maximize his own interests by taking advantage of opponents. Therefore, the invisible hand doesn't necessarily work to the benefit of participants; Adam Smith's invisible hand ensuring that individual pursuits bring about group well being is, at least in this simple situation, cast in doubt.

The second, related flaw in the mechanistic argument follows from the increased competition that characterizes today's economy. Put simply, the larger the number of competitors the greater the uncertainty of competitors' choices, which in turn pushes players toward self-interest. Self-interest increases because of heightened competition. Earlier this century, founders of great, industry-dominating corporations had far fewer competitors. This situation may have allowed managers like Watson at IBM, Procter at P&G, or

---

[18] Adam Smith pointed out that free actions by profit seeking individuals benefit society as a whole, but only if the transactions are bounded. For example, cheating, fraud, and theft should be forbidden.

[19] Adam Smith's justification for this approach was based on the efficiency of broad markets rather than the welfare of the individual firm; if all firms pursue economic values, then society as a whole benefits.

[20] Dennis P. Quinn and Thomas M. Jones (1995) ibid.

Johnson at Johnson & Johnson, all companies that have been heralded as models of social responsibility, the freedom to maximize social goals and at the same time make a substantial profit. Today's hypercompetitive industries force managers into an analysis that is far more complicated. In theory, a monopolist can build a perfect organization. As soon as a competitor comes into the picture, moral dilemmas arise. Extending the situation to many players, each with a choice—Do I make a minuscule contribution to public good like cleaner water or increased employment, or do I make a large contribution to private gain?—may help explain which choices lead competitors to cooperation and betterment of society and which do not.

The third and final flaw of the invisible hand approach is that it offers no solution to the question, "If I can clearly see an economic benefit from defying an ethical principle, should I disobey"? Actions governing the invisible hand are not specified in any underlying moral theory and, as a result, these is no internally prescribed penalty for immorality. At the same time, the invisible hand sets up conditions that make disobedience attractive and discovery difficult and imposes severe penalties for unethical behavior.[21] While it is not irrational or immoral to try to improve one's position, choices not grounded in ethical principles will inevitably lead to other problems. For example, maximizing economic outcomes means the organization is often seen as driving out individual dignity, a characteristic of the organization of the 1990s, which is beset with problems like low employee loyalty and increased employee violence.

Stakeholder Analysis

He who wills the end, wills the means.

Immanuel Kant

Stakeholder analysis relies on the ethical principle grounded in the Golden Rule, do as you would be done by, taking only those actions that you would impose on everyone. Do not override any stakeholder's reason as though it counted for nothing.[22] At least theoretically, this principle is applied to every stakeholder group. In practice, stakeholder groups are analyzed using a grid like the one shown in Figure 1. In the grid, stakeholders' interests in important outcomes are compared with their relative power to influence the outcome. Management attention to different groups is based on grid positions. For example, if product innovation is an important goal, employees have a strong effect on innovation and, in most situations, a high interest in the objective. Owners have a high interest in increased returns and, as a group, high power

---

[21] Federal guidelines for corporate crime now extract a penalty for internal use of the invisible hand.

[22] This principle is based on a much deeper philosophy of Kant's. Briefly, it states that decision makers should treat people always as ends in themselves and never as means only. This leads to the definition of an ideal community where every right is respected and every duty is fulfilled. People cannot be exploited, abused, or manipulated in any way since they are equal members of an ideal community (to the extent that they obey the moral law themselves). Every person is owed the same respect that moral law is owed. The role of morality is to coordinate our individual actions by setting limits to them.

FIGURE I   **The Stakeholder Analysis Grid**

Stakeholders to be
mapped include:

• Owners

• Employees

• Customers

• Suppliers

• Government and regulators

• Special interest groups
(environmental)

• Competitors

• The financial community

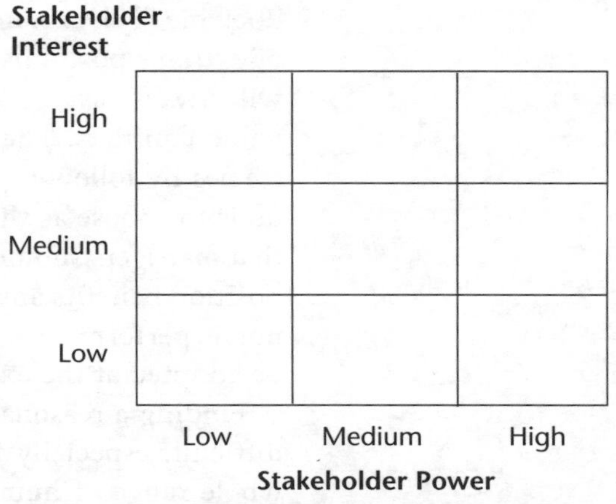

• ...

**Stakeholder
Interest**

High

Medium

Low

Low   Medium   High

Stakeholder Power

to influence this outcome. Employees have a lower interest in this outcome and are less likely to oppose reduced payouts. Mapping important stakeholder groups onto the grid also gives a complete picture of the effects of value choices on the status of stakeholder positions. This is clearly useful decision input.

But conflicts in the form of unavoidable harms to one group at the expense of others still occur because of a fundamental flaw in the stakeholder approach. The question is, Whose happiness is to be increased when stakeholders are in opposition? Answers today seem to favor stockholders at the expense of other groups, so stakeholder analysis has become somewhat synonymous with the invisible hand. But the arguments are more complicated and can be summarized with the following questions.[23]

1. Whose happiness will be increased?

2. How much happiness will our actions produce? And when?

3. Are managers ever entitled to sacrifice one group's or person's happiness for the sake of a greater quantity all around?

4. Can we measure the happiness that our actions will produce?

All four are deep philosophical questions that have been debated through the ages. They attempt to direct managers' choices about which group's position to improve through a rational analysis of stakeholder's interests and power to influence outcomes in their favor. The final end is presumed to be stakeholder happiness or fulfillment. The approach still relies on answering two important questions: What should I do now? and What position should I adopt to make that choice?

The Reasonable Man Argument

The stakeholder approach sets up an inevitable competition between vested groups but offers no guidance for resolution. Is there, practically, ever a rational

---

[23] Roger Scruton (1994) *Modern Philosophy* (New York: The Penguin Press), p. 282.

argument for choosing the interests of one group over another? For example, why should managers ever choose employee over stockholder interests? The doctrine of the mean states that value choices can always be framed in terms of extreme positions, e.g., we will always maximize shareholder value or we will always have a no-layoff policy. An extreme stance, however, leads to clear value conflicts. The reasonable man achieves the mean between these extremes by following the course that reason recommends. The right thing to do is to choose as the virtuous person would choose. This doctrine assumes that managers should always take a compromise position whether or not that position benefits any one group. Community would not be sacrificed for economic performance. Lifetime employment, a community building tactic, may be adopted at the expense of increased profit.

Finding a reasonable position among extreme competing interests is very difficult, especially in business, where these fundamental choices span the whole range of human emotions from greed to altruism. While part of this tradeoff can be traced to the rule that one can't serve two masters, it is a much more complex issue, ultimately coming down to balancing goals to ensure that the varied interests of major stakeholders are met. This has been done in well known cases like the Tylenol poisoning and product recall at Johnson & Johnson. More recently, the 3M Company provides a good example of how economic, environmental, and employee development goals can be met simultaneously.[24] Like any efficient business, 3M stresses the productivity of labor, capital, and resources. Innovation is key: 30 percent of sales come from products introduced within the last four years. 3M also emphasizes environmental responsibility and uses environmental champions equivalent to its internal product champions. Generally, every environmental project adopted by 3M must eliminate or reduce pollutants; benefit or improve the environment through reduced energy use or more efficient use of material or resources: demonstrate technological innovation; and show real cost savings. 3M is able to maintain a reasonable balance among stability in community, performance of people, change, competence, and profits without sacrificing any one. This balance is often achieved by using value choices as challenges for maintaining profitability.

Relying on the reasonableness of decision-makers is a sound addition to the invisible hand and stakeholder approaches, but, like the others, it has some inherent flaws. Decision-makers are all subject to temptation or weakness of will. Reasonableness offers a middle ground for compromise on dilemmas; but does not resolve them. Because reasonableness is difficult to define, it often reverts to the earlier positions. All of the following are themselves reasonable questions: Is pursuing only profit reasonable? If so, how much profit is enough? Is community more valuable than short-term profit? How much more? Is building a better society the best answer? Using the reasonable man approach raises the question, What is the cost/benefit to the organization of making the human situation better?

---

[24] Paul Shrivastava (1995) "Environmental technologies and competitive advantage," *Strategic Management Journal*, vol. 16, 183–200.

Shaping Competitor Behavior

Decision-makers will control dilemmas if competitors can be forced to hold a reasonable position that does not take advantage of actions benefiting the larger system (e.g., see the above payoff matrix). Shaping competitor behavior is accomplished with a strategy called tit-for-tat (TFT). The logic is that someone has to assume the leadership role in the competitive game by preempting competitor moves or responding to competitor moves in a way that forces them into a desired position. Statements like, "We will not abandon this market," "We will match competitor prices," or "It is important for this industry to protect the environment," are examples of preempting announcements. Matching every competitive move in the payoff matrix once it is made would eventually send the signal that not expanding is the most lucrative position to hold. According to Axelrod,[25] TFT combines three important properties: (1) it never abandons the cooperative outcome first; (2) it immediately punishes a rival who leaves the cooperative position by matching the rival's defection in the next period; and (3) if the rival returns to the cooperative strategy, TFT will too. Unfortunately, the success of the tit-for-tat strategy depends on competitors playing the same game over time. They must correctly perceive the sent message and act rationally in their own and the system's best interests; TFT requires a leap of faith on the part of the decision leader.

Enlightened Self-Interest

Enlightened self-interest—taking an action because it allows one to reach a goal controlled at least in part by others—may hold the most promise for building values-based positions in business because it requires serious examination of competing goals for their interactive effects on outcomes and it is under the control of the decision maker. Enlightened self-interest defines dilemmas in terms of resolving competing goals in order to have freedom to operate in the marketplace. For example, building a stable community allows freedom to expand creatively in different directions or to use the labor force in novel ways; ends chosen by the community as well as ends chosen by managers bind all decision makers.

The value statements shown in Appendix 1 are formal examples of enlightened self-interest. Their content is largely derived from individual ethical principles, although these principles are restated in personal terms unique to the organization.[26] These statements address a few clear, unifying themes that are the fundamental measuring sticks against which strategies are first tried and tested. Along with economic measures, these themes build a goal structure. In practice, organizations have chosen values to make profit and community compatible. At W. L. Gore, fairness, commitment, freedom, and waterline (how serious are the financial consequences of the decision) are used to test strategic initiatives with the intention of building increased individual responsibility for performance and financial results. Johnson & Johnson's Credo prioritizes profit and shareholder wealth with other goals.

---

[25] Robert Axelrod (1984) *The Evolution of Cooperation,* New York, Basic Books.
[26] Larue Tone Hosmer (1994) ibid. and Dennis P. Quinn and Thomas M. Jones (1995) ibid.

Resolving the Dilemmas

This section briefly revisits the dilemmas surrounding community using the five decision positions. The most telling dilemmas often occur in economic hard times and are often resolved in ways that sacrifice community for profit, using mechanistic, market forces arguments. But this solution comes with a price, often sacrificing future growth. The other four positions lead to different decision frames that expand the range of options managers should consider when facing and resolving these dilemmas.

The Organization as Community and Economic Performance

Since for-profit organizations should pay attention to building substantial shareholder wealth, does community enhance or detract from increased returns to owners? The invisible hand argues that pursuing economic gain at the firm level results in maximum benefit for society. However, within the organization there is a disparity of individual economic interests. Therefore, organizations need a defined sense of community to assure there is a common approach to resolving difficult issues that might lead to disagreement among reasonable people. It is very time consuming and, possibly, inconsistent for an organization to try to resolve every value-based issue anew. By providing the guidance inherent in values-based management, management assures an efficient and consistent response to most problems.

Community also provides a necessary counterpoint and precedence to financial goals, since it has a different appeal to basic needs, motives, and instincts; it enlarges the range of each person's competence, control, initiative, and commitment, which are root causes of economic success. While the invisible hand places community and profit at opposite ends of a continuum, reasonableness and enlightened self-interest search for a middle ground where community is necessary to reach specific economic goals.[27] Both are enhanced through value-based management. Building an organization parallels building economic performance. By itself, shareholder wealth provides an incomplete sense of identity and uniqueness, and does not motivate long-term creativity the same way community does. Coupling strong communities with high economic performance comes closer to assuring the overall health of the organization. Business success is grounded in a stable organization community.

The Organization as Community and Competence

The challenge of building an organization capable of competing in the global economy should be compatible with the simultaneous challenge of cultivating a community that will sustain the organization in periods of changes. Generally, stakeholder mapping and enlightened self-interest positions expand the decision frame so that strong communities provide competitive advantages

---

[27] N. Craig Smith (1995) "Marketing strategies for the ethics era," *Sloan Management Review,* Summer, vol. 36, no. 4, 85–97. This article develops a "marketing ethics continuum." At one end is caveat emptor where profit maximization is only subject to legal constraints. At the other end is caveat venditor where consumer interests and satisfaction are favored and producer interests are less favored.

equal in importance to high quality, efficient production, and effective processes.[28] Individual and team performance should improve through the stability and security of community.[29] Community increases speed of response and maintains the commitment of individuals to stretch themselves because they can be relied on to make decisions using consistent principles and a common understanding of the world to sort out alternatives.[30] By engaging people's hearts and minds and retaining expertise, community affects such important functions as the design of products and services and the creation of new technology. In this way, community enhances the most formidable entry barriers to competition, barriers based on ideas. Ideas flow from the minds of bright people who are more easily recruited and retained when they identify with and internalize value choices. Ideas lead to sustainable advantage; product or service growth opportunities are developed by internal entrepreneurs before competitors can act. The time frame for decision making is compressed. Actions are taken closer to when events begin (e.g., when mainframe computers start to decline as a percentage of the market rather than when PCs are already dominant). Rebuilding these advantages, if lost, should add costs higher than the profits from short-term efficiencies.

The Organization as Community and the Learning Organization

Evaluating the community/learning dilemma from all five positions expands a manager's breadth of options. A stable community increases the chances for serious decentralization and learning by specifying behaviors for people in widely separated units where other kinds of control are impractical. Internal, personal controls are used. More than ever, managers at lower levels must determine where and how the organization will compete, what competencies it will build, and how it will add customer benefit. The probability of getting people in independent, entrepreneurial units to pull together in the same direction is increased if they use the same decision making apparatus. When things become more complex, individuals are more likely to experiment and implement new ideas in groups that are closer to the market and that have less red tape and bureaucracy. This is especially important in situations requiring the most creativity (R&D at Microsoft, developing buyer relationships at Johnson & Johnson, overseas growth at Ben & Jerry's, or new strategies for increasingly diverse competition at The Body Shop). If community becomes embedded in the systems of the organization, it should increase learning. In the long run it will attract better people and continue

---

[28] Mark A. Huselid (1995) "The impact of human resource management practices on turnover, productivity, and corporate financial performance," *The Academy of Management Journal*, vol. 38, no. 3, June, 635–672; Jay B. Barney and Edward J. Zajac (eds.) (1994) "Competitive organizational behavior," *Strategic Management Journal*, vol. 15, Special Issue, Winter; Thomas M. Jones (1995) "Instrumental stakeholder theory: a synthesis of ethics and economics," *Academy of Management Review,* vol. 20, no. 2, 404–437.

[29] Kenneth R. Andrews devoted two chapters to this issue in K. R. Andrews, *The Concept of Corporate Strategy* (Homewood, IL: Richard D. Irwin, Inc., 1987, Chaps. 4 and 5).

[30] W. G. Ouchi (1980) "Markets, bureaucracies, and clans," *Administrative Science Quarterly,* vol. 25, 129–141.

the cycle of preeminence.[31] Over the long term, entrepreneurial decisions in this spoke and wheel organization add up to new market and/or technical directions, but the essence of the corporation, its underlying philosophy, remains stable.[32]

The advantages of hierarchy, standardizing and coordinating behavior are captured but dependence on such legitimate power as top-down directives is reduced. Decision practices relying on fear as a primary motivator are a poor substitute for community. But the cumbersome controls and routines of most organizations are also dispensable. Formal systems like goal/incentive or MBO, in which people exchange time and effort for money, position, or other tangible rewards, can lead to solid performance, but these systems rely on detached computations. The superficial use of annual goal setting, measurement, and review does not ensure that people use their minds, energy, commitment, and creativity to identify the right problems and to craft imaginative solutions. After-the-fact measurement and reward is simply too late in today's environment. Motivating actions to improve learning is more likely when people buy into community choices as well as economic rewards.

Prescriptions

Using all five philosophical positions increases the understanding of managers and others of the effects of their choices. Consistency can be better maintained over a sequence of decisions, avoiding confusion among the ranks and among stakeholders. Managers can objectively judge and incorporate the options of others, especially when their preferred decisions do not have widespread acceptance.

Using all five positions ensures compatibility between individual and organization values. People are inherently moral and believe in the goodness of what they are doing. They do not separate business and personal lives. They do not compartmentalize economics, religion, and morality. Resolving dilemmas using all five approaches captures creativity, community, and economic outcomes.

A formal statement of values (see those highlighted in the Appendix) should be drafted to legitimize value choices. Organizations are built on a foundation of value choices cemented in the framework of ethical principles. Value choices are legitimized in a formal value statement that is the most fundamental organization document. (See Figure 2.) The values statement should be used to maintain stability, trust, and teamwork; what it expresses is central to the organization's character. Further, preexisting statements or codes preclude having to establish a new policy or rule on the spur of the moment or worry about later defense before owners or the

---

[31] Gary Hamel and Airne Heeme (1994) *Competence Based Competition* (New York: John Wiley & Sons); Alan Farnham (1993) "State your values, hold the hot air," *Fortune,* April 19, p. 21.

[32] Charles Handy (1992) "Balancing corporate power: a new federalist paper," *Harvard Business Review,* November–December, 59–72; Christopher A. Bartlett and Sumantra Ghoshal (1993) "Beyond the M-form: toward a managerial theory of the firm," *Strategic Management Journal,* Special Issue, Winter, vol. 14, 23–46.

FIGURE 2   **Five Levels of Documents**

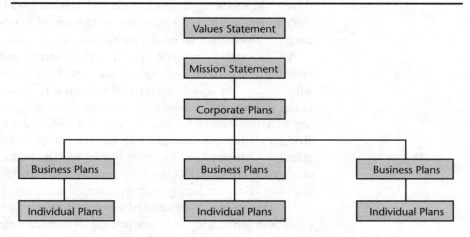

The first step in implementing values-based management is formalizing—writing down—the organization's value choices. The diagram shows where the values statement fits in the hierarchy of documents a typical organization might generate and how values statements precede and are different from mission statements, corporate plans, and other formal, commonly used goal setting approaches.

1. A values statement drives the goals and actions listed in the following documents. A values statement has a longer time frame than the documents listed below. As shown in the Appendix, values statements are built on ethical principles.

2. Mission statements describe the business arena for the corporation. Products, markets, and desirable financial results may be included. This statement begins the process of defining actions and outcomes that is continued in more specific terms in the following documents.

3. Corporate plans include the definition of various businesses, specific financial goals for them, time frames for accomplishment, and new directions that will be pursued.

4. Business plans are similar, but at the business level. Quantifiable, short-term results are stated.

5. Finally, function, team, or individual plans specify actions and goals at operational levels for the immediate future.

Depending on the size of the organization, one or more of these documents can be eliminated, but the statements of values, mission, and one level of operational planning are essential.

media. The companies included in the Appendix have sustained long-term high performance by legitimizing value choices and then living by these preferences.

Value statements should remain stable over time. Mission statements are better targets for change. An accurate mission means understanding technologies, markets, industry and competitive dynamics, and the motives of the people expected to share in them. Although both require intimate knowledge of the organization's situation and conferred trust from other managers and employees that years of experience bring, it is likely that stakeholders would accept changes in product and market choices more quickly than they would changes in fundamental values. Take Louis Gerstner's 1993 statement: "The last thing IBM needs right now is a vision." Gerstner was correct in the sense that in complex, high-tech situations, values shouldn't be changed by outsiders until they get a handle on the intricacies of the business and the people in it.

A value statement must appeal to the current audience and its language, meaning it has to be reenergized and rewritten from time to time. Style in a value statement should be refined to keep it relevant to the changing nature of the workplace, to who is in the organization, to what management is trying to achieve, and to what external stakeholders expect. One of the most studied challenges took place in the late 1970s at Johnson & Johnson when managers from around the world rewrote The Credo. In 1994, the Credo was changed again to reflect the important role of fathers in family affairs and the growing effects of family responsibilities in the workplace.

Serious problems are created when companies do not live up to their lofty choices or when they redefine principles in hard times. Businesses are value-laden institutions that are not above the common moral code of a free society. Articulated value choices raise stakeholder expectations, which, if they aren't met, undermine the credibility of the organization. For example, The Body Shop has been investigated for its franchising practices and has been forced to alter its claim that its ingredients were not tested on animals. Ben & Jerry's is recruiting executives who will not fit into its historic seven-to-one pay scale ratios. At Johnson & Johnson, some of the more than 160 divisions put profit ahead of The Credo. Downsizing in times of record profits violates the principle of justice, honesty, and fairness. There are no raises for some rank and file, while executives receive millions, thus violating the principle of individual dignity.

All of these practices are targets for a skeptical public. The original value choices are seen by some as too idealistic; they should be tempered by the realities of business, which include a large dose of periodic creative destruction. Changing them in hard times brings an "I told you so!" response. Others criticize the widespread publication of lofty ideals as a form of public relations. These ads are viewed with suspicion, in part because advertising one's values violates the fundamental principle of humility. Finally, the popular business press often labels practices like tithing at Ben & Jerry's as welfare, promoting the well being of people outside the firm at the expense of profits, wages, and benefits to other stakeholder groups.

On the other hand, value choices play a more complicated role in providing a call to a higher purpose, to be more and better than we are, and to improve the human condition. In this way, value choices rely on idealism and the uplifting moral debate about what is right and good. Even if they aren't ever reached, they complete the process of personal fulfillment. Proponents point out that pursuing perfection leads to higher performance even though perfection cannot be attained. Pursuing perfect values benefits the entire organization in the same way that pursuing zero defects benefits production or pursuing total customer satisfaction benefits marketing. Honesty doesn't always pay, but the moral benefits always outweigh the economic costs.

◨ Summary

Values-based management has been largely ignored in recent business practice, except for discussions of right and wrong and some well-publicized examples in which benefiting society is put ahead of profit or economic efficiency is put ahead of employee interests. The emphasis today is clearly on building world-class organizations by applying techniques like TQM and process engineering to decentralized units, increasing their efficiency, and using efficiencies to justify a wave of downsizing. Now lean and mean, these organizations are poised to create growth for the remainder of the decade. While it is clear that plenty of opportunities for growth exist (e.g., Eastern Europe or the Chinese mainland), very few companies have been able to steer their well-oiled corporate machines on a common course toward these growth targets. Challenging people in independent operating units to create their own growth opportunities by inventing specific responses to competition and, at the same time, gluing these units together in order to take advantage of synergies, remain among the most troublesome of organization problems. A piece of the puzzle still seems to be missing.

The missing piece is a coherent method for considering and resolving value dilemmas. An emphasis on neutral market forces does not, by itself, build advantage in a competitive world. The market forces doctrine aims at understanding, manipulating, and capitalizing on things. Values-based management shifts the attention to the connections between things: compassion, justice, and frugality. Both are necessary for effective decision making.

Further, the internal logic of management decision making requires moral content. Business decision making without a discussion of values is incomplete. People do not separate their work and materialistic lives from their religious and moral lives. If business leaders are to be both strategists and philosophers, if they are to articulate the company's financial goals while also encouraging employees to be moral, socially conscious, creative, and loyal, then they must set goals for community, competence, and learning that are equal in importance to economic goals. The manager who defines the economic strategy must elicit confidence in his or her value judgments, especially if the strategy is risky, because others who implement the strategy will also have to assume the risk.[33]

Since any of the value judgments mentioned in this paper represent honest choices, it could be argued that the direction of the tradeoff doesn't really matter. Managers should make a decision, implement it, and stakeholders will eventually adapt. But the tradeoffs do make a difference; some choices position the organization without conscience. Eventually this eats into the legacy of trust as community bonds break down. When there is no community, trust and respect are hard to maintain and performance is even more difficult to reinforce. This may have happened in many organizations already. For example, young people begin their careers highly motivated, willing to contribute and to go beyond the basic requirements of the job. Many, within a few months, are

---

[33] This has always been a part of the strategic management framework as defined by Barnard, Learned, Christensen, Andrews, and others.

turned off because there is no imagination, passion, and trust—the things that bond people to any organization. Managers don't need to provide security and a safe haven, but they do need to provide answers to questions like what should I do, what is important, why, what are the consequences of my actions beyond financial rewards, and are these consequences predictable? The right answers to these questions build trust in the institution, the only kind of trust that lasts, not blind trust in legitimate authority or trust resulting from charisma. Asking for right answers is to ask a great deal of management. In the relative freedom accompanying business decisions, value considerations are necessary and equal in importance to analysis and facts. Resolving value dilemmas sets the connections for our organizations and society.

Over the last fifteen years, many managers have defined the market forces doctrine in the narrowest way, as self-interest exploited through laissez-faire economics. In the most extreme cases, using ethical principles in decision making is seen as a sure path to ruin in the Darwinian fight for survival. Competing within an open system is stressed, but preserving the competitive system itself is not.[34] Businessmen and business women have a stake in analyzing systems as a whole, thinking about the overall good of the society in which we are to live. Stakeholder analysis, reasonableness, and enlightened self-interest force decision-makers to consider the situation of the worst off in society as well as of the owners who are obvious targets of attention.

Through their decisions, business leaders influence the directions their organizations take. Ultimately, organizations are good because they emphasize the plural; members belong to something greater than themselves, which is a source of reassurance and continuity as well as of higher productivity. Business institutions are persons not just in legal/financial ways, but in moral ways as well. They are expressions of their members' beliefs, rights, and obligations. Organizations that focus only on financial results can easily crumble under the weight of indifference as people retreat into themselves. In this sense, business is an important agent in the great human march toward a civilized society. That is a fundamental argument for building a model organization that helps all stakeholders develop into productive members of a pluralistic community.

---

[34] George Soros (1995) *Soros on Soros: Staying Ahead of the Curve* (Wiley).

APPENDIX 1

Examples of Value Judgements and Value Statements Derived from Individual Principles

Six categories of individual ethical principles form the basis of most value statements.[35] The first five cut across cultural boundaries while the sixth is unique to western society. Value choices are grounded in these principles.

1. *General beneficence* ("Don't murder," "Don't bring misery to others," "Follow the Golden Rule," and "Self-sacrifice for a worthwhile end is a good thing") or "doing good," benefiting the human condition by making things better

---

[35] This list does not include three principles commonly cited in texts: (1) self-interest, taking actions that are in one's own long-term self-interests; (2) universal standards, taking actions that others take when faced with the same situation (e.g., industry standards); and (3) government legal requirements, obeying the law. These three principles are usually assumed in most business situations. For a review see Larue Tone Hosmer (1994) ibid.

than they were before. In business organizations, beneficence is usually translated to purpose; what the organization does that will make a contribution to society beyond profit. A sense of purpose allows people to build an identity to meet challenges they could not master by themselves.

It is easier to develop a sense of purpose where the products and services have high moral content. For example, hospitals and ethical drug companies ease pain and suffering and postpone death. They have an easier time communicating purpose than do soft drink or cigarette manufacturers. On the other hand, Ben & Jerry's, a mundane ice cream company, has defined its purpose in terms of acting like a model business rather than in terms of the products it manufactures.

2. *Justice, honesty, and fairness* ("Don't steal," "Behave honestly," "Assume a loss over shameful gains," "Don't take bribes," and "Don't rely on falsehoods and trickery") affect how groups and individuals are treated. Justice can be translated to development of outstanding products and services, skill development, competency development, teamwork, and fair and honest treatment of all stakeholder groups.

3. *Mercy or compassion* ("Everyone, including the weak, have worth" and "Take care of others"). In business organizations, compassion is often translated to developing people, recognizing what people contribute, responding to family and community problems, and sourcing from disadvantaged groups.

4. Frugality or economic efficiency ("Don't waste resources," "Protect the environment," and "Buy only essential items") is often communicated in a sense of stewardship.

5. *Humility* supports teamwork and communication, increases sensitivity to customers and suppliers, and avoids the development of bureaucracy. It seems to be especially important in high tech and professional fields where education or individual skills may breed arrogance.

6. *Individual dignity* ("People are unique," "People control their own destinies," "Recognize the competence of the individual," and "The organization exists for the individual"). Western culture values self-governance, self-control, individual uniqueness, and the right of individuals to make decisions that affect them personally.

I have selected five well known and well publicized companies to illustrate value choices, formalized in value statements, based on these ethical principles. The statement is followed by examples of ethical principles contained in the statement.[36]

1. Johnson & Johnson, *Our Credo*

We believe our first responsibility is to the doctors, nurses and patients, to mothers and fathers and all others who use our products and services. In meeting their needs, everything we do must be of high quality. We must constantly strive to reduce our costs in order to maintain reasonable prices. Customers' orders must be serviced promptly and accurately. Our suppliers and distributors must have an opportunity to make a fair profit.

We are responsible to our employees, the men and women who work with us throughout the world. Everyone must be considered as an individual. We must respect their dignity and recognize their merit. They must have a sense of security in their jobs. Compensation must be fair and adequate, and working conditions clean, orderly, and safe. We must be mindful of ways to help our employees fulfill their family responsibilities. Employees must feel free to make suggestions and complaints. There must be equal opportunity for employment, development and advancement for those qualified. We must provide competent management, and their actions must be just and ethical.

We are responsible to the communities in which we live and work and to the world community as

---

[36] The companies cited in this section were selected using the following criteria: (1) each of these companies realized significant growth or turnaround resulting in industry leadership; (2) each company had a formal statement of organization values at the time of growth or turnaround; (3) the values statement included a wide variety of values, not just social responsibility or general beneficence; (4) the values statement was used, specifically, as a management tool to improve individual performance and enhance growth; and (5) top management made a specific connection between the values statement and overall performance.

well. We must be good citizens—support good works and charities and bear our fair share of taxes. We must encourage civic improvements and better health and education. We must maintain in good order the property we are privileged to use, protecting the environment and natural resources.

Our final responsibility is to our stockholders. Business must make a sound profit. We must experiment with new ideas. Research must be carried on, innovative programs developed and mistakes paid for. New equipment must be purchased, new facilities provided and new products launched. Reserves must be created to provide for adverse times. When we operate according to these principles, the stockholders should realize a fair return.

Examples of Ethical Principles in the Credo

There must be equal opportunity for employment, development and advancement for those qualified. (Justice, Honesty, Fairness)

We must be mindful of ways to help our employees fulfill their family responsibilities. (Mercy and compassion)

We must constantly reduce our costs in order to maintain reasonable prices. ... We must maintain in good order the property we are privileged to use, ... (Frugality)

Everyone must be considered as an individual. (Individual dignity)

2. Cray Research, The Cray Style

At Cray Research, we take what we do very seriously, but don't take ourselves very seriously.

We have a strong sense of quality—quality in our products and services, of course; but also quality in our working environment, in the people we work with, in the tools that we use to do our work, and in the components we choose to make what we make. Economy comes from high value, not from low cost. Aesthetics are part of quality. The effort to create quality extends to the communities in which we work and live as well.

The Cray approach is informal and nonbureaucratic. Verbal communication is key, not memos. "Call, don't write" is the watchword.

People are accessible at all levels.

People also have fun working at Cray Research. There is laughing in the halls, as well as serious discussion. More than anything else, the organization is personable and approachable, but still dedicated to getting the job done.

With informality, however, there is also a sense of confidence. Cray people feel they are on the winning side. They feel successful, and they are. It is this sense of confidence that generates the attitude of "go ahead and try it, we'll make it work."

Also, there is a sense of pride at Cray. Professionalism is important. People are treated like and act like professionals. Cray people trust each other to do their jobs well and with the highest ethical standards. They take what they do very seriously. But Cray people are professional without being stuffy. They take a straightforward, even simple, approach. They don't take themselves too seriously.

Because the individual is key at Cray, there is a real diversity in the view of what Cray Research really is. In fact, Cray Research is many things to many people. The consistency comes in providing those diverse people with the opportunity to fulfill themselves and experience achievement. The creativity, then, that emerges from the company comes from the many ideas of the individuals who are here. And that is the real strength of Cray Research.

Examples of Ethical Principles in The Cray Style

People are treated like and act like professionals. ... The consistency comes in providing those diverse people with the opportunity to fulfill themselves and experience achievement. (Justice, Honesty, Fairness)

At Cray Research, we take what we do very seriously, but don't take ourselves very seriously. ... More than anything else, the organization is personable and approachable, but still dedicated to getting the job done. (Humility)

The creativity, then, that emerges from the company comes from the many ideas of the individuals who are here. (Individual dignity)

3. The Body Shop International, What We're All About

The Body Shop manufactures and sells naturally-based cosmetics, skin and hair care products, using high quality ingredients to make original and exclusive products.

The Body Shop believes in an honest approach to selling cosmetics. We don't promote idealized notions of beauty, nor do we claim our products will perform miracles. Our products are straightforward, designed to meet the real needs of real people. That is why they're sold in five sizes. Through our refill bar and minimal packaging, we conserve resources, reduce waste and save customers money.

The Body Shop practices basic good housekeeping: energy efficiency, waste minimization, and utilization of renewable resources whenever possible. This is the very least we can do while we continue the search for ways to reduce our impact on the environment.

The Body Shop believes that profits and principles should go hand in hand. We are against animal testing in the cosmetics industry. We campaign for human and civil rights. We are committed to establishing trading partnerships with indigenous peoples and grass roots communities. And we seek alternatives to the conventional ways of doing business.

The Body Shop aims to be sensitive to the local needs of communities in which we work. At the top of our social agenda are our community projects. We are also committed to education, not just for staff but for customers. We value an open exchange of information because knowledge is a healthy step towards responsibility and self-empowerment.

Examples of Ethical Principles in What We're All About

We are against animal testing in the cosmetics industry. We campaign for human and civil rights. (General beneficence)

The Body Shop believes in an honest approach to selling cosmetics. (Justice, Honesty, Fairness)

The Body Shop aims to be sensitive to the local needs of communities in which we work. ... We are committed to establishing trading partnerships with indigenous peoples and grass roots communities. ... We are also committed to education, not just for staff but for customers. (Mercy and Compassion)

The Body Shop practices basic good housekeeping: energy efficiency, waste minimization, and utilization of renewable resources whenever possible. (Frugality)

4. Ben & Jerry's *Statement of Mission*

Ben & Jerry's is dedicated to the creation and demonstration of a new corporate concept of linked prosperity. Our mission consists of three interrelated parts:

* *Product mission.* To make, distribute and sell the finest quality all natural ice cream and related products in a wide variety of innovative flavors made from Vermont dairy products.

* *Social mission.* To operate the company in a way that actively recognizes the central role that business plays in the structure of society by innovative ways to improve the quality of life of a broad community: local, national, and international.

* *Economic mission.* To operate the company on a sound financial basis of profitable growth, increasing value for our shareholders and creating career opportunities and financial rewards for our employees.

Underlying the mission of Ben & Jerry's is the determination to seek new and creative ways of addressing all three parts, while holding a deep respect for individuals, inside and outside the company, and for the communities of which they are a part.

Examples of Ethical Principles in Statement of Mission

Ben & Jerry's is dedicated to the creation and demonstration of a new corporate concept of linked prosperity. ... To operate the company in or way that actively recognizes the central role that business plays in the structure of society by innovative ways to improve the quality of life of a broad community: local, national, and international. (General beneficence)

... while holding a deep respect for individuals, inside and outside the company, and for the communities of which they are a part. (Individual dignity)

5. Liz Claiborne Inc., *Priorities*

Behind every LIZ CLAIBORNE product is an organization that thrives on a unique value system described here as LIZ CLAIBORNE PRIORITIES. At the heart of these PRIORITIES is the development of every individual's enthusiasm, vitality, and commitment. We are motivated to maintaining these qualities through professionalism, entrepreneurial spirit, and flexibility; demanding excellence in all we do. Our spirit keeps our company progressive, encouraging constant reevaluation of what can be done to make the best even better.

We are committed to maintaining a consumer dedicated and design oriented company that respects the unique relationship between the consumer and our products. Our commitment ensures that, throughout our operation, we pay enormous attention to details both aesthetic and technical. Consumer satisfaction guides all our efforts. Through quality, value, service and fashion leadership, original and innovative ideas will ensure that our products continue to meet the needs of our consumers.

We value and constantly cultivate the close partnerships we share with suppliers, customers and one another. Our relationships with these partners are based on trust, fairness, and mutual respect. Respect for one another ensures a successful team effort. Trust encourages honest communications for the best exchange of ideas. Fairness in our dealings ensures a balanced perspective, always working with the future in mind.

Examples of Ethical Principles in Priorities

Our relationships with these partners are based on trust, fairness, and mutual respect. ... Trust encourages honest communications for the best exchange of ideas. (Justice, Honesty, Fairness)

At the heart of these PRIORITIES is the development of every individual's enthusiasm, vitality, and commitment. (Individual dignity)

Coping with Hypercompetition: Utilizing the New 7S's Framework[1]

RICHARD A. D'AVENI

This business is intensely, vigorously, bitterly, savagely competitive.

Robert Crandall, CEO, American Airlines

Major sustainable competitive advantages are almost non-existent in the field of financial services.

Warren Buffett

I don't believe in friendly competition. I want to put them out of business.

Mitchell Leibovitz, CEO of auto parts retailer Pep Boys

Declare business war. This *is the enemy.*

Statement over a photo of Northern Telecom CEO Paul Stern
on posters at an AT&T plant in Denver[2]

We have seen giants of American industry, such as General Motors and IBM, shaken to their cores. Their competitive advantages, once considered unassailable, have been ripped and torn in the fierce winds of competition. Technological wonders appear overnight. Aggressive global competitors arrive on the scene. Organizations are restructured. Markets appear and fade. The weathered rule books and generic strategies once used to plot our strategies no longer work as well in this environment.

Source: R. A. D'Aveni, "Coping with hypercompetition: utilizing the new 7S's framework," *Academy of Management Executive,* vol. 9 (1995), no. 3, pp. 45–57.

Richard A. D'Aveni (Ph.D., Columbia University) teaches business strategy at the Amos Tuck School at Dartmouth College and consults for several *Fortune 500* corporations. He received the A. T. Kearney Award for his research on why big companies fail, and has been profiled as one of the next generation's promising new management thinkers by *WirtschaftsWoche,* Germany's equivalent to *Business Week.*

[1] Adapted from: R. A. D'Aveni, *Hypercompetition: Managing the Dynamics of Strategic Maneuvering* (New York: NY: The Free Press, 1994).

[2] R. Crandall, quoted in *Business Week,* July 6, 1992; W. Buffett, quoted in *Harvard Business Review,* September–October 1986; M. Leibovitz, quoted in *Fortune,* February 22, 1993; Northern Telecom poster, *Newsweek,* December 28, 1992.

The traditional sources of advantages no longer provide long-term security. Both GM and IBM still have economies of scale, massive advertising budgets, the best distribution systems in their industries, cutting-edge R&D, deep pockets, and many other features that give them power over buyers and suppliers and that raise barriers to entry that seem impregnable. But these are not enough any more. Leadership in price and quality is also not enough to assure success. Being first is not always the same as being best. Entry barriers are trampled down or circumvented. Goliaths are brought down by clever Davids with slingshots. Welcome to the world of hypercompetition.

Hypercompetition

Hypercompetition results from the dynamics of strategic maneuvering among global and innovative combatants. It is a condition of rapidly escalating competition based on price-quality positioning, competition to create new know-how and establish first-mover advantage, competition to protect or invade established product or geographic markets, and competition based on deep pockets and the creation of even deeper pocketed alliances. In hypercompetition the frequency, boldness, and aggressiveness of dynamic movement by the players accelerates to create a condition of constant disequilibrium and change. Market stability is threatened by short product life cycles, short product design cycles, new technologies, frequent entry by unexpected outsiders, repositioning by incumbents, and radical redefinitions of market boundaries as diverse industries merge. In other words, environments escalate toward higher and higher levels of uncertainty, dynamism, heterogeneity of the players, and hostility.

It is not just fast-moving, high-tech industries, such as computers, or industries shaken by deregulation, such as the airlines, that are facing this aggressive competition. There is evidence that competition is heating up across the board, even in what once seemed the most sedate industries. From software to soft drinks, from microchips to corn chips, from packaged goods to package delivery services, there are few industries that have escaped hypercompetition. As Jack Welch, CEO of General Electric, commented, "It's going to be brutal. When I said a while back that the 1980s were going to be a white-knuckle decade and the 1990s would be even tougher, I may have understated how hard it's going to get."[3]

There are few industries and companies that have escaped this shift in competitiveness. Even such seemingly comatose industries as hot sauces or such commodity strongholds as U.S. grain production have been jolted awake by the icy waters of hypercompetition.

Movement Toward, but Failure to Reach, Perfect Competition

American corporations have traditionally sought established markets wherein sustainable profits were attainable. They have done so by looking for low or moderate levels of competition (see Exhibit 1). Low and moderate-intensity

---

[3] Stratford Sherman, "How to prosper in the value decade," *Fortune,* November 30, 1992, p. 91.

EXHIBIT 1 Different Levels of Competition Within an Industry

Low-Intensity Competition ⇨	Moderate Competition ⇨	High-Intensity Competition ⇨	Extreme Competition

No Competition
- Monopoly
- Legal monopoly through patents
- Excessive profits are sustainable for years

Competition Avoidance
- Firms position around each other but not directly against each other.
- Segmentation of markets occurs so there is only one player in each segment.
- Barriers to entry are used to limit entry of markets by competitors.
- If some small degree of segment/niche overlap occurs, firms tacitly cooperate to restrict this overlap or restrain competitive behavior.
- Long-term sustainable advantage and profits are possible, but only as long as all the competitors cooperate or respect the entry barriers.

Hypercompetition
- Firms aggressively position against one another by attempting to disadvantage opponents.
- Firms create new competitive advantages which make obsolete or match opponents' advantages in one or more of the four arenas.
- Firms attempt to stay ahead of their competitors in one or more of the four arenas.
- Firms create new competitive advantages that make the opponents' advantages irrelevant by moving to compete in another arena.
- Temporary advantage and short periods of profit are achievable until competitors catch up with or outmaneuver the aggressor's last competitive move.

Perfect Competition
- All four of the traditional competitive advantages have been eliminated so the players are equal in all four arenas.
- Firms compete on price until no one makes abnormal profits.
- Normally, perfect competition is not preferred over lower levels of competition because lower levels of competition lead to more opportunity for profits.

The Trends

Monopoly (one player) ⇧	**Oligopoly** (small number of players) ⇧	**Dynamic Competition** (several players) ⇧	**Perfect Competition** (many players) ⇧
Excessive Profits ⇧	Sustainable Profits ⇧	Intermittent or Low Profits ⇧	No Abnormal Profits ⇧

competition occurs if a company has a monopoly (or quasi monopoly protected by entry barriers) or if competitors implicitly or explicitly collude, allowing each other to "sustain" an advantage in one or more industries or market segments. Collusion or cooperation, while it can be useful in limiting aggressiveness, is limited because there is incentive to cheat on the collusive agreement and gain advantage. Entry and mobility barriers are destroyed by firms seeking the profit potential of industries or segments with low or moderate levels of competition. Gentlemanly agreements to stay out of each other's turf fall apart as firms learn how to break the barriers inexpensively. As competition shifts toward higher intensity, companies begin to develop new advantages rapidly and attempt to destroy competitors' advantages. This leads to a further escalation of competition into hypercompetition, at which stage companies actively work to string together a series of temporary moves that undermine competitors in an endless cycle of jockeying for position. Just one hypercompetitive player (often from abroad) is enough to trigger this cycle.

At each point firms press forward to gain new advantages or tear down those of their rivals. This movement, however, takes the industry to faster and more intense levels of competition. The most interesting aspect of this movement is that, as firms maneuver and outmaneuver each other, they are constantly pushing toward perfect competition, where no one has an advantage. However, while firms push toward perfect competition, they must attempt to avoid it because abnormal profits are not at all possible in perfectly competitive markets. In hypercompetitive markets it is possible to make temporary profits. Thus, even though perfect competition is treated as the "equilibrium" state in static economic models, it is neither a desired nor a sustainable state from the perspective of corporations seeking profits. They would prefer low and moderate levels of competition but often settle for hypercompetitive markets because the presence of a small number of aggressive foreign corporations won't cooperate enough to allow the old, more genteel levels of competition that existed in the past.

◼ The New 7S's

Paraphrasing George Bernard Shaw, while reasonable people adapt to the world, the unreasonable ones persist in trying to adapt the world to themselves. Thus, all progress depends upon the unreasonable person. In hypercompetition the reasonable strategies that focus on sustaining advantages do not lead to progress. It is not enough to merely adapt to the environment. Companies make progress in hypercompetition by the unreasonable approach of actively disrupting advantages of others to adapt the world to themselves. These strategies are embodied in the New 7S's.

My studies of successful and unsuccessful companies in hypercompetitive environments reveal seven key elements of a dynamic approach to strategy. Unlike the old 7S framework, originally developed by McKinsey and Company, the new framework is based on a strategy of finding and building temporary advantages through market disruption rather than sustaining advantage and perpetuating an equilibrium. It is designed to sustain the momentum through a series of initiatives rather than structure the firm to achieve internal fit or fit with today's external environment, as if today's external conditions will persist for a long period of time.

The New 7S's are:

- Superior stakeholder satisfaction
- Strategic soothsaying
- Positioning for speed
- Positioning for surprise
- Shifting the rules of the game
- Signaling strategic intent
- Simultaneous and sequential strategic thrusts

Because of the nature of the hypercompetitive environment, the New 7S's are not presented as a series of generic strategies or a recipe for success. Instead, these are key approaches that can be used to carry the firm in many different directions. They are focused on disrupting the status quo through a series of temporary advantages rather than maintaining equilibrium by sustaining advantages. The exact strategic actions formulated under this system will depend on many variables within the industry and the firm. Many types of strategic initiatives can be carried out using the New 7S's, and there are many variations.

As shown in Exhibit 2, the New 7S's encompass three factors for effective delivery of a series of market disruptions: vision, capabilities, and tactics. What is being called for is an increased emphasis on the first two levels (vision and capabilities) and more creative approaches to the last level (tactics) than many firms currently use.

▇ Vision for Disruption: The First Two S's

Successful firms learn how to disrupt the status quo. A key to their choice of a disruption is the realization that not all disruptions are good. The disruptions that work are those that involve the first S—the creation of a temporary ability to serve the customer better than competitors can.

To create this type of disruption, successful firms prioritize customers as the most important stakeholder. This implies that employees and investors are prioritized less highly. Thus, to create successful disruptions, the firm must find a way to satisfy employees and investors even though their interests have been subordinated to customers.

Before the Pentium chip, Intel rarely asked customers what they wanted, but now they have instituted a process of concurrent engineering to get customers (and internal manufacturing) involved as early as possible. Now, when designing new chips, Intel designers visit every major customer and major software houses to ask them what they want in a chip. Intel has also provided early software simulations of its new chips to computer makers, allowing them to get a jump on designing their new machines, and has produced software compilers to help software companies use the new chip.

EXHIBIT 2   Disruption and the New 7S's

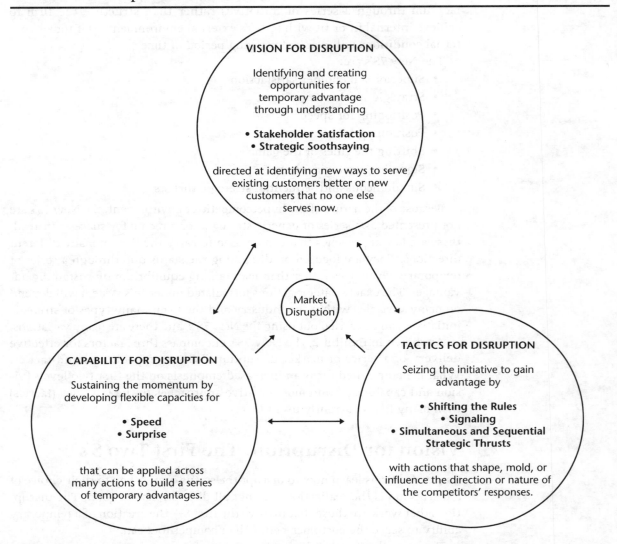

VISION FOR DISRUPTION

Identifying and creating opportunities for temporary advantage through understanding

- **Stakeholder Satisfaction**
- **Strategic Soothsaying**

directed at identifying new ways to serve existing customers better or new customers that no one else serves now.

Market Disruption

CAPABILITY FOR DISRUPTION

Sustaining the momentum by developing flexible capacities for

- **Speed**
- **Surprise**

that can be applied across many actions to build a series of temporary advantages.

TACTICS FOR DISRUPTION

Seizing the initiative to gain advantage by

- **Shifting the Rules**
- **Signaling**
- **Simultaneous and Sequential Strategic Thrusts**

with actions that shape, mold, or influence the direction or nature of the competitors' responses.

CEO Andrew Grove holds regular meetings with employees from all parts of the organization to brainstorm about the future, competitive challenges, and customer needs. Employees are motivated and empowered to serve customers' priorities above their own. Employees have a right to demand AR—"action required"—of any executive. Over the years Intel has also worked to avoid layoffs through asking staff to put in overtime or cut back on hours, so employees remain motivated to serve customers.

Disruptions that satisfy current customer needs are not enough. Constantly improving customer satisfaction is now so standard that firms that once led the pack on customer satisfaction now find themselves without any lead at all. Thus, the key to achieving real advantage from customer satisfaction is to:

- Identify customer needs that even the customer cannot articulate for him/herself
- Find new, previously unserved customers to serve
- Create customer needs that never existed before
- Predict changes in customer needs before they happen

To do this, firms are now engaging in the second S, strategic soothsaying. This allows firms to see and create *future* needs that they can serve better than any competitor does, even if only temporarily. The ability to see and create these future need depends upon the firm's ability to predict future trends, to control the development of key technologies and other know-how that will shape the future, and to create self-fulfilling prophecies.

Intel CEO Grove has quipped that the company bets millions on science fiction.[4] As pressure builds from clonemakers and rival systems, engineers are brought together to consider the emerging technological capabilities and the performance needed to keep ahead of competitors. Intel has also expanded into other areas such as supercomputers, flash memories, video chips, and networking boards. Its sales in these areas are climbing at an average rate of 68 percent per year.[5] It has gained 85 percent of the emerging market for flash memory chips and practically owns one third of the market for massively parallel computers. This experience provides knowledge that Intel can then apply to standard chips, adding features such as video.

The second S, strategic soothsaying, is concerned with understanding the future evolution of markets and technology that will proactively create new opportunities to serve existing or new customers. This arise contributes to the firm's vision of where the next advantage will be discovered and where the company should focus its disruption.

Capabilities for Disruption: The Next Two S's

To act on this vision, companies need two key capabilities: speed and surprise. As in fencing, speed and surprise are key factors in gaining an advantage before competitors are able to do so and in delaying competitor reactions to the new advantage.

If two companies recognize the opportunity to create a new advantage at the same time, the company that can create the advantage faster will win. Because success depends on the creation of a series of temporary advantages, a company's ability to move quickly from one advantage to the next is crucial. Speed allows companies to maneuver to disrupt the status quo, erode the advantage of competitors, and create new advantages before competitors are able to preempt these moves.

Intel used to bring out one or two new chips each year and a new microprocessor family every three or four years. In 1992 it drove out nearly thirty new variations on its 486 chip and introduced the next generation of chip, the Pentium. To stay ahead of clonemakers, Intel plans to create new families of

---

[4] Robert D. Hof, "Inside Intel," *Business Week,* June 1, 1992, p. 88.
[5] Ibid., p. 90.

chips every year or two throughout the 1990s.[6] Instead of waiting until the current generation of chip is rolled out before working on the next one, Intel now develops several generations of chips at once. It is already working on making its chips obsolete before they have even hit the market. Intel has created design-automation software that allows it to add two or three times the transistors to each new chip design with no increase in development time. It also has achieved a breakthrough in modeling systems that promises to cut the four-year product-development cycle by six months. The new Quickturn system will allow Intel to perform engineering tests up to thirty thousand times faster.

If a competitor is unaware of the opportunity to create a new advantage, surprise can maintain that lack of awareness. While this is not a source of sustainable advantage (once the competitor recognizes the advantage, it can usually move quickly to duplicate it), surprise allows the company to create the advantage and to extend the period in which the advantage is unique. Surprise also allows companies to act to undermine competitor advantages before the competitors can take defensive actions.

Intel's multiple capabilities—with strengths in microprocessors, other chips, flash memories, personal computers, and supercomputers—keep competitors guessing about its next move. Since its early days, it has often pursued a strategy of simultaneously pursuing alternative technology, and it currently has its own versions of the competing RISC-based chip (Reduced Instruction-Set Computing) although it continues to defend its stronghold of CISC (Complex Instruction-Set Computing), which offers more software. Not wanting to compete with its customers, Intel hasn't entered the personal computer market under its own name, but it has developed the capabilities to do so as the only supplier to computer manufacturers with a brand name—so competitors never know when it might decide to enter the PC market.

Intel has used advances in modeling and design of new chips to surprise competitors. Its new modeling system gave it a strategic victory over a competing RISC-based chip. At a technology forum in 1991, an Intel executive demonstrated a working model of the Pentium chip, using a link to the model, before an actual chip was ready. In what may have been a response to Intel's signal, six months later Compaq Computer Corporation canceled plans to launch a RISC-based personal computer.[7] And it is still unclear whether new research efforts in RISC chips will surprise Intel.

Intel also maintains a flexible workforce, shifting employees to different projects and keeping operations lean. Despite its continued growth in revenues, the number of Intel employees declined between 1984 and 1992 to maintain flexibility.

Capabilities for speed and surprise are therefore key elements for successfully disrupting the status quo and creating temporary advantages. These capabilities are flexible in that they can be deployed across a wide range of specific actions.

---

[6] Ibid., pp. 86–94.
[7] Ibid., p. 89.

◼ Tactics for Disruption: The Last Three S's

The final three S's—shifting the rules of the game, signaling, and simultaneous and sequential strategic thrusts—are concerned with the tactics used in delivering a company's disruptions, especially tactics that influence the flow of future dynamic strategic interactions among competitors. These three S's follow the vision developed by the first two S's and use the potential for speed and surprise from the third and fourth S's.

In contrast to static approaches to strategy, these final three S's are concerned with a dynamic process of actions and interactions. Most planning is concerned with the company's next move to gain advantage. It usually analyzes potential competitive responses but doesn't shape those responses to its advantage.

The view presented here is a set of tactics designed to disrupt the status quo and create temporary advantage. Tactics such as actions that shift the rules of competition create or sudden and discontinuous move in the industry, reshaping the competitive playing field and confusing the opponent.

Intel's move into new areas such as supercomputers, interactive digital video, and flash memory has helped shift the rules of competition. Flash memory provides an alternative to the standard memory market, where Intel lost out to Japanese competitors. Intel is adding ancillary products, such as networking circuit boards and graphic chips, that make it easier for computer makers to add these features. It has also designed a personal computer with workstation power, the Panther, which it is licensing to computer makers. This shifts the rules by creating a machine that Intel is not marketing itself. The purpose of the design is to take full advantage of Intel's Pentium chip.

Signaling can delay or dampen the competitor's actions to create advantage, throw the competitor off balance, or create surprise. Grove has signaled Intel's intent to fight the clonemarkers "with everything we've got."[8] It has also stated a vision of making the company the center of all computing, from palmtops to supercomputers. Its precise strategy for doing this is less visible. Although it has clearly revealed that it has 686 and 786 chips in the works, what these chips will be able to do is still open to speculation. As discussed, Intel used signaling to shift the rules of competition by transforming computer chips from a hidden commodity to a marketing asset through its Intel Inside campaign. By making the chip visible and using branding in marketing PCs, it made major gains in its battle against the clones. But the brand is only as powerful as the computer chip behind it.

Competitive thrusts in this environment are rapid—either a sequence of moves or a set of simultaneous actions—to upset the equilibrium of the industry, disrupt the status quo, and open opportunities for new advantage. As an example of a set of simultaneous thrusts, a company might feint a move in one direction and then move forcefully in another direction, creating surprise and temporary advantage from the misdirection of the opponent. One can think of sequential thrusts as being akin to the sequence of plays used in a football game. One team may run the ball several times until the defense is conditioned to expect a run

---

[8] Ibid., p. 87.

play. Then the offense switches to the long bomb at a time that should call for a run. The sequence of actions create surprise and temporary advantage, since once the play is used, the defense will watch out for the long bomb in future plays.

Intel has used a variety of simultaneous and sequential strategic thrusts to seize the initiative. In the late 1970s, struggling with its 8086 microprocessor chip, Intel launched an all-out assault—code-named Operation Crush—against Motorola and other competitors. Intel set up war rooms to work toward making the 8086 the industry standard. It was this effort to simultaneously attack several segments of the market that helped lead to IBM's decision to adapt the 8088 as the center of its personal computer.[9] Intel rode the wave of the PC's growth to dominance in the microprocessor industry.

Intel also participated in both the memory and microprocessor markets at various points in time. In a way, Intel's retreat from the memory chip market and return with flash memory might be seen as a sequential set of moves akin to a strategic retreat followed by regrouping and counterattack. It has used multiple exploratory attacks to develop a variety of know-how and technology capabilities and gauge competitor and customer reactions (for example, its simultaneous development of RISC and CISC technology). It has also explored promising markets (such as video and massively parallel computing) and moved into those with the highest potential for growth. It has built its businesses by using a sequential strategy, moving from memory chips to microprocessors, to boards, to building personal computers (although not marketing them).

These three tactics reflect the increasing speed and intensity of hypercompetition. Although these actions sometimes push companies into the gray areas of antitrust because the behaviors could be construed as exclusionary or anticompetitive actions, companies are increasingly seeing them as necessary for competitive survival.

Putting All the S's Together

Exhibit 2 illustrates how the New 7S's work together to develop a vision, capabilities, and tactics for disruption.

As suggested earlier, while the traditional 7S's are concerned with capitalizing on creating a static strategic fit among internal aspects of the organization, the New 7S's are concerned with four key goals that are based on understanding dynamic strategic interactions over long periods of time.

1. *Disrupting the status quo.* Competitors disrupt the status quo by identifying new opportunities to serve the customer, signaling, shifting the rules, and attacking through sequential and simultaneous thrusts. These moves end the old pattern of competitive interaction between rivals. This requires speed and surprise; otherwise, the company's competitors simply change at the same rate.

2. *Creating temporary advantage.* Disruption creates temporary advantages. These advantages are based on better knowledge of customers,

---

[9] Ashish Nanda and Christopher A. Bartlett, "Intel Corporation—leveraging capabilities for strategic renewal," working paper, Graduate School of Business, Harvard University, November 25, 1992, p. 3.

technology, and the future. They are derived from customer orientation and employee empowerment throughout the entire organization. These advantages are short-lived, eroded by fierce competition.

3. *Seizing the initiative.* By moving aggressively in each arena, acting to create a new advantage or undermine a competitor's old advantage, the company seizes the initiative. This throws the opponent off balance and puts it at a disadvantage for a while. The opponent is forced to play catch-up, reacting rather than shaping the future with its own actions to seize the initiative. The initiator is proactive, while competitors are forced to be reactive.

4. *Sustaining the momentum.* Several actions in a row to seize the initiative create momentum. The company continues to develop new advantages and doesn't wait for competitors to undermine them before launching the next initiative. For example, while U.S. manufacturers are doing remedial work in quality improvement, Japanese manufacturers are now building key advantages in flexibility. This succession of actions sustains the momentum. This is the only source of sustainable competitive advantage in hypercompetitive environments.

In hypercompetition it is not enough to build a static set of competencies. Good resources are not enough. They must be used effectively. This is precisely why successful firms pay attention to tactics as well as capabilities and vision in an environment of traditional competition and to competencies in an environment of hypercompetition. In slower and less aggressive competitive environments, companies could concentrate primarily on making great swords. In hypercompetition, they have been forced to concentrate much more on the skills of fencing. It is these dynamic skills that are the most significant competencies of the firm. Thus, a company's success depends equally upon its swords and its fencing skills, and the New 7S's are intended to guide firms towards making the right swords, learning how to fence, and pointing them in the right direction.

◼ Some Tradeoffs

One final analysis can be done using the New 7S's. In choosing which to concentrate on, companies are forced to make tradeoffs among them. This makes it difficult for companies to do all seven equally well. Companies choose among the seven to confront different challenges and opportunities that present themselves.

Thus, it is possible to analyze a competitor (or one's own company) to see what types of tradeoffs have been made. Once these are identified, the weakness of the competitor (or one's own company) is apparent. Furthermore, the tradeoff means that the competitor can't plug the weakness without giving up something else. Thus, it is possible to identify weakness, which, if attacked, forces the competition to be slow to respond or to give up some other strength in order to respond. Either way the competitor loses.

Among the tradeoffs implied by the New 7S's are the following:

- *Tradeoffs at the expense of stakeholder satisfaction (S-1)* can be undermined by speed (S-3), as companies may sacrifice product or service quality to gain speed or push employees to work harder and faster. Speeding products to market with little testing could also reduce customer satisfaction. Similarly surprise (S-4), shifting the rules (S-5), signaling (S-6), and simultaneous and sequential strategic thrusts (S-7) also have the potential to confuse customers, employees, and shareholders as well as competitors.

- *Tradeoffs at the expense of future orientation/soothsaying.* Strategic soothsaying (S-2) can be hurt by speed (S-3), which often leaves little time for reflecting on what lies ahead, and surprise (S-4), which is sudden and unpredictable enough to make prognostication irrelevant or impossible. Shifting the rules (S-5) often reshapes competition in a way that unpredictably changes future opportunities so that soothsaying becomes difficult. To the extent that competitor reactions are not anticipated, simultaneous and sequential strategic thrusts (S-7) sometimes make soothsaying more difficult.

- *Tradeoffs at the expense of speed.* Speed (S-3) can be eroded through the slowness of decision making in an organization such as the ones used to increase stakeholder satisfaction (S-l). Also, strategic alliances used to shift the rules (S-5) sometimes reduce speed because of negotiations. Shifting the rules of competition (S-5) may require a tradeoff with speed. It can temporarily reduce speed (S-3), for example, because of the confusion and time it takes to regroup and retool to create the new rules. Simultaneous and sequential strategic thrusts (S-7) can reduce speed (S-3) because they require more effort than single thrusts.

- *Tradeoffs at the expense of surprise.* The flexibility and stealth of surprise (S-4) can be eroded by strategies to increase capabilities for speed. For example, just in time systems could decrease the company's flexibility while increasing speed. Alliances to shift the rules sometimes also decrease surprise because the alliances are usually public. Signaling can also reduce the element of surprise because it often involves revealing the strategic intent of the company. Sequential thrusts can reduce surprise (S-4) by committing the company to a clear set of actions.

These tradeoffs mean that firms can't always do all of the New 7S's equally well, even if they are above a reasonable threshold on each one of them. Thus, a competitor can do a tradeoff analysis to identify the maneuvers it can do through use of the S's that the opponent can't do well because the opponent can't respond without depleting its strength in one of the other S's. Other firms will creatively switch among the New 7S's to shift the rules of competition, sometimes focusing on the opponent's weaker S's, sometimes using several in concert.

Moreover, firms have limited resources, so they can't acquire all seven of the New S's at once. They must prioritize them and make tradeoffs. Thus, it will be rare that a firm is equally good at all of the New 7S's. This will create opportunities for a new type of hypercompetitive behavior whereby firms use the resource investment tradeoffs made by a competitor to determine which of the New 7S's should be invested in first. Finally, truly hypercompetitive firms, like Intel, will find ways to eliminate the tradeoffs. Tradeoffs exist only if firms believe that tradeoffs are necessities and stop looking for ways to do both alternatives. After all, it was once said that firms could not achieve low cost and high quality at the same time. Now it is not just a reality but a necessity for survival in many industries.

Will Advantages from Using the New 7S's Eventually Erode?

Like all know-how, knowledge of how to use the New 7S's might eventually be expected to erode as it becomes widely assimilated. As knowledge of these approaches becomes increasingly widespread and all competitors begin using them—this is already taking place—one might expect that any advantage would be neutralized. In particular, this erosion may be seen in the temporary advantages of a customer focus. As customer focus (a central part of S-l) has been driven through U.S. organizations by the total quality movement and other forces, it has become less of an advantage and more of a requisite to succeed in business.

While the impact of the New 7S's may be diminished somewhat by their widespread adoption, there are several factors that promise to continue to make them a source of advantage even after they are widely used. First, the New 7S's have some inherent flexibility so that different companies using the New 7S's can take very different strategies. The use of simultaneous and sequential strategic thrusts (S-7) presents a wide range of options and variations. There are many other thrusts that can be designed for specific opportunities, making it difficult for firms to exactly replicate a competitor's use of the New 7S's.

Second, the New 7S's are dynamic. Companies use them in different ways over time. Stakeholder satisfaction changes, competitive opportunities change, sources of temporary advantage change. The New 7S's and their goals of creating disruption and seizing the initiative remain constant, but the methods companies use to achieve these goals constantly change. In this way, even if all competitors in an industry are using the New 7S's, their moves will continue to be unpredictable.

Third, companies usually cannot use all of the New 7S's at once because of inherent tradeoffs among the S's. Companies perform a balancing act in weighing these tradeoffs. This adds to the unpredictability of competitive moves, because companies can use any of the New 7S's in developing their next strategic move, and the tradeoffs may make it difficult to respond.

As more competitors focus on disrupting the status quo and seizing the initiative, this intent may become fairly predictable. Companies will know that their competitors will be actively working on their next competitive move. But this intent does little to reveal the actual strategies of competitors. All it does is make it clear that the company will not pursue one strategy: namely, sustaining its current advantage. This leaves every action other than that one open.

The one certain impact is that as the New 7S's become more widespread, competition will become more aggressive. Instead of having one or two competitors seeking to disrupt the status quo, every competitor will be looking for the next source of temporary advantage. With this further intensification of hypercompetition, one might expect an increased interest in alliances and other forms of cooperation to dampen the intensity of competition (as has already been seen). Ultimately, however, the only way out of this dilemma is for companies to become more aggressive in seizing the initiative. Cooperative attempts to end this cycle of aggression will be seen as either illegal (collusive antitrust violations), or futile, since it is like shoveling sand against the tide. Leading firms will be wary of cooperative efforts that ask them to be less aggressive and give up their temporary advantage. Lagging firms with the fire in their bellies to be number one will not be satisfied with their permanent status as second-class citizens. So the New 7S's will be used more aggressively and more frequently in the future world of hypercompetition.

While the New 7S's will continue to be important, especially with the intensifying competition of the future, there may be even newer S's that emerge as keys to competitive success. Hypercompetitive companies will continue to monitor and define these new strategic approaches in new attempts to provide temporary advantages and sustain momentum with a series of successful short-term advantages.

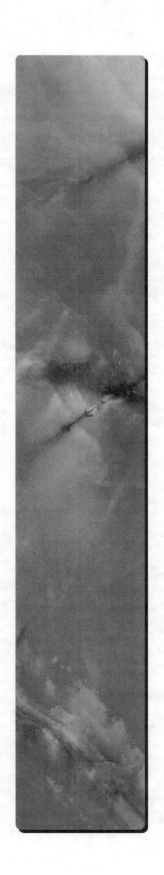

SECTION

III

Cases

CASE 1

Aer Lingus— ATS (A)

On July 15, 1985, Denis Hanrahan was flying from Dublin to Toronto, as he had many times over the past 11 months, to meet with Klaus Woerner, the owner and president of Automation Tooling Systems (ATS), a robotics firm based in Kitchener, Ontario. Mr. Hanrahan's job was to expand the "non-air-line" activities of Aer Lingus and ATS was a company in which he wanted to acquire an equity position.

The negotiations between Denis and Klaus had been friendly but protracted, and it appeared that they were finally nearing an end. The deal, which both sides had agreed to orally, was that Aer Lingus would purchase 75 percent of the shares of ATS and that Klaus would stay on and manage the company. The price that he would receive for his shares would depend on the earnings of ATS in the years ending September 30, 1985 and 1986. If ATS met the profit forecast that Klaus had prepared for it, he would receive a total of $4.6 million in cash, and retain a 25 percent interest in the company.

Aer Lingus

Aer Lingus was the Irish international airline, wholly owned by the Irish government. As shown in Figure 1, Aer Lingus, like many airlines, had difficulty producing a consistently high level of earnings. The early 1980s in particular were not good years for the airline (nor for any other) and only the consistent profitability of the group's hotels, airline-related businesses (maintenance and overhaul of the other firm's aircraft, training of flight crews and so on), and financial and commercial businesses kept the company's overall losses in check.

A small group of managers under the leadership of Gerry Dempsey were responsible for managing and expanding Aer Lingus' non-airline activities. Denis Hanrahan, second in command, commented:

> We all recognize that the airline business is a cyclical one, and our goal is to create a stable base of earnings which will see the airline safely through

Case material is prepared solely as a basis for classroom discussion. This case was prepared by Peter Killing, Associate Professor. © 1989 Ivey Management Services and the IMEDE Management Development Institute, Lausanne, Switzerland, version 9-89-M004.

FIGURE 1   Aer Lingus Financial Results (millions of Irish pounds—years ending March 31)

	1985		1984		1983		1982		1981	
	Revenue	Profit	Revenue	Profit	Revenue	Profit	Revenue	Profit	Revenue	Profit
Air transport	281	0.5	270	1.4	244	(2.7)	218	(11.2)	164	(15.9)
Ancillary Operations										
Airline-related	110	12.7	82	11.1	66	9.0	62	8.6	47	7.5
Hotel and leisure	79	11.7	82	7.7	82	6.0	71	7.8	54	7.7
Financial and commercial	33	5.4	24	4.5	11	3.6	8	2.0	6	1.3
Net profit after head office expenses, interest, tax*		11.6		4.9		(2.5)		(9.2)		(13.6)

Note: In 1985 the Group total assets stood at £285 million. A breakdown of assets employed in each business area was not publicly reported.

Note re Exchange Rates: **Canadian Dollars per Irish Pound**
1981: 1.90
1982: 1.75
1983: 1.54
1984: 1.41
1985: 1.44

*The company earned a positive net profit in each of the four years preceding 1981.

the bottom of the cycles. We have been successful so far so we don't know if the government would bail us out if we did make continued heavy losses, and we don't want to have to find out! The mission of our "ancillary activities" is to increase the Group's reported earnings and to strengthen its balance sheet.

The "financial and commercial" results shown in Figure 1 include a data processing firm, an insurance company, a helicopter company, a hospital management firm, a land development company, and a 25 percent interest in GPA, formerly Guiness Peat Aviation. Many of these firms, with the exception of the hotels, were founded by former Aer Lingus employees. Although most of the companies were performing well, the undoubted star was GPA. A manager explained:

In 1975 or so, Tony Ryan, our New York station manager, was transferred back to Ireland and asked to lease out a 747 which we did not need for the winter. In looking at the leasing market, he thought he saw a very good business opportunity, and he convinced us and a related British company to each put up 45 percent of the capital required to start an aircraft leasing company. He kept the remaining ten percent. As things have developed, he was certainly right about the opportunity. In the ten intervening years, we have received almost 20 million Irish pounds from that business, and our initial investment was only 2.2 million! We still own 25 percent of the company, and now have firms like Air Canada and the General Electric Credit Corporation as partners. GPA is one of *the* Irish success stories of the past decade.

◼ The Move into Robotics

In 1983 Denis Hanrahan began an informal search for a new area of investment which could provide healthy financial returns to Aer Lingus for at least the next decade. By January 1984 he had concluded that robotics was an extremely interesting field. Robots had been used in Japan since the 1960s but were not adopted in Europe and the United States until the late 1970s. Many analysts expected a robotics boom, with growth rates as high as 30 percent per annum, as Western firms strove to catch up.

Although robot manufacturing appeared to Denis to be an overcrowded field, he was excited about the possibility of becoming a developer of the ancillary technology and components that were required by firms wanting to install robot-based flexible manufacturing assembly lines. His figures suggested that the market value of ancillary systems was at least equal to the value of the robots themselves. Although the volume of business being done in this new area was impossible to quantify with any degree of precision, it appeared to be growing quickly and offer high margins. There were as yet no major companies in the business.

Denis described Aer Lingus' initial entry into the field:

> The first company we looked at was in the UK. We fairly quickly decided that it was too big, too sexy, and considering its size, depended too heavily on a single supplier of robots. One thing you have to watch out for in this business is guys in very classy suits who know more about doing deals and driving for the initial public offering which is going to make them rich than they do about robotics. It turned out that we were right about that company, as it went bankrupt afterwards.
>
> The company we did buy was Airstead Industrial Systems of the U.K. This is a very small company, much smaller than ATS, but it has the rights to distribute Seiko robots in England. Seiko, in addition to producing products such as watches and Epson computer printers, is a prominent robot manufacturer and was doing very well in some fast-growing niches.

After the acquisition of Airstead, Aer Lingus dispatched an analyst to North America to examine six companies that Seiko had identified as the most promising North American robotics systems firms. On August 15 Denis received a telex containing a thumbnail sketch of ATS, indicating that it was the best of the three firms the analyst had seen to date, and was worth a closer look. On August 28 Denis was in Kitchener for his first meeting with Klaus Woerner.

Klaus Woerner and ATS

Born in Germany in 1940, Klaus Woerner emigrated to Canada at age 20 after serving an apprenticeship in the tool and die business. He subsequently worked for a variety of manufacturing firms in Canada but, tired of the "hierarchies and rigidities of large corporations," founded ATS in 1978. The new company was not successful, however, until Klaus turned it away from manufacturing and into systems work. The move into robotics was made in late 1981.

By the summer of 1984 ATS had grown to employ 44 people, including 26 tool makers, 15 hardware and software designers, and 3 in sales and administration. Denis was encouraged to see that Klaus was a technically oriented, "hands on" manager whose elegant and creative solutions to systems problems played a major role in the company's success. Klaus, Denis observed, was more at home on the shop floor than talking to accountants, bankers, or lawyers. In his summary of their first meeting, Denis made the following points:

1. Mr. Woerner was an easy individual to get along with, though I would anticipate that he is used to getting his own way. He is the key decision maker in the company, although he does solicit the opinions of his senior colleagues.

2. The company currently turns over approximately $3.5 million per year and expects to double its sales this year on last year, after a number of years of relatively slow growth. Woerner reports a current backlog of $3 million.

3. The major financial problem with the business is that there is a significant working capital requirement. I have heard a rule of thumb that suggests 40 percent of turnover is required in this business, but Klaus thought that was far too high. The practical problem is that the final payment of 30 percent of systems cost tends to be delayed for several months after completion of the work while fine-tuning is being performed.

4. Mr. Woerner recently came very close to selling ATS to Berton Industries,[1] a major Canadian corporation in the automotive components business. One hundred percent of ATS was to be acquired and, depending on results, it would have been valued at $3 to $4 million. Mr. Woerner got very concerned, however, at what he perceived to be the inordinate length of time being taken in detailed negotiations and at the aggressive attitude of the other party's attorneys. In addition Berton would not give him any assurances about future investment in ATS and apparently Woerner learned that plans had been made to move ATS to another location without any consultation with him. When the president of Berton then ignored Woerner's request that a number of written commitments be made within one week, the deal was off.

5. Mr. Woerner's proposal was that Aer Lingus would take 50 percent of the company for an undetermined amount, that 50 percent of this money would be left in the company and that he would take 50 percent out. I indicated to him that 50 percent would probably be the minimum share that we would require and it could be that we would want considerably more. However, any deal that we would do would be structured in such a way that he and his key people would be committed to staying with the company. He had no difficulty with this point and conceded that he was not wedded to the 50:50 formula which was clearly an ideal going-in position from his point of view.

6. On balance, I found ATS to be very impressive. Although operating in cramped facilities it does appear to have a real technical depth and undoubtedly has an established customer base. The company appears to be an appropriate size to take over since it is neither so

---

[1] Disguised name.

small as to be extraordinarily risky nor so big as to be extraordinarily expensive.

The meeting ended with the two men agreeing to continue discussions and to try to reach a gentlemen's agreement reasonably quickly rather than getting bogged down in protracted technical or legal discussions. Mr. Woerner promised to send some financial information as soon as he could get it put together, although he warned that his business plan should not be taken unduly literally as "these things are more exercises than necessarily forecasts of reality."

Subsequent Meetings

Over the next six months Denis Hanrahan held a number of meetings with Klaus Woerner, bringing with him on occasion Gerry Dempsey and Larry Stanley, another of Aer Lingus' ancillary business managers. Both men subsequently supported Denis' view that ATS would be a good acquisition. This positive feedback was also strengthened by comments from Seiko's North American sales manager who stated that in ten years ATS would be "one of the top three robot systems integrator firms in North America" if it grew to its potential. The meetings with Klaus also yielded more information about his expectations and the operations of ATS. The following excerpts are taken from Denis Hanrahan's notes and comments on various meetings, all of which were held in Kitchener or Toronto.

Meeting of November 6

Present: G. P. Dempsey, Denis Hanrahan, Klaus Woerner, and Peter Jones,[2] who was Klaus Woerner's personal financial advisor and company accountant.

1. Mr. Woerner outlined his expectations for growth of the automation and robotics industry and for ATS. It seems clear that they have not done very much forward planning ... Mr. Woerner quoted Laura Conigliaro of Prudential-Bache as suggesting growth from $250 million in 1984 to $1 billion by 1987, but these figures were not very convincing since they relate to the total industry rather than to the sub-segment in which ATS is involved.

2. Mr. Woerner stated that he expected ATS revenues to total $4 million for the year ending September 1984, $6 million for 1985 (rather than the $5 million he had earlier been projecting) and to reach $10 million in three years' time. He believed that growth to $10 million could be financed through a combination of retained earnings and bank debt.

3. Northern Telecom (a major Canadian multinational firm) apparently accounts for approximately 40 percent of ATS revenues. Mr. Woerner indicated that this proportion would fall to one-third in 1985 due to the growth of ATS. He stated strongly that in spite of the company's high dependence on Northern Telecom he could, if necessary, survive a total loss of Northern's business by falling back on traditional

---

[2] Disguised name.

non-flexible production line work ("hard" automation). However, he expressed the view that Northern Telecom could not break the relationship with him since they were dependent on ATS for maintenance and software updates.

4. There was an extensive discussion on the subject of control. Mr. Woerner's recent negotiations with Berton have left him very uneasy about the behaviour of large corporations, and he again expressed his strong preference for a 50:50 partnership. Mr. Dempsey responded that our whole approach to subsidiaries was to work in partnership with the management of them and that this approach was not altered whether the shareholding was 2 percent, 50 percent, or 99 percent. Mr. Woerner appeared to implicitly accept that we might go to 75 percent or higher of the equity as long as we were concerned only with issues such as overall earnings and growth rather than the detailed operating practices involved. Mr. Dempsey suggested that Mr. Woerner should write to us in simple, non-legal terms outlining those issues upon which he believed he would require assurance from us. Mr. Woerner accepted this suggestion.

5. Mr. Woerner also expressed concern that his was a small company and in danger of being "trampled on" by Aer Lingus. While he was happy enough with the people he currently knew in Aer Lingus, he felt that these individuals could change and he could thus find himself exposed to changes of policy or personality. Mr. Dempsey responded that we could not fully reassure him on this issue. We had now had a wide range of relationships with subsidiaries over a long period of time and as this had not occurred historically he saw no reason why it should happen in the future.

6. There were no specific discussions on the matter of price. Mr. Dempsey stated on a number of occasions that it was purposeless to discuss price until the financials were available and had been reviewed. Mr. Woerner concurred.

7. The meeting ended on a positive and progressive note. It was agreed that we would appoint Peat Marwick to review the affairs of ATS and they would contact Mr. Jones as necessary. It was also agreed that Mr. Jones would shortly produce a three-year forecast for ATS.

Meeting of January 10

The next meeting between Klaus and Denis included Bill Harcourt[3] of Peat Marwick Mitchell. During this meeting the ATS financial statements and projections (see Exhibits 1 and 2) were given to Denis. These were to have been sent to Ireland several weeks earlier.

Denis learned during this meeting that Klaus had not written the promised letter concerning his specific issues of concern because he preferred to discuss them face to face. Further discussion ensued during which Klaus reiterated his

---

[3] Disguised name.

EXHIBIT I

ATS FINANCIAL STATEMENTS
(Cdn$000)

	1980	1981	1982	1983	1984
Sales	332	765	1,210	1,753	4,168
Cost of sales	187	491	902	1,450	3,197
Gross margin	145	274	308	303	971
Overheads	58	127	188	243	451
Operating profit	87	147	120	60	520
Interest	2	10	20	26	71
Tax	11	22	4	0	18
Net profit	74	115	96	34	431
Balance Sheets					
Assets:					
Fixed assets	106	211	308	390	517
Current assets	113	282	384	457	1,300
Current liabilities	(35)	(129)	(209)	(252)	(390)
Working capital	78	153	175	205	910
	184	364	483	595	1,427
Funded By:					
Share capital	1	6	5	3	3
Revenue reserves	79	114	177	(160)	164
Shareholders' funds	80	120	182	(157)	167
Loan capital	104	244	301	752	1,260
	184	364	483	595	1,427

general unease at the prospect of being controlled and repeated his desire for a 50:50 deal. While still not raising any specific concerns, Klaus repeatedly referred to the Berton deal and how lucky he was to have avoided it. Denis commented after the meeting:

All of this was territory that we had covered several times previously with him and we essentially just covered it again. It was clear that as the discussion progressed, Klaus began to get more comfortable and his fears began to recede. I have no doubt that after I depart from Canada he begins to get uneasy again at the unknown. He reiterated that he was quite comfortable working with Mr. Dempsey or myself but that he could naturally have no assurance that we would be around forever.

In the earlier part of the meeting when Klaus was appearing very reluctant, Bill Harcourt asked him directly if he, in fact, wanted to sell ATS. Klaus replied that he didn't really want to—he had devoted all of his time in the last few years in building up the company, and wished to continue to do so in the future—but because ATS would not be producing large amounts of cash in the short term he had no choice. He believes that ATS can and must grow very rapidly to forestall the competition—the opportunities are there

EXHIBIT 2

PROJECTED ATS FINANCIAL STATEMENTS
(Cdn$000)

	1985	1986	1987	1988
Sales	8,000	11,000	14,000	17,000
Cost of sales	5,920	8,360	10,920	13,260
Gross margin	2,080	2,640	3,080	3,740
Overheads	1,040	1,430	1,750	2,210
Operating profit	1,040	1,210	1,330	1,530
Interest	70	120	200	300
Tax	427	480	497	541
Net profit	543	610	633	689
Dividends (projected)	0	0	250	300

Projected Balance Sheets

	1984 (actual)	1985	1986	1987	1988
Assets:					
Fixed assets	517	680	1,030	1,310	1,860
Development				1,000	1,000
Current assets	1,300	2,417	4,904	5,740	6,580
Current liabilities	(390)	(760)	(1,720)	(1,886)	(2,260)
Working capital	910	1,657	3,184	3,854	4,320
	1,427	2,337	4,214	6,164	7,180
Funded by:					
Share capital	3	750	2,000	2,300	2,700
Revenue reserves	164	707	1,317	1,701	2,090
Shareholders' funds	167	1,457	3,317	4,001	3,790
Loan capital	1,260	880	897	2,163	3,390
	1,427	2,337	4,214	6,164	7,180

Note: These projections were prepared by Klaus Woerner and Peter Jones.

and if ATS does not take advantage of them someone else will. In this vein he mentioned that he had just revised his estimate of the current year's sales from $6 million to $9 million.

The other reason that Klaus feels that he has to sell ATS is that important customers like Northern Telecom are nervous of becoming too dependent on him, as long as he does not have a major corporate backer. Klaus told us in the meeting that Northern had in fact deliberately cut back their orders to him for this reason, and we independently checked that this was indeed the case.

The meeting ended on a very friendly note with Denis again encouraging Klaus to make up a list of his specific concerns so that they could be addressed, and Klaus inviting Bill Harcourt to visit the ATS plant before the next meeting so that he could develop a better understanding of what they were doing.

Meetings of January 24 and February 20

The meetings of January 24 and February 20 were devoted to discussions of a deal whereby Aer Lingus would acquire 75 percent of ATS stock, with Klaus Woerner holding the remaining 25 percent. At the January 24 meeting Klaus appeared to accept the idea that he would sell the 75 percent of the company, but, apparently as a result of his earlier negotiations with Berton, was adamant that ATS was worth at least $6 million. In the February 20 meeting Denis finally agreed that ATS could be worth $6 million if the company met Klaus' new projections for it, but at the moment it was not. As a consequence, Denis proposed that the amount paid to Klaus should depend on the company's performance in 1985 and 1986. The details, spelled out in a letter from Denis to Klaus following the February meeting, were as follows:

1. We propose that a valuation be established for ATS as of September 30, 1986. This valuation will be calculated by taking 3.5 times the pre-tax income for the fiscal year ended September 30, 1985, and adding to it 3.5 times the incremental pre-tax income earned in the fiscal year ending September 1986. By incremental income here, I mean the excess of pre-tax income in fiscal 1986 over that earned in fiscal 1985.

2. In determining pre-tax income, research and development costs shall be charged at the rate contained in your financial projections or at a higher rate if so incurred. Profit sharing to employees shall be charged at 10 percent of pre-tax income before profit sharing or such higher rate as may be incurred. In addition, we would require the company to maintain a key-man insurance policy on yourself in the amount of $5,000,000 and the cost of such coverage would be borne as a charge before striking pre-tax income.

3. On the basis of the pre-tax income figures outlined above, the company would have a total value of $6,835,000 as of September 30, 1986.

4. Under the above formula, the maximum value that we would be prepared to put on ATS would be $7,000,000 even if the results are better than projected.

5. It is our view that the company is in need of significant additional funds to allow it to develop to the sales and income levels in your projections. Accordingly, we are willing to inject $2,000,000 into ATS for agreed working capital and investment use in the form of a secured debt with a 10 percent interest rate. It would be our intention to make available $750,000 at time of closing, $750,000 at time of completion of the 1985 audit, and the remaining $500,000 as needed by the company on an agreed basis during 1986.

6. It would be our intention that this loan would be used to purchase treasury stock from ATS at the end of 1986 using the valuation for the company as established by the formula outlined above. In other words, if the company was valued at $6,835,000, the $2,000,000 loan would convert to give us 22.6 percent of the enlarged equity in the company. The attraction of this arrangement from your point of view is that it provides you with the money now to grow but that the shares are ultimately purchased in ATS at the valuation achieved in 1986 rather than at a current valuation.

EXHIBIT 3

REVISED INCOME PROJECTIONS
(Cdn$000)

	1985	1986	1987	1988
Sales	8,000	14,000	20,000	30,000
Gross margin	2,080 (26%)	3,360 (24%)	4,400 (22%)	6,000 (20%)
General and administrative	862	1,190	1,578	2,159
Income	1,218	2,170	2,822	3,841
Profit sharing	120	217	282	384
Pre-tax income	1,098	1,953	2,540	3,457
Tax @ 45%	494	879	1,143	1,556
After-tax income	604	1,074	1,397	1,901

Note: These revisions were dated February 20, 1985. They were prepared by Klaus Woerner, working with Bill Harcourt.

Depending upon the ultimate valuation of the company, the percentage of its enlarged equity that would be bought by the $2,000,000 referred to above would vary. It would then be our intention to purchase directly from you existing shares held by you in ATS such as would give us 75 percent of the then-enlarged equity of the company. In the example quoted above, we would need to purchase 67 percent of your shareholding to give us a total of 75 percent of the enlarged equity. Using the value above, this would cost $4,600,000. In other words, what you would receive would be $4,600,000 in cash plus 25 percent interest in the $2,000,000 injected by us, for a total of $5,100,000 which is 75 percent of $6,835,000.

7. We propose that you would be paid for these shares as follows: on closing, $500,000; in March 1986 and March 1987, further payments of $500,000; in March 1988 and March 1989, further payments of $1,000,000 each; the balance payable on March 1990. To the degree that the final value of the company is larger or smaller than the $6,835,000 figure, the above payments would be prorated.

◼ Moving Forward

On March 16 Bill Harcourt phoned Denis to report that he had met with Klaus subsequently to the February 22 meeting. Denis recalled the discussion:

Apparently Klaus was initially very unhappy with the limit of $7 million that we put on the company, although he is now willing to live with it and in fact has become very positive about doing a deal with Aer Lingus. He appears to have overcome his hesitancy and concern at another party becoming the majority shareholder of ATS. This may be due to the fact that he has taken advice from a friend named Bob Tivey who is the retired president of Monarch Canada.[4] Some minor improvements are required, however.

---

[4] Disguised name.

One of these is that Klaus wants us to increase the $500,000 coming to him on closing so that he can pay employee bonuses—these will come out of his own pocket—and have more for himself. He also wants us to pay interest on the portion of the purchase paid which remains unpaid until the earn out is completed. Finally, he would like a personal contract which will last five years, and include a good salary plus a bonus that is 2 percent of pre-tax earnings, and a car.

Other news included the fact that Klaus is in the process of hiring a financial person, and is considering a second-year registered industrial accountancy student. Bill suggested that he discuss this matter in some detail with us, as it might be advisable to opt for a more high-powered person. Bill also told me that Klaus was facing an immediate decision with respect to new premises for ATS—the major question being whether the company should rent or buy. Purchase cost will be close to one million dollars.

Shortly after this phone call Denis received a letter from Klaus which began, "I wish to advise you that I am prepared to accept the proposal as outlined … subject to the following changes." As expected, the most important of the requested changes were an increased initial payment, the payment of interest on the unpaid portion of the purchase price, and a five-year employment contract.

After some negotiation, Aer Lingus agreed to increase its initial payment to allow Klaus to pay employee bonuses and to increase the initial funds going to his own pocket by approximately 50 percent, which was less than he had requested, but was deemed satisfactory.

In early April Klaus travelled to Ireland for a meeting with the Chief Executive of Aer Lingus, and later that month the Aer Lingus board approved the purchase of a 75 percent shareholding of ATS on the terms agreed on with Klaus.

At the end of April Denis was once again in Kitchener, where he and Klaus held a most amicable meeting. Denis learned that Klaus and Bob Tivey had prepared a new business plan which they had used to obtain an increase in the ATS credit line. Also, Klaus had decided to proceed with the acquisition, his only objection being that eight board meetings a year was too many. Denis concluded his notes on the meeting with the following:

> We discussed at length the need for ATS management to develop credibility with me and for me to develop credibility on ATS subjects in Dublin which he seemed to accept. All in all, the discussions were satisfactory and straightforward and have put to rest a significant number of my fears concerning Mr. Woerner's independence and his unwillingness to accommodate the requirements of a major corporate shareholder. In my view, he will accept direction provided that the direction is fast-paced and is seen by him as being responsive to ATS's needs.

Due to some apparent foot-dragging on the part of Klaus' lawyers and intervening vacations, it was July before Denis arrived in Kitchener to review the drafts of the sale contracts and bring the deal to a conclusion.

◼ The Meeting of July 16

Klaus attended this meeting with Ron Jutras, his new financial controller (who had been hired without consultation with Aer Lingus), and Bob Tivey, who was acting as a consultant to Klaus. Denis recalled the meeting as follows:

They opened the meeting by tabling a number of requirements which they said were critical to the deal going ahead. These were:

1. A reluctance to hand over control to us before the valuation date of September 1986.
2. A five-year guaranteed contract for Klaus, with a ten-year period before we can force him out of share ownership.
3. A degree of protection against the possibility that one-off costs may depress 1986 earnings—specifically a *minimum* buyout price of $6 million!

I was very distressed to find such a total about-face on something that we had agreed three months earlier, and when faced with this Klaus acknowledged that he was changing his mind, but said that he could not afford the possibility of one bad year depressing his buyout price. As for the contract length, Klaus was very emotional when the possibility of anything shorter than a five-year contract was raised.

The question facing me as I sat in that meeting was how to react. Was it time to give up on this long and apparently fruitless process, or should I continue—and if so, how?

Airview Mapping Inc.

In early March 1994, Rick Tanner, the principal of Airview Mapping Inc., started drafting plans for the upcoming summer season. For him, late winter typically involved making sales calls on the company's established and potential clients for the purpose of determining the expected demand for his services and then drafting his sales forecasts for the upcoming year.

Airview, which had traditionally dominated the aerial surveying markets of Central and Eastern Canada, had recently been faced with increasing competition in its traditional territories from other air surveyors from across Canada. The protracted recession of the early 1990s, combined with the anti-deficit measures introduced by all levels of government, had reduced the overall demand for geomatic services in Canada, producing significant overcapacity in the industry, including the particular markets in which Airview was involved.

This situation had already reduced the company's profits, but the real threat lay in the fact that the new competitors, once established in Airview's region, would stay there, permanently capturing a significant share of the Central Canadian market. These competitors, typically larger than Airview, could expand their market coverage, even if it meant creating a temporary operating base in a distant location. At the same time, their home markets were extremely difficult for small companies from other regions to penetrate due to their fierce price competition.

Rick realized that his company might face difficult times if he could not redirect his attention to some new areas of opportunity. His view was that these opportunities had to be found in international markets. He had already gathered some information on several foreign markets which looked promising from the company's perspective. It was now time to review the overall situation and decide whether to attempt penetrating any of the identified foreign markets, and, if so, what entry strategy to choose.

Prepared by Kris Opalinski and Walter S. Good of the University of Manitoba, Canada as a basis for classroom discussion rather than to illustrate either effective or ineffective handling of an administrative situation.

The name of the company and its officers have been disguised. Support for the development of this case was provided by the Centre for International Business Studies, University of Manitoba, Canada.

◼ The Company

Airview Mapping Inc. was incorporated in November 1979 by a group of former employees of Aerosurvey Corporation Ltd., with Tom Denning and Rick Tanner as the principal shareholders of the new entity. For the first two years, the company operated without an aircraft, providing mapping services based on externally developed photogrammetric images to clients in Central Canada. Airview's early success provided sufficient capital to acquire an aircraft and a photographic processing laboratory, which in 1981 was initially placed under the company's subsidiary, Airtech Services Ltd. The two operations were amalgamated in November 1983 under the parent company's name.

When Tom Bruise retired in 1990, Rick took over his duties as president. He acquired Tom's shares in the company and offered 40 percent of them to his employees.

Airview's sales grew steadily throughout the 1980s, from an annual level of $500,000 in 1981 to $1.2 million in 1989. Sales stabilized during the 1990s at a level of just over $1.1 million.

Airview had traditionally maintained an advanced level of technical capabilities, investing in the most up-to-date photographic, film processing, data analysis, and plotting equipment. This, combined with the technical expertise of the company's staff, had enabled them to build an excellent reputation for the quality, reliability, and professionalism of its services.

◼ Product Line

With its extensive technological capabilities, Airview provided a range of services associated with the development of spatial images of terrain, referred to (in Canada) as geomatics. The company's primary specialization was to make, process, and analyze airborne photographs of the earth's surface.

The major groups of services provided by Airview included:

Aerial Photography and Photogrammetry.   Aerial photography occupied a pivotal place in Airview's business. The majority of the complex services provided by Airview were initiated by taking photographs from the air. However, aerial photography was also a separate product, that, depending on the light spectrum applied in taking the photograph, could provide information on forest growth and diseases, quality of water resources, wildlife migration, land erosion, and other physical features.

Photogrammetry involved a number of image processing techniques using aerial photographs as a basis for the development of maps, composite views, or spatially referenced databases. Photogrammetry was distinguished from aerial photography by its capability to identify three-dimensional coordinates for each point on the captured image.

Aerial photography/photogrammetry was very capital intensive, requiring a specially prepared aircraft with specialized cameras and sophisticated photo-laboratory equipment. Airview was considered one of the best equipped aerial photography companies in Canada. Its Cessna 310 L aircraft with 25,000 feet photo ceiling was capable of producing photographs at scales of up to 1:10,000. A recently (1992) acquired Leica camera represented the latest in optical technology, meeting all calibration and accuracy requirements set by North American mapping agencies, and accommodating a wide variety of specialized aerial film. Finally, Airview's photo laboratory, which was certified by the National Research Council, processed all types of aerial film used by the company.

Aerial Surveying.   Aerial surveying involved taking photographs with the purpose of defining and measuring boundaries and the configuration of particular areas on the earth's surface for a variety of uses, such as establishing ownership rights (cadastre), triangulation,[1] locating and appraising mineral resources, forests, and wild habitat, and detecting earth and water movements.

Mapping.   This service group comprised the development of maps from either internally or externally acquired photographic images. Before the 1980s, map making had largely been a manual process of drawing the terrain's contours and elevations, and then inserting the accompanying descriptive information. From the early 1980s, however, the process had been increasingly computer-driven. This resulted in a reduction in the manual labor required and increased accuracy of the images produced. The new technology also permitted the storage of maps in an easily accessible, digital format, which created demand for converting maps from the traditional, analog format into a computer-based one.

CADD.   This area also dealt with map making, but was based on computer-operated scanners supported by CADD/CAM (Computer-Aided-Design and Drafting/Computer-Aided-Mapping) software. With this technology, the digitizing of analog images, such as existing maps or photographs, was fully automated. The scanners interpreted the subject image as a series of dots identified by their coordinates, colours, and illuminance, and then produced their digital presentation. The computer-stored images could then be enhanced by adding descriptive information, using a process still performed manually by the CADD operators.

Consulting.   Over its 15-year history, Airview had developed a multidisciplinary team of specialists, whose expertise was also employed in providing consulting services associated with the planning and execution of comprehensive mapping projects. Consulting involved advising clients on the optimal method of gathering spatial information, the interpretation of client-provided data, and supervising data gathering projects conducted by the client or his or her subcontractors.

Data capture (aerial photography/photogrammetry) and data processing (mapping and CADD) projects had traditionally generated (in equal proportions) around 90 percent of Airview's sales. The remainder had come from consulting projects (9 percent) and surveying (1 percent).

By 1994, this sales distribution of sales did not reflect the changing structure of the marketplace where data capture had become a relatively small part of the overall scope of geomatic activities.

---

[1] A specialized technique for defining an accurate three-dimensional coordinate system for determining the location and dimensions of objects on the earth's surface.

◼ Customer Base

Airview Mapping Inc. provided services to a variety of clients locally and nationally. The majority of the company's sales had traditionally come from the public sector. Over the period of 1991/93, government agencies (both federal and provincial), local municipalities, and regional utilities in Ontario, Manitoba, and Saskatchewan had accounted for between 65 percent and 75 percent of the company's total dollar sales.

Energy, Mines, and Resources Canada; Transport Canada; the Department of Indian Affairs; Manitoba Hydro; and Manitoba Telephone System were Airview's most significant clients. Procurement by public tender, the significant size of individual contracts (from $50,000 to $100,000+), and clear specifications of requirements characterized these clients' approach to project management.

The private sector, accounting for the remaining 25 percent to 35 percent of sales, was represented predominantly by clients from the mining sector (such as Hudson Bay Mining and Smelting Company; Inco; Delcan; Noranda; and Placer Dome), whose contracts were typically in the range of $20–40,000. Companies representing such diverse areas as construction, recreation, and environmental protection provided projects valued at up to $20,000 each. Companies from the private sector did not apply a rigorous procurement procedure, and frequently needed guidance in defining (or redefining) project requirements.

◼ Geographic Coverage

Airview concentrated its activities within a 1,200-mile radius of its Brandon, Manitoba, headquarters. This was the area where the company was able to deal directly with its clients and had a cost advantage over its competitors from other provinces. It included northwestern Ontario, Manitoba, Saskatchewan, and Alberta, each contributing equally to the company's revenues.

The company had never attempted to expand beyond the national market, even though the sizable market south of the U.S.-Canada border was well within its defined geographic radius. In the past, this was justified by the abundance of opportunities available in Canada and restrictions on foreign access to the U.S. market. However, this situation had recently changed on both counts, which caused Rick to consider changing his company's geographic orientation.

◼ Organization and Staff

The production process associated with the services provided by Airview involved grouping activities into three functional areas: airplane operation and maintenance (two staff members), film development (two staff members), and image processing/output (ten staff members). Managerial, marketing, and administrative activities required four additional staff members.

Each production area (aircraft operations, photo lab, data capture, and data conversion) was assigned a coordinator, responsible for quality assurance and overall coordination of the work load. These coordinators also provided expert advice to their staff and were responsible for individual projects within their respective production areas.

Airview's production activities were characterized by the relatively small number of concurrent projects (4–6) and their modest size. This, combined with the well-trained staff (13 out of 18 had completed postsecondary education in geomatics-related fields), enabled the company to apply a skeleton project management structure.

Coordination of project work among different production areas was the responsibility of the production coordinator, Sean Coleman. Garry Howell was in charge of marketing. Tim Conners, who occupied the position of vice-president, also acted as the general manager responsible for all projects. Rick, who was the company's president, oversaw general administration and communication with customers.

Pricing

Each price quotation was based on Garry Howell's assessment of the scope of work required to complete it. This was broken down by category of activity (aircraft operation, film processing, digitization of images, or image analysis). For each of these activity categories a budget hourly rate was developed, based on historical cost figures (both direct and fixed), the budgeted number of hours for a given planning period, and the company's profit targets. Recently, rates had ranged from $25 for digitization of images to over $900 for aircraft flying time, with an overall average of $70.

The initial price was determined by multiplying the estimated number of hours required in each category by its budgeted rate, and than adding these figures for all activity categories involved in the project. This price was later adjusted by Rick's assessment of the competitive situation (in the case of a tendered bid) or his negotiations with the customer.

Generally, Airview's budgeted rates, and consequently prices, were within average values prevailing in Canada. This situation reflected their general knowledge of the cost structure of the industry. Any undercutting of price tended to raise suspicions of lower standards. This being the case, the competition between bidders had severely squeezed profit margins, with many firms trying to survive by quoting their services on a break-even basis.

Financial Results

In the late 1980s and early 1990s, Airview had acquired advanced photographic and mapping equipment, and computer hardware and software with a total value of close to $900,000. Financing for these acquisitions had been provided by bank loans and capital leases at interest rates ranging from 12.25 percent to 17.25 percent.

During the past two years, the cost of servicing this debt load had created a real strain on the company's cash flow, requiring an annual outlay of $200,000, split evenly between interest expenses and repayment of the principal. This was extremely difficult for a company traditionally only generating a free annual cash flow in the range of $100,000 to $150,000.

Airview's operating cost structure was characterized by a high proportion of fixed costs. Currently, some 75 percent of direct costs and 83 percent of total costs did not vary with changes in their sales level. This cost structure might seem surprising for a business with some 60 percent of its direct expenses associated with wages and salaries. However, considering the unique nature of the professional qualifications of the company's staff, it was extremely difficult, if not impossible, to vary the number of staff in line with fluctuations in sales levels.

This situation reduced the company's profitability at their current sales level, but, at the same time, created significant profit potential with the possibility of a sales increase. It was estimated that the company, barely breaking even at its current sales of $1.1 million, could make over $200,000 in profits by increasing sales to $1.4 million.

◼ Overall Strategic Profile

Viewed from a strategic perspective, Airview could be characterized as a locally based company with strong technical capabilities, but limited expertise in marketing, particularly outside its traditional markets. Rick recognized the importance of having a clear view of his company's current position, as well as its goals for the next few years.

Analysis of Airview's structure and performance led him to develop the corporate profile presented in Exhibit 1.

◼ Industry Trends

The term "geomatics" was widely used in Canada to describe a variety of fields which acquired, managed, and distributed spatially referenced data. The term was applied to generally refer to several disciplines, including the following:

- Aerial photography
- Ground-based (geodetic) and aerial surveying, i.e., assessing and delimiting boundaries of land
- Mapping, i.e., cartography (map making based on ground measurements) and photogrammetry (converting photographic images and measurements into maps)
- Geographic Information Systems (GIS), i.e., computer-based systems for the storage and processing of spatial information
- Remote sensing, i.e., satellite-borne images and measurements; quite often, airborne images were included in the remote sensing category

The use of this general term, however, was limited to Canada. In other countries these disciplines were referred to by their individual names. On the other hand, the term "remote sensing" was frequently used to describe all satellite and airborne observations of the earth's surface, regardless of their purpose and the techniques applied.

EXHIBIT 1   Airview's Corporate Profile, Current Versus Target (5-year perspective)

	Current	Target
Rank and size	$1,100,000 sales $0–$25,000 profits 18 employees Medium-sized aerial surveying company No export sales	$2,000,000+ sales $300,000+ profits 30+ employees Medium-sized GIS company $700,000+ export sales
Product line	Aerial photography—40% Mapping—30% Surveying—1% CADD—20% Commercial—9% 5–10 concurrent projects	Aerial photography—30% GIS—40% Mapping—20% Commercial/consulting—10% 3–5 concurrent projects
Geographic coverage	Canada—100%	Canada—60% International—40%
Performance goals	Maintenance of cash flow Profit margin Protecting market share	Sales/profit growth Market penetration Technology adoption New product development Productivity
Strengths	Customer goodwill Technological expertise: • Aerial photography • Digital imaging	Customer goodwill Active marketing Geographical diversification Flexible offerings Technological expertise: • Digital imaging • Aerial photography • System development
Weaknesses	Marketing Narrow product line Balance sheet	International exposure
Strategy	Passive	Active

Although traditionally distinct, these disciplines were becoming increasingly integrated due to the commonality of the computer tools employed to acquire and process spatial information, and generate the final product.

The emergence of satellite-based remote sensing had also affected the geomatics industry worldwide. Its impact on air-based services had been largely positive, despite the fact that the two technologies served the same user segments. Advances in satellite technology had received a lot of publicity, which sensitized users of geomatic services to the cost advantages of remote sensing in general, and aerial photography/photogrammetry in particular. Consequently, those users who could not use satellite-based services turned to airborne imagery. In many cases, satellite trajectories limited the frequency at which information on a particular earth location could be gathered. This problem was exacerbated by the prevalence of cloud cover over certain territories. It was expected that, despite recent plans to increase the overall number of remote sensing satellites, aerial photography/photogrammetry would maintain its advantage in applications requiring high resolution capabilities (aerial images could produce resolutions in a 2-to-3-inch range versus a 10-metre range available from most satellites) and full colour capabilities.

Airview's Market

In the first half of the 1990s, the Canadian geomatics industry comprised over 1,300 firms from all geomatic disciplines employing some 12,000 people. The largest numbers of firms were located in Quebec and Ontario, followed by British Columbia. The distribution of primary activities within the industry was as follows:

Major Line of Business	Percent of Establishments	Percent of Billing
Geodetic (ground) surveying	65%	53%
Mapping	9	16
Remote sensing	5	11
Consulting	10	4.5
GIS	7	12
Other	4	3.5

The vast majority (86 percent) of geomatic firms were small establishments generating sales of less than $1 million. However, the remaining, small number of larger firms generated the majority (68 percent) of the industry's revenues. Airview belonged to the growing category of medium-sized businesses (10 percent of all establishments) with sales of between $1 million and $2 million.

The overall market size in Canada was estimated at $630–650 million, and was dominated by local companies. The industry also generated some $120 million in foreign billings (mainly GIS hardware and software). Interestingly, export of services had traditionally been directed outside of North America and Europe, and concentrated in Africa, Asia, and the Middle East.

Competition

Competition in the Canadian geomatics industry was on the increase. The overall economic climate, characterized by fiscal restraint in both the private and government sectors, had reduced the growth rate of the demand for services provided by the industry. As a result, geomatic companies, with their increased production capacities and reduced costs, had become more active in competing for the constant volume of business. This had resulted in a decrease in profitability. Overall industry profit levels were the same as in the early 1980s despite a doubling of overall industry demand.

Global Opportunities Overview

By March 1994, Rick had spent considerable time reviewing global market opportunities for his company. He had taken a general look at several foreign markets, identifying such major factors as their overall size and growth prospects, political stability and entry barriers, competition, and the availability of funding for geomatic projects.

This step had resulted in rejecting the possibility of entering Western European markets, which—despite their size—were characterized by ferocious competition and limited growth prospects. Eastern Europe was felt to be too unstable politically (the countries of the former USSR), lacked funding, and was fragmented along national borders.

Rick also felt that the distances associated with dealing with markets in Southeast Asia and Oceania would put a significant strain on the company's financial and human resources, particularly in view of increasing competition from locally based companies. On the other hand, other Asian markets lacked either the size or the financing required to support Airview's long-term involvement.

Finally, he decided that Sub-Saharan Africa, although in dire need of the services offered by Airview, was either dominated by companies from their former colonial powers, or could not afford any significant level of geomatics-related development, particularly in view of the declining level of support received from international financial institutions like the World Bank.

On the other hand, Rick found the characteristics of some of the remaining regions quite interesting. Consequently, he decided to concentrate his deliberations on these markets, which included North America (the United States and Mexico), Latin America, and the Arab World (North Africa and the Middle East).

■ American Market

The U.S. market was somewhat different from its Canadian counterpart in that it had a larger proportion of geodetic and GIS firms among the 6,300 businesses in its geomatic industry. The larger proportion of geodetic firms in the United States was due to its higher population density, which increased the need for cadastral surveying. At the same time, faster adaptation of computers in a variety of industrial applications in the United States had stimulated demand for GIS applications and related services.

On the other hand, in view of the relative size of the U.S. and Canadian economies, the Canadian market was disproportionately large. The American market was estimated at $3 billion in 1994, only five times the size of its Canadian counterpart, or only half the relative difference in the size of the economies between the two countries. This disparity could be largely attributed to structural differences between the economies of the two countries. Canada's economy was largely dependent on the mineral and forestry sectors; both industries supported a high level of geomatic activity.

The demand for geomatics services in the U.S. market was growing at a 15 percent annual rate, and was particularly dynamic in the areas of airborne photography and (satellite) remote sensing, digital conversion of existing data, and consulting.

Access to U.S. Markets.   In 1994, there were few tariff obstacles when entering the U.S. market. Previously existing barriers related to licensing and local presence requirements were being removed as a result of the passage of the North American Free Trade Agreement. In some cases, Canadian companies who had succeeded in penetrating the U.S. market indicated that it had been easier for them to cross the national border than to overcome provincial barriers within their home country.

Although there had been some opportunities in the U.S. geomatics market during the 1980s, Canadian firms had traditionally been reluctant to pursue them. For aerial surveying companies like Airview, one of the reasons was the fact that aircraft maintenance and licensing requirements were much more lenient in the United States than they were in Canada. As a result, a company operating an aircraft out of Canada was not able to compete with American firms on price if there was any significant amount of flying time involved. Although these differences still remained, the recently falling value of the Canadian dollar had all but nullified the cost advantage previously enjoyed by U.S. companies.

In general, the level of competition in the United States was not much different from that in Canada except that the American firms, particularly the larger ones, marketed their services much more aggressively than their Canadian counterparts.

User Segments.   It was estimated that local and state governments accounted for some 25 percent of the total U.S. market for geomatics products and services, and that close to half of all local/state budgets allocated to the acquisition of geomatic services was allocated for data capture purposes.

The greatest potential lay with the 39,000 municipal/county governments. A trend to modernize land records and registration systems which document the 118 million land parcels in the United States was the most significant factor in stimulating the demand for data capture, their conversion into a digital format, their subsequent analysis, and graphical presentation.

The average contract performed for local/state governments ranged from $60,000 to $190,000 for aerial photography/photogrammetry services. Although the northeast, southeast, southwest, and states bordering the Pacific Ocean accounted for the greatest demand, there was also an abundance of opportunities in the states closer to Airview's base, such as Minnesota (3,529 local government units), North Dakota (2,795), and South Dakota (1,767).

Federal government agencies represented the second-largest user group, accounting for slightly less than 25 percent of the total U.S. geomatic market. Digital mapping was the major area of demand within this segment. This corresponded closely to Airview's principal area of expertise.

Contracts with the federal government ranged from $30,000 for surveying projects to $1.5 million for data digitizing projects. On average, they tended to be larger in size than those with state and local governments and were typically awarded to larger firms. As a result of the U.S. federal government policy of decentralizing contracting for services, the demand from this user sector was spread across the country.

The third-largest segment in the U.S. geomatic market was the demand from regulated industries, such as communication firms and gas and electric utility companies which traditionally generated between 20 percent and 25 percent of the overall U.S. demand for geomatic services. Customers from this category were interested in more cost-efficient management of the large infrastructures under their administration. Consequently, they had been among the early adopters of GIS technology, and their major thrust was in implementing AM/FM (Automated Mapping and Facilities Management) systems, which combined digital maps with information on the operation of their facilities.

The utilities market for geomatic services was spread across the United States, with the size closely related to the population density of individual regions. These regional markets were dominated by large companies, such as Baymont Engineering and AT&T, which—due to economies of scale—became very price-competitive in catering to the utility sector.

Finally, the rest of the demand for geomatic services came from the private sector, with the most significant segments being the resource industries, mining, and forestry. The rate of adoption of GIS technology in this sector was rather slow, and remote sensing of data and basic mapping were the primary services contracted out by resource companies.

The Mexican Geomatics Market

Overview.   By the early 1990s, Mexico had developed significant capabilities in geomatics. Between 40,000 and 50,000 people were employed in all surveying- and mapping-related disciplines. Yet, in view of the country's problems with rapid urbanization, deforestation, and land use change, local demand for geomatics products and services in the early 1990s exceeded the available supply in some product and service categories.

The primary demand for geomatics services in Mexico was created by cartographic agencies of the federal and state governments. The National Institute of Statistics, Geography, and Informatics (INEGI) had the primary responsibility for integrating the country's geographical data, carrying out the national mapping project, and developing the National Geographic Information System.

Each state in Mexico was responsible for undertaking and maintaining a land survey of its territory and maintaining land cadastre. Therefore state markets were the second-largest in volume after the federal market.

Several large municipalities also purchased geomatics products and services. In 1993/94, they were in the process of establishing databases of property boundaries, partly in cooperation with SEDESOL (Directorate of Cartography and Photogrammetry) under the One Hundred Cities Program.

The private sector was also a significant user of spatially referenced information. PEMEX, the state oil monopoly, was by far the largest of those users. It was also in the strongest position to acquire the most technologically advanced products and services in this area.

The total size of the Mexican market for geomatics services in 1993 was estimated at between $160 million and $200 million.

There were two cycles which affected the volume of geomatics work available in Mexico. First, there was the annual rainy season (June to September) during which the inclement weather had a negative impact on aerial surveying. Second, there was the change in Mexico's presidency every six years. As government agencies were the main purchasers of geomatic services, the political environment had a profound effect on business. In general, the first three years of any presidency resulted in minor projects, while the final three years were noted for major works.

The demand for geomatics services in Mexico was increasing. In addition, most Mexican companies competing for this business were interested in foreign participation, particularly if these relationships carried with them better technology and more modern equipment.

Mexico offered a significant operating benefit to Canadian aerial photography firms in that its weather patterns (the rainy season between May and September) counterbalanced those in Canada. This could enable Canadian exporters to utilize their aircraft and photographic equipment during the slow season in Canada (December–March).

Competition.   The Mexican geomatics industry was well developed in the traditional areas of ground surveying and cartography. However, its technological and human resource capabilities in the more technical areas, such as digital mapping and GIS, were generally limited.

In the area of aerial mapping and surveying, there were about 20 companies, located principally in Mexico City. Six of these companies owned their own aircraft, and dominated the national market. The remaining 14 were quite small, did not have their own aircraft, and were fairly new to the industry.

Market Access.   Public tender was the normal method for obtaining projects in Mexico. Most tenders were open to all companies, but some were by invitation only. The tendency was for contracts to go to those companies that had their own aircraft and the proper equipment. Subcontracting was a popular way for smaller companies to obtain a portion of larger projects.

If a foreign company was awarded a contract, it had to obtain permission from the state geography department and from the Mexican Defense Department. In addition, until 1996, foreign companies were not allowed to operate aircraft over Mexican territory without local participation.

◼ The Latin American Geomatics Market

In the early 1990s, the geomatics market in Latin America was at an early stage of transition from traditional to digital technologies for data capture, analysis, and storage. Although general awareness of GIS and remote sensing was widespread, their adoption was largely limited to international resource exploration companies and some public institutions.

The market for geomatics products and services was dominated by the public sector on both the supply and demand sides. However, the private sector was becoming the primary growth area, particularly in the resource sector (agriculture, forestry mining, and energy), where significant investment programs created demand for cadastral surveying, mapping, and GIS. This potential demand, in turn, was providing a growth opportunity for the local surveying and mapping industry. The industry had traditionally been dominated by government organizations (mostly military-controlled), that over the previous few years had gained a significant degree of business autonomy and were actively competing in both local and international markets.

International Financial Institutions (IFIs), such as the World Bank and the Inter-American Development Bank, were very active in Latin America. Their major concern was economic development of the region, thus they concentrated on the less-developed nations of the region. The IFIs recognized the importance of infrastructure projects and their geomatics components and provided financial support for such basic services as topographic and property mapping and cadastral information systems. As a result of this fundamental focus, the geomatics contract activity was not confined to the more economically advanced countries of the region. From the point of view of foreign-based geomatics companies attempting to enter the Latin American market, the IFI-sponsored contracts provided a very attractive opportunity, since they were open for public tender.

It was anticipated that the Latin American market for geomatic products and services would grow significantly in the near term. Over the 1993–1998 period, the total demand for geomatics products and services in the region was anticipated in the range of US$650 million to US$1,500 million (the low and high estimates).

The provision of spatial information and its conversion to a digital format, as well as the delivery of GIS applications and the provision of training to local staffs, constituted the major demand area, expected to comprise three-quarters of the region's market.

Geographic Distribution.   Brazil was by far the largest market for geomatics products and services, with an estimated 50 percent of the total demand in the region.

Argentina, with the second-largest territory and population in the region, was also the second-largest market for geomatics products and services, accounting for 20 percent of Latin American demand.

Chile, with its significant resource sector, was the third significant geomatics market in the region with a 5 percent share of total demand.

Interestingly, Bolivia, with its relatively small population and economy, had a disproportionately large market for geomatics products and services (4 percent of the overall demand).

The other 13 countries of the region shared the remaining 21 percent of the Latin American market, with Venezuela and Colombia leading the group.

Competition.   By the 1990s, Latin American companies had developed substantial capabilities in the areas of surveying and mapping. The mapping sector in the region had originated from the military and until recent years had been protected from foreign competition by trade barriers. Consequently, the capabilities of local firms were significant, particularly in larger countries such as Brazil and Argentina. More significantly, larger surveying and mapping companies had already invested in digital mapping technology and remote sensing. With their developed expertise and low labour and overhead costs, these firms had a significant advantage over their competitors from North America, Europe, and

Australia. Their knowledge of the local market was an additional factor placing them ahead of competitors from other continents.

Larger Brazilian and Argentinean firms had used this advantage to penetrate the markets of the smaller countries of the region. Since each national market was characterized by wide fluctuations in demand, the markets in other countries provided them with an opportunity to stabilize and, possibly, expand their sales.

In view of this situation, service firms from outside the region had to compete on the basis of their technological and managerial advantage. Large-scale projects, possibly involving digital imaging, provided the best opportunity to compete with local companies.

Despite all these impediments to foreign participation in the Latin American market, European companies had succeeded in capturing a significant share of the region's business. Their success was built on the strong business network established in the region by their home countries. Their penetration strategy was to establish their presence initially (through international assistance programs and the provision of training and education), and then to develop ties with local government agencies and companies from the private sector. European firms were also characterized by their ability to form consortia to pursue larger contracts. These combined European technology and equipment with local labour and market experience.

American firms had obtained a significant degree of penetration of these markets for GIS hardware and software. However, their presence in the other sectors was less pronounced, probably due to their uncompetitive cost structure.

Australian geomatics firms involved in Latin America were typically affiliated with Australia's mining and forestry companies active in resource exploration activities in the region.

The Arab World (North Africa and the Middle East)

Countries of the Arab World were characterized by the dominance of their oil and gas industries in the market for geomatics-related projects. Their economies and political systems were relatively stable and provided a good foundation for establishing long-term penetration plans by a foreign geomatics company. In terms of economic development, countries in this region were less dependent on international aid than was the case of the countries of Latin America. Consequently, their approach to the development of topographic, cadastral, and administrative mapping was based more on long-term planning.

With generally higher levels of resource allocation, countries of this region had developed their own companies, typically originating from the national cartographic agencies. In the early 1990s, these agencies still dominated the industry in the region, employing from 30 percent to 60 percent of the total number of personnel working in the geomatics field. However, their role had been steadily declining over the past few years.

At the same time, the level of saturation of the industry with locally-based manpower differed significantly among individual countries. Egypt, Iran,

Jordan, Kuwait, Lebanon, Qatar, Syria, and Tunisia each had a substantial number of local specialists in the field (relative to their populations and territory), whereas Algeria, Libya, Iraq, Saudi Arabia, and Yemen had rather limited geomatics capability. Even more significantly, this latter group also had a relatively low proportion of geomatics specialists with a university education.

The combined market size for geomatics services in the region was estimated at between $400 million and $600 million in the commercial sector. Some of the markets restricted foreign access. Libya and Iraq, for example, were not open to Canadian companies. Also Syria, with its militarized economy, was of limited attractiveness to Canadian companies.

Iran was the country with the best opportunity for geomatics firms. The climate for Canadian firms was favourable due to Canada's position as a politically non-involved country and the technological advancement of the Canadian geomatics industry.

Major opportunities in Iran were associated with several national development programs in the areas of energy production (construction of hydro-electric and nuclear power stations and upgrading the country's power distribution system); expansion of the mining industry (production of iron ore, copper, aluminum, lead/zinc, and coal); the oil and gas sectors; and construction of the country's railway system.

Kuwait and Saudi Arabia had traditionally been the target markets for several Canadian geomatics firms. The expansion of the two countries' oil production and refining capacity had triggered major investment outlays in both countries (for a total of over $20 billion between 1992 and 1994) and would continue (albeit at a slower rate) for a number of years. These two national markets were dominated by American companies and any penetration effort there would require cooperation with Canadian firms from the construction, mining, or oil and gas sectors.

Tunisia represented an example of a country which had developed its own expertise in the area of cartography, which in turn had created demand for external assistance in the provision of more sophisticated products and services, such as digital mapping and GIS applications.

Egypt represented yet another type of geomatics market in the region. Its major thrust was now on environmental concerns. The country had developed an environmental action plan which addressed problems with water and land resources management, air pollution, marine and coastal resources, and global heritage preservation, all of which had a significant geomatic component. The cost of implementing phase 1 of the plan was estimated at some $300 million over the period of 1993–1995.

Egypt also provided opportunities created by a $3 billion power generation and distribution project, and some $2 billion in construction projects associated with the expansion of the country's gas production and oil processing capacity. Although the majority of work in the geomatics-related field was conducted by local companies, subcontracting opportunities were significant.

Egypt was also a significant market from another perspective. Historically, Egypt had exported its geomatics expertise to other Arab states. Consequently, penetration of this market could be used to leverage access to other markets in the region, particularly in conjunction with Egyptian partners.

Market Evaluation.   In order to evaluate each of the four geographic regions from Airview's perspective, Rick developed a summary of the primary characteristics of each market under consideration. This summary is presented in Exhibit 2.

EXHIBIT 2   Market Review

	Market			
Characteristics	**United States**	**Mexico**	**Latin America**	**North Africa and the Middle East**
Economic and political environment	Stable	Stabilizing	Stabilizing	Fluctuating
Access restrictions	None	Local agent required, no flying in Mexico	All mapping on-site in Brazil	Language, culture
Market size	Large	Small	Medium	Medium-large
Entry and operating costs	Low	Medium	Medium	Medium-high
Growth	Slow, stable	High	High	High
Financing	Cash, immediate	Transfer, delays	Transfer problems, IFI	Ranging from cash to IFI's financing
Contract procurement	Transparent, fair	Ambiguous, improving	Frequently ambiguous	Ambiguous
Major products	Digital mapping, GIS	Cadastral mapping, GIS	Topographic and cadastral mapping	Topographic mapping, surveying
Long-term advantage (technology, expertise)	Limited advantage	Diminishing, but not disappearing	Slowly diminishing	Sustainable
Primary customers	State and municipal governments	Federal and state governments	Federal governments, resource sector	Central cartographic agencies, resource sector
Pricing	Competitive, but based on high local costs	Competitive, based on low local costs	Extremely competitive, based on low local costs	Relatively high
Competition	Local, very high	Local, U.S. high	Local, international, extremely high	Local, international, moderate
Entry strategies	Direct bidding, local partner	Local partner or subsidiary	Network of agents or local partner, IFI's projects	Local partner or agent, IFI's projects
Strategic advantages	Close, similar to the Canadian market	Entry to South America, technological, advantage, active during Canadian slack	Technological fit, active during Canadian slack	Technological advantage, growing, less competition, long-term prospects
Expansion opportunities	GIS consulting systems, integration	Acquisition of local subsidiary	Training	CIDA project, Libya (with restrictions)

EXHIBIT 3   Airview Entry Strategies

Project-Oriented Penetration

This is a strategy suitable for small, niche-oriented firms. The company would have to target a specific area and seek a specific contract. Involvement would be limited to the scope of the specific contract. The main barrier to this approach could be associated with local presence requirements.

Establishing a network of local agents in the countries of interest in the region may provide access to information on upcoming tenders and allow for participation in the binding process. Bidding for local contracts may serve as a foundation for establishing the company's presence in the region and could be treated as part of an entry strategy.

Subcontracting to Local Firms

This strategy offered the advantage of overcoming local presence restrictions.

Strategic Alliances

An alliance with a Canadian or foreign partner can work quite effectively provided the firms complement one another in resources and business philosophies.

Establishment of a Branch Office

This could be an effective way of overcoming local presence restrictions provided the firm was sufficiently financed to undertake the costs of setting up such an operation. The choice of location would also be crucial in determining the success of such a venture.

A Corporate Buyout

This seemed a somewhat risky proposition, requiring both adequate financing, business acumen to succeed, and lack of restrictions on foreign ownership of local companies. If successful, however, the result would be an immediate presence in the selected market.

Establishment of Head Office Outside of Canada

Although this could enable a company to access the selected market, this possibility could only be considered for large and stable markets, such as the United States.

Foreign Ownership

Like the strategic alliance option, this could offer opportunities, particularly with U.S. firms, provided this route is in keeping with the long-term goals of the firm and the two firms are compatible.

Alliances with Local Geomatics Firms

An alliance with a local partner could be beneficial if based on the combination of local experience and inexpensive labour with Airview's equipment and data processing and mapping capabilities.

Joint Ownership of a Local Company

Acquiring a local company in partnership with another Canadian company may provide some advantages if the partners' product lines complement each other. A provider of GIS software or system integrator may be a good candidate for joint ownership with Airview.

He also reviewed several ways of establishing Airview's presence in the regional national markets, as indicated in Exhibit 3.

Discussion.   Regarding the choice of Airview's optimum target area, Rick assumed that once he had arrived at a sensible, coherent marketing plan, Airview could apply for financial support from the government. In fact, he had already discussed this possibility with Western Economic Diversification (WED) and the Federal Business Development Bank (FBDB). In addition, he could expect some assistance from the Program for Export Market Development if he chose to establish an office or participate in bidding for projects in a selected market. This assistance could cover 50 percent of the cost of travel and setting up a permanent foreign office.

His overall concerns included not only the immediate costs of implementing his marketing plan but also the process he should use to select the best market in view of its salient characteristics and the company's goals.

Rick's view of the American market was generally positive. His major concern was with price competition from local firms and possible fluctuations in the exchange rate, which over a short period of time might undermine Airview's cost structure. At the same time, he felt that Airview's technological advantage in the United States was less significant than in other markets. Finally, he assumed that his best opportunity south of the border would be in GIS-related areas, which would require either a substantial investment in obtaining greater expertise in this area or a joint effort with a GIS company.

The Mexican market was also viewed positively, particularly after the lifting of restrictions in 1996. However, Rick felt that due to the high cost of his staff, Airview would probably be competitive only in complex projects involving both data capture and their conversion into a computer format. At the same time, he was attracted by the operating advantages of having the company's flying season extended beyond the current few summer months.

Latin America seemed to be too competitive to support Airview's solo entry. On the other hand, the region's fragmentation into many small national markets could prove challenging from an operating point of view. Rick felt that seeking an alliance with Canadian mining and resource companies, thereby successfully establishing their operations, might prove to be attractive, particularly if Airview's entry could be supported by the provision of some elements of GIS. As in Mexico's case, the countries of Latin America provided the possibility of operating the company's aircraft during the Canadian off-season.

Finally Rick regarded the markets of the Arab world with particular interest. Airview would definitely have a technical advantage over its local competitors in these markets. At the same time, pricing in this region seemed to be generally less competitive than in the other areas, whereas the similarity of the individual national markets, in most cases based on the demand created by the resource sector, would allow for gradual penetration of the region. At the same time, Rick realized that Airview's lack of experience in international markets in general, and in the Arab world in particular, would create a very challenging situation for the company's staff.

Argyle
Diamonds

In 1995 the Argyle Diamond joint venture of CRA and Ashton Mining was bracing itself for the toughest round of sales negotiations in its history in a determined bid to squeeze a better deal from the De Beers–owned Central Selling Organization (CSO). De Beers had dominated the diamond industry as a monopoly cartel for most of the century and was an experienced negotiator. The existing five-year contract expired in June 1996 and in mid-1995 the posturing and maneuvring on both sides were well under way.

Argyle's contract required it to sell approximately 80 percent of its production through the CSO, while the rest was marketed through its office in Antwerp. The partners were concerned about the CSO's performance over the past few years, particularly in relation to deferred purchases and a 10 percent cut in the price of smaller diamonds in a "realignment" exercise from July 1, 1995.

The outcome of the renegotiations was equally critical to De Beers which was anxious to maintain the delicate structure of organized sales while trying to cope with a flood of diamonds from Russia, Angola, and Zaire. In addition, new mines were being planned by strong players such as BHP and Ashton Mining, which could further threaten the CSO's dominance in the market.

◼ History

Diamonds were first discovered in Western Australia at Nullagine in the far northwest, but serious exploration did not begin until the mid-1960s. In 1978 the first significant diamond deposit in Australia was discovered in the Kimberley region, in the far north of the State. The find followed systematic exploration efforts throughout the Kimberley region by several organizations, most notably the Kalumburu Joint Venture, which was established in 1972. In 1976 CRA (Conzinc Riotinto of Australia), one of the largest mining groups in the country, became involved through CRA Exploration (CRAE). The Kalumburu Joint Venture was reformed as the Ashton Joint Venture, and CRA assumed the role of manager in 1977. In 1993 CRA owned 59.7 percent of Argyle Diamonds and the remainder was held by Ashton.

This case was prepared by André Morkel and Joanne Simpson at the University of Western Australia, 1995. The cooperation of Argyle Diamonds is gratefully acknowledged. The case is based in part on an earlier version prepared by Alvin Cameron under the supervision of André Morkel.

Exploration

In September 1979 the joint venturers, led by CRAE, set up camp 80 kilometres from the Argyle region for what was to be an "undercover" exploration mission. The tenements which contained the diamond-rich AKI (Argyle pipe) were held by other explorers, but were due to expire within weeks. The CRAE geologists avoided radio communication and developed secret codes for telephone messages to ensure that their presence remained hidden. Mr. Grant Boxer, then Argyle Diamond Mines' senior geologist at the "secret camp," explained: "We had helicopters on standby so that as soon as we confirmed the find and the other tenement had expired, we could stake our claim."[1]

During September 1979 the CRAE team uncovered many stones from the Smoke Creek alluvial diamond deposits before they discovered the 45-hectare AKI pipe on October 2. The geologists needed to maintain their secrecy for a further six weeks, because another tenement had still not yet expired. However, to their relief the CRAE cover was not blown, and after further investigation their geologists were confident that a mine could be economically developed on the site.

The Argyle Diamond Joint Venture

In 1982 the Argyle Diamond Joint Venture was established by CRA (56.8 percent), Ashton Mining Group (38.2 percent), and the Western Australian government through the WA Diamond Trust (WADT) (5 percent). At a later stage CRA and Ashton took over the WADT's interests, raising their shareholdings to 59.7 percent and 40.3 percent, respectively.

The Argyle project was managed by a wholly owned CRA subsidiary, Argyle Diamond Mines Pty Ltd. (ADM). Marketing was managed through Argyle Diamond Sales Ltd. (ADS), owned 60 percent by CRA and 40 percent by Ashton. ADS was established in 1982.

CRA Ltd. was in 1994 one of the five largest mining companies in the world and had one of the largest mineral exploration budgets of any mineral resources company worldwide. It was active in the mining of iron ore, coal, bauxite, copper, and gold in Australia and neighbouring countries, as well as being a producer of aluminum metal. Its consolidated total assets in 1994 came to more than $9 billion dollars, supporting sales revenue of $5.8 billion. Its main shareholder at 49 percent was the United Kingdom mining house RTZ. In 1995 the two companies merged their operations to form the world's largest mining concern.

Ashton Mining in 1994 had consolidated assets of over $670 million, with sales exceeding $186 million. The company was active primarily in diamond exploration and production, though it also maintained interests in opal and gold mining and owned a high-grade rare earth project at Mt. Weld in Western Australia. Its main shareholder was Malaysian Mining Berhad at 47 percent.

---

[1] *Australia's Mining Monthly,* December 1989—January 1990, "Major upgrade for Argyle Diamond Mine," p. 19.

EXHIBIT 1   **Argyle Diamonds 1992–1994 (US$ millions)**

	1994	1993	1992
Net sales revenue	$ 497	$518	$591
Total assets	745	720	650
Capital expenditure	57	97	45
Employees	1,006	930	929

Source: CRA annual reports 1993 and 1994.

● Production and Operations

Total proven and probable ore reserves in 1993 amounted to 83 million tonnes at 3.42 carats per tonne at the Argyle site.[2] ADM commenced commercial mining of alluvial deposits downstream from the AK1 pipe in 1983 and continued until late 1985. There were 17.3 million carats of diamonds recovered during this phase. ADM resumed alluvial mining in 1989 to augment production from the AK1 pipe.

Following a feasibility study and the State government's approval of proposals for mining the ore body, construction and development work on the pipe mining phase of the Argyle project commenced in 1983. This involved the design and construction of the mine, the processing plant, the airstrip, and all associated infrastructure at the mine site. The mine was remote, more than 2,000 kilometres from Perth, the capital of Western Australia, and 120 kilometres south of the nearest town, Kununurra. Capital investment in this stage of the project was around $465 million.[3] Despite industrial problems associated with union protests against the company's proposed marketing association with De Beers of South Africa, the plant came into operation ahead of schedule, in December 1985. Potential disputes with the local Aboriginal population were managed through a policy of involving the local community in decision making.

The plant processed ore mined from the pipe by open-cut methods. After crushing, screening, and heavy media concentration, diamonds were recovered through X-ray technology, and were cleaned in acid before being sent to Perth for sorting and classifying prior to sale. Although the plant was designed to process throughput of 3 million tonnes of ore a year, Exhibit 2 indicates that this figure was consistently exceeded.

In April 1994 a second major expansion and upgrade of the mine's processing facilities was completed. Capital expenditure of $100 million included the purchase of conveyor belts and a power generator, as well as ore-handling and processing equipment such as heavy-media separation facilities and high-pressure roller crushers. The haulage fleet was upgraded from 120-tonne to 150-tonne trucks. The upgrade in production throughput was expected to help compensate for the declining grade, which had fallen from an initial 8 carats per tonne to 5 carats per tonne.

---

[2] Ashton Mining, annual report 1993, p. 17.
[3] *Australia's Mining Monthly,* July 1986, "Diamond production hits target," p. 15.

EXHIBIT 2   Argyle Diamonds Production 1989–1994

	1994	1993	1992	1991	1990	1989
AK1 Pipe						
Ore treated (million tonnes)	7.9	7.0	6.8	6.0	5.1	4.9
Waste mined (million tonnes)	34.6	33.3	26.1	28.2	27.3	19.2
Grade (carats/tonne)	5.0	5.8	5.4	5.6	6.1	6.7
Diamonds produced (million carats)	39.7	38.4	36.6	33.4	31.7	32.8
Alluvials						
Ore treated (million tonnes)	4.6	3.9	3.5	1.3	1.9	0.8
Grade (carats/tonne)	0.7	0.7	0.7	1.2	1.1	1.4
Diamonds produced (million carats)	3.1	2.5	2.4	1.6	2.1	1.6
Total diamond production (million carats)	42.8	40.9	39.0	35.0	33.8	34.4

Source: Ashton Mining annual reports 1993 and 1994.

In 1994 estimates of the open-cut mine's remaining operating life ranged from seven to ten years. Research was being carried out in late 1994 to determine the feasibility of extending the mining operations underground, which would extend the mine's life by up to seven years.

Work Force Arrangements

By late 1994 Argyle Diamonds employed a work force of approximately 1,000 people. Under its principles of equal employment opportunities, Argyle achieved a level of female employment of 20 percent, and Aboriginal employment at the minesite of 10 percent. These figures were exceptionally high for the mining industry. In 1993 Argyle was the overall winner of the *Business Review Weekly* Affirmative Action Awards.[4]

The company employed 650 people at the mine site, most of whom commuted to the mine from Perth on a two-week rotation system. On-site accommodation consisted of single motel-style units with extensive recreational facilities. The Perth office had 250 employees in 1995, who were responsible for general administration and diamond sorting, cutting, polishing and marketing. Additional staff were employed in Argyle's overseas offices in Antwerp and Bombay.

Argyle Diamond Mine spent about 8 percent of wages on training. According to former Managing Director David Karpin, the company led the way among the mining companies of Western Australia in terms of percentage of gross wages spent on training.

Diamonds in Australia

The only other diamond mine in Australia, Bow River Diamonds, commenced alluvial production in 1988. It yielded 0.58 million carats in the 1988/89 financial

---

[4] *Business Review Weekly,* March 12, 1993, "Argyle Diamonds sets shining example," pp. 62–66.

year (compared with 34 million carats produced by Argyle), after treating 2.5 million tonnes of ore.[5] In 1993 Bow River was returning about US$30 per carat, about three times the value per carat of the giant Argyle mine. Assessed on the basis of per-carat value, sites further down the kimberlite pipeline appeared to be smaller but richer than the Lake Argyle deposit.

Active exploration in the Kimberley during the early 1990s raised the possibility of further competition in the region. Ashton Mining revealed evidence of a substantial diamond discovery in its Northern Territory Merlin exploration prospect in April 1994. Sampling on the prospect identified an area 10 kilometres by 2 kilometres containing diamonds of a commercial size. Grades were in excess of 20 carats per 100 tonnes which was considered suitable for commercial mining provided the gem quality was sufficiently high. The early indicators were that the stones from Merlin were "clear and colourless," that is, of higher quality than the Argyle deposit.

Exploration by a Triad Minerals Ltd. joint venture in the Philips Range of the Kimberleys in the late 1980s and early 1990s produced small parcels of stones with an expected value of between US$150 and US$350 per carat.

Smaller exploration companies such as Cambridge Gulf began exploring the Kimberley coastline for subsea diamonds. Several successful mining operations on the African coast had showed that alluvial diamonds could be gradually eroded out of the kimberlite pipes and carried out to sea by rivers. They would then be concentrated in rocky crevices on the shallow seabed by wave action. Cambridge Gulf hoped to find seabed diamonds in Western Australia that had been deposited by the same process. They reported their first diamonds recovered in December 1993. Their explorations were also helped by the gentler and more favourable conditions off the West Australian coast.

BHP, CRA, and junior explorers were also investigating large regions on the east coast of Australia, on the basis of a new theory about the formation of diamonds.

● Overseas Exploration by Australian-Based Companies

Northwest Territories, Canada

Ashton Mining's 60%-owned subsidiary, Ashton Mining Canada, reported in June 1994 that it had promising evidence of diamonds in the Cross River and Attawapiskat River regions of Canada's Northwest Territories.[6] This followed significant discoveries by BHP and its Canadian partner, Dia Met, in nearby Lac de Gras. Lac de Gras was in the Tundra area of Canada's Northwest Territories. It was insect-ridden swampland in summer and extremely cold in winter, presenting considerable challenges for mining and protecting the fragile ecology. BHP and Dia Met recovered 3,885 carats, mainly gem or near-gem quality, from 905 tonnes of material from their Misery pipe. By December 1994 BHP

---

[5] "Argyle diamonds sparkle for investors," p. 15.
[6] *Australian*, June 6, 1994, "Diamond recovery excites Ashton."

had sufficient evidence to announce that it would commence production in mid- to late 1997. The project was estimated at A$1.2 billion and BHP expected to generate $500 million a year in revenue over its 25-year life span. The company planned to extract 9,000 tonnes of ore initially, increasing to 18,000 a day at full capacity, to produce up to 10 million carats of diamonds a year. Indications were that the Lac de Gras mines could become the second-richest diamond mine in the world, after Botswana's Jwaneng deposit.[7]

Namibia

In May 1994 BHP formed a joint venture with Benguela Concessions Limited to explore an alluvial concession off the Namibian coast. The Namibian coastal waters had been a rich source of diamonds for De Beers for many decades and had the potential for more discoveries. Several companies were actively exploring this area.[8]

Finland, Karelia, and Arkhangelsk

A number of groups were competing actively for the right to explore for diamonds in the Karelia region of Siberia. Ashton Mining had also won the right to explore large tracts of Finland after eight years of top-secret negotiations.[9] According to John Robinson, Chief Executive of Ashton Mining, 14 of the 22 kimberlite bodies found in Finland were diamond-bearing, and four were considered of commercial significance. Pipe 21 was the most promising and yielded up to 66 carats per 100 tonnes of drill core samples.[10]

India

A number of groups were actively competing for access to mining territory in India, including CRA, BHP, and De Beers.[11]

◼ The World Diamond Industry

Diamonds are a crystalline form of carbon and are the hardest natural substance known. They are formed in the earth's mantle under conditions of extreme temperature and pressure and brought to the surface by small volcanic pipes which tap these depths. The principal host rock for diamonds is kimberlite or lamproite, a hard blue-grey rock. Alluvial and subsea diamonds occur when kimberlite or lamproite pipes erode, washing the diamonds into riverbeds and to the sea.

By 1995, up to 5,000 diamond pipes have been identified worldwide, but only a tiny percentage of these pipes contain diamonds in commercial quan-

---

[7] *Australian Financial Review,* July 26, 1995, "Canadian $1.2bn diamond mine firms up," p. 22.

[8] *Australian Financial Review,* May 18, 1994, "BHP's venture off Namibia."

[9] *Australian Financial Review,* August 31, 1994, "Explorer lifts lid on sparkling prospect."

[10] *Australian Financial Review,* May 20, 1995, "Finland, NT stake claims as Ashton's new diamond mine," p. 21.

[11] *Australian Financial Review,* August 25, 1994, "De Beers set to gain Indian mining rights."

tities. Fewer than 0.5 percent of kimberlite or lamproite deposits have developed into major producers and it typically took five to ten years to develop a viable deposit into a producing mine. It took an average of 250 tonnes of ore to provide one carat of polished diamond.[12]

From the late 19th century until 1954 the African continent was the only major diamond producer. The Soviet Union discovered its first major Siberian pipe in 1954, and the Argyle AK1 pipe represented Australia's only major diamond discovery. The major world producers are presented in Exhibit 3. Although Australia was ranked number one in the world as the leading volume supplier of diamonds, it was only ranked fifth in terms of value, behind the former USSR, Botswana, South Africa, and Namibia.

While beauty and durability are important, a steady price which increases over the years is also part of the attraction of diamonds in the marketplace. In reality, diamonds are not scarce and the main role of the Central Selling Organization (CSO) has been to regulate supply and demand to bring stability to the diamond markets.

De Beers Consolidated Mines Limited was formed in 1888 to take over the assets of the De Beers Mining Company Limited and the Kimberley Central Diamond Mining company Limited. However, before the late Sir Ernest Oppenheimer forged the CSO and its many trading arms during the 1930s, there were several periods in which South African diamonds flooded the market and severely depressed prices.

About 80 to 90 percent of all rough diamonds marketed in the world were sold through the CSO, and its sales for 1986 (uncut production) amounted to $2,562 million.[13] De Beers was proud that it had never announced a reduc-

---

[12] "De Beers and the diamond industry," De Beers promotional material, England.
[13] *Mining Journal,* London, March 18, 1988, "Record profits for De Beers," p. 231.

EXHIBIT 3   **World Natural Rough Diamond Production 1989 and 1993 (million carats)**

	1989	1993
Australia	37.00	41.00
Zaire	20.00	16.50
Botswana	15.20	14.70
CIS (Russia)	12.00	11.50
South Africa	9.00	9.80
Namibia	0.90	1.10
South America	0.90	2.90
Ghana	0.20	0.70
Central African Republic	0.60	0.40
Sierra Leone	0.60	0.35
Liberia	0.30	0.00
Angola	1.20	1.00
Guinea	0.20	0.40
Other countries	0.40	0.50
WORLD TOTAL	98.50	100.85

Source: Australia's Mining Monthly, December 1989–January 1990, p. 21.

tion in prices, although in 1978 temporary surcharges were progressively removed. However, it has become increasingly difficult to maintain this record. Since 1992 restraints have been placed on suppliers, and on July 1, 1995 the CSO decided to "realign" its pricebook, which effectively decreased prices of smaller and lower-grade diamonds by 10 percent.

De Beers, through the CSO, maintained the price of diamonds by controlling supply and demand. The company's chairman, Harry F. Oppenheimer, defended De Beers against the accusation that it constituted a classic monopoly:

> Whether this measure of control amounts to a monopoly, I would not know. But if it does it is certainly a monopoly of the most unusual kind. There is no one concerned with diamonds, whether as producer, dealer, cutter, jeweller or customer who does not benefit from it. It protects not only the shareholder in the big diamond companies but also the miners they employ and the communities that are dependent on their operations. The well-being of tens of thousands of individual diamond diggers of all races is dependent on its maintenance.[14]

The United States government has viewed De Beers and the CSO as violating its antitrust laws. Though North America has always been one of its most important markets, it was said that no executive or official from the De Beers group ever visited the United States, to avoid the possibility of initiating a court case. In 1973 De Beers was accused of engaging in a conspiracy to suppress competition in the diamond drill bit market. The United States Justice Department appeared to have a strong case for a violation of antitrust laws, but De Beers avoided prosecution by selling all its United States interests in the offending company. Not until 1975 were two distributors involved in the purported arrangement convicted. They received relatively modest fines.[15] In 1993 De Beers Centenary AG, General Electric, and two individuals were charged by the United States Justice Department with an alleged conspiracy to raise the price of synthetic industrial diamonds. In the words of De Beers chairman Julian Ogilvie Thompson:

> We do not do business in the United States and are therefore not within the jurisdiction of its courts for the purposes of this action. There has been no price fixing. G.E. and De Beers/Centenary have always been in direct and fierce competition and G.E. has stated that it intends to defend the action vigorously.[16]

CSO's Influence over Supply

During a major downturn in the diamond industry in the early 1980s, the CSO saved the industry from collapse when they held a stockpile between 1983 and 1984 of nearly US$2,000 million, demonstrating their enormous power and financial resources.[17]

---

[14] *Register of Australian Mining, 1981,* Ross Louthean Publishers, p. 215.

[15] Stefan Kanfer, 1993, *The Last Empire: De Beers, Diamonds and the World,* Hodder & Stoughton, p. 317.

[16] De Beers annual report, 1993, p. 6.

[17] *Mining Journal,* London, February 5, 1988, "A good year for diamonds," p. 98.

EXHIBIT 4   De Beers Diamond Stocks and Earnings 1984–1993 (US$ million)

	1993	1992	1991	1990	1989	1988	1987	1986	1985	1984
Diamond stocks	4,124	3,765	3,034	2,684	2,476	2,003	2,303	1,847	1,898	1,950
Group earnings	595	491	759	950	1127	877	536	349	252	168

Source: De Beers annual report 1993.

While the CSO's administration of rough diamond supplies provided a stability that benefited all producers, most producers and their governments sought to retain some control over their output by either establishing local polishing industries or by marketing a proportion of output independently. Producers who attempted to split from the CSO cartel altogether, however, in general did not succeed.

In the late 1970s the booming diamond-cutting industry in Israel attempted to pull free of the cartel by creating their own stockpile of diamonds. De Beers retaliated by placing a temporary surcharge on their uncut diamonds of 40 percent, putting pressure on Israeli banks to increase interest rates to diamond buyers and forcing Israeli cutters to dip into their stockpiles to survive. By 1980 some 350 smaller dealers had been forced into bankruptcy.

Zaire attempted to operate independently in 1981–1983 but failed to achieve any significant price benefit, in spite of the efforts of independent market dealers. It was claimed that De Beers broke Zaire's bid for independence by exploiting the country's active diamond smuggling. By positioning dealers across the border in the Congo and offering large premiums to smugglers, De Beers caused the flow of legitimate diamonds out of Zaire to almost completely dry up. Consequently, Zaire was obliged to return to the CSO fold.[18] Similarly, Botswana tried to take an independent position, but was also forced to rejoin the CSO by selling its US$500 million stockpile to De Beers. In 1990 the then Soviet Union reaffirmed its links with De Beers in an exclusive five-year contract to sell its rough diamonds through the CSO. The value was estimated at $5,000 million over the period of the contract.[19]

These deals put the stamp of De Beers firmly on the diamond market. Output from the Aredor mine in Guinea was marketed independently with some success, but its production was relatively modest and characterized by larger, high-quality diamonds for which there was considerable demand. The agreement between the CSO and Argyle diamonds was unusual in that ADS was able to sell a portion of the Argyle output on its own while continuing to market the bulk of its production through the CSO.

In the early 1990s, however, the multiple discoveries of viable diamond pipes outside Africa and the increasing activity of other large international players such as CRA and BHP weakened De Beers' grip on the world diamond market. The flood of diamonds from Russian sites and the high volume of uncontrolled smuggled diamonds coming out of politically unstable countries

---

[18] Kanfer, pp. 343–344.
[19] *Australian,* July 27, 1990, "Soviets sign $66 million diamonds agreement," p. 1.

such as Angola were difficult for the CSO to absorb. The Russian stockpile had reached levels estimated at between $2 and $4 billion and the Russians were increasing pressure on De Beers for a larger share of official sales, from 26% to 36% of the CSO's sales as well as a seat on the De Beers board and a hand in running the CSO. The Russian activities were important to Argyle because the Russian production was similar to Argyle's output in terms of grade and colouring.[20]

By 1993 De Beers' diamond stockpile had increased well above the rate of inflation to nearly double that of the 1981 crisis. Some of the company's older South African mines had almost reached the end of their useful life, while others were becoming uneconomic to operate. Though the company was developing new prospects in Siberia and India, it was in an uncertain position.[21] Some analysts claimed that in 1995 CSO's share of the rough diamond trade had dwindled to 63 percent.[22]

The CSO exercised strong control downstream in the diamond trade. In addition to its own production, the CSO sold rough diamonds from other producers for a levy of about 12 percent on sales. Rough diamonds were supplied only to accredited dealers in a highly formalized procedure. Dealers were invited to buy preselected parcels of diamonds called "sights" at prices set by the CSO. No haggling over price was allowed and the dealer either accepted or rejected the parcel unconditionally. Dealers who rejected parcels could find that lesser parcels were allocated to them at future sights or they could be dropped from the invitation list. From acceptance of the sights, the rough diamonds proceeded to the diamond-cutting industry and on to the jewellers who created the settings for the final customers.

CSO's Influence over Demand

In addition to regulating supply, De Beers also excelled in marketing, creating large demand for diamonds in markets where little existed before.

In the mid-1930s, as a result of the depression, De Beers were holding stock worth over four times their annual sales. In 1939 the company embarked on a marketing campaign to increase sales, particularly of the smaller diamond categories. De Beers established the near-universal tradition of diamond engagement rings and popularized the slogan "A diamond is forever." By the early 1960s, almost 80 percent of U.S. males "made it official" by buying a diamond engagement ring. However, the market in the United States matured as de facto lifestyles became more popular and people became less subject to the sentimental appeals of a diamond engagement ring.[23]

De Beers' marketing accomplishments in the United States paled in comparison with its achievements in Japan and West Germany. Thirty years ago there was no Japanese word for diamond. In 1966, only 5 percent of Japanese brides

[20] *Australian Financial Review,* April 24, 1995, "Russia in a capitalist frenzy over diamonds," p. 18.

[21] *Australian Financial Review,* September 19, 1994, "The dig's up for De Beers cartel," pp. 1–24.

[22] *Financial Times,* London, February 12, 1996, "Analysts question De Beers cartel's claimed share of world diamond trade," p. 21.

[23] D. E. Koskoff, 1981, *The Diamond World,* Harper and Row Publishers, New York, p. 273.

received a diamond engagement ring, which played little part in Japanese culture. An advertising initiative by De Beers through advertising agency J. Walter Thompson discovered a cultural niche called *Yuino*—the exchange of gifts between bride and groom. As a result of marketing efforts, 60 percent of Japanese brides received diamond rings in 1979. Much the same trend occurred in Germany, where it was a Teutonic tradition that two gold bands symbolized undying love. In 1967 De Beers introduced the concept of a third band—this one studded with diamonds. West Germany became the third-biggest market behind the United States and Japan. More recent marketing attempts by De Beers to increase diamond demand included the "eternity ring" for women and diamond-studded cufflinks and tiepins for men.

In 1995, the CSO spent US$168 million to launch its "Shadows" campaign created by J. Walter Thompson in London. After much research, De Beers concluded that diamonds are addictive. The more diamonds a woman owns, the more likely she was to have acquired diamonds in the last year and to want to buy more. Tiffany's Ms. Jacqueline Carniato said, "Madam will get her first taste as a teenager with a gift from her parents like little diamond studs. When she gets engaged she receives a diamond engagement ring, then a wedding ring. For her birthday her partner will buy a diamond pendant or earrings and so on."[24]

The Investment Market

Because of the diamond's value, portability, and attractiveness, it is often viewed as a promising medium for investment. The remarkable rise in the price of the "D-flawless" in the late 1970s could be largely attributed to a general lack of confidence in all paper currencies, encouraging investment in inflation shelters. However, the smaller investor who paid a retail price for a diamond, which often included sales tax, found on resale to the trade that it had to compete with similar gems freely available at wholesale prices from the CSO.

Another important problem for investors was that diamonds are not a homogeneous commodity. While its size and weight could be established unambiguously, every diamond was an individual gem with subtle differences in terms of colour and lack of flaws. Even experts disagreed on the exact classification of a particular diamond. Thus diamonds which had investment value were largely confined to top-quality and unusual stones which had scarcity value. Lower-quality diamond investments often relied on certification to determine a stone's grade. Yet even at the most respected laboratories, diamond grading remained an inexact art.

The diamond industry was ambivalent about widespread investment in diamonds and an active resale market. High prices paid for spectacular gems enhanced the mystique and appeal of diamonds. However, as more polished diamonds entered investment portfolios, this stockpile was becoming a threat to the ability of De Beers to control the market. Major fluctuations in the price of diamonds only occurred in cases where De Beers had, temporarily, lost control over the supply of diamonds.

---

[24] *Australian,* June 6, 1995, "Feeding the diamond addiction," p. 28.

This happened in the mid-1980s during a flurry of investment into diamonds. Some highly geared investors used investment diamonds as collateral. After the 1987 stock-market crash De Beers had to use its persuasive skills to discourage banks from panic-selling these diamonds to recoup losses from defaulted loans. In addition, the former USSR dumped diamonds on the world market during this period in order to secure much-needed foreign exchange. These incidents caused some industry observers to contend that De Beers had already lost control of the top-quality gem market (D-flawless) as a result of investor trading.

Industrial Diamonds

In sharp contrast to gems and near-gems, industrial diamonds were commodities used in the manufacture of drill bits for rock cutting and for surface treatments of cutting and polishing tools where extreme hardness was required. Prices were determined by the normal supply/demand market mechanisms and natural diamonds competed with synthetic industrials. Because of oversupply, prices of industrial diamonds were low. No diamond which had the potential to be cut and polished would be sold as industrial.

The industrial diamond market was very competitive and characterized by high technology and product innovation. Prices of naturally occurring industrial diamonds faced ever-increasing competition from synthetic diamonds and consisted of about 20 percent of the industrial market in 1982.[25]

General Electric announced in 1954 that it had fully synthesized industrial diamonds and by the 1960s both GE and De Beers were manufacturing large quantities of industrial diamonds. However, since 1954, the price of industrial diamonds (both natural and synthetic) has decreased almost annually, and in dollar terms the economic significance of industrials to the diamond industry has been greatly reduced.

Natural industrial diamonds are preferred in some applications for technical reasons, but in most applications they compete against synthetics only through price competition. The recession of the early 1980s, plus the defection of Zaire from the CSO at that time, caused a fall in the price of industrials. Zaire subsequently reentered ties with De Beers.

The mid-1980s saw some major developments in the production of synthetic diamonds, particularly in the United States, the USSR, and Japan. Some of the uses for synthetic diamonds included abrasion-resistant drills and other cutting tools, as well as superfast diamond integrated circuits.[26]

Despite some reports, synthetic diamonds were not actively sold as gems, because of their flaws and distinct yellow colour. Imitation diamond gems such as glass and cubic zirconium created a potential threat to the diamond gem industry, but did not, in fact, cause discernible damage. However, threats of substitutes continued and reports emerged in mid-1994 of Russian processes for enhancing the colour of brown and other dark-coloured diamonds.[27]

---

[25] Economist Intelligence Unit 1993, "Inflation shelters: diamonds, gold, silver, platinum," Special Report no. 136, Spencer House, London.

[26] *Business Week,* February 12, 1990, "Diamonds could be high tech's best friend," pp. 58–59.

[27] *Business Review Weekly*, May 9, 1994, "Russia refines art of faking gems."

Cutting, Polishing, and Trading

The major centres for the processing of rough diamonds include Belgium (Antwerp), India (Surat and Bombay), Israel (Tel Aviv), and the United States (New York).

By 1990 India was the world's largest diamond cutting and polishing centre with an estimated 800,000 people employed in the industry.[28] Exports of cut and polished diamonds were India's second-largest foreign exchange earner after textiles. Because of its low labour costs, India was cost-effective at cutting and polishing the smaller, lower-quality stones.

Antwerp was widely acknowledged as the centre for trading both rough and polished stones since the early part of the century, and was the chief market for non-CSO sales. Antwerp's cutting industry numbered around 5,000 individuals who specialized in the better-quality diamonds, particularly those that are difficult to cut.

Israel employed around 12,000 cutters and the industry was the country's most important source of foreign exchange. Israel specialized in commercial quality and medium to smaller-sized diamonds. New York employed about 400 diamond cutters. Because of their expertise and high labour costs, the American cutters specialized in the largest and best-quality stones.

Because of their relative specialities, processing in India added 43 to 47 percent to the value of rough diamonds, processing in Israel added 22 percent value, and Antwerp and New York added even less value.[29] Diamond processing also took place to a lesser extent in the former USSR, South Africa, and Brazil.

Diamond Grading

Diamonds are graded according to weight, colour, clarity, and proportion into over 5,000 categories. Diamond sorting is a demanding occupation which requires extensive training. However, in the end there always remains an element of subjectivity and judgement.

The first major factor affecting the price of a diamond is the carat weight, a carat being equal to 200 milligrams.

Second, the colour of a diamond also greatly affects its value. When diamond graders discuss "colour," they are in most cases referring to its "discolouration" or "tinges" of yellow of a colourless stone (see Exhibit 5). According to one common classification system, there are several grades of colour ranging from "D," a perfectly colourless stone, through to "Z," a decidedly yellow or brown stone. The lower down the alphabet the letter, the lower the price of the diamond. The gems further down the colour scale were difficult to sell in the United States, despite retailers' efforts to promote them as "champagne-hued" or "honey-coloured." Apart from the yellow and brown stones, there were also naturally occurring pink, red, green, and blue diamonds which are extremely rare and very valuable.

---

[28] Employment figures are based on P. Temple, "The investor's best friend," *Accountancy,* September 1989, pp. 60–61.

[29] Koskoff, p. 247.

Third, a diamond's clarity refers to its internal qualities, that is, the number, kind, size, location and overall significance of flaws and imperfections within the stone. Diamonds are graded for clarity on an elaborate scale, ranging from "Flawless" or top quality to "Imperfect" or industrial quality.

Finally, the cut of the diamond is determined by the proportions of the stone, and this also affects the weight of the final product.

To the ordinary eye a flawless "D" gem may look identical to an "SI" (slight imperfect) stone, but the difference in price is staggering. In 1981 the first article sold for $40,000 per carat wholesale, while the second article commanded only $429.50.[30]

Polished Diamond Traders

The trader in the diamond business provided the age-old function of matching sellers (the diamond processors) with buyers (the jewellery manufacturers and retailers) throughout the world.

The diamond processing centres (particularly Antwerp) were also major centres for world trading. Because of the nature of the product, establishing trusting business relationships was vital in the diamond trade. After all, how can you be sure that the diamond you purchased was the one that has been delivered? The following quotes by diamond traders illustrated some of the problems: "Yes, this is a business of trust but that doesn't mean that it doesn't get violated," and "If I send a parcel to Tel Aviv and by the time it gets there prices had dropped, the Israelis will decline to accept the goods."[31]

---

[30] Koskoff, p. 283.
[31] Koskoff, pp. 290–91.

EXHIBIT 5   Diamond Grades—Colour and Clarity

Colour (CSO Grading System)	Argyle Coloured Diamond Grading	Clarity Grades
D, E, F Fine White (colourless)	C1 Light champagne	IF Internally flawless
G, H, I, J White (near-colourless)	C2 Medium champagne	VVS 1/2 Very, very slightly included
K, L Slightly Tinted (light yellow/champagne)	C3 Dark champagne	VS 1/2 Very slightly included
M, N Tinted (light yellow/champagne) Light Cognac	C4 Slightly included	SI 1/2
	C5 Medium cognac	P 1/2/3 Visible inclusions
	C6 Dark cognac	
	FC Fancy cognac	

Source: De Beers brochure.

Jewellery Manufacturers and Retailers

The retail diamond-jewellery market has developed to a substantial size over the years, largely due to the marketing efforts of De Beers. However, retail sales of diamond jewellery are also affected by diamond prices and economic conditions. During economic recessions retailers face the choice of either increasing markups, reducing sales, or reducing margins (to gain volume) in order to maintain profitability. The choice of pricing strategy depends, largely, on the size and price-sensitivity of market segments.

◼ Argyle Diamonds Taking on the World?

In 1995, 45 percent of Argyle's production was of "industrial" quality, and 52.5 percent of the mine's output was "near-gem" quality, and 25 percent represented "gem" quality production. The term "near-gem" was used only for rough uncut diamonds. Over the years the industry had developed techniques to cut gems (usually small) from diamonds which due to flaws or their small size would otherwise have been relegated to the industrial market. The ability to cut and polish marginal stones was a particular speciality of the Indian industry, partly because of lower labour cost. The boundaries between gem and near-gem stones were ambiguous and changed over time. On this point ADS general manager, Mr. Mike Mitchell, noted:

> An important impact on the company's business and marketing strategies arises from the production mix, with the dominance of near-gem and industrial diamonds in volume terms. As a consequence, much of Argyle's material is labour intensive and difficult to process (near-gem), or faces strong competition from synthetic diamonds [industrials].[32]

The different categories varied markedly in their ability to raise revenues. In 1995, gems accounted for 32 percent of Argyle's revenue, while near-gems and industrials represented 60 percent and 8 percent of revenue, respectively. The company's five-year contract with the CSO required ADS to sell 78 percent of its near-gem diamonds, 75 percent of its industrials, and almost all of its gem-quality diamonds (excluding the pinks) to the CSO. Once again, Mike Mitchell explained:

> The near-gem and industrial rough sold independently are marketed by ADS through its sales office in Antwerp. The main customers for Argyle goods sold in Antwerp are Indian dealers and representatives of the Indian cutting and polishing factories. The highest value gem goods go to the cutting and polishing factory in Perth. These polished goods are then sold either through Perth or Antwerp offices.[33]

---

[32] *Australia's Mining Monthly,* December 1989–January 1990, "Major upgrade for Argyle Diamond Mine," p. 28.

[33] Ibid.

Product Development

Although Argyle produced 40 percent of the world's diamonds by volume in the early 1990s, the mine's output was highly skewed toward lower-quality and coloured stones and its output represented significantly less than 40 percent of world's value. In common with many other diamond mines around the world, about 40 percent of Argyle's production was coloured diamonds with yellow to brown tones. The high proportion of coloured stones presented ADS with a major marketing challenge. Based on De Beers' marketing and grading structure, the industry had grown accustomed to the view that good-quality diamonds are white (colourless) in the sense of the absence of a yellow or brown tint. Traditionally, these colours realized about 30% lower retail prices than white stones or the rare deeply coloured pink, green, or blue "fancies."

To build awareness and change consumers' attitudes toward coloured diamonds, ADS embarked on its own extensive marketing campaign. The words "yellow" and "brown" were not popular in the company and had been replaced by "champagne" and "cognac." To enhance the credibility of champagne and cognac diamonds, ADS commissioned Stuart Devlin, jeweller to the Queen, to design and produce a two-hundred piece jewellery collection, featuring about 10,000 Argyle gems. The centrepiece of the collection, known as the "Champagne Diamond Exhibition," was a $2.9 million golden Fabergé-style egg studded with 4,000 champagne and cognac gems, and which opened to reveal diamond-studded golden horses on a revolving carousel. The exhibition received widespread attention and media coverage, both in Australia and overseas.

The original egg was sold to a collector and in 1990 the company commissioned a second, much larger egg from Kutchinsky jewellers. The 70-centimetre, 23-kilogram egg featured 20,000 diamonds, including 348 carats of tiny pink diamonds arranged in a complex pattern. The egg opened to reveal a diamond-studded library and miniature portrait gallery.

In 1992 the Kutchinsky egg as part of a $20 million exhibition of coloured diamonds, jewellery, and objets d'art was displayed in the Australian Pavilion at the Universal Expo held in Seville, Spain.

In addition to champagnes and cognacs, Argyle also produced limited numbers of pink, green, blue, red, and purple gems. Argyle's rare pink diamonds generated considerable international interest. The company produced about 40 carats of tender-quality polished pinks per annum, about one carat of tender-quality pink for every 2.5 million carats of annual world production. ADS sold the pink by auction and tender, and at its annual tender at Geneva in 1989, ADS sold 67 pink diamonds totalling 64.38 carats for $9 million.

Cutting, Polishing, and Trading

ADS established an office in Antwerp in 1985 to market its quota of gems and industrial stones. This provided Argyle with knowledge of the diamond industry, a useful network of contacts, and trading experience in this important part of the diamond world.

Cutting and polishing in Perth began in 1985 as a feasibility study and became a permanent fixture in 1987. Due to high labour costs in Australia,

ADS only considered this operation economical for the treatment of top-quality gems. In 1995, the company sold approximately 9,000 carats of polished gem-quality diamonds, one-third of which were polished in the Perth facility. ADS sold its polished production through its European sales office in Antwerp, servicing European and North American customers, and through its Perth sales office which focused on customers in Australia, Southeast Asia, and Japan.

ADS opened an office in Bombay in 1989 to service the Indian diamond-cutting industry and also to further investigate marketing opportunities in India. The Indian industry originally faced technical difficulties processing Argyle diamonds because of the hardness and structural complexity of these stones. The company expended considerable resources to introduce new technology to the Indian industry to overcome these problems, and assisted the Indians with the development and manufacture of diamond-impregnated scaifes (polishing discs) for the Indian industry. David Fardon, then Manager Corporate Affairs, commented:

> We are assisting in the upgrade of diamond polishing technology in India, where technical improvements will result in increased efficiency for the industry. The thinking here is that achieving lower production costs through improved polishing technology will result in higher demand for the Argyle goods being processed in India. Argyle's aim in India will be to transfer polishing technology in an effort to manufacture scaifes for the largest cutting and polishing centres in the world.[34]

Commenting on the Indian market, former Ashton Mining Chief Executive David Tyrwhitt stated: "No doubt Argyle has been a stimulant (for Indian expansion). ... The Argyle project would never have succeeded to the extent it has without the phenomenal entrepreneurial activity by the Indian trade. They've developed a new market in Japan."[35]

In conjunction with the government's Australian International Development Assistance Bureau, ADS co-funded, set up, and managed a diamond-cutting training centre in Beijing. In the long term, Argyle wished to establish the country as a processor for Argyle's diamonds. Argyle also provided technical assistance to people setting up processing facilities in Thailand.

Expansion

Argyle embarked on an expansion program and major upgrading of operating facilities which raised the capacity of the AK1 treatment plant to 6.6 million tonnes in 1990 compared with 4.9 million tonnes achieved in 1989. This was part of Argyle's plans to maintain the company's steady production trend and to help the company further capitalize on its growing international profile. In 1994, a further expansion increased plant throughput capacity to 8.6 million tonnes per annum.

---

[34] Ibid.

[35] *Australian Business Monthly*, June 6, 1990, "Argyle gets down to marketing nitty-gritty," p. 18.

Negotiations with De Beers

Argyle's relationship with De Beers and the CSO started in 1986 when the mine commenced production. Pressure by the Australian government and the trade unions contributed to a historic five-year contract which allowed the joint venture partners to market approximately 25 percent of the mines production on their own and channel 75 percent through the CSO.

The contract was renegotiated in 1991 and after extended discussions its essential features were rolled over for another five years. Argyle gained total control over the marketing of its rare and valuable pink diamonds, and new marketing powers for its other coloured stones. Its allocation of gems was also substantially increased. In return, the CSO's share of gem and near-gem stones (excluding the pinks and the stipulated quantity of high-quality gems) was increased from 75 percent to 78 percent. An unusual aspect of the agreement was an escape clause for Argyle which gave it the right to cancel the agreement if they were not satisfied with the CSO's method of sorting and classifying its diamonds.

The agreement with the CSO was due to expire in June 1996 and by mid-1995 preparations for the renegotiations of the agreement were well under way at Argyle and the joint venture partners. By now the circumstances and mood of the negotiating parties had changed. Large quantities of diamonds from Russia and various African countries found their way into markets beyond the CSO's influence. The Russian authorities were demanding a greater market share and direct involvement in the running of the CSO. Ashton Mining, one of the Argyle joint venture partners, had announced substantial new deposits in Australia and Finland. BHP had announced major finds in Canada's frozen north and active exploration was under way on the coast of Namibia. The CSO was in danger of losing the tight control it had historically exercised over demand and supply in the industry.

In mid-1995, the CSO was particularly concerned about the extent to which the Russians were destabilizing the market by selling diamonds from its large stockpiles outside their agreement with the CSO. The agreement with Russia was due to expire on December 1, 1995. Tim Capon, an executive director of De Beers and a member of the CSO executive committee, commented, "We have bought US$1 billion of rough diamonds from them for each of the past five years."[36] Despite the substantial volumes bought by the CSO under the agreement, it was clear that sales outside the agreement were continuing. It was estimated that in 1994 Russian diamonds worth between US$700 million and US$900 million bypassed the CSO.

Capon indicated that the CSO had to review its pricing system which had more than 5,000 price categories. The prices ranged from US$0.20 a carat for industrial-grade diamonds to US$8,000 a carat at the top. The CSO price book only covered diamonds up to 10 carats, beyond which prices were negotiable. Given its production mix, the July 1995 "realignment" exercise disadvantaged Argyle. "In this particular instance, Argyle had a disproportionate

---

[36] *Bulletin,* July 25, 1995, "Stones in the sward," p. 85.

volume in those areas of the price book in which there were reductions. The smaller size was the area which was hit."[37] The CSO had also sought to stem the oversupply of diamonds from 1992 on by deferring purchases, originally by 25 percent of contracted sales and later by 15 percent.

These recent actions by the CSO did not please Argyle Diamonds and the joint venture partners. According to Argyle spokesperson Andrew Murray: "Argyle has certainly been disappointed with the deferred purchases having gone on for so long and we were disappointed with the recent price changes."[38] He declined to comment on whether there was likely to be a big cut in the portion of Argyle's production channelled through the CSO. "Argyle is certainly capable of doing it itself. We have the competence and we have substantial history in selling to our own customer base—we are mine to market competent."[39]

Ashton Mining's chief executive, John Robinson, indicated that studies were under way in Bombay and Antwerp to determine whether it should break away from the CSO.

> Any new contract would need to provide significant benefits to Argyle before the partners would sign up again. When we renegotiated the contract last time we recognized there was an opportunity cost involved. At this stage that cost appears to have outweighed the benefits of dealing through the CSO. Included in that cost was about $130 million worth of Argyle diamonds held in store because of the CSO's decision to cut back 15 percent on deliveries under its supply contracts.[40]

John Robinson said that the CSO apparently had not sufficiently recognized the growth potential of the "six-point market." These small diamonds, ranging from 0.01 to 0.06 of a carat in size, had become the fastest-growing sector of the world jewellery trade.

> What is happening is that Indian polishers are democratising the demand for diamond jewellery, making it more affordable. This new market which has developed over the past 10 years or so, now accounts for about 30 percent of the world polished diamond trade. The CSO, with its jewellery promotions, has relied on a trickle-down effect from high value stones.[41]

---

[37] Ibid.
[38] *West Australian,* July 25, 1995, "Argyle to put pressure on CSO for better deal," p. 33.
[39] Ibid.
[40] Ibid.
[41] *Australian,* September 1, 1995, "Ashton confirms CSO split option," p. 21.

Canadian Tire Corporation (condensed)

In November 1981 Dean Muncaster, president and CEO of the Canadian Tire Corporation (CTC), was assessing the position he should take with respect to the takeover of White Stores, Inc., which was headquartered in Wichita Falls, Texas. Since 1977 CTC had been looking for an opportunity to expand to the United States and preferably into the Sunbelt states. For a price that was not to exceed $45 million (U.S.) pending a year-end audit, CTC would acquire White's 81 retail stores, four warehouses, trucking fleet, and access to more than 425 independent dealer-owned stores centred in Texas, Louisiana, Oklahoma, and 11 other states. It was now up to Dean Muncaster to decide if he should recommend to the board that Canadian Tire proceed with the purchase.

History of Canadian Tire

In 1922, two brothers, Alfred and John Billes, invested $1,900 and formed Hamilton Tire and Garage Ltd. in Hamilton, Ontario. They dealt primarily in automobile parts and servicing. The firm, renamed Canadian Tire, grew quickly and in 1927 had three stores in Toronto. During the 1930s, the company started supplying other automobile parts and service centres in Ontario. Prior to World War II, six stores existed in Ontario.

The Billes family demonstrated significant innovation during their early years, a trademark that remained as one of the cornerstones of the firm's success. For instance, the first CTC store on Yonge Street in Toronto in 1937 had stockroom clerks on rollerskates moving parts to the sales counter for faster customer service time. CTC adopted computer-aided accounting and inventory control procedures as early as 1963. Throughout the 1970s, CTC built one of the most modern distribution networks in the country, utilizing the latest technology in warehousing and inventory control.

By the end of 1981 the firm had grown to 348 retail stores and 83 gasoline stations. The product line had been expanded to include hardware products, lawn-care products, sporting goods, and small household appliances. Internationally, CTC had purchased a 36 percent controlling interest in McEwan's Ltd. of Australia in 1979.

This case was written primarily from published sources by Mark C. Baetz and Ralph Troschke, School of Business and Economics, Wilfrid Laurier University. © 1986 by Mark C. Baetz; condensed, 1989.

Much of the success of CTC was attributed by some observers to the leadership of Dean Muncaster, age 48, who had been involved with CTC since he was 12 years old. Muncaster had worked in his father's store in Sudbury during the summers while attending the University of Western Ontario and Northwestern. In 1957 he was hired by Canadian Tire as a financial analyst. Approximately two years later, he left Canadian Tire in Toronto and returned to Sudbury to be the manager of the Sudbury dealership held by his father. He returned to Toronto in 1961 as a vice-president and became president in 1966. During his presidency, CTC's sales rose from $100 million to over $1.3 billion (1981), and after-tax net income reached $51.4 million or $4.05 per share. He was well liked and respected by CTC's dealer network and by Canadian financial experts.

Muncaster was faced with managing three divergent groups while steering CTC. The three groups were, first, Alfred Billes and his family; second, the heirs of John Billes headed by John's son, Dick; and third, the dealer network. The two factions of the Billes family collectively controlled 60.8 percent of the voting shares in the corporation (representing only 8.5 percent of all outstanding shares) and were not always in agreement with one another. For example, Muncaster's decision to enter the Australian market was heavily contested between the two family groups, with Dick Billes in favour and Alfred Billes in opposition. The decision left its scars.

The Billes family was active in the corporation. They managed several stores and held directorships on the board. Their influence was not always evident to the general public, as they shunned the limelight and the media.

◼ The Canadian Tire Success Formula

CTC was extremely successful due to the corporation's emphasis on the dealer-run network, advantages incurred from its highly modernized distribution system, and a marketing program that clearly established its desired image in the minds of the consumers. The dealer-manager network was the cornerstone of CTC's success and essential in an understanding of corporate values and strategies.

The dealer-run stores were a type of franchise operation. CTC usually owned the building (87 percent of the time) and acted as the central buyer, distributor, national advertiser, and dealer recruiter. The dealer ran the store as his or her own business. He would buy all of his goods from CTC (approximately 6,000 of 32,000 products were mandatory), and most operational decisions (for example, personnel, local advertising, and so forth) were his or hers to make. CTC wanted to blend the entrepreneurial spirit with that of a corporate manager. It was hoped that this arrangement would provide individual dealers with enough incentive to turn their stores into a success. The dealers did not have to pay franchise fees but had to invest a minimum of $50,000 into their location. They were free to reap as much profit as they could from their stores.

The corporation was very careful in its selection of prospective dealers. The ability to invest at least $50,000 was not the only criterion. Exhaustive examinations and interviews were utilized to trim the 1,000–1,200 applicants down to the final 50 trainees. The trainees spent three months of in-class training followed by six months of in-store training before posting to a store. Corporate support was always available after the training period on any retailing issue, and dealer-support group meetings were numerous. The system worked so well, in fact, that virtually no dealer failure was encountered by CTC.

The desire for revenues and profits was instilled through the dealer-run network. The advanced distribution system ensured that the parent corporation managed its costs to make its own profit. As well, by having the right merchandise in the right store at the right time, the system ensured customer satisfaction. The key ingredients in this distribution system were three fully automated one-storeyed warehouses (one in Edmonton and two in Toronto) that utilized robotics, conveyor belts, and computerized cataloguing of parts. The inventory levels of the warehouses, as well as those of individual retail operators, were monitored by computers. Reorder points of the retail and wholesale levels were automatically triggered on a nightly basis. This ensured a maximum delivery time of two days to retail outlets.

The result of CTC's advanced distribution system, from a customer's point of view, was constant availability and selection of thousands of products that CTC carried. This became a trademark of the firm. Inventories were also reduced, increasing CTC's inventory turnover and decreasing its carrying charges. This made profitability easier to attain for CTC and its retailers.

The constant availability and broad selection of numerous products were part of an image that CTC had built for itself through an effective marketing campaign. Consumers also came to know Canadian Tire as a retail outlet offering value with a reputation for low price. This was especially important during 1981 as inflation, interest rates, and unemployment all rose. The value–low price appeal attracted a lot of people who had turned into "do-it-yourselfers" during this period. The average purchase at a Canadian Tire store was $15, and these purchases were said to be interest-rate-proof as they were small "must" expenditures. While the average purchase seemed low, CTC would see approximately 2 million customers per week according to Muncaster.

The typical customer found it difficult to enter the store and buy just one item. Due to the firm's low prices and broad product lines, it was not uncommon to witness the typical customer filling up a shopping basket with various products.

Muncaster identified several additional key factors to CTC's success: (1) CTC became known as a place for "more than just tires," a theme employed in its advertising. Traditionally, 80 percent of CTC's customers had been male, but by 1981, the split was almost even. (2) To lure customers back to the store, the firm employed "Canadian Tire money," which was a form of discount coupons given to customers after each cash purchase. (3) Twice per year, 7 million catalogues listing the entire CTC product line were published and distributed to households across Canada.

These factors led to unusually high growth rates and startling financial successes for CTC. Exhibit 1 highlights the performance of the corporation during this period of high growth and image development. Walter Hachhorn, general manager of Home Hardware Stores Ltd., CTC's major Canadian competitor, explained the success of CTC in the following way: "Canadian Tire has succeeded

EXHIBIT 1 Four-Year Review of Performance (dollars in thousands except per-share amounts)

	1981	1980	1979	1978	1977
Comparative Income Statement					
Gross operating revenue	$1,340,764	$1,057,536	$935,753	$798,717	$718,114
Pre-tax income	100,432	72,240	69,583	53,938	52,240
Taxes on income	48,966	34,513	33,070	25,163	23,750
Income before extraordinary gain	51,466	37,727	36,513	28,775	28,490
Extraordinary gain	2,212	901	2,195	694	1,000
Net income	53,678	38,628	38,708	29,469	29,490
Cash dividends	9,936	8,487	7,017	10,435	5,800
Income retained and reinvested	43,742	30,141	31,691	19,034	23,690
Comparative Balance Sheet					
Current assets		435,183	343,372	312,831	277,894
Investments		44,151	49,371	1,823	1,014
Net property and equipment		266,854	244,496	235,989	218,209
Other assets		2,213	2,582	3,620	4,026
Total assets		748,401	639,821	554,263	501,143
Current liabilities		279,451	211,903	165,040	134,511
Long-term debt		136,387	136,361	138,377	142,317
Deferred income taxes		3,599	3,822	3,382	1,512
Shareholders' equity		328,964	287,753	247,464	222,803
Per-Share Data					
Income before extraordinary gain	4.05	3.07	3.07	2.49	2.50
Net income	4.22	3.14	3.26	2.55	2.59
Dividends	.78	.69	.59	.90	.51
Shareholders' equity	30.44	26.75	24.20	21.40	19.59
Statistics at Year-End					
Number of associate stores		333	319	314	314
Number of gasoline stations		71	64	62	61
Number of Class A shareholders		8,665	9,310	10,435	10,035
Number of common shareholders		1,252	1,315	1,450	1,417

Source: For years 1977–1980: Canadian Tire annual report, 1980; for 1981: estimated.

because of excellent marketing and superior merchandising combined with the fact that they were the first to fill a void in the Canadian retailing market. They happened to come along at the right time and place."

Suppliers to CTC were also impressed with CTC operations. One supplier noted: "We've been impressed by the energy levels exhibited by the CTC head office when negotiating contracts, and although they have pushed the cost of advertising our product in their catalogue on to us, we consider their organization as top-notch."

Despite the phenomenal growth, it was apparent to Muncaster and other senior CTC executives that CTC growth could not be sustained indefinitely. Since 1977 CTC had been following a master plan prepared by Muncaster for future growth. The strategy in 1977 was to blanket the Canadian market by expanding into British Columbia, as yet untapped, and by establishing retail outlets in any community or suburban area that could support a regular-size CTC store. It was estimated in 1980 that 65 percent of Canadians lived within 15 minutes of a Canadian Tire store, and it was felt that by 1985, the maximum penetration of 400 stores would be reached.

The strategy also called for growth into other countries and markets with an English language/cultural component as well as a similar economic base. The Australian entry had taken place in 1979, and the United States was earmarked for entry in 1981. Carrying the CTC concept into these countries was not expected to be difficult, and consumer acceptance was anticipated to be high.

The need to expand was foremost in the mind of Muncaster. Without further expansion, an adverse impact on operating performance was anticipated. Expansion in British Columbia was well under way by 1981, and CTC had attempted to diversify somewhat by getting into gasoline stations and a small automobile engine remanufacturing plant for resale of the engines at its stores. These developments merely put off the inevitable total market saturation by CTC.

The Australian venture into McEwan's, a hardware chain, was intended to allow CTC to enter Australia to gain a foothold, then to expand its operations and to conquer Australia as Canada was conquered. The Australian venture was a small one, involving only a $2.2 million investment for a 36 percent interest. However, McEwan's suffered losses of $1,837,000 (Canadian) in 1980 and $548,000 in 1981. While performance was improving, CTC was disappointed. The Foreign Investment Review Board of Australia had also made it clear that it would prohibit CTC from acquiring a greater than 50 percent share in the Australian firm. CTC decided to sell off the investment in 1982 and use the funds of the sale toward the costs of an entry into the United States.

The Australian experience put some pressure on the president of CTC to seek out a successful expansion opportunity whereby the firm could parachute its Canadian success formula and reap large rewards. The original timetable called for an expansion to the U.S. market. Muncaster had favoured the Sunbelt states as they had exhibited the fastest growth in populations and incomes. Demographic trends from 1973 to 1981 definitely pointed to this area of the United States as a ripening market. Some disagreement existed in CTC management, as some favoured expansion to the northeast, where climatic conditions and automobile models tended to parallel those of the Canadian market more closely.

■ American/Sunbelt Retail Market Considerations

In their analysis of the Sunbelt area, CTC managers felt that no competitors had a stranglehold on the things that CTC did well. Given the successes in Canada which CTC had enjoyed even when the retailing was on a decline, the general consensus among the management in Toronto was that the Sunbelt market was a "sure-fire success." Long-term demographic studies were undertaken, and a heavy reliance was placed on their favourable findings (see Exhibit 2).

It was noted that only six major competitors existed for Canadian Tire in the Texas and Sunbelt markets: Sears Roebuck, Montgomery Ward, Kmart, Builders Square, Home Depot, and Handy Dan. The first three competitors did, however, carry a lot of clout within the market. For example, Sears was heavily involved in auto parts and services, and it was not unusual for Sears to have 16 or more auto bays as opposed to 5 or 6 at White's. Wal-Mart, a potential entrant to this market and a major U.S. retailing force, had chosen at this point in time to forgo expansion into the major metropolitan areas in the state of Texas.

EXHIBIT 2   Sample Demographics for Texas

1. Texas was the second-largest state in retail sales.

2. Houston was the eighth and Dallas was the ninth in terms of ranking the size of metropolitan statistical areas.

3. Dallas was expected to increase by 12.9 percent in population from 1980 to 1984; Houston by 14.2 percent; the U.S. average was only 5.2 percent.

4. Mean income (1977):

	Dallas	$19,443
	Houston	18,340
	New York	16,714
	U.S. average	17,137

On a television documentary, one prominent retail market analyst in Houston described the market characteristics of the United States, and in particular the Sunbelt states, as follows:

1. In any U.S. market, three markets were at work: a national one, a regional one, and one based on local climate.

2. Retailing in the United States, and more so in the Sunbelt, was highly competitive and dynamic (the rate of change was far greater than in Canada).

3. The Sunbelt market was witnessing an ever-increasing number of retail entrants who were scrambling to get into very specific market niches.

4. Corporate image and advertising had to be slanted to two very different groups: the English- and the Spanish-speaking population.

5. Promotional campaigns should take into account a high degree of illiteracy and a variety of racial problems (for example, white versus black, white versus Mexican, Mexican versus black).

6. The impact of revenues flowing from oil after 1973 had created a "gold rush" where even poorly run businesses could make money. New people were arriving every day.

7. Every neighbourhood in this area varied due to its ethnic composition.

8. Shopping malls predominated since most consumers preferred one-stop shopping.

9. Sunbelt consumers were sophisticated, however, and would visit a variety of shops (usually specialty stores) within one mall to accomplish their shopping needs.

10. Stores in the United States tended to be far larger, especially department stores, where 25,000 square feet (about 2,300 square metres) would be considered a small area.

11. The U.S. consumer enjoyed a wide option of shopping choices (for example, it would have been typical to see 40 brands of an automotive product available on one shelf).

12. Older downtown areas were considered marginal and these "strip centres" tended to cater to the neighbourhood traffic.

13. Hardware and sporting goods stores in Texas were a rarity, as every major store sold this kind of merchandise.

14. Some observers considered the Houston area the toughest market in the United States.

15. Consumers needed to identify with a firm's message (i.e., a reason for its existence) in order for it to survive and prosper.

◼ White Stores, Inc.

The White Stores were held by Household International Ltd. of Chicago, which was one of the largest retailers in the United States. At approximately $150 million (U.S.) in annual sales, White's represented only 4 percent of Household's revenues. It was an insignificant holding to this large firm and thus received very little attention from its owners.

Although White's was losing money, CTC felt that if the price was low enough, it could refurbish the units and have them take on a CTC philosophy and market appeal. It was felt that a time frame of two or three years would be necessary before White's could break even and start to contribute to corporate profits. It was felt that the added top management attention and CTC's successful Canadian strategy could turn this firm around and represent a springboard for further U.S. expansion.

With White's, CTC would be acquiring 81 retail outlets, access to supply 425 independent dealer-owned stores, and four warehouses. The chain of stores covered Texas (the majority), Louisiana, New Mexico, and Oklahoma as well as ten other states. Approximately half of the White-owned outlets were on leased properties, while all of the real estate (i.e., land and buildings) of the other half were owned by White Stores. The price tag of a maximum of $45 million (U.S.) seemed reasonable to CTC executives when compared to recent costs of $2.5 million per store to establish new outlets in British Columbia. Exhibit 3 shows a proposed financing scheme for the acquisition.

CTC saw other positive factors in the purchase option. The White Stores name was long established, and therefore CTC assumed the name would be a source of loyalty and brand recognition. White's had a store size (approximately 25,000 square feet) similar to that of the typical CTC store. As well, like CTC, White's had only a few brands for their products. In general, White Stores did many of the same things that CTC did, such as automotive service and parts sales; and other broad product lines were available which were similar to CTC except that White's carried furniture as well. This probably would be dropped if the purchase was made. Plenty of warehouse capacity existed. It was estimated that the four warehouses could conduct two to three times their existing volumes without any further capital. The current warehouse utilization rate varied between 30 and 50 percent. The infrastructure for expansion, therefore, was in place.

There were some concerns with an acquisition of White Stores. The locations of many of the stores were not in prime commercial or retail areas but, rather, in local neighbourhoods. In some of these neighbourhoods, the people were Mexican and could not read or understand English. CTC proposed to gradually relocate these by establishing a greater concentration of stores in prime retail space in the lucrative Dallas–Forth Worth market. Further, the 81 stores owned by White Stores were not dealer-operated but company-owned

EXHIBIT 3   **Purchase of White Stores—Financing (Canadian dollars in thousands)**

Net working capital to be acquired		$12,134
Property, equipment, and leasehold obligations	$35,658	
Long-term portion of short-term portion of obligations	(287)	35,371
Other assets		208
Net assets to be acquired		$47,713
The effect on consolidated working capital is:		
Use of working capital:		
Payment on closing		$15,904
Promissory note due December 31, 1982		10,603
		26,507
Working capital to be acquired		(12,134)
Net use of working capital		$14,373

and -operated. CTC felt that this would have to change and become a number one priority in terms of introducing its philosophy and corporate objectives. Although CTC would prefer a dealer network to replicate the strategy in Canada, some of the states containing White Stores locations prohibited exclusive distributor-dealer relationships because of antitrust legislation. Finally, most of the stores were in desperate need of refurbishing. A lot of the outlets were 20 to 30 years old and looked it. CTC did not feel that this would be a problem, as it had anticipated having to pour up to an additional $100 million (U.S.) over the following $2^{1}/_{2}$ years into the project.

◼ Other Options

Other growth options had been tossed around CTC's corporate office in Toronto. One option being considered was to access the U.S. market by building a new chain from the ground up and, therefore, not be confined by an existing organization's limitations and problems. However, costs and the time commitment to establish a major foothold made this a difficult option to pursue. Another option was to search out an acquisition in the nearby northeastern U.S. states. One CTC executive who favoured this option noted: "We should expand to a market that is similar to our own—with the same climate, the same autos, and the same kind of products. A place that is close enough, that if there is a problem we can do something about it." But this meant ignoring the fastest-growing segment of the United States, namely the Sunbelt. A third option involved oil and gas opportunities in Canada. The existing Liberal government in Ottawa heavily favoured Canadian involvement in this industrial sector. The difficulty here was a lack of expertise on the part of CTC's management in this field. A fourth option was vertical integration. The manufacture of CTC products would require a massive capital investment into a field where CTC again had little expertise, and production runs for only CTC dealers would not always prove economical. Furthermore, due to CTC's large size, it already controlled a fair amount of power in distribution channels and could, therefore, already influence prices to some extent. Finally, CTC could turn to real estate sales. The firm had already engaged in some of this type of business and had made a small amount of money at it. Interest rates, however, were disturbingly high and unstable. Furthermore, the risk involved in a massive venture of this nature might not have been acceptable to CTC shareholders.

Muncaster had a difficult decision ahead of him. Growth in Canada for CTC would peak in approximately three to four years, so the groundwork for a new growth spurt would have to be laid down shortly. Shareholders would not react favourably to a flattening out of earnings per share after 1985. The White Stores acquisition would involve a major refurbishing program to bring the White Stores up to par, and this would create a temporary short-term drain on CTC's earnings.

The Turnaround Strategy

As the president and executive vice-president of CTC more closely examined White Stores, they agreed on the following turnaround strategy if they were to acquire White's:

- There would be an aggressive renovation schedule at a cost of $100 million (U.S.) to be completed by the end of 1983. Up to 22 stores would be closed at any one time for up to two months for the renovation.

- CTC dealers would be brought in to run some of the stores with a goal of 81 dealer-run stores by the end of 1983.

- The merchandise mix (currently at 23,000 items) would be phased in gradually. (See Exhibit 4 for existing mix and other information on the typical store.)

- More money would be spent on advertising than was spent by the average U.S. retailer in order to develop a clear image. The predominant form of advertising would be flyers.

EXHIBIT 4   **Typical White's Store/White's Auto Centre**

Typical store size in square feet (excluding auto bays):	
Gross area	24,000 sq. ft.
Selling area	14,000 sq. ft.
Percent selling area to gross area	58%
Number of auto service bays	5–6
Store focus and sales mix:	
Auto	10–50%
Hardware	15–20
Lawn and garden	15
Sporting goods	15
Housewares	10
Electronics, miscellaneous	5
Percentage of products under promotion discounts	50
Typical inventory (at cost)	US$900,000
Number of products carried	22,000
Final retail gross margin	16–22%
Store sales per year (breakeven point)	US$2.5 million

- The White Stores name would be retained to take advantage of existing customer loyalty.

- In order to gain market share and increase store traffic, White's would use loss leaders.

- In order to help dealers finance their inventories, credit would be given quite freely, although at the prevailing interest rates. If a dealer could not afford a shipment of goods, the price to the dealer would be lowered and the difference added to the notes payable to White's.

- No additional capital would be required to upgrade warehousing facilities, since the four warehouses were remaining at 30 to 35 percent capacity.

- The independent dealer network would be reduced from the existing 425 to 300 stores by cutting off the outlying dealers.

Muncaster summarized the strategy: "We plan to change their [White's] merchandise offering substantially. ... We believe the appeal will be in a merchandise offering which you see in a Canadian Tire Store." With this strategy, CTC expected White's to break even by the third year.

CIBC Wood Gundy in Asia: An Evolving Regional Strategy

CASE

5

In late December 1996, Singapore-based Russell Cranwell pondered how expansion opportunities in Asia fit with CIBC CEF's[1] Asia-Pacific strategy and what his recommendation would be at the monthly senior management meeting regarding expansion into Malaysia. Cranwell, most recently one of the architects of the CIBC Wood Gundy's strategy in Europe, knew that making decisions about expansion in Asia was dynamic and required extensive research. The firm's understanding of the opportunities in Asia was still developing, and the constant challenge Cranwell and his counterparts in Asia faced was the ongoing education of their colleagues in North America and Europe. Reviewing the expansion team's analysis, Cranwell confirmed that there were numerous opportunities; growth rates in the region outstripped those of all the G-7 countries, and infrastructure spending over the next five years was estimated to be in excess of US$1 trillion. Presenting growth rates was the easy part, the details of an expansion were much harder—was the firm ready for another expansion? Did CIBC CEF have the right products and people to be successful in Malaysia? In the event that Malaysian expansion was pursued, should the office be located in the capital of KL (Kuala Lumpur), or the newly developing International Offshore Financial Center in Labuan?

The discussion at the management meetings had frequently focused on how the firm could best capitalize on the growth prospects in the region including developing new products and expanding the current number of locations. The approval process for increasing investments in Asia was the joint responsibility of senior management in the region and CIBC Wood Gundy in Canada.

Bruce Moore has prepared this case under the direction of Professor Paul Beamish solely to provide material for class discussion. The authors do not intend to illustrate either effective or ineffective handling of a managerial situation. Certain names and other identifying information may have been disguised to protect confidentiality. © 1998, Ivey Management Services. Case 9A98G004, version 1998-05-22.

The Richard Ivey School of Business gratefully acknowledges the generous support of The Richard and Jean Ivey Fund in the development of this case as part of the Richard and Jean Ivey Fund Asian Case Series.

[1] CIBC Wood Gundy operated in non-Japan Asia under the name CIBC CEF. CIBC CEF represented the combined resources of CIBC and CEF. It was not a legal entity.

IVEY

Richard Ivey School of Business
The University of Western Ontario

CIBC

The Canadian Imperial Bank of Commerce (CIBC), with assets of Cdn$199 billion and $12.6 billion in capital as of 1996, was Canada's second-largest financial institution and the ninth-largest bank in North America. CIBC Wood Gundy, 85 percent owned by CIBC, operated as the bank's investment banking arm. CIBC Wood Gundy was a fully integrated global investment firm with offices in Toronto, New York, London, Singapore, Hong Kong, Tokyo, and principal cities across North America.

The market had recognized CIBC Wood Gundy's world-class capabilities, awarding the firm top industry ranking for derivatives, sales and trading, high-yield finance, public and structured finance, mergers and acquisitions, global loan underwriting and syndication, and economics research. Of particular note was CIBC Wood Gundy's recognition by the investment banking periodical, *International Financing Review* (IFR), as the lead project finance arranger in the Americas and the more recent announcement about the *Global Finance's* Project Finance All Star Team for its innovative work in supporting airport construction projects.

CIBC Wood Gundy was aligned in three main regions: North America, Europe and Asia-Pacific. The breakdown of the size of the regions by employees was approximately: North America—70 percent, Europe—20 percent, and Asia-Pacific—10 percent. The firm remained primarily a North American investment bank with a clear focus on providing clients with a true global partner that would deliver financial solutions around the world.

Over the past two years, CIBC Wood Gundy had taken an aggressive stance in growing its franchise. The results had been highly successful. In 1996, CIBC Wood Gundy recorded its best results ever with net income in excess of $500 million (see Exhibit 1); unless otherwise stated, all figures are in Canadian dollars.

CIBC in Asia-Pacific

CIBC and CIBC Wood Gundy operated in non-Japan Asia under the name CIBC CEF (CIBC Wood Gundy operated under its own name in Japan). CEF was a joint venture between CIBC and Cheung Kong (Holdings) Ltd. of Hong Kong (see Exhibits 2 and 3). Cheung Kong's principal activities were investment holding

EXHIBIT 1   **CIBC Wood Gundy Results—Years Ended October 31 (Cdn$ millions)**

	1996	1995
Net interest income	$1,217	$876
Non-interest income	1,193	834
Non-interest expenses	(1,488)	(1,087)
Provision for credit losses	(23)	(223)
Net income before taxes	899	400
Taxes	(370)	(162)
Minority interests	(1)	—
Net income	$528	$238

Source: CIBC, annual report, 1996.
Note: The breakdown of revenue by region was approximately: North America 60 percent, Europe 25 percent, and Asia 15 percent.

and project management. Its subsidiaries were active in the field of property development and investment, real estate agency and management, the production of cement and ready-mixed concrete, quarry operation, and investment holding. The CIBC–Cheung Kong joint venture had been operating in Asia for over 25 years. The CIBC CEF partnership provided an invaluable combination of local market knowledge and global financial expertise. CIBC CEF had a significant presence throughout Asia as a leading expert in the aerospace, energy, media, and telecommunication industries, and for derivatives and structured finance. CIBC Wood Gundy had become Taiwan's preferred source of finance for the energy industry and was regarded as the leading house for Asian airline financing. CIBC Wood Gundy attributed the growing successes in Asia to the transferability of its North American reputation, its concentrating on a limited number of businesses, and its having the support of senior management to fully develop the key businesses.

More recently, CIBC Wood Gundy had been transferring significant resources to the Asia-Pacific region. Specifically, (1) over the last two years, the firm's regional employment had increased by 50 percent to approximately 500 employees, (2) the Taipei office was experiencing similar growth, (3) new products (derivatives, project finance) had been added; and (4) large numbers of highly skilled employees had been transferred from offices outside Asia or hired directly by the regional office(s). In summary, the firm was in a phase of dramatic growth.

Over the past year, management had made decisions on three expansion opportunities:

- *Australia.* The Sydney office was opened in the spring of 1996. The bank had a history in Australia and once had a large operation but closed it in the early 1990s as there was not enough activity to support the infrastructure. Reentry had been on a select basis with a small operation (six people) and an emphasis exclusively on project finance opportunities in the mining industry. The longer-term strategy included the potential acquisition of an Australian brokerage house.

EXHIBIT 2   Joint Venture Structure

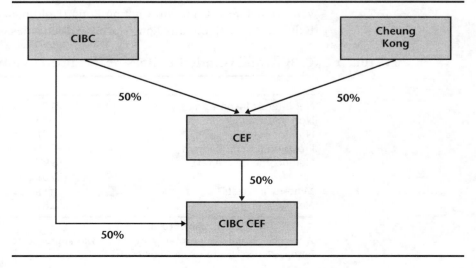

EXHIBIT 3

CHEUNG KONG (HOLDINGS) LIMITED
GROUP FINANCIAL SUMMARY

	1991	1992	1993	1994	1995
Profit and Loss Account (HK$ million)					
Turnover	9,990	10,278	10,693	14,841	12,122
Profit before extraordinary items	4,886	6,266	9,781	10,113	11,125
Extraordinary items	403	−48	—	—	—
Profit attributable to shareholders	5,289	6,218	9,781	10,113	11,125
Dividends	1,494	1,758	2,198	2,417	2,727
Profit for the year retained	3,795	4,460	7,583	7,696	8,398
Balance Sheet (HK$ million)					
Fixed assets	1,944	2,021	2,733	3,763	4,574
Investments	17,102	23,835	33,963	47,164	48,000
Net current assets	6,395	4,297	6,952	11,815	10,577
	25,441	30,153	43,648	62,742	63,151
Deduct:					
Long-term bank loans	1,628	1,241	3,346	7,650	271
Other loans	—	—	3,870	9,179	8,274
Deferred items	936	893	26	12	47
Minority interests	129	684	989	2,648	2,560
TOTAL NET ASSETS	22,748	27,335	35,417	43,253	51,999
Representing:					
Share capital	1,099	1,099	1,099	1,099	1,099
Share premium	2,752	2,752	2,752	2,752	2,752
Reserves and retained profits	18,897	23,484	31,566	39,402	48,148
TOTAL SHAREHOLDERS' FUNDS	22,748	27,335	35,417	43,253	51,999
Earnings per share (HK$)	2.22	2.85	4.45	4.60	5.06
Dividend per share (HK$)	0.68	0.80	1.00	1.10	1.20
Net asset value per share (HK$)	10.35	12.44	16.12	19.68	23.66

Source: Cheung Kong web site.

- *India.* In the recent past, an Indian banker was hired by the bank to write a proposal on opportunities in India. While the report confirmed relevant opportunities, the bank decided that until there was evidence of sufficient deal flow, they wouldn't consider opening a new office. The rationale for postponing direct investment in India also included the high cost of office space in Bombay[2] and the relative ease of travelling to most Indian destinations from Singapore. For now, the country deals in India would be run from the Singapore office. Similar decisions had been made regarding Indonesia and Thailand.

- *China.* The expansion of the Beijing representative office was deferred indefinitely. The firm's Hong Kong office was having continued success in nearby Guangdong province and thus made further expansion unnecessary at this time. Furthermore, the handover of Hong Kong to China in 1997 would further clarify if a greater exposure to mainland China was necessary or if the existing Hong Kong operation was sufficient.

---

[2] "Economic indicators," *The Economist,* August 31, 1996, p. 82.

Strategy

CIBC Wood Gundy was positioned in Asia-Pacific as a niche, regional player providing expertise in selected products and services, to clients in selected markets. Specifically, the firm had chosen products and services that offered an immediate competitive advantage. The recent awards in Project Finance and Financial Products offered excellent opportunities to generate further revenues. Furthermore, the firm did not intend to replicate the large infrastructure investments that direct competitors such as ABN-Amro and Deutsche Morgan Grenfell[3] had created in Asia.

Products/Services

CIBC Wood Gundy's major business activities in Asia included the following:

Global Capital Markets (GCM).   Commonly known as the trading floor, GCM combined traditional trading and sales activities in fixed income, money markets, and foreign exchange with the research activities supporting these areas and the development of new products, including securitization, private placements, and structured products. The group concentrated on large corporate clients and central banks. In 1996, GCM expanded its customer base by 100 percent.

Financial Products (FP).   FP developed and marketed innovative financial structures for regional governments, fund managers, financial institutions, corporations, and wealthy individuals. Products included over-the-counter interest rate, currency and equity derivatives (including swaps, forwards, and futures transactions), and options contracts and other, similar types of contracts and commitments based on interest rates, currency rates, the price of equities, and other financial market variables. The group was started in 1994, and in 1996 had over 60 professionals on staff. FP focused on dealing with large corporations in both the local and G-7 currencies. In 1996, *Global Finance* named FP the number one structured derivatives house in Asia.

Project Finance.   The group had focused primarily on energy and commodity-based industries (mining and forestry), and now was actively involved in telecommunication, electric power, natural gas storage, and transmission businesses. In 1996, the group was the lead on a US$600 million telecommunications project in Java, Indonesia. The deal was considered to be a major success and was named "Asian Deal of the Year" by *Project Finance International*. Also in 1996, the group was engaged as an advisor to the Taiwanese government to assist with the development of a plan for the country's energy grid. The efforts of 1996 were expected to result in numerous opportunities.

The key skill that the group provided to clients was the unique combination of engineering and financial expertise. The projects ranged from oil refineries, hydroelectric dams, and fixed telephone wire installations to highway and airport construction, and to compete effectively the engineering skills provided

---

[3] ABN-Amro has approximately 3,000 employees in Asia. Deutsche Morgan Grenfell has approximately 4,000 employees in Asia.

the necessary edge. The success of Project Finance often resulted in additional business for the FP and GCM groups. The group, based in Singapore, was a collection of various nationalities, with representation from India, the United States, England, the Philippines, Australia, Singapore, and Taiwan, and included one Canadian. The long-term plans included establishing an Infrastructure group (roads, airports) and an Airline Finance group.

The CEF Group.   The CEF group, a preeminent Asian holding and financial services group of companies, serviced strategic local, regional, and overseas clients. CEF's capabilities included mergers and acquisitions, equity underwriting, and debt underwriting. The group also co-managed a number of CIBC CEF-originated transactions.

Other Products.   Included: securitization and structured trade finance.

The four largest product/service groups (GCM, FP, Project Finance, CEF) combined for more than 90 percent of gross revenues.

Locations in the Asia-Pacific Region

The firm had just under 500 employees in the region. The offices ranged in size from approximately 250 employees at the regional head office in Singapore to the six-person mining team in Sydney. The other locations included Hong Kong, Tokyo, Taipei, and Beijing.

The Decision

As Cranwell, Managing Director of Origination and Structuring, was preparing his presentation he reviewed the analysis his team had prepared one more time and noted the group's inclination to recommend expansion into Labuan, Malaysia, which he located on the map (see Exhibit 4).

Expanding into Malaysia would provide the firm with the opportunity to compete for significant transactions. Mr. Cranwell recollected an ongoing Malaysian deal that continued to offer project finance opportunities, the US$10 billion Bakun project, a hydroelectric dam and transmission system in Sarawak, East Malaysia. The firm had an excellent reputation in energy financing, but without a Malaysian presence they were virtually shut out.

Finally, Cranwell reflected on the expectations of CIBC CEF's key stakeholder, CIBC Wood Gundy in Toronto. CIBC Wood Gundy had invested considerable resources (both financial and human) in the Asia-Pacific region and expectations were high that the current fiscal year would generate exceptional returns.

Expansion Team's Analysis

This section gives the expansion team's analysis.

Asian Overview

The opportunities in Asia are numerous. In an effort to summarize some key points we have attached a table outlining the basic strengths and weaknesses

EXHIBIT 4   Detailed Map of Malaysia

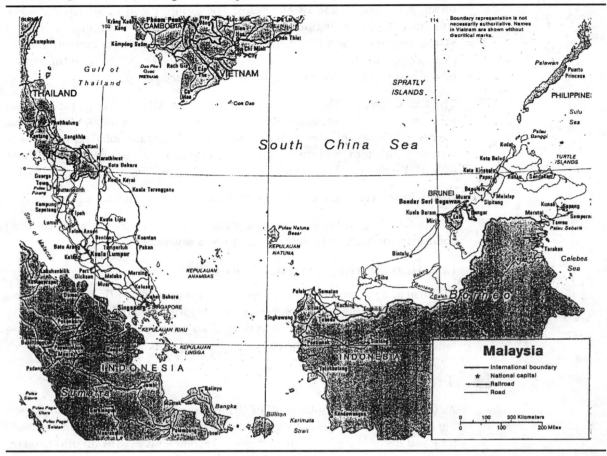

of the potential markets for expansion [see Exhibit 5]. We have concluded from our analysis, and given the firm's existing locations in Asia, that our attention should be focused on opportunities in Southeast Asia.

EXHIBIT 5   Asian Overview

Country	Strengths	Weaknesses
China	• Consumer demand growing • Private sector growing and more open to foreign investment • Improving investment climate • Currency and banking sectors less regulated • Access to foreign exchange improving	• Potential leadership struggle in 1997 • Pace of economic reform subject to change • Piracy rampant • Tax incentives being removed
Hong Kong	• Good location • Excellent communications and transportation infrastructure • Low government interference or red tape • Stable government • Low corporate and personal taxes	• Political uncertainty • High inflation, high cost of living • Pollution • High turnover of labour

EXHIBIT 5 *continued*

Country	Strengths	Weaknesses
India	• Democracy with independent and fair courts making contractual agreements secure • Foreign investment usually welcome • Good capital markets • English widely spoken • Well-educated work force	• Poor infrastructure • Business hurdles complicated • Support services very poor • Duty rates high
Indonesia	• Growing economy requiring a multitude of product and services • Foreign investment welcome • Tax incentives • Few foreign exchange controls • Low labour costs	• Potential for political upheaval • Weak judiciary • High red tape and corruption • Poor infrastructure • Shortage of skilled labour, especially managers
Japan	• Independent and high-quality judiciary • Efficient civil service • Infrastructure • Labour supply • Reducing market barriers	• Highly regulated economy • Immense power of bureaucrats • Operation and property costs are high • Harsh attitudes toward transfer pricing
Malaysia	• Competitiveness ranked very high • Infrastructure • English widespread • Low labour costs relative to skill level • Liberal exchange controls • Government incentives increasing • Location • Political stability, widespread support growing for UNMO (government)	• Lack of technical knowledge • Acute shortage of labour coupled with pressure on wages • Ethnic quotas in jobs and equity ownership
New Zealand	• Efficient civil service • Absence of corruption • Very open and competitive economy • Encourages foreign investment • Good economic conditions • Weak trade unions • Low labour costs • Low corporate and personal taxes	• Isolated location with small population • Absence of investment and tax incentives • Skill shortages in some areas
South Korea	• Fast-growing domestic economy • Ever-improving level of technological ability • Well-educated and young work force	• Bureaucracy not overly welcoming of foreign investors • Chaebol conglomerates continue to dominate the economy • Labour costs are increasing
Thailand	• High economic growth • Trade liberalization increasing • Good investment incentives	• Coalition politics undermines government efforts • Poor infrastructure, especially Bangkok • Frequent labour disputes • Shortage of skilled workers
Taiwan	• Advanced democracy with developing judiciary • Commitment to free enterprise • High-tech industries developing quickly • Well-educated work force	• Ongoing dispute with China, recent withdrawal of support by South Africa • Infrastructure problems • Intellectual piracy • Labour costs high

Source: Economist Intelligence Unit.

EXHIBIT 6   Expected Growth Rates in Southeast Asia

Country	Expected GDP Growth Rate 1997 (%)	Per Capita GDP (US$)	Country Credit Risk Rating	Infrastructure Investment 1995–2004 (US$ billion)
Malaysia	8.5	3,160	26	55
Indonesia	8.0	730	44	190
Singapore	6.1	19,310	8	Negligible
Philippines	6.0	830	NA	55
Vietnam	4.8	170	NA	NA
Thailand	8.0	2,040	36	150
Brunei	NA	NA	NA	Negligible
China	9.5	NA	44	740
Taiwan	5.5	NA	16	NA
India	6.8	NA	40	340

Sources: World Bank and Economist Intelligence Unit.

Southeast Asia

The ASEAN[4] economies are estimated to continue to record high real growth rates. The upgrading of key infrastructure investments such as roads, telecommunication systems, and power grids are critical to sustaining these growth rates (summarized as [in Exhibit 6]).

Malaysia[5]

Politics.   The political scene has been dominated by the United Malays National Organization (UMNO) party headed by the current prime minister, Dr. Mahathir Mohamad. Dr. Mahathir has retained the post since 1981 and has recently announced his successor as leader of the party, Anwar Ibrahim. The party has widespread support throughout the country and retains control over all 13 of the Malaysian states with the exception of Kelantan. The Parti Islam SeMalaya (PAS) is the main opposition party. The issues of central importance in Malaysian politics are gaining developed nation status by 2020, continued economic growth, and the inclusion of Islamic principles in daily life.

External Relations

In terms of external relations, Malaysia's most important affiliations are with ASEAN and the Asia-Pacific Economic Community (APEC). Malaysia is also a member of the United Nations and a shareholder in the World Bank and the International Monetary Fund.

Industrial Policy

The National Development Policy (1991) set out a 30-year vision that defines how the Malaysian economy will reach developed status by 2020. Included in the policy are plans to increase privatization of a number of government-owned entities. Government policies are also directed toward attracting foreign investment, with a view to further developing the industrial base of the country. The current focus is on infrastructure industries (for example, telecommunication,

---

[4] Association of Southeast Asian Nations. Burma (Myanmar), Cambodia, and Laos were expected to be admitted in 1997 or 1998.
[5] Internal CIBC CEF document.

power, ports, roads, airports) with total spending from 1996–2000 estimated at M$68.3 billion[6] (Cdn$37.6 billion).

Of great importance to CIBC CEF is that the government's focus on developing all aspects of the economy has resulted in banks with Malaysian branches being heavily favoured to win deals over those with no infrastructure in Malaysia.

Monetary and Economic Policy

The inflation target for 1997 is under 4 percent, compared to an actual rate of 3.5 percent for 1996. This number is high for Malaysia, as a number of items included in the index are controlled. The indications are that the government is having difficulty controlling inflation.

The outstanding feature of the economy has been the very high growth rate, with growth of 8.2 percent for 1996 and average annual growth from 1990 to 1995 of 8.7 percent. The target for the next five years is 8 percent per annum. The plan is also aiming to transform the economy from one that is investment-driven to one that is productivity-led through increased investment in human capital. Price pressures and the current account deficit are the two main areas of concern, and the central bank (Bank Negara) is addressing the overheating.

Foreign Investment

The government's ambitious plans require a substantial flow of foreign investment. As an example, a number of incentives have been created to lure foreign investors to the new multimedia super corridor, which encompasses three of Malaysia's megaprojects—the Kuala Lumpur City Centre, the new KL airport, and the new administrative centre, Putrajaya.

Location Alternatives

Labuan

The island of Labuan is located off the northwest coast of Borneo, not far from the Kingdom of Brunei Darussalam. The island is 92 square kilometres, with a population of approximately 60,000. It is located on the major shipping and air routes of the ASEAN region, being roughly equidistant from Bangkok, Hong Kong, Jakarta, Kuala Lumpur, Manila, and Singapore. It is a free port where no sales tax, surtax, or excise, import, or export duties are levied.

The Malaysian government established Labuan as an International Offshore Financial Centre (IOFC) to enhance the flow of capital into Malaysia. The island is intended to be the Channel Islands or Cayman Islands of Asia. Labuan has the necessary conditions for a successful IOFC: political stability, stable currency with limited exchange controls, banking secrecy, minimum rules and regulations, good infrastructure support facilities such as excellent communication with other financial centres, and access to a professionally qualified and experienced work force. The government's commitment to the development of Labuan as an IOFC is reflected in the preferential tax treatment of banking, trust and fund management, offshore insurance, and offshore investment holding companies. The reduced corporation tax rate is 3 percent of audited net profits or a flat tax of M$20,000 (Cdn$11,000).

---

[6] Exchange rate: US$1 = 2.52 Ringgit or 1 RM = US$0.39 as at December 10, 1996.

Costs/Benefits

The principal benefit to offshore banks operating from Labuan is the opportunity to deal directly with Malaysian corporations and government-related companies. Currently, foreign banks without a Malaysian presence are subject to various restrictions, including outright exclusion from government transactions. The establishment of an office in Labuan is often a prerequisite for bidding on infrastructure projects.

The increase of intra-Asian and intra-ASEAN trade enhances the attractiveness of investing in Malaysia. The five biggest investors in Malaysia included four Asian countries: Taiwan ($1,150 million); Japan ($706 million); the United States ($501 million); Singapore ($425 million); and Hong Kong ($350 million).

Based on interviews with existing offshore banks in Labuan, local government authorities, the landlord of the Financial Park (office space) and KPMG of Kuala Lumpur, the estimated annual costs for operating a six-person office are US$652,800 [see Exhibit 7]. The biggest cost differentials between Singapore and Labuan are the salaries for administrative staff. In Singapore a mid-level administrative employee earns approximately US$40,000. In comparison, the same person would earn $US25,000 in Labuan.

Infrastructure

The Labuan government indicates that projects totalling M$4 billion (Cdn$2.2 billion) are under development, including 4,000 housing units, road upgrades, new airport, new international school, light industrial park, and improvements to the power supply. The Financial Park, the main business centre, has adequate facilities, including dedicated telephone lines.

Competition

Labuan has attracted over 40 other foreign banks, including Chase Manhattan Bank, ABN-AMRO Bank, Bank of America, and Citibank Malaysia [see Exhibit 8].

EXHIBIT 7

ESTIMATED EXPANSION COSTS (all costs in US$)			
		Labuan	KL
Staff (housing and benefits)			
Professional staff (expatriate)	2 each @	200,000	250,000
TOTAL PROFESSIONAL STAFF		400,000	500,000
Support staff	4 each @	25,000	40,000
TOTAL SUPPORT STAFF		100,000	160,000
TOTAL STAFF		**$500,000**	**$660,000**
Premises			
Office space (lease rate per month)	2,000 sq. ft. @	$2.20/sq. ft.	$15/sq. ft.
TOTAL PREMISES		**$52,800**	**$360,000**
Annual licence fee	M$60,000	$ 25,000	$ —
Professional and other fees	M$60,000	$ 25,000	$ 25,000
Business development expenses	M$60,000	$ 25,000	$ 25,000
Miscellaneous (travel, office)		$ 25,000	$ 25,000
TOTAL ANNUAL EXPENSES		**$652,800**	**$1,095,000**
U.S. dollar/Ringgit exchange rate	$2.40		

Source: Interviews with officials in Labuan, landlord of Financial Park, other banks in Labuan.

EXHIBIT 8   **Offshore Banks in Labuan, December 1996**

• ABN-Amro Bank	• AMMB International
• Asahi Bank	• Bank Brussels Lambert
• Bank of Commerce	• Banque Nationale de Paris
• Bank of America	• Banque Indosuez
• Banque Paribas	• Barclays Bank
• Bayerische Landesbank Girozentrale	• BBMB International
• Credit Suisse	• Chase Manhattan Bank
• Citibank Malaysia	• Daiwa Bank
• Dao Heng Bank	• DCB Bank
• Development Bank of Singapore (DBS)	• Dresdner Bank AG
• Fuji Bank	• Industrial Bank of Japan
• Overseas Chinese Banking Corporation	• Overseas Union Bank (OUB)
• Public Bank	• Long-Term Credit Bank of Japan
• Maybank International	• National Westminster
• Rabobank Netherland	• Sakura Bank
• Sanwa Bank	• Schroeders Malaysia
• Skandia AFS Southeast Asia	• Standard Chartered Bank
• Société Générale	• Sumitomo Bank
• Tat Lee Bank	• The Bank of Tokyo Mitsubishi
• The Dai-Ichi Kangyo Bank	• The Development Bank of Singapore
• The Hong Kong and Shanghai Banking Corp.	• The Keppel Bank
• The Mitsubishi Bank	• Tokai Bank
• UMBC International Bank	• Union Bank of Switzerland
• United Overseas Bank	• Yasuda Trust & Banking

Miscellaneous

- Dividends are non-taxable in Malaysia if paid from a Labuan company to an out-of-country company.
- The expatriate tax rates include a 50 percent rebate until December 2002.
- Revenue Canada has not passed judgement on the acceptability of Labuan's preferential tax treatment. If Revenue Canada rules against the tax treatment, all repatriated earnings will be subject to Canadian corporate tax of 33 percent.

Kuala Lumpur

The capital of Malaysia is located on the west coast of the Malaysian peninsula. Kuala Lumpur (KL) has a population of approximately 3,000,000, making it Malaysia's largest city. The area surrounding KL is home to the majority of Malaysia's largest domestic- and foreign-controlled corporations. The city is undergoing numerous projects in preparation for the Commonwealth Games in 1998. The projects include a new international airport, extensions to various highways, and a new national stadium.

Costs/Benefits

The principal benefits to locating in KL are:

- The proximity to major corporations. The head offices of Malaysia's largest corporations are almost exclusively in KL.
- Concentration of economic activity. Various projects, such as the multi-media corridor in adjacent Purtajaya, are expected to attract increased foreign direct investment.

- The city is a major hub, with connecting flights to all major Asian, European, and North American cities.
- The distance from Singapore is a one-hour flight or four-hour drive.
- The city shares many cultural similarities with Singapore.

The principal costs or drawbacks of locating in KL are:

- The corporate tax rate averages 30 percent of income.
- Office space leases for US$10–$20 per square foot.
- The labour costs are the highest in Malaysia.
- Locating in KL does not support the government's initiative in developing Labuan.

Infrastructure

KL is considered to have a good level of infrastructure development. The on-going improvements will serve to ensure that the city can support continued growth into the next century.

Competition

KL has attracted a large number of the major investment banks.

◼ Location Decision

In the event that a decision was made to proceed with either location in Malaysia, Cranwell needed to consider the various implementation issues.

Human Resources

Who would staff the firm at the new office? The new location would require at least one expatriate for the first year. How would he interest one of his people in going? Was Labuan an attractive post? Cranwell also had to consider the need for attracting qualified support staff. Labour turnover in Asia was becoming a worrisome and time-consuming trend (see Exhibit 9). Increasingly, the norm was for support staff to switch jobs for nominal amounts (often less than a 5 percent increase in salary). Would locating in KL make attracting staff easier?

Infrastructure/Services

Labuan was essentially under construction. Cranwell wondered how certain the improvements were. For instance, the island had only one foreign school, expatriate housing was being developed, and the airport's runways were scheduled to be extended to handle larger aircraft. Finally, flying to Labuan from Singapore involved connections via KL, Brunei, or Kota Kinabalu in the Eastern Malaysian state of Sabah. Could the other 40 competitors have overlooked these points?

EXHIBIT 9   Labour Turnover for 1995 (percentage of total)

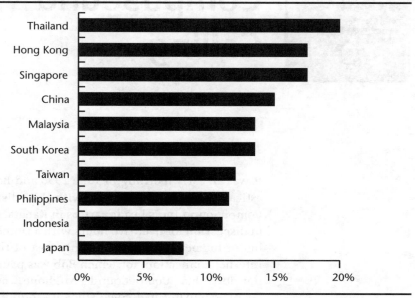

Source: The Economist, March 1996.

Summary

Finally, Mr. Cranwell was considering the regional strategy of CIBC CEF. Did another office make sense? CIBC Wood Gundy had established itself as a niche player in the Asia-Pacific region. Did a Labuan or KL office complement or contradict that strategy? Were there any other benefits of a Malaysian office? Would having an office in Malaysia create any cultural barriers? Did the group have anyone who spoke Malaysian Bahasa? Should the senior manager be Malay, Chinese, or Indian? Should he or she be Malaysian?

CASE 6

CompuSound Calling

It was an early morning in June 1996 and Bob Norman was talking enthusiastically over the Internet with his distributor in Amsterdam. From CompuSound Inc.'s headquarters in Kanata, Ontario, the president had been in discussion for over two hours with a Dutch manager regarding the marketing of his new product. The only cost of this transatlantic call was a local Internet connection, for which Bob was paying approximately US$2. As Bob put down his "CompuSound Pro Phone," he smiled as he reflected on how far his company had come since its founding in 1992. Then he paused to think about the challenges that lay in store for CompuSound.

CompuSound's first product was the CompuSound Pro, which was introduced to the market in the spring of 1994. This was a high-quality sound board for personal computers. Sound boards enabled computers to play music, provided the sound effects for computer games, and allowed businesspeople to make multimedia presentations. The CompuSound Pro received major critical acclaim throughout the computer industry. Bob was extremely pleased by these international reviews, but the resulting sales were disappointing. At the end of 1994, Bob hired a vice-president of marketing, Pierre Charest, to help him achieve better market penetration. After two years of commercization, Bob was faced with total sales of approximately 5,000 sound boards or US$900,000. By this time, the financial resources expended to gain adequate distribution and retail shelf space had been nearly depleted.

On a brighter note, by 1995 CompuSound had signed lucrative licensing agreements with two major multinational firms, Sunrise Corporation of Japan and Network Electronics of the Netherlands, for part of the proprietary technology of the CompuSound Pro. Bob understood how vital his international licensing agreements were to CompuSound and he made every effort to keep his alliance partners satisfied. He believed that he had to continually develop new products and technology in order to remain attractive in this fast-moving industry.

In line with this strategy, Bob had extended the CompuSound Pro technology to include the ability to transmit voice over computer networks, including the

---

This case was prepared by James L. Bowey at Bishop's University, with the help of Kimberly I. McKell, for the sole purpose of classroom discussion. Case material has been disguised; however, essential relationships are maintained. It is not intended to illustrate either an effective or ineffective handling of a managerial situation. © 1997 by Bishop's University. Not to be reproduced without permission.

Internet. The resulting product was a hardware board called the CompuSound Pro Phone, which was installed in personal computers. The trade press was just starting to pick up on the potential of the Internet telephony market. Bob believed that there could be an excellent position for CompuSound in this emerging industry, as his team was staffed with experts in PC sound technology.

Bob realized that he must continue to grow his company, but was unsure what direction should be taken. He realized that CompuSound had developed a high-quality hardware solution for voice calls over computer networks; however, he was not sure if and how his small company should expand into the Internet telephony industry. Bob knew that CompuSound would be the first company to try to market a hardware solution for Internet telephony, but the best way to proceed was less than clear. He sensed that decisions had to be made about marketing channels quickly and decisively, due to the constrained nature of CompuSound's financial situation. Perhaps he could use his past alliance strategy to be successful in this new industry? Bob decided to review both the history of CompuSound and the research Pierre Charest had done on the Internet telephony competition, before making any decisions.

Company History

Since starting CompuSound in 1992, Bob Norman had grown the company from a two-person basement operation to a staff of 12. Headquartered in Kanata, Ontario, amid numerous high-technology companies, CompuSound was in a prime locale for new developments in the computer and telecommunications industries. Kanata offered first-rate product and software engineering, product manufacturing, and assembly outsourcing alternatives.

The inspiration for starting CompuSound stemmed from Bob's love of sound and technology. Bob had experienced extremely poor quality sound from his personal computer. Therefore he decided to revolutionize the evolving PC audio industry by introducing a sound board that would provide computer sound that would rival compact disc players. He teamed up with AudioTech, an engineering firm that had been involved in the production of the first sound board ever, the AdLib sound board. Bob formed an alliance with the AudioTech engineers, who were located only two hours away from Kanata.

Starting in 1992, Bob and his personal assistant worked with AudioTech to develop the CompuSound Pro technology. This product development phase took approximately 18 months, and the CompuSound Pro was ready for market in the spring of 1994. It was manufactured locally by a circuit board assembly company called FLEX Assemblers. CompuSound enjoyed the high quality and flexible manufacturing schedule that FLEX Assemblers provided, although the costs were somewhat higher than Bob had anticipated.

In 1994, the CompuSound Pro was positioned at the very top end of the sound board market. The first sound board had appeared in 1988. Creative Labs of Singapore dominated the sound board market with 65 percent of the world's market share. The sound quality of Creative Labs' Sound Blaster sound boards was undoubtedly inferior to that of the CompuSound Pro, yet Creative Labs fiercely controlled the marketing channels. The sound board market was projected to decline after 1995 (see Exhibit 1) because of the increase in sales of multimedia computers, which had inclusive sound capabilities. PC audio technology was also moving toward a chip that, when installed on the computer's motherboard, eliminated the need for sound boards altogether.

By 1996, monthly sales at CompuSound were levelling out at 400 units. The retail price of the CompuSound Pro was approximately US$250, while the total direct cost of the sound board was US$140. At a distributor price of US$180, Bob was not receiving much contribution from CompuSound Pro sales toward his US$1.5 million in R&D investment spent to date.

Technology Licensing Agreements

The VP Marketing, Pierre Charest, dealing with difficult shelf penetration issues, recognized that the true strength of CompuSound was not marketing, but the superior audio technology that Bob had developed in alliance with AudioTech. Fortunately, Bob had begun to adjust his strategy by using his extensive industry contacts to develop licensing possibilities for CompuSound. During 1995, Bob signed two licensing agreements with Sunrise Corporation and Network Electronics for CompuSound's proprietary PC audio technology. The contracts helped offset the extensive R&D, operational, and marketing costs involved in developing the CompuSound Pro business.

The international press for the CompuSound Pro attracted much attention from large music and computer companies, including Sunrise Corporation. Bob flew to Japan on several occasions over a six-month period to give demonstrations to Sunrise's engineers. Sunrise wanted to purchase CompuSound's technology and to co-develop new technology based on Sunrise's MXZ line of chipsets. The Sunrise MXZ6 chip was an integral component of the CompuSound Pro. Sunrise would pay CompuSound royalties based on the number of products that Sunrise sold that incorporated CompuSound's technology. Sunrise also wanted CompuSound to custom-design new technology and products, and was willing to pay for the ensuing R&D costs for these projects. Bob was unsure of the next strategic moves of Sunrise; however, Sunrise had just produced its own sound board, which was receiving some good trade press.

Network Electronics also wanted to incorporate CompuSound's technology into their product line. Bob, along with the AudioTech engineers, visited

EXHIBIT I   **Worldwide Sound Board Sales**

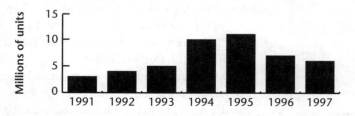

Note: 1991–1993 sales: actual; 1994–1997 sales: projected.
Source: Dataquest, February 1994 worldwide estimates.

the headquarters of Network Electronics in the Netherlands, where they were very warmly received. The Network Electronics agreement was also based on royalty revenue, along with lump-sum payments for the CompuSound technology. Any custom-made products and technology development would be funded by Network Electronics. This funding would enable CompuSound to develop the high-quality, customized product that Network Electronics expected. Sunrise and Network Electronics were each developing different facets of PC sound, which challenged the engineers at AudioTech and kept them working on numerous different projects concurrently.

In addition to Sunrise and Network Electronics, the trade shows that CompuSound attended always generated new potential partners for CompuSound's technology. The maintenance of these alliance relationships seemed to be Bob's main focus as he was constantly communicating with Japan, the Netherlands, and AudioTech in order to coordinate each party's needs. AudioTech's resources were stretched as CompuSound tried to fulfill their large alliance partners' orders and their own commercial product side of the business. Often, the commercial products took on secondary importance, resulting in delayed prototypes and final products.

The Internet Telephony Industry

One major trend that seemed to be hitting the computer industry was the convergence of telephones and computers. Internet telephony software solutions, such as VocalTec's Internet Phone, allowed people to use their computers to talk over network lines previously used only for data (e.g., e-mail). When these solutions were used over the Internet, people could talk to each other for free, only paying their local connection fees to the Internet. The Internet telephony software programs, when installed on PCs, needed sound boards and microphones in order to work. The popularity of this type of software was booming as Internet Phone users had sprung up around the world. The players in the telecommunications industry were also jumping into Internet telephony as the threat to their long-distance business demanded a competitive response.

Internet telephony products offered extraordinary savings in long-distance charges. However, there had been much controversy concerning the various software packages. In the United States, the America's Carriers Telecommunications Association (ACTA) had recently petitioned the Federal Communications Commission (FCC) to ban the use of Internet telephony products. The FCC is an independent U.S. government agency that regulates interstate and international communications by radio, television, wire, satellite, and cable. The FCC indicated that it would as yet not interfere with the usage of the Internet, which was growing rapidly.

The market reports on Internet telephony reflected extraordinary growth potential (see Table 1). Of course, the continued growth rate would be dependent on the reactions of long-distance carriers, Regional Bell Operating Companies (RBOCs), cable companies, and regulatory institutions to the potential of Internet telephony.

TABLE I   **Worldwide Internet Telephony Statistics, 1995–1999**

	1995	1996	1997	1998	1999
Active consumer Internet telephony users (000s)	475	1,500	2,500	4,000	6,000
Active business Internet telephony users (000s)	25	500	2,500	6,000	10,000
User spending on Internet telephony software (M$)	3.5	70.0	175.0	350.0	560.0

Note: Estimated average revenue per unit over the projected time frame is $35.
Source: International Data Corporation, 1996.

If ACTA forced the FCC to rule against the use of Internet telephony products, there would not be much growth in Internet telephony software sales, and the above figures would be grossly overstated. However, if the telephone and cable companies embraced the idea of Internet telephony, and became a dominant distribution channel for the products, the figures could be vastly understated. The above projections for Internet telephony usage were potentially volatile.

◼ Software Versus Hardware Internet Telephony Solutions

There were currently 15 different software packages on the market that enabled voice conversations over networks. These software solutions offered varying sound quality and voice delay times. The majority of these Internet telephony software solutions crackled and crunched the voice, resulting in conversations that hardly resembled a regular telephone call. The voice quality of the software packages related directly to the type of technology that was used to compress the voice to send it over the network; several different types were currently being used. One large drawback of the software solutions was that they were incompatible with each other. Therefore, if one person had VocalTec's Internet Phone software and another had Quarterdeck's WebPhone software, they could not talk to each other.

One advantage of a hardware Internet telephony solution was that it usually provided better sound quality than a software solution could offer. Hardware solutions did not require the use of the computer's CPU (central processing unit) resources in order to function. The latter quality meant that computers could run many more software applications at the same time as their Internet Phones, without their computers becoming unstable or crashing. Bob believed that there could be a large market for a high-end Internet telephony hardware solution.

◼ Internet Telephony Software Marketing

Software Internet telephony solutions were distributed in several different ways. Most of the Internet telephony companies allowed customers to sample the capabilities of their software by making it available for free downloading on the Internet on their World Wide Web pages. Pre-commercial or "beta" versions of Internet Phone were available for one-month free trials on VocalTec's home page at **http://www.vocaltec.com.** A consumer could therefore easily test out the product before paying for the software. These trials posed no risk for the customer, and allowed VocalTec to attain valuable feedback on software features before releasing a commercial package. Most recently, Netscape and Microsoft had bundled their Internet telephony software within their Internet browser software packages, which were used by most Internet users to navigate on the World Wide Web. Consumers using these browsers did not need to pay a separate price for their Internet telephony software.

Several companies were selling the software as a boxed product that was found in computer stores, similarly to video games. Internet telephony software was also bundled with personal computers, modems, and sound boards. Other sound board manufacturers were using the different Internet telephony software packages to promote their products. Consumers who purchased bundled Internet telephony software did not pay a separate price, as it was hidden in the overall cost of the hardware.

Advertisements were springing up for sound boards, including the CompuSound Pro and the Creative Labs AWE32, that promoted their full-duplex capability. Full-duplex was a feature of these high-end sound boards which allowed Internet telephony software users to experience true two-way conversation. Consumers that did not have full-duplex sound boards, would be limited to using Internet telephony software on a half-duplex basis. This meant that their conversations behaved like a walkie-talkie; only one person could speak at a time. The combined sound board and Internet telephony software solution was considered only a software solution, since all of the processing required for Internet telephony was located in the software. The CompuSound Pro Phone was a true hardware solution; all of the processing needed for Internet telephony was done with hardware. At this point, the CompuSound team believed that there was no other hardware Internet telephony solution on the market.

Internet Telephony Competition

Of the 500,000 Internet telephony software users (see Table 1), VocalTec currently had 94 percent of the market. VocalTec's Internet Phone competed primarily against Camelot Corporation's DigiPhone, NetSpeak's WebPhone, Quarterdeck's WebTalk, and Voxware's TeleVox (see Table 2). Recently, IBM had introduced its own Internet telephony software, called Internet Connection Phone. Netscape had teamed up with InSoft to bring consumers CoolTalk, which was integrated with their Netscape Navigator Internet browser software. To counteract this move, Microsoft introduced NetMeeting with its Internet Explorer browser software.

All of these companies wanted their software to become the standard technology for making phone calls over the Internet. The main reason why technologies became standard in the Internet business was a market-driven

TABLE 2   **Leading Internet Telephony Market Products, 1995**

Company	Software	1995 Market Share
VocalTec	Internet Phone	94%
Camelot Corporation	DigiPhone	3%
NetSpeak	WebPhone	2%
Quarterdeck	WebTalk	1%
Voxware	TeleVox	New
IBM	Internet Connection Phone	New
Netscape/InSoft	CoolTalk	New
Microsoft	NetMeeting	New

Source: International Data Corporation, 1996.

process, whereby the technology with the most usage became standard. It was not always the best technology that was successful.

Competition among Internet telephony software products was based on their ease of connection to another user; ability to work with other Internet telephony software packages; and provision of telephony features (e.g., call waiting, voice messaging, and call forwarding). Superior voice compression technology, which made the sound quality of the voice transmission better, was an essential element for success in the Internet telephony market. Bob had examined the qualities of the software packages before starting his own product development and he was determined to make a superior solution.

The CompuSound Pro Phone

With his product manager, Bob guided AudioTech into designing an add-on piece of hardware for the CompuSound Pro. This expansion board was called the CPP or CompuSound Pro Phone. When both the CPP and the CompuSound Pro boards were combined, they allowed people to talk over networks, including LANs (local area networks), WANs (wide area networks), and the Internet.

While building the CPP solution, Bob had teamed up with a nearby Canadian university to incorporate their state-of-the-art voice compression technology. The technology was far superior to any used by the software solutions currently available on the market. The technology enabled the voice quality produced by the CPP to sound exactly like a regular telephone conversation. Similarly to other Internet telephony software packages, however, the CPP could not be used to call anyone who did not have another CPP and CompuSound Pro at their end of the telephone line. Also, as Bob and Pierre discovered in their early testing of the product, connections were not always easily made. At this point in the product development, users had to be quite competent with computers before they would be comfortable using the CPP.

The primary advantage of the CPP was that it provided a hardware solution to Internet telephony. One drawback of the CPP was the fact that its voice compression technology was not proprietary to CompuSound, as it belonged to the Canadian university; the technology was therefore freely available for licensing by any of CompuSound's competitors. Nevertheless, CompuSound had a six-month head start on its competitors, in terms of incorporating the voice compression technology into a consumer product.

In early summer 1996, the CPP board was tested at a trade show in the Netherlands with CompuSound's Dutch distributor. CompuSound and the Amsterdam Computer Group talked for over three hours on the Internet, for a cost of approximately US$3. The voice quality was amazingly clear, and parties on both ends were extremely excited. Bob talked with the media in the Netherlands, who wanted to know when CompuSound was shipping the CPP boards. In June, Bob shipped prototypes to a networking distributor in Japan and the resulting product demonstration went exceedingly well. Production of 500 units of the CPP could not begin for four weeks, due to manufacturing scheduling conflicts at FLEX Assemblers.

The CompuSound Network Telephone

Initially, the combined CompuSound Pro sound board and CPP expansion board solution was developed as an interim test-market product before an all-in-one-board solution called the CNT or CompuSound Network Telephone could be developed. The CPP would be used by customers who already had the CompuSound Pro installed in their computers, making it an upgrade product, while the CNT would attract an entirely new group of customers for CompuSound.

The CompuSound Network Telephone was slated for production only in September 1996, after the test-marketing phase of the CompuSound Pro Phone was complete. The direct competition for the CNT hardware solution was not easily identifiable. CompuSound's product manager believed that CompuSound had no competition, and that the product was about to conquer the world. The growth of the Internet was deemed very attractive by CompuSound as the possibilities for the CNT could only increase (see Table 3).

CompuSound Distribution Challenge

By spring 1996, Pierre Charest had begun investigating the distribution and marketing of a hardware product in the Internet telephony channel. It seemed very complex (see Exhibits 2 and 3). Unlike Internet telephony software packages, which could be demonstrated by downloading the software from the Internet, a hardware solution posed very different sales challenges. Most of all, Pierre was concerned about the retail sales price of a hardware solution, versus the average software price of US$35 (see Table 1). At the estimated regular retail price of approximately US$500, the CompuSound Pro with CPP expansion board would be a significantly more expensive solution.

TABLE 3   **World Wide Web (WWW) Statistics, 1995–1999**

	1995	1996	1997	1998	1999
Number of WWW users (millions)	8	30	62	92	125
WWW user breakdown: United States	78%	74%	66%	60%	55%
WWW user breakdown: International	22%	26%	34%	40%	45%

Source: International Data Corporation, 1996.

The Computer Network Telephone board would retail at approximately US$400, while direct cost estimates for the CNT were around US$200. Those customers who already owned a CompuSound Pro sound board would merely add the CPP expansion board onto their sound board, while new customers would buy the CNT solution.

It seemed clear to Bob and Pierre that key relationships with major international computer companies, telephony companies, cable companies, networking manufacturers, or integrators would be very important in the Internet telephony market. This would be especially true when competing against Microsoft and Netscape, who had excellent product distribution through their browser software.

Pierre thought that a test market of 500 CPP boards should be aimed at networking distributors, CompuSound's existing international distributors, Internet Service Providers, key media contacts, and several universities. Some of these contacts would be shipped the board at no charge, while others would be charged a special promotional price of US$299. This strategy would enable CompuSound to almost break even, while providing an attractive testing ground of influential customers. Pierre recognized that many more boards might have to be given away, in order to encourage adoption of the hardware solution. The breakdown of the test market costs was as shown in Table 4.

When the experiment with the Amsterdam Computer Group worked, Bob was very encouraged. He wanted to bundle the CPP with the CompuSound Pro and sell the solution for a retail price of US$500 (US$250 for each part). Each person who wanted to acquire the solution had to purchase it for their computer. Similarly to the software solutions, a computer on each end of the conversation had to have both the CompuSound Pro and the CPP in order for the solution to work. It also meant that the owner would have to open up their computer and install the hardware solution, as opposed to simply downloading or installing a software solution. Pierre was concerned that the CPP and CNT solutions did not seem to belong in a retail shop because the technology

TABLE 4   **Costs and Sales Projections of Test-Market CPP Bundles**

COSTS	
	Cost (US$)
Cost of CompuSound Pro sound board	$132.38
Cost of CPP expansion board	$125.00
TOTAL BUNDLE COST	**$257.38**
Trial Unit Bundle Price for 420 Trial Users	**$299.00**
SALES PROJECTIONS	
	Revenue (US$)
80 evaluation unit bundles (no charge)	—
420 trial unit bundles (US$299 each)	$125,580
TOTAL REVENUE	**$125,580**
Product costs (500 units)	$128,690
GROSS PROFIT (LOSS)	**($ 3,110)**

Source: CompuSound Inc., internal report, May 1996.

EXHIBIT 2   Internet Telephony Distribution Channel Overview

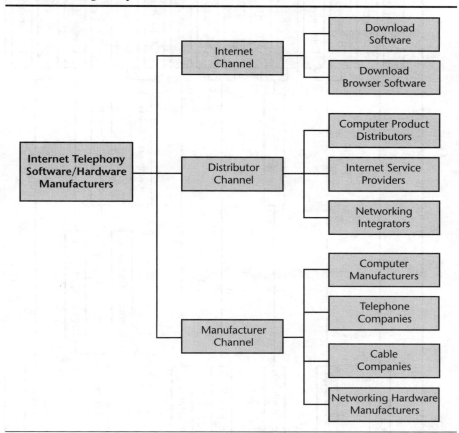

was too complex for both consumers and retail salespeople. CompuSound had already experienced (with the CompuSound Pro sound board) the lack of retailer enthusiasm for products that did not sell themselves. The poor quality of the in-store servicing of these technical products could also pose a problem for a retail approach.

Internet Telephony: Consumer Markets

The consumer market for Internet telephony was reached via computer retailers, Internet service providers, telephone companies, and cable companies (see Exhibit 3). The CompuSound staff assumed that consumers who purchased Internet telephony products were adept in computer use and looked for low-cost products to get the job done. The typical Internet telephony consumer was most likely an enthusiast who enjoyed tinkering with the various software programs, in order to conduct conversations with friends and with Internet chat groups around the world.

The most convenient way for these users to obtain Internet telephony capability was to download software from the Internet. If the users liked the pre-commercial versions of the Internet telephony software, they would then

EXHIBIT 3 Internet Telephony Distribution Channel

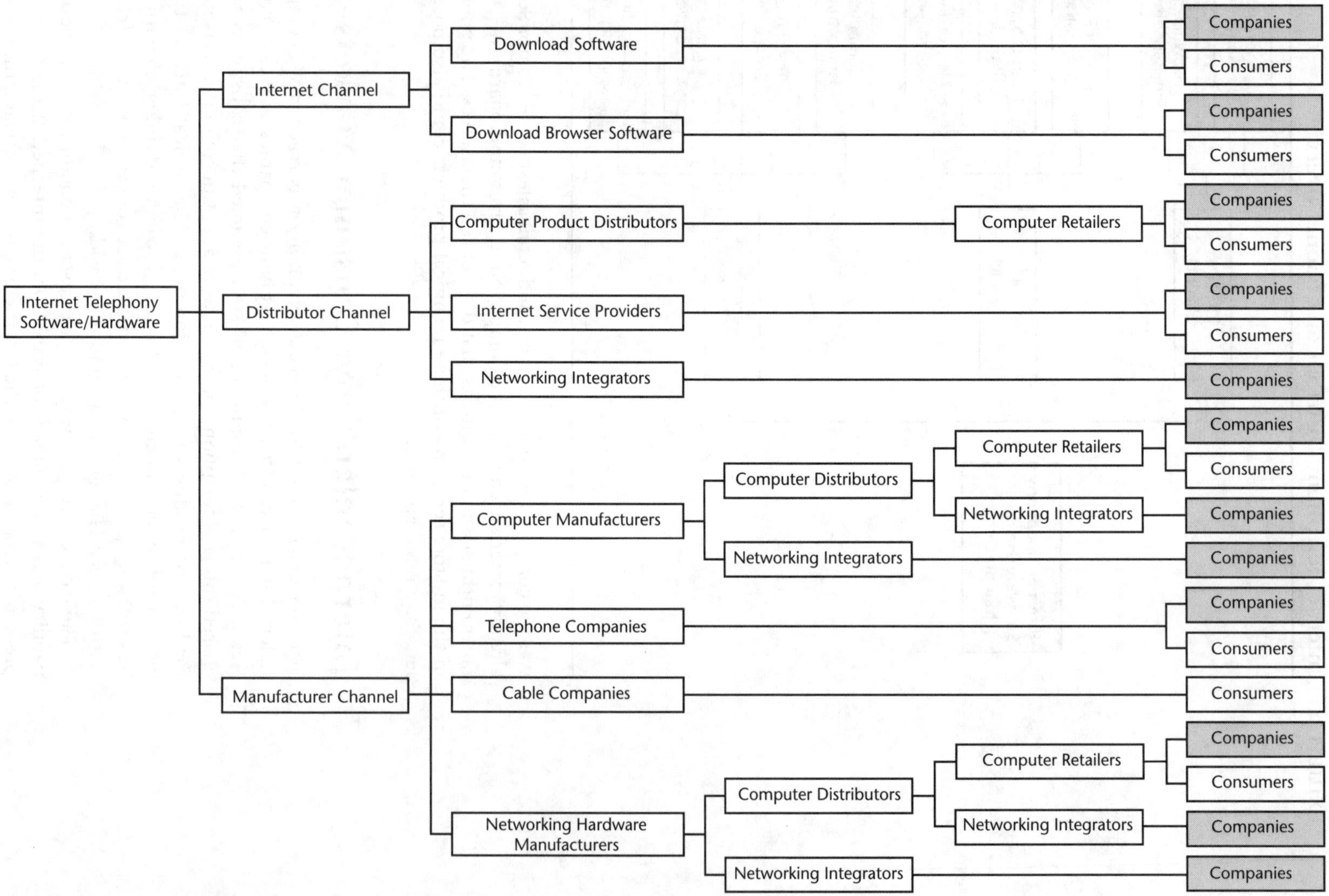

go out and buy the commercial package, usually from a computer retailer. Unfortunately, CompuSound did not have the ease of distribution of a software product, with the hardware CPP and CNT solutions.

Bob seemed to think that cable companies would be the best way to reach the Internet telephony enthusiasts with a hardware product, because they were working to supply multimedia into the home markets. Canadian and international cable companies had large pipelines already installed into homes, which provided consumers with television shows. They were currently altering their technology so not only would content be able to be sent directly to a consumer sitting in the living room, but also the consumer would be able to send back information over the cable lines. This would allow Internet access almost instantaneously unlike the comparatively snail-like pace of Internet access via a computer's modem. The cable companies were very interested in learning about how the Internet telephony solutions could be adapted to their markets. With this technology, cable companies worldwide could potentially enter the long-distance telephone business, another factor that was threatening the traditional telephone companies. CompuSound could easily adapt its CNT technology to meet the needs of the cable companies.

Another very attractive way to reach these end users was to sell Internet telephony products through computer superstores. The informed buyers wanted the lowest price possible for their solutions, and the superstores were very cost-competitive. The computer retailers were supplied with Internet telephony products from computer distributors, computer manufacturers, and networking hardware manufacturers. CompuSound was already working with numerous distributors in Europe, Canada, and the United States who were marketing its CompuSound Pro sound board. Pierre realized that some of his distributors would have some use for the Internet telephony solution. However, the majority of his distributors supplied music stores, which would hardly be an attractive market for the CPP or CNT. The lack of technical knowledge on the part of the retail salespeople would probably inhibit sales of these products.

Multimedia computers were also targeted at the home market. The major computer companies, such as IBM and Compaq, were starting to bundle Internet telephony software solutions with their multimedia computers. IBM had developed its own software, the Internet Connection Phone, which provided the same capability as VocalTec's Internet Phone. Many of the computer companies were testing solutions and trying to determine what would best meet the needs of their customers. Those that could not develop the technology in-house were outsourcing or buying solutions through licensing or alliance partnerships. Pierre thought that with the declining price trend in the personal computer market, that it would be difficult for CompuSound to sell an expensive hardware solution. Also, interoperability was a problem, because only those computers that had the CNT installed would be able to talk to each other.

Perhaps telephone companies could be used to reach home users. While most people in the United States were equipped with telephones, personal computers in the home only reached a penetration level of approximately 30 percent. This figure was much lower internationally. In addition, there were problems implementing the solution in foreign countries, where the existing telephone infrastructure varied and was tied up by government legislation. Bob believed that the telephone companies would not want to give up their lucrative long-distance market before it was absolutely necessary. On the other hand, they would want access to this technological threat.

Finally, the Internet Service Providers were an attractive market for getting the Internet telephony solutions to the home market. Since the Internet Service Providers reached everyone who was using the Internet, they could prove to be a valuable marketing channel for these products. Internet telephony software makers used the providers as a marketing tool, by setting up advertisements on their World Wide Web pages. Although the Internet service providers were more likely to distribute a software solution, they perhaps could be targeted with a hardware board. Bob was unsure of the viability of this market, because the small Internet service providers in Canada often seemed to be unstable financially.

Internet Telephony: Corporate Markets

The corporate market for Internet telephony was reached via computer retailers, Internet Service Providers, telephone companies, and networking companies (see Exhibit 3). Corporate networks were a very attractive target for the Internet telephony products, with their higher margins, compared to the cost-conscious consumer market. The "Intranet" market (internal company networks) was booming. The Intranet was exactly like the Internet, except that it was closed off to company outsiders. For example, an AT&T representative in Malaysia would have instantaneous access to internal pricing changes made in the United States, by logging on to AT&T's Intranet. By setting up a voice Intranet using Internet telephony products, companies with international offices could save huge money on their internal communications.

Internet telephony within the corporation was not well known as yet. Some proactive company technicians had started experimenting with the technology. However, corporate-wide adoption of Internet telephony was a long way from becoming reality. Although the current Internet telephony software did not provide the voice quality and reliability that most corporations required for their inter-firm communications, there was potential for future growth (see Table 1). Corporate users would soon outnumber the home users. Telecommuting was increasing and so was the need for international communications, which made the market very attractive for Internet telephony suppliers, who could back up quality products with superior service.

Pierre thought that the networking integrators would be the most direct route to reach the potentially lucrative corporate market, as they did not focus on the consumer, but prepared complete solutions for corporations. Networking integrators pieced together computer systems for corporations and they were starting to explore how they could meet the corporations' communications needs with Internet telephony solutions. The networking integrators could be targeted directly, or else reached through the computer distributors, computer manufacturers, and networking hardware manufacturers.

The networking product makers who serviced the networking integrators could also be targeted at source. These players made the routers, hubs, and software that linked PCs. The manufacturers of LAN and WAN equipment were good customers for an Internet telephony solution. Cisco Systems was the dominant player in the LAN networking market. By the end of April 1996, Cisco had acquired Stratacom, the leader in the WAN networking market. Some industry experts predicted that the Cisco/Stratacom alliance would become to the networking industry what IBM was to the computer industry. Meanwhile, the other big LAN players, such as Bay Networks, Cabletron, and 3Com were scrambling to find WAN partnerships, to counteract this surprise merger.

The telephone companies were possibly an attractive market for the CPP or CNT in a corporate setting. However, these companies did not know where to position themselves in the Internet telephony software market, because many were also trying to become Internet service providers. Bell Canada had recently started its own Internet service called Sympatico. Both AT&T and MCI were keeping a low profile on this issue, and they had not signed the ACTA petition. Internet telephony solutions could be dangerous for the telephone companies, because they threatened their traditional long-distance market. At the same time, any increase in the use of phone lines, whether it be for traditional phone calls or for Internet telephony calls, would be good for their business. The progressive telephone companies realized that they must enter this market early, before they were shut out of the potentially lucrative business.

To a lesser extent, the corporate market could be reached through computer retailers and Internet service providers. Companies who were too small to deal with networking integrators would also buy from computer retailers. The Internet service providers for large companies could also be targeted at source to meet the corporations' needs.

A Fading Sound Board Market

Bob Nornan was acutely aware that the revenue generated by the CompuSound Pro sound board had not met the expectations of CompuSound management. The company had to rely on licensing revenue to meet the deficit in its sound board sales. However, the need for full duplex sound boards was arising from the use of Internet telephony software. CompuSound could reposition the sales of the CompuSound Pro to meet these users' needs. Bob would be able to reduce the large amount of inventory which was presently being held at FLEX Assemblers. However, this strategy would include having to support the existing channels with extensive advertising and promotional materials.

Also, CompuSound could actively develop higher-end sound boards for even more demanding consumers. The AudioTech engineers would be relied upon to come up with better products, guided by the customer feedback that CompuSound had gathered from the CompuSound Pro sales. CompuSound would have to be very careful in positioning a new sound board, due to the declining nature of the sound board industry.

As yet, the manufacturers of multimedia computers did not have high-quality sound boards installed in their computers. There could be an opportunity to place the CompuSound Pro in the hands of these manufacturers. With consumers becoming ever more demanding in terms of the quality of PC sound, this might prove to be an attractive market.

◼ Resources

Pierre Charest presently spent most of his time dealing with the sound board sales within CompuSound. He was trying to find a way to easily maintain the CompuSound Pro business, while being able to move on to other important projects. The monthly costs involved in maintaining the sound board business were approximately US$70,000, including the salaries of the majority of CompuSound's employees, office expenses, and promotional costs. Pierre seemed to be worried about incurring a big inventory loss at FLEX Assemblers, which had CompuSound Pro-related components in stock (see Exhibit 4). Meanwhile, existing distributors were demanding new products to replace the CompuSound Pro in their product lineups. Both Bob and Pierre were concerned that a lack of product innovations could be perceived by retailers and distributors as an exit strategy.

Bob was working very hard at maintaining and extending the licensing agreements while still promoting PC sound technology to potential partners. Bob was feeling the pressure of conflicting commitments. He was trying to keep everyone happy: the partners he had brought in to finance CompuSound, his licensing partners, AudioTech, FLEX Assemblers, and his staff. Bob was somewhat overwhelmed by the possibilities of trying to market the CompuSound Internet telephony solution to the consumer and corporate markets. However, he realized that because of the versatility of CompuSound's solutions, there would be plenty of opportunity to create international alliances throughout the numerous channel opportunities.

In the meantime, Bob's young product manager was trying to guide CompuSound to a new chapter in its history. The product manager believed that the future of CompuSound lay within its ability to produce "tools," not "toys." The sound board industry had been seen as a "toy" industry; the boards were mainly used by a very small exclusive group of people who tinkered with their computers to produce music. The product manager wanted CompuSound to develop a "tool" that everyone would use on a daily basis to be productive. He believed the future of the company would be to produce a tool that enabled people to make phone calls using their computers, namely the Computer Network Telephone solution.

Beyond Pierre and the product manager, the remaining employees at CompuSound supported the sound board business. This group was composed of two technical support specialists, a video game tester, a product tester, a sales representative, a marketing assistant, a secretary, a receptionist, and a shipping clerk. The major human resource deficiency that CompuSound had was its lack of software programming expertise. The specialty of the AudioTech engineers was hardware; they lacked the capability to develop software to complement the new Internet telephony technology. The entire staff at CompuSound realized that without an attractive and functional software user interface for the

CPP and CNT, the products would never reach non-technical or mainstream consumers. The software would include telephony features, such as call waiting and a caller ID. The investment in qualified software engineers was of concern to Bob, as was the immediate need for attractive software for his new products. Bob estimated that he would require four software programmers, at a salary of Cdn$30,000 each. He expected overall costs of approximately Cdn$200,000 for the first year of CompuSound's investment in the Internet telephony industry.

Bob could not make these large financial decisions autonomously. Initially, Bob had sole control of CompuSound and was the only shareholder. However, in order to fuel the growth of the company, Bob had brought in additional investors. The finances of the company were extremely tight, although the outside parties seemed patient and confident in the capabilities of CompuSound and AudioTech. As at August 31, 1995, CompuSound had no cash in the bank

EXHIBIT 4

COMPUSOUND INC.
BALANCE SHEET (Cdn$)
As at August 31, 1995

Current Assets		Current Liabilities	
Bank account	$ 0	Bank overdraft	$ 19,650
Accounts receivable—trade	493,837	Bank loan	680,000
Accounts receivable—other	50,998	Accounts payable—licensing	154,364
Investment tax credit receivable	332,604	Accounts payable—other	347,276
Inventory	556,616	Payable to shareholders	20,000
Prepaid expenses	11,122	Deductions at source	92,799
		Current portion of long-term debt	250,079
TOTAL CURRENT ASSETS	1,445,177	TOTAL CURRENT LIABILITIES	1,564,168
Property and equipment	138,737	**Long-Term Liabilities**	
Other assets:		Deferred credits	381,497
Development costs	697,786	Notes payable	474,437
Startup costs	3,982		
Trademarks	5,213	TOTAL LIABILITIES	$2,420,102
		Equity	
		Common stock	1,399,065
		Retained earnings	(1,528,272)
		TOTAL LIABILITIES AND	
TOTAL ASSETS	$2,290,895	**SHAREHOLDERS' EQUITY**	$2,290,895

Key Financial Data	US$	Cdn$
Average selling price to distributor/unit of CompuSound Pro	$180	$250
Average retail selling price/unit of CompuSound Pro	$250	$345
Actual sound board sales to date	$900,000	$1,250,000
Direct cost/unit of CompuSound Pro	$140	$190
Average monthly variable costs*	$69–76,000	$95–105,000
Gross margin**	10%–15%	10%–15%

*Including salaries, marketing, distributor maintenance, and advertising costs.
**Depending on special discounts.

and a large overdraft, and the shareholders were owed cash (see Exhibit 4). The company was also saddled with nearly Cdn$400,000 of CompuSound Pro–related inventory at FLEX Assemblers. CompuSound's current portion of its long-term debt had reached Cdn$250,000, and the bank was starting to call regularly regarding the company's bank loan of Cdn$680,000.

Bob's Reflections

After reviewing the CompuSound situation, Bob left for vacation without the answers he wanted. Just before his departure, Bob received a fax from Sunrise indicating that they were interested in having CompuSound design a new sound card, one with capabilities superior to those of the CompuSound Pro. Finally a major consumer products company had recognized the extraordinary value that CompuSound's sound board provided. Bob thought that there could possibly be a market for this new sound board now that Sunrise was requesting one. Maybe he should be thinking about designing a new sound board that could be marketed under the CompuSound name.

Bob was uncertain how to advise Pierre and his product manager as to the priorities of CompuSound. Several critical questions continued to haunt him. What should he do with the declining CompuSound Pro business? Should CompuSound market a new sound board under its own name or focus on Sunrise's latest sound board request? What kind of alliance partner would best suit his growing company? Should a small company like CompuSound enter the Internet telephony industry? Which channel would be the most effective way to enter this extraordinary market, given its size and limited resources? Where would the financing for these maneuvers come from? Bob recognized that the answers and the resulting direction would likely change CompuSound forever.

Cooper Canada
Limited

In late 1982, CCM Canada, a manufacturer of bicycles, skates, and hockey equipment, was put into receivership and the business put up for sale. While CCM's competitors had noted the company's accumulating problems with some satisfaction and relief, they were now faced with new questions: Who would acquire the assets of CCM? What would be the impact on the competitive structure of the industry?

In the meantime, the CCM receiver was pressing for action. John Cooper, vice-chairman of Cooper Canada Ltd., one of the interested competitors, described the situation:

> Our people visited the CCM plant and offices last week and they had no sooner returned than the receiver called wanting to know how soon we could make a bid. He said that speed was critical because he expected other bids at any moment and that the creditors wanted action since CCM's situation was worsening every day. We will have to act fast … we have a meeting set for next Monday to make an offer if we want to. It is too bad we are under such time pressure but that's the way this deal is.

Cooper was interested only in the skate and hockey equipment part of the CCM business. Here some elements of the fit between Cooper and CCM's winter goods business were obvious. Cooper could completely outfit a hockey player except for sweaters and skates. CCM's skate line was still one of the most respected in the business. The value of CCM's competing lines of hockey sticks and protective equipment, however, was less clear. The bicycle line was of no interest but Cooper had made arrangements with another prospective buyer to pick up this part of the CCM operation in a joint bid. The question facing Cooper management, under time pressure, was whether they wished to proceed with their side of the bid and, if so, with what price and conditions?

This case was prepared by Professor Donald H. Thain for the sole purpose of providing material for class discussion at the Ivey Business School. Certain names and other identifying information may have been disguised to protect confidentiality. It is not intended to illustrate either effective or ineffective handling of a managerial situation. Any reproduction, in any form, of the material in this case is prohibited except with the written consent of the School. © 1988 Ivey Management Services. Case 9-84-M010, version 10/26/93.

Richard Ivey School of Business
The University of Western Ontario

The Skate and Hockey Equipment Industry

There were four basic product lines in the industry: skates, protective equipment (e.g., helmets, gloves, pads), sticks, and apparel. Cooper management estimated the industry's 1981 value of shipments for these lines was as follows:

	($000)
Ice skates	78,000
Hockey equipment	31,500
Hockey sticks	29,000
Apparel	27,000

The overall demand for hockey-related products had grown slowly in the 1970s and little or no growth was expected in the 1980s. Population trends in the prime hockey-playing age groups were not favourable and participation rates were under pressure. A major problem with participation was the increasing cost of equipping a player: from $100 to $200 for beginners including used equipment and up to $1,500 for a professional.

The rapidly changing technology of hockey equipment was one reason for the high cost of equipment. Product innovation was driving toward lighter, safer, and more comfortable gear. As a 1982 article in the Maple Leaf Gardens program described it:

> Space-age hockey equipment is speeding up the game and cutting down on injuries. Technological breakthroughs are sending the NHL where it has never gone before—to lighter, cooler, stronger, tighter-fitting one-piece body protection; aluminum or fibreglass and plastic-laminated sticks; and, zircon-guarded, carbon-bladed skates encased in ballistic and nylon-wrapped boots. Leaf trainer Danny Lemelin thinks skates have "changed most dramatically" in the past few years. He points out that most are four ounces lighter because of the plastic blade holder and nylon boot.
>
> This space-age equipment has speeded up the game and cut down on injuries. And, it's made the felt and fibre shin, shoulder, elbow and pant pads, one-piece ash sticks and leather tube skates so popular only a decade ago, obsolete. ...
>
> The evolution turned revolution in NHL gear is the by-product of by-products. New foams, plastics, nylon and fibreglass (many invented in Korea during the fifties to keep fighting forces warm and protected) have made things "lighter and stronger," says one long-time equipment manufacturer. All these new inventions have been developed to conform to the game of hockey. ...

Canadian brands had established an international reputation for product excellence, and exports of hockey equipment had increased from $20 million in 1971 to $41.5 million in 1980. The United States was the largest market, but Scandinavia and western Europe were also strong. Japan and Australia were newly developing markets.

The market shares of the major competitors in the industry by product line are given in Exhibit 1. The skate business was dominated by three firms: Warrington Industries Ltd. (with three brands—Bauer, Lange, and Micron), CCM, and Daoust. Cooper was the primary company in hockey equipment. The

EXHIBIT 1   Products and Estimated Market Shares of Major Competitors in the Canadian Hockey Equipment Market, 1981

	Market Share (%)			
Company	Skates	Hockey Equipment	Sticks	Apparel
Cooper		69	7	31
Canadien		7	12	
CCM	25	7	6	
D & R		7		
Jofa		3		
Koho		2.5	10.5	
Sherwood			25	
Victoriaville			11	
Louisville			6.5	
Titan			11	
Maska				42
Bernard				11
Sandow				10
Bauer*	33			
Lange*	5			
Micron*	13			
Daoust	17			
Orbit	5			
Roos	1			
Ridell	1			
Others		4.5	11	4
	100%	100%	100%	100%
($ millions)	$78	$31.5	$29	$27

*Brands of Warrington Industries Ltd.
Source: Rough estimates by Cooper product managers.

stick business was shared by half-a-dozen significant competitors, of which the largest was Sherwood-Drolet. Cooper and Sport Maska were the two most significant competitors in apparel. A brief description of the companies that Cooper considered interested and capable of bidding for CCM is given in Appendix A.

Skates

The demand for skates in Canada had for several years fluctuated between 1 and 1.3 million pairs. There were two basic types of skate boots: sewn and molded. Leather had been the first boot material and was still used in most high-quality, high-priced skates. Over 90 percent of NHL players wore leather skates. However, in the 1970s molded boots had entered the market and, in the low-priced market particularly, had become competitive with leather-booted skates.

Information on the total Canadian hockey skate market and the shares of major competitors segmented by sewn and molded boots is presented in Exhibit 2. Hockey skates could also be segmented by price point as follows:

Range	Retail Price	1982 Estimated Share (Units)
High	More than $200	15%
Medium	$120–$180	20%
Low	Less than $90	65%

EXHIBIT 2

CANADIAN HOCKEY SKATE PRODUCTION
(000s of pairs)

Year	Sewn	Molded	Total
1977	1,050	50	1,100
1978	775	150	925
1979	1,050	250	1,300
1980	850	300	1,150
1981	970	400	1,370
1982 (forecast)	750	300	1,050
1983 (forecast)	900	350	1,250

1982 FACTORY SALES AND MARKET SHARES OF LEADING COMPETITORS
(000s of pairs)

	Sewn	%	Molded	%	Total	%	(000s)	%	$ Average of Total
Bauer	305	42.9	50	13.7	355	32.9	$20,265	35.4	$57.08
Micron	—		185	50.5	185	17.2	8,690	15.2	46.97
Lange	—		100	27.3	100	9.3	3,280	5.8	32.80
Daoust	205	28.7	—		205	19.0	9,780	17.0	47.70
CCM	147	20.6	6	1.6	153	14.2	12,050	21.0	78.76
Orbit	55	7.8	25	6.8	80	7.4	3,205	5.6	40.06
	712	100	366	100	1,078	100	$57,270	100	$53.13

1982 HOCKEY SKATE SALES BY GEOGRAPHIC MARKET
(000s of pairs)

Manufacturer	Canada	U.S.A.	Europe	Far East	Total
Canadian	785	238	67	15	1,105
Non-Canadian	—	312	233	25	570
Totals	785	550	300	40	1,675

Source: Estimates based on industry information and case writer's estimates.

Industry observers noted that the high- and low-end market shares were increasing and the medium range decreasing. The breakdown of CCM's total unit skate sales in the high, medium, and low price ranges was approximately 60 percent, 25 percent, and 15 percent, respectively, while that of Bauer, the largest brand, was thought to be 20 percent, 30 percent, and 50 percent, respectively.

Skate blades were another factor in the market. They were available from three sources in Canada. The largest manufacturer, the St. Lawrence company of Montreal, sold mainly to CCM and Daoust. Canpro Ltd., owned by Warrington, sold mainly to Bauer, Micron, and Lange. CCM manufactured its own Tuuk blades and sold some to other skate makers. While blade technology had changed significantly in the late 1970s with the introduction of plastic mounts to replace tubes, the major current change was the trend back to carbon steel from the newer stainless steel.

Protective Equipment

Protective equipment included the list shown in Table 1 with typical retail prices. Continuous research and development was necessary to ensure

TABLE 1   Price Ranges for Protective Equipment

Equipment Item	Typical for Hockey Equipment	
	Men's	Boys'
Pants	$ 40 –$130	$30 –$60
Gloves	50 – 140	25 – 70
Helmet	27 – 45	27 – 45
Cooperall	115 – 125	98
Shin pads	20 – 75	20 – 75
Elbow pads	19 – 50	7 – 25
Shoulder pads	25 – 70	14 – 40
Pants	40 – 130	30 – 60
Gloves	50 – 140	25 – 70
Helmet	27 – 45	27 – 45

maximum protection and comfort. Cooper dominated the market with a 69 percent share.

Sticks

The composition of sticks was continually changing. What had started out as a one-piece blade and handle developed into a two-piece solid-wood handle and blade, and later a laminated handle and curved blade with fibreglass reinforcement. The most recent development was an aluminum handle with a replaceable wooden blade. Changes were intended to improve strength passing and shooting accuracy. Sherwood-Drolet led in this market with a 25 percent share.

Apparel

Differences in prices of sweaters and socks were due basically to the material used in the product. The most popular sweater materials were polyester and cotton knits because of their strength and lightness. Designs of sweaters were fairly standard, with lettering and cresting done separately. Socks were a standard product with little differentiation. Sport Maska controlled 42 percent of this market because of its quality product, excellent distribution, and good rapport with dealers.

Distribution

Skates and hockey equipment were sold in a wide range of retail outlets including specialty, independent, department, discount, chain, and catalogue stores. Although specific numbers were not available, the split of business between these outlets followed a common retail pattern. The specialty independents and chains dominated the higher-priced items where product knowledge and service were essential. The mass merchandisers were dominant in the lower-priced product areas.

In Canada, the most common route from manufacturer to retailer was through distributors who used sales agents. Manufacturers wanted agents who would represent their product aggressively, seek out new orders, and provide them with market feedback. Usually these agents either were, or had been, actively involved in sports. However, since the agents sold multiple lines, it was difficult to control their activities and mix of sales. Most companies used a sales force of 10 to 12 reps to cover most of Canada. A few small companies utilized wholesalers to supplement their sales force.

Retail outlets had experienced little real growth in sales and were finding themselves with increasing inventories. Therefore, retailers started carrying shallower stocks, ordering more frequently, and relying on manufacturers or distributors to provide backup inventories. This trend meant that bargaining power had shifted from the manufacturers to the retailers who were trying to gain volume discounts and delivery advantages by reducing the number of suppliers.

Promotion

Three types of promotion were used: company and product promotion, media advertising, and trade show participation. Product and image promotion seemed to be the most effective avenue for stimulating sales. Because professional players set industry trends, it was important to get popular players to use and endorse products. To recruit these players, professional "detail men" from sports equipment manufacturers were assigned to players to make sure their equipment fit perfectly and that the player was loyal to the brand. It was also important to get as many players as possible wearing the products so that the brand name would enjoy good exposure during televised games. Therefore, the detail men also tried to work through team trainers to supply most of the team with the brand. While some competitors used financial incentives to push a product, Cooper relied on high quality, fast service in fitting and repairs, and intensive sales efforts, and was not involved with special deals or endorsement contracts.

Media advertising was primarily confined to the larger firms. Print advertising in the concentrated population areas was the most common approach.

Trade shows significantly influenced retail buyers. Many sales took place at the shows, bookings were made for orders, and sales were made on followup calls by sales reps. The Canadian Sporting Goods Association organized two shows annually.

◼ Cooper Canada

In 1946, Jack Cooper left Eaton's to join General Leather Goods Ltd., as its first, and until 1951, only salesperson. Subsequently Cooper and Cecil Weeks bought out the company's original owner and changed the name to Cooper-Weeks. In 1954, Cooper acquired Cecil Weeks' interest and the company became the exclusive Canadian manufacturer of Burton leather goods. In the following years the company grew through internal development and acquisitions to encompass a wide range of leather and sporting good products. In 1970, the company changed its name to Cooper Canada Ltd. and went public. By 1981, revenues were almost $63 million, but Cooper experienced its first loss in years. Cooper management expected a return to profitability in 1982 in spite of a recession and high interest rates. Financial statements for Cooper Canada from 1977 through 1981 are presented in Exhibits 3 and 4.

EXHIBIT 3

CONSOLIDATED STATEMENT OF INCOME AND RETAINED EARNINGS
Years Ended December 31
($000s)

	1981	1980	1979	1978	1977
Net sales	62,827	62,183	55,810	49,429	42,803
Less: Operating costs	57,049	55,901	51,844	44,364	38,538
Net before depreciation etc.	5,778	6,282	3,966	5,064	4,265
Less:					
Depreciation and amortization	724	746	748	626	609
Long-term debt interest	1,905	934	1,022	929	778
Other interest	2,933	2,866	2,068	1,138	941
Add:					
Foreign exchange gain	(105)	369	(107)	216	173
Earnings, discontinued operations	929	—	—	—	—
Less income taxes:					
Current	14	176	20	525	518
Deferred	208	48	454	21	58
Net income, operations	818	1,977	455	2,039	1,650
Add: Extraordinary item	(1,543)	76	—	—	—
Net income	(725)	2,053	455	2,039	1,650
Shares outstanding:					
Common ($000)	1,486	1,483	1,483	1,404	1,388
Net income per share	(0.49)	1.38	0.31	1.45	1.18

Source: Company financial reports.

In 1982, Cooper was engaged in two major lines of business: sporting goods (hockey equipment, apparel, golf bags, baseball gloves, inflated goods, etc.) and leather goods and finishing (wallets, carrying bags, etc.). The relative scale and performance of these businesses are illustrated in Table 2. Cooper also had a significant sales and distribution operation in the United States as indicated by the geographic segmentation of the business in Table 2.

TABLE 2   **Cooper Canada Revenue and Profits by Business Segment, 1991 ($000)**

INDUSTRY SEGMENTS

	Sporting Goods	Leather Goods and Finishing	Consolidated
Revenue	$46,913	$16,076	$62,827
Operating profit	7,434	1,678	8,939
Identifiable assets	28,703	8,001	40,870*

GEOGRAPHIC SEGMENTS

	Canada	United States	Consolidated
Revenue	57,122	11,321	62,827
Operating profit	7,823	1,289	8,939
Identifiable assets	30,403	6,301	40,870*

*Includes corporate assets of $4,549.
Source: Cooper annual reports.

EXHIBIT 4

CONSOLIDATED BALANCE SHEET
As at December 31
(000s)

Assets	1981	1980	1979	1978	1977
Current:					
Short-term bank deposit	—	1,790	—	22	95
Accounts receivable	9,726	10,625	10,315	9,185	8,340
Inventories:					
Raw materials	6,177	8,792	13,064	5,675	5,535
Work in process	1,593	1,758	1,817	1,006	1,379
Finished goods	15,954	11,669	10,530	10,937	10,839
Prepaid expenses etc.	580	691	545	886	706
	34,030	35,325	39,271	27,714	26,897
Fixed assets at cost:					
Buildings	6,179	6,145	6,145	6,117	6,078
Machinery, equipment, etc.	4,191	4,521	4,171	3,354	3,174
Dies, molds, etc.	235	567	619	435	284
Land	91	91	91	90	90
Less: Accumulated depreciation	5,351	5,104	4,518	4,000	3,712
	5,345	6,220	6,508	5,998	5,914
Deferred financing expenses	—	—	—	—	76
Investment in non-consolidated subsidiaries	1,122	—	—	—	—
Deferred income taxes	373	581	533	—	—
	40,870	42,126	46,312	33,713	32,889
Liabilities					
Current:					
Bank indebtedness	10,373	15,853	17,423	8,283	6,955
Accounts payable	3,463	3,380	6,380	3,153	3,576
Income and other taxes payable	1,002	695	641	352	314
Long-term debt due	16	233	603	1,134	1,059
	14,854	20,161	25,047	12,924	11,905
Long-term debt:					
Bank loan	9,000	4,000	5,375	5,875	6,900
10% sinking fund debentures, due 1990	1,582	1,892	1,920	2,053	2,148
6.5% mortgage, due 1992	248	265	273	291	280
Notes payable to shareholders	—	125	437	504	—
Less: Amount due 1 year	16	233	603	1,134	1,059
Deferred taxes	—	—	—	418	397
Shareholders' Equity					
Capital stock:					
Common	3,403	3,392	3,392	2,764	2,716
Retained earnings	11,799	12,524	10,471	10,016	9,600
	40,870	42,126	46,312	33,713	32,889

Source: Company financial reports.

Management Goals

Jack Cooper, "the chief," and his two sons, John and Don,[1] owned 82 percent of the company's outstanding common stock. Jack Cooper, who retained voting control, was chairman and chief executive officer and Henry Nolting was president and chief operating officer. John Cooper was vice-chairman and deputy chief executive officer. They worked closely together, meeting for frequent discussions daily. The company's organization is shown in Exhibit 5.

Management's immediate concerns were to increase sales and margins; to implement a badly needed information system; to strengthen control over activities in marketing, production, and finance; to reduce short-term bank debt and high interest expenses; and to iron out troublesome technical and production problems in J. B. Foam, a manufacturer of plastic foam pads and products that had recently been purchased and moved to Cooper's Toronto plant.

Long-term goals called for further development of sporting goods to increase growth and utilize the great strengths of the Cooper name. Additions

---

[1] Don, who had managed the leather goods division for several years, left the company in 1980 and started a women's sportswear retailing company. He remained a director.

EXHIBIT 5   Organization Chart

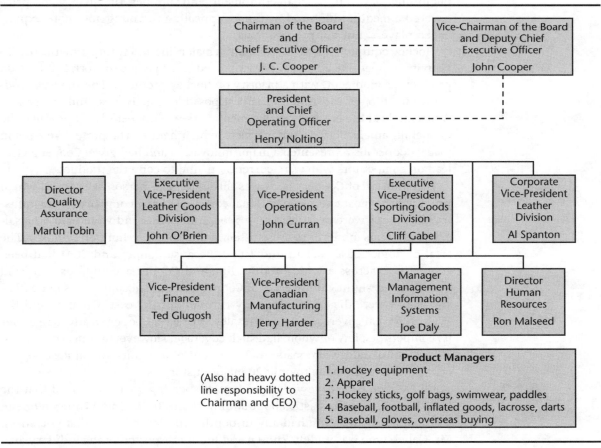

to the product line were sought through new product development and/or acquisition. Cooper was also developing more export markets for its sporting goods products.

Performance

Growth had always been foremost among Jack Cooper's goals. Sales had increased continuously since 1969, except in 1975. However, earnings had fluctuated widely over the same period. Earnings dropped in 1979 because of problems in absorbing the purchase of Winnwell Sports. In 1981, high interest rates, the recession, and the disposal of Cooper's unsuccessful production operations in Barbados all hurt the bottom line. However, interim 1982 figures indicated much stronger performance. Although there was little growth in sales, tight inventory and cost controls implemented by Henry Nolting had helped to increase earnings.

Marketing

Cooper products covered a wide range of quality and price points in hockey equipment. For example, the Cooper line ranged from high-end items, used by top professional teams around the world, to medium-low items for the beginning player. In baseball equipment, and supplies, the quality and price covered a medium-high to low range, appealing to young and more experienced players, but not professionals.

Hockey equipment was the company's major line and future growth area. To keep its competitive edge, Cooper employed eight people to work full-time on product development, with a priority on hockey products. The aim was product leadership, giving athletes the best possible effectiveness and protection. An example of the product development work was Cooper's latest product, the Cooperall, an elasticized body garment which held all the protective pads in place. Cooperalls represented a major innovation and had given Cooper a clear lead on competitors who were currently trying to copy the product.

Distribution of Cooper goods was through its 25-person sales force, which provided the most extensive national coverage of any company in the industry. Sales reps were organized on a geographic basis and were paid on a salary plus bonus minus expenses system, with no upper limit on bonuses. The total customer base was around 1,600. Because Cooper and CCM had been competitive across a wide product line and Cooper accounts usually sold Bauer skates, significant overlap of Cooper and CCM accounts was not extensive. Sales were distributed equally throughout the east, Ontario, and the West. National coverage by its own sales force gave Cooper an advantage over its competitors, few of whom had such coverage. However, a concern was that 90 percent of sales were made to 20 percent of accounts and almost 40 percent of sales were made to only 20 major customers.

Cliff Gabel, executive vice-president of sporting goods, reported that the sales force was enthusiastic about adding skates to its line. While no one in the Cooper organization had any in-depth experience in the skate business, Mr. Gabel, who was widely known and highly respected in the industry, had maintained a good relationship with several key marketing managers at CCM, some of whom were not retired. He believed that one man in particular, who had an outstanding reputation as perhaps the "best skate man around," would welcome the opportunity to help Cooper take over and manage CCM should the opportunity arise. A respected and now retired manager from the Bauer Company who was a good friend of John Cooper was also thought to be available.

Cooper was the largest national advertiser in the sporting goods industry and had won awards for the quality of its television and print ads. The latest campaign had featured the Cooperall and was aired during the 1982 Stanley Cup telecasts.

Manufacturing and Distribution

Cooper had two manufacturing facilities. A plant in west Toronto did the bulk of the work but an older woodworking plant in Cambridge produced hockey sticks, baseball bats, and canoe paddles. Each facility manufactured hundreds of separate products that involved thousands of parts, requiring control procedures that were complex and numerous.

There was an excess of relatively expensive manufacturing space in the Toronto plant because it was built larger than necessary in 1976. In addition, several products, previously produced in Canada, had since been contracted to offshore manufacturers at lower costs. These manufacturers were primarily in the Orient and did contract work for most of Cooper's competitors. As a result, Cooper's designs were widely and easily copied by the other companies.

In distribution, Cooper chose to act as a "stockhouse," filling as many customer orders as possible on request. Speedy response was a major factor in maintaining customer loyalty. Cooper had a policy of providing a fill rate of 90 percent in non-peak seasons and 80 percent in peak seasons. This required substantial working capital, as Cooper's line encompassed over 12,000 stock-keeping units (SKUs). The sporting goods division carried 65 percent to 80 percent of the total company inventory. Finished sporting goods inventory reached as high as $18 million each April for deliveries of fall lines. A company objective was to reduce year-end inventories from $23.7 million in 1981 to a more manageable $18 million by the end of 1982. One manager indicated that a recent reduction in the past company policy of producing 120 percent of forecast sales to a level of 100 percent of forecast sales would be a major factor in reducing inventory.

Information Systems

A monthly report of sales and gross profit for each SKU and product line was available to each product manager. Quarterly reports provided by cost accounting attempted to determine actual margins realized by each division on each product line. Product managers were expected to make decisions on pricing and provide input on production levels based on the information provided by these reports.

Product managers were evaluated on the basis of sales, market share, and product margins. The market share was expected to be maintained or increased to achieve sales growth. Product-line margins were compared to the company aver-age. However, a major argument between the department and product managers, particularly for leather goods, was that allocated overheads were not fair or accu-rate. The cost accounting department had struggled with this problem for years.

Financing

A bank operating loan and other term loans were the company's major sources of financing. Banking services for Canada were provided by the Ca-nadian Imperial Bank of Commerce (CIBC) and for Cooper International by Marine Midland Bank of Buffalo, New York. The CIBC provided an operating loan to a maximum line of $16 million at $1/4$ percent above prime and a term loan at $3/4$ percent above prime to be paid in $1 million per year installments in the first five years and $2 million per year thereafter. The bank prime rate was currently 12 percent but had been as high as 20 percent in mid-1982.

A combination of high working capital requirements and high interest rates in the early 1980s had prompted Cooper to seek to minimize capital expenditures without adversely affecting manufacturing or productivity. The payback requirement approval of capital expenditures was 2.5 years or bet-ter. Typical annual capital expenditures were additions of new dyes and molds and the purchase of manufacturing equipment.

CCM

Incorporated in 1899 as the Canadian Cycle and Motor Company, CCM was Canada's oldest sporting goods manufacturer. Over its history, CCM had been engaged in three separate businesses: bicycles; automobiles; and skates, hockey sticks, and equipment.

The skate business was entered in 1905 to even out the seasonal sales and production of bicycles. Originally, CCM manufactured high-quality blades and riveted them to the best available boots purchased from George Tackaberry of Brandon, Manitoba, to make the skates used by virtually all professional and high-level amateur hockey players. Later, to fill out the line, it purchased lower-quality boots from two small shoe companies in Quebec and its hockey equip-ment from other manufacturers. By 1967, all winter goods were manufactured by the company in what was then a large, modern, efficient plant in St. Jean, Quebec.

Through industry-leading product innovation, CCM became the world's premier hockey skate manufacturer. For years, customers in Europe equated Canada with hockey and hockey with CCM.

Performance

Starting in 1961, CCM went through an unfortunate series of ownership and management changes. This resulted at various times in serious labour problems, inadequate attention to marketing and distribution, and a general deterioration of the company's reputation for quality and service. Despite sales growth in recent years, profitability had been erratic and in 1982 devastatingly poor, since an operating loss of $4.3 million was expected.

The company's financial position, on September 30, 1982, was summarized by the interim receiver as follows: CCM owed two secured creditors $33 million—the Royal Bank $28 million and the Enterprise Development Board $5 million—while the liquidation value of the company was $11.6 million less than its total debts of $41 million. Preferred creditors were owed $1.2 million and product liability claims amounted to almost $13 million, $12 million of which rested on the resolution of a New York civil suit lodged by a hockey player who suffered an injury while wearing a CCM helmet.

The financial information available to Cooper on CCM's winter goods operation is presented in Exhibits 6 and 7.

Marketing

CCM's world-class strength was in leather skates. Like other leading skate manufacturers, CCM concentrated heavily on supplying skates to professional players because they were the trend-setters. Three special pro detail men were employed to sell and service these players, who were often given custom-fitted skates free of charge.

Up to the mid-1970s, when it began to slide, CCM's share of the Canadian and worldwide hockey skate markets had been approximately 60 percent, 30 percent,

EXHIBIT 6

	CCM INC. WINTER GOODS OPERATIONS ($000s)							
	Actual Year Ended						**Projected Year Ending**	
	Sept. 30/80		**Sept. 30/81**		**Sept. 30/82**		**Dec. 31/83**	
Sales:								
Skates	17,148		16,530		14,304		16,500	
Sticks	1,413		2,307		1,445		2,000	
Helmets	1,774		1,814		1,714		2,000	
Protective	3,681		5,047		6,455		6,000	
Sundries	1,250		838		787		1,000	
	25,266		26,536		24,705		27,500	
Gross margins:		%		%		%		%
Skates	5,985	35.0	5,604	34.0	4,577	32.0	5,940	36.0
Sticks	(230)	(16.3)	(30)	(1.3)	(267)	(18.5)	—	—
Helmets	415	23.4	424	23.4	492	28.7	600	30.0
Protective	482	13.1	934	18.5	1,556	24.1	1,350	22.5
Sundries	381	30.5	262	31.3	215	27.3	300	30.0
	7,033	27.8	7,194	27.1	6,573	26.6	8,190	29.8
Expenses:								
Selling							1,291	
Administration							661	
Warehouse and distribution*							1,086	
Financial							618	
							3,656	
Net before income taxes							4,534	

* Figures not available for actual year ended 1980–82.

Source: 1980–1982: from audited financial statements; 1983: projections estimated by CCM management.

EXHIBIT 7

SUMMARY OF CCM WINTER GOODS ASSETS
(at cost)
October 29, 1982
($000s)
Inventories

Finished goods:		
Skates	1,861	
Sticks	407	
Helmets	264	
Protective	1,476	
Sundries	349	
		4,357
Raw material:		
Skates	1,264	
Protective	798	
Blades	1,604	
		3,666
Work in process:		
Skates	216	
Sticks	250	
Protective	234	
Blades	25	
		725
		8,748
Fixed Assets		
St. Jean	1,200	
Hudson	70	
Nylite	867	
		2,137
		10,885

Source: CCM management estimates.

and 20 percent of the high-, medium, and low-priced markets, respectively. Because of its domination of the top end of the market, Supertack, its long-established premium brand name, was better known around the world than CCM. Although skate sales were the largest contributor to fixed costs, they declined from 68 percent of winter goods sales in 1980 to 58 percent in 1982. At the same time, protective equipment sales roughly doubled from 14 percent to 26 percent, with gross margins of 24 percent. Total gross margin as a percent of sales decreased from 27.8 percent in 1980 to 26.6 percent in 1982.

Distribution

From 1945 to 1982 CCM's dealer network had shrunk from 2,500 to 1,500 and its sales force from 21 to 12. All dealers sold the total CCM line but spent most of their time on winter goods. Up to 1970 the sales reps had been paid salary plus car and expenses and had been encouraged to service dealers and customers. However, industry sources reported that by 1982, the sales reps were strictly on a commission basis and, pressured to get orders through as many dealers as possible, spent little time on service.

Although CCM's reputation for service was suffering, its reputation for quality had been maintained fairly well. A quick survey of a few present or past CCM dealers in November 1982 indicated that approximately one-third said they would never carry CCM again; one-third would consider carrying CCM again if they could be assured of delivery and service; and one-third would stick with CCM through thick and thin because they were enthusiastic about the product and the name.

Manufacturing

Early in November, Henry Nolting, president, and Jerry Harder, vice-president of manufacturing at Cooper Canada Ltd., visited CCM's winter goods plant in St. Jean. Following are excerpts from their reports on the visit:

> The woodworking facility is not modern, looks somewhat like ours as far as equipment and machinery are concerned, and it is not surprising that they do not turn a profit in that part of their operation. The roof in the stick-making facility is leaking and that part of their plant is badly maintained.

> The protective equipment manufacturing has nothing in it which we do not know, there is nothing innovative being done and, as far as I am concerned, it is worth very little.

> The skate manufacturing operation seems reasonable despite the fact that there are no great innovations. The boot-making part is something which is easily transferable to our location. Jerry feels he would like to have it and can run it. The whole layout seems relatively simple but modern enough and efficient. The equipment is not new but is in good repair.

> The existing machine shop is old and dirty and there is nothing in it which I would like to buy. They have, at present, approximately 100 people working, but cleaning up work is in process. The people are very slow, they seem to be puzzled, unenthusiastic, and listless.

> There seems to be a lot of old stock in the finished goods warehouse.

> The major lasting machines are leased from United Shoe Machinery which is normal in this trade. However, they apparently work. They say they have 3,000-plus pairs of lasts (many are specials for individual players) at about $25 per pair. The lasts I saw were in very good repair.

> The R&D department has two employees. They have had tremendous problems with their Propacs (copies of Cooperall) and are constantly trying to improve the product. They are working very closely with the Quebec Nordiques in perfecting this product. They have never done any helmet-related work at that facility.

> We think their sporting goods division lost approximately half-a-million dollars each year, in '80 and '81, sharing equally in the total company loss of $4.3 million at the end of September '82.

> The offices are in terrible condition. They are old and in an unbelievable mess.

The president's assessment of the situation is that somebody will buy the assets and he feels that they might go for book value. His opinion is that nobody could pick it up for less.

Not counting raw material storage we would need at least 25,000 sq. ft., which excludes cutting to accommodate the skate-making operation. This is equal to 42 of our present 600 sq. ft. bays. To give you another perspective, this area would be slightly larger than the whole area now devoted to apparel. Because of the size, we would have to do major relocations of our existing floors (in the Toronto plant). Also, we must be careful of the existing electrical supplies—I would make a cautious estimate of a $25,000 rewiring charge.

Organization

As a result of natural attrition and dim prospects, the CCM organization had shrunk to skeleton status. While it was reportedly limping along, many of the best and most experienced managers had either retired or moved on to better opportunities.

◼ Deciding to Bid

In reviewing a list of possible bidders for CCM (Appendix A), John Cooper felt that the strongest competitive threats would be Warrington and Sport Maska. Both companies had strong management teams, well-established distribution systems, and adequate financial strength. In addition, both companies were Canadian-owned and would not face possible delay and veto of their offer by the Foreign Investment Review Agency. Of further concern was the realization that the St. Jean plant represented up to 200 politically sensitive jobs and that the Quebec government might become involved directly or indirectly in the proceedings. Immediate decisions and actions were essential, however, if Cooper wanted to acquire CCM. Two questions puzzled John Cooper: If we don't buy CCM, who will? And how will it affect our business?

APPENDIX A

Competitors in the Skate and Hockey Equipment Industry

There were many manufacturers of hockey equipment, helmets, skates, and sticks in Canada. Some were Canadian-owned, others were foreign-owned with manufacturing facilities in Canada, while others were foreign-owned with only a marketing organization in Canada. Not all of the companies produced and marketed a full line of hockey equipment. Some chose to specialize in two or three product lines. Several of the Canadian companies were small and privately owned, especially

those which produced hockey sticks and skates.

There were seven businesses that Cooper management considered capable and perhaps interested in the CCM winter goods assets:

1. *Canadian Hockey Industries*. CHI was a small company that made high-quality hockey sticks. Its use of fibreglass technology and other materials such as graphite, plastics, laminates, and aluminum had resulted in the most unique stick line in the market. It also

marketed a full line of hockey equipment, including a helmet, but no skates or apparel.

Located in Drummondville, Quebec, it had sales of $10 million in 1981, which had been growing rapidly for the past five years. In the factory it employed approximately 120 workers. It was owned by Amer Industries, a Finnish company which also owned Koho.

2. *Koho.* Koho was owned by Amer Industries of Finland, and shared marketing, distribution, and some hockey stick manufacturing with Canadian Hockey Industries. It was thought to be the largest hockey stick manufacturer in the world. It also manufactured and marketed hockey equipment and helmets, but no skates or apparel.

Koho had sales of approximately $14 million from about 800 or 900 dealers, serviced by six or seven commission agents who primarily sold Koho and Canadian. Major accounts included large department stores, for example, Eaton's, Simpsons, and Sears; sporting goods chains, for example, Collegiate Sports; and other stores such as Canadian Tire.

Sticks were manufactured in the Canadian plant in Quebec; sticks and some hockey equipment were manufactured in Finland; and some hockey equipment was purchased in the Orient.

Koho's organization in Canada was headed by a sales manager who reported to a president for North America. The United States also had a sales manager who reported to the North American president. This president reported to the head office of Amer, a very large and profitable Finnish corporation that was involved with ship building, steel, food, and tobacco.

3. *Jofa.* A Volvo-owned company, Jofa manufactured and marketed hockey equipment, hockey sticks, and skates, but not apparel. It had one factory in Sherbrooke, Quebec, and others in Sweden. The rest of its products were purchased in the Orient.

Sales of $10 million were achieved through 700 to 800 dealers and approximately seven commissioned sales agents. Major accounts included large department stores and sporting goods stores and Canadian Tire.

The organization of the company was thin, with one director of marketing responsible for all of North America. Supporting him was a sales manager and a small number of commissioned sales agents.

4. *Sherwood-Drolet.* Sherwood-Drolet was a Quebec company, 80 percent owned by an American firm, ATO Inc. ATO was the world's largest integrated producer of fire protection equipment and also owned Rawlings and Adirondack sporting goods in the United States.

Sherwood, a producer of high-quality hockey sticks, had been an industry leader in sales and in the introduction of new materials and production processes. It had one of the most automated plants in the industry, enabling it to produce large volumes of sticks of consistent quality. In 1981, its share of the Canadian market was 25 percent.

Sales of around $15 million came from approximately 600 dealers. The company's direct sales were aided by ten sales agents who sold to 300 dealers.

5. *Hillerich and Bradsby.* Hillerich and Bradsby's head office and manufacturing facility were located in Wallaceburg, Ontario. The company was a wholly owned subsidiary of H & B, Louisville, Kentucky, the world's top baseball bat manufacturer. Besides producing the Louisville Hockey stick and being a market leader in brightly coloured goalie sticks, it was making aggressive inroads into the baseball glove and accessory markets. It had also earned a good name for itself in manufacturing golf clubs that were sold primarily through club professionals. The plant employed 62 people.

Sales in 1981 were about $6 million. H & B's distribution system included warehouses in Richmond, B.C.; Dorval, Quebec; Winnipeg, Manitoba; and Concord, Ontario. The sales were achieved primarily by commission sales agents through approximately 400 dealers. Management was reportedly very strong.

6. *Warrington Industries.* Warrington produced Bauer, Micron, and Lange skates. Bauer had been in the skate business for many years, and was CCM's major competitor. This Canadian-owned company was located in Kitchener, Ontario, and produced only skates and shoes. It employed 400 in the skate business and 150 in the shoe business.

   Sales of approximately $30 million were generated by 12 to 15 agents through a dealership of 1,200 stores. Warrington was, in turn, owned by Cemp Investments, a firm representing the interests of the Bronfman family.

7. *Sport Maska.* Maska was a high-quality hockey jersey manufacturer. Good distribution resulted in Maska being the exclusive supplier to the NHL. Besides hockey jerseys and apparel, its business consisted of spring and summer ball uniforms and apparel, soccer jerseys, and leisure wear. The plant in St. Hyacinthe, Quebec, employed approximately 175 people.

   Sales in Canada were achieved by nine commissioned agents through 1,200 to 1,500 dealers across Canada. The agents did not carry Maska exclusively. It was distributed coast to coast across the United States through the use of commission agents. Recently, Maska had purchased Sandow, another Canadian athletic apparel company, and had consolidated the manufacturing into its own plant.

   Sport Maska was a private company that appeared to be profitable and to have a strong equity base. Industry sources felt that the management team, directed by president Denny Coter, was strong and had good depth.

Coral Divers Resort

CASE 8

Jonathon Greywell locked the door on the equipment shed and began walking back along the boat dock to his office. He thought about the matters that had weighed heavily on his mind during the last few months. Over the years, Greywell had established a solid reputation for the Coral Divers Resort as a safe and knowledgeable scuba diving resort. It offered not only diving, but a beachfront location. As a small but well-regarded all-around dive resort in the Bahamas, many divers had come to prefer his resort to other crowded tourist resorts in the Caribbean.

However, over the last three years, revenues had declined and, for 1995, bookings were flat for the first half of the year. Greywell felt he needed to do something to increase business before things got worse. He wondered if he should add some specialized features to the resort that would distinguish it from others. One approach was to focus on family outings. Rascals in Paradise, a travel company that specialized in family diving vacations, had offered to help him convert his resort to one which specialized in family diving vacations. They had shown him the industry demographics that indicated that families were a growing market segment (see Exhibit 1) and made suggestions about what changes would need to be made at the resort. They had even offered to create menus for children and to show the cook how to prepare the meals.

Another potential strategy for the Coral Divers Resort was adventure diving. Other resort operators in the Bahamas were offering adventure-oriented deep depth dives, shark dives, and night dives. The basic ingredients for adventure diving, reef sharks in the waters near New Providence and famous deep water coral walls, were already in place. However, either of these strategies, family or adventure, would require changes and additions to his current operations. He was not sure whether any of the changes were worth the time and investment or whether he should instead try to improve upon what he was already doing.

A final option, and one which he had only recently thought about, was to leave New Providence and try to relocate. At issue here was how much he

Richard Ivey School of Business
The University of Western Ontario

Professors Kent E. Neupert of the University of Houston and Paul W. Beamish of the Ivey School of Business prepared this case solely to provide material for class discussion. The research assistance of Tara Hanna is gratefully acknowledged. The authors do not intend to illustrate either effective or ineffective handling of a managerial situation. The authors may have disguised certain names and other identifying information to protect confidentiality. © 1996 Ivey Management Services Inc. Case 9-96-M001, version 1996-04-08.

EXHIBIT 1   **U.S. Population Demographics and Income Distribution: 1970, 1980, and 1990**

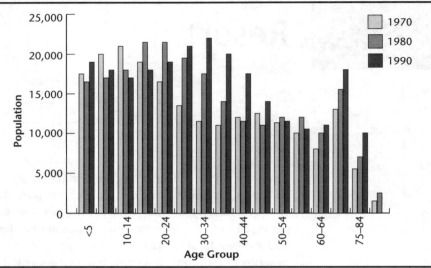

Note: Numbers are in the thousands.
Source: American Almanac, 1994–1995, from U.S. Bureau of Census.

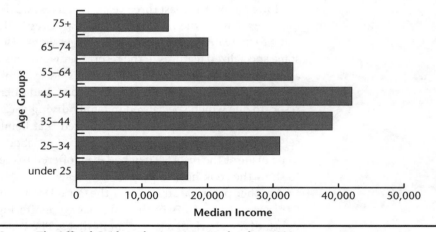

Source: The Official Guide to the American Marketplace, 1992.

might be able to recover if he sold Coral Divers and whether better opportunities existed elsewhere in the Bahamas or around the Caribbean.

Scuba Diving Industry Overview

Skin diving is an underwater activity of ancient origin in which a diver swims freely, unencumbered by lines or air hoses. Modern skin divers use three pieces of basic equipment: a face mask for vision, webbed rubber fins for propulsion, and a snorkel tube for breathing just below the water's surface. The snorkel is a plastic tube shaped like a J and fitted with a mouthpiece. When the opening of the snorkel is above water, a diver will be able to breathe. For diving to greater depths, the breath must be held; otherwise, water will enter the mouth through the snorkel.

Scuba diving provides divers with the gift of time to relax and explore the underwater world without having to surface for their next breath. "Scuba" is an acronym for "self-contained underwater breathing apparatus." While attempts to perfect this type of apparatus date from the early 20th century, it was not until 1943 that the most famous scuba, or Aqualung, was invented by the Frenchmen Jacques-Yves Cousteau and Emil Gagnan. The Aqualung made recreational diving possible for millions of nonprofessional divers. Scuba diving is also called free diving, because the diver has no physical connection with the surface. Although some specially trained commercial scuba divers descend below 100 metres (328 feet) for various kinds of work, recreational divers rarely go below a depth of 40 metres (130 feet) because of increased risk of nitrogen narcosis, a type of intoxication similar to drunkenness, or oxygen toxicity, which causes blackouts or convulsions.

The scuba diver wears a tank that carries a supply of pressurized breathing gas, either air or a mixture of oxygen and other gases. The heart of the breathing apparatus is the breathing regulator and the pressure-reducing mechanisms that deliver gas to the diver on each inhalation. In the common scuba used in recreational diving, the breathing medium is air. As the diver inhales, a slight negative pressure occurs in the mouthpiece, which signals the valve that delivers the air to open. The valve closes when the diver stops inhaling, and a one-way valve allows the exhaled breath to escape as bubbles into the water. When using a tank and regulator, a diver can make longer and deeper dives and still breathe comfortably.

Along with scuba gear and its tanks of compressed breathing gases, the scuba diver's essential equipment includes a soft rubber mask with a large faceplate; a soft rubber diving suit for protection from cold; long, flexible, swimming flippers for the feet; buoyancy compensator device (known as a BC or BCD); weight belt; waterproof watch; wrist compass; and diver's knife. For protection from colder water, neoprene-coated foam rubber wet suits consisting of jacket, pants, hood, and gloves are worn.

Certification Organizations[1]

There are several international and domestic organizations that train and certify scuba divers. PADI (Professional Association of Diving Instructors), NAUI (National Association of Underwater Instructors), SSI (Scuba Schools International), and NASDS (National Association of Scuba Diving Schools) are the most well known of these organizations. Of these, PADI is the largest certifying organization.

PADI (Professional Association of Diving Instructors) is the largest recreational scuba diver training organization in the world. Founded in 1967, PADI has issued more than 5.5 million certifications since it began operation. Since 1985, seven of every ten American divers and an estimated 55 percent of all divers around the

---

[1] Information on certifying agencies drawn from materials published by the various organizations.

world are trained by PADI instructors using PADI's instructional programs. At present PADI certifies well over half-a-million divers internationally each year and has averaged a 12 percent increase in certifications each year since 1985. In 1994, PADI International issued 625,000 certifications, more than in any other single year in company history.

PADI's main headquarters are in Santa Ana, California. Its distribution centre is in the United Kingdom and it has seven local area offices in Australia, Canada, Japan, New Zealand, Norway, Sweden, and Switzerland with professionals and member groups in 175 countries and territories. PADI is made up of four groups: PADI Retail Association, PADI International Resort Association, Professional Members, and PADI Alumni Association. The three association groups emphasize the "three Es" of recreational diving: education, equipment, and experience. By supporting each facet, PADI provides holistic leadership to advance recreational scuba diving and snorkel swimming to equal status with other major leisure activities, while maintaining and improving the excellent safety record PADI has experienced. PADI offers seven levels of instruction and certification ranging from entry-level to instructor.

NAUI (National Association of Underwater Instructors) first began operation in 1960. The organization was formed by a nationally recognized group of instructors that was known as the National Diving Patrol. Since its beginning, NAUI has been active worldwide, certifying sport divers in various levels of proficiency from basic skin diver to instructor. In addition, NAUI regularly conducts specialty courses for cave diving, ice diving, wreck diving, underwater navigation, and search and recovery.

Industry Demographics[2]

Scuba diving has grown steadily in popularity, especially in recent years. For the period 1989–1994, increases in the number of certifications averaged over 10 percent per year. The total number of certified divers worldwide is estimated to be over 10 million. Of these newly certified scuba divers, approximately 65 percent are male and 35 percent are female. Approximately half are married. Approximately 70 percent of them are between the ages of 18 and 34, while about 25 percent are between 35 and 49 (see Exhibit 2). They are generally well educated with 80 percent having a college education. Overwhelmingly, they are employed in professional, managerial, and technical occupations. Their average annual household income is $75,000. Forty-five percent of divers travel most often with their families. Another 40 percent travel with friends or informal groups.

Divers are attracted to diving for various reasons: seeking adventure and being with nature are the most often cited reasons (over 75 percent for each). Socializing, stress relief, and travel also are common motivations. Two-thirds of divers travel overseas on diving trips once every three years, while 60 percent travel domestically on dive trips each year. On average, divers spend $2,816 on dive trips annually, with an average equipment investment of $2,300. Aside from upgrades and replacements, the equipment purchase could be con-

---

[2] This section draws from results of surveys conducted by scuba diving organizations and publications for the years 1991–1993.

EXHIBIT 2   Diver Demographics: Age of Divers

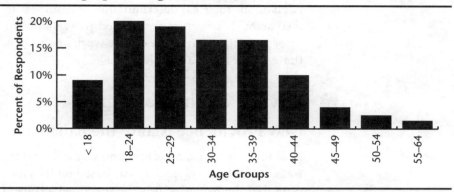

Source: Information taken from the *PADI 1991 Diver Survey Results and Analysis,* preliminary draft.

sidered a one-time cost. Warm-water diving locations are generally chosen 2 to 1 over cold-water diving sites. Cozumel in Mexico, the Cayman Islands, and the Bahamas are the top three diving destinations outside the continental United States for Americans.

According to a consumer survey, the "strongest feelings" that divers associate with their scuba diving experiences are "excitement" and "peacefulness." In a recent survey, the two themes drew an equal number of responses. However, there seem to be very distinct differences in the two responses. One suggests a need for stimulation, while the other suggests relaxation and escape. Visual gratification ("beauty") is another strong motivation for divers. The feelings of "freedom, weightlessness, and flying" were also popular responses.

Under PADI regulations, twelve is the minimum age for certification by the majority of scuba training agencies. At age twelve, the child can earn a Junior Diver certification. The Junior Diver meets the same standards as an Open Water diver but generally must be accompanied on dives by a parent or other certified adult. At age 15, the Junior Diver certification can be upgraded to Open Water status by an instructor. This upgrade may require a skills review and evaluation. Pre-dive waiver and release forms require the signature of a parent or guardian until the minor turns 18.

A cautious approach to young divers is based on the concept of readiness to dive. An individual's readiness to dive is determined by physical, mental, and emotional maturity. Physical readiness is easiest to assess: Is the child large and strong enough to handle scuba equipment? An air tank and weight belt can weigh over 40 pounds (18 kilograms), although most dive shops can provide equipment specially sized for smaller divers. Mental readiness refers to whether the child has the academic background and conceptual development to understand diving physics and perform the arithmetic required for certification. The arithmetic understanding focuses on allowable bottom time, which requires factoring in depth, number of dives, and length of dives. Emotional readiness is the greatest concern. Will the junior diver accept the responsibility of being a dive buddy? Divers never dive alone and dive buddies are supposed to look out for and rely on each other. Do they comprehend the safety rules of diving and willingly follow them? Most dive centres accept students from age twelve, but the final determination of readiness to dive rests with the scuba instructor. Instructors are trained to evaluate the readiness of all students prior to completion of the course work and will only award a certification to those who earn it, regardless of age.

Diving in the Bahamas[3]

New Providence Island, the Bahamas

New Providence Island is best known for its major population centre, Nassau. Nassau's early development was based on its superb natural harbour. As the capital of the Bahamas, it is the seat of government, also home to 400 banks, elegant homes, ancient forts, and a wide variety of duty-free shopping. It has the island's most developed tourist infrastructure with elegant resort hotels, casinos, cabaret shows, and cruise ship docks. More than two-thirds of the population of the Bahamas live on New Providence and most of these 150,000 people live in or near Nassau, on the northeast corner of the island.

With thousands of vacationers taking resort courses (introductory scuba courses taught in resort pools), Nassau has become known as a destination that is as good for an exploratory first dive as it is for more advanced diving. There are many professional dive operations in the Nassau/Paradise Island area (see Exhibit 3). While all offer resort courses, many also offer a full menu of dive activities designed for the more advanced and experienced diver. Within a 30-minute boat ride of most operations are shipwrecks, beautiful shallow reefs, and huge schools of fish.

In contrast to the bustle of Nassau, the south side of New Providence Island is quieter and more laid-back. Large tracts of pine trees and rolling hills dominate the central regions, while miles of white sand beach surround the island. At the west end of the island is Lyford Cay, an exclusive residential area. Nearby, the winding canals of the Coral Harbour area offer easy access to the sea. While golf and tennis are available, the primary attraction is good scuba diving and top-quality dive operators.

The southwest side of the island has been frequently used as an underwater movie/film set. The "Bond wrecks" are popular diving destinations for divers and operators. The Vulcan Bomber used in *Thunderball* has aged into a framework draped with colourful gorgonians and sponges. The freighter *Tears of Allah,* where James Bond eluded the Tiger Shark in *Never Say Never Again,* remains a popular dive attraction in just 40 feet (12 metres) of water. The photogenic appeal of this wreck has improved with age as more and more marine life congregates on this artificial reef.

There are also natural underwater attractions. Shark Wall and Shark Buoy are popular dive spots. Drop-off dives like Tunnel Wall feature a network of

---

[3] Based on information drawn from *The Islands of the Bahamas: 1994 Dive Guide,* published by the Bahamas Ministry of Tourism, Commonwealth of the Bahamas, in conjunction with the Bahama Diving Association.

EXHIBIT 3   **Names and Location of Diving Operators in the Bahamas (based on the Bahamas Diving Association membership)**

Abaco
- Brendal's Dive Shop
- Dive Abaco
- Walker's Cay Undersea Adventures

Andros
- Small Hope Bay Lodge

Bimini
- Bimini Undersea Adventures

Cat Island
- Cat Island Dive Center

Eleuthera/Habour Island
- Romora Bay Club
- Valentine's Dive Center

Exuma
- Exuma Fantasea

Long Island
- Stella Maris Resort

New Providence Island/Nassau
- Bahama Divers
- Coral Divers Resort
- Custom Aquatics
- Dive Dive Dive
- Diver's Haven
- Nassau Scuba Center
- Stuart Cove's Dive South Ocean
- Sun Divers
- Sunskiff Divers

San Salvador
- Riding Rock Inn

Live-Aboard Dive Boats
- Blackbeard's Cruises
- Bottom Time Adventures
- Nekton Diving Cruises
- Out Island Voyages
- Sea Dragon
- Sea Fever Diving Cruises

crevices and tunnels beginning in 30 feet of water and exiting along the vertical wall at 70 or 80 feet. Southwest Reef offers magnificent coral heads in only 15 to 30 feet of water, with schooling grunts, squirrelfish, and barracuda. A favourite of the shallow reef areas is Goulding Cay, where broad stands of Elkhorn coral reach nearly to the surface.

Types of Diving

A wide array of diving activities are available in the Bahamas. These include shark dives, wreck dives, wall dives, reef dives, drift dives, night dives, and so forth. Illustrative examples follow.

Shark Diving

The top three operators of shark dives in the Caribbean are in the Bahamas. While shark diving trips vary with the operators running them, there is at least one common factor in the Bahamas: the Caribbean Reef Shark (*Carcharhinus perezi*). When the dive boat reaches the site, the sound of the motor acts as a dinner bell. Even before the divers are in the water, the sharks gather for their handouts.

Long Island in the Bahamas was the first area to promote shark feed dives on a regular basis. This method began 20 years ago and has remained relatively unchanged. The feed is conducted as a feeding frenzy. Sharks circle as divers enter the water. After the divers position themselves with their backs to a coral wall, the feeder enters the water with a bucket of fish. This is placed in the sand in front of the divers and the action develops quickly. At Walker's Cay, in

Abaco, the method is similar except for the number and variety of sharks in the feed. While Caribbean Reef Sharks make up the majority, Lemon Sharks, Bull Sharks, Hammerhead Sharks, and other species also appear.

The shark feed off Freeport, Grand Bahama, is a very organized event in which the sharks are fed either by hand or off the point of a polespear. The divers are arranged in a semicircle with safety divers guarding the viewers as the feeder is positioned at the middle of the group. If the sharks become unruly, the food is withheld until they calm down. The sharks then go into a regular routine of circling, taking their place in line and advancing to receive the food. Although the sharks come within touching distance, most divers resist the temptation to reach out.

Shark Wall, on the southwest side of New Providence, is a pristine dropoff decorated with masses of colourful sponges along the deep-water abyss known as the Tongue of the Ocean. Divers position themselves along sand patches among the coral heads in about 50 feet of water as Caribbean Reef Sharks and an occasional Bull or Lemon Shark cruise mid-water in anticipation of a free handout. During the feeding period, the bait is controlled and fed from a polespear by an experienced feeder. There are usually six to twelve sharks present, ranging from four to eight feet in length. Some operators make two dives to this site, allowing divers to cruise the wall with the sharks in a more natural way before the feeding dive.

The Shark Buoy, also on the southwest side of New Providence, is tethered in 6,000 feet of water. Its floating surface mass attracts a wide variety of ocean marine life such as dolphin fish, Jacks, Rainbow Runners, and Silky Sharks. The Silky Sharks are typically small, three to five feet long, but swarm in schools of 6 to 20, with the sharks swimming up to the divemasters' hands to grab the bait.

From the operator's standpoint, the only special equipment needed for shark dives is a chain mail diving suit for the feeder's protection, some type of feeding apparatus, and intestinal fortitude. The thrill of diving among sharks is the main attraction for the divers. For the most part, the dives are safe, with only the feeder taking an occasional nick from an excited shark.

Divers participating in shark dives were required to sign waivers prior to the actual dive. As the fine print in most life insurance policies noted, claims for any scuba-related accidents were not payable. However, there did exist specialty insurers such as Divers Alert Network.

Wreck Diving

Wreck diving is divided into three levels: non-penetration, limited penetration, and full penetration. Full penetration and deep wreck diving should be done only by divers who have completed rigorous training and have extensive diving experience. Non-penetration wreck diving refers to recreational diving on wrecks without entering an overhead environment that prevents direct access to the surface. Divers with open-water certification are qualified for this type of diving without further training as long as they are comfortable with the diving conditions and the wreck's depth. Limited penetration wreck diving is defined as staying within ambient light and always in sight of an exit.

Full penetration wreck diving involves an overhead environment away from ambient light and beyond sight of an exit. Safely and extensively exploring the insides of a wreck involves formal training and mental strength. On this type of dive, the first mistake could be the last.

Wall Diving

In a few regions of the world, island chains, formed by volcanos and coral, have been altered by movements of the earth's crustal plates. Extending approximately due east-west across the central Caribbean Sea is the boundary between the North American and Caribbean crustal plates. The shifting of these plates has created some of the most spectacular diving environments in the world, characterized by enormous cliffs, 2,000 to 6,000 feet high. At the cliffs, known as walls, the diver experiences the overwhelming scale and dynamic forces that shape the ocean more than in any other underwater environment. It is on the walls that a diver is most likely to experience the feeling of free motion, or flying, in boundless space. Many of the dives in the Bahamas are wall dives.

Reef Diving

Reefs generally are made up of three areas: a reef flat, a lagoon or bay, and a reef crest. The depth in the reef flat averages only a few feet with an occasional deeper channel. The underwater life on a shallow reef flat may vary greatly in abundance and diversity within a short distance. The reef flat is generally a protected area, not exposed to strong winds or waves, making it ideal for novice or family snorkellers. The main feature distinguishing bay and lagoon environments from a reef flat is depth. Caribbean lagoons and bays may reach depths of 60 feet but many provide teeming underwater ecosystems in as little as 15–20 feet. This is excellent for underwater photography and ideal for families or no-decompression-stop diving. The reef's crest is the outer boundary that shelters the bay and flats from the full force of the ocean's waves. Since the surging and pounding of the waves is too strong for all but the most advanced divers, most diving takes place in the protected bay waters.

▮ Family Diving Resorts

The current average age of new divers is 36. As the median age of new divers increased, families became a rapidly growing segment of the vacation travel industry. Many parents are busy and do not spend as much time with their children as they would prefer. Many parents who dive would like to have a vacation that would combine diving and spending time with their children. In response to increasing numbers of parents travelling with children, resort operators have added amenities ranging from babysitting services and kids' camps to dedicated family resorts with special facilities and rates. The resort options available have greatly expanded in recent years. At all-inclusive self-contained resorts, one price includes everything: meals, accommodations, daytime and evening activities, and water sports. Many of these facilities offer special activities and facilities for children. Diving is included or available nearby.

For many divers, the important part of the trip is the quality of the diving, not the quality of the accommodations. But for divers with families, the equation changes. Children, especially younger children, may find it difficult to do without a comfortable bed, television, or VCR, no matter how good the diving promises to be. Some resorts, while not dedicated to family vacations, do make accommodations for divers with children. Condos and villas are an economical and convenient vacation option for divers with children. The additional space of this type of accommodation allows parents to bring along a babysitter. Having a kitchen on hand makes the task of feeding children simple and economical. Most diving destinations in the Bahamas, Caribbean, and Pacific offer condo, villa, and hotel-type accommodations. Some hotels organize entertaining and educational activities for children while parents engage in their own activities.

As the number of families vacationing together has increased, some resorts and dive operators have started special promotions and programs. On Bonaire, part of the Netherlands Antilles, August has been designated Family Month. During this month, the island is devoted to families, with a special welcome kit for children and island-wide activities including "eco-walks" at a flamingo reserve, snorkelling lessons, and evening entertainment for all ages. In conjunction, individual resorts and restaurants offer family packages and discounts. Similarly, in Honduras, which has very good diving, a resort started a children's dolphin camp during summer months. While diving family members are out exploring the reefs, children between ages 8 and 14 spend their days learning about and interacting with a resident dolphin population. The program includes classroom and in-water time as well as horseback riding and paddle boating.

One travel company, Rascals in Paradise (1-800-U-RASCAL), specializes in family travel packages. The founders, Theresa Detchemendy and Deborah Baratta, are divers, mothers, and travel agents who have developed innovative packages for diving families. Theresa says, "The biggest concern for parents is their children's safety, and then what the kids will do while they're diving or enjoying an evening on the town." The Rascals people have worked with a number of family-run resorts all over the world to provide daily activities, responsible local nannies, and child-safe facilities with safe balconies, playgrounds, and children's pools.

They have also organized Family Weeks at popular dive destinations in Belize, Mexico, and the Cayman Islands. Family Week packages account for over 50 percent of Rascals' bookings each year. On these scheduled trips, groups of three to six families share a teacher/escort who brings along a fun program tailored for children and serves as activities director for the group. Rascals Special Family Weeks packages are priced on the basis of a family of four (two adults and two children, age 2–11) and include a teacher/escort, one babysitter for each family, children's activities, meals, airport transfers, taxes, services, and cancellation insurance (see Exhibit 4). For example, in 1995, a seven-night family vacation at Hotel Club Akumal, on the Yucatan coast, was US$2,080–$3,100 per family.[4] Rascals also packages independent family trips to

---

[4] Lunch and airport transfer not included. Prices reflect seasonal fluctuations and are subject to change. Airfares not included.

EXHIBIT 4   **Rascals in Paradise Pricing Guide: Rascals Special Family Weeks**

Destination	Duration	Price	Notes
Bahamas			
South Ocean Beach	7 nights	$3,120–$3,970	Lunch not included
Small Hope Bay	7 nights	$3,504	Scuba diving included; local host only
Mexico			
Hotel Buena Vista	7 nights	$2,150–$2,470	
Hotel Club Akumal	7 nights	$2,080–$3,100	Lunch and airport transfer not included

Prices are based on a family of four with two adults and two children aged 2–11. All packages include the following (except as noted): accommodations, Rascals escort, meals, babysitter, children's activities, airport transfers, taxes and services, and a $2,500 cancellation insurance per family booking. Airfares not included.

57 different condos, villas, resorts, or hotels which offer scuba diving. An independent family trip would not include a teacher/escort (see Exhibit 5). A seven-night independent family trip to Hotel Club Akumal ran US$624–$1,779.[5]

Rascals' approach is unique in the travel industry because they personally select the resorts with which they work. "We try to work with small properties so our groups are pampered and looked after," says Detchemendy. "The owners are often parents and their kids are sometimes on the property. They

[5] Based on a family of four with two adults and two children age 2–11. Rates are to be used as a guide only. Each booking is quoted separately and will be dependent on season, type of accommodation, ages and number of children, meal and activity inclusions. All prices are subject to change. Some variations apply. Airfares not included.

EXHIBIT 5   **Rascals in Paradise Pricing Guide: Independent Family Trips**

Destination	Duration	Price	Notes
Bahamas			
South Ocean Beach	7 nights	$1,355–$1,771	
Small Hope Bay	7 nights	$2,860–$3,560	All meals, bar service, babysitter, and diving included
Hope Town Harbour Lodge	7 nights	$ 962–$1,121	
Treasure Cay	7 nights	$ 875–$1,750	
Stella Maris, Long Island	7 nights	$1,547–$2,597	
Mexico			
Hotel Buena Vista	7 nights	$1,232–$1,548	All meals included
Hotel Club Akumal	7 nights	$ 624–$1,779	
Hotel Presidente	7 nights	$1,120–$1,656	
La Concha	7 nights	$ 655–$ 963	
Plaza Las Glorias	7 nights	$ 632–$1,017	

Prices are based on a family of four with two adults and two children aged 2–11. Rates are per week (seven nights) and include accommodations and applicable taxes. These rates are to be used as a guide only. Each booking is quoted separately and will be dependent on season, type of accommodation, ages and number of children, and meal and activity inclusions. All prices are subject to change. Some variations apply. Airfares not included.

understand the characteristics of kids." Typically, Detchemendy and Baratta visit each destination, often working with the government tourist board in identifying potential properties. If the physical structure is already in place, it is easy to add the resort to the Rascals booking list. If modifications are needed, the two sit down with the management and outline what needs to be in place so that the resort can be part of the Rascals program.

Rascals evaluates resorts according to several factors: (1) Is the property friendly toward children and does it want them? (2) How does the property rate in terms of safety? (3) What are the facilities and is there a separate room to be used as a Rascals Room? (4) Does the property provide babysitting and child care by individuals who are screened and locally known? A successful example of this approach is Hotel Club Akumal, in Akumal, Mexico. Detchemendy and Baratta helped the resort expand its market reach by building a family-oriented resort that became part of the Rascals program. Baratta explained, "In that case, we were looking for a place close to home, with a multi-level range of accommodations, that offered something other than a beach, that was family-friendly, and not in Cancun. We found Hotel Club Akumal, but they didn't have many elements in place, so we had to work with them. We established a meal plan, an all-inclusive product and designated activities for kids. We went into the kitchen and created a children's menu and we asked them to install a little kids' playground that's shaded." The resort became one of their most popular family destinations.

Rascals offered two types of services to resort operators interested in creating family vacations. One was a consulting service. For a modest daily fee plus expenses, Baratta or Detchemendy, or both, would conduct an on-site assessment of the resort. This usually took one or two days. They would provide a written report to the resort regarding needed additions or modifications to the resort to make it safe and attractive for family vacations. Possible physical changes might include the addition of a Rascals room, child-safe play equipment, and modifications to existing buildings and structures, such as rooms, railings, and docks, to prevent child injuries. Rascals always tried to use existing equipment or equipment available nearby. Other non-structural changes could include the addition of educational sessions, playtimes, and other structured times for entertaining children while their parents were diving. The report also included an implementation proposal. Then after implementation, the resort could decide whether or not to list with the Rascals for bookings.

Under the second option, Rascals provided the consulting service at no charge to the resort. However, they asked that any requests for family bookings be referred back to Rascals. Rascals would then also list and actively promote the resort through its brochures and referrals. For resorts using the Rascals booking option, Rascals would provide premiums such as hats and T-shirts, in addition to the escorted activities. This attention to the family was what differentiated a Rascals resort from other resorts. Generally, companies who promote packages receive net rates from the resorts which are from 20 percent to 50 percent lower than "rack" rates. Rascals, in turn, promoted these special packages to the travel industry in general and paid a portion of their earnings out in commissions to other travel agencies.

Rascals tried to work with its resorts to provide packaged and prepaid vacations. This approach created a win-win situation for the resort managers and the vacationer. Packages or an all-inclusive vacation was a cruise ship approach. It allowed the inclusion of many activities in the package. For example, such a package might include seven nights' lodging, all meals, babysitting, children's activities, and scuba diving. This approach allowed the vacationer to know, up front, what to expect. Moreover, the cost would be included in one set price, so that the family would not have to pay for each activity as it came along. The idea was to remove the surprises and make the stay enjoyable. It also allowed the resort operator to bundle activities together, providing more options than might otherwise be offered. As a result, the package approach was becoming popular with both resort owners and vacationers.

In its bookings, Rascals required prepayment of trips. This resulted in higher revenues for the resort since all activities were paid for in advance. Ordinarily, resorts on their own might only require a two- or three-night room deposit. Then, the family would pay for the rest of the room charge on leaving, after paying for other activities or services as they were used. While the vacationer might think they had a less expensive trip this way, in fact, prepaid activities were generally cheaper than à la carte activities. Moreover, they potentially yielded lower revenues for the resort. Rascals promoted prepaid vacations as a win-win, low-stress approach to travel. Rascals had been very successful with the resorts it listed. Fifty percent of their bookings were repeat business, and many inquiries were based on word-of-mouth referrals. All in all, Rascals provided a link to the family vacation market segment that the resort might not otherwise have. It was common for Rascals-listed resorts to average annual bookings of 90 percent.

Coral Divers Resort

Coral Divers Resort had been in operation ten years. Annual revenues had reached as high as $554,000. Profits generally had been in the 2 percent range, but for the past two years, losses had been experienced. The expected turn-around in profits in 1994 had never materialized (see Exhibit 6). While not making them rich, the business had provided an adequate income for Greywell and his wife, Margaret, and their two children, Allen, age 7, and Winifred, age 5. However, revenues had continued to decline. From talking with other operators, Greywell understood that resorts with strong identities and reputations for quality service were doing well. Greywell thought that the Coral Divers Resort had not distinguished itself in any particular aspect of diving or as a resort.

The Coral Divers Resort property was located on a deep-water channel on the southwest coast of the island of New Providence in the Bahamas. The property occupied 3 acres (1.2 hectares) and had beach access. There were six cottages on the property, each having a kitchenette, a full bath, a bedroom with two full-size beds, and a living room with two sleeper sofas. Four of the units had been renovated with new paint, tile floors, microwave, colour TV, and VCR. The two other units ranged from "adequate" to "comfortable." Greywell tried to use the renovated units primarily for families and couples, while putting

EXHIBIT 6

COMPARATIVE BALANCE SHEETS
As at June 30 (US$)

	1994	1993	1992
Assets			
Current assets:			
Cash	5,362	8,943	15,592
Accounts receivable	2,160	8,660	2,026
Inventories	5,519	6,861	9,013
Prepaid expenses	9,065	8,723	8,195
Total current assets	22,106	33,187	34,826
Fixed assets:			
Land	300,000	300,000	300,000
Building	200,000	200,000	200,000
Less: Accumulated depreciation	(70,000)	(60,000)	(50,000)
Boats	225,000	225,000	225,000
Less: Accumulated depreciation	(157,500)	(135,000)	(112,500)
Vehicles	54,000	54,000	54,000
Less: Accumulated depreciation	(32,400)	(21,600)	(10,800)
Diving equipment	150,000	150,000	150,000
Less: Accumulated depreciation	(90,000)	(60,000)	(30,000)
Total fixed assets	579,100	652,400	725,700
TOTAL ASSETS	601,206	685,587	760,526
Liabilities			
Current liabilities:			
Accounts payable	1,689	4,724	1,504
Bank loan	20,000	0	2,263
Mortgage payable, current portion	25,892	25,892	25,892
Note payable, current portion	40,895	40,895	40,895
Total current liabilities	88,476	71,511	70,554
Long-term liabilities:			
Mortgage payable, due in 1996	391,710	417,602	443,494
Note payable, five-year	81,315	122,210	163,105
Total long-term liabilities	473,025	539,812	606,599
TOTAL LIABILITIES	561,501	611,323	677,153
Shareholders' Equity			
Jonathon Greywell, capital	44,879	44,879	44,879
Retained earnings	(5,174)	29,385	38,494
Total shareholders' equity	39,705	74,264	83,373
TOTAL LIABILITIES AND SHAREHOLDERS' EQUITY	601,206	685,587	760,526
Revenues:			
Diving and lodging packages	482,160	507,670	529,820
Day diving	11,680	12,360	14,980
Certifications	5,165	5,740	7,120
Lodging	2,380	1,600	1,200
Miscellaneous	1,523	1,645	1,237
Total revenues	502,908	529,015	554,357

EXHIBIT 6   *continued*

Expenses:	1994	1993	1992
Advertising and promotion	15,708	15,240	13,648
Bank charges	1,326	1,015	975
Boat maintenance and fuel	29,565	31,024	29,234
Cost of goods sold	762	823	619
Depreciation	73,300	73,300	73,300
Dues and fees	3,746	4,024	3,849
Duties and taxes	11,405	18,352	17,231
Insurance	36,260	34,890	32,780
Interest, mortgage, note, and loan	40,544	40,797	41,174
Management salary	31,600	31,600	31,600
Office supplies	12,275	12,753	11,981
Professional fees	11,427	10,894	10,423
Repairs and maintenance, building	15,876	12,379	9,487
Salaries, wages, and benefits	196,386	194,458	191,624
Telephone and fax	9,926	9,846	7,689
Trade shows	14,523	14,679	14,230
Utilities	20,085	19,986	17,970
Vehicles, maintenance and fuel	12,753	12,064	11,567
Total expenses	537,467	538,124	519,381
Net income	(34,559)	(9,109)	34,976
Retained earnings, beginning	29,385	38,494	3,518
Retained earnings, ending	(5,174)	29,385	38,494

Note: Bahama$1 = US$1.

groups of single divers in the other units. Also on the property was a six-unit attached motel-type structure (see Exhibit 7 for prices). Each of these units had two full-size beds, a pullout sofa, sink, refrigerator, microwave, and TV. The resort had the space and facilities on the property for a kitchen and dining room, but it had not been used. However, there was a small family-run restaurant and bar within walking distance.

Greywell had three boats, which could carry from eight to twenty passengers each. Two were 40-foot fibreglass V-hull boats powered by a single diesel

EXHIBIT 7   **Coral Divers Resort Pricing Guide: Family Dive Vacations**

Destination	Duration	Price	Notes
Bahamas			
Coral Divers Resort	7 nights	$1,355–$1,455	Standard accommodations, continental breakfast, and daily two-tank dive included
Coral Divers Resort	7 nights	$1,800–$1,950	Deluxe accommodations, continental breakfast, and daily two-tank dive included

Prices are based on a family of four with two adults and two children aged 2–11. Rates are per week (seven nights) and include accommodations and applicable taxes. Rates will be dependent on season, type of accommodation, and ages and number of children. All prices are subject to change. Airfares not included. Prices dropped to $600–$700 per week for the standard package and $800–$900 for deluxe accommodation if diving was excluded.

inboard with a cruising speed of 18 knots and protective cabin, with dry storage space. The third was a 35-foot covered platform boat. Greywell also had facilities for air dispensing, equipment repair, rental and sale, and tank storage.

Coral Divers Resort, affiliated with PADI and NAUI, had a staff of eleven, which included four scuba diving instructors. Greywell, who worked full-time at the resort, was a certified diving instructor by both PADI and NAUI. The three other diving instructors had various backgrounds. One was a former U.S. Navy SEAL working for Coral Divers as a way to gain resort experience. Another was a local Bahamian whom Greywell had known for many years. The third was a Canadian who had come to the Bahamas on a winter holiday and never left. There were two boat captains and two mates. Given the size of the operation, the staff was scheduled to provide overall coverage, with all of the staff rarely working at the same time. In addition, there was a housekeeper, a groundskeeper, and a person who minded the office and store. Greywell's wife, Margaret, worked at the business on a part-time basis, taking care of administrative activities such as accounting and payroll. The rest of her time was spent looking after their two children and their home.

A typical diving day at Coral Divers for Greywell began around 7:30 a.m. He would open the office and review the activities list for the day. If there were any divers that needed to be picked up at the resorts in Nassau or elsewhere on the island, the van driver would need to leave by 7:30 a.m. to be back for the 9 a.m. departure. Most resort guests began to gather around the office and dock about 8:30. By 8:45, the day's captain and mate began loading the diving gear for the passengers.

The boat left at 9 a.m. Morning dives were usually "two-tank dives," that is, two dives utilizing one tank of air each. The trip to the first dive site took about 20–30 minutes. Once there, the captain would explain the dive, the special attractions of the dive, and tell everyone when they were expected back on board. Most dives lasted 30–45 minutes, depending on depth. The deeper the dive, the faster the air consumption. A divemaster always accompanied the divers on the trip down. The divemaster's role was generally to supervise the dive. The divemaster was responsible for the safety and conduct of the divers while under water.

Once back on board, the boat would move to the next site. Greywell tried to plan dives that had sites near each other. For example, the first dive might be a wall dive in 60 feet of water, while the second would be a nearby wreck 40 feet down. The second would also last about 40 minutes. If things went well, the boat would be back at the resort by noon. This allowed for lunch and sufficient surface time for divers who might be going back out in the afternoon. Two morning dives were part of the resort package. Whether the boat went out in the afternoon depended on whether enough non-resort guest divers had contracted for afternoon dives. If they had, Greywell was happy to let resort guests ride and dive along free of charge. If there were not enough outside paying divers, there were no afternoon dive trips and the guests were on their own to swim at the beach, go sightseeing, or just relax. When space was available it was possible for non-divers (either snorkellers or bubble-watchers) to join the boat trip for a fee of $15–$25.

EXHIBIT 8 A Canadian Vacation Comparison: Diving in Nassau Versus Skiing in Whistler/Banff

NASSAU—SEVEN NIGHTS*

	January 5–11 (CAN$)			February 16–22 (CAN$)		
	Dbl/Person	Child	Family (3)	Dbl/Person	Child	Family (3)
Average cost for 12 packages	1,201	711	3,113	1,429	723	3,582
Range	$919–$1,377	$667–$737	$2,575–$3,461	$1,217–$1,687	$707–$737	$3,157–$4,081

*Includes quotes for select hotels only.
*Includes transportation and accommodation (some taxes may be additional) and estimated cost for five two-tank dives (CAN$337.50).

SKI VACATION—SEVEN NIGHTS*

	January 5–11 (CAN$)			February 16–22 (CAN$)		
	Dbl/Person	Child	Family (3)	Dbl/Person	Child	Family (3)
Average for 20 packages	1,161	566	2,888	1,270	567	3,107
Range	$757–$1,645	$454–$1,166	$2,087–$3,845	$824–$1,739	$454–$1,172	$2,221–$4,031

*Includes quotes for select hotels only.
*Includes transportation, accommodation, and lift passes. Some taxes may be additional.
*Air Canada Vacations includes four lift passes/person. Canadian holidays includes five lift passes/person.
*Does not include airfare.

EXHIBIT 9 A U.S. Vacation Comparison: Diving in the Caymans/Cozumel Versus Skiing in Vail/Breckenridge/Winter Park

SEVEN NIGHTS*

	January 5–11 (US$)			April 16–22 (US$)		
	Dbl/Person	Child	Family (3)	Dbl/Person	Child	Family (3)
Cayman Islands						
7 Mile Beach Resort	1,099	Free	1,998	949	Free	1,698
Seaview Hotel	899	Free	1,628	799	Free	1,428
Hyatt Regency	1,499	Free	2,856	1,299	Free	2,198
Radisson	1,299	Free	2,398	1,149	Free	1,998
Cozumel						
Casa del Mar	899	Free	1,648	799	Free	1,248
Suites Colonia	799	Free	1,538	719	Free	1,278
Average cost	933	Free	2,011	952	Free	1,641

*Includes quotes for select hotels only.

SKI VACATION—SEVEN NIGHTS*

	January 5–11 (US$)			February 16–22 (US$)		
	1 to a Room	2 to a Room	3 to a Room	1 to a Room	2 to a Room	3 to a Room
Average for 18 packages	945	678	659	1,250	880	821
Range	420–2,766	298–1,489	391–1,215	830–1,935	533–1,304	492–1,304

*Includes quotes for select hotels only.
*Includes lodging and lift passes. Some taxes may be additional.
*Mountain vacations include rental cars.
*Does not include airfare.

Greywell's Options

Greywell's bookings ran 90 percent of capacity during the high season (December through May) and 50 percent during the low season (June through November). Ideally, he wanted to increase the number of bookings for the resort and dive businesses during both seasons. Adding additional diving attractions could increase both resort and dive revenues. Focusing on family vacations could increase revenues since families would probably increase the number of paying guests per room. Breakeven costs were calculated on the basis of two adults sharing a room. Children provided an additional revenue source since the cost of the room had been covered by the adults and children under 12 incurred no diving-related costs. However, either strategy, adding adventure diving to his current general offerings or adjusting the focus of the resort to encourage family diving vacations, would require some changes and cost money. The question became whether the changes would increase revenue enough to justify the costs and effort involved.

Emphasizing family diving vacations would probably require some changes to the physical property of the resort. Four of the cottages had already been renovated. The other two also would need to be upgraded. This would run $10,000 to $20,000 each, depending on the amenities added. The Bahamas had duties up to 50 percent which caused renovation costs involving imported goods to be expensive. The attached motel-type units also would need to be refurbished at some point. He had the space and facilities for a kitchen and dining area, but had not done anything with it. The Rascals in Paradise people had offered to help set up a children's menu. He could hire a chef or cook and do it himself or offer the concession to the nearby restaurant or someone else. He would also need to build a play structure for children. There was an open area with shade trees between the office and the cottages that would be ideal for a play area. Rascals would provide the teacher/escort for the family vacation groups. It would be fairly easy to find babysitters for the children as needed. The people, particularly on this part of the island, were very family-oriented and would welcome the opportunity for additional income. In asking around, it seemed that $5 per hour was the going rate for a sitter. Toys and other play items could be added gradually. The Rascals people had said that, once the program was in place, he could expect bookings to run 90 percent capacity annually from new and return bookings. While the package prices were competitive, the attraction was in group bookings and the prospect of a returning client base.

Adding adventure diving would be a relatively easy thing to do. Shark Wall and Shark Buoy were less than an hour away by boat. Both of these sites offered sharks that were already accustomed to being fed. The cost of shark food would be $10 per dive. None of Greywell's current staff were particularly excited about the prospect of adding shark feeding to their job description. But these staff could be relatively easily replaced. Greywell could probably find an experienced divemaster who would be willing to lead the shark dives. He would also have to purchase a special chain mail suit for the feeder at a cost of about $10,000. While there were few accidents during the feeds, Greywell would rather be safe than sorry. His current boats, especially the 40-footers, would be adequate for transporting divers to the sites. The other shark dive operators might not be happy about having him at the sites, but there was little they could do about it. Shark divers were charged a premium fee. For example, a shark dive would cost $100 for a two-tank dive, compared to $25–$75 for a normal two-tank dive. He figured that he could add shark dives to the schedule on Wednesdays and Saturdays without taking away from regular business. He needed a minimum of four divers on a trip at regular rates to cover the cost of taking out the boat. Ten or twelve divers was ideal. Greywell could usually count on at least eight divers for a normal dive, but he did not know how much additional new and return business he could expect from shark diving.

A third option was for Greywell to try to improve his current operations and not add any new diving attractions. This would require him to be much more cost-efficient in his operations. Actions such as strictly adhering to the minimum required number of divers per boat policy, along with staff reductions might improve the bottom line by 5–10 percent. He would need to be very attentive to materials ordering, fuel costs, and worker productivity in order to realize any gains with this approach. However, he was concerned that by continuing as he had, Coral Divers Resort would not be distinguished as unique from other resorts in the Bahamas. He did not know what would be the long-term implications of this approach.

As Greywell reached the office, he turned to watch the sun sink into the ocean. Although it was a view he had come to love, a lingering thought was that perhaps it was time to relocate to a less crowded location.

Corel's Acquisition of WordPerfect (A)

Introduction

"To buy or not to buy" was the question confronting Dr. Michael Cowpland, founder, chairman, president, and CEO of Corel Corporation early in 1996. Corel had contemplated buying WordPerfect a month ago. A Corel team had reviewed the program code and technical operations, but negotiations had fallen apart when Novell's investment bankers demanded a high price—well in excess of US$200 million cash. At this point Cowpland had scuttled the deal. Then ten days ago, Novell phoned Cowpland urging him to take a second look. Novell's negotiating position had changed. WordPerfect's market share had declined sharply since their announced selloff and corporate customers, in particular, had become wary because of the uncertainty surrounding the company and product. Furthermore, many of the potential buyers did not meet Novell's criteria of continuing to operate WordPerfect as an operation in Utah. These issues constrained the price Novell was going to get for WordPerfect.

WordPerfect

During the 1980s, WordPerfect had developed into the world's foremost supplier of word processing software, and by the 1990s, it had become the world's fourth-largest software company. Then in the early 1990s sales began to stagnate as management was having trouble transitioning from a small, family-controlled firm to a large, professionally managed firm. More specifically, costs were too high and there was a general lack of product and strategic planning.

In 1994, Novell Corporation, a network operating software company, bought WordPerfect for $1.4 billion.[1] Novell thought they could turn around the company using their depth of professional management staff and combining

---

G. Meredith, Professor C. P. Woodcock, and Professor D. Large prepared this case solely to provide material for class discussion. This case is not intended to illustrate either effective or ineffective handling of a managerial situation. Certain names, information, and facts may have been altered to protect confidentiality. Any reproduction, in any form, of the material in this case is prohibited unless permission is obtained from the copyright holder. © 1997 C. Patrick Woodcock.

[1] About two times its 1993 revenues of $700 million.

synergies of the two companies. From a technical and market perspective, WordPerfect had many strengths. It had a large installed base of 20 million users, and until recently was the undisputed leader of the word processing application market. It was particularly strong in some institutional markets such as the legal and government segments, as well as the standalone word processor market segment.

To complement the WordPerfect deal, Novell acquired Borland's spreadsheet business for $145 million, and incorporated this into the applications division. This provided WordPerfect with a suite of software products that could compete directly with Microsoft and Lotus, in the fast-growing "desktop suite" market segment.

Over the next year, Novell made numerous changes, but WordPerfect continued to have problems. Product development release dates were being missed badly, costs were too high, and the technical and marketing synergies had not materialized. In fact, WordPerfect's businesses fit poorly into Novell's. Novell's business focused on high-margin products which were marketed to MIS specialists, while WordPerfect sold a relatively low-margin, high-volume product through many distribution channels. Thus, when Novell disbanded WordPerfect's marketing and sales department, they discovered that their sales personnel did not want or know how to sell lower-margin desktop applications. Furthermore, much shorter product development cycle times were required in the desktop application business. Because of this, WordPerfect had developed an informal entrepreneurial decision making culture that emphasized quick decisions, but Novell's was quite formal and hierarchical. This diversity created immediate and deep cultural clashes, and WordPerfect managers were continually frustrated with Novell's slow decision making. Clearly, Novell had overestimated the unifying bond of Mormonism and the two companies' shared Utah location.

These problems led to numerous planning and execution mistakes. A critical mistake during this period was WordPerfect's late introduction of a Windows 95 version (it was over a year late). With all these difficulties, combined with the uncertainty surrounding the announced selloff, their sales were estimated to have dropped to $200 million annually by early 1996. In October 1995, Novell announced they intended to sell WordPerfect.

The Desktop Word Processing and Suites Software Market

Ownership of WordPerfect meant participation in a word processing and integrated suite application[2] market worth in excess of $5 billion. Table 1 estimates the market shares for the various companies and segments. The big growth markets were in the Windows 95 and suite markets. In particular, customers were attracted to suite software because of its integrated capabilities and its cheaper price relative to multiple software purchases.[3]

---

[2] Suite application software was a bundled product that included not only word processing, but also spreadsheet, presentation, and possibly other software products.

[3] Generally these products included word processing, presentation, database, and spreadsheet software.

TABLE I   Worldwide Word Processing Revenue and Market Share

	1994		1995	
	Revenue (US$m)	Segment Share	Revenue (US$m)	Segment Share
DOS-based				
Microsoft	$ 59	12%	$ 59	15%
Novell/WP	394	81	336	85
Other	34	7	NA	NA
TOTAL (DOS-based)	$487	100%	$395	100%
Windows 3.x				
Microsoft	$ 977.7	68.8%	$ 960.5	73.6%
Novell/WP	340	23.9	250	19.2
IBM/Lotus	100	7	90.8	7
TOTAL (Windows)	$1,420	100%	$1,304	100%
Windows 95				
Microsoft	NA	NA	$379.5	99.4%
Novel/WP	NA	NA	NA	NA
IBM/Lotus	NA	NA	2.2	0.6
TOTAL (Windows 95)	NA	NA	$381	100%
Suites				
Microsoft	$1,600	83%	$2,652	88.5%
Novel/WP	50	3	110	4
IBM/Lotus	275	14	235	7.5
TOTAL (suites)	$1,925	100%	$2,997	100%
TOTAL MARKET	$3,885	100%	$5,177	100%

Note: NA=not available.

The word processing market could be divided into two market segments based on end user needs: the corporate and the personal/small business (PSB) segment. The corporate segment was an estimated 75 percent of the total market for word processing and suite software (on a unit basis). This market relied heavily on licensing which provided buyers with multiple copies at lower unit cost. Software companies now were using professional sales teams to sell to this segment. These teams would put together customized packages and licences involving prices, services (i.e., training and tech support), and possibly other, complementary software products. Generally, corporate buyers looked for software with stability, reputation, compatibility, and lower overall costs. Recent studies had shown that the software and hardware acquisition costs for a PC averaged $1,000 annually, but operation costs[4] were in excess of $7,000 annually. Thus, operating costs were an important consideration, and changing word processing software would increase costs dramatically in the short term because secretaries would become less efficient, and demand for technical support would increase dramatically. For this reason, corporations had to be offered a compelling reason to change software, and sellers had to work with buyers very closely during this decision making process.

[4] This includes training, support, programming, and technical assistance for hardware and software.

Customers in the PSB market segment usually bought software from the local software store, or directly from the software maker. Buying decisions were based on prior experience, advertising, product features, product reviews, and price. And although this market was differentiated from the corporate market, compatibility with the corporate market was important for many PSBers because many of them wanted to have software compatible to that which their corporation had purchased, or, in the case of small businesses, wanted compatibility with companies they interfaced with.

In general, these two segments are supplied product through several distribution channels that tend to have very different characteristics, some of which are more fully described in Table 2.

Competition

Three companies competed in this software market. Microsoft dominated the word processing applications market, capturing nearly 78 percent of the market worldwide in 1995, up from 68 percent the year before. WordPerfect remained the second-largest in terms of market share, but probably had an installed base very close to that of Microsoft.[5] IBM, through its Lotus products, was a distant third. (See Table 1.)

IBM's competitive advantage was its size, its strength in the corporate sector, and the breadth and scope of its products and services.[6] IBM's most recent product entry in this market was Lotus' word processor and desktop

---

[5] "Installed base" represents the number of users that have purchased a product historically and have it installed on their computers.

[6] IBM was the largest computer software and hardware company in the world, but Microsoft was catching IBM in size. Its capitalization was expected to surpass IBM's in the next several years.

TABLE 2   Major Distribution Modes for Software

Mode	Description of Mode	Characteristics
OEM (original equipment manufacturer)	• Sell to PC makers to that they can preinstall software on the PC.	• Large volumes, but margins are nil. • OEMs buy on basis of ability to sell hardware. They generally don't want too many variations of a software category. • Only widely used software is preinstalled.
Direct licence	• Licences are sold directly to institutions or companies for multiple-site usage.	• Mostly sold to corporate users. • Margins small, but volumes can be high if the software is widely used in organizations.
Direct upgrade	• Software owners purchase a newer version directly from the software company.	• A very important mode because margins are high and repetitive volume purchases can be anticipated. *Note:* Some upgrades are sold through retail mode.
Retail	• Sold to individual purchasers in the store. This market also included retail upgrade sales.	• Largely for personal or small business use.

TABLE 3   **CorelDRAW Units Shipped: Full Kits (000s)**

Version	1992	1993	1994	1995	Total
DRAW 1 and 2	NA	NA	NA	NA	241
DRAW 3	163	357	379	816	1,715
DRAW 4	0	106	379	968	1,453
DRAW 5	0	0	113	201	314
DRAW 6	0	0	0	54	54
TOTAL	163	463	871	2,039	3,777

suite, which it purchased two years ago. However, during this time, IBM had focused on non-PC-related network services and hardware markets. Their word processor and suite customers were feeling neglected. At this point in time market analysts were wondering if and when IBM might address this concern, or possibly they viewed these markets as secondary relative to their more profitable non-PC businesses.

Microsoft had a strong presence in most segments of the PC software market. Its revenues were in excess of $8.6 billion annually with over $3.4 billion coming from applications software alone. An important advantage for Microsoft was its dominance in the PC operating system[7] (OS) market where they had over 90 percent market share. Microsoft's accumulated skills and knowledge in the OS business gave them synergies in their applications software business. However, the most important advantage appeared to be the economies of scale and access to distribution channels. In fact, the interrelated scope of their businesses had triggered several antitrust investigations by the U.S. Department of Justice, and in 1995, Microsoft had settled out of court on one antitrust charge.

Microsoft's product breadth and marketing power was backed up with considerable sales strength. They used distributors to access the retail channels, but they had built their own sales force that focused on corporate accounts. In Canada Microsoft had corporate sales offices in Halifax, Quebec City, Montreal, Ottawa, Toronto, Winnipeg, Calgary, Edmonton, and Vancouver. Microsoft's development of these offices during the past five years was just beginning to pay off with increased penetration of some of their more sophisticated products. Microsoft also supported local corporate users by licensing trainers and technical support staff on their products. The outsourcing of these functions lowered the cost, but the licensing ensured that high-quality support was available in virtually every town in Canada and the United States.

Presently, Microsoft's greatest challenge was in the Internet market. They had belatedly realized the opportunities in this market, and Netscape, the market leader, had built a dominant market position and a technological lead. Microsoft was now attempting to close that lead. In addition, a new Internet programming language, called Java, posed a threat to Microsoft's OS dominance. A number of companies, including IBM and Sun, had been trying to

---

[7] An operating system is the base software that allows all application software to run on the computer hardware. Developing application software, therefore, requires intimate knowledge of the operating system in which it is design to run.

develop network-based computer systems, which would drastically lower operating costs because they would require less administration and technical support. Java could potentially support such a network computing approach. In fact, some industry leaders were hailing Java as revolutionary. Though the approach had some perceptual and technological hurdles, experts suggested it would gain adoptive momentum over the next five years, and at that time one would have an idea of its potential. Pundits, however, thought that Microsoft, with its competitive agility and market strength, could counter almost any type of attack on its competitive core.

Corel Corporation

Corel was founded in 1985 by Cowpland to develop and manufacture computer hardware integrating devices. Previous to this, he had co-founded Mitel, a very successful multimillion-dollar telephone exchange manufacturer.

In its first three years, Corel struggled with a core product line. A wide variety of hardware and software products were developed in three product divisions (Graphics Software, Optical Technology, and Integrated Systems), but none were clear successes. Then in 1989, Corel launched CorelDRAW, a program for creating, manipulating, and outputting graphics. It was an instant success and growth in revenue and income levels far exceeded financial analysts' projections. Corel then developed Versions 2, 3, 4, and 5 on an annual basis, and by 1995, DRAW had garnered over 230 international awards. Corel now enjoyed an installed base of nearly 4 million DRAW users (see Table 3).

TABLE 4   **Corel's Competitors**

Product Category/Application	Company
Illustration and graphics software	• Adobe Systems • Claris • Micrografx • Macromedia • Deneba Systems
Photo editing/painting	• Adobe • Claris • Micrografx
Desktop publishing	• Adobe • Claris • Quark • Aldus
PhotoCD	• Westflight • Digital Zone • Aris Entertainment
Charting/presentations/slideshow software	• Software Publishing Corp. • Claris • Microsoft • Adobe • Micrografx • Lotus/IBM

An important factor in this success was Corel's unique marketing approach. A standard practice in the industry was to discontinue selling previous software versions and force customers to buy the new version. Corel's approach was to offer the previous versions at a discount. This had a remarkable effect on sales, because the lower-priced versions helped penetrate price-sensitive, high-volume segments of the market (see Table 5). Furthermore, it brought with it the prospect of customers buying upgrades in the future. This strategy propelled Corel's revenue growth spectacularly, averaging over 50 percent from 1989 through to 1994.

By 1992, DRAW accounted for over 80 percent of Corel's sales. On this basis, Cowpland decided product diversification was vital to the long-term survival and growth of the company,[8] so they developed or acquired the rights to many different programs. By 1995, with the diversification plan in gear, Corel had several product lines, of which the main ones were *Graphics and Publishing* (including the DRAW family, CorelFLOW, Corel GALLERY, Corel PhotoPaint, Corel Print House, Corel Ventura, and Corel Xara); *Multimedia* (including home and children's titles—16 titles with 35 new ones planned—CD Creator hardware and software, the SCSI group, and the Corel Photo CD series); and *Desktop Video Communications* (the CorelVIDEO product).

Almost all of these products were available in 17 languages, and Arlen Bartsch, Executive Director of Marketing, estimated that Corel now had in the range of 5,000 separate stockkeeping units (SKUs) at the retail level, a remarkable output for the approximately 550 employees at Corel. In 1995 alone, the company released over 30 multimedia titles aimed at the mass home market. The thrust of all of these products was to home users and small businesses through retail outlets. Yet, Corel's revenues continued to be dominated by the DRAW graphics product line, which accounted for over 90 percent of Corel's overall revenues in 1995 (see Table 6).

R&D

Corel's product development speed[9] was an important competitive advantage. Their development cycle was one of the shortest in the industry and generally

---

[8] Growth is important in most high-tech companies, because workers are paid in stock options and only companies having high growth prospects can attract the best workers at a relatively inexpensive wage rate (i.e., base salary).

[9] Product development speed represents the speed at which programmers can produce a new product version.

TABLE 5   **Average Selling Prices, CorelDRAW, 1995 (Windows platform)**

DRAW 3	Kit	$ 74.33
	Upgrade	NA
DRAW 4	Kit	$145.98
	Upgrade	NA
DRAW 5	Kit	$467.89
	Upgrade (from 4)	$208.56
DRAW 6	Kit	$453.78
	Upgrade (from 5)	$234.07

TABLE 6   Corel Sales by Major Product Line, 1989–1995 (000s of US$)

	1989	1990	1991	1992	1993	1994	1995
Graphics software—new licences	NA	NA	NA	$45,440	$ 70,367	$ 93,573	$114,530
Graphics software—existing users	NA	NA	NA	14,168	26,873	55,170	63,595
Subtotal, graphics software				$59,608	$ 97,240	$148,732	$178,125
Other	NA	NA	NA	7,907	7,778	15,570	18,254
TOTAL SALES				$67,515	$105,018	$164,313	$196,379

New Users Versus Existing Users as a Percentage of Graphics Software Sales

	1989	1990	1991	1992	1993	1994	1995
Graphics software—new licences	NA	93%	90%	76%	72%	63%	64%
Graphics software—existing users	NA	7%	10%	24%	28%	37%	36%
TOTAL GRAPHICS SOFTWARE				100%	100%	100%	100%

Graphics Versus Other Sales as a Percentage of Total Corel Sales

	1989	1990	1991	1992	1993	1994	1995
Total graphics software	77%	82%	87%	88%	93%	91%	91%
Other	23%	18%	13%	12%	7%	9%	9%
TOTAL	100%	100%	100%	100%	100%	100%	100%

Note: NA=not available.

costs were tightly controlled, making the company very efficient in reprogramming a new version of a product.

However, successful new product innovation, including market introduction, was an area where Corel had shown mixed results. After approximately ten years and many different new product introductions, Corel could only boast one significant product, CorelDRAW. Product innovation took place on an informal basis. Usually products were conceived from a combination of Cowpland's enthusiasm and top programmers' ideas. Generally, either the new products were related to the DRAW product or they used Corel's cost-efficient distribution channels and the Corel name to get shelf space.[10] Either new products were developed or the rights to the product were purchased from another company or party. In fact, the majority of products in Corel's product line had been purchased from other small companies or individuals that were not able to make a go of the competitive marketing environment for their product. This approach was very cost-effective, because many of these products were purchased at low prices; the downside was that most did not have a strong market presence. Many of these ancillary products had small market shares in their respective market classes compared to CorelDRAW.

An analyst summed this problem up as follows:

Corel has become very adept at developing and selling new CorelDRAW versions, but it has not successfully developed any strong secondary products as yet. This clearly points to the competitive nature of most segments in the desktop market, but it also points to Corel's focus on efficiency rather than market sophistication. Corel's success in the future may depend

---

[10] Recently, however, some unrelated products were being developed such as a network computer and personal digital assistant.

more upon market sophistication and understanding the many graphics customer segments' needs than efficiency.

Although traditional R&D spending had previously averaged 9 percent of sales, in 1995 this increased to 13 percent of sales.[11] From 1993 to 1994, gross expenditures on R&D, before tax credits, rose 68 percent, and by a further 106 percent in the next fiscal year. The company attributed these increases to support for an increasingly broad range of products, plus introduction of new products such as Corel Ventura 5, CorelFLOW, and Corel PhotoPaint 5. Development costs were important part of this industry, making up a significant part of overall fixed costs of the final product. (*Note:* Fixed costs averaged 80 percent and variable costs 20 percent in this industry.) Despite these cost increases, Corel was still above average in efficiency when compared to many other software companies. Thus, two of Corel's most important competitive advantages were getting code out quickly and relatively inexpensively. (See Tables 7 and 8.)

[11] Microsoft spent about 16.5 percent of sales on R&D in fiscal 1996 ($1.43 billion on revenues of $8.67 billion) up from 13 percent in 1994 and 14 percent in 1995.

TABLE 7

COREL CORPORATION
CONSOLIDATED STATEMENTS OF INCOME AND RETAINED EARNINGS, 1992–1995
Year ended November 30 (000 US$)

	1992	1993	1994	1995
Sales	$67,515	$105,027	$164,313	$196,379
Cost of sales	$19,459	$24,310	$35,940	$47,352
Gross profit	$48,056	$80,717	$128,373	$149,027
Expenses:				
Advertising	$15,067	$19,136	$31,891	$55,099
Selling, general and administrative	$13,266	$18,005	$30,833	$40,292
Research and development	$5,368	$7,699	$13,387	$27,232
Depreciation and amortization	$2,810	$4,079	$6,137	$9,468
Loss (gain) on foreign exchange	($2,366)	($480)	$1,546	$136
	$34,145	$48,439	$83,794	$132,227
Income from operations	$13,911	$32,278	$44,579	$16,800
Interest income	$1,229	$2,389	$2,861	$5,023
Income before income taxes	$15,140	$34,667	$47,440	$21,823
Income taxes current	$5,811	$12,574	$14,799	$7,174
Income taxes deferred	$127	$1,240	$138	$165
	$5,938	$13,814	$14,937	$7,339
Net income from continuing operations	$9,202	$20,853	$32,503	$14,484
Loss from discontinued operations	($824)	—	—	—
Net income	$8,378	$20,853	$32,503	$14,484
Retained earnings, start of year	$13,487	$21,865	$42,718	$75,221
Retained earnings, end of year	$21,865	$42,718	$75,221	$89,705
Earnings per Share				
Net income per share, basic	$0.26	$0.49	$0.70	$0.30
Net income per share, fully diluted	$0.24	$0.45	$0.63	$0.26
Weighted-Average Number of Common Shares Outstanding (000s)				
Basic	35,415	42,201	46,558	48,412
Fully diluted	38,667	46,146	51,768	55,174

TABLE 8

COREL CORPORATION
CONSOLIDATED BALANCE SHEETS
As at November 30 (000 US$)

	1993	1994	1995
Assets			
Current assets:			
Cash and short-term investments	$ 57,000	$ 85,618	$ 81,816
Accounts receivable			
Trade	36,327	50,586	58,797
Other	2,185	2,264	3,322
Inventory	7,361	13,417	16,224
Income taxes recoverable	—	—	3,306
Prepaid expenses	812	1,348	8,881
	$103,685	$153,233	$172,346
Capital assets	28,605	38,189	49,000
	$132,290	$191,422	$221,346
Liabilities and Shareholders' Equity			
Current liabilities:			
Accounts payable	$ 5,391	$ 8,487	$ 12,896
Accrued liabilities	6,073	10,722	10,097
Income taxes payable	7,400	4,930	—
	$ 18,864	$ 24,139	$ 22,993
Deferred income taxes	$ 2,192	$ 2,330	$ 2,495
Shareholders' equity:			
Share capital	$ 67,792	$ 89,380	$105,801
Accumulated foreign currency translation	372	—	—
Contributed surplus	352	352	352
Retained earnings	42,718	75,221	89,705
	$111,234	$164,953	$195,858
	$132,290	$191,422	$221,346

Marketing and Advertising

Cowpland, along with Arlen Bartsch, managed sales and marketing from Corel's head office in Ottawa, Canada.[12] Again the focus was on cost-efficiency. Almost all marketing decisions, including all product design, advertising copy and design, and product packaging design, were implemented in-house. This minimized the costs and turnaround time.

Product was sold primarily through retail channels, focusing on the personal and small office segments. They also sold corporate site licences, but these did not constitute a significant portion of Corel's overall market. Products were sold in 60 countries, through 160 distributors, but an overwhelming percentage of the product volume was sold by three top distributors. Corel tried to manage these channels by pushing product inventory using various incentives and relying on their brand name. For the most part, Corel allowed the distributors to manage the retail channels, and Corel supported

---

[12] Corel did have a small Irish office that handled European technical support and some marketing.

them with promotional and advertising programs. In 1995, Corel expanded its retail channel focus by broadening into major mail order accounts and broader consumer outlets like Wal-Mart, Virgin, and Toys-"R"-Us stores.

An important part of Corel's marketing strategy was their approach to promotion and advertising. They spent about 20 percent of sales on advertising. In 1995, this ballooned to 28 percent partly as a result of the diversification strategy, and lower than forecast revenues from DRAW 6. Their approach to advertising was often alarmingly colourful and full of products and product features. Corel was also very successful at managing promotional events.[13] They were now a major sponsor of the Women's Professional Tennis circuit, and had recently acquired the right to name the Ottawa NHL team's arena The Corel Centre.

Manufacturing and Logistics

Corel was very fast and efficient at manufacturing and logistics. They outsourced all manufacturing and kept in-house product-related operations that were costly or time-consuming if outsourced. For example, when a product required packaging, Corel would quickly adapt their standard packaging in a matter of hours and at little cost while other software companies hired marketing and packaging consultants who would take months to design a package and ultimately cost a small fortune. One person handled all of the manufacturing logistics decisions in the company, with consultation of course from Cowpland.

The Corel Organization

In many respects, Corel was a study in contrasts. It was fast-moving, yet centralized. The people had a tremendous range of responsibility, yet the CEO was involved in most major decisions. It marketed its products in more than 60 countries and 17 languages, yet a tiny headquarters staff directed virtually everything. The pace was frantic, and Mike demanded huge dedications of time and effort from his staff.

Corel was "Mike's company," no doubt about that, but the significance of that statement went well beyond his status as the major shareholder and founder. Mike left his personal imprint on everything. He ran a flat organization that was very collegial, had very few hierarchical levels, and almost no support staff. Senior managers had no secretarial staff, and often greeted visitors themselves. Mike's office was open, and a range of employees, down through to product managers, met with him regularly to make financial, technological, and marketing decisions. To instill an openness in the organization, Mike made a point of meeting every new employee, and was once quoted as saying that he preferred Corel to remain relatively small, say under 1,000 employees, in order to maintain the entrepreneurial spirit that had made it successful. Corel's employees tended to be young and eager; even most of the top managers were under 40 years old. This created a work force that lacked the breadth of business experience found in some companies, but Corel found

---

[13] The Annual DRAW Contest awarded the best CorelDRAW picture artist a multimillion-dollar prize. The contest had become popular with designers and artists and provided the program with well-targeted promotional coverage.

these younger employees worked long hours for less money, thus making the firm very efficient from the point of view of getting a task done. The unofficial company motto had become "Do what it takes to get the job done."

Corel compensated its employees with both salaries and stock options. The salaries were modest, but the generous options were the key to employee motivation and loyalty.[14] The modest salaries and demanding pace of work made Corel very efficient, but also increased employee turnover to rates slightly higher than the industry norm. In fact, in 1994 Corel had one of the highest sales-per-employee ratios in the software industry, and it also had one of the fastest product development cycle times.

The Graphics Market Competition

Corel competed in a number of different software markets, the most important being graphics, a market in which Corel had an 87 percent market share. The competitors in graphics were numerous, but many were small niche players. The top four major players are included in Table 9. Claris, an Apple Computer subsidiary, had good graphics programs and was large, but their market was

---

[14] Stock options were critical too for the wealth generation of employees. Options allowed the employees to buy stock at the issue date value and sell at the fully vested date price. (*Note:* The option has a value, but it is given to the employee.) Thus, after three years with the company (the time it takes for options to become fully vested) an employee could use his or her first-year options to buy stock at the price of three years ago and sell it now or for a limited time in the future.

It should be noted that it is critical for the stock to be appreciating at a relatively fast level for options to be of value to employees. For example, at Microsoft, employees fully vested over five years' employment were millionaires due to the increased value of their options.

TABLE 9 The Major Competition in the Illustration and Graphics Market

Competitor	Estimated Market Share*	Size	Notes
Corel	80%	(See attached financials.)	(See case.)
Claris	10%	A subsidiary of Apple Computer	It is a highly diversified software company that produces software for the Macintosh, which makes up about 10% of the personal computer market. For Macintoshes it has the majority share of the market, but in PCs it has not captured a huge part of the graphics software market.
Macromedia	7.5%		
Adobe	3.4%	Revenues $207 million in 1996	This profitable company has many products. Its revenues are derived mainly from the printing and desktop publishing software products.
Micrografx	1%	Revenues $72 million in 1996	This company is probably Corel's greatest competitor for CorelDRAW. It is a smaller mirror image of Corel in that it targets many of Corel's segments. The company was unprofitable last year and revenues declined slightly.

*This estimate is by PC data and represents unit sales in the drawing and painting software category.

principally for Macintosh computers, which made up only 10 percent of all personal computers. Their focus on—in fact, dominance—in the Macintosh, combined with their wide product breadth, blunted their competitiveness in the Windows/PC sector, which was Corel's principal sector.

Macromedia was an important competitor in the drawing and painting market segment. They had started out as the premier package for the Macintosh, which provided them with a small market but considerable prestige, and had recently developed their drawing and painting programs for the Windows PC market. They had less than half the revenues of Corel, but their growth had been extremely strong. They were an effective competitor because of their ability to collaborate with other computer companies and their development of products enabling third parties to develop add-on products.

Micrografx was another important competitor. They focused on a line of graphics products that mirrored Corel's product line. This made them a strong competitor from the perspective of their understanding the market and the features desired by the customers. They were also known as an innovative company. Their weakness was their size and lack of resources. Being one-third the size of Corel Limited, their marketing prowess and ability to get good shelf space at the retail level was much less. Micrographx had had the same problems with stagnant sales that Corel had in the past year, and they were presently losing money.

As regards revenues, Adobe was almost the same size as Corel. However, they were more focused on a variety of other software lines, such as printing, Internet browsing, and desktop publishing, and were latecomers to the main graphics market, with only a small share of it. Adobe was expected to continue to focus on their growing browser segment, as they were clearly the market leader and resources were being demanded of them in this sector if they wanted to maintain their market leadership.

In its other market areas, Corel faced considerable competition, either because competitors were well established in the sector or because there were low barriers to entry. For example, Corel Venture and Corel Video both had well-established competitors with strong brand recognition and capabilities. Other markets, such as the PhotoCD segment, were highly price-sensitive because of low entry barriers. Here, Corel competed on price as well as the breadth and quality of photos available. In general, Corel's lean structure allowed it to compete in the segments with moderately low prices as long as they could differentiate to some degree through breadth of features and advertising support.

The Growth Imperative

Throughout its history Corel had developed many ancillary products, but as discussed earlier, developing a product as successful as DRAW had proven difficult. Cowpland considered diversified growth to be vital for Corel's long-term well-being. Two problems might arise if Corel continued to strategically focus on the graphics market. First, the market could stagnate, which would mean its fast product development cycle capability would become less advantageous; stock options would become less valuable and programmers—a software company's core competence—might begin leaving. Second, a company relying on one product would be more vulnerable to competition from the likes of Microsoft.

Unfortunately, there were signs the graphics market was beginning to slow, as sales were down and profit margins were being squeezed. Cowpland was also worried that such a singular product focus exposed Corel to competitive threats if the graphics market became popular and a major competitor decided to enter. Corel had no ancillary revenues and income from other sources to protect its cash flow. Thus, in late 1995, Cowpland promised shareholders that 50 percent of Corel revenues in 1996 would come from other than the graphics software line. This was a major commitment to change.[15]

Cowpland also realized that acquisition of WordPerfect would instantly diversify the company. He felt that with Corel's marketing and WordPerfect's strong product, Corel could grab 20 to 30 percent or more of the market for suites and standalone word processors. This would double or triple Corel's current revenues almost instantly, and he thought it would provide an excellent base from which to diversify further in the years to come.

Analyzing the Deal's Potential

Corel had spent considerable time reviewing WordPerfect's programming code and operations. Eid Eid, VP Technology, with his technology manager, Carey Stanton, examined the potential deal from a technical perspective. Their report to Cowpland was that the core technology was superb and compatible with Corel's graphics expertise. The product was robust, with features and a richness that surpassed Microsoft's wares. WordPerfect Presentations—the presentation and slide show program—was "four times more powerful" than PowerPoint, Microsoft's offering. It could fully replace their own Corel Presents. The Quattro Pro product was also strong; though the development team was demoralized under Novell's ownership, both managers thought they could get them motivated.

They also examined the new Windows 95–based WordPerfect Office suite and found it was at least half a generation ahead of Microsoft's present suite technology. Furthermore, it was, at most, a couple of months from being ready to ship. On the R&D side, however, Eid thought Novell's costs were out of whack, and this was an area where Corel could bring value to shareholders. Corel knew how to get code written quickly and efficiently. Thus, from Eid and Carey's perspective, the WordPerfect acquisition made sense. Corel's technical capabilities and marketing prowess were exactly what the WordPerfect products needed.

Arlen Bartsch, Executive Director of Sales and Marketing, although not as active in the acquisition analysis as the technology and financial people, thought the strongest reason to consider the deal was that Corel had reached the market saturation point in the graphics software segment. Corel needed growth opportunities. WordPerfect had tremendous brand equity, and a base

---

[15] Microsoft had incorporated some graphic capabilities in its latest word processing software.

of 20 million users. Furthermore, Novell had fired the WordPerfect marketing team and had assigned the sales and marketing to the NetWare division. Arlen referred to this as a mistake that could be corrected by Corel. Furthermore, Novell's sales incentive program was biased toward NetWare sales, and they used little or no advertising. Arlen felt it was vital to invest in building brand equity.

In contrast, Arlen pointed out that Corel spent heavily on advertising and used more push strategies in the channels than Novell. Corel was strong in marketing to resellers and the shrinkwrap retail segment. Eventually, they may have to set up a corporate sales staff, but for the most part he wanted to maintain Corel's approach of turning sales over to channel members. Keeping them happy was important. The OEM segment was another one where the WordPerfect suite might have some attractiveness, and although Corel had few OEM deals, Arlen planned to expand this effort if the WordPerfect deal closed.

Cowpland and Arlen thought Corel's approach to DRAW would not have to be changed radically for WordPerfect. As negotiations went on, Arlen developed plans to compete on price, value (more features for the money), third-party support, and commitment to multiple platforms. He needed to reignite some excitement in the brand name, and instill confidence in the market that Corel was here to stay. This could be done with a big advertising campaign. In addition to competing on features and price in the suite and standalone segments, Arlen felt Corel would have to begin distinguishing itself from Microsoft, probably through an Internet/Java-based strategy. Corel had already begun to position itself in the Internet and intranet markets through net-focused vector graphics tools (CorelXara) and a suite of net utilities. If Corel were to position itself as unique from Microsoft, it would have to push the net angle and embrace Java as an alternative system. To accomplish these tasks, Arlen figures that the sales and marketing group would have to grow by 80 to 200 people in the Ottawa-based headquarters to support the increased breadth and volume.

Chuck Norris, Chief Financial Officer and Director of Finance, was one member of the team that had significant experience in a large company outside of Corel. He had joined the company in 1991. Chuck's main concern was the financial structure of the deal.

Chuck's thinking about the reasons for buying WordPerfect reflected the Corel way of thinking. It was there, had a huge following, and strong code, so buy it and make it work. Developing financial projections for WordPerfect in Corel was going to require considerable judgement and estimating because the financials and organization of WordPerfect were so interwoven with Novell's. One had to forecast the costs of WordPerfect as a part of Corel. There were many uncertainties, but Chuck with Cowpland estimated that Corel could probably break even with WordPerfect sales levels at the $500 million level. And if Corel could grab 20 percent of the market, which was then estimated at about $5 billion, they would be extremely profitable. This latter target was not too far from the levels of sales that WordPerfect had a year ago.

Kerry D. Williams, Director of Operations, was the guy who would have to turn the code into saleable product and move it through the distribution channels. He was brought in at the last moment to consider the operational logistics of transferring ownership. In negotiation and preliminary due diligence meetings, Kerry saw lots of opportunity for cutting costs, reducing bureaucracy, and streamlining decision making. During conference calls Kerry was often the only Corel representative, while Novell would have a half-dozen or more. He would make a decision, with Cowpland's endorsement, but the Novell team would have to consult elsewhere in the organization, often taking days to do so. He figured that if Corel bought WordPerfect, he would need no new people to run the show, even though he expected to ship thousands of units initially, quickly turning into millions. Novell had devoted 19 or more people to WordPerfect logistics. Kerry figured he would need none of them.

Part of this efficiency was Corel's subcontracting approach to manufacturing. But a large part was Corel's leanness and can-do approach. For example, Kerry noted that Novell's operation had a seven-week quality assurance phase in their manufacturing where a mock run would be done, quality assessed, and then the line would begin real manufacturing; Corel would cut this step entirely, focusing any quality assurance on the code itself. From cutting a master disk to packaging and shipping would take Corel 2 1/2 weeks tops. Kerry saw some other dimensions where the Corel culture and style would be a better match to WordPerfect than Novell had been. For example, Novell's WordPerfect developers felt very much out of the Novell mainstream. In Corel, they would get the best toys (computers) and would be treated like the core of the company. That's one reason why Kerry felt confident that the deal could work for Corel.

The deal would mean more than doubling the size of Corel's development staff, and reestablishing a sales organization that had been left to atrophy under Novell. It would entail merging a distant and by all indications a troubled applications division, situated 2,000 miles away in Orem, Utah, with the lean, centralized, Ottawa-based Corel operation. Reports were that Orem's 300 developers and approximately 300 other members of the WordPerfect division were not happy with the management of Novell and how the WordPerfect brand had been handled. Not only was integrating them and managing them as a division a challenge, it ran in a different direction from Corel's normal approach, which was to acquire programming code, not people. And if forecasts were accurate, Corel would have to grow from a company generating slightly over $200 million a year to one generating over $200 million a quarter. This would mean more people, more R&D, more market and sales support, more training, greater operating liquidity, and, without doubt, more intense competition.

From Cowpland's viewpoint, these were minor hurdles. He knew his team and they knew his style—flat out all the time, hungry, competitive, youthful, and energetic. Cowpland also knew that Novell's greatest problems in making WordPerfect work were areas where Corel was strongest. Novell/WordPerfect's margins were slim, its development costs high, and its product cycles long; Corel, on the other hand, was a model of efficiency and rigorous development cycles in the industry. Corel generated among the industry's highest revenues per employee, in the range of $355,000 in 1995, compared to Novell's $262,000. Where Novell was stodgy and bureaucratic, Corel was lean and fast. Where Novell had given WordPerfect's engineers the feeling they were second-rate players, Corel treated its R&D staff as critical to the company's success.

Cowpland knew Microsoft could not be ignored, but to those in the industry who questioned why Corel would want to pick a fight with Microsoft by buying WordPerfect, Cowpland's response was simple. He would point out that if Microsoft at any time decided it wanted a bigger slice of the graphics business, Corel could quickly be encircled in its core line. Microsoft could buy Micrografx, or Adobe, for example, and compete head-on with Corel in the graphics business. Or the Seattle-based behemoth might go after Claris in the desktop publishing segment, and quickly become Corel's number one competitor there. In the past year, several medium-sized software companies had gone under because of Microsoft's encroachment on their market. Why wait for that? As for other potential competitors, such as IBM with its newly acquired Lotus division, Cowpland was unimpressed. IBM, he said, was slow and bureaucratic. If Corel bought WordPerfect, it would be a two-horse race with Microsoft.

Cowpland had the predictable questions in mind when Corel was first approached about the deal in late 1995. Was the technology right? Were the critical Windows 95 products ready? Were WordPerfect's customers going to stick with the wounded developer, or use the sale as an opportunity to bail out? Were the people in Orem capable of competing the way Corel liked to compete? Could Corel reignite enthusiasm for WordPerfect in the marketplace? Cowpland thought he knew the answers to most of these questions. The programming code of word processing was similar to the code Cowpland's own people knew and understood. In fact, it was a subset of graphics code, and Cowpland figured that if it were of high quality it could be adapted to Corel's torrid development cycles. On the marketing side, Corel knew how to get product out the door onto shelves fast, where people would see it and buy it. They knew how to gain a presence in the market and in people's minds.

A final consideration for the acquisition was Cowpland's knowledge that CorelDRAW's sales had been significantly lower than forecast during the past year, and recent quarterly sales had been particularly poor. The possible causes for this were manifold. Some suggested that Corel had flooded the market with cheap older versions of its very powerful products, creating a market that was reaching maturity early. Another oft-cited cause was related to the introduction of Windows 95 and the subsequent confusion due to lack of backward compatibility.[16] (However, if this were the cause a period of low demand would be followed by a recovery in the market.) Others suggested that competitors were slowly eating away at Corel's massive market share. Whatever the reason, Cowpland realized that product diversification would help Corel overcome unstable growth problems.

All these factors played a role in Cowpland's thinking. Naturally, the deal had its risks. But passing it up also jeopardized Corel's long-term growth prospects—and what if one of Corel's competitors (such as Computer Associates) took the deal? Table 10 provides a summary of the highlights of the deal from Corel's perspective, and Table 11 provides Corel's recent quarterly results.

---

[16] Corel's latest DRAW version only worked on Windows 95. So only those having Windows 95 could purchase and use the product. This would limit the market potential until the OS was more widely accepted.

TABLE 10   Notes on Benefits of the Deal

The Potential
- Size and growth potential of the suite/word processing market, a market in excess of $4.6 billion in 1995 compared to $200-million-plus for business graphics.

WordPerfect Growth Potential
- Substantial WordPerfect brand equity and installed base, and estimated 20 million users worldwide.

WordPerfect Product
- Underlying robust technology that was competitive with the market share leader.

Corel Synergies
- More efficient Corel cost structure, which would increase product line profitability.
- Common engineering culture with the WordPerfect division.
- Low price, particularly low cash outlays, which enabled Corel to buy the WordPerfect division without risking the company.
- Opportunity for Corel to grow from a niche developer into a central player in a mainline software segment.

The Deal

Chuck Norris phoned saying he thought they had a reasonable deal from a value perspective. The deal was as follows:

- WordPerfect and all of Novell's suite desktop applications software was included in the sale. This included the spreadsheet purchased from Borland less than a year ago, and a highly rated presentation software program.
- Corel would pay $10.75 million cash to Novell immediately upon closing the deal.
- Corel would pay royalties to Novell for its NetWare and other supporting products, to a value of not less than $70 million over five years (net present value of $30–$40 million).
- Corel would give 9.95 million Corel common shares issued from treasury stock upon closing the deal. This would give Novell a 15 percent

TABLE 11   Corel Quarterly Results

	3 Months to Nov. 30, 1995	3 Months to Nov. 30, 1994
Revenue	$62,083,000	$48,840,000
Net profit	($956,000)	$11,186,000
Average shares	49,000,000	47,495,000
Net profit/share	($0.02)	$0.24
Net profit/share (diluted)	($0.02)	$0.21

COREL FISCAL YEAR RESULTS		
	Year to Nov. 30, 1995	Year to Nov. 30, 1994
Revenue	$196,379,000	$164,313,000
Net profit	$14,484,000	$32,503,000
Average shares	48,412,000	46,558,000
Net profit/share	$0.30	$0.70
Net profit/share (diluted)	$0.26	$0.63

interest in Corel. Novell could not sell the stock for ten months. Corel's stock was fluctuating considerably, but was now trading in the $10 to $11 range.

- Novell would get one seat on Corel's board of directors.

Overall, the deal was valued at an estimated $157 million, and it would make Novell Corel's largest shareholder (owning 15 percent of the outstanding stock while Cowpland owned 14 percent). However, on a cash basis, the deal was very affordable for Corel, who had over $80 million in cash and no debt—i.e., $10 million now and $30 to $40 million (present value) over the next five years. There was also the potential of trying to cross-sell Corel and WordPerfect's products to each other's users. The joint licensing agreement provided some potential benefits for both companies in technological developments and marketing.

Cowpland had to decide in the next 24 hours, or less, whether to accept or walk away from this deal. It was clear that Novell could be pushed no further. In fact, Cowpland wondered how they could justify the deal to their shareholders. From a value perspective, it seemed incredible that a company, having been sold for over $1.5 billion[17] a little more than a year ago, could be acquirable for less than $50 million cash (on a NPV) plus some shares.

---

[17] This includes the value of the Borland spreadsheet purchase.

Fishery Products International

In late January 1989, Vic Young, Chief Executive Officer of Fishery Products International (FPI), was considering the future of their new venture in Japan. Following several years of research and development, FPI had launched eleven value-added products in Japan in February 1988 and sales to date had exceeded all expectations. Despite this early success, questions had been raised about FPI's future involvement in Japan, particularly in the light of the dramatically reduced fishing quotas that had just been announced by the Canadian government. As he reviewed an internal report on the profitability of the new venture, Vic realized that the company had to decide if it should stay in the Japanese market.

◼ The Canadian East Coast Fishing Industry

There were two main sectors in the east coast fishery—the inshore and the offshore. The inshore fishery was based on independent fishermen who supplied fish on a daily basis to primary processing plants. These fishermen owned and operated small to medium-sized vessels that fished close to the shore. The offshore fishery was serviced by large company-owned trawlers (up to and including factory freezer trawlers) which fished further from shore for periods up to ten days before returning to unload their catches.

Under the terms of the Northwest Atlantic Fishery Organization (NAFO) Convention, the waters off Canada's Atlantic coast were divided into three divisions and 16 individual zones. The government of Canada, as part of its management plan for the Atlantic fishery, used an Enterprise Allocation system under which each zone was given an annual allocation, or quota, of fish by species that could be caught during the fishing season.

This case was prepared by R. William Blake and Diane M. Hogan, Faculty of Business Administration, Memorial University of Newfoundland, with the assistance of Louise Handrigan Jones. It is intended as the basis for classroom discussion rather than to illustrate either effective or ineffective handling of an administrative situation. This case was made possible in part by financial assistance from the Pacific 2000 program of External Affairs and International Trade Canada as arranged by Professor Paul Beamish of the Ivey School of Business. Any reproduction, in any form, of the material in this case is prohibited except with the written consent of the school. © Ivey Management Services. Case 9-93-M003, version 01/25/93.

IVEY

Richard Ivey School of Business
The University of Western Ontario

Three main fish species groupings were used in the allocation system: groundfish including cod, flounder, sole, and redfish; pelagics made up of capelin, mackerel, and salmon; and the shellfish group of crab, shrimp, and lobster. The quota system was subdivided into allocations for the inshore and offshore fishery, with the offshore quota further subdivided into allocations for the various fishing companies.

In the early 1980s the fishing industry off the east coast of Canada was in a dismal state. Poor fishery management practices, an increase in the number of plant closures, and escalating labour unrest had led to a sharp increase in the number of government bailouts.

As consumer tastes and diets changed, the market had increasingly demanded a higher-quality fish product. The east coast fishery had been slow to respond to this trend and, despite access to the world's greatest fishing grounds and projections of a continuing increase in cod stocks, had been having difficulty increasing its sales in the Canadian market.

To address these issues, the Atlantic Canada Fisheries Restructuring Act was adopted in November 1983. This act authorized the Minister of Fisheries to invest in, and provide financial assistance for, the restructuring of the Atlantic fishery. One of the mandates the government set for the restructuring was that, following the stabilization of the Atlantic fishing industry, it was to move from government control back to the private sector.

In the restructuring, two of the larger independent companies, National Sea Products and Fishery Products, were chosen as the vehicles to create an economically viable and competitive industry. In December 1984, Fishery Products became the basis for the formation of Fishery Products International Ltd. This new company was formed from twelve individual companies that had been involved in the fishing industry off the Atlantic coast of Canada. In 1986, Fishery Products International was given the largest allocation of fish off the east coast of Canada (Exhibit 1).

▣ Fishery Products International (FPI)

Prior to the creation of FPI, Fishery Products operated six primary processing plants and one small secondary processing plant in Atlantic Canada. After the merger, FPI, from its head office in St. John's, Newfoundland, undertook a major modernization program. Marginal plants were closed and a program of intensive capital investment in processing plants and trawler equipment was implemented. Fourteen of FPI's inshore plants were targeted for sale to independent processors leaving FPI to own and operate sixteen primary and three secondary processing plants[1] (Exhibit 2).

---

[1] Primary processing involves the conversion of raw fish into fillets or blocks for sale as an end product or for transfer for secondary processing. A "block" is an international standard and consists of 16.5 pounds (about 7.5 kilograms) of fish which has been processed and frozen in a freezing frame of exact dimensions. Forty percent of FPI's cod was processed into block, and half of this block was sold to other processors. Secondary processing plants are devoted to the production of value-added finished products, such as fish burgers, fish sticks, and frozen fish dinners, for use by the end customer.

EXHIBIT I Groundfish Allocations (in thousands of tonnes)

Species		1986	1987	1988	1989
Cod	Inshore	326.7	320.6	309.7	306.9
	Offshore	192.5	193.1	213.7	150.1
FPI quotas		84.6	82.1	86.3	68.0
Percentage of TAC caught		88%	81%	85%	
Haddock	Inshore	19.2	19.2	14.3	11.6
	Offshore	18.0	8.3	10.6	11.5
FPI quotas		1.6	1.6	1.7	4.0
Percentage of TAC caught		94%	3%	4%	
Redfish	Inshore	20.6	22.1	19.7	24.9
	Offshore	119.2	121.2	121.2	108.1
FPI quotas		27.2	26.9	23.7	23.4
Percentage of TAC caught		54%	8%	9%	
American plaice	Inshore	18.9	17.4	17.4	16.4
	Offshore	59.0	53.4	46.5	37.9
FPI quotas		53.0	47.3	38.7	33.0
Percentage of TAC caught		61%	29%	25%	
Yellowtail	Inshore	—	—	—	—
	Offshore	17.6	17.6	17.6	7.8
FPI quotas		13.2	13.1	13.1	4.3
Percentage of TAC caught		80%	13%	10%	
Witch	Inshore	3.0	3.0	2.5	2.5
	Offshore	9.8	9.7	8.1	8.1
FPI quotas		7.7	7.6	6.3	6.3
Percentage of TAC caught		39%	4%	5%	
Flounder	Inshore	5.4	6.4	5.4	6.6
	Offshore	8.4	7.3	8.3	7.1
FPI quotas		0.6	0.5	0.5	0.4
Percentage of TAC caught		53%	0.1%	0.2%	
Greenland halibut (turbot)	Inshore	41.6	45.5	47.2	47.2
	Offshore	30.7	38.7	38.7	28.7
FPI quotas		17.1	17.1	12.0	15.9
Percentage of TAC caught		22%	2.2%	0.6%	
Pollock	Inshore	20.0	23.0	24.5	25.5
	Offshore	20.0	21.5	23.8	22.8
FPI quotas		0.3	0.3	0.6	0.5
Percentage of TAC caught		108%	0.4%	0.5%	

Notes: Inshore: vessels less than 100 feet; offshore: vessels larger than 100 feet; TAC=total allowable catch.

To service their plants FPI operated 58 company-owned trawlers that harvested over 260 million pounds of cod, flounder, sole, perch, haddock, and turbot annually. The company also purchased crab, shrimp, capelin, and herring from some 2,500 independent inshore fishermen in Newfoundland. FPI had traditionally not fully harvested its quotas of underutilized species, such as redfish (ocean perch) and turbot. Redfish was not as lucrative in its markets as Atlantic cod, and Canadian companies lacked the deep-water-harvesting technology to fully utilize the turbot quotas.

EXHIBIT 2   FPI Plant Locations

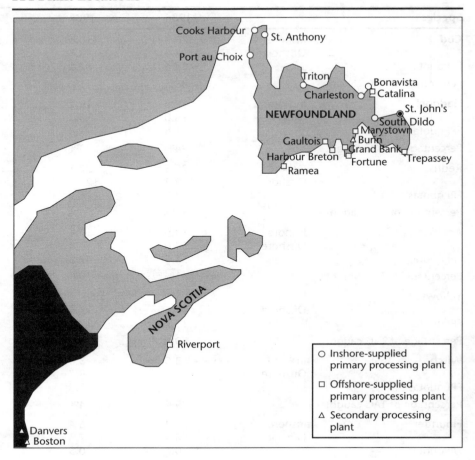

Under the restructuring, FPI became a vertically integrated seafood company, catching and processing fish, developing new seafood products, and marketing them in the international marketplace. Through this process, FPI emerged as a major international player, with sales of $260 million, and a loss of $35 million in 1984, its first year of operation. Although the company recorded another loss in 1985, it reported healthy profits of $46 million and $58 million in 1986 and 1987, respectively (Exhibit 3). In 1987 Canada accounted for 16 percent of FPI's sales, the United States 77.6 percent, and other countries (Europe, Australia, and Japan) 6.7 percent.

FPI's approach to the market differed from country to country. FPI was the largest foreign supplier of frozen seafood to the United States and supplied the value-added component of that market from two secondary processing plants in Massachusetts through a subsidiary company, Fishery Products Inc.

In Europe, FPI principally supplied fish-blocks to other processors and finished products to food service companies, using sales offices which employed local people with specific market knowledge in sales and distribution. These subsidiaries were located in West Germany (Fishery Products GmbH) and Great Britain (Fishery Products of Canada Ltd.). The market in Europe

EXHIBIT 3

FISHERY PRODUCTS INTERNATIONAL
SUMMARY OF FINANCIAL STATEMENT
(thousands of dollars)

	1988	1987	1986	1985
Sales	366,611	395,705	388,664	298,182
Net income (Loss)	16,755	57,963	46,596	(20,160)
Cash flow (1)	29,275	71,298	56,731	(8,357)
Working capital	99,467	94,035	55,404	41,192
Long-term debt	38,593	17,487	14,471	24,531

(1) Cash flow from operations before net changes in non-cash working capital balances.

Segmented Information

Sales	1988	1987	1986	1985
Canada (a)	338,328	367,051	354,149	252,111
Inter-company (b)	(272,563)	(317,055)	(300,661)	(205,047)
	65,765	49,996	53,488	47,064
United States	264,263	314,342	304,490	231,282
Other (c)	36,583	31,367	30,686	19,836
	366,611	395,705	388,664	298,182
Profit (Loss) (d)				
Canada	16,969	58,951	44,757	(15,396)
United States	1,097	7,001	3,945	(4,831)
Other	300	37	(52)	67
	18,366	65,989	48,650	(20,160)

Identified Assets

	1988	1987	1986	1985
Canada	281,662	286,416	238,485	208,516
United States	50,009	56,029	42,085	50,726
Other	9,409	4,626	3,212	5,060
Inter-company accounts	(31,931)	(68,815)	(59,730)	(62,924)
	309,149	278,256	224,052	200,376

(a) Canadian sales includes sales to customers in the United States and other geographic regions.
(b) Transfer pricing: Inter-company sales are at market prices less commissions.
(c) "Other" includes sales to Europe, Australia, and Japan. Sales to Japan were $3 million of capelin product only.
(d) Profit (Loss): Profit is income before provision for profit sharing, income taxes, and extraordinary items.

was fiercely competitive and Canadian value-added products were subject to high tariffs which made it difficult for them to compete. Marketing and all other related activities for the European operations were handled by headquarters in St. John's.

Prior to the restructuring of the industry, independent fishing companies had placed less emphasis on quality than on increasing the catch. In the light of forecasts of shifting consumer preferences toward higher-quality products, FPI management realized that the company needed to catch and process fish more effectively. The company also needed higher-quality fish for many of the new products being produced in its secondary processing plants.

Improved quality was to be achieved through a capitalization program and an increasing emphasis on quality control. FPI had invested heavily in its fleet and processing facilities. To complement this capitalization program, and to increase productivity and motivation, it had also invested heavily in its work force. This had been accomplished through the implementation of such programs as employee ownership, the use of an FPI newsletter, and Employee of the Month awards. The company adopted the motto "Excellence through people, productivity, and profits." It was realized that attempts to increase quality had to be reflected in the employees' attitude and the employees slowly began to realize that if they could not produce a higher-quality fish product, their jobs could be lost.

FPI management had become increasingly concerned about the company's financial vulnerability to fluctuations in the exchange rate of the American dollar. Over 75 percent of FPI's sales were in the United States, and management was looking for ways to reduce their reliance on this market. An integral part of the new strategy was to diversify into new markets and to place an increased emphasis on secondary processing.

Fishery Products' expertise prior to the creation of FPI (1984) had been in the supply of both raw and finished products to the food service industry with little emphasis placed on retail sales. The new emphasis on research and development of new value-added products had led to several Canadian awards for innovative products.

To meet its corporate goal of increasing emphasis in the area of secondary processing, FPI had developed a world-class secondary processing capability in its plant in Burin, Newfoundland. The newly modified plant, which reopened in June 1987, had the capacity to process 15 million pounds of finished product per year. Given the fact that the Canadian market would not immediately utilize the new plant's capacity, part of the company's strategy included steps to explore the Japanese market.

The Japanese Seafood Market

The market development division of FPI had continued the collection of information about the Japanese market that had been started by Fishery Products. As part of their ongoing analysis of the potential of the Japanese marketplace, a team from FPI, including Randy Bishop, Director of International Marketing Sales, participated in a government-sponsored trade mission to Japan in late 1985. During this mission FPI's representatives learned about the characteristics of the Japanese marketplace and had the opportunity to meet with various seafood marketers. Upon returning to Canada and reviewing their findings, the team concluded that, despite the fact that FPI had been exporting unprocessed capelin, squid, and cod to Japan for years, it knew very little about the Japanese domestic market.

The FPI research found that, on a per capita basis, Japan had the highest fish consumption in the world at 68 kilograms per year compared to the United States at 7.2 kilograms and Canada at 7 kilograms. Because local resources were insufficient to meet the high demand for fish, Japanese fishing companies used factory freezer trawlers outfitted to fish, freeze, and store while operating worldwide. Historically Japan had been a major fishing nation harvesting in excess of 15 percent of the total world catch and exporting far more than it imported. Recently, however, the increasingly restrictive policies of many nations had limited access to their fishing grounds and Japan had become a fish-importing nation (Table 1).

Since World War II, Japan had used very restrictive import policies as a way of developing its economy. Approximately 20 percent of Japanese imports were finished goods, compared to 50 percent for the United States and 40 percent for the European Economic Community. In the fishing industry a focus on the importation of raw product allowed Japan to continue to utilize the massive fish processing infrastructure developed when it was a major fishing nation.

In recent years Japan, as a member of GATT (General Agreement on Tariffs and Trade), had been working at reducing both tariff and non-tariff barriers. Despite this trend, companies still found it difficult to enter the Japanese market as government regulations and non-tariff barriers were used as deterrents. The quality control standards applied to imports were examples of such non-tariff barriers. The FPI team realized during their investigation that there was no central governing body in Japan that it could access to determine product standards. Although there had been a movement to centralize these standards, the process was very slow.

The retail market for frozen seafood in Japan in the large chain grocery stores alone was worth Cdn$1.3 billion annually; in the three major regions of Tokyo, Osaka, and Nagoya, there were 40 of these chains with approximately 2,000 stores. The rest of the retail market, which represented approximately 30 percent of the seafood market, was split among the food sections of department stores and convenience stores with approximately one store per 68 people in the country. Each of these stores had a very small section devoted to frozen food, and there was tremendous competition among brands.

The introduction of new food products in Japan was done very methodically with new releases occurring primarily in February and October. As many as 2,000 new entries would be released each time, of which approximately 300 would be in the frozen food category, the sector FPI would be entering. The success rate for new products was approximately 15 percent and, in general, new products faced a very short product life cycle—often less than two years.

The Japanese consumer demanded high-quality foods and sought a wide variety of choice in products; as Randy Bishop noted, "The Japanese eat with their eyes." Portion size had to be uniform and be composed of top-quality fish. This would have considerable ramifications for FPI if it decided to enter the market

TABLE I   **Fish Consumption in Japan in Thousands of Tonnes**

	1965	1970	1975	1980	1984	1986*
Production	5,547	6,857	7,522	7,421	7,352	—
Imports	109	294	752	1,027	1,746	2,300
Exports	618	791	755	817	624	—
Apparent domestic consumption	5,048	6,356	7,549	7,666	8,251	8,600
Imports as a percentage of total market	2.3	4.6	9.9	13.3	21.1	26.7

*Estimated consumption.

with value-added products. FPI felt that many current top products (as classified by North American and European standards) would not pass the Japanese quality standards for importation.

Japan was becoming more Westernized in its tastes and placed a high demand and value on imported products. Once a foreign product was adopted in the domestic market, it usually commanded a high price. Despite the high demand for imported products, FPI realized that the Japanese had very distinct tastes. It was common knowledge that companies such as Nestlé and Heinz had entered the Japanese domestic market with their standard products and failed. The experience of such companies had earned Japan the reputation of being a very difficult market to enter successfully.

The distribution network in Japan reflected many characteristics of a hierarchical and closed society. A greatly simplified version of a Japanese distribution chain is provided in Exhibit 4. Imports of raw materials were handled by large trading companies through their import/export divisions. Foreign companies wishing to sell value-added products to the Japanese domestic market would have to do so through the domestic marketing division of the trading company. Given the nature of the trading companies, the import/export division and the domestic marketing division were independent operations. Even though FPI had been exporting raw materials to Japan for years, it had no contacts in the domestic marketing division, and therefore no access to the domestic retail market or the larger food service market. From its research, FPI realized that the sale of imported value-added fish products was essentially unknown in these markets.

In addition to increased Japanese demand for foreign products and the potential size of the Japanese market, FPI was encouraged by two other factors: the change in value of the Japanese currency and the Japanese fish consumption

EXHIBIT 4   **Simplified Diagram of the Japanese Distribution Chain for Imported FPI Value-Added Products**

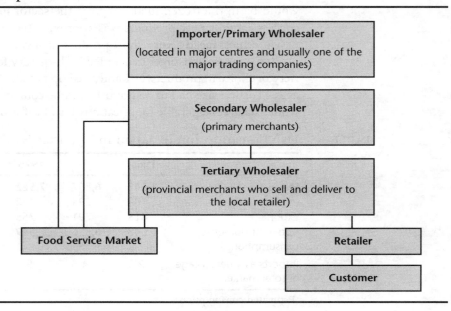

EXHIBIT 5 **Average Quarterly Exchange Rate of Japanese Yen to Canadian Dollar, 1980–1989**

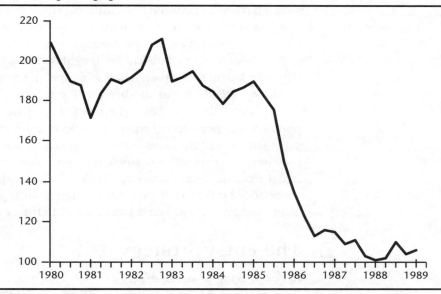

pattern. In 1982, the Canadian dollar was worth close to 200 yen, but by 1987, the exchange rate was approximately 100 yen to the dollar (Exhibit 5). This would allow FPI to set prices on its products that would be attractive to the Japanese consumer and would generate returns equivalent to its sales in other markets. In terms of consumption, the Japanese were keenly interested not only in cod and sole, but also in species such as redfish and capelin, neither of which played a significant part in the North American diet. Exports of fish products from Canada had increased significantly in recent years as Japan actively sought supplies to satisfy its domestic demands (Table 2). This fact was of particular interest to FPI, since the quotas for these species were not being fully utilized (Exhibit 1).

The Japanese were very uncomfortable doing business with individuals that they had not known for extended periods of time. They desired to develop *ningen kankei*—a sense or feeling of good human relations, before they established any relationship (business or otherwise). Even if FPI were able to establish such relationships, it was recognized that the Japanese would require

TABLE 2 **Japanese Fish Imports by Major Supplier**

	1985		Rank		
	US$ (millions)	% share	1985	1983	1981
United States	915.0	18.5	1	1	1
Korea	688.4	13.9	2	2	2
Taiwan	578.4	11.7	3	3	3
Canada	269.7	5.5	4	6	8
India	232.7	4.7	5	4	4
Indonesia	226.2	4.6	6	5	5
Australia	198.8	4.0	7	7	7

a high degree of personal contact in order to maintain the relationship. Because of the hierarchical nature of the Japanese culture, these relationships would have to be between individuals at equal levels in the organization; that is, a Canadian vice-president of marketing would not be able to establish such a relationship with a CEO of a Japanese company.

FPI's experience to date had not taught it to deal with the subtleties of negotiation in Japan. In the past, it had sold capelin, squid, and cod to the Japanese, and more recently it had also been selling some redfish, an underutilized species. If FPI wished to sell excess catches of raw fish, this was done by placing a phone call to the import/export division of a Japanese trading company. FPI management had no experience in negotiating contracts in Japan, although they were aware that the Japanese consensus style of negotiating was very different from the North American style. If FPI decided to enter Japan with its value-added products, it would entail significantly more management involvement, money, and long-term commitment to the development of the market.

The Entry Strategy

In considering possible strategies for the Japanese market, three alternatives were considered. The first was for FPI to maintain the status quo by continuing exports of raw materials. This alternative was attractive, as the Japanese demand for raw materials was high, the infrastructure was available to process this material, and the price that could be commanded for quality fish would be favourable. Second, FPI could set up an independent sales office in Japan to market its products, while maintaining corporate control. The third alternative was to develop a cooperative venture with an existing Japanese seafood marketing company to allow FPI value-added produces to be exported to the Japanese market.

After reviewing the alternatives, top management decided to seek an arrangement with one of the larger Japanese seafood marketing firms dealing in both the food service and the retail market. The decision was based on the belief that, despite a lower return on investment, this approach would allow it to penetrate the market more quickly than would be possible if it attempted to set up its own operations in Japan. Through 1986, FPI actively researched Japanese seafood marketing companies, including Toyo, Nippon Su, and Nichiro, in an attempt to identify a potential partner. The analysis led FPI to approach Nichiro Gyogyo Kaisha (Nichiro), the third-largest of the seafood marketing companies, with a proposal for them to market FPI's value-added products in the Japanese domestic market. Nichiro was one of the five Japanese companies purchasing ocean perch and capelin from FPI and was hoping to get exclusive access to FPI's quota for these underutilized species.

After the preliminary meetings of corporate representatives, the CEOs of the two companies met in Boston in September 1986 and agreed that some type of arrangement would be mutually beneficial. The details of the arrangement were to be left to the marketing departments of the companies to complete.

In order to further assess the Japanese market potential, FPI requested that Nichiro provide detailed information on the Japanese distribution system and consumer needs. In addition, a team from FPI, headed by Randy Bishop, made three trips (two lasting a week to ten days, the other three weeks) to Japan over the following year to become more familiar with the Japanese market and to define the parameters of the agreement. As well, the domestic marketing team from Nichiro visited the FPI plants in Burin, Newfoundland, and Danvers, Massachusetts, to aid in its evaluation of the FPI operations.

In June 1987, Vic Young, CEO of FPI, and Mr. Junzo Sasaki, CEO of Nichiro, signed a formal agreement. It was agreed that Nichiro would market FPI's value-added products in Japan and that FPI would provide Nichiro with exclusive access to the purchase of raw fish species traditionally supplied by FPI to the Japanese market.

Development of Product Specifications

In the summer 1987 FPI's corporate R&D department, headed by Nancy Wilson, began to develop products for potential release in the Japanese market. In order to maximize effectiveness, research, and development into new products was conducted by teams from both partners. The initial contact between the R&D representatives from FPI and Nichiro was a week-long meeting to address product issues, specifications, and consumer demands. Nichiro had advised FPI that a February release date was much preferable to October in the Japanese market. The teams met frequently through the summer in Newfoundland, and although FPI was not obligated by its agreement with Nichiro to produce a specific number of products, eventually twenty were developed for possible release with new Nichiro products in February 1988. Nichiro typically introduced between 40 and 50 of their own new products at a time.

FPI's first efforts were aimed at producing a bread coating mix specifically for products for the Japanese market. The Japanese deep-fry at lower temperatures than North Americans, a factor which had to be addressed in developing breaded and battered products. FPI already produced breaded products, but the standard coating used did not meet the Japanese requirement of a crunchy look with a soft bite. FPI's initial efforts to develop a new batter to meet Japanese standards were unsuccessful, and it was not until late October 1987 that a suitable coating was developed that met both the needs of the Japanese consumer and FPI production requirements and abilities. Of the eleven products eventually included in the final release, seven were breaded products.

Packaging requirements presented a number of problems. Japanese package sizes, which averaged 180 grams and contained portion sizes of 20 to 40 grams each, were much smaller than the 300-gram packages FPI was currently producing for its North American and European markets. Product packaging also caused concern as FPI planned to maintain its use of cardboard, a type of packaging uncommon in the Japanese marketplace. During the fall of 1987, there was a shortage of cardboard in Canada, which further complicated the production of appropriate packaging. FPI also wanted to ensure that the FPI logo and the Canadian flag were prominent on the package itself. The design of the package was made more difficult because the products to be released in February 1988 were not chosen until October 1987.

Although initial product development was done at FPI's head office, sample production runs were performed at the Burin plant (a four-hour drive from St. John's) to assess the capability of equipment and determine productivity standards. It was also critical to determine whether the stringent Japanese quality standards could be met. The initial sample production runs had reject rates as high as 30 percent, due largely to the Japanese tolerance level of approximately 30 percent on portion sizes compared to a North American standard of approximately 10 percent. All of the rejects from the sample run for the Japanese market would have been considered first-quality in the American or European markets.

Concurrently with product development, FPl's marketing department was attempting to determine a pricing strategy for the products to be marketed in Japan. This was complicated by the fact that, although production costing could normally be accurately estimated, the Japanese product would be subject to Japanese quality control standards, the impact of which was impossible to estimate accurately until full-scale production was under way. Moreover, the pricing estimates were to be based on positioning the product as unique and premium in the market, rather than simply on the cost of production. Although contributions appeared to be highest for the cod-based products, cod was relatively unknown to the Japanese consumer. Sole (or flatfish) was well known and liked, and it was hoped that sole-based products could be used as a part of a "pull" strategy to market the cod products (Exhibit 6).

Most of FPI's previous experience had been in negotiating sales to the food service industry rather than the retail market. It did produce some "house brand" retail packages, but this would be the first significant retail market outside North America that FPI had entered. Japan was perceived as a growth market, particularly for frozen products, although the potential for FPI products in the Japanese market was unknown. Given a per capita fish consumption

EXHIBIT 6   **FPI Japan Value-Added Contribution Plan, 1988**

Item	Price ($/lb.)	Direct Cost	Total Cost	Contribution ($/lb.)
Retail Market				
Cod nuggets	2.88	1.97	2.32	0.56
Cod strips	2.84	2.02	2.35	0.49
Sole dinner	2.67	2.18	2.50	0.17
Food Service Market				
Cod nuggets	2.38	1.58	1.91	0.43
Cod sticks	2.42	1.55	1.96	0.46
Scotch sole	2.22	1.86	2.15	0.07
Sole boat	2.72	2.39	2.71	0.01
Sole portion	2.72	2.61	2.89	(0.17)
Fresh-formed sole	2.15	1.51	1.91	0.24
Cod wedge, 50 g	2.23	1.56	1.91	0.31
Cod wedge, 65 g	2.21	1.52	1.87	0.34

Notes: Cod block raw material costed at US$1.50 rate versus current price of $1.30. Direct cost of raw fish based on transfer price.

of 68 kilograms, it was not unrealistic to believe that this market could absorb more of the increased capacity of the Burin plant over time. Conscious of the market potential, FPI priced the product without detailed cost information.

The Burin Plant

When FPI was created in 1984, the Burin plant was redundant to the needs of the new organization. Although it had once been a productive primary processing plant, it had not been well maintained. However, federal and provincial government money was available to help the community of Burin and the decision was made to renovate the plant. Because there was inadequate secondary processing capacity in Canada, some value-added products were being imported from the United States at considerable cost. Accordingly, the decision was made to convert the plant to secondary processing. After the renovations the Burin plant would be able to supply value-added products to the Canadian and international markets. In June 1986, the plant was closed, and renovations to turn it into a state-of-the-art secondary processing facility began. When the renovations were completed in June 1987, staff were recalled and production resumed. During the first two months, production and productivity were low as the plant geared up and the plant workers were trained on the new equipment and production lines, but by October 1987, all 108 people on the seniority list had been recalled.

FPI had contributed approximately $7.3 million of the $11.3 million cost of the Burin plant renovation. While some major equipment, including the deep fryer and cold storage facility, was retained, new equipment, including extensive conveyor equipment, two spiral freezers, and breading lines, was also installed. The renovation increased the plant's capability to process and freeze finished products from 5 million pounds to 15 million pounds annually.

Through the summer and early fall 1987, R&D efforts at Burin were intensified as products were developed for the Japanese market. In test production runs wastage of fish continued to be high, as much as 10 percent on certain products, due mainly to products not being shaped properly. It was recognized that until the Burin plant could install additional specialized equipment, part of the processing for some of the Japanese products would have to be transferred to the Danvers plant, since Danvers possessed the only prototype of an acceptable cutting machine in existence.

Staff at the Burin plant were well aware of the importance that corporate headquarters was placing upon the new products they were producing. This was illustrated in late 1987 when the decision was made to ship sole, which was then in short supply, to Burin for processing for the Japanese market, rather than supplying traditional customers in the United States. With the pressure to produce a quality product, extra staff had been placed on the breading lines and the number of quality control personnel was increased. The workers were not accustomed to such strict standards; however, they realized that it was important to produce a quality product, or their jobs and the future of the plant would be jeopardized.

By far the greatest pressure was felt by the management team, who had to ensure the coordination of activities so that everything was available in time for production. Because partial processing for some products had to be temporarily carried out at Danvers, management spent considerable time scheduling and coordinating the transfer of fish to the United States, working it into the production schedule at the Danvers plant and transporting back to Burin for final processing. It was not unusual for the Burin plant to be waiting on a shipment of semi-processed fish from Danvers and/or packaging materials from Toronto to allow the daily production schedule to be established. There was a considerable amount of time pressure as well, given Nichiro's advice to aim for a February release date.

There was considerable pressure on the Burin workers and management to keep to production schedules and produce a top-quality product, one that met the stringent Japanese quality control standards. During the production stage, three quality control specialists from Nichiro worked at the plant on a full-time basis alongside FPI's quality control employees. The groups provided constant feedback to the workers in relation to the control standards.

The first consignments of the eleven products produced at Burin for the February launch into the Japanese market were completed in December and shipped immediately to allow for the six-week lead time. The Burin plant planned to ship products twice a month via Halifax to Japan. Demand for the product was not yet known and neither Nichiro nor FPI was able to predict if these products would be accepted by the Japanese consumer.

With the first shipment of products to Japan completed, management undertook a general assessment of Burin operations, including the production for the Japanese market, and concluded that the plant would have to invest in capital equipment, including the installation of a microwave tempering and block-pressing system, to improve overall productivity. With respect to the Japanese product, Burin management questioned if some of the products currently being produced could be made profitable at the negotiated prices, even with additional equipment.

Release of Products in Japan

The release of value-added products for the Japanese domestic market took place in February 1988 with a press conference and a reception and display of products in Tokyo, jointly hosted by Mr. Young and Mr. Sasaki. This was followed by similar promotions in six additional cities in Japan during February. All of the products were well received and one, sea strips, was noted by many to be the best product to be produced in the frozen seafood class in the previous ten years. Demand for the products in Japan through the first six months after the release date was strong.

Review of the Japanese Product Line

A detailed financial review of the Japanese venture was conducted in September 1988 (Exhibit 7). The sales of value-added product to the Japanese market for the period from the February release date to September 3, 1988, were over $4 million, more than one-third of the estimated total sales to Japan for that year and significantly higher than expected.

EXHIBIT 7

FPI JAPAN SALES
ANALYSIS OF VALUE-ADDED PRODUCTS
To September 3, 1988*

Product	Pounds (000s)	Cdn$ (000s)
Retail Market		
Nuggets	306.1	$830
Sea strips (cod)	324.9	925
See dinner (sole)	286.8	765
TOTAL RETAIL	917.8	$2,520
Food Service		
Nuggets	99.4	233
Fish sticks	59.4	158
Scotch sole	52.4	116
Fresh-formed	140.2	302
Sole boat	190.4	517
Cod boat	31.8	89
Cod loin	24.1	69
Sole portion	104.3	284
TOTAL FOOD SERVICE	702.0	$1,770
TOTAL VALUE-ADDED	1,620.0	$4,290

*The date corresponds to Nichiro's fiscal year. FPI uses the calendar year.

A contentious issue was the pricing of the raw materials used in the finished product. FPI treated Burin as a profit centre and used open market prices to determine the transfer price charged by its primary production plants to Burin. If, for example, one pound (about 454 grams) of cod cost $1 on the open market, that was the transfer price used, irrespective of the actual production cost, which might be as low as $0.65. Utilizing this cost accounting approach, FPI had determined that certain of the products produced for the Japanese market were marginally profitable or unprofitable for Burin at the prices negotiated in the original arrangements (Exhibit 6). FPI's management knew, however, that when an alternative system of cost allocation was used, some of those products were profitable because production costs were lower than market prices. Despite the oversupply of cod in the market and the resulting buildup in inventory, the determination of the profitability of the Japanese products continued to be based on market pricing.

Management at the Burin plant knew that, although their existing equipment could freeze up to 15 million pounds of fish annually, they could not produce that amount of packaged finished product, particularly for the retail market. With the purchase of $640,000 worth of specialized equipment, Burin would be able to improve its overall productivity, including productivity on the Japanese line and operate independently of the Danvers plant. That investment was expected to yield an annual saving of $195,000, solely on the basis of the projected volumes of sales for 1989 for established Nichiro products.

Because of the innovative nature and high quality of the FPI products, they had been positioned in the premium price range. Although the products had proven to be popular, the fact that the Japanese consumer did not seem to be able to differentiate between premium Atlantic cod and Alaskan pollock, which was being sold for 25 percent less in the ultracompetitive Japanese retail market, had caused some concern.

Conclusion

FPI had made a significant commitment to the Japanese venture and was developing an in-house expertise that would allow it to continue in that market. Although the company realized it was capable of developing products for the Japanese domestic market, it was unsure what its strategy should be, given that not all of its products were profitable. Although the corporate R&D department of FPI continued to research additional new products, the company needed to forecast its long-term opportunity in the Japanese market. The per capita consumption of 68 kilograms of fish was very inviting, but the market share that FPI could realistically hope to achieve was unknown.

On January 30, 1989, the Canadian government announced new fish quotas and allocations, based on research which had shown a major depletion in the cod stock (Exhibit 1). The situation was considered serious and fisheries experts predicted that further cuts would be necessary in subsequent years. The quota reduction hit FPI hard, and virtually overnight cod moved from a position of oversupply to one of undersupply. FPI now had to consider whether it might be wiser to market its limited resource in traditional markets, rather than attempt to maintain the company's presence in Japan. Foreign exchange markets were also causing some concern. The yen, which had moved from 200 to the dollar to as low as 99 to the dollar in January 1988, had reversed its downward trend. In January 1989, it stood at 109 yen to the dollar and experts were predicting further increases. Because the prices had been negotiated in Canadian dollars, Nichiro was absorbing the resulting costs, but it was unclear how long it would continue to do so, or what the future financial implications might be for FPI.

As Vic again reviewed the report from Randy Bishop, he acknowledged that, although sales to Japan were higher than FPI had anticipated, this had not been achieved without strain on the company. FPI was growing rapidly; in 1986 and 1987, profit had been $22,330,000 and $31,004,000, respectively. Although the company had been successful in Japan, the nature of that market would require the ongoing development of new and innovative products and a commitment to the venture which might call for a disproportionate amount of management time. Nichiro was already pushing for the development of new products for October 1989. With currency exchange fluctuations and a major drop in quotas, Vic wondered what the strategy should be for the Japanese market and how it fit with the future growth and direction of FPI.

GAMETRONICS

Early Wednesday morning, August 10, 1994, Tom Katz, the new CEO and president of GAMETRONICS (a manufacturer of video game software), settled into his chair at his office in San Jose, California, and began to scan the morning newspaper when the phone rang. It was Martin Fueller, a controlling shareholder and chairman of the board of GAMETRONICS. Fueller told Katz that he had just received a call from a close friend in New York with some troubling news. Rumours were circulating in the arbitrage department of one of the large securities firms that a hostile takeover of GAMETRONICS was being planned by Sony Corp. Fueller said that he did not believe a takeover could be achieved without his consent, since he held 42.5 percent of GAMETRONICS' shares. He also told Katz that while he had not yet been contacted by Sony, if the rumors proved correct, he could anticipate that a call would be forthcoming within the next week. As the conversation progressed, Fueller acknowledged that over the past year he had grown increasingly concerned about the company's lacklustre performance. "Of course you know, Tom," he said, "you have my full support. But we have to act. I am giving you one week to put together a plan. One that we can live with, not only now, but into the future." When Katz hung up the phone he called his secretary and cancelled all meetings for the day. Then he sat staring out his fourth-storey window, wondering why only two months earlier he had been so happy to assume his new position as president.

The Video Game Industry

The video game industry was composed of a wide range of small, medium, and large companies in both software and hardware segments. Both sides of the industry were closely tied through their mutual dependence on technological innovation and an often fickle market. Over its short twenty-year life, the industry suffered cycles of enormous prosperity followed by often-significant downturns. In the early 1970s the industry sprang to life with *Pong* as well as several derivative products. During the late 1970s and early 1980s, the industry

---

This case was prepared by Professor Allen Morrison with assistance from Jan Visser, Andres Maldonado, and Heather Leonard. The name of the real company which served as the basis for this case as well as financial data have been disguised. © 1994 The American Graduate School of International Management.

experienced a major boom led by upstart Atari. After 1982, the bottom fell out of Atari's sales as a consequence of its inability to come up with new, interesting, and appealing software games. In 1985, the industry began recovering and during the late 1980s and early 1990s, video game hardware and software sales and profits boomed.

The industry's recovery in the late 1980s was led by Japan-based Nintendo which offered an array of innovative games based on 8-bit technology. To entice parents to purchase their machines, Nintendo sold hardware at prices close to its costs. Only after the machines were purchased did parents learn that an enormous investment would be required in new software to maintain their children's interests. Nintendo's strategy of squeezing most of its profits out of the software side of the business became a model for other competitors. To maximize returns, only the most critical hardware and software design and marketing functions were kept in-house. In 1992, Nintendo employed just 892 people and generated sales of $5.5 billion.

In 1989, Sega a medium-sized Japanese video game manufacturer, entered the market with *Genesis*. *Genesis* employed superior 16-bit technology which resulted in more realistic and complex graphics compared to the Nintendo system. Sega also attracted consumers with rock-bottom hardware prices. They combined this approach with lower licensing fees for software suppliers. Lower fees attracted some of the best software developers in the industry and the resulting line of new games led to soaring sales. In 1992, Sega's sales topped $4 billion.

By 1994, the worldwide video game hardware and software industry revenues topped $11.3 billion. The industry was effectively controlled by Nintendo with 46 percent market share and Sega with 36 percent market share. The remaining 18 percent share was split among several other minor players. By 1994, both Nintendo and Sega had an installed base of approximately 65 million machines across the United States, Europe, and Asia Pacific.

Despite an enormous boom in sales during the late 1980s and early 1990s, the industry in 1994 was starting to show signs of another downturn. Beginning in early 1993 and continuing through mid-1994, Sega and Nintendo had been engaged in an ongoing price war which emerged from the growing software inventories that the two firms had been unable to sell. The failure of both companies to introduce new, innovative games appeared to be a major problem. As Mike Anderson, account manager at one major retail outlet indicated:

> Consumers are tired of having to pay large amounts of money for the same games; both Sega and Nintendo thought lowering prices was the way to get rid of inventories by stealing market share from one another or by attracting new consumers. This has not been the answer. ... What customers want is new technology. The current generation of video games is losing steam; consumers are waiting for a new line of video games that should be ready for late 1994 or for the beginning of 1995.

Exacerbating the problems for both Sega and Nintendo was the arrival of several new competitors. The evolution of video games into virtual reality capabilities attracted the interest of other high-tech companies seeking a place in the new information superhighway. Sony, for example, announced that it would be entering the market in late 1994 in Japan and early 1995 in the United States with compact disk (CD) technology. Sony's new machine, called the *Playstation,* was equipped with 32-bit chips which could support even more complex software and sophisticated graphics programs. In bringing CD games to the market, Sony planned to tap its enormous Hollywood movie library. Atari also reentered the market with a new hardware game system called *Jaguar;* Commodore and Phillips were also getting ready with CD-based game systems. Beyond these dedicated video game competitors was the growing threat of personal computer (PC)–based games. While in 1994 it was estimated that about 85 percent of video games were sold in cartridge format, the rapidly escalating graphics and sound quality of PCs suggested that PC-based video game sales would grow at a disproportionate rate. The movement toward PC-based games was also attracting a variety of new software entrants. For example, in the fall of 1994 Walt Disney entered the software fray by introducing two interactive, multi-media PC-based games: *Aladdin Activity Center* and *Disney's Animated Storybook: The Lion King.*

Nintendo and Sega Strike Back

Motivated by fear of fleeing sales, both Sega and Nintendo began developing their own CD-based systems in the early 1990s. To cut development time and incorporate the most advanced technology available, Sega established a series of collaborative agreements with leading technology companies. Agreements were made with AT&T to develop telephone communication capabilities for the games, with Hitachi to manufacture microprocessor chips, with Yamaha to produce greater sound capabilities, and with JVC to assemble the machines. Sega was also holding discussions with Microsoft to develop a range of new software. The result was a prototype 3-D, combination CD and cartridge system called *Saturn.* By mid-1994, Sega was reported to have a $200 million annual R&D budget, much of it going toward *Saturn.* While the company hoped to have the system on the market by late 1994, the coordination of software and hardware development was proving to be a significant challenge.

Nintendo's strategy for the mid- and late 1990s centred around *Project Reality,* which was intended as a 32-bit replacement for *Super Nintendo.* In proceeding with *Project Reality,* the company announced it would be sticking to cartridges as opposed to CD technology. According to one company spokesperson:

> CD technology takes longer than cartridges to seek out and display images on the screen and, therefore, does not test hard trigger reflexes. The format is very complex and that is why there are so few good CD games.[1]

Despite this concern, CD-ROM games were cheaper to manufacture than cartridge games—roughly two dollars to make one CD-ROM game, compared with ten dollars to make a cartridge. For consumers, however, cheaper games were offset by significantly more expensive CD-ROM hardware.

---

[1] "Sega trying video component strategy," *Television Digest,* March 21, 1994, p. 11.

Not surprisingly, many in the industry debated the attractiveness of CD-ROM technology. Even within companies, opinions differed. For example, at Electronic Arts Inc., a major manufacturer of game software, Bing Gordon, an executive vice-president, argued that "although the whole industry believes CD-ROM is the wave of the future, there is reason to believe that the mass market is not going to understand the value of the improved play as justification for the higher price CD-ROM-equipped console."[2] This view was not shared by his boss, Lawrence Probst, chairman of Electronic Arts, who actually set company strategy. According to Probst, "our strategy is to get there (CD-ROM based games) early, be prolific and carve out market share."[3] Even Nintendo seemed to be hedging its bets. Despite its public statements of disinterest in CD-based games, the company was negotiating a partnership with Silicon Graphics Incorporated to develop unspecified multimedia (PC/CD-ROM–based) applications.

Software Developers

Individual software companies developed from as few as one to as many as fifteen or more games per year. Games were typically developed specifically for either Nintendo or Sega. Once developed, game manufacturers would approach the target company for licensing opportunities. If a game was not accepted, the approval process began all over again after repackaging in an alternative format. With few exceptions, Nintendo and Sega insisted that outside software companies sign exclusive contracts and pay royalties which could amount to as much as 30 percent for the privilege of writing games for Nintendo and Sega systems. Even in cases where developers were not required to sign exclusivity contracts, they risked losing all future sales if either Nintendo or Sega found out they had been double-dealing.

Software played a major role in determining the fate of the major hardware vendors. Of the software used by Nintendo, approximately 65 percent was developed externally; for Sega, this figure was 55 percent. With software development costs soaring due to increasingly complex operating systems, many industry observers predicted that both Nintendo and Sega would promote fewer, more expensive games in the future.

In many cases, both Nintendo and Sega relied on the same software development companies. Sega's growing market share was generally well received by software companies because it meant that they would be less reliant on Nintendo. In 1994, Nintendo had begun changing its rigid licensing stance in the face of increased competition. In exceptional circumstances, Nintendo had even begun paying development fees to certain software companies plus royalties which ranged between 2 and 12 percent.

In 1994, only about 30 percent of the games developed were accepted by Sega and Nintendo. Part of the problem was that software companies had to consider the constantly changing tastes of end users who were, as Bobby

---

[2] *Business Week,* p. 43.

[3] Jim Carlton, "Electronic arts shifts focus to CD-ROM video games," *The Wall Street Journal,* September 7, 1994, p. B6.

Kotick, CEO of Activision, defined, "boys from six to sixteen and guys who can't get a date on Saturday night."[4] Terry Munson, a Nintendo employee who answered telephone questions from stumped players, believed that a really successful title was one that kids enjoyed for a month. The impact of a fickle market was perhaps best summed up by Nintendo of America president Minoru Arakawa: "If we don't supply kids with interesting and new products all the time, we'll get killed and buried."[5]

A combination of both design talent and an eye for ever-changing market demands was essential in developing winning software. Many industry observers were increasingly convinced that market research was producing too many "me-too" games and that true blockbusters could only come from design genius. While market research could indicate an insatiable demand for hit games like *Mortal Kombat* and *Street Fighter II,* many copycat games had only limited appeal. Totally new game concepts frequently came from within the mind of the designer. This view was expressed by Sigeru Miyamoto, the chief developer of Nintendo's *Super Mario Brothers*: "I am not creating a game, I am in the game. The game is not for children, it is for me."[6]

Despite the demand for highly innovative software designers, these individuals were often difficult to work with. Many designers were perfectionists who became so obsessive in the design process that they had enormous problems getting up to speed on new projects. In addition, top designers often lacked interpersonal skills and had a difficult time working in design teams. Finally, good designers commanded top salaries and reciprocated with limited company loyalty.

■ GAMETRONICS

GAMETRONICS manufactured and developed video game software that was distributed throughout the United States and several European and Asian countries. In 1993, net company sales reached $58.34 million and operating profits topped $7.98 million. (See Exhibits 1, 2, and 3 for a review of GAMETRONICS' performance.) The company had 156 employees worldwide divided primarily between software development, operations, sales and service. In 1994, all GAMETRONICS video game software was licensed or sold to Sega and Nintendo which added their own labels and distributed the product worldwide.

GAMETRONICS was started in 1980 as a wholly-owned affiliate of Fueller's Corporation. Fueller's was itself begun by Martin Fueller in 1963 with inheritance money received from his grandfather who had built a sizable fortune in the 1920s and 1930s in the textile industry. During much of the 1960s and 1970s, Fueller's was engaged in plastic production with plants in West Virginia, New York, and Illinois. In 1978, the company started manufacturing plastic floppy disk covers for the computer industry and became a principal supplier

---

[4] V. Rice and B. Snyder, "Busy going Hollywood," *PC Week,* November 29, 1993, p. A6(1).

[5] *Fortune,* p. 110.

[6] As quoted in David Sheaf, *Game Over: How Nintendo Zapped an American Industry, Captured Your Dollars, and Enslaved Your Children* (New York: Random House, 1993), p. 51.

EXHIBIT 1

INCOME STATEMENT
GAMETRONICS
(in millions)

	1985	1990	1991	1992	1993
Net sales	12.81	39.09	47.81	54.02	58.34
Cost of goods sold	6.40	19.74	24.29	27.50	30.12
GROSS PROFIT	6.41	19.35	23.52	26.52	28.22
Selling and administrative expenses	2.31	7.94	9.75	11.07	12.26
R&D expenses	1.26	3.91	5.88	6.64	6.87
Depreciation, amortization	0.35	0.72	0.80	1.07	1.12
OPERATING PROFIT	2.49	6.78	7.09	7.74	7.97
Total interest	0.12	0.43	0.48	0.70	0.76
Non-operating income/expenses	0.21	1.13	1.27	1.43	1.50
PRETAX INCOME	2.16	5.22	5.34	5.61	5.71

EXHIBIT 2

UNIT AND DOLLAR SALES
GAMETRONICS
(in millions)

	1985	1990	1991	1992	1993
Unit sales	1.42	3.55	4.20	4.16	3.89
Sales	13.26	41.32	50.68	58.13	63.01

EXHIBIT 3

BALANCE SHEET 1993
GAMETRONICS
(in millions)

Assets		Liabilities	
Cash and equivalents	3.70	Notes payable	1.20
Accounts receivable	3.52	Accounts payable	4.96
Inventories	7.12	Accrued expenses	3.96
Other current assets	6.56	Taxes payable	1.81
TOTAL CURRENT ASSETS	20.90	Other current liabilities	1.21
		TOTAL CURRENT LIABILITIES	13.14
Gross plant	6.74		
Accumulated depreciation	1.75	Deferred taxes	0.90
Net plant	4.99	Long-term debt	8.20
Deferred charges	0.46	Other long-term liabilities	0.62
Intangible assets	36.49	TOTAL LIABILITIES	22.86
Other long-term assets	0.32	**Equity**	
TOTAL ASSETS	63.16	Preferred stock	27.00
		Common stock	7.00
		Retained earnings	5.70
		Other liabilities	0.60
		TOTAL EQUITY	40.30
		TOTAL LIABILITY AND EQUITY	63.16

for Apple II computers. At the end of the same year, Fueller's floppy disk business was incorporated under the name of Protoinfo Inc. This company operated with relative success until heightened competition in the mid-1980s pushed Protoinfo out of the floppy disk cover business. Protoinfo then refocused on its roots—the manufacturing of plastic parts for computer components. In 1994, Protoinfo had sales of $32 million in plastic computer keys, laptop computer casing, and floppy disk carrying cases.

With growing contacts in the computer industry, Martin Fueller had become convinced that the real profits in the industry lay in software development. Concern that the giant computer companies would be hard to work with combined with Atari's spectacular profits in the late 1970s convinced Fueller that niche, game-based software would offer the easiest avenue to success. In 1979, a separate software development division was created at Protoinfo. Six software engineers were hired, each recent university graduates in computer science. One of these engineers, Harold Green, age 26, was appointed general manager of software operations. After nine months of development, the company entered the market with *Martian Invasion*. Within six months, 320,000 copies had been sold with an average retail price of $19.95. Protoinfo received about $7 for each game cartridge.

With this initial success, the video game business at Protoinfo was spun off into GAMETRONICS, a wholly owned affiliate of Fueller's. Harold Green was appointed president. By 1983, the engineering staff had tripled to eighteen people. An additional fifteen people had been hired in manufacturing and shipping, and an additional six employed as full-time sales representatives.

In 1985, after several years of good returns, Martin Fueller took GAMETRONICS public, selling some 57.5 percent of his shares in the process. At the time, net sales were near $12.8 million, and operating profits were almost $2.5 million. In looking back on the events surrounding the public offering, Martin Fueller commented:

> We decided to take it public because the industry had such a promising future. Prices were going wild. At the time of the initial offering, the stock was trading at 32 times its earnings. My other businesses weren't doing anywhere near that well. In retrospect, it was almost certainly a mistake. Back then, Microsoft only had sales of $140 million. Look at Bill Gates today. I actually thought that I needed the money. A friend had me convinced of a great opportunity to buy into an underutilized plastics resin plant that Monsanto had put on the block. I thought it would be a great fit with Protoinfo. I ended up buying a 20 percent share. Yet resin prices have been very volatile and I have never been satisfied with its performance.

In taking GAMETRONICS public, Fueller was able to maintain effective control, because no other single shareholder held more than 20 percent of the stock.

Sales climbed each year during the next eight years. They were helped by highly favourable industry conditions and a string of software hits including *Alligator Warrior, Super Racer, Cliff Diver,* and *Jungle Warfare.* As performance picked up, Martin Fueller devoted more and more of his time to outside interests. While he would come every month to check the books, Harold Green was left to make critical decisions.

Changes in Top Management

In May 1994, Harold Green announced that he would be stepping down as president of GAMETRONICS to assume a senior management position at a major Utah-based software development company. One month later, Martin Fueller appointed 42-year-old Tom Katz to the vacated position of president and CEO of GAMETRONICS. Katz, who was at the time serving as vice-president of sales and marketing, assumed his new duties on June 6.

Tom Katz was raised in the New York City borough of Queens and in 1975 graduated from City University of New York with an undergraduate degree in Computer Science. Upon graduating, he immediately entered the MBA program at Fordham University and placed in the top 5 percent of his 1977 graduating class. Interested in working in the computer industry, Katz accepted an offer from a major Boston-based software manufacturer. Over the next three years, Katz became the top performer at the company, where his responsibilities included selling preinstalled software packages to large accounts including Wang, IBM, Toshiba, and Compaq.

Katz first became acquainted with GAMETRONICS and Green at a software trade show in Las Vegas in 1983. Over the next two years both men kept in contact and in November 1985 Green asked whether Katz would ever be interested in working for GAMETRONICS. One month later Katz joined the company in the newly created position of vice-president of sales. When Green left the company, Fueller turned to Katz as the obvious replacement: "He has the experience and the results behind him to become a successful leader to take the company through the changing future of the video manufacturing industry."

The majority of employees were also delighted at the news. Gerry Oswald, head of production, was quoted at the time as saying:

> This is the right decision. The president needs to be someone who will move GAMETRONICS towards the future of the video game industry. Tom is the person who will initiate changes and listen to the ideas of not only the customers but employees as well.

Emerging Challenges

In assuming his new position, Katz was aware of several challenges facing the company. One problem was that sales increases seemed to be much more a function of title proliferation than of market hits. The company's best-selling game, *Jungle Warfare,* accounted for 18 percent of GAMETRONICS' sales, representing approximately 700,000 units at $15 each. While this resulted in a solid market position, it was not a blockbuster. True blockbuster games generated sales of over one million cartridges and provided enormous cash flow. Cash flow was essential for funding new games. Development costs in the industry averaged well over $1 million for each new game; in some well-publicized cases, game development costs exceeded $3 million. Of GAMETRONICS' library of 138 games, only six had been introduced within the last 12 months.

GAMETRONICS was also having internal problems with production and inventory control. All sales of video games to Nintendo and Sega were subject to extensive performance parameters, and rejected games became the sole financial burden of GAMETRONICS. In 1993, rejection rates were twice that of industry averages. The rejections were primarily the result of packaging and labelling problems. In addition, company managers felt that GAMETRONICS' prototype games were often rejected on the apparent whims of Nintendo and Sega purchasing agents. When a decision *was* made to buy from GAME-TRONICS, Nintendo and Sega demanded almost overnight deliveries. The result was that GAMETRONICS often overproduced batches of cartridges in expectation of escalating demand that in many cases never materialized.

Internal friction mounted when sales did not materialize. In most cases the sales staff blamed the software developers for producing inferior games. Software developers, in turn, blamed the sales and marketing staff for ineffective research and for weak customer contacts. The production department was often blamed for either overproducing or not having the right products available when needed. When Katz met individually with managers to discuss possible solutions, he was disappointed with their responses. Gerry Oswald argued:

> pressure from the sales staff to have new products developed or production increased is unrealistic. I don't think they understand what goes into developing the product and preparing it for distribution. Even if some of them do, they don't seem to care.

Paul Frierson, vice-president of development, argued:

> we are falling behind on R&D compared with the others. The budget just isn't there to hire the new talent coming on the market. Furthermore, whatever we do doesn't seem good enough. A lot of my people are getting demoralized.

Before Fueller's call on June 1, Katz had intended to focus his short-term efforts on the mounting internal problems facing GAMETRONICS. This priority now seemed to fade.

Weighing Options

As Katz considered where to turn, his thoughts shifted to an initiative that Green had explored but which had been cut short by his departure. It was the option of moving the company into educational software. The idea had come to Green quite unexpectedly during the summer of 1993 when Green heard his neighbours complain that their children spent too much time playing video games. This comment made Green realize that a movement to educational games could represent a good business opportunity for the company. Green called Fueller early the next day and told him the idea. Fueller agreed:

> This sounds great. It could be the solution that would help us offset the weak demand for video games we seem to be facing. It would also help diversify some of the risk involved in being in a particular segment of the industry. Education seems like a low-risk option.

Green started researching the educational software industry and found that it had an entirely different structure from the video game segment. A number of small companies had been able to survive in the market, thanks to very specialized software development. While most educational software was distributed through medium-size and large companies, these small firms were able to deliver the product directly to the end consumer typically through mail order distribution. Since the late 1980s, the industry had expanded greatly, fuelled in large part by a surge in home computer sales. After reviewing the files prepared by Green, Katz determined that the cost of developing educational software capabilities from scratch would require a capital investment of approximately $4 million over two years.

Another alternative was to buy an existing educational software company. Green had already done some preliminary research into this possibility. About three months before he left GAMETRONICS, Green had taken a trip to Bombay, India, to follow up on a lead to buy a small educational software development company called Educomp. Educomp's software was developed by four Indian nationals who shared ownership of the company. Total sales for Educomp were approximately $5.2 million, with about $1 million coming from exports to the United States and England. After-tax profits had averaged between 20 percent and 25 percent for the last three years. These returns were significantly higher than industry norms for educational software companies, which averaged between 17 percent and 18 percent. While Katz had not had any direct contact with Educomp, he had been in recent phone contact with Green who indicated that he would be happy to make formal introductions. In their telephone conversation, Green also offered some additional commentary:

> Tom, although it has now been a couple of months since I left, one of my big disappointments was in not getting closure on Educomp. Things just got too busy at the end. They are good people with world-class talents. I am sure they would still be happy to talk. I was also impressed with the abundance of inexpensive, talented programmers in India. ... It is obviously your call. My guess is that with the right arguments you could quite easily get Fueller to go along.

In addition to considering a move into educational software, Katz was weighing an option to sell the company's game library. This option was the result of a recent inquiry by a software distributor who was interested in buying GAMETRONICS' library of cartridges in order to turn them into PC-based games. Under the proposal, GAMETRONICS would receive $2.6 million in cash for the library with additional annual royalty payments of 4 percent. Only existing games would be covered; new titles would not be included. Katz estimated that royalty payments might amount to as much as $400,000 in the first year, declining each year thereafter.

Another option was to focus efforts on strengthening the existing development team at GAMETRONICS. It was clear that the company needed a constant stream of winning software titles and that pressure to do so would only increase. By focusing on the engineering core and investing in new computing facilities and manpower, GAMETRONICS could maximize its chances of staying at the forefront of software development. Katz figured that if he increased the R&D budget by 20 percent and allocated one-half of the additional money to new benefits such as bonuses and other incentives to the designers, morale and, quite possibly, output would improve significantly. The remaining new money could also fund the hiring of possibly four new software designers.

A final solution would be to attempt to form an alliance with some as yet to be determined large company in the industry. GAMETRONICS was dwarfed in sales by some of its larger software game competitors such as Virgin Interactive Entertainment (a unit of Viacom, Inc.), Acclaim Entertainment Co., and Electronic Arts Inc., which had sales that ranged from $100 million to $1 billion. By working with a company like NEC or Microsoft, GAME-TRONICS would have access to the latest technologies and benefit from their distribution channels. Katz was uncertain whether an ideal partner would be one in the software side or one in the hardware side of the industry. He was also aware of a number of instances where alliances led to a significant loss of autonomy on the part of the smaller company and wondered how Martin Fueller might perceive this risk.

With so many options, Katz was uncertain how to proceed. He realized that involving his top managers in a discussion of the options was highly risky. If word of the potential acquisition of GAMETRONICS slipped out, the impact on employee morale might be disastrous. In the back of his mind, Katz wondered whether being acquired would not be such a bad idea for him personally. New investment would lead to more responsibility and expanded career options. However, Katz knew that such thoughts could not be shared with Fueller who was certain to fight any appearance of an acquisition. As he sat at his desk, Katz realized that Fueller expected a plan of action. He had maybe a week to put it all together.

GT's Medical Equipment Division & IMed Inc. (A)

Bob Shepard was sitting at his desk contemplating what action he should take. He had met with outside legal counsel earlier that day. During this meeting, the lawyers had outlined possible actions (see Exhibit 1). Yet, in spite of this meeting, Bob felt frustrated and angry. His tenure as manager of the division had been nothing but a variety of unpleasant surprises.

Bob was general manager of the Medical Equipment Division within General Technologies (GT) Inc. GT was a major U.S.-based conglomerate that had approximately a dozen large divisions, all of which were major corporations unto themselves. These divisions were mostly in the telecommunications, electrical, and high-tech businesses. The Medical Equipment Division was the newest and smallest division, one that had been born out of orphan medical product lines from other divisions plus some new product development projects. GT was known for its aggressive as well as progressive management style.

Two years ago, Bob was promoted to GM of the Medical Equipment Division. This was after a very successful sojourn at the larger Telecommunications Equipment Division. He was hired into GT as a marketing representative, after having completed an MBA at a top Midwestern U.S. business school. In marketing, he initiated new approaches to customer relations and services, which gave him with the fastest sales growth in the division. This success had translated into promotions, first to sales group manager and then to product group manager. During this time, he had built the group into one of the most competitive and profitable segments in the division by aggressively cutting costs, maintaining relatively low prices, and more effectively targeting customers. When he took over as head of the Medical Equipment Division his mandate was clear—*make the division profitable.*

The Medical Equipment Division's History

The Medical Equipment Division had evolved over a period of years from a variety of products and projects in the Electronic and Scientific Equipment

EXHIBIT 1   The Lawyers' Briefing

The lawyers advised Bob of the following potential actions. These actions were presented to Bob in order of legal risk and cost, the first option having no legal cost and risk, while the latter options have considerable legal costs and risks.

Costs and risks were uncertain. However, the lawyers estimated the second option would probably cost less than one hundred thousand dollars (at least initially); the third option would probably cost several hundred thousand dollars to begin to proceed with (the final cost would depend on how far the charges proceeded); and the last option probably would cost in excess of several million dollars. The legal risks of the first two options would be relatively minimal, but the legal risks of the last two options could be significant because almost certainly countercharges would be forthcoming. The liability and costs of fighting these countercharges would be very difficult to estimate, and they would be clearly the highest if option four were selected.

The lawyers also noted that these escalating risks and costs could be similarly applied to the opposing party in the suits—that is, option four would carry more risks and costs for Keith and IMed too.

1. Do nothing.

2. Begin to investigate charges or possible charges but do not charge Keith and IMed yet. Attempt to find out what happened and whether IMed is using any of the technology that Keith worked on at GT. The action taken would be to hire both internal and external investigators to find out who is using what technology, where Keith's missing personnel documents are, and who developed what technologies.

3. Advise the lawyers to draft charges against Keith and his company. This would allow GT's lawyers and experts to cross-examine, under oath, Keith and other IMed employees. It would also give GT a peek at their technology although they had some idea of the technology through searches of the patent filings. This approach would be much more expensive than option two, but it would give GT all of the information categorically and it would possibly let GT get a peek at how their patent ideas fit into their working sensor.

4. Aggressively attempt to inflict the maximum damage to Keith and IMed. This would involve hiring an investigator to seek all damaging information on IMed and Keith (i.e., financial, legal, etc.). As many lawsuits as possible would be filed against both Keith and IMed. In addition, find out about the IPO. The lawyers advised that filing charges against Keith and IMed and getting a cease and desist court order against IMed during the IPO would be very damaging. However, they warned that GT would have to go into the cease and desist court hearings with very strong statements of misconduct against both Keith and IMed. This was because such a restraining order would constrain Keith and IMed from doing any business at all for a certain amount of time. For a judge to grant such an order, the evidence would have to be persuasive. Furthermore, such a move would tend to inflict the maximum legal damage to IMed, because it would demonstrate to the new shareholders that IMed had not provided full and accurate information in their IPO. Almost certainly shareholders would begin a class action suit against IMed.

Divisions. Initially, the division started as an intrepreneurial R&D unit. Then, when Bob was assigned as GM of the division, the distribution and marketing rights of medical equipment products made by other divisions were transferred into this division. The aim was to develop revenues and income support for new R&D projects as well as building marketing, sales, and service support resources in the division.

GT decided to put medical products into a separate division because the other divisions were clearly not providing adequate product development and marketing support. Product development initiatives and sales were being lost in other departments because the engineers and sales support staff were not knowledgeable about the diverse medical specialties and the complex purchasing decisions in medical institutions (see Exhibit 2 and Exhibit 3). Yet, the business looked attractive. The population was aging and medicine was turning more and more to technological solutions. GT felt that their technological knowledge and abilities could provide them with an important advantage in this market.

From a competitive stance, the new division faced a variety of problems. Competitors were of two types. Large competitors, such as Toshiba, Siemens, Hewlett-Packard, Beckman Instruments, and Abbot Laboratories, were all billion-dollar-plus companies having large, highly knowledgeable sales forces, huge R&D budgets, a broad product scope, and usually several critical patents. Where these companies did not have patent protection they competed on strong customer relationships. In fact, the market for some of these products had evolved to the point where the products were of similar quality, but customer relationships differentiated the better competitors in the market. In addition, after sales, service and support in the form of providing ancillary products and quick repair and replacement (i.e., within hours) was very important.

There were also numerous small companies in the medical equipment market. These generally worked through distributors and relied on patents, market focus, or specialization to protect themselves from the larger competitors.

Approximately seven years ago, executives at GT were grappling with the decision with what to do with medical products because the barriers to entry were high and increasing rapidly. Yet, they had not developed a medical business large enough or products unique enough to provide them with such barriers to entry. They considered divesting the business, but because it was not a business unto itself, selling it would be difficult. Another argument against selling it was that the market segment looked quite attractive, having a growth rate in excess of 20 percent annually.

EXHIBIT 2   **Partial List of Medical Specialities**

• Surgery	• Immunology
• Radiology	• Neurology
• Pharmaceutical	• Oncology
• Cardiology	• Endocrinology
• Genetics	• Anesthesiology

EXHIBIT 3   **List of Medical Equipment Markets**

• Cardiovascular devices	• Medical lasers
• Pacemakers and defibrillators	• Medical plastics
• Health care products and commodities	• Monitors and instrumentation
• Home testing and test kits	• Surgical instruments
• Biomaterials	• Clinical lab equipment and instrumentation
• Medical imaging equipment	

Fortunately, the decision was aided by the fact that a successful product developer in the medical sensing field, Keith Fischer, approached them with an idea. He suggested that GT fund the development of a new medical product, a blood analyzing sensor. GT was very enthusiastic about the idea, because it would potentially allow them to develop R&D capabilities, customer servicing capabilities, and sales and marketing abilities, based upon this product and its patent; then they could leverage these strengths as new products were developed.

Keith had developed the scientific basis for a sensing device while doing his Ph.D. at a California university. During these studies he realized the potential of a blood sugar sensor for diabetics. Therefore, he quit the program and began developing the device on his own. Relatives and several government business/research grants subsidized the development of the product. The resulting product gave a diabetic patient blood sugar results within seconds and without the messy chemical strips that were normally required. When the sensor was introduced it was well received and within weeks a major medical equipment distributor purchased the rights to the technology.

Keith, out of a job and still only in his late 20s, had become a relatively wealthy man due to the success of this prior sensor (estimated wealth $5 million to $10 million). Yet, since he was a scientist at heart, his inventive drive had merely been whetted. Thus, Keith began considering extensions to his previous sensor work. When the idea of a complete blood analysis sensor evolved, he approached GT, where he proceeded to convince them of the merits of his new idea. He talked avidly of how a more general blood chemical analysis device should and could be developed.

GT managers saw the enormous potential of this product. Presently, chemical blood analysis took up to two weeks; even in the case of emergencies it often took several hours. The problem with present approaches was that before every analysis a variety of fresh chemicals had to be mixed to calibrate the electronic sensing device. Then other chemicals had to be used to treat the blood prior to having the machine analyze the results. This procedure always had to be done by highly qualified lab technicians to ensure accurate results. Furthermore, many small hospitals and most doctors' clinics did not have the facilities or the technicians to perform such an analysis. Therefore, a sensor that could produce blood analysis results quickly, with no expensive calibration procedure, would be an enormous product breakthrough.

All those who listened to Keith loved his idea, and GT immediately offered him a position as manager of a new R&D unit. The research unit's initial objective would be to develop the blood sensing device. Then, when the product reached the commercial stage a Medical Equipment Division would be formed. GT made its desires clear to Keith: they wanted to become a leading medical equipment supplier, and they saw this as a rare opportunity to build such a business.

Keith accepted the position because he felt that GT's technological resources could allow him to develop a variety of new medical sensing devices. Furthermore, the position satisfied his immediate desire to be a scientist, yet also gave him the opportunity to evolve into a variety of management roles, if he so desired in the future. Keith clearly felt that GT was offering him a future with enormous potential.

The project started with tremendous enthusiasm. Keith hired a core of top scientists. Lab and office space was established and for three years they methodically researched and developed various components of the complex sensing device. Compared to the blood sugar sensor, this device was many times more complex because of the variety of tests that had to be performed simultaneously and the complex relationships between blood gases, solubles, and organics. The research was extremely difficult and at times the team ran into problems that initially appeared to be insurmountable. However, with time and patience, research led them to work-around solutions.

During the fourth year progress slowed dramatically. In particular, the team could not find a comprehensive solution to a sensor calibration problem. The sensor would not stay calibrated between tests. The dilemma was that it had to be very sensitive to measure the various blood chemicals, yet this sensitivity also created calibration problems. The most minute environmental changes affected the results. To use the sensor in its present state meant that a lab technician would have to recalibrate it after each test. They had tried a wide variety of solutions, most of them extremely expensive and complex, but each solution had only corrected parts of the problem and combining them had proven to be impossible—at least so far.

At this point in time, Keith was beginning to feel some pressure for progress. Clearly the problem was a major hurdle for the project and team. To this end, Keith had begun considering a wide variety of potential new avenues of research. And after much research, Keith felt a solution might lie in an ion battery technology used in a new CO_2 gas analyzer for liquids. Approximately a month ago he had met the inventor of the analyzer, Dr. Jim Slatery, at a conference. The two immediately struck up a scientific kinship, and after several visits and long discussions Keith began to be quite excited about the potential for this new avenue of research. However, the other researchers, all having Ph.D.s, were quite reticent about this technical approach. First, it would mean throwing out much of the prior work and starting afresh. Second, the team would have to acquire new skills in a scientific area called gas-liquid ion battery technology. This would take both time and money. And finally, the other researchers pointed out that this technology had a long research history that was littered with failures and difficulties. Even the simplest of gas-liquid ion batteries were extremely difficult to keep stable for any length of time, and manufacturing them had proven to be virtually impossible. The complex battery that would be required in this case was unheard of in such research.

In the meantime, top management in the Electrical Equipment Sector was becoming worried about the lack of progress. The project was consuming almost $4 million annually in operating costs, and the accumulated capital costs were not being amortized against any profits. To date they had sunk over $25 million in the project and it seemed to be stalled. Based on these concerns, they decided to bring a professional manager into the project. Bob Shepard volunteered for the position and he was quickly promoted into it.

Bob realized that if he were successful it would have a very positive effect on his career in the company. However, he also realized that marketing and business management was his forte, not management of R&D projects. Therefore, he accepted the position on the condition that the unit be turned into a division, and marketing, sales, and service groups that represented medical products in other divisions be rolled into the new division within three months. This would give the division a chance to build some revenue and profit streams to offset the ongoing research costs.

Upon taking the job, Bob met with research staff to try and understand the depths of the project problems. He quickly realized that the project was incurring a variety of difficulties all stemming from the calibration problem. For example, the underlying disagreement over a solution to the calibration problem was factionalizing the group into two camps, particularly because Keith, their leader, was absent most of the time, either visiting Dr. Slatery or devoting time to researching the new technology—nobody in fact knew which. Bob realized he had to provide some direction to the project or it might disintegrate. He also understood that the team could not afford to pursue both lines of research, because one line of research was expensive enough. Therefore, he decided to defuse the issue by having a democratic vote. The vote was held and the solid state approach won over the gas-liquid ion battery.

Within the day Keith handed in his resignation. He felt not only betrayed by GT and its initial commitment to fund his research, but also slighted that they would bring in a manager who knew nothing about the technology and allow that person to make unilateral decisions without consulting him.

Pushing for a Commercial Product

Bob asked the remaining team to concentrate on two objectives: develop a prototype, and then attempt to incrementally improve the calibration problem. His first objective of developing a prototype was aimed at getting a marketable product out as soon as possible. He felt that they could compete initially with the machine in its present state, because, although it had calibration problems, it was smaller than competitive machines. They could then introduce sensor upgrades as the calibration problem was solved. He saw it as largely a marketing problem.

The product came on to the market halfway through 1992. The division spent a great deal on marketing, billing it as the newest technology of its kind in modern medicine. As shown in Exhibit 4, sales increased slowly during the remainder of 1992. However, in 1993 sales responded to various marketing initiatives and promotional deals. Clearly the market had become interested in the "revolutionary solid state" device. Revenues increased by 30 percent. The downside to this was that considerable expenses were being incurred because of a higher-than-expected return rate and a high service cost associated with the product. Customers were calling service technicians because the product required a slightly different approach to calibration than previous equipment. In the meantime the research team was kept busy trying to fix the calibration problem. They had made some improvements, but medical technicians in the labs still had to calibrate it after each test to ensure accuracy.

The real surprise was in 1994 when the market, despite greater marketing and promotional efforts, was not particularly taken with the new product. The problem appeared to be that technicians were familiar with the calibration

EXHIBIT 4

INCOME STATEMENT FOR MEDICAL EQUIPMENT DIVISION
(in thousands $)

	1990*	1991*	1992*	1993	Actual 1994	Budgeted 1994
Revenue	10,238	11,671	14,006	21,008	19,958	25,210
Manufacturing costs	6,040	7,003	8,123	13,235	13,571	15,126
Gross margin	4,198	4,669	5,882	7,773	6,387	10,084
Research expenses	4,097	4,192	4,687	5,007	4,256	3,942
Administration expenses	245	269	487	483	479	490
Sales and marketing	789	907	1,815	2,722	3,539	3,362
Depreciation	788	946	1,135	1,362	1,634	1,961
PROFIT	(1,721)	(1,645)	(2,241)	(1,801)	(3,521)	329

*The first three years' income statements are consolidated to account for the various activities that were integrated into the Medical Equipment Division in 1992. It does not include the $25 million development costs for the sensor. This is the report that top managers in the Electrical Equipment Division were looking at when they met with Bob.

process used on the old machines. The new machines, although smaller and very slightly cheaper, required a new calibration technique that required additional training and different chemicals. Thus, medical managers had a hard time justifying the cost benefits of the product, and technicians and doctors were not actively supporting the product because it did not provide them with any key advantage.

The majority of technicians appeared to be telling their managers that they would rather stick with old technology because it made the process easier and more consistent for them. However, there was also a more subtle issue, revealed to Bob when he attended a sales convention: a medical technician quite bluntly stated that "he was not about to support the decision to buy a product that was ultimately aimed at putting him out of business." Due to these problems, sales actually declined slightly in 1994 and compared to Bob's budgeted breakeven situation, the division was faced with a very large loss.

▉ Keith's Endeavours During This Time

Bob had heard that, since his departure from GT two years ago, Keith had been doing research on gas-liquid ion battery technology with Dr. Jim Slatery. Then approximately three months ago, Bob heard they had incorporated as International Medical Systems (IMed) Inc., and were trying to get funding to build a blood chemical sensor prototype. Bob approached his boss and got the authority to talk to Keith in attempt to investigate how the research was going, and possibly discuss GT's involvement as venture partner. Keith refused to meet with Bob. Then just last week Bob heard they had successfully developed a blood chemical sensor prototype based on the gas-liquid ion battery technology. Furthermore, they were trying to go public—that is, sell stock on the stock markets through an Initial Private Offering (IPO)—with the hopes of introducing a product in six months to a year.

At this point Bob realized he had to do something. He felt that Keith had clearly violated any anti-competition contracts that he had signed while at GT, something that all employees were asked to sign when they joined. Furthermore, IMed's new product could contain a variety of technologies that Keith had developed while at GT. Again this could be deemed as stealing GT's knowledge assets that they had paid him to work on and develop. GT also required employees to sign a proprietary knowledge and technology agreement giving them the rights to any technology developed in their labs.

Bob also understood that his business division would be in big trouble if IMed's product was successful as rumours suggested it might be, if and when it came to market. Furthermore, what would his superiors say when they found out that the product they had been counting on had walked out from under their noses—possibly due to Bob's decision to intervene in the project?

Bob's superiors were already concerned with the financial trends in the new division. The unit was consuming valuable resources, yet it was not progressing, financially, in the way they had hoped. Furthermore, completion of the technological breakthrough that they had sought to develop in their labs was nowhere in sight.

Two days ago, Bob had felt he had to start considering some alternative actions. In particular, he felt that he had to consider the legal implications of Keith leaving the company with assets and technological secrets, and using them to IMed's benefit. Bob went back and asked for Keith's prior personnel file. He found that the confidentiality and proprietary information and technology agreements were missing from the file, as were the five-year anti-competition contract. This concerned him enormously and the lawyers told him that this would make prosecution more difficult—although not impossible as long as the necessary evidence was there. He also talked to several of the scientists that been involved in the research efforts during Keith's employment, but they did not know whether Keith had taken research knowledge from GT because they did not know what technologies were in IMed's product. Bob instructed one of the junior scientists to begin cataloguing the technologies and patents that had been worked on during Keith's employment.

The lawyers had indicated to Bob that a fast decision was essential if any action was to be taken. Bob decided that he had to make a decision before the end of the day.

IKEA (Canada) Ltd. 1986 (Condensed)

Founded as a mail order business in rural Sweden in 1943, IKEA had grown to more than US$1 billion in sales and 70 retail outlets by 1985, and was considered by many to be one of the best-run furniture operations in the world. Although only 14 percent of IKEA's sales were outside Europe, the company's fastest growth was occurring in North America.

Success, however, brought imitators. In mid-1986, Bjorn Bayley and Anders Berglund, the senior managers of IKEA's North American operations, were examining a just-published Sears Canada catalogue, which contained a new 20-page section called "Elements." This section bore a striking resemblance to the format of an IKEA Canada catalogue (see Exhibits 1 and 2 for sample pages), and the furniture being offered was similar to IKEA's knock-down, self-assembled line in which different "elements" could be ordered by the customer to create particular designs. Bayley and Berglund wondered how serious Sears was about its new initiative, and what, if anything, IKEA should do in response.

The Canadian Furniture Market

Canadian consumption of furniture totalled more than $2 billion in 1985, an average of well over $600 per household. Imports accounted for approximately 18 percent of this total, half of which originated in the United States. The duties on furniture imported into Canada were approximately 15 percent.

Furniture was sold to Canadian consumers through three types of stores: independents, specialty chains, and department stores. Although the independents held a 70 percent market share, this figure was declining due to their inability to compete with the chains in terms of advertising, purchasing power, management sophistication, and sales support. The average sales per square metre in 1985 for furniture stores of all three types was $1,666 (the figure was $2,606 for stores which also sold appliances) and the average cost of goods sold was 64.5 percent.

IVEY

Richard Ivey School of Business
The University of Western Ontario

Professor Paul W. Beamish prepared this case, condensed by Peter Killing, solely to provide material for class discussion. The author does not intend to illustrate either effective or ineffective handling of a managerial situation. The author may have disguised certain names and other identifying information to protect confidentiality. © 1988, Ivey Management Services. Case 9-88-M010, version 1992-09-03.

While the major department stores such as Eaton's and Sears tended to carry traditional furniture lines close to the middle of the price/quality range, chains and independents operated from one end of the spectrum to the other. At the upper end of the market, specialty stores attempted to differentiate themselves by offering unique product lines, superior service, and a specialized shopping atmosphere. The lower end of the market, on the other hand, was dominated by furniture warehouses which spent heavily on advertising, and offered lower price, less service, and less emphasis on a fancy image. The warehouses usually kept a larger inventory of furniture on hand than the department stores, but expected customers to pick up their purchases. Over half the warehouse sales involved promotional financing arrangements, including delayed payments, extended terms, and so on.

The major firms in this group—both of whom sold furniture and appliances—were The Brick and Leon's. The Brick had annual sales of $240 million from 15 Canadian stores, and was rapidly expanding from its western Canada base. With 30 additional stores in California under the Furnishings 2000 name, The Brick intended to become the largest furniture retailing company in the world. Leon's had annual sales of $160 million from 14 stores, and was growing rapidly from its Ontario base. These 14 stores were operated under a variety of names. Leon's also franchised its name in smaller cities in Canada. For part of their merchandise requirements, The Brick and Leon's often negotiated with manufacturers for exclusive products, styles, and fabrics and imported from the United States, Europe, and the Far East. Although both firms had had problems earlier with entry to the U.S. market, each intended to expand there.

Most furniture retailers in Canada purchased their products from Canadian manufacturers after examining new designs and models at trade shows. There were approximately 1,400 Canadian furniture manufacturers, most of whom were located in Ontario and Quebec. Typically, these firms were small (78 percent of Canadian furniture plants employed fewer than 50 people), undercapitalized, and minimally automated. One industry executive quipped that one of the most significant technological developments for the industry had been the advent of the staple gun.

Canadian-produced furniture typically followed American and European styling, and was generally of adequate to excellent quality but was often more costly to produce. The reason for high Canadian costs was attributed to a combination of short manufacturing runs and high raw material, labour, and distribution costs. In an attempt to reduce costs, a few of the larger manufacturers such as Kroehler had vertically integrated—purchasing sawmills, fabric warehouses, and fibreboard and wood frame plants—but such practices were very much the exception in the industry.

The IKEA Formula

IKEA's approach to business was fundamentally different from that of the traditional Canadian retailers. The company focused exclusively on what it called "quick assembly" furniture, which consumers carried from the store in flat packages and assembled at home. This furniture was primarily pine,

EXHIBIT I   **Sample Page from IKEA Catalogue**

GUTE. EIGHTEEN DIFFERENT CHESTS   OF DRAWERS TO FIT IN ALMOST ANYWHERE.

GUTE chests of drawers ●möbelfakta White lacquered or pine veneered particleboard, natural or nutbrown stained. W80 cm, D40 cm. QA.
49/2. 2 drawers. H49 cm. White $94. Natural or nutbrown $98.
49/6. 6 drawers. H49 cm. White $115. Natural or nutbrown $125.
87/4. 4 drawers. H87 cm. White $130. Natural or nutbrown $145.

87/8. 8 drawers. H87 cm. White $170. Natural or nutbrown $185.
126/6. 6 drawers. H126 cm. White $175. Natural or nutbrown $195.
126/10. 10 drawers. H126 cm. White $215. Natural or nutbrown $225.

had a clean, European-designed look to it, and was priced at 15 percent below the lowest prices for traditional furniture. Its major appeal appeared to be to young families, singles, and frequent movers, who were looking for well-designed items that were economically priced and created instant impact.

According to company executives, IKEA was successful because of its revolutionary approach to the most important aspects of the business: product design, procurement, store operations, marketing, and management philosophy, which stressed flexibility and market orientation rather than long-range strategy. Each of these items is discussed in turn.

Product Design

IKEA's European designers, not the company's suppliers, were responsible for the design of most of the furniture and accessories in IKEA's product line, which totalled 15,000 items. The heart of the company's design capability was a 50-person Swedish workshop which produced prototypes of new items of furniture and smaller components such as "an ingenious little snap lock for

EXHIBIT 2 **Sample Page from Elements Section of Sears Catalogue**

Dressers and chests whose quality and practicality are inherent—
in the colors and sizes you want. Assemble them yourself with ease.

Your choice of clear knot-free pine veneer over non-warp platewood core
or White baked-on European-quality low gloss enamel on a platewood core.

3 Drawer Units. 38 cm deep, 54 cm high (15 x 21¼"). Wide. 75 cm wide (29½").	4 Drawer Units. 38 cm deep, 69 cm high (15 x 27¼"). Wide. 75 cm wide (29½").	6 Drawer Units. 38 cm deep, 99 cm high (15 x 39"). Wide. 75 cm wide (29½").
012 065 012 DLT – Pine Each.139.98	012 065 011 DLT – Pine Each.159.98	012 065 010 DLTJ – Pine Each.219.98
012 065 002 DLT – White Each.139.98	012 065 001 DLT – White Each.159.98	012 065 000 DLTJ – White Each.219.98
Narrow. 50 cm wide (19½").	Narrow. 50 cm wide (19½").	Narrow. 50 cm wide (19½").
012 065 015 DLT – Pine Each.119.98	012 065 014 DLT – Pine Each.139.98	012 065 013 DLT – Pine Each.189.98
012 065 005 DLT – White Each.119.98	012 065 004 DLT – White Each.139.98	012 065 003 DLT – White Each.189.98

table legs which makes a table stronger and cheaper at the same time" and a "clever little screw attachment which allows for the assembly of a pin-back chair in five minutes." IKEA's designers were very cost-conscious, and were constantly working to lower costs in ways that were not critical to the consumer. "The quality of a work top, for example, would be superior to that of the back of a bookshelf which would never be seen. "Low price with a meaning" was the theme.

Although it was not impossible to copyright a particular design or process, IKEA's philosophy was "if somebody steals a model from us we do not bring a lawsuit, because a lawsuit is always negative. We solve the problem by making a new model that is even better."

Procurement

IKEA's early success in Sweden had so threatened traditional European furniture retailers that they had promised to boycott any major supplier that shipped products to the upstart firm. As a result, IKEA had no choice but to go to the smaller suppliers. Since these suppliers had limited resources, IKEA began assuming responsibility for the purchase of raw materials, packaging materials, storage, specialized equipment and machinery, and engineering. What began as a necessity soon became a cornerstone of IKEA's competitive strategy, and by 1986 the firm had nearly 100 production engineers working as purchasers. Together, with IKEA's designers, these engineers assisted suppliers in every way they could to help them lower costs, dealing with everything from the introduction of new technology to the alteration of the dimensions of a shipping carton.

Although IKEA sometimes leased equipment and made loans to its suppliers, the firm was adamant that it would not enter the furniture manufacturing business itself. In fact, to avoid control over—and responsibility for—its suppliers, the company had a policy of limiting its purchases to 50 percent of a supplier's capacity. Many products were obtained from multiple suppliers, and frequently suppliers produced only a single standardized component or input to the final product. Unfinished pine shelves, for example, were obtained directly from sawmills, cabinet doors were purchased from door factories, and cushions came from textile mills.

In total, IKEA purchases goods from 1,500 suppliers located in 40 countries. About 52 percent of the company's purchases were from Scandinavia, 21 percent from other countries of western Europe, 20 percent from eastern Europe, and 7 percent elsewhere.

Store Operations

IKEA stores were usually large one- or two-storey buildings situated in relatively inexpensive standalone locations, neither in prime downtown sites nor as part of a shopping mall. Most stores were surrounded by a large parking lot, adorned with billboards explaining IKEA's delivery policy and product guarantee, and contained a coffee shop and/or restaurant.

On entering a store, the customer was immediately aware of the children's play area (a room filled with hollow, multicolored balls), a video room for older children, and a receptionist with copies of IKEA catalogues, a metric conversion guide, index cards for detailing purchases, and a store guide. The latter, supplemented by prominent signs, indicated that the store contained lockers and benches for shoppers, a first-aid area, rest rooms, strollers and a baby-care area, an "As-Is" department (no returns permitted), numerous checkouts, suggestion boxes, and in many cases a restaurant. All major credit cards were accepted.

Traffic flow in most IKEA stores was guided in order to pass by almost all of the merchandise in the store, which was displayed as it would look in the home, complete with all accessories. Throughout the store, employees could be identified by their bright red IKEA shirts. Part-time employees wore yellow shirts which read "Temporary Help—Please Don't Ask Me Any Hard Questions." The use of sales floor staff was minimal. The IKEA view was that "salesmen are expensive, and can also be irritating. IKEA leaves you to shop in peace."

While IKEA stores were all characterized by their self-serve, self-wrapping, self-transport, and self-assembly operations, the company's philosophy was that each new store would incorporate the latest ideas in use in any of its existing stores. The most recent trend in some countries was an IKEA Contract Sales section, which provided a delivery, invoicing, and assembly service for commercial customers.

Marketing

IKEA's promotional activities were intended to educate the consumer public on the benefits of the IKEA concept and to build traffic by attracting new buyers and encouraging repeat visits from existing customers. The primary promotional vehicle was the annual IKEA catalogue which was selectively mailed out to prime target customers—who, in the Toronto area for instance, had the following characteristics:

- Income $35,000+
- Owner condominium or townhouse
- University degree
- White collar

- Primary age group 35–44
- Secondary age group 25–34
- Husband/wife both work
- Two children
- Movers

With minor variations, this "upscale" profile was typical of IKEA's target customers in Europe and North America. In Canada, IKEA management acknowledged the target market, but felt that, in fact, the IKEA concept appealed to a much wider group of consumers.

IKEA also spent heavily on magazine advertisements, which were noted for their humorous, slightly off-beat approach. In Canada, IKEA spent $2.5 million to print 3.6 million catalogues, $2 million on magazine advertising, and $1.5 million on other forms of promotion in 1984.

Management Philosophy

The philosophy of Ingvar Kamprad, the founder of IKEA, was "to create a better everyday life for the majority of people." In practice, this creed meant that IKEA was dedicated to offering, and continuing to offer, the lowest prices possible on good-quality furniture, so that IKEA products were available to as many people as possible. Fred Andersson, the head of IKEA's product range for the world, stated: "Unlike other companies, we are not fascinated with what we produce—we make what our customers want." Generally, IKEA management felt that no other company could match IKEA's combination of quality and price across the full width of the product line.

IKEA also made a concerted effort to stay "close to its customers," and it was not unusual for the general manager of IKEA Canada, for instance, to personally telephone customers who had made complaints or suggestions. Each week an employee newsletter detailed all customer comments, and indicated how management felt they should be dealt with.

Another guiding philosophy of the firm was that growth would be in "small bites." The growth objective in Canada, for instance, had been to increase sales and profits by 20 percent per year, but care was given to sequence store openings so that managerial and financial resources would not be strained.

Internally, the company's philosophy was stated as "freedom, with responsibility," which meant that IKEA's managers typically operated with a good deal of autonomy. The Canadian operation, for instance, received little in the way of explicit suggestions from head office, even in the one year when the budget was not met. The Canadian management team travelled to head office as a group only once every several years. As Bjorn Bayley explained:

> We are a very informal management team, and try to have everyone who works for us believe that they have the freedom to do their job in the best way possible. It's almost impossible to push the philosophy down to the cashier level, but we try.

IKEA in Canada

IKEA's formula had worked well in Canada. Under the direction of a four-man management team, which included two Swedes, the company had grown from a single store in 1976 to nine stores totalling 800,000 square feet (about 7.4 hectares) and, as shown in Exhibit 3, predicted 1986 sales of more than $140 million. The sales of IKEA Canada had exceeded budget in all but one of the past five years, and usually by a wide margin. Net profits were approximately 5 percent of sales. Profit and loss statements for 1983 and 1984, the only financial statements available, are presented in Exhibit 4.

IKEA Canada carried just less than half of the company's total product line. Individual items were chosen on the basis of what management thought would sell in Canada, and if IKEA could not beat a competitor's price by 10 to 15 percent on a particular item, it was dropped. Most of the goods sold in the Canadian stores were supplied from central warehouses in Sweden. To coordinate this process a five-person stock supply department in Vancouver provided Sweden with a three-year forecast of Canada's needs, and placed major orders twice a year. Actual volumes were expected to be within 10 percent of the forecast level. As Bayley noted, "you needed a gambler in the stock supply job."

Individual stores were expected to maintain 13.5 weeks of inventory on hand (10.5 weeks in the store and three weeks in transit), and could order from the central warehouse in Montreal, or, if a product was not in stock in Montreal, direct from Sweden. Shipments from Sweden took six to eight weeks to arrive,

EXHIBIT 3   IKEA Canada Sales by Store (including mail order; Cdn$000s)

	1981	1982	1983	1984	1985	1986 (forecasted)	Mail Order* (%)
Vancouver	$12,122	$11,824	$12,885	$19,636	$ 19,240	$ 25,500	6.8%
Calgary	7,379	8,550	7,420	7,848	9,220	11,500	8.6
Ottawa	5,730	6,914	8,352	9,015	10,119	12,500	1.8
Montreal			8,617	12,623	15,109	22,000**	2.2
Halifax	3,634	4,257	4,474	6,504	7,351	9,000	22.9
Toronto	11,231	13,191	16,249	18,318	22,673	30,500	1.8
Edmonton	6,506	7,474	8,075	8,743	9,986	16,000	15.4
Quebec City		5,057	8,284	9,027	10,037	12,000	6.1
Victoria					2,808	3,500	
TOTAL	$46,602	$57,267	$74,356	$91,714	$106,543	$142,500	6.7%

*1984 most recent data available.
**Projected growth due to store size expansion.

EXHIBIT 4

STATEMENT OF EARNINGS AND RETAINED EARNINGS
Year Ended August 31, 1984
(with comparative figures for 1983)

	1984	1983
Sales	$92,185,188	$74,185,691
Cost of merchandise sold	49,836,889	38,085,173
Gross profit	42,348,299	36,100,518
General, administrative, and selling expenses	28,016,473	23,626,727
Operating profit before the undernoted	14,331,826	12,473,791
Depreciation and amortization	1,113,879	1,066,286
Franchise amortization	257,490	257,490
Franchise fee	2,765,558	2,225,571
	4,136,927	3,549,347
Earnings from operations	10,194,899	8,924,444
Rental income	769,719	815,683
Less: Rental expense	245,803	258,296
	523,916	557,387
Interest expense	2,453,116	3,042,471
Less: other income	438,683	65,757
	2,014,433	2,976,714
Earnings before income taxes	8,704,382	6,505,117
Income taxes:		
Current	3,789,773	2,716,645
Deferred	(70,400)	175,500
	3,719,373	2,892,145
Net earnings for the year	4,985,009	3,612,972
Retained earnings, beginning of year	5,501,612	1,888,640
RETAINED EARNINGS, END OF YEAR	$10,486,621	$5,501,612

Source: Consumer and Corporate Affairs, Canada.

shipments from Montreal two to three weeks. In practice, about 50 percent of the product arriving at a store came via each route.

IKEA's success in Canada meant that the firm was often hard pressed to keep the best-selling items in stock. (Twenty percent of the firm's present line constituted 80 percent of sales volume.) At any given time in Canada IKEA stores might have 300 items out of stock, either because actual sales deviated significantly from forecasts or because suppliers could not meet their delivery promises. While management estimated that 75 percent of customers were willing to wait for IKEA products in a stock-out situation, the company nevertheless began a deliberate policy of developing Canadian suppliers for high-demand items, even if this meant paying a slight premium. In 1984, the stock control group purchased $57 million worth of goods on IKEA's behalf, $12 million of which was from 30 Canadian suppliers, up from $7 million the previous year.

As indicated in Exhibit 3, IKEA Canada sold products, rather reluctantly, by mail order to customers who preferred not to visit the stores. A senior manager explained:

> To date we have engaged in defensive mail order—only when the customer really wants it and the order is large enough. The separate handling, breaking-down of orders, and repackaging required for mail orders would be too expensive and go against the economies-through-volume approach of IKEA. Profit margins of mail order business tend to be half that of a store operation. There are more sales returns, particularly because of damages—maybe 4 percent—incurred in shipping. It is difficult to know where to draw the market boundaries for a mail order business. We don't want to be substituting mail order customers for store visitors.

In 1986, the management team which had brought success to IKEA's Canadian operations was breaking up. Bjorn Bayley, who had come to Canada in 1978, was slotted to move to Philadelphia to spearhead IKEA's entry into the U.S. market, which had begun in June 1985 with a single store. With early sales running at a level twice as high as the company had predicted, Bayley expected to be busy, and was taking Mike McDonald, the controller, and Mike McMullen, the personnel director, with him. Anders Berglund, who, like Bayley, was a long-time IKEA employee and had been in Canada since 1979, was scheduled to take over the Canadian operation. Berglund would report through Bayley to IKEA's North American sales director, who was located in Europe.

New Competition

IKEA's success in Canada had not gone unnoticed. IDOMO was a well-established Toronto-based competitor, and Sears Canada was a new entrant.

Idomo

Like IKEA, IDOMO sold knocked-down furniture which customers were required to assemble at home. IDOMO offered a somewhat narrower selection than IKEA but emphasized teak furniture to a much greater extent. With stores in Hamilton, Mississauga (across from IKEA), Toronto, and Montreal, IDOMO appeared to have capitalized on the excess demand that IKEA had developed but was not able to service.

The products and prices offered in both the 96-page IDOMO and the 144-page IKEA catalogues were similar, with IKEA's prices slightly lower. Prices in the IKEA catalogues were in effect for a year. IDOMO reserved the right to make adjustments to prices and specifications. A mail order telephone number in Toronto was provided in the IDOMO catalogue. Of late, IDOMO had begun to employ an increased amount of television advertising. IDOMO purchased goods from around the world and operated a number of their own Canadian factories. Their primary source of goods was Denmark.

Sears

The newest entrant in the Canadian knocked-down furniture segment was Sears Canada, a wholly owned subsidiary of Sears Roebuck of Chicago and, with $3.8 billion in annual revenues, one of Canada's largest merchandising operations. Sears operated 75 department stores in Canada, selling a wide range (700 merchandise lines comprising 100,000 stockkeeping units) of medium price and quality goods. Sears Canada also ran a major catalogue operation which distributed 12 annual catalogues to approximately four million Canadian families. Customers could place catalogue orders by mail, by telephone, or in person through one of the company's 1,500 catalogue sales units, which were spread throughout the country.

A quick check by Bayley and Berglund revealed that Sears' Elements line was being sold only in Canada and only through the major Sears catalogues. Elements products were not for sale, nor could they be viewed, in Sears' stores. In the fall/winter catalogues that they examined, which were over 700 pages in length, the Elements line was given 20 pages. Although Sears appeared to offer the same "type" of products as IKEA, there was a narrower selection within each category. Prices for Elements products seemed almost identical to IKEA prices. One distinct difference between the catalogues was the much greater emphasis that IKEA placed on presenting a large number of coordinated settings and room designs.

Further checking indicated that at least some of the suppliers of the Elements line were Swedish, although it did not appear that IKEA and Sears had any suppliers in common.

The IKEA executives knew that Sears was generally able to exert a great deal of influence over its suppliers, usually obtaining prices at least equal to and often below those of its competitors, because of the huge volumes purchased. Sears also worked closely with its suppliers in marketing, research, design and development, production standards, and production planning. Many lines of merchandise were manufactured with features exclusive to Sears and were sold under its private brand names. There was a 75 percent buying overlap for the catalogue and store and about a 90 percent overlap between regions on store purchases.

Like any Sears product, Elements furniture could be charged to a Sears charge card. Delivery of catalogue items generally took about two weeks, and for a small extra charge catalogue orders would be delivered right to the consumer's home in a Sears truck. If a catalogue item was out of stock, Sears policy was either to tell the customer if and when the product would be available or to substitute an item of equal or greater value. If goods proved defective (10 percent of Sears Roebuck mail order furniture purchasers had received damaged or broken furniture), Sears provided home pickup and replacement and was willing, for a fee, to install goods, provide parts, and do repairs as products aged. Sears emphasized that it serviced what it sold, and guaranteed everything that it sold—"satisfaction guaranteed or money refunded." In its advertising, which included all forms of media, Sears stressed its "hassle-free returns" and asked customers to "take a look at the services we offered ... they'll bring you peace of mind, long after the bill is paid."

In their assessment of Sears Canada, Bayley and Berglund recognized that the company seemed to be going through something of a revival. Using the rallying cry that a "new" Sears was being created, Sears executives (the Canadian firm had ten vice-presidents) had experimented with new store layouts, pruned the product line, and improved customer service for catalogue orders. Richard Sharpe, the chairman of Sears Canada, personally addressed as many as 12,000 employees per year, and the company received 3,000 suggestions from employees annually. Perhaps as a result of these initiatives, and a cut in the work force from 65,000 to 50,000 over several years, Sears Canada posted its best-ever results in 1985.

◼ Conclusion

With the limited data they had on Sears, IKEA management recognized that their comparison of the two companies would be incomplete. Nonetheless, a decision regarding the Sears competitive threat was required. Any solution would have to reflect Kamprad's philosophy:

> Expensive solutions to problems are often signs of mediocrity. We have no interest in a solution until we know what it costs.

International Decorative Glass

In June 1996, Delta, British Columbia, remained overcast and rainy. Frank Lattimer, vice-president of operations of International Decorative Glass (IDG), mused that it really didn't matter, as there would be little time for golf this year. Rapidly increasing demand for decorative glass panels by steel door manufacturers in the United States, IDG's primary market, had its two production facilities in Delta and Shuenyi, China, scrambling to keep up.

Lattimer had been asked to develop a recommendation for capacity expansion for consideration by the board of directors. The board had emphasized the need to move quickly as sales were increasing faster than IDG's ability to meet them. Although either existing plant could be expanded, IDG also had recently been approached about considering further offshore sourcing in the rapidly developing country of Vietnam. Frank knew that any decision would have significant ramifications for the company's long-term positioning and ability to meet its ambitious goals for growth.

The Industry

Decorative glass panels typically are inserted into residential steel doors, and were increasingly being used by builders and home renovators to add architectural interest and a customized appearance to doorways (Exhibit 1). Growth in the industry was being fuelled by the general trend away from wooden exterior doors to steel doors. Forestry restrictions, lumber prices, energy-efficiency, and increasing criminal activity all contributed to the growing demand for retrofitting wood doors with steel replacements, often with decorative glass panels. In addition, the lower price of steel doors relative to the traditional wood door, with wholesale prices starting as low as Cdn$300, further eroded market share in new home construction. Decorative glass was now being incorporated into 10 percent of new home construction.

IVEY

Richard Ivey School of Business
The University of Western Ontario

Jim Barker prepared this case under the supervision of Professors Robert Klassen and Paul Beamish solely to provide material for class discussion. The authors do not intend to illustrate either effective or ineffective handling of a managerial situation. The authors may have disguised certain names and other identifying information to protect confidentiality. © 1997 Ivey Management Services. Case 9A97D010, version 1988-07-02.

EXHIBIT I   Sample of Decorative Glass Panel Applications

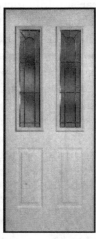

The total North American sales for decorative glass panels was conservatively estimated at $2 billion in 1995 (all figures are reported in Canadian dollars), and the market showed signs of continued strong growth. Industry experts predicted that annual sales could reach $4.5 billion in the United States alone, within five years. Canada's weighting of the North American market was disproportionately high, at 15 percent, reflecting the somewhat earlier development of the market here for these panels. By 1996, panels were found in approximately 85 percent of steel doors in western Canadian homes.

Manufacturers in Canada tended to be more vertically integrated than their U.S. counterparts, with plants fabricating both the steel door and the decorative panel. Locally, British Columbia's supply capacity grew well past the sustainable growth rate during the late 1980s and early 1990s as new market entrants scrambled to ramp up production capability to capitalize on the residential construction boom. The result was steadily eroding margins, followed quickly by industry consolidation, with high-cost producers closing or being absorbed by more competitive operations. In spite of these changes, Canadian industry continued to be characterized by oversupply, underutilized capacity, and commodity pricing. Lattimer had recently completed a basic competitive assessment of several key Canadian competitors as part of IDG's business plan (Exhibit 2).

By contrast, U.S. manufacturers of decorative glass panels acted as original equipment manufacturers (OEMs) for large residential steel door fabricators and retail chains. The industry was quite fragmented, with the largest three producers in the United States each having less than 6 percent of the total market. Unfortunately, information on these producers was limited (Exhibit 3). Manufacturers ship panels to predetermined central warehousing and assembly points where their panels are fitted into the steel doors and distributed by the customer through their retail channels. In general, the U.S. marketplace demanded high quality, fast service, and, increasingly, low price.

At this time, the United States, unlike Canada, was rapidly growing and underserved. In addition, Canadian manufacturers typically were three years ahead of their U.S. counterparts in product functionality and design, and thus able to exploit this market through strategic partnerships with steel door manufacturers. A depreciating Canadian currency also provided domestic suppliers, such as IDG, with an initial competitive advantage. Combined, these factors

EXHIBIT 2   Summary of Major Canadian Competitors

Company	Accent	JCX Glass	Roseview
Target market	Small regional distributors	Anyone who calls	Small regional distributors
Supply	Custom: None Volume: Langley, B.C., and Tacoma, Wash.	Custom: None Volume: New Westminster, B.C., Georgia; buy from China	Custom: None Volume: Surrey, B.C.
Positioning	Good quality	Copy designs of others	Design leader Lower quality
Cost base	• Two locations, 38,000 sq. ft. • Heavy overheads • Non-union • Small orders, but purchase materials in volume • Thus, very high raw material and finished goods inventory • Efficient production system	• Two locations, 105,000 sq. ft. • Heavy overheads • One year left on collective agreement • Volume purchase • Finished goods inventory of $3.2 million • Efficient production system	• One location, 38,000 sq. ft. • Heavy overheads • Non-union • High raw material costs • Finished goods inventory of $1.6 million
Sales (est. 1995)	• $11 million • Down, some of their lowest months	• $14 million • Up 39%	• $3 million • Down
Warranty	1 year	10 years	1 year
CAD	Yes	No	No
MRP	Some implementation	Some implementation	No
Reputation/customer relations	Very good in Pacific Northwest with the "old boys'" network	Generally poor, can let the customer down	Generally poor, always lets customer down
Management	Good, but have lost their spark and desire	Aggressive, but weak in the middle management	Generally weak

EXHIBIT 3   Summary of Major U.S. Competitors

Company	Spanner Door	Western Design	Billings	New England Glass
Target market	National (U.S.)	National (U.S.)	National (U.S.)	Eastern (U.S.)
Positioning	• Good quality • Simple, high-volume panels	Broad product line	Broad product line; focus on high-volume commodities, although some lower-volume panels	Fast delivery, high quality
Supply	Good operations in Mexico, with long-term commitment	Plants in Mexico and Thailand	No offshore production	• High-cost producer • Focus on automation
Est. 1995 sales	$120 million	$85 million	$60 million	$25 million
Reputation/ customer relations		Extensive distribution system	Product line is narrower than IDG	Strong, dependable supplier
Management		Three top managers have left recently		

created a significant market opportunity for any Canadian supplier who could meet rigorous quality standards and maintain a high level of customer responsiveness to design customized panels.

Early attempts by Canadian firms to develop their export sales quickly revealed that a customer would pay only so much for quality, service, and product differentiation, and price was becoming an increasingly important driver in the purchase decision. In response, manufacturers on both sides of the border began to source production of the glass panels at lower cost to facilities located abroad. Because labour represented a large portion of cost of goods sold, production was increasingly being moved to countries with low labour costs, such as Mexico, Thailand, and China. At this time, only a few Canadian manufacturers had been able to address all of these challenges successfully.

Production of Decorative Glass Panels

The production process for decorative glass panels was quite standardized, with little variation among firms and plants. As might be expected with a product that until recently was considered a "craft," the process was very labour-intensive, with the equivalent of up to two person-days required for each panel. Production equipment was generally quite flexible, and could be purchased from a number of suppliers.

Decorative glass panels essentially consist of multiple glass panes of different sizes, colours, and grades assembled between soldered brass rods to form a decorative picture. The production of the panels used a multistep process that cuts and forms the glass and brass components, and assembles the parts into sealed decorative glass units that could withstand the harsh exposure needed for exterior doors.

The manufacturing process begins with the cutting of raw glass sheets of various colours and finishes into pieces of the precise shape and size needed for the final design. Some of these pieces are then bevelled to give a more attractive final appearance. Both the specialized cutting and the bevelling of the glass pieces were the most capital-intensive steps in the production process.

In a separate area, brass rods were cut and formed into segments that ultimately serve to hold and separate the glass pieces. The correct set of glass pieces and brass rods were then grouped into panel-specific "kits." These kits were assembled and soldered into predetermined patterns that formed semifinished panels.

Several cleaning and touch-up steps followed, after which the glass was tempered to improve its durability. Next, clear solid glass panes were added to each side of the inlay, creating a "sandwich" that protected the more delicate decorative inlay. Swizzle, a sealant material, was added around the edge to insulate and protect the panel from water damage. The panel was then put through an automated sealing machine, washed, and inserted into a frame. Finally, the finished panel was labelled and packaged for shipment. These operations typically were performed in small batches of panels.

■ The Company

Located near Vancouver, British Columbia, IDG was founded in 1984 by Michael Jeffrey, decorative glass designer and entrepreneur. Initially, the company started as an integrated manufacturer of steel doors and decorative glass panels, and IDG enjoyed modest prosperity through the 1980s as the housing market boomed in that province. During this period, numerous firms entered the market, hoping to share in the prosperity of the industry. As real estate development slowed and even stagnated in the early 1990s, and the competitive basis shifted to cost, Jeffrey realized that the company was losing money in their manufacturing of steel doors. He felt that IDG could significantly enhance profitability by concentrating exclusively on decorative glass panels.

Jeffrey also recognized the need for a senior operations and business development person to make the operations more competitive in that market. Lattimer was hired in 1991 with the mandate to grow the international market, to improve cost-efficiency, to set up a fully integrated management information system, and to create a corporate structure and culture that would support continued expansion. To meet these objectives, contacts and sales were further developed with several U.S. steel door manufacturers, the largest being Midwest. Lattimer also gained concessions in wage rates and flexibility in staffing requirements during collective bargaining with the union. Finally, a management information system, including materials requirements planning (MRP), was installed and brought on line to improve access to timely information and to raise customer responsiveness.

Historically, IDG's sales had been driven by custom orders for the glass panels. However, with recent efforts to increase sales volume, an increasing number of higher-volume orders were being pursued, although often at much lower margins. In spite of labour concessions, high rates and limited flexibility continued to make IDG's plant in Delta increasingly less cost-competitive. To reduce production costs, Lattimer was forced to explore alternative, offshore sources of production.

◼ Century Glass

In January 1995, International Decorative Glass began sourcing some of its high-volume, low-skill production through a strategic partnership with Century Glass, located in Shuenyi, approximately an hour's drive outside of Beijing, China. This manufacturing facility was developed solely to meet the production needs of IDG, although the actual plant was owned and operated by the father of a former employee Jianwei (Jerry) Lo. Lo had returned to China to set up the joint venture with IDG.

When IDG first arrived, the Shuenyi facility was little more than a deserted warehouse, situated across the highway from Jerry Lo's village of 2,000 people where Lo had been born. The Lo family was well respected in the area, even though they came from modest means relative to Canadian standards. There was no electricity, telephone, or plumbing in the village, and fresh water was unavailable.

With minimal infrastructure in place, power requirements, communication, and capital equipment challenges all needed to be addressed. Co-generation power supplies and inverters were supplied by IDG, satellite and cellular phones were used until Century received a land line (faxes were sent from Beijing in the interim). Basic production equipment needed to cut glass sheets and brass rods were sourced locally; however, one large panel sealing machine was imported from Korea. Practically everything else at the facility was built by the local work force. Approximately one-third of the workers lived in four-person dormitory rooms located on the premises, and the production plant also included space for the workers to grow their own food in the courtyard.

Family ties of the Los facilitated the shipment of goods, as Chinese bureaucracy was legendary. Jerry's uncle was the police chief of the local district, and thus extremely well connected politically; IDG benefited from the association. The movement of raw materials into China and finished goods out of China, via Tientsin to the Gulf of Chihli, was expedited through Jerry's uncle.

Because of differences in proximity to the market and cost structure, the Chinese production facility concentrated on producing high-volume, low-cost glass panels for IDG. These panels were then shipped in bulk to the Delta production facility for final processing, followed by packaging and shipment to U.S. or Canadian customers. The additional processing in Canada resulted in a change in product classification under the North American Free Trade Agreement (NAFTA), which allowed the finished product to be imported duty-free into the U.S. market. (By contrast, if complete, sealed panels were to be imported directly from China into the United States, a 60 percent duty would apply.)

For some customers, the standardized panels produced at Shuenyi were modified and further assembled at Delta to form larger, more complex, customized panels. By necessity, these arrangements required a long lead time, currently in the range of 18 to 20 weeks (Exhibit 4), well above that of the Delta plant, where lead times averaged one month.

Initial startup problems in 1995 centred on logistics and quality. Rather than allow IDG's reputation for excellent customer service to suffer by missing delivery dates, orders of panels were, at times, air-freighted to Delta from

EXHIBIT 4   **Order Cycle Time for Production at Shuenyi Plant**

Raw materials ordered and received for shipment	2–4 weeks
Components in transit to China facility	5 weeks
Raw materials conversion to WIP and semi-finished goods	4 weeks
Sub-assemblies shipped to Canada	5 weeks
Final assembly completed at Richmond, B.C., facility	2 weeks
Finished goods shipped to customer	$^{1}/_{2}$ week
Total Time	**18–20 weeks**

China, at an extra cost of $250,000 in the first year. These problems were gradually overcome as typical production lead times were reduced to their current levels. Low yields and high waste/breakage also plagued the startup. However, as the skill levels of the local work force improved, yields increased dramatically. By mid-1996, finished panel yields consistently surpassed 99 percent, although in-process breakage and other losses remained a problem.

Current Status

By June 1996, Century Glass produced 80 percent of IDG's panels, representing 60 percent of revenues. The remaining somewhat more specialized, lower-volume panels were produced by 70 employees in the Delta plant. The Century plant was operating close to capacity, with approximately 100 employees producing 8,000 panels per month. Dorms were overcrowded and people were elbow to elbow in the manufacturing area.

The joint venture agreement specified that IDG purchase all materials, own all inventories, and specify all finished product standards. The production arrangement with Century stipulated a fixed charge per employee and a variable cost per finished panel. Specifically, IDG paid $140 per employee, per month. In addition, IDG also paid Century a product transfer price of $4 for each panel that met IDG's rigorous quality standards for finished panels. Employment levels could be varied as needed to match sales volumes; employees worked seven eight-hour days per week, every week.[1]

By comparison, in Canada, unionized employees received $9.75 per hour, based on a 40-hour work week. Combined, these differences in labour translated into a significant cost advantage for Shuenyi, without accounting for the operational advantages of increased labour flexibility. Relative product costs are provided for three illustrative products in Exhibit 5.

Labour savings were offset to some degree by a higher working capital investment necessary to finance larger inventories and longer payment cycles. For example, inventory turnover at Century Glass was only two turns per year in 1995, whereas Delta averaged six. In addition, banks refused to finance or factor raw material and work-in-process (WIP) inventories located in, or in transit to or from, China as the risk of recouping funds in the case of insolvency was considered too high. This risk varied by country. Some developing countries, such as

---

[1] The average worker takes only a couple of days off each year to celebrate the Chinese New Year. Seven-day work weeks are high by Chinese standards, where the six-day work week was more common.

EXHIBIT 5   **Typical Production Costs**

Product	Production Location	
	Shuenyi	Delta
#677, Oval–San Marino		
Materials	95.19	92.97
Labour	6.61	69.44
Freight	7.82	1.25
Total direct costs	**$109.62**	**$163.66**
#936, 22" × 36" panel		
Materials	44.27	44.27
Labour	3.18	40.27
Freight	7.08	1.25
Total direct costs	**$54.53**	**$85.79**
#445, 7$^{1}/_{2}$" × 18$^{1}/_{2}$" panel		
Materials	15.51	15.51
Labour	1.10	10.13
Freight	1.08	0.50
Total direct costs	**$17.69**	**$26.14**

Mexico, were viewed as less risky, while others, such as India, offered government guarantees for export-oriented manufacturers.

The Los were anxious to keep 100 percent of IDG's business at their facility. Lattimer was very concerned about having only a single supplier in China, where political risks remained significant, for such a large portion of their production. For example, the repatriation of Hong Kong in 1997, adverse trade tensions, and possible trade restrictions between China, the United States, and Canada all indicated that a move to establish another production source might have strategic and operational merits.

Financial Results

IDG's revenue growth had been impressive since 1990, increasing from $2.6 million to $5.4 million for fiscal 1995. Financial results for the last two years are summarized in Exhibits 6 and 7. Revenues were projected to reach $10.5 million this year, with 95 percent of sales being made in the United States. As noted earlier, margins had eroded during the early 1990s as residential construction slowed, and competition increased. Sales levels had risen significantly in 1995 as new production capacity became available at Shuenyi. However, profitability fell as a result of poor initial yields and air freight shipment costs at this new plant. Looking forward, Lattimer expected margins to increase as productivity further improved in Shuenyi.

Both Jeffrey and Lattimer strongly felt that the market for strong growth by IDG was there. IDG had already been turning away business as they struggled to meet existing customer commitments from their two production facilities. Current plans called for revenue growth to $30 million by the year 2000. Critical to achieving these long-term results was an increase in production capacity to match the forecasted sales volumes.

EXHIBIT 6

INCOME STATEMENT FOR INTERNATIONAL DECORATIVE GLASS
As of September 30
(all figures reported as $000s)

	1995	1994
Sales	$5,404	$3,634
Cost of sales	4,365	2,610
Gross profit	1,039	1,024
Expenses:		
Administration and marketing	388	413
Travel and promotion	97	44
Rent and assessment	120	138
Amortization of debt	48	55
Bank charges and interest	141	48
Interest on long-term debt	18	17
Other expenses	182	258
SUBTOTAL	994	973
Income (loss) from operations	45	51
Other income	28	0
Income (loss) before taxes	73	51
Income taxes:		
Current	24	0
Deferred	(6)	11
NET INCOME (LOSS) FOR THE YEAR	$ 55	$ 40

This aggressive growth necessitated access to additional capital to finance investment in new capacity and additional working capital. In August 1995, IDG approached a venture capital firm, Working Opportunity Fund, for $2 million of equity financing. The structure of the investment was negotiated, due diligence conducted, and the deal finalized in November of that year. In addition, IDG paid down its line of credit from the bank by financing its inventory in China with a guarantee from the Export Development Corporation. This effectively reduced IDG's investment in working capital and made the sourcing of manufacturing to Asian facilities increasingly attractive. Combined, these additional sources of capital enabled IDG to increase its operating flexibility, and further develop its presence in the U.S. market.

Capacity Expansion

Lattimer had narrowed the options for expansion of production to three alternatives. Expansion was possible at either existing plant. In addition, another strategic partnership could be developed in another low-labour-cost country, similar to IDG's earlier decision to expand into China. After exploring options in other developing nations with low labour costs, Lattimer, in consultation with senior management, had narrowed the candidate list of countries to one: Vietnam. This country offered a critical advantage in Lattimer's mind over other developing nations: a potential local partner, Dan Kim. Kim's firm currently supplied raw glass to IDG, and Kim had approached Lattimer about establishing a manufacturing joint venture.

EXHIBIT 7

BALANCE SHEET FOR INTERNATIONAL DECORATIVE GLASS
As of September 30
(all figures reported as $000s)

	1995	1994
Current:		
Cash	$ 1	$ 2
Accounts receivable	1,513	474
Income taxes recoverable	15	22
Inventories	1,422	988
Prepaid expenses	54	28
	3,005	1,514
Capital assets	233	296
	3,238	1,810
Current:		
Bank loans	1,435	593
Accounts payable	886	482
Income taxes payable	17	0
Current portion of long-term debt	32	39
	2,370	1,114
Long-term debt	152	177
Deferred income taxes	13	20
Due to (from) affiliated company	522	372
	3,057	1,683
Share capital	0.1	0.1
Contributed surplus	45	45
Retained earnings	136	82
	$3,238	$1,810

Expansion in Delta

At this time, company-wide capacity could be doubled by investing a relatively modest amount of capital, $30,000, in the Delta plant. Labour costs would rise according to existing wage levels. Given the proximity of this plant to the U.S. market, the existing production planning system could be further leveraged and customer responsiveness further improved.

Expansion in Shuenyi

Because production at the Shuenyi plant was already very tight, any expansion would involve a significant increase of middle management and support staff, and an expanded production planning system, mirroring the earlier MRP investment made in Delta. Existing arrangements for labour would be maintained, whereby IDG would pay a flat monthly fee per person, plus a variable rate per panel.

Although some of the existing production equipment still had excess capacity, additional equipment would be needed. In total, an estimated capital investment of $30,000 would be needed in new cutting equipment to double company-wide capacity. Incremental manufacturing overhead costs would be approximately $150,000 per year. Direct labour costs would increase proportionately with production volumes. These costs did not include either a desperately needed new building or additional inventory carrying charges. Timing for ramp-up to this volume level would be approximately six to eight months.

The most significant concerns with expansion at Shuenyi were related to further dependance on a single supplier and issues related to political risks associated with production in China. Trade uncertainties between China and the United States also aggravated long-term planning efforts. Management was apprehensive that existing tensions could escalate over any, or all, of repatriation of Hong Kong in 1997, intellectual property rights (software piracy and patents), dissident protests, strained relations with Taiwan, and a general trade imbalance.

Smaller manufacturers that supply the U.S. market, like IDG, inadvertently have been punished by short-term high tariffs, customs delays, and other non-tariff barriers. Although quite unlikely now, the worst-case scenario would be a ban on importation from China. Unfortunately, because of the general income levels in China and construction norms, there was little local market for IDG's products at this time, although it did look promising in the longer term.

Foreign Operations in Vietnam

Situated in the heart of the rapidly developing Pacific Rim, Vietnam had only recently begun to exhibit the economic growth characteristic of other countries in this region. Like many developing countries, infrastructure at this time was terribly inadequate. Lattimer estimated that development was at least five years behind China, and conditions were even more challenging than those first faced by IDG when they established their joint venture in China.

In recent years, Vietnam had been plagued by internal political problems, and foreign investors were apprehensive about investing in the economy. This situation now was beginning to change, as the United States had moved to reestablish diplomatic relations with the Socialist Republic of Vietnam in 1995. In turn, this thawing of the political climate encouraged foreign investors to consider Vietnam as a country in which to do business and invest capital. Foreign investment had grown rapidly as a result. Vietnam also had a strategic location for reexport to other markets in Asia.

Although a Communist state, the central government had instituted the beginnings of *Doi Moi or* "open door" policy as early as 1986. The objectives of *Doi Moi* were to develop export-oriented production capabilities that create jobs and generate foreign currency, to develop import substitutes, to stimulate production using natural resources, to acquire foreign technology, and to strengthen Vietnam's infrastructure. Incentives offered included: the option to establish wholly owned foreign subsidiaries; favourable corporate income tax and tax holidays; waivers on import/export duties; and full repatriation of profits and capital.

With 75 million citizens and a labour force of 32 million, Vietnam had the second-lowest wage rate in the Pacific Rim. Only about 11 percent of the working population was employed in manufacturing, another 19 percent in the service sector, and the remainder in agriculture. Inflation was high, at 14 percent in 1995, partially because of the devaluation of the "new dong" as the government had allowed the currency to float in world markets for the first time. The primary industries of Vietnam included food processing, textiles, machinery, mining, cement, chemical fertilizers, tires, oil, and glass. Vietnamese companies already supplied some of the standard glass and bevelled glass components used by IDG.

Generally, the labour force was energetic, disciplined, and hardworking, although unemployment remained high, at 20 percent. English and French were widely spoken but literacy was relatively low, at 88 percent. Unfortunately, basic human rights and freedoms had received little attention. There was widespread conflict between local and central governing bodies with extensive corruption and exhaustive bureaucracy at both levels.

Production of Decorative Glass Panels in Vietnam

The State Committee for Cooperation and Investment (SCCI) identified seven areas of the Vietnam economy where foreign investment would receive preferential tax treatment. Of particular relevance to IDG, labour-intensive manufacturing was one such area. The SCCI would assist the new venture in whatever way they could, typically through the development of contacts with customers and suppliers, as well as guiding the investor through the government bureaucracy that approved any business venture.

The Vietnamese government also had legislated five approaches for establishing a business venture in the country. Of the five, the international business community and the government widely favoured the joint venture approach. Under this approach, a foreign firm such as IDG would sign a contract with one or more Vietnamese parties to create a new legal entity with limited liability. Foreign capital had to constitute at least 30 percent of the new entity's total capital. A foreign investor could then leverage the local partner's contacts, knowledge of the local market, and access to land and resources.

The Vietnamese had a saying; "*Nhap gia tuy tuc*," which means "When you come into a new country, you have to follow the culture." Clearly, identification of a strong local partner would be critical for meeting the cultural norms in Vietnam and ensuring the success of any investment by IDG; this had been a major obstacle for many other foreign firms.

Lattimer saw many parallels with the earlier joint venture into China. That investment had succeeded largely as a result of IDG's strategic partnership with Century Glass and the Lo family. IDG had been able to limit their investment risk to supplying capital equipment for the facility and inventories. By contrast, other decorative glass suppliers operating in China were paying higher costs, and making larger investments in plant and infrastructure. The partnership with Century also had provided IDG with additional political clout and allowed them to bypass much of the Chinese bureaucracy.

One obvious choice for a local partner was IDG's bevel glass supplier, managed by Dan Kim. Kim operated a glass plant in Da Nang, which was well under capacity, and had an oversupply of qualified labour. Kim had approached both IDG and government authorities and essentially paved the way for IDG to begin joint venture operations within a six-to-twelve-month time frame. Labour and product transfer prices were likely to be significantly lower than either the Delta or Shuenyi plants, with these costs being approximately half those of Shuenyi. Additional overhead costs were estimated at $50,000 annually. Finally, a significant investment would be needed in new equipment to reach the same, company-wide production volume possible with the other options (Exhibit 8). Lattimer wondered whether he might be able to extract more favourable terms for any joint venture relationship, such as shifting responsibilities for financing inventories to Kim.

The Decision

As Lattimer was putting together his proposal for the board, he reflected on a conversation he had with Jerry Lo last month. Lo had indicated that Century would soon expect their piecework compensation to increase from $4 to $7 per finished panel. While seemingly a small fraction of total production costs, Lattimer worried that further requests for increases would follow unless other alternatives were developed. He also was only too aware that with up to $1 million invested in inventory at Century at any given time, IDG was in a very precarious position. Single-sourcing had given Century a level of bargaining power that might limit IDG's future options and cost-competitiveness.

Lo had become agitated as Lattimer described IDG's exploring additional manufacture sourcing arrangements, but had to agree it made sense from IDG's perspective. Lattimer reassured Lo that IDG was looking to add capacity, not replace it. This discussion had reinforced the need to delicately handle IDG's existing relationships. Any recommendation for locating new production capacity would have to take into account the skilled Canadian work force, Century Glass and the Lo family, and Dan Kim's offer for an expanded relationship in Vietnam.

EXHIBIT 8 **Production Equipment Required for Startup in Vietnam**

Production Equipment	Cost
Electrical backup generator	$ 13,000
Air compressor	1,500
Glass equipment:	
Two-shape cutter (pneumatic, from Korea)	7,000
Shape cutter (CNC, from Canada)	110,000
Glass washer	60,000
Brass equipment:	
Roll-former	55,000
Roll-forming dies	21,500
Circle rollers (large and small)	5,000
Table saws (2)	1,400
Chop saw	700
Mitre saw	500
Saw blades for startup	400
Blade sharpener	500
Bevelling equipment:	
Straight-line beveller	125,000
Curved bevelling machines (12)	30,000
Miscellaneous equipment:	
Small forklift	7,000
Pallet jack	2,000
Computer, fax, etc.	3,500
Hand tools, tables, etc.	5,000
TOTAL CAPITAL EQUIPMENT	$449,000

CASE 15

International UNP Holdings Ltd. (1994)

In early October 1994, George Bonar, the president and CEO of International UNP Holdings Ltd. (IUNP), arrived in Poland to participate in the annual shareholders' meetings of IUNP's subsidiaries. During his visit he also planned to negotiate new investments and discuss his company's future role in the Mass Privatization Program with government representatives.

His first task on arriving in IUNP's Warsaw office was to analyze the most recent quarterly reports of Biawar, IBIS, and Unipak, the three subsidiaries his company had acquired over the preceding two years. George had already skimmed the documents, and was quite satisfied with the results presented by Biawar and Unipak. IBIS's performance, however, was disappointing. This was not entirely surprising to him because, for some time, he had been concerned with the pace and direction of post-privatization changes taking place in this subsidiary.

He had a clear view of what steps would be needed to bring IBIS back in line with IUNP's expectations. He also felt that by taking a closer look at all three companies he might be able to discern some patterns which could help him to avert similar situations in the future.

Company History

IUNP was formed in Vancouver, Canada, to establish a pool of capital for investment in Poland's manufacturing sector.[1] The idea of creating an investment fund for this purpose had first crossed Stan Lis' mind in early 1989. Changes in the politics and the economies of central Europe had just begun, but it seemed apparent to Stan that, as a result of a collapse of the communist system, countries of the region would increasingly open their doors to the West. Consequently, farsighted Western entrepreneurs and investors could capitalize on what might be enormous profit opportunities by getting an

This case was prepared by Kris Opalinski and Walter Good of the University of Manitoba, Canada, as a basis for classroom discussion rather than to illustrate either effective or ineffective handling of an administrative situation. © Canadian Consortium of Management Schools, 1994.

[1] The startup of IUNP was discussed in a 1990 business case study entitled "International UNP Holdings Ltd." available from the authors at the Faculty of Management, University of Manitoba.

early foothold in these new markets. For Stan, it seemed natural to concentrate on Poland. Not only was it his native country, but it was at the forefront of the trend toward adopting the free market system.

Stan had settled in Canada in 1976 and had been involved in the Vancouver investment community since then. He presented his idea to Bill Hudson, a close friend and business associate who also committed himself to the venture.

The initial efforts of the partners to raise the capital for their investment fund were unsuccessful. Stan and Bill decided they needed to include a successful business executive in their venture to work out the details of the company's business plan, contribute a higher level of professionalism to its operations, and lend more credibility to the concept. Their search led to George Bonar, a seasoned business executive, also of Polish decent.

George was initially somewhat skeptical of the opportunities described by Stan and Bill and wanted to investigate the viability of the idea himself before fully committing himself to the venture. He agreed to sign on as a consultant to investigate the situation before making a decision. The preliminary search George conducted in Canada indicated that investing in Poland had considerable merit. In order to confirm these initial findings, George continued his investigation in Poland. This visit confirmed his view that the country offered the opportunity of a lifetime for Western investors and, upon his return, he joined the company as president, CEO, and significant shareholder. One of his initial acts was to develop the following short-term organizational objectives for IUNP:

1. Improve the company's credibility (which he perceived as the major factor in attracting investment capital)
2. Raise $5 to $10 million in equity capital
3. Develop UNP's overall strategy
4. Develop procedures for the identification of investment opportunities and their subsequent screening, as well as guidelines for managing the company's investment portfolio
5. Search for investment opportunities and allocate a portion of any acquired funds to Poland

It took him more than a year and $1 million of his and his partner Bill Hudson's money to obtain the capital needed to implement his strategy. He later commented on the company's early days:

> At the beginning, IUNP was just a concept, a dream, the legitimacy of which had yet to be proved to potential investors. To sell this concept, we had to portray ourselves as a credible company. This was not easy for a one-person business operating out of a borrowed office. We had to build our credibility based on the reputation of people associated with us. We brought in some of the most reputable Canadian business executives on our board while retaining the services of legal and accounting advisors with names recognizable worldwide. This may have seemed an extravagant strategy but it worked.

By 1991, the company had managed to raise $8.5 million in equity funding, an amount sufficient to finance the acquisition of two or three Polish subsidiaries. Large financial institutions, such as the British branch of U.S.-based Fidelity

Investments, Murray Johnstone International Ltd. of Glasgow, and Fleming International Investment Ltd., were the major investors, who, in addition to their money, contributed additional credibility to the company.

With the newly obtained capital, IUNP could strengthen its operating base. In May 1991, the company founded a Dutch subsidiary, UNP Holdings B.V., that was to be used as the acquisition vehicle for making investments in Poland.[2] In the second half of 1991, IUNP opened a permanent office in Poland.

The Investment Process

By early 1992, George had scanned some 250 companies, of which he found 75 attractive enough to warrant a more detailed investigation. His approach to evaluating potential Polish investments followed a carefully designed set of guidelines (Exhibit 1) and procedures (Exhibit 2), which were to ensure the consistency and efficiency of the process.

With his previous experience in dealing with prospective acquisitions, George had developed a fairly good feeling of what to look for. Obviously, the primary investment criteria had to be met in each case, but, in his direct dealings with the managers of his prospect companies, he was also looking for some indication of their openness to new ideas, a positive attitude, and a

---

[2] Under the terms of the Netherlands-Poland Income Tax Convention, the withholding tax on dividends paid by a Polish company to a Netherlands-based investor (generally set at up to 15 percent) is waived if the investor holds more than 25 percent of the capital of the Polish company. This compares favourably with the terms of the Canada-Poland Income Tax Convention, which does not allow for such a waiver.

EXHIBIT 1   **IUNP Investment Guidelines***

IUNP generally intends to invest in businesses in Poland which are profitable and will only make an investment if an investee company meets any seven of the following Investment Guidelines:

1. It operates in the manufacturing sector.
2. It is operated by management which IUNP believes to be competent.
3. It manufactures goods that have a sizable demand in Poland and are competitive with domestic and imported products in Poland.
4. It has fewer than 1,000 employees.
5. It does not operate in an industrial sector which has a high visibility or social or environmental sensitivity.
6. It manufactures goods with a high labour content such that it takes advantage of current wage rates which are low relative to wage rates in similar industries in other developed countries.
7. It has a significant market share in its product area.
8. It manufactures goods that do not have a high brand visibility or a large marketing content.
9. It uses mature technologies instead of high technology unless the high technology is available in "packaged" form.
10. It has established and secured domestic access to supplies and materials.

*Quoted from the July 28, 1993, offering of IUNP shares.

EXHIBIT 2   IUNP Investment Procedure*

Sourcing of Investments

IUNP seeks potential investments through the use of existing contacts in Poland and contacts developed by management on an ongoing basis. The typical sources of information on investment opportunities include state administration, consultants, trade development offices of foreign embassies, international organizations operating in Poland, and commercial and investment banks.

Screening and Due Diligence of Investments

1. *Initial screening.* A company identified as a potential investment opportunity is contacted personally by IUNP executives. Based on information provided by the management of the potential investee company and review of generally available sources of information, IUNP's management decides whether the prospective investment satisfies the Investment Guidelines.

2. *Initial due diligence.* Initial due diligence involves a review of legal, financial, and technical operations of the potential investee company. Outside expertise is used if required, particularly in translating the financial statements of the company into the Canadian format. If this stage results in a positive evaluation of the potential investment, the two sides enter into a letter of intent.

3. *Letter of intent.* Generally, letters of intent entered into by IUNP include an agreement in principle as to IUNP's investment, a right for IUNP to conduct further due diligence of the investee company, and an agreement by the investee company not to consider investment proposals from any party other than IUNP for a specified period of time, usually six months.

4. *Due diligence.* Due diligence is initiated by detailed discussions with the management and, if one exists, the Employees' Council of the investee company. If appropriate, the relevant Polish authority, usually the Ministry of Industry, is involved in the investment discussions at this point. Should these discussions proceed in a satisfactory manner, then the due diligence review is formally undertaken and pursued to completion. This review encompasses a review of the following aspects of operations of the investee company:

   - The business plan
   - Historical operating results
   - Financial and marketing projections
   - Customer base and competition
   - Technology, operations, and quality control
   - Environmental impact (if deemed necessary)

IUNP's Investment Approval Process

Following a positive result of due diligence, an investment proposal is prepared by IUNP's management and submitted to the Board's Investment Committee for approval. The Investment Committee reviews each investment proposal and makes a recommendation to the IUNP Board of Directors to approve or reject the investment.

Negotiations with the Polish State

An investment proposal approved by the Board becomes the subject of negotiations with the Polish State. The valuation and capitalization of the prospective investee company are the major issues negotiated with the State. IUNP prefers to base its initial valuation of the investee company upon a multiple of not more than 1.5 times the historical annual earnings, after the payment of interest but prior to depreciation and any mandatory payments to the Polish State and excluding any changes to noncash working capital.

The actual negotiated value assigned to the assets and liabilities contributed by the Polish State to the new company may differ from IUNP's initial valuation. In addition, IUNP may choose to increase its contribution beyond ECU 2 million (Cdn$3.2 million), the amount required to qualify an investment by a foreign company for a 3-year tax holiday. In such a case, IUNP would acquire a larger share of the new company.

Completion of Investment

The investment may be completed if the following requirements have been met:

1. Approval is obtained from the Polish Ministry of Privatization, the Anti-Monopoly Commission, and any other applicable authority (often the Ministry of Industry or a provincial governor).

2. The constituting documents of the newly formed investee company are signed before a notary and registered.

*Based on the relevant section of the June 28, 1993, offering of IUNP shares.

gleam in their eye suggesting their commitment to their companies, all intangible qualities. George stated:

> I know after five minutes of a conversation with a general manager of a company interested in joining us if there is common ground on which we can build our relationship. If there is not, I spend an hour with him just to be polite, but then let him know that I don't see us working together.

Two of these companies, Biawar Bialystok, a producer of water boilers, and IBIS Bydgoszcz, Poland's leader in the manufacture of baking equipment, were considered viable investments. However, negotiations regarding their privatization proved to be quite a challenge for IUNP. The management of Biawar and IBIS were wholeheartedly supportive of the idea of privatization with IUNP's participation but had to overcome resistance from their Employees' Councils to their privatization plans. This was readily overcome at IBIS, but came very close to derailing negotiations with Biawar and delayed the process significantly.

The approval process at the state level further delayed IUNP's investments. In the early 1990s, Poland had just begun implementing a newly designed privatization program. The idea of foreign participation in the privatization of State-Owned Enterprises (SOEs), although approved by several consecutive governments, was fiercely contested by nationalist parties viewing foreign money as a threat to the country's political and economic independence. This made government agencies involved in privatization very defensive in considering agreements involving foreign capital. On the other hand, state administrators did not have any experience in managing the process, which often resulted in uncertainties about the relevant regulations and implementation guidelines. Consequently, the approval process was riddled with confusion and uncertainty, both causing significant delays.

As a result of these circumstances, IUNP had to wait until 1992 to complete its first two investments. In April 1992, the IBIS agreement was finalized, while negotiations on the takeover of Biawar continued until November before all necessary approvals were obtained.

IUNP as an Investor

With over Cdn$5 million invested in IBIS and Biawar, George could be assured of IUNP's future as a holding company. To further enhance its credibility, he initiated the process to list IUNP's securities on the Toronto Stock Exchange (TSE). He then hired Justin Bonar, his son, with a background in computers and business administration, to take over the administrative duties at the Toronto office, including the handling of the company's application for the listing on the TSE. Later in the year, Marek Scibor-Rylski, a British-born venture capital executive of Polish descent, joined the company as a full-time replacement for John Wleugel.[3] Mr. Scibor-Rylski, with an engineering and business

---

[3] John Wleugel, a retired executive from Bata Limited (the Czech shoe manufacturer reestablished in Canada after World War II) had previously performed the duties of vice-president of finance on a part-time basis.

background as well as fluency in Polish, was also to assist George in sourcing, selecting, and screening investments in Poland.

At the end of 1992 IUNP's long-term prospects seemed excellent, but, in the short run, the company faced a severe cash flow problem. Of the $8.5 million raised in 1991, $5 million was spent on the two acquisitions, more than $2.5 million on ongoing operations (in 1991 and 1992), $800,000 on securities issue costs, and some $800,000 on the partial repayment of liabilities. Although in April and May of 1992 George raised an additional $1 million through the private placement of 1.3 million IUNP shares, the company's cash position in early 1993 was very weak.

George, who always tried to ensure the long-term stability of his company, had anticipated this situation well in advance. However, he felt that the company's chances of raising new equity capital would be better after obtaining the listing of its shares on the TSE. The listing was approved in November 1992, which set the stage for a new offering of IUNP's securities.

This public offering was an anxious event for George, but in the end it was a real breakthrough for the company. After five months, during which IUNP ran out of cash, the first tranche of the offering was closed. J. P. Morgan and Morgan Stanley, two financial institutions of international stature, joined the roster of IUNP's shareholders, further validating the company's strategy. Subsequent closings came in quick succession in May, June, and September of 1993, bringing a total of Cdn$20 million in gross proceeds.

George further exploited the momentum created by the success of the second offering, and, immediately after its closing, issued yet another offering, which closed in January 1994 bringing an additional $12.5 million in equity capital. In the end, the company's total capitalization reached $42 million, an amount firmly securing its future needs.

During 1993, IUNP continued its search for new investment opportunities. In the early part of the year it signed a letter of intent with Unipak Gniezno, Poland's leading manufacturer of packaging equipment. Six months later, the acquisition was completed, marking quite a significant improvement in the pace of the approval process.

With an increased level of activity in Europe, the company could no longer effectively operate from its Toronto headquarters. In August 1993, it moved its head office to London where its staff was expanded to six. The Warsaw office was also expanded by the addition of four employees. In George's view this structure could serve the company's needs for the next few years.

Throughout the second half of 1993 and 1994, George and Scibor-Rylski were busy identifying prospective investee companies in Poland, negotiating deals, and getting governmental approval. After securing the company's financial well-being, George had more time to explore some additional opportunities created by IUNP's unique position as the only foreign holding company operating in Poland. He was particularly interested in the planned Mass Privatization Program, which would affect some 600 of Poland's SOEs. In anticipation of the final approval of the program, he teamed up with one of IUNP's shareholders, Murray Johnstone of Glasgow, and, with the additional participation of Bank Gdanski, formed Hevelius Management, a consortium hoping to become one of the managers of the National Investment Funds.

In August 1994, the new consortium was ranked (unofficially) as the ninth of the 19 candidates who applied to become NIF managers. This meant that its chances to become one of 15 managers to be selected were reasonably good. If, in fact, the consortium became a NIF manager, IUNP would have an additional growth opportunity. Besides receiving management fees for its services, Hevelius could also obtain up to 15 percent of its NIF's ownership. This latter component of the remuneration package could mean significant growth for IUNP, which held a 65 percent share of Hevelius.

In mid-October 1994, IUNP was just a few steps from completing several new acquisitions. Negotiations with a glass container maker, Antoninek, and FADA, a Gniezno manufacturer of industrial lifts, were already completed and the acquisition agreements were awaiting approval from the Ministry of Privatization. Two other investment opportunities were being negotiated with companies from the timber processing and electronics industries. In addition, IUNP was close to completing an agreement with Polbita, a distributor of cosmetics and household chemicals. In this deal, IUNP was engaged in a complex arrangement involving a $5.5 million loan with an option to convert it into equity. Part of the capital to be provided to Polbita came from Wasserstein Emerging Markets, a New York–based financier. This transaction, once finalized, would signify IUNP's first foray into the service sector and first agreement with a private company.

◼ Investment Climate in Poland[4]

In the second half of 1994, Poland's economic prospects looked promising. It was the first country in post-communist East and Central Europe to have pulled out of the deep recession caused by the collapse of the region's previous regime. It was expected that its growth in 1994 would at least match the 4 percent achieved in 1993, while inflation would be reduced from 36 percent to 27 percent. With its 38.5 million population, a 1993 GDP of US$85 billion, and choice location (astride major east-west and north-south communication routes), Poland had emerged as the single most important market in Central Europe, ripe for treatment as a Big Emerging Market (BEM). However, experts agreed that this growth, largely fuelled by domestic consumption, might be difficult to sustain without an increase in exports and investments. It was hoped that foreign capital would contribute significantly to both of these growth factors.

A more significant role for foreign investment in the country's expansion would become possible after its foreign debt had been significantly reduced in early 1994. An agreement with the Paris club on a 50 percent reduction of the $33 billion owed to its members was followed by an agreement with 300 commercial banks who had agreed to reduce the $13.2 billion owed to them by 42.5 to 45 percent.

---

[4] Based on Colin Jones, "First over the Wall," *The Banker,* May 1994, pp. 58–60.

As a result of these two debt-reduction agreements, Poland could reenter the international capital market on normal commercial terms instead of relying upon loans from foreign governments and international financial institutions like the World Bank. It was expected that the Polish government would be able to raise funds from the syndicated loan market on more favourable terms.

It was also anticipated that the improved financial situation would provide a more stable, less risky investment environment, increasing the attractiveness of equity investment in Poland. In the early 1990s, Poland was not very successful in attracting a proportionate share of Central Europe's relatively modest inflow of direct investment. By the end of 1993, the overall value of foreign investment in Poland did not exceed US$2.8 billion, with a further $4.6 billion in forward commitments. This compared unfavourably with the much smaller and more heavily indebted Hungary which attracted $7 billion.

Foreign direct investment in Poland was heavily skewed toward Italy and the United States as countries of origin. In 1993, Fiat and Coca-Cola, with their investments in new production facilities, accounted for this dominance. Interestingly, Germany, which accounted for one-third of Poland's external trade, provided only just above 7 percent of all foreign investment in 1993. Japan largely refrained from investing in Poland.

In particular need of equity capital was the country's fast-growing private sector, which accounted for 60 percent of national output in 1993 but attracted very little interest from foreign investors, who concentrated their interest on joint ventures with SOEs.

The Privatization Program

Poland's privatization program had two goals: first, to transform and redistribute property rights to different categories of economic agents (employees, managers, private and institutional investors, foreign companies, and banks) and, second, to restructure state-owned enterprises. It was initiated in 1990 by the Sejm (the lower chamber of Parliament) which adopted a series of laws defining the legally acceptable ways of transferring ownership of economic entities from the state to private investors.

The principal methods of privatization under the Law of 1990 on Privatization were as follows:

A. Individual privatization:
    1. *Capital privatization.* Sale of an enterprise through public offering, employee buyout, or trade sale by tender.
    2. *Privatization by liquidation.* Winding up of a state enterprise in order to (a) sell its assets, (b) contribute its assets into a new company owned in whole or in part by private capital (foreign or domestic), or (c) lease its assets to employees and/or management. Privatization by liquidation was reserved for SOEs showing good profit performance and favourable growth prospects.
    3. *Liquidation under bankruptcy.* The sale or leasing of assets of SOEs placed under bankruptcy proceedings due to their insolvency.

4. *Commercialization*. Transformation of an SOE into a joint-stock company owned by the State Treasury and managed through a Supervisory Board controlled by the state (2/3) and an Employees' Council (1/3). Commercialized enterprises could be viewed as hybrid firms, owned by the state, but managed for commercial purposes.

B. Mass privatization:

5. *The Mass Privatization Program*. Provided for privatization of several hundred larger, relatively healthy SOEs. After preliminary selection, SOEs participating in the program were to be transformed into companies owned by the State Treasury. At the same time, a number (10–20) of "National Investment Funds" were to be set up (as joint-stock companies) to manage the portfolios of securities of the firms participating in the program. Each fund would then receive a small share (1–3 percent) in many of the privatized SOEs and a large share (33 percent) in a few (10–15). Ultimately, 33 percent of the shares of each SOE participating in the program would be owned by a single fund, 27 percent by all the remaining funds, 10 percent by employees, and the remaining 30 percent by the State Treasury. Authorized adult Polish citizens would receive investment certificates representing one share in each investment fund.

IUNP used "privatization by liquidation" to acquire its subsidiaries. From IUNP's perspective, this method provided several advantages over the alternative methods. First, as a result of the process, the newly established entity was legally separate from its predecessor, limiting IUNP's exposure to the liabilities of the old entity. Second, the approval process for privatization through liquidation was much simpler than for capital privatization. Third, and most importantly, by applying this method (a "money in" deal), IUNP could channel its investment to the new subsidiary instead of transferring it to the State Treasury.

◼ Management of IUNP Subsidiaries

The relationship between IUNP and its subsidiaries was defined by the terms of their privatization agreements. These agreements provided IUNP with the power necessary to affect all major aspects of corporate governance in IBIS, Biawar, and Unipak. However, IUNP viewed these agreements primarily as a safeguard and did not want to use them to interfere with the ongoing management of its subsidiaries. Of course, all company officers were always available to assist in resolving specific problems raised by the managers of these subsidiaries. Advice, discussion, and persuasion were the major methods applied by IUNP's executive staff.

IUNP was formally required to provide its subsidiaries with "the most far-reaching assistance in the organization and development of export products." It was also obliged to "ascertain that they receive assistance and training in management and the organization of production, marketing, and other expertise." IUNP was to receive Cdn$50,000 per year from each company for its services, subject to the company meeting its profit target for the year.

In 1993 and 1994, George was very active in negotiating licensing agreements on behalf of IUNP's subsidiaries. His international corporate experience was of tremendous help, especially in the early days, when Polish executives had to overcome their timidity in dealing with representatives of major international companies. One of these managers commented on George's role in forming his attitude toward business:

> Mr. Bonar has helped me a lot in changing my way of dealing with problems. He rarely gives you a direct solution to your problem, but puts you on the right track in analyzing it. I once asked him for advice on some technical problem. He answered, "Do you know who would know the answer?" I said, "Probably someone at a German company." "So, take your car and go there," he said. For me, it was an eye opener: Just go?!

Supervisory Boards[5] provided IUNP with a formal way of influencing the direction of its subsidiaries. Their composition reflected the relative share of each company held by IUNP and the state. George Bonar, Marek Scibor-Rylski, and the company's comptroller, Adam Michon, represented IUNP, in some cases complemented by Polish business executives. The state was represented by members nominated by the Ministry of Industry or appropriate government authority.

These boards met quarterly to review the company's operating results and deal with other matters of significance. They had the power to preapprove all fixed asset transactions, capital investment plans, credit facilities, and changes in banks and banking arrangements. The boards also nominated members to the company's Management Board (for a two-year period), and approved annual business plans and quarterly performance reports.

Since one of the principal factors used by IUNP in assessing investment prospects was the competency of their management, it was assumed that the change in ownership would not lead to any major changes in their managerial staff. This was consistent with George's view that IUNP could not afford to fire the managers of its subsidiaries as it would discourage the management of other prospective investee companies from seeking his involvement.

The company provided some training in areas crucial to the growth of its subsidiaries, such as marketing, information systems, and general management. Managers of IBIS, Biawar, and Unipak had participated in corporate seminars where they shared information and experience on organizing their operations in these crucial areas. IUNP also invited keynote speakers who discussed areas of particular interest to the companies.

IUNP planned to implement a common financial reporting system in all three of its subsidiaries. This system was to be based on a MIS package adapted to Polish accounting regulations. IBIS and Unipak were chosen as the pilot sites with scheduled January 1995 implementation. Biawar, which had already adopted a locally developed system, was to switch to the new system

---

[5] The management structure of private companies in Poland typically consisted of non-executive supervisory boards (the equivalent of boards of directors) and management boards consisting of company executives.

later. Production planning and reporting modules were to be implemented once the core accounting modules/functions had been fully adopted.

By mid-1994, IUNP had also implemented a corporate-wide e-mail communications system and distributed database. Lotus Notes was the core of this system. It enabled IUNP corporate offices in London and Warsaw and the three investee companies to automatically replicate and exchange information on sales, costs, and orders.

IUNP's staff were in constant communication with their subsidiaries. Their major concern was with translating financial results from Polish to Canadian (international) standards. The new reporting system, which was designed to produce two sets of records (in both the Polish and Canadian format), was intended to relieve the Warsaw staff of the bulk of these tasks.

Transition Goals

IUNP's investment in each of its Polish subsidiaries was expected to contribute to their transformation from production-oriented entities operating in a planned economy to market-driven businesses functioning in a competitive environment. Obviously, the primary objective for each subsidiary was to increase its profits to a level sufficient to provide a superior return on IUNP's investment. Considering the risk involved in investing in Poland, IUNP required a cash payback of 2–3 years.

It was felt that, in order to meet this primary objective, all three companies had to adjust their mode of operations in three major areas:

1. *Developing a market orientation.* This goal was common for all three subsidiaries and presupposed both the organizational and cultural changes required to improve responsiveness to market signals. A better customer service system, improved market research capabilities, and, most of all, closer alignment of corporate activities with marketing objectives were the practical measures of progress in this area.

2. *Upgrading production technology, modernizing, and expanding product lines.* Capital contributed by IUNP was expected to address the most immediate investment needs of each company. Further, the technological gap between IUNP's subsidiaries and its Western competitors was to be closed through the acquisition of licences from leading manufacturers. Therefore, the ability of each subsidiary to adopt foreign licences and accelerate the new product development process was viewed as a primary success factor.

3. *Changing corporate culture.* IUNP viewed internal communication as a primary factor determining a business's ability to achieve its goals. Improved communication was fundamental in fostering the culture of shared goals, open discussions, and transparent responsibilities among the company's staff. Information technology was considered a major factor in opening up communication routes, and a company's ability to adopt it was considered an important measure of its success in the transition process.

IUNP did not develop a formal policy for managing the transition in each of its subsidiaries. It was felt that this would be difficult if not impossible, for a diverse set of entities operating in different industries and markets, and with different histories. Consequently, no formal compliance requirements or evaluation criteria were set. The evaluation process was expected to come naturally as part of the ongoing supervision of the three entities.

The General Impact of Privatization

IUNP's investments had a profound impact on all three subsidiaries. The most important change resulted from the fact that private ownership put an end to the question of who was in charge of the company. This relieved management from having to satisfy multiple conflicting objectives set by various stakeholders, which included the state administration, trade unions, and the workers' councils.

The new ownership set the stage for implementing a rational management system in which corporate goals, responsibilities, and evaluation criteria were clearly defined and well understood by all parties involved. Under the new system, managers had their hands untied and could set goals for their subordinates and demand performance while being responsible for their own decisions. This also allowed for a more rational human resource policy. Qualifications and performance were becoming the determinants of an employee's place in the corporate hierarchy, which was also reflected in a compensation structure which favoured skills, responsibility, and achievement.

These managerial changes induced a markedly different attitude toward work among employees. Better discipline as expressed by a willingness to follow orders and established procedures, decreased absenteeism and tardiness, and greater attention to the quality of work performed were just a few qualities of the new spirit brought about by the change. Obviously, the fear of losing relatively well-paying jobs in a country affected by high unemployment was certainly a factor in enforcing these new attitudes as well. However, it was generally agreed that the major impact could be attributed to the introduction of a sensible and fair management system.

Organizational changes emphasized the new strategic direction embraced by the three companies. The driving force behind their activities switched from production to marketing. This was reflected in the leading position given to the marketing and sales departments relative to their production and administrative counterparts. The marketing departments were the only ones that grew in size, despite a general trend to reduce employment in other areas due to increased productivity. Business plans, marketing research, customer satisfaction, product positioning, and distribution channels were being quickly adopted as part of management's vocabulary.

In addition, increased foreign competition stressed the importance of quality of production and customer service. Foreign licences obtained with the funds contributed by IUNP addressed this problem, but were not sufficient to entirely change a system which traditionally turned out goods generally below international standards. In response to this challenge, all three companies implemented quality management programs which concentrated on developing production systems with built-in quality. They were also developing a system of rewards and penalties tied to the quality of output at each stage of the production process.

Privatization had an immediate effect on the subsidiaries' financial position. Equity capital provided by IUNP was used to reduce their significant debt burden, which immediately improved profitability. In addition, the privatized companies were relieved from the surtax on excessive salaries and wages (*popiwek*), and the tax on fixed assets (*dywidenda*). In addition, foreign investment above 2 million ECU qualified investee companies for a three-year tax holiday.

George was generally satisfied with the transition process taking place in Unipak and Biawar (Exhibits 3 and 4). Within a relatively short time, these two companies were able to meet the objectives established by IUNP. They

EXHIBIT 3   Biawar—Corporate Profile Before and After Privatization

	1991	1994

IUNP investment and share	• SOE	• IUNP investment (1992)—ZI $37 billion ($2.8 million)
		• Ownership (1994):*
		  • IUNP—86%
		  • State—10%
		  • Employees—4%

Rank and size	• Medium-sized manufacturer • ZI 68 billion sales • ZI 1 billion after-tax profit • 275 employees	• Medium-sized manufacturer • ZI 220 billion sales • ZI 35 billion net profit • 285 employees
Culture	• Confrontation	• Collegiality
Product line	• Water heating tanks—100%	• Water heating tanks—75% • Instant water heaters—25% • Kitchen oven hoods—<0.5% • Hot-dog cookers—<0.5%
Geographic coverage	• Poland—99% • Export—1%	• Poland—99% • Export—1%
Evolution	• SOE with no future	• Dynamic private company
Organization	• Four departments • Four layers of management	• Three departments • Three layers of management
Performance goals	• Survival • Cash-flow maintenance	• Domination of domestic market • Profit growth • New product development
Strengths	• Good quality of products • Low cost	• Strong distribution network • Good quality of products • Broad product line • Collegial management style
Weaknesses	• Financial instability • No marketing capabilities • Poor morale	• Production bottlenecks • Inadequate working capital
Strategy	• Maintenance of market share	• Market leadership

*After the employee buyout of 4 percent of the Biawar shares.

could now be viewed as truly market-oriented manufacturers of significantly improved products. Also, their manufacturing, although still less productive than their foreign counterparts, was no longer inferior technologically. Most important, their corporate cultures fostered a spirit of achievement, cooperation, and openness to new ideas.

At the same time, George was seriously concerned with the developments taking place at IBIS. This company, which was initially considered a jewel among his acquisition targets, could not shake off its past. Although it implemented many changes consistent with IUNP's expectations, George and his colleagues felt that IBIS's employees only paid lip service to the new system, while still continuing to act in the old manner. Their marketing, although consuming the same proportion of sales as in the other two companies, did not produce the expected results as measured by the quality of their market

EXHIBIT 4   Unipak—Corporate Profile Before and After Privatization

	1992	1994 (projected)
IUNP investment and share	• SOE	• IUNP investment (1993)—ZI 45 billion ($3.75 million) • Ownership (1994): • IUNP—51% • State—49%
Rank and size	• Medium-sized batch manufacturer • ZI 80 billion sales • ZI 15 billion after-tax profit • 600 employees	• Medium-sized batch manufacturer • ZI 135 billion sales • ZI 24 billion net profit • 578 employees
Product line	• Based on technology from the 1970s: • Packaging machines—70% • Milk separators—6% • Spare parts, services—24%	• 15% sales—new or modernized products: • Packaging machines—79% • Milk separators—4% • Spare parts, services—17%
Culture	• Indifference • Strong departmentalization	• Motivation • Collegiality
Geographic coverage	• Poland—95% • Export—5%	• Poland—90% • Export—10%
Evolution	• Stagnating SOE	• Growing private company
Organization	• Five departments (directors) • Five layers of management	• Three departments • Three layers of management
Performance goals	• Survival	• Profit growth • Technological improvement • Market-share growth
Strengths	• Strong production base • Relatively good product quality • Low cost	• Knowledge of the marketplace • Low cost • Strong financial base • Customer franchise
Weaknesses	• No clear mandate for management • Internal conflicts • Lack of working capital • Obsolete product line	• Low productivity • Shortage of specialized marketing skills • Narrow product line
Strategy	• Price leadership	• Value leadership

analysis and, foremost, the company's ability to align its production activities with its marketing objectives.

◼ The Situation at IBIS

Overview of the Business

IBIS had traditionally occupied a dominant position in the manufacture of bakery production equipment in Poland. Over the postwar period, bakery production in Poland was dominated by large, state-owned producers, often serving entire urban centres with a limited range of basic products. Under the centralized structure of the Polish economy, IBIS (then part of the Spomasz group, an industrial combine for manufacturing food processing equipment) was assigned a monopolistic position for the manufacture of bakery equipment.

With the introduction of market forces into the food processing sector, large bakeries began to lose market share to small, local, more responsive bakeries offering a greater variety of products of superior freshness. Consequently, by the early 1990s the demand for equipment for large bakeries was significantly reduced. At the same time, thousands of small bakeries were opening, each requiring bakery equipment. Obviously, these small bakeries required equipment suited for small production volumes and specific types of bakery products, such as baguettes and croissants, which were becoming increasingly popular.

IBIS was in a relatively good position and made an effort to introduce a new product line responding to these needs. However, its success was limited as Poland became the target of a number of foreign manufacturers of bakery equipment. Their products, although more expensive, were superior in esthetics, reliability, and durability, and—most importantly—labour-saving controls. Faced with this competition, IBIS's products, although less expensive, could not obtain a significant market share. Although the company was able to survive, it could not prosper without new products and technologies. This, of course, was impossible without additional capital, not readily available to a company generating hardly any profit. Consequently, for IBIS, privatization, with its potential for bringing in additional equity capital, was the only real chance for long-term survival.

Management and Employees

The management of IBIS included a core group of 15- to 20-year company veterans supported by recent appointees recruited from outside of the company. The group was dominated by engineers with degrees from Bydgoszcz Technical University. In terms of age, it was a balanced mix of people in their mid-50s and those in their early 40s.

Jerzy Gorzynski, the company's president (in his mid-50s) was an economist with a long career in management even prior to joining IBIS in 1979 as economic director. He was appointed to his current post in 1990. His management style was a little autocratic, emphasizing the importance of corporate hierarchy and formal organization. His central role was indispensable in dealing with problems, but his domination over his team members may have limited their ability to make their own decisions.

The Privatization Process

The lack of growth prospects under state ownership made the company's management consider privatization. It was initially felt that "strategic investors," that is, foreign manufacturers of bakery equipment, would be the best match for the company. However, not one of a number of strategic investors contacted by IBIS in 1990 wanted to transfer technology to a potential competitor. They were more interested in converting the Polish company into a supplier of components for their own products. This method of privatization was rejected.

Although this attempt at privatization was unsuccessful, it caused members of the Employees' Council and the trade unions to accept the general idea of privatization with foreign capital. This proved quite important when, in early 1991, IUNP contacted the company and decided that its situation merited further review.

The results of this review were positive and in July 1991 IUNP and IBIS signed a standstill agreement which set the stage for subsequent negotiations. Over the next five months, IUNP conducted its due diligence while negotiating the monetary terms of its investment with the state administration. By November 1991, the negotiations were completed, and their results awaited final approval from the ministries of privatization and industry. That this stage was completed in only five months was later attributed by Mr. Gorzynski, IBIS's president, to his persistent lobbying of the ministries involved, culminated by a visit of a busload of his workers to the ministerial offices in Warsaw. This action apparently eliminated all the existing barriers, and resulted in an immediate approval of the privatization deal.

The Effects of Privatization

The funds invested by IUNP were largely used to pay off most of IBIS's existing debt burden. However, the most significant impact on the company's situation came as a result of its newly obtained ability to acquire foreign technology and new machinery for those processes with the most impact on the quality of its products. In 1992, with George's participation, IBIS negotiated a licensing agreement with Zucchelli Forni SPA and Sancassiano SPA, two major Italian manufacturers of bakery equipment. With these licences, IBIS could add modern ovens and mixers to its offering, significantly improving its product line for small bakeries.

With its expanded financial and technological capabilities, IBIS's management could concentrate on improving operations. Their efforts focused on three areas: marketing, corporate organization, and production quality.

In marketing, top priority was assigned to changing the corporate image. IBIS was generally perceived as an unresponsive, low-quality producer, a picture quite inconsistent with the company's new orientation. The task of changing this negative image was assigned to the newly created Marketing and Sales Department. Significant resources were allocated to a promotional campaign featuring a new corporate logo and licensed products, and providing information on the expanding network of regional sales and service offices (four in Poland, one in Russia, and one in Germany).

As part of its overall attempt to rebuild the company's image, Mr. Gorzynski decided to refurbish IBIS's corporate offices. He began with his own office, which was substantially expanded and equipped with expensive furniture, all intended to communicate a new corporate style to his visitors. The Marketing and Sales Department was next in line for upgrading of its facilities. By late 1994, however, only a visitors' room in the section of the corporate headquarters housing the marketing department had been rebuilt.

These steps were accompanied by changes in the company's organizational structure, which became less fragmented and flattened. Some departments were consolidated, most notably production and technology, while the number of management levels was reduced from five to four.

IBIS also put a great deal of effort into bringing the quality of its products up to international standards. In 1992, the company initiated an application for the ISO 9000 certification, a process typically taking two years. A number of technological processes were also upgraded in order to match the quality offered by foreign competitors.

The changes brought significant results (Exhibit 5). IBIS's sales in 1993 increased almost threefold, with a further 60 percent increase planned for 1994. At the same time, its profits rose from the 1992 figure of Zl 4.5 billion to almost Zl 13 billion in 1993, and Zl 28 billion budgeted for 1994. The geographic orientation of the company's sales pattern shifted from east to southwest, with close to 50 percent coming from Germany, the Czech Republic, Slovakia, Hungary, and Lithuania.

Problem Areas

Although the above facts would suggest a healthy operation poised for further expansion, by 1994 some disquieting signs had begun to appear. There seemed to be a problem with the company's management style, which was characterized by secrecy, fragmentation, and a lack of direction. Each department appeared to be driven independently, with only limited communication with the rest of the company. Access to information on corporate performance as well as other issues affecting the entire company was confined within departmental lines. For example, the corporate business plan was kept confidential, the individual copies locked in the desks of a privileged few. Communication with IUNP suffered from this lack of openness, sometimes resulting in delays, distortions, and conflicting information.

Besides general managerial problems, George also identified marketing as a functional area with major weaknesses. There was no clear direction in IBIS's overall marketing program. The company's understanding of the forces shaping the market in Poland seemed to be inadequate. George also suspected that the departmental divisions within the company adversely affected IBIS's responsiveness to market signals, even when they were accurately interpreted by their marketing people.

EXHIBIT 5 IBIS—Corporate Profile Before and After Privatization

	1991	1994

IUNP investment and share	• SOE	• IUNP investment (1992)—ZI 30 billion ($2.9 million)
		• Ownership:
		  • IUNP—53%
		  • State—47%

Rank and size	• Medium-sized manufacturer • ZI 47 billion sales • ZI 1 billion after-tax profit • 540 employees	• Medium-sized batch manufacturer • ZI 200 billion sales • ZI 20 billion net profit • 420 employees
Culture	• Autocratic	• Autocratic

Product line	• Full line of bakery equipment:
	  • Ovens—27%
	  • Mixers—22%
	  • Formers/dividers—16%
	  • Trolleys—13%
	  • Parts/service—22%
	• Majority of products technologically outdated
		• Full line of bakery equipment:
		  • Ovens—32%
		  • Mixers—28%
		  • Formers/dividers—7%
		  • Trolleys—19%
		  • Parts/service—14%
		• 25% of sales from licensed products (ovens, mixers, and trolleys); most products modernized

Geographic coverage	• Poland—90% • Export—10%	• Poland—60% • Export—40%
Evolution	• Deteriorating SOE	• Growing private company
Organization	• Five departments • Five layers of management	• Three departments • Four layers of management
Performance goals	• Maintenance of cash flow • Sustaining sales levels	• Sales/profit growth • Development of marketing • Quality improvement
Strengths	• Low cost/price • Large capacity • Technical competence	• Good quality of products • Product-market fit • Financial stability • Low cost
Weaknesses	• Marketing capabilities • Lack of product-market fit • Product quality/esthetics • Low productivity	• Deficient marketing • Poor internal communication
Strategy	• Price leadership	• Value leadership

These problems were further evidenced by IBIS's management views on IUNP's involvement in the company's operations. They felt that IUNP interfered too frequently in their internal operations while providing too little support in areas which could directly affect IBIS's results, such as developing international distribution for IBIS's products.

All these symptoms caught IUNP's attention within the first year after the acquisition. However, at that time, they were difficult to validate. The company's 1992 and 1993 results were excellent and IUNP's policy not to interfere in the ongoing operations of its subsidiaries made it very difficult to influence these mostly intangible aspects of IBIS's corporate governance. This was not made any easier by the reluctance of IBIS's officers to openly discuss their problems. For the time being, IUNP limited its action to communicating its concern to IBIS's management.

However, as the company's revenues plummeted in the third quarter of 1994, it became obvious that the situation required IUNP to take immediate steps. IBIS's management attributed this to the overall decline in demand for bakery equipment in the Polish market, a situation precipitated by the low prices for bakery products which made new investments in equipment unprofitable. This was not a convincing argument to IUNP, especially since there had been no hint of this possibility in the company's 1994 business plan.

In October 1994, IBIS's marketing director resigned. A new director was to be appointed by the supervisory board at its next meeting. Further changes in the company's top management could be undertaken following the board's recommendations.

◼ Final Considerations

George attributed IBIS's situation to a communication problem stemming from a deeply rooted culture of interdepartmental competition, secrecy, and fear of reprisal for going against the established ways. His concern was not only with addressing this problem at this particular company, but also with adjusting IUNP's policies in such a way that similar situations could be avoided at other acquired companies. His options included the following:

1. A more active role by his company in assigning management staff within its subsidiaries. He regarded this option as undesirable in view of his long-term acquisition goals, which could be jeopardized if managers of his prospective investee companies were to receive a chilling message of possible management dismissals following an acquisition agreement.

2. Assignment of on-site advisors to top management of problem subsidiaries. This approach could be difficult to implement due to its cost and the problem of finding consultants with the required level of expertise and language capabilities. Moreover, the effectiveness of an outside advisor in companies with internal communication problems could be limited.

3. Developing a set of clearly defined transition goals for each company and the evaluation of management on the basis of their ability to meet those goals. This would also be a costly approach, particularly considering the growing number of IUNP's subsidiaries. It would have to be applied indiscriminately, because problems with transition related mainly to intangible aspects of corporate governance and were difficult to identify before the acquisition was completed. On the other hand, IUNP's own expertise could allow it to deal with a variety of specialized industries. This would require hiring external consultants for each acquisition once it had been effected, with all the related costs and uncertainties.

4. Maintaining the status quo. IBIS's performance could well improve with the overall growth of the Polish economy. Possibly, it was simply a matter of time for the cultural change to take effect. The existing means of influence through the supervisory board could be used more effectively while IUNP's contacts with its problem-ridden subsidiaries could be extended and increased. Later on, more emphasis could be put on analyzing corporate culture as a significant predictive factor in the due diligence phase leading to an acquisition.

George felt that the current problems at IBIS could be addressed within the existing set of guidelines and policies. However, he realized that with an increasing number of subsidiaries, the company would have to identify the most effective way of directing and handling their transition to private companies.

Kolapore, Inc.

In January 1986 Adriaan Demmers, president and sole employee of Kolapore, Inc., a firm based in Guelph, Ontario, specializing in the importation, processing, and sale of high-quality souvenir spoons, was becoming increasingly frustrated with the pace at which his business was developing. Over a two-year period, Demmers had taken his idea of importing souvenir spoons from the Netherlands to Canada to annual sales of nearly $30,000. He believed the potential existed for well over $100,000 in Canadian sales plus exports to the United States. This success to date had been a strain, however, on Demmers' limited financial resources and had not provided any compensation for the long hours invested. Demmers was beginning to question if he was ever going to have the major breakthrough which he had always believed was "just around the corner."

Recently, Demmers had accepted a full-time position with another firm in an unrelated business. While Demmers realized that he could continue to operate Kolapore, Inc., on a part-time basis he wondered if he should "face reality" and simply fold up the business or try to sell it. Alternatively, Demmers could not occasionally help wondering if he should be devoting himself full-time to Kolapore.

Company Background

In February/March 1984, Demmers conducted a feasibility study of starting a business to market souvenir spoons. His idea was to offer a high-quality product depicting landmarks, historic buildings, and other unique symbols of the area in which the spoons were to be sold.

There were numerous spoons on the market, but most tended to be representing Ontario rather than local sites of interest, and were generally poorly made and not visually appealing. There were few quality spoons, and the ones that did exist were priced in the $15 to $40 range.

Sources of spoons were examined and quotations were received from firms in Canada, the United States, and the Netherlands (Holland). The search process for a country from which to source the spoons was a limited one and was settled quickly, thanks to Demmers' Dutch heritage, the existence of a well-recognized group of silversmiths in Schoonhoven, plus a particular company which already had over 40 Canadian-specific dies and lower prices.

Demmers thought the key factors for success were good-quality product, designs of local landmarks, and an eyecatching display. He felt displays should be located in a prominent position in retail stores because souvenir spoons are often bought on impulse.

Feasibility Study

As part of his feasibility study, Demmers conducted a market analysis (including customer and retailer surveys) and a competitive analysis (both manufacturers and distributors), and developed an import plan, marketing plan, and financial projections (including projected breakeven and cash flows). Excerpts from this study follow.

Market Analysis

The market for souvenir spoons consisted of several overlapping groups—primarily tourists and the gift market. There were also groups interested in spoons for more specialized purposes such as church groups, service clubs, associations, and others. These were very specialized and for special occasions.

A random telephone survey conducted in March 1984 of 50 people in Guelph revealed that 78 percent owned souvenir spoons; 46 percent of those people had purchased the spoons themselves, while 54 percent had received them as gifts. In total, almost 25 percent of the people in the sample collected souvenir spoons or had a rack on which to hang them. Retailers indicated that sales occurred primarily during the summer months and at Christmastime. Twelve retail outlets were visited to obtain information regarding quality, sales, and prices. Background on a selection of these retailers is summarized in Appendix 1.

There was a high awareness of souvenir spoons in the market, but the product quality was generally at the low end of the market. For example, rough edges on the bowls were common, and the crests on the spoons were often crooked. In fact, one manufacturer's spoon had a picture of Kitchener City Hall which was out of focus and off-centre. (Terms concerning souvenir spoons are explained in Appendix 2.)

A limited variety of spoons was often available, and few of the spoons were of local points of interest even though these were the spoons that were most in demand. One retailer noted that of a total of 140 spoons sold in 1983, 106 were one variety, a spoon with a relief design in plastic of a Connestoga wagon. This was the only unique spoon Demmers found in the area "other than the cheap picture spoons."

There was no advertising for souvenir spoons due to the nature of the product and the lack of identification with a particular brand.

Souvenir spoons appeared to be a low priority in many producing companies, with little marketing effort made to push the products. Even the packaging was of poor quality; often, boxes were not supplied for gift wrapping.

The sale of spoons was viewed as seasonal by some retailers. In many instances, point-of-purchase displays were removed once the summer rush was over.

Spoons were not prominently displayed in most stores, yet they were largely an impulse item. In several stores they were kept in drawers and only taken out when requested.

Competitive Analysis

Souvenir spoons essentially served two customer functions: as gifts or commemoratives. They could be used as gifts for family, friends, or special occasions such as Christmas. They could also serve as a commemorative token of visiting somewhere or celebrating a special anniversary (for example, the Province of Ontario's 200th anniversary). They could be either functional (used for coffee or tea) or decorative (hung in a spoon rack or put in a cabinet).

Competition came from all other gift items and all other souvenir items in approximately the same price range.

Demmers identified 11 companies that distributed souvenir spoons in the southwestern Ontario area and gathered what data he could—much of it anecdotal—on each. This process had provided encouragement for Demmers to proceed. Background on these suppliers is summarized in Appendix 3.

Southwestern Ontario contained a number of large urban areas including Toronto (over 2 million people), Hamilton-Burlington, Kitchener-Waterloo, and London, with over 300,000 people in each, plus many smaller cities such as Guelph. Guelph was located roughly in the centre of the triangle formed by Toronto, Waterloo, and Burlington and was within an hour's drive of each.

Import Plan

To import goods into Canada on a regular basis in amounts over $800, an importer number was required. This was available from Revenue Canada, Customs and Excise. Requirements for customs were an advise notice from the shipper and a customs invoice. These were available in office supply stores. A customs tariff number and commodity code were also required to complete the customs B3 form.

Souvenir spoons of either sterling silver or silver plate were listed in the customs tariff under number 42902-1. Because the Netherlands had Most Favoured Nation status, the duty was 20.3 percent. On top of the cost of the merchandise (excluding transportation and insurance but including duty), there were a further 10 percent excise tax and a 10 percent federal sales tax.

A customs broker could be hired to look after the clearing of goods through customs. Rates were approximately $41 plus $3.60 for every thousand dollars of value, duty included.

Insurance on a shipment of less than $10,000 cost a fixed fee of about $150 with insurance brokers. This could be reduced if insurance were taken on a yearly basis, based on the expected value of imports over the year. Freight forwarders charged approximately $2 per kilogram regardless of the total weight of the shipment.

The importing could be easily handled without help on small shipments such as spoons. The product could be sent by air mail and insured with the post office. It could also be sent to a small city like Guelph rather than Toronto, thereby avoiding the busy Toronto customs office and possible delays of several days. The customs office in Guelph could easily clear the goods the same day they arrived.

Product

The proposed souvenir spoons would be a high-quality product with detailed dies made to give them a relief design far superior to any competitive spoons (except for those retailing in the $30 range). These spoons were available in silver plate and alpacca which made them similar to jewellery.

Designs would be of specific points of interest. In the Kitchener-Waterloo area, for example, possible subjects would include Seagram Museum, Schneider House, Doon Pioneer Village, university crests, and city crests. Kitchener-Waterloo would be printed under the picture, also in relief in the metal, along with the title of the particular picture.

Marketing Plan

Price Points

$2.25	• Metropolitan Supplies—nickel-plated.
4.50–6	• Breadner Manufacturing—rhodium-plated and silver-plated. Candis Enterprises; Gazelle Importers.
7–8	• Oneida or Commemorative—simple designs with engraved insignia. • Appear to be made of a silver alloy.
10–14	• Proposed price range for retail. • Quality comparable to $30 spoons, but silver content is lower. • Detailed designs of local landmarks. • Variety of 6–10 spoons in each market.
30 and up	• Breadner. • Sterling silver. • Fine workmanship. • Very limited variety of designs.

Place

Because souvenir spoons were purchased on impulse, locations with high traffic were essential. Jewellery stores and gift stores in malls and tourist areas were probably most suitable in this respect.

Due to the price range proposed and the quality of the merchandise, the quality and image of the store had to be appropriate. This would eliminate discount jewellery stores and cheap souvenir shops for the aforementioned reasons. Secondly, it would not please higher-end retailers if the same spoons were sold for less in the same area and would likely restrict distribution in the appropriate channels.

FIGURE I

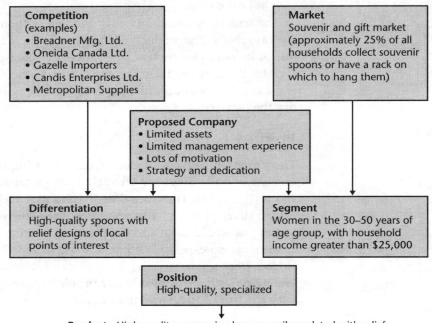

Competition
(examples)
• Breadner Mfg. Ltd.
• Oneida Canada Ltd.
• Gazelle Importers
• Candis Enterprises Ltd.
• Metropolitan Supplies

Market
Souvenir and gift market (approximately 25% of all households collect souvenir spoons or have a rack on which to hang them)

Proposed Company
• Limited assets
• Limited management experience
• Lots of motivation
• Strategy and dedication

Differentiation
High-quality spoons with relief designs of local points of interest

Segment
Women in the 30–50 years of age group, with household income greater than $25,000

Position
High-quality, specialized

Product. High-quality spoons in alpacca or silver-plated with relief designs of local points of interest

Price. To retail in the $10 to $14 range and therefore sell to retailer at $5 to $7 per spoon

Place. Distribution in jewellery stores primarily and selected gift shops

Promotion. Label on store window, saying spoons are available; oak countertop display rack; prominent position near store entrance

Jewellery stores were perceived by many people as selling expensive, luxury items that were not part of one's everyday needs. For this reason it would be helpful for these stores to have a window display.

Promotion

Each retail location would carry a minimum product line of six varieties of spoons: one with a Canadian theme, one with a provincial theme, and at least four spoons with designs of local landmarks or points of interest.

The packaging would be suitable for giftwrapping, so would likely consist of a small box with a clear plastic cover.

Each retail location would have an oak countertop display rack. There would be a relatively high cost to the displays initially, but the price would attract attention and convey the quality of the spoons. Different sizes could be made depending on the number of spoons required for a particular market.

Because souvenir spoons were primarily an impulse purchase, location in the store was important and should be near the entrance or in a window. This factor could be controlled only by persuading the retailer that good promotion would increase the turnover and, consequently, profits.

TABLE 1

FORECAST VARIABLE COSTS AND MARGINS OF SPOONS

	Alpacca	Silver Plate
Quote by Dutch manufacturer (Zilverfabriek) (in guilders) 1 guilder = Cdn$0.43	2.20 guilders	3.10 guilders
Factory cost in $Cdn	$0.95	$1.33
Duty (@ 20.3 percent)	0.19	0.27
Cost, duty included	$1.14	$1.60
Federal sales tax (@ 9 percent)	0.10	0.14
Federal excise tax (@ 10 percent)	0.11	0.16
Freight and insurance	0.10	0.10
Cost	$1.45	$2.00
Contribution margin	$2.05 to $3.55	$1.50 to $3.00
Cost to retailer	3.50 to 5.00	3.50 to 5.00
Retailer markup	3.50 to 5.00	3.50 to 5.00
Retail price	7.00 to 10.00*	7.00 to 10.00

*These prices are lower than originally forecast due to Demmers' recognition that a $10 to $14 retail price was too high.

Financial Projections

Contribution margin per spoon was calculated using the most conservative numbers and at a wholesale price of $3.50. Typically, retailers would mark prices up by 100 percent (see Table 1). The contribution margins worked out to $2.05 on alpacca spoons and $1.50 on silver-plated spoons.

The breakeven, assuming costs of $25,250 per year and a contribution margin of $2.05, would be sales volume of 12,317 spoons with sales value of $43,110 (see Table 2). Assuming the spoons would be introduced in the Toronto market and distribution obtained in 100 retail locations, this means sales of 124 spoons per store.

Upon graduating from a university business school in April 1984, Demmers planned to devote his efforts to Kolapore. He estimated that, while there could

TABLE 2

FORECAST BREAKEVEN

Distribution costs (transportation)	$ 4,000
Rent expense (work from home)	0
Salary	15,000
Office supply costs (including telephone)	1,000
Inventory costs	1,000
Merchandising expenses (displays and boxes)	3,000
Investment in dies (10 @ $125 each)	1,250
TOTAL FIXED COSTS	$25,250

$$\$25.250/\$1.50 = 16.833 \text{ spoons}$$
$$\$25.250/\$2.05 = 12.317 \text{ spoons}$$
$$\$25.250/\$3.00 = 8.416 \text{ spoons}$$

be a short-term financial drain, his cash balance would be positive at the end of the second month of operation (see Table 3).

Subsequent Events

Soon after graduating in April, Demmers became aware that Kolapore was not going to realize forecast sales of $28,100 by September 1984. Due to delays in getting shipments from the Netherlands and difficulty in obtaining distribution in Canada, sales were only $1,830 over the summer. A number of assumptions in the original feasibility study (as described in the first section) had proven incorrect:

1. The number of dies ultimately required (each of which cost $125) was not going to be 10 but closer to 50.

2. The federal sales tax rate had increased to 10 percent from 9 percent.

3. Duty was payable on the dies themselves as well as on the spoons at the rate of 20.3 percent excise tax plus federal sales tax.

4. Delivery time for new dies was closer to six months than the forecast 10–12 weeks (the artist had been ill for several months). Several orders were cancelled during this period as a result.

5. Packaging costs per spoon were closer to $0.32 per unit than the estimated $0.10.

6. Distribution had been difficult because the large chain stores which dominated the market all had established suppliers.

7. The target market was not nearly as upscale as originally envisioned. Although Kolapore's spoons were readily identifiable as being of superior quality, most customers would only pay a maximum of $7 to $8 retail for any spoon. Demmers had estimated the total Canadian souvenir spoon market at about $1.5 million annually. Within that, a very small portion was for sterling silver (where Demmers could not compete), about $450,000 was at the $7 retail price point where Demmers was selling (some of his competitors were promoting similar

TABLE 3

FORECAST CASH FLOW, MAY–AUGUST 1984				
	May	June	July	August
Cash	$3,000	$ (750)	$1,000	$ 7,500
Disbursements:				
Molds	1,250	—	—	—
Purchases	—	7,250	—	7,250
Promotion expenses	2,000	1,000	—	—
Car expenses	500	500	500	500
TOTAL DISBURSEMENTS	3,750	8,750	500	7,750
Net cash	(750)	(9,500)	500	(250)
Receipts:				
Accounts receivable		10,500	7,000	10,500
Cash balance (to be borrowed)	$ (750)	$ 1,000	$7,500	$10,250

(Terms n/30)

or poorer-quality spoons at the same price), with the balance of the market reserved for lower-priced/lower-quality spoons.

The goal of 100 stores by September 1984 was still a long way off.

Demmers had also discovered that the chain stores planned all their buying from six to twelve months in advance. Because many of the spoons he had designed did not arrive until September 1984, this meant that he had missed much of the tourist season (and nearly all of the Christmas market).

On the positive side, the Dutch guilder had depreciated relative to the Canadian dollar. In September 1984, it cost Cdn$0.39 for 1 guilder rather than $0.43 as forecast. In addition, delivery times for spoons from existing dies required three to four weeks rather than the expected four to six weeks, and the cost of display cases was only about $16 each. These were made of plastic rather than the originally envisioned oak.

Although Kolapore was showing a negative cash balance at the end of August 1984 (see Table 4), sales began to improve in September (see Table 5), growing to nearly $16,000 by the end of the first full year of operation (see Tables 6 and 7 for financial statements). A financial loss of $1,800 was incurred for the first year of operation, and this took no account of the countless hours Demmers had invested.

Since the business was not yet self-supporting, in September 1984 Demmers had begun to look for other sources of income.

Between September 1984 and January 1986 Demmers worked for five months in a fibreglass factory, acquired a house in Guelph in which he was

TABLE 4

ACTUAL CASH FLOW, 1984

	May	June	July	August
Cash	$2,600	$1,000	$950	$ 530
Disbursements:				
Purchases	1,000	550	870	1,460
Expenses	1,000	80	300	300
TOTAL DISBURSEMENTS	2,000	630	1,170	1,760
Net cash	600	370	(220)	(1,230)
Receipts:				
Accounts receivable	400	580	750	1,100
Cash balance	$1,000	$ 950	$530	$ (130)

TABLE 5

ACTUAL SALES, 1984–1985

May	$ 400
June	580
July	750
August	1,100
September	2,600
October	2,540
November	1,500
December	1,400
January–March	4,923

TABLE 6

BALANCE SHEET
As at March 31, 1985
(unaudited—see notice to reader)

Assets

Current assets:

Cash	$1,708
Accounts receivable	1,763
Inventory	2,873
Total current assets	6,344
Incorporation expense	466
TOTAL ASSETS	$6,810

Liabilities

Current liabilities:

Accounts payable and accruals	$ 268
Due to shareholder (note)	8,342
TOTAL LIABILITIES	8,610

Shareholders' Equity

Retained earnings (deficit)	(1,800)
TOTAL LIABILITIES AND SHAREHOLDERS' EQUITY	$6,810

Notice to reader: These financial statements have been compiled solely for tax purposes. I have not audited, reviewed, or otherwise attempted to verify their accuracy or completeness.

Guelph, Ontario
Chartered Accountant   May 2, 1985

able to live and to rent out rooms, sold Bruce Trail calendars on a commission basis, worked at organizing and selling several ski tours (which did not take place), and opened an ice cream store in a regional resort area (Wasaga Beach). Due to a low volume of traffic, this latter venture in the summer of 1985 resulted in an $8,000 loss. In the fall of 1985 Demmers accepted a position as production manager for a weekly newspaper in Guelph.

By this time, Demmers was selling direct to retailers in 20 towns and cities in Ontario and through five chains: Simpsons and United Cigar Stores and, to a much smaller extent, Eaton's, Birks, and Best Wishes. Other chains such as The Bay, Sears, and Woolco had been approached but so far without success. Demmers was hoping to find the time so that he could approach the buyers at Kmart, Zeller's, Consumers Distributing, Robinson's, Woodwards, and others.

Kolapore spoons were sold in Simpsons stores from Windsor, Ontario, to Halifax, Nova Scotia, and in 18 United Cigar Store locations in southern Ontario.

Four months after Demmers' first delivery to the chain outlets in the summer of 1985, about half the stores were sold out of Kolapore spoons. None of the chains would reorder stock partway through the year.

To sell direct in some of the smaller cities, Demmers' practice had been to drive or walk through the main shopping areas, stopping at jewellery stores or other likely retail outlets. If he was unable to meet with the store owner, he would usually leave a sample and a letter with some information. (See Exhibit 1 for a copy of the letter.) Demmers's experience had been that unless he personally met with the right person—which sometimes took three or more visits—no sales would occur. When he was able to meet with the owner, his

TABLE 7

STATEMENT OF INCOME
Year Ended March 31, 1985
(unaudited—see notice to reader)

Sales	$15,793
Cost of sales:	
Inventory at beginning of year	—
Purchases	8,453
Duty and freight	2,288
Dies	3,034
	13,775
Less: Inventory at end of year	2,873
Cost of sales	10,902
Gross profit	4,891
Expenses:	
Office	657
Samples	582
Auto expenses	1,137
Car allowance	3,900
Bank interest and charges	139
Advertising	26
Accounting	250
Total expenses	6,691
NET PROFIT (LOSS) FOR THE YEAR	$(1,800)

Notes:

1. Significant accounting policies: Kolapore, Inc., is a company incorporated under the laws of Ontario on April 6, 1984, and is primarily engaged in the importing and selling of souvenir spoons. The accounting policies are in accordance with generally accepted accounting principles. Inventory is valued at lower of cost or net realizable value. Incorporation expense is not amortized.
2. Due to shareholder is non-interest-bearing and payable on demand.

success rate was over 70 percent. To sell direct in larger centres such as Toronto (where he had 40 customers), Demmers had focused his efforts on hotel gift shops. Having established these customers, he could now visit all 40 customers in Toronto personally in two to three days.

By year-end, Demmers had access to a pool of 89 Canadian-specific dies. Demmers' supplier in the Netherlands had 46 dies in stock which another Canadian from western Canada had designed. Spoons based on these dies were no longer being sold anywhere, as far as Demmers could tell.

For the most part Demmers was selling spoons based on his own designs. (For those spoons which Demmers had designed, he had exclusive rights in Canada.) In less than two years he had 43 more dies made up. (See Exhibit 2 for a complete list.) In some cases Demmers had asked a particular company/ group to pay the cost of the dies; in others, such as for universities, he had built the die cost into his price for the first shipment; while in others he had simply gone ahead on his own with the hope that he could achieve sufficient sales to justify the investment.

There was a wide variability in the sales level associated with each spoon. Sales from his best seller—the Toronto skyline (which depicted major buildings

EXHIBIT I   **Letter of Introduction**

Kolapore, Inc.
P.O. Box 361
Guelph, Ontario
N1H 6K5

Dear

Kolapore, Inc., would like to offer you the opportunity to have your own
design on a spoon made up in metal relief, for example, a logo, code of arms,
crest, building, or whatever you would like.

There is always a large market for souvenir spoons of unique design and high
quality. Kolapore Collection Spoons fit this category extremely well and are
priced very competitively.

The spoons are available in silver plate at $3.50 per spoon. This price
includes a gift box, federal sales tax, and shipping.

The minimum order is 100 spoons to get a new design made up, and there is
also a one-time die charge of $125 to help offset the cost of making the new
die. Delivery time is approximately three months if a die has to be made up;
subsequent orders will take four to six weeks.

The dies for Kolapore Collection Spoons are made by master craftsmen in
Schoonhoven, Holland, the silversmith capital of the world. The spoons
themselves are made in Canada. As a result, the quality of the spoons is
exceptional and recognized by the consumer at a glance.

I trust that this is sufficient information. I look forward to hearing from you.
If you have any questions or concerns, please don't hesitate to contact me.
Thank you for your time and consideration.

Sincerely,

Adriaan Demmers
President

and the CN Tower)—were about 1,000 spoons a year. Demmers's second-best-
selling spoon in Toronto was 300 units of Casa Loma. (For a list of some of the
major tourist sites in Toronto, see Exhibit 3.) This spoon had quickly sold out
on-site in ten days. (However, the buyer had been unwilling to order more
partway through the year.) Spoons with other Toronto designs were selling less
than 50 units a year.

By December 1985 inventories had increased and Kolapore, Inc., was still
showing a small loss (see Table 8). Any gains from changes in the rate of import
duty on spoons (20.3 percent in 1984 to 18.4 percent in 1986) had been negated
by changes in federal sales tax (9 percent in 1984 to 11 percent in 1986) and ex-

EXHIBIT 2   Kolapore Collection Spoons—Designs Available

Canada
Deer
Elk
Caribou
Cougar
Mountain Goat
Moose
Bighorn Sheep
Grizzly Bear
Salmon
Coast Indian
Indian
Coat of Arms
Mountie
Maple Leaf

Province of Ontario
✓ Trillium
✓ Windsor, Ambassador Bridge
✓ Sarnia, Bluewater Bridge
✓ Chatham, St. Joseph's Church
✓ London, Storybook Gardens
✓ Woodstock, Old Town Hall
✓ Stratford, Swan
✓ Kitchener, Schneider Haus
✓ Waterloo, The Seagram Museum
✓ Waterloo County, Mennonite Horse & Buggy
✓ Elora, Mill Street
✓ Guelph, Church of our Lady
✓ Guelph, Credit Union
✓ Guelph, St. Joseph's Hospital
✓ Kitchener-Waterloo, Oktoberfest
✓ St. Catharines, Old Court House
✓ Niagara Falls, Falls, Brock Monument,
   and Maid of the Mist
✓ Acton, Leathertown (hide with buildings)
✓ Toronto Skyline
✓ Toronto, City Hall
✓ Toronto, St. Lawrence Hall
✓ Toronto, Casa Loma
✓ Kingston, City Hall
✓ Ottawa, Parliament Buildings
✓ Collingwood, Town Hall
✓ Owen Sound, City Crest

**University & Community College Crests/
   Coats of Arms**
✓ Wilfrid Laurier
✓ Waterloo

✓ Carleton
✓ Guelph
✓ York
✓ Western
✓ Windsor
✓ McMaster
✓ Brock
✓ Fanshawe
✓ Humber

Province of Quebec
Montreal, skyline
Montreal, Olympic Stadium

Province of Nova Scotia
Bluenose (schooner)

Yukon Territory
Coat of Arms
Gold Panner

Province of British Columbia
Coat of Arms
Prince George
Victoria, Parliament Buildings
Victoria, Lamp Post
Victoria, Empress Hotel
Nanaimo, Bastion
Dogwood (flower)
Totem Pole
Kermode Terrace
Smithers
Northlander Rogers Pass, Bear
Northlander Rogers Pass, House
Kelowna, The Ogopogo
Vancouver, Grouse Mountain Skyride/Chalet
Vancouver, Grouse Mountain Skyride
Vancouver, Grouse Mountain Skyride/Cabin
Vancouver, Cleveland Dam
Vancouver, The Lions
Vancouver, The Lions Gate Bridge

Province of Alberta
Banff, Mount Norquay
Banff, Mount Rundle
Banff, Banff Springs Hotel
Calgary, Bronco Rider
Edmonton, Klondike Mike
Wild Rose (flower)
Oil Derrick
Jasper
Jasper Sky Tram

Note: Check mark denotes those made up on Demmers' initiative.

EXHIBIT 3   Some Major Tourist Sites in Toronto

1. Metro Zoo	6. Art Gallery of Ontario (AGO)
2. CN Tower	7. Canada's Wonderland
3. Casa Loma	8. Ontario Place
4. Royal Ontario Museum (ROM)	9. The Ontario Science Centre
5. Black Creek Pioneer Village	

change rates. The fluctuating Dutch guilder was at a two-year high relative to the Canadian dollar. From a March 1984 value of Cdn$0.43, the guilder had declined to $0.36 in February 1985 and climbed to $0.50 by December 1985. Partially due to these exchange fluctuations, during the past eight months Demmers had also arranged for the spoons to be silver-plated in Ontario at a cost $0.40 each. This had resulted in a saving of $0.15 a spoon (which varied with the exchange rate). More significantly, because many spoons were purchased as souvenirs of Canada, by adding sufficient value by silver-plating in Canada, the imported product no longer had to be legally stamped "Made in Holland." In fact, the packaging could now be marked "Made in Canada." Demmers was quite optimistic regarding the implications of this change, as a number of potential store buyers had rejected his line because it did not say "Made in Canada." Demmers' supplier was quite upset, however, with the change.

◼ The Decision

Meanwhile, the feedback he was receiving from many of his customers was positive; in most cases they were selling more of his spoons than any other brand. Some customers, in fact, had enquired about other products. Since he had so far not experienced any competitive reactions to his spoons, Demmers was thinking of investigating the possibility of adding ashtrays, letter openers, key chains, lapel pins, and bottle openers to the product line in 1986—if he stayed in business. Each one of these products could have a crest attached to it. These crests would be the same as those used on the spoons and would thus utilize the dies to a greater extent. The landed costs per metal crest from the same supplier would be $0.85. Demmers contemplated attaching these crests himself onto products supplied by Canadian manufacturers. However, initial investigations had revealed no obvious economical second product line.

Demmers also planned to phase out alpacca imports—all products would now be silver-plated. In fact, Demmers was also wondering if he should acquire the

TABLE 8

STATEMENT OF INCOME
Eight Months* Ending November 30, 1985
(unaudited)

Sales	$21,000
Cost of sales:	
Inventory at beginning of year	2,873
Purchases	12,000
Duty and freight	3,500
Dies	1,950
	20,323
Less: Inventory at end of year	5,000
Cost of sales	15,323
Gross profit	5,677
Expenses	6,500
NET PROFIT (LOSS) FOR THE YEAR TO DATE	$ (823)

Note: Annual sales expected to be $30,000.

equipment and materials in order to do this silver-plating and polishing himself.

With no lack of ideas, Demmers nevertheless experienced many of the original frustrations. The buyers at major chains such as Eaton's and Simpsons had changed once again, and because they did not use an automatic reorder system, new appointments had to be arranged. This was as difficult as ever. Also, Demmers still had not been able to draw anything from the firm for his efforts. These factors, coupled with his lack of cash and the demands of his new full-time position, had left Demmers uncertain as to what he should do next. With the spring buying season approaching—when Demmers would normally visit potential buyers—he realized that his decision regarding the future of Kolapore could not be postponed much longer.

APPENDIX I

Survey of Spoons Carried by Local Retailers in Guelph and Kitchener-Waterloo Region

A Taste of Europe—Delicatessen and Gift Store, Guelph Eaton Centre
- A selection of spoons from Holland with Dutch designs.
- One with the Canadian coat of arms which looked good.
- Rhodium-plated spoons—$5.98 per spoon.
- Well displayed at front of store.

Eaton's—Guelph Eaton Centre
- Breadner spoons with maple leaf or Canadian flag and "Guelph" stamped in the bowl.
- Rhodium-plated—$4.98.
- No display and hard to find.

Pequenot Jewellers—Wyndham Street, Guelph
- Carry Candis spoons, which look cheap and do not sell very well.
- $4.98.
- Poorly displayed.

Smith & Son, Jewellers—Wyndham Street, Guelph
- Do not carry souvenir spoons because they are not in line with the store's image. They often get requests for them.

Franks Jewellers—King Street, Waterloo
- Carry Breadner spoons with the Waterloo coat of arms.
- Rhodium-plated spoons—$4.50 per spoon.
- Not on display but kept in drawer.
- Sell less than 12 per year.

Copper Creek—Waterloo Square Mall, Waterloo
- Candis spoons—$5 each.

Birks—King Centre, Kitchener
- Carry Oneida and Breadner spoons.
- Rhodium-plated spoons for $5.98.
- Oneida spoons were $8.95 and looked like a silver alloy.
- Sterling silver Breadner spoons for $31.95.
- Displayed in a spoon rack, looked good.
- Birks Regency spoons with crest of each province, $12.50.

Eaton's—Market Square, Kitchener
- Breadner spoons, two types for Canada only.
- Rhodium-plated—$4.98 each.

Young's Jewellers—King Street, Kitchener
- Rhodium-plated Breadner spoons, $4.50 each.

Walters Jewellers
- Against chain policy to carry souvenir spoons because of poor quality and low turnover.

Peoples Jewellers
- Do not carry souvenir spoons.

Engels Gift Shop—King Street, Kitchener
- Carry Breadner, Oneida, Gazelle, and Metropolitan.
- Altogether about 20 varieties.
- Well displayed near entrance of store; prices range from $2.25 for Metropolitan spoons to $7.98 for Oneida spoons.
- Saleslady said they sell hundreds every year, mostly in the summer.

APPENDIX 2

Terms Concerning Souvenir Spoons

Crest	Emblem, either metal, plastic, or enamel, that is affixed to a standard spoon.
Picture spoon	Spoon with a picture under plastic which is heat-molded to the spoon.
Relief design	Spoon with an engraving or picture which is molded into the metal of the spoon.
Enamel	Opaque substance similar to glass in composition.
Plated	Thin layer of metal put on by electrolysis.
Rhodium-plated	Shiny "jeweller's metal" which does not tarnish (no silver content).
Silver-plated	Silver covering on another metal (such as steel).
Sterling silver	Alloy of 92.5 percent silver and 8.5 percent copper, nickel, and zinc.
Alpacca	Alloy of 82 percent copper and 18 percent nickel.

APPENDIX 3

Souvenir Spoon Suppliers

Breadner Manufacturing Ltd.

Breadner appears to have national market distribution and includes two major retailers, Birks and Eaton's. According to some of the store managers interviewed, their sales of souvenir spoons in each location were low. Several retailers also expressed dissatisfaction with the Breadner line because of the slow turnover. Typically, there was a basic design for the spoon which did not change except for a different crest glued on for the different locale.

Breadner has been in the jewellery business since 1900 and has a plant in Hull, Quebec. The company manufactures to order various types of pins, medals, and advertising specialties but advised Demmers that in general it uses its entire output of souvenir spoons for its own sales.

Breadner has many varieties of spoons in its catalogue and an established distribution system across the country. Demmers recognized the possibility that Breadner could upgrade its selection in a short time span to compete directly with his intended selection of spoons.

Typical retail prices for Breadner spoons were $4.50 and up; the cost to the retailer was $2.25 and up. Breadner's high-end sterling silver spoons were available at Birks for $31.95, with the cost to Birks estimated at about $15 per spoon. Both rhodium-plated and silver-plated spoons were available, but rhodium-plated was more common. Silver-plated spoons were not carried.

Candis Enterprises Ltd.

Candis is located in Willowdale, Ontario. This company has good distribution in gift shops (for example, the 650-outlet United Cigar Store chain) and in some jewellery stores, selling a line of rhodium-plated spoons marketed under the MAR-VEL name and silver-plated spoons under the Candis name.

Candis' strategy appears to be one of putting out a large variety of spoons for each place in which the company sells. However, the quality seems to be toward the low end: many of the spoons have rough edges on the bowls and there is no detail in the dies.

Wholesale cast ranges from $2 per spoon for a rhodium-plated picture spoon to $3.25 for a silver-plated spoon with a five-colour ceramic crest.

Metropolitan Supplies Ltd.

Metropolitan Supplies is located in Toronto and distributes its goods across Canada primarily to gift shops and souvenir shops in tourist areas. This company deals with all sorts of souvenirs and novelty items. It has a large selection of spoons, each of which can be crested to suit the buyer. The quality of the spoons is at the low end. Prices range from $0.55 per spoon (wholesale) for iron and nickel-plated spoons to $2 per spoon for silver-plated spoons.

Gazelle Importers and Distributors

Gazelle Importers and Distributors is located in Grimsby, Ontario. The company previously imported spoons from Holland but later manufactured them in Ontario. The spoons are sold under the Gazelle name, and retail for $5.95 and therefore presumably cost the retailer about $3. Spoons have designs for Ontario and Canada but nothing local. Quality seems about the same as Breadner's less expensive line.

Oneida Canada Ltd.

Oneida is located in Niagara Falls, Ontario, and is a division of Oneida Ltd. in the United States. The Niagara Falls plant manufactures stainless steel and silver-plate flatware which is distributed in several jewellery stores including Birks and gift shops. The quality is better than any other spoons except for Breadner's sterling spoons. Prices are also somewhat higher with a retail price of $7.98, giving a probable cost to the retailer of about $4 per spoon. There is little variety. All spoons come in one design with a different engraving in the top of the spoon.

Commemorative Spoons

This firm is located in Ottawa and sells spoons in the $6.95–$8.95 range, with three basic designs (supplied by Oneida). It has large accounts with Simpsons and Cara and frequently deals with clubs requiring special spoons for fundraising.

Hunnisett and Edmunds

This is a distribution company which specializes in selling to card shops and variety stores, using a somewhat unique packaging system consisting of fly-top displays of 12 spoons.

Parsons-Steiner

This firm is located in Toronto. The quality of the product is low. Retail prices range from $1.99 to $5.98. Spoons tend to be picture spoons, and the least expensive ones appear to be made of cast iron with a decal attached.

Boma

This company is located in Vancouver, British Columbia. The quality is very good. Spoons are made out of pewter with designs of such things as totem poles. Retail prices range from $10 to $20.

Aalco Souvenirs

Located in Vancouver, this company carries over 300 "three-dimensional" models of spoons. They are made in Canada and are nickel-plated with a white gold flash. Aalco's products are distributed across Canada. The company also carries other souvenir items such as bells, bottle openers, key chains, lapel pins, and charms. Prices for spoons range from $2.50 to $3 each.

Souvenir Canada

Located in Downsview, Ontario, and operating throughout Canada and the United States, this company carries spoons with plastic decals, key chains, bottle openers, bells, lapel pins, mugs, plates, glasses, clothing, and special promotional items. It has been in business for about ten years and uses standardized spoons with crests attached. Retail price per spoon is $3.

London Telecom Network

On a snowy Thursday in December 1995, Rob Freeman, chairman and sole owner of London Telecom Network Inc. (LTN), was driving to Hamilton for his biweekly meeting with senior management. LTN was one of Canada's more prominent long-distance resellers, servicing over 22,000 customers and generating annualized revenues of $23 million. Profits had improved in the past year from a breakeven in the first five months to a cumulative $1 million forecast by the end of December. (See Exhibit 1 for further financial information).

Rob and his management team were encouraged by the developing profitability of the business. They were now turning their attention to longer-term issues, and particularly to opportunities for further growth. The problem here was not one of generating new ideas, but rather of deciding which ideas made sense. Rob's aims were high—to pursue the prospect of offering "flat-rate long-distance to everyone" and becoming a billion-dollar, debt-free telecommunications corporation.

The Canadian Long-Distance Telecommunications Industry

Overview

The 1995 Canadian market for telephone telecommunications services was estimated at $16 billion per year. Of this amount, $8 billion was for local service and $8 billion was for long distance. The local service market included local phone service and phone equipment. The long-distance market—including phone calls, data transmission, and fax—encompassed all calls that originated and terminated in Canada and the Canadian portion of calls that originated or terminated outside Canada. Overall, the long-distance market was growing at a rate of 5 to 10 percent per year.

IVEY

Richard Ivey School of Business
The University of Western Ontario

John Bogert prepared this case under the supervision of Professor Joseph N. Fry solely to provide material for class discussion. The author does not intend to illustrate either effective or ineffective handling of a managerial situation. The author may have disguised certain names and other identifying information to protect confidentiality. © 1996 Ivey Management Services. Case 9-96-M002, version 1997-04-25.

EXHIBIT 1   London Telecom Networks: Financial Statements 1992–1995

	Jan. 31, 1992	Jan. 31, 1993	Jan. 31, 1994	Jan. 31, 1995	11 Months Ending Dec. 31, 1995
INCOME STATEMENT					
Revenue	253,387	1,625,012	5,899,065	12,368,252	20,036,062
Line costs	127,987	860,832	3,919,194	8,836,132	13,273,814
Gross margin	125,400	764,180	1,979,871	3,532,120	6,762,248
Sales, general and admin	117,678	906,566	1,820,178	4,007,550	5,305,266
Amortization	9,514	49,785	100,428	704,110	456,725
Operating profit	(1,792)	(192,170)	59,265	(1,179,540)	1,000,257
Other income	2,240	0	0	92,465	0
Unusual item (1)	0	0	0	(1,000,000)	0
Taxes	0	0	0	0	0
NET PROFIT	448	(192,170)	59,265	(2,087,075)	1,000,257
BALANCE SHEET					
Assets:					
Cash	17,948	0	354,037	299,450	1,675,700
Accounts receivable	32,716	471,915	1,330,838	1,983,534	3,138,090
Prepaids	0.00	3,273	13,348	51,660	560,004
Due from shareholders	0	0	31,233	96,630	201,980
Total current assets	50,664	475,188	1,729,456	2,431,274	5,575,774
Capital assets (net)	69,944	296,663	509,452	772,134	1,469,330
Due from related companies	0	0	15,487	286,465	908,358
Other assets	63,058	56,591	50,123	43,657	0
TOTAL ASSETS	183,666	828,442	2,304,518	3,533,529	7,953,462
Liabilities:					
Short-term debt	0	48,162	0	0	0
Accounts payable	139,278	198,184	614,073	1,069,528	2,672,297
Deferred revenue	45,268	456,014	1,163,008	2,043,873	3,393,849
Customer deposits	0	313,810	658,343	1,638,109	2,105,040
Shareholders' advance	(2,880)	2,443	0	0	0
Non-competition A/P	0	0	0	1,000,000	1,000,000
TOTAL LIABILITIES	181,666	1,018,613	2,435,424	5,751,510	9,171,186
Equity:					
Capital stock	2,000	2,000	2,000	2,000	2,000
Retained earnings	0	(192,170)	(132,906)	(2,219,981)	(1,219,724)
TOTAL LIABILITIES AND EQUITY	183,666	828,442	2,304,518	3,533,529	7,953,462

Notes:
(1) Unusual item in 1995: non-competition agreement paid to past shareholder.
Source: LTN internal documents.

Background

Until the mid-1980s, Canadian telecommunications services had been controlled by a series of regulated provincial monopolies. A notable exception to this situation was Bell Canada, which was a public company that operated as a regulated monopoly in southern Ontario and southern Quebec (60 percent of the total market). Bell and the provincial monopolies were organized into a consortium called the Stentor Alliance, which provided a unified front for them to lobby on regulatory matters and other industry-wide issues. The Stentor Alliance comprised: BCTel (British Columbia), SaskTel (Saskatchewan), AGT (Alberta), MTS (Manitoba), Bell Canada (Ontario and Quebec), Quebec-Tel (northern Quebec), IslandTel (Prince Edward Island), MT&T (New Brunswick and Nova Scotia), NewfoundlandTel (Newfoundland), and NorthwestTel (Northwest Territories and Yukon).

The CRTC

Radio, television, and telecommunications in Canada were controlled by the Canadian Radio-television and Telecommunications Commission (CRTC). In the late 1980s the CRTC had come under immense pressure from industry to deregulate the long-distance market. Canadian industry, which had watched long-distance rates in the U.S. drop some 40 percent in the five years since U.S. deregulation, wanted the same opportunities in Canada. In addition, some companies were using technical and legal loopholes to enter the long-distance market. This practice undermined the CRTC's control. As a result, the CRTC passed Ruling 90-3 in the spring of 1990, deregulating 90 percent of all long-distance services, and Ruling 92-12 in late 1992, deregulating the remaining 10 percent. These revisions forced the Stentor Alliance to rent long-distance lines and time to registered resellers.

The CRTC's mandate had thence become one of ensuring the smooth deregulation of the telecommunications market. In this passage, rate rebalancing became a major issue. Under regulation, the Stentor Alliance companies had been charged with providing all Canadians with "affordable" local phone service. As a result residential users paid $11–$15 per month for a service that cost $38 to deliver. Long-distance charges subsidized local service costs. As lower prices and competition cut into the Stentor Alliance's long-distance income, it became difficult to continue to cross-subsidize local residential service. Therefore, the CRTC decided to allow the Stentor Alliance to phase in rate rebalancing. Over a five-year period, long-distance charges would drop 35 to 50 percent, while local residential line charges would go up 30 to 40 percent.

It was thought that the CRTC's increase in local access charges would pave the way for deregulation of the local loop (lines that run from individual houses to the main switch). Local charges needed to reflect actual costs if competition was to be successful. Most recently, the CRTC had ruled to allow the Stentor Alliance to deliver cable television and the cable companies to deliver local telephone service. Experts were curious as to what would happen to phone charges as local loops were privatized. If the cable companies could deliver an individualized movie to a house for $5, how would they justify charging $0.20/minute for a phone call that used 1/10,000 of the bandwidth?

The Canadian Long-Distance Market

There were three basic ways in which a company could provide long-distance service:

- *Buy time on a per-minute basis.* Renting the use of another carrier's network, one call at a time.

- *Rent lines and switch space*. Stentor Alliance companies and alternative carriers had excess capacity on their switches and fibre optic lines. Alternative carriers rented a dedicated amount of capacity for a flat monthly fee, to supplement their dedicated networks.
- *Build a dedicated network*. Buying lines and switches was very capital-intensive, but resulted in the lowest cost per minute, once capacity was filled.

There were three types of companies that provided long-distance service to end users: the Stentor Alliance, the resellers, and the alternative carriers. The Stentor Alliance controlled 82 percent of the $8 billion long-distance market, with the remaining 18 percent divided among 270 resellers and the alternative carriers.

Stentor Alliance

The Stentor Alliance companies had traditionally controlled 100 percent of the long-distance market. With the advent of deregulation, however, they had lost 18 percent of the market to resellers and alternative carriers. The Alliance continued to control 100 percent of the market for local phone service, however, and were the only providers of long-distance that reached into all the small towns and cities across Canada. Therefore, many resellers and alternative carriers bought long-distance services from the Stentor Alliance.

Resellers

There were 265 resellers of long distance in Canada which had collectively captured about 9 percent of the end user market. They were called resellers because they rented time from Bell or the alternative carriers. Take, for example, a reseller which buys time from Bell. When a customer places a long-distance phone call, Bell carries the call, tracks the fact that this was customer of the reseller, and invoices the reseller instead of the customer. Bell forwards individualized call data to the reseller when invoicing, so that the reseller could repackage it to the customer's needs. Typically, the reseller bought time at a 50 percent discount and then resold it at a 35 percent discount. These businesses, with low overheads and low advertising, focused on capturing mid-size businesses which were looking for additional services such as calling cards, data lines, and customized billing.

Resellers lived in a constant cash crunch. They often had to pay their provider in advance for service (at least until they built up a credit history), and had to wait 30 to 60 days to collect from their customers. It was easy to enter the industry, and easy to fail as well.

Alternative Carriers

There were four major alternative long-distance carriers in Canada, Sprint, fonorola, ACC, and Unitel (see Table 1). These companies had all started as resellers, but over the past five years they had invested in their own dedicated networks, which were typically installed between major hubs, and connected to their U.S. parent. The alternative carriers all supplemented their networks

TABLE I   **Canadian Alternative Carriers—Revenue and Performance**

1995 Data	Sprint	fonorola	ACC	Unitel
Revenue ($MM)	457	209	109	1,118
Profits ($MM)	–65	–7.2	0.6	–181

Source: Company financial statements; Unitel figures are estimates.

by leasing lines and space on switches from the Stentor Alliance companies. Each firm had its own discount plan, often complicated by different discounts for specific areas, and customers. Although competition was stiff, customers could generally expect to receive up to 25 percent off Bell rates. (See Exhibit 2 for an example of discounts).

Alternative carriers had financed their network expansion with equity and debt issues (see Exhibits 3 and 4 for financial data on ACC and Sprint Canada). These funds were spent to install fibre optic cable between major hubs and

EXHIBIT 2   **Comparison of Competitive Long-Distance Prices and Costs**

	Cost/Min. (cents)
1. Bell Canada: Prices	
Base rate (Quebec-Windsor corridor):	37.0
Residential	
Evening discount (6–11 p.m.)—35%	24.1
Late-night (after 11 p.m.)/weekend discount—60%	14.8
Business	
Large business (over $300,000/month):	
Day rate	14.8
Late-night rate	10.4
Medium business (over $2,500/month):	
Day rate	16.7
Late-night rate	11.7
Bell Canada: Costs	
Cost per MOU (minute of use)—average	8.0
2. Large Alternative Carriers (ACC, fonorola, Unitel, Sprint): Prices	
Business and Residential	
Best discount—25% off Bell rate:	
Day rate	27.8
Evening	18.0
Late-night/weekend	11.1
Large Alternative Carriers: Costs	
Cost per MOU (minute of use)—average	12.0–16.7
3. Small Resellers: Prices	
Business and Residential	
Best discount—35% off Bell rate:	
Day rate	24.1
Evening	15.6
Late-night/weekend	9.6
Small Resellers: Costs	
Cost per MOU (minute of use)	77% of selling price

Source: Discount rates based on literature search. Better discounts may be available to key clients.

switches. The expectation was that lower costs per unit would result once the network was filled. All of these companies (with the exception of Unitel) were expected to start turning a profit in 1996.

◼ London Telecom Network

History

In 1988, Rob Freeman, a real estate broker living in Strathroy, Ontario, was bothered by the $0.35 per minute charge for calling London, only 12 miles away. Rob knew something about telecommunications (telecom) switches, having studied two years of electrical engineering at the University of Waterloo and having toyed with telecom as a hobby for years.

EXHIBIT 3   **ACC TelEnterprises Overview and Financial Statements 1994–1995**

OVERVIEW

ACC TelEnterprises was a subsidiary of ACC Corp. of Rochester, New York. ACC rented all of its long-distance equipment, but had invested in switching technology and frame relay equipment to ensure that it was able to offer a full range of services to its customers. As a part of this, the Canadian ACC network was interconnected with ACC's networks in the United States and in the United Kingdom. In 1995, ACC TelEnterprises spent $4.2 million on switches and equipment.

ACC's motto was to be "all things to some people." ACC ended 1995 with 136,000 residential and 25,000 commercial customers, an increase of 58,000 over December 1994. ACC had exclusive marketing rights at 30 universities in Canada, provided private label services to The Bay, and had recently introduced Internet services.

INCOME STATEMENT
(amounts in 000s)

	Dec. 31, 1994	Dec. 31, 1995
Revenue	95,511	120,002
Network costs	65,482	76,130
Operating expenses	36,729	40,231
EBITDA	(347)	10,005
NET PROFIT	(11,002)	631
Balance Sheet		
Assets:		
Current	17,350	23,147
Fixed	13,604	16,017
Other	10,997	20,317
TOTAL ASSETS	41,951	59,481
Liabilities and Equity		
Accounts payable	15,350	20,612
Debt	354	3,437
Due to affiliates	20,440	28,167
Other	185	1,008
Capital stock	22,990	22,994
Deficit	(17,368)	(16,737)
TOTAL LIABILITIES	41,951	59,481

Source: ACC TelEnterprises annual report.

EXHIBIT 4   **Call-Net (Sprint Canada) Overview and Financial Statements 1994–1995**

OVERVIEW

Call-Net Enterprises (Sprint Canada) was 25 percent owned by Sprint U.S., and had signed special distribution agreements with Sprint U.S. that ensured Call-Net exclusive Canadian rights to Sprint U.S.'s switched voice network and trademarks. Sprint Canada had over 700,000 circuit miles of company-owned fibre optic cable, and state-of-the-art switching equipment in Vancouver, Toronto, Calgary, and Montreal. Call-Net had spent $110 million on network expansion over the last two years and had planned an additional $50 million for 1996.

Sprint Canada was involved in all areas of the Canadian long-distance market, including residential and business long-distance services, toll-free services, bill analysis software, global frame relay (for interconnecting LANs), private line, data packet switching, and Internet access services.

Over the past two years, most of Sprint's new revenues had come from residential and small/medium business clients, but in 1996 Sprint had planned to focus more effort on large business clients, and on the cellular market.

INCOME STATEMENT
(amounts in 000s)

	Dec. 31, 1994	Dec. 31, 1995
Revenue	176,287	457,461
Network costs	125,093	302,016
Operating expenses	82,382	171,238
EBITDA	(31,188)	(15,793)
NET PROFIT	(55,359)	(64,751)
Balance Sheet		
Assets:		
Cash	157,730	179,626
Other current	41,507	92,643
Fixed	85,290	132,008
Other	115,446	120,481
TOTAL ASSETS	399,973	524,758
Liabilities and Equity		
Accounts payable	53,498	104,367
Debt	139,634	164,853
Due to affiliates		
Other	2,587	5,900
Capital stock	262,638	372,593
Deficit	(58,384)	(123,135)
TOTAL LIABILITIES	399,973	524,578

Source: Call-Net Enterprises annual report.

Through a friend who worked at Bell Canada, he inquired about the legality of setting up a phone in Mount Bridges, halfway between Strathroy and London, to forward phone calls. He could then make a local call to Mount Bridges from Strathroy. The phone in Mount Bridges would forward a second local call from Mount Bridges to London. The net effect was that a long-distance call would be converted into two local calls, and no long-distance charges would apply.

Bell, of course, claimed that such a system was illegal. Rob disagreed; his research had not revealed any preventative regulations. He decided to proceed without Bell's permission. Selling long-distance was illegal in 1988, so he started a sharing group, and convinced 100 Strathroy residents to join. Because he had no money, he asked the members to prepay two months. He then set up a switch in Mount Bridges with ten lines in and ten lines out. Later, he added Exeter and St. Thomas.

Bell filed a complaint with the CRTC. The ruling came out in Rob's favour: as long as the call was forwarded only once, he could continue. However, call forwarding more than once was ruled to be illegal.

In 1990, when the CRTC deregulated the Canadian long-distance market, Rob acquired the interests of the other members of the sharing group, and formed London Telecom. Rob knew that, to survive, LTN had to grow. Therefore, he established a line through Oakville to link Burlington to Toronto, and rented his first trunk line to carry long-distance calls. In the first week LTN signed up 400 customers. By the end of 1991, the company had 1,000 customers. From this starting point LTN grew rapidly, and by December 1995, the company provided services to over 22,000 customers.

The Organization

LTN was a flat organization. A group of six managers—Jim Weisz, president; Rob Belliveau, vice-president, sales and marketing; Gary Campbell, vice-president, finance and information services; Greg Cope, manager, regulatory issues and special projects; Maureen Merkler, manager, human resources; and Randy Patrick, vice-president, network services—handled virtually all the business operating decisions and the supervisory activities for a roster of about 100 employees. Rob Freeman, as chairman, confined his involvement primarily to policy issues and to developing the management group. Jim Weisz explained the management approach:

> We try to keep ourselves lean. We need to keep costs down in this market and at the same time we need to be able to make decisions quickly. The CRTC keeps us on our toes. That's why I have Greg Cope keeping an eye on the CRTC for us.
>
> The organization is growing and Rob Freeman would like LTN to hire from within whenever possible. Maureen Merkler was hired a year ago to help in this area. We are working to get job descriptions down for all positions, and have sent a few employees who were not performing out for training.

LTN's Product Offering

As of late 1995 LTN operated a network connecting 41 Canadian cities (see Exhibit 5). LTN rented all of its equipment and lines at flat monthly rates from the Stentor Alliance companies. Between different cities, depending on call traffic, LTN could vary the amount of bandwidth rented on lines and switches. There were significant economies of scale in renting long-distance bandwidth. For example, a DS-0 line could carry 12 calls at a time at a cost of $4,100 per month, while a DS-3 line could carry 504 calls and at a cost $37,800 per month. To ensure customer service levels, LTN had an agreement with fonorola to carry overflow calls.

EXHIBIT 5   LTN Network and Network Access

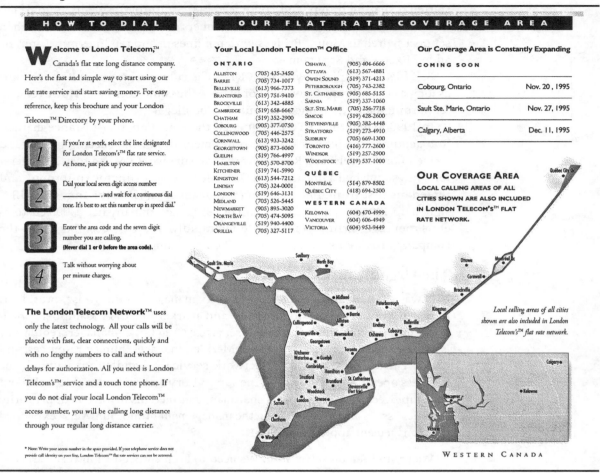

Source: LTN promotional brochure.

LTN had been rapidly increasing the scope and capacity of its network. Randy Patrick commented:

> We had a problem last January with growth. The network was growing faster than marketing could keep up. Bell requires that we give them two months' notice on changes to the network, so we have to order the lines before we know for sure if the sales are going to materialize. Up until then, we had been growing at a rate of one city a week. We have cut back to one city every three weeks. Of course, our network still has a lot of empty space on it, but unfortunately our technology doesn't allow us to pin down exactly where very easily.
>
> We are Bell's second-largest customer. None of the long-distance resellers get the kind of discounts we do. While Bell's sales guys might not like us because we are stealing business from them, they realize that losing a sale to us is better than losing a sale to Unitel.

Unlike its competitors LTN charged a flat rate for its long-distance service: $74.95 per month to residential customers and $94.95 per month to business customers. For this customers received 40 hours of long-distance covering calls placed any time of the day. If they exceeded the 40 hours, customers were automatically sold time in additional five-hour blocks. LTN's service included a reverse calling feature; for example, relatives could call the customer using the customer's LTN account.

There were regulatory and economic reasons why few companies charged a flat rate like LTN. Until recently, the Stentor Alliance, Sprint, and Unitel had not been allowed to do so; as inter-exchange carriers they had been limited by the CRTC in the way in which they could bill for services. In September 1995, the CRTC decided to allow Sprint and Unitel to charge in whatever way they pleased, leaving only the Stentor companies strictly controlled by pricing tariffs. Resellers, which could legally sell flat-rate services, usually sold on a per-minute basis because they bought their services on a per-minute basis and avoided the risk associated with fixed-cost line rentals.

LTN also departed from industry norms in not offering direct-access service. To use LTN, customers first had to call the LTN network using a local access number, and then dial the number of the party they wanted to reach (see brochure, Exhibit 5). LTN had configured its network this way to take advantage of the lower rates set by the CRTC for non-direct access service.

The net result of buying services on a flat rate and operating a non-direct access network was that LTN's costs were lower than those of a reseller buying time on a per-minute basis, providing LTN could achieve a minimum utilization of 40 percent.

Rob Belliveau summed up how the customers felt about the flat rate, and the extra dialing:

> Our product is simple to understand. The flat-rate concept sets us apart from the other resellers. We offer the security of a constant long-distance phone bill and we don't try to force our customers to make their calls in the middle of the night if they want to save money. In fact, our nights are full. We wish more customers would call during the day.
>
> Customers don't mind dialing the extra numbers. With speed dialing it's just not a big deal. As far as I'm concerned, it's actually a bonus. A customer can sign up with Unitel for overseas calls and still keep us for Canadian calls.

Billing

Since the inception of the call-sharing group, Rob had always required that customers pay first and last month when joining. As the business grew, he saw no reason to change this system, although recently LTN had been hearing complaints about the high up-front cost to join. For example, a residential customer joining LTN would have pay to $150 in advance ($75 for the first month, and $75 for the last month).

LTN billed every day of the month, based on the day the customer signed up. This helped the accounting staff to smooth the workload. Billing was further simplified by the fact that all customers received a one-line invoice for either $74.95 or $94.95. The occasional customer who used more than 40 hours in a month received a second invoice. This procedure was quite different from the industry standard of multi-line invoices detailing the length and cost of every call.

Marketing

LTN relied heavily on advertising through direct mail. As each new city was added to the network, LTN would blanket the area with brochures. More recently, Rob Belliveau had begun experimenting with focused mailing efforts directed at certain demographic pockets and had run a 30-second TV spot in the World Series. LTN used sales representatives to follow up on leads:

- *Sales agents.* Ten sales agents across the country went door to door, cold-calling residential and small business customers.
- *Inside sales.* LTN had 15 people in its call centre who answered enquiries and received a commission for customers that they closed.
- *Direct sales.* Two full-time sales representatives handled enquiries from business prospects and made site visits to close sales.

Most of LTN's customers fell into three categories (see Table 2):

- Residential customers, calling primarily within Canada
- Small and medium-sized businesses, especially home-based businesses and outbound telemarketers
- Large businesses willing to use more than one company to minimize costs

The Call Centre

The 15 employees in LTN's call centre handled all inbound calls, with customers often waiting 10–15 minutes for service. Monday mornings were especially busy because potential customers would be calling after seeing advertisements on the weekend. Simultaneously, customers with billing problems would be calling, wondering why they had received two, and sometimes three, invoices. When call loads were especially heavy, the call centre would forward calls related to invoices to the accounting department.

TABLE 2   LTN's Current Canadian Market Segmentation and Share

	High Use Residential	Med. Use Residential	Low Use Residential	Small/Med. Business	Large Business	Total
Total Market						
% accounts (residential only)	5%	35%	60%			
Spending per month	>$100	$10–100	<$10			
Total (millions)	$750	$1,680	$432	$2,000	$3,138	$8,000
% market	9.4%	21.0%	5.4%	25%	39.1%	100%
LTN						
# customers	14,000	0	0	9,300	1	23,300
Revenue (millions)	$12.6	0	0	$10.2	$0.2	$23.0
Current market share	1.7%	0.0%	0.0%	0.5%	0.01%	0.3%

Source: Consultant estimates.

Gary Campbell, vice-president finance and information systems, commented:

> We are still using the ACCPAC accounting package. It was designed for a few thousand customers at most, and we have 22,000. We figure that 50 percent of the calls received by the call centre are related to billing problems. We are hoping to have a new accounting system in place in the next few months. Once that is done, call centre traffic should drop substantially.
>
> Confounding the problem was that we are adding 1,000 customers a month. The computer system can't handle it. Call centre staff trying to add a new customer over the phone typically wait five minutes to pull up a file on the computer.

Wintel

Wintel was a separate company controlled by LTN management that was established in the summer of 1995 to deal with startup competitors in the Toronto area. These companies were using the call forwarding technique that Rob Freeman had originally developed. LTN had been looking for a way to compete effectively with these new competitors without cannibalizing its own product line. The Wintel startup provided the solution by offering a package of $29.95 flat rate for 40 hours, covering a limited area around Toronto. By December 1995, Wintel had 600 customers of its own.

Looking Ahead

The LTN senior management team had several ideas for continued expansion. The options included:

1. Going public
2. Expanding into the United States
3. Expanding the Canadian product offering
4. Introducing new products
5. Building a permanent network

Going Public

LTN senior management had approached Rob Freeman with the idea of going public. They felt that this option would provide funding for some of the ideas they were considering. One plan, which had been discussed in a preliminary way with an investment banker, involved issuing $10 million worth of shares: $5 million would be new issue, with funds to be used by the company, while $5 million would be sold by Rob Freeman. After the issue, Rob Freeman would retain 46 percent of the shares, the public would hold 46 percent, and the remaining 8 percent would be divided equally among the senior managers.

Expanding into the United States

The management team had been working on and off on this expansion possibility for months. Originally, they had been interested in the possibility of providing Canadian customers with access to the United States; however, they had been looking more recently at full entry into the U.S. market.

The $80 billion U.S. long-distance market had been deregulated five years longer than the Canadian market. Twenty-eight percent of all long-distance traffic was carried by 150 alternative carriers, 7 percent by the 3,800 resellers, and the remainder by AT&T. The regulatory aspects of the long-distance market were controlled by the Federal Communications Commission (FCC). This body was similar to the CRTC in mandate; but unlike the CRTC, its rulings had to be passed by Congress before they became law.

LTN had two potential plans for entry. The first was to ease into the market, growing slowly as it had in Canada, by starting in upstate New York, or around Chicago, and expanding outward. Advertising would be primarily by direct mail, and word of mouth. The second possibility was to go after traffic between the major centres by connecting the six biggest cities in the United States. The advantage of this option was that LTN would immediately cover 30 percent of the population of the United States. The network would gradually expand out to the smaller centres.

In either case, LTN expected to offer a flat-rate service. Although some competitors were already offering flat rates per minute, none was offering a flat monthly rate. LTN hoped to manage the network from Canada, but realized it would need a U.S. call centre to give customers service with a local feel. Randy Patrick (network) and Greg Cope (regulatory) had been working hard to determine whether FCC regulations would allow LTN to set up a low-cost network similar to the one in Canada. Even without favourable FCC regulations, LTN was optimistic. With over 100 alternative carriers in the United States, the competition to sell to resellers was intense. LTN had been quoted a cost of $0.05 a minute for nationwide coverage, and anticipated that it would be able to sell time for $0.08 a minute.

Expanding the Canadian Product Offering

The average customer used only 20 of the 40 hours available. Management was concerned that they might lose some customers who decided that they were not getting their money's worth. Therefore, they were considering two new products, five hours for $29.95 and ten hours for $49.95.

Rob Freeman, who was concerned about cannibalization, was also excited about the prospect of expanding the customer base by offering packages with more universal appeal. Rob Belliveau (marketing) had inquired with marketing research companies, but data on new customer potential were not available. Management was also considering automatic billing for the new products. Customers who submitted their credit card numbers would be billed automatically once a month.

Introducing New Products

Jim Weisz had recently been in contact with Calldex Inc., the manufacturer of a new technology: a calling card with a digital display that showed a new PIN number every minute. The advantage of this system was that the calling card number could not be stolen by someone looking over the shoulder of a caller entering the code.

LTN intended to use this new technology to target the cellular market. LTN could not offer cellular long-distance service with their current network setup. Regular phone calls carried with them the number from which they had originated, which was used for services like call display. LTN used this number to verify that calls into their network came from registered customers. Unfortunately for LTN, cellular calls did not carry this number. LTN planned to reconfigure the network so that customers could input a calling card number, in this way solving the cellular problem.

LTN wanted to charge a flat rate for long-distance calls placed with the calling card. The Calldex card was perfect for this, because the user could not pass the number around to friends or coworkers; the customer had to have the card in hand to place a call. LTN's proposal was that customers would use the Calldex cards to circumvent per-minute long-distance charges by using the local access numbers to call the LTN network. Once connected, they would input their calling card number, the PIN number currently being displayed, and the number they want to reach. Customers would pay a flat amount in advance, as well as an additional $160 to buy the card.

An alternative idea was to sell disposable calling cards with a fixed amount of long-distance time pre-loaded with amounts of $10, $25, or $50. Disposable cards were popular in Europe, where people paid a per-minute charge for local calls. LTN hoped to sell the cards directly to current customers, as well as to packaged goods companies which might want to put $2 worth of long-distance credit into every cereal box as a promotion.

Building a Permanent Network

With projectability building and the possibility of going public, management felt LTN should plan on building a permanent network. To transmit calls, the company was considering using microwave towers which, although susceptible to weather, were much cheaper than fibre optic cable. Rob Freeman thought that LTN could easily arrange a contract with one of the alternative carriers to carry calls when the weather was bad.

■ Decision

Rob Freeman had almost reached the Hamilton office, where he would be meeting with his management team to discuss the options at 10 a.m. Although each option had potential, he was uncertain about how to make a choice and unwilling to take any big risks.

Lonely Planet Publications

Steve Hibbard reflected on the irony of life. The case study he and his fellow students had written as an assignment during the final year of his MBA had led to his current job as General Manager, Business Administration, of Lonely Planet Publications—a job that was now leading him to question much of what he had learnt during the MBA.

Since joining Lonely Planet, Steve Hibbard had implemented a number of significant changes, but he was now wondering how far he could go before, as he put it, "the introduction of 'management science' ruined the place." On the other hand, Lonely Planet was a rapidly growing, global business and Steve sensed it would run into trouble if it did not become more formalized and systematic in the way it operated.

The immediate issue was the introduction of a mission statement, a process Steve had started over a year ago. He now saw the first draft (Figure 1) as his own attempt to come to terms with the essence of the highly successful publisher of travel guides. The second draft (Figure 2) was more specific, but did not fully capture the spirit of the company. And besides, many people in the organization questioned the point of the exercise.

In fact, Steve had run into a lot of flack in attempting to introduce a formal mission statement. The process had brought to the surface a great deal of disagreement about what the "mission" of Lonely Planet actually was. His MBA training suggested that it was important for these things to be clear, that they should not be vague—his notes from Strategic Management reminded him that "clarity and constancy of purpose was critical." And yet, many people in Lonely Planet argued that more definition would just limit things and that it was better if people had their own feeling about what the purpose of Lonely Planet was and why people bought their books. What surprised Steve was how well this vague, informal approach seemed to work.

The dilemma he faced regarding the mission statement was a specific example of the broader sense of unease he felt about what seemed to be a tradeoff between a disciplined and systematic approach and the costs and, in

This case was prepared by Geoffrey Lewis. It is based on an earlier case developed by students at Melbourne Business School. The assistance of Claude Calleja, MBA 1993, in preparing an earlier draft is gratefully acknowledged.

some ways, constraints that this more professional approach entailed. A management information system and regular reporting cost money; job descriptions limited what people did.

When Steve first arrived at Lonely Planet, he had made the mistake of putting things into "MBA categories." Lonely Planet was not doing any formal market research and did not have a marketing plan. The editors and publishers just talked about "making the books nicer." He had been convinced it was a "product-driven organization." As time went on, however, Steve came to realize that the people at Lonely Planet were more in tune with their customers

FIGURE 1   **Draft Mission Statement (May 1994)**

Why Are We Doing This?
Best Guess

To be the planet's best source of interesting, down-to-earth information for the independent traveller.
  To operate a business which is environmentally and socially responsible, by:

- Encouraging responsible travelling practices
- Recognizing the impact of our material, and striving to ensure it has a positive impact on the places we encourage people to visit
- Making a positive contribution to the communities in which we work

We want to foster a working environment which is productive, creative, participatory, and fun. One which will attract and retain people committed to quality, and which will encourage them to grow and learn and feel positive about our role in the global community.
  We must be an effective, profitable business. Profit is a prerequisite for our continuing ability to pursue the above goals.

FIGURE 2   **Draft Mission Statement (January 1995)**

Aim

  To be the planet's preferred choice for useful, accurate, interesting, entertaining, and down-to-earth information for the independent traveller.
  To achieve this we will:

- Gather, store, filter, and communicate up-to-date information relevant to independent travellers
- Facilitate the exchange of information between independent travellers
- Encourage cross-cultural understanding and responsible travel practices; provide the information necessary for "aware" travellers to make responsible choices
- Make a positive contribution to the destinations we cover and the communities in which we work
- Develop an international organization working in an interactive and responsive partnership with an international audience
- Foster a working environment that is productive, challenging, creative, participatory, fun, and financially rewarding
- Attract and retain motivated and talented people and encourage them to grow and learn
- Operate a profitable business to enable the continued pursuit of these goals

than any of the "customer-focused" organizations he had studied during the MBA.

At Lonely Planet, Steve gained some insights into what a brand franchise really meant:

> To build a brand requires real values, integrity, and consistency. Lonely Planet publishes information for travellers. Tony Wheeler is still the quintessential traveller and remains one of the best, and most prolific, authors we have.
>
> Valuable brands engender real loyalty in customers—often beyond the rational level. Lonely Planet engages the customer at every opportunity—with letter correspondence, by putting contributors' names in books, by getting into the media at every opportunity with the direct, personal style of the authors. We also engage the industry through debates, travel summits, bookstore talks, radio appearances, etc. We engage the trade with long-term loyalty, mutually supportive arrangements, sales conferences, and square dealings.
>
> We often turn down opportunities for quick profit because it would dilute the brand. We constantly decline invitations to accept advertising in books, or to endorse travel products such as backpacks, etc.
>
> Independence is required for brand building. Financial stakeholders have often required short-term rewards. We are doing stuff now that cannot be explained with a spreadsheet or in terms of cash flow, but we are maintaining and building the value of the brand, which may only be fully realized over 10–20 years or with the sale of the whole thing.
>
> Another reason independence is required relates back to the integrity argument. We have turned down very attractive offers to work with other companies to co-produce a product, because their brand conveys a different message than ours and co-branding would send confusing messages about what we stand for.
>
> You have to love what you are doing to build a brand; it's a long, hard slog.

Steve stared out of the window of his small office—one of the few in Lonely Planet—at the wintery Melbourne weather and pondered. "How much do you try to implement what you learned in the MBA? How much chaos and inefficiency do you tolerate? Particularly when people like it that way."

◼ The Lonely Planet Story

The Early Years: Lonely Planet Finds a Niche

In 1972 a young and adventurous newly married English couple, Tony and Maureen Wheeler, then 26 and 22 years old, respectively, walked, hitched, and backpacked their way to Australia across Asia from England. They arrived in Sydney on Boxing Day 1972 with precisely $0.27 in their pockets. In order to survive, Tony pawned his camera and Maureen got a job in a milk bar.

Soon the numerous "How did you do it?" inquiries from friends inspired them to write down their travel experiences. With virtually no publishing knowledge (although Tony had worked or a university newspaper in his student days) and working from a kitchen table in the basement of a Sydney flat, they converted their meticulously kept travel notes into a publication—a cut and paste job they called *Across Asia on the Cheap*.

Tony Wheeler described those early days:

> We did everything. We wrote the books, we edited them, we sold them, and we delivered them. When *Across Asia* was published, I took a day off work in Sydney to come sell it in Melbourne. I loaded up a suitcase with books, flew to Melbourne, took a bus to the city, put the books in the left luggage office at the train station, went around the book shops and sold the books, went back to the station, picked up the suitcase and then delivered them.

Across Asia on the Cheap became an instant success, with the initial print run of 1,500 copies becoming sold out in ten days. It inspired thoughts of a second trip to Asia. Encouraged by their success and driven by their love of being "on the road," they postponed their return to England and set out again for Southeast Asia.

This trip resulted in *Southeast Asia on a Shoestring*. Cobbled together in a cheap Singapore hotel between fortnightly visits to the authorities to renew their visas, *Southeast Asia on a Shoestring* was published in 1973. Fifteen thousand copies were sold in Australia, New Zealand, Britain, the United States, and Asia. Its meticulously researched information, communicated in a down-to-earth style, was to create an entirely new genre of travel-guide writing.

Tony Wheeler, reflecting on this early success, observed:

> Now I can look back and think that was a really clever idea, but at the time I didn't realize it. It was just a nice thing to do. As soon as we saw how well the first book went we thought, "Let's do another." We grew very slowly at first. It took us five years to get to ten titles.

The name "Lonely Planet" surfaced while working on their first book over pizza and red wine. They were musing about names: "It came out of a song by Joe Cocker from the album *Mad Dogs and Englishmen*. There's a line in it about a lovely planet and we just changed it to Lonely Planet."

With the success of its second publication the fledgling company expanded its title list with books on Nepal and Africa, and guides to New Zealand and Papua New Guinea. The early growth, however, was not without difficulties—financing expansion was a real problem in the early days. According to Maureen:

> Once you're in debt to the bank for a couple of million, you can borrow as much as you want. But when you're getting started and you want to borrow maybe a thousand to buy a car to get around the city to sell your books, or a two thousand dollar overdraft to pay your print bill, you can go on your hands and knees and kiss their feet but, boy, you won't get it.

The first ten years were a real struggle as Tony and Maureen tried to keep the business going. Exploring Third World countries in the region, living out of a backpack, and writing in cheap hotels for weeks and months on end became a normal way of life. Despite its promise of adventure and excitement, life "on the road" was, more often than not, a less than salubrious experience. Their obsession with detail, and their insistence on experiencing life as a traveller, often took them to regions where few Westerners had been, much less written about.

Jim Hart: A New Partner

The year 1980 was an important one for Lonely Planet. Jim Hart, a friend of the Wheelers with a mixture of travel and publishing experience, joined Lonely Planet from a major publishing house in Adelaide, South Australia. With Jim's involvement, the Wheelers' shoestring operation gradually took on more permanence, allowing them more time to travel and to undertake the intensive, year-long research effort necessary for the production of an India guide. When the first edition of *India: A Travel Survival Kit* came out in 1981, it marked a major turning point for Lonely Planet. Previously, books priced at A$3.95 had sold up to 30,000 copies; by 1981 books priced at A$14.95 sold 100,000 copies. The India guidebook provided the steady income desperately needed for the company to finance its operations.

By the time Jim joined, Tony and Maureen had already established the Lonely Planet name and set up the beginning of an international distribution system. With Jim's involvement, and with the publication of the India guide, Tony and Maureen could look forward to a period of stability.

Shortly after Jim joined the company, however, disaster struck. He became critically ill and was out of action for almost eight months. Also, during this time Maureen gave birth to her first child, which left Tony with the main responsibility of running their growing business, while supporting a new family and their sick friend in hospital.

Doing It Tough: The First Overseas Office

The Wheelers came close to throwing it in on several occasions: "There were a couple of awful times when no money was coming in and nothing was happening and you look at each other and think how long can we keep this going for."

One such time was during 1984–85, when the Wheelers set out to open an office in the United States. Originally Tony and Maureen went to the United States for a few weeks intending to arrange warehousing, but it didn't take them long to realize that they needed to spend more time there to set up a full distribution operation. Their direct involvement in the United States lasted more than a year.

Setting up the United States office turned out to be a very difficult experience. The cutthroat competitive environment in that country, coupled with a lack of appropriate personnel, looked as if they would sink Lonely Planet. Maureen reflected on the personal toll:

> It was a terrible time. The U.S. became a big hole into which we poured money for well over a year and from which we wondered if we'd ever get out. In order to try and make it work, Tony and I had to spend time there trying to run the office ourselves, which of course affected our operations in Australia, because we could not be in two places at one time. To cap it all, the Americans threw us out because of some visa technicality. The situation came close to unbearable. Tony became ill and started to suffer high blood pressure.

Internationalizing the Business

It was only after some major staff changes, numerous trips across the Pacific, and the installation of an accountant to run the United States office that things began to stabilize and improve. By 1991, Lonely Planet was in a position to open another office overseas.

The United Kingdom was the natural choice, given its status as the centre of English-language publishing in the large European market, and Lonely Planet's decision to commence publishing guides to European destinations. Lonely Planet had been represented in the United Kingdom for many years by a small specialist distributor, but there was potential to do much more. They opened a small office in London to promote the books and to handle distribution in the United Kingdom and on the continent.

Lonely Planet's expansion into Europe was another major test for the company. In Asia Lonely Planet was preeminent, but in the "Old World" such long-established guides as *Frommer's, Let's Go, Baedackers,* and *Fodor's* battled for superiority. Furthermore, Lonely Planet, which had create a name for itself by publishing guidebooks to the world's more out-of-the way places, did not have an image as a provider of travel information about the industrialized countries of the West. Lonely Planet expected to meet fierce competition in the European market, which was dominated by the big American-produced guides.

Opening the English office turned out to be much easier than the United States experience. This was in large part due to the efforts of an enthusiastic young Englishwoman who, after working for a number of years with Lonely Planet in Melbourne, was charged with the task of setting up the United Kingdom operation. The United Kingdom market had always been important to Lonely Planet and establishing a dedicated sales and promotions office there ensured the continuation of high levels of sales (see Figure 3).

FIGURE 3   **Lonely Planet Sales by Region**

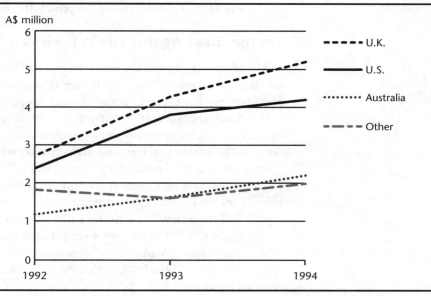

Two years later, heartened by its United Kingdom experience, Lonely Planet set up an office in France. The French office marked a significant development for the company in that, unlike its other overseas offices, its role was not limited to promotion and distribution, but included production of French translations.

The opening of Lonely Planet's French office was also significant because it marked the company's first attempt to diversify into non-English-speaking markets and at controlling the content, presentation, and marketing of its products and brand in those markets.

Until this time, Lonely Planet had considered itself to be exclusively an English-language publisher. The translation of its books into other languages had been undertaken by foreign publishers under various licensing arrangements.

Lonely Planet Comes of Age

In November 1994 Lonely Planet turned 21. The celebrations the Wheelers organized reflected the creativity and spontaneity with which they had infused the organization. What started out as a party for a few of the staff grew into a weekend bash that attracted some of the world's leading travel writers, journalists, and publishing bosses to Lonely Planet's hometown of Melbourne. Rather than waste such a pool of talent, the Wheelers organized a one-day travel summit, which was open to the public. "We thought 'Wouldn't it be nice to get all our staff from all over the world together in one space and just have a party,'" recalled Maureen. "And then we thought of all the people who have worked with us for years—booksellers, journalists, etc.—so we began to expand it out to other people we'd like to have. And then we thought, 'We have some fantastic names coming, why don't we have a public event?'"

"Party guests" included English author Eric Newby, freelance writer Pico Iyer, travel writers from the *San Francisco Examiner, The Times, The Independent,* and *The Sunday Mail,* and bosses of some of the world's leading publishing houses. That Lonely Planet could attract such big names to the far side of the world showed the esteem in which the company was held.

On the Road Again: The Wheelers in the 1990s

While continuing to run the business, much of the Wheelers' time was still spent on the road—researching, which they described as "dawn-to-dusk hard work and not without some annoyances." Typically they travelled overseas half-a-dozen times a year, investigating new places, double-checking facts from one of their books, or simply enjoying life on the road. In 1994, for example, they went to Queensland, Tahiti, and made two trips to the United States. Tony also spent time in Britain researching Lonely Planet's first guide to that country.

In typical Wheeler fashion the United States trips were anything but ordinary. They bought a 1959 Cadillac and drove from San Francisco to Boston in April, and then flew back to the United States in July to make a return trip to San Francisco. "The car was so big it took a mile to stop and used fuel like a 747, but it was a load of fun," remembered Tony. The car was featured on the front cover of Lonely Planet's 1994 product catalogue. Tony explained the reasons for their travel:

With Lonely Planet preparing guidebooks on each U.S. state, the trip was important to get a feel for the country.

It's never really a holiday. We always travel with all the guidebooks, others' as well as our own, and are always checking facts.

All trips are a potential source of new ideas. A few years ago we went outback in Australia—up the Birdsville track and then crossed the Simpson desert. It was the kids' vacation (the Wheelers have two teenage children) and we hadn't intended to make a book at all. But we came back so enthusiastic we ended up with an "Outback Australia" guide.

For the book about Britain, Tony made two trips to the country, travelling mostly on foot with a rucksack and often staying at the cheapest B&Bs he could find.

Can they ever see the time when they run out of projects or ideas? "No way," says Tony. "They keep making new countries. Every time we turn around they create a whole new country. We are doing Slovenia right now. The potential for city guides hasn't been tapped yet, either." And when it comes to their favourite destinations they are not easy to pin down. They both love Nepal and the wide-open spaces of the Australian outback. But deep down they simply enjoy being on the road. "I always love the last place I've been to," says Tony. "I always like the next place we're going to," laughs Maureen.

The primary passion of the Wheelers was always to produce good travel information. Profit was important, but mainly because it was the means to grow and do more for travellers. Until recent years, when the accountants forced change, the owners drew a salary lower than the average first-year MBA.

According to Maureen the fairy tale was a long time coming: "It took us a long, long time. It is a fairy tale existence now, but it took a lot of years of scrimping and scraping and watching other people fly way beyond us."

Maureen gives this advice to anyone starting their own business:

Find something that you love to do, so that the fact that you're not earning a lot of money for a long time, and the fact that you're working eighteen hours a day for an awful long time ... is not a hassle. If you're doing it for the money, and you're doing all the right things laid down by accountancy principles, you might do well and you might do well faster but you wouldn't have any fun.

The Wheelers planned to live in Paris during 1996—because they had always wanted to.

The Publishing Industry

Emerging Trends

During the late 1980s and early 1990s a number of important changes occurred in the book publishing industry. Dramatic worldwide rationalization saw smaller, regionally based publishers who, until this time, had operated independently in many countries around the world taken over by powerful international publishing houses. This trend was evident first in America and Europe, but soon spread to Australian publishing houses, which were seen as strategic launching pads for English-language books into the rapidly growing Asia Pacific region.

The 150 members of the Australian Book Publishers Association in 1995 represented an industry with $1.5 billion turnover. Eighty percent of members had a turnover of less than $2 million. The top five competitors dominated the industry. These large publishers had their own distribution capabilities and were often part of a larger communications conglomerate covering electronic as well as the print media.

The trends toward global consolidation of the industry appeared to be part of the large players' corporate strategies. Control of newspapers, printing works, film libraries and production, databases, book retailing and publishing, radio and television broadcasting, satellite television, and magazines began to converge in the expectation of massive economies of scale.

These global companies were also at the forefront of the implementation of new technologies that offered the possibility of increasing audience size and, hence, further leveraging the returns from their "information stores." In this climate, smaller publishers survived by catering for specialist niche markets, which the large corporates could not service economically.

In the mass-market segment of the book trade, paperbacks had to compete with a multitude of other "entertainment" products for the consumer dollar, with the result that some publishers anticipated that, by the end of the 1990s, the growth in the sale of books would become stagnant in many countries. In 1994, however, the book market was still growing (Figure 4).

Lonely Planet had been protected, to a large degree, from these industry trends. Its products provided readers with factual information with a specific purpose and did not have to compete solely on entertainment value. In addition, although the international recession had slowed the growth of tourist travel, there always seemed to be a demand for travel information by Lonely Planet's particular target niche, the independent traveller.

Book Distribution

The difficulties faced by small publishers following consolidation of the industry were exacerbated by changes in distribution channels.

In the late 1980s the owner-operators of independent bookstores numerically dominated the market. In Australia, for instance, 75–80 percent of bookstores

FIGURE 4   Demand Trends for Books

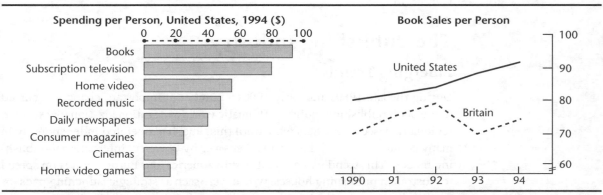

Source: Economist, September 30, 1995, from information supplied by Veronis, Suhler & Associates and the Publishers Association.

were owner-operated stores, or small chains with two to five stores. The majority of these were not commercially aggressive and books were generally sold at the publishers' recommended retail prices (RRP). This pricing structure was supported by a 100-year-old international publishing cartel. Book retailers competed on the basis of convenience and service rather than price. As in most markets overseas, there were few independent book wholesalers in Australia. Books were generally distributed to retailers directly by publishers or their exclusive licensees.

By the early 1990s however, bookstore chains and large department stores were becoming increasingly dominant in the book-retailing segment throughout the world. Book superstores had emerged in the United States to compete with discount stores—Wal-Mart alone had 18 percent of the United States book retail market. These stores were much more commercially oriented. They offered a wide selection of books, and their size and buying power allowed them to negotiate large margins with publishers, who often had no choice but to comply or be denied access to their readers. Lower prices were, in part, then passed on to consumers through heavy discounting of many titles. Discounting of hardback bestsellers was starting to occur in the United States.

Travel Guide Publishing

In the early 1990s the competitive environment facing Lonely Planet varied from country to country. While there were a large number of travel-guide publishers all around the world, there were only a few which operated internationally.

Rough Guides

Rough Guides is a United Kingdom–based publisher that focused initially on the British independent traveller, predominantly to European destinations and gradually to a wider readership. It was, however, expanding its subject coverage to a broader range of destinations. Certainly, Rough Guides looked as if they would pose a greater threat to Lonely Planet's position with Asian destinations, and would continue to be a strong competitor in European destinations. Rough Guides were Lonely Planet's closest competitor in terms of target customers and style of book.

The Let's Go Series

A United States series that targeted young budget travellers, predominantly students from the United States and Canada. It covered all the major destinations within the United States and Europe and parts of northern Africa. Let's Go concentrated on its specific market segment and destinations. It used student researchers to update its books annually in time for the United States summer break. Let's Go was owned by St. Martin's Press.

Frommer's

Frommer's is a United States publisher (owned by Prentice Hall), popular with the "traditional" North American traveller. Its books focused on middle-class, middle-aged travellers going to major destinations. While it had guides covering the emerging destinations that were Lonely Planet's stronghold, its target audience was quite different.

Fodor's

Fodor's tended to compete directly with Frommer's. It was United States–based and aimed at wealthier American travellers with limited time. It had, however, a wider international perspective than Frommer's, with good coverage of all destinations except Africa. Its 180 titles, all in a recognizable format, were updated annually. In 1992 Fodor's released a budget-conscious series called *Berkeley Guides* in an attempt to tap this growing segment, and in direct competition with *Let's Go*. Fodor's was owned by Random House.

Traditionally, travel guide publishers enjoyed regional strongholds and/or unique customer niches. Lonely Planet, for example, primarily published books about Asia for independent travellers from the English-speaking West (Europe, the United States, and Australia). By the 1990s, however, most of the popular destinations had been covered and travel guide publishers began moving out of their traditional range of titles and into new regions formerly the exclusive domain of other publishers. As a consequence, sales were becoming less regional and the market was becoming more global.

This globalization drove industry rationalization and alliances. For example, Rough Guides formed an alliance with "deep-pocketed" Penguin for access to technology, distribution, marketing, and financial resources. Similarly, Fodor's entered into a partnership with Worldlink, a global travel information network that could provide customers with supplemental current events and destination guides. The supplemental guide information was time-sensitive and geared to a particular customer's interests and itinerary. Fodor's expansion into new geographical and demographic markets, and its experimentation with new information technology, was a result of a very aggressive international expansion strategy.

In non-English-speaking countries, the market for travel guides was serviced by local companies publishing in their native language and competing aggressively against one another. Many of these publishers were long-established and they tailored their products to the particular needs of their local markets. Most did not publish in English.

Technological Change

In addition to industry consolidation and major changes in distribution channels that occurred in the early 1990s, the whole publishing industry was on the brink of a technological revolution. The introduction of electronic media and the convergence of communication and computer technologies, creating the "information superhighway," was reshaping the entire industry.

The basic concept of presenting prepackaged information via the printed page in book form, the primary method of communicating information since the discovery of printing, was being challenged. Publishers of travel information were frantically trying to assess the implications of new technologies, which saw an entire collection of books, weighing several kilograms, stored on one compact disk weighing no more than a few grams. The significance of this was not lost on Lonely Planet, which had been using lightweight paper in its bigger editions for several years in an effort to keep weight and volume down. Nonetheless, the practice of ripping out and discarding irrelevant sections in the company's regional guides was common among its prime back-packer market.

Further, the Internet allowed virtually free access to information from anywhere in the world and, significantly for Lonely Planet with its two-year recycle time, allowed users to gain instant access to current information. By 1990 it was possible to download current information on train timetables and weather patterns for most European cities from anywhere in the world.

Tourism Trends

By 1993 there were almost 500 million tourist arrivals worldwide. While Europe had by far the largest number, Asia had the fastest rate of growth (see Table 1).

Tourism had been booming worldwide since the 1950s (Figure 5). Tourism trends revealed that Asia was the fastest-growing destination market, with some industry observers predicting that tourist arrivals to the region would equal those to Europe by the year 2001.

Many social, political, and demographic factors contributed to the rapid worldwide growth in tourism since the early 1970s. Among the most important were:

- Greater competition among airlines, resulting in decreased real costs of international travel
- Easing of political restrictions on travel by many countries attempting to capture part of the estimated US$2 trillion (1993) worldwide travel market
- Demographic shifts in developing countries, such as an increase in dual-income families, later marriage, and fewer children

The travel guide market could be segmented in terms of customer needs—ranging from the "armchair traveller" with a strong desire to learn, but little desire (or ability) to experience a foreign culture, to the hardened, independent traveller with a strong desire for both. In between were those travellers, more commonly referred to as tourists, who through lack of resources or personal disposition wanted to learn about and experience a foreign culture, but were less likely to travel off the beaten path. Independent travellers required very specific and detailed information of a practical nature, for example local road

TABLE 1   **World Tourism Trends**

Continent	Share of Total Tourists (%)	Growth Rate (%)
Africa	5	9.6
Latin America	6	3.4
North America	11	2.6
Asia	19	12.1
Europe	57	2.7

Source: "Worldwide Travel and Tourism Review," *Economist,* 1991.

FIGURE 5   **Development of World Tourism (1950–1992)**

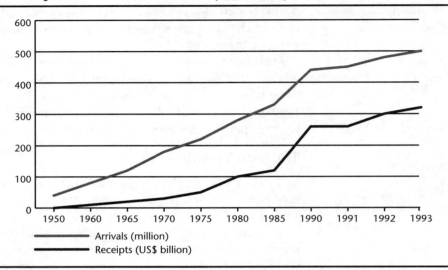

Source: WTO.

conditions, the nature, availability, and types of transport, and the availability and range of accommodation.

Lonely Planet's Operations

Lonely Planet in 1995

By 1995 Lonely Planet's publishing process had come a long way from the husband and wife operation working on a kitchen table. The company produced 180 titles (some of which were in their seventh edition), covering some of the most inaccessible regions in the world. It employed over 150 staff in four offices on three continents, though the largest proportion (around 80 percent) were still employed in Melbourne, where the company continued to undertake the production of all its English-language books. Lonely Planet also had 20 full-time writers with another 80 authors who worked occasionally, and had an annual turnover in excess of A$17 million.

The financial performance of Lonely Planet was impressive by almost any measure. During the early 1990s the company enjoyed rapid growth and high profitability. For example, in 1993 sales were up 38 percent over the previous year to $12 million, while EBIT (earnings before interest and tax) was up 50 percent to $3.1 million. Ninety-two percent of sales came from guidebooks (*Shoestring Guides* and *Travel Survival Kits*), the remainder coming from its newer lines such as *City Guides* and *Phrase Books*.

Lonely Planet donated approximately 1 percent of sales to charities in the countries it covered, funding small-scale projects such as cornea transplants in Nepal, as well as larger organizations like Greenpeace and Amnesty International.

In spite of the change in the nature of the organization as it grew, the books retained their chatty style and practical format, with much material being sent in from backpackers on the road.

Product Range

During the late 1980s Lonely Planet began to rapidly diversify its product lines, as well as its destination titles. Its two main travel guide series, *Shoestring Guides* and *Travel Survival Kits* remained, however, its core product lines. (See Appendix A for a brief description of Lonely Planet's product range.)

Lonely Planet attributed its success to a large range of titles, brand loyalty, and the best form of advertising that accompanied that loyalty—word of mouth. Inherent to its brand franchise were the integrity and consistency of the product. Lonely Planet guidebooks were thoroughly revised on average every two to three years. By contrast, most of the company's competitors updated only small sections of their books, some on a yearly basis. Each Lonely Planet book was in a constant state of revision. New editions incorporated not only the latest research by writers sent out into the field specifically for the purpose, but also comments and suggestions sent into the company by travellers using the previous version of the book. The company maintained its reliance on its far-flung readers for information and ideas, with in excess of 10,000 letters arriving at its office every year. Some argued that Lonely Planet knew as much about conditions in other countries as the Department of Foreign Affairs.

Lonely Planet's readers' letters department made sure that an acknowledgement was sent to every person who wrote to Lonely Planet, and awarded a free book to all those who supplied important updated information. Every writer to Lonely Planet was mentioned in the following edition of the relevant guide and received "Planet Talk," a free, bimonthly publication with information and experiences drawn from readers.

Editors in Melbourne kept an eye on competitors' products and made suggestions about ways the books could be enhanced. Lonely Planet believed that its consumers were primarily independent Western travellers, between the ages of 20 and 40, but market research had never been carried out to confirm this belief.

During the 1970s and 1980s, while the large publishers concentrated on the established North American or European destinations, Lonely Planet had the market for Asian titles virtually to itself. By the 1990s, however, travel guide publishing was globalizing and had become so competitive that the main guidebook publishers were looking to each others' traditional regional strongholds for both new destination titles and markets.

Although the Lonely Planet guidebook "formula" was developed with English-speaking Westerners in mind, the company has had some success in foreign translations. Lonely Planet books have been translated into nine languages including Italian, German, Japanese, and French. The company's policy was to sell translation rights to third parties for a small royalty. These publishers were then allowed to "repackage" the company's information as they liked. Translated books were not marketed under the Lonely Planet logo. Other than an acknowledgement of the source of information, which was carried inside the translated version of its books, the company did not have a translation policy. Consequently, there was a large variation in the way Lonely Planet translations reappeared in non-English versions. Some bore little resemblance to the standard format of a Lonely Planet book. Others, however, copied the format to the smallest detail, including the full-colour picture on the front cover and the hallmark banner at the top of the page, but replacing the Lonely Planet logo with their own.

The Publishing Process

Most of the research and writing for Lonely Planet was done by a small army of freelance, experienced travellers with a proven ability to collect and present information. Lonely Planet supplied a "style guide" which described the format that writers had to follow. Most authors are not salaried, but are contracted for individual books. They are paid by flat fee and, occasionally, by a royalty on sales.

All authors are featured prominently in the front pages of each Lonely Planet book. Black-and-white photographs, often taken on the road, accompany a short tongue-in-cheek biographical paragraph describing how the writer (invariably) "dropped out" and became a writer-traveller. Some Lonely Planet writers "went feral"—they "dropped out" so seriously that they never returned from a "life on the road."

Lonely Planet prides itself on being an early adopter of new technology. Computers have long been used at Lonely Planet in all stages of production, and a "techo" group of three full-time computer experts maintain the company's computer network in Melbourne. Computer backups are made weekly and duplicate copies of all the information in the company's system is stored off-site.

Printing and binding of finished books is mostly done in Hong Kong and Singapore. Apart from cost considerations and delivery time to major overseas markets, printers have to be able to "section sew" books. This type of binding, which prevents pages from falling out and book spines from being broken, guarantees that Lonely Planet books stand up to the hard treatment that they receive on the road.

Bulk distribution is decentralized through regional warehouses located in Melbourne, San Francisco, London, and Singapore. From these locations, books are supplied to wholesale distributors in each country except Australia and the United States, where sales and distribution to retailers is done directly by Lonely Planet.

Organization and Management

The Lonely Planet culture is often described as "funky." It has a non-commercial feel to it and is often perceived as an organization of "travellers helping travellers." Employees are generally younger people, and editors often work to the sound of their favourite music, with earphones connected to portable CD players.

Lonely Planet seems to attract creative people. Apart from writers, there are musicians, actors, and other artists, several of whom are very successful in their artistic careers outside of Lonely Planet. The people employed by Lonely Planet were, almost without exception, travellers. The people the Wheelers intentionally employed were, like themselves, their own customers.

Lonely Planet's two-storey headquarters in suburban Melbourne is an open-plan office on two floors, with just glass walls to define meeting rooms. Dress code is relaxed in the extreme. Well-loved jeans are the standard dress from the directors down. In summer, staff walk around in shorts and T-shirts and are often barefooted. Staff are encouraged to cycle to work or take public transport, and daypacks can be seen everywhere.

A door separates the office from a large warehouse, which is a hive of activity—often to the sound of the latest rock or heavy metal hit—during working hours. The warehouse doubles as a meeting place for staff "general meetings." Every Friday evening the company ships in cartons of beer and bottles of champagne and throws a party. This Friday ritual had started as a celebration of sending the latest book to the printer.

The relaxed atmosphere at Lonely Planet, which often catches visitors by surprise, belies the professionalism of the company's staff. Virtually everyone at Lonely Planet has at least one university degree, including two in 1995 who had Ph.D.s. There were, however, only two with MBAs (one of whom was Tony Wheeler, who completed an MBA at London Business School in the early seventies).

New Technology: The Internet

Lonely Planet went its own way in developing applications in response to the rapid developments in technology. In 1994, in its typical "try it first and fix it later if something goes wrong" operating style, it created a position which it called Manager, Information Systems. One of the editors in the Melbourne office was invited to take the position.

Within a short while the new manager had gathered a small group of editors and cartographers to develop applications for a Lonely Planet Internet site. None of the group had any previous programming experience. In fact, one member of the team had started at Lonely planet a few years earlier as a packer in the warehouse. Baptising themselves "The e-Team," they had to unlearn much of what they learnt from book publishing. In a few months this group of half-a-dozen "experimenters" had developed what became one of the largest Internet sites in Australia.

While they were delighted with the result, which was generally considered to have very successfully translated Lonely Planet's youth-oriented culture to the new medium, everyone was still trying to figure out what could be done with it. As one of the directors said:

> It's fun. But what are we going to do with it? I can't see anybody using anything but books on their travels well into the future. Sometimes I wonder if we're wasting our time and money going down this path.

Tony Wheeler, it was said, just could not get himself excited about multimedia and sometimes wished the new technology would "go away." This sentiment was not shared by the younger staff, who were more comfortable, if not outright enthusiastic, with the developments resulting from the convergence of computer and communication technologies.

Lonely Planet Attracts Attention

The Wheelers' work had a pioneering quality and the company acquired a reputation for blazing trails—where Tony and Maureen went one day (and later their writers), others were soon to follow. An industry observer commented that "Tony's books transformed the overland hippie trail to Asia and its grapevine more surely than if he'd hammered in signposts." The pathfinding skills of the young couple led, in fact, to one of the main—if scarcely logical—criticisms levelled at Lonely Planet; namely, that it had helped open up and commercialize what were previously "pristine places" known only to a deserving and adventurous few.

It didn't take long for the drawing power of Lonely Planet books to be appreciated by tourist operators in the budding tourist industry of the region. Self-titled "Lonely Planet" restaurants and touring companies began to sprout up in several developing countries from India to Kenya. And a mention of one's restaurant, hotel, or nightspot in a Lonely Planet book became a virtual guarantee of success. Because of this, Tony and Maureen were careful, when out in the field, not to reveal their identities.

The Wheelers' insistence on providing accurate information on the commercial establishments mentioned in their guides was a cornerstone on which they built Lonely Planet's reputation for unbiased, factual, down-to-earth travel information. To this day, Lonely Planet authors tend to travel incognito when they are in the field and, unlike most of its competitors, Lonely Planet continues to abhor the notion of carrying any form of advertising in its publications.

It wasn't only commercial establishments that began to take an interest in the company. As they became better known among more and more travellers, they also began to attract the attention of governments keen to capitalize on the growth in tourism. Sometimes, however, Lonely Planet's down-to-earth, no-holds-barred, somewhat irreverent writing style attracted unfavourable attention from governments. In Malawi, for instance, president-for-life Banda took a dislike to certain references to his country in *Africa on a Shoestring* and banned it. Vietnam also banned *Vietnam: a Travel Survival Kit* soon after it was published, citing as the reason a number of references, including one which informed travellers that its police force was "one of the best money could buy." Despite this action, a few weeks after it was banned, pirated copies of the book appeared for sale in government book shops with the offending passages intact.

Reaction to what Lonely Planet was saying and the way it was said was not limited to developing countries:

> The British press has hit back at an Australian tourist guide which is scathingly critical of some of London's most popular historical attractions.
>
> The latest Melbourne-compiled Lonely Planet guide, released last week, suggests the best way to aggravate the English is to tell them what they have always known—that their food is inedible, their weather an embarrassment and their beer a joke.
>
> And Auberon Waugh, an arch-conservative commentator, was oozing subtle sarcasm when he described the guide's editor thus: "It was written by

an Australian originating in Bournemouth called Tony Wheeler, who wears spectacles."

But Tony Wheeler naturally is delighted by all the free publicity. "I'm totally happy about it ... I expect it's going to be a very good seller for us," he said.[1]

Some of the observations in the guidebook about Britain included:

Looking at Margate, God got so depressed she created Torremolinos.

[Buckingham Palace] bad kitsch to tasteless opulence, like being trapped inside a chocolate box.

Manchester ... a city so ugly it can almost be exhilarating.

Lonely Planet also attracted the attention of the corporate giants of the publishing industry. During the late 1980s, the Wheelers began to receive lucrative buyout offers from a number of large organizations who, as Maureen explains, "after leaving us alone for all those years had finally woken up to our existence and the dynamism of our niche market." The offers kept coming. "People would drop in 'on the way somewhere' and casually ask us whether we were for sale. Everybody knows that Australia is not on the way to anywhere," laughed Maureen.

One organization which courted Lonely Planet was the software giant Microsoft, whose activity in multimedia and the "information superhighway" led it to approach Lonely Planet about joint development of multimedia travel publications. Although flattered by Microsoft's interest, Tony, Maureen, and Jim declined the offer, feeling that an association with such a large and powerful organization could compromise Lonely Planet's independence. As Tony said: "It really felt like we would be going to bed with an elephant and if it rolled over we would be crushed."

When asked why they didn't "take the money and run," Maureen said:

I don't know if I'd like to travel without a reason, and I really, really like the books we do. I always did, right from the very first book. On a day-to-day basis I really like all the people who work here, and who still enjoy working here. I suppose I just love the books.

Steve Hibbard Joins Lonely Planet

Restructuring the Organization

Steve Hibbard was completing his MBA at the Melbourne Business School in 1993. He had decided he didn't want to make a career in a large corporation. His plan was to identify a high-growth company he could join and perhaps later get some equity in.

A group case-writing assignment during the final year of the MBA introduced him to Lonely Planet. Steve described what happened:

---

[1] Ed Rush, *The Advertiser*, Adelaide, March 3, 1995.

I was intrigued by Lonely Planet—it seemed to be a great company—so I called the owner, Tony Wheeler, and said, "Remember me? I interviewed you for a business school project. Can I come and do some projects for you?"

So Tony, Jim, and I ended up sitting around a little black table. There was a long silence ... so I started to probe them about their "list of worries" and suggested I spend a week or two talking to people and then tell them where I might be able to help.

Anyway, I found lots of things were going on, but nobody was looking after them. Management information was inaccurate or unobtainable. They were licensing the Lonely Planet name for a television program, with too little control on the use of the name. The sales system and inventory system were out of date and it wasn't clear even who I should talk to about these issues. I tried to draw the organization chart. No one could agree how it should look ... the telephone list had things like "PC Guru." The organization seemed to be like this [see Figure 6].

Steve suggested to the directors that they should consider a reorganization and that he should be engaged to look after it. To his surprise "they bought it." Later, Tony and Maureen admitted to Steve that they felt, "We're big enough now that nothing you can do can damage it."

Steve recalled the first "interview" as an introduction to Tony's style:

I had to drive the meeting, that's Tony's style. He trusts people and if it's 70 percent what he thinks, he says do it your own way.

Take atlases, for example. Tony wanted to do it, but he wouldn't drive it. He would say, "Wouldn't it be a good idea to do atlases," and then waited for someone to pick it up.

As Steve went around and talked to people he encountered a lot of sentiments such as, "It (Lonely Planet)'s not as good as it gets bigger," and "We need to preserve the good things while putting in place an information struc-

FIGURE 6   Lonely Planet's Organization Structure, 1993

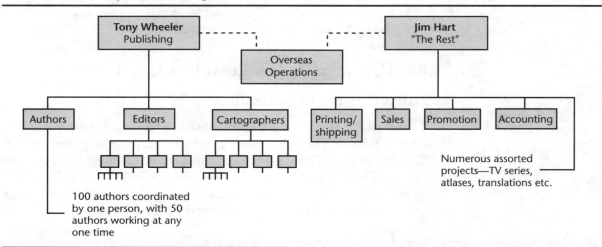

ture." As he started to understand the business better, a concept of what the organization structure should be started to emerge:

> I talked to everyone and I must have drawn the proposed structure on the whiteboard a thousand times. Gradually it got refined. There was a person looking after the authors, someone looking after the editors, and someone for the cartographers. They were in "departments" but they were getting too large and a "hands-off mentality" was starting to form. There were barriers to the process flow and the U.S. and France offices were like satellites hanging off the structure. Signs of strain from the relentless growth were everywhere.

Out of all the conversations emerged the idea of restructuring along process flow lines (see Figure 7). The regions Lonely Planet covered were divided between three groups, who were named Venus, Mars, and Pluto (other names had been considered, for example Itchy and Scratchy, and Laurel and Hardy). There was no management ruling on the names; they just came into common usage.

One person suggested she set up a Travel Literature section (to publish travel stories); it was something she (and Tony) had always wanted to do. The former head of editors decided he would rather be an author, and the person who was head of the cartographers took responsibility for design and ensuring consistency of "look."

The departments under Steve still had "functional heads," including Steve himself, who headed up Sales. In Steve's terms, the organization was now "a classic matrix." The other general manager, Richard Everist, had been an author and, before that, an editor. He and Steve formed a close working relationship and "made sure it all pulled in the same direction."

FIGURE 7   Lonely Planet's New Organization Structure

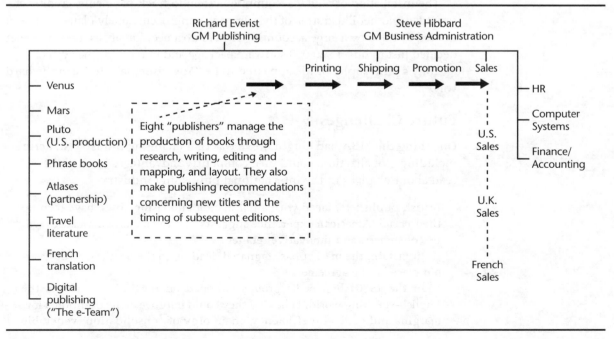

The objective of the restructuring was to maintain small teams while overcoming the barriers to the process flows: "It was commonsense. The MBA gets you in touch with your commonsense. You get used to laying things out on paper. Tony (Wheeler) uses his MBA more than he likes to admit—it's a way of thinking."

Tony, Maureen, and Jim expressed skepticism about the restructuring. Steve had to first convince them, and deal with their concerns about "too much bureaucracy and extra layers in the organization." Steve had to be careful to avoid "technical" language and to use a commonsense approach. Frequent use of the whiteboard earned him the title "The Whiteboard Kid." No whiteboards existed at Lonely Planet before Steve ordered one.

The new structure took about six months to be implemented, with a lot of consultation—too much, in Maureen's opinion. A lot of sorting out of relationships in Richard Everist's areas was done, and a new Financial Controller was employed. Steve continued to work on making his side of the organization more effective.

The new structure allowed Tony and Jim to step back from the day-to-day running of the business. Tony defined his responsibilities in terms of being an author, quality control ("trying out the books to see if they work"), the public face of the company, and visionary ("what's next").

Management control in Lonely Planet was described by Steve as being "like herding sheep; you come along after the fact and just try to shape the general direction." The United States publishing office was an example of this approach to management control. It was set up without any clear guidelines and in the early stages experienced its share of problems, but was now up and running beyond anyone's expectations: "Sometimes it is better to get it running and fix it when it comes off the rails, than to try to plan everything."

The installation of a new accounting system to track payments, credits, etc. provided another illustration of the company's approach. Lonely Planet had been quoted $12,000 by a large accounting firm to do a needs analysis. Lonely planet decided just to buy a $20,000 software package and implement the system.

Tony's philosophy of life appeared to be "You often have to learn the hard way."

Future Challenges

One thing the MBA had taught Steve was that changing industry structures, including globalization, could turn competitive advantages into liabilities. He read about changes in the international publishing industry:

> British publishers, faced with a flat market and rising costs, have torn up their cartel. American experience suggests that the main beneficiaries will be consumers, and innovative retailers.
>
> In Britain, the market has stagnated, leading to the death of a 100-year-old price-fixing agreement.
>
> In the 1980s big media groups swooped on the industry across the English-speaking world, believing they could improve on its traditional low margins and genteel inefficiency. In an orgy of consolidation, venerable

imprints were swept into big groups such as Rupert Murdoch's HarperCollins or Bertelsmann's Bantam Doubleday Dell.

Not everyone is persuaded that amalgamation has achieved much. "Paradoxically, the editorial aspect of publishing works better as a cottage industry but finance and distribution are better done on a big scale," says Anthony Cheetham who founded Orion, a British house. But in America, bigger, more professionally managed publishers have combined with discount retailers to transform the economics of the industry. There, publishers now make money by selling huge quantities of books at low prices, mostly through big, specialist chains or other large retailers.[2]

Steve, along with others, was concerned that Lonely Planet was being crowded out by increasing competition and that it was becoming increasingly difficult to "shine through" as the industry changed. Would Lonely Planet be able to continue to compete in the globalizing publishing industry without changing? Steve's dilemma was how he could change Lonely Planet to ensure it could continue to compete in the changing global industry without destroying the essence of its competitive advantage in the process.

Steve was wondering what role the mission statement might play in the change process when Tony Wheeler dropped into his office and said, "Steve, Microsoft want to come and see us again."

---

[2] *Economist,* September 30, 1995.

APPENDIX A

Lonely Planet's Products

Travel Guides

These fall into four categories. The main ones are the *Shoestring Guides,* which are targeted specifically at backpackers travelling on a tight budget, and *Travel Survival Kits,* which are the company's general-purpose travel guidebooks to individual countries. The company also produces a *Walking Guide* series covering some of the world's most interesting bush-walking and trekking routes. More recently, Lonely Planet began production of small pocket-sized *City Guides.* These provide in-depth travel coverage to some of the world's most exciting cities. All guides share a common format and down-to-earth writing style which has become the hallmark of the company's products and which has endeared the company to its loyal readership base.

Phrase Books and Audiopacks

Lonely Planet produces pocket-sized phrasebooks for some of the world's less-known languages (e.g., *Thai Hill Tribes Phrasebook*) as well as for some of its more common ones. Language audiopacks (on cassette or CD) complement its phrasebook series, offering a fun and practical way of learning a foreign language.

Travel Atlases

The company recently began production of travel atlases. These are produced for some of the most remote regions in the world, regions for which good roadmaps are generally nonexistent.

Multimedia Applications

The company has recently developed a fully functioning Internet site which has quickly become one of Australia's largest sites. It is also considering other multimedia applications such as compact disc technology and fax-back services.

APPENDIX B

Critical Acclaim, Awards, etc.

1982
- Australian Export Award
- Victorian Small Business Award
- Winner, Thomas Cook Award for Best Guidebook of the Year (*India: A Travel Survival Kit*)

1984
- Finalist, Thomas Cook Award for Best Guidebook of the Year (*Thailand: A Travel Survival Kit*)

1986
- Australian Export Award
- Runner-up, Lowell Thomas Award for Travel Journalism (*Fiji: A Travel Survival Kit*)

1991
- Finalist, Thomas Cook Award for Best Guidebook of the Year (*Vietnam, Laos, and Cambodia*)
- Grand Award Winner, Pacific Asia Travel Association Award for Best Guidebook (*Islands of Australia's Great Barrier Reef*)
- Nominated, European Book Awards (*India: A Travel Survival Kit*)
- Finalist, Ben Franklin Award USA (*Islands of Australia's Great Barrier Reef*)

- First Runner-up, SATW Lowell Thomas Award for Travel Journalism (*La Ruta Maya: Yucatán, Guatemala, and Belize*)
- Special Commendation, Reference Review Awards, Best Specialist Reference Work (*Nepal*)

1992–93
- Victorian State Winner, Australian British Chamber of Commerce Small Business Award for Export Growth, Initiative and Innovation
- Gold Medal Winner, SATW Lowell Thomas Award for Travel Journalism (*Costa Rica*)

1994
- Business Review Weekly, Top 100 Fastest-Growing Private Companies (Lonely Planet ranked number 67)
- Silver Medal Winner, Best Guidebook, SATW Lowell Thomas Award for Travel Journalism (*Guatemala, Belize, and Yukatán*)

1995
- Gold Award, Pacific Asia Travel Association Award for Best Guidebook (*Outback Australia*)

Magna International and NAFTA

Government must attract successful business people with a social conscience who have the capability and commitment to improve the living standards for all citizens.

Frank Stronach, CEO of Magna International, on his decision to run for the Canadian parliament in 1988

To be in business, your first mandate is to make money, and money has no heart, soul, conscience, homeland.

Frank Stronach, Chairman of Magna International, quoted in *Newsday*, August 7, 1992

"We're a Canadian company with a European heritage," said Fred Jaekel, president and chief operating officer of Cosma International, the second-largest of Magna International's four Automotive Systems Groups.

> Most of Magna's plants are in Ontario. Half our General Managers are originally from Germany or Austria. But the geography of the auto industry is changing. As a supplier to the industry we need to make sure we understand these changes and make the right investments—without repeating the mistakes we made in the 1980s.

Like Magna's chairman Frank Stronach, Fred Jaekel was a tool and maker by trade. Although he grew up in Argentina, Jaekel was born in Germany and had returned there at the age of 19 to undertake an apprenticeship. Several years later a vacation brought him to Canada and he decided to stay.

Now an 11-year veteran of Magna, Jaekel and several executives at Cosma were meeting to discuss the preparation of their long-term business plan, "Year 2000: Paving the Road." A central item on the agenda was the recent signing of the North American Free Trade Agreement (NAFTA) by the governments of Canada, the United States, and Mexico. In the wake of the heated political

© 1994 by the Sloan School of Management, MIT. This case was prepared by Tony Frost, Doctoral Candidate, International Management, and Ann Frost, Doctoral Candidate, Industrial Relations, both Sloan School of Management, MIT. It is intended for classroom use and may be reproduced without permission. Financial support was provided the Business Fund for Canadian Studies in the Unitied States, and is gratefully acknowledged. Thanks to Rose Batt, Mauro Guillen, Don Lessard, Gil Preuss, and Eleanor Westney for valuable comments.

battles that had eventually led to NAFTA's ratification in the three countries, Jaekel's team was trying to understand what the agreement meant for Cosma, which specialized in steel stampings for automotive frames and parts.

Would the further integration of 85 million Mexican consumers into the regional economy provide a key source of long-term growth? Would Mexican wage rates, in some cases less than one-tenth of those in the United States and Canada, spur a massive southward shift in production by Cosma's customers and competitors? And how would other changes brought about by NAFTA—in local content rules, for example—affect the industry and Cosma's growth strategy? Answers to these questions would form an important part of Cosma's business plan that Jaekel was due to present to Frank Stronach and Magna's executive management. The first task was to sketch out Cosma's most realistic alternative strategies. From there, Jaekel would have to decide on a course of action that would carry Cosma through to the turn of the century.

Magna International

Origins and Growth

In 1954, Frank Stronach, Magna International's mercurial and charismatic chairman, arrived in Canada from his native Austria with little more than his skills as a tool and die maker. Three years later, at the age of 25, Stronach founded the company that would eventually make him a wealthy man, using a Cdn$2,000 bank overdraft to buy a few basic tools. Over the next three decades, the company grew at an exceptional pace, driven by the energies of the young, competitive, and entrepreneurial group of expatriate Austrian and German tool and die makers Stronach attracted to work with him.

By 1992, the company had developed a reputation as one of the premier suppliers of automotive components and systems in North America, ranking fourth in auto parts sales behind only the components divisions of GM and Ford, and Du Pont Automotive. Its 68 plants produced over 5,000 different parts (the broadest range of any independent supplier in the industry), employed 15,000 people, and generated over Cdn$2.4 billion in sales. Exhibit 1 summarizes Magna's financial performance since 1984.

Organization

Frank Stronach's personal stamp was visible on virtually every aspect of Magna's operations, from the technical sophistication of the company's products and manufacturing processes to the extreme decentralization of its organizational structure. Stronach had even given a name to the set of ideas that guided his approach to business: Fair Enterprise. Enshrined in Magna's Corporate Constitution (Exhibit 2), Fair Enterprise aimed to motivate employees—both workers and managers—through equity and profit-sharing incentives, at the same time that it kept greed in check by limiting management's share of company profits to a fixed 6 percent and allocating up to 2 percent to charities and societal institutions. Central to Stronach's philosophy were the principles of individual autonomy and entrepreneurialism, both of which were encouraged

EXHIBIT 1   Magna Financial Review 1984–1993 (millions of Cdn$)

	1992	1991	1990	1989	1988	1987	1986	1985	1984
Operations Data									
Sales	2,359	2,017	1,927	1,924	1,459	1,152	1,028	690	494
Cost of goods sold	1,885	1,622	1,567	1,535	1,133	886	789	524	370
SG&A	156	154	203	204	179	125	101	74	45
Interest expense	50	82	86	73	50	28	15	4	5
Taxes	50	27	24	23	13	28	39	30	26
Net income	98	17	(224)	34	20	40	47	38	29
Balances									
Current assets	500	486	740	601	550	356	293	258	177
Fixed assets	752	841	918	1,101	1,000	881	590	359	180
Current liabilities	407	472	1,363	545	496	298	225	194	97
Long-term debt	81	381	NA	589	518	370	280	104	97
Convertible	165	201	NA	96	98	100			
Shareholders' equity	590	268	231	464	446	449	346	295	149
Other Information									
Employees	14,500	15,000	16,900	17,500	15,000	12,000	10,300	7,500	5,800
% sales from Canadian operations	67	70	75	80	81	86	85	86	88
Sales per North American auto produced (Cdn$)	190	173	NA	NA	NA	NA	66	44	38
Number of divisions	68	71	112	126	120	107	85	70	NA

through an organizational structure that kept divisions small (most were less than 200 employees) and pushed responsibility and accountability to the lowest possible level.

Each of the company's 68 plants—known as *divisions* inside Magna—was separately incorporated and run as a profit centre by a General Manager (GM) who was rewarded on divisional performance. Within broad company guidelines, GMs had discretion over most aspects of their business, from hiring and pay standards to decisions about which contracts the division would compete for. The decentralized structure and the small unit size not only fostered interpersonal communication and a sense of ownership among employees, but it also encouraged competition between Magna's divisions.

Magna's divisions were clustered into four "Automotive Systems Groups" according to their technical and product specializations: Atoma (doors, interiors, and electronics); Cosma (metal stamping, rust proofing, and sunroofs); Decoma (plastics and trim); and Tesma (engines and transmissions). Exhibit 3 provides a list of the four groups' product lines. Each group had its own technical sales force and product development engineers located in Detroit, as well as its own management team, all of whom provided technical and commercial guidance to the divisions. Group sales engineers also had dotted-line responsibility to corporate marketing to ensure a coordinated approach to Magna's customers and to provide headquarters with important information about industry trends and changes in OEMs'[1] product and process strategies.

---

[1] OEM stands for *original equipment manufacturer,* and refers to auto assemblers, such as the Big Three, Toyota, and BMW.

EXHIBIT 2   Magna's Corporate Constitution

Board of Directors
Magna believes that outside directors provide independent counsel and discipline. A majority of Magna's Board of Directors will be outsiders.

Employee Equity and Profit Participation
Ten percent of Magna's profit before tax will be allocated to employees. These funds will be used for the purchase of Magna shares in trust for employees and for cash distributions to employees, recognizing both performance and length of service.

Shareholder Profit Participation
Magna will distribute, on average, 20 percent of its annual net profit to shareholders.

Management Profit Participation
In order to obtain a long-term contractual commitment from management, the Company provides a compensation arrangement which, in addition to a base salary comparable to industry standards, allows for the distribution to corporate management of up to 6 percent of Magna's profit before tax.

Research and Technology Development
Magna will allocate 7 percent of its profit before tax for research and technology development to ensure long-term viability of the Company.

Social Responsibility
The Company will contribute a maximum of 2 percent of its profit before tax to charitable, cultural, educational, and political institutions to support the basic fabric of society.

Minimum Profit Performance
Management has an obligation to produce a profit. If Magna does not generate a minimum after-tax return of 4 percent on share capital for two consecutive years, Class A shareholders, voting as a class, will have the right to elect additional directors.

Major Investments
In the event that more than 20 percent of Magna's equity is to be committed to a new unrelated business, Class A and Class B shareholders will have the right to approve such an investment with each class voting separately.

Constitutional Amendments
Any change to Magna's Corporate Constitution will require the approval of the Class A and Class B shareholders with each class voting separately.

Staff at Magna's corporate headquarters was also kept to a bare-bones minimum, again reflecting Stronach's philosophy and the company's steadfast aversion to bureaucracy: only about 70 people, mostly in legal, accounting, and human resource functions, worked out of Magna's headquarters in Ontario. There were also about a dozen executives at corporate headquarters who coordinated activities across groups, raised and allocated capital, and analyzed industry trends and growth opportunities. The long-term and strategic plans developed by the executive management team were utilized by the groups in the development of their own business plans. Recently, the company had also established a centralized purchasing function to leverage Magna's corporate-wide buying power. A purchasing director negotiated pricing agreements with suppliers of commodities such as steel, plastics, and lubricating oils, the terms of which were made available to each of the divisions, regardless of its size, input requirements, or location.

Human Resources

Magna employed a range of skilled and semi-skilled employees within its divisions. Each division typically employed two or three engineers who solved

EXHIBIT 3   Magna's Product Lines by Automotive System Group

Seating Systems
Modular Seat Assemblies
Seat Adjusters
Seat Frames
Seat Risers
Headrest & Armrest Supports
Release Handles
Molded Seat Cushions
Integrated Child Safety Seat

Panel Systems
Interior Panels
Wood and Polyurethane
   Substrates

Sunroof Sunshades

Electronics
Interior Lamp Assemblies
Switch Plate Assemblies
Integrated Alarm and
   Control Modules ICAM
Audible Alarms
Printed Circuit Board
   Assemblies
PRNDL—Modules
Switches
ABS-Coil Assemblies
Fuel Sender Assemblies

Door Systems
Door Hinges Stamped,
   Cast and Profile
Door, Hood & Deck Latches
Door Checkers
Release Cables
Door Strikers
Mirror Assemblies Manual/
   Power and Breakaway
Cable and Padded Remote
   Mirrors
Mirror Remote Controls
Window Regulators Manual,
Power and Cable

Modular Door Assemblies

Hardware
Fuel Filler Doors
Pedal Assemblies
Parking Brake Assemblies
Shift Selectors
Headlamp Assemblies
Vehicle Emblems
Stamped Parts

Chassis Stampings
Crossmember Assemblies
Engine Compartment Panels
Floor Pans
Radiator Supports
Shock Towers
Transmission Supports

General Stampings
Armrest Supports
Seat Belt Anchor Plates
Instrument Panel Supports

Bumper Stampings
Aluminum Impact Bars
High-Tensile Steel Impact
   Beams
Stamped and Roll-Formed
   Bumper Beams

**Engine and Brake
Related Stampings**
Oil Strainers
Oil Pans
Heat Shields

Water Pumps
Brake Backing Plates
Master Cylinder Vacuum
   Shells

Body Sheet Metal
Body Side Assemblies
Door Assemblies
Hood & Deck Assemblies
Roof Panels
Rear Quarter Panels
Medium/Large Stamping Dies

Sunroofs
Large Stamping Dies
Electric Sliding and Tilting
Electric Spoiler
Manual Sliding
Pop Up

Finishing
E-Coating

Decoma Plastics
Complete Bumper Systems
Vertical and Horizontal
   Body Panels
Hard Tops and Roof Systems
Complete Body Dress-up Kits
Airdams
Body Cladding
Clear Hard-Coated Glazing
   Panels

Grilles
Headlamp Lenses
Rocker Panels
Spoilers
Bumper Beams
Energy Absorbers
Acrylic Backlites

Decoma Trim
Complete Body Trim Systems
Body Front, Rear and Side
   Moldings
Bright Metal Moldings
Bumper Guards
Co-extruded PVC and
   EPDM Moldings
Door/Window Channels
Fuel Tank Straps

Headlamp Bezels
Headlamp Retainers
Rocker Panel Moldings
Scuff Plates
Tail Light Bezels
Wheel House Opening
   Moldings
Roof Drip Moldings
Dynamic Sealing Systems

Engine
Air Conditioning Clutch
   Rotor Assemblies
Automatic Belt Tensioners
Engine Timing Belt
   Tensioners and Sprockets
Flywheels
Heat Shields
Idler Pulleys
Aluminum Pulleys
Alternator Pulleys

Timing Gears
Oil Pickup Tubes
Plastic Pulleys
Poly-V Pulleys
Starter Ring Gears
Timing Chain Covers
Torsional Isolators/
   Decouplers
Torsional Vibration Dampers
Water Pump Accessories

Transmission
Clutch Housings and Hubs
Clutch Pistons
Stamped Covers and
   Housings

Systems
Automatic Belt Tensioner
   Systems
Front End Accessory Drive
   Systems

Timing Belt Systems
Clutch Pack Assemblies

Other Products
Aluminum Die Castings
Collapsible Drive Shafts
Fine Blanked Components

problems on the shop floor and interfaced with group engineers in Detroit over design and quality issues. Magna placed a great deal of emphasis on shop floor quality and productivity, and virtually all of its GMs and AGMs had at one time worked on the production line at a Magna division. Many GMs and AGMs were, in fact, skilled tool and die makers, and it was well understood that the path to management lay in the acquisition and development of solid technical skills. In 1991, the company employed over 1,600 skilled tradespeople, and an additional 300 were completing apprenticeships as tool and die makers in various Magna divisions.

Operators of the actual machines used on the shop floor came from diverse backgrounds and were generally less skilled, although Magna trained many of these workers in continuous improvement techniques such as SPC and team problem solving. Average hourly wage rates for shop floor employees were around US$10 in 1992. In addition to the Corporate Constitution, Magna had also developed an Employee Charter of Rights, which laid out a set of principles regarding safety, training and assistance, and employment equity that Magna strove to uphold. These principles were supported in practice by a number of different programs and procedures, such as a toll-free hotline that could be used by employees to lodge complaints, and a grievance process that provided for a binding vote by a panel of workers and management—with workers forming the panel majority.

Magna's human resource practices, along with its extremely decentralized structure, served an additional purpose: they helped to preserve the company's non-union status. Magna believed small divisions were less tempting targets for union organizing, and, further, that they fostered the development of close personal relationships between employees and management, an outcome that significantly reduced the likelihood of successful union organizing drives.

Strategy

Magna positioned itself as a full-line supplier to the automotive industry. Through its four systems groups, the company claimed it had the capability to develop an entire car from concept to clay model to full prototype. In 1989, *Automotive News* even reported that Magna was designing *and* assembling small lots of Lamborghinis for Chrysler, which had taken over the marque in the mid-1980s. Although several Magna executives saw design and development of niche cars as a potential growth area, the bulk of Magna's business came from supplying integrated modules and systems—bumper systems, seating systems, vehicle frames—to OEMs.

Central to the company's strategy was an emphasis on innovation, which provided a critical source of competitive differentiation. Several of Magna's product innovations, such as its integrated child safety seat (co-developed with Chrysler), door intrusion beams, and electronic sun roof, had enabled Magna to carve out distinct and lucrative product niches. Magna further prided itself on numerous process innovations that had led to greater production efficiencies, higher quality, and even entirely new products. One such innovation, known as polyurethane vacuum molding, provided a method of fabricating car seats that eliminated cutting, sewing, and gluing, thus providing a major reduction in labour costs over traditional cut-and-sew methods. The company attributed much of its innovativeness to its organizational structure and culture, which encouraged and rewarded ideas from the shop floor.

Perhaps equally important to Magna's strategy was its careful targeting of OEM product lines. Dennis Bausch, senior vice-president of marketing and strategic planning, explained:

> It's the old 80:20 rule. In North America, the top ten selling vehicles account for about 25 percent of total automobile production. What we try to do is pick those winners. Right now, 50 percent of our sales come from parts we produce for the ten best sellers.

Bausch continued:

> We average about Cdn$190 worth of parts for every vehicle produced in North America, but on cars like the Ford Taurus, Cadillac Seville, and Jeep Grand Cherokee we do a lot better than that. We've got over Cdn$1,000 of parts on the Chrysler Minivan and over Cdn$700 on the new Chrysler LH—those are key models for us. We're building our presence with the Japanese, too; right now, transplants only account for about 5 percent of our sales, but we've made good inroads on models like Toyota Camry and Honda Accord.

Bausch's analysis began by looking at forecasts and trends for various segments of the industry, both cars (compact, midsize, luxury) and light trucks (sport utility, full size, minivans). The next step was to analyze the potential of particular "body types"—for example, Taurus/Sable—within these segments. Bausch looked at the OEM's estimates for each of the body types as a starting point, but then did his own analysis using data from consultants and other industry experts.

> What we look for first is volume—that's got to be there. Our contracts stipulate that we've got to have enough capacity to meet the OEM's forecast, so if we don't think they're going to hit their sales numbers on a particular model, we've got to factor in the cost of excess capacity when we're putting together a bid.
>
> After volume, we look at the expected margin on the car. If the OEM had good margin, it's likely there will be less margin pressure on us. Chrysler makes over $6,000 (U.S.) on each minivan. We do all right on that model, too. The other factor is the life cycle of the model. Taurus is in its eighth year. That means less development outlays and fewer startups and die changes.

Once the demand for each body type had been estimated, Bausch then looked at the capabilities Magna had to add to that car: Could it do the plastic body panels required by the design? Did the car require intrusion beams, one of Magna's technical specialties? Did one or more divisions have the capacity to take on this business? Were they located close enough to the OEM's production facility to be competitive on transportation costs and delivery standards? Was it business that was "strategic"—leading to future business or to new and promising areas of technology? On the basis of this analysis, Bausch categorized OEM request for proposals into three categories—red, yellow, and green—signalling the level of effort divisions should expend in obtaining a particular piece of business.

Magna's Experience in the 1980s

By 1980 Magna had grown from its roots as a small toolmaking shop to a Cdn$180 million parts supplier with over 40 divisions in Canada and the United States. Over the course of the next decade, the number of divisions mushroomed to 126, sales reached Cdn$1.9 billion, and the company invested over Cdn$1 billion in new facilities, real estate, equipment, and technology. Consistent with its culture and operating structure, Magna's expansion exceeded on a highly decentralized basis.

Top management's guidance was even more hands-off than usual after April 1988, when Frank Stronach stepped down as CEO of Magna to run for the Canadian parliament in that year's federal election. Stronach set out to convince voters that his Fair Enterprise system was "perhaps the most important chapter in Western industrial society in many years" and he predicted it would "have an enormous bearing on the future structure of corporations [and] law making." Political insiders speculated that Stronach was a top candidate for Minister of Industry if the Liberal Party he was running for were elected.

Although pro–free trade by nature, Stronach nonetheless came down against the impending Canada-U.S. Free Trade Agreement (FTA), arguing that the country was ill prepared for an open trading relationship with the much larger United States, especially without an industrial policy to facilitate Canadian adjustment. In the end, Stronach, along with the anti-FTA Liberal Party, lost the election.

Returning to Magna in the fall of 1989, Stronach soon discovered that the company he had founded more than 30 years before had taken a rapid turn for the worse. The competitiveness problems of the Big Three—which accounted for the vast majority of Magna's business—and the general downturn in the North American automotive market had taken a heavy toll on Magna's bottom line. At the same time, a number of Magna's new facilities had not yet come fully on-line, causing the company to operate at low capacity levels. Diversification into non–auto parts businesses such as magazine publishing and radio stations also distracted the company's attention and proved a large financial drain.

In 1990, Magna found itself in the red for the first time. That year the company lost Cdn$224 million—more than it had earned in the previous ten years combined. Worse, the company's expansion had been financed largely through debt, especially after the 1987 stock market crash, and the combination of operating losses and high interest payments plunged the company into default on virtually all of its outstanding loans.

What followed was a drastic restructuring as Magna worked with its customers and creditors to repair its operational and financial woes. The company's plan called for a return to its core auto parts business. Employment dropped from a high of 17,500 in 1989 to 15,000 in 1992, by which time the company had streamlined its operations to 68 divisions—40 in Canada, 20 in the United States, and an additional 8 overseas. On the finance side, Magna's major focus was its debt problem, and it set the ambitious objective of eliminating its long-term debt by the end of 1994. Future growth would be financed by equity or out of cash flow from operations.

By the end of 1992, Magna appeared to have regained its momentum. *Ward's Auto World,* an influential trade journal, called Magna's recovery the "comeback of the year" in the auto parts industry. Graham Orr, senior vice-president of corporate development and investor relations, summed up Magna's situation:

> What we're focused on now is bottom-line-oriented growth. Before we were totally focused on growth. The key question for us is what investments to pursue—in products, customers, geographic markets—to ensure disciplined growth. We made mistakes in the 80s because we didn't do strategic planning. Now we're putting the process of strategic planning into place. This time we'll look very carefully before we leap.

The Automotive Industry

The Competitiveness Crisis of the 1980s

Over the 15-year period from the late 1970s to the early 1990s, the North American automobile industry experienced sweeping changes in market structure, production methods, and buyer-supplier relations. Long the dominant force in the worldwide production of automobiles, U.S. assemblers had seen their share of the North American market fall from over 97 percent in the late 1960s to around 60 percent by 1991. In a period of just under 15 years, Japanese auto makers collectively increased their share to more than 30 percent of the North American market.

The penetration of the North American market by the Japanese producers was initially accomplished through the export of small, competitively priced vehicles that proved reliable over the long haul. Having established a reputation for quality and value with entry-level vehicles, the Japanese producers gradually moved up market toward the more lucrative mid-size and luxury car segments. Through a superior organizational model—often referred to as "lean production"[2]—Japanese auto makers were able to design vehicles that consumers demanded, and bring them to market faster, with fewer defects, and at a lower cost than their American competitors.

By the early 1980s, however, the competitiveness crisis of the Big Three had produced a political backlash against the Japanese auto producers. This resulted, initially, in attempts to limit Japanese penetration of the North American market through the 1981 "voluntary restraint agreement" between the United States and Japan and four years later through "voluntary export restraints" initiated by the Japanese. These trends toward protectionism, along with appreciation of the yen, were instrumental in moving Japanese producers to establish assembly operations in North America—the so-called "transplants."

---

[2] The hallmarks of this model include design for manufacturability, the use of teams of multiskilled workers, flexible machinery, the absence of buffering inventory (just-in-time delivery), and the dedication to continuous improvement in quality, efficiency, and cost.

Led by Honda in 1982 with its Marysville, Ohio, plant, the Japanese were producing over 1.5 million vehicles in ten plants in the United States and Canada less than a decade later—more than 20 percent of total North American production. The inflow of direct investment by the Japanese automobile producers also led to a second wave of investment, this time by Japanese parts suppliers, who were operating more than 300 plants in the United States and Canada by 1992.

By the late 1980s there were signs that many of the principles of lean production were beginning to diffuse to the Big Three. Through joint ventures with the Japanese, visits to Japanese production facilities, and the intense scrutiny given to the Japanese transplants by journalists, consultants, and academics, the Big Three appeared to be slowly learning and adopting techniques such as statistical process control, just-in-time delivery, total quality management, concurrent engineering, and design for manufacturability. With time these changes in the way cars were designed and produced began to have visible effects, both in the quality ratings received by new American models, and, most importantly, in the marketplace. In 1992, an American car, the Ford Taurus, regained the title of top-selling passenger vehicle, edging out the Honda Accord, which had taken the title the previous few years. In 1992, for the first time in over a decade, the Japanese share of the U.S. market actually declined, dropping 3 percent, while the Big Three's share rose by 11.5 percent.

For North American automotive suppliers such as Magna, the restructuring of the Big Three also brought major changes in the way they conducted their businesses. Not only were suppliers required to learn and adopt the techniques of lean production in their own factories; in many cases they faced a fundamental transformation of their traditional relationships with the OEMs. By the early 1990s, these changes were having dramatic effects on the structure and operation of the North American automobile parts industry.

The Changing Buyer-Supplier Relationship

Perhaps the biggest change in the buyer-supplier relationship was the movement to outsourcing by the OEMs. Under the old mass production system, many of the nearly 10,000 parts contained in a car were designed and produced in-house by the Big Three. In contrast, under the emerging system, responsibility for entire subsystems, from design and engineering to just-in-time delivery, was being transferred to outside suppliers. Components were also increasingly being sourced from a single supplier, a major break with traditional sourcing practices in the North American industry. In 1992, Magna estimated that fully 3/4 of its revenues came from parts on which it was the sole supplier. The objectives of the new sourcing strategies—reduced cycle times, improved quality, and decreased costs—were basic to the competitive recovery of the Big Three.

The movement to subsystem sourcing from single suppliers led directly to the consolidation of the auto parts industry and the emergence of "tiers" of suppliers. First-tier suppliers were the elite cadre of suppliers such as Magna that contracted directly with the OEMs. In addition to their engineering and production responsibilities, first-tier suppliers also served as integrators, managing networks of second- and third-tier subcontractors who supplied them with components for the subsystem that would eventually be delivered to the OEM. The OEMs chose their first-tier suppliers for their track record in meeting cost, technical, quality, and delivery standards as well as their ability and willingness to adopt the new practices associated with lean production. The financial stability of the supplier was also an important consideration in achieving first-tier status, since single-sourcing of major vehicle subsystems created potential vulnerabilities for the OEMs.

Although the industry shakeout had caused the number of North American parts suppliers to decline by an estimated 35 percent in the decade of the 1980s, there were still more than 2,000 companies involved in the industry the early 1990s. The vast majority were second- and third-tier suppliers, generally small companies that tended either to specialize in a narrow range products for the auto industry or to produce a wider variety of products for several industries, including autos. Magna's direct competitors in the first tier could be classified into three main groups: parts divisions of the OEMs themselves, including GM's Automotive Components Group, Ford's Automotive Components Group, and Chrysler's Acustar; automotive divisions of large, diversified companies such as Du Pont, ITT, Rockwell, and TRW; and specialized parts suppliers such as Budd, A. O. Smith, and Robert Bosch.

Beyond the structural changes that were sweeping the parts industry as a result of the changing sourcing strategies of the OEMs, a new set of practices also governed the relationship between the OEM and the first-tier supplier. Not surprisingly, many of these practices were variants of the Japanese model of buyer-supplier relations that were believed to have contributed so greatly to the competitive success of the Japanese.

Chrysler's launch of its new LH models was illustrative of the direction buyer-supplier relations in the auto industry appeared to be headed. Approximately two years before production was scheduled to begin, Chrysler selected its suppliers for the LH. Whereas under the old mass production system the car might have had over 1,000 parts and materials suppliers, Chrysler had contracted with only 230 suppliers for the LH. Although most of the suppliers were responsible for the total design of the system they were producing, Chrysler engineers on the LH team worked with engineers from the parts suppliers to ensure that finished subsystems were tightly integrated with the rest of the design and could be efficiently assembled by workers on the production line. Additional goals were also pursued through this common effort: reductions in the number of parts in each subsystem, decreased component weight, and efficient material usage.

In the case of Magna and several of the other major parts suppliers, location of technical facilities near Chrysler's LH headquarters at Auburn Hill, Michigan, facilitated close interaction between supplier and OEM engineers. In other cases, parts engineers worked out of LH headquarters for the design phase of the project, or Chrysler temporarily transferred key individuals to suppliers' technical facilities.

For each of the components, Chrysler set "target prices" based on value analysis it conducted prior to production. Chrysler then worked with the supplier to meet these cost targets. In addition to the initial target price, Chrysler negotiated annual price reductions in the 3 to 5 percent range for each of the components, reflecting an estimate of the cost reductions achievable through experience effects. Chrysler also provided incentives for suppliers to exceed their cost targets in the form of additional content in the subsystem or gain sharing.

On the LH, as in virtually all Big Three models in production by the early 1990s, primary responsibility for component quality rested with the suppliers. Parts inspection by OEMs was greatly reduced or eliminated altogether. Virtually all first-tier suppliers had implemented SPC on their production lines, and many had moved toward team-based assembly, job rotation, and multi-skilling of shop floor employees. The OEMs had also launched grading systems for their suppliers that rated supplier performance along a wide spectrum of quality metrics, usually over an extended period of time. Some had even initiated programs to improve their suppliers' production processes directly by sending specially trained teams to suppliers' production sites.

The same concern for quality and cost was also driving first-tier suppliers to work with second- and third-tier suppliers to implement many of the same practices. In many cases, first-tier suppliers were acquiring suppliers of key components to ensure that the capability for complete subsystems was in-house and to prevent supply disruptions due to inefficient or financially troubled suppliers. Changes originated by the OEMs were thus having ripple effects throughout the industry value chain.

The responsibility of the parts supplier did not end with production of the subsystem. An integral part of the movement toward lean production was delivery of the subsystem just in time and, increasingly for parts incorporating trim and colour options, in sequence.[3] For Magna, which supplied front and rear fascias, exterior moldings, and side panel and floor pan stampings on the LH, just-in-time and in-sequence delivery were facilitated by the location of its stamping division, which was only ten miles from Chrysler's LH assembly plant in Bramalea, Ontario. During the ramp-up to full production, suppliers such as Magna frequently placed engineers in the OEM's production facility to ensure that their parts were meeting the quality and delivery standards of the new production system. Having suppliers' engineers on-site ensured that problems could be more easily identified, traced back to their source, and remedied. On the LH, suppliers of complex subsystems continued to provide on-site engineers to Chrysler a year after production had begun.

North American Economic Integration

Politics had long played an important role in shaping the geography of the North American automobile industry. Canada and Mexico were locations for automobile production largely as a result of government policies that required companies to produce locally in exchange for market access. However, despite the heavy hand of government, trade in autos and auto parts remained relatively unfettered

---

[3] In-sequence delivery refers to the practice of delivering parts to the assembly line that match the requirements of individual vehicles. For example, if the interior colours on the next three vehicles on the line are blue, black, blue, then the supplier of seats for that model was expected to arrange delivery such that the seats arrived to the line in the same sequence—blue, then black, then blue.

by protectionist barriers compared to sectors such as agriculture, textiles and apparel, and steel. At the onset of NAFTA negotiations, automotive products constituted the single largest component of trade between each of the three NAFTA countries, accounting for about 1/3 of total Canada-U.S. trade and about 1/6 of U.S.-Mexico trade.

Integration of the North American automobile market was achieved through three distinct phases of intergovernmental bargaining: the 1965 Canada-U.S. Auto Pact, the 1988 Canada-U.S. Free Trade Agreement, and the 1992 North American Free Trade Agreement.

The 1965 Auto Pact

In response to an escalating trade dispute between the United States and Canada over Canadian export subsidies, governments of the two countries negotiated the Auto Pact, which eliminated tariffs on autos and parts produced with least 50 percent local content. Although the Auto Pact effectively created an integrated market for autos and parts, the agreement also contained several Canadian safeguards designed to ensure autos would continue to be produced in Canada. The most important of these provisions was the production-to-sales ratio test, which required companies to produce in Canada autos or parts worth at least 3/4 of their Canadian sales. Companies that met this requirement would qualify for duty-free status on their exports to Canada, even on goods originating from third countries such as Mexico or Japan.

The 1988 Canada-U.S. Free Trade Agreement

In 1988, Canada and the United States negotiated a comprehensive free trade agreement (FTA) designed to secure and extend open trade between the world's two largest trading partners. The Canada-U.S. agreement was also the direct precursor to, and model for, NAFTA, which added Mexico to the bilateral free trade zone. In the auto sector, the 1988 agreement included provisions designed to relieve tensions that had emerged as a result of changes in the worldwide automobile industry since the negotiation of the Auto Pact. Inside the industry, the FTA became known as "Auto Pact Plus."

The most important feature of the FTA pertaining to autos was the freeze placed on new participants to the Auto Pact, a measure that resulted in the exclusion of Japanese producers, all of whom had elected not to join the Auto Pact prior to 1988 because of the onerous Canadian production requirements. The freeze on membership, along with the elimination of Canadian export-based duty drawbacks,[4] ensured that non–Auto Pact producers would pay at least some duty on vehicles or parts imported into the region. Prior to the agreement, the Big Three were alarmed that Japanese producers could export vehicles or parts to Canada duty-free under the drawback scheme, while using

---

[4] In the early 1970s, Canada began a policy of remitting duty to non–Auto Pact producers who exported goods manufactured in Canada. This "parallel benefits" policy was an important factor in inducing investment into Canada by non–North American auto assemblers such as Honda, Toyota, Suzuki, and Hyundai; it was also a major source of tension in the trade relations between the two countries.

their Canadian production facilities to export vehicles to the large U.S. market under the duty-free provision of the Auto Pact. After passage of the FTA, Japanese cars produced in Canada could only be exported duty-free to the United States if they met the 50 percent North American content requirement. Many industry observers believed these changes had significantly reduced the attractiveness of Canada as a location for transplants.

The other significant change brought about by the FTA concerned the basis for calculating the 50 percent North American content requirement needed for duty-free status. Prior to the agreement, parts manufacturers had lobbied for a 65 percent local content requirement as a way of increasing North American sourcing by OEMs. Instead, the FTA imposed a tougher standard by which the existing 50 percent would be calculated: only labour and direct processing costs—factory costs—would be included, not advertising or overhead costs. This change was believed to have increased domestic sourcing by OEMs, especially transplant producers who still imported a large number of parts.

NAFTA

The addition of Mexico to the Canada-U.S. FTA introduced a fundamentally new dynamic into the North American political economy. In the United States and Canada, the uncertainty about NAFTA's consequences—it was the first free trade agreement between large developed and developing nations during the postwar period—led to fears that the industrial core of each country's economy would be lost to Mexico due to low wages and lax enforcement of labour and environmental standards.[5]

In November 1993, after one of the most fiercely contested battles in the history of U.S. trade politics, NAFTA was finally ratified by the U.S. Congress. From Tuktoyaktuk to Tapachula, more than 360 million people would be linked together in the world's largest free trade area.[6]

Auto sector provisions under NAFTA reflected the complex configuration of interests involved in the negotiations. Exhibit 4 provides a summary of the main features of the agreement pertaining to autos.

Perhaps the most important objective of the Big Three was improved access to the Mexican consumer market, which at the time of the NAFTA negotiations was the fastest-growing automobile market in the world. Liberalization of the Mexican market was ensured through three NAFTA provisions: (1) an immediate halving of Mexico's 20 percent tariff on autos and light trucks, and a ten-year phaseout of the remaining tariff; (2) a ten-year phaseout of Mexico's requirement that vehicles sold in Mexico contain 36 percent domestic content;

---

[5] Different economic models produced widely disparate forecasts of NAFTA's impact on trade flows, economic growth, employment gains and losses, and wage rates in each country. For example, projections about the impact of NAFTA on Mexican employment ranged from a net loss of 158,000 jobs to a net gain of 1,464,000 jobs, depending on the assumptions contained in the model (*Source:* Institute for International Economics).

[6] In 1989, the EC and EFTA countries *together* were home to 358 million people. The European project is not technically a free trade area. Formed in 1958 as a customs union with a common external tariff, the EC (now the EU) had recently embarked on a much more ambitious process of economic union.

EXHIBIT 4   NAFTA Provisions Pertaining to the Automotive Sector

	United States		Canada		Mexico	
Tariffs	*Now*	*NAFTA*	*Now*	*NAFTA*	*Now*	*NAFTA*
Cars	2.5%	0% by 1994	9.2%	4.6% to 0% by 2004	20%	10% to 0% by 2004
Light trucks	25%	10% to 0% by 1999	9.2%	4.6% to 0% by 1999	20%	10% to 0% by 1999
Other trucks	25%	25% to 0% by 2004	9.2%	9.2% to 0% by 2004	20%	20% to 0% by 2004
Parts	3 to 6%	0% for some parts; 5- or 10-year elimination Cdn.-U.S. FTA schedule for Canada		9.2%; will match Mex. offer Cdn.-U.S. FTA schedule for U.S.	10–15%	75% of parts to 0% by 1999; remainder to 0% by 2004
Import Quotas	Light vehicles: none		Light vehicles: none		*Now:*	<15% of domestic production
					NAFTA:	None by 1994
	Heavy vehicles: none		Heavy vehicles: none		*Now:*	Equivalent to local content
					NAFTA:	None by 1994
Trade Balancing	None		None		*Now:*	No deficit; $1.75 of exports for $1 of imports
					NAFTA:	$0.80—$0.55 of exports for $1 of imports; none by 1994
Local Content	None		None		*Now:*	36% of total domestic production plus net exports
					NAFTA:	1992 level or declining % (starting at 34%), whichever lower; none by 1994
Manufacturing Requirement	None		None		*Now:*	Required
					NAFTA:	None by 2004
Equity Restriction	None		None		*Now:*	<40% foreign equity in parts
					NAFTA:	<49% by 1994; none by 1999
Care Rules	NAFTA: Mexican production counts as domestic fleet		None		*Now:*	<40% foreign equity in parts
					NAFTA:	<49% by 1994; none by 1999

and (3) an immediate reduction in Mexico's trade balancing requirement from $2 of automotive exports for every dollar's worth of imports, to $0.80, and to zero by 2004. The automotive industry hailed this last provision as "the single most significant accomplishment of the NAFTA automotive negotiations."

The gradual phaseout of tariff and non-tariff barriers was designed, in part, to ensure that the budding Mexican parts industry would not be wiped out by immediate exposure to international competition, a key Mexican objective. Still, some analysts were predicting that as many as 80 percent of Mexican parts companies would be forced to exit the market as a result of NAFTA.[7] Many

---

[7] Kay G. Husbands, "Strategic alliances in the Mexican auto parts industry," IMVP Working Paper, MIT, 1993.

Mexican suppliers were scrambling to form alliances with their U.S. and Canadian counterparts as a way of obtaining badly needed capital and technology.

The terms of the transition also reflected one of the Big Three's major priorities, namely to ensure that Mexico could not easily be used as an "export platform" to the U.S. market by foreign producers. The gradual phaseout clearly benefited producers with established Mexican facilities, primarily Chrysler, Ford, and General Motors, as well as Nissan and Volkswagen, since new entrants were required to establish sourcing relationships with Mexican suppliers just as the established OEMs had done. NAFTA ensured that there were no "late-mover advantages" conferred on companies such as Toyota and Honda that had yet to establish Mexican production facilities.

North American parts suppliers also stood to gain by several NAFTA provisions, especially the increase in the North American content requirement from 50 percent to 62.5 percent over an eight-year period. Furthermore, the method of calculating local content was again changed to a system that effectively created a more onerous requirement for assemblers: rather than counting a part as 100 percent regional if its domestic content exceeded 50 percent as under the FTA (the so-called "roll-up" method), under NAFTA the value-added of 69 key components (e.g., engines, transmissions, bumpers) would be traced and counted according to their actual percentage of domestic or foreign content. Japanese producers, who were on record as calling the auto provisions of the agreement "a giant step in the wrong direction," were expected to have the most difficulty meeting the new content requirements.

Cosma's Response to NAFTA

Cosma's Business

Fred Jaekel had been COO of Cosma since 1991, four years after the group was created in a reorganization that brought together Magna's metal stamping and assembly capabilities under the management of one group. Since the reorganization, Cosma had positioned itself as a supplier of complete body components and systems to OEMs, with capabilities spanning the range from design to tooling to production. By 1992, Cosma had sales of Cdn$781 million and was one of the largest, most complete stamping companies in North America. Its presses, ranging from 60 to 3,500 tons (54 to 3,175 tonnes), could produce virtually any body part made of sheet steel: engine compartments, bumpers, hoods, and body panels, for example. Cosma's ability to design and construct its own die-making tools was a capability that had long been an integral part of Magna's competitive thrust.

Cosma operated 19 divisions in the United States and Canada: 12 in southern Ontario and 7 in the United States (5 in Iowa, 1 in Maryland, and 1 in Tennessee). In addition, the group had a design and engineering centre in Detroit, where teams of engineers worked with OEMs to create drawings, feasibility studies, working prototypes, and full-scale testing programs for new products. Cosma had also recently opened Magna's first Mexican division, a stamping facility servicing the VW assembly plant in

Puebla.[8] Jaekel himself had managed startup of the Mexican facility. In 1993 Cosma was also constructing a new plant in Greensville, South Carolina, to supply frames just in time to the new BMW assembly facility that was slated to open the following year.

The stamping business was highly capital-intensive. Labour accounted for about 9.5 percent of Cosma's costs. The dies and presses used in Cosma's stamping facilities were among the most complex and expensive tools in the industrialized world: even the slightest deviation was enough to tear or melt the part being stamped. Servicing and maintenance of the presses was thus a critical factor in ensuring component quality and machine uptime. In addition to high capital costs, stamping operations also required large inputs of raw materials, especially steel, which made up 50 percent of Cosma's costs. Because of Cosma's focus on body systems, much of the steel it used was of automotive grade, one of the most stringent grades on the market and only available from large, integrated steel makers such as U.S. Steel or Canada's Dofasco. The major steel makers were also increasingly providing stampers with important value-added services such as computer simulations that compared weight and stress tolerances of parts using alternative steel specifications.

The Impact of Mexico

Cosma's executive team had agreed to divide the preparation of their business plan into several parts. Because of Jaekel's firsthand experience in Mexico, he chose to tackle the question of what effect, if any, NAFTA was likely to have on Cosma's future strategy, operations, and growth plans. Returning to his office, Jaekel pulled out a report prepared by Magna's executive management on NAFTA, as well as a report he had obtained from the U.S. Government's Office of Technology Assessment (OTA).[9]

The OTA report had an especially interesting chapter on the likely impact of NAFTA on the auto and auto parts industry. Two tables, in particular, caught Jaekel's eye, the first a comparison of production costs in Mexico and the United States for auto assemblers, and the second a similar comparison for parts suppliers to the industry—in the OTA's example, suppliers of wire harnesses. These are reproduced in Exhibits 5 and 6.

According to the OTA, Mexican wages in the auto industry ranged from a low of about US$2 per hour for the assembly of wire harnesses, which typically took place in maquilladoras,[10] to a high of about US$5 per hour for assembly operations at Big Three facilities. Jaekel recalled that his own costs in Mexico were closer to the OEMs'. However, despite Mexico's low wage costs, Jaekel had encountered several difficulties setting up Cosma's stamping facility there. Engineers and other skilled employees had to be transferred to Mexico—some

---

[8] A Magna division in Europe had previously designed and developed the tools for the Golf platform that VW had now decided to produce in Mexico. VW had encouraged Magna to open a Mexican division to supply parts for the VW Puebla factory.

[9] *Pulling Together or Pulling Apart* (Washington, D.C.: Office of Technology Assessment, 1992).

[10] Maquilladoras are foreign-owned plants located on the Mexican-U.S. border. Inputs for production are imported tariff-free; all output is exported.

EXHIBIT 5   **Cost of Automobile Production, United States and Mexico**

	United States	Mexico
Labour*	$ 700	$ 140
Parts and subassemblies	7,750	8,000
Component shipping costs	75	600
Finished vehicle shipping	225	400
Inventory costs	20	40
TOTAL	$8,770	$9,180

Note: All figures in $US.

*Assumes 20 hours of labour per U.S.-made car, 30 hours per Mexican-made car.

temporarily, some for an extended period of time. Equipment downtime had also been a problem, since few of the press and machine tool vendors that supplied Cosma had a service network that extended to Mexico, and Mexican workers had not yet developed the skills to adequately maintain the equipment. A company like Cosma, whose customers suffered losses of hundreds of thousands of dollars an hour when their just-in-time delivery schedules were interrupted, stood to lose contracts if it were the cause of customers' downtime.

Jaekel also knew that Mexican steel makers were unable to provide the automotive grade steel necessary for most of his stamping operations, a situation that was unlikely to change in the near future, even with NAFTA. Fortunately for Cosma, prices in the steel market were soft enough that they had been able to negotiate a deal with Dofasco to supply the Puebla facility from southern Ontario without additional transportation costs. How long this agreement would last was unclear, however. Finally, there were the added costs and difficulties associated with Mexico's notoriously poor infrastructure. The shipment of supplies and finished goods into, and out of, Mexico would increase Cosma's transportation costs and would greatly increase the likelihood of damaged goods.

The major question in Jaekel's mind was what the OEMs would do as a result of NAFTA: Would they relocate existing capacity to Mexico? Or simply add capacity there? Which models were likely to be produced in Mexico? And in what volumes?

According to both the OTA and Magna's internal report, the future of the Mexican automotive industry looked bright in 1993. In addition to the eight assembly plants already in Mexico (see Exhibit 7), several new investments had recently been announced. Ford was expected to invest US$700 million to

EXHIBIT 6   **Cost of Wiring Harness Production, United States and Mexico**

Assembly cost (40 minutes):	
Mexico (maquilladora plant)	$1–2
United States:	
Big Three internal supplier (@ $35/hour)	$23
Unionized supplier (@ $26/hour)	$17
Non-union supplier (@ $18/hour)	$12
Added shipping costs for Mexican assembly	$7
Extra inventory costs for Mexican production	$0.50
Mexican cost advantage	$2.50–14.50

EXHIBIT 7   Auto Assembly Plants in Mexico

Company	Location	Models	Annual Capacity
Ford	Cuautitlan:		
	Cars	Tempo/Topaz; Thunderbird	60,000
	Trucks	F Series; B200; P350	50,000
	Hermosillo	Escort/Tracer	160,000
General Motors	Ramos Arizpe	Century/Cavalier/Cutlass	100,000
	Mexico City	Suburban; Blazer; pickups	60,000
Chrysler	Toluca	LeBaron; New Yorker; Shadow/Sundance; Acclaim/Spirit	120,000
	Lago Alberto	Ramcharger; D Series pickups	50,000
Nissan	Cuernevaca:		
	Cars	Sentra	80,000
	Trucks	Pickups; vans	50,000
Volkswagen	Puebla:		
	Cars	Beetle; Golf; Jetta	200,000
	Trucks	Pickups; vans	15,000

Source: Pulling Together or Pulling Apart (Washington, D.C.: Office of Technology Assessment, 1992).

expand its Chihuahua engine plant for production of Escort and Tracer engines by 1994. GM was planning a new assembly facility for building up to 200,000 light trucks annually. Chrysler had plans for a new large facility in northern Mexico. Nissan was spending US$1 billion to expand its current facilities to build 120,000 (and eventually 150,000 to 200,000) Sentras per year for export to Japan and South America. VW Mexico had also begun to expand its capacity from 250,000 vehicles per year to 350,000 to 400,000 units per year by 1994.

In addition to these relatively concrete plans published in the trade press, there were other, less definite pieces of information circulating about the future of the automobile industry in Mexico. Foreign parts suppliers were expected to invest as much as US$4.2 billion between 1992 and 1996. Many economists were predicting rapid growth of the Mexican consumer market over the next decade as Mexican standards of living rose, creating increased demand for autos, which in 1990 alone had grown by 17 percent.

Industry analysts also pointed to the potential migration of small car production from Canada and the United States to Mexico, an outcome that was facilitated in part by NAFTA's provision allowing OEMs to count their Mexican production as "domestic" for the purposes of fuel-efficiency (CAFE) regulations. Examples of models that were thought likely to migrate to Mexico included the Ford Tracer and the Pontiac LeMans, which GM was currently producing in Korea. The Big Three had always struggled to make money on small cars, and it was thought that a combination of low Mexican wages and labour-intensive production technology might prove an advantage for the production of small cars. The same logic led some observers to predict that Mexico would become a prime location for producing niche vehicles, those with a short expected lifespan and limited market penetration, but high margins.

Despite these press releases and industry rumours, Jaekel was not yet convinced that the path to profitability for the OEMs ran to Mexico. First there was the excess capacity that had long plagued the Big Three's North American operations. Also, Jaekel knew that for every Mexican success storey, such as Ford's Hermosillo plant and GM's Ramos Arizpe plant, both of which were world-class in terms of quality and productivity, there was a failure. He had firsthand knowledge of VW's problems in Mexico: the company was forced to delay startup of its Puebla facility for over a year while it battled strikes and undertook a massive training program so that its Mexican workers could produce Golfs at the quality levels required for sale to the North American market. The OTA data, too, seemed to indicate little cost advantage for OEMs in Mexico, although Jaekel recalled having seen other reports that pegged the bottom-line advantage to producing in Mexico at between 4 and 10 percent.

The Impact of Local Content Rules

Jaekel turned next to the second set of potential opportunities he saw stemming from NAFTA, namely increased North American investment by foreign OEMs. Jaekel knew that the higher local content requirement under NAFTA and the new method by which it was calculated would create difficulties for many of the Japanese transplants. Most would be forced to increase their local sourcing, a trend Jaekel believed was likely to continue regardless of NAFTA's fate in the U.S. Congress. Political pressures and the rising yen were creating inexorable pressures in that direction.

Most of the Japanese OEMs had, in fact, publicly stated their intentions to increase their purchases from North American suppliers. In late 1991, for example, Toyota announced it would increase its U.S. purchases by 40 percent to US$5 billion annually beginning in 1994. At the same time Nissan had announced that it would also increase U.S. purchases by 40 percent during the next few years. Honda, too, although it had already increased its U.S. purchases in 1991, pledged to reach US$4.5 billion in domestic purchases by 1994. Finally, Mazda announced it would double its U.S. purchases by 1994, up to US$3 billion from US$1.43 billion in 1990.

Jaekel believed Cosma was well positioned to capture a greater share of the business from Japanese OEMs. Many of the Japanese suppliers that had followed the transplants to North America were known to be struggling. Most were unable to obtain significant business from the Big Three, and many had also experienced difficulties adapting their managerial practices to the new business environment. Moreover, Cosma had recently won several sizable contracts with Japanese OEMs, and was gradually establishing its reputation with the Japanese as an innovative supplier of high-quality components. In 1992, several of Cosma's divisions had won quality awards from the Japanese OEMs, including Toyota's prestigious Grand Slam Award.

Another potentially important development was the inflow of investment from Europe. The European automobile makers were building North American production facilities for a number of different reasons. Not only were they coming to ensure market access under NAFTA; they were also seeking lower labour costs and direct experience operating a lean production system, something that had proved difficult to implement in Europe.

Cosma had already leveraged its European links to land the contract to supply BMW's new South Carolina plant with complete framing systems. Mercedes, too, had recently announced that it would build a new production facility in Alabama, and Audi was thought to be considering a similar move. Jaekel believed Cosma also had an excellent chance of supplying these new facilities.

"Year 2000: Paving the Road"

Fred Jaekel's deadline was fast approaching and he had now digested the contents of the two reports. NAFTA, he reflected, seemed to offer a lot of different avenues for growth. But what, exactly, was the strategic vision he would put forward in Cosma's long-term business plan? Jaekel knew he needed to come up with a specific set of recommendations and be clear about the assumptions that underlay them. If there was one lesson Magna had learned from its experience in the 1980s it was to make sure that its investment plans were focused, strategic, and represented the best use of company resources.

Jaekel also knew there was still one stone he had left unturned. He turned in his chair toward the scale model of a Magna-designed niche car that sat on his desk. He reached forward and pushed a speed dial button on his office phone. Two rings later Frank Stronach was on the line.

"Hello, Frank? Ya, it's Fred," Jaekel said, still with a trace of German accent. "NAFTA—What do ya think?"

Metropol Base-Fort Security Group

Pat Haney, president of Metropol Base-Fort Security Group (Metropol), was sitting in his office contemplating the future direction of his company. Metropol, a leading Canadian security firm whose services included the provision of uniformed security guards, mobile security patrols, polygraph testing, insurance and criminal investigations, and a broad range of specialized services, was faced with a number of challenges that threatened its future profitability. "Increasing competition, especially from large multinationals such as Pinkertons, is further reducing already low industry margins," offered Pat. He was also concerned about Metropol's reliance on the commodity-like security guard business for 90 percent of its revenue. "We have to find some way to meaningfully differentiate our services from those of our competitors," Pat observed. "That is essential if we are to achieve the kind of growth we desire."

Company Background

Metropol was founded in 1952 by George Whitbread, a former RCMP officer. In 1975, Whitbread sold the company to former Manitoba premier Duff Roblin. Haney came aboard in 1976 to run the Winnipeg operation, which was then 80 percent of Metropol's business. In the late 1970s and early 1980s, Metropol expanded into Saskatchewan and Alberta. In 1984, it took over the leading Alberta security firm, Base-Fort Security Group, Inc. Pat believed this move offered economies of scale and helped to make Metropol a national company. Of Metropol's $30 million in 1985 revenues, 70 percent were in western Canada. Offices were maintained in all four western provinces as well as in the Northwest Territories, Quebec, and Newfoundland.

The Security Industry

Security products and services were purchased by individuals and businesses as a means of reducing the risk of loss or damage to their assets. The amount of

This case was written by Stephen S. Tax under the supervision of Professor W. S. Good. © 1988 by the Case Development Program, Faculty of Management, University of Manitoba. Support for the development of this case was provided by the Canadian Studies Program, Secretary of State, Government of Canada.

security purchased depended upon individual risk preferences, their perception of the degree of risk involved, and the value of the assets to be protected. Security, therefore, was very much an intangible product subject to individual evaluation.

The industry offered such services as unarmed uniformed security guards, mobile patrols, investigations, consulting and education, as well as hardware products such as alarms, fences, locks, safes, and electronic surveillance devices (ESDs) and monitoring equipment. Most companies purchased a package combining various services and hardware systems. "It would not make much sense to have 50 television monitors and only one person watching them," Pat pointed out, "nor would it be wise to have 50 security guards roaming around a building which had no locks on the doors."

There were a number of factors which contributed to the competitive nature of the security industry. All a firm needed to enter the business was to open an office. Startup costs were minimal and no accreditation was required by the company or its employees. Clients considered the cost of switching from one firm to another quite low so the business often went to the lowest-cost provider. Most customers really did not understand the difference in services provided by the various competitors in the security business, which made differentiation very difficult. Pat found in studying the financial statements of the large multinational security firms that most security companies earned pre-tax profit margins of about 4 percent on gross sales.

The 1985 security guard and private investigation markets in Canada were worth about $400 million retail. ESDs and other types of hardware added close to another $400 million to this figure at retail prices.

Growth was expected to continue in the security field for a variety of reasons including a general increase in the level of risk around the world, the rising cost of insurance, economic growth, technological innovation that created new security problems, and an increasing sophistication among security system purchasers. The ESD and security guard segments were expected to outpace basic hardware sales growth (Exhibit 1).

On the negative side was the industry's poor reputation for the quality and reliability of its services. This perception threatened to limit growth and provide an opportunity for new competitors to enter the market.

◼ Competition

Metropol's competition came in both a direct and an indirect form from a variety of competitors. "We compete with other firms who primarily offer security guard services as well as a number of companies that provide substitute products and services," observed Pat.

There were hundreds of security guard businesses in Canada, ranging in size from one or two ex-policemen operating out of a basement to large multinational firms such as Pinkertons, Burns, and Wackenhut. Metropol was the third-largest firm in the country with a 7 percent market share (Exhibit 2). It was the leading firm in western Canada with a 25 percent share of that market.

EXHIBIT I   Forecasted Market Growth for Security Guard and Private
Investigation Services, Electronic Security Devices (ESDs), and
Hardware Products in the United States, 1958–1995*

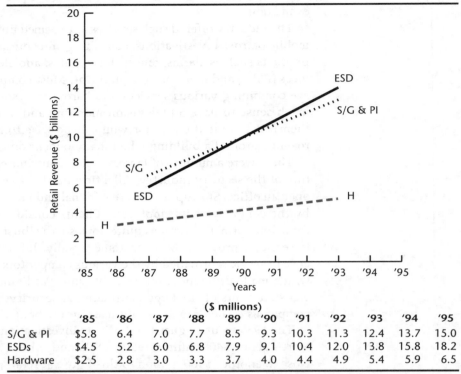

	($ millions)										
	'85	'86	'87	'88	'89	'90	'91	'92	'93	'94	'95
S/G & PI	$5.8	6.4	7.0	7.7	8.5	9.3	10.3	11.3	12.4	13.7	15.0
ESDs	$4.5	5.2	6.0	6.8	7.9	9.1	10.4	12.0	13.8	15.8	18.2
Hardware	$2.5	2.8	3.0	3.3	3.7	4.0	4.4	4.9	5.4	5.9	6.5

*The Canadian growth rate for each type of service/product was expected to be similar to the
U.S. pattern.
Source: Metropol Research.

Hardware products served as the foundation of a good security system.
While items such as fencing, lighting, alarms, safes, and locks were to some
extent complementary to the security guard business, they also competed
with it—firms could substitute some proportion of either their security
guard or hardware expenditures for the other.

Insurance had long been a favourite substitute for security and other loss
prevention services. Business spent more on insurance than all forms of security products combined. However, falling interest rates, a series of major
disasters around the world, and a trend to more generous damage awards by
the courts were making insurance a more expensive alternative. Faced with
higher premiums, lower limits, and higher deductibles, businesses were
likely to consider spending more on loss-prevention products and services.

The various levels of government also provided some basic protection services to companies (fire, police, etc.). However, their services were geared
more to personal than business protection. These government services tended
to set the base level of risk in a community. Tight budgets were not permitting these services to keep pace with the growth in crime and the increase in
the value of corporate assets. This provided the private security business
with an opportunity to fill the void.

EXHIBIT 2   **The Largest Security Guard Companies Operating in Canada Ranked by Market Share**

Company Name	Canadian Revenue ($ millions)	Employees	Market Share
1. Pinkertons	$ 50	4,600	12.5%
2. Burns	30	4,500	7.5
3. Metropol Base-Fort	30	2,000	7.0
4. Wackenhut	12	2,000	3.0
5. Canadian Protection	12	1,700	3.0
6. Barnes	12	1,500	3.0
7. Phillips	10	1,200	2.5
CANADA TOTAL	$400	40,000*	100%

*In-house guards could raise this figure by as much as 100 percent. However, a better estimate would be 50 to 60 percent, as in-house accounts use more full-time staff. This means that there are more than 60,000 people working as guards or private investigators at any time. Further, with turnover at close to 100 percent annually, there are over 100,000 people working in this field over the course of a year.
Source: Metropol Research.

Businesses were spending almost as much for ESDs and related services as for security guard services. There were a number of different ESD products ranging from small electronic gadgets to the very popular central station monitoring systems. ESDs were the fastest-growing segment of the security industry. The principal attribute of these products was that they provided accurate and reliable information to whomever was responsible for responding to a problem situation. Thus, to a large extent, these products were really productivity tools that enhanced the performance of security guards, the fire department, and/or the police force. They did tend to reduce the amount of security guard service needed. Some security-conscious firms with large-scale security needs hired their own internal (in-house) specialists. In most cases, they would also hire guards from companies like Metropol to do the actual patrolling.

The primary basis of competition in the security business was price. However, this was as much the fault of small, poorly managed firms and large multinationals trying to purchase market share as it was a fundamental characteristic of the industry. "I've seen companies bid under cost," observed Pat, "and they did not necessarily know they were doing it. It is a very unprofessional business in that sense. If you offer superior service and give a customer what he wants, in most cases you don't have to offer the lowest price. Just recently the Air Canada Data Centre job went to the highest bidder. Lowering your price is very easy but not the way to succeed in this business." However, since price was a key factor in getting jobs, cost control became crucial if profits were to be made. Pre-tax margins of 4 to 8 percent quickly disappeared if unanticipated costs occurred.

Market Segments

The market for security products and services could be segmented in a variety of ways, such as by type of service, type of business, geographic location, sensitivity to security needs, government versus private companies, and occasional versus continuous needs. Metropol segmented their customers and the rest of the market, using a combination of the above bases, as outlined below and in Exhibit 3.

Large, Security-Conscious Organizations (Private and Public).   The common feature among these companies was that they had the potential for heavy losses if security was breached. They typically had high-value assets, such as computers or other high-tech equipment, or valuable proprietary information, as in the case of research and development firms. These buyers were usually quite knowledgeable about security and rated quality over price. This group included firms in both local urban and remote, rural locations.

Organizations for Whom Security Was a Low Priority.   This group was dominated by local companies, commercial property management companies, and branches of firms that were headquartered elsewhere. They were less knowledgeable about security and tended to have limited security programs. They were price-sensitive and principally utilized low-cost security guards.

Government Organizations.   Government organizations (non-hospital) typically awarded contracts based on a tendered price for a predetermined period of time, usually one to two years. The price for these contracts was commonly in the vicinity of the minimum wage plus 5 percent.

Occasional Services.   These included anything from sporting or entertainment events to social or emergency services. For example, this might include seasonal contracts, as with a CFL or NHL sports team, or one-time affairs. Wages paid to the security personnel were usually quite low, but profit margins to the firm were above average.

EXHIBIT 3   **Security Guard Service Market Segmentation by Gross Margins and Guard Wages**

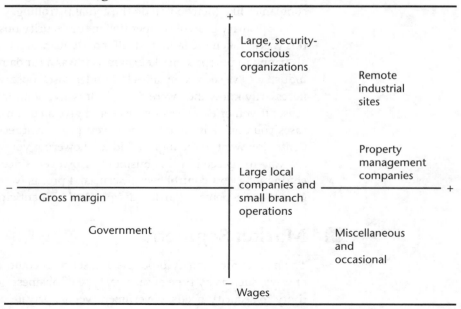

Buyer Behaviour

The buyer of security services was commonly in the stronger position. This resulted from a multitude of firms offering what buyers perceived to be largely undifferentiated products and services, and sellers trying to win business by providing the lowest price. Further, the cost of switching suppliers was low because of the customers' perceived similarity of their services. It was also quite simple for firms to bring the security function in-house if they believed they could achieve substantial cost savings or other improvements in their security programs. In addition, some buyers tended to give security considerations a low priority in their budgeting.

Firms purchasing security products and services had three levels of decisions to make: (1) a general policy on the role and risk-cost framework that security would play in their firm, (2) a decision regarding the types of products and services to be purchased, and (3) the selection of suppliers.

Each decision level involved new groups or individuals within the organization. Policy decisions were generally made at the senior executive level while the product/service and supplier decisions tended to be made at the local level.

Most purchases were straight tender purchases based on a sealed bidding process. Firms with whom security was a low priority, and most government agencies, tended to choose the lowest bidder. Companies who took a greater interest in the quality of their security program considered attributes other than price when deciding upon their security supplier.

As part of a study on the security industry, Metropol surveyed buyers' ratings of the importance of several factors in choosing a security firm. They also had buyers rate Metropol's performance on those performance factors. Among the most significant decision-making criteria identified were consistency and reliability, availability of service representatives, and price. Metropol scored highest on the quality of their representatives and the customers' view of the firm's reputation (Exhibits 4 and 5).

EXHIBIT 4   **Customer Decision-Making Criteria—Survey Results**

How important are the following attributes to you when making a decision on security services?

	Not Important 1	2	3	4	Very Important 5	Average Score
Consistency and reliability	—	—	—	3	14	4.824
Quality of service representatives	—	—	—	5	12	4.706
Price-competitiveness	—	—	3	8	6	4.176
Company reputation	1	1	—	7	8	4.176
Emergency services	—	2	4	7	4	3.765
Full range of products and services	—	4	2	6	5	3.706
Consulting services	—	6	6	3	2	3.059
National coverage	4	4	6	2	—	2.375

Note: The survey was a convenience sample of Metropol customers.
Source: Metropol Research.

EXHIBIT 5   **Customer Decision-Making Criteria—Survey Results**

How would you rate Metropol Security on the following attributes?

	Poor 1	Fair 2	Sat. 3	Good 4	Excellent 5	Average Score
Consistency and reliability	1	1	5	7	3	3.588
Quality of service representatives	—	2	—	11	4	4.000
Price-competitiveness	—	1	4	10	2	3.765
Company reputation	—	—	2	10	5	4.176
Emergency services	1	1	6	7	3	3.556
Full range of products and services	1	2	7	6	1	3.235
Consulting services	—	4	5	5	2	2.944
National coverage	1	—	7	3	—	3.091

Metropol

Metropol organized its operations on a regional (provincial) basis. The Manitoba headquarters developed a centralized policy and operating guidelines procedure that was instituted in all offices. While sales representatives dealt with the day-to-day needs of customers, top management was involved in making sales presentations to large accounts.

Services

Despite Metropol's variety of services, supplying unarmed, uniformed security guards accounted for most of their revenue. Their sales revenue breakdown by service type was:

Security guards	90%
Mobile security checks	8
Other (investigation, polygraph testing, retail services, consulting, and education)	2
	100%

Providing security guard services involved more than just sending guards to industrial or office sites. Metropol had to train, pay, uniform, and insure the guards. They also had to supervise and dispatch their people as well as provide reports to their clients.

"We have attempted to provide greater value to our customers than our competitors have," stated Pat. "For example, we have a 24-hour dispatch service while all the other firms use an answering service. There is a $100,000 (annual) difference in cost, but we can respond much faster to any situation. Some customers will say they just consider price in their purchase decision but end up liking and buying the extra service."

Metropol also gave their guards special training on the procedures to follow in the case of such emergencies as bomb threats, hostage takings, and fire evacuations. Again, this was an attempt to differentiate their services from those of other security guard companies.

The mobile security business was contracted out to local firms. This market was not considered to be a growth area, and Metropol did not invest a great of deal of resources in it.

Investigative and polygraph services were contracted out to a couple of ex–RCMP officers. Metropol had maintained these investigators on its staff at one time but found that demand for these services was not great enough to justify having the high-salaried people as full-time employees.

Education programs were another means Metropol used to create added value and increase switching costs for their customers. Pat explained, "We give seminars on such topics as 'The Protection of Proprietary Information' for our clients and even invite some companies we don't currently serve. We want our clients to realize that if they switch security firms they will be losing something of value."

Metropol did not sell hardware products such as fences, alarms, and locks. However, it could arrange the purchase of such equipment for their clients. It was presently considering working in conjunction with a systems engineer so the company would be able to provide a total security package to their customers.

Costs

Metropol divided its costs into two groups, direct and administrative. A typical job had the following cost characteristics:

Direct costs	83–86%
Selling and administrative costs	8–9%
Pre-tax profit margin	4–7%

Given the above figures, cost control was a key success factor for Metropol and the security industry in general. Metropol's margins were, in fact, higher than the industry average of approximately 4 percent. "We use a job-costing process," volunteered Pat. "Every pay period (two weeks) we look at what we made on each job. We consider and analyze every expense item very closely to see if there was any deviation from what was budgeted."

Direct costs included wages, uniforms, bonding, transportation, and supervision. Metropol did a good job of keeping its costs as low or lower than its competitors despite offering a higher level of service. Some of this was a result of economies of scale in purchasing such items as uniforms, achieved because of their comparatively large size. The company also did a superior job in collecting their outstanding receivables within a two-week period.

Pricing

Prices were determined by identifying the direct costs associated with a job, allowing for a contribution to selling and administrative overhead and providing for a profit margin. Consideration was also given to any particular reason there may be for pricing a bid either particularly high or low. "We once bid at very close to our direct cost for a job in a town where we had no competition in order to discourage other firms from entering that market," noted Pat. He also suggested that it was important to anticipate competitors' likely pricing strategy when bidding on a job as well as recognizing that some projects had greater potential for cost overruns.

Promotion

Metropol individually identified the companies in each of their trading areas that were potential clients and concentrated their promotional efforts on that group. In Manitoba, this "club" amounted to about 500 firms.

Once these firms were identified, strategies were developed to either sell to those potential accounts which presently had no security service or to become the logical alternative for those businesses who were using competitive services. "We want to put pressure on these incumbent firms to perform," explained Pat.

Metropol used, among other things, their educational seminars to stress to their clients that they offered superior service. At times, firms using competing security companies were invited as a means of encouraging them to switch to Metropol.

Employees

Metropol employed almost 2,000 people, 1,900 of whom were security guards and 100 who were selling, administrative, or management personnel.

Security guards came principally from three backgrounds: (1) young people (18–25) who could not find other work, (2) older people (50–65) looking for a second career, or (3) ex-military or police personnel who liked the quasi-military nature of the job.

Annual employee turnover in the security guard industry was very high, estimated to be in the vicinity of 100 percent. Metropol's turnover rate was in the same range. Reasons for the high level included a combination of low wages, generally boring work, and a lack of motivation or support from senior management.

"We have some employees who have been with the company for 15 years," Pat pointed out. "However, the wages we pay are based on our billing rate which often only allows for minimum wages to be paid to our employees." Intense competition and clients who wanted to pay a bare minimum for security guard services forced companies to pay their guards the legal minimum wage. This caused high turnover rates which, evidently, did not bother some clients. Other customers, concerned with employee turnover, specified a higher minimum wage rate which the security company had to pay its guards. Pat liked this attitude because it allowed him to pay his people a higher wage and still be competitive.

Metropol's supervisors and customer service representatives (salespeople) did a good job servicing their accounts and handling any crisis that arose. They helped maintain Metropol's reputation as a competent and reliable security company despite the generally poor reputation of the industry.

The Future

Pat turned his attention to the future. He believed that the way business was conducted in the security guard industry would not significantly change in the near future. He did expect the business to become somewhat more professional with guards being trained in formal, standardized programs. The pressure on profit margins was expected to continue and perhaps even intensify as the larger, multinational firms fought for market share and smaller independents struggled for survival. Pat was thinking about how he could use Metropol's present position and reputation in the security guard sector to expand into more profitable segments of the industry or improve the company's general standing within the guard sector. Some of the opportunities he was considering included:

- Geographic expansion
- A focused strategy
- Expanding the range of security products and services offered by the company
- Diversification into other service areas outside the security field
- Serving the consumer home security market

Geographic Expansion

"To be a national company in Canada you need a presence in Southern Ontario," observed Pat. Even though many companies' security needs were handled at the local level, there was considerable potential for a national accounts program. To be involved in providing a national service, a company had to be active in the Toronto area, where most national companies' security decisions were made. In addition, the Ontario market offered substantial local business. Pat explained, "We handle Northern Telecom's security guard needs throughout western Canada, but not in Ontario. Northern Telecom has three times the business volume there as it does in all of the western provinces combined."

There were three ways Metropol could enter the Ontario market: (1) by purchasing a local security firm, (2) by merging with another company, or (3) by bidding on contracts in Ontario and opening up an office once a contract was obtained.

Pat believed that the merger method was the most appealing, since it offered the potential for increased profits with virtually no additional cash investment. He had discussed the possibility with two firms that had head offices in Ontario and were also minor competitors in the Winnipeg, Edmonton, Calgary, and Vancouver markets. The western offices of the merged firm could be closed down, and the business operated under the Metropol name. "The gross margin on their western contracts would go right to the bottom line," suggested Pat, "because all the current Metropol offices could meet their administrative needs and absorb any incremental expenses."

A restricting factor in this strategy was Metropol's limited product/service line. To provide a "complete" security package for any company on a national basis, it was necessary to offer the hardware and ESD packages in addition to the security guards.

A Focused Strategy

This alternative was really a continuation of Metropol's current strategy. Following this approach, Metropol's principal objective would be to become the fastest-growing security guard firm in western Canada, with the highest profit margin and return on equity, the lowest employee turnover, and the most satisfied customers in the business of providing contract, unarmed security personnel. This strategy required an increased emphasis on developing a formal marketing program and increasing the value-added of Metropol's security guard and support services. Tighter control of costs and employee motivation would be critical success factors as would be the need to carefully segment the market and identify the most profitable clients.

The strategy would be designed to match the distinct competencies and resources of Metropol with the needs of the marketplace. Pat believed that while the strategy "sounded good," it would be very difficult to implement. "Even if you offer the highest-quality service you might not get the job," he offered. "Too many contracts, particularly those involving the government sector and Crown corporations, are based solely on price, and simply supplying a higher service level in the provision of security guards is not likely to change that."

Expansion of Security Products and Services

From the customer's point of view, there was an advantage to having one firm coordinate and provide the complete security coverage required by his business; the security system was more effective and efficient. If the customer had to contract with different firms for guards, fences, locks, lights, alarms, and ESDs, there was likely be a lot of overlap and, in some cases, gaps in the overall system. Also, it was likely to be more expensive. Pat considered an investment in the product of hardware equipment much too costly, given his firm's limited resources, but he was investigating the possibility of arranging a deal with a large multinational distributor of security hardware and ESD products.

Pat explained, "We would like to have an exclusive relationship whereby they [large multinationals] would provide us, at wholesale, with all the hardware and ESD equipment we needed on a private-label basis [Metropol brand] and they would train our people. We could offer them our monitoring services and access to new markets." Metropol would package the system, which would include hardware, software, and people in whatever mix its clients needed. The products would be sold to the client or leased on a five-year arrangement.

The expanded product-line strategy would deliver significant benefits to Metropol. Hardware and ESD equipment offered better margins than security guard services and, in some cases, were subject to becoming obsolete. This provided opportunities to sell upgraded systems. For example, television monitoring devices had already gone through several generations of change despite their relatively recent entry into the security product mix. Service contracts to maintain the equipment would provide another source of additional revenue. Finally, the need of these systems for close monitoring and servicing increased the dependence of the customer on Metropol. This higher dependence meant that switching costs for the customer were much higher than with security guard services. This would be especially true if the equipment was leased for a five-year period.

Diversification into Other Service Areas

This alternative would capitalize on Metropol's skills in hiring people for contract-type jobs and administering a payroll. Their current product line could be expanded to include one or all of the following additional services, which could be provided on a contractual basis: secretarial services, nursing care, janitorial services, or landscaping services. The commercial sector would continue to be their primary target market.

Several years ago Metropol got into the commercial cleaning business with poor results. "Businesses such as janitorial and landscaping services are beyond our particular expertise," revealed Pat. "However, we are looking at providing people and handling the payroll for temporary clerical or nursing services. In those cases, we would be taking our established skills to another market." Pat cited Drake International's experience as evidence that the strategy could work. That company went from providing temporary help to the provision of security guards.

The Consumer Market

Another alternative for Metropol would be to expand into the consumer market for security products and services. The major products of interest to residential customers were locks, supplementary lighting, fences, mobile home checks, house sitting, and alarm systems. This segment was growing more slowly than the business sector, but still offered substantial opportunity.

Pat was currently exploring Metropol's opportunities as a franchisor of home alarm systems to the numerous small Canadian alarm system dealers. "We would become the Century 21 of the alarm business," Pat suggested.

The alarm business in Canada was made up of a large number of small independent dealers and a few large multinationals. The "small guys" would buy their alarms from wholesalers in small lots which precluded much discounting. They also had to contract out their alarm monitoring to their competition, the large multinationals, because they could not afford the central station monitoring equipment. In most cases, advertising and financing of installations for customers was too expensive to be carried out on a significant basis.

Pat thought a Metropol alarm franchise offered a number of important strategic advantages to independent alarm dealers: (1) by arranging with a large alarm manufacturer to produce a private-label Metropol brand alarm line, they could pass on volume discounts to their dealers, (2) franchises would have the Metropol name behind them, (3) co-op advertising would provide greater exposure, (4) an arrangement for consumer financing could be established, and (5) Metropol would set up a central monitoring system.

Consideration was also being given to making locksmiths subdealers of Metropol alarm systems. "Normally a customer must call a locksmith and an alarm specialist to secure his home," suggested Pat. "It would be more effective, especially from a selling perspective, if the locksmith could do both."

◼ Conclusion

Pat realized that the alternatives he was considering were not merely incremental changes in Metropol's strategy. In fact, each option represented a distinct direction for the firm's future development. "We have to define our business mission more specifically," Pat thought to himself. "Then we can choose and implement the strategy that best suits that mission."

Mr. Jax Fashion Inc.

It was 6:30 am., Monday, January 16, 1989. Dawn had not yet broken on the Vancouver skyline, and Louis Eisman, president of Mr. Jax Fashion Inc., was sitting at his desk pondering opportunities for future growth. Growth had been an important objective for Eisman and the other principal shareholder, Joseph Segal. Initially, the company had focused on the professional/career women's dresses, suits, and coordinates market, but by 1986 it had virtually saturated its ability to grow within this market segment in Canada. Growth was then sought through the acquisition of four companies: a woollen textile mill and three apparel manufacturing companies. The result of this decade-long expansion was a company that had become the sixth-largest apparel manufacturer in Canada.

In the future, Eisman felt continued growth would require a different approach. A good option appeared to be expansion into the U.S. market. Strong growth was forecast in the women's career/professional market, Mr. Jax's principal market segment, and the recently ratified Free Trade Agreement (FTA) provided an excellent low-tariff environment for expansion into the United States. Yet, Eisman wanted to ensure the appropriate growth strategy was selected. He was confident that, if the right approach was taken, Mr. Jax could become a major international apparel company by the end of the next decade.

The Industry

The apparel industry was divided into a variety of market segments based upon gender, type of garment, and price points. As regards price points, the women's segments ranged from low-priced unexceptional to runway fashion segments. Low-priced segments competed on a low-cost manufacturing capability, while the higher-quality segments tended to compete on design and marketing capabilities. Companies in the higher-priced segments often contracted out manufacturing.

Richard Ivey School of Business
The University of Western Ontario

C. Patrick Woodcock and Professor J. Michael Geringer prepared this case solely to provide material for class discussion. The authors do not intend to illustrate either effective or ineffective handling of a managerial situation. The authors may have disguised certain names and other identifying information to protect confidentiality. © 1991 Ivey Management Services. Case 9-89-M008, version 1992-01-01.

The professional/career women's segment ranged from the medium to medium-high price points. During the late 1970s and early 1980s, this segment had undergone strong growth due to the demographic growth in career-oriented, professional women. In the United States, it had grown by 50 percent annually during the first half of the 1980s, but had slowed to about 20 percent in 1988. Experts predicted that by the mid-1990s, growth would drop to the rate of GNP growth. The U.S. professional/career women's segment was estimated to be $2 billion in 1988. The Canadian market was estimated to be one-tenth this size and growth was expected to emulate the U.S. market. Yet, the exact timing of the slowing of growth was difficult to predict because of extreme cyclicality in the fashion industry. During difficult economic times, women tended to delay purchases, particularly in the mid-priced, fashionable market sectors. Then, during times of economic prosperity, women who would not otherwise be able to afford fashionable items tended to have more resources to devote to these items.

Competition

Some of the more prominent Canada-based companies competing in the professional/career women's segment included:

- *Jones New York of Canada,* a marketing subsidiary of a U.S.-based fashion company that was thought to share the leadership position with Mr. Jax in the Canadian professional/career women's market. The company focused exclusively on marketing clothes to this market segment. Manufacturing was contracted out to Asian companies.

- *The Monaco Group,* which had become a major Canadian designer and retailer of men's and women's fashions during the 1980s. By 1988, the company had sales of $21 million and a rate of return on capital of over 20 percent. The company designed their own fashion lines, which were merchandised through their own retail outlets as well as major department stores. Manufacturing was contracted out to Asian companies. Recently, the company had been purchased by Dylex Inc., a large Canada-based retail conglomerate with 2,000 retail apparel stores located in both Canada and the United States.

- *Nygard International Ltd.,* with revenues of over $200 million, which was Canada's largest apparel manufacturer. Approximately one-third of their sales and production were located in the United States. This company had historically focused on lower-priced clothing, but they had hired away Mr. Jax's former designer to create the Peter Nygard Signature Collection, a fashion line aimed at the professional/career women's market. This new line had been out for only six months, and sales were rumoured to be moderate.

Additional competition in this Canadian segment included a wide variety of U.S. and European imports. These companies generally manufactured garments in Asia and marketed them in Canada through independent Canadian sales agents. Historically, most had concentrated their marketing resources on the rapidly growing U.S. market, yet many had captured a significant share of the

Canadian market on the basis of strong international brand recognition. Prominent U.S.-based competitors included:

- *Liz Claiborne,* which, as the originator of the professional/career women's fashion look, had utilized their first-mover advantage to build a dominant position in this segment. This company, started in 1976, grew tremendously during the late 1970s and early 1980s, and by 1988 they had sales in excess of US$1.2 billion, or nearly two-thirds of the market. Claiborne generally competed on price and brand recognition, a strategy copied by many of the larger companies which had begun to compete in this segment. To keep prices low, Claiborne contracted out manufacturing to low-cost manufacturers, 85 percent of which were Asian. The company's large size allowed them to wield considerable influence over these manufacturing relationships. Recently, the company had diversified into retailing.

- *J. H. Collectibles,* a Milwaukee-based company with sales of US$200 million, which had one of the more unique strategies in this segment. They produced slightly upscale products which emphasized an English country-sporting look. Using facilities in Wisconsin and Missouri, they were the only company to both manufacture all of their products in-house and to produce all of them in the United States. In addition to providing stronger quality control, this strategy enabled J. H. Collectibles to provide very fast delivery service in the United States. Limiting distribution of their product to strong market regions and retailers also enabled them to maintain production at levels estimated to be at or near their plants' capacities.

- *Jones of New York,* the parent company of Jones New York of Canada, which was a major competitor in the U.S. market. In fact, the majority of their US$200 million in sales was derived from this market.

- *Evan-Picone,* a U.S.-based apparel designer and marketer which had become very successful in the slightly older professional/career women's market. This company contracted out their manufacturing, and had annual sales in excess of US$200 million.

In addition, there were myriad other apparel designers, marketers, and manufacturers competing in this segment. They included such companies as Christian Dior, Kasper, Pendleton, Carole Little, Susan Bristol, J. G. Hooke, Ellen Tracy, Anne Klein II, Perry Ellis, Adrienne Vittadini, Tahari, Harve Bernard, Norma Kamali, Philippe Adec, Gianni Sport, Regina Porter, and Herman Geist.

Profitability in this segment had been excellent. According to data from annual reports and financial analyst reports, Liz Claiborne led profitability in the apparel industry with a five-year average return on equity of 56 percent and a 12-month return of 45 percent, and J. H. Collectibles had averaged over 40 percent return on equity during the last five years. This compared to an average return on equity in the overall apparel industry of 12.5 percent in the United States, and 16 percent in Canada during the past five years.

Distribution

The selection and maintenance of retail distribution channels had become an important consideration for apparel manufacturers in the 1980s. The retail industry had gone through a particularly bad year in 1988, although the professional/career women's segment had been relatively profitable. Overall demand had declined, and retail analysts were predicting revenue increases of only 1 to 2 percent in 1989, which paled beside the 6 to 7 percent growth experienced in the mid-1980s. The consensus was that high interest rates, inflation, and somewhat stagnant demand levels, were suppressing overall profitability.

Although initially considered a mild downturn, recent market indicators suggested that this downward trend was relatively stable and long-lasting. Industry analysts had begun to suspect that permanent market changes might be occurring. With baby boomers reaching their childbearing years, further constraints on disposable income might result as this group's consumption patterns reflected increasing emphasis on purchases of homes, or the decision by many women to permanently or temporarily leave the work force to raise their children. In addition, the effects of rampant growth in the number of retail outlets during the 1980s were beginning to take their toll. Vicious competition had been eroding margins at the retailer level, and the industry appeared to be moving into a period of consolidation. As a result of these developments, a shift in power from the designers to the retailers appeared to be under way.

To counter the retailers' increasing power, some apparel designers had been vertically integrating into retailing. The attractiveness of this option was based on controlling the downstream distribution channel activities, and thus enabling an apparel company to aggressively pursue increased market share. The principal components for success in the retail apparel industry were location, brand-awareness, and superior purchasing skills. The apparel companies which had integrated successfully into retailing were the more market-oriented firms, such as Benetton and Esprit.

The Free Trade Agreement

Historically, developed nations had protected their textile and clothing industries through the imposition of relatively high tariffs and import quotas. Tariffs for apparel imported into Canada averaged 24.5 percent, and 22.5 percent into the United States. Tariffs for worsted woollen fabrics, one of the principal ingredients for Mr. Jax's products, were 40 percent into Canada, and 22.5 percent into the United States. Import quotas were used to further limit the ability of developing country manufacturers to export to either country. Despite these obstacles, Canadian apparel imports had grown from 20 percent to 30 percent of total shipments during the 1980s, most of which came from developing countries. Shipments into Canada from the United States represented an estimated $200 million in 1988, while Canadian manufacturers exported approximately $70 million to the United States.

The FTA would alter trade restrictions in North America considerably. Over the next ten years, all clothing and textile tariffs between the two countries would be eliminated, but stringent "rules of origin" would apply. To qualify, goods not only had to be manufactured in North America, but they also had to utilize raw materials (i.e., yarn, in the case of textiles, and fabric, in the case of apparel) manufactured in North America. Unfortunately, these "rules of origin" favoured U.S. apparel manufacturers, as 85 percent of the textiles they used were sourced in the United States, while Canadian manufacturers utilized mostly imported textiles. To ameliorate this disadvantage, a clause was appended to the agreement which allowed Canadians to export $500 million worth of apparel annually into the United States that was exempt from the "rules of origin" but would have a 50 percent Canadian value-added content. There was much speculation as to how this exemption would be allocated when, in approximately five years, exports were projected to exceed the exemption limit. Experts expected the companies successfully demonstrating their ability to export into the United States would have first rights to these exceptions.

Many industry experts had contemplated the consequences of the FTA. There was some agreement that in the short term, the FTA would most severely impact the lower-priced apparel segments in Canada because of the economies of scale which existed in the U.S. market (the average U.S. apparel manufacturer was ten times larger than its Canadian counterpart). Yet, long-term prospects for all segments were restrained, because the industry was slowly being pressured by the Canadian government to become internationally competitive. The question was when international negotiations would eliminate more of the protection afforded to the industry. It was with this concern in mind that Eisman had been continuously pushing the company to become a major international fashion designer and manufacturer.

Overall, Eisman considered the FTA a mixed blessing. Competition in Canada would increase moderately over time, but he felt that the lower tariff rates and the company's high-quality, in-house woollen mill presented an excellent opportunity for expansion into the U.S. market.

Mr. Jax Fashions

In 1979, a venture capital company owned by Joseph Segal acquired a sleepy Vancouver-based apparel manufacturer having $3 million in sales, 70 percent of which was in men's wear. Segal immediately recruited Louis Eisman, a well-known women's fashion executive, who proceeded to drop the men's clothing line, and aggressively refocus the company on the career/professional women's market segment.

Eisman appreciated the importance of fashion, and for the first three years he designed all of the new lines. In 1982, he recruited an up-and-coming young Canadian fashion designer, yet he continued to influence the direction of designs considerably. He travelled to Europe for approximately two months annually to review European trends and procure quality fabrics appropriate for the upcoming season. He personally reviewed all designs. The combined women's fashion knowledge and designing abilities provided Mr. Jax with a high-quality, classically designed product which differentiated it from most other Canadian competition. In 1989, the designer resigned, and Eisman recruited a New York–based fashion designer, Ron Leal. Leal had excellent experience in several large U.S. design houses and, unlike the previous de-signer, he brought considerable U.S. market experience and presence.

Eisman's energy and drive were also critical in establishing the merchandising and distribution network. He personally developed relationships with many of the major retailers. He hired and developed sales agents and in-house sales staff, and in 1983 recruited Jackie Clabon, who subsequently became vice-president, marketing and sales. The sales staff were considered to be some of the best in the industry. Clabon's extensive Canadian sales and merchandising experience, com-bined with Eisman's design and marketing strength, provided Mr. Jax with con-siderable ability in these critical activities.

Initially, acceptance by Eastern fashion buyers was cool. The fashion "estab-lishment" was highly skeptical of this new Vancouver-based apparel designer and manufacturer. Thus, Eisman focused on smaller independent retail stores, which were more easily swayed in their purchasing decisions. As Mr. Jax gained a reputation for high quality, classic design, and excellent service, larger retail chains started to place orders. By 1988, Mr. Jax's products were sold in over 400 department and specialty stores across Canada. Major customers in-cluded The Bay, Eaton's, Holt Renfrew, and Simpson's and, although initial marketing efforts had been aimed at the smaller retailer, the majority of Mr. Jax's sales were now to the larger retail chains. The apparel lines were sold through a combination of sales agents and in-house salespersons. Ontario and Quebec accounted for 72 percent of sales. In addition, two retail stores had re-cently been established in Vancouver and Seattle; the Vancouver store was very profitable, but the Seattle store was very unprofitable. Industry observers had suggested a number of factors to explain the two stores' performance differ-ences. These factors included increased competition in U.S. metropolitan areas due to increased market density, lower levels of regulation and other entry barriers, greater product selection, and more timely fashion trend shifts com-pared to the Canadian market, which often exhibited lags in fashion develop-ments of six months or more. Mr. Jax also had a local presence in Vancouver, which was believed to have helped their store by way of reputation, ancillary promotions, and easier access to skilled resources.

Many industry experts felt that Mr. Jax's product line success could be at-tributed directly to Eisman. He was known for his energy and brashness, as well as his creativity and knowledge of the women's fashion market. In his prior merchandising and marketing experience, he had developed an intuitive skill for the capricious women's apparel market. This industry was often considered to be one of instinct rather than rationality. Eisman was particularly good at design, merchandising, and marketing (Exhibit 1). He worked very closely with these departments, often getting involved in the smallest details. As Eisman said, "It is the details that make the difference in our business." Al-though Eisman concentrated a great deal of his effort and time on these func-tions, he also attempted to provide guidance to production. The production function had been important in providing the service advantage, particularly in terms of delivery time, which Mr. Jax held over imports. By 1988, Mr. Jax's professional/career women's fashion lines accounted for $25 million in revenues and $3 million in net income (Exhibit 2).

EXHIBIT I   **Eisman Helping in a Promotional Photo Session**

Diversification Through Acquisitions

In 1986, Segal and Eisman took Mr. Jax public, raising in excess of $17 million although they both retained one-third equity ownership. The newly raised capital was used to diversify growth through the acquisition of four semi-related companies.

Surrey Classics Manufacturing Ltd., a family-owned Vancouver-based firm, was purchased in 1986 for $2 million. This company was principally a manufacturer of lower-priced women's apparel and coats. The acquisition was initially made with the objective of keeping the company an autonomous unit. However, the previous owner and his management team adapted poorly to their position within the Mr. Jax organization and, upon expiration of their non-competition clauses, they resigned and started a competing company. Unfortunately, sales began to decline rapidly because of this new competition and the absence of managerial talent. To stem the losses, a variety of designers were hired under contract. However, Surrey's poor cash flow could not support the required promotional campaigns and the new fashion lines faired poorly, resulting in mounting operating losses.

EXHIBIT 2

INCOME STATEMENT
(000s)

	1981	1982	1983	1984	1985	1986	1987 (9 months)	1988
Sales	4,592	4,315	5,472	7,666	13,018	24,705	53,391	72,027
Cost of sales	2,875	2,803	3,404	4,797	7,885	14,667	38,165	49,558
Gross profit	1,717	1,512	2,068	2,869	5,133	10,038	15,226	22,469
Selling and general administration	1,172	1,117	1,458	1,898	2,434	4,530	9,071	18,175
Income from operations	545	395	610	971	2,699	5,508	6,155	4,294
Other income	22	25	25	10	16	564	418	117
Loss from discontinued operations								(554)
Income before taxes	567	420	635	981	2,715	6,072	6,573	3,857
Income taxes:								
Current	150	194	285	432	1,251	2,874	2,746	1,825
Deferred	47	2	(5)	28	24	57	245	(195)
Net income	370	224	355	521	1,440	3,141	3,582	2,227
Share price range						$7.5–11	$8–18	$7.5–14

Note: In 1987, the accounting year-end was changed from February 1988 to November 1987. This made the 1987 accounting year nine months in duration.

BALANCE SHEET
(000s)

Assets	1981	1982	1983	1984	1985	1986	1987	1988
Current assets:								
Short-term investments	—	—	—	—	—	5,027	1,794	495
Accounts receivable	709	874	961	1,697	2,974	6,430	16,133	14,923
Inventories	464	474	684	736	1,431	3,026	15,431	16,914
Prepaid expenses	11	15	20	22	201	398	404	293
Income taxes recoverable	—	—	—	—	—	—	—	1,074
Property, plant, and equipment	318	349	424	572	795	4,042	7,789	13,645
Other assets	—	—	—	—	—	273	526	513
TOTAL ASSETS	1,502	1,712	2,089	3,027	5,401	22,196	42,077	47,857
Liabilities								
Current liabilities:								
Bank indebtness	129	356	114	351	579	575	1,788	4,729
Accounts payable	490	435	678	963	1,494	3,100	4,893	6,934
Income taxes payable	126	58	86	153	809	1,047	546	
Deferred taxes	84	86	81	109	133	217	462	267
Shareholder equity:								
Share equity	127	7	13	5	4	12,252	26,577	26,577
Retained earnings	546	770	1,125	1,446	2,347	5,005	7,811	9,350
TOTAL LIABILITIES	1,502	1,712	2,097	3,027	5,401	22,196	42,077	47,857

Note: Years 1981 to 1984 were estimated from change in financial position statements.

In late 1988, Eisman reassigned Mr. Jax's vice-president, finance, as interim manager of Surrey Classics. As Eisman stated, "The company needed a manager who knew the financial priorities in the industry and could maximize the effectiveness of the company's productive capacity." Several administrative functions were transferred to Mr. Jax, including design, pattern making, sizing, and scaling operations. Marketing and production continued to be independent operations housed in a leased facility just outside of Vancouver. Surrey Classics now produced a diversified product line which included Highland Queen, a licensed older-women's line of woollen apparel, and Jaki Petite, a Mr. Jax fashion line patterned for smaller women. During this turnaround, Eisman himself provided the required industry-specific management skills, which demanded a considerable amount of his time and attention. Eisman kept in daily contact and was involved in most major decisions. During this time Surrey's revenues had declined from $12 million in 1986 to $10.8 million in 1988, and net income had dropped from $100,000 in 1986 to a loss of approximately $2 million in 1988. Eisman felt that, in the next two years, Surrey's operations would have to be further rationalized into Mr. Jax's to save on overhead costs.

West Coast Woollen Mills Ltd. was a 40-year-old, family-owned, Vancouver-based worsted woollen mill. Mr. Jax acquired the company for $2.2 million in 1987. Eisman was able to retain most of the previous management, all of whom had skills quite unique to the industry. West Coast marketed fabric to customers across Canada. In 1986, its sales were $5 million, profits were nil, and its estimated capacity was $10 million annually. The company was the smallest of three worsted woollen mills in Canada, and in the United States there were about 18 worsted woollen manufacturers, several being divisions of the world's largest textile manufacturing companies.

Both Mr. Jax and West Coast had benefited from this acquisition. The affiliation allowed Mr. Jax to obtain control of fabric production scheduling, design, and quality. In particular, Mr. Jax had been able to significantly reduce order lead times for fabric produced at this subsidiary, although the effects of this on West Coast had not been studied. West Coast benefited from increased capital funding which allowed it to invest in new equipment and technology, both important attributes in such a capital-intensive industry. These investments supported the company's long-term strategic objective of becoming the highest-quality, most design-conscious worsted woollen mill in North America. This objective had already been reached in Canada.

Mr. Jax was presently fulfilling 30 to 40 percent of its textile demands through West Coast. The remainder was being sourced in Europe. By 1988, West Coast's revenues were $6.5 million and profitability was at the breakeven point.

Olympic Pant and Sportswear Co. Ltd. and *Canadian Sportswear Co. Ltd.,* both privately owned companies, were acquired by Mr. Jax in 1987 for $18.3 million. The former management, excluding owners, was retained in both of these Winnipeg-based companies.

Olympic manufactured lower-priced men's and boys' pants and outerwear as well as some women's sportswear. Canadian Sportswear manufactured low-priced women's and girls' outerwear and coats. Canadian Sportswear was also a certified apparel supplier to the Canadian Armed Forces and, although these types of sales made up a minority of their revenue base, such a certification provided the company with a small but protected market niche. The disparity in target markets and locations between these companies and Mr. Jax dictated that they operate largely independently. The expected synergies were limited to a few corporate administrative functions such as finance and systems management.

Combined revenues for these companies had declined from $35 million in 1986 to $30 million in 1988. Both of these companies had remained profitable during this period, although profits had declined. In 1988, combined net income was $1.2 million. Management blamed declining revenues on increased competition and a shortage of management because of the previous owners' retirement.

The Corporation's Present Situation

Diversification had provided the company with excellent growth, but it had also created problems. The most serious was the lack of management control over the now-diversified structure (Exhibit 3). By 1988, it had become quite clear that without the entrepreneurial control and drive of the previous owners, the companies were not as successful as they had been prior to their acquisition. Therefore, in late 1988, Eisman recruited a new CFO, Judith Madill, to coordinate a corporate control consolidation program. Madill had extensive accounting and corporate reorganization experience, but had limited operating experience in an entrepreneurial environment such as the fashion industry. Madill suggested that corporate personnel, financial, and systems management departments be established to integrate and aid in the management of the subsidiaries. Eisman was not completely convinced this was the right approach. He had always maintained that one of Mr. Jax's competitive strengths was its flexibility and rapid response time. He thought increased administrative overhead would restrict this entrepreneurial ability, and that extra costs would severely restrict future expansion opportunities. Thus, he had limited the administrative expansion to two industrial accountants for the next year.

Consolidation was also occurring in the existing organization. Eisman was trying to recruit a vice-president of production. Mr. Jax had never officially had such a position and, unfortunately, recruiting a suitable candidate was proving to be difficult. There were relatively few experienced apparel manufacturing executives in North America. Furthermore, Vancouver was not an attractive place for fashion executives, because, not being a fashion centre, it would isolate him or her from future employment opportunities. Higher salaries, as well as lower taxes, tended to keep qualified individuals in the United States. Yet, a manager of production was badly needed to coordinate the internal production consolidation program.

Originally, production had been located in an old 22,000 square foot (2,044 square metre) facility. By 1986, it had grown to 48,000 square feet located in four buildings throughout Vancouver. Production flow encompassed the typical apparel industry operational tasks (Exhibit 4). However, the division of

EXHIBIT 3   Organizational Chart

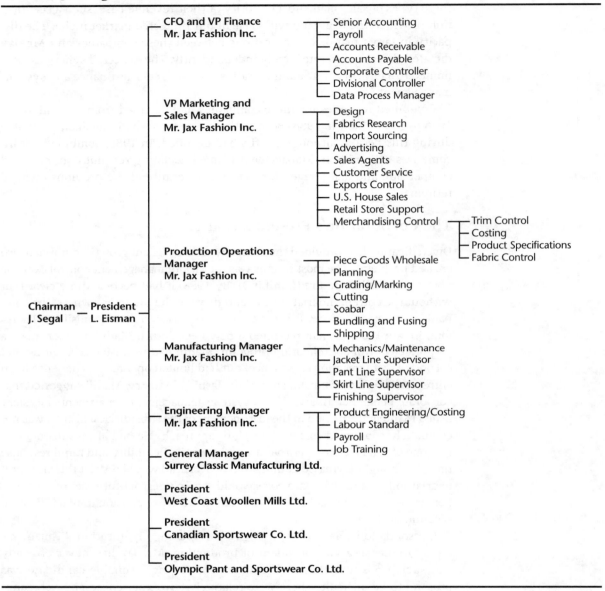

tasks between buildings made production planning and scheduling very difficult. Production problems slowly accumulated between 1986 and 1988. The
problems not only restricted capacity, but also caused customer service to deteriorate from an excellent shipment rate of approximately 95 percent of orders
to recently being sometimes below the industry average of 75 percent. Mr. Jax's
ability to ship had been a key to their growth strategy in Canada. Normally,
apparel manufacturers met between 70 percent and 80 percent of their orders,
but Mr. Jax had built a reputation for shipping more than 90 percent of orders.

Consolidation had begun in the latter part of 1987. An old building in downtown Vancouver was acquired and renovated. The facility incorporated some

EXHIBIT 4   Production Flowchart

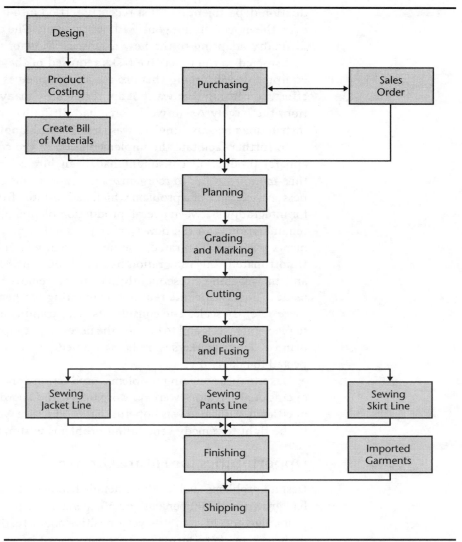

of the most modern production equipment available. In total, the company had spent approximately $3.5 million on upgrading production technology. Equipment in the new facility included a $220,000 Gerber automatic cloth cutting machine to improve efficiency and reduce waste; $300,000 of modern sewing equipment to improve productivity and production capacity; a $200,000 Gerber production moving system to automatically move work to appropriate workstations as required; and a computerized design assistance system to integrate the above equipment (i.e., tracking in-process inventory, scheduling, planning, and arranging and sizing cloth patterns for cutting). The objectives of these investments were to lower labour content, improve production capacity, and reduce the time required to produce a garment.

In the last quarter of 1988, Mr. Jax had moved into this new head office facility. The building, which was renovated by one of Italy's leading architects, represented a design marvel with its skylights and soaring atriums. The production department had just recently settled into its expansive space. However, the move had not gone without incident. The equipment operators had difficulty adapting to the new machines. Most of the workers had become accustomed to the repetitive tasks required of the old technology. The new equipment was forcing them to retrain themselves and required additional effort, something that was not appreciated by many of the workers. In addition, the largely Asian work force had difficulty understanding retraining instructions because English was their second language.

To further facilitate the implementation of the consolidation program, an apparel production consultant had been hired. The consultant was using time-motion studies to reorganize and improve task efficiency and effectiveness. An example of a problem which had resulted from the move was the need for integration between overall production planning, task assignment, worker remuneration, and the new Gerber production moving system. If these elements were not integrated, the new system would in fact slow production. Unfortunately, this integration had not been considered until after the move, and the machine subsequently had to be removed until adjustments were made. The adjustments required converting workers from a salary base to a piece-rate pay scale. The consultants were training all the workers to convert to piece-rate work and to operate the necessary equipment in the most efficient manner. Three workers were being trained per week. The conversion was expected to take two years.

Despite these ongoing problems, production appeared to be improving and operational activities were now organized and coordinated with some degree of efficiency. Eisman was hopeful that production would gain the upper hand in the fight to remedy scheduling problems within the next six months.

Opportunities for Future Growth

Despite problems such as those detailed above, Mr. Jax's revenues and profits had grown by 1,500 percent and 500 percent, respectively, over the past eight years. Further, Eisman was very positive about further growth opportunities in the U.S. market. During the past two years, Eisman had tested the Dallas and New York markets. Local sales agents had carried the Mr. Jax fashion line, and 1988 revenues had grown to US$1 million, the majority of which had come from Dallas. Followup research revealed that retail purchasers liked the "classical European styling combined with the North American flair."

This initial success had been inspiring, but it had also exposed Eisman to the difficulties of entering the highly competitive U.S. market. In particular, attaining good sales representation and excellent service, both of which were demanded by U.S. retailers, would be difficult. Securing first-class sales representation required having either a strong market presence or a promising promotional program. In addition, Mr. Jax had found U.S. retailers to be extremely onerous in their service demands. These demands were generally a result of the more competitive retail environment. Demands were particularly stringent for smaller apparel suppliers because of their nominal selling power.

These demands ranged from very low wholesale prices to extremely fast order filling and restocking requirements. Eisman recognized that Mr. Jax would have to establish a focused, coordinated, and aggressive marketing campaign to achieve its desired objectives in this market.

Eisman had studied two alternative approaches to entering the U.S. market. One approach involved establishing a retailing chain, while the other involved starting a U.S.-based wholesale distribution subsidiary responsible for managing the aggressive promotional and sales campaign required.

Establishing a retail chain would require both new capital and skills. Capital costs, including leasehold improvements and inventory, would be initially very high, and an administrative infrastructure as well as a distribution and product inventorying system would have to be developed. Yet, starting a retail chain did have benefits. The retail approach would provide controllability, visibility, and rapid market penetration. It was the approach taken by many of the aggressive apparel companies in the women's professional/career market segment, such as Liz Claiborne, Benetton, and Esprit.

Furthermore, Mr. Jax's marketing strength fit well with this approach. It was estimated that the initial capital required would be about $10 million to open the first 30 stores, and then cost $300,000 per outlet thereafter. Sales revenues would grow to between $300,000 and $750,000 per outlet, depending upon the location, after two to five years. Operating margins on apparel stores averaged slightly less than 10 percent. Experts felt that within five years the company could possibly open 45 outlets; 5 the first year, and 10 each year thereafter. In summary, this option would entail the greatest financial risk, but it would also have the greatest potential return.

The alternative approach was to establish a U.S. distribution subsidiary. This alternative would require capital and more of the same skills the company had developed in Canada. In general, the company would have to set up one or more showrooms throughout the United States. The location of the showrooms would be critical to the approach eventually implemented. Exhibit 5 illustrates regional apparel buying patterns in North America.

A wholesale distribution approach could be carried out in one of two ways: either on a regional or on a national basis. A regional approach would involve focusing on the smaller regional retail stores. These stores tended to attract less competitive attention because of the higher sales expense-to-revenue ratio inherent in servicing these accounts. The approach required the new distributor to provide good-quality fashion lines, and service the accounts in a better manner than established suppliers. An advantage to this approach was that regional retailers demanded fewer and smaller price concessions compared to the larger national chains. The obstacles to this approach included the large sales force required and the superior service capability. Even though Mr. Jax had utilized this strategy successfully in Canada, success was not assured in the United States, because of the very competitive environment. These factors made this approach difficult to implement and slow relative to other approaches. Experts estimated fixed costs to average $1 million annually per region, of which 75 percent would be advertising and 25 percent other promotional costs. Additional operating costs would consist of sales commissions (7 percent of

EXHIBIT 5   North American Apparel Consumption by Region

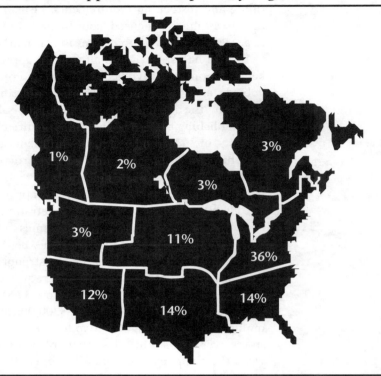

Source: U.S. and Canadian governments.

sales) and administrative overhead costs (see below). Revenues would be dependent upon many factors, but an initial growth rate of $1 million annually within each region was considered attainable over the next five years. In summary, this approach would minimize Mr. Jax's risk exposure, but it would also minimize the short-term opportunities.

The national approach was also a viable option. The greatest challenge in a national strategy would be the difficulty in penetrating well-established buyer/seller relationships. Floor space was expensive, and national chains and department stores tended to buy conservatively, sticking with the more reputable suppliers who they knew could produce a saleable product and service large orders. They also tended to demand low prices and rapid reorder terms. In summary, the national approach provided significant entry barriers, but it also provided the greatest potential for market share growth. Clearly, if economies of scale and competitive advantage in the larger North American context were the desired goals, this had to be the eventual strategy.

The principal costs of this approach would be the advertising and promotional expenses. National apparel companies had advertising expenditures of many millions of dollars. In discussions with Eisman, industry advertising executives had recommended an advertising expenditure of between $3 and $5 million annually in the first three years and then, if successful, increasing it by $1 million annually in the next two successive years. Additional operating costs would be required for sales commissions (7 percent of sales) and administrative overhead (see below). The results of this approach were very uncertain and two outcomes were possible. If the approach was successful, Eisman expected that one or two accounts grossing $1 to $2 million annually could be captured in the first two years. Eisman then felt the sales would expand to about $5 million in the third year, and increase by $5 million annually for the next two successive years. However, if the expected quality, design, or service requirements were not sustained, sales would probably decline in the third year to that of the first year and then virtually disappear thereafter.

Both the national and regional approaches would require an infrastructure. Depending upon the approach taken, the U.S. head office could be located in a number of places. If a national approach was taken, Mr. Jax would have to locate in one of the major U.S. apparel centres (e.g., New York or California). Eisman estimated that the national approach would require a full-time director of U.S. operations immediately, while the regional approach could delay this hiring until required. Such a managing director would require extensive previous experience in the industry, and be both capable and compatible with Mr. Jax's marketing, operating, and strategic approach. To ensure top-quality candidates, Eisman felt that a signing bonus of at least $100,000 would have to be offered. The remuneration would be tied to sales growth and volume, but a continued minimum salary guarantee might be necessary until the sales reached some minimum volume. In addition, a full-time sales manager would be required. Eisman estimated that the subsidiary's administrative overhead expense would be $500,000 if a regional approach was taken, versus $1 million for a national approach in both cases. These overhead costs would then escalate by approximately $500,000 annually for the first five years.

Eisman had now studied the U.S. growth options for over six months. He felt a decision had to be made very soon, otherwise the company would forgo the window of opportunity which existed. The new FTA environment and the growth in the professional/career women's market segment were strong incentives, and delaying a decision would only increase the costs as well as the possibility of failure. Eisman realized the decision was critical to the company's evolution toward its ultimate goal of becoming a major international fashion company. The challenge was deciding which approach to take, as well as the sequencing and timing of the subsequent actions.

Neilson International in Mexico

In January 1993, Howard Bateman, vice-president of international operations for Neilson International, a division of William Neilson Limited, was assessing a recent proposal from Sabritas, a division of Pepsico Foods in Mexico, to launch Neilson's brands in the Mexican market. Neilson, a leading producer of high-quality confectionery products, had grown to achieve a leadership position in the Canadian market and was currently producing Canada's top-selling chocolate bar, Crispy Crunch. In the world chocolate bar market, however, Neilson was dwarfed by major players such as M&M/Mars, Hershey/Lowney and Nestlé-Rowntree. Recognizing their position as a smaller player with fewer resources, in a stagnant domestic market, Neilson in 1990 formed its International Division to develop competitive strategies for their exporting efforts.

Recent attempts to expand into several foreign markets, including the United States, had taught them some valuable lessons. Although it was now evident that they had world-class products to offer to global markets, their competitive performance was being constrained by limited resources. Pepsico's joint branding proposal would allow greater market penetration than Neilson could afford. But at what cost?

Given the decision to pursue international opportunities more aggressively, Bateman's biggest challenge was to determine the distributor relationships Neilson should pursue in order to become a global competitor.

The Chocolate Confectionery Industry[1]

The "confectionery" industry consisted of (1) the "sugar" segment, including all types of sugar confectionery and chewing gum and (2) the "chocolate" segment, which included chocolates and other cocoa-based products. Most large

Gayle Duncan and Shari Ann Wortel prepared this case under the supervision of Professors P. W. Beamish and C. B. Johnston solely to provide material for class discussion. The author does not intend the case to illustrate either effective or ineffective handling of a managerial situation. The author may have disguised certain names and other identifying information to protect confidentiality. © 1995 Ivey Management Services. Case 9-95-G003, version 1995-07-06.

[1] Some information is this section was derived from J. C. Ellert, J. Peter Killing, and Dana Hyde, "Nestlé-Rowntree (A)," in *Business Policy: A Canadian Casebook,* Joseph N. Fry et al. (eds.) (Scarborough, Ont.: Prentice Hall Canada Inc., 1992), pp. 655–667.

IVEY

Richard Ivey School of Business
The University of Western Ontario

chocolate operations were dedicated to two major products, boxed chocolates and bar chocolates, which represented nearly 50 percent of the confectionery industry by volume.

Competition from imports was significant with the majority of products coming from the United States (39 percent). European countries such as Switzerland, Germany, the United Kingdom, and Belgium were also major sources of confectionery, especially for premium products such as boxed chocolates. (See Exhibit 1 for a profile of chocolate-exporting countries.) In order to maintain production volumes and to relieve the burden of fixed costs on operations, Canadian manufacturers used excess capacity to produce goods for exporting. Although nearly all of these products were traditionally exported to the United States, in the early 1990s, the world market had become increasingly more attractive.

Firms in the confectionery industry competed on the basis of brand name products, product quality, and cost of production. Although Canadian producers had the advantage of being able to purchase sugar at the usually-lower world price, savings were offset by the higher prices for dairy ingredients used in products manufactured for domestic consumption. Other commodity ingredients, often experiencing widely fluctuating prices, caused significant variations in manufacturing costs. Producers were reluctant to raise their prices due to the highly elastic demand for chocolate. Consequently, they sometimes reformatted or reformulated their products through size or ingredient changes to sustain margins. Three major product types were manufactured for domestic and export sales:

- *Blocks*. These products are molded blocks of chocolate that are sold by weight and manufactured in a variety of flavours, with or without additional ingredients such as fruit or nuts. Block chocolate was sold primarily in grocery outlets or directly to confectionery manufacturers.

EXHIBIT 1   **World Chocolate Exports, 1990 (% of total)**

	1987	1988	1989	1990
Africa	x1.5	x1.0	x1.1	x0.7
Americas	8.1	9.1	9.2	x9.1
LAIC [1]	2.1	1.9	1.4	x1.4
CACM [2]	0.1	x0.1	x0.1	x0.1
Asia	2.5	3.2	3.4	2.9
Middle East	x0.5	x0.5	x0.7	x0.4
Europe	86.4	85.0	84.2	85.4
EEC (12) [3]	73.3	71.8	71.3	73.5
EFTA [4]	12.5	12.7	12.1	11.5
Oceania	x1.5	1.8	x2.1	x1.8

Note: Figures denoted with an "x" are provisional or estimated.
Source: Adapted from The United Nations, *International Trade Statistics Yearbook,* vol. II, 1990.
[1] LAIC = Latin American Industrialists Association.
[2] CACM = Central American Common Market.
[3] EEC (12) = The 12 nations of the European Economic Community.
[4] EFTA = European Free Trade Association.

(Examples: baking chocolate, Hershey's Chocolate Bar, and Suchard's Toblerone.)

- *Boxed chocolates*. These products included a variety of bite-sized sweets and were generally regarded as "gift" or "occasion" purchases. Sales in grocery outlets tended to be more seasonal than for other chocolate products, with 80 percent sold at Christmas and Easter. Sales in other outlets remained steady year-round. (Examples: Cadbury's Milk Tray, Rowntree's Black Magic, and After Eight.)
- *Countlines*. These were chocolate-covered products sold by count rather than by weight, and were generally referred to by consumers as "chocolate bars." The products varied widely in size, shape, weight, and composition, and had a wider distribution than the other two product types. Most countlines were sold through non-grocery outlets such as convenience and drug stores. (Examples: Neilson's Crispy Crunch, Nestlé-Rowntree's Coffee Crisp, M&M/Mars' Snickers, and Hershey/Lowney's Oh Henry!)

Sweet chocolate was the basic semi-finished product used in the manufacture of block, countline, and boxed chocolate products. Average costs of sweet chocolate for a representative portfolio of all three product types could be broken down as follows:

Raw material	35%	
Packaging	10	
Production	20	
Distribution	5	
Marketing/sales	20	
Trading profit	10	
TOTAL	100%	(of manufacturer's selling price)

For countline products, raw material costs were proportionately lower, because a smaller amount of cocoa was used.

In value terms, more chocolate was consumed than any other manufactured food product in the world. In the late 1980s, the world's eight major markets (representing over 60 percent of the total world chocolate market) consumed nearly three million tonnes with a retail value close to $20 billion. During the 1980s countline was the fastest-growing segment with close to 50 percent of the world chocolate market by volume and an average annual rate of growth of 7 percent. An increasing trend towards indulgence in snack and "comfort" foods strongly suggested that future growth would remain strong.

Competitive Environment

In 1993, chocolate producers in the world included M&M/Mars, Hershey Foods, Cadbury-Schweppes, Jacobs Suchard, Nestlé-Rowntree, United Biscuits, Ferrero, Nabisco, and George Weston Ltd. (Neilson). Chocolate represented varying proportions of these manufacturers' total sales.

For the most part, it was difficult to sustain competitive advantages in manufacturing or product features due to a lack of proprietary technology.

There was also limited potential for new product development since the basic ingredients in countline product manufacturing could only be blended in a limited variety of combinations. This forced an emphasis on competition through distribution and advertising.

Product promotion played a critical role in establishing brand name recognition. Demand was typified by high-impulse and discretionary purchasing behaviour. Since consumers, generally, had a selection of at least three or four favourite brands from which to choose, the biggest challenge facing producers was to create the brand awareness necessary to break into these menus. In recognition of the wide selection of competing brands and the broad range of snack food substitutes available, expenditures for media and trade promotions were considerable. For example, Canadian chocolate bar makers spent more than $30 million for advertising in Canada, in 1992, mostly on television. This was often a barrier to entry for smaller producers.

Major Competitors

M&M/Mars

As the world leader in chocolate confectionery M&M/Mars dominated the countline sector, particularly in North America and Europe, with such famous global brands as Snickers, M&Ms and Milky Way. However, in Canada, in 1992, M&M/Mars held fourth place with an 18.7 percent market share of single bars. (Exhibits 2 and 3 compare Canadian market positions for major competitors.)

M&M/Mars' strategy was to produce high-quality products which were simple to manufacture and which allowed for high volume and automated production processes. They supported their products with heavy advertising and aggressive sales, focusing marketing efforts on strengthening their global brands.

Hershey/Lowney

Hershey's strength in North America was in the block chocolate category in which it held the leading market position. Hershey also supplied export markets in Asia, Australia, Sweden, and Mexico from their chocolate production facilities in Pennsylvania. In Canada, in 1992, Hershey held third place in the countline segment with a 21.6 percent share of the market.

Hershey's strategy was to reduce exposure to volatile cocoa prices by diversifying within the confectionery and snack businesses. By 1987, only 45 percent

EXHIBIT 2   **Single Bars, Canadian Market Share, 1991–1992**

Manufacturer	1992	1991
Neilson	28.1%	29.4%
Nestlé-Rowntree	26.9%	26.2%
Hershey/Lowney	21.6%	21.9%
M&M/Mars	18.7%	19.0%
Others	4.7%	3.5%

Source: Neilson News, Issue 1, 1993.

EXHIBIT 3   **Top Single Bars in Canada, 1991–1992**

Bar	Manufacturer	1992	1991
Crispy Crunch	Neilson	1	1
Coffee Crisp	Nestlé-Rowntree	2	3
Kit Kat	Nestlé-Rowntree	3	2
Mars Bar	M&M/Mars	4	4
Caramilk	Cadbury Schweppes	5	6
Oh Henry!	Hershey/Lowney	6	5
Smarties	Nestlé-Rowntree	7	7
Peanut Butter Cups	Hershey/Lowney	8	8
Mr. Big	Neilson	9	11
Aero	Hershey/Lowney	10	10
Snickers	M&M/Mars	11	9
Crunchie	Cadbury Schweppes	12	12

Source: Neilson News, Issue 1, 1993.

of Hershey's sales came from products with 70 percent or more chocolate content. This was down from 80 percent in 1963.

Cadbury Schweppes

Cadbury was a major world name in chocolate, with a portfolio of brands such as Dairy Milk, Creme Eggs, and Crunchie. Although its main business was in the United Kingdom, it was also a strong competitor in major markets such as Australia and South Africa.

Cadbury Schweppes diversified its product line and expanded into new geographic markets throughout the 1980s. In 1987, Cadbury International sold the Canadian distribution rights for their chocolate products to William Neilson Ltd. Only in Canada were the Cadbury brands incorporated into the Neilson confectionery division under the name Neilson/Cadbury. In 1988, Cadbury sold its U.S. operations to Hershey.

Nestlé-Rowntree

In 1991, chocolate and confectionery made up 16 percent of Nestlé's SFr 50.5 billion revenue, up sharply from only 8 percent in 1987. (In January 1993, 1SFr = Cdn$0.88 = US$0.69.) This was largely a result of their move into the countline sector through the acquisition in 1988 of Rowntree PLC, a leading British manufacturer with strong global brands such as Kit Kat, After Eight and Smarties. In 1990, they also added Baby Ruth and Butterfinger to their portfolio, both "Top 20" brands in the United States. Considering these recent heavy investments to acquire global brands and expertise, it was clear that Nestlé-Rowntree intended to remain a significant player in growing global markets.

◼ Neilson

Company History

William Neilson Ltd. was founded in 1893, when the Neilson family began selling milk and homemade ice cream to the Toronto market. By 1905 they had erected a house and factory at 277 Gladstone Avenue, from which they shipped ice cream as far west as Winnipeg and as far east as Quebec City. Chocolate bar production was initiated to offset the decreased demand for ice cream during the colder winter months and as a way of retaining the skilled labour pool. By 1914, the company was producing 1,000,000 pounds of ice cream and 500,000 pounds of chocolate per year.

William Neilson died in 1915, and the business was handed down to his son Morden, who had been involved since its inception. Between 1924 and 1934, the Jersey Milk, Crispy Crunch, and Malted Milk bars were introduced. Upon the death of Morden Neilson in 1947, the company was sold to George Weston Foods for $4.5 million.

By 1974, Crispy Crunch was the number-one-selling bar in Canada. In 1977, Mr. Big was introduced and became the number one teen bar by 1986. By 1991, the Neilson dairy operations had been moved to a separate location and the ice cream division had been sold to Ault Foods. The Gladstone location continued to be used to manufacture Neilson chocolate and confectionery.

Bateman explained that Neilson's efforts under the direction of the new president, Arthur Soler, had become more competitive in the domestic market over the past three years, through improved customer service and retail merchandising. Significant improvements had already been made in administration and operations. All of these initiatives had assisted in reversing decades of consumer share erosion. As a result, Neilson was now in a position to defend its share of the domestic market and to develop an international business that would enhance shareholder value. (Exhibit 4 outlines the Canadian chocolate confectionery market.)

Neilson's Exporting Efforts

Initial export efforts prior to 1990 were contracted to a local export broker— Grenadier International. The original company objective was to determine "what could be done in foreign markets" using only working capital resources and avoiding capital investments in equipment or new markets.

EXHIBIT 4   **Canadian Confectionery Market, 1993**

	Dollars (millions)	%
Total confectionery category	$1,301.4	100.0
Gum	296.5	22.8
Boxed chocolates	159.7	12.3
Cough drops	77.0	5.9
Rolled candy	61.3	4.7
Bagged chocolates	30.3	2.3
Easter eggs	22.0	1.7
Valentines	9.4	0.7
Lunch pack	3.6	0.3
Countline chocolate bars	641.6	49.3
Total chocolate bar market growth	+ 8%	

Source: Neilson Marketing Department estimates.

Through careful selection of markets on the basis of distributor interest, Grenadier's export manager, Scott Begg, had begun the slow process of introducing Neilson brands into the Far East. The results were impressive. Orders were secured for containers of Mr. Big and Crispy Crunch countlines from local distributors in Korea, Taiwan, and Japan. Canadian Classics boxed chocolates were developed for the vast Japanese gift (*Omiyagi*) market. Total 1993 sales to these markets were projected to be $1.6 million.

For each of these markets, Neilson retained the responsibility for packaging design and product formulation. While distributors offered suggestions as to how products could be improved to suit local tastes, they were not formally obliged to do so. To secure distribution in Taiwan, Neilson had agreed to launch the Mr. Big bar under the distributor's private brand name "Bang Bang" which was expected to generate a favourable impression with consumers. Although sales were strong, Bateman realized that since consumer loyalty was linked to brand names, the brand equity being generated for Bang Bang, ultimately, would belong to the distributor. This put the distributor in a powerful position from which they were able to place significant downward pressure on operating margins.

Market Evaluation Study

In response to these successful early exporting efforts Bateman began exploring the possible launch of Neilson brands into the United States (discussed later). With limited working capital and numerous export opportunities, it became obvious to the International Division that some kind of formal strategy was required to evaluate and to compare these new markets.

Accordingly, a set of weighted criteria was developed during the summer of 1992 to evaluate countries that were being considered by the International Division. (See Exhibit 5 for a profile of the world's major chocolate importers.) The study was intended to provide a standard means of evaluating potential markets. Resources could then be allocated among those markets that

EXHIBIT 5   **World Chocolate Imports, 1990 (% of total)**

	1987	**1988**	**1989**	**1990**
Africa	x0.7	x0.7	x0.7	x0.7
Americas	x15.6	x15.0	x13.9	x13.2
LAIC [1]	0.2	0.4	1.1	x1.3
CACM [2]	x0.1	x0.1	x0.1	x0.1
Asia	ll.7	x13.9	x15.6	x12.9
Middle East	x3.5	x3.3	x3.9	x2.8
Europe	70.8	68.9	67.7	71.4
EEC (12) [3]	61.1	59.5	57.7	59.3
EFTA [4]	9.3	9.0	8.9	8.4
Oceania	x1.3	x1.7	x2.1	x1.8

Note: Figures denoted with an "x" are provisional or estimated.
Source: Adapted from The United Nations, *International Trade Statistics Yearbook,* vol. II, 1990.
[1] LAIC = Latin American Industrialists Association.
[2] CACM = Central American Common Market.
[3] EEC (12) = The 12 nations of the European Economic Community.
[4] EFTA = European Free Trade Association.

promised long-term incremental growth and those that were strictly opportunistic. While the revenues from opportunistic markets would contribute to the fixed costs of domestic production, the long-term efforts could be pursued for more strategic reasons. By the end of the summer, the study had been applied to 13 international markets, including the United States. (See Exhibit 6 for a summary of this study.)

Meanwhile, Grenadier had added Hong Kong/China, Singapore, and New Zealand to Neilson's portfolio of export markets, and Bateman had contracted a second local broker, CANCON Corp. Ltd, to initiate sales to the Middle East. By the end of 1992, the International Division comprised nine people who had achieved penetration of 11 countries for export sales (see Exhibit 7 for a description of these markets). As of January 1993, market shares in these countries was very small.

EXHIBIT 6   Summary of Criteria for Market Study, 1992

Criterion	Weight	Aus-ralia	China	Kong Hong	Indo-nesia	Japan	Korea	Malay-sia	New Zealand	Singa-pore	Taiwan	Mexico	EEC	U.S.A.
* U.S. countline	—	4	4	4	4	4	4	4	4	4	4	4	4	4
1 Candybar economics	30	20	20	30	20	20	28	20	15	25	15	20	10	10
2 Target market	22	12.5	14	13	15.5	19	15	10	7	9.5	12.5	21	22	22
3 **Competitor dynamics**	20	12	15	8	7.5	11	13.5	10	12	14.5	12	**11**	20	6.5
4 Distribution access	10	9	4	4	3.5	5	6	6.5	9	3.5	7.5	9.5	9	9
5 Industry economics	9	2.5	3.5	6	5.5	2	5	2.5	7	4.5	3	3.5	3.5	4.5
6 Product fit	8	7	6	6	6	3	7.5	7.5	7.5	8	4	8	5	8
7 Payback	5	4	4	1	2.5	4	5	2.5	4	2	2	5	2	1
8 Country dynamics	5	5	1	4	3	5	3.5	4.5	4.5	5	4	3	2	4
TOTAL	109	72	67.5	72	63.5	69	83.5	63.5	66	72	60	81	73.5	65

Due to Neilson/Cadbury's limited resources, it was not feasible to launch the first Western-style brands into new markets. The basic minimum criterion for a given market, therefore, was the presence of major Western industry players (e.g., Mars or Hershey). Countries were then measured on the basis of 8 criteria which were weighted by the International Group according to their perceived importance as determinants of a successful market entry. (See above table.) Each criterion was then subdivided into several elements as defined by the International Group, which allicated the total weighted score accordingly. (See table, right.)

This illustration depicts a single criterion, subdivided and scored for Mexico.

Competitor Dynamics	Score	Mexico
Financial success of other exporters	0–8	5
Nature (passivity) of competition	0–6	2.5
Brand image (vs. price) positioning	0–6	3.5
SCORE/20	/20	11

Source: Company records.

EXHIBIT 7   Neilson Export Markets, 1993

Agent (Commission)	Country	Brands
Grenadier International	Taiwan	Bang Bang
	Japan	Mr. Big, Crispy Crunch, Canadian Classics
	Korea	Mr. Big, Crispy Crunch
	Hong Kong/China	Mr. Big, Crispy Crunch, Canadian Classics
	Singapore	Mr. Big, Crispy Crunch
CANCON Corp. Ltd.	Saudi Arabia	Mr. Big, Crispy Crunch, Malted Milk
	Bahrain	Mr. Big, Crispy Crunch, Malted Milk
	U.A.E.	Mr. Big, Crispy Crunch, Malted Milk
	Kuwait	Mr. Big, Crispy Crunch, Malted Milk
Neilson International	Mexico	Mr. Big, Crispy Crunch, Malted Milk
	United States	Mr. Big, Crispy Crunch, Malted Milk

Source: Company records.

 # The U.S. Experience

In 1991, the American chocolate confectionery market was worth US$5.1 billion wholesale. Neilson had wanted to sneak into this vast market with the intention of quietly selling off excess capacity. However, as Bateman explained, the quiet U.S. launch became a Canadian celebration:

> Next thing we knew, there were bands in the streets, Neilson T-shirts and baseball caps, and newspaper articles and TV specials describing our big U.S. launch!

The publicity greatly increased the pressure to succeed. After careful consideration, Pro Set, a collectible trading card manufacturer and marketer, was selected as a distributor. This relationship developed into a joint venture by which the Neilson Import Division was later appointed distributor of the Pro Set cards in Canada. With an internal sales management team, full distribution and invoicing infrastructures, and a 45-broker national sales network, Pro Set seemed ideally suited to diversify into confectionery products.

Unfortunately, Pro Set quickly proved to be an inadequate partner in this venture. Although they had access to the right outlets, the confectionery-selling task differed significantly from card sales. Confectionery items demanded more sensitive product handling and a greater amount of sales effort by the Pro Set representatives who were used to carrying a self-promoting line.

To compound these difficulties, Pro Set sales plummeted as the trading-card market became oversaturated. Trapped by intense cash flow problems and increasing fixed costs, Pro Set filed for Chapter 11 bankruptcy, leaving Neilson with huge inventory losses and a customer base that associated them with their defunct distributor. Although it was tempting to attribute the U.S. failure to inappropriate partner selection, the United States had also ranked poorly relative to other markets in the criteria study that had just been completed that summer. In addition to their distribution problems, Neilson was at a serious disadvantage due to intense competition from the major industry players in the form of advertising expenditures, trade promotions, and brand proliferation. Faced with duties and a higher cost of production, Neilson was unable to maintain price-competitiveness.

The International Division was now faced with the task of internalizing distribution in the United States, including sales management, broker contact, warehousing, shipping, and collections. Neilson managed to reestablish a limited presence in the American market using several local brokers to target profitable niches. For example, they placed strong emphasis on vending machine sales to increase product trial with minimal advertising. Since consumer purchasing patterns demanded product variety in vending machines, Neilson's presence in this segment was not considered threatening by major competitors.

In the autumn of 1992, as the International Division made the changes necessary to salvage past efforts in the United States, several options for entering the Mexican confectionery market were also being considered.

Mexico

Neilson made the decision to enter the Mexican market late in 1992, prompted by its parent company Weston Foods Ltd.'s own investigations into possible market opportunities which would emerge as a result of the North American Free Trade Agreement (NAFTA). Mexico was an attractive market which scored very highly in the market evaluation study. Due to their favourable demographics (50 percent of the population was within the target age group), Mexico offered huge potential for countline sales. The rapid adoption of American tastes resulted in an increasing demand for U.S. snack foods. With only a limited number of competitors, the untapped demand afforded a window of opportunity for smaller players to enter the market.

Working through the Ontario Ministry of Agriculture and Food (OMAF), Neilson found two potential independent distributors:

- *Grupo Corvi,* a Mexican food manufacturer, operated seven plants and had an extensive sales force reaching local wholesalers. They also had access to a convoluted infrastructure which indirectly supplied an estimated 100,000 street vendor stands or kiosks (known as *tiendas*) representing nearly 70 percent of the Mexican confectionery market. (This informal segment was usually overlooked by marketing research services and competitors alike.) Grupo Corvi currently had no American- or European-style countline products.

- *Grupo Hajj,* a Mexican distributor with some experience in confectionery, offered access to only a small number of retail stores. This limited network made Grupo Hajj relatively unattractive when compared to other distributors. Like Grupo Corvi, this local firm dealt exclusively in Mexican pesos, historically a volatile currency. (In January 1993, 1 peso = $Cdn0.41.)

While considering these distributors, Neilson was approached by Sabritas, the snack food division of Pepsico Foods in Mexico, who felt that there was a strategic fit between their organizations. Although Sabritas had no previous experience handling chocolate confectionery, they had for six years been seeking a product line to round out their portfolio. They were currently each week supplying Frito-Lay-type snacks directly to 450,000 retail stores and *tiendas*. (The trade referred to such extensive customer networks as "numeric distribution.") After listening to the initial proposal, Neilson agreed to give Sabritas three months to conduct research into the Mexican market.

Although the research revealed strong market potential for the Neilson products, Bateman felt that pricing at two pesos (at parity with other American-style brands) would not provide any competitive advantage. Sabritas agreed that a one-peso product, downsized to 40 grams (from a Canadian-U.S. standard of 43–65 grams), would provide an attractive strategy to offer "imported chocolate at Mexican prices."

Proposing a deal significantly different from the relationships offered by the two Mexican distributors, Sabritas intended to market the Mr. Big, Crispy Crunch, and Malted Milk bars as the first brands in the Milch product line. *Milch* was a fictitious word in Spanish, created and owned by Sabritas, and thought to denote goodness and health due to its similarity to the word "milk." Sabritas would offer Neilson 50 percent ownership of the Milch name, in exchange for 50 percent of Neilson's brand names, both of which would appear on each bar. As part of the joint branding agreement, Sabritas would assume all responsibility for advertising, promotion, distribution, and merchandising.

The joint ownership of the brand names would provide Sabritas with brand equity in exchange for building brand awareness through heavy investments in marketing. By delegating responsibility for all marketing efforts to Sabritas, Neilson would be able to compete on a scale not affordable by Canadian standards.

Under the proposal, all Milch chocolate bars would be produced in Canada by Neilson. Neilson would be the exclusive supplier. Ownership of the bars would pass to Sabritas once the finished goods had been shipped. Sabritas in turn would be responsible for all sales to final consumers. Sabritas would be the exclusive distributor. Consumer prices could not be changed without the mutual agreement of Neilson and Sabritas.

Issues

Bateman reflected upon the decision he now faced for the Mexican market. The speed with which Sabritas could help them gain market penetration, their competitive advertising budget, and their "store door access" to nearly a half million retailers were attractive advantages offered by this joint venture proposal. But what were the implications of omitting the Neilson name from their popular chocolate bars? Would they be exposed to problems like those encountered in Taiwan with the Bang Bang launch, especially considering the strength and size of Pepsico Foods?

The alternative was to keep the Neilson name and to launch their brands independently, using one of the national distributors. Unfortunately, limited resources meant that Neilson would develop its presence much more slowly. With countline demand in Mexico growing at 30 percent per year, could they afford to delay? Scott Begg had indicated that early entry was critical in burgeoning markets, since establishing market presence and gaining share were less difficult when undertaken before the major players had dominated the market and "defined the rules of play."

Bateman also questioned their traditional means of evaluating potential markets. Were the criteria considered in the market evaluation study really the key success factors, or were the competitive advantages offered through ventures with distributors more important? If partnerships were necessary, should Neilson continue to rely on independent, national distributors who were interested in adding Neilson brands to their portfolio, or should they pursue strategic partnerships similar to the Sabritas opportunity instead? No matter which distributor was chosen, product quality and handling were of paramount importance. Every chocolate bar reaching consumers, especially first-time buyers, must be of the same freshness and quality as those distributed to Canadian consumers. How could this type of control best be achieved?

CASE 23

A Note on the Malaysian Pewter Industry

May 3, 1994, was another hot and humid afternoon in Kuala Lumpur (KL), the capital city of Malaysia. About five kilometres from the city, several busloads of tourists arrived at the largest pewter factory in Malaysia, reputedly the largest in the world. The factory, operated by Royal Selangor Sdn Bhd[1] (RS), was a major attraction for foreign visitors to KL. At RS, pewter alloy was handcrafted into high-quality, esthetic products such as decorative household utensils, giftware items, and souvenirs. They were sold under the brand name Royal Selangor Pewter (RS Pewter).

At the conclusion of the 20-minute factory tour, visitors at the RS facility could make purchases from among the many products in the showroom. A few visitors, seeing the crowds and knowing that pewter was made mostly of locally abundant tin, could not help wondering whether investment opportunities existed in the Malaysian pewter industry. For them, at issue was the need to assess how attractive the industry was, and whether export opportunities existed.

Historical Perspectives of the Industry

Pewter is an alloy of tin. During the Middle Ages, the composition of pewter ranged from 65 to 75 percent tin, 20 to 30 percent lead, and small amounts of copper. English pewter was then considered the finest pewter, as it contained 75 percent tin and only 2 to 3 percent lead.

The lead content in the pewter alloy caused pewter items to tarnish easily, giving it an unappealing appearance. Lead could also separate easily from the alloy to contaminate drinks or food in pewter containers such as beer mugs, plates, and bowls. The toxic nature of lead caused alarm among pewter consumers and subsequently affected the demand for pewter utensils.

In the 1770s, English pewterers invented a new pewter alloy named Britannia metal which contained tin, copper, and antimony as a replacement for

R. Azimah Ainuddin prepared this case under the supervision of Professor Paul Beamish solely to provide material for class discussion. The authors do not intend to illustrate either effective or ineffective handling of a managerial situation. The authors may have disguised certain names and other identifying information to protect confidentiality. © 1995 Ivey Management Services. Case 9A94M014, version 1995-09-12.

[1] *Sdn Bhd* is an abbreviation for *Sendirian Berhad,* which means "Private Limited."

Richard Ivey School of Business
The University of Western Ontario

lead. This alloy then became the standard pewter alloy. High-quality pewter was set to contain 84 percent tin with variable amounts of antimony and copper. Since tin was abundant in Malaysia, Malaysian pewter was able to exceed the standard by producing finer-quality pewter with 97 percent tin and very small amounts of copper and antimony. Tin used in Malaysian pewter is refined (Malaysian) Straits Tin, which is 99.85 percent pure. Although the tin content determined the quality of pewter, copper and antimony had to be added to make tin, a soft and brittle metal, harder and malleable.

The use of pewter dated back to at least the time of the Roman Empire. Artifacts found in ancient Egyptian tombs indicated the existence of pewter since 1300 B.C. The use of pewter utensils had flourished during medieval Europe. Although these utensils were used initially by the richer households to replace wood and coarse pottery, pewter had then become the most common material suitable for daily use by most households. Some of the most common utensils made of pewter were tankards, plates, bowls, flagons, and spoons.

At that time, pewter guilds were formed to ensure the credibility of the pewterer and his products. The guilds regulated the quality of metal used, checked on prices and wages, and organized apprenticeships. An apprenticeship could last for at least seven years before the apprentice could become a pewterer and set up his own business. A pewterer usually used marks called touches or touchmarks to identify the maker and to guarantee the quality of his work. Pewter guilds were known to have been established in Germany, Sweden, France, and England.

By the end of the 17th century, throughout Europe and America, pewter's popularity as tableware began to decline steadily as new materials such as glass, porcelain, and good-quality earthenware became more favoured. While most pewter items had simple and dull designs, the new materials were more appealing with their brightly coloured and decorative designs. Nevertheless, the pewter industry persisted and pewterers began to manufacture pewter items for decorative purposes. Pewter guilds were replaced by new organizations such as the Association of British Pewter Craftsmen, the Gutegemeinschaft Zinngart of Germany, and the Belgian Pewter Association. In North America, the American Pewter Guild was founded in 1958 to actively promote trade in the region.

Pewter also had a history of use in Japan when it was introduced into the country from China over 1,000 years ago. This was evidenced by a 1,200-year-old pewter piece currently displayed at an ancient treasure house at Nara Perfecture in Japan. During the early days, pewter was a highly valued material used for making utensils for the nobility in the imperial courts. In particular, pewterware was used to keep sake (Japanese wine) warm and the tin content was believed to "soften" the flavour of the wine. A similar belief was prevalent among the German pewter users who said that beer tasted better when drank from a pewter mug.

The Industry in Malaysia

The pewter industry began during the 19th century when Malaysia (then known as Malaya) was ruled by the British. The British had exploited the large tin resources in the country to meet the demand for tin by British industries. Over the years, as the tin industry expanded, Malaysia became the world's largest tin producer until the late 1980s. (See Exhibit 1 for information on the world's tin production.)

Apart from the abundance of the raw tin, there was also a small demand from England for finished pewter products (particularly pewter tankards, wine goblets, and flower vases). The local demand for pewter was almost negligible, because the use of pewter was not in the tradition of the local population. In addition, pewter was not highly regarded, because it was made mostly of tin, a cheap and abundant local resource in the country. Consequently, interest in pewter-making was nonexistent. As well, the skills in pewter-making had always been confined to the pewterer and passed down to family members. Thus the pewter industry could not expand easily.

Among the first pewterers who capitalized on the small demand for Malaysian pewter was an immigrant pewtersmith from China who set up a pewter business in the tin-rich state of Selangor. The Chinese had used pewter items such as incense burners and joss-stick holders, but were limited mostly for ceremonial purposes. The business, established in 1885, was later known as

EXHIBIT 1   World Tin Production

For the past century, about two-thirds of the world's tin production came from Southeast Asia, particularly Indonesia, Malaysia, and Thailand. Tin deposits could also be found in Europe, Australia, Canada, and certain parts of Africa. Tin was first discovered in Brazil in the 1970s, and by 1990 Brazil had become one of the largest tin producers in the world (see table below for a list of tin-producing countries). China and Russia were noted as potential large producers of tin.

In 1985, world tin prices declined by about 50 percent, from an average price of US$11,500 per tonne to US$6,200 per tonne. The decline was the result of a supply glut attributed to a large increase in tin production from Brazil and the release of the U.S. tin stockpile. Tin analysts predicted that tin prices would remain low and would never reach the pre-1985 level.

The 1985 tin crisis led to the closure of tin mines in Malaysia, the world's largest tin producer, when tin prices were too low to support the cost of production. The tin content in Malaysian mines had depleted, making it relatively more costly to extract tin now than in previous years. The average cost of tin production in Malaysia had increased to more than US$6,000 per tonne compared to Brazil whose production cost was estimated at around US$5,000 per tonne. In Indonesia and Thailand, the average costs of tin production were around US$6,000 per tonne but there were still areas in these countries where the cost of tin production could be as low as US$3,000 per tonne.

Estimates of Tin Deposits in Selected Countries

Country	1987–1990 Average (tonnes)
Australia	8,000
Brazil	31,500
Canada	3,500
Germany	3,900
Indonesia	10,700
Malaysia	32,800
Portugal	100
South Africa	1,400
Thailand	16,000
United Kingdom	4,000

Source: IMD & World Economic Forum, *The World Competitiveness Report,* 1992.

Selangor Pewter Sdn Bhd, and today as Royal Selangor Sdn Bhd (RS). It had since become the leading pewter company in the country and synonymous with the Malaysian pewter industry. In 1993, RS captured 75 percent of the Malaysian market and was one of the largest pewter manufacturers in the world.

When the British rule ended in 1957, there was continued demand for Malaysian pewter from the former British residents. Consequently, local pewter companies began exporting their products to England. As these companies gained experience in the export market, they started to explore other markets in Europe, where traditionally, there was a strong demand for pewter. By the 1970s, the pewter industry in Malaysia was export-driven and local companies were producing quality pewter products that met the tastes and preferences of their customers overseas. Locally, pewter was positioned as a high-end gift item.

In 1985, the Malaysian economy was hit by a recession due to its excessive dependence on the export of commodities such as tin, rubber, and palm oil. A ten-year Industrial Master Plan was implemented to diversify into the manufacturing sector. Several industries were identified for development via a pragmatic foreign investment policy. Consequently, there was an influx of foreign companies and expatriates to the country which led to increased demand for pewter products. In 1987, increased living standards and purchasing power among the local population after the recession further boosted the demand for pewter gifts and souvenirs.

The rapid growth of the Malaysian economy in the late 1980s could not, however, overcome the consistent deficits in the country's balance of payments. Consequently, in 1990, the government undertook programs to develop the tourism industry in Malaysia. A "Visit Malaysia Year" campaign in 1990 resulted in a marked increase of tourist arrivals to the country. Tourists had since become a major market for the pewter industry in Malaysia. Tourists were attracted to Malaysian pewter souvenirs because pewter was considered a national heritage and a local handicraft.

In 1993, the retail sales of pewter in Malaysia was estimated at about RM40 million[2] (equal to approximately US$16 million). Although there was an increase in the local demand, there were only six Malaysian companies known to be actively involved in the manufacture of pewter. This included a recent entrant to the industry, JS Pewter Sdn Bhd (JS). The excess demand had encouraged new entrants to the industry but their presence was short-lived. The owner of JS explained:

> At least two other companies established in KL in 1992 had left the industry. Although these companies were knowledgeable about the market, they lacked the skills in pewter-making. Basically, pewter-making is still a handicraft industry that requires skillful hands to ensure high-quality products. In addition, new pewter companies must be able to produce products that are comparable in quality to that of RS pewter and subsequently compete on price. Although buyers tend to be price-sensitive, sometimes they are not willing to give up on quality for a small difference in price.

Exhibit 2 describes the processes involved in making pewter.

---

[2] The Malaysian currency is the Ringgit Malaysia (RM). On December 31, 1993, US$1 = RM2.73.

EXHIBIT 2 The Methods of Making Pewter

There are two main methods of making pewter: casting and spinning. Cast pewter is usually preferred to spun pewter, because it is made from molten pewter and is perceived to be of the best quality. Spun pewter, made from thin pewter sheets, is light and considered to be of lower quality. However, spun pewter is easier to mass-produce than cast pewter and is becoming more popular as improvements in quality, designs, and finishes are made.

Casting

The casting methods commonly used in the Malaysian pewter industry are die casting and centrifugal casting using a rubber mold. The traditional method of pewter-making in Europe is die casting, using a gun-metal (bronze) mold. Pewter companies in Malaysia had instead used steel molds in casting pewter.

In die casting, a pewter maker pours molten pewter from a ladle into a preheated steel mold. Holding the mold at an angle, molten pewter is ladled into the mold as the mold is slowly brought to an upright position. This technique requires skill and experience to know exactly at which angle to hold the mold as the molten pewter is poured. This is to ensure that the molten pewter flows smoothly to obtain a smooth, hardened pewter with minimal rough edges. Although the casting is done by hand, the process takes only a few seconds as the molten pewter inside the mold solidifies very quickly. The hardened pewter is removed from the steel cast and rough edges are scraped and polished. Polishing removes a layer of pewter oxide left on the surface and this process is done using a fine sandpaper or a buffing wheel. The pewter is rotated on a lathe as a thin coating is peeled off the surface of the pewter. This process requires steady hands, as a sharp steel blade is used to peel off the coating while it is rotated.

The different parts of a finished pewter product are cast separately, polished, and then joined by soldering the separate pieces such as handles, spouts, or hinges to a pewter mug or pitcher. Soldering pewter is especially difficult because of its low melting point. This process requires skill and experience to ensure neat joints. In a well-soldered piece, the joints are almost invisible to the naked eye. The final product is then polished with a soft flannel and a dried stone leaf (a wild tropical leaf with fine, abrasive texture) to obtain a satin shine.

Another casting technique used by pewter makers in Malaysia is centrifugal casting. This method uses two halves of a flat circular mold which are clamped together. The upper half of the mold has a central hole from which channels run into cavities which are filled with molten pewter. The mold is rotated at very high speed on a turntable while molten pewter is poured. A few seconds later the pewter hardens and is removed from the mold. This technique has the advantage of using the less expensive rubber mold, but its use is limited to the production of small items only such as figurines and keychains.

Spinning

In this process, a circular pewter alloy sheet is placed in a lathe, then pressure is exerted by a spinning tool and forced into the required shape. This method requires skilled workers to model the metal while it is spinning. It is more efficient than die casting, particularly in making hollow and cylindrical items such as vases, tumblers, and pitchers. The spun product is finished on the lathe by high-speed polishing using a greased mop. Compared to casting, the spinning method is faster, more efficient, and has been used to make some of the cheapest pewter mugs.

◖ The Product

Malaysian pewter companies offered a wide selection of pewter products. In 1993, RS produced more than 1,000 different items ranging from designer pewter collections to pewter sets and small pewter souvenirs.

The esthetic value of pewter seemed to be a very important factor in determining the success of a product. Thus it was common for pewter companies to employ in-house designers to create new designs and improve on the existing ones. For example, RS employed a team of 15 designers to design the company's standard and custom-made products. Investments were also made in engaging well-known designers in other industries such as jewellery and fashion apparel to design pewter collections.

In the early 1970s, RS began to penetrate foreign markets in a planned and aggressive fashion. It took a multidomestic approach in terms of the design of its pewter products. The company developed designs that suited the tastes and preferences of the market within a specific country. For example, wine goblets of the Roemer design were produced for the German market and Oxford-styled goblets for the Australian market. In recent years, although RS continued to produce pewter designs according to cultural tastes, such as the sake sets for the Japanese and the four seasons Oriental design for the Chinese, these products were marketed on a global basis.

RS developed at least four new product lines each year. For example, in 1993, RS introduced the following products: a collection of figurines based on the mythical fantasy of unicorns and sorcerers launched in Australia, Hong Kong, and Singapore; the Meridian Collection for travelling male executives comprising a shaving kit crafted from pewter, a range of pewter desk accessories called the "corporate jungle" featuring letter openers, bookends, and business card holders with animal designs; and a collection created by a Japanese fashion designer comprising pewter plates, picture frames, and trays finished with wood-grain patterns.

Large capital investments in design and product development were beyond the financial capability of the other local companies. Occasionally, these companies would capitalize on RS designs and produce a similar range of products and subsequently compete on price. Others focused on special orders and custom-made designs. A pewterer commented:

> A pewter company could take advantage of a new product design for, at most, six months. Designs can easily be copied by the other companies and vice versa. Unless some new form of technology was used for a particular design of a pewter item, a company could not sustain its advantage based solely on a particular design for a very long period of time.

In response to the demand for pewter souvenirs, the local pewter companies turned to designs reflecting Malaysian culture in the form of local landmarks, people in traditional costumes, and various scenes of Malaysian life. These designs were inscribed on the flat surface of a pewter plate, a keychain, or the handles of a letter opener. There were also pewter figurines of Malaysian people and local landmarks and scenes carved out of pewter.

Pewter Substitutes

A major and continuing challenge faced by Malaysian pewter companies was the threat of substitute products. In place of pewter gifts, a customer could choose a wide range of gift products ranging from hand-crafted jewellery to textiles, electronic gadgets, ceramics, crystal, porcelain, wood-based products, glassware, and earthenware products. Within the fabricated metal product category, pewter had to compete with silver, brass, and even gold and gold-plated products.

Pewter as a Malaysian souvenir was only one of many Malaysian handicrafts which reflected the local culture and national heritage of the country. Malaysian batik, a fabric material handpainted with attractive designs, appealed to many tourists. Batik prices ranged widely, due in part to the fabric used. Batik could be made from relatively cheap cotton material or the best-quality Italian, Chinese, or Korean silk. These batik materials were sewn into traditional dresses, shirts, ties, handkerchiefs, and purses.

On a global perspective, another potential pewter substitute was a pewter-lookalike alloy made of statesmetal which was used by companies in the United States to produce souvenir and gift items. Some of these items, which went under the name Armetelle, looked like pewter, but were much more scratch-resistant. One company, Carson Industries Inc., produced about 100 different items and the product range appeared to be quite similar to that of pewter products offered by most pewter companies: letter openers, picture frames, candle holders, wind chimes, etc. These items were available in gift outlets that carried various other giftware products. At a glance, both retailers and customers could easily be deceived by these products, because they looked very much like pewter especially when they were given a stained, antique finish.

The Pewter Market

The Malaysian market for pewter consisted of several groups: corporate purchasers, tourists, and the gift market. Corporate purchasers included private companies, government agencies, associations, sports and recreation clubs, and non-profit organizations. Engraved pewter plates were popular among corporate purchasers as gifts to foreign visitors and pewter trophies were common as prizes in competitive events.

Increased prosperity among Malaysian companies led to increased demand for high-end gift items. These companies tended to give away high-end gifts and souvenirs to their valued customers. For example, at the launch of a new car model in the local market, the local distributor of a Japanese automobile company switched from plastic to pewter keychain souvenirs for its new car purchasers.

To meet corporate purchasers' demand, prompt delivery, quality, and competitive prices seemed to be the key success factors. As the market leader, RS set the industry standard for quality and price of pewter products. RS was also an efficient producer and paid particular attention to prompt delivery. For a May 1993 special order, RS formed a special team to run additional shifts for several days to meet the delivery of an order of 7,000 tankards within eight days. Smaller companies that offered competitive prices but could not deliver on time would not pose much competition to RS.

Another major market segment in the Malaysian pewter market consisted of tourists and foreign visitors (participants in international conferences and sporting events, and corporate guests). This segment was characterized by impulse buying, although there were some foreign purchasers who had planned their purchase prior to their visit to Malaysia. It was common for foreign visitors to request a visit to the pewter factory or a pewter outlet to make their purchase. They seemed to be aware of the product from sources within their own country. Such visitors usually ended up making large purchases which sometimes required the pewter company to make special shipments back to their home country.

Although there were some items which seemed to be a bargain when bought in Malaysia, the price differences of other pewter items were not significantly large (see Exhibit 3 for a comparison of RS prices in Malaysia and prices of similar items in Canada). Nevertheless, there was a wider selection of items in the RS showrooms in Malaysia compared to the very limited range of RS pewter displayed in gift shops overseas.

Generally, tourists preferred low- to medium-priced pewter souvenirs with cultural motifs to commemorate their visit to Malaysia. Malaysians also purchased such pewter items as gifts for their foreign friends and acquaintances. Among the local population, pewter was positioned as high-end gift items and was popular for special occasions—birthdays, weddings and anniversaries.

The Export Market

Since the 1960s, the export market had been a major one for Malaysian pewter companies. The most common markets among these companies were Singapore, Japan, Australia, and the United States. RS exported about 60 percent of its production directly to 20 countries and about 15 percent more was exported indirectly through foreign visitors.

Although the pewter industry had not been identified as one of the priority industries for development under the Industrial Master Plan, a pewter company could enjoy many privileges provided to any manufacturing concern, in the form of tax allowances for capital expenditure in the expansion of a production facility or in R&D activities.

Additional incentives were available for companies that exported and promoted their products overseas. Incentives in the form of tax deductions were given to companies that incurred expenses for overseas advertising, market research in foreign countries, maintenance of sales offices, and participation in trade or industrial exhibitions. The availability of such incentives, coupled with the high demand for pewter in foreign countries, had encouraged Malaysian pewter companies to emphasize the export market.

EXHIBIT 3   **RS Retail Prices in Malaysia and Canada for Selected Items (in Cdn$)**

Product	Prices in Malaysia	Prices in Canada
Erik Magnusson Collection		
Candlestand	34.00	39.00
Bowl (small)	120.00	125.00
Large coffee pot	207.00	275.00
Gerald Benney Collection		
Bowl (5.75 centimetres high)	37.00	45.00
Coffee pot (122 centilitres)	235.00	275.00
Tankard (45 centilitres)	46.00	85.00
Water goblet (23 centilitres)	30.00	45.00
Hip flask (9.5 centilitres)	44.00	55.00
Sugar bowl (9.5 centimetres high)	55.00	85.00
Vase (15 centimetres high)	22.00	28.00
Vase (20 centimetres high)	27.00	35.00
Picture frame	22.00	32.00

Source: Royal Selangor, retail price lists.

Another factor that induced Malaysian companies to export was the reduced tariff rates resulting from most favoured nation (MFN) status. Consequently, Malaysian pewter were more competitive in certain foreign markets than pewter from countries that did not enjoy the MFN privilege. However, in markets such as Canada, Malaysian pewter would be less competitive than pewter imports from the United States. Even before the implementation of NAFTA, the import duty for American pewter was only 9.1 percent compared to 10.2 percent imposed on Malaysian pewter imports.

RS established sales offices in its major foreign markets, while the smaller companies like JS would usually sell its products on a free-on-board basis. The importer would take the responsibility to make arrangements to ship the products into a particular country and bear the costs of freight and handling and the insurance charges. An importer from Canada explained:

> The easiest way to import 500 pieces of Christmas ornaments, each weighing 20 grams and priced at Cdn$4, from a pewter company in Malaysia is to appoint a broker who makes further arrangements with an agent in Malaysia. The agent picks up the package from the Malaysian producer and has it transported to Canada either by sea or by air. Shipment by sea will take about $3^1/2$ weeks to reach Vancouver but only five days to reach Toronto by air. The costs involved to transport it by air included Cdn$75 for freight and handling charges in Kuala Lumpur, Cdn$55 for airport terminal handling in Toronto, Cdn$80 for customs clearance charges, Cdn$204 for import duty based on a rate of 10.2 percent of Cdn$2,000 and the federal 7 percent Goods and Services Tax charge is added to all goods sold in Canada.

Marketing Practices

Pricing

As the leader in the Malaysian pewter industry, RS set the prices of Malaysian pewter. RS pewter were sold at standard prices throughout the country to maintain the perception of high quality and to ensure that retailers do not undercut prices or give unnecessary discounts. The other pewter companies based their pricing on RS prices and subsequently priced their products slightly lower to ensure a share in the market. This pricing strategy guaranteed their continued existence in the industry. While RS enjoyed large markups, the smaller companies were willing to accept smaller profit margins. In 1993, RS keychains with Malaysian cultural motifs were retail-priced at RM20 while the JS wholesale price was RM10 and retail-priced at RM15. The cost of producing such an item was estimated at only RM6.

In the export markets, RS prices had to be competitive in view of the large variety of products offered by local pewter companies as well as those from other foreign companies. For example, in Canada, an RS pewter photo frame was retail-priced at Cdn$31.95 compared to an equivalent item with almost similar design made by Seagull, a Canadian pewter manufacturer, retail-priced at Cdn$33.95. However, an almost similar pewter item made in Korea was retail-priced at only Cdn$24.95.

A retailer commented:

Pewter is now produced in many countries and not limited to tin-producing countries. In fact, there are pewter companies in Belgium that operate tin mines in African countries to supply the raw material to its manufacturing facility in Belgium. In addition, customers are not too particular about the pewter brand. For example, a customer looking for a letter opener made of pewter would settle for one that is made in Thailand with an antique finish priced at Cdn$29.95 rather than the shiny RS letter opener displayed in a wooden box priced at Cdn$39.95.

Distribution

By the end of 1992, RS had established more than 40 pewter showrooms in the major cities and main towns throughout Malaysia. These places were the best markets because of the large concentration of government agencies, institutions, private companies, and tourist attractions. These showrooms were equipped with engraving facilities and RS employees conducted pewter-making demonstrations for tourists.

At the showrooms, pewter items were displayed on open racks where customers could take a closer look at the design and material. Once a customer decided on an item, a brand-new one would be presented to him/her. Most customers would be amazed to see the difference between the item on display and the fresh new item in the box. Due to constant handling by various customers, the pewter items displayed on open racks tended to lose their lustre and shine unless fingerprints were wiped off immediately. In fact, a special cleaning agent was needed for the long-term maintenance of pewter.

In places within Malaysia where RS had not established its own showroom, the company appointed more than 250 authorized retailers, particularly giftware outlets and book stores, to carry their products. In such outlets, pewter brands other than RS pewter were also available. In these outlets, buyers were able to compare RS pewter with those of the other pewter companies. In comparing the products, price-conscious buyers who were not too concerned over brand image would usually settle for products other than RS pewter.

In foreign markets, RS had established its own representative offices and outlets in Australia, Singapore, Hong Kong, Japan, Switzerland, and Denmark. There were about 2,500 agents and distributors of RS pewter overseas. Currently, many international exclusive shops carried RS pewter. They included Harrods in London, Ilum Bolighus in Denmark, Birks of Canada, Myer of Australia, and Mitsukoshi of Japan. The other Malaysian pewter companies had also ventured into foreign markets in their own small way, mainly through foreign agents.

There was a significant advantage for pewter companies that established their own retail outlets or distributed their products through appointed retailers that sold exclusively the products of a particular pewter company. In general retail outlets, not only was competition intense when pewter products of competing companies were displayed side by side, shelf space available for each company was also very limited.

Promotion

To obtain international exposure, it was common for pewter companies to participate actively in trade shows and exhibitions, particularly in international gift fairs. Numerous fairs were held in major cities all over the world throughout the year: for example, the Toronto Gift Fair, the Birmingham Fair, Formland Fair in Denmark, the Frankfurt International Gift Fair, and the Sydney Gift Fair. Fairs provided new and existing companies the opportunity to promote their products to leading retailers in the giftware industry.

RS had made heavy investments in export promotion by consistent participation in international trade fairs. Since the mid-1980s, RS maintained a permanent stand at the spring and autumn international fairs in Frankfurt, which meant paying an annual rental for about ten days of use in a year when the fair was on. As one RS manager said, "This seems like a very expensive investment but these fairs act as a springboard for our new products. Such commitment also helps to enhance our image as a serious exporter among the international business community."

Participation in trade shows and exhibitions also enabled companies to evaluate their own positions in the industry. Pewter companies took advantage of these occasions to keep up with the designs of their competitors and to seek new ideas in designing their own products.

◼ The Malaysian Pewter Companies

Besides RS, there were four other pewter companies in Malaysia that sold pewter under their own specific brands. These companies were Penang Pewter & Metal Arts Sdn Bhd (Penang pewter), Oriental Pewter Sdn Bhd (Oriental pewter), Zatfee (M) Sdn Bhd (Tumasek pewter), and Selex Corporation (Selwin pewter), a subsidiary of RS. JS, a new pewter company, produced generic pewter items which were custom-made for marketing agents or individual orders.

Apart from RS, the other Malaysian companies were niche players and are less well-known among the Malaysians. They had established their own markets within the locality where they operate. Penang Pewter and Oriental Pewter served markets in the northern states of Peninsular Malaysia (Penang and Perak), JS in Melaka, and Zatfee and Selex in KL and Selangor. These companies had also ventured into the export markets. The following discussion describes RS as the leader in the industry and JS as the new entrant, and gives brief accounts of some of the other Malaysian pewter companies.

Royal Selangor

RS, established more than 100 years ago, operated as a family business with a paid-up capital of RM16 million. The company had grown dramatically in the late 1980s. In 1988, RS profits doubled from RM1.0 million in 1987 to RM2.2 million in 1988. The number doubled again in 1989 when profits jumped to RM4.9 million. In the following years, growth averaged about 14 percent.

RS was a major consumer of local tin, using about 250 tonnes of the commodity annually. RS produced its own pewter alloy by melting tin ingots and adding copper and antimony to the molten metal. In 1993, Malaysia's tin production dropped to 10,000 tonnes compared to an annual production of about 60,000 tonnes in the 1960s. Although RS was a major consumer of tin, the decline in the Malaysian tin industry would not significantly affect the profitability of the company. An RS manager commented, "Even if the tin production in Malaysia declines, tin is readily available from the international commodity market. Furthermore, our products are many times value-added. Thus the price of the commodity has no direct effect on our costs."

RS had positioned itself in the market as a producer of high-quality pewter products. In 1991, the company was conferred the use of the word "Royal" in its name by the ruler of the state of Selangor, where RS was established. According to an RS manager, the name change from Selangor Pewter to Royal Selangor was a move toward exclusivity. RS predicted that over the next 12 years, more than 12 million pieces of its pewter items would be exported to various parts of the world, accounting for about 60 percent of the company's total production. RS pewter was sold in more than 20 countries and had been particularly successful in Europe, Canada, Australia, and Hong Kong. RS had won several international awards for the design and quality of its products and its innovative packaging. In the late 1970s, RS invested in designing unique packaging to accompany the image of its high-quality products.

In 1993, RS employed about 1,000 workers in its pewter factory. The workers were highly skilled in performing specific tasks such as casting the molten pewter, soldering parts of an item together, and creating hammering finishes on pewter mugs. Although RS operated a modern factory, traditional methods of craftsmanship were retained where most of the individual tasks are done by hand.

Industry observers commented that as an established pewter company, RS had invested large amounts of money in training its workers in specific skills. This was to ensure that these workers became more productive as they became more skillful. However, such specialization served two other important purposes. First, specialization helped deter new entrants. Workers specializing in casting would not be skillful enough in the other aspects of pewter-making. Thus it would be difficult for them to take advantage of their skills and entrepreneurial spirit to set up their own pewter business. This had prevented the entry of new competitors into the industry.

Second, because there were very few pewter companies, RS could further ensure its leadership by maintaining a strong bargaining power over its skilled workers. These workers were skillful in a particular craft which had very limited use in the other industries. Thus their mobility was limited to jobs in other pewter companies which might not be able to offer better pay and incentives than RS.

JS Pewter

JS was established in January 1993 by C. Y. Tay and his two brothers. Tay's brothers were former employees of RS. They had worked as pewter makers at RS for more than ten years and had acquired the skills of pewter-making.

With a paid-up capital of RM100,000, JS incurred a loss during its first year of operation. However, Tay was positive that JS would be able to recover its losses in 1994. Tay attributed the losses to JS's lack of experience in the industry. He said, "Last year, we were still new and had to sell cheap and provide better terms to our customers. We are slowly gaining their trust and when we get ourselves established, then we can seek better deals."

Upon entering the industry, JS positioned itself as a niche player by fulfilling small corporate and special orders. Tay believed that JS was filling a gap in the industry by taking jobs which RS would have turned down:

> JS is willing to accept small orders of even fewer than 100 pieces which RS would not be willing to fill. We are not competing for the same business as RS. Our target customers are those who could not afford RS pewter and are not particular about the brand. We use RS's price for a similar item as a guide and price our products 30 to 40 percent lower.

JS operated a factory in Melaka, about 200 kilometres from its sales office in KL. The factory was a rented shop measuring 20 by 50 feet (about 6 by 15 metres). Rental and energy charges amounted to about RM2,000 per month. Other overheads included insurance premium and capital investments on a casting machine costing about RM50,000. JS did not produce its own pewter alloy but purchased pewter bars from local metal-based companies. In 1994, the price of a pewter bar containing 97 percent tin, weighing 4 kilograms, was RM72. Tay said that the price of pewter bars had not changed much since he ventured into the business.

JS used the less expensive rubber mold production process. Since JS served specific orders, the rubber mold could be discarded once an order had been fulfilled. Rubber molds were cheaper but their application was limited to the production of figurines and smaller items such as key holders. JS charged RM300 for the cost of making a mold for an order of less than 500 pieces. The company had not ventured into the production of large and hollow items such as mugs and vases, which required the use of steel molds.

JS employed ten workers who were paid a monthly salary of RM300 to RM400 depending on their skills and experience. The factory operated daily from nine to five, six days a week. During busy periods, JS had to pay overtime at more than double the daily wage of the workers. On average, a worker earned up to RM500 to RM600 per month on overtime. Tay said:

> We have only ten workers and our factory is still too small to cope with large orders. Although we would like to take advantage of scale economies by filling large orders for just a few clients, it would be too risky to be dependent on a few large orders. At this stage, we are trying to develop a wide customer base and gain experience in producing a wide range of products.

JS also employed two sales personnel, one to handle sales in KL, the other to establish markets in Melaka. Melaka was a major tourist attraction known for its historical sites including the remains of a Portuguese fortress and buildings reflecting Dutch architecture, preserved to retain the state's heritage. In 1994, Melaka also joined in the country's pace of industrialization and undertook various activities to woo local and foreign investors to the state. By the end of 1993, rents in Melaka increased 100 percent and labour was scarce. Businesses in the plantation and construction industries had already turned to imported labour from Indonesia, the Philippines, and Bangladesh.

Other Malaysian Pewter Companies

Penang Pewter & Metal Arts was one of the better-known pewter companies. The company served the markets in Penang, an island off the northern coast of Peninsular Malaysia. Penang, known as the Pearl of the Orient, is a major tourist attraction in Malaysia because of its beaches. In recent years, the state had developed industrial parks to attract foreign investment which further boosted the demand for pewter in the area. Locally, Penang was the major geographical market for Penang pewter although the products were readily available in gift outlets in major cities, particularly KL. With an employment of about 100 workers, the company produced a wide range of pewterware which were exported to markets such as Australia, Singapore, Japan, and the United States.

Zatfee produced a wide range of pewter under the brand name Tumasek Pewter, which were exported to Canada, the United States, and Japan. The company had expanded gradually from 90 employees in 1987 to 200 in 1993. In 1993, the company increased its global market penetration by entering new markets such as Australia, Hong Kong, Korea, New Zealand, and Singapore. Zatfee's annual turnover of RM1.5 million in 1987 had grown to RM6.5 million in 1993.

Oriental Pewter was located in Perak, formerly another tin-rich state in Malaysia. With a work force of about 100 employees, the company produced modern and unique pewterware which was exported to Canada, New Zealand, Singapore, Australia, the United Kingdom, and Japan.

◼ Global Competition

The export market had always been the thrust of the Malaysian pewter industry. However, in recent years, the world market had become increasingly competitive with the emergence of pewter companies even in countries where tin was an unknown metal. For example, the pewter industry had flourished in Sweden and pewter items were manufactured in Korea, Taiwan, and Belgium.

Pewter companies had initiated the establishment of pewter-making concerns in Taiwan and Korea to take advantage of the relatively cheap and skilled labour in these countries. Thailand and Indonesia seemed to have the potential for the establishment of a competitive pewter industry in view of the presence of large tin deposits and cheap work force. Pewter was presently manufactured in Thailand while PT Tambang Timah, an Indonesian tin producer, was planning to set up a pewter plant which would consume at least half of its tin supplies for the production of high-value-added pewter products. (See Exhibit 4 for hourly compensations of the work force in fabricated metal industries in selected countries.)

In Sweden, the pewter industry began about 150 years ago. In 1994, there was a strong market demand particularly for pewter trophies. Prizes for most

EXHIBIT 4   **Hourly Compensation in Fabricated Metal Products, 1990**

Country	US$
Belgium	15.07
Brazil	1.12
Canada	15.90
Germany	19.88
Korea	3.94
Portugal	2.90
South Africa	3.05
Sweden	20.31
Taiwan	3.80
United Kingdom	11.84
United States	14.98

Source: IMD & World Economic Forum, *The World Competitiveness Report 1992.*
Note: The average daily wage rate for an unskilled factory worker was estimated at US$1.60 in Indonesia, US$5.50 in Malaysia, and US$2.90 in Thailand. The average monthly wage rate in China and India was estimated at US$51 and US$43, respectively.

sporting events such as yachting, skiing, ice hockey, and swimming were made of pewter and Swedish sportsmen were known to have built a collection of pewter trophies. Other pewterware produced by the Swedish pewter companies included household items, jewellery, and gifts.

Scandiapresent was the largest pewter manufacturer in Sweden and was noted for its antique finished pewter. Another company was Arktis Smedgen, formed in 1980 and employing four workers, which produced a range of pewterware with engraved patterns. AB Harryda Adelmetallsmide produced the Harryda Tenn pewter products such as tankards, bowls, and goblets with a shiny finish.

Other pewter companies in Sweden included AB Koppar & Tennsmide, Jokkmok Tenn AB Sigurd Ahman, Metallum AB, and several other companies which mostly operated as small concerns employing four to eight workers. Metallum AB in Stockholm, set up in 1988, produced small pewter gifts and jewellery; it was also the agent in Sweden for the supply of pewter sheets and ingots from a U.K. supplier, George Johnson & Company (Birmingham) Limited.

In the United Kingdom, where the pewter industry had a long history, there was a high concentration of pewter companies in Sheffield. Of 14 pewter manufacturers in the United Kingdom, two were located in London, three in Birmingham, one in Glasgow, and the rest in Sheffield. Sheffield Pewter, noted for its highly polished and hammered finishes, was distributed in large retail outlets as an exclusive product, usually displayed in glass cases. The product line was, however, quite narrow, limited to tankards, mugs, and hip flasks.

Canada was one of the countries that produced pewter and had quite a large retail market. In 1994, Seagull Pewter and Silversmiths Ltd. (Seagull) was one of the most successful Canadian pewter companies. Exhibit 5 gives a brief description of Seagull to provide an insight on the operations of a pewter company in a foreign country. Seagull had recently grown rapidly to become one of the top ten pewter manufacturers in North America and posed a major threat to the Malaysian pewter companies in the global market.

EXHIBIT 5   Seagull Pewterers & Silversmiths Limited (Seagull)

Seagull, located in Pugwash, Nova Scotia, was established in 1979 by a husband-and-wife team, John Caraberis and Bonnie Bond, who were seeking a more peaceful lifestyle and less expensive place to live. In a town with a population of 1,000 people, they expanded their original basement operation to a 6,000-square foot (557.5 square metre) factory ten years later. Their business line had developed from silver and pewter jewellery to pewter giftware. In 1994, Seagull produced 1,000 different items and was constantly adding new products and refining existing ones.

Seagull employed 100 pewter makers, designers, and sales representatives. The company had a wide product line of pewter giftware ranging from picture frames to letter openers, mugs, and a large selection of Christmas ornaments. The Caraberises ranked their company's pewter line as the broadest in North America.

The business was booming at Seagull and for most of the year the workers worked two separate shifts (ten-hour days, four days a week). Several methods were employed to produce different pewter products. Jewellery was hand-made from twisted pewter wire and thin pewter plates. Seagull's hollowware was made by spinning while a majority of its other items were made in rubber casts. In rubber casting, original items were designed and several copies of the models were made by hand. These models were then used to make several thousand rubber molds. The company used over 400 molds a week and each mold lasted for between 100 and 200 casts.

Seagull was very aggressive in promoting its products and claimed to have a total of 10,000 accounts spread across every state and province in North America. The accounts included independent retail shops, tourist shops, country and craft shops, and jewellery stores. Aggressive selling was undertaken by Seagull's 12 sales representatives and strengthened by dozens of other giftware distributors. In 1988, the United States accounted for about 70 percent of Seagull's total sales and the company was looking for opportunities in Australia, Japan, and Europe, particularly Germany.

In the Canadian market, Seagull would appoint an exclusive retailer who carried only Seagull pewter together with a range of giftware, except pewter from other companies. Seagull pewter would occupy a corner of the retail gift outlet where a wide selection of the pewter items was displayed in open racks. Customers were able to handle the product without having to seek assistance from the salesperson. Items purchased were taken off the rack and packed in boxes, or plastic sleeves for the smaller items. Seagull's pewter bookmark was retailed at Cdn$7, a keychain at Cdn$13, a photo frame at Cdn$34, and a Christmas ornament at Cdn$8.

For the past several years, Seagull had invested heavily in giftware design to ensure that its product line was current, comprehensive, and consumer-oriented. "Given the giftware industry, which typically launches two product lines a year, that can be hectic. The development of new products does not require new technology but is very demanding and takes a lot of work and money," said Caraberis.

The owners of Seagull Pewter had also attributed the company's success to their active participation in trade shows. Seagull attended and displayed its products at 40 to 50 shows throughout North America each year, at show locations such as Boston, Washington, D.C., New York, Dallas, Kansas City, Toronto, Montreal, Edmonton, and Halifax. "We're a little more rigorous in getting out there in the marketplace for a small business. You've got to be there to build up your reputation, to build up your clientele," explained Caraberis.

There were at least eight other Canadian pewter manufacturers. They were located in Nova Scotia (Amos Pewterers), Newfoundland, Quebec (Val David's Pewter), New Brunswick (Aitkens Pewter), Ontario (Morton-Parker Ltd.), Alberta, and British Columbia (Boma Manufacturing Ltd.). In the Canadian market, the products of Malaysian pewter companies such as Tumasek Pewter, Oriental Pewter, RS Pewter, and Selwin Pewter faced intense competition from the local and foreign pewter companies.

To understand the global nature of supply on the retail side, the experience in Stratford, Ontario, is illustrative. Stratford is a small town with a major tourist attraction in Canada, famous for its annual Shakespearean Festival. In Stratford, only The Touchmark Shop carried RS pewter and Selwin pewter. Although RS pewter and Selwin pewter were among Touchmark's best-selling items, there was intense competition from pewter made in Brazil

(John Sommers Pewter), Thailand, Belgium (Riskin Pewter), and England (Sheffield Pewter), and the locally produced pewter, particularly Boma Pewter and Lindsay Claire Pewter. A salesperson at Touchmark commented, "Pewter is an impulse item; thus, customers look for items with attractive designs that are reasonably priced. Only customers who have prior knowledge of pewter are conscious of pewter brands and their country of origin."

Seagull pewter was sold exclusively at three large gift shops in Stratford; Bradshaws, La Crafe, and Christmas and Country Gift Shop. Bradshaws, however, had on display a very small selection of pewter made in Korea and Metzke pewter from the United States. Since these shops did not carry pewter of other manufacturers, Seagull pewter occupied a relatively large shelf space and purchasers could not make spontaneous comparison in terms of product design and price with competitors' products.

Touchmark was reported to have sold more than Cdn$500 worth of pewter per month during the summer season. In contrast, the retailer of a large gift shop in Kitchener complained that the pewter items were selling much slower than the rest of the other gift items such as crystal, silver, and porcelain. As a result, the Kitchener shop maintained a limited range of pewter products, mainly Riskin pewter and John Sommers pewter from Brazil.

◼ Future Outlook

Based on the current situation in the pewter industry in Malaysia, RS leadership in the industry was indisputable and was expected to remain so for the next decade at least. RS had been a family-owned business and there were no immediate plans for the company to go public. Such a strategy shielded the company from acquisition threats and leakages of trade secrets. Although RS had captured a major share of the Malaysian pewter market, RS, together with the other Malaysian pewter companies, faced a major challenge from existing and emerging pewter companies from all over the world. At issue for new entrants was whether they could compete globally by emphasizing efficient production and targeting the low-to-medium-priced giftware market segment. But was this realistic? And overall, was this an attractive industry for investment?

Ontario Hydro and the Mattagami Project[1]

Part I: The Mattagami Complex[2]

A. The Challenge

It was December 1991, and Debbie Smith sat quietly in her chair reflecting on the task that faced her. Debbie was the recently appointed Manager of Aboriginal and Northern Affairs, a senior-level management position which had just been established by Ontario Hydro. The work of the committee, for which she was responsible, had finally been completed. It was now her task to prepare and present a final report to the Board of the corporation. She had set aside a day without interruption to develop a presentation strategy that would identify clearly for the Board the nature, and significance, of the decision that Ontario Hydro faced. It was not the size of the project that was crucial in this case, though the project was not inconsiderable—a four-dam redevelopment

This case was prepared by Mark Schwartz (Ph.D. candidate) and Professor Wesley Cragg, York University, as the basis for class discussion and not to illustrate either effective or ineffective management practices. © 1997 York University. All rights reserved. No part of this publication may be reproduced by any means without permission.

[1] Funding support for this research was provided by the Social Sciences and Humanities Research Council (Strategic Grants Program), York University's National Management Education Project in Business and the Environment, and York University's Schulich School of Business Small Research Grants Program.

[2] This case study is a product of an interdisciplinary environmental ethics research project studying four situations involving the use or extraction of natural resources in Ontario and northern British Columbia. The authors wish to acknowledge the contribution of: Maria Radford, who did much of the original document research; David Pearson, a project co-investigator, Ralph Wheeler (Ministry of Natural Resources), and Mario Durepos (Ontario Hydro), who are project partners; Paul Wilkinson and Associates; the Ontario Aboriginal Research Coalition, created to direct research into the effects on Ontario's First Nations of Ontario Hydro's Twenty-Five Year Plan, who financed the collection of oral histories assembled to which we refer in a number of places; Chief Ernest Beck and David Fletcher of the Moose Factory First Nation, Chief Randy Kapashesit of the Mocreebec First Nation, and John Turner of the Mushkegowuk Tribal Council, who provided guidance and site visit assistance; and Ontario Hydro, who arranged a site visit to the Mattagami Complex. Without the assistance of all of these people, this research would not have been possible. Also acting as co-investigators for the project and involved in other aspects of the research were John Lewko and Craig Summers (Laurentian University).

project along the Mattagami River in northern Ontario. Rather, the final report she would put to the Board would be the first major test of the new environmental and ethical policies of the corporation, policies that she knew were destined to change in dramatic ways the corporation's understanding of its environmental and social responsibilities.

Integrating the policy changes into the strategic planning process had been a challenge for senior management. But management had been a part of the evolution of those policies and had had ample opportunity to develop an understanding of their implications for strategic planning as well as day-to-day operations. The Board had not had the same immersion experience. They had approved the new directions and indeed had participated in their articulation, yet they had not been working with them intensively since their formulation. Debbie knew that her first challenge was to present the final report in a way that allowed the Board members the opportunity to retrace the reasons for the changes in corporate policy and their application to development strategy.

Debbie knew that the redevelopment project, known as the Mattagami Complex, was only a small part of an extensive operation. Ontario Hydro was currently one of Canada's largest corporations generating annual revenues of over $7 billion and holding assets of over $43 billion. It was now the largest electric utility in North America. The corporation employed approximately 30,000 people (Ontario Hydro, 1991a) and served over 3 million retail customers (Ontario Hydro, 1991b). Ontario Hydro was able to produce the required power through a combination of nuclear, fossil, and hydroelectric sources. Nuclear generating stations were supplying just over half of the total system energy requirements, while fossil-fuelled generation and hydroelectric stations each contributed approximately one-quarter of the remaining power (Ontario Hydro, 1991a). In terms of hydroelectric power, over 65 generating stations were producing approximately 34 million megawatt-hours of energy a year (Ontario Hydro, 1991a).

Despite its tremendous growth over the years, the Crown corporation had continued to struggle in making energy development decisions that were acceptable to all of its stakeholders. In this case, the decision regarded not only whether to proceed with the extension of four hydroelectric dams along the Mattagami River in northeastern Ontario, but how to proceed. The project had gone through an environmental assessment. Subsequent public evaluation of that assessment had raised a number of significant issues for the corporation. Ontario Hydro's historical approach to making development decisions based on least-cost planning was clearly under attack. Indeed, the new environmental and ethical policies now in place had been developed as a response to what in retrospect were now acknowledged by the corporation to be well-founded criticisms. The challenge was now to apply these new policies creatively and constructively to the situation at hand.

Having examined the issues the Board would have to discuss, Debbie made her first decision. She would first review the case and remind the Board of the weaknesses inherent in Ontario Hydro's historical approach to hydroelectric generation. She would then review the position that had been set out in the environmental assessment prepared by management for public discussion. The position taken by management had reflected what Ontario Hydro officials, guiding the process, had identified as the interests of the project's key stakeholders. The public response to the environmental assessment had been positive with one exception: the Aboriginal reaction had been bitterly critical.

In response to the corporation's environmental assessment a First Nation coalition developed a counterproposal that they submitted directly to the Ontario government. A crucial period of discussion and negotiation had followed which led to the creation of a working group—50 percent of whose members came from the Native community. This group had been assigned the task of attempting to build a consensus on the proposed development. Debbie and her committee at Ontario Hydro had been deeply involved in that process. Indeed, their recommendations were built around the proposals created by the working group that the government had established.

It was now Debbie's task to write a report that would draw the Board into a discussion that would help them to understand the recommendations they would then have to evaluate. She knew that to accomplish this goal she would have to review both the facts of the case and the limitations of the corporation's historical approach to the development of hydroelectric generating stations. Without an understanding of that history, a balanced evaluation of the Report's recommendations would not be possible. She would then have to review the Mattagami Complex proposal, the Aboriginal reaction to it, their counterproposal, and the nature and results of the involvement of the Ontario government.

With this plan to guide her, Debbie began to review the facts of the case[3] before setting out to write her report.

B. The Mattagami River Area

i. Geography

The Mattagami River is one of several rivers draining the Moose River Basin, an area of approximately 108,000 square kilometres, a region larger than Ireland (Ontario Hydro, 1991c). The Mattagami river itself is 491 kilometres long and drains a sub-basin area of 41,672 square kilometres (Ontario Hydro, 1990). The river flows in a northerly direction and empties into the Moose River 96 kilometres upstream from James Bay.

The Mattagami River runs through the Pre-Cambrian Shield and the Hudson Bay Lowlands. Vegetation in the vicinity of the hydroelectric stations along the river consists mainly of boreal forests. Downstream from the dams, the boreal forest of the Canadian Shield transforms into the Hudson Bay Lowlands where poor climate and drainage retards tree growth. The basin's wildlife population includes moose, bear, beaver, fox, otter, and numerous species of birds, amphibians, and fish (Ontario Hydro, 1991c).

ii. The Local Inhabitants

The non-Native population in the Moose River Basin numbers approximately 80,000, with over half of these people living in Timmins (DeLauney, 1992).

---

[3] The account that follows is based on Ontario Hydro's Environmental Assessment, Aboriginal Witness Statements (Adams, Conway, Roderique, J. Sutherland, P. Sutherland), and an exhibit by J. Morrison used during the Demand/Supply Plan Environmental Assessment Hearing.

The area most directly affected by the hydroelectric development supports a non-Native population of approximately 17,000 and includes the communities of Kapuskasing (10,850), Smooth Rock Falls (2,100), Moonbeam (1,250), Val Rita-Harty (1,200), Fauquier-Strickland (815), and Opasatika (400) (Ontario Hydro, 1990).

The Aboriginal population in the Basin and along the James Bay coast numbers approximately 10,000. Some live in isolated communities, and others live close to, or within, urban centres (DeLauney, 1992). The two largest Aboriginal communities are Moosonee and Moose Factory Island, which are located 5 kilometres apart at the mouth of the Moose River. Of the 1,500 residents living in Moosonee, approximately 900 are of Aboriginal descent (Ontario Hydro, 1990). Approximately 2,200 Aboriginal inhabitants live on Moose Factory Island (DeLauney, 1992).

The political organization of the Aboriginal communities living in the Moose River Basin is complex. The majority of Aboriginals are members of recognized "First Nations" and are represented by different Tribal Councils. However, other Aboriginals are not members of recognized First Nations and are considered "non-status" Aboriginals.

There are nine Cree and Ojibway First Nations in the Basin. Six of these First Nations (Wagoshig, Matachewan, Mattagami, Brunswick House, Chapleau Ojibway, and Chapleau Cree) are members of the Wabun Tribal Council and are located in the southern end of the Basin. The other three First Nations in the Basin (New Post, Moose Factory, and Mocreebec) are members of the Mushkegowuk Tribal Council. The New Post First Nation is located in the southern end of the Basin near Cochrane. The Moose Factory and Mocreebec First Nations are located in the northern end of the Basin, on Moose Factory Island along the James Bay coast (DeLauney, 1992).

All the First Nations involved in this discussion, with the exception of the Mocreebec, are among the 46 First Nations covered by Treaty #9, signed in 1905, and are represented by the Nishnawbe-Aski Nation (NAN), which was founded in 1973 (DeLauney, 1992). The Mocreebec First Nation is a special case, as it is not recognized as a band by the federal government, does not have a reserve, and does not receive federal government payments (DeLauney, 1992).

C. The Origins of the Mattagami Complex Redevelopment Proposal

i. Early Development in the Moose River Basin

Though human activity in the Moose River Basin dates back 2,500 to 5,000 years, the first European trading post was not established until 1776 in Moose Factory by the Hudson Bay Company (Ontario Hydro, 1991c). In the early 1900s, railway lines opened up portions of the Basin to agricultural settlement, mining, and lumbering (Morrison, 1992). Between 1911 and 1932, a total of nine private hydroelectric developments were established on the Mattagami and Abitibi rivers to supply power to the new industries. One such development was the Smoky Falls Station on the Mattagami River (described below). During the 1930s, the Hydro-Electric Power Commission of Ontario (the precursor to Ontario Hydro) purchased a number of these private generating systems in order to increase the Commission's hydroelectric capacity (Morrison, 1992).

Early mining and lumbering development in the Moose River Basin provided some benefits to the Aboriginal people, such as casual or wage labour and easier access to traditional hunting grounds in some cases. However, there were profound negative consequences as well which included the loss of lands and resources used for traditional harvesting, exposure to infectious disease, and other, related social problems (Morrison, 1992).

The early hydroelectric projects also had significant environmental and social consequences. Among the outcomes: Aboriginal lands were partially flooded; graves and campsites disappeared; traditional lifestyles were disrupted by construction; the incursion of hunters and fishers resulted in a growing non-Native population; improved access by roads and railway transportation facilitated development; and fish and wildlife habitats were polluted and destroyed.

Available evidence suggests that only very limited attempts to mitigate the damaging effects of development had been undertaken. The attitudes of developers had been dominated by a simple belief in the benefits of development and the economic opportunities it provided (Morrison, 1992).

ii. The Smoky Falls Generating Station

In 1922, the "model" town of Kapuskasing was built around the creation of a pulp and paper mill. The mill was operated by the Spruce Falls Power and Paper Corporation (SFPP) owned by Kimberly Clark and The New York Times. The plant had been established to provide a reliable supply of newsprint for the newspaper. Over 700 people were hired to operate the pulp and paper plant while another 3,500 were employed to fell the wood (Morrison, 1992). At that time it took almost two days' production and 225 acres (91 hectares) of forest to make the Sunday edition of The New York Times (Morrison, 1992).

In 1928, the SFPP constructed the Smoky Falls Generating Station on the Mattagami River for the principal purpose of supplying power to their plant in Kapuskasing (Ontario Hydro, 1991c). The Smoky Falls Station was one of the earliest hydroelectric power stations in the Moose River Basin on the Mattagami River. The building of the station replaced a natural waterfall having a drop of approximately 80 feet (24 metres) (Morrison, 1992). The plant was operated as a "run-of-river" or "base load" station (see Appendix A). Electrical power was transmitted via an 80 kilometre 115 kV transmission line from the Smoky Falls Station directly to SFPP's mill in Kapuskasing 24 hours a day (Ontario Hydro, 1990).

The development of the Smoky Falls Station caused some environmental damage. Aboriginal reports indicate that a spawning ground upriver from the dam was destroyed as fish access to it was blocked. Noise from the plant's operations was reported to have caused wildlife to move away from what had been a traditional trapping area. Native hunters reported a deterioration in the quality of the fish, geese, and ducks (Morrison, 1992). However, as the station was a "run-of-river" operation flooding and erosion damage was not extensive.

Despite the environmental problems, access to an inexpensive electrical supply played a crucial role in ensuring the economic viability of the SFPP

Corporation, leading in turn to growth and stability for the town of Kapuskasing.

iii. The 1960s Development

In order to increase its hydroelectric production, Ontario Hydro constructed several facilities on the Mattagami River in the 1960s: the Little Long Station (1963), Harmon Station (1965), and Kipling Station (1966) (Ontario Hydro, 1991c). The Little Long Station is upstream from the Smoky Falls Station, while the Harmon and Kipling Stations are both downstream. The stations are between 60 and 100 kilometres north of Kapuskasing. Beginning in 1963, a small trout stream known as Adam Creek was used to divert excess water around the hydroelectric stations. The three stations and the Adam Creek Diversion became known as the Mattagami Complex (Ontario Hydro, 1990).

The three new stations, Little Long, Harmon, and Kipling, were built with a quite different function from the Smoky Falls Station. The Smoky Falls Station was designed as a base load station to provide a continuous supply of energy to the SFPP mill in Kapuskasing. The other three stations were to be "peaking" stations, operating for approximately five hours per day (Ontario Hydro, 1990). These stations were designed to provide electrical power only during the periods of peak electrical demand from Ontario Hydro's consumers.

The functioning of each of the four dams depends on the buildup and subsequent release of a headpond through the dam structure. The headponds for each station differ in size, the largest being Little Long (7,167 hectares), followed by Harmon (251 hectares), Smoky Falls (213 hectares), and Kipling (141 hectares). By agreement with SFPP, Ontario Hydro discharges sufficient water from the Little Long Station to restore the Smoky Falls headpond to its full level each day. Due to the different operating patterns between Smoky Falls and the other three stations, the headpond water levels of the four stations fluctuate daily up to 3 metres (Ontario Hydro, 1990).

As mentioned above, the Adam Creek Diversion was an important element of the Mattagami Complex. The 37 kilometre long creek extends from the mouth of the Little Long headpond, 2.5 kilometres east of the Little Long Station, and runs back into the Mattagami River 17 kilometres downstream of the Kipling Station (Ontario Hydro, 1990). A control structure (or spillway) was constructed at the mouth of the creek as a means of rerouting excess water around the four generating stations along the Mattagami River. Each time water flows exceed 541 cubic metres per second, the creek is used to bypass excess water around the generating stations (Ontario Hydro, 1990). The most extensive use of Adam Creek occurs with winter runoff—from mid-April to the end of June (Ontario Hydro, 1990). At this time of year the volume of water flowing down the creek is similar to that which flows over Niagara Falls.

The use of the creek as a spillway had profound environmental consequences. At one time, Adam Creek was a tiny trout creek that a person could jump across (Roderique, 1992). Over the intervening 30 years, the small creek was transformed into a wide river channel by the erosion of approximately 27 million cubic metres of soil resulting from the increased water flow. The eroded banks at the mouth of the creek grew to be 20 to 30 metres high

(Ontario Hydro, 1990) with pools of water varying in depth from 2 to 6 metres (Ontario Hydro, 1990). As a result, the creek has changed to the point where it is hardly recognizable to local Cree residents (Conway, 1992).

iv. Impacts of 1960s Development

Hydroelectric developments along the Mattagami River in the 1960s had certain positive consequences for the Aboriginal people. Some Native people benefited economically as they were hired to work on the construction of the dams (Morrison, 1992). In addition, though not a direct consequence of the dams on the Mattagami, the towns of Moose Factory and Moosonee were finally connected to the Ontario power grid in 1973, alleviating the need to use diesel generators to produce electricity (Morrison, 1992).

On the negative side, construction and use of the Mattagami Complex resulted in damaging environmental and social impacts as reported by the Native people affected.[4] Aboriginal witness statements collected during the Demand/Supply Plan Environmental Assessment hearings indicated that the dams had had a deleterious impact on the wildlife in the Basin. Population declines in a number of bird species were observed, including owls, woodpeckers, songbirds, grouse, and chickadees. Cree hunters also observed a decline in the number of geese. The decline was partly attributed to the decreased availability of underwater food for the geese to eat resulting from mud and silt deposits caused by the dams. According to Cree Elders, the dams have made the river so polluted that geese and ducks have become too contaminated to eat (Conway, 1992; Sutherland, J., 1992; and Roderique, 1992).

Elders have also observed major declines in otter, mink, and fox populations. Noise from the dams' generators is said to have driven wildlife away (MacDonald, 1992). Other animal populations such as caribou, white-tailed deer, and moose appear to have declined (Linklater, 1992). Herbicide spraying along Ontario Hydro transmission lines is reported by Natives and their elders to have adversely affected moose and other animals that eat the sprayed berry plants (Conway, 1992).

The flooding of plant communities and feed beds caused by the release of water has resulted in less food for beavers (Conway, 1992). This has caused a reduction in beaver populations in riverbanks (Conway, 1992). Beavers have drowned or frozen to death in their lodges as a result of releases of winter water creating additional layers of ice (Mugiskan, 1992). The quality of beaver, muskrat, and otter fur is reported to have deteriorated.

Natives have observed that downriver from the Mattagami dams there has been a decline in the number of fish and fish habitat, as well as the discovery of sick fish, all resulting in a net loss of fisheries (Conway, 1992). These environmental effects have also extended upriver above the dams where traditional fisheries have been lost and important spawning beds flooded or silted over. Native people report that all of this has resulted from the unnaturally low and fluctuating water levels caused by the operation of the dams (Conway, 1992).

---

[4] See Aboriginal Witness Statements, DSP Environmental Assessment Hearing, Exhibits 829–886, 947–951, 1018–1019.

The dams also have had significant direct and indirect social impacts on the Native population. Water quality deterioration has made the rivers unsuitable as a source of drinking water (Sutherland, J., 1992). Individuals who swam in the Moose River near Moose Factory sometimes developed skin infections. Families ceased washing clothes in the Moose River (Conway, 1992).

The flooding caused by the operation of the dams destroyed a number of historic Cree settlement sites, historic portages, fur trade sites, and cemeteries (Conway, 1992; Adams, 1992; and Roderique, 1992). Oral histories record an Elder as complaining:

> A number of cemeteries where my people were buried are now beneath the Little Long Dam reservoir. We can't visit them anymore because they are underwater (Sutherland, J., 1992).

In order to construct the dams, roads were built which created additional pressures on the traditional Aboriginal way of life. The improved access for non-Native hunters generated additional competition between subsistence and sport hunters (Conway, 1992). The roads allowed increased access by game wardens causing increased incidents of harassment for Natives in their practice of subsistence fishing and hunting (Conway, 1992, and Sutherland, P., 1992). The access roads were also used to expand logging activities into new areas. The logging companies' use of clearcutting was detrimental to fur-bearing mammals and fish, and thus created difficulties for Cree families pursuing subsistence trapping (Conway, 1992).

Travel problems were caused by the dams releasing an unnatural cycle of water. For Native users the river was their highway (Jones, 1992), yet the fluctuating river levels made boat travel difficult or impossible. Above the dam, former rapids, islands, and portages were flooded, making navigation confusing for travellers (Roderique, 1992; Conway, 1992; and Sutherland, P., 1992). The construction and use of the dams created dangerous travel conditions because of tree stumps in the flooded areas, flooded traditional campsites, and flooded travel routes (Conway, 1992). During the summer the unnaturally low water levels made the river too dry for travel (Roderique, 1992). During the winter, the river ice broke up much earlier, thus shortening the late-winter travel period and hindering the ability of the Cree people to reach trapping grounds (Cheena, 1992).

According to Aboriginal sources, Aboriginal communities were not consulted about the planning or construction of the Hydro dams (Morrison, 1992, and Conway, 1992). Neither is there evidence of serious efforts at mitigation nor compensation for the social, economic, or heritage impacts resulting from the construction and operation of the dams (Morrison, 1992).

v. Ontario Hydro's Twenty-Five Year Demand/Supply Plan

By 1984, Ontario Hydro was predicting that new electrical power options were going to be required as electricity demand increases of 60 to 200 percent by the year 2014 were projected (Sears and Paterson, 1991). In response to these forecasts and to ensure a sufficient energy supply to meet Ontario's future needs, Ontario Hydro developed what became known as the Twenty-Five-Year Demand/Supply Plan (DSP).

The DSP consisted primarily of the rehabilitation and development of hydraulic, nuclear, and fossil generating stations (Ontario Hydro, 1989a). As part of the DSP, Ontario Hydro stated that it wanted to proceed with 12 hydraulic projects in the Moose River Basin: six new dams, five extensions of existing dams, and the redevelopment of one dam. In December 1989, Ontario Hydro submitted its plans to the Ontario Ministry of the Environment. An Environmental Assessment Hearing commenced shortly afterwards. As one small part of the hydraulic component of the DSP, Ontario Hydro submitted an Environmental Assessment for the Mattagami Complex in November 1990. The Environmental Assessment examined the extension of three hydroelectric stations on the Mattagami River (Little Long, Harmon, and Kipling) and the redevelopment of the Smoky Falls Station (still owned at that time by the SFPP corporation).

vi. Ontario Hydro's Mattagami Complex Proposal

Ontario Hydro's Mattagami Complex proposal was developed as a means to increase the hydroelectric generation capacity on the Mattagami River. The existing four-station complex produced 450 MW of power (Little Long (2 units × 61 MW), Smoky Falls (4 units × 14 MW), Harmon (2 units × 68 MW), and Kipling (2 units × 68 MW) (Ontario Hydro, 1990). The proposal called for the addition of one unit to the Little Long (61 MW), Harmon (68 MW), and Kipling (68 MW) generating stations, and the construction of a new (3 units × 80 MW) power station adjacent to the existing Smoky Falls Station (Ontario Hydro, 1990). The current Smoky Falls Station would be retired. The redevelopment would provide an additional 381 MW of capacity to help meet Ontario's peak electrical requirements. A new 230 KV transmission line would be built between the Smoky Falls and Little Long Stations stretching 7 kilometres. It would replace the existing 110 KV transmission line between Smoky Falls and Kapuskasing. The small community of workers currently living at Smoky Falls would be relocated to Kapuskasing, as the dam would be operated remotely.

The major benefit of the project was that it would provide for the sequential or "in-step" operation of the four hydroelectric plants. Currently, this was impossible, as the Smoky Falls Station was a "base load" station operating continuously, while the other three operated only five hours a day as "peaking" stations (see Appendix A). In-step operation could only take place when the plants had similar discharge capacities and generated electricity for the same period of time each day. By retiring the current station at Smoky Falls and the building a "peaking" station in its place the hydraulic potential of the river could be maximized (Ontario Hydro, 1990).

vii. Sale of the Smoky Falls Station to Ontario Hydro

By early 1991, SFPP had determined that it was no longer in their financial interests to continue operating their mill in Kapuskasing, as it had produced dismal profits since 1986 (Philp, 1991). Following an unsuccessful attempt to sell the mill, SFPP began to prepare to shut down most of its operations. The loss of SFPP would have turned Kapuskasing into a ghost town (Mackie,

1991). Approximately 1,200 direct jobs and 6,200 indirect jobs in a town of about 11,000 people would have been lost (Nation and Noble, 1991). A political crisis erupted placing pressure on the Ontario government to intervene (Allen, 1991).

In August 1991, as a result of the Ontario government's intervention, the majority of the shares in the SFPP corporation were sold by Kimberly Clark and the New York Times to SFPP's employees. As part of the buyout arrangements, the Smoky Falls Generating Station was to be sold to Ontario Hydro. The purchase price for the station included an immediate payment by Ontario Hydro of $140 million to Kimberly Clark and the New York Times plus a $34 million cash payment to help finance upgrading the mill. Ontario Hydro would also provide the mill with ten years of free power (Noble, 1991). Ontario Hydro only agreed to purchase the Smoky Falls Station on the condition that the environmental assessment to redevelop the site be approved by the Ontario government. Without such redevelopment, the site was considered useless to Ontario Hydro (Philp, 1991). The Ontario government agreed to pay Ontario Hydro $247 million if the environmental assessment was not approved (Noble, 1991).

D. Reassessing the Planning Process

A number of issues surfaced as a result of Ontario Hydro's decision to redevelop the Mattagami Complex. Previous hydroelectric development had left a serious residue of anger and resentment on the part of the Aboriginal communities negatively affected. It was clear that overcoming this resentment would require significant changes in planning and project implementation than what had occurred in the past.

For much of the century, Ontario Hydro's study and exploitation of the hydraulic potential of the great rivers draining the Canadian Shield had been governed by its mandate: "to provide a reliable supply of electrical power and energy to the people of Ontario at the lowest feasible long-term costs" (Ontario Hydro, 1991c). To fulfill this mandate, dams were constructed on northern rivers that altered in environmentally significant ways the flow of rivers so as to create huge new reservoirs. Such reservoirs were needed to ensure reliable energy that could be produced over long time periods in response to fluctuating demand. The resulting energy was delivered at a relatively low monetary cost and considerable economic benefit to the residents of Ontario. However, the developments imposed substantial costs on Native communities in the absence of meaningful consultation and countervailing benefits recognizable as such by those affected.

The legacy of these developments was reflected in an acute sense of grievance which now dominated discussion of northern Ontario resource use. It was reflected as well in substantial environmental problems that now confronted Native and non-Native communities in the North. These problems were all mirrored in the Mattagami Complex debate.

In Debbie's view, it was crucial that the Board realize the nature of these problems if they were to understand subsequent events as they unfolded as well as the committee's final recommendations.

⬛ Part II: Reconceptualizing the Planning Process

The task that now faced Debbie was to explain clearly to the Board the new principles underlying project planning for the Mattagami Complex and how they might affect the decision-making process. Some decision-making tools, the mandate and the principle of "least-cost planning" for instance, remained as important considerations. Ontario Hydro's mandate stated that the corporation must "provide a reliable supply of electrical power and energy to the people of Ontario, at the lowest long-term feasible cost" (Ontario Hydro, 1990). The proposed redevelopment of the Mattagami Complex had much to recommend it in light of this mandate. If realized, the redeveloped complex would allow the utility to extract substantially more of the energy potential of the river with positive financial benefits when measured against the direct costs of the project. Proceeding with the project was clearly consistent with the mandate and the principle of "least-cost planning."

However, two crucial changes had been made with respect to how projects were to be evaluated at Ontario Hydro. The first had been forced by legislation. Ontario Hydro was now required to take into account the *Environmental Assessment Act* (R.S.O. 1980, c.140).[5] This legislation had as its stated aim "the betterment of the people of Ontario by providing for the protection, conservation and wise management in Ontario of the environment" (s.2). The environment was defined to include the natural environment as well as "the social, economic and cultural conditions that influence the life of man or a community" (s.1[c]).[6] This act modified in significant ways the regulatory setting in which energy planning, on the part of Ontario Hydro, now had to take place. For example, the corporation was now required by law to take into account costs that historically it had externalized, thereby passing them onto the public at large.

This aforementioned change was clearly of importance in evaluating the proposed development. However, of even greater significance was the policy decision taken by the corporation to endorse the principle of sustainable development in its planning and project activities.[7] Senior management had concluded that commitment to sustainable development required four things:

---

[5] Presently the *Environmental Assessment Act* R.S.O. 1990, c.E.18.

[6] More specifically, the *Environmental Assessment Act* defines the environment to include:
    i) air, land or water,
    ii) plant and animal life, including man,
    iii) the social, economic and cultural conditions that influence the life of man or a community,
    iv) any building, structure, machine or other device or thing made by man,
    v) any solid, liquid, gas, odour, heat, sound, vibration or radiation resulting directly or indirectly from the activities of man, or
    vi) any part or combination of the foregoing and the interrelationships between any two or more or of them (Revised Statutes of Ontario, 1980, s.1[c]).

[7] Note that in 1993 Ontario Hydro announced a new mandate, namely:
To recommend an overall corporate strategy that will enable Ontario Hydro to become the world leader in the pursuit of more sustainable forms of energy production, development and use, in response to Agenda 21; to help Ontario achieve a more innovative, energy efficient and internationally competitive economy by applying the principles of sustainable development (*Ontario Hydro Report*, p. vii).

1. *All direct costs associated with the project were to be internalized in the planning process.* This meant that regardless of what the law might say on the subject, Ontario Hydro's planners had to identify who was likely to be negatively impacted by a project, what the nature of that impact would be, and then to build the costs of those impacts into the cost-benefit analysis used to assess the viability of the project.

2. *Social and environmental impacts were to be included in the cost-benefit calculations.* That is that the impact on people as well as on the natural environment would have to be assessed. Project planning had to consider the costs and benefits of environmental protection and conservation, regional economic stability, recreation, health, heritage protection, and Aboriginal concerns.

3. *Future as well as present social and environmental costs and benefits had to be factored into the analysis.* This element takes into consideration that the desire to meet the energy needs of present generations cannot compromise the ability of future generations to meet theirs.

4. *Generally, it was preferable that those who bore the risks of a project also shared equitably in the benefits* (Ontario Hydro, 1989b).

Consideration of these four principles led internally to a new planning and environmental assessment process for Ontario Hydro. The corporation's new guidelines, formulated to allow Ontario Hydro *to meet the electrical power needs of the province in the most sustainable or least unsustainable manner,* could be summarized as follows:

1. Integrating environmental, social, and economic costs in all cost calculations

2. Informing and consulting the public in identifying benefits and costs

3. Mitigating all adverse impacts where economically feasible

4. Substituting offsetting benefits for losses where economically feasible for all residual impacts

5. Compensating fairly for all adverse residual impacts, where mitigation or substitution was not possible

A. Assessing the Mattagami Project Under the New Planning Guidelines

The above changes had a significant impact on strategic planning. They required, among other things, that Ontario Hydro identify and consult with project stakeholders. Research revealed the existence of both primary stakeholders, those likely to be directly affected by the project, and secondary stakeholders, those for whom any impacts were likely to be more indirect.

i. Primary Stakeholders

Ontario Hydro, the Aboriginal communities of Moosonee and Moose Factory, the Ontario government, the Spruce Falls Pulp and Paper Corporation, and the town of Kapuskasing were identified as primary stakeholders in the process.

Ontario Hydro's stake was based on the desire to produce more cost-effective and efficient energy from the Mattagami River than was presently the case. Also at stake for the corporation were relationships with northern Ontario's Aboriginal populations. Although the 1960s hydroelectric development had generated large revenues for Ontario Hydro, it had also caused a great deal of environmental damage. This situation led to a great deal of mistrust on the part of the Aboriginal community toward the corporation (DeLauney, 1992). That mistrust was now a significant obstacle in effectively involving the Aboriginal communities in the new planning process.

The *Aboriginal communities living in Moosonee and Moose Factory* had been most affected by previous development. They had suffered more than other Aboriginal communities in the Basin as a result of being located downstream from the Mattagami Complex. These Aboriginal communities still relied heavily on traditional resource harvesting activities for both commerce and food (Ontario Hydro, 1990). Research available to the corporation indicated that one-third of the Native population continued to be directly involved with fishing and hunting. Approximately 50 percent of the protein consumed by native residents of Moose Factory was obtained from the wild (ESSA, 1992).

Thus, the Aboriginal communities were a critical primary stakeholder in the project. Their oral culture was replete with stories about the negative environmental impacts of previous development upon hunting, fishing, trapping, gathering wild plants, and other traditional pursuits. They were concerned that further development would accelerate the destruction of their way of life. As one Aboriginal stated:

> I think and wish that the building of the dams had never happened, because here and now we are already losing a lot of our culture and our ways of life. Those dams would end our culture. They would break the Circle of Life (Faries, 1992).

The Aboriginal First Nations were concerned about the planning process, resource development, the cumulative effects of development in the basin as a whole, and compensation for damage done by past development. The Aboriginals were as a consequence now making self-government a critical issue. Furthermore, they had decided that given their distinct status as original inhabitants, negotiations must be on a government-to-government basis (DeLauney, 1992).

The provincial government and its ministries were also primary stakeholders. The government was ultimately responsible for the environmental assessment process and would inevitably be held politically accountable for the resolution of the conflict. As well, the Ontario government had agreed to pay Ontario Hydro $247 million if the Environmental Assessment of the proposed redevelopment of the entire Mattagami Complex did not obtain project approval (Noble, 1991). Issues for the government were job creation, energy production, Aboriginal self-government, and past grievances. Two ministries were principally responsible for overseeing the approval process, the Ontario Ministry of the Environment and Energy and the Ontario Ministry of Natural Resources.

The Spruce Falls Pulp and Paper Corporation was also directly affected. If the development did not proceed the result might well be higher energy costs for the corporation which ultimately might make the company's products less competitive in the marketplace. If the project did proceed, SFPP would switch from exclusive use of the Smoky Falls Generating Station to drawing power from the Ontario Hydro Bulk Energy System. This would result in a more reliable energy supply for the corporation, less downtime from poor energy supply, and lower operating costs as a result of not having to operate and maintain the generating station and the community of workers that lived there, as well as receiving free power from Ontario Hydro for ten years (Keir, 1991).

If the SFPP were to close, *the entire community of Kapuskasing* with a population approximately 10,840 people (Keir, 1991) would be in jeopardy as SFPP employed around 30 percent of the community's work force (Keir, 1991). As well, 52 percent of the shares of SFPP were now owned by the pulp and paper company's employees. A further 9 percent of the shares were held by area residents. Many of the employees had invested their life savings into the future of the corporation (Fowlie, 1991).

SFPP also provided significant indirect economic benefits to the community in Kapuskasing. Many of the approximately 358 businesses, the majority of which were quite small, provided services directly or indirectly to SFPP or its employees. If SFPP were shut down, so would the vast majority of these businesses (Keir, 1991).

Alternatively there would be a positive economic benefit for Kapuskasing from the proposed development. Up to 2,035 person-years of direct project employment would be made available to qualified people over the five-year construction period, resulting in a peak labour force of 650 workers. As well, approximately 250 indirect jobs would be generated. Local businesses would benefit from direct project purchases of goods and services (Keir, 1991). Kapuskasing could experience additional net revenues of between $25,000 to $35,000 per year during the construction period as a result of additional property taxes and provincial grants (Keir, 1991).

It was clear, therefore, that the town of Kapuskasing was also a primary stakeholder in the project.

ii. Secondary Stakeholders

Identified secondary stakeholders included other municipalities in the area, labour groups, independent power producers, tourist operators, and environmental groups.

The municipalities likely to be indirectly affected by the project included the *towns* or the *residents* of Smooth Rock Falls, Val Rita-Harty, Moonbeam, and Fauquier. These communities were primarily concerned with promoting economic growth and stability. New hydroelectric development would provide additional jobs and training, and some stimulation in spending. In the past they had benefited from Ontario Hydro development, through job creation and indirectly through access to cheaper electric power. The communities had expressed environmental concerns and had indicated that they would be opposed to development that would result in further deterioration. However, since they had been assured by Ontario Hydro that this was unlikely, they wanted the hydroelectric development to be approved (Submission Letters, 1992).

Labour groups such as the International Union of Operating Engineers and the Labourers' International Union of North America had been and would continue to be directly affected by hydroelectric development. Future construction would result in increased direct and indirect employment opportunities for their members (Submission Letters, 1992).

There were several *independent power producers* in the Basin. These proponents of non-utility generation (NUGs) were concerned about economic opportunities for power development. The resolution of the conflict would establish conditions for further development and would therefore affect their ability to negotiate with Ontario Hydro and the Aboriginals for approval of future projects. They were represented by the Independent Power Producers' Society of Ontario (IPPSO) (DeLauney, 1992).

Tourist operators would also be impacted. For example, if wildlife were harmed, hunting and fishing outfitters would be negatively affected. On the other hand, any development that improved access would benefit those same outfitters, as well as operators of snowmobile tours, motel operators, and so on. (DeLauney, 1992).

Environmental groups such as the Coalition of Environmental Groups, Energy Probe, and Northwatch were concerned about the hydroelectric development. Their main apprehension was over the cumulative effects of the development, now and in the future (Submission Letters, 1992).

B. Project Assessment

Ontario Hydro's own assessment had led to the conclusion that tested against its historical criteria the Mattagami proposal represented a lowest-cost development option for the corporation. Management had also concluded that the planning criteria that had evolved from the corporation's understanding of what was required by the Environmental Assessment Act and its commitment to sustainable development constituted a fair basis for responding to the concerns of all those likely to benefit or suffer as a result of the development. The redevelopment would allow a more efficient and productive use of the hydraulic potential of the river. The construction phase would benefit local communities economically through the creation of employment and related purchasing of goods and services. Permitting the redevelopment would justify the purchase of the Smoky Falls Station from the Spruce Falls Pulp and Paper Corporation saving tax dollars and strengthening the economic viability of the mill and consequently the town of Kapuskasing. Equally importantly, in light of their commitment to sustainable development, these economic benefits would be accompanied by potential for certain environmental improvements (Ontario Hydro, 1991c). Ontario Hydro indicated that the planned redevelopment would have little deleterious impact on soil, vegetation, wildlife, and aquatic habitat. The project would, however, lead to a reduction in shoreline erosion in headponds, in downstream erosion in Adam Creek, and in the passage of fish through the Adam Creek control structure, all of which pointed in the direction of environmental remediation.

Ontario Hydro was aware that some negative environmental impacts would result from the redevelopment that it was proposing. However, it was publicly committed to mitigating those impacts where possible. For example, although there would be additional angling and hunting pressure on fish and wildlife populations from the construction work force, the corporation had proposed measures to both restrict and discourage excessive hunting and angling activities during the construction period (Ontario Hydro, 1991c). Although the peaking operations would increase the water-level fluctuation downstream of the Kipling Station, Ontario Hydro was proposing to maintain minimal water levels to prevent the dewatering of aquatic habitat. A new spawning habitat would be created in the Smoky Falls tailrace[8] (see Appendix A) to compensate for the loss of spawning grounds as a result of the redevelopment (Ontario Hydro, 1991c). Ontario Hydro's environmental assessment also acknowledged that there would be some residual impacts for which compensation would be required. For example, Ontario Hydro was proposing to "co-operate with trappers to identify yields before the project and compensate financial losses resulting from project activities" (Ontario Hydro, 1990). Ontario Hydro also offered to compensate for impacts on Aboriginal harvesting activities. Through its environmental assessment Ontario Hydro had publicly stated both that it would:

> seek to provide fair compensation for all subsistence users and licensed trappers in the project area for any losses that may result from the undertaking. With their co-operation, funding will be provided to area First Nations to define both pre- and post-development levels of Aboriginal harvesting (Ontario Hydro, 1990).

and that:

> Should impacts be identified, options such as financial compensation, replacement of losses in kind (e.g., provision of fish, fowl, etc. from other sources) or other equivalent impact management measures (e.g., to establish new trap lines, relocate cabins, etc.) will be offered (Ontario Hydro, 1990).

The commitment to inform and consult was reflected in "public information and feedback" which "were the cornerstones of the public involvement program for the Mattagami River Extensions Environmental Assessment Study" (Ontario Hydro, 1990). Although its relationship with the Nishnawbe-Aski First Nations was acknowledged as strained,[9] attempts were being made to rectify the situation including the appointment of a Corporate Aboriginal Affairs Coordinator (Ontario Hydro, 1990).

Finally, Ontario Hydro had undertaken to deal with the grievances to which the earlier developments on the river had given rise. However, it had rejected the view that settling those grievances was, or should be, an element in any environmental assessment carried out under the *Environmental Assessment Act*. Its views in this matter had been sustained against legal challenges.

---

[8] A tailrace is a channel that carries away water which has passed through the generating station.

[9] The First Nations in the Moose River Basin refused to cooperate with Ontario Hydro's environmental assessment.

Almost certainly, given the new environmental philosophy of the corporation and the public commitments that were entailed, the Board would be surprised and upset to learn that the Aboriginal communities affected continued to be angrily opposed to the development as proposed by the corporation. Debbie understood clearly that explaining why this was the case would be an important component of her presentation.

Part III: An Aboriginal Counterproposal

Debbie's next task would be to carefully lay out the First Nations' response to Ontario Hydro's proposed redevelopment of the Mattagami Complex. That response had three components. First was a commitment to sustainable development that the Native People's Circle on Environment and Development (established to bring an Aboriginal perspective to the Ontario Round Table on Environment and Economy) suggested had always been a guiding concept for Native people. This commitment, they went on to say, was reflected in the Native view that "the land and its resources be preserved for the benefit of past, present, and future generations" (Native People's Circle, 1992).

As with Ontario Hydro, sustainability for the Aboriginal people was closely linked to economic well-being. This apparent agreement, however, masked important differences. Randy Kapashesit, Chief of the Mocreebec First Nation, had underlined these differences in pointing out that:

> Ontario Hydro's notion of economic development is not supportive of the kind of economy that is reflective of our own culture, values, traditions and environment (Kapashesit, 1992).

Underlying these distinct perspectives were different ways of assessing the impacts of hydraulic development on the land. For Ontario Hydro, the land was a resource to be used. From a Native perspective, the land was something deserving great respect, a source of cultural, esthetic, and spiritual as well as economic value. The land was seen as possessing great value in its own right. Its health was viewed as directly linked to human well-being (Native People's Circle, 1992). From an Aboriginal perspective, sustainability was impossible in the absence of respect for the land. The implications of these two perspectives for dealing with the concept of sustainability were striking. For Ontario Hydro, impacts were discussed with a view to replacing losses with equivalent substitutes and failing that providing financial compensation; however, these same impacts were seen by the Aboriginal people as affecting their capacity to sustain a way of life.

The second component in the First Nations' response was the insistence that historical grievances associated with past development be addressed as a condition of future development. This view is captured succinctly by Chief Kapashesit in a statement to the Environmental Assessment Board created to evaluate Ontario Hydro's Twenty-Five-Year Demand/Supply Plan. As he put it:

> Justice requires that ... past grievances be settled before future projects are even considered. It is immoral for Ontario Hydro to be talking about future projects when they have not entered into settlements to compensate for the damage they inflicted by past projects (Kapashesit, 1992).

For the First Nations involved, sustainable development had a historical dimension that they were not prepared to ignore.

The third component of the Aboriginal position on the proposed Mattagami Complex extensions was the demand that there should be no further development until the rights of the First Nation communities to self-government had been recognized. Recognition was to include control over the development of natural resources in areas of Native jurisdiction. The logic behind this demand stemmed directly from the importance of preserving the traditional native way of life and sustainability, and the consistent failure to date on the part of those developing the North to respect values of central importance to the Native communities affected by change. Aboriginal control over the land and its use would ensure that future development was appropriately responsive to those values.

Part IV: The Ontario Government's Option

Debbie knew that historically Ontario Hydro had been closely linked to the Government of Ontario. For example, the Board's Chair and CEO were appointed by the premier of the province. At the same time, the corporation had always tried to operate on business principles at arm's length from the government. Hence, taking the Board through an evaluation of the results of what was essentially a government-inspired initiative in which the corporation had played only a supporting role would certainly be difficult. Debbie decided to set her explanation in the context of the government's substantial financial, economic, and political interest in resolving the conflict that emerged in response to the Mattagami Complex proposal.

The government's response to the conflict was to create a consultative process designed to lead to a consensus on redevelopment. In response to a report it commissioned in July 1991, the provincial government attempted to facilitate problem solving in two distinct ways. Both were designed to resolve the conflict over the Mattagami Complex Proposal fairly while laying the framework for constructive resolution of the longer-term resource use planning issues. The process reflected the view that there could be no adequate resolution of the problems without addressing both the economic interests of the non-Native stakeholders and Aboriginal concerns about the right to equitable participation on their part in resource development and resource management.

First, the Ontario government proposed the creation of a "technical group" with a mandate to review "how the design and/or operation of the [Mattagami Complex] Project could be modified to achieve the primary objective of environmental enhancement as well as the production of energy." The government proposed that the group have four members: two appointed by the government and two by the Moose River and the New Post First Nations. The government also committed itself to providing the financial and technical resources the group would need to assess the Mattagami Complex project, as well as consult broadly and report their findings to the government and the elected chiefs and councils of the New Post, Moose Factory, and Mocreebec First Nations (Ontario Ministry of Natural Resources, 1993a). In addition, the technical group's mandate was to make recommendations on any issues of concern identified in the consultative process. In proposing the committee, the Minister implied a willingness to be guided in his decisions on the project in the event that a consensus report that was able to win First Nation support was forthcoming.

Second, the government proposed the collection of data establishing the existing biophysical, social, cultural, and economic environmental conditions in the Moose River Basin. This data could then be used to establish a baseline against which the cumulative impacts of resource development in the basin could be measured (Ontario Ministry of Natural Resources, 1993b). The government proposed that "traditional knowledge" as well as scientific data be included in the database.

In calling for a baseline data study, the government was responding to a fundamental Native environmental concern, namely that the environment should be looked at holistically. In responding to resource development proposals, Native spokespeople argued that what matters is not the aggregate environmental impact of any particular development looked at in isolation but the cumulative impact of resource development in the Moose River Basin looked at as a whole. Native groups also argued that cumulative impacts could only be calculated against preestablished environmental benchmarks. Identifying benchmarks for the Moose River Basin before further development was approved was therefore a fundamental demand which the government hoped in this way to satisfy.

Part V: The Recommendations

If she succeeded in her goal of explaining the evolution of management thinking, Debbie knew the Board would be in a position to determine the fate of the Mattagami project. Her final task was now to set out the committee's analysis and recommendation to the Board. She had an afternoon to complete this most crucial part of her task. She sat down to write.

APPENDIX A

Components of a Hydroelectric Generating Station

The main components of a hydroelectric generating station are the dam or diversion weir, the powerhouse, and the water passages. The dam or diversion weir directs the flowing water into a canal or turbine inlet. The water then passes through a turbine, causing it to spin with enough force to create electricity in a generator. The water is then returned to the river via a tailrace channel. When the supply of water exceeds the plant's capacity, it is redirected around the station via a sluiceway (Bennett, 1992).

There are two main types of generating stations. The first type is a "run-of-river" or "base load" operation which harnesses the natural flow of the river. The power output of such a plant fluctuates with the stream flow and operates 24 hours a day. The second type of station is known as a "peaking" operation.

Unlike a base load station, a dam is used to build up a reservoir of water or "headpond." During periods of peak power demand, the water is released through the turbines of the power station. As a result, both headpond and downstream water levels fluctuate greatly each day which can cause downstream flooding and the erosion of riverbanks (Bennett, 1992).

Both types of operation require an electrical transmission system to transport the electricity to the bulk electrical system. The electrical transmission system consists of transformers at each generating station, and overhead transmission lines that must be kept clear of brush and trees, a task that is accomplished through the use of herbicides and in other ways.

BIBLIOGRAPHY

Adams, T. "Witness statement." DSP Environmental Assessment Hearing, Exhibit #855. December 1992.

Allen, G. "Ontario backs mill buyout plan." *Globe and Mail,* June 20, 1991, A4.

"Bay and basin bulletin." *The Moose River Basin Project Newsletter,* vol. 1, no. 2, January 1995.

Bennett, Kearon. "Small hydro research summary report." Appendix G, DSP Environmental Assessment Hearing, Exhibit #926, November 1992.

Cheena, G. "Witness statement." Ontario Hydro. DSP Environmental Assessment Hearing, Exhibit #833, December 1992.

Conway, T. "Impacts of prior development." DSP Environmental Assessment Hearing, Exhibit #890, December 1992.

Cragg, A. W. *Contemporary Moral Issues* (4th edition). Toronto: McGraw-Hill Ryerson, 1997.

Cragg, A. W., and Schwartz, M. "Sustainable development and historical injustice: lessons from the Moose River Basin." *Journal of Canadian Studies,* vol. 31, no. 1, Spring 1996.

Cragg, A. W., Wellington, A., and Greenbaum, A., *Applied Environmental Ethics in Canada.* Peterborough: Broadview Press, 1997.

DeLauney, D. "Report of the provincial representative: Moose River Basin consultations." Report prepared for the Ministry of Natural Resources, April 1992.

Environmental Assessment Act, R.S.O. 1980, c.140.

Environmental Assessment Act, R.S.O. 1980, c.E.18.

ESSA (Environmental and Social Systems Analysts Ltd.). "Hypotheses of effects of development in the Moose River Basin workshop summary—final report." DSP Environmental Assessment Hearing, Exhibit #719, March 1992.

Faries, B. "Witness statement." DSP Environmental Assessment Hearing, Exhibit #876, December 1992.

Fowlie, L. "Town that refused to die." *Financial Post,* December 28–30, 1991, p. 16.

Friedman, M. "The social responsibility of business is to increase its profits," *The New York Times Magazine,* September 13, 1970.

Great Whale Public Review Support Office. *Guidelines, Environmental Impact Statement for the Proposed Great Whale River Hydroelectric Project.* Evaluating Committee, Kativik Environmental Quality Commission, Federal Review Committee North of the 55th Parallel, Federal Environmental Assessment Review Panel. Montreal: Great Whale Public Review Support Office, 1992.

Hydro Quebec, *Grande Baleine Complex: Feasibility Study.* Part 2—Hydroelectric Complex, Book 8—Key Issues, August 1993.

Jones, I. "Witness statement." DSP Environmental Assessment Hearing, Exhibit #950, December 1992.

Kapashesit, R. "Evidence in chief." DSP Environmental Assessment Hearing, Exhibit #1019, December 1992.

Keir, A. "Socio-economic impact assessment: reference document of hydroelectric generating station extensions Mattagami River." Prepared for Ontario Hydro Corporate Relations Branch, vols. 1 and 2, January 1991.

Linklater, M. "Witness statement." DSP Environmental Assessment Hearing, Exhibit #877, December 1992.

Litchfield, J., Hemmingway, Leroy, and Raphals, P. "Integrated resource planning and the Great Whale public review." Background Paper No. 7, Great Whale Environmental Assessment, Great Whale Public Review Office, 1994.

MacDonald, R. "Witness statement." DSP Environmental Assessment Hearing, Exhibit #852, December 1992.

Mackie, R. "Cant's afford mill bailout, premier says." *Globe and Mail,* July 15, 1991, A8.

McDonald, M., Stevenson, J. T., and Cragg, A. W. "Finding a balance of values: an ethical assessment of Ontario Hydro's Demand/Supply Plan." Report to the Aboriginal Research Coalition of Ontario, November 1992.

Mittelstaedt, M. "Hydro looking to end environmental hearing," *Globe and Mail,* November 13, 1992, A5.

Mittelstaedt, M. "Ontario gives hydro project go-ahead." *Globe and Mail,* October 6, 1994, B10.

Morrison, J. "Colonization, resource extraction and hydroelectric development in the Moose River Basin: a preliminary history of the implications for aboriginal people." DSP Environmental Assessment Hearing, Exhibit #869, November 1992.

Mugiskan, Chief W. "Witness statement." DSP Environmental Assessment Hearing, Exhibit #866, December 1992.

Nation, K., and Noble, K. "U.S. firm rejects newsprint mill deal." *Globe and Mail,* June 29, 1991, B1 and B4.

"Native people's circle on environmental and development." Report prepared for the Ontario Round Table on Environment and Economy, 1992.

Noble, K. "Kapuskasing deal best for everybody." *Globe and Mail,* August 15, 1991, Section B1 and 4.

Ontario Hydro, *Demand/Supply Plan Report,* DSP Environmental Assessment Hearing, Exhibit #3, December 1989a.

Ontario Hydro. *Demand Supply Plan Environmental Analysis.* DSP Environmental Assessment Hearing, Exhibit #4, December 1989b.

Ontario Hydro, *Environmental Assessment: Hydroelectric Generating Station Extensions Mattagami River,* October 1990.

Ontario Hydro. *Annual Report,* 1991a.

Ontario Hydro. *The Gifts of Nature,* May 1991b.

Ontario Hydro. *Environmental Assessment Summary: Hydroelectric Generating Station Extensions Mattagami River,* February 1991c.

Ontario Hydro. *Report of the Task Force on Sustainable Energy Development: A Strategy for Sustainable Energy Development and Use for Ontario Hydro,* October 18, 1993.

Ontario Ministry of Natural Resources. "Draft terms of reference work plan for the technical group." July 28, 1993a.

Ontario Ministry of Natural Resources. "Moose River Basin baseline data collection project, background report." August 1993b.

Philp, M. "Spruce Falls mill may close." *Globe and Mail,* March 20, 1991, B3.

Roderique, J. "Witness statement." DSP Environmental Assessment Hearing, Exhibit #875, December 1992.

Sears, S. K., and Paterson, M. "Integrated ecosystem-based planning for hydroelectric generation development in a remote northern Ontario river basin." DSP Environmental Assessment Hearing, Exhibit #382, May 1991.

Submission Letters re: Review of Environmental Assessment for the Proposed Hydroelectric Generating Station Extensions on the Mattagami River. Ministry of the Environment, Environmental Assessment Branch, 1992.

Sutherland, J. "Witness statement." DSP Environmental Assessment Hearing, Exhibit #873, December 1992.

Sutherland, P. "Witness statement." DSP Environmental Assessment Hearing, Exhibit #874, December 1992.

Prince Edward Island Preserve Co.

In August 1991, Bruce MacNaughton, president of Prince Edward Island Preserve Co. Ltd. (P.E.I. Preserves), was contemplating future expansion. Two cities were of particular interest: Toronto and Tokyo. At issue was whether consumers in either or both markets should be pursued, and if so, how. The choices available for achieving further growth included mail order, distributors, and company-controlled stores.

Background

Prince Edward Island Preserve Co. was a manufacturing company located in New Glasgow, P.E.I., which produced and marketed specialty food products. The company founder and majority shareholder, Bruce MacNaughton, had realized years earlier that an opportunity existed to present P.E.I. strawberries as a world-class food product and to introduce the finished product to an "upscale" specialty market. With total sales in the coming year expected to exceed $1.0 million for the first time, MacNaughton had made good on the opportunity he had perceived. It had not been easy, however.

MacNaughton arrived in Prince Edward Island from Moncton, New Brunswick, in 1978. Without a job, he slept on the beach for much of that first summer. Over the next few years he worked in commission sales, waited tables in restaurants, and then moved to Toronto. There he studied to become a chef at George Brown Community College. After working in the restaurant trade for several years, he found a job with Preserves by Amelia in Toronto. After six months, he returned to P.E.I., where he opened a restaurant. The restaurant was not successful and MacNaughton lost the $25,000 stake he had accumulated. With nothing left but 100 kilograms of strawberries, Bruce decided to make these into preserves in order to have gifts for Christmas 1984. Early the following year, P.E.I. Preserves was founded.

IVEY

Richard Ivey School of Business
The University of Western Ontario

Professor Paul W. Beamish prepared this case solely to provide material for class discussion. The author does not intend to illustrate either effective or ineffective handling of a managerial situation. The author may have disguised certain names and other identifying information to protect confidentiality. © 1991 Ivey Management Services. Case 9A91G005, version 1991-12-12.

The products produced by the company were priced and packaged for the gift/gourmet and specialty food markets. The primary purchasers of these products were conscious of quality and were seeking a product which they considered tasteful and natural. P.E.I. Preserves felt their product met this standard of quality at a price that made it attractive to all segments of the marketplace.

Over the next few years as the business grew, improvements were made to the building in New Glasgow. The sense of style which was characteristic of the company was evident from the beginning in its attractive layout and design.

In 1989 the company diversified and opened The Perfect Cup, a small restaurant in P.E.I.'s capital city of Charlottetown. This restaurant continued the theme of quality, specializing in wholesome, homemade food featuring the products manufactured by the company. The success of this operation led to the opening in 1990 of a small tea room at the New Glasgow location. Both of these locations showcased the products manufactured by the P.E.I. Preserve Co.

In August 1991, the company opened a small (22 square metres) retail branch in the CP Prince Edward Hotel. MacNaughton hoped this locale would expand visibility in the local and national marketplace, and serve as an off-season sales office. P.E.I. Preserves had been given very favourable lease arrangements (well below the normal $275 per month for space this size) and the location would require minimal financial investment. As Table 1 suggests, the company had experienced steady growth in its scope of operations.

Marketplace

Prince Edward Island was Canada's smallest province, both in size and in population. Located in the Gulf of St. Lawrence, it was separated from Nova Scotia and New Brunswick by the Northumberland Strait. The major employer in P.E.I. was the various levels of government. Many people in P.E.I. worked seasonally, in either farming (especially potatoes), fishing, or tourism. During the peak tourist months of July and August, the island population would swell dramatically from its base of 125,000. P.E.I.'s half-million annual visitors came "home" to enjoy the long, sandy beaches, picturesque scenery, lobster dinners, arguably the best-tasting strawberries in the world, and slower pace of life. P.E.I. was best known in Canada and elsewhere for the books, movies, and (current) television series based on Lucy Maud Montgomery's turn-of-the-century literary creation, *Anne of Green Gables*.

TABLE 1

	Year Opened				
Operation	1985	1989	1990	1991	Projected 1992
New Glasgow—manufacturing and retail	•	•	•	•	•
Charlottetown—restaurant (Perfect Cup)		•	•	•	•
New Glasgow—restaurant (Tea Room)			•	•	•
Charlottetown—retail (CP Hotel)				•	•
Toronto or Tokyo?					•

P.E.I. Preserves felt they were competing in a worldwide market. Their visitors were from all over the world and in 1991 they expected the numbers to exceed 100,000 in the New Glasgow location alone. New Glasgow (population 200) was located in a rural setting equidistant (15 kilometres) from Charlottetown and P.E.I.'s best-known North Shore beaches. In their mailings they planned to continue to promote Prince Edward Island as "Canada's Garden Province" and the "little jewel it was in everyone's heart!" They had benefited, and would continue to benefit, from that image.

Marketing

Products

The company had developed numerous products since its inception. These included many original varieties of preserves as well as honey, vinegar, mustard, and tea (repackaged). (Exhibit 1 contains a 1990 price list, ordering instructions, and a product picture used for mail order purposes.) The company had also added to the appeal of these products by offering gift packs composed of different products and packaging. With over 80 items, it felt that it had achieved a diverse product line and efforts in developing new product lines were expected to decrease in the future. Approximately three-quarters of total retail sales (including wholesale and mail order) came from the products the company made itself. Of these, three-quarters were jam preserves.

With the success of P.E.I. Preserves, imitation was inevitable. In recent years, several other small firms in P.E.I. had begun to retail specialty preserves. Another company which produced preserves in Ontario emphasized the Green Gables tie-in on its labels.

Price

P.E.I. Preserves were not competing with "low-end" products, and felt their price reinforced their customers' perception of quality. The 11 types of jam preserves retailed for $5.89 for a 250 millilitre jar, significantly more than any grocery store product. However, grocery stores did not offer jam products made with such a high fruit content and with champagne, liqueur, or whisky.

In mid-1991, the company introduced a 10 percent increase in price (to $5.89) and, to date, had not received any negative reaction from customers. The food products were not subject to the 7 percent national Goods and Services Tax or P.E.I.'s 10 percent Provincial Sales Tax, an advantage over other gift products which the company would be stressing.

Promotion

Product promotion had been focused in two areas—personal contact with the consumer and catalogue distribution. Visitors to the New Glasgow location (approximately 80,000 in 1990) were enthusiastic upon meeting Bruce, "resplendent in the family kilt," reciting history and generally providing live entertainment. Bruce and the other staff members realized the value of this "island touch" and strove to ensure that all visitors to New Glasgow left with both a positive feeling and purchased products.

EXHIBIT 1   **P.E.I. Preserves Mail Order Catalogue**

Mail Order
Canada

Prince Edward Island Preserve Co.
RR# 2 Hunter River
Prince Edward Island
Canada
C0A 1N0

Tel. (902) 964-2524
Fax. (902) 566-5565

PRODUCTS

Preserves
1. Strawberry & Grand Marnier 250ml 5.69
2. Raspberry & Champagne 250ml 5.69
3. Wild Blueberry & Raspberry in Champagne 250ml 5.69
4. Strawberry, Orange & Rhubarb 250ml 5.69
5. Raspberry & Peach 250ml 5.69
6. Blueberry, Lemon & Fresh Mint 250ml 5.69
7. Black Currant 250ml 5.69
8. Gooseberry & Red Currant 250ml 5.69
9. Sour Cherry Marmalade 250ml 5.69
10. Orange Marmalade with Chivas Regal 250ml 5.69
11. Lemon & Ginger Marmalade with Amaretto 250ml 5.69
12. Strawberry & Grand Marnier 125ml 3.60
13. Raspberry & Champagne 125ml 3.60
14. Wild Blueberry & Raspberry in Champagne 125ml 3.60
15. Raspberry & Peach 125ml 3.60
16. Black Currant 125ml 3.60
17. Orange Marmalade with Chivas Regal 125ml 3.60

Honeys
18. Summer Honey with Grand Marnier 250ml 5.95
19. Summer Honey with Amaretto 250ml 5.95
20. Summer Honey with Grand Marnier 125ml 3.50
21. Summer Honey with Amaretto 125ml 3.50

Mustards
22. Hot & Spicy Mustard 250ml 3.95
23. Champagne & Dill Mustard 250ml 3.95
24. Honey & Thyme Mustard 250ml 3.95
25. Hot & Spicy Mustard 125ml 2.75
26. Champagne & Dill Mustard 125ml 2.75
27. Honey & Thyme Mustard 125ml 2.75

Vinegars
28. Raspberry Vinegar 350ml 5.95
29. Black Currant Vinegar 350ml 5.95
30. Peach Vinegar 350ml 5.95
31. Raspberry Vinegar 150ml 3.50
32. Black Currant Vinegar 150ml 3.50
33. Peach Vinegar 150ml 3.50

Specials
34A. Catharines Hors d'oeuvre & Pasta Sauce . 250 ml 6.49
35. Catharines Hot Antipasto .... 250 ml 5.69
36. Catharines Antipasto .... 250 ml 5.69

Spices *(recipes included)*
37A. Bloody Mary, Bloody Caesar Mix 3.95
38A. Apple Spices - for pies, butters, chutneys............3.95
39A. Mulling Spices - for wine, cider, or ale............4.95
40A. Hot Chocolate - rich & tasty, just add hot water 4.95

Tea - *No tea is fresher than ours*
41. a) Monks Blend   b) Strawberry   c) Raspberry
41. d) Earl Grey   e) English Breakfast   f) Blackcurrant
42. Sachets ....50 g   2.95
43. Tea by the Pound, all blends ....1 lb 14.95

Maple Products
44A. Pure Maple Syrup ....100 ml   3.95
45A. Pure Maple Syrup ....250 ml   5.95
46A. Pure Maple Syrup ....500 ml 10.95
47A. Maple Syrup with Light Rum ....250 ml   5.95
48A. Maple Butter, excellent on pancakes, toast or baking
....250 ml   5.95

Coffees - *We think this is the best coffee available*
First Colony - ground coffee, available 8 oz. and 2 oz.
49A. Columbian Supremo ....8 oz.   6.49
50A. Irish Cream   50B. Swiss Chocolate Almond
....8 oz.   6.49
50C. Chocolate Raspberry Truffle............8 oz.   6.49
51A. Special House Blend.........................2 oz.   2.25
52. All flavours available in 2 oz. packs
    (order coffee by # and letter, i.e. 52C is a 2 oz Chocolate Raspberry Truffle)

Teapots - *If you've had tea with us, these are the ones!*
56. Executive Tea set Black with Sterling Silver   49.95
57.   Sky Blue with Sterling Silver   49.95
58. [1-2 cup teapot, 1 cup & saucer]   Fern Green with Gold Inlay   49.95
59.   Rust with Gold Inlay 49.95
60. Romance Tea set Black with Sterling Silver   59.95
61.   Sky Blue with Sterling Silver   59.95
62. [1-2 cup teapot, 2 cups & saucers]   Fern Green with Gold Inlay   59.95
63.   Rust with Gold Inlay 59.95
64. Gift Packages - We pack all for long journeys!
A. P.E.I.Summer House 24.99
B. Taster's Choice Duo ....2-125 ml Preserves Crated 8.25
C. Taster's Choice Trio .2 -125 ml Preserves,1-125 Honey Crated 11.95
D. Crated vinegars ....2-150ml Fruit Vinegars Crated 7.49
E. Crated Preserves (2 jars) ....250 ml 12.49
F. Crated Preserves (3 jars) ....250 ml 17.95
G. Tea-for-Two ....1-125 ml Preserves, Tea, 1-125 ml Honey 11.95
75. 8" Brass Planter - filled with Swiss Chocolate, Hot
    Chocolate, Chocolate Coffee and more
    Chocolate 23.99
76. 6" Brass Planter - 1-125 ml Preserve, 1-125 ml
    Honey with Liqueur, Honey Dipper and
    Chocolate 16.50
77. 4" Brass Planter - 125 ml Honey with Liqueur and
    Honey Dipper 10.95
78. Wicker House - 2-250 ml Preserves with Liqueur,
    1-250 ml Honey with Liqueur, 100 ml Maple Syrup,
    Irish Cream Coffee, Strawberry Tea 39.95
79. 14" Wicker Hamper - 1-125 ml Preserve, 1-125 ml
    Honey with Liqueur, 1 Raspberry Tea, 1 Irish
    Cream Coffee, Honey Dipper 32.95
80. Hunter Green S M L XL Sweatshirt 29.95
    87% Cotton, 13% Poly, Preshrunk
81. Deep Lavender S M L XL Sweatshirt 29.95
    87% Cotton, 13% Poly, Preshrunk

Shipping cost per Address

Value of Order	*Shipping Cost
$ 0. - $30.	5.00
$31. - $40.	6.00
$41. - $55.	7.00
$56. - $65.	8.00
$66. - $75.	9.00
$76. - $100.	10.00
$101. & over	5% of order

All packages are packed well for shipping. We use double strength corrugated boxes and finish the packages with a heavy brown paper wrap.

Please note that if the postage cost is less than the amount charged to you, we then will charge you the least amount. That is why we prefer if you paid by credit card. Thank you, Bruce.

Gift Wrapping
$3.50 per package

Using the appropriate gift wrap for the season, we'll give your package that little extra. We can supply a small card with your salutation, or if you send us your card with your order, we will include it.

Gift Packaging
Friends, we have many packaging ideas, too many for our catalogue. If you wish us to do up a basket in a certain price range, or any special order for that matter just give us a call, fax or mail in your request. We are here for you!

Method of Payment
□MasterCard □Visa

CREDIT CARD NUMBER

Cardholder Name
Please Print

We require a signature

mo./ yr.
Expiry Date

① **SOLD TO:**   □Mr. □Mrs. □Ms.
Name _____ Please Print
Address _____
City _____ Prov _____ PostalCode _____
May we have your phone number in case of a question about your order?
Home ( ) _____   Work ( ) _____

Send to me at the above address.
Ship to arrive: □Now □Christmas □Other.............

Prod.#	Quantity	Price Each	Gift Wrap	Total Price
			3.50☐	
			3.50☐	
			3.50☐	
			3.50☐	
			3.50☐	
			3.50☐	
			3.50☐	
			3.50☐	
		Shipping		
		Total Cost		

② **Send to:**   □Mr. □Mrs. □Ms. □Firm
Name _____ Please Print
Address _____
City _____ Prov. _____ Postal _____
Greetings from:
Ship to arrive: □Now □Christmas □Other.........

Prod.#	Quantity	Price Each	Gift Wrap	Total Price
			3.50☐	
			3.50☐	
			3.50☐	
			3.50☐	
			3.50☐	
			3.50☐	
			3.50☐	
			3.50☐	
		Shipping		
		Total Cost		

Dear Shopper,
If you have visited our store recently, and wish to purchase an item which is not on this list, please feel free to do so.
On a separate sheet of paper, write a description of the item to the best of your ability, and we will do our best to satisfy your request.

sincerely,

Bruce MacNaughton

For *FAST* delivery call:
(9:00 am to 5:00 pm A.S.T.)
(902) 964-2524
Fax (902) 566-5565

Prices subject to change without notice.

EXHIBIT I   *continued*

Visitors were also encouraged to visit the New Glasgow location through a cooperative scheme whereby other specialty retailers provided a coupon for a free cup of coffee or tea at P.E.I. Preserves. In 1991, roughly 2,000 of these coupons were redeemed.

Approximately 5,000 people received their mail order catalogue annually. They had experienced an order rate of 7.5 percent with the average order being $66. They hoped to devote more time and effort to their mail order business in an effort to extend their marketing and production period. For 1991/92, the order rate was expected to increase by as much as 15 percent because the catalogue was to be mailed two weeks earlier than in the previous year. The catalogues cost $1 each to print and mail.

In addition to mail order, the company operated with an ad hoc group of wholesale distributors. These wholesalers were divided between Nova Scotia, Ontario, and other locations. For orders as small as $150, buyers could purchase from the wholesalers' price list. Wholesale prices were on average 60 percent of the retail/mail order price. Total wholesale trade for the coming year was projected at $150,000, but had been higher in the past.

Danamar Imports was a Toronto-based specialty food store supplier which had previously provided P.E.I. Preserves to hundreds of specialty food stores in Ontario. Danamar had annually ordered $80,000 worth of P.E.I. Preserves at

30 percent below the wholesale price. This arrangement was amicably discontinued in 1990 by MacNaughton due to uncertainty about whether he was profiting from this contract. P.E.I. Preserves had a list of the specialty stores which Danamar had previously supplied, and was planning to contact them directly in late 1991.

Over the past few years, the company had received numerous enquiries for quotations on large-scale shipments. Mitsubishi had asked for a price on a container load of preserves. Airlines and hotels were interested in obtaining preserves in 28 or 30 gram single-service bottles. One hotel chain, for example, had expressed interest in purchasing 3,000,000 bottles if the cost could be kept under $0.40 per unit. (Bruce had not proceeded due to the need to purchase $65,000 worth of bottling equipment, and uncertainty about his production costs.) This same hotel chain had more recently been assessing the ecological implications of the packaging waste which would be created with the use of so many small bottles. They were now weighing the hygiene implications of serving jam out of multi-customer-use larger containers in their restaurants. They had asked MacNaughton to quote on $300,000 worth of jam in 2 litre bottles.

Financial

The company had enjoyed a remarkable rate of growth since its inception. Sales volumes had increased in each of the six years of operations, from an initial level of $30,000 to 1990s total of $785,000. These sales were made up of $478,000 from retail sales (including mail order) of what they manufactured and/or distributed, and $307,000 from the restaurants (the Tea Room in New Glasgow, and Perfect Cup Restaurant in Charlottetown). Exhibits 2 and 3 provide income statements from these operations, while Exhibit 4 contains a consolidated balance sheet.

This growth, although indicative of the success of the product, has also created its share of problems. Typical of many small businesses which experience such rapid growth, the company had not secured financing suitable to its needs. This, coupled with the seasonal nature of the manufacturing operation, had caused numerous periods of severe cash shortages. From Bruce's perspective, the company's banker (Bank of Nova Scotia) had not been as supportive as it might have been. (The bank manager in Charlottetown had last visited the facility three years ago.) Bruce felt the solution to the problem of cash shortages was the issuance of preferred shares. "An infusion of 'long term' working capital, at a relatively low rate of interest, will provide a stable financial base for the future," he said.

At this time, MacNaughton was attempting to provide a sound financial base for the continued operation of the company. He had decided to offer a preferred share issue in the amount of $100,000. These shares would bear interest at the rate of 8 percent cumulative and would be non-voting, non-participating. He anticipated that the sale of these shares would be complete by December 31, 1991. In the interim he required a line of credit in the

EXHIBIT 2

P.E.I. PRESERVE CO. LTD.
(Manufacturing and Retail)
STATEMENT OF EARNINGS AND RETAINED EARNINGS
Year ended January 31, 1991
(unaudited)

	1991	1990
Sales	$478,406	$425,588
Cost of sales	217,550	186,890
Gross margin	260,856	238,698
Expenses:		
Advertising and promotional items	20,632	6,324
Automobile	7,832	3,540
Doubtful accounts	1,261	—
Depreciation and amortization	11,589	12,818
Dues and fees	1,246	2,025
Electricity	7,937	4,951
Heat	4,096	4,433
Insurance	2,426	1,780
Interest and bank charges	5,667	17,482
Interest on long-term debt	23,562	9,219
Management salary	29,515	32,600
Office and supplies	12,176	10,412
Professional fees	19,672	10,816
Property tax	879	621
Rent	—	975
Repairs and maintenance	6,876	9,168
Salaries and wages	70,132	96,386
Telephone and facsimile	5,284	5,549
Trade shows	18,588	12,946
	249,370	242,045
Earnings (loss) from manufacturing operation	11,486	(3,347)
Management fees	—	7,250
Loss from restaurant operations—Schedule 2	3,368	—
Earnings before income taxes	8,118	3,903
Income taxes	181	1,273
Net earnings	7,937	2,630
Retained earnings, beginning of year	9,290	6,660
RETAINED EARNINGS, END OF YEAR	$ 17,227	$ 9,290

amount of $100,000 which he requested to be guaranteed by the Prince Edward Island Development Agency.

Projected sales for the year ended January 31, 1992, were:

New Glasgow Restaurant	$ 110,000
Charlottetown Restaurant	265,000
Retail (New Glasgow)	360,000
Wholesale (New Glasgow)	150,000
Mail order (New Glasgow)	50,000
Retail (Charlottetown)	75,000
TOTAL	$1,010,000

EXHIBIT 3

SCHEDULE 2
P.E.I. PRESERVE CO. LTD.
SCHEDULE OF RESTAURANT OPERATIONS
(Charlottetown and New Glasgow)
Year ended January 31, 1991
(unaudited)

	1991
Sales	$306,427
Cost of sales:	
Purchases and freight	122,719
Inventory, end of year	11,864
	110,855
Salaries and wages for food preparation	42,883
	153,738
Gross margin	152,689
Expenses:	
Advertising	2,927
Depreciation	6,219
Electricity	4,897
Equipment lease	857
Insurance	389
Interest and bank charges	1,584
Interest on long-term debt	2,190
Office and supplies	2,864
Propane	2,717
Rent	22,431
Repairs and maintenance	3,930
Salaries and wages for service	90,590
Supplies	12,765
Telephone	1,697
	156,057
LOSS FROM RESTAURANT OPERATIONS	$ 3,368

◼ Operations

Preserve production took place on-site, in an area visible through glass windows from the retail floor. Many visitors, in fact, would videotape operations during their visit to the New Glasgow store, or would watch the process while tasting the broad selection of sample products freely available.

Production took place on a batch basis. Ample production capacity existed for the $30,000 main kettle used to cook the preserves. Preserves were made five months a year, on a single-shift, five-days-per-week basis. Even then, the main kettle was in use only 50 percent of the time.

Only top-quality fruit was purchased. As much as possible, P.E.I. raw materials were used. For a short period the fruit could be frozen until time for processing.

The production process was labour-intensive. Bruce was considering the feasibility of moving to an incentive-based salary system to increase productivity

EXHIBIT 4

P.E.I. PRESERVE CO. LTD.
BALANCE SHEET
As at January 31, 1991
(unaudited)

	1991	1990
Current Assets		
Cash	$ 5,942	$ 592
Accounts receivable:		
Trade	12,573	6,511
Investment tax credit	1,645	2,856
Other	13,349	35,816
Inventory	96,062	85,974
Prepaid expenses	2,664	6,990
	132,235	138,739
Grant receivable	2,800	1,374
Property, plant, and equipment	280,809	162,143
Recipes and trade name, at cost	10,000	10,000
	$425,844	$312,256
Current Liabilities		
Bank indebtedness	$ 2,031	$ 9,483
Operating and other loans	54,478	79,000
Accounts payable and accrued liabilities	64,143	32,113
Current portion of long-term debt	23,657	14,704
	144,309	135,300
Long-term debt	97,825	99,679
Deferred government assistance	54,810	—
Payable to shareholder, non-interest-bearing,		
no set terms of repayment	43,373	49,687
	340,317	284,666
Shareholders' Equity		
Share capital	55,000	5,000
Contributed surplus	13,300	13,300
Retained earnings	17,227	9,290
	85,527	27,590
	$425,844	$312,256

and control costs. Because a decorative cloth fringe was tied over the lid of each bottle, bottling could not be completely automated. A detailed production cost analysis had recently been completed. While there were some minor differences due to ingredients, the variable costs averaged $1.25 per 250 millilitre bottle. This was made up of ingredients ($0.56), labour ($0.28), and packaging ($0.20/ bottle, $0.11/lid, $0.03/label, and $0.07/fabric and ribbon).

Restaurant operations were the source of many of Bruce's headaches. The New Glasgow Restaurant had evolved over time from offering "dessert and coffee/tea" to its present status where it was also open for meals all day.

Management

During the peak summer period, P.E.I. Preserves employed 45 people among the restaurants, manufacturing area, and retail locations. Of these, five were managerial positions (see Exhibit 5). The company was considered a good place to work, with high morale and limited turnover. Nonetheless, most employees (including some management) were with the company on a seasonal basis. This was a concern to MacNaughton, who felt that if he could provide year-round employment, he would be able to attract and keep the best-quality staff.

Carol Rombough was an effective assistant general manager and bookkeeper. Maureen Dickieson handled production with little input required from Bruce. Kathy MacPherson was in the process of providing, for the first time, accurate cost information. Natalie Leblanc was managing the new retail outlet in Charlottetown, and assisting on some of the more proactive marketing initiatives Bruce was considering.

EXHIBIT 5   Key Executives

President and General Manager: Bruce MacNaughton, age 35

Experience:	• Seventeen years of "front line" involvement with the public in various capacities
	• Seven years of managing and promoting Prince Edward Island Preserve Co. Ltd.
	• Past director of the Canadian Specialty Food Association
Responsibilities:	• To develop and oversee the short-, mid-, and long-term goals of the company
	• To develop and maintain quality products for the marketplace
	• To oversee the management of personnel
	• To develop and maintain customer relations at both the wholesale and the retail level
	• To develop and maintain harmonious relations with government and the banking community

Assistant General Manager: Carol Rombough, age 44

Experience:	• Twenty years as owner/operator of a manufacturing business
	• Product marketing at both the wholesale and the retail level
	• Personnel management
	• Bookkeeping in a manufacturing environment
	• Three years with the Prince Edward Island Preserve Co. Ltd.
Responsibilities:	• All bookkeeping functions (e.g., Accounts Receivable, Accounts Payable, Payroll)
	• Staff management—scheduling and hiring
	• Customer relations

Production Manager: Maureen Dickieson, age 29

Experience:	• Seven years of production experience in the dairy industry
	• Three years with the Prince Edward Island Preserve Co. Ltd.
Responsibilities:	• To oversee and participate in all production
	• To plan and schedule production
	• To requisition supplies

Consultant: Kathy MacPherson, Certified General Accountant, age 37

Experience:	• Eight years as a small business owner/manager
	• Eight years in financial planning and management
Responsibilities:	• To implement an improved system of product costing
	• To assist in the development of internal controls
	• To compile monthly internal financial statements
	• To provide assistance and/or advice as required by management

Store Manager: Natalie Leblanc, age 33

Experience:	• Fifteen years in retail
Responsibilities:	• To manage the retail store in the CP Hotel
	• To assist with mail order business
	• Marketing duties as assigned

Bruce felt that the company had survived on the basis of word-of-mouth. Few followup calls on mail order had ever been done. Bruce did not enjoy participating in trade shows—even though he received regular solicitations for them from across North America. In 1992, he planned to participate in four *retail* shows, all of them in or close to P.E.I. Bruce hoped to be able eventually to hire a sales/marketing manager, but could not yet afford $30,000 for the necessary salary.

The key manager continued to be MacNaughton. He described himself as "a fair person to deal with, but shrewd when it comes to purchasing. However, I like to spend enough money to ensure that what we do—we do right." Financial and managerial constraints meant that Bruce felt stretched ("I haven't had a vacation in years") and unable to pursue all of the ideas he had for developing the business.

■ The Japanese Consumer

MacNaughton's interest in the possibility of reaching the Tokyo consumer had been formed from two factors: the large number of Japanese visitors to P.E.I. Preserves, and the fact that the largest export shipment the company had ever made had been to Japan. MacNaughton had never visited Japan, although he had been encouraged by Canadian federal government trade representatives to participate in food and gift shows in Japan. He was debating whether he should visit Japan during the coming year. Most of the information he had on Japan had been collected for him by a friend.

Japan was Canada's second most important source of foreign tourists. In 1990, there were 474,000 Japanese visitors to Canada, a figure that was expected to rise to 1,000,000 by 1995. Most Japanese visitors entered through the Vancouver or Toronto airports. Within Canada, the most popular destination was the Rocky Mountains (in Banff, Alberta, numerous stores catered specifically to Japanese consumers). Nearly 15,000 Japanese visited P.E.I. each year. Excluding airfare, these visitors to Canada spent an estimated $314 million, the highest per capita amount from any country.

The Japanese fascination with Prince Edward Island could be traced to the popularity of *Anne of Green Gables*. The Japanese translation of this and other books in the same series had been available for many years, and the adoption of the book as required reading in the Japanese school system since the 1950s had resulted in widespread awareness and affection for "Anne with red hair" *and* P.E.I.

The high level of spending by Japanese tourists was due to a multitude of factors: the amount of disposable income available to them, one of the world's highest per-person duty-free allowances (200,000 yen), and gift-giving traditions in the country. Gift giving and entertainment expenses at the corporate level are enormous in Japan. In 1990, corporate entertainment expenses were almost 5 trillion yen, more than triple the U.S. level of 1.4 trillion yen. Corporate gift giving, while focused at both year-end (*seibo*) and the summer (*chugen*), in fact occurred throughout the year.

Gift giving at the personal level was also widespread. The amount spent would vary depending on one's relationship with the recipient; however, one

EXHIBIT 6   Jam Distribution Channels in Japan

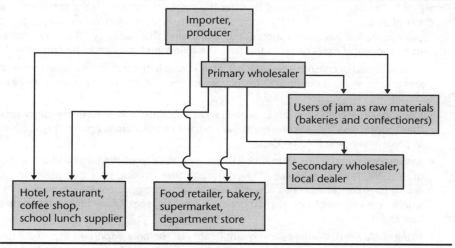

Source: Access to Japan's Import Market, Tradescope, June 1989.

of the most common price points used by Japanese retailers for gift giving was offering choices for under 2,000 yen.

The Japanese Jam Market

Japanese annual consumption of jam was approximately 80,000 tonnes. Imports made up 6 to 9 percent of consumption, with higher-grade products (470 yen or more per kilogram wholesale CIF) making up a third of this total. Several dozen firms imported jam, and utilized a mix of distribution channels (see Exhibit 6). Prices varied, in part, according to the type of channel structure used. Exhibit 7 provides a common structure. Import duties for jams were high—averaging about 28 percent. Despite such a high tariff barrier, some firms had been successful in exporting to Japan. Excerpts from a report on how to access Japan's jam market successfully are contained in Exhibit 8.

EXHIBIT 7   Example of Price Markups in Japan

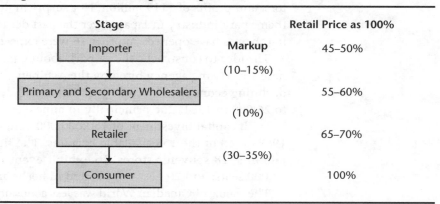

Source: Access to Japan's Import Market, Tradescope, June 1989.

EXHIBIT 8   The Japanese Jam Market

To expand sales of imported jam or to enter the Japanese market for the first time, it is necessary to develop products after precise study of the market's needs. Importers who are making efforts to tailor their products to the Japanese market have been successfully expanding their sales by 10 percent each year. On the basis of the analysis of successful cases of imported jam, the following factors may be considered very important.

- *Diversification of consumer preferences.* Strawberry jam occupies about 50 percent of the total demand for jam and its share is continuing to rise. Simultaneously, more and more varieties of jam are being introduced.

- *Low sugar content.* European exporters have successfully exported low-sugar jam that meets the needs of the Japanese market. Jam with a sugar content of less than 65 percent occupies a share of 65–70 percent of the market on a volume basis.

- *Smaller containers.* Foreign manufacturers who stick to packaging products in large-sized containers (650 grams, 440 grams, 250 grams), even though their products are designed for household use, have been failing to expand their sales. On the other hand, foreign manufacturers who have developed products in smaller containers (14 grams, 30 grams, 42 grams) specifically for the Japanese market have achieved successful results.

- *Fashionable items.* Contents and quantity are not the only important aspects of jam. The shape and material quality of the containers and their caps, label design, and product name can also influence sales. It is also important that the label not be damaged in any way.

- *Development of gift items.* Sets of various types of imported jams are popular as gift items. For example, there are sets of ten kinds of jam in 40 gram mini-jars (retail price 2,000 yen) sold as gift sets.

- *Selection of distribution channel.* Since general trading companies, specialty importers and jam manufacturers each have their own established distribution channels, the selection of the most appropriate channel is of the utmost importance.

Source: Access to Japan's Import Market, Tradescope, June 1989.

Canadian World

In spring 1990, P.E.I. Preserves received its biggest-ever export order; $50,000 worth of product was ordered (FOB New Glasgow) for ultimate shipment to Ashibetsu, on the northern Japanese island of Hokkaido. These products were to be offered for sale at Canadian World, a new theme park scheduled to open in July 1990.

In 1981, Japan's first theme park was built outside Tokyo. Called Tokyo Disneyland, in 1989 it had an annual revenue of $815 million, 14.7 million visitors, and profits of $119 million. Not surprisingly, this success has spawned a theme park industry in Japan. Over the past decade, 20 parks with wide-ranging themes have opened. Another 16 were expected to open in 1991/92.

The idea to construct a theme park about Canada was conceived by a Japanese advertising agency hired by the Ashibetsu city council to stop the city's declining economy. The city's population had decreased from 75,000 in 1958 to 26,000 in 1984, due principally to mine closures.

With capital investment of 750,000,000 yen, construction started in mid-1989 on 48 of the 156 available hectares. The finished site included six restaurants, 18 souvenir stores, 16 exhibit event halls, an outdoor stage with 12,000 seats, and 20 hectares planted in herbs and lavender.

The theme of Canadian World was less a mosaic of Canada than it was a park devoted to the world of *Anne of Green Gables.* The entrance to Canadian World was a replica of Kensingston Station in P.E.I. The north gateway was Brightriver Station, where Anne first met with Matthew. There was a full scale copy of the Green Gables house, Orwell School where you could actually learn English like Anne did, and so forth. Canadian World employed 55 full-time and 330 part-time staff. This included a high school girl from P.E.I. who played Anne—complete with (dyed) red hair—dressed in Victorian period costume.

In late August 1991, Canadian World still had a lot of P.E.I. Preserves' products for sale. Lower-than-expected sales could be traced to a variety of problems. First, overall attendance at Canadian World had been 205,000 in the first year, significantly lower than the expected 300,000. Second, the product was priced higher than many competitive offerings. For reasons unknown to Canadian World staff, the product sold for 10 percent more than expected (1,200 yen versus 1,086 yen).

Wholesale price in P.E.I.	$3.50
Freight ($4.20/kilogram, P.E.I. to Hokkaido)	0.80
Duty (28% of wholesale price plus freight)	1.20
Landed cost in Japan	5.50
Importer's margin (15%)	0.83
Price to primary wholesaler	6.33
Wholesaler margin (10%)	0.63
Price to retailer	6.96
Canadian World markup (30%)	2.09
Expected retail price	$9.05
Exchange (Cdn$1 = 120 yen)	¥1,086

Third, the product mix chosen by the Japanese buyers appeared to be inappropriate. While it was difficult to locate any of the company's remaining strawberry preserves in the various Canadian World outlets which carried it, other products had not moved at all. Canadian World personnel did not have a tracking system for product-by-product sales. Fourth, the company's gift packs were not always appropriately sized or priced. One suggestion had been to package the preserves in cardboard gift boxes of three large (250 millilitres) or five small (125 millilitres) bottles for eventual sale for under 2,000 yen.

An increasing portion of all of the gifts being sold at Canadian World were, in fact, being made in Japan. Japanese sourcing was common due to the high Japanese duties on imports, the transportation costs from Canada, and the unfamiliarity of Canadian companies with Japanese consumer preferences.

◻ The Tokyo Market

With ten million residents, Tokyo was the largest city in Japan and one of the most crowded cities anywhere. Thirty million people lived within 50 kilometres of Tokyo's Imperial Palace. As the economic centre of the nation, Tokyo also had the most expensive land in the world—US$150,000 per square metre in the city centre. Retail space in one of Tokyo's major shopping districts would cost $75–$160 per square metre or $1,600–$3,400 per month for a shop equivalent in size to that in the CP Prince Edward Hotel. Prices in the Ginza were even higher. In addition to basic rent, all locations required a deposit (guarantee money which would be repaid when the tenant gave up the lease) of at least $25,000. Half of the locations available in a recent survey also charged administrative/maintenance fees (5–12 percent of rent), while in about one-third of the locations a "reward" (gift) was paid by tenants to the owner at the time the contract was signed. For a small site it might amount to $10–15,000.

The Toronto Market

With three million people, Toronto was Canada's largest city and economic centre. It contained the country's busiest airport (15 million people used it each year) and was a popular destination for tourists. Each year, roughly 20 million people visited Toronto for business or vacation.

MacNaughton's interest in Toronto was due to its size, the local awareness of P.E.I., and the high perceived potential volume of sales. The company did not have a sales agent in Toronto.

The Toronto market was well served by mass-market and specialty jam producers at all price points. Numerous domestic and imported products were available. Prices started as low as $1 (or less) for a 250 millilitre bottle of high-sugar/low-fruit product. Prices increased to $2–$2.50 for higher-fruit, natural brands and increased again to $3–$3.50 for many of the popular branded imports. The highest-priced products, such as P.E.I. Preserves, were characterized by even-higher fruit content, highest-quality ingredients, and a broader selection of product offerings.

The specialty domestic producers were from various provinces and tended to have limited distribution areas. The specialty imports were frequently from France or England. The Canadian tariff on imports was 15 percent for most countries. From the United States, it was 10.5 percent and declining.

The cost of retail space in Toronto varied according to location but was slightly lower than that in Tokyo. The cost of renting 22 square metres would be $100 per square metre per month (plus common area charges and taxes of $15 per square metre per month) in a major suburban shopping mall, and somewhat higher in the downtown core. Retail staff salaries were similar in Toronto and Tokyo, both of which were higher than those paid in P.E.I.

Future Directions

MacNaughton was the first to acknowledge that, while the business had been "built on gut and emotion, rather than analysis," this was insufficient for the future. The challenge was to determine the direction and timing of the desired change.

Raymark Technologies Inc.

Raymark Technologies Inc. (Raymark) had just completed another extremely successful year. Founded in 1976, Raymark, an Ottawa, Ontario–based company that produced hardware and software interfaces for industrial control equipment, had grown from 15 employees in 1983 to 425 employees and sales of almost $50 million in 1993. Nevertheless, in April 1994, Steve Thomas, founder and president of Raymark, was not entirely sure if the current structure of the partnership with Sentor Equipment (Sentor) was in the best long-term interests of the firm. There was little question but that the relationship with Sentor was a major part of Raymark's success. However, Raymark was no longer a struggling young firm in search of markets and customers. Several acquisitions in recent years had allowed Raymark to lessen its dependence on Sentor as a customer, although sales to Sentor still represented 75 percent of total Raymark sales. The question now facing Thomas was what shape the relationship should take in future years. Perhaps, Thomas thought, it was time to restructure the ten-year-old agreement between Sentor and Raymark.

Raymark Technologies

Raymark was a world leader in products used for a range of applications as diverse as semiconductor manufacturing, airline baggage handling, integrated building control, retail point-of-sale terminals, blood analysis machines, and industrial process control for a variety of industries including brewing, food processing, and hazardous chemical disposal.

The firm was founded in 1976 by Steve Thomas. After earning a doctorate in Engineering Physics from the University of Toronto and working for several years as a consulting engineer, Thomas decided to start his own business. Using microprocessors, Raymark was able to enter the industrial control market. With Steve Thomas as the creative force at Raymark, the firm created new computer alternatives to the traditional pushbutton control market.

From the outset, Raymark developed products able to facilitate the exchange of information between computers and direct manufacturing processes. Using

---

This case was prepared by Andrew Inkpen for the sole purpose of providing material for class discussion. © 1995 Andrew Inkpen.

innovative graphics and communication devices, manufacturing processes could be monitored and controlled. The company's monitors, computers, and real-time software were used to simplify the interface between people and their control systems by providing easy ways for users to effectively interact with computer-controlled machines and processes. A continuing objective was the modification of the controls to make them even more sensitive and sophisticated. In recent years, this had led Raymark into the manufacturing of sensors for robotic hands.

Raymark management viewed the firm as both a software and a hardware firm, and for many products Raymark's software and hardware skills were equally important. For example, Raymark manufactured a line of touch control systems that incorporated a touch-screen computer with high-quality graphics capabilities. The product was housed in a rugged case impervious to chemicals and cleaning solutions. The computer was a complete PC that operated in a DOS and Microsoft Windows environment. Standard off-the-shelf software development tools could be used to create unique applications. The product could be customized with a variety of different-colored cases, buttons, and function keys. Raymark utilized advanced computer-aided design and simulation tools to design and manufacture the touch-screen computers in Raymark in-house facilities.

Underlying the success at Raymark was a corporate culture dedicated to innovation. Steve Thomas was largely responsible for the innovative spirit in his talented employees. As a business press article emphasized, constant innovation drove the culture of Raymark:

> Like so many other firms making leading-edge products, Thomas understands the innovative treadmill Raymark walks. A high-tech item has a short life cycle. A company must redemonstrate its ingenuity about every year and a half. But, risky product development expenditures eat up revenues. For example, half of Raymark's payroll goes for developmental work. According to Thomas, one can't simply keep the faith that new ideas will bear fruit.

◼ The Industrial Controls Industry

Considered a mature market in the mid-1980s, technological advances in computer hardware and software were driving the industrial controls industry in many new directions. Industrial controls were found in virtually every manufacturing location and, increasingly, in a range of service industries. At their most basic, controls were used to start, regulate, stop, and protect electric motors. Other industry controls were used in factory floor applications requiring logic, data transfer, machine diagnostics, computer interfacing, and distributed control. The automation of many industrial processes was facilitated by the use of sophisticated control devices.

The traditional control market covered such products as starters, controls for adjustable speed drives, motor control centres, mechanical positioning sensors, and relays. In many industries, these traditional products had been replaced by electronic and computer-based controls using operator interfaces (such as those produced by Raymark). Computer-based controls with enormous information-gathering and -processing capabilities could be used in large-scale industrial control environments in which hundreds of variables had to be continuously controlled. These type of controls eliminated the use a conventional application-specific and general industrial controls.

With the changes in the technological nature of industrial controls there has been a consolidation in the controls industry in the United States. The largest companies included Allen-Bradley, Sentor, Texas Instruments, and Eaton. Each of these companies was spending large sums of money on the development of in-house computer expertise. Competition from firms in Japan, the United Kingdom, Germany, and Switzerland was also increasing.

The Sentor-Raymark Partnership

The relationship between Sentor and Raymark began in the early 1980s. At that time, Raymark was a struggling young high-tech company with plenty of ideas and initiative, little capital, and few products. The company had only 15 customers and minimal infrastructure, and was relying on sales representatives and distributors to market its products.

Sentor, a firm with $1.6 billion in sales in 1994, was based in Rochester, Michigan, a Detroit suburb. Sentor was a leading firm in the industrial control industry with sales channels throughout the world. More than 30 percent of Sentor sales were exports. Sentor was founded in 1921 as a manufacturer of electric motors and electric motor parts. In 1994, Sentor offered specialized control and automation expertise for virtually every industry. Sentor produced more than 250,000 control products and variations. Sentor was an industry leader in plant floor automation, with a focus on helping customers become more competitive through increased manufacturing flexibility. Some of Sentor's automation and control product categories were programmable controls, communications networks, sensing and motor control devices, machine vision, and computer numerical control systems.

In 1982, a large automation equipment and industrial controls manufacturer, Sterling Automation (Sterling), developed an innovative computerized technology for operating and controlling equipment. Sentor, a direct competitor of Sterling, had not yet developed a similar technology for its products. Without this operator interface technology and as rapid developments in microprocessors began to occur, Sentor was in danger of being leapfrogged in technology by its competitors.

Sentor's industrial automation group decided it could not take the time to develop new operator interface technology in-house. Sentor management began discussions with a number of outside firms to supply operator interface hardware and software. Steve Thomas heard through the grapevine that Sentor was looking for a partner and was able to get Raymark on the short list of potential Sentor suppliers. Sentor's objective in soliciting bids was to find a supplier to carry them for a few years until the technology could be developed in-house.

Raymark was selected as the firm to develop and supply the products to Sentor. After a year of negotiating, an agreement between Sentor and Raymark was signed in November 1983. The deal had two parts. One part was a commercial agreement for Raymark to supply a line of human-machine interface products to Sentor. Under the agreement, Raymark designed and manufactured products that were brand-labelled by Sentor and sold as if they were Sentor's own products. These products were designed specifically to the requirements of Sentor customers. For example, in 1986 Raymark developed a family of intelligent plant floor terminals with integrated touch screens that were more functional and cost-effective than controls with pushbuttons and indicators. Raymark also manufactured a set of realtime software products that integrated process control, data management, and graphical operator interface for industrial personal computers. Raymark had been able to maintain its innovative lead in control products that could perform a very wide variety of graphics and depended on the development of both software and hardware devices.

Sentor used many Raymark products as integral elements of its industrial control systems. For products distributed by Sentor, Raymark relied largely on Sentor to keep them up to date on customer and market developments. With the exception of a few visits to large Sentor customers in conjunction with Sentor marketing personnel, Sentor preferred that Raymark not interact directly with Sentor customers. While Raymark was free to sell to Sentor competitors outside the United States, the firm had never done so. Recently, with Sentor's permission, Raymark had started selling to a U.S.-based competitor of Sentor. The product involved was not directly competitive with the products sold to Sentor.

The deal provided Sentor with exclusive U.S. rights to certain Raymark products. Raymark was prohibited from selling the specified products to any Sentor competitors in the United States. Raymark was free to sell these products to customers outside the United States. The commercial agreement was initially for five years. After five years, each party to the agreement would have the right to end the agreement 90 days before the end of the Raymark fiscal year. As of early 1994, the commercial agreement was still in place.

Sentor's Purchase of Raymark Stock

The second part of the Sentor agreement involved Sentor acquiring 25 percent of Raymark stock for $1.5 million. After Sentor's purchase, there were four Raymark shareholders, each with a one-quarter interest. Not long after the Sentor agreement was signed, the other two shareholders were bought out by Thomas and Sentor. Since Thomas had little capital, payment to the two shareholders was via Raymark earnings. This left two Raymark shareholders each with 50 percent equity: Thomas Holdings Inc., a company wholly owned by Steve Thomas, and Sentor.

Although the ownership was equal between Thomas and Sentor, voting on the board of directors was not. When Steve Thomas founded Raymark he opted not to use a lawyer. Instead, he used a $15 "do-it-yourself" articles of incorporation. In these articles, the president had an extra vote on the board of directors. As president of Raymark, Thomas retained the extra vote. The articles of incorporation clearly specified the decisions that could be made at the board level and those to be voted on by shareholders. Decisions on new share issues, stock options, and major sales of shares had to be voted on by shareholders. Decisions involving product lines, marketing, corporate acquisitions, and capital expansions were to be made at the board level.

Within Raymark, the deal with Sentor was not seen as a case of "do a deal with Sentor or die." The partnership was viewed as a means of getting a channel to North American and worldwide markets with a high-quality firm. Sentor controlled as much as 40 percent of the U.S. and Canadian markets. Thomas had looked at other options and this looked like the best one. As far as Thomas was concerned, the critical piece missing in Raymark's strategy was a way to the market. The products and technology were in place; Sentor provided market access. A relationship with a well-known and highly respected company like Sentor provided Raymark with instant credibility. In a sense it was a way for Thomas to buy market share. The deal also forced Raymark to develop new management processes and systems, without which Raymark would have been unable to meet Sentor's very strict customer expectations.

Sentor's objectives in forming the relationship were very straightforward. Sentor needed an inexpensive visual interface that was competitive with other products on the market. Since the product was not going to be developed in-house, at least initially, an outside supplier was required. The commercial agreement with Raymark guaranteed supply and its non-competition clause meant that Raymark would have to work very closely with Sentor.

R&D and Innovation at Raymark

Raymark products often had life cycles of less than two years. Although some products remained installed for up to ten years, a continual process of improvement resulting in automatic obsolescence was under way in the industrial controls industry. Consequently, the creation of new products and the improvement of existing products was critical for Raymark. As evidence of the emphasis on innovation, Raymark allocated 15 percent of sales revenue to research and development. Of the 86 people in the R&D group, more than half were software engineers or computer scientists. As Thomas explained, "This company has grown because we are committed to the development of new products. We reinvest our money and develop new products. So far, we have managed to grow steadily and it has worked very well."

For Raymark, labour empowerment was a central feature of the business. All employees were treated as part of a team. Raymark had a single cafeteria where everybody ate together, including Thomas and other senior managers. Thomas described his ideas about empowerment and the Raymark corporate culture:

> High-tech companies require a certain kind of culture. If we do something which interferes with that culture, Raymark will not be successful and we will lose our best people. We need highly responsive teams that can work closely together.
>
> Raymark has annual awards of excellence. [The reception room walls were decorated with photographs of employees receiving awards of excellence.] The objective of the awards is to recognize people who have done outstanding things. Everyone at Raymark is eligible for an award. The awards are peer-judged and moderated by the Raymark VPs. We don't want to sprinkle favours and reward our favourites. We want people to be judged as outstanding by their colleagues.

Under various categories, peer committees decide who has done an outstanding job. We then hand out about $10,000 worth of cash bonuses to the winners. In my opinion, people deserve to be recognized and that is the culture we have tried to build at Raymark. After the winners have been chosen, the results are released to the media because people thrive on recognition.

Personnel turnover at Raymark was very low, averaging about 2 percent per year. At the management level, the same team had been in place for almost ten years. In contrast, the Sentor managers interacting with Raymark changed regularly. According to a senior manager at Raymark, credit for the durability of the Raymark management team must be given to Thomas:

He is a very bright person with a high IQ. He has excellent management skills and is an excellent person to work for. Even though he is very smart and capable, he is willing to use outsiders for help when necessary.

Raymark Performance

Prior to signing the agreement with Sentor, Raymark's sales were less than $1 million per year. In 1984, sales jumped to just under $3 million. Sales reached $10 million in 1989 and almost $50 million in 1993. Of this total, 15 percent could be attributed to software and the remainder to hardware. In 1994, sales were expected to reach $67 million. Average sales growth over the past ten years was 28 percent. Almost 75 percent of Raymark sales were through Sentor channels, down from 100 percent a few years earlier.

The end user value of Raymark's 1993 sales was approximately $100 million. Almost 90 percent of the end users of Raymark products were locate outside Canada. As Thomas explained, "We are competing with firms that are primarily located in the United States. Therefore, we have to compete with U.S. cost structures. And, we have to be careful that our cost structures stay in line."

Raymark's main facility in Ottawa was 92,000 square feet (8,548 square metres) and two additional 18,000-square-foot areas were leased in Ottawa. Negotiations were under way to build a new 150,000-square-foot plant beside the existing one.

Acquisitions

In 1992, Raymark acquired a division of an electronics firm based in Boston. This division was established as a subsidiary of Raymark called Raysys Inc. The division manufactured a complementary line of control products and had a solid base of domestic and international customers. Because the products sold by this new division would not be sold to Sentor, they were considered outside the Sentor-Raymark commercial agreement. Sentor management did not support this acquisition and voted against it at a Raymark board meeting. For the first time, Thomas exercised his majority vote on the board and the acquisition was made at a cost of $10 million, supported in part by a low-interest loan from the Ontario government.

In early 1994, Raymark purchased a business from a firm based in Chicago. After investing more than $15 million in the business, the Chicago firm decided to exit the business and sold it for $1.5 million. When the business was purchased, there were about 30 employees; after a few months Raymark had built the business up to 75 employees. The business manufactured components used in custom products and computer screens. This business provided Raymark with the opportunity to expand into new markets and strengthen its technological expertise. With the acquisition, Raymark acquired state-of-the art equipment, several patented processes, and a highly qualified team of designers and manufacturing personnel. This new business was also set up as a Raymark subsidiary. Management in Chicago had a small minority interest in this division.

In both acquisitions, Raymark wasted little time in making its decision. According to Dan Wilson, Raymark's finance VP, one of the reasons the acquisitions were quickly and successfully executed is that "Raymark has faster lawyers than some of their competitors—that is one of our strategic competences."

The products in the new divisions, and other products not sold through Sentor channels, were marketed in various ways. Some products were sold directly to end users, OEMs, and systems integrators. Geographic regional manufacturers' representatives were also used and in Europe, independent dealers were used for several products. At trade shows, Raymark products were shown at both a Raymark booth and Sentor exhibits. Raymark and its divisions had 41 people involved in sales, marketing, and publications. The marketing personnel regularly interacted with Raymark R&D people.

Sentor and Raymark

The relationship with Sentor had lasted more than ten years, which was quite unusual for Sentor. When Sentor made equity investments in small firms, one of two things usually happened. One, if Sentor was satisfied with the relationship and saw some strategic value in continuing it, Sentor would buy out the smaller firm and fold the company into the Sentor organization. Two, Sentor often ended its relationships after a few years because of conflict between the partners or because the original goals of the relationship were not achieved. By lasting ten years, the Raymark-Sentor relationship was unusual and a survivor.

Dan Wilson referred to the relationship with Sentor as a strategic partnership that benefited both sides. Sentor was by far Raymark's largest customer. To a large degree, Raymark relied on Sentor for its market intelligence. The Sentor relationship provided additional purchasing leverage for Raymark and internationally, Raymark was able to capitalize on its relationship with a large, well-known firm like Sentor.

The relationship was beneficial to Raymark in other ways. For example, in 1986 Raymark was developing a new product line. Development costs were expected to run into the millions of dollars. Raymark management were seriously concerned that the company might exhaust its liquidity and be forced to lay off staff. After discussing the situation with Sentor, Sentor agreed to buy some products to help Raymark's cash flow. As a result, the new product line was successfully developed and no layoffs were necessary.

A primary concern for Raymark was that when Sentor saw a product or part of the business becoming lucrative or "strategic," Sentor tended to act like a

Raymark competitor rather than a partner. In 1988, Sentor established its industrial computer and communications group to manufacture industrial computers and develop operator interface software for IBM personal computers. In the early 1990s, Sentor set up two engineering teams with the explicit goal of outdesigning Raymark.

> One team was going to design us out of one product and the other team was going to design us out of another product. That would be the bulk of our product line. They spent about $50 million but we kept coming out with products faster. Finally, they gave up and eliminated the teams.

Despite Sentor's inability to replicate Raymark's products successfully, Raymark management were convinced that Sentor continued to view their relationship with Raymark as a stopgap measure. Wilson described Sentor objectives:

> We were a temporary fix for Sentor. We would come in until Sentor could do it right and use their massive technology to displace us. They are working on products that could put us out of the market. We were a two-year fix. But, every two years we have become another two-year fix. Our goal is to stay forever with our two-year mandate.

Wilson identified some other negative aspects of the relationship:
- Changes in both partners' managements created significant time demands in managing the relationship.
- Sentor's size sometimes resulted in conflicting messages. "Lower-level staff want one thing and upper levels want something else. All sorts of different people have to be kept happy at the different levels."
- Politics on both sides was sometimes difficult to deal with.
- The cultures of the two companies were very different, sometimes leading to inconsistent expectations in the two companies.
- Raymark management often felt as if the firm were being treated as a subsidiary of Sentor rather than a partner.
- The relationship created some strategic marketing constraints for Raymark.
- It was sometimes hard to get good business opportunities from Sentor because Sentor had their own engineering software groups also looking for new products.

Clearly, the partnership with Sentor had played an important role in Raymark's success. But would the partnership payoff be as great in the future? Wilson described the dilemma facing Raymark:

> We would like to have our cake and eat it, too. We want to keep our sales to Sentor and expand our non-Sentor business. We think the partnership is pretty solid but Sentor would prefer that we concentrate on them and they have made that clear to us. They were not very happy when we purchased the Raysys business. We know, because Sentor has told us that if they can develop the same technology in-house, they will get rid of the commercial agreement with Raymark. A Sentor VP described our relationship like this: Raymark is like a minnow swimming around a whale. One day the whale will flip its tail and squash the minnow.

Russki Adventures

On July 15, 1991, Guy Crevasse and Andrei Kakov, the two major partners in Russki Adventures (Russki), contemplated their next move. They had spent the last year and a half exploring the possibility of starting a helicopter skiing operation in the USSR. Their plan was to bring clients from Europe, North America, and Japan to a remote location in the USSR to ski the vast areas of secluded mountain terrain made accessible by the use of helicopters and the recent business opportunities offered by *glasnost*.

During the exploration process, Crevasse and Kakov had visited a number of potential locations in the USSR, including the Caucasus Mountains near the Black Sea, and the Tien Shen and Pamir ranges north of Pakistan in the republics of Kazakistan and Tadzhikistan, respectively. After close inspection of the three areas, and consideration of many issues, the partners had decided upon the Caucasus region.

After almost two years of planning and research, the thought of making a solid commitment weighed heavily on their minds. Their first option was to accept the partnership offer with Extreme Dreams, a French company that had started a small ski operation in the Caucasus Mountains during the 1991 season. Their second option was to enter a partnership with the USSR's Trade Union DFSO and a Russian mountaineer, and establish their own venture in a Caucasus Mountains area made available to them by a Soviet government agency. Their final option was to wait, save their money, and not proceed with the venture at this time.

The Partners

Andrei Kakov, 27, was born in Russia. His family emigrated to Italy, and then to Canada when he was 17 years old. After completing an undergraduate degree in economics at the University of Toronto, he worked with Sebaco for two years before enrolling in 1989 in the Masters of Business Administration (MBA) program at the University of Western Ontario (Western). Sebaco was

Ian Sullivan prepared this case under the supervision of Professor Paul Beamish solely to provide material for class discussion. The author does not intend to illustrate either effective or ineffective handling of a managerial situation. The author may have disguised certain names and other identifying information to protect confidentiality. © 1992 Ivey Management Services. Case 9-92-G002, version 1992-03-24.

IVEY

Richard Ivey School of Business
The University of Western Ontario

a Canadian-Soviet joint venture that, since 1980, had been facilitating business ventures in the Soviet Union by acting as a liaison between the foreign firms and the different levels of Soviet government and industry. This job gave Kakov extensive contacts in the Soviet Union and in many of the firms, such as McDonald's and Pepsico, which were doing business in the Soviet Union. Kakov was fluent in Russian, Italian, English, and Japanese.

Guy Crevasse, 28, had an extensive ski racing career which began at a young age and culminated in the World Cup with the Canadian National Ski Team. His skiing career took him to many countries in Europe, North America, and South America. During his travels he learned to speak French, Italian, and some German. After retiring from competitive ski racing in 1984, Crevasse remained active in the ski industry as a member of the Canadian Ski Coaches Federation. He led the University of Western Ontario Varsity Ski Team to four consecutive Can-Am titles as a racer/coach while pursuing an undergraduate degree at Western. Before returning to Western to complete an MBA, Crevasse worked for Motorola Inc. in its sales and marketing departments, where he worked on key accounts, set up product distribution channels, and developed product programs with original equipment manufacturers in the automobile industry. Crevasse had also worked with a ski resort planning and development firm on a number of different projects.

◼ Overview of the Skiing and Helicopter Skiing Industries

Development of the Ski Resort Industry

In 1990, the world wide ski market was estimated at 40 million skiers. The great boom period was in the 1960s and 1970s when growth ran between 10 to 20 percent annually. However, the growth stagnation which began during the 1980s was expected to continue during the 1990s. Some of this decline was attributable to increased competition for vacationers' time, the rapidly rising real costs of skiing, and baby boom effects. The only growth segment was female skiers, who represented 65 percent of all new skiers. The total revenue generated by ski resorts in the United States for 1990 was estimated at $1.5 billion. This figure did not include any hotel or accommodation figures.

Prior to World War II, most skiing took place in Europe. Since there were no ski lifts, most skiing was essentially unmarked wilderness skiing, requiring participants who enjoyed the thrill of a downhill run to spend most of their time climbing. There were no slope-grooming machines and few slopes cut especially for skiing.

The development of ski lifts revolutionized the sport, increased the accessibility to many previously unaccessible areas, and led to the development of ski resorts. After the skiing market matured, competition for skiers intensified and resort operators shifted their efforts away from the risk sport focus toward vacation and entertainment. In order to service this new market and to recover their large capital investments, the large resorts had developed mass-market strategies, and modified the runs and the facilities to make them safer and easier to ski in order to serve a greater number of customers.

Introduction of Helicopter Skiing

This change in focus left the more adventurous skiing segments unsatisfied. For many, the search for new slopes and virgin snow was always a goal. The rapid rise in the popularity of skiing after World War II increased demand on existing ski facilities and thus competition for the best snow and hills became more intense. Those who wanted to experience the joys of powder skiing in virgin areas were forced to either get up earlier to ski the good snow before the masses got to it, or hike for hours from the top of ski areas to find new areas close to existing cut ski runs. Hiking to unmarked areas was tiring, time-consuming, and more dangerous because of the exposure to crevasses and avalanches.

This desire to ski in unlimited powder snow and new terrain away from the crowds eventually led to the development of the helicopter skiing industry. The commonly held conception was that powder skiing was the champagne of all skiing, and helicopter skiing was the Dom Perignon. The first helicopter operations began in Canada. From the beginning of the industry in 1961, Canadian operations have been typically regarded as the premium product in the helicopter skiing industry for many reasons, including the wild, untamed mountains in the western regions. For many skiers worldwide, a trip to a Western Canadian heli-ski operation is their "mecca."

Operators used helicopters as a means of accessing vast tracts of wilderness areas which were used solely by one operator through a lease arrangement with the governments, forest services, or regional authorities. The average area leased for skiing was 2,000 to 3,000 square kilometres in size, with 100 to 150 runs. Due to the high costs in buying, operating, maintaining, and insuring a helicopter, the vast majority of operators leased their machines on an as-needed basis with rates based on hours of flight time.

In the 1970s and early 1980s, the helicopter skiing industry was concentrated among a few players. During 1990 and 1991, the number of adventure/wilderness skiing operators increased from 41 to over 77. The industry could be divided between those operations that provided day trips from existing alpine resorts (day-trippers) and those operations that offered week-long trips (destination-location).

By 1991, the entire global market for both day-trippers and destination-location was estimated to be just over 23,000 skiers per year, with the latter group representing roughly 12,000 to 15,000 skiers. Wilderness skiing represented the largest area of growth within the ski industry in the 1970s and 1980s. Market growth in the 1980s was 15 percent per year. Only capacity limitations had restrained growth. The addictive nature of helicopter skiing was illustrated by the fact that repeat customers accounted for over 75 percent of clients annually. The conservative estimate of total margin available to the destination-location skiing industry (before selling and administration costs) was US$12.4 million in 1990. Table 1 gives typical industry margin figures per skier for heli-skiing.

From a cost standpoint, efficient management of the helicopter operations was essential. Table 2 provides a larger list of industry key success factors.

TABLE 1   **Helicopter Skiing Margin per Skier Week (North America)**

Price	$3,500	100%
Costs:		
Helicopter*	1,260	36%
Food and lodging	900	26%
Guides	100	3%
Total operating costs	2,260	65%
TOTAL MARGIN	$1,240	35%

*Helicopter costs were semi-variable, but were based largely on a variable basis (in-flight hours). The fixed nature of helicopter costs arose through minimum flying hours requirements and the rate negotiations (better rates were charged to customers with higher usage). On average, a helicopter skier used seven hours of helicopter time during a one-week trip. A typical all-in rate for a 12-person helicopter was $1,800 per flying hour. Hence the above figure of $1,260 was calculated assuming full capacity of the helicopter using the following: $1,800 per hour for 7 hours for 10 skiers + pilot + guide.

Combination of Resort and Helicopter Skiing

The number of resorts operating day facilities doubled in 1990. Competition in the industry increased for a number of reasons. Many new competitors entered because of the low cost of entry (about $250,000), low exit barriers, the significant market growth, and the rewarding margin in the industry. The major growth worldwide came mainly from the day operations at existing areas, as they attempted to meet the needs for adventure and skiing from their clientele. The major concentration of helicopter operators was in Canada; however, competition was increasing internationally. Industry representatives thought that such growth was good because it would help increase the popularity of helicopter skiing and introduce more people to the sport.

In Canada, where helicopter skiing originated, the situation was somewhat different. Out of the twenty wilderness skiing operations in Canada in 1991, only two were tied to resorts. However, for the rest of the world, roughly 80

TABLE 2   **Helicopter Skiing Industry Key Success Factors**

Factors Within Management Control
- Establishing a safe operation and reliable reputation
- Developing great skiing operations
- Attracting and keeping customers with minimal marketing costs
- Obtaining repeat business through operation's excellence
- Providing professional and sociable guides
- Obtaining operating permits from government
- Managing relationships with environmentalists

Location Factors
- Accessible destinations by air travel
- Available emergency and medical support
- Favourable weather conditions: annual snowfall, humidity, altitude, etc.
- Appropriate daily temperature, sunshine, daylight time
- Suitable terrain
- Quality food and lodging

percent of all the operations were located and tied closely to existing ski operations. Both Crevasse and Kakov realized that there were opportunities to create partnerships or agreements with existing resorts to serve as an outlet for their helicopter skiing demand.

Russki's Research of the Heli-Ski Industry

Profile of the Skier

The research that the Russki group had completed revealed some important facts. Most helicopter skiers were wealthy, independent, professional males of North American or European origin. Increasingly, the Japanese skiers were joining the ranks. The vast majority of the skiers were in the late-30s-to-mid-60s range. For them, helicopter skiing provided an escape from the high pace of their professional lives. These people, who were financially secure with lots of disposable income, were well educated and had done a great many things. Helicopter skiing was a good fit with their calculated-risk-taker image. Exhibit 1 describes a typical customer. It was not unusual for the skiing "addict" to exceed 100,000 vertical feet of skiing in a week. A premium was then charged to the skier.

Buyers tended to buy in groups rather than as individuals. They typically had some form of close association, such as membership in a common profession or club. In most cases, trips were planned a year in advance.

Geographically, helicopter skiers could be grouped into three segments: Japan, North America (United States and Canada), and Europe: in 1991, they represented 10 percent, 40 percent (30 percent and 10 percent), and 50 percent of the market, respectively. There were unique features associated with each segment and Crevasse and Kakov knew that all marketing plans would need to be tailored specifically to the segments. In general, they felt that the European and North American customers placed more emphasis on the adventure, were less risk-averse, and had a propensity to try new things.

Analysis of the Competition

Crevasse and Kakov had thought that more detailed information on their competitors would help answer some of their questions. During the winter of 1991, they conducted a complete physical inspection of skiing and business facilities of many helicopter skiing operations. As a result of the research, Russki determined that the following companies were very significant: Rocky Mountain Helisports (RMH), Cariboo Snowtours, and Heliski India. RMH and Cariboo Snowtours were industry leaders and Heliski India was another new entrant trying to establish itself in the market. A close analysis had provided Crevasse and Kakov with some encouraging information.

Rocky Mountain Helisports, the first operation to offer helicopter skiing, was started in 1965 in Canada by Gunther Pistler, a German immigrant and the "inventor" of helicopter skiing. In 1991 his operation, servicing 6,000 skiers, represented roughly 40 to 50 percent of the worldwide destination-location market. He followed a strategy which cloned small operating units at seven different sites in the interior of British Columbia. RMH's strategy was designed

EXHIBIT 1   Description of a Typical Helicopter Skiing Addict

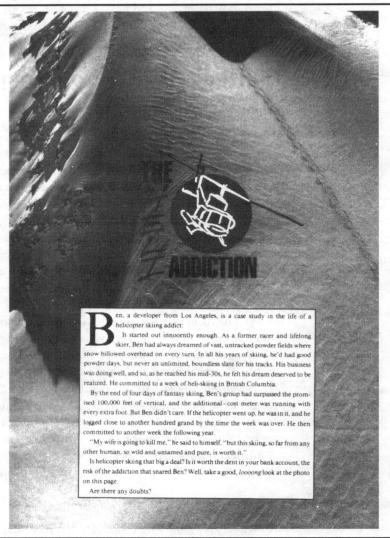

Ben, a developer from Los Angeles, is a case study in the life of a helicopter skiing addict:

It started out innocently enough. As a former racer and lifelong skier, Ben had always dreamed of vast, untracked powder fields where snow billowed overhead on every turn. In all his years of skiing, he'd had good powder days, but never an unlimited, boundless slate for his tracks. His business was doing well, and so, as he reached his mid-30s, he felt his dream deserved to be realized. He committed to a week of heli-skiing in British Columbia.

By the end of four days of fantasy skiing, Ben's group had surpassed the promised 100,000 feet of vertical, and the additional–cost meter was running with every extra foot. But Ben didn't care. If the helicopter went up, he was in it, and he logged close to another hundred grand by the time the week was over. He then committed to another week the following year.

"My wife is going to kill me," he said to himself, "but this skiing, so far from any other human, so wild and untamed and pure, is worth it."

Is helicopter skiing that big a deal? Is it worth the dent in your bank account, the risk of the addiction that snared Ben? Well, take a good, *loooong* look at the photo on this page.

Are there any doubts?

Source: Powder, The Skier's Magazine, November 1990.

to offer a product that catered to a variety of different skier abilities and skiing experiences. The company serviced all segments that could afford the $4,000 price of admission, including introducing less able skiers to the experience of helicopter skiing. Compared with the revenue of traditional Canadian ski resorts, such as Whistler Resorts in British Columbia, RMH's gross revenue for the 1990 season was larger than any resort in Canada at over $21 million. RMH, which had developed a loyal following of customers in North America and Europe, enjoyed significant competitive advantage because of proprietary client lists, a loyal consumer base, and economies of scale due to its large size.

Cariboo Snowtours, the second-largest operation in the world, was established by another German immigrant, Fritz Mogler, at Blue River, British Columbia. In 1991, Cariboo Snowtours served over 2,000 skiers, a number which represented roughly 18 percent of the market. Mogler developed a strategy of one mega-operation and enjoyed economies of scale in the operations area. Similar to RMH, Cariboo Snowtours had a loyal following from North America and Europe, and catered to a variety of skiing abilities and price levels.

Heliski India was a new entrant to the helicopter skiing business. In 1990, the first year of operation, the company serviced 30 skiers in a three-week period, increasing to 120 skiers during the 1991 season. Heliski India followed a more exclusive and adventurous strategy aimed at the experienced helicopter skiing enthusiast. To cover the high costs and low volume, the operation charged $5,500.

Russki estimated margins and profit dynamics for these three operations. Exhibit 2 contains the projection for RMH. These projected statements were

EXHIBIT 2

RUSSKI'S 1991 PROJECTIONS*
PROFIT DYNAMICS OF TYPICAL RMH OPERATION

Revenues

Ski season duration:			
Peak	20 weeks		
Regular	0 weeks		
Total season duration	20 weeks		
Revenue per skier:			
Peak		$3,500	
Weekly group size (10 skiers + 1 guide × 4)	44 people		
Total season regular revenue (3,500 × 40 skiers × 20 weeks)		$2,800,000	
Revenue from skiers exceeding 100,000 virtual feet (10%)		280,000	
TOTAL REVENUE			$3,080,000

Expenses
Variable

9 nights lodging/person/night	$80	$ 720	
9 days meals/person/day	50	450	
Total variable cost/person/week		$ 1,170	
Total annual variable costs (20 weeks × 44 × $1,170)			$1,029,600
Contribution margin			$2,050,400

Fixed

Helicopter cost @ $50,000 per week (20-week season)		$1,000,000	
Guides—1 guide per 10 skiers @ $50,000 per guide/year	4 guides	$ 200,000	
Support staff—5 employees @ $20,000 per employee		$ 100,000	
Promotional		$ 250,000	
TOTAL DIRECT FIXED COSTS			$1,550,000
TOTAL MARGIN			
(Revenue – Direct variable costs – Direct fixed costs)			$ 500,400

Annual overhead:			
Communication		$ 20,000	
Staff travel		50,000	
Office branch	20,000		
Office North America		100,000	
Insurance @ $5/day/person		50,000	
TOTAL OVERHEAD			$ 240,000
Operating profit			$ 249,600
Number of operations	7		
TOTAL OPERATING PROFIT			$1,747,200

*These projected statements were best-guess estimates based on discussions with a wide range of industry experts, managers, and investors.

best-guesses based on discussions with a wide range of industry experts, managers, and investors. Cariboo Snowtour's total profit was estimated as slightly over $2 million, while Heliski India was projected to turn a small profit. Crevasse and Kakov found these figures very encouraging.

■ Land Usage and Environmental Concerns in the Industry

The helicopter skiing industry was facing some land use issues which were tough on many operators, but which also created new opportunities on which Russski wanted to capitalize. Of particular concern to many helicopter skiing operations, especially European, were pressures from environmentalists who were concerned that noise from helicopters could adversely affect wildlife habitat and start avalanches.

As a result, severe downsizing or complete shutdown of existing European operations had recently occurred, leaving only eight helicopter skiing operations in continental Europe in 1991. The one Swiss and one Austrian operation were under pressure to close, and a 1992 season for the latter was already doubtful. The six small operations in Italy, which worked in conjunction with existing ski areas, were basically the only helicopter skiing available in Western Europe. Flying for skiing in France was illegal due to environmentalists' concerns about a negative impact on the limited areas in the Alps. In Sweden, a few companies operated with a shorter season due to the high latitude, and provided less-expensive daily services for visitors who skied within the existing lift systems, but week-long packages were not part of their program.

The North American industry had not been exposed to the same environmental and limited area constraints as the European, mainly because of the vast size of the mountain ranges and good relationships with all interested parties. The American operators, who were associated mostly with the large ski areas, had good working relationships with the forest services, which controlled the areas and issued the working permits.

Canadian operators received their permits from the Ministry of Lands and Forests and the provincial governments. Helicopter skiing had been encouraged because of its ability to bring money into the regions. Due to the vast size of the Canadian mountain ranges and the limited competition for the land use, pressure on the operators in any form had been minimal or nonexistent.

Crevasse and Kakov realized that the environmental and capacity constraints in Europe provided helicopter skiing operators worldwide with significant opportunities. Thus far, it had been mainly the North American operators who had capitalized on this situation, and Russski wanted to find a way to capture unsatisfied demand.

■ Russian Environment

The Political Environment

Crevasse and Kakov knew that starting a venture in the Soviet Union at this time would be complex. The political situation was very unstable in July

1991, and most expert predictions were not encouraging, including the possibility that the Soviet Union might not exist in the near future. There was a major power struggle going on: the hardliners, most of whom were from the old guard of the Communist Party, were trying to hang onto power; and others, such as Russian President Boris Yeltsin, wanted sweeping democratic changes. The new buzzword on the streets was not *glasnost* or *perestroika* but *razgosudarstvo,* which refers to the breakup of the Soviet state. Secession pressures from many of the republics, such as the Baltics, tested the mettle of the political leaders, *perestroika,* and the strength of the union itself.

On a regional basis, the future status of some of the regions and republics where the physical conditions met the requirements for helicopter skiing, such as Georgia and Kazakhistan, was unknown. However, Crevasse and Kakov were encouraged by the fact that experts predicted that, no matter what the state of the whole union, Russia would remain intact and continue to function as a unit. This was one of the many reasons why the Russian republic was selected for the potential initial location.

The Economic Environment

The economy of the Soviet Union was in dire straits. Confusion, lack of focus, and compromise were crippling the process of change from a government-controlled economy to a market-based one. Real Gross Domestic Product was projected to drop anywhere from 3 to 11 percent or more in 1991. Soviet President Mikhail Gorbachev had been given authority to overhaul the economy. However, what changes he would initiate, and whether he still had the support and power to see the process through to completion, were questionable.

Therefore, developing a helicopter skiing operation in the Soviet Union presented Russki with a difficult business environment. Marshall Goldman, Director of Harvard's Russian Research Centre, summed up part of the dilemma facing any new venture in the Soviet Union at this time:

> for those entrepreneurs who think chaos is an ideal environment, this is a perfect time, but for others it is a scary time. The society is collapsing. The economy—both the marketing portion and the planning and administrative sector—is a shambles.

Russki's research indicated that only 20 percent of the 1,300 joint ventures signed since 1987 were operational because of currency exchange problems, bureaucratic delays, and lack of legal framework to make agreements. Also, it had been very hard for the few operational ventures to realize a return on their investment. In 1991, any business in the Soviet Union had to be viewed with a long-term bias in mind. The big question for many businesses was getting hard currency out of Soviet ventures, because there was no international market for the Soviet currency, the ruble. Those who were operating business ventures in the Soviet Union suggested to Russki that it was not an area for the fainthearted to tread. PlanEcon's Keith Crane advised that "even after the agreement has been signed it can be very difficult to get down to specifics and venture into working entities. It took McDonald's 14 years to do it." Due to the political and economic realities of the Soviet environment, firms were making deals with republics, with city agencies, directly with Soviet firms or factories, and sometimes with all of them. More and more frequently, firms had to go to the enterprise level to find the right people and partners. Additionally, foreign firms found the business environment difficult because the concept of business that Westerners had was very different from the one that the Soviets had after 70 years of a controlled Marxist economy. The addition of cultural differences made for a demanding business climate. Russki thought long and hard about the fact that doing business in the Soviet Union had never been easy. In 1991, as the nation wrestled with the gargantuan task of restructuring the country, most firms were finding it more confusing than ever. No roadmap or blueprint for business development existed.

In addition, without the significant financial resources of a highly capitalized firm that could overlook short-term profits for long-term gains, Crevasse and Kakov realized they would be in a more exposed position if they decided to go ahead with the venture. Political unrest or civil war in the Soviet Union, especially in Russia, could destroy their business and investment. Without a steady supply of repeat and new customers, the venture would be finished as an ongoing concern. They knew that credibility from an existing operation or established name would make the task of attracting customers to an uncertain environment easier but, in a time of crisis, would guarantee nothing.

The Opportunities

Despite all the negatives, Crevasse and Kakov thought that helicopter skiing in the Soviet Union would be developed on a large scale in the next few years for a number of reasons. The sport was experiencing tremendous growth, environmental pressures were great in Europe, and capacity at all of the good locations was already stretched.

Therefore, a current opportunity existed in the industry. The partners speculated about how fast they could proceed with their business plan and whether they were exposing themselves to too much risk for the return. Would the opportunity still exist in a couple of years? Could a business of this nature function with the future of the Soviet Union being so unstable? The complete answer to these questions was unknown. Crevasse and Kakov felt as if they were doing a case back at business school where someone had left out half the facts. Regardless, this was a real-life situation, and a decision had to be made on the knowledge available.

After looking closely at their competition and the general environment, they concluded that, despite the instability in the Soviet environment, there were a number of strong points that suggested that they might be able to make this venture work. On a positive note, the Canadian prime minister, Brian Mulroney, had recently signed the Foreign Investment Protection agreement to ensure stability of Canadian ventures in the USSR. Also encouraging to entrepreneurs wanting to enter the Soviet Union was the new law that allowed for full ownership of Soviet subsidiaries by foreign firms. Experts suggested that these agreements would be honoured by whatever form of government was in place.

The critical factor in the minds of the Russki partners was the fact that they would be taking in all revenue in hard currency. Thus, the absence of profit repatriation risk decreased this business exposure dramatically. Russki would operate all of the sales and administrative tasks outside of the Soviet Union and, as a result, all of its revenues would be collected in the West in hard currency, thereby eliminating the currency risk completely. This was a position that would be envied by any firm attempting to do business in the Soviet Union. Also, Russki was attractive to all levels of government because the venture would bring desperately needed hard currency into the country.

Mt. Elbrus, the highest peak in Europe and the Caucasus mountain region, was where Russki had options to locate. It was well known throughout Europe and its high altitudes and warm climate offered ideal skiing conditions. Because a strong allegiance already existed between the European customers and the Canadian operators, Russki's Canadian background would sit well with customers. In addition, Russki would deliver comparative cost advantage for the Europeans in a Soviet operation, as shown in Exhibit 5, even if Russki charged similar costs for a week of skiing.

The uniqueness of the region and mystique of Russia offered an interesting alternative for tourism. Russia had a 2,000-year history and a rich culture, which was reflected in the traditions of the local people and the architecture. Furthermore, the Black Sea area which was close to the Caucasus Mountains had been used as a resort area for centuries. The dramatic changes during the early 1990s in the Soviet Union and Eastern Europe had resulted in tremendous interest in these areas.

Since Russki already had the money required for startup, the company could move quickly without having to take time to raise the capital. The low cost of leasing Soviet helicopters, pilot salaries, service, and fuel as compared with North America was a distinct advantage, and one of the original attractions of Russia. Negotiations with the Russians had shown that this cost advantage was obtainable. The high costs of helicopter operations represented the largest part of the operating costs in helicopter skiing. Lower helicopter costs in Russia would result in cost savings in the range of 50 percent or more in this expense relative to North American competitors.

The Russki management team was strong. Both men were business-school-trained individuals with international work experience, language skills, and ski industry background. Additional hard-to-copy assets, including access to the "Crazy Canucks" (a World Cup ski team) and European ski stars as Guest Guides, and Soviet knowledge, would be tough for anyone to match in the short term.

Positioning and Marketing of Russki Adventures

Positioning and Pricing

The Russki team had considered two positioning strategies, a high and a low pricing strategy. A premium pricing and service strategy like that of Heliski India at around US$6,000 would require superior service in every aspect of the operation. The lower-priced strategy at $3,500 to $4,000 was $500 below the US$4,000-to-US$4,500 pricing of Canadian operators like RMH for the initial season. The second positioning strategy would be designed to target a larger market and concentrate on building market share during the first few years, allowing more time and flexibility to move down the learning curve.

Even with parallel pricing of US$4,000, the "all in" (as shown in Exhibit 5) would give a cost advantage to the European and Japanese customers. Crevasse and Kakov knew that this situation would help challenge customers' traditional allegiance to the Canadian operators.

Based on a "best-guess scenario," profit models for the two pricing strategies using conservative sales levels are shown in Exhibits 3 and 4. Though the higher-priced strategy was more lucrative, Crevasse and Kakov felt that they had a higher capacity to execute the lower-price strategy during the first few years of operations regardless of which partner they chose. They were not sure that they could meet the sales volume for the premium strategy as shown in Exhibit 4, regardless of the realization of savings from use of Russian helicopters. (In the unlikely event that the projected helicopter saving could not be realized, the discounted cash flow in Exhibit 3 dropped from $526,613 to $293, and in Exhibit 4 from $597,926 to $194,484.)

EXHIBIT 3   Profit Dynamics, Low-Price Strategy with Low Helicopter Costs

	Year 1	Year 2	Year 3	Year 4	Year 5
Revenues					
Total season duration	10 weeks	15 weeks	15 weeks	20 weeks	20 weeks
Revenue per skier—peak	$ 4,000	$ 4,000	$ 4,000	$ 4,000	$ 4,000
Weekly group size	10	15	20	25	25
TOTAL SEASON REVENUE	$400,000	$900,000	$1,200,000	$2,000,000	$2,000,000
Expenses					
Total variable cost					
(variable cost/skier @ $1,000)	$100,000	$225,000	$ 300,000	$ 500,000	$ 500,000
Contribution Margin	$300,000	$675,000	$ 900,000	$1,500,000	$1,500,000
Fixed					
Helicopter cost (assumes Soviet costs					
of $10,000/week)	$100,000	$150.000	$ 150,000	$ 200,000	$ 200,000
Guides—1 guide per 10 skiers @					
$50,000 per guide/year	$ 50,000	$ 75,000	$ 100,000	$ 125,000	$ 125,000
Soviet staff—3 employees @					
$5,000 per employee	$ 15,000	$ 15,000	$ 15,000	$ 15,000	$ 15,000
Promotional	$100,000	$100,000	$ 100,000	$ 100,000	$ 100,000
TOTAL DIRECT FIXED COSTS	$265,000	$340,000	$ 365,000	$ 440,000	$ 440,000
TOTAL MARGIN (Revenues – Direct					
variable costs – Direct fixed costs)	$ 35,000	$335,000	$ 535,000	$1,060,000	$1,060,000
TOTAL OVERHEAD	$ 35,000	$115,000	$ 115,000	$ 115,000	$ 115,000
OPERATING PROFIT	0	$220,000	$ 420,000	$ 945,000	$ 945,000

	Year 0	Year 1	Year 2	Year 3	Year 4	Year 5
Investment	$–230,000					
Operating profit		0	$220,000	$ 420,000	$ 945,000	$ 945,000
N.A. partner's share: 100%		0	$220,000	$ 420,000	$ 945,000	$ 945,000
Profit (taxes @ 30%)	$–230,000	0	$154,000	$ 294,000	$ 661,500	$ 661,500
DCF Year 1–5 PV @ 20.00%		$526,613				
IRR	71.86%					

These estimates were extremely conservative. One helicopter could service 44 people per week (four groups comprising ten skiers and one guide). All projections for the profit dynamics were made with the number of skiers per week below capacity. In addition, the first two years were estimated using 10 and 15 skiers, respectively. In subsequent years, the number of skiers was increased, but never to full capacity, in order to keep estimates conservative. Russki realized that operating at or close to capacity on a weekly basis would increase its efficiency and returns dramatically.

Russki also built in an additional $250 in the variable costs per skier per week for contingent expenses such as the cost of importing all foodstuffs.

If Russki proceeded with the lower-priced approach, it would position its product just below the industry standard at $4,000 initially. The intent would be to attack the market as the Japanese automobile manufactures had done when entering into the North American luxury car market.

Crevasse and Kakov were encouraged by the numbers, because the conservative sales estimates using the low-price positioning strategy would allow

EXHIBIT 4 Profit Dynamics, Premium-Price Strategy with Low Helicopter Costs

	Year 1	Year 2	Year 3	Year 4	Year 5
Revenues					
Total season duration	5 weeks	10 weeks	10 weeks	20 weeks	20 weeks
Revenue per skier—peak	$ 6,000	$ 6,000	$ 6,000	$ 6,000	$ 6,000
Weekly group size	10	10	15	15	20
TOTAL SEASON REVENUE	$300,000	$600,000	$900,000	$1,800,000	$2,400,000
Expenses					
Total variable cost					
(variable cost/skier @ $1,000)	$ 50,000	$100,000	$150,000	$ 300,000	$ 400,000
Contribution Margin	$250,000	$500,000	$750,000	$1,500,000	$2,000,000
Fixed					
Helicopter cost (assumes Soviet costs of $10,000/week)	$ 50,000	$100,000	$100,000	$ 200,000	$ 200,000
Guides—1 guide per 10 skiers @ $50,000 per guide/year	$ 50,000	$ 50,000	$ 75,000	$ 75,000	$ 100,000
Soviet staff—3 employees @ $5,000 per employee	$ 15,000	$ 15,000	$ 15,000	$ 15,000	$ 15,000
Promotional	$100,000	$100,000	$100,000	$ 100,000	$ 100,000
TOTAL DIRECT FIXED COSTS	$215,000	$265,000	$290,000	$ 390,000	$ 415,000
TOTAL MARGIN (Revenues – Direct variable costs – Direct fixed costs)	$ 35,000	$235,000	$460,000	$1,110,000	$1,585,000
TOTAL OVERHEAD	$ 35,000	$115,000	$115,000	$ 115,000	$ 115,000
OPERATING PROFIT	0	$120,000	$345,000	$ 995,000	$1,470,000

	Year 0	Year 1	Year 2	Year 3	Year 4	Year 5
Investment	**$–230,000**					
Operating profit		0	$120,000	$345,000	$ 995,000	$1,470,000
N.A. partner's share: 100%		0	$120,000	$345,000	$ 995,000	$1,470,000
Profit (taxes @ 30%)	$–230,000	0	$ 84,000	$241,500	$ 696,500	$1,029,000
DCF Year 1–5 PV @ 20.00%		$597,926				
IRR	70.78%					

them to generate a profit in the second year of operations if they could realize the projected savings with Russian helicopters. However, if they didn't,
the strategy would still show a profit in the third year. They thought that the
return on their investment would be sufficient as far as the internal rate of
return was concerned, but they wondered whether the risk of the Soviet environment should increase their demands even more.

Product

Crevasse and Kakov planned to model the Russki product after the RMH operation, which was the best in the industry, by evaluating what RMH had
built and improving on its processes. Although Russki wanted very much to
differentiate itself from the rest of the industry, the partners were not sure
how far they could go within the constraints of the Soviet environment.

Geographical Distribution

Although Russki would focus on the European and North American markets, the
former segment was most important. Both Crevasse and Kakov realized that they
would need a strong European operation in marketing and sales if they were going to capitalize on the opportunity available. Developing these functions
quickly, especially in Europe which was not their home turf, was a major concern. They had to decide on the best sales and marketing channels immediately
and set them up as soon as possible if they decided to go ahead with the venture.

Promotion

Due to the small size of the target market and promotion budgets, the new company would have to make sure that the promotional dollars spent were directed
effectively. Russki would do this by direct mail, personal selling by the owners, travel agents, and free tour incentives to trip organizers and guides. Long-
term word of mouth would be the best promotional tool, but it had to be
supplemented, especially in the startup phase of the business.

Additionally, Crevasse and Kakov planned to increase the value to customers by inviting business and political speakers to participate in the skiing activities with the groups in return for their speaking services. Celebrity skiers
such as Canadian Olympic bronze medallist and World Cup champion Steve
Podborski, would be used as customer attractions. As outlined in Table 3, they
budgeted $100,000 for promotional expenses.

TABLE 3   **Marketing Promotion Budget, Year 1**

Information nights with cocktails @ $1,000/night in 20 cities	$ 20,000
Travel expenses	10,000
Trip discounts (one free trip in ten to groups)	25,000
Direct mail	5,000
Brochures	5,000
Commissions	15,000
Celebrity	20,000
TOTAL	$100,000

EXHIBIT 5   Cost Comparison by Geographic Location

North America

Costs for customer to go heli-skiing in North America from different geographic locations:

Origin of Skier	Trip	Transportation	Total
Japan	$4,000	$2,500	$6,500
Europe	$4,000	$2,000	$6,000
North America	$4,000	$ 750	$4,750

Russia

Cost for customer to go heli-skiing in Russia from different geographic locations:

Origin of Skier	Trip	Transportation	Total
Japan	$4,000	$2,000	$6,000
Europe	$4,000	$1,000	$5,000
North America	$4,000	$2,500	$6,500

Conclusion: This comparative analysis of all-in costs to the consumer shows that the Russian operation offers a 20% cost advantage to the European customers.

Labour

Where possible, Russki planned to employ Russians and make sure that they received excellent training and compensation, thereby adding authenticity to the customers' experience. Providing local employment would also ensure the Canadian company's existence and create positive relations with the authorities.

Currency

Through Kakov's contacts, Russki had worked out a deal to purchase excess rubles from a couple of foreign firms which were already operating in the Soviet Union but which were experiencing profit repatriation problems. Russki would pay for as many things as possible with soft currency.

■ The Partnership Dilemma

During the exploration period, Crevasse and Kakov had well over a dozen offers from groups and individuals to either form partnerships or provide services and access to facilities and natural resources. They even had offers from people who wanted them to invest millions to build full-scale Alpine Resorts. Many of the offers were easy to dismiss, because these groups did not have the ability to deliver what they promised or their skill sets did not meet the needs of Russki. Crevasse and Kakov's inspection and site evaluation helped them to determine further the best opportunities and to evaluate first-hand whether the site and potential partner were realistic. This research gave Russki a couple of excellent but very distinct partnership possibilities. They knew that both options had tradeoffs.

Extreme Dreams

A partnership with the Extreme Dreams group had some definite strengths. This French company, located in Chamonix, a town in the French Alps, had been running the premier guiding service in and around Mont Blanc, the highest peak in the Alps, for 11 years. Chamonix was the "avant garde" for alpinists in Europe and one of the top alpine centres in the world. Extreme Dreams had a 5,000-person client list, mostly European but with some North American names.

What Extreme Dreams had was the operational expertise Russki needed to acquire in order to run the helicopter skiing and guiding side of the business. During the 1991 winter season, it had run a three-week operation servicing 50 skiers in the Elbrus region in the Caucasus Mountains. The Soviet partner facilitated an arrangement with a small resort villa in the area. The facilities, which had just been upgraded during the summer, now met Western standards.

The French company had invested roughly US$100,000, and although it did not have a capital shortage, the partnership agreement that was outlined would require Russki to inject the same amount of capital into the business. The firm would be incorporated in the United States and the share split would be equal amounts of 45 percent of the stock with 10 percent left over for future employee purchase. The Soviet partner, a government organization that helped facilitate the land use agreements and permits, would be paid a set fee for yearly exclusive use of the land.

However, Extreme Dreams lacked experience in the key functional areas of business. Possibly this situation could be rectified by the partnership agreement whereby the management team would consist of three members. Marc Testut, president of Extreme Dreams, would be in charge of all operations. Guy Crevasse would act as president for the first two years and his areas of expertise would be sales and marketing. Andrei Kakov would be chief financial officer and responsible for Soviet relations.

Extreme Dreams had overcome the lack of some foodstuffs by importing, on a weekly basis, products not securely attainable in Russia. These additional costs were built into the variable cost in projected financial statements. Russki would do the same if it did not choose Extreme Dreams as a partner.

Trade Union DFSO

The other potential partnership had its strengths as well. The partnership would be with the All-Union Council of Trade Union DFSO, and with a mountaineer named Yuri Golodov, one of the USSR's best-known mountaineers, who had agreed to be part of the management team. Golodov, who had been bringing mountaineers from all over the world to parts of the Soviet Union for many years, possessed valuable expertise and knowledge of the Caucasus area. One of his tasks would be coordination of travel logistics for Soviet clientele. Sergei Oganezovich, chief of the mountaineering department, had made available to Russki the exclusive rights to over 4,000 square kilometres in the Caucasus Mountain Range about 50 kilometres from the area awarded to Extreme Dreams. A small user fee per skier would be paid to the trade organization in return for exclusive helicopter access to the area.

A profit-sharing agreement with Golodov, which would allow him to purchase shares in Russki and share in the profits, was agreed to in principle by Russki, the Trade Union DFSO, and Golodov. Under this agreement, Crevasse and Kakov would remain in control of the major portion of the shares. Capital requirements for this option would be in the $230,000 range over the first two years. The two Canadians would perform essentially the same roles as those proposed in the Extreme Dreams agreement. If Crevasse and Kakov selected this option, they would need to bring in a head guide, preferably European, to run the skiing operations. On a positive note, a small resort centre that met the standards required by Western travellers had been selected for accommodations in the area.

As regards medical care in case of accidents, both locations were within an hour of a major city and hospital. Less than an hour was well within the industry norm. In addition, all staff were required to take a comprehensive first-aid course.

After discussions with many business ventures in the Soviet Union and with Extreme Dreams, Russki concluded that having the ability to pay for goods and services with hard currency would be a real asset if the situation were critical. Russki would use hard currency, where necessary, to ensure that the level of service was up to the standard required by an operation of this nature.

Crevasse and Kakov knew that selecting a compatible and productive partner would be a great benefit in this tough environment. Yet, they had to remember that a partnership would not guarantee customer support for this venture in the Soviet environment or that the USSR would remain stable enough for them to function as an ongoing concern.

The Decision

Crevasse and Kakov knew that it would take some time for the business to grow to the level of full capacity. They were willing to do whatever it took to make ends meet during the early years of the business. Because helicopter skiing was a seasonal business, they realized that they would need to find a supplementary source of income during the off-season, especially in the startup phase.

However, they also were confident that, if they could find a way to make their plan work, they could be the ones to capitalize on the growing market. The Soviet Union had the right physical conditions for helicopter skiing, but the business environment would present difficulties. Moreover, the two partners were aware that starting a venture of this nature at any time was not an easy task. Starting it in the present state of the Soviet Union during a recession would only complicate their task further. Yet the timing was right for a new venture in the industry and, in general, they were encouraged by the potential of the business.

Crevasse and Kakov had to let all parties involved know of their decision by the end of the week. If they decided to go ahead with the venture, they had to move quickly if they wanted to be operational in the 1992 season. That night they had to decide if they would proceed, who they would select as partners if they went ahead, and how they would go. It was going to be a late night.

Samsung and the Theme Park Industry in Korea

In March 1994, Her Tae-Hak, president of Samsung's Joong-Ang Development Company, was driving to his office, past the Yongin Farmland (Farmland), an amusement complex sprawling over 3,700 acres (1,497 hectares) in the Yongin valley. Her was spearheading a major drive within the company to position the theme park as one of the world's leading vacation resort towns. His master plan called for an investment of about US$300 million over the next five years, to be internally funded by the Samsung Group. Despite the booming Korean economy and the increasing demands for leisure attractions, the global competitive environment of the theme park industry raised several concerns. Should Samsung invest in such an aggressive expansion plan for Farmland? Was this an attractive industry for investment? Her was scheduled for a meeting with the chairman of the Samsung Group for a formal presentation of the proposal at the end of the month.

The Global Theme Park Industry

The early 1990s saw the emergence of theme parks as a major source of family entertainment, not just in the United States but around the world. The earliest evidence of a business where people "paid money to be terrified" was in the early 1600s when several Russians operated a sled ride with a 70-foot vertical drop. In the late 1800s, several theme parks were set up in Coney Island (New York) in the United States. The first roller coaster was set up in 1884, followed by an indoor amusement park called Sealion Park. In the 1930s, the amusement industry had to contend with alternative entertainment offered by the movie houses as well as setbacks due to economic depression. However, with the Disneyland Park opening in 1955 in California, the industry was revived, and Walt Disney was credited with raising the profile, as well as the profitability, of the industry to a new height.

Charles Dhanaraj (Ivey) and Young Soo Kim (Samsung) prepared this case under the supervision of Professor Paul Beamish solely to provide material for class discussion. The authors do not intend to illustrate either effective or ineffective handling of a managerial situation. They may have disguised certain names and other identifying information to protect confidentiality. © 1996 Ivey Management Services and Samsung HRDC. Case 9A96M006, version 1996-10-23.

Richard Ivey School of Business
The University of Western Ontario

There was a variety of parks and attractions, each with a different approach to drawing crowds and showing them a good time:

- *Cultural and education parks* were a remnant of the old-fashioned type of European park. Such parks featured formal greens, gardens, and fountains. Generally they incorporated historical and educational exhibits.
- *Outdoor amusement parks* were small parks that served a metropolitan or regional market. These parks featured traditional thrill rides, carnival midways, and some entertainment. Most amusement parks did not have a theme to the architecture, rides, and entertainment.
- *Theme parks* were generally family-oriented entertainment complexes that were built around a theme. Theme parks were larger and had a greater variety of rides and attractions than amusement parks.
- *Water theme parks* were a recent phenomenon, a special type of theme parks centred on water activities. Large water parks featured wave-action pools, river rides, steep vertical-drop slides, and a variety of twisting flume slides.

Most of the theme parks were members of the International Association of Amusement Parks and Attractions which tracked the attendance at various theme parks. In 1993, North American parks accounted for 48 percent of the worldwide attendance, Asian parks 33 percent, European parks 14 percent, and Central and South American parks 4 percent (see Table 1).

North America

The Walt Disney Company was the largest park chain in the world with three major theme parks in the United States. Time Warner's Six Flags Corporation was the second-largest with seven parks spread out in the United States. Paramount, Anheuser-Busch, Cedar Fair were some of the other conglomerates who owned theme parks. In mid-1993, Paramount bought Canada's Wonderland theme park originally developed by Taft Broadcasting Company in 1981. Despite the mature nature of the industry in the United States, a number of theme parks were investing heavily in upgrading their facilities, and extending the theme parks' services.

Europe

In 1980, Alton Towers, a 60-year old park in North Staffordshire (England), comprising primarily historic gardens, repositioned itself as a theme park by adding a roller coaster and some other attractions. The park was extremely successful within a very short span of time. The success of Alton Towers led to a number of new theme parks in the late 1980s and the early 1990s, including Blackpool Pleasure Beach (England) which featured the world's tallest roller coaster. In France alone, three major theme parks emerged in the early 1990s: Walt Disney's $3 billion EuroDisney, the $150 million Parc Asterix located northeast of Paris, and the $110 million Big Bang Schtroumpf (Smurfs) theme park just north of Metz. Six Flags Corporation and Anheuser-Busch both recently opened new theme parks in Spain coinciding with the 1992 Barcelona Olympics.

TABLE I   **Top 50 Amusement/Theme Parks Worldwide, 1993**

Rank	Park and Location	Attendance (millions)
1	DISNEYLAND, Tokyo, Japan	16.030
2	MAGIC KINGDOM of Walt Disney World, Florida, U.S.	11.200
3	DISNEYLAND, Anaheim, California, U.S.	10.300
4	JAYA ANCOL DREAMLAND, Jakarta, Indonesia	9.800
5	EPCOT at Walt Disney World, Florida, U.S.	9.700
6	EURO DISNEYLAND, Morne la Voltée, France	8.800
7	YOKOHAMA HAKKEIJIMA SEA PARADISE, Japan	8.737
8	DISNEY-MGM STUDIOS, Walt Disney World, Florida, U.S.	8.000
9	UNIVERSAL STUDIOS FLORIDA, Orlando, Florida, U.S.	7.700
10	BLACKPOOL PLEASURE BEACH, England	7.000
11	YONGIN FARMLAND, Kyonggi-Do, South Korea	6.071
12	UNIVERSAL STUDIOS HOLLYWOOD, California, U.S.	4.600
13	SEA WORLD OF FLORIDA, Florida, U.S.	4.600
14	LOTTE WORLD, Seoul, South Korea	4.433
15	CHAPULTEPEC, Mexico City, Mexico	4.200
16	HUIS TEN BOSCH, Sosebo, Japan	3.902
17	TOSHIMAEN AMUSEMENT PARK, Tokyo, Japan	3.800
18	KNOTT'S BERRY FARM, Fuona Park, California, U.S.	3.800
19	SEA WORLD OF CALIFORNIA, San Diego, California, U.S.	3.700
20	BUSCH GARDENS, Tampa, Florida, U.S.	3.700
21	CEDAR POINT, Sandusky, Ohio, U.S.	3.600
22	SIX FLAGS MAGIC MOUNTAIN, Valencia, California, U.S.	3.500
23	SEOUL LAND, Seoul, South Korea	3.311
24	PARAMOUNT'S KING'S ISLAND, Ohio, U.S.	3.300
25	OCEAN PARK, Hong Kong	3.200
26	SIX FLAGS GREAT ADVENTURE, Jackson, New Jersey, U.S.	3.200
27	SANTA CRUZ BEACH BOARDWALK, California, U.S.	3.100
28	NAGASHIMA SPA LAND, Kuwona, Japan	3.008
29	TIVOLI GARDENS, Copenhagen, Denmark	3.000
30	SIX FLAGS OVER TEXAS, Arlington, Texas, U.S.	3.000
31	ALTON TOWERS, North Staffordshire, United Kingdom	3.000
32	SIX FLAGS GREAT AMERICA, Gumee, Illinois, U.S.	2.900
33	PARAMOUNT CANADA'S WONDERLAND, Maple, Canada	2.850
34	TAKARAZUKA FAMILY LAND, Japan	2.796
35	SIX FLAGS OVER GEORGIA, Atlanta, U.S.	2.600
36	DE EFTELING, The Netherlands	2.550
37	PLAYCENTER, Sao Paulo, Brazil	2.500
38	DUNIA FUNTASI, Jakarta, Indonesia	2.500
39	PARAMOUNT'S GREAT AMERICA, California, U.S.	2.500
40	KNOTT'S CAMP SNOOPY, Bloomington, Minnesota, U.S.	2.500
41	EUROPA PARK, Germany	2.450
42	KORAKUEN, Tokyo, Japan	2.423
43	PARAMOUNT'S KING'S DOMINION, Virginia, U.S.	2.400
44	SIX FLAGS ASTROWORLD, Houston, Texas, U.S.	2.400
45	PLAYCENTER, Sao Paulo, Brazil	2.400
46	BUSCH GARDENS THE OLD COUNTRY, Virginia, U.S.	2.300
47	DAKKEN, Klampenborg, Denmark	2.300
48	LISEBERG, Gothenburg, Sweden	2.200
49	TOEI UZUMASA EIGAMURA, Kyoto, Japan	2.146
50	BEIJING AMUSEMENT PARK, China	2.050

Asia

Tokyo Disneyland was opened in 1983 by Walt Disney as a joint venture with the Oriental Land Company (OLC). The success of Tokyo Disneyland set off a wave of theme park developments in Asia. OLC and Disney had agreed to open a second theme park, Tokyo Disney Sea, in 2001. Ocean Park in Hong Kong, started in 1977, was the largest water park in Asia, with an annual attendance of 3.2 million. Jaya Ancol Dreamland, located in North Jakarta, Indonesia, was one of the largest recreation complexes in southeast Asia. Dreamland had a theme park (Dunia Fantasi), a waterpark complex, an oceanarium, a golf course, a beach, and several hotels. China was a major growth market. Beijing Amusement Park, started in 1981, reported that between 1990 and 1993 revenues increased over 2,000 percent and earnings before interest and taxes were up 200 percent. Over the next five years, six regional theme parks were to be developed with a total investment of over $100 million.

◼ Financial Issues

The theme park business required a large-scale initial investment, typically ranging from $50 million to $3 billion. Depending on the real estate markets, the cost of the land value itself could be very high. Theme parks required over 50 acres of land for a full-scale development, with some of the theme parks utilizing 10 to 30 thousand acres. Since accessibility of the park location was a key success factor in the industry, theme park developers chose land sites in a central area which was relatively expensive. Alternatively, they could choose a remote area at a low cost and develop the transportation network. In either case, the land development costs constituted nearly 50 percent of the overall investment. The amusement machinery constituted 20 to 30 percent of the total investment, and the working capital requirements took up the remaining 20 to 30 percent. The amusement equipment required for the park was also expensive, most of it going from $1 million to $50 million. Businesses that had an in-house land development expertise or equipment technology had better control of these costs.

Many parks periodically added new attractions or renovated existing ones to draw repeat customers. The parks typically reinvested much of their revenue for expansion or upgrading purposes. The economies of scale and scope were significant in the industry. Increasingly, parks got larger and larger to generate more operating revenues. Also, companies had multiple parks to take advantage of the learning-curve effects in the management of theme parks and the increased economies of scope. Most of the operating expenses for theme parks (about 75 percent) were for personnel.

Admission fees[1] constituted over 60 percent of the total revenues of a theme park, while the rest came primarily from food, beverage, and merchandise sales. To handle the admissions revenue a centralized ticket system was generally preferred. An all-inclusive admission price entitled customers to as

---

[1] Admission fees varied from $5 to $25 depending on the location and reputation of the park.

many rides and shows as they desired. This approach led to longer stays at parks resulting in increased food and beverage sales. Another centralized admission method was to sell ride/show tickets in sets or coupon books (e.g., five coupons for $5, but twelve coupons for $10). Both approaches to centralized ticket sales minimized the number of employees handling money throughout the park, resulting in improved efficiency and control.

Walt Disney Company's financial profile was generally used to assess the return on investment within the industry. The revenues for the theme parks segment of the Walt Disney Company were at US$2.042 billion in 1988 and grew to US$3.4 billion in 1993. Operating income was pegged at US$565 million in 1988 and US$747 in 1993. The return on equity for the Walt Disney Company was pegged at 17 to 25 percent. One of the analysts remarked on the theme parks segment of Walt Disney, "Theme parks are going to become increasingly stable and annuity-like, with the ability to generate $700 to $750 million in cash flow a year."

There were signs of declining profitability in the U.S. operations, since the market was maturing and the competition was getting more intense. In contrast, Tokyo Disneyland, the Japanese operations, were showing continuing growth. However, EuroDisney, the European theme park, was a disaster for the company with huge losses since operations began in 1992. The company was expecting a breakeven in 1995.

Marketing and Social Issues

The traditional appeal of theme/amusement parks was to preteens, teens, and young adults. Changing demographics were causing most parks to think in terms of a broader market, particularly families, corporate groups, and even senior citizens. There were five major market segments for theme parks:

- *Local families*. People within a day's drive who visited mostly on weekends; most parks focused exclusively on this segment, which generally constituted 60–75 percent of the attendance
- *Children's groups*. Schools, churches, recreation agencies, Scouts, and other groups who travelled in buses on summer weekdays
- *The evening market*. Teens and young adults who came for entertainment, concerts, and romancing at night
- *Corporate groups*. Including consignment sales and group parties
- *Tourists*. A substantial market for large theme parks in destination areas such as Florida

Customer satisfaction was a critical issue in theme parks management. Successful park managers used extensive marketing research to understand their customers and also spent a lot of effort in promoting the park. To reach the diverse groups, parks emphasized increased beautification and the range of entertainment and food services offered. Theme park managers were working with tour operators and government tourist promotion boards to draw the tourist crowds to their parks. Theme parks spent about 10 percent of their annual revenues for advertising. Radio, newspaper, Yellow Pages advertisements, family and group discounts, and direct mail were the most common promotional methods. Among large theme parks, television advertising was an excellent visual medium to capture the excitement. Some parks expended a major portion of their advertising budget for television promotion.

An issue for the theme parks industry was the seasonal and intermittent nature of the business. Theme parks' attendance peaked in the spring/summer and in the school holidays. Even in the holiday season, bad weather could adversely affect the attendance. The seasonal fluctuations put a lot of strain on the theme parks' management. During the peak season, the requirement for employees shot up; quite often the management had to find employees beyond the domestic territory and provide housing for out-of-town employees. The sudden surge in demand often choked the service systems such as transportation, building management, etc.

It was the availability of leisure time and a high discretionary income that drove the commercial recreation industry. Economic downturns had a severe impact on industry revenues. Also, consumers could substitute a visit to theme parks with other modes of entertainment. Consumers substituted products/services in order to try something new, different, cheaper, safer, better, or more convenient. Free admission parks and beaches, camping trips, or even video-movies at home were competing options for leisure time.

Regulatory Issues

Government regulations were quite strict because of the extensive land use, and the potential for serious accidents. Licensing requirements and methods of ascertaining operational expertise to ensure visitors' safety varied from country to country. In some countries, where land was scarce, governments limited the area of the land that the developers could take up for theme parks. Park administration was dependent on the government for utilities such as power, gas, and water. A typical period required for arranging government approval for a theme park could be as high as two to five years, depending on the country.

A related issue was insurance premiums. Given the likelihood of accidents in the amusement parks and the possibility of serious injury, 100 percent insurance coverage was a must in the industry. Although safety records in the industry were very good, the insurance premiums were extremely high in some parts of the world, particularly in the United States, and the large premiums often drove the small players in the industry out of business. Countries in Asia did not have this handicap.

Technology Issues

The theme park industry had three classes of inputs: the building and construction services that provided landscaping and architectural support; the hardware providers that supplied amusement machinery; and the software providers that supplied management know-how.

The amusement machinery industry had grown over the years. Most of the large rides, such as the Hurricane or the Giant Wheel, were manufactured in Japan, Europe, or the United States. There were fewer than ten suppliers who were capable of developing quality machinery, such as DOGO of Japan, HUSS of Germany, and ARROW of the United States. Most of these suppliers worked globally, and the machinery was custom-designed and made to order to fit the particular market and environmental conditions. There were a large number of suppliers for the smaller machines, and quite often, they could be manufactured domestically. Special simulators for amusement purposes using proprietary technology were being developed by technology-intensive companies such as Sega Japan and Simex Canada.

The park management expertise commonly referred to as the "software" in the industry was not easily available. Leading theme park companies, such as Walt Disney Company, charged huge licensing fees which were over 10 percent of the revenues. Also, they were very selective in choosing joint ventures in other countries. Disney went through an extensive market analysis and partner profile analysis for over three years in Europe before finalizing the venue in France with the joint venture partner. Mr. Yu, director in charge of the Farmland project, commented:

> We wanted to go for a joint venture with Walt Disney Corporation. But they somehow were not interested in Korea. So we had to go it alone. It takes a long time for theme park managers to develop service delivery of world-class quality.

Although Walt Disney offered a number of educational programs to train other managers in the "Disney management" style, the know-how seemed to be too sophisticated for the competitors to emulate.

Virtual reality (VR) was increasingly becoming a highly lucrative mass-market entertainment phenomenon. A new entry that was due to open in July 1994 was Joypolis, a $70 million interactive theme park owned by Sega Enterprises, with projected revenues of $37 million per annum. Sega had plans to open 50 such parks in Japan, and was negotiating with Universal Studios, California, for its first U.S. installation of a VR theme park.

Yongin Farmland

Yongin Farmland (Farmland), opened in 1976, was the first amusement park in Korea. It was managed by Joong-Ang Development Company, one of the wholly owned subsidiaries of Samsung with a mission to provide a better quality of life through healthy open-air leisure activities. In addition to the Farmland management, Joong-Ang was responsible for the building maintenance at all Samsung's offices, as well as maintaining two golf courses. Farmland was located about an hour south of Seoul, and was owned by the Korean conglomerate, the Samsung Group (see Exhibit 1). The 3,700-acre attraction began as an agricultural centre to demonstrate how mountainous land could be used productively for growing food products. Mr. Lee of Joong-Ang said:

At that time, we had trouble raising enough food for our country. We created a model farm of how to work with an abandoned mountain by building a pig farm and planting fruit orchards. We changed the land use gradually through the years as we added entertainment elements.

The Wild Safari was opened in 1980, and the Rose Festival, an impressive rose garden filled with 6,000 rose bushes of 160 different varieties arranged according to various themes, opened in 1985. To provide for winter entertainment, the Sled Slope was opened in 1988. A drastic departure from the traditional theme parks was taken when Yongin Farmland opened a Motor-Park in late 1993. The Motor-Park operations incurred a loss in the first year (see Table 2 for the profit and loss statement).

In November 1993, Her took over as the president and chief executive officer of the Joong-Ang Development Company. Prior to his assignment to

EXHIBIT 1   Samsung Group

The late Chairman Lee Byung-Chul founded the Samsung Group in 1938. Though started as a trading firm to supply rice and agricultural commodities to neighbouring countries, Samsung moved quickly into import substitution manufacturing activities such as sugar refining and textiles. In the 1960s Samsung moved into electronics by establishing Samsung Electronics that developed VCRs, integrated circuits for televisions and telephone exchanges, electron guns for cathode ray tubes (CRTs), and cameras. The 1980s marked a major expansion for Samsung with its evolution into high-tech industry, such as semiconductors, telecommunications, computers, factory automation systems, and aerospace. Samsung had accomplished remarkable growth (see table below). The 1994 revenues were expected to be about US$70 billion.

Samsung, with 206,000 employees operating in 65 countries, had recently reorganized the group into four core business subgroups, Electronics, Machinery, Chemicals, and Finance & Insurance, and one subgroup of independent affiliates. While the core groups represented specific technological area, the independent affiliates subgroup represented a diverse mosaic that included the trading activities of the company, Korea's highest-rated hotel, Korea's leading newspaper publisher, state-of-the-art medical and research institutes, and cultural and welfare foundations. The Joong-Ang Development Co. Ltd., the developer of the Yongin Farmland, came under this subgroup.

Samsung Group Financial Highlights (billions of Korean Won)

	1992	1993	1994 (projected)
Domestic sales	23,680	24,609	27,736
Export sales	14,531	16,755	23,578
Total assets	38,016	40,964	50,491
Stockholders' equity	5,089	5,900	8,440
Return on equity	6%	7%	16%
Employees (thousands)	189	191	206

Note: Exchange rates, Korean Won/US$: 1992, 773; 1993, 808; 1994, 806.

In 1987, Lee Kun-Hee, son of the late Lee Byung-Chul, was appointed the chairman of the Samsung group. Lee accelerated the pace of growth at Samsung by pursuing aggressively high-technology areas and pushed the group to change from a quantity-oriented company to a quality-oriented company. Samsung's goal was to become one of the world's top ten corporations by the year 2000 by achieving annual sales of US$200 billion, and by producing products and services of the highest quality. Service quality and customer satisfaction became key phrases in all Samsung's activities, and all the companies in the group were taking active part in the "quality revolution" initiated by Lee.

TABLE 2

PROFIT AND LOSS STATEMENT FOR YONGIN FARMLAND
(millions Korean Won)

	1991	1992	1993
Revenue			
Net sales:			
Admissions	24,829	30,885	35,004
Merchandise	3,255	3,684	5,378
Restaurants	10,309	12,604	14,835
TOTAL	38,393	47,173	55,217
Expenses			
Park operations	26,209	33,487	40,409
Sales and administration	8,524	8,980	10,145
Others	1,215	1,350	1,433
TOTAL	35,948	43,817	51,987
Operating profit	2,445	3,356	3,230
Less interest expense	(1,724)	(1,100)	(3,417)
Profit (Loss) After Interest	**721**	**2,834**	**(18)**

Joong-Ang, Her was the CEO of Cheju Shilla, a luxury hotel on Cheju Island in Korea. Her was credited with developing a world-class sea resort at Cheju Shilla, which in customer service surpassed established hotel chains such as Hotel Hilton. Since taking over the reins of the company, Her had focused on improving the customer satisfaction level at Farmland, and had also been developing the plans for Farmland's expansion. One of the major challenges was to see how the expansion plans for Farmland would match with the corporate strengths of the Samsung group. Her was aware that earlier attempts by previous management to expand Farmland had not met with the approval of the group's chairman. There were concerns in many quarters that the theme park industry did not fit well with the "high-tech" and the "global" image of the Samsung group, and also that the profitability might be very low.

The theme park industry was still in its early stages in Korea, and had a history of less than two decades. Though indications were that the industry was growing globally, with more players entering, some of the managers did not see profitable growth opportunity. One of the managers in Joong-Ang said:

> Theme parks may be a growing industry worldwide. That does not mean that it should be so in Korea. In Korea, we work five and a half days a week and we have annual vacation of only four to five days a year. Where do Korean people have time for theme parks?

⬛ Farmland Customers

Traditionally, Farmland focused on the local customers. Most of its customers came from surrounding areas within two hours' drive (see Table 3). The economic growth in Korea had been a major driving force in industry growth (see Exhibit 2).

Despite the early stage of growth in the Korean leisure industry, there were six theme parks in the Seoul area including Farmland. Most notable among

TABLE 3   Target Segments—Attendance and Population Data

Market Type	Percent of Total Attendance from the Market Type[2] (%)	Population from the Market Type (millions)	Estimated Current Capture Rate[3] (%)	Projected Population in A.D. 2000 (millions)[4]
Primary resident market[1]	73	19.2	19.30	20.2
Secondary resident market	20	13.8	7.30	14.7
Tertiary resident market	8	12.5	4.10	12.3
TOTAL	100	43.5	11.30	47.2

[1] The primary resident market is within one hour's drive from Farmland, typically in a radius of up to 60 miles (96.6 kilometres). The secondary market is within one to two hours, and the tertiary market is outside the two-hour drive limit but within driving distance.

[2] Percentage of total attendance is based on three repeat surveys of visitors to Farmland in early 1994.

[3] The estimated capture rate is based on statistical projections from the survey respondents.

[4] The analysis does not include overseas visitors, which constituted 25 percent of the total attendance in 1993. Visitors were mostly from other Asian countries, such as Japan and Singapore.

these were Lotte World and Seoul Land. Lotte World, started in 1989, prided itself on having the world's largest indoor theme park with adjoining hotel, department store, shopping mall, folk village, and sports centre. Commenting on Lotte's strategy, one of the managers at Lotte World said:

> We focus on a segment different from Farmland. Since we are located downtown, we cater to a clientele who want to drop by for a shorter period. Typically, we get office people who want to relax after a hard day's work or couples who would like to spend some time in a romantic environment.

Seoul Land, located near Seoul at Kyungkido, was also a key competitor to Farmland. With attendance at 3.37 million, Seoul Land ranked 23rd in the "Top 50 theme parks worldwide." Mr. Woon, one of the managers at Seoul Land, remarked:

EXHIBIT 2   Korea in the Nineties

Korea, with its population of 44 million people, had seen tremendous economic growth over the 1980s and 1990s, despite the political difficulties. Over 10 million Koreans lived in Seoul, and along with the other five metropolitan cities the urbanization rate was at 74.4 percent. Korean economic growth has often been dubbed an "economic miracle." The per capita GNP had risen from US$4,210 in 1989 to US$7,513 in 1993. The growth rate for the second half of the 1990s was expected to be 8 to 9 percent. The growth of the Korean economy was accompanied by an increasing prominence of large business groups, commonly known as chaebol—privately held industrial conglomerates involved in a wide range of businesses. Samsung, Hyundai, Sunkyong, Daewoo, Lucky-Goldstar, and Ssangyong were some of the better-known chaebols.

Korean weather was a temperate climate, since it was in the transitional zone between continental climate and subtropical maritime climate. The winter stretched from December to mid-March when intense, cold, dry spells alternated with spells of milder weather. Temperatures dropped to –20 degrees Celsius in some places. Heavy snow was expected in the mountains. Summer, stretching from June to early September, was hot and humid with temperatures rising to 35 degrees Celsius with heavy showers in June and July. Mid-July to mid-August was the peak of Korean vacation season. Many festivals came together in October. Despite the pressing political problems, the country was successful in attracting international events to the country—the most prominent being the 1988 Olympics in Seoul. Tourist growth had been steady, approximately one-third of the tourists in Seoul using a travel package from some travel agencies.

The park has a good reputation for quality special events and the people enjoy coming to the park because of its fresh air, beautiful scenery, and easy access.

Despite the competition from other parks, Farmland had the highest growth rate within the Korean industry (Table 4). The seasonal nature of the theme park industry affected all the competitors, not necessarily in the same pattern (Table 5).

▣ Pricing

Farmland was also going through a major change in its pricing structure. The pricing strategy in place (Table 6) was a combination of "pay as you go" and "pay one price." Users had the option of paying the admission fees and buying separate tickets for rides ("pay as you go") that were available as coupons (Big 5 for five rides). Membership in the park was available for a price, which provided free admission for a year. The other option was to buy a "passport" ("pay one price") that provided admission as well as unlimited rides for one full day. The passport users were estimated at 17.4 percent of the attendance in 1993, and the membership holders were estimated at 75 percent. Farmland wanted to switch gradually to the pay-one-price scheme, which was the most common pricing scheme in the leading markets.

TABLE 4   **Comparative Attendance, Seoul-Area Amusement Parks (thousands)**

	1990	1991	1992	1993
Yongin Farmland	3,786	4,300	4,810	5,113
Lotte World	4,578	4,529	4,605	4,476
Seoul Land	2,198	2,819	2,834	2,648
Dream Land	971	1,319	1,236	1,325
Children's Grand Park	2,107	2,334	2,263	2,159
Seoul Grand Park	1,356	1,431	1,590	1,772

TABLE 5   **Comparable Monthly Attendance, Seoul-Area Theme Parks, 1993 (thousands)**

Month	Farmland	Lotte World	Seoul Land
January	641	618	220
February	158	390	93
March	190	290	115
April	844	380	378
May	952	363	460
June	801	241	171
July	220	406	182
August	392	646	413
September	193	226	184
October	351	323	302
November	99	214	54
December	270	381	75
	5,111	4,478	2,647

TABLE 6   Yongin Farmland Pricing Policy (Korean Won)

	Adult	Teen	Child
Admission			
Individual	3,200	2,250	500
Group	2,550	1,150	500
Big 5	12,000	10,000	7,000
Passport	17,000	14,000	10,000
Membership Public			
Individual	39,000	31,000	29,000
Family 3		85,000	
Family 4		95,000	
Group 3		75,000	
Group 4		85,000	
Ski Sled Passport	13,000	13,000	10,000
Snow Sled Common		7,000	
Grass Sled		3,000	
Swimming Pool			
Admission	1,850	1,350	1,000
Rides			
Suspended Coaster	3,200	2,700	2,200
Major Rides	3,000	2,500	2,000
Medium Rides	2,500	2,000	1,700
Secondary Rides	2,000	1,700	1,400
Tertiary Rides		1,400	
Kiddy Rides		800	
Pony Rides		1,700	
Time Machine	2,000	5,000	8,000
Lift	550	450	350

The prices across the major competitors were comparable. In 1993, average admissions and ride fee per person was 6,667 Korean Won in Farmland, 7,279 in Lotte World, and 6,494 in Seoul Land. Theme parks also monitored the amount a visitor spent on food, beverages, and souvenirs. In 1993, average per capita expenditure on food and beverage in the three parks was 2,874 Won in Farmland, 2,017 in Lotte World, and 1,804 in Seoul Land; merchandise sales per capita were 996, 1,319, and 722 Won, respectively.

Operational Issues

While there was some indication that the Samsung Group would be willing to consider a proposal for expansion of the Farmland, Her had to contend with a number of operational issues at Farmland. Based on discussions with a number of managers and customers, Her had some idea of the various issues involved in the operation of Farmland.

Transportation

One major issue was accessibility to the park. Yongin was 60 kilometres south of Seoul, and during peak hours, it took as long as two hours to drive from Seoul to Farmland due to traffic jams. One resident who lived very close to the Yongin area said:

Actually, it should take only 15 minutes to drive from my home to Farmland. But the traffic jam is so intense that if I go to Farmland, it may take almost an hour of crawling in the traffic. That's one main reason why I have not visited it so far.

One of the managers in the marketing group commented on the critical nature of this problem:

In Korea, we work five and a half days a week. Most of the time on the working days the travel time is long. All the house chores have to be done only on the weekends. Given this fact, it is only to be expected that Korean customers would not be so keen to travel on a Sunday or on a holiday if the traffic is heavy.

However, many managers in Joong-Ang believed that the accessibility problem was only a temporary issue. Mr. Yu, director of personnel at Joong-Ang, commented:

Travel difficulties are part of our life in Korea, given the small land and the large number of people. The government has plans to bring the subway up to Yongin, in which case Farmland would have a subway terminal, which will provide a lot of convenience to our people.

This was echoed by one of the visitors to Farmland, who commented:

I hate sitting inside my house all day. I have to get out somewhere. Seoul is too crowded and I would like to go to some place to breath some clean air. Beaches are closed most of the season, and if I want to go for some mountains or Pusan, it is too far away. So, I don't mind driving down to Yongin to spend a relaxed day. I will skip the rush hour by leaving early from the park.

Parking

Another, related issue was parking. Farmland had ample parking space for about 8,000 cars at one time around the four sides of the park. One of the managers who conducted an extensive analysis of the parking space said:

What we have now is more or less enough for the time being. We have enough space for about 8,000 cars and at four people per car we can accommodate about 32,000 people. If we assume the lot turning over at 1.7 times a day (at an average stay of six to eight hours), we can handle a peak attendance of 52,000. But the real problem is the seasonality. On peak days, we may get more visitors and quite often people may spend more time. If we are going to expand, this will be a major bottleneck.

Part of the expansion plan included augmenting the parking spaces and also providing a "Park and Ride" scheme for visitors so that they could travel comfortably from the various car parks to the entrance.

Environmental Issues

Expanding Farmland meant taking over more of the land mass available in the Yongin valley. A farmer living in the Yongin valley, who was vehemently opposed to the expansion ideas, said:

They [Samsung] just want to expand their business. But they don't realize that one of the problems with cutting down the trees and levelling the ground will cause potential flooding in the surrounding region. This will damage all our crops. How will they compensate us?

Organizational Inertia

It was also a challenge to introduce a dynamic environment within the Farmland organization. In order to succeed in the industry, Farmland had to go through a major reorientation in its organizational style. Farmland had initiated customer satisfaction surveys recently and it was brought to the attention of the management that the customer satisfaction levels were lagging behind the key competitor, Lotte World. As one of the marketing managers noted:

Repeat business is very important to our survival. If we don't satisfy our customers, they won't come back and we won't have any business left. But, it is not in our Korean nature to smile at strangers. We are very serious people. So it becomes all the more difficult to get the type of service you can see at Disneyland.

Mr. Yu, who had pioneered a number of changes within the organization, recalled one event that demonstrated the type of organizational inertia the management had to deal with:

Previously we had the head office at Seoul and we were managing the Farmland by "remote control." We were faxing information and directives up and down. But I somehow did not see that this would be the best way to work. I insisted that the head office had to be located where our products are and only after much persuasion could we move to this place.

Among other things, management was also considering a change in the recruitment process. Traditionally, Farmland had gone after the "academically best" graduates and students, which was the standard practice at Samsung. The management felt that they needed more service-oriented people. The management wanted to recruit more female workers, the level of which at that time was below 25 percent, but anticipated problems since most Korean women stopped working after marriage. Mr. Yu said:

I think times are changing. For that matter, even if we have a high turnover, it may be good for us since fresh blood always brings in fresh ideas and we would be able to preserve some dynamism in our organization.

▣ The Master Plan

Based on a tentative analysis, the management had put together a master plan to invest about $300 million in revamping Farmland. There were also suggestions of changing the name to provide a better image of the company. A master plan, for a phased investment of about $300 million over the next five years, was being developed. Everland, Green Country, and Nature Land were some of the names proposed for the new "mountain resort." Included in the master plan were:

- A waterpark to be built adjacent to the existing theme park, at an estimated cost of US$140 million, with a Caribbean theme
- A Global Fair, a fun-fair indicative of the major countries in the world, at an estimated cost of $85 million
- Expansion of the existing zoo, and parks including a nighttime laser show and a fable fantasy garden at an estimated cost of $50 million

The funding would come mainly from the parent, Samsung Group, and also through corporate sponsorship of the other companies within the Samsung Group. The master plan also indicated that if the first phase is successful, there would be a second phase of developing a resort town in Yongin, with luxury hotels, golf courses, and resort accommodations. (An exact budget for the second phase was not available at that stage.) A number of managers within the company who were closely involved in developing the master plan felt strongly that the theme park expansion not only was a priority but also would be a profitable venture. The general manager of the planning group commented:

> What we want to create is a destination resort town and a residential community where people can come, relax and enjoy themselves in a low-stress environment. Samsung employs more than 180,000 people here in Korea. This will give them a place to come and be proud of. There will be plenty here for all members of the family as they grow.
>
> We feel it is time to change from a farm-oriented name to a name which represents our new mission, which is to create a zeal for long-lasting life that is combined with the harmony of nature. If this plan is approved, we will become the prototype destination resort town in the entire world. We have visited them all, and when we're finished, there won't be any better!

Her wanted a comprehensive analysis of the theme park industry to ascertain the profitability of the industry. He wanted to present to the chairman of the Samsung Group a clear rationale for Samsung's proposed investment in this industry.

Scotch-Brite (3M)

In June 1990, the 3M operating committee met in world headquarters in St. Paul, Minnesota, to consider a proposal to rationalize the North American production and distribution of Scotch-Brite hand scouring pads. Due to increased consumer demand, the decision had been made to upgrade the equipment which converted the jumbo-sized rolls into consumer and industrial-sized packages and quantities. At issue was where this upgraded processing equipment would be located.

Currently, most of the conversion took place in Alexandria, Minnesota, from jumbo rolls supplied from Perth, Ontario. The Alexandria facility then shipped finished goods to eight distribution centres around the United States. (See Exhibit 1.)

The Canadian division of 3M was now proposing that all production and distribution for Scotch-Brite hand pads take place from Perth. This would mean $4 million in new equipment would go to Perth, the current Scotch-Brite work force in Alexandria would be shifted to different responsibilities, and Perth would now ship directly to the various distribution centres. (See Exhibit 2.) This proposal to grant a regional product mandate to Perth had not gone unopposed. The Alexandria plant felt it would be preferable to place the new converting equipment in their facility, and to maintain the existing relationship with Perth.

3M Background

3M was a multinational enterprise with 80,000 employees, subsidiaries and operations in 50 countries, and worldwide annual sales in excess of US$10 billion. During the past decade, 3M's outside-the-U.S. (OUS) sales had climbed from about one-third to nearly one-half of total sales. This growth was a result

This case was prepared by Professor Paul W. Beamish for the sole purpose of providing material for class discussion at the Ivey Business School. Certain names and other identifying information may have been disguised to protect confidentiality. It is not intended to illustrate either effective or ineffective handling of a managerial situation. Any reproduction, in any form, of the material in this case is prohibited except with the written consent of the School. This case was made possible through the support of the Task Force on Investment from the Ontario Premier's Council on Economic Renewal. © 1993 Ivey Management Services and the Ontario Premier's Council on Economic Renewal. Case 9-93-G003, version 02/01/94.

IVEY

Richard Ivey School of Business
The University of Western Ontario

EXHIBIT 1   **Present Scotch-Brite Product Flow Chart**

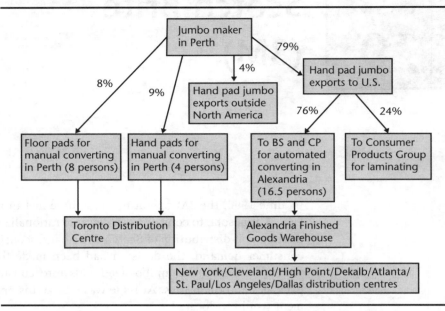

of a conscious strategy of global expansion. The company was organized into four divisions: Industrial and Consumer, Electronic and Information Technologies, Life Sciences, and Graphic Technologies.

Among the more familiar products were Scotch brand transparent tapes, magnetic tapes, cassettes, and cartridges. Abrasives and adhesives were early products of the company and still formed a very important portion of the business.

Developing other technologies and applying them to make problem-solving products was the basis on which 3M had been able to grow. So many new products were produced on an ongoing basis that 25 percent of any year's sales were of products that did not exist five years before.

EXHIBIT 2   **Proposed Scotch-Brite Product Flow Chart (all hand pad)**

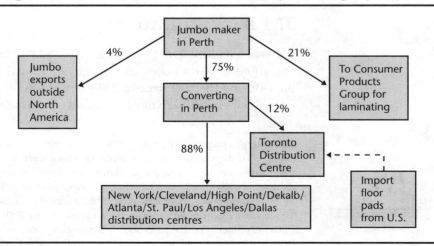

3M Canada Inc., like its parent company, was a highly diversified company which manufactured thousands of different products for industry, business, the professions, and the consumer. The head office and main plant were located in London, Ontario, with sales and service centres across the country. 3M Canada was established as part of the newly founded International Division in 1951. Additional subsidiaries were set up at that time in Australia, Brazil, France, West Germany, Mexico, and the United Kingdom. 3M Canada employed about 2,000 people. In addition to operations in London and Perth, the company had manufacturing plants in Toronto; Havelock; Simcoe, Ontario; and Morden, Manitoba. 3M Canada was the sixth-largest of 3M's subsidiaries.

With the exception of two or three people from the worldwide organization, everyone working for 3M Canada was Canadian. The Canadian subsidiary annually lost 10 to 15 people to the worldwide organization. Although a high proportion of the professional management group in Canada had a career goal to work in the worldwide organization at some stage, this was not a requirement. For example, several managers at the plant manager level and above had indicated a preference to stay in Canada despite offers within the worldwide organization.

The Canadian subsidiary, under the direction of its president, Jeffery McCormick, was expected to generate sales growth and to produce an operating income on Canadian sales. Increasingly, emphasis was being placed on achieving certain target market share levels.

Within Canada, the 25 individual business units were split among eight groups, each of which operated as a profit centre. Variability existed in each with respect to the amount of divisional input from the United States.

The headquarters perception of the competencies of the Canadian subsidiary varied according to the business and functional area. For example, Canadian manufacturing and engineering had a solid reputation for getting things done.

In terms of research, Canada specialized in three somewhat narrow areas. These dealt with polymer chemistry, materials science, and electromechanical telecommunications. Several dozen scientists pursued research in these areas within Canadian laboratories.

The Canadian subsidiary did not have a critical mass in R&D for all the technologies necessary to support Scotch-Brite. In addition it was not deemed feasible to move (or built) a pilot plant to Canada for Scotch-Brite testing purposes, since pilot plants tended to serve a multitude of products.

Partly as a consequence of the 1988 Canada-U.S. Free Trade Agreement, the overall level of company harmonization between the two countries had risen. Some U.S. divisions were asking for more direct control over their businesses in Canada. The Canadian president needed to deal with these issues and to develop the necessary organizational response.

The Canadian subsidiary had placed a lot of importance on building intercompany sales. Over 20 percent of its sales were of this type, and further increases were intended.

3M Canada sales in 1990 were over $500 million while after-tax earnings were in the range of 10 percent. (See Exhibits 3 and 4 for financial statements.)

EXHIBIT 3

3M CANADA INC.
CONSOLIDATED STATEMENT OF EARNINGS AND RETAINED EARNINGS
For the Year Ended October 31, 1989

	1989 (000s)	1988 (000s)
Revenue:		
Net sales*	561,406	516,663
Other income	8,823	3,536
	570,229	520,199
Costs and expenses:		
Cost of goods sold and other expenses	451,298	412,826
Depreciation and amortization	16,908	15,921
Interest	312	239
Research and development	1,876	2,010
	470,394	430,996
	99,835	89,203
Provision for income taxes	41,636	38,339
Net earnings for the year	58,199	50,864
Retained earnings—beginning of year	215,960	185,496
	274,159	236,360
Dividends	28,046	20,400
RETAINED EARNINGS—END OF YEAR	246,113	215,960

*Includes net sales to parent and affiliated companies of 106,773 and 89,709, respectively.

The Perth Scotch-Brite Plant

The $5 million Perth plant went into operation in 1981, employing 22 people. The plant covered 36,000 square feet (3,345 square metres) on a 78-acre (32 hectare) site and was the first Canadian production facility for this product line. It was built to supplement the jumbo output of Alexandria, which was nearing capacity. The plant was designed with sufficient capacity to produce enough hand pads and floor pads to eliminate imports, but with exports in mind. In 1981, the Canadian duty on shipments from the United States to Canada was 13.5 percent, while shipments from Canada could enter the United States duty-free.

Over the next decade, the plant was expanded several times, and employment grew to 80 people. Throughout this period, the plant exclusively produced Scotch-Brite. Scotch-Brite was a profitable, growing product line in a core business area. The total scouring pad market in which Scotch-Brite competed was estimated to be $60 million in the United States and nearly $5 million in Canada.

Scotch Brite material was a web of non-woven nylon or polyester fibres impregnated throughout with abrasive particles. The result was a pad, disk, or wheel used to scour, clean, polish, or finish materials such wood, metal, plastic, and many other surfaces.

As Scotch-Brite material wears down it exposes more abrasives so that it continues to be effective all through its life. Because it is made of a synthetic fibre it does not rust or stain. Some types of Scotch-Brite have a sponge backing so that

EXHIBIT 4

3M CANADA INC.
CONSOLIDATED BALANCE SHEET AS AT OCTOBER 31, 1989

	1989 (000s)	1988 (000s)
Assets		
Current assets:		
Interest-bearing term deposits	66,998	52,896
Accounts receivable	73,524	69,631
Amounts due from affiliated companies	18,050	13,670
Other receivables and prepaid expenses	5,472	4,592
Inventories:		
Finished goods and work in process	67,833	63,745
Raw materials and supplies	9,321	10,601
	241,198	215,135
Fixed assets:		
Property, plant, and equipment—at cost	180,848	164,313
Less accumulated depreciation	85,764	75,676
Other assets	9,590	8,856
	345,872	312,628
Liabilities		
Current liabilities:		
Accounts payable—trade	21,600	18,388
Amounts due to affiliated companies	18,427	17,985
Income taxes payable	9,394	12,437
Deferred payments	1,437	1,422
Other liabilities	20,832	18,367
	71,690	68,599
Deferred income taxes	14,669	14,669
	86,359	83,268
Shareholders' Equity		
Capital stock:		
Authorized—unlimited shares		
Issued and fully paid—14,600 shares	13,400	13,400
Retained earnings	246,113	215,960
	259,513	229,360
	345,872	312,628

---

both scouring and washing can be done with the one product. Other versions of this material have integral backing pads and handles made of strong plastic to enable the user to scour and clean flat surfaces and corners with ease.

Scotch-Brite products were made in sheet, roll, and wheel shapes, and used in a wide variety of applications in the metal-working, woodworking, and plastics industries, as well as in the hotel and restaurant trade, and the home.

Floor and carpet cleaning companies, schools, hospitals, and building maintenance personnel used a wide variety of Scotch-Brite disks and pads for floor maintenance. Other smaller hand-held pads were used for cleaning painted surfaces such as door frames, stairs, walls, sinks, and tiled surfaces. Scotch-Brite products were used in hotels and restaurants for griddle and grill cleaning, deep fat fryer scouring, as well for carpet and floor maintenance. Several types of Scotch-Brite products were available for home use. These ranged from a gentle version designed for cleaning tubs, sinks, tile, and even fine china, to a rugged scouring pad with a built-in handle for scouring barbecue grills.

● The Perth Proposal

During the 1980s as the Perth plant grew in size and experience, its reputation as a work force with a demonstrated ability to work effectively began to develop. With increased confidence came a desire to assume new challenges. An obvious area for potential development would be to take on more of the Scotch-Brite value-added function in Perth, rather than to ship semi-finished goods to the United States.

In the mid-1980s, the Perth managers advocated that they should now supply finished goods to the United States for certain mandated products. The Scotch-Brite manufacturing director during this period opposed this approach. He claimed that nothing would be saved as all the finished goods would have to be sent to Alexandria anyway, for consolidation and distribution to the customer.

The U.S.-based manufacturing director also argued that mandating products could reduce the utilization of the larger, more expensive maker at Alexandria which would increase the unit burden costs on other products there. During this period, the Perth maker operated as the swing maker with utilization cycling in order to keep the Alexandria maker fully loaded.

With a change in management came a willingness to take a fresh look at the situation. The new manager, Andy Burns, insisted that a more complete analysis of all the delivered costs be provided. To that end, a study was initiated in December 1989 to determine the cost of converting and packaging Scotch-Brite hand pads in Perth, rather than shipping jumbo to Alexandria for converting and packaging.

The task force struck in Canada was led by Len Weston, the Perth plant manager. Procedurally, any proposal would first go to Gary Boles, manufacturing director for Canada, and Gord Prentice, executive vice-president of manufacturing for Canada. Once their agreement had been obtained, the Perth plant manager would continue to champion the project through the 3M hierarchy, although people such as Prentice would facilitate the process.

The proposal would next go to the Building Service and Cleaning Products (BS + CP) division for review and agreement. If successful, the proposal would then be sent back to Canadian engineering to develop an Authority for (Capital) Expenditure, or AFE. It would then be routed through senior Canadian management and U.S. division and group levels. The final stage was for the AFE to go the operating committee at the sector level for assessment. See Exhibits 5 and 6 for partial organization charts for 3M Worldwide and International.

The Perth proposal acknowledged that Alexandria was a competently managed plant and that putting the new equipment in either location would reduce costs from their current levels. At issue was where the greater cost savings would be generated. The Perth proposal argued that these would occur in Perth (see Exhibit 7) through a combination of reduced freight and storage costs, and faster and more efficient manufacturing. The Perth proposal's

EXHIBIT 5   3M International—Partial Organization Chart

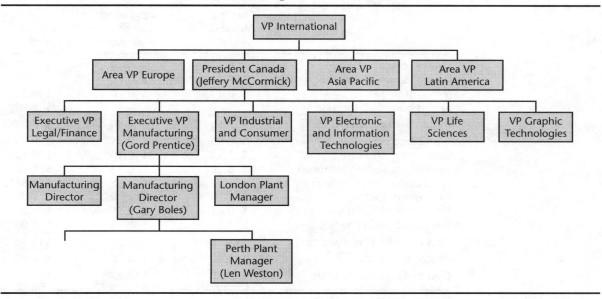

overall approach was to emphasize what was best for shareholders on the basis of total delivered costs.

Overall employment needs were expected to increase by 8 persons in Canada yet decline by at least double that in Alexandria. (See Table 1.)

EXHIBIT 6   3M Worldwide—Partial Organizational Chart

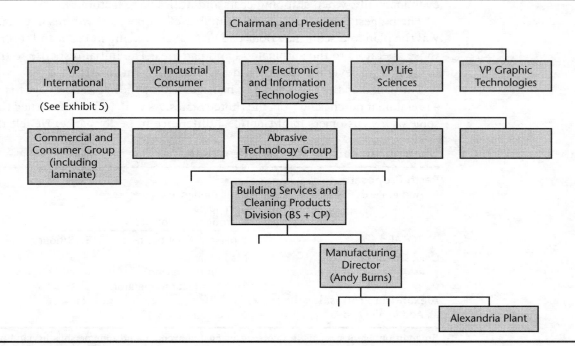

Note: Operating Committee made up of the four sector vice-presidents, the VP International, and several other key executives.

EXHIBIT 7   Sample Unit Cost Comparison (US$ per Case)

	Current Alexandria Operation	Upgraded Cutter Alexandria	Upgraded Cutter Perth
Jumbo cost ex Perth	$ 6.20	$ 6.20	$ 6.20
Jumbo freight to Alexandria	$ 0.70	$ 0.70	—
Jumbo storage	$ 0.70	$ 0.70	$ 0.05
Jumbo burden absorption	—	—	($ 0.20)[1]
Input cost to converting	**$ 7.60**	**$ 7.60**	**$ 6.05**
Converting waste	$ 0.95	$ 0.65	$ 0.45
Converting labour	$ 1.35	$ 0.30	$ 0.15[2]
Variable converting overhead	$ 0.60	$ 0.45	$ 0.30
Fixed converting overhead	$ 1.00	$ 0.55	$ 0.85[3]
Packaging supplies	$ 1.20	$ 1.20	$ 1.20
Fin. goods whse./mat. hand	$ 0.45	$ 0.45	$ 0.25
Fin. goods direct charges	$ 1.15	$ 1.15	$ 0.90
Cost including converting	**$14.30**	**$12.35**	**$10.10**
Freight to branch	$ 0.90	$ 0.90	$ 1.05
Cost delivered to branch	**$15.20**	**$13.25**	**$11.15**

[1] Volume savings through equipment usage.
[2] Lower than Alexandria due to faster equipment speed and smaller production teams.
[3] Higher than Alexandria due to larger investment in equipment.
Source: Perth proposal.

Some of the modest employment increases in Canada could be traced to the fact that the small amount of manual converting in Perth would now be automated. It had been viable to convert a small quantity of hand pads in Canada, even manually, when shipping costs and duties were factored in.

The biggest reason for the small number of proposed new hires in Canada was the plan to discontinue floor pad manual converting in Perth and to shift those operators to the automated hand pad area. The initial response to this in Canada, in several quarters, had been less than enthusiastic.

The Canadian floor pad business manager felt that he might now have to pay a premium if purchasing from the United States. As well, he was concerned that some of his customers might notice a difference in performance. He felt the

TABLE 1   Changes in Staffing for Each Proposal

Perth Proposal

Add in Perth	1 maintenance
	3 shippers
	4 production operators*
TOTAL	8 persons @ labour rate US$13.18/hour
Delete in Alexandria	Maintenance?
	Shipping/receiving?
	16.5 production operators

Alexandria Proposal

Add in Alexandria	6 operators @ 15.43

*In addition, eight persons in floor pad manual conversion and four persons in hand pad manual conversion would now be shifted to hand pad automated conversion in Perth.

manually converted floor pads from Perth were of slightly higher quality than the automatically converted ones from Hutchinson, Minnesota. The Canadian business manager had built a higher market share for 3M floor pads in Canada than his U.S. counterparts, and he did not wish to see this jeopardized.

A shift from floor pad manual converting to hand pad automated converting would also have immediate implications for the operators. Currently most of the manual floor pad (and hand pad) jobs were on a one-shift (day) basis. A second, evening shift was sometimes required, but no one worked the midnight-to-morning shift. With automation, all operators would now need to work a three-shift rotation in order to maximize machine utilization. In a non-union plant, with a ten-year tradition of day jobs in converting, and with a no-layoff policy, this could be an emotional issue. The task of selling it to the operators would fall to Weston.

◖ The Alexandria Response

The Alexandria response was less a proposal, and more a reaction to the Perth initiative. A variety of concerns, some old and some new, were raised.

- First, the increased production volume in Canada and the resultant reexports to the United States would cause an increased vulnerability to currency fluctuations.
- Second, lengthening the supply distance would make it more difficult to guarantee delivery to U.S. customers.
- Third, the Perth plant would now need to be interfaced with the 3M-USA computer-based materials management system in order to have effective transportation. This would require the Canadian information technology group to work with the logistics people in order to develop a program which would allow for cross-border integration of information.
- Fourth, cost of shipping finished goods to the branches would increase in both Perth *and* Alexandria. In Perth it would be due to the smaller volumes, and increased distances associated with shipping a single product line. In Alexandria it would now take longer to make up a truckload without the hand pads.
- Fifth, since Scotch-Brite converting was already well established in Alexandria, and there would be savings wherever the new equipment was located, it was safer to keep it where the manufacturing experience already existed rather than to rely on optimistic projections from Perth.

◖ Conclusion

In part, due to the distances involved, regional production mandates on various products had been granted as early as the 1970s by 3M in Europe. Scotch-Brite, in fact, was already also being produced in Europe, Asia, and Mexico. However, unlike these other production mandates, the Perth proposal was to supply the core U.S. market. For the operating committee, the decision would come down to how much confidence they had in the Perth proposal.

Seagram and MCA

In early March 1995, Edgar Bronfman, Jr., the 39-year-old president and chief executive of Seagram Company Ltd. (Seagram), was flying from Osaka to New York. He had just concluded a round of meetings with the senior management team of Matsushita Electric Industrial Company Ltd. (Matsushita). The meetings were held to discuss Seagram's possible acquisition of MCA Inc. (MCA), the entertainment company. Matsushita, the largest consumer electric manufacturer in the world, had acquired MCA in 1990 for $6.59 billion. Matsushita was clearly interested in selling a portion or possibly all of MCA.

At the meetings, designed as get-acquainted sessions, the two sides agreed to negotiate exclusively for a possible sale. Although the meetings had gone well, Bronfman had some major reservations. An acquisition of MCA could cost as much as $9 billion. To finance the acquisition, Seagram would have to sell its stake in Du Pont Company (Du Pont). This investment was worth an estimated $9–10 billion at current market prices. Because dividend and equity income from these shares accounted for nearly three-fourths of Seagram's 1995 income, a sale of the Du Pont shares could result in an adverse reaction from Seagram shareholders. Although Bronfman saw huge potential in the entertainment industry, he was concerned that besides cash, Seagram would bring little to the acquisition of MCA in terms of entertainment assets or management. Hollywood had a legacy of treating newcomers badly. Would Seagram fare any better in the unpredictable world of entertainment, where relationships in the Hollywood network were just as important as creativity, technology, and business experience?

Background History of Seagram

In 1916, Samuel Bronfman, a Russian immigrant, bought the Bonaventure Liquor Store Company in Montreal and began selling liquor by mail order, the only way liquor could be sold legally during Canadian prohibition. In 1924, along with his brother Allan, Bronfman opened a distillery and named

---

This case was prepared by Andrew Inkpen for the sole purpose of providing material for class discussion. It is not intended to illustrate either effective or ineffective handling of a managerial situation. Any reproduction, in any form, of the material in this case is prohibited unless permission is obtained from the copyright holder. © 1995 Andrew Inkpen.

his company Distiller's Corporation. In 1928, he purchased Joseph E. Seagram and Sons Ltd. and changed the name of his company to Distillers Corporation-Seagram Limited.

During the 1920s and after Canadian prohibition ended, Bronfman established a lucrative business smuggling whiskey to the "dry" United States. Anticipating that Prohibition would soon end, Bronfman began stockpiling whiskey. In 1933 when prohibition ended, Bronfman had the world's largest supply of aged rye and sour mash whiskey. He then purchased three U.S. distillers to add to his Canadian operations.

During the 1930s and 1940s the company expanded its product line. Seagram's 7 Crown whiskey was introduced in 1934 to honour the Canadian visit of King George VI and Queen Elizabeth and Crown Royal was developed in 1939. In 1942, distilleries in the West Indies were purchased and after World War II, several acquisitions were made: Mumm and Perrier-Jouet (champagne), Barton & Guestier and Augier Frères (wine), and Chivas Brothers (scotch).

In 1959, Edgar Bronfman succeeded his father as president. The company diversified into many new businesses, including Texas gas fields and Israeli supermarkets. In the late 1960s, Seagram bought, and then sold, 5 percent of the MGM film studio. Bronfman produced several Broadway plays during this period. In 1980, after a battle with Du Pont to acquire the oil and gas company Conoco, Seagram ended up with a 20.2 percent share in Du Pont. Additional shares of Du Pont were acquired through open-market purchase, bringing Seagram's ownership to 24.2 percent. In 1988, Seagram acquired Martell, the cognac firm, for $850 million and 28 times earnings. Tropicana, a manufacturer of fruit juices, was acquired for $1.2 billion. In 1991, the company was realigned into spirits and non-spirits groups. The same year, Seagram began purchasing shares in Time Warner, the huge entertainment and media company. Seagram eventually spent $2 billion to acquire a 14.95 percent stake, leading Time Warner to adopt a poison pill anti-takeover device to prevent Seagram from increasing its ownership.

Seagram Operations in 1995

In 1995, Seagram was the second-largest distiller in the world (Grand Metropolitan was the largest). The Seagram Spirits and Wine Group produced, marketed, and distributed more than 230 brands of distilled spirits and 195 brands of wines, champagnes, ports, and sherries. Spirits and wine were produced and bottled by the group at facilities located in 22 countries in North America, South America, Europe, Asia, and Australia. Subsidiaries and affiliates marketed products in 36 countries, while the company's brands were sold through independent distributors in virtually all other markets in which spirits and wine were sold. Some of Seagram's best-known brand names, such as Chivas Regal Premium Scotch Whisky, Martell Cognac, and Mumm Champagne, were sold throughout the world, while others were produced primarily for sale in specific markets. In addition to marketing company-owned brands, the firm distributed spirits and wine produced by others. In late 1993, V&S Vin and Sprit of Sweden awarded Seagram global marketing rights to Absolut Vodka, the best-selling premium vodka in the United States.

The Tropicana unit produced and marketed one of the leading brands of orange juice in the world. Tropicana pioneered not-from-concentrate orange juice in the United States with Tropicana Pure Premium Orange Juice. Tropicana offered a number of other juices not made from concentrate plus several brands of juices made from concentrate and frozen concentrate juices.

Seagram was actively looking for expansion opportunities around the world. For example, in 1993 Seagram became the only company to receive approval from the Indian government to establish a wholly owned subsidiary to produce and market a range of spirits, wine, and juice beverages.

The financial results of the recent diversification were mixed (see Exhibits 1 and 2 for Seagram financial statements and Exhibit 3 for product segment information). The financing costs on the Time Warner shares exceeded the dividends and the share value was stuck at $2 billion. In 1994, Seagram offered to invest a further $1 billion in Time Warner but this offer was rejected by Time Warner management. Estimated annual earnings for Tropicana were less than $100 million and senior executive turnover was very high.

The New CEO

The Bronfman family continued to play a major managerial and ownership role in Seagram. The descendants of Samuel Bronfman and trusts established for their benefit controlled 36.4 percent of the company. In 1994, 38-year-old

EXHIBIT I

SEAGRAM INCOME STATEMENTS
(US$000,000)

	Year Ending January 31:				
	1995	**1994**	**1993**	**1992**	**1991**
Sales and other income	6,399	6,038	6,101	6,345	6,127
Cost of sales	3,654	3,451	3,535	3,794	3,632
Net sales	2,745	2,587	2,566	2,551	2,495
Selling, general and administrative expenses	2,020	1,833	1,804	1,791	1,787
Operating income	725	754	762	760	708
Gain on divestitures	0	0	0	201	0
Dividend income	318	295	286	276	266
Interest expense	396	339	326	334	338
Income before income taxes and unremitted					
Du Pont earnings	647	710	722	903	636
Provision for income taxes	189	171	176	229	160
Income from beverage operations and dividends	458	539	546	674	476
Equity in unremitted Du Pont earnings	353	−160	−72	53	280
Net income under Canadian GAAP	811	379	474	727	756
Cumulative effect of accounting changes, Seagram	0	0	−195	0	0
Cumulative effect of accounting changes, Du Pont	0	0	−1,179	0	0
Cumulative effect of accounting changes for U.S. GAAP	−75	0	0	0	
Net income under U.S. GAAP	**736**	**379**	**−900**	**727**	**756**
Average number of shares outstanding (000,000)	372	373	376	378	376
Net income per share under U.S. GAAP	1.98	1.02	−2.38	1.92	2.01

EXHIBIT 2

SEAGRAM BALANCE SHEETS
(US$000,000)

	1995	1994	1993	1992	1991
Assets					
Cash and short-term investments at cost	157	131	116	266	131
Receivables	1,328	1,170	1,135	1,250	1,064
Beverages	2,398	2,234	2,341	2,562	0
Materials and supplies	121	116	106	114	127
Inventories	2,519	2,350	2,447	2,676	5,141
Prepaid expenses	172	143	138	135	141
TOTAL CURRENT ASSETS	**4,176**	**3,794**	**3,836**	**4,327**	**3,970**
Common stock of E. I. du Pont de Nemours and Co.	3,670	3,154	3,315	4,566	4,504
Common stock of Time Warner Inc.	2,043	1,769	0	0	0
Land	137	133	135	131	0
Buildings	505	453	444	433	0
Machinery and equipment	805	726	680	673	0
Furniture and fixtures	137	135	130	122	0
Other, including construction in progress	541	522	486	473	0
Property, plant, and equipment, at cost	2,125	1,969	1,875	1,832	1,775
Less: Accumulated depreciation	858	749	660	618	566
Net property, plant, and equipment	1,267	1,220	1,215	1,214	1,209
Excess of cost over fair value of assets acquired	1,547	1,520	1,511	1,526	1,558
Sundry assets	253	261	227	243	236
TOTAL ASSETS	**12,956**	**11,718**	**10,104**	**11,876**	**11,477**
Liabilities					
Short-term borrowings and indebtedness	2,475	1,844	851	568	1,752
Payables and accrued liabilities	1,423	1,011	1,023	1,116	1,122
Income and other taxes	193	141	129	212	170
Indebtedness payable within one year	0	0	0	0	86
Total current liabilities	4,091	2,996	2,003	1,896	3,130
Long-term indebtedness	2,841	3,053	2,559	3,013	2,038
Deferred income taxes and other credits	515	668	612	484	357
Common shares	638	617	595	583	444
Cumulative gain on equity securities	−85	46	0	0	0
Cumulative currency translation adjustments	359	479	369	87	13
Retained earnings	5,315	4,817	4,704	5,987	5,521
Total shareholders' equity	5,509	5,001	4,930	6,483	5,952
TOTAL LIABILITIES AND SHAREHOLDERS' EQUITY	**12,956**	**11,718**	**10,104**	**11,876**	**11,477**

Source: Seagram annual report.

EXHIBIT 3

1994 SEAGRAM SEGMENTED INFORMATION

By Region	Sales	Operating Income
United States	43%	14%
Europe	36	55
Canada	2	20
Other countries	19	11
TOTAL	100%	100%
By Product Category		
Spirits and wine	75%	
Fruit juices, coolers, and mixers	25	
TOTAL	100%	

Source: Hoover's Handbook of World Business, 1995–1996.

Edgar Bronfman, Jr., became president and CEO of Seagram. Bronfman had spearheaded the Martell, Tropicana, and Time Warner acquisitions.

When he was 16, Bronfman left his family in New York to board with movie producer David Puttnam in London. In his early twenties, Bronfman worked in Hollywood, producing several movies and a play. He was also involved in songwriting; Dionne Warwick and Ashford and Simpson are among the artists who recorded songs co-authored by Bronfman (under the pseudonym Junior Miles). Although he joined the family business in 1982, Bronfman maintained close ties with the people he had met in Hollywood. Later, he became friends with David Geffen, chairman of Geffen Records, and Michael Ovitz, influential Hollywood talent agent (Ovitz' father was a Seagram distributor). At Bronfman's recent wedding, guests included actor Michael Douglas, entertainment industry executive Barry Diller, and Michael Ovitz.

Matsushita Electric Industrial and the Purchase of MCA

In 1918, Konsuke Matsushita, a 23-year-old grade school dropout and inspector for the Osaka Electric Light Company, invested 100 yen to start production of electric sockets in his home.[1] Matsushita Electric Industrial (Matsushita) grew by developing inexpensive lamps, batteries, radios, and motors in the 1920s and 1930s. In 1953, Matsushita began producing televisions, refrigerators, and washing machines. This was followed by stereos, tape recorders, and air conditioners in 1959; and colour TVs, dishwashers, and electric ovens in 1960. Manufactured under the National, Panasonic, and Technics names, the company's products were usually not leading-edge, but they were manufactured efficiently in huge quantities at low prices.

By the late 1960s, Matsushita produced 5,000 products and sold them in Japan in more than 25,000 company-owned retail outlets. Matsushita's transition from a predominantly Japanese company to a global giant can be largely attributed to the firm's success with the videocassette recorder (VCR). After a fierce battle with Sony, Matsushita's VHS format became the accepted VCR standard in the late 1970s. In 1980, Matsushita's international sales grew by 52 percent, and in 1981 by 35 percent.

Although Matsushita was the largest consumer electric company in the world, the firm had earned the nickname "Maneshita," or copycat, for its practice of introducing products only after its competitors had created a market for them.[2] Traditionally very conservative, the firm was said to be run by bureaucrats, not innovators. In surveys of Japanese businessmen and consumers, Matsushita had fallen from the top of preeminent Japanese firms. Matsushita's main rival, Sony (which acquired Columbia Pictures in 1989 for $3.5 billion), was usually ranked first or second. In addition, Japanese customers were starting to switch from Matsushita retail stores to lower-priced discount outlets.

---

[1] Robert W. Lightfoot and Christopher A. Bartlett, *Philips and Matsushita: A Portrait of Two Evolving Companies,* Harvard Business School Case #388-144.

[2] *Wall Street Journal,* November 26, 1990, A1.

To move beyond consumer electric products, Matsushita began investing in areas such as semiconductors, industrial robots, high-definition TV, and computers. In 1989, Matsushita senior managers began a series of meetings with talent agent Michael Ovitz about a possible acquisition in the entertainment industry. These meetings culminated in Matsushita's acquisition of MCA for $6.59 billion in November 1990.

MCA History

MCA was founded in 1924 as Music Corp. of America by Jules Stein, a Chicago ophthalmologist who had worked his way through medical school by organizing bands to play one-night stands. In 1936 he hired Lew Wasserman, a Cleveland theatre usher and former publicity director for a local nightclub. Wasserman became president in 1946. By 1937, when the company moved to Hollywood, MCA was managing talent for radio, TV, and motion pictures. In 1952, MCA began producing television shows when the Screen Actors Guild and its president and MCA client, Ronald Reagan, gave the firm a waiver from the rule prohibiting talent agencies from producing television shows. In 1959, MCA purchased Universal Studios, and in 1961 purchased Universal Pictures and its parent, Decca Records. Universal would subsequently release some of the top-grossing movies of all time, including *Jaws*, *E.T.*, and the *Indiana Jones* series. In 1964, MCA created its Universal Studios tour business. In 1986, MCA acquired a 42 percent stake in Cineplex Odeon, a large movie theatre chain, and in 1990 it acquired Geffen Records from David Geffen for $545 million in stock. This made Geffen MCA's largest shareholder prior to the Matsushita acquisition.

MCA began searching for a partner or a buyer in the mid-1980s. The decision to sell the company was driven by concerns that MCA needed greater access to investment capital. With three major studios—Warner Bros., 20th Century Fox, and Columbia—owned by large media conglomerates, MCA risked losing future business opportunities to its richer competitors. In particular, MCA's international presence lagged behind that of its rivals. The takeover by Matsushita, the largest acquisition of an American firm by a Japanese firm, seemed ideal from both sides. Prior to making the acquisition, Matsushita had $10 billion in cash. According to MCA Chairman, Lew Wasserman, the acquisition by Matsushita would provide MCA with many opportunities for expansion, especially in the global arena.[3] David Geffen indicated that "this [MCA] will be the most acquisition minded company in the world."[4]

While there were questions about the cultural fit between conservative, bureaucratic Matsushita and Hollywood, analysts generally agreed that Matsushita acquired MCA for a bargain price, perhaps as much 25 percent lower than recent valuations. For Matsushita, the strategic benefits of the acquisition seemed clear. The deal would combine MCA's entertainment "software"—movies, music, and TV shows—with Matsushita's wide range of hardware—TVs, VCRs, CD players, etc. There was much talk about the synergy that would allow Matsushita to revolutionize the marketing of new technologies

---

[3] *Wall Street Journal,* November 28, 1990, A3.
[4] *Wall Street Journal,* November 28, 1990, A3.

738 SECTION III   CASES

such as high-definition TV and laserdisc players. The acquisition would also counter rival Sony's push into new product areas.

In negotiating the sale, both Lew Wasserman and president Sydney Sheinberg agreed to five-year employment contracts. No significant changes in MCA personnel or policies were planned and Matsushita's president, Akio Tanii, pledged never to interfere with the creative independence of MCA.

MCA and Matsushita Fours Years Later

Not long after the acquisition, Japan's "bubble" economy burst, hitting Matsushita especially hard. In 1993 and 1994 Japan, Matsushita sales and profits dropped substantially (see Exhibit 4 for Matsushita financial information and Exhibit 5 for product segment information). Matsushita's president and architect of the MCA acquisition was ousted because of poor results. The new president, Yoichi Morishita, was pushing a "revitalization strategy focused on electrical consumer goods." For these and other reasons, Matsushita was unable to support MCA's expansion goals. Matsushita vetoed MCA's 1992 proposed acquisition of Virgin Records and 1994 plans to join with ITT to bid for CBS.[5] The predicted seamless blending of Matsushita hardware and MCA software was not happening.

Cultural clashes added to the problems. Matsushita executives spoke little or no English, rarely visited the United States, and had little contact with MCA managers other than to turn down requests for funds.[6] These clashes boiled over in October 1994. MCA chairman Wasserman, now 81 and the industry's most revered elder statesman, told Matsushita that he would resign when his contract expired at the end of 1995 unless MCA was granted more management control and sufficient capital to compete with the other movie studios. Sydney Sheinberg indicated that he would also leave. There were rumours that as many as 100 MCA employees might defect, along with Wasserman and Sheinberg.[7] In addition, film director Steven Spielberg, one of the most successful directors in history, said that he would stop working for MCA if Sheinberg left.[8] Sheinberg was a close friend and mentor of Spielberg, having given Spielberg his first directing job. In the previous year Spielberg had released *Jurassic Park,* the biggest-grossing film in history, and the Academy Award–winning *Schindler's List,* both with Universal Pictures.

Spielberg's formation of a new entertainment company with former Disney Studio chief Jeffrey Katzenberg and David Geffen was of further concern to Matsushita. The equity in the new company, Dreamworks, would be split equally between the three founders, who together had an estimated net worth of more than $2 billion. Both Wasserman and Sheinberg endorsed the plans for the new company, although there were many unanswered questions. The films made by Dreamworks would have to be distributed through one of the established studios, such as Universal. According to one report, Spielberg sent a letter to Matsushita

---

[5] *Los Angeles Times,* April 10, 1995, A12.
[6] *Wall Street Journal,* April 10, 1995, A8.
[7] *Wall Street Journal,* April 10, 1995, A14.
[8] *Wall Street Journal,* November 18, 1994, A11.

EXHIBIT 4

MATSUSHITA FINANCIAL INFORMATION
(000,000 yen)

	Year Ending March 31:			
	1994	1993	1992	1991
Income Statement Information				
Net sales	6,623,586	7,055,868	7,449,933	6,599,306
Cost of sales	4,573,964	4,831,572	5,068,877	4,393,502
Gross profit	2,049,622	2,224,296	2,381,056	2,205,804
Selling, general and administrative expenses	1,876,016	1,988,466	1,997,784	1,733,214
Operating profit	173,606	235,830	383,272	472,590
Interest & dividend income	79,832	118,310	170,915	266,634
Interest expenses	99,790	133,363	177,324	161,371
Income taxes	99,878	128,388	193,784	304,994
Net income	24,493	37,295	133,904	258,914
Net income per common share	11.67	17.66	61.13	117.12
Balance Sheet Information				
Total current assets	4,073,697	4,349,559	4,440,439	4,402,929
Net property	1,395,454	1,499,568	1,496,507	1,158,252
Total assets	8,192,632	8,754,979	9,019,707	8,761,143
Total current liabilities	2,578,737	2,962,571	3,262,876	3,177,287
Total noncurrent liabilities	1,767,266	1,708,579	1,565,646	1,513,057
Stockholders' equity	3,288,945	3,406,303	3,495,867	3,434,747

Source: Matsushita annual report.

EXHIBIT 5

MATSUSHITA SALES

By Product Category

Communications and industrial equipment	25%
Video equipment	20
Home appliances	13
Electronic components	12
Entertainment	9
Audio equipment	8
Batteries and appliances	5
Other products	8
TOTAL	100%

By Region

Japan	68%
Other countries	32
TOTAL	100%

Source: Hoover's Handbook of World Business, 1995–1996.

executives indicating an interest in an MCA distribution deal only if Sheinberg and Wasserman remained with MCA.[9] If the company were to produce records, David Geffen's potential role raised a further question for Matsushita. Geffen was chairman of MCA's Geffen Record division, and in 1994 the division was having its most successful year. If Geffen left MCA and started a new label, top MCA recording artists and executives might follow him.

[9] *Los Angeles Times,* April 8, 1995, D8.

Wasserman and Sheinberg's concerns were reported publicly in the *Wall Street Journal,* the *Los Angeles Times,* and other newspapers. Matsushita executives reacted with surprise at the MCA managers' public announcement of their unhappiness with Matsushita. Matsushita president Yoichi Morishita was quoted, "I am surprised at the report in the U.S., as it is a bolt from the blue"[10] and "the relationship with MCA remains unchanged ... at this moment we have no plan to sell MCA."[11] On October 18 Matsushita executives met with Wasserman and Sheinberg in a meeting that ended acrimoniously and left both sides frustrated.[12] In December, Matsushita hired Michael Ovitz and the New York investment banking firm of Allen & Co. to explore alternatives for MCA. In January in Osaka, Ovitz and several associates from his firm, Creative Artists Associates, met for eight hours with Matsushita's senior management team.

MCA Operations and Performance in 1995

MCA had 1994 estimated revenues of $5 billion and a profit of $400 million from six businesses: movies ($2.3 billion in revenue), music ($1.4 billion), television ($600 million), theme parks ($350 million), publishing and software ($240 million), and Cineplex Odeon theatres ($150 million).[13]

In recent years MCA's movie business, Universal Pictures, had been highly dependent on movies produced and/or directed by Steven Spielberg, to the extent that MCA had been called the "House of Steven." These movies had made Spielberg immensely wealthy; his typical deal involved taking 15 percent of the revenue of every film he made. Other than the Spielberg movies, Universal had created few recent hits. Universal was also in the process of making *Waterworld,* a film that at a cost of $175 million was on its way to becoming the most expensive of all time. Universal also controlled a library of more than 3,000 films, including classics such as *Psycho* and *To Kill a Mockingbird.* The value of these films was uncertain. If MCA could strike a deal with a broadcast or cable TV network, the value could increase substantially.

MCA's Music Entertainment Group, the smallest of the six leading music conglomerates, had an estimated profit of $220 million and was growing at more than 10 percent annually.[14] MCA's largest music label was Geffen Records, which had sales of $500 million and estimated profits of $90 million. Geffen Records had a reputation as one of the best in the business at discovering new talent. Among its biggest sellers in 1994 were bands such as Counting Crows and Nirvana. Geffen Records was also the label for veteran acts such as Peter Gabriel, Aerosmith, and the Eagles. In 1994, the president of Geffen Records signed a long-term agreement to run the company after David Geffen's contract expired in April 1995. MCA also owned a concert division, and the 6,000-seat Universal Amphitheatre. The estimated market value for the music division ranged from $2.3 to $3 billion.

[10] *Wall Street Journal,* October 14, 1994, A5.
[11] *Wall Street Journal,* October 17, 1994, A5.
[12] *Los Angeles Times,* April 10, 1995, A12.
[13] *Business Week,* April 24, 1995.
[14] *New York Times,* April 10, 1994, D8.

The MCA Television Group produced series such as *Northern Exposure* and *Murder, She Wrote*. The group had produced few new hits in recent years and was rumoured to be poorly managed. The group also owned 50 percent shares in the cable networks USA Network and Sci-Fi Channel.

The Theme Park Division owned Universal Studios Hollywood and 50 percent of Universal Studios Florida. Both parks included major TV and film production facilities. Although highly profitable, both parks would require upgrades in the coming years. In February 1995, MCA submitted a plan to municipal authorities for a $3 billion development at the Hollywood park that would include expansion of the theme park, new film production facilities, and new shops, restaurants, and resort hotels. In the Florida park, a *Jurassic Park* ride was under development that could cost several hundred million dollars.

The Publishing and Software Group included two publishing houses, Putnam and Berkeley, and published books by bestselling authors Dean Koontz and Tom Clancy. The Universal Interactive unit distributed multimedia and video games. MCA owned 42 percent of Cineplex Odeon, a Canadian firm with 2,800 movie screens and revenues of about $350 million. The Bronfman family was also involved as a minority shareholder in Cineplex Odeon. Finally, MCA owned Spencer Gifts, a retail gift store chain with more than 500 outlets.

The Entertainment Industry

Movies

Besides MCA, the film industry was dominated by six other major studios and had been for 50 years. Warner Bros. was owned by Time Warner, in which Seagram had a major stake. In recent years, Warner Bros. had realized the highest U.S. market share among the major studios. Warner Bros.' television unit was the largest producer of successful TV shows for other networks and the firm was moving aggressively into merchandising to take advantage of its animated characters such as *Bugs Bunny* and the *Road Runner*. In addition to its movie and television business, Time Warner was involved in periodicals publishing, book publishing, music, and cable TV operations. Because of its major acquisitions, Time Warner was burdened by about $15 billion in debt and had lost money in the past few years.

Paramount Studios was acquired by Viacom in 1994 for $10 billion. Viacom, a diversified entertainment company, owned television and radio stations, cable TV operations, the publisher Simon and Schuster, MTV, and Blockbuster Video. One of Paramount's strongest assets was its *Star Trek* franchise, which had generated a reported $1.3 billion for the studio in combined revenues from films, syndication rights, and merchandising. Paramount produced the 1994 box office winner *Forrest Gump,* which generated more than $300 million at the box office.

Walt Disney Studios, the most financially sound of the major studios, was divided into three units: Walt Disney Motion Pictures Group, which produced live action movies; Walt Disney Television and Telecommunications Group, which handled TV, home video, and new technology; and the Feature Animation Group, which developed Disney's animated feature films. In recent years, Disney was the leading studio in terms of the number of new film releases and had a string of highly successful animated films, including *The Lion King,* the most successful film in Disney's 73-year history. With the success of this film and others (*Aladdin, Beauty and the Beast,* and *The Little Mermaid*), Disney was recharging its theme parks, consumer products, television, and video divisions with fresh characters. Although with limited success to date, Disney was building music and publishing divisions and was committed to capitalizing on the strength of the Disney name.

Sony Pictures Entertainment, and its studios Columbia Pictures and TriStar Pictures, was owned by Sony Corp. Sony Pictures was reeling from box office failures, executive turnover, and according to industry insiders, a succession of bad creative and financial decisions. Sony had recently taken a $3.2 billion charge for writeoffs at its Columbia and TriStar Studios and was reportedly seeking an investor to buy at least 25 percent of the business.

Twentieth Century Fox was a division of Rupert Murdoch's News Corp. More than the other studios, Fox was aggressively trying to become integrated into the worldwide media network. Fox had formed several international distribution joint ventures and was planning its first overseas production facility in Sydney, Australia. News Corp.'s global operations included the Hong Kong–based satellite network Star TV, which covered much of Asia; the London-based satellite service British Sky Broadcasting, covering Britain; the Los Angeles–based cable channel El Canal Fox, servicing 18 countries in Latin America; and the Fox network in the United States.

MGM/United Artists was owned by the French bank Credit Lyonnais. The studio had lost money annually since 1987 and was on its third management team since being acquired by Credit Lyonnais in 1992. In 1995, the latest management team appeared to be making progress in getting the studio back to profitability.

In 1994, the major studios released 185 films, compared with 161 in 1993. The average film cost $34 million to produce and $16 million to market, a 15 percent jump over the previous year. Top box office draws such as Sylvester Stallone and Arnold Schwarzenegger were able to earn $20 million a film. In addition to rising costs, the movie business was well known for attracting outsiders who went on to suffer huge losses. For example, in the 1970s, the San Francisco financial services firm Transamerica bought United Artists. Faced with huge writeoffs after the most expensive film fiasco up to that point, *Heaven's Gate,* Transamerica sold the studio to Metro-Goldwyn-Mayer (MGM), which was controlled by financier Kirk Kerkorian. Italian financier Giancarlo Parretti purchased MGM from Kerkorian after Kerkorian had little success in the film business. After major losses, Credit Lyonnais foreclosed on Parretti and took over MGM. Credit Lyonnais was forced to remove $800 million in bank debt from MGM's books in early 1994 and provided an additional $400 million credit line. The Japanese firm Pioneer Electronics was expected to write off its $60 million investment in the independent film studio Carolco Pictures.

An area of very positive growth for the film studios was overseas sales and distribution. There was a huge and growing international market for American films, to the extent that several European countries were restricting the market share of American films. As an example of the kind of deal the studios were involved in, MCA was one of the overseas distributors for the movie *True Lies,* a film produced and released in the United States by Twentieth Century Fox. *True Lies* grossed $145 million in the United States. Because Twentieth Century Fox wanted to spread its risk, MCA was distributing *True Lies* in various countries, including Australia, Brazil, Mexico, and South Korea. The gross in MCA's territory was estimated to be $115 million, with MCA spending about $20 million on marketing.[15] As another example, Warner Bros. in 1994 signed a movie distribution deal with China's exclusive film import agency, China Film Distribution, Exhibition, Export & Import Corp. The films were to be dubbed in Mandarin. Also in 1994, Turner Broadcasting's TNT Network announced that it would introduce a 24-hour movie channel in Asia. The program was to be beamed from a Chinese satellite and dubbed initially in Mandarin and Thai.

Music

Like the film industry, the recorded music industry was also dominated by a small number of large companies. MCA's music business, with a 1994 market share of 10.7 percent, was the smallest of the six major distributors. The other major firms were: WEA, owned by Time Warner, 21.1 percent share; Sony, 15.2 percent; Bertelsmann, 12.9 percent; PolyGram, owned by Philips Electronics, 12.9 percent; and Thorn EMI, 11.2 percent. Independent distributors had a 16 percent share.[16]

Music differed from films in several respects. Most important, the average album cost a few hundred thousand dollars to produce, which allowed a music company to produce several hundred titles a years and spread its risk. In contrast, the major movie companies released an average of 26 films each in 1994. Movie companies had to wait years to see a revenue stream; music companies could start making money within months of recording. Unlike movie stars, few recording artists could command multimillion-dollar fees, and when they did it was usually spread over several projects. Because music fans tended to be loyal, once an artist became established there was a fairly predictable sales base with each new album. For some records, sales never seemed to end. Pink Floyd's *Dark Side of the Moon* spent a record 741 weeks on Billboard's Top 200 after its release in 1973 and sold more than 500,000 copies in 1994. *The Eagles Greatest Hits: 1971–75* sold 662,000 copies in 1994 and outsold all but 119 of the more than 5,000 new releases.[17]

The movie and music industries also differed when it came to developing new artists. Moviegoers tended to be loyal to their favourite stars, and as a result the studios were reluctant to use lesser-known actors and actresses in their films. Nevertheless, there was never a guaranteed film success, even when the most well-known stars, directors, and screenwriters were involved. In contrast, the music business relied heavily on new artists. Each year, dozens of new music acts had successful records. Although about 85 percent of all acts signed never made money for the music companies, the other 15 percent plus sales of

---

[15] *Wall Street Journal,* November 22, 1994, B1.
[16] *New York Times,* April 10, 1995, D8.
[17] *Los Angeles Times,* April 10, 1995, F1.

previously released records more than made up for the losses. New acts could be huge moneymakers for the music companies because of their low costs and because of the high profit margins for bestselling records. When a record sold in the millions, manufacturing costs became pennies per unit. At this point, operating margins could be as high as $7 per unit.

At many of the large entertainment conglomerates, including MCA, the music business was more profitable and consistent than the film business. For example, Time Warner's film division in 1994 generated $565 million in operating income on $5 billion in revenue. Its music business did much better, earning $720 million on revenue of $4 billion.[18] In 1994, Sony's music unit earned $550 million on $4.5 million in revenue.

A recent trend in the global music business was the linkages between the record companies and music videos. Music video broadcasting, pioneered by Viacom's MTV, reached 60 million homes in the United States. MTV International reached 250 million homes in 67 countries. A competing channel in Europe, Viva, was partially owned by Thorn EMI, Sony, Warner Germany, and PolyGram. In early 1995, Bertelsmann, Thorn EMI, Sony Pictures, and Warner Music Group joined as equity partners in an Asian music video channel. MTV Mandarin, a partnership between MTV and PolyGram, was set to launch in April 1995 in Asia. This was the first MTV channel to have an outside partner. In 1994, when Warner, Sony Pictures, Thorn EMI, PolyGram, and Ticketmaster announced plans to start a rival U.S. service to MTV, Viacom chairman Sumner Redstone threatened an antitrust suit and declared that Viacom and MTV would compete with its suppliers and start a record company.

Seagram and MCA

Seagram's chief financial officer, Stephan Banner, had worked as a mergers and acquisitions lawyer in New York prior to joining Seagram. As a mergers lawyer, Banner had worked on Matsushita's acquisition of MCA. In January 1995, Banner talked with a lower-level Matsushita executive and indicated that Seagram might be interested in acquiring MCA.[19] For the next month, Seagram executives debated the pros and cons of the possible acquisition. The main attraction of MCA was the opportunity to become a controlling shareholder of one of the major firms in the entertainment industry. If the industry was able to continue its international expansion and if the merging of entertainment, telecommunications, and computers happened as many analysts predicted, the rewards for those in the "software" side of entertainment could be enormous. The downside was the high-risk nature of the business and Seagram's lack of entertainment industry experience.

On March 6 in Osaka, Bronfman met with Matsushita president Morishita and other senior executives to discuss the possible purchase. At the meeting, the two sides agreed to negotiate exclusively for a possible sale. For Seagram, an exclusive negotiation would preclude the deal from turning into an auction.

---

[18] *New York Times,* April 10, 1995, D8.
[19] *Los Angeles Times,* April 10, 1995, A12.

For Matsushita, the company would be spared public embarrassment if the deal fell through. At this point, MCA's Wasserman and Sheinberg were not involved in the discussions and were not even aware they were going on.

The meetings had gone well and Bronfman was convinced that Matsushita was genuinely interested in selling all or a majority of MCA. He knew that he would have to come back to Matsushita with a firm offer fairly quickly or risk losing the exclusive negotiation privilege. He also knew there would be some heated debate with his father and other Seagram board members. In particular, selling the Du Pont shares would surely be a very contentious issue. Reports that Seagram was interested in selling the Du Pont shares surfaced publicly in June 1994, at a meeting between financial analysts and Seagram management (including Edgar Bronfman). There was speculation that Seagram would sell the shares if they hit a price of $80–$85. Although Seagram, when asked about the Du Pont shares, did not say it planned to sell the stock, it did not deny the possibility either. According to a Seagram spokeswoman, "We're not looking to sell the Du Pont stock. You never say never—this is our position now."[20] By January 1995 and before the first discussions with MCA, discussions with Du Pont about selling the shares back to Du Pont were under way.

Du Pont

Du Pont was the largest chemical company in the United States, with revenue of $40 billion in 1994, and the fourth-largest in the world (Exhibit 6). Du Pont was founded in 1802 as a manufacturer of gunpowder by a French immigrant, E. I. du Pont de Nemours. Over the years, Du Pont had invented many products, such as neoprene, nylon, Teflon, Orlon, and Dacron, and diversified into many areas. In 1995, Du Pont had five major divisions: chemicals (fluorochemicals, specialty chemicals, pigments), fibres (textiles, flooring, non-wovens, nylon, polyester, lycra), polymers (films, finishes, elastomers), petroleum (Conoco—exploration, production, refining, marketing, petrochemicals), and diversified businesses (agricultural herbicides and insecticides, medical products, printing and publishing materials). The largest unit was Conoco with $17.2 billion in sales and $1.1 billion in operating profit. Fibres, which accounted for $6.8 billion in sales and more than $1 billion in profit, was growing rapidly. The polymers division was also doing well, with sales of $6.5 billion and profit of more than $1 billion.

In 1991, Du Pont initiated a major reengineering effort. Since then, Du Pont had cut 37,000 employees, sold $1.8 billion in assets, and eliminated more than $2 billion in annual expenses. Operating margins increased from 5.4 percent in 1992 to 8 percent. In 1994, Du Pont had the highest earnings in its history and net cash flow (operating cash flow after dividends and capital expenditures) was $1.6 billion and was projected to be $2 billion for the next two years. International sales increased from 39.8 percent in 1989 to 47 percent in 1994. Du Pont was actively looking for new projects and acquisition targets in the Asia Pacific region. In early 1994, Du Pont was evaluating more than 30 projects in China alone.

---

[20] *Financial Post,* June 10, 1994, Sections 1, 3.

EXHIBIT 6

DU PONT FINANCIAL INFORMATION
(000,000,000)

	Year Ended December 31:			
	1994	**1993**	**1992**	**1991**
Income Statement				
Revenue	39.33	37.84	38.35	39.52
Cost of goods sold	21.98	21.40	21.86	22.52
Selling, general and administrative expenses	2.88	3.31	3.74	3.58
Restructuring charges	–1.42	–1.845	–0.48	
Changes in accounting principles	NA	–4.83		
Net income	2.73	0.56	–3.93	1.40
Balance Sheet				
Total current assets	11.11	10.90	12.23	11.32
Total assets	36.89	37.05	38.87	36.56
Long-term debt	6.38	6.53	7.19	6.46
Shareholders' equity	12.82	11.23	11.77	16.74
Employees	NA	107,000	124,916	132,578

Source: Du Pont annual report, *Wall Street Journal.*

After dropping below $30 in 1989, Du Pont shares were trading at about $60. Seagram owned 164 million Du Pont shares, which, at market value of $60 each, were worth $9.8 billion. Seagram acquired the shares for $3.28 billion.

◼ Bronfman's Decision

Selling the Du Pont stake would have an enormous impact on Seagram's bottom line. Without the Du Pont shares, Seagram would lose more than 70 percent of its net income. MCA's earnings would make up some of the difference but not all. For the next few years it looked as if the Du Pont shares would provide a steady source of income and cash flow for Seagram. However, Bronfman saw some problems with Du Pont's business lines. Most were cyclical, highly capital-intensive, and fraught with potential environmental problems. Although Seagram had three positions on the 15-member Du Pont board of directors, it had only minimal control over strategy. MCA represented an opportunity to acquire a controlling interest in one of the largest entertainment companies in the world. As well, Bronfman felt that Seagram management would be comfortable with MCA because its businesses were customer-driven and moving toward global expansion. Bronfman now had to decide if MCA was the right opportunity for Seagram.

The Pepsi Challenge— Russia 1992

CASE 31

In May 1992, economic output in Russia was declining 20 percent on an annual basis and the monthly inflation rate was in double digits. Nonetheless, a number of Western businesses were hopeful that economic liberalization, though occurring in turbulent and unpredictable steps, would eventually produce opportunities. Pepsi, with its relatively long history in Russia, was among the most optimistic.

William A. Shaddy, director of human resources for Pepsi International in Eastern Europe, had only been in Russia for two weeks. Bill was tasked with the critical responsibility of building a Russian organization to implement Pepsi's business strategy.

Pepsi in Russia

In October 1959, the world was in the middle of the Cold War. In Moscow, the American International Exposition was being held to highlight consumer goods which were abundant in the United States, but scarcer in the USSR. Donald Kendall, then head of Pepsi-Cola's international operations, made sure Pepsi was present. Arch-rival Coca-Cola had ignored the event. During the fair, Premier Nikita Khrushchev and Vice-President Richard Nixon had their famous "kitchen debate." Nixon said, "We are richer than you are." Khrushchev would retort, "We are catching up and we will surpass you."

Later, as international reporters and photographers watched, Nixon and Khrushchev walked by the Pepsi-Cola booth. Kendall pushed his way through a phalanx of bodyguards, audaciously pressed a bottle of Pepsi into the Soviet leader's hand and urged him to try it. "Good stuff! We should have this here,"[1] Khrushchev remarked upon tasting it. The Premier of the Soviet Union liked it so

This case was prepared by Honorio Todino with assistance from Professor Paul Beamish and Professor Marina Kalinina of the Moscow State Academy of Management for the sole purpose of providing material for class discussion at the Ivey Business School. Certain names and other identifying information may have been disguised to protect confidentiality. It is not intended to illustrate either effective or ineffective handling of a managerial situation. Any reproduction, in any form, of the material in this case is prohibited except with the written consent of the School. Funding support was provided by Foreign Affairs and International Trade Canada. © 1994 Ivey Management Services. Case 9-94-G001, version 09/23/94.
[1] *Newsweek*, June 22, 1992, p. 45.

much that he proceeded to finish off six more bottles. It was a publicity coup as media around the world showed the leader of the communist bloc drinking Pepsi.

Twelve years later, Richard Nixon, now U.S. President, had initiated the first real thaw in superpower relations with his policy of "detente." Khrushchev was gone; Leonid Brezhnev and Alexei Kosygin held the reigns of power. Kendall, now CEO of Pepsi, was in Moscow as part of an American trade mission. Just before a Kremlin meeting, Kendall showed and played a portable radio in the shape of a Pepsi-Cola can to Premier Kosygin, eliciting a laugh from the Soviet leader. At the reception later that evening, Kosygin said to Kendall, "I understand that you want to trade Pepsi-Cola for vodka." Kendall immediately replied, "Yes, sir."[2] Kosygin and Kendall shook hands and Pepsi was in the Soviet Union.

◼ Corporate Background[3]

The first Pepsi-Cola drink was formulated by North Carolina pharmacist Caleb Bradham in 1893. The company almost went bankrupt several times in its first three decades. In the 1930s, although Coca-Cola already dominated the U.S. soft drink market, Pepsi grew rapidly by underpricing Coke and by catchy radio advertising. Both companies followed the growth strategy of signing up regional bottlers and selling them concentrate.

Immediately after World War II, Coke outsold Pepsi by a large margin due in part to the fact that Coca-Cola bottling plants, with the aid of the U.S. government, had followed victorious G.I.s around the globe. In 1950, Alfred Steele, a former Coca-Cola marketing executive, became Pepsi-Cola CEO. He made "Beat Coke" his theme and focused efforts on supermarket takehome sales in the rapidly expanding phenomenon of the American suburb. Pepsi introduced the first 24-ounce bottle for family use and launched several successful advertising sales campaigns. Sales grew over 300 percent from 1950 to 1958.

Kendall became CEO in 1963, renamed the company PepsiCo and diversified the company. Acquisitions included Frito-Lay in snack foods and Pizza Hut and Taco Bell in restaurants. The "Pepsi Generation" advertising theme, featuring the drink as the choice of the young and young-at-heart, was very successful. PepsiCo focused on the aggressive management of its store delivery operations. Throughout the 1960s and 1970s, Pepsi's unit sales and profits increased faster than Coca-Cola's.

In 1974, Pepsi introduced the "Pepsi Challenge" marketing campaign. It featured blind comparison taste tests which had shown that a majority of consumers preferred Pepsi to Coke. The hugely successful program used advertising, store displays, and in-store challenge booths. By 1975, Pepsi had gained market share leadership in U.S. food store sales, beating Coke for the first time.

In most European and Asian markets, Coke had a higher market share than Pepsi. In 1976, Coca-Cola's CEO stated that Coke's largest growth would come from international sales. By 1980, the international market accounted for 62 percent of Coke's soft drink volume, compared to 20 percent for Pepsi.

---

[2] J. C. Louis and H. Yazijian, *The Cola Wars* (New York: Everest House, 1980).

[3] Draws from R. Wayland and M. E. Porter, *Coca-Cola Versus Pepsi-Cola and the Soft Drink Industry,* Harvard Business School Case 9-391-179.

● Internationalization

Pepsi started internationalizing in the 1930s. Its first non-U.S. plant opened in Canada in 1934 followed a year later by plants in Cuba and the Dominican Republic. It was under Kendall's leadership that Pepsi started expanding outside of the United States. By the 1980s Pepsi had over 500 bottling operations in more than 140 countries.

Both Pepsi and Coke expanded internationally by repeating their national growth strategies. They relied on local investors, mainly businesspeople already successful in banking, mining, trading, and other enterprises. Pepsi granted national and area franchises to local business people and assisted with the construction of bottling plants and the installation of modern, high-speed bottling lines. Pepsi assisted the franchisee in setting up distribution and transportation systems, sales forces, and marketing and advertising programs. Reliable supplies of bottles, can containers, and purified water for each market were arranged with Pepsi's help. Pepsi laboratories provided quality control, while PepsiCo plants sold the concentrate to franchisees.

With the combination of modern mass-marketing techniques developed in the United States and the local partner's resources and knowledge of the market, Pepsi usually overwhelmed local soft drink competitors. Moreover, soft drinks were a quintessential part of modern Americana and with the spread of American pop culture, the world developed a thirst for Pepsi or Coke.

Coca-Cola preceded Pepsi into affluent Western Europe, entering the United Kingdom as early as 1900. Pepsi tried to beat Coke into new markets such as low-income countries in Asia, Africa, and Latin America. Both companies eyed the potential of the Eastern European markets with great interest in the 1960s. In 1965, PepsiCo announced a deal with the government of Romania to bottle Pepsi-Cola in Constanta, Romania. It was its first entry behind the Iron Curtain. However, Kendall always thought that the biggest prize lay in the Kremlin.

● Back in the USSR

After the handshake between Kosygin and Kendall, Pepsi executives and Soviet trade officials painstakingly worked on the details of the deal, which was finally announced with much publicity in November 1972. It was a milestone in U.S.-Soviet commercial relations. Pepsi would engage in a joint venture with the Soviet government, providing technological and managerial know-how in installing several bottling plants. Pepsico would sell concentrate from its Western European plants to the joint venture and in return would receive premium Stolichnaya vodka in a novel countertrade arrangement.

At this time, U.S.-Soviet joint ventures were not permitted by law but an exception was made for Pepsi. Just as importantly, Pepsi had shut out Coke from the Soviet market, gaining an exclusive deal for cola drinks until 1984.

In 1974, the first bottle of Soviet Pepsi came off the Novorossisk production line. It was the first licenced foreign consumer product to be made in the Soviet Union. Later that year, the PepsiCo board of directors met in Abrau-Durso, in the Black Sea region of the Crimea, in an important symbolic gesture. Pepsi first went on sale in Moscow in 1979. Sales outlets included red, white, and blue kiosks.

Mikhail Gorbachev came into power in the Soviet Union in 1985. He soon launched the policy of *perestroika,* literally "reconstruction," signifying liberalization of Soviet society. In practice, this applied more to political reform than to the economy, which continued to be centrally planned. Another period of rapprochement with the West, called *glasnost,* started.

In connection with the 1986 Goodwill Games in Moscow which PepsiCo sponsored, Pepsi's commercials became the first from the West to appear in Soviet television. In 1988, PepsiCo was the first advertiser of any kind to buy time on state-owned television. It aired five 60-second commercial spots on the five-part program *Pozner in America,* including two that featured Michael Jackson. A new TV commercial was filmed in the USSR, featuring 20 Soviet teenage actors and actresses speaking in Russian. The advertisement emphasized the commonality between American and Soviet teens including the fact that they both drank Pepsi.

That same year, PepsiCo launched Fiesta, a lemon-flavoured soft drink, and Tanez, which means "dance" in Russian, an orange-flavoured soft drink. The two products were developed specifically for the Soviet market.

From its base in the USSR, PepsiCo steadily expanded into the markets of the Soviet satellites, in some cases keeping Coke out and greatly outselling its rival in the Eastern European region. By the time the Iron Curtain came crashing down in 1989, Pepsi had the highest market share in soft drinks in Poland, Czechoslovakia, Hungary, Bulgaria, and Romania.

In 1990, PepsiCo signed an agreement extending its reciprocal trade arrangement with the Soviet Union to the year 2000. In the most innovative and far-ranging deal between a U.S. corporation and the Soviet government, it provided for 26 new bottling plants in the USSR which would be buying concentrate from Pepsi, in exchange for increased purchases of vodka by PepsiCo, and the purchase of ten Soviet commercial shipping vessels by PepsiCo to be sold or leased in international markets. The entire transaction represented more than $3 billion over the decade. Kendall reportedly said, "I think anybody who has a product that can be marketed in the Soviet Union is a damn fool if they don't go over there now and get started. If they wait until all the conditions are right, someone else will have the business."[4]

◼ Bill Shaddy

William Shaddy was born in Manitoba, a central Canadian Prairie province with a population of a little over a million people. He attended the University of Manitoba and graduated in 1981 with a Commerce degree major in marketing. After graduation, Bill joined Procter & Gamble Canada in Grand Prairie, Alberta, where the headquarters of the Cellulose Division was located. Later, he transferred to the Procter & Gamble detergent plant in Hamilton, Ontario, as production supervisor. Shaddy joined Pepsi Canada in

---

[4] J. L. Hecht, *Rubles and Dollars* (New York: HarperBusiness, 1991).

Toronto in 1984 as employee relations manager for Canada. He was responsible for developing and executing the human resources acquisition strategy for 7-Up Canada in 1986 when Pepsi purchased 7-Up International.

In early 1987, Shaddy was transferred to Pepsi's U.K. office in London and stayed there until early 1989, covering parts of Europe and the Middle East. He recalled:

> In Europe, I learned the ability to be effective and to make an impact among different cultures and backgrounds. Though cultures, business practices, and politics may be different, there are common threads to motivating people and this was true as well in Africa and the Middle East. People everywhere want interesting and exciting work; they want to be rewarded for what they do; they want to be respected and recognized as individuals.

In 1989, Bill was transferred to India to put together a greenfield startup operation. A couple of months before his transfer, PepsiCo had asked him to work on how to build an organization in India. Pepsi had been aggressively lobbying the Indian government for years to get back into India. There had been no multinationals in the soft drink industry since 1977 when Coke left. India was a large untapped market. PepsiCo wanted to preempt Western competition and targeted the 150 million middle-class Indians with disposable incomes.

Bill reflected on his experience:

> First, I learned in India how to go in and sort out reality and fiction. In the Indian environment, there was a lot of background noise surrounding every issue but when you scratched and got down to the base, it was a nonissue. I developed the ability to sort through and come up with what was important and achieve what we had to do. Second, it was important that we maintained our code of conduct or corporate integrity on how we operated. In a lot of countries in the world, when faced with a lot of challenges or difficulties, there are easy ways, not necessarily the right way, that might conflict with the company's ethical codes.

Bill Shaddy was assigned to Hong Kong from late 1989 to late 1991 as personnel director for Asia, which included India, Pakistan, China, Korea, Taiwan, Indonesia, Australia, and New Zealand. PepsiCo had 49 percent ownership of a joint venture in Taiwan but insisted on managing control. A single local partner had 51 percent of the company. Shaddy recalled:

> Our partner was a very successful Taiwanese business that had a very traditional operating style to the point where they had employment for life. This was substantially different from Pepsi management culture that was high-reward, aggressive, performance-driven. Trying to blend these two cultures was a big challenge.

⬤ Bill Shaddy in Russia

Shaddy was assigned to Cyprus in February 1992 where he was director of human resources development for the Middle East, Africa, and Eastern Europe. By late April 1992, Bill was in Russia following only a single one-week trip in March. Bill explained his mission:

My top-line mandate is to spend three to six months to build an organization consistent with what we want to do from a business strategy point of view and to make sure our personnel strategy is tied to business strategy. Human resources is high-profile in Pepsi compared to other companies. We are expected to be involved with general managers in every step of their business strategy and in their development. We are in key meetings and key business presentations so that they have an understanding of where we are coming from. We then develop our human resources objectives and link them with business objectives to make sure of long-term consistency.

We have a fairly detailed human resources planning process. We try to map out where the business is going in three or four years with the talent that we have today. Here is our bench of talent today; here is where the business is today; here is where the business strategy is taking us—how do we grow that bench of foreign service employees and locals to meet future needs? Is the organization we have today right for five years from now? For Russia, where's the organization going to be six months, a year, five years from now? We're trying to align the organization with strategy. How are we going to recruit people for our strategy? Where are we going to find them; how are we going to compensate them; how do we train them; how do we motivate them throughout their careers?

Shaddy was also responsible for putting together the organization chart, including reporting relationships with the Russia-area vice-president based in Vienna, his director of finance, and key technical people. He was also to determine the total number of staff, on the basis of input from functional areas and of Pepsi's policy of being tight on head count. At the time, Pepsi had only six Russian employees based in Moscow including the driver, and two secretaries. Recently, Pepsi formed a joint stock company, which was the vehicle that allowed foreigners to hire Russians directly. Formerly, they employed Russians through one of the government employment bureaus, which seconded them.

Shaddy explained further:

One of the key things is to hire a 22-to-28-year-old Russian who is as Western as we can get. Maybe an MBA from the West. Maybe with some work exposure in the West. The person could currently be living either in the West or in Russia, but still a Russian passport holder. Once hired, we'll immediately put him in the U.S. for 12 to 18 months for training. The person will have an aggressive development program to learn the state of the art in Pepsi systems, the Pepsi way of doing business, of managing an organization. Then we'll bring him or her back to Moscow as country manager for Russia. We tried to hire a 28-year-old Russian MBA student at the London Business School, but he ended up taking an offer by one of the investment banks. In the future, we might send two Russians to MBA programs in North America or Europe.

Pepsi International had what they called Foreign Service Employees (FSEs), a population of individuals who were flexible and had a functional skill set. They formed a cadre of internationally mobile executives. Pepsi formally kept a list of FSEs. They were measured against internal benchmarks on functional skills, impact, and technical knowledge. FSEs were different from locals.

They were primarily Americans, Canadians, and Britons. They were there to watch Pepsi's investments in certain countries and to develop people. Shaddy explained:

> There will always be a need for that type of talent. One day they could be in a two-year assignment in India, the next a two-year assignment in Brazil. Our expats that we move around are pretty savvy at being able to adapt to different cultures and markets. To focus in on key things, they rely heavily on local resources and local consultants to develop and tailor a system that will work locally. The international organization needs people who can learn quickly.
>
> You have to make sure before you send people international that they will be successful. They need to have the right skill set, the right cultural mindset, and the right set of values. You have to make sure from the family point of view that there aren't any pressures that could derail the assignment; the family has to be flexible and adaptable, and the spouse should not have to worry about the kids' safety.

Shaddy thought that an FSE would probably come in as country manager of Russia in January 1993. When the Russian from the U.S. training came back, he or she was going to work in tandem with this FSE; then the FSE would leave, having put in the systems, business strategy, and policies, and having transitioned with the Russian designate country manager. The FSE country manager would have Pepsi functional expertise in sales and distribution. The FSE was likely to be a European who had been in the Pepsi system several years. Another FSE in production/manufacturing might also be brought in. Shaddy continued:

> I'm learning very quickly that here in Russia the most basic business fundamentals are just not developed to what we are used to. What we find in other markets is not here or is not developed to the extent that we would like to see. We realize that is something that is going to take time. At least in India they have a well-developed business system and the people have a well-developed business sense. Here it's not quite as developed. Traditionally, we'd like to get people with packaged food or consumer goods backgrounds. But the right type of educational skills that we look for may not be here, so we have to be flexible. We like to hire people who have a certain impact, people who come into a room and look confident, not wallflowers. Here, you may find that it's difficult for people to really be individuals. To go out and sell themselves and make an impact, that's not really part of the culture. So we realized that we may have to be flexible with our recruiting profile.
>
> Language and cultural issues compound the problem. Hopefully, the people we'll be looking at will have some knowledge of English. An English-speaking Russian may make a nice presentation to the president of the international division if he comes and visits tomorrow. I could go out and hire a dozen Russians who speak good English. But are they smart? Do they have the right skills—do they have the right potential? My process in hiring people will involve a lot of direct networking and talking with other foreign company representatives here, like chartered accounting firms, legal firms, our advertising agency BBDO. They're here too, trying to plug in to people they know.

I'm using a couple of local recruiting consultants-headhunters. One of them is affiliated with Korn Ferry Budapest. They have two Russians here who used to work for government ministries in a personnel function. We're working with them for a couple of advertisements. There's another consultant who's Vienna-based. An Austrian, who speaks Russian, been here for years, has very good contacts. To find the country manager designate for Russia, I'll use a London-based recruiter who's done substantial work in this part of the world. We don't have the structure to directly recruit ourselves.

Shaddy gave an example of Pepsi's organizational moves in the Ukraine:

A Ukrainian-American of Ukrainian descent who speaks fluent Ukrainian was hired in the U.S. to work in Kiev for Pepsi. She had several years of package goods experience in the U.S. and had been in Kiev several times over the last few years. Her brother was a lawyer for Baker Mackenzie who had been seconded to the Ukrainian government to translate, and redraft their laws and regulations. She has a strong understanding of how it works in the Ukraine and we'll build a local organization around her. She has the right functional skills from her work experience, the language skills, and the adaptability profile. She will be business development manager for Ukraine, effectively running Ukraine and reporting to the vice-president in charge of the C.I.S. from Vienna. We can't have her reporting to Moscow because of the current sensitivities regarding the two now independent countries—Russia and Ukraine. I'll be hiring four to five people for the Ukraine in the next ten days.

Bill talked about his dilemmas:

In my two weeks here I've learned it takes a significant amount of time to get things done, that you have to cut through the baggage to find out what the issues really are and what has to be done. It's a challenge due to the language barrier. Cultural sensitivity is something which you have to be aware of. You have to be very careful how you approach people, how you phrase or word things so you don't get the individual giving you the answer they think you want to hear. It's being able to cut through that.

Another issue is managing confidentiality in terms of what we pay people and confidential career decisions because there are no secrets here. Everyone talks and shares information about what they are earning or did not earn. I want to be sensitive that what we do in compensation does not disrupt or cause long-term difficulties. We also want to make sure our compensation respects local regulations and taxation as it stands today and as it may develop in the future. We want to make sure we have enough flexibility as the situation changes so we can stay one step ahead in terms of adapting our policies and programs. I've talked to other Western managers and their compensation is all over the map. There is no rationale over anything. Some companies have paid in hard currency which fuels expectations of locals. Other companies have paid only in rubles and have been able to attract some very good people with a ruble package.

At some point I'm going to have to decide on a compensation policy as we hire people. How much? Hard currency compensation or not? Some prospects might say, "I only want hard currency," but you can get good

Russians who will want to work for a Western company for rubles because of the development aspect, to learn. In other countries, you have to adapt to local conditions and a lot of questionable practices but you can cut through all that and design something that's going to be right for your code of conduct. We're using our public accounting firm to come up with creative solutions, but like everybody else here, they are also on a steep learning curve. So what we try to do is aggressively talk to other companies here and use vehicles like the American business association or the American embassy and come up with frameworks on how things should be done.

Another big issue is office space. I can't hire people without an office. Pizza Hut has no more room so we have to go out and find a suitable office but we have to fund renovations from the profits generated in Russia. You go out and talk to real estate agents and they say, "Oh yeah—Pepsi-Cola. You want to be here (in this building) where Mercedes is and Mitsubishi and these sexy high-profile companies." But we can't afford that. That office space is US$800 to US$1,200 per square metre, but I'm looking for US$200 per square metre, which is consistent with how we want our offices in the field. Simple but big, functional. You can get three floors of space but then you need to negotiate with 28 landlords to get a common consensus. You need to hire consultants for international communications facilities and telex hookups.

I want to come up with a strategy that moves us from an expensive Vienna-based organization of 50 people managing the former Soviet Union from afar to a more cost-effective Russian organization with just a couple of people in Vienna in key positions. It's a transition over three or four years. We're opening a Kiev office in the Ukraine Republic in the third or fourth quarter of this year, a St. Petersburg office in the first quarter of 1993, and a Tashkent office in Kazakstan in the second quarter of 1993. [See map in Exhibit 1.] That is a rough plan in mind in building the organization and strategy and having the right people in place.

If you come in and start aggressively recruiting, if you don't take the time to follow your screening procedures, and you're perhaps pushed by the pressure of filling a job, you might compromise a little bit; then you might make mistakes and unknowingly get someone who is not ready for business. You try to get reference checks, preemployment physicals, but how do you get references in Russia? You can use police records but then again there are things which may have been illegal in the past like "making money."

We have to accomplish a lot of things quickly, rely upon outside resources but at the same time, we have a strong bottom line that we have to meet. Every dollar and ruble I spend is being scrutinized by the Vienna office. It all hinges on when we can get the vodka flowing [laughter].

Shaddy described the hiring process:

What makes people successful in Pepsi International? We studied how to identify a success profile. Also, why people fail in international, either foreign service or local employees. We came up with 11 or 12 success factor measures that people who are successful in Pepsi over a length of time demonstrate. We use the measures as a tool to help manage their careers in Pepsi. We also use them as a predictive tool in hiring people. We structure interviews so that we each look at a group of these factors to see what the candidate has done in the past to demonstrate capability in these areas. It's a consistent profile; we tweak it a little bit for various markets but basically it cuts across culture, language, religion, origin, economics. It has been proven to work in different cultures.

Our hiring criteria include dynamic personality, loyalty, confidentiality, potential for development, an active person, career-oriented and eager to learn, with hopefully a little bit of exposure to joint venture accounting

EXHIBIT 1

practices. For example, the accounting manager for Pizza Hut is a Russian woman. We're looking for the same type recognizing that we won't be finding anyone like the typical accounting manager in the West. Experience in Russian accounting and finance may be the closest thing we could get. This is a critical position because we need somebody to run the day-to-day books, to make sure stuff isn't disappearing or being siphoned off.

They're a valuable tool, these benchmarks, to help assess and judge candidates. They've been used in the interviewing process. We rely on a series of interviews using five Pepsi people from different functions. Each person focuses on portions of the success profile. We call it a Fast Focus interview process. I think these success factors are here in Russia, people who have a high drive to succeed, who are smart, are not afraid of challenge, are honest about themselves and can admit their mistakes, who can get along with people, who can make an impact and influence people. The problem is how do we find them?

The Russian Market

Pepsi's sales in the former Soviet Union were concentrated in Russia, Ukraine, and Kazakstan, the three largest republics. In 1992, the population in Russia was estimated to be around 149 million with a per capita GNP of US$5,400. Ukraine had a population of 52 million and a per capita GNP of US$4,400. Kazakstan had a population of 17 million and GNP pet capita of US$3,800. To give some perspective, Russia's population and total economic output were roughly similar to Brazil's.

It was estimated by Moscow News that Pepsi had around 6 percent of the market in total soft drink sales. This figure should be interpreted in light of the fact that sales and market share figures were very unreliable in an economy in which the words "market" and "marketing" were novel and not fully understood, and statistics were educated guesses at best, complete fabrications at worst. A trade official had been quoted as saying, "We know more about space research than market research."[5] The same estimate had Coke with about 3 percent of the market, which was surprising considering that Coke was a much more recent entrant in the former Soviet Union.

The main competition consisted of local soft drink brands with mainly citrus flavourings. These were not advertised or promoted, their packaging was drab and they did not compete on price. Pepsi, Coke, and the local competition sold for roughly the same price, around 75 rubles or the equivalent of US$0.60 in May 1992 for an 8-ounce (0.2 litre) bottle. Soft drinks were sold in small roadside kiosks which also sold other goods, and by enterprising individuals who simply stood on street corners and sidewalks with a few bottles, boxes of cigarettes, used personal items, and whatever else they could get their hands on to sell on an ad hoc basis. In Moscow, Pepsi-Cola was also dispensed out of sidewalk fountain machines, which Pepsi leased to the city government.

Pepsi-Cola was produced by 50 franchised bottlers in the republics of the former Soviet Union with concentrate imported from a PepsiCo plant in Ireland.

---

[5] M. N. Rajan and J. L. Graham, "Nobody's grandfather was a merchant," *California Management Review,* vol. 33, no. 3: 40–57.

Local state enterprises who were the joint venture partners owned and operated the automated bottling plants. Pepsi provided quality control to ensure that the product was not being diluted and met Pepsi's uniform international product standards. Random samples were sent to testing labs in Vienna and Pepsi technicians trained the partners on quality control. The distribution system was also state-owned and -controlled. The partners did not do any advertising and promotions, which were PepsiCo's domain. Advertising was done through newspapers and magazines, outdoor and kiosk displays, and the occasional TV commercial. Pepsi also sponsored promotions in sports, entertainment, and cultural events.

One of the biggest problems in the old Soviet economy was distribution. It was estimated that up to a third of all food produced was wasted through the supply and distribution system. In market economies, Pepsi relied on shelf space and positioning, as well as convenience packaging, pricing tactics, and the pull exerted by advertising and promotions to generate food store sales volume. Russian stores did not compete on service, convenience, prices, or promotions. Availability of Pepsi in the inefficient Russian food stores was currently very limited. Pepsi relied solely on 8-ounce glass bottles, as did the competition. Pepsi could try to push restaurant sales but at present restaurants in Russia were extremely scarce. The country lacked a legal framework for property rights, a financial system, social traditions, and knowledgeable businesspeople to encourage the formation of privately owned stores and restaurants.

It was conceivable that the state-owned enterprises that owned and operated all the means of production and distribution in the different stages of the business system in the former Soviet Union would eventually be privatized. However, as of May 1992, the pace of privatization was agonizingly slow, fraught with controversy, opposed by the managers, unpredictable, and proceeding unevenly between the different republics. As contracts with franchise bottlers came up for renegotiation, it was often a problem to determine who were the right people to negotiate with in the turbulent situation.

▣ Pizza Hut

Pizza Hut International, which was wholly owned by Pepsico, employed 300 Russians in a 50:50 joint venture with the Moscow City government. There were currently two restaurants and the entire operations were headed by a Russian and fully staffed by Russians. Certainly, the only soft drink choice in the menu was Pepsi-Cola.

The first two Pizza Hut restaurants opened in Moscow in September 1990. One was along the Nevskaya Prospect (formerly Gorky Street), the busiest boulevard in the city. It had a takeout counter that accepted payment in Russian rubles and a small sit-down area for U.S.-dollar customers. Outside the restaurant, Russian youths would frequently eat pizza and drink Pepsi on the top of the hoods of their cars parked along the curb while playing loud Western rock and roll music. It was only a block away from the huge McDonald's restaurant on Pushkin Square which served as a beacon to young Russians with a taste for Western culture.

The second outlet was larger and was located on Kutuzovesky Prospect. Pepsi and Pizza Hut's administrative offices occupied the second floor of this small building. The restaurant on the ground floor was divided into two sit-down sections of equal size. One side accepted Russian rubles, while the other was for U.S. dollars. There were frequent half-hour lineups to get in on the ruble side which was much cheaper. Patrons could always go straight in and get a seat immediately on the dollar side. The young Russian employees usually spoke some English.

Coke and McDonald's

For years, the main impediment to Pepsi toppling Coke in total soft drink sales in the United States was Coke's dominance in fountain outlets. Its contract with McDonald's, the leading fast food chain in the world, was pivotal in this battle. In 1990, the largest single McDonald's restaurant in the world opened in Moscow. By May 1992, it was serving about 40,000 customers each day. It only served Coca-Cola.

Coca-Cola first made its presence known in Russia when it was one of the major sponsors of the 1980 Olympics in Moscow. Unfortunately for Coke, this Olympics was boycotted by the United States and some other Western countries in protest against the Soviet invasion of Afghanistan. Now, it seemed that Russia was part of Coke's plans to dominate the market in Eastern Europe. In May 1992, Coke announced it would invest $1 billion in Eastern Europe over the next four years. Already, Coke had made big moves in former East Germany.

The Coca-Cola company's sole joint venture partner in Russia was millionaire Dr. Valentin Fyodorov, who owned 3 percent of the joint venture. Fyodorov invented laser surgery for myopia and ran 12 clinics around the world. In the past, Coke had used countertrade in Lada cars to repatriate its ruble profits. Now the joint venture was a ruble-only operation. Craig Cohon, an aggressive Canadian with a degree from the Western Business School, headed the joint venture and was also busy recruiting people for Coke. He planned to build a vertically integrated plant across the street from McDonald's' huge vertically integrated production facility. Craig was the son of George Cohon, chairman of McDonald's Canada, the person who got McDonald's into Russia.

Pepsico Inc.

In 1991, PepsiCo had total sales of $19.6 billion, placing them 17th in the Fortune 500. Total net income amounted to $1.1 billion. PepsiCo products in nearly 150 countries had estimated retail sales value of $50 billion. Total soft drink revenues were $6.9 billion, of which $1.7 billion was international. International revenues had grown 25 percent from the previous year compared to 3 percent for the U.S. side. Worldwide soft drink profits were $863 million, of which international was $117 million. PepsiCo was one of the most successful large companies in the United States in growth, having increased sales and net income at a rate of nearly 15 percent over the last 26 years. In fact, PepsiCo was cited by *Fortune* as having created the most number of new jobs, 218,000, among all Fortune 500 companies from 1981 to 1991, and PepsiCo was also consistently rated by executives among the ten most admired companies in America.

Excerpts from the 1991 annual report's messages from the chairman said:

Up until a few years ago, we were basically a strong U.S. company with a solid but limited international presence. In 1991, nearly one out of every four sales dollars came from our international operations, nearly double the level five years ago. When you consider that 95 percent of the world's population is outside the U.S., you can see what that means in terms of opportunity. And this is doubly true for our kinds of products, which are in great demand everywhere on earth, with almost no economic or cultural barriers.

I believe there's a consumer revolution taking place across the globe and that's why we must redefine how we do business. Fuelled by economic and cultural trends, the revolution involves people seeking more control of their lives, more value in the things they do, and more personal freedom.

From Tbilisi[6] to Bangkok and Guadalajara, consumers are emerging by the billions, literally. Our worldwide goal is to take advantage of this enormous opportunity. Our strategies include supporting our superior brands, leading in emerging markets, building on our strong bottling relationships and using our well-honed operating skills to improve our ability to compete. Our goal is to double our international soft drink business over the next five years.

Pepsi had a reputation of having a strong corporate culture. It was reported to be a combative, aggressive, adventurous, and achievement-oriented culture. It valued personnel selection, socialization, and training more than most big companies. The development of this culture was thought to be strongly linked to the influence of almost mythic leaders in PepsiCo's history like Kendall. It had also been cited by analysts as one of the main reasons for Pepsi successes over Coca-Cola during the last two decades. One executive who was familiar with the cultures of both cola companies compared them:

Pepsi is much quicker to say what it thinks, much quicker to argue. It's hard to disagree at Coke. Pepsi is made up of fast-track MBAs, who take nothing for granted. Coke values loyalty. Pepsi says let's get something done or be done. At Pepsi you don't have to like somebody to play with them.[7]

The Russians

During May 1992 there was a palpable air of optimism in Moscow. Another harsh winter was over. Democracy was a novel experience like the blossoming of a spring flower. Unlike the past, the May Day celebrations in Red Square had not been a parade of ballistic missiles and tanks before a stonefaced group of old men, the Politburo, atop the Kremlin walls. Instead, a rock concert held by Western musicians blared in the middle of Red Square just yards away from Lenin's tomb. On one of the buildings surrounding Red Square a huge white sign with blue letters covered an entire wall, proclaiming "Freedom Wins," in English and Russian Cyrillic, which had been paid for by an American foundation. On another side of Red Square, colourful banners promoted tourism in a Caribbean Island (though few if any Russians could afford the trip). The Russian government had

---

[6] Capital city of former Soviet Georgia.
[7] Thomas Oliver, *The Real Coke, the Real Story* (New York: Random House, 1986).

sold advertising space around Red Square to Western companies for $500,000. The Kremlin walls were available for $1,000,000 but found no takers.

Despite the outward symbols of capitalism, there was reasonable doubt about how well the Russian people could change after 70 years of communist statism. The state-planned economy had created an environment described as:

> ruled by monopolies with no competition, where state enterprises were guaranteed profit, and government regulation and control were pervasive and stifling. Internally, organizations were described as heavily staffed bureaucracies, with managers who were skilled at implementing but not developing strategy; workers had a welfare mentality; overstaffing and nepotism were rampant; rewards were not tied to performance; efficiency was not measured; and emphasis was on loyal, "right-thinking" employees.[8]

An American research team quoted one manager in 1990 as saying:

> The Soviet worker is lazy, doesn't want responsibility, and doesn't want to even be at work. There is no incentive to work and no reason to be a good performer. There is widespread alienation, disaffection, and apathy among workers. Managers have very few solutions that can overcome years of apathy, disgust, and undisciplined practices.[9]

A Russian academic observed, "Perhaps the biggest problem for Russians in a free market economy is making decisions and choices. Under communism all our decisions and choices were made for us by the state."

There were examples of successful managers in the old Soviet system. However, success often was arrived at by expertise in beating the system. Production supplies were obtained through bribes or through the exchange of personal favours. Involvement with the sinister Russian Mafia which controlled or intimidated many business channels was also existent.

Perhaps the most optimistic signs of the Russians' capacity to adjust to capitalism were the huge street markets that spontaneously had sprung up in Moscow. These markets covered several blocks and impeded traffic on several streets. Hordes of men and women forced by necessity to find a way to survive, patiently stood on sidewalks hawking everything from a new pair of shoes, used clothing, bottles of vodka, nylon hosiery, Snickers bars, children's dolls, old military uniforms and medals, to puppies and kittens. The young *perestroika*-era Russians also offered some hope. Perhaps their generation had more in common with their video culture cohorts around the world than with the older generations of their country.

The Human Resources Challenge

Bill Shaddy was in the process of recruiting a sales manager to develop accounts and a technical engineering manager to work with the bottling franchisees. He was worried that the increasing number of multinationals in Moscow might be competing for a small pool of select people. Bill had to keep in mind Pepsi's code

---

[8] J. Shaw and C. Fisher, "From materialism to accountability: the changing cultures of Ma Bell and Mother Russia," *Academy of Management Executive,* vol. 5, no. 1 (1991).

[9] J. Ivancevich, R. DeFrank, and P. Gregory, "The Soviet enterprise director: an important resource before and after the coup," *Academy of Management Executive,* February 1992.

of conduct (see Exhibit 2 for excerpts from Pepsi's Code of Worldwide Business Conduct) and organizational values (see Exhibit 3). He wondered how to go about finding Russians that could become successful "Pepsi people." How would he select them? How should they be compensated, trained, and managed?

EXHIBIT 2   PepsiCo Inc.'s "Code of Worldwide Business Conduct" (excerpts)

Public Responsibility

Pepsico firmly believes that, in fostering economic growth, international commerce strengthens both understanding and peace. Our goal is to achieve commercial success by offering quality and value to our customers, to continue to provide products that are safe, wholesome, economically efficient, and environmentally sound, and to provide a fair return to our investors while adhering to the highest standards of integrity.

International Investment

As a company with operations in most nations of the world, PepsiCo obeys all laws and regulations and, to the maximum extent feasible, respects the lawful customs of host countries. In managing our financial commercial operations, we take into account the established objectives and related rules and regulations of host countries regarding balance of payments and credit policies.

We seek to reinvest locally a reasonable portion of earnings produced by our investment in a host country. We also consider the staffing of host country operations with national personnel at every level to be an important objective which includes the providing of training programs to facilitate advancement.

Political Activities and Contributions

We will, within the framework of the laws, regulations, and customs of each host country, act in a manner consistent with the highest standards of business integrity. We will not seek improper advantage through contributions of Pepsi funds, equipment, or facilities or the provision of other gifts or benefits to public officials or political organizations. We will not make an illegal or improper payment to any person or entity.

EXHIBIT 3   PepsiCo Inc.'s "Our World-Wide Values"

Integrity
- Say what we think, do what we say—communicate openly and directly.
- Treat others with respect as we would wish to be treated.
- Take ownership of one's mistakes—don't blame others.
- Set a personal example in everything we do.

Customer Service
- Understand our customers' needs and exceed them.
- Implement processes that add value to our customer.
- Respond with urgency to customer problems.
- Always analyze situations and take actions from a customer perspective.

Operational Excellence
- Understand the whole business and how your expertise adds value across the system.
- Constantly strive to improve quality and minimize costs to provide value products/services.
- Utilize operating systems to drive and measure results.

Innovation
- Demonstrate outside-of-the-box thinking.
- Challenge assumptions to generate new ideas and approaches.
- Develop creative ways to use existing processes, technology that benefit Pepsi and the customer.
- Motivate and reward creative people on your team.

Continuous Improvement
- Always review the way things get done to improve efficiency.
- Commit to and deliver better-quality solutions that add value to the customer.
- Take the initiative to eliminate activities that do not add value.
- Have clear objectives, measure performance, and keep "raising the bar."
- Learn from mistakes to do better next time.

TV Asahi Theatrical Productions, Inc.

In April 1996, Kenji Sudo, vice-president of TV Asahi's Theatrical Productions, Inc., was in a pensive mood. He had just heard that one of their musicals had been nominated for a variety of Tony Awards.[1] This was tremendous news. It was the 50th anniversary of the Tony Awards and this year's televised show was expected to be a spectacular event. Even in a run-of-the-mill year, getting a Tony nomination almost guaranteed that the musical would be profitable, and possibly very profitable because of the TV exposure.

Yet, there was also some unsettling news. During the past week he had been talking to several top managers in TV Asahi (pronounced *ah-saw-hee*), the Japanese parent company of the Theatrical Productions unit. All of the managers had voiced some doubt about the role of the Theatrical Productions subsidiary in TV Asahi. Through these conversations, Kenji realized that they didn't understand the business, and inevitably they didn't know what to do with it.

This lack of commitment was clearly a concern for Kenji. He had spent 14 years of his life building the subsidiary into a profitable musical theatre production company and the number one Asian company in the U.S. live theatre business. Last year the subsidiary had been very profitable and Kenji thought these results would go a long way toward improving the attitude of top management toward the subsidiary, but this appeared not to be the case. He wondered what Asahi would do about the Theatrical Productions unit, and of course the ultimate question for him was: What should he do about it?

TV Asahi and the Newspaper and Broadcasting Industry in Japan

TV Asahi Theatrical Productions, Inc., was part of TV Asahi's Special Events Division whose parent company was Asahi National Broadcasting Co., Ltd. (TV Asahi), of Japan (see Figure 1 for an organizational chart). TV Asahi was part of

Professors Patrick Woodcock and Paul Beamish prepared this case solely to provide material for class discussion. The authors do not intend to illustrate either effective or ineffective handling of a managerial situation. The authors may have disguised certain names and other identifying information to protect confidentiality. © 1996 Ivey Management Services. Case 9A96G004, version 1996-10-07.

Richard Ivey School of Business
The University of Western Ontario

[1] The Tony Awards are the most prestigious live theatre awards in the world, and are quite literally the Academy Awards of the theatre industry.

a small *keiretsu*[2] involving interlocking ownership of three other companies: Asahi Shimbun (newspapers), Toei (movies and TV production), and Obunsha (publishing). The Asahi group of companies was privately owned by the employees and three Japanese families. The largest company in this group was the Asahi Shimbun, the largest newspaper company in Japan. This newspaper company dominated the other two companies in a variety of ways, including having the largest revenues, profits, and ownership in them. The presidents of the smaller companies were appointed by the Asahi Shimbun and had always been former Asahi Shimbun managers.

The Japanese Newspaper Industry

The Japanese newspaper industry was tightly controlled and dominated by a few privately owned firms. There were five major players in the industry, with Asahi being the largest. Most of these companies had some degree of regional focus, while others differentiated themselves by focusing on specialized news such as business or sports. None of these companies faced any direct international competition since foreign firms faced enormous entry barriers related to the Japanese language, culture, and distribution, all of which were critical to the business. None of these companies had newspaper interests outside of Japan.

In general, the industry had been slow to respond to the technological changes and related shifts in economies of scale and scope which had been the rage of English-language-based newspapers around the world. The retiring competitive environment had produced organizations that were quite conservative and bureaucratic. Historically, the industry had been very profitable, but the recession of the early 1990s had affected all sectors, including this one.

The Japanese Television Industry

The television broadcasting industry was also relatively concentrated. Yet, it was clearly more competitive and dynamic than the newspaper industry. This was due to a variety of factors including the continual demand for creativity in programming, and technological developments, as well as both national and international competition. National competition was significant in comparison to the newspaper industry because the incremental costs of broadcasting nationally versus regionally were relatively small. Therefore, a company tended to broadcast in as many regions as its licence allowed. International competition was moderate, but some English TV programming was broadcast in the populated regions (e.g., CNN news), and very popular international programs were dubbed into Japanese (e.g., Dallas). The larger broadcasting companies all had international divisions which were largely unprofitable.

There were four large national TV broadcasting companies in Japan. They were, in order of size, Nippon Hoso Kyokai (NHK), Fuji Television Network,

---

[2] A *keiretsu* is a group of Japanese firms that usually has joint ownership and operates to varying degrees as one large firm. The degree of interlocking ownership can be quite small (e.g., 5 percent). The operational linkages can include sharing of capital, exchange of technology and personnel, and joint management decision making.

FIGURE 1   TV Asahi Organizational Chart

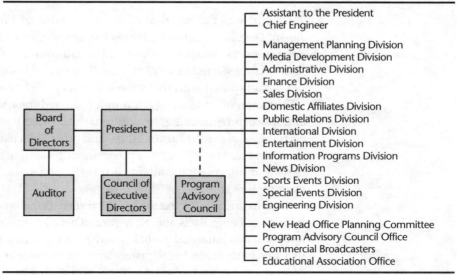

Source: TV Asahi publications, 1996.

Inc. (Fuji TV), Tokyo Broadcasting System (TBS), and TV Asahi. In addition, there was a variety of smaller, regional companies (e.g., TV Tokyo and Kansai TV) and some pay television channels (e.g., Japan Satellite Broadcasting). A summary description of the top three firms is provided in Table 1.

TABLE 1   **Summary Description of Top Three Competitors**

NHK is the largest national broadcasting company, and because of its size and dominance in the industry it is often referred to as the Japanese Broadcasting Corporation. NHK is focused entirely on television and radio broadcasting in Japan, although NHK does license some of its news, cultural, and business programs to broadcasters in other countries who desire some Japanese content for their local audiences. This company is very research- and development-oriented. It was the major force behind Japan's development of the high-definition television standards and broadcasting equipment. Now it is the only company in the world that broadcasts high-definition digital signals. From a programming perspective, NHK is known for its sports programming. Finally, this company has considerable technical and programming skills compared with the other competitors. The large market share and historical government support allowed it to develop these skills and consequently build market share that could support the skills.

Fuji TV is owned by a company called Jujisankei Communications Group. It is the second-largest television broadcaster in Japan and it is particularly well known for its animation, children's programming, and variety shows. This company is a largely diversified mass-media company. It has taken an aggressive approach to international development through acquisitions and joint ventures with companies such as US Today. It acquired a number of companies in Europe relating to creative software production and licensing rights. It also produced Japanese musical productions. It owns its own theatre hall for live theatre as well as an art gallery with many of Picasso's sculptures. The company is into publishing computer software and multimedia, computer magazines, and Internet shopping, and it owns a few regional newspapers, and a film business. Its core competence is its creative programming capabilities.

TBS is a national television and radio broadcasting company. TBS is a relatively aggressive company that tends to produce racy shows, at least by Japanese standards. It is in all types of production, from drama to news broadcasting. Recently, it got itself into trouble with its investigative reporting of a "Tokyo bombing cult." TBS is the third-largest broadcaster, just slightly larger than Asahi.

Source: Company Internet sites and Time Warner documents on the Japanese media industry.

TV Asahi

TV Asahi was the smallest of the four national broadcasting companies in Japan. Despite its ranking, it was a sizable organization. Its revenues for 1995 were in excess of US$1 billion and it had over 1,300 employees worldwide.

TV Asahi started in 1959 as a small news and information educational channel. It had quite naturally evolved into its present niche, which was news and information programming, although it carried some variety, drama, animation, and sports programming. In addition, the company produced or promoted concerts, musical theatre, art exhibits, and other international cultural events. Yet, over 50 percent of TV Asahi's programming was live broadcasting reflecting its news and information content. It was the first station to introduce prime-time evening news.

Internationally, TV Asahi had 21 international news bureaus, the two most important being Paris and New York. These 21 international offices were used to establish a balanced global coverage of international news events, to establish ties with other broadcasters around the world, to develop international coproductions, and to sell Asahi's programming to non-Japanese broadcasters.

TV Asahi had been involved in cooperative international programming and news reporting for over a decade. In 1982 it signed an exclusive agreement with CNN (U.S.) centred around joint news and information programming. It had also collaborated with a number of other foreign news broadcasters, including TF1 (France), RTL (Germany), BBTV (Thailand), CTV (Taiwan), CCTV (China), RTRC (Russia), and RTM (Malaysia). In addition, Asahi offered Japanese news, culture, and entertainment to television stations that broadcast to a Japanese audience in New York, San Francisco, Los Angeles, and Hawaii, although this was a very small part of its broadcasting business.

However, Asahi was in the process of trying to broaden its scope of broadcasting skills and products into the non-news sectors of the industry. For example, it was currently trying to build a reputation in children's animation shows; it had developed a very popular children's animation show in Japan and it was selling this show, with some success, to foreign broadcasters. The managers believed that the only way Asahi would grow and challenge some of its rivals was to add non-news-related shows. In their opinion, they had as much of the news market as they were going to capture in Japan, and moving into non-Japanese news broadcasting in a foreign country would be very difficult, if not impossible. So their one avenue for growth was in the more popular TV shows such as variety, drama, etc. Thus, they were slowly exploring ways of developing some of the skills that their rivals had in this aspect of broadcasting.

Organizational Characteristics

TV Asahi's organizational chart is shown in Figure 1. The chairman was a former newspaper executive appointed from Asahi Shimbun, as were all previous chairmen. In addition, a few other top managers were from Asahi Shimbun. This gave the company a distinctive "news culture."

Organizationally, the company was relatively conservative and bureaucratic in both its systems and its structures. None of the employees, including Kenji, was paid on the basis of performance. The reporting systems tended to be quite formal and seniority was clearly an important issue in career advancement. In fact, Asahi had all of the classical Japanese organizational attributes. Lifetime employment was the norm and personnel got to know each other through socializing during work and the frequent (often biweekly) after-work "get togethers" for drinks. Socializing was important, because it made the cooperative Japanese decision-making and working environment function smoothly. It also provided workers with mentors and management contacts which could later prove valuable when the person moved into a management position. This system also inculcated the organizational culture (e.g., group decision-making approach) into the employees.

TV Asahi's conservative organizational style was due, in part, to its heritage in the news industry and ownership roots in Asahi Shimbun. The news programming format provided the least amount of motivation for innovation and change, simply because a news report was a news report in any language and station. News stations tended to differentiate themselves on the operational aspects of gathering and reporting news. In essence, the depth and speed of coverage differentiated a good station from an "also-ran." In this respect, TV Asahi was clearly an extension of Asahi Shimbun. Yet, such a culture had clearly gotten in the way of the move toward a more creative broadcasting format and content.

Such a classical Japanese organizational approach had proven to be very effective in producing organizational efficiency, decision making leading to very effective implementation, and a focused organizational strategy. Yet, it had also created some concerns. The biggest worry was the lack of creativity and specialization leading to a lack of fundamental research and development in the organization. A cooperative and generalist approach tended to attenuate the ability of the organization to take risks in decision making and to try creative ideas. In some Japanese industries, this had clearly been a problem.

New Forces Acting on the TV Industry

Governmental controls on the industry had also contributed to the tempered competitive environment. The Japanese government had historically controlled the industry through regulatory policies that restricted channel ownership. Channels were awarded on the basis of availability and the owners' perceived honour, reverence, and trustworthiness in Japanese society. Historically, it had been very important for the owners to be standard-bearers of cultural honour, probity, and respect because they were reporting the news. Unlike North Americans, the Japanese were very concerned about what was televised. In particular, they did not condone programming that brings shame to them or their society. To a large extent the government had used ownership as a method of self-monitoring. This had resulted in an industry that had historically been concentrated in a few hands. Such a restrictive industry structure was wonderful for the companies. They enjoyed a stable competitive environment and commensurate levels of profitability.

However, a number of forces were changing the nature of the business. The recession, which began in 1992 and still continued, had reduced profitability dramatically in the broadcasting business, due to the "shrinkage" in advertising volume and rates. TV Asahi and Fuji TV had both delayed the development of their new headquarters office buildings. TV Asahi's was to be a 50-floor office building with a large theatre and retail shopping mall at the ground level. All of the broadcasters were searching for ways to save money and reorganize to improve efficiency. Some companies had even laid off workers for the first time since their inception some 40 years ago. Bankruptcies were at an all-time high and this was expected to continue for the near term. The financial crisis had forced two banks into bankruptcy and more were expected to follow.

The government was also looking at ways to deregulate the broadcasting industry in the next two years. The change in policy was being driven by the availability of many more channels and the merging of a variety of technologies, including telecommunications, satellite dishes, computers, digital broadcasting, and international competition. If Japan did not implement this deregulation, there was the potential that a wide variety of competitors would circumvent the present regulations, creating chaos. Furthermore, the government had come to view competition as essential to the development of new technologies and innovations in this fast-changing industry.

The four national broadcasters were, however, not pleased with this movement toward deregulation. They had been fighting the deregulation movement in a number of ways, but the predominant approach was to use political suasion. Having come from such a non-competitive environment, it was about the only response that they knew and had practised over the years. It now appeared that some sort of deregulation was going to occur within the next several years, and ultimately full deregulation was viewed as a distinct possibility in the long term.

The Special Events Division

The Special Events Division of TV Asahi, which the Theatrical Productions unit was part of, employed approximately 50 people. The mandate for this division was to enhance the image of TV Asahi through the sponsoring of various special events. A few of these events had been turned into TV specials and/or publications. The division had become involved in a wide and eclectic number of activities:

- It published a number of different magazines and educational videos.
- It had created The Sakura Campaign to further world peace, in which cherry trees had been planted annually for the last five years at the former site of the Berlin wall.
- It had funded and produced several art exhibitions; the latest one was an exhibition of Vincent van Gogh. A variety of publications had resulted from this show.
- It had brought a variety of musical talent, both classical and popular, to Japan. Some of the recent performers included Prince, New Kids on the Block, and Van Halen. It brought the Vienna Boys Choir to Japan annually for a series of concerts.
- In addition, it had brought Broadway musical productions to Japan through the Theatrical Productions subunit.

The Special Events Division was not perceived as one of the more dynamic divisions in TV Asahi. Its objective was primarily to "give back" to the community and Japanese society, and secondarily, to create unusual and different TV programming material. The primary objective, although unusual by Western standards, was considered an important aspect of Japanese business and represented the cooperative interface between business and Japanese society. Most Japanese companies accomplished this in some manner.

Despite this honourable objective, the Special Events Division was not considered one of the more exciting places to work in Asahi. In fact, a transfer to the division was jokingly referred to as early retirement. A number of managers in the division were "burnt out" TV Asahi managers who had transferred to the division to get out of the hustle and bustle of the demanding TV business. An indication of the instability in this division was the turnover of its president. For long as Kenji could remember, the president of the Special Events Division had been replaced yearly due to either retirement or transfer.

TV Asahi Theatrical Productions, Inc.

Asahi Theatrical Productions was founded because of a fondness for music by TV Asahi's second-highest manager, Mr. Hidedata Nishimura. In particular, Hidedata loved western-style musicals and he felt that the Japanese public would also enjoy this form of entertainment if they were exposed to it. His idea was to bring these musicals to Japan using Asahi's Special Events Division. However, the division did not have the staff or skills to do this. Therefore, in 1982 he recruited Mr. Kenji Sudo and Mr. Yasu Kata Nishimura, his younger brother, to manage the selection and licensing of the musicals in New York and to manage the operational aspects in Japan, respectively.

Kenji Sudo was well suited to the position. He had been employed at Fuji TV in New York for the previous 20 years. During this time he had developed strong Western management skills including an entrepreneurial bent, something that would become quite useful in his new position.

Kenji immediately went to work and was able to license the Japanese rights to the musical *Sophisticated Ladies,* which toured Japan during 1983. After that Asahi licensed *My One and Only* in 1984 and *Dreamgirls* in 1986. The first two were not financial successes, but they provided Asahi with some fame, particularly with young Japanese girls who loved this form of entertainment. *Dreamgirls,* was a major hit. It ran almost double the length of the previous two productions in Japan and with every show sold out it more than paid for itself. From it, Asahi received considerable publicity and recognition. The top managers in TV Asahi especially got tremendous adulation, and were often asked by top managers in other large companies and institutions if they could get some tickets for them.

At this point, both Kenji and Hidedata knew they had developed an interesting business opportunity. Furthermore, Kenji was starting to develop some important contacts and musical-theatre-specific knowledge. On this basis and the success of *Dreamgirls,* Asahi formalized the Theatrical Productions Unit into TV Asahi Theatrical Productions, Inc., in 1988. Mr. Hidedata assumed the role of president, little more than a Japanese figurehead of the corporation. He left all operational details to the two vice-presidents, Kenji and Yasu Kata, who ran their separate operations in the United States and Japan, respectively.

Additionally, in 1988 Asahi began investing in musical productions rather than just buying the Japanese rights to them. As a producer,[3] Asahi would now have more favourable access to the licensing rights of top musicals, although it would have to select its investments during the inception stages of the project, prior to the knowledge of whether the musical would be a hit or not. Its first investment was in an off-Broadway production called *Blues in the Night*. It was not a financial success, and from this Kenji realized that he must concentrate on major investments and top Broadway musicals, not off-Broadway productions.

In 1991, Kenji's associate and sponsor in Japan, Hidedata set up a company, called International Musical, Inc. (IMI), to handle secondary and amateur performance rights and licensing in Japan. Hidedata was retiring in 1994, and IMI would allow him to continue to work in a business that had been his hobby for more than ten years. IMI complemented Asahi Theatrical Production's work by focusing on secondary musical rights and licences, and it would work with Asahi whenever possible. Furthermore, IMI would leave the Broadway and West End[4] musical rights and licences to Asahi.

In 1991, Kenji managed to convince Asahi to make another investment in a musical production. This time it was a Broadway musical entitled *The Secret Garden*. This was a considerable breakthrough for Asahi Theatrical Productions. Investing in Broadway or West End theatre production was a risky business for anyone. Only two out of ten investments made money, another one out of ten would break even, and the other seven would lose money. These were very poor odds and some top managers in Asahi were not terribly comfortable making such an investment. To become a investor, or a producer as they were called in the business, a company had to invest $250,000 to $500,000. The producers then had no real rights to the musical other than to the profits derived from the show. In other words, this did not give the investor the right to take the show to Japan. These rights had to be negotiated separately, and a producer had no more legal claim to the rights than a non-producer, although investing in a musical obviously gave the investor an inside track on getting the rights.

On average, about five Broadway and West End musicals were shown annually. There were almost 100 theatres on Broadway and in the West End (split about half-and-half, and only a half-dozen in each location focused on musicals). Most of these theatres searched out directors who had creative ideas, or, less often, were presented with creative ideas. Directors having successful track records, such as Andrew Lloyd Webber, were widely sought after, because they could attract talent, money, and ultimately a paying audience. While the directors looked after the creative and artistic side of the production, the theatres managed the business aspects of the show: financing, advertising, selling of tickets, etc.

Broadway theatre management was a difficult business and many of the theatres were jointly owned because of the rarity of skills and assets necessary. A successful theatre owner was a rare commodity; the position required a unique

---

[3] Investors are called "producers" in the musical theatre business.

[4] Broadway and West End are the theatres, in New York and London (U.K.), respectively, that produced the best plays and musicals in the world.

TABLE 2   Asahi's Theatrical History

Year	Title	Involvement	Japanese
1983	Sophisticated Ladies	Japanese Tour	32 Performances
1984	My One and Only	Japanese Tour	32 Performances
1986	Dreamgirls	Japanese Tour	53 Performances
1988	Blues in the Night	Producer	
	West Side Story	Japanese Tour	43 Performances
1989	Can-Can	Japanese Tour	35 Performances
	Blues in the Night	Japanese Tour	48 Performances
1990	South Pacific	Japanese Tour	32 Performances
1991	The Secret Garden	Producer	
1991	Grand Hotel	Japanese Tour	48 Performances
1992	Jelly's Last Jam	Producer	
	Guys and Dolls	Producer	
1993	The Secret Garden	Japanese Tour	60 Performances
	Guys and Dolls	Japanese Tour	61 Performances
	The Who's Tommy	Producer	
	Blues in the Night	Japanese Tour	46 Performances

mix of skills, including excellent communication skills, good contacts in the business, adroit intuition as to the wishes and desires of the audience, and hardcore business acumen. Needless to say, few people had such a complex mix of skills. Thus, the few successful theatre companies tended to buy up those that failed. On Broadway only about three to four owners had been successful at developing musicals with any sort of consistency. Ultimately the directors could take their talent anywhere and Andrew Lloyd Webber, the most successful musical director in the world, often selected a theatre not on its past record but on its willingness to pay royalties and provide financial support for the production.

Unfortunately, musicals tended to be either big hits or big busts. A show that received poor reviews on opening night might not even last a week. A big hit that had garnered Tony Awards might play for over a year on Broadway, and subsequently in different international locations. The Tony Awards were important to a show because a nomination provided four minutes of television air time for the show during prime-time viewing. Such coverage would be unaffordable to all but the largest and most successful shows, yet it contributed enormously to the awareness and image of the musical.

⬤ Bringing a Musical to Japan

Getting the rights to a musical and bringing it to Japan was a very involved process. First the rights to the music and/or story had to be purchased. Then the talent (performers) had to be "acquired." The easiest way to do this was to wait until the show ended its Broadway run and then bring the actors to Japan. Signing the performers involved dealing with their managers and unions. Star performers often required separate negotiations, while regulars had more standard contracts. Then the unions had to be satisfied that the theatre was up to standard and that the appropriate care (e.g., flight, travel, hotel, food, rest) was provided to its members. The union negotiations often represented the most frustrating part of the negotiation process because of their restrictive rules, and at times their perceived confrontational approach. In addition to all of this, theatres had to be secured (they had to be rented two years in advance of the actual show in Japan because of the lack of appropriate venues), sets had to be transported and/or built, backstage personnel had to be acquired and/or trained. Thus, getting a show to Japan was not only time-consuming but also expensive. To bring a Broadway production to Japan cost US$7 to $8 million.

Asahi had developed some skill in putting on these musical productions in Japan. Mr. Yasu Kata Nishimura, the manager of the Japanese operations, had developed excellent liaisons, and where necessary, contracts in the Japanese theatre industry. Finding an appropriate theatre was one of the most difficult obstacles to overcome in putting on live theatre in Japan. Large Broadway-type theatres were very rare in Japan, and often another type of venue had to be adapted for the situation. Yasu Kata had become quite proficient at managing the Japanese tours. He had developed relationships with the large theatre owners. He understood the needs and desires of the various Western directors, actors, and workers. He also had developed considerable knowledge in the business aspects of the production such as advertising, promotion, ticket sales, etc. In addition, Yasu had developed a subtitling system that allowed the Japanese audience to follow the story in Japanese, and some of the stories were published using Asahi's publishing subsidiary. Clearly, Kenji and Yasu had become a very effective team.

To aid with the financing of the Japanese tours, Asahi got sponsors. These sponsors would usually contribute about US$1 million, a sum that would help defray some initial costs. Then, the remaining costs would be covered, if possible, by ticket sales. In general, because of the enormous costs of most productions that Asahi brought to Japan, it was lucky to break even, although the odd one had been profitable. It should also be noted that although Asahi had purchased the rights for a Japanese musical theatre tour, that did not give it the right to broadcast the show on television. The TV rights involved further negotiations of licensing agreements which were even more complex and costly than those of the Japanese tour rights. Usually, after a musical had been televised, the potential for live theatre runs to that audience was limited. Therefore, any royalty payments for television rights had to consider the opportunity costs of losing any subsequent live theatre royalties.

The success of the investment in *The Secret Garden* motivated Kenji and Asahi into becoming more involved in the investment side of the business. One of Kenji's more important associations was with Mr. Landesman, president of Jujamcyn Theatres, who was one of the top Broadway theatre owners that tended to specialize in musicals. Through Kenji's close association with Mr. Landesman, he actively sought new musical productions in which he could invest. This relationship developed into a formal agreement in the early 1990s by which Asahi agreed to invest $1 million annually in Jujamcyn Theatre productions over the next three years. This non-exclusive agreement was due to expire in the next year. In this agreement, Asahi, through Kenji, was to be offered investments in every Broadway musical that Jujamcyn Theatres developed. Kenji would decide whether to invest or not, on the basis of Landesman's recommendations. Then Kenji would submit a formal investment proposal to TV Asahi and Asahi would usually take about three to four months to officially give the okay for the investments. So far, head office had never said no to a show that Kenji had committed to, and in fact, Kenji often wondered on what basis they would turn down a project that he recommended.

From 1992 to 1996, Kenji had committed Asahi, as producer, to seven musicals. Most of them were profitable and some were very successful. During that time, only three musicals were brought to Japan and a fourth was scheduled to begin a Japanese Tour this year (1996). All of the musicals that toured Japan were ones in which Asahi had initially been a producer. Furthermore, during this time, all of the musicals that they had invested in had received some sort of Tony Award whether for a singer, a song, or the musical itself. The 1992 musical *Guys and Dolls* received the coveted Tony's Best Revival Musical. Clearly, the investment aspect of the business was going very well.

Asahi's success was also due to Kenji's induction as a voting member for the Tony's in 1993, the only Asian to be given such an honour. This provided Kenji with considerable fame, which allowed him to establish a broad network of relationships in this rather cliquish and exclusive business.

Asahi's managers clearly did not understand the business, but some of them were enjoying the successes of the theatre division. Presidents of other major Japanese corporations had asked them for tickets to performances. Kenji had also been able to introduce TV Asahi's top executives to several top U.S. executives. For example, the Kennedy Center had been a Jujamycn investor, and when the president of the Kennedy Center, a very well-known figure in U.S. business circles, came to Japan, Kenji arranged a dinner with him and the president of TV Asahi. All of this brought considerable honour to TV Asahi top managers. However, Kenji wondered whether this was enough to keep them interested in the business.

Kenji was the principal person behind the success of Asahi's Theatrical Productions investing. He had the contacts and the understanding of the business skills and entrepreneurial attitudes necessary in the business. He even had a good sense of humour which stood him in good stead when he had to mix with his business peers in New York.

The only employee in Asahi Theatrical Productions besides Kenji was Kenji's assistant, a Japanese woman who looked after office details while Kenji developed business opportunities. Kenji negotiated which musicals they would invest in and usually committed Asahi to a dollar figure for each production. Other legal and financial aspects were handled by either outside help or by TV Asahi in its head office.

The Question of the Future

TV Asahi Theatrical Productions, Inc. had been very successful in 1995, making a profit of approximately $1.5 million on revenues of about US$15 million. Needless to say, such revenues and profits were small compared to TV Asahi's annual revenues (less than 1 percent). However, in Kenji's eyes there was considerable opportunity for further growth. This included additional investment in musicals, investments in other types of live entertainment, and attempts to move more into the theatre management and creative side of the business. There was also the considerable, yet untapped, opportunity of musicals in the West End theatres in London. Demand for Broadway musicals had exploded, particularly outside of Broadway and the West End. If Asahi could tap into this growth, it could become a significant player in the business. There was also the potential of trying to integrate the creative and artistic talent represented in this business into the TV business.

The problem was that Kenji and Yasu Kata, his Japanese counterpart, didn't actively support any growth opportunities since Hidedata had retired from TV Asahi, although they had not actively dissuaded growth in the past. Neither Kenji or Yasu Kata had actively trained others in TV Asahi, so their specialized skills were quite unique. Now, Yasu Kata was scheduled to retire in less than two years and Kenji had inquired about a replacement for Yasu Kata. He found out that TV Asahi had no plans in place for replacing Yasu Kata—in fact they really had not thought about it. Kenji was in his mid-50s and, as a U.S. resident, did not have to, and did not want to, retire at the mandatory Japanese retirement age of 60. He felt that he had considerable energy left to devote to this business over the next decade. Kenji was also involving some young Japanese located in New York, largely university musical and theatre students, in his business dealings and associations. He saw his role as an informal mentor and friend to these Japanese associates, none of whom were formally employed by Asahi.

Unfortunately, Kenji realized that part of the problem was that since Nishimura's retirement neither he nor Yasu Kata had developed a strong set of new relationships with TV Asahi's top managers. Prior to Nishimura's retirement, Kenji had been in constant contact with Nishimura. Each understood the business and the other's desires and attitudes about a decision. However, Kenji had not been a lifetime employee of TV Asahi, and in fact had not even been employed with TV Asahi in Japan. This was a disadvantage, because he now had few contacts with whom he could develop a relationship in TV Asahi. Not only was he not a TV Asahi person, but he had lived outside of Japan for over three decades.

While Kenji pondered his fate, he wondered what must be going through the minds of the top TV Asahi executives in Tokyo. They appeared not to understand the business. It represented a relatively small amount of their deployed assets, yet he felt strongly that it could contribute more to TV Asahi's future. Disney Corporation had just invested in a Broadway theatre and some of the other Japanese broadcasting corporations had been actively getting involved in theatre during the last several years.

Two recent musical successes in Japan were motivating other broadcasters to consider this type of unusual and highly desirable source of entertainment as an investment and potential broadcasting opportunity. Asahi had a tremendously successful run of *The Secret Garden,* which had won a Tony Award prior to its Japanese tour. Then Japan Broadcasting (JBS) invested nearly $2 million in the Broadway show *The Will Rogers Follies,* winner of the 1991 Tony award for best musical. JBS had negotiated the rights to broadcast the show to its TV audience in late 1995, and it was expected that the show would complete a Japanese tour after its five-year stint on Broadway. JBS had accomplished this feat by hiring a

New York–based media consultant and paying a lot of money. NTV, a subsidiary of NHK, had also become involved in televising Broadway musicals. They had produced and televised the musical *Annie* in Japan solely for the purpose of a television production, and they were continuing to try to work with top directors to find new shows to be televised. Suntory, Inc., Japan's largest liquor company, had also invested in musicals during the past four years. They had developed an agreement with another Broadway and off-Broadway theatre owner, Shubert Theatres. This relationship had produced eight shows, including *The Grapes of Wrath, The Heidi Chronicles,* and *Cities of Angels.* Suntory was expected to sign another long-term agreement with Shubert in the upcoming months. The message was quite simple that Japanese money was willing to invest in top Western musicals. It also indicated to Kenji that considerable opportunity existed for this business and his talents within a variety of Japanese companies.

Televising the shows in Japan was viewed as a tremendously risky business. But the financial risks were moderated in some decision-makers' eyes by the realization that it would provide recognition and very high advertising ratings to the channel. Financially, some felt that a musical broadcast might break even if it was combined with an Asian tour followed by an Asian-only broadcast of the show, as long as the show was a hit. However, this was a difficult thing to manage and it clearly posed a variety of risks. The key to any musical was getting the right one. Clearly, the Japanese were most interested in top Broadway and West End musicals. In this regard, the audiences were quite discerning and they knew the difference between a first- and a second-rate show. In addition, the musicals best suited to Asian audiences were those that had little conversation and lots of music because much of the audience did not understand English.

◼ The Future

Every year Asahi had renewed the contract that employed Kenji. However, Kenji was now wondering what the company would do when this year's or possibly next year's contract renewal came up. Furthermore, what should he do? Kenji realized that the key to figuring out what he should do really lay in figuring out what TV Asahi would do, given its options.

Kenji realized that TV Asahi had a variety of options available to it. It could withdraw financial support now; it could do nothing; or it could get actively involved in further developing the Theatrical Production's activities. Ultimately, Asahi's decisions would affect his decision. Yet, there was also the broader question of whether he should be proactive or reactive? These were complex questions with many cultural ambiguities. He knew that he had become partially Western and partially Japanese in his management attitudes, something that made his decision even more complex. Should he manage this situation as a Westerner or as a Japanese manager? He had worked, and he thought he always would work, for a Japanese company, yet he also realized that he would have to continue to work in this business in the United States. In this regard, his brain was telling him one thing, but his heart was telling him something quite different.

CASE 33

University Hospital— 1987

"Finding a better way."

UH's motto; attributed to Thomas Edison.

In the fall of 1987 University Hospital (UH) had just completed, with the assistance of outside consultants, an extensive strategy review culminating in a formal strategic plan. The original stimulus for the plan had been to better understand the growth patterns and potential of the hospital's services in order to forecast the need for and justify a significant expansion of the hospital's facilities. However, the final document had gone beyond this original intention, raising questions about the hospital's "service portfolio" and its future potential.

The strategic plan had seven key recommendations (see Exhibit 1), several of which represented significant departures from past practice. As part of the planning process, the hospital's services had been put into different categories, a portfolio approach, with apparent implications for future emphasis and resource allocation. As one UH vice-president commented:

> The plan has forced us to establish some priorities for our different services. Not everything we do is, or will be world-class and the plan will help us allocate our increasingly scarce resources, capital, and operating funds towards our premier services.

Further, the plan recommended organizing business units around these "service clusters" (or product lines), and continuing the planning process as an ongoing, in-house activity, As Pat Blewett, President and CEO of UH, reviewed the report and its recommendations, he was satisfied with both the process and the results. Blewett was widely recognized as a highly positive, entrepreneurial type of administrator willing to try new ideas and promote

IVEY

Richard Ivey School of Business
The University of Western Ontario

This case was prepared by Mary Crossan, Research Assistant, and Rod White, Associate Professor, for the sole purpose of providing material for class discussion at the Ivey Business School. Certain names and other identifying information may have been disguised to protect confidentiality. It is not intended to illustrate either effective or ineffective handling of a managerial situation. Any reproduction, in any form, of the material in this case is prohibited except with the written consent of the School. © 1989 Ivey Management Services. Case 9-89-M003, version 08/15/91.

EXHIBIT 1   Key Recommendations from the Strategic Plan

Recommendation 1:
Pursue a Service Cluster/Product Line Development Approach
Product line management is a system that organizes management accountability and operations around discrete service or product lines. Service clusters are those groups of services that are provided to distinct market segments.

By shifting management focus to product line development, hospitals can increase their market share by improving the efficiency of their services and by tailoring services to specific market needs.

Recommendation 2:
Adopt an Appropriate Bed Complement for UH in the 1990s
To facilitate the implementation of a service cluster or product line concept for University Hospital it will be essential to adopt an appropriate bed complement (for each service).

Recommendation 3:
Address Facility Considerations Through a Medical Mall Implementation Strategy
The purpose of the medical mall is multifold:
- It compartmentalizes functions and services to allow an optimum level of capital expense by type of service.
- It targets and controls traffic by patient type while ensuring convenience and accessibility.
- It provides a "one-stop" location for multiple levels of inpatient and outpatient support services.

Recommendation 4:
Pursue a Networking Strategy as Part of the Role of Tertiary Care
Pursuit of a networking strategy asserts that the role of University Hospital in tertiary care should represent a "hub" within the Canadian and international health care system.

As such, options have been developed to ensure University Hospital is able to accept patients who need to be "stepped up" from community hospitals and outpatient settings and also "step down" patients who no longer require UH's intensity of services.

Recommendation 5:
Adopt a Diversification Strategy
To encourage management to investigate which type of integration makes most sense for UH, given its tertiary nature and commitment to research and education, diversification efforts can be adopted. This can be done in basically three ways: vertical integration, horizontal integration, or geographic dispersion.

Recommendation 6:
Implement an Organizational Enhancement Strategy
Due to the complexity and dynamic nature of University Hospital, ongoing strategic planning and administrative support and leadership will be essential. The recommended organizational enhancement strategy has, as its focus, to:
- Pursue process planning and implementation by adopting an ongoing annual planning cycle
- Assign responsibility/authority for successful ongoing strategic planning
- Address management/medical staff succession
- Exploit the benefits of University Hospital's relationship with HCA

At the heart of this strategy is the need to formalize and integrate current planning mechanisms into an ongoing process.

Recommendation 7:
Continue an Aggressive Financial Strategy: Preserve/Enhance Financial Resources
The objectives of this recommendation are twofold:
- To enhance financial resources
- To preserve financial resources

---

innovative services. Results had been impressive. New services had contributed substantially to UH's growth and cash flow. However, the facility was straining within its existing physical space. In addition UH, like other hospitals in the province of Ontario, had to cope with increasing budgetary pressures from the Ministry of Health, while demand for all services continued to grow. Blewett hoped the recommendations from the strategic plan would allow the hospital to deal with these issues while maintaining the institution's innovative and entrepreneurial spirit.

Background

While a separate institution, UH was part of a larger health sciences complex of the University of Western Ontario. UH had been an educational and research, as well as a health care delivery facility since opening in 1972, the newest of the three major acute-care hospitals in London, Ontario, a community of about 300,000 in southwestern Ontario. UH had been established in 1909, and was owned and operated by the London Health Association (LHA).

The LHA's activities had changed dramatically over the years. Originally, it had operated a tuberculosis sanatorium on the outskirts of the city. As the number of tuberculosis patients declined, the LHA made plans to diversify into chest diseases and purchased property adjacent to the university for a new hospital. However, in the decade of the 1960s, the university was growing rapidly, especially in the health sciences, and wanted a full-fledged teaching/research hospital attached to it. The LHA was persuaded to undertake this more ambitious task but stipulated that their institution would remain administratively separate from the university.

Planning for the new facility began in 1966. An innovative spirit was evident from the outset. Hospitals tend to be very traditional institutions, but the planning group, in its efforts to create an outstanding medical facility, were willing to deviate from conventional practices. The UH motto, "Finding a better way," was applied to facilities design, organizational practice, as well as patient care and research activities. The hospital layout was guided by a philosophy of "Form follows function." The result was revolutionary, with physicians' offices, research areas, inpatient and outpatient departments, and teaching space all on the same floor. Essentially each of the floors operated as a specialized mini-hospital sharing support services within a larger hospital setting. UH's deviation from accepted hospital practices were wide-ranging, from the use of noise-deadening carpeted floors—a hospital blasphemy at the time—to the decentralized organizational structure with an unconventional division of tasks.

The Health Care Environment

Canada's health care system was one of the most comprehensive in the world, providing equal access to all Canadians. The publicly funded system was the responsibility of the provincial governments, although a substantial portion of the funding came from the federal level by way of transfer payments. In Ontario, the Ministry of Health (MOH) was the department concerned with hospitals. Health care costs accounted for 32 percent of the province's $32 billion budget, the single largest category of expenditure with the most rapid growth. As a result, the province was becoming increasingly active in its efforts to contain these costs. Examples included the banning of extra-billing by doctors, cuts in the number of medical residency positions, and provision for the MOH to take over any hospital in a deficit position.

Health care funding had evolved in a piecemeal fashion into an extremely complex and often ambiguous system. Basically, the MOH contracted with the hospitals to provide services, in an approved plant, at an approved ("global") budget. Further, the Ministry expected each hospital to show an excess of revenue over expenses sufficient to provide for a reasonable accumulation of funds for future capital requirements. Program or service reductions or bed closures which related directly to patient care required the agreement of the Ministry. However, under pressure to balance budgets, some hospitals were reducing services without the formal agreement of the Ministry. Using a universal formula based largely on history, the Ministry arrived at a hospital's global operating budget. Most MOH revenues were *not* directly tied to actual expenditures or the provision of services. New programs could be initiated by the hospital, but incremental capital and/or operating costs could be incorporated into the existing global funding base. Additional funds were forthcoming only if approved by the Ministry.

In the approval of new programs District Health Councils had a prominent voice. They provided the forum for ensuring that changes met the health care needs of the *local* community. The Thames Valley District Health Council (TVDHC) was responsible for the 18 hospitals in the London area. New program proposals submitted to TVDHC were very diverse, ranging from a $400,000 request from UH for a four-bed epilepsy unit, to Victoria Hospital's $94 million expansion request. Evaluating programs on a regional basis, according to community need, did not allow much consideration of the type of care provided or the referral base they served. UH frequently went outside this process, appealing directly to the Ministry, or failing that, by funding projects from their own accumulated surplus.

The government's influence upon hospitals extended well beyond the control of global operating budgets and new programs. It also affected the supply of nurses, residents, and physicians by controlling the number of available positions in nursing and medical schools, by influencing the certification of immigrants, and by limiting the number of hospital residency positions funded. The MOH had recently reduced, province-wide, the number of medical residency positions for physicians doing postgraduate specialty training. Essentially, medical residents learned a specialty while providing patient care in a hospital, freeing physicians to do teaching, research, and other activities. Reduction in residency positions created a gap in the provision of service in larger, teaching hospitals, and would ultimately lead to a decline in the number of indigenously trained medical specialists and researchers.

Pressures on the health care system were increasing. Because of an aging population demand for basic services was expected to increase into the 21st century. Further, increasingly sophisticated and expensive new medical technologies not only improved existing services, but also developed new treatments for previously untreatable illnesses—all at a cost, however. While gross measures of productivity, like patient days in hospital per procedure, had been improving, the increasing sophistication of treatments appeared to be increasing costs at a faster rate than offsetting gains in productivity. Further, most gains in productivity came about by requiring fewer personnel to do the same tasks, rather than reducing the number of tasks. The increasing stresses and turnover that naturally resulted were present in all hospital health care professionals but especially evident in the exodus from the nursing profession. Although not as severe in the London area, it was estimated six to eight hundred beds in Toronto hospitals were closed because of lack of nursing staff. Shortages of staff existed in other areas, such as occupational and physical therapists, radiologists, and pharmacists.

The province's basic approach to managing demand (and costs) appeared to be by limiting supply. As a result, waiting lists were growing, especially for elective procedures. Certain serious, but not immediately life-threatening, conditions had waiting lists for treatment of six months to a year, and were getting longer.

Social and political expectations also put pressures on the system. Universal, free access to a health care system offering equal, high-quality care to all had become a societal expectation and a political sacred cow. Politically acceptable ideas for fundamentally restructuring the industry were not obvious. There was no apparent way to reconcile increasing demand and costs with the governmental funding likely to be available. As a result many observers felt that the health care system was out of control. And the Ministry was under tremendous pressure to control costs and account for its expenditures, while at the same time providing more, new, and enhanced services. Without an overall approach to the health care situation it was not clear how the Ministry would allocate funds in the future. Choices between high-technology, expensive procedures, such as heart transplantation and intensive care for premature infants and basic care for the aged, were difficult to make and politically sensitive.

◼ University Hospital

UH was a well-designed and -maintained facility. It was located in north London, Ontario. Rising from a three-floor service podium, each of its seven tower floors was divided into two basic components—one an inpatient area, the other an outpatient, office, research, and teaching area. Each inpatient area, except pediatrics, had a corresponding outpatient department for initial assessment and followup, and the performance of minor procedures. UH had 463 inpatient beds with an average occupancy rate of over 90 percent, which effectively meant 100% utilization. The occupancy rate and number of beds had been fairly constant over the past few years. Although space was severely constrained within the hospital, there was a land bank available for future expansion.

In the past, UH had employed some creative solutions to its problem of space constraints. Services had been reviewed to determine whether they could be more effectively provided in one of the other London hospitals, or, as in the case of the Occupational Health Centre, whether they could be better served in an off-site location. Some specialization had already occurred within the city. For example, since another major acute-care hospital specialized in maternity, UH did not duplicate this service. However, UH did have an in vitro fertilization program (popularly known as the test-tube babies program). In a major move during 1986, the Robarts Research Institute (RRI) was opened adjacent to UH. A separate but affiliated institution with its own board, the RRI specialized in heart and stroke research. Moving researchers from UH to this new facility helped to alleviate, at least temporarily, some of the hospital's space pressures. The five-floor, 69,000-square-foot (6,411 square metre) institute housed 35 labs. By the end of 1987, it was expected 80 RRI researchers would be active in conducting basic research into stroke and aging, heart and circulation, and immunological disorders relating to transplantations.

UH housed some of the latest medical technology. For example, a magnetic resonance imaging (MRI) machine costing $3 million was added in 1986. One of the most powerful machines in Canada, the MRI provided unparalleled images of all body organs. Interestingly, neither funding for the total capital cost nor the majority of the ongoing operating costs for this advanced technology instrument was assumed by the Ministry. However, this had not deterred Blewett, and UH was considering other high-technology equipment, such as a $3 million gamma knife which would enable neurosurgeons to operate without having to cut the skin surface.

Mission and Strategy

UH's mission involved three core activities: research, teaching, and patient care. And in this way it did not differ from other university-affiliated teaching hospitals. What made it more unique was the emphasis on innovative, leading-edge research. Clinical and teaching activities were expected to reflect and reinforce this focus. This strategy had implications for UH's product/market scope and its service portfolio.

Product/Market Scope

UH attempted to serve the needs of three related, but different markets: teaching, research, and the health care needs of the community. Local community and basic teaching needs generally required a broad base of standard services. On the other hand, research needs argued for focus and specialization of products offered with a physician's clinical activities related to their research and necessarily drawing from a large patient referral base.

With three different markets, service focus was not easy to achieve. The initial design of UH had included only a small emergency service, because another hospital in the city specialized in trauma. However, in response to local community pressure, a larger emergency department was incorporated. Balancing the product/service portfolio under increasing space constraints, funding pressure, and demand for basic health care services was becoming ever more challenging.

Overall UH's mix of cases had a high proportion of acute cases, very ill patients requiring high levels of care. UH had approximately 1 percent of the approved hospital beds in Ontario, as well as 1 percent of discharges and patient days in acute-care public hospitals. However, when broken down by the acuity/difficulty of the procedure, UH's tertiary focus was clear. (See Table 1.)

Geographically, 81 percent of UH's admitted patients came from the primary service area of southwestern Ontario, with one-third of all patients originating from the hospital's primary service area of Middlesex County. Fifteen percent of

TABLE I   **Market Share of Ontario Patients by Acuity***

Level I: Primary	0.7%	8,092
Level II: Secondary	1.4%	2,616
Level III: Tertiary	4.2%	2.783
Examples:		
Heart transplant	66.0%	31
Liver transplant	30.8%	175
Kidney transplant	27.0%	71
Craniotomy (age > 18 years)	15.7%	388

*As classified by a scheme developed in the United States designed to reflect intensity of nursing care required.

all patients came from the secondary service area, which consisted of all parts of Ontario outside the primary region. The remaining four percent of patients came from outside the province of Ontario. However, because these cases tended to be more acute than the norm they accounted for a disproportionate share of patient days, approximately 6 percent, and an even larger proportion of revenues. Exhibit 2 provides a breakdown of current patient origin by service. For the future, the strategic plan had identified transplantation, in vitro fertilization, neurosciences, diabetes, cardiology/cardiovascular surgery, epilepsy, orthopedics/sport injury, and occupational health care as services with high out-of-province potential.

EXHIBIT 2   **Patient Origin by Service, 1986 (percent)**

	Origin			
	Primary	Secondary	Tertiary	
Service	(S-W Ont.)	(Remainder of Ont.)	Canada (except Ont.)	International
Cardiology	71.9	22.3	3.9	1.9
Cardiovascular and thoracic surgery	61.4	28.8	7.8	2.1
Chest diseases	88.1	10.8	0.6	0.5
Dentistry	89.1	10.8	0.0	0.1
Endocrinology	83.2	15.4	0.0	1.5
Gastroenterology	80.1	15.7	2.5	1.0
General surgery	87.5	11.1	0.6	0.8
Gynecology	70.9	24.4	3.8	1.0
Hematology	92.2	6.8	0.0	1.0
Immunology	90.0	10.0	0.0	0.0
Internal medicine, infectious diseases	85.6	10.1	0.2	2.0
Nephrology	76.8	20.4	0.2	2.5
Neurology	70.0	26.2	2.4	1.4
Neurosurgery	42.6	36.3	2.4	18.6
Ophthalmology	75.9	23.7	0.0	0.4
Orthopedic surgery	85.6	13.4	0.3	0.7
Otolaryngology	92.2	7.0	0.4	0.0
Pediatrics	42.6	45.0	0.0	12.4
Plastic surgery	86.8	12.4	0.2	0.6
Psychiatry	91.0	6.7	0.3	2.0
Rheumatology	91.9	7.7	0.0	0.4
Urology	92.9	7.1	0.0	0.0

Source: UH Strategic Plan.

To help manage the service/product portfolio, the strategic plan called for the following designation of products: *premier product lines* were designated on the basis of the world-class, cutting-edge nature of the service; *intermediate product lines* represented those services that were approaching premier status or that stood alone as a service entity; *service support clusters* were services that supported the intermediate and premier product lines; *ambulatory/ emergency services* included outpatient clinics, emergency services, and regional joint-venture arrangements; and *diversification/collaboration ventures* were standalone services that generated revenue for UH. The services for premier and intermediate categories are listed in Exhibit 3. A more detailed profile of the premier product lines is provided in Appendix A.

Product Innovation

Developing new and improved leading-edge treatments for health problems was a key element of UH's mission relating to research and teaching. And while the institution, over its relatively brief history, had participated in a number of medical innovations, this success did not appear attributable to formal planning. Rather new programs and services developed at UH in a seemingly ad hoc fashion. As Ken Stuart, Vice-President, Medical, observed, "New services happen because of individuals—they just grow. There is some targeted research, but it is not the route of most [activities] because it would

EXHIBIT 3	Services by Strategic Category

Premier Product Lines
- Cardiology/Cardiovascular Surgery
  - Arrythmia Investigation and Surgery
  - VAD
- Clinical Neurological Sciences (Neurology/Neurosurgery)
  - Epilepsy Unit
  - Stroke Investigation
  - Multiple Sclerosis
  - Aneurysm Surgery
- Multiple Organ Transplant Centre (Adult and Pediatric)
  - Kidney
  - Liver
  - Heart
  - Heart/lung
  - Other
  - Pancreas
  - Small bowel
  - Bone marrow
  - Whole joint and bone
- Reproductive Biology
  - IVF Clinic

Intermediate Product Lines
- Chest Diseases
- Endocrinology/Metabolism
- General Internal Medicine
- Hematology
- Nephrology—Dialysis Unit
- Orthopedic Surgery
- Pediatrics
- Physical Medicine and Rehabilitation
- Rheumatology
- Dentistry
- Gastroenterology
- General Surgery
- Immunology
- Ophthalmology
- Otolaryngology
- Plastic/Reconstructive Surgery
- Psychiatry
- Urology

stifle people's ideas. They need to fiddle with things and be able to fail." The development of the Epilepsy Unit, outlined in Appendix B, describes an example of this process.

Blewett commented on the development of new programs at UH:

> The fact that the hospital is so small—everyone knows everyone—I can get around. Everyone knows what's going on in the hospital. ... People just drop in to see me. Someone will come down and tell me that they've found a real winner and they just have to have him/her, and so we go out and get them. There's always room for one more; we find a way to say yes.
>
> When it impacts other resources, Diane [Stewart, Executive Vice-President] becomes involved. She says it's easy for me to agree, but her people have to pick up the pieces. In order to better identify the requirements for new physicians and new programs Diane came up with the idea of the Impact Analysis [a study of how new or expanded programs affected hospital staffing, supplies, and facilities]. But even when the study is done we don't use it as a reason to say no; we use it to find out what we have to do to make it happen.

Diane Stewart was sensitive to the need for continued innovation. She had stated, "We like to leave the door open to try new things. We go by the philosophy that to try and fail is at least to learn." A UH vice-president commented:

> People here are well-read. When ideas break, anywhere in the world, they want them. There is a lot of compromising. But things get resolved. It just takes some time. We haven't learned the meaning of the word "no." But we're at a juncture where we may have to start saying no. We're just beginning to be [in the tight financial position] where many other hospitals have been for several years.

Revenue and Costs

UH's revenues and costs could not be neatly assigned to its major areas of activity. As shown in Exhibit 4a, in 1983, 73 percent of UH's sources of funds were a "global allocation" from the MOH; by 1987 this amount had been reduced to 70 percent. For the most part these funds were not attached to specific activities, acuity of patients, or outcomes. Over the past few years, UH, like another hospitals, had simply been getting an annual increase in its global allocation to offset inflation. The stipulation attached to MOH funds was that there could be no deficit.

Some small part of MOH funding was tied to activity levels. Increases in outpatient activity did, through a complex formula, eventually result in increased funding to the hospital. Further, the Ministry had established a special "life support fund" to fund volume increases for specified procedures. However, this fund was capped and the number of claims by all hospitals already exceeded funds available, so only partial funding was received. The MOH also funded the clinical education of medical students and interns. This accounted for most of the $5.8 million in revenue from MOH programs (Exhibit 4a).

Approximately 30 percent of UH's revenues did not come directly from the Ministry of Health through its global funding allocation. A large percentage of these self-generated revenues originated from servicing out-of-province patients.

EXHIBIT 4A

STATEMENT OF REVENUES AND EXPENSES
For the year ended March 31
($000s)

	1983	1984	1985	1986	1987
Revenue					
MOH allocation	$47,067	$51,527	$56,329	$61,103	$69,502
Inpatient services	5,355	7,482	9,986	13,945	14,771
Accommodation differential	1,548	1,624	1,746	2,277	2,537
Outpatient services	1,692	2,069	2,033	2,428	3,135
MOH programs	4,908	5,083	5,405	5,503	5,811
Other revenue	3,626	3,471	4,079	4,510	4,836
	64,196	71,256	79,578	89,766	100,592
Expenses					
Salaries and wages	35,779	39,480	43,505	47,450	53,581
Employee benefits	3,869	4,441	4,711	4,866	5,628
Supplies and other services	10,312	11,751	13,640	15,289	18,960
Ministry of Health programs	4,978	5,376	5,701	5,976	6,099
Medical supplies	3,679	3,915	4,842	5,506	6,547
Drugs	2,226	2,079	2,871	3,846	5,220
Depreciation	2,444	2,818	3,121	3,398	3,843
Bad debts	192	205	165	197	141
Interest	75	137	144	122	420
	63,554	70,202	78,699	86,650	100,439
Excess of Revenue over Expenses from Operations	642	1,054	878	3,116	153
Add (deduct) unusual items:					
Debenture issue cost					(154)
Gain on asset sale					466
EXCESS OF REVENUE OVER EXPENSES	642	1,054	878	3,116	465
Operating Statistics					
Inpatient days (000)	137.5	138.5	139.7	140.4	142.0
Inpatient admissions (000)	11.8	11.9	12.5	12.9	13.1
Average inpatient stay (days)	11.7	11.6	11.2	10.9	10.8
Occupancy (percent)	89.5%	89.9%	90.3%	91.0%	90.9%
Outpatient visits (000)	96.5	101.9	108.4	113.1	122.4
Total patients seen	NA	NA	221,090	233,688	254,001
Equivalent patient days	NA	NA	208,932	214,980	222,137
Bookings ahead:					
Urgent				294	584
Elective				650	724
UH Employees					
Number of beds:					
Approved	421	424	424	428	436
Rated	451	451	451	463	463

For patients from other provinces the MOH negotiated with the paying provinces, a per diem charge for services provided. Even so, because out-of-province patients generated incremental revenues, above and beyond the global allocation, they were a very attractive market. For out-of-country patients UH could set their own price for services provided, thereby ensuring that the full cost of providing health care was recovered. But, as shown in Table 2, the out-of-province and out-of-country revenue appeared to have reached a plateau at around 14 percent of

TABLE 2   **University Hospital Revenue Breakdown**

Fiscal Year	MOH Global Base	Other Revenue	Out-of-Province and Out-of-Country
1983	74.6%	25.4%	7.4%
1984	73.7%	26.3%	8.7%
1985	72.1%	27.9%	11.3%
1986	69.3%	30.7%	13.8%
1987	70.5%	29.5%	13.9%

total revenue. There was also a sense the mix of this component was shifting away from out-of-country patients toward out-of-province.

Additional funds also came from the University Hospital Foundation of London and other entrepreneurial activities. The numerous fundraising appeals by the Foundation included sales of operating room greens in sizes ranging from doll-size through to a small child, and a specially produced record and music-video. The Foundation was a separate financial entity and funds flowing to UH appeared as an addition to UH equity (and cash) with no effect on revenues.

Salaries, wages, and benefits made up the single largest cost category. (The base salary of medical staff, who were employees of the university, were not directly included in this number.) As a proportion of total revenues these costs had declined marginally over the last five years. Other costs had, however, increased, in particular medical supplies and drugs. Much of this increase was due to the MOH's unwillingness to pay for certain drug therapies. For example, drugs used to prevent rejection of transplanted organs were not paid for by the MOH because the drugs were considered experimental and therefore the cost of these drugs had to be covered under the hospital's global budget. Similar funding limitations had evolved with other drugs and medical apparatus (e.g., implantable defibrillators). The boundary between clinical research and clinical practice was often difficult to draw. Research funding bodies, such as the Medical Research Council, would not pay for medical procedures beyond the purely experimental stage. And often the MOH would not immediately step in and fund procedures after research grants expired.

On balance UH had never recorded a deficit year. However, its operating surplus had been decreasing (see Exhibit 4a). Blewett felt the key to UH's future financial success was reduced reliance on Ministry funding. (UH's reliance on Ministry funding was already less than that of most hospitals.) UH was actively pursuing opportunities with the potential to generate funds. One recent development was the Occupational Health Centre (OHC), which opened in 1986 as a separate private, for-profit organization to provide occupational health care services to the business community. By the end of 1987, it had 30 companies with 11,000 employees as clients. However, like most startups the OHC had required an initial infusion of cash and was not expected to generate net positive cash flow for several years.

Not all of the activity undertaken at UH was reflected in its financial statements and operating statistics. Research grants and many of their associated costs were not included in the hospital's statements; even though they were administered by the university and much of the activity was conducted at UH.

EXHIBIT 4B

BALANCE SHEET
As of March 31
($000)

Assets	1983	1984	1985	1986	1987
Integrated Funds*					
Current:					
Cash and securities	$ 2,795	$ 1,580	$ 1,562	$ 1,799	$ 1,541
Accounts receivable:					
Province	3,095	3,341	4,324	6,068	7,508
Other	2,299	3,119	3,742	6,394	7,006
Inventories	1,005	1,147	1,130	1,127	1,064
Prepaid expenses	101	109	99	78	100
Total current assets	9,231	9,296	10,857	15,466	17,219
Funds available to purchase plant, property, and equipment	2,099	3,701	3,086	2,764	6,800
Fixed assets:					
Property, plant, and equipment	36,884	37,873	38,511	40,325	48,223
Capital leases	173	144	141	40,249	48,114
	37,057	38,017	38,652	40,325	48,223
	48,387	51,014	52,596	58,555	72,242
Special Funds*					
Cash and deposits	19	21	35	40	90
Marketable securities (cost)	4,256	5,042	5,948	7,105	7,817
Accrued interest	57	103	108	123	141
Mortgage receivable	59	56	53	49	46
Advance to integrated fund	1,264	1,004	744	734	1,775
	5,655	6,227	6,888	8,051	9,869
	54,042	57,241	59,485	66,606	82,112
Liabilities and Equity					
Integrated Funds					
Current:					
Account payable	2,941	4,490	4,153	5,618	6,987
Accrued charges	2,401	2,074	2,580	2,988	3,668
Current portion of leases and loans	417	401	400	260	307
Total current liabilities	5,759	6,965	7,133	8,866	10,962
Long-term:					
Debentures**					5,629
Advances from special funds	1,265	1,004	744	734	1,775
Capital lease	175	141	95	18	12
	1,440	1,145	839	752	7,417
Less principal due	417	401	400	260	307
	1,023	744	439	492	7,109
Integrated equity	41,605	43,305	45,025	49,196	54,170
	$48,387	$51,014	$52,597	$58,554	$72,241
Special Fund					
Equity	5,656	6,227	6,888	8,052	9,870
Total Equity and Liabilities	54,042	57,241	59,485	66,606	82,111

*Revenue and expenses relating to the day-to-day activities of the Hospital are recorded in the statement of revenue and expenses and the integrated fund statement of assets. Activities relating to funds made available to the LHA under conditions specified by the donor are recorded in the special funds statement. Most of these monies were donated to the LHA prior to the establishment of the Foundation.

**In February 1987 the Hospital issued debentures to finance the new parking garage and attached office facility.

Note: The hospital has received the following advances from the Special Fund, repayable with interest:

Year	Amount	Purpose
1983	$1,264,000	New telephone system
1986	$ 250,000	Establishment of Occupational Health Centre
1987	$1,400,000	Financing of MRI building

EXHIBIT 4B

STATEMENT OF CHANGES IN EQUITY
Year Ended March 31

	1983	1984	1985	1986	1987
Integrated Funds					
Balance, beginning of year	$40,386	$41,605	$43,305	$45,025	$49,196
Add (Deduct) MOH settlements	(1,114)				
	39,272	41,605	43,305	45,025	49,196
Donations and grants	1,692	646	842	1,054	4,509
Excess of revenue over expenses	641	1,054	878	3,117	465
	2,333	1,700	1,720	4,171	4,974
Balance, end of year	$41,605	$43,305	$45,025	$49,196	$54,170
Special Funds					
Balance, beginning of year	$ 5,044	$ 5,651	$ 6,227	$ 6,888	$ 8,052
Add:					
Donations and bequests	1	1	11	409	835
Net investment income	606	575	650	755	983
Balance, end of year	$ 5,651	$ 6,227	$ 6,888	$ 8,052	$ 9,870
Represented by:					
Non-expendable funds	$ 492	$ 492	$ 492	$ 492	$ 492
Expendable funds	5,139	5,734	6,396	7,560	9,378
	$ 5,651	$ 6,227	$ 6,888	$ 8,052	$ 9,870

During 1986/87, UH physicians and researchers were involved in over 200 projects with annual funding of $9.5 million. Table 3 lists the services most involved in research. In an effort to capitalize on the revenue potential of the innovations developed at UH, an innovations inventory was being developed and the potential for licensing explored. It was expected this activity, if it demonstrated potential, would be spun out into a private, for-profit corporation.

Staffing and Organization

UH was a large and diverse organization employing 2,600 personnel. There were 128 medical clinicians and researchers, 70 residents, 44 interns and research fellows, 875 nursing staff, 140 paramedical, 312 technical, 214 supervisory and specialist, 444 clerical, and 379 service staff.

The relationship with UH's medical staff was especially unique. *All* UH physicians held joint appointments with UH and the university, and were technically university employees. As well, they did not have a private practice outside

TABLE 3   **Clinical Services with Largest Research Budgets**

Service	Amount ($000)
Transplantation and nephrology	$1,979
Gynecology	1,454
Neurology	1,105
Endocrinology	923
Cardiology	678

Source: Research Annual Compendium; does not include the Robarts Research Institute.

of University Hospital. As a consequence, all patients (except those admitted through the emergency department) were referred to UH by outside physicians. At most other hospitals physicians were not salaried employees. They had hospital privileges, and spent part of their time at the hospital and the rest at their own clinics/offices, usually separate from the hospital. These physicians billed the Ontario Health Insurance Plan (OHIP) directly for *all* patient care delivered. At UH the "GFT"[1] relationship with physicians was very different. They were paid a base salary by the university. Physicians negotiated with the Dean of Medicine and the department chairperson for salaries in excess of this base. This negotiated portion was called the "if earned" portion. UH physicians were expected to make OHIP billings from clinical work inside the hospital at least up to the level of their "if earned" portion. Any additional billings were "donated" to the university, and were placed into a research fund. Although arrangements varied, the physicians who contributed their billings usually had some say in the allocation of these research funds.

Because of this GFT relationship, the medical staff at UH generally developed a stronger identification and affiliation with the institution. Even so, retaining medical staff was not easy. Most could make significantly higher incomes if they gave up their teaching and research activities and devoted all their efforts to private practice. While the salary of UH physicians was competitive with similar institutions in Canada, many research hospitals in the United States were perceived to offer higher compensation and often better support for research. To further complicate matters the available number of university positions in the medical faculty and the dollar amount of the salary had been frozen for several years. As a result, the base salaries for any net new positions or salary increases were funded entirely by UH.

Structure

The physicians were by nature highly autonomous and independent. Nominally at least medical staff were responsible through their clinical service head (e.g., Neurology) or a department head (e.g., Neurosciences) to Ken Stuart, Vice-President Medical. The role of service and department head was a part-time responsibility rotated among senior clinicians in the specialty. The heads of services and departments in the hospital, often, but not always, held parallel appointments in the Faculty of Medicine at the university.

The division of services and departments was in most instances determined by traditional professional practice. However, "product offerings" that crossed traditional departmental boundaries were common. At UH, the only one with formal organizational recognition was the multi-organ transplant service (MOTS). It had its own medical head, manager, and budget. Other multidisciplinary units, such as the Epilepsy Unit, did not have formal organizational status, even though the strategic plan recommended organizing around product lines (or business units).

In general, the hierarchy could best be described as loose and collegial. Although it varied from individual to individual, most physicians, while they

---

[1] "Geographic full-time."

might consult with their service and department heads when confronted with a problem or pursuing an opportunity, felt no requirement to do so. Typically they dealt directly with the persons concerned. Most chiefs of services supported this laissez-faire approach, since they wanted to encourage initiative and did not wish to become overly involved in administration, coordination, and control.

At an operational level the primary organizational difference between UH and traditional hospitals was its decentralized approach. Each floor acted as a mini-hospital. A triumvirate of medical, nursing, and administrative staff were responsible for the operation of their unit. In many hospitals, nurses spent much of their time doing non-nursing tasks, including administrative duties such as budget preparation, and coordinating maintenance and repairs. At UH, a service coordinator located on each floor handled non-nursing responsibilities for each unit and interfaced with centralized services such as purchasing, housekeeping, and engineering. Whenever possible, the allied health professionals, such as psychologists, occupational therapists, and physiotherapists, were also located on the floors. In traditional hospitals, hiring, staff development, quality assurance, and staff assignment of nurses were done on a centralized basis. At UH, a nursing manager, located in each service, handled the nursing supervision responsibilities. A nursing coordinator handled the clinical guidance and supervision of the nurses.

Organizationally service coordinators and allied health professionals reported through their respective managers to the newly created, and as yet unfilled, position of Vice-President Patient Services. Nursing reported through nursing managers to the Vice-President Nursing. In practice, the physicians, nurses, and service coordinators on each floor formed a team that managed their floor. Ideally, integration occurred and operational issues were addressed at the floor level, only rarely being referred up for resolution.

Non-medical personnel working in centralized laboratories and services but not directly involved in patient care reported to the Vice-President Administration. Activities dealing with financial, accounting, and information were the responsibility of the Vice-President Finance. While final hiring decisions for non-physician positions were decentralized to the units concerned, job description, posting, and initial screening was done in the human resources department. In addition, some employee education and health services were handled through this department. The hiring of physicians, even though they were technically university employees, was usually initiated within UH. Typically service or department heads would identify desirable candidates. If the person was being hired for a new position (as opposed to as a replacement), then after discussion of the physician's plans, an impact analysis would be prepared identifying the resources required. Generally, Pat Blewett was very much involved in the recruitment of physicians.

UH was considered progressive in its staffing and organization, having recorded many firsts among Canadian hospitals. Over the years, they had been one of the first to introduce service coordinators, paid maternity leave, dental benefits, 12-hour shifts, job sharing, workload measurement, and productivity monitoring. The concern for employees was reflected in UH's relatively low turnover, in the 9 percent range. Exit interviews indicated very few people went to another health care job because they were dissatisfied with UH. Aside from normal attrition, the biggest reason for leaving was lack of upward job mobility, a situation caused by UH's flat structure and low turnover among its management.

Committees at all levels and often across departments were a fact of life at UH and reflected the organization's decentralized and participative approach to decision making. Diane Stewart, for example, was a member of 48 different hospital and board committees. Medical staff were also expected to be involved, as Ken Stuart explained:

> Committee work is not a physician's favourite activity. But it's important they be involved in the management of the hospital. I balance committee assignments amongst the medical staff and no one can continually refuse to do their part. This is a demand UH makes of its GFT physicians that other hospitals do not.

UH's management group had recently undergone a reorganization, reducing the number of direct reports to Pat Blewett from five to three. Now the Vice-President Human Resources and the Vice-President Administration along with the Vice-Presidents of Patient Services and Nursing reported to the Executive Vice-President, Diane Stewart (Exhibit 5). The reorganization centred control of operations around Stewart, allowing Blewett to concentrate on physicians, external relationships, and the future direction of UH.

Budgets

There were five groups that submitted budgets to administration: support services, nursing, allied health, diagnostic services, and administrative services. The annual capital and operating budgetary processes involved a lot of meetings, and give and take. As one manager described:

> The budget of each department is circulated to the other departments within our service. We have a meeting with ... VP Administration and ... VP Finance and all the department heads. Although the department heads are physicians, often the department managers will either accompany or represent the department head. In that meeting we review each department's budget, questioning any items which seem out of place. The department will either remain firm on its budget, back down, or decide to postpone the expenditure to the following year. People do back down. If we can't get our collective budgets within the budget for our service, the vice-presidents will either make tradeoffs with the other service categories, or speak with the department heads privately to try and obtain further cuts. The majority of cuts are made in the meeting. ... It works because the department heads are fiscally responsible, and there is a lot of trust between the departments and between the departments and administration.

Operating budgets were coordinated by the service coordinator on each floor but really driven by the plans of the medical staff. Each year physicians were asked about their activity levels for the upcoming year; these were translated into staffing and supplies requirements, in terms of number of hours worked and the physical volume of supplies consumed. Costs were attached and the overall expense budget tabulated later by the finance depart-

EXHIBIT 5 Organizational Chart, October 1987

Board Committees
Audit
Business Development
Ethics
Executive
Finance
Joint Conference
and Patient Care
Joint Relations
LHA/UWO
Medical Advisory
Parking
Personnel
Planning
Property
Public Relations
Volunteers

Board of Directors
University Hospital
Foundation of London

Board of Directors

President and
Chief Executive Officer

Executive
Vice-President

Vice-President
Fund Development

Secretary
to the Board

Vice-President
Public Relations

Curator
Medical Museum

Manager
Volunteer Services

Manager
Communication Services

Manager
Administrative Projects

Manager
Quality Assurance

Vice-President
Finance

Manager Computer Services
Manager Financial Services
Manager Hospital Management Information System
Manager Patient Accounts
Manager Payroll Services
Manager Telecommunication Services

Vice-President
Administration

Manager Audio/Visual Services
Manager Biomedical Engineering Services
Manager Housekeeping Services
Manager Library Services
Manager Management Engineering Services
Manager Nutrition and Food Services
Manager Planning & Development and Property Services
Manager Purchasing Services
Manager Security Services

Director Cardiac Investigation Unit
Director EEG Services
Director EMG Services
Director Lipid Investigation
Director Pulmonary Function Laboratory
Director Synovial Fluid Laboratory
Director Transplant Immunology Laboratory
Director Dialysis Technical Services

Vice-President
Nursing

Manager—Nursing Service
• Chest Medicine and Surgery
• ENT
• Intensive Care Unit
• Coronary Care Unit
• Transplant Unit
• IV Team
• Medicine
• Nephro Urology and Dialysis
• Neurosciences
• Operating and Recovering Rooms
• Orthopedics, Gynecology, and Ophthalmology
• Pediatrics
• Adult Neurology
• Psychiatry
• Rehabilitation
• RDU and Medicine
• Surgery and Emergency
Clinical Nurse Specialists

Vice-President
Patient Services

Manager Psychological Services
Manager Respiratory Therapy Services
Manager Service Coordination
Manager Social Work
Manager Speech Pathology Services
Manager Supply Processing and Distribution

Manager Clinical Perfusion Services
Manager Occupational Therapy Services
Director Otologic Function
Manager Pastoral Services
Manager Pharmacy Services
Manager Physiotherapy Services

Vice-President
Human Resources

Manager Educational Services
Manager Employee Health Services
Manager Occupational Health Centre
Manager Occupational Health and Safety

Vice-President
Medical

Administrative Assistant

Director Medical Education
Director Medical Research
Chief Dentistry
Chief Emergency Services
Chief Clinical Biochemistry
Chief Clinical Immunology
Chief Hematology/Blood Bank
Chief Microbiology
Chief Nuclear Medicine
Chief Pathology
Chief Diagnostic Radiology
Manager Admitting Services
Manager Medical Record Services

Medical Services
Anesthesis
Gynecology
Medicine
• Cardiology
• Chest
• Clinical Pharmacology
• Dermatology
• Endocrinology
• Gastroenterology
• General Medicine
• Hematology
• Immunology and Allergy
• Infectious Diseases
• Nephrology
• Rheumatology
Neurosciences
• Neurology
• Neurosurgery
Ophthalmology
Otelaryngology
Pediatrics
Psychiatry
Rehabilitation Medicine
Surgery
• Cardiothoracic
• General
• Orthopedic
• Plastic
• Urological
Multi-Organ Transplant Service
GFT Secretaries

ment. In the last fiscal year when the overall budget was tabulated it exceeded the estimated revenues of the hospital by over $10 million, roughly 10 percent. Ross Chapin, Vice-President Finance, explained what happened:

> We went back to each of the clinical services and looked at their proposed level of activity. The hospital had already been operating at 100-plus percent of its physical capacity. Most of the services had not taken this into account in preparing their plans. They had assumed more space and more patient beds would be available. Since this just wasn't going to happen, at least in the short term, we asked them to redo their budgets with more realistic space assumptions. As a result our revenue and expense budgets came more into line.

While the activity of the medical staff drove the operating expenditures of the hospital, physicians were not in the ongoing budgetary loop. If expenditures were exceeding budget physicians might not even be aware, and if aware had no incentive to cut expenses and reduce activity levels in order to meet budget. Aside from the number of physicians and the limits of their own time, the major constraint on expenditures was space and the availability of support services. A patient could not be admitted unless a bed was available; an outpatient procedure could not be conducted unless a consultation room was free and the needed support services (e.g., radiology, physical therapy, etc.) could be scheduled.

Because of MOH funding and space constraints, the hospital had a set number of inpatient beds. The allocation of beds among services was determined by a committee made up of the manager of admitting and several physicians and chaired by the Vice-President Medical. Since bed availability affected the activity level of the services and their physicians, this allocation was a sensitive area. Services would often lend an unused bed to another, usually adjacent, service. However, the formal reallocation of beds was done infrequently. And when done, it was based on waiting lists (by service) and bed utilization rates.

New Programs

While capital and operating budgets for ongoing activities originated with the managers on the floors, the medical staff usually initiated requests for *new* programs and equipment. Money to fund large outlays associated with new or expanded programs would be requested from the MOH or might be part of a special fundraising campaign. (Private charitable foundations had made significant contributions to the Epilepsy Unit, the MOTU (see Appendix A), and the MRI facility.) When proposals for a new program or the addition of a new physician were made an impact analysis was undertaken. These studies detailed the resource requirement—space, support staff, supplies, etc.—of the initiative and summarized the overall financial impact. The analysis did not, however, identify the availability or source of the required resources should the initiative be pursued. As one vice-president explained:

> The impact analysis might show that if we bring on a new orthopedic surgeon, we'll need two more physical therapists [PTs]. But there is no space (and probably no money) for the PTs. Quite often the physician is hired anyway, and the PTs currently on staff have to try and manage the additional

workload. We *know* what a new physician will need beforehand, but we don't always ensure it's there before they come on board.

Recently a new physician had arrived after being hired, and office space was not available.

Basis for Success

UH attributed its success to several factors. A primary factor was the GFT status of the medical staff, which cultivated a high degree of loyalty and commitment to the hospital, and supported the integration of excellence in teaching, research, and practice. The ability of the medical staff to attract out-of-province patients contributed to the hospital's revenues. The strong entrepreneurial orientation of management, its ability to identify and create additional sources of revenue, and a widely shared understanding of the mission of UH helped to foster commitment to the organization's goals.

Early in its development, UH had attracted physicians/researchers capable of developing major internationally recognized research and clinical programs: Doctors Drake and Barnett in neurosciences and Dr. Stiller in transplantation. These physicians and their programs had developed international recognition and generated patient referrals from all over the country and around the world.

UH's product portfolio required a delicate balance. It was natural for products to evolve and mature. As innovative procedures became more commonplace, they tended to diffuse to other hospitals. Indeed, UH contributed to this process by training physicians in these procedures (as part of their teaching mission). As a consequence, UH's patient referral base would shrink, and so too would out-of-country, out-of-province revenues from maturing service. UH required a constant inflow of innovative, internationally recognized clinical procedures in order to sustain its out-of-province referral base.

◼ The Strategic Plan

UH did not have an internal ongoing strategic planning process. In 1985, a change occurred. UH signed an affiliation agreement with the Hospital Corporation of Canada (HCC), an affiliate of the Hospital Corporation of America (HCA), a large, publicly owned international health care company, which gave UH access to HCA strategic planning expertise. For UH's existing service portfolio, the consultants assessed underlying demand, UH's share of market, and its capability base and abilities relative to other research and teaching hospitals. They did not specifically consider MOH funding policy.

Senior management wanted a process that would enable people to buy into the emerging plan, so they conducted a series of planning sessions. The first information session was conducted in the fall of 1986, when general information about the health care environment was presented to the chiefs of services and administration. In December, a daylong retreat was held to disseminate information and to provide some education on key strategic concepts such as market share and product life cycle. In January 1987, a second retreat was held. The chiefs of services were asked to come prepared to make a presentation on the direction of their department, resource requirements, and priorities. Blewett commented on the meeting:

> The chiefs did an outstanding job. They really got into it; using business ideas to look at their services and where they are going. They were talking about market share and product life cycles. I believe it gave them a new way to think about things. Really, the chiefs were presenting to each other and they wanted to do a good job and make their best case. A lot of information sharing occurred.

In late February, the consultants' initial recommendations were presented to administration. One of the recommendations was to adopt a portfolio approach to planning. A preliminary designation of products into portfolios of premier, intermediate, and service support clusters was provided. The initial criteria used to determine premier status were: geographic "draw," "leading edge" service, consensus as a priority, and future orientation of its people. Subsequent meetings with the medical staff led to some modifications of these designations. Blewett reflected on the process of identifying the product/service portfolio.

> I never thought we would do it. But when it came down to making the hard decisions, it didn't take that long. I give a lot of credit to the planners and to our administrative person, who kept in close contact with everyone, and made sure that concerns were taken care of. ... The GFTs are committed to this institution; therefore, it's easier to mobilize these people. ... We also made it clear that services could move between categories, which provides some incentive.

Indeed, Sport Medicine had not initially been categorized as a premier service, but in the final version of the plan it was placed in this category.

The final strategic plan, a 150-page document, was approved by both the Medical Advisory Committee of the hospital and its Board of Directors. As Blewett reflected on the process, he was pleased with the results of the effort which had taken over a year to complete. Blewett knew many of his senior managers had applauded the direction the report had taken in providing a more solid foundation on which to make difficult resource allocation decisions. However, he was concerned that the plan not be used as a reason to say "no," to stifle initiative and the emergence of new areas of excellence. He wondered how an ongoing planning process would have affected the evolution of the Epilepsy Unit (described in Appendix B). With this in mind, he was wondering where to go from here. How could the plan, its recommendations, and the following activities be used to help guide the hospital?

APPENDIX A

Profile of Premier Service Categories

The premier product lines fell into four categories: cardiology/cardiovascular surgery, clinical neurological sciences, multiple organ transplant, and reproductive biology. More detailed descriptions follow.

Cardiology/Cardiovascular Surgery

The two major programs in cardiology/cardiovascular surgery were Arrythmia Investigation and Surgery and the Ventricular Assist Device (VAD). *Arrythmia investigation* received a major breakthrough when in

1981 the world's first heart operation was performed to correct life-threatening right ventricular dysplasia. In 1984, UH entered into a collaborative relationship with Biomedical Instrumentation Inc., a Canadian research and development firm based near Toronto, to produce a sophisticated heart mapping device, which greatly advanced the surgical treatment of patients suffering from life-threatening heart rhythm disorders. The computer-assisted mapping system, which fit over the heart like a sock, enabled doctors to almost instantaneously locate the "electric short circuit" in the hearts of patients afflicted with cardiac arrhythmias. Physicians were then able to more easily locate and destroy the tissue which caused the patient's heart to beat abnormally.

The *ventricular assist device (VAD),* which UH began using in 1987, was functionally no different from some life support machines, such as the heart-lung machine already in use. In assisting the heart to pump blood, the VAD was used for patients waiting for transplants, those needing help after open-heart surgery, and hearts weakened after a severe heart attack. The VAD worked outside the patient's body, carrying out approximately 50 percent of the heart's work. When the patient's heart recovered sufficiently or when a donor organ became available for those who required a transplant, the pump could be disconnected without difficulty. Other than UH, there was only one other hospital in Canada using the VAD.

Clinical Neurological Sciences (CNS)

There were four major programs in CNS: the Epilepsy Unit, Stroke Investigation, Multiple Sclerosis, and Aneurysm Surgery.

The *Epilepsy Unit,* discussed at length in Appendix B, was one of only a few of its kind in North America. The demand for its services had extended the waiting time for a bed to over a year.

The *Stroke Investigation Unit,* a four-bed unit, was established at UH in 1983 to improve the diagnosis and treatment of stroke. In 1986, UH and the University of Western Ontario collaborated in the development of the Robarts Research Institute, which focused its efforts on stroke research.

The *Multiple Sclerosis (MS) clinic* at UH conducted exploratory research to study the causes

and incidence of MS, a chronic degenerative disease of the central nervous system. One study involved 200 MS patients in ten centres, coordinated by UH, to determine whether cyclosporin[2] and prednisone, either alone or in combination with repeated plasma exchange treatments, could prevent further deterioration in MS patients.

Aneurysm Surgery became a centre for excellence and internationally renowned early on, when in 1972 Dr. Charles Drake pioneered a technique for surgically treating a cerebral aneurysm. In October of 1979, vocalist Della Reese underwent neurosurgery at UH. She returned to London the following year to give a benefit concert to raise funds for UH.

Multi-Organ Transplant Service

The first kidney transplant at UH was performed in 1973, followed by its first liver transplant in 1977. In 1979, UH was chosen as the first centre in North America to test the anti-rejection drug Cyclosporin A. In 1981, the first heart transplant at UH was performed. In that same year, UH became the site of the Canadian Centre for Transplant Studies. In 1984, Canada's first heart-lung transplant was performed at UH.

In 1984, the provincial government announced that they would partially fund a multi-organ transplant unit (MOTU) at UH. The 12-bed MOTU, which opened in 1987, was one of the first units of its kind in the world. With the help of leading-edge computer technology, transplant patients were closely monitored for the first signs of organ rejection. A highly specialized team of transplant experts including surgeons, physicians, nurses, technologists, and physiotherapists came together in the MOTU to care for transplant patients.

Reproductive Biology

The primary work in Reproductive Biology was the *In-Vitro Fertilization (IVF) program.* The program was launched in 1982, with the first birth occurring in 1985. By 1987, the 100th child was

---

[2] Cyclosporin was the drug originally used to minimize the body's rejection of transplanted organs. Because of its transplantation experience, UH had a considerable expertise with this drug and immunology in general.

born to parents who previously had been incapable of conceiving a child. The pregnancy rate was 27 percent using this method, with a birth rate of 22 percent. These results were comparable to those of well-established clinics worldwide. It was anticipated that with the combination of continually increasing experience together with basic science and clinical research interests in IVF, the success rate in the program would continue to increase. There was a two-year waiting period to participate in the program.

APPENDIX B

The Process of Innovation at UH: The Epilepsy Unit

Research and service innovations had been important to UH. This appendix describes how one of these came about.

The Epilepsy Unit probably had its genesis when Dr. Warren Blume, a neurologist, joined Dr. John Girvin, a neurosurgeon at UH in 1972. Girvin had trained under a founding father in epilepsy treatment at the Montreal Neurological Institute (MNI). Blume had done postgraduate work in epilepsy and electroencephalography (EEG)[3] at the Mayo Clinic. Girvin was unique among neurosurgeons in that he had also gone on to obtain a Ph.D. in neurophysiology.

In 1972, the primary treatment for epilepsy was through drug therapy. However, there were many patients whose epilepsy could not be effectively treated this way. For those patients, the only hope was a surgical procedure to remove that part of their brain which caused the epileptic seizure. This required an EEG recording of a patient's seizure to identity the focus of the problem. Blume was one of the few individuals trained in the use of EEG to study epilepsy; furthermore, Girvin had the training in neurosurgery to carry out the procedure. Neither physician, however, was recruited specifically to do work in epilepsy. It was an interest they shared and developed over time.

A number of factors united Blume and Girvin, providing the impetus for the dedicated Epilepsy Unit that was eventually opened in May 1986. One was the integration within UH of neurosurgery and neurology under the umbrella of neurosciences. In most hospitals the two departments were separate, neurosurgery being part of surgery and neurology being its own service. At UH, they were integrated organizationally and located on the same floor. Many attribute this unique relationship to the leadership and friendship of Doctors Barnett and Drake, the original chiefs of neurology and neurosurgery.

In 1974, a young Italian boy and his father arrived on the doorstep of UH seeking help to control the boy's epilepsy; this was the precipitating factor that brought Blume and Girvin together. It was a complex case, requiring the expertise of both Blume and Girvin. The surgery was successful, and Blume and Girvin realized that by pooling their expertise they could make a significant contribution to the field. Prior to that time, Blume's efforts had been focused on providing EEG readings for epileptic patients that would either be treated with medication or referred to the MNI for possible surgical treatment. Girvin's efforts had been directed at neurosurgery in general, having no special contact with epileptic patients.

Blume and Girvin began to draw together a team. The technique of removing part of the brain for the treatment of epilepsy was based on the fact that most human functions were duplicated in both temporal lobes of the brain. In the early days of surgical treatment of epilepsy at the MNI, there was no method of ensuring that both temporal lobes were functioning normally. As a result in some cases where a malfunctioning temporal lobe could not duplicate the function of the part of the brain that had been removed, patients were left with serious brain dysfunction such as loss of memory capacity. Later, a procedure was developed whereby neuropsychologists were able to assess the level of function of one temporal lobe, while the other temporal lobe was anesthetized. It so happened that a neuropsychologist

---

[3] The mapping of electrical activity in the brain.

with this expertise was working at UWO's psychology department. She was asked to join the team. For Blume and Girvin, adding a neuropsychologist was essential to their ability to deal with more complex cases. The addition of full-time researchers also served to enhance the team's capability.

Capability was further enhanced when in 1977 Blume and Girvin were successful in obtaining funding to purchase a computer that would facilitate the recording and reading of the EEG. This was a significant step, since to obtain funding they positioned themselves as a Regional Epilepsy Unit. This was the first formal recognition of their efforts as an organized endeavour. The computerized monitoring could benefit from a dedicated unit; at the time, beds and staff were still borrowed from other departments as needed. Epileptic patients were scattered around the neurosciences floor.

As the volume of patients increased, it became increasingly apparent that a unit was needed. In order to identify the focus of the brain that triggered the epileptic seizure, it was necessary to record a seizure. As a result, EEG recording rooms were tied up for several hours in the hope that a patient would have a seizure. There were a number of problems with this approach. The patient had to have a seizure while in a recording room, and the patient or technologist had to activate the recorder. It was estimated that over 50 percent of seizures were missed using this method. Furthermore, leaving the patient unattended without the benefit of medication to control their seizures was dangerous. A unit that would provide full-time monitoring in order to get the vital EEG recordings, and ensure patient safety, was needed.

Blume, Girvin, and the manager of EEG developed a proposal for a four-bed epilepsy unit. The beds that they had been using on an ad hoc basis were the neuroscience overflow beds which "belonged" to pediatrics. Pediatrics was located on the same floor as EEG, so when Blume, who was also a member of the department, heard pediatrics was downsizing, he had approached the chief to negotiate for four beds. As well, the pediatric nurses, who had been responsible for the overflow beds, had become comfortable with providing care for epileptic patients, and it was agreed that they would provide continued support for the unit. Blume and Girvin approached Blewett with a plan requiring funding of $400,000 for equipment and renovations. There was no provision for an annual budget, since pediatrics was prepared to cover the nursing salaries and supplies.

Blewett and his senior management group supported the plan, and it was submitted as a new program to the TVDHC for funding in February 1984. The proposal was ranked 10th, which meant it was not one of the top few submitted to the Ministry for consideration. A revised proposal was resubmitted the following February. In the meantime, Blewett, Girvin, and Blume met with the Assistant Deputy Minister of Health to make a plea for funding—to no avail. They subsequently received news that the TVDHC had given the proposal a ranking of 6th. Blume and Girvin did not lose hope. After exhausting all alternatives, Blewett decided to fund the program out of the hospital's operating surplus. However, compromises were made in the plans by cutting the budget back as far as possible. The Board approved the allocation, and shortly thereafter the unit was opened.

Victoria Heavy Equipment Limited (Revised)

Brian Walters sat back in the seat of his Lear Jet as it broke through the clouds en route from Squamish, a small town near Vancouver, British Columbia, to Sacramento, California. As chairman of the board, majority shareholder, and chief executive officer, the 51-year-old Walters had run Victoria Heavy Equipment Limited as a closely held company for years. During this time Victoria had become the second-largest producer of mobile cranes in the world, with 1985 sales of $100 million and exports to more than 70 countries. But in early 1986 the problem of succession was in his thoughts. His son and daughter were not yet ready to run the organization, and he personally wanted to devote more time to other interests. He wondered about the kind of person he should hire to become president. There was also a nagging thought that there might be other problems with Victoria that would have to be worked out before he eased out of his present role.

◼ Company History

Victoria Heavy Equipment was established in 1902 in Victoria, British Columbia, to produce horse-drawn log skidders for the forest industry. The young firm showed a flair for product innovation, pioneering the development of motorized skidders and later, after diversifying into the crane business, producing the country's first commercially successful hydraulic crane controls. In spite of these innovations, the company was experiencing severe financial difficulties in 1948 when it was purchased by Brian Walters, Sr., the father of the current chairman. By installing tight financial controls and paying close attention to productivity, Walters was able to turn the company around, and in the mid-1950s he decided that Victoria would focus its attention exclusively on cranes, and go after the international market.

At the time of Walters Sr.'s retirement in 1968, it was clear that the decision to concentrate on the crane business had been a good one. The company's sales

Richard Ivey School of Business
The University of Western Ontario

Paul W. Beamish and Thomas A. Poynter prepared this case solely to provide material for class discussion. The authors do not intend to illustrate either effective or ineffective handling of a managerial situation. The authors may have disguised certain names and other identifying information to protect confidentiality. © 1986 Ivey Management Services. Case 9-86-M003, version 1993-04-26.

and profits were growing, and Victoria cranes were beginning to do well in export markets. Walters Sr. was succeeded as president by his brother James, who began to exercise very close personal control over the company's operations. However, as Victoria continued to grow in size and complexity, the load on James became so great that his health began to fail. The solution was to appoint an assistant general manager, John Rivers, through whom tight supervision could be maintained while James Walters' workload was eased. This move was to no avail, however. James Walters suffered a heart attack in 1970 and Rivers became general manager. At the same time, the young Brian Walters, the current chairman and chief executive officer, became head of the U.S. operation.

When Brian Walters took responsibility for Victoria's U.S. business, the firm's American distributor was selling 30 to 40 cranes per year. Walters thought the company should be selling at least 150. Even worse, the orders that the American firm did get tended to come in large quantities, as many as 50 cranes in a single order, which played havoc with Victoria's production scheduling. Walters commented, "We would rather have ten orders of ten cranes each than a single order for 100." In 1975, when the U.S. distributor's agreement expired, Walters offered the company a five-year renewal if it would guarantee sales of 150 units per year. When the firm refused, Walters bought it, and in the first month fired 13 of the 15 employees and cancelled most existing dealerships. He then set to work to rebuild—only accepting orders for ten cranes or less. His hope was to gain a foothold and a solid reputation in the U.S. market before the big U.S. firms even noticed him.

This strategy quickly showed results, and in 1976 Walters came back to Canada. As Rivers was still general manager, there was not enough to occupy him fully, and he began travelling three or four months a year. While he was still very much a part of the company, it was not a full-time involvement.

◨ Victoria in the 1980s

Victoria entered the 1980s with sales of approximately $50 million and by 1985, partly as a result of opening the new plant in California, had succeeded in doubling this figure. Profits reached their highest level ever in 1983, but declined somewhat over the next two years as costs rose and the rate of sales growth slowed. Financial statements are presented in Exhibits 1 and 2. The following sections describe the company and its environment in the 1980s.

Product Line

The bulk of Victoria's crane sales in the 1980s came from a single product line, the LTM 1000, which was produced both in the company's Squamish facility (the firm had moved from Victoria to Squamish in the early 1900s) and its smaller plant in California, built in 1979. The LTM 1000 line consisted of mobile cranes of five basic sizes, averaging approximately $500,000 in price. Numerous options were available for these cranes, which could provide uncompromised on-site performance, precision lifting capabilities, fast highway travel, and effortless city driving. Because of the numerous choices available, Victoria preferred not to

EXHIBIT 1

VICTORIA BALANCE SHEET
For the Years 1981–1985
($000s)

	1981	1982	1983	1984	1985
Assets					
Current assets:					
Accounts receivable	$ 8,328	$ 7,960	$ 9,776	$10,512	$10,951
Allowance for doubtful accounts	(293)	(310)	(282)	(297)	(316)
Inventories	21,153	24,425	24,698	25,626	27,045
Prepaid expenses	119	104	156	106	129
Total current assets	29,307	32,179	34,343	35,947	37,809
Advances to shareholders	1,300	1,300	1,300	1,300	1,300
Fixed assets: property, plant, and equipment	6,840	6,980	6,875	7,353	7,389
TOTAL ASSETS	$37,447	$40,459	$42,518	$44,600	$46,598
Liabilities and Shareholders' Equity					
Current liabilities					
Notes payable to bank	$ 7,733	$ 8,219	$ 9,258	$10,161	$11,332
Accounts payable	9,712	11,353	10,543	10,465	10,986
Accrued expenses	1,074	1,119	1,742	1,501	1,155
Deferred income tax	419	400	396	408	345
Income tax payable	545	692	612	520	516
Current portion of long-term debt	912	891	867	888	903
Total current liabilities	$20,395	$22,674	$23,418	$23,943	$25,237
Long-term debt	6,284	6,110	6,020	6,005	6,114
TOTAL LIABILITIES	26,679	28,784	29,438	29,948	31,351
Shareholders' Equity					
Common shares	200	290	295	390	435
Retained earnings	10,568	11,385	12,790	14,262	14,812
TOTAL SHAREHOLDERS' EQUITY	10,768	11,675	13,080	14,652	15,247
TOTAL LIABILITIES AND SHAREHOLDERS' EQUITY	$37,447	$40,459	$42,518	$44,600	$46,598

EXHIBIT 2

VICTORIA INCOME STATEMENT
For the Years 1981–1985
($000s)

	1981	1982	1983	1984	1985
Revenue:					
Net sales	$63,386	$77,711	$86,346	$94,886	$100,943
Costs and expenses:					
Cost of sales	49,238	59,837	63,996	71,818	75,808
Selling expense	7,470	9,234	10,935	11,437	13,104
Administrative expense	2,684	3,867	5,490	5,795	7,038
Engineering expense	1,342	1,689	1,832	1,949	2,109
Gross income	2,652	3,084	4,093	3,887	2,884
Income taxes	1,081	1,281	1,630	1,505	1,254
NET INCOME	$1,571	$ 1,803	$ 2,463	$ 2,382	$ 1,630

build them to stock. The company guaranteed 60-day delivery and "tailor-made" cranes to customer specifications. This required a large inventory of both parts and raw material.

Walters had used a great deal of ingenuity to keep Victoria in a competitive position. For example, in 1982, he learned that a company trying to move unusually long and heavy logs from a new tract of redwood trees in British Columbia was having serious problems with its existing cranes. A crane with a larger than average height and lifting capacity was required. Up to this point, for technical reasons, it had not been possible to produce a crane with the required specifications. However, Walters vowed that Victoria would develop such a crane, and six months later it had succeeded.

Although the LTM 1000 series provided almost all of Victoria's crane sales, a new crane had been introduced in 1984 after considerable expenditure on design, development, and manufacture. The $650,000 A-100 had a 70-tonne capacity and could lift loads to heights of 61 metres, a combination previously unheard of in the industry. Through the use of smooth hydraulics even the heaviest loads could be picked up without jolts. In spite of these features, and an optional ram-operated tilt-back cab designed to alleviate the stiff necks which operators commonly developed from watching high loads, sales of the A-100 were disappointing. As a result, several of the six machines built were leased to customers at unattractive rates. The A-100 had, however, proven to be a very effective crowd attraction device at equipment shows.

Markets

There were two important segments in the crane market—custom-built cranes and standard cranes—and although the world mobile crane market was judged to be $630 million in 1985, no estimates were available as to the size of each segment. Victoria competed primarily in the custom segment, in the medium- and heavy-capacity end of the market. In the medium-capacity custom crane class Victoria's prices were approximately 75 percent of those of its two main competitors. The gap closed as the cranes became heavier, with Victoria holding a 15 percent advantage over Washington Cranes in the heavy custom crane business. In heavy standard cranes Victoria did not have a price advantage.

Victoria's two most important markets were Canada and the United States. The U.S. market was approximately $240 million in 1985, and Victoria's share was about 15 per cent. Victoria's Sacramento plant, serving both the U.S. market and export sales involving U.S. aid and financing, produced 60 to 70 cranes per year. The Canadian market was much smaller, about $44 million in 1985, but Victoria was the dominant firm in the country, with a 60 percent share. The Squamish plant, producing 130 to 150 cranes per year, supplied both the Canadian market and all export sales not covered by the U.S. plant. There had been very little real growth in the world market since 1980.

The primary consumers in the mobile crane industry were contractors. Because the amount of equipment downtime could make the difference between showing a profit or loss on a contract, contractors were very sensitive to machine dependability, as well as parts and service availability. Price was important, but it was not everything. Independent surveys suggested that Washington Crane, Victoria's most significant competitor, offered somewhat superior service and reliability, and if Victoria attempted to sell similar equipment at prices comparable to Washington's, it would fail. As a result, Victoria tried to reduce its costs through extensive backward integration, manufacturing 85 percent of its crane components in-house, the highest percentage in the industry. This drive to reduce costs was somewhat offset, however, by the fact that much of the equipment in the Squamish plant was very old. In recent years, some of the slower and less versatile machinery had been replaced, but by 1985 only 15 percent of the machinery in the plant was new, efficient, numerically controlled equipment.

Victoria divided the world into eight marketing regions. The firm carried out little conventional advertising, but did participate frequently at equipment trade shows. One of the company's most effective selling tools was its ability to fly in prospective customers from all over the world in Walters' executive jet. Victoria believed that the combination of its integrated plant, worker loyalty, and the single-product concentration evident in their Canadian plant produced a convinced customer. There were over 14 such visits to the British Columbia plant in 1985, including delegations from the People's Republic of China, Korea, France, and Turkey.

Competition

Victoria, as the world's second-largest producer of cranes, faced competition from five major firms, all of whom were much larger and more diversified. The industry leader was the Washington Crane Company with 1985 sales of $400 million and a world market share of 50 percent. Washington had become a name synonymous around the world with heavy-duty equipment and had been able to maintain a sales growth rate of over 15 percent per annum for the past five years. It manufactured in the United States, Mexico, and Australia. Key to its operations were 100 strong dealers worldwide with over 200 outlets. Washington had almost 30 percent of Canada's crane market.

Next in size after Victoria was Texas Star, another large manufacturer whose cranes were generally smaller than Victoria's and sold through the company's extensive worldwide equipment dealerships. The next two largest competitors were both very large U.S. multinational producers whose crane lines formed a small part of their overall business. With the exception of Washington, industry observers suggested that crane sales for these latter firms had been stable (at best) for quite some time. The exception was the Japanese crane producer Toshio, which had been aggressively pursuing sales worldwide and had entered the North American market recently. Sato, another Japanese firm, had started in the North American market as well. Walters commented:

> My father laid the groundwork for the success that this company has enjoyed, but it is clear that we now have some major challenges ahead of us. Washington Cranes is four times our size and I know that we are at the top of their hit list. Our Japanese competitors, Toshio and Sato, are also going to be tough. The key to our success is to remain flexible—we must not develop the same kind of organization as the big U.S. firms.

Organization

In 1979, a number of accumulating problems had ended Brian Walters' semi-retirement and brought him back into the firm full-time. Although sales were growing, Walters saw that work was piling up and things were not getting done. He believed that new cranes needed to be developed, and he wanted a profit-sharing plan put in place. One of his most serious concerns was the development of middle managers. Walters commented, "We had to develop middle-level line managers, we had no depth." The root cause of these problems, Walters believed, was that the firm was overly centralized. Most of the functional managers reported to Rivers, and Rivers made most of the decisions. Walters concluded that action was necessary. "We have to change," he said. "If we want to grow further we have to do things."

Between 1979 and 1982 Walters reorganized the firm by setting up separate operating companies and a corporate staff group. In several cases, senior operating executives were placed in staff/advisory positions, while in others, executives held positions in both operating and staff groups. Exhibit 3 illustrates Victoria's organizational chart as of 1983.

By early 1984 Walters was beginning to wonder "if I had made a very bad decision." The staff groups weren't working. Rivers had been unable to accept the redistribution of power and had resigned. There was "civil war in the company." Politics and factional disputes were the rule rather than the exception. Line managers were upset by the intervention of the staff VPs of employee relations, manufacturing, and marketing. Staff personnel, on the other hand, were upset by "poor" line decisions.

As a result, the marketing and manufacturing staff functions were eradicated with the late-1985 organizational restructuring illustrated in Exhibit 4. The services previously supplied by the staff groups were duplicated to varying extent inside each division.

In place of most of the staff groups, an executive committee was established in 1984. Membership in this group included the president and head of all staff groups and presidents (general managers) of the four divisions. Meeting monthly, the executive committee was intended to evaluate the performance of the firm's profit and cost problems, handle mutual problems such as transfer prices, and allocate capital expenditures among the four operating divisions. Subcommittees handled subjects such as R&D and new products.

The new organization contained seven major centres for performance measurement purposes. The cost centres were:

1. Engineering; R&D (reporting to Victco Ltd.)
2. International Marketing (Victoria Marketing Ltd.)
3. Corporate staff

The major profit centres were:

4. CraneCorp. Inc. (U.S. production and sales)
5. Victco Ltd. (supplying Victoria with components)
6. Craneco (Canadian production and marketing)
7. Victoria-owned Canadian sales outlets (reporting to Victoria Marketing Ltd.)

EXHIBIT 3   Victoria Organizational Structure, 1979–1983

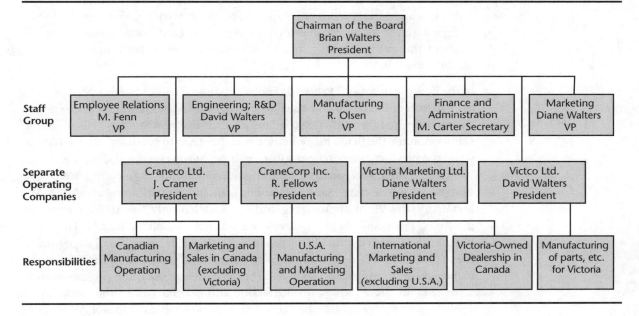

The major profit centres had considerable autonomy in their day-to-day operations and were motivated to behave as if their division was a separate, independent firm.

By mid-1985, Brian Walters had moved out of his position as president, and Michael Carter, a long-time employee close to retirement, was asked to take the position of president until a new one could be found.

EXHIBIT 4   Victoria Organizational Structure, Late 1985

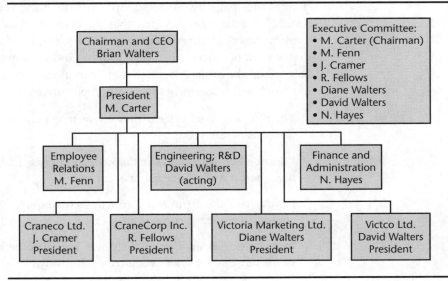

Walters saw his role changing.

> If I was anything, I was a bit of an entrepreneur. My job was to supply that thrust, but to let people develop on their own accord. I was not concerned about things not working, but I was concerned when nothing was being done about it.

In the new organization Walters did not sit on the executive committee. However, as chairman of the board and chief executive officer, the committee's recommendations came to him and "they tried me on six ways from Sunday." His intention was to monitor the firm's major activities rather than to set them. He did have to sit on the product development subcommittee, however, when "things were not working ... there was conflict ... the engineering group (engineering, R&D) had designed a whole new crane and nobody, including me, knew about it." Mr. McCarthy, the VP of engineering and R&D, called only five to six committee meetings. The crane his group developed was not to Walters' liking. (There had been a high turnover rate in this group, with four VPs since 1983.) Recognizing these problems, Walters brought in consultants to tackle the problems of the management information system and the definition of staff/line responsibilities.

In spite of these moves, dissatisfaction still existed within the company in 1986. The new organization had resulted in considerable dissension. Some conflict centred around the establishment of appropriately challenging budgets for each operating firm and even more conflict had erupted over transfer pricing and allocation of capital budgets. In 1985/86, even though requested budgets were cut equally, lack of central control over spending resulted in overexpenditures by several of the profit and cost centres.

The views of staff and the operating companies' presidents varied considerably when they discussed Victoria's organizational evolution and the operation of the present structure.

Diane Walters, the president of Victoria International Marketing, liked the autonomous system because it helped to identify the true performance of sections of the company. "We had separate little buckets and could easily identify results." Furthermore, she felt that there was no loss of efficiency (due to the duplication of certain staff functions within the divisions), since there was little duplication of systems between groups, and each group acted as a check and balance on the other groups so that "manufacturing won't make what marketing won't sell." Comments from other executives were as follows:

> The divisionalized system allowed me to get closer to my staff because we were a separate group.

> We ended up with sales and marketing expertise that was much better than if we had stayed under manufacturing.

> If you (run the firm) with a manufacturing-oriented organization, you could forget what people want.

> In a divisionalized system there was bound to be conflict between divisions, but that was not necessarily unhealthy.

Some executives saw the decentralized, semiautonomous operating company structure as a means of giving each person the opportunity to grow and develop without the hindrance of other functional executives. Most, if not all, of the operating company presidents and staff VPs were aware that decentralization brought benefits, especially in terms of the autonomy it gave them to modify existing practices. One senior executive even saw the present structure as an indicator of their basic competitive stance: "Either we centralize the structure and retract, or we stay as we are and fight with the big guys." With minimal direction supplied from Brian Walters, presidents were able to build up their staff, establish priorities and programs, and essentially were only held responsible for the bottom line.

Other executives believed that Victoria's structure was inappropriate. As one executive put it, "The semi-independence of the operating companies and the lack of a real leader for the firm has resulted in poor coordination of problem solving and difficulty in allocating responsibility." As an example, he noted how engineering's response to manufacturing was often slow and poorly communicated. Even worse, the executive noted, was how the priorities of different units were not synchronized. "When you manufacture just one product line all your activities are interrelated. So when one group puts new products first on a priority list, while another is still working out bugs in the existing product, conflict and inefficiencies have to develop."

The opposing group argued that the present organization was more appropriate to a larger, faster-growing and more complex company. As one senior executive put it, "We're too small to be as decentralized as we are now. All of this was done to accommodate the Walters' kids anyway, and it's now going to detract from profitability and growth." Another of these executives stated that rather than being a president of an operating company he would prefer to be a general manager at the head of a functional group, reporting to a group head. "If we had the right Victoria Heavy Equipment president," he said, "we wouldn't need all these divisional presidents." Another continued:

> Right now the players (divisional presidents and staff VPs) run the company. Brian Walters gives us a shot of adrenaline four or six times a year, but doesn't provide any active leadership. When Brian leaves, things stop. Instead, Brian now wants to monitor the game plan rather than set it up for others to run. As we still only have an interim president [Carter], it is the marketplace that leads us, not any strategic plan or goal.

■ The New President

Individual views about the appropriate characteristics of a new president were determined by what each executive thought was wrong with Victoria. Everyone realized that the new president would have to accommodate Brian Walters' presence and role in the firm and the existence of his two children in the organization. They all generally saw Brian as wanting to supply ideas and major strategies, but little else.

All but one of Victoria's executives agreed that the new president should not get involved in day-to-day activities or in major decision making. Instead, he should "arbitrate" among the line general managers (subsidiary presidents) and staff VPs and become more of a "bureaucrat-cum-diplomat" than an aggressive leader. As another put it, "The company will drive itself—only once in a while he'll steer a little."

■ The 1986 Situation

Industry analysts predicted a decline of 10 percent in world crane sales, which totalled 1,200 units in 1985, and as much as a 30 percent decrease in the North American market in 1986. Victoria's sales and production levels were down. Seventy-five shop floor employees had been laid off at Squamish, bringing total employment there to 850, and similar cuts were expected in Sacramento. Worker morale was suffering as a result, and the profit-sharing plan, which had been introduced in early 1985 at Walters' initiative, was not helping matters. In spite of the optimism conveyed to workers when the plan was initiated, management had announced in October that no bonus would be paid for the year. Aggravating the problem was the work force's observation that while certain groups met their budget, others did not, and hence all were penalized. This problem arose because each bonus was based on overall as well as divisional profits.

Many of the shop floor workers and the supervisory staff were also disgruntled with the additions to the central and divisional staff groups, which had continued even while the work force was being reduced. They felt that the paperwork these staff functions created was time-consuming and of little benefit. They noted, for example, that there were four or five times as many people in production control in 1986 as there were in 1980 for the same volume of production. In addition, they pointed out that despite all sorts of efforts on the part of a computer-assisted production control group, inventory levels were still too high.

Brian Walters commented as follows on the 1986 situation and his view of the company's future:

> What we are seeing in 1986 is a temporary decline in the market. This does not pose a serious problem for us, and certainly does not impact on my longer-term goals for this company, which are to achieve a 25 percent share of the world market by 1990, and reach sales of $250 million by 1999. We can reach these goals as long as we don't turn into one of these bureaucratic, grey-suited companies that are so common in North America. There are three keys for success in this business—a quality product, professional people, and the motivation for Victoria to be the standard of excellence in our business. This means that almost everything depends on the competence and motivation of our people. We will grow by being more entrepreneurial, more dedicated, and more flexible than our competitors. With our single product line we are also more focused than our competitors. They manage only by the numbers—there is no room in those companies for an

emotional plea, they won't look at sustaining losses to get into a new area, they'll turn the key on a loser. ... we look at the longer-term picture.

"The hazard for Victoria," Walters said as he looked out of his window toward the Sacramento airstrip, "is that we could develop the same kind of bureaucratic, quantitatively oriented, grey-suited managers that slow down the large U.S. competitors. But that," he said, turning to his audience, "is something I'm going to watch like a hawk. We need the right people."